# Intercultural
## Communication: A Reader

**LARRY A. SAMOVAR**
*San Diego State University, Emeritus*

**RICHAR…**
*California…*

**EDWIN …**
*San Dieg…*

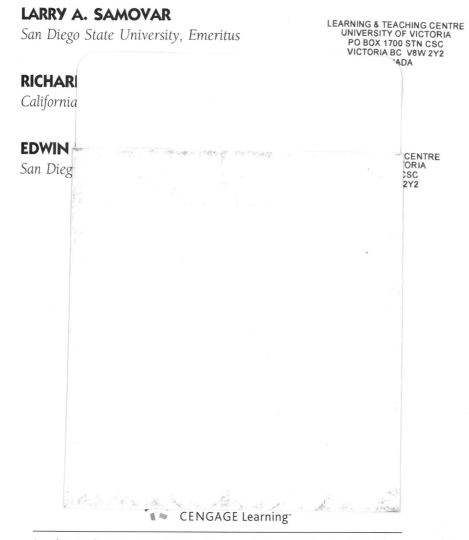

CENGAGE Learning

Australia • Brazil • Japan • Korea • Mexico • Singapore • Spain • United Kingdom • United States

# WADSWORTH
## CENGAGE Learning™

**Intercultural Communication: A Reader, Thirteenth Edition**

**Larry A. Samovar, Richard E. Porter, Edwin R. McDaniel**

Publisher/Executive Editor: Lyn Uhl

Executive Editor: Monica Eckman

Assistant Editor: Rebekah Matthews

Editorial Assistant: Colin Solan

Media Editor: Jessica Badiner

Marketing Manager: Amy Whitaker

Marketing Coordinator: Gurpreet Saran

Marketing Communications Manager: Caitlin Green

Project Management: PreMediaGlobal

Art Director: Linda Helcher

Print Buyer: Denise Powers

Rights Acquisition Specialist (Text): Katie Huha

Rights Acquisition Specialist (Image): Amanda Grozsko

Production Service: PreMediaGlobal

Cover Designer: Rokusek Design

Compositor: PreMediaGlobal

For product information and technology assistance, contact us at
**Cengage Learning Customer & Sales Support, 1-800-354-9706**

For permission to use material from this text or product, submit all requests online at **www.cengage.com/permissions.** Further permissions questions can be e-mailed to **permissionrequest@cengage.com.**

Library of Congress Control data is on record at the Library of Congress.

ISBN-13: 978-0-495-89831-3

ISBN-10: 0-495-89831-7

**Wadsworth**
20 Channel Center Street
Boston, MA 02210
USA

Cengage Learning is a leading provider of customized learning solutions with office locations around the globe, including Singapore, the United Kingdom, Australia, Mexico, Brazil and Japan. Locate your local office at **international.cengage.com/region**

Cengage Learning products are represented in Canada by Nelson Education, Ltd.

For your course and learning solutions, visit **www.cengage.com.**

Purchase any of our products at your local college store or at our preferred online store **www.cengagebrain.com.**

**Instructors:** Please visit **login.cengage.com** and log in to access instructor-specific resources.

Printed in the United States of America
2 3 4 5 6 7 14 13 12 11

# Table of **Contents**

## Chapter 8
### Ethical Considerations: Prospects for the Future    473

# Preface

*I know quite certainly that I myself have no special talent; curiosity, obsession and dogged endurance, combined with self-criticism have brought me to my ideas.*
—ALBERT EINSTEIN

*Precision of communication is important, more important than ever, in our era of hair-trigger balances, when a false or misunderstood word may create as much disaster as a sudden thoughtless act.*
—JAMES THURBER

## A SIMPLE "THANK YOU"

We begin, as we do with every new edition, with a simple "thank you." Our gratitude is directed at all those educators and students who have seen our book through twelve previous editions. We are not being prosaic or trite when we make known our pride in this extraordinary honor. Hence, we trust you can understand why we are excited about this new edition and want to begin by expressing our appreciation to the thousands of individuals who have found something of value in past presentations.

## BLENDING THE NEW AND THE OLD

We approached this new edition with the twin feelings of exhilaration and prudence. The excitement, as noted, was due to the recognition we have received during the last forty years—enough acknowledgment to warrant yet another new edition. Still, our sense of pride is moderated with a heavy dose of caution. As we proceeded, we wanted to preserve the basic framework and philosophy that has sustained us through the previous editions, while at the same time we needed to include topics that are new to the field. Here in our thirteenth edition we have balanced these two complementary positions—the past and present.

First, the new version of the book continues to reflect our belief that the basic core of the discipline should not be changed for the sake of being novel; such change would deprive the book of those fundamental concepts that we have infused into all previous editions. Second, a new book needs to reflect how intercultural theory has evolved since the last edition. We needed to present essays that mirror that change. We believe we have accomplished the blending of the old with the new in this edition. We have, as is the case in all past editions, even staked out some fresh territory for the field.

## A POINT OF VIEW

A constant theme in this edition is "globalization," a term that can no longer be applied solely to international economic activities. Globalization has stimulated the growth of all developed nations and vastly increased the economic, political, and in many cases military aspirations of what are now called "emerging markets." For instance, Brazil, Russia, India, and China, the "BRIC nations," have issued joint communiqués indicating they expect developing nations to be given more influence over how world international financial systems are managed and increased participation in world affairs. Russia has openly called for a new international currency to replace the U.S. dollar as the world reserve currency. India's population reached 1.2 billion in 2010, and that country continues to invest heavily in industrialization and education. China continues to assert itself across all aspects of international relations, and its military growth and modernization have become a concern to the United States.

As these emerging-market nations increase their economical and political influence, they will expect to play a larger role in the management and direction of the world community. This will exert pressure on the established world order and currently normative behaviors. The dominant nations of the West, led by the United States, will be faced with little choice but to engage these new players.

The changes and challenges brought about by globalization are not limited to the international sphere. Within the United States, people from a host of diverse cultures are coming together by both chance and design. These "meetings" are taking place in workplaces, classrooms, health care facilities, tourist venues, and numerous other locations. Most encounters are positive and lead to productive relationships, but not all. For example, Arizona's 2010 passage of legislation targeting illegal immigrants led to protests, sometimes destructive, across the country. Here was a conflict that clearly calls out for cultural awareness and understanding. Developing that awareness and transforming it into understanding is at the core of this book.

As a member of this multicultural globalized world, your ability to engage successfully in intercultural communication may be one of the most important skills you will ever develop, because now, more than ever before, you are being challenged by a future in which you will interact with people from a wide range of dissimilar cultural backgrounds.

Developing effective intercultural communication skills will require that you acquire new ways of thinking and interacting. This will not be easy, for two very important reasons. First, because your view of the world is shaped by the perspective of your own culture, it is often difficult to understand and appreciate many of the actions originating from other people, groups, and nations. Your cultural perceptions tend to condition you to see people and events through a highly selective lens. Second, to be a successful intercultural communicator you must be open to new and different communication experiences, have empathy toward cultures different from your own, develop a universalistic, realistic worldview, and learn to be tolerant of views that differ from your own. These communication characteristics may be easy for you to read about, but translating them into action is a very difficult task. Yet training in intercultural communication does offer you an arena in which to work on these skills. In short, it is your ability to change, to make adjustments in your communication habits and behavior, which gives you the potential to engage in successful and effective intercultural contacts.

## OUR APPROACH

The basic energizing motive for this book has remained the same since we became interested in the topic of intercultural communication over forty years ago. We believe that the ability to communicate effectively with people from other cultures and co-cultures benefits each of us as individuals and has the potential to benefit the nearly seven billion people with whom we share this planet. We have intentionally selected materials that will assist you in understanding those intercultural communication principles that are instrumental to success when you interact with people from diverse cultures. Fundamental to our approach is the conviction that *communication is a social activity; it is something people do to and with one another.* The activity might begin with ideas or feelings, but they are manifested in our behaviors, be they verbal or nonverbal. In both explicit and implicit ways, the information and the advice contained in this book are usable; the ideas presented can be translated into action.

## NEW FEATURES

We have already noted that the study of intercultural communication is a vibrant and energetic discipline. As intercultural contacts became more intense and widespread, the field has been forced to adapt to these new dynamics. As it has continued to evolve, we have attempted to mature and adapt with it. In 1972, the first edition contained thirty-four articles and essays. In this new edition, we included forty-five, of which twenty-four are new to this volume. Of these, twenty were written exclusively for this edition. Furthermore, six authors from earlier editions have made revisions to their selections for this new volume.

In one sense, we could say that these twenty-five new essays are "new features." But that point is obvious. There are, however, two other changes that are deserving of the title of "new features." First, in an attempt to broaden our theoretical base, we have incorporated the work of international scholars from Russia, Germany, Korea, China, Japan, Kenya, Israel, Canada, United Kingdom, the Netherlands, and India who were able to complement and counterbalance the research of the academic community in the United States. Second, because of our long-held conviction that it is the deep structure of a culture that dictates how members of each culture view themselves and others, we have added a number of new essays that look at religion, worldview, identity, and spirituality. These enduring deep-structure elements carry a culture's most important beliefs, and are emotional, deeply felt concepts. They also have a profound influence on how perceptions are shaped and how people communicate. For these reasons, we have added new selections that examine the deep structure elements of culture. Finally, realizing that we have been editing this book for over forty years, we have chosen to include the voices of new, young scholars who have added a fresh perspective that we have been able to combine with the basic core of the field.

## UTILIZING THE BOOK

As in the past, we intend this anthology to be for the general reader who is interested in learning about intercultural communication. Therefore, we have selected materials that are broadly based, comprehensive, and suitable for both undergraduate and graduate students. Although the level of difficulty might fluctuate from essay to essay, we have attempted to select essays aimed at the level found in most textbooks directed toward college and university students.

Intercultural Communication: A Reader is designed to meet three specific needs. The first comes from a canon that maintains that successful intercultural communication is a matter of highest importance if humankind and society are to survive. Events during the past forty years have created a world that sees us becoming increasingly linked together in a multitude of ways. From pollution to economics to health care, what happens to one culture potentially influences many other cultures. This book, then, is designed to serve as a basic anthology for courses concerned with the issues associated with human interaction. Our intention is to make this book both theoretical and practical so that the issues associated with intercultural communication can be first understood and then acted upon.

Second, the book may be used as a supplemental text to existing service and basic communication skill courses and interpersonal communication courses. Third, the text provides resource material for courses in communication theory, small-group communication, organizational and business communication, and mass communication, as well as for courses in anthropology, health care, sociology, social psychology, social welfare, social policy, business, and international relations. The long list of possible uses only underscores the increased level of intercultural interaction that is characteristic of what is often now called the "global village."

## ORGANIZATION

The book is organized into eight closely related chapters. In Chapter 1, "Approaches to Understanding Intercultural Communication," our purpose is twofold: We acquaint you with the basic concepts of intercultural communication while at the same time arousing your curiosity and interest in the topic. Hence, the essays in this chapter are both theoretical and philosophical. The selections explain what intercultural communication is, why it is important, and how it operates. Chapter 2, "Cultural Identity: Issues of Belonging," has essays that demonstrate how different cultural and ethnic identities influence role expectations, perceptions, and intercultural interaction. By reading various stories, you will be able to get an appreciation of how a person's cultural identity helps shape his or her view of the world. Chapter 3, "International Cultures: Understanding Diversity," describes the communication patterns of six cultures. We offer a sampling of cultures found in East Asia, India, Russia, the Middle East, Africa, and even the United States. We should add that in many other chapters of the book we examine additional international cultures in the health care, business, and educational setting. Chapter 4, "Co-Cultures: Living in Two Cultures," moves us from the international arena to co-cultures that exist within the United States. For many of you these will be the groups you interact with on a daily basis. We need to point out once again that space constraints have limited the total number of co-cultures we could include. Yet we believe that through the selection of groups such as Latinos, African Americans, Asian Americans, persons with disabilities, and the LGBT community, you will get a summary of the cultural diversity found in those groups. In addition to those appearing in this chapter, additional international cultures and co-cultures are examined in other chapters of the text

In Chapter 5, "Intercultural Messages: Verbal and Nonverbal Communication," we study how verbal and nonverbal symbols are used (and vary) in intercultural communication. We offer readings that will introduce you to some of the difficulties you might encounter when your intercultural partner uses a different verbal or nonverbal coding system. We will look at how verbal idiosyncrasies and distinctions influence problem solving, speaking, perception, and understanding. As noted, this chapter is also concerned with nonverbal symbols and explains some of the cultural differences in movement, facial expressions, eye contact, silence, space, time, and the like.

Chapter 6, "Cultural Contexts: The Influence of Setting," continues with the theme of how culture modifies interaction. This time, however, the interaction is examined within a specific context and environment. The assumption is that the "rules" that influence how members of a culture behave in certain settings will fluctuate across cultures. To clarify this important issue, we have selected "places" such as Japan, Germany, Jamaica, Mexico, and the like where the cultures often follow rules that differ from those found in North America. More specifically, we look at settings related to business groups, negotiations, health care, and education.

In Chapter 7, "Communicating Interculturally: Becoming Competent," readings are offered that are intended to make you a more competent intercultural communicator. To help accomplish that purpose the chapter highlights some problems inherent in intercultural communication. These problems range from cultural differences in dealing with conflict to variations in interpersonal rituals. In addition, solutions are advanced that are intended to provide you with knowledge about and suggestions for responding to these and other difficulties you might face when communicating with "strangers."

Chapter 8, "Ethical Considerations: Prospects for the Future," presents essays that deal with ethical and moral issues as well as the future directions and challenges of intercultural communication. It is the intent of this chapter to ask you not to conclude your study of intercultural communication with the reading of a single book or the completion of one course. We believe that the study of intercultural communication is a lifetime endeavor. Each time we want to share an idea or feeling with someone from another culture, we face a new and exhilarating learning experience.

## ASSISTANCE

As in the past, many people have helped us rethink and reshape this project. We express appreciation to

our Executive Editor, Monica Eckman, who managed to balance being amicable with being firm while guiding the manuscript from inception to conclusion. We also wish to thank our Assistant Editor, Rebekah Matthews, who was always able to anticipate our needs. From beginning to end, she saw to it that the manuscript was free of problems. Her being part of "our team" made this thirteenth edition a pleasurable experience. And, as we do with each edition, we must call attention to our first editor, Rebecca Hayden. Becky had enough courage and insight forty years ago to decide that intercultural communication should and would become a viable discipline. We also need to recognize the contribution of our publisher, Wadsworth Cengage Learning. Although "corporate dynamics" and major alterations in the publishing business, have forced us to adapt to a never-ending stream of new people and "philosophies," Wadsworth Cengage Learning has nevertheless been consistent in its determination to produce and market a quality textbook.

In a culture that values change, this anthology would not have survived for nearly 40 years if we had not been fortunate enough to have so many scholars willing to contribute original essays to each edition. Here in the thirteenth edition, we acknowledge the work of Peter A. Andersen, Polly Begley, Mira Bergelson, Charles Braithwaite, Dawn Braithwaite, Aaron Castelan Cargile, Justin Charlebois, Guo-Ming Chen, Peggy Cooke, Lynda D. Dixon, William F. Eadie, Donald G. Ellis, Richard J. Evanoff, Mary Fong, Maurice Hall, Michael David Hazen, Michael Hinner, Satoshi Ishii, Wenshan Jia, Xuanzi X. Jia, Eriko Katsumata, Young Yun Kim, Donald Klopf, Ifat Maoz, Yoshitaka Miike, Ann Neville Miller, Kazuo Nishiyama, Peter Nwosu, Debbie A. Ockey, Merry C. Pratt, Steven B. Pratt, Steven E. Quasha, Carolyn Roy, Bernard Saint-Jacques, Rui Shi, Brian H. Spitzberg, Dexin Tian, Fumiko Tsukada, John T. Warren, and Xiasosui Xiao. We thank all of you for letting us share your voices with thousands of other people who share your commitment to intercultural matters.

Finally, we conclude the preface the way we started it. We again express our gratitude to the thousands of users of previous editions who have given the opportunity to "talk to them." Although the contact has been somewhat intangible, we appreciate it all the same.

# Approaches to Intercultural Communication

**1**

*I don't much like him. I think I need to get to know him better.*                **Abraham Lincoln**

*The curse of the human race is not that we are so different from one another, but that we are so alike.*                **Salman Rushdie,** *The Enchantress of Florence*

Although the ability to communicate effectively has long been an important aspect of any social interaction between people from different cultures, within the past two decades it has become essential. In the wake of the Berlin Wall falling on November 9, 1989, the power structure of the international community moved from a bipolar (United States and the Soviet Union) to a unipolar (United States) position. Now, the movement is rapidly toward a multipolar international arrangement. Responsible world leaders are working toward greater cooperation on all fronts—economic, political, and military. President Obama's policy of engaging other nations, even when their aims appear counter to U.S. interests, demonstrates this trend toward increased international integration and cross-cultural interaction.

Movement to a more global, interconnected community has been abetted by dramatic technological changes, such as digital communication advances that permit the uninterrupted transfer of large amounts of data across national borders and breakthroughs in transportation that facilitate the rapid, economical movement of people and goods over vast distances. These events, often referred to collectively as "globalization," have brought about unprecedented levels of interaction among people from different national, ethnic, and religious cultural backgrounds. Media originating in one country are generally available throughout the world. Multinational and transnational organizations, replete with multicultural workforces, are now commonplace. An increasing number of international nongovernmental organizations (NGOs) are engaged in emergency relief, humanitarian assistance, and charitable service work around the globe. World tourism, once available only to the wealthy, is a growth industry, with package tours to international destinations tailored to almost any budget. Nations with declining birthrates and aging populations are recruiting health care workers from abroad. Immigration, international marriage, and inter-country adoptions have added to U.S. cultural diversity. For example, for the ten-year period 1999–2010, U.S. State Department statistics report that over 178,000 children from other nations were adopted by U.S. families ("Total Adoptions," 2010)[1].

Broadly speaking, globalization has brought about the realization that modern societies must learn to cooperate in order to prevent their mutual self-destruction. There is a growing perception that employment of force may result in near-term solutions but will ultimately create problems that are more complex. Increased concern over the planet's ecological degradation

> **Broadly speaking, globalization has brought about the realization that modern societies must learn to cooperate in order to prevent their mutual self-destruction.**

resulting from climate change and pollution has raised awareness of the need for international cooperation on a scale previously unseen. There is also a recognition of the need to engage in global cooperative efforts on a number of other issues—nuclear arms, terrorism, over-population, world poverty, and escalating competition for natural resources. Closer to home, the United States is faced with such culturally related domestic concerns as immigration, an aging population, growth of minority groups, and ideological divisions. Solutions, either whole or partial, to these circumstances will require increased intercultural understanding.

Before moving further into the study of culture and communication, we need to specify our approach to intercultural communication and recognize that other people investigate quite different perspectives. For example, some scholars who examine mass media are concerned with international broadcasting, worldwide freedom of expression, the premise of Western domination of media information, and the use of electronic technologies for instantaneous worldwide communication. Other groups study international communication with an emphasis on communication between national governments—the communication of diplomacy, economic assistance, disaster relief, and even political propaganda. Still others are interested in the communication needed to conduct business on a global basis. Their concerns include such issues as cross-cultural marketing, negotiation

---

[1]Total Adoptions to the United States. (2010). Intercountry Adoption: Office of Children's Issues, U.S. Department of State. Retrieved 13 April 2010 from http://adoption.state.gov/news/total_chart.html#

styles, management, and conflict resolution, as well as daily communication within domestic, multinational, and transnational organizations.

Our focus, however, relates to the more personal aspects of communication: What happens when people from different cultures interact face to face? Thus, our approach explores the interpersonal dimensions of intercultural communication across different contexts. The essays we have selected for this edition focus on the variables of culture and communication that are most likely to influence an intercultural communication encounter—those occasions when you attempt to exchange information, ideas, or feelings with someone from a culture different from your own.

Something as simple as an awareness of cultural variations in eye contact can help teachers achieve greater communication effectiveness in their multicultural classroom. An international businessperson who realizes that other cultures have different negotiation styles is more likely to acquire a contract satisfactory to both parties. Health care workers who understand that some people place more faith in traditional, natural remedies than in modern pharmaceuticals may be able to provide better medical treatment. In a culturally diverse workforce, the manager who understands that there are variations in cultural values is more apt to be successful. United States Border Patrol agents working with their Mexican counterparts to stem the flow of narcotics and violence across the border will be well served by knowledge of Mexican etiquette and customs.

Succinctly, we believe that many cross-cultural problems can be resolved or avoided through an awareness and understanding of the components of intercultural communication. This book, by applying those components to numerous cultures and contexts, is an effort to promote that understanding.

Your exploration of intercultural communication begins with a series of varied articles designed to (1) introduce the philosophy underlying our concept of intercultural communication; (2) provide a general orientation to, and overview of, intercultural communication; (3) theorize about the linkage between culture and communication; (4) offer insight into innovations in the study and teaching of intercultural communication; and (5) demonstrate how perception can vary in contemporary society. Our objective is to give you an introduction to the diverse dimensions of intercultural communication that will help you to approach subsequent chapters with a mindset that makes further inquiry interesting, informative, and useful.

# Using Intercultural Communication: The Building Blocks

EDWIN R. MCDANIEL • LARRY A. SAMOVAR • RICHARD E. PORTER

*The initial essay, by the three editors of this text, is titled "Understanding Intercultural Communications: The Working Principles." This essay will introduce you to many of the specific subjects and issues associated with the study of intercultural communication. As a prologue, we use the context of "globalization," our rapidly integrating global community, to demonstrate the importance of intercultural communication, both at home and abroad. Next, we discuss the purpose of communication, define it, and provide a review of its characteristics. Third, we offer an overview of culture—what it is and what it does. We then focus on some specific dimensions of culture that are germane to human communication—those components that constitute the study of intercultural communication. We examine a number of major variables—perceptual elements, cognitive patterns, verbal and nonverbal behaviors, and social contexts—to help you better understand what happens when people from different cultural backgrounds engage in communication. By understanding, at the outset of the book, what the study of intercultural communication entails, you will have a greater appreciation for subsequent essays.*

> The requirement to understand cultural differences and communicate across cultural borders has increased exponentially.

## INTERCULTURAL COMMUNICATION IN A DYNAMIC WORLD

You live in an era where intercultural communication skills are not just an asset; they are a requirement. Never before has it been so easy for people from different nations and ethnicities to meet and interact. This increased intermingling is largely the product of the stunning advances in technology that now allow people to move quickly and easily across vast distances, both physically and virtually. As one example, 54.9 million international travelers visited the United States in 2009, a phenomenon that produced approximately $17 billion in tax revenues (Office of Travel, 2010).

In addition to international travel, technology has vastly increased the number of virtual interactions. People all over the world now interact daily with others through the medium of modern telecommunications—telephones, Internet, teleconferencing, etc. Not only has this facilitated international commerce and tourism, but it has also made transborder interpersonal relations increasingly frequent. Your authors know of an international couple where one works in California and the other in Japan. They use e-mail to communicate daily, talk via Skype several times a week, and travel to visit each other every two to three months, all the while dealing with their cultural and linguistic differences. Long-distance intercultural relationships, such as theirs, are becoming increasingly commonplace as distances across the global community continue to shrink.

"Globalization," "global society," "world community," "homogenized culture," and similar terms have become catchphrases used to characterize the increased economic and social integration of national populations and ethnicities. As a result, the requirement to understand cultural differences and communicate across cultural borders has increased exponentially. To help you understand the importance of this requirement, it is worthwhile to first look back and then look forward. By looking back to your grandparents and parents' generations, you can discover how much more intercultural the world *has* become. And by looking at future projections of world events, you will realize how much more intercultural the world *will* become.

# Looking Back

One of the most noticeable changes over the past two generations is just how international the world has become. As a result of media and transportation advances, you now have access to a wide variety of products and services from abroad. Depending on your location, U.S. cable TV companies now offer channels in Chinese, Japanese, Tagalog, Hindi, Punjabi, Spanish, Russian, and many other languages. For example, DISH TV has available more than 170 international channels in 28 different languages ("International," 2010). A visit to your local supermarket will reveal a variety of ethnic foods, many imported from other parts of the world. In urban areas, small ethnic food stores have become the norm. For instance, in La Jolla, California, a small Iranian market sells a selection of fresh feta cheeses imported from France, Bulgaria, Denmark, and Greece, as well as delicious pistachios from Iran.

A heightened awareness of culture in the U.S. armed forces is another significant change from the past. During the Vietnam conflict (1961–73) and the first Gulf War (1990–91), culture was an afterthought at best. However, fighting in Iran and Afghanistan has brought the importance of cultural understanding into the spotlight and several programs designed to instill cultural awareness have been developed. The U.S. Army has instituted the Human Terrain System, which co-locates civilian socio-cultural experts with commanders and staff to provide a source of knowledge on local peoples and their culture ("Human," 2010). In order to acquire and effectively employ cultural knowledge, the U.S. Marine Corps established the Center for Advanced Operational Cultural Learning, which has the mission of training personnel in the application of language and culture to operations ("Center," 2010).

Globalization has brought profound changes to the commercial sector, including the creation of numerous transnational corporations whose reach influences markets around the world. For example, Yum! Brands, the parent company of KFC, Pizza Hut, Taco Bell, Long John Silver, and others, employs over one million workers in more than 110 countries ("Taking", 2009). In earlier years, international corporate managers came to

*People born outside the United States constitute 13 percent of the total U.S. population, the largest percentage among the developed nations.*

the United States to launch their careers, but now it is common to see U.S. managers heading to foreign locations. In 2009, for instance, 24 percent of the graduates from MIT's prestigious Sloan School of Management took positions abroad ("Job," 2009). Among U.S. employers, workplace diversity is a continuing source of concern, and training courses designed to make employees aware of cultural differences and varied communication behaviors have become routine.

Residence abroad has also increased "because the globalization of industry and education tramples national borders," and among the developed nations, the foreign-born population exceeds 8 percent on average ("Others," 2009). This international movement also includes students in higher education. Current estimates are that over three million students are studying in a country other than their own, and some 672,000 foreign students were attending U.S. universities in 2008 ("Leagues," 2010; "And," 2009).

Contemporary U.S. demographics probably represent the most easily noticeable change relating to cross-cultural issues. Quite simply, the United States has become much more multicultural over the past fifty years. A glance around your classroom will probably reveal a mix of people from different ethnicities, nationalities, age groups, and, less obvious, sexual preferences. Most of these classmates will be U.S. born, but some may be from other countries. This is because people born outside the United States constitute 13 percent of the total population, the largest percentage among the developed nations ("Ponzi," 2009). And lest you think all immigrants work in low-wage, dirty jobs, the 2000 census indicated that "47 percent of scientists and engineers in America with PhDs" were foreign born ("Economics," 2009, p. 84). Immigrants in the United States often group themselves together in urban areas, where they retain their language and culture, unlike their predecessors in the early twentieth century who were expected, and indeed often forced, to assimilate to the dominant U.S. culture. A particularly vivid example of contemporary U.S. cultural diversity was the 2010 census website, which could be accessed in over fifty languages ("United States," 2010).

The preceding overview of selected changes arising from globalization was intended to make you aware of how culture has become an important consideration in modern society. Now we turn our attention to the future, where culture and communication promise to play an even more vital role in our lives.

## Looking Forward

The financial crisis that began in 2007, which brought about the collapse of several large U.S. financial firms and weakened many international institutions, is a particularly salient example of how interrelated the world economy has become. Although the problems initially started in the United States, they quickly spread worldwide. Almost no nation, and certainly no developed country, has been unaffected by the problems. This economic interconnectedness will continue and grow in complexity. Already we see old icons taking on new personas—the Volvo brand, originally Swedish, is now owned by a Chinese company; an Indian firm now owns Land Rover and Jaguar, once U.K. brands. Even greater changes are on the horizon as the members of the BRIC group of nations (Brazil, Russia, India, and China) continue their economic growth. According to some predictions, the BRIC group "will surpass the current leading economies by the middle of this century, a tectonic shift that by this reckoning will eventually nudge the United States and Western Europe away from the center of world productivity and power" (Kramer, 2009, p. 2). This ever-increasing interconnectivity and shifting of the world economy will necessitate greater cultural awareness among the workforces. The ability to work effectively with people from other nations and ethnicities, speaking different languages and possessing varied values and beliefs, will become a common requirement.

Information technology has greatly increased public awareness of the seriousness of worldwide environmental issues. Climate change, whether natural or human induced, is producing often-catastrophic human disasters, such as the prolonged drought in southern Sudan, which has left thousands on the brink of starvation. Altered rainfall patterns are accelerating desertification in China and Africa. Pelagic pollution is having a detrimental impact on ocean marine life. Coral reefs are dying due to rising ocean temperatures, overfishing, and excessive runoff of silt and farm fertilizer. International efforts to slow and eliminate these environmentally enervating practices are proving problematic.

The December 2009 climate summit in Copenhagen, Denmark was attended by over 100 heads of state and government, "[y]et from its opening the conference was marked by bitter divisions, confusion, and setbacks." ("Summary," 2009). The many global environmental issues will not be easily solved, but any successful resolutions will also require competent intercultural communication skills.

Changing environmental conditions are also creating "environmentally induced" migration—people driven from their traditional homelands as a result of environmental degradation ("New," 2009). The International Organization for Migration estimates there may be upwards of 200 million environmental migrants by 2050, and as their means of livelihood are destroyed, many are likely to become long-term migrants (Warner et al., 2009).These refugees will be in addition to the numbers of immigrants motivated by traditional causes—economic, religious and political persecution; armed conflict; and ethnic discrimination.

The likelihood of cultural conflicts arising from growing immigrant populations is obvious, and the potential is particularly high in Western Europe. There, immigrants already represent 10 percent of the total population, and antipathy toward immigrant communities appears to be on the rise ("Treacherous," 2009). Evidence of the growing anxiety includes France's barring of the Muslim veil and headscarf from public buildings and state schools ("War," 2010), Switzerland's decision to prohibit construction of minarets at mosques ("Swiss," 2009), and consideration by Belgium of banning Islamic veils that cover the face ("Belgian," 2010).

### United States Demographics

| Year | 2005 | 2050 |
|---|---|---|
| Total population (millions) | 296 | 438 |
| Population Groups[*] | | |
| White (non-Hispanic) | 67% | 47% |
| Hispanic | 14% | 29% |
| Black | 13% | 13% |
| Asian | 5% | 9% |

*Native American and Pacific Islanders not included.

Source: Passel & Cohen, 2008

Changing demographics in the United States also present fertile ground for future clashes between people of varied cultures. According to multiple reports, minorities will represent the collective majority by 2050, and 19 percent of the total population will be foreign born (Passel & Cohen, 2008; "U.S. Census," 2008). This demographic shift is expected to produce considerable social change as members of minority ethnicities continue to replace the white majority in political, commercial, and educational positions of power.

In the commercial sector, changes are already occurring. In states such as New Mexico and California, where Hispanics constitute over 30 percent of the population, Spanish-language media programs are common, and several large U.S. retailers, including Walmart, have opened stores in Texas and Arizona specifically catering to the Hispanic market. According to a Walmart press release, the new stores "feature a layout and product assortment designed to make it more relevant to local Hispanic customers" (Moreno, 2009; "New Supermercado," 2009). This is an excellent example of how culture influences our lives. We are comfortable with the things we know and are drawn to them, but we are often uncomfortable with things we do not know and frequently avoid them.

---

### Food for Thought

A review of various websites containing information about the opening of the Walmart Supermercado stores revealed instances of vitriolic comments, with calls for people living in the United States to learn English and adopt the U.S. culture. Think about the following: Have you ever traveled abroad? Did you see any U.S. fast food outlets such as those listed below?

- Starbucks in Berlin
- Pizza Hut in Beijing
- Denny's in Tokyo
- Taco Bell in Bangalore
- Burger King in London
- KFC in Paris
- Wendy's in Mexico City

How did you feel? How do you think the local residents might have reacted when those restaurants were opened in their home country? Why?

---

This contemporary mixing of people from varied nationalities and ethnic groups, brought about by immigration, global business connections, the ease of international travel, Internet social networking sites, and increased societal acceptance is also dramatically increasing the number of international interpersonal relationships. In Europe, international marriages (also referred to as interracial marriage, biracial marriage, cross-cultural marriage, intercultural marriage, interethnic marriage, and intermarriage) are growing in number (Pulsipher & Pulsipher, 2008), no doubt abetted by the European Union's emphasis on cultural diversity. A recent report indicates that in the United States "7 percent of America's 59 million married couples in 2005 were interracial, compared to less than 2 percent in 1970" (Crary, 2007, para. 4). These cross-cultural unions are expected to increase, and such couples will encounter a host of challenges, both within society and between themselves. Cultural issues such as identity, gender roles, religious traditions, language, communication behaviors, conflict styles, child-rearing practices, family acceptance, and many, many more, including some as mundane as food choices, will have to be managed.

The issues of the future we have mapped out in this section represent only a portion of the cultural challenges you will need to confront in the increasingly globalized social order. Others problem areas requiring intercultural skills include the following:

- Religious fundamentalism will continue to present inflexible opinions on a variety of U.S. domestic subjects—gay rights, same-sex marriage, pro-life/pro-choice, etc.—which can lead to violent confrontation.

- International fundamentalism remains the motivation for many terrorists and underlies the Israeli–Palestinian problem.

- Aging populations coupled with declining birthrates will create a shortage of indigenous workers in many developed nations, requiring a still greater influx of immigrants. These new, younger arrivals will be needed to fill vacant jobs and to contribute to the tax base supporting national social welfare programs.

- The preference for male children is already creating a gender imbalance in some countries (e.g., India, China, and Korea). The lack of available indigenous brides in these nations raises the potential for a host of problems.

- The continuing empowerment of women is creating widespread societal change as traditional gender roles evolve.

- International competition for declining natural resources carries the potential for violent conflict. The availability of water, humankind's most vital resource, is already such a serious concern in many areas of the world that it was the subject of a special issue of *National Geographic* magazine ("Water," 2010).

- The struggle between rich nations and poor nations, coupled with world poverty, will continue to require cross-cultural mediation skills.

Measures to solve many of the existing and future problems will create distrust and acrimony, and perhaps even lead to open conflict among the participants due to cultural variations. Solving problems usually entails changing something, and when applied to culture, change can be quite frightening. People's lives are guided by their cultural perspectives, and when their worldview, beliefs, and values come under assault through social change, they can feel threatened and resort to extreme measures to maintain the status quo. A knowledge of intercultural communication, and the ability to use it effectively, can help bridge cultural differences, mitigate problems, and assist in achieving more harmonious, productive relations.

The essays in this text are designed to help you achieve the awareness and ability necessary to become a more skilled intercultural communicator. Each chapter introduces you to a topic considered critical to acquiring and improving intercultural competence. As the first step on that path, we begin with a fundamental definition: *Intercultural communication occurs whenever a person from one culture sends a message to be processed by a person from a different culture*. While this may seem simple and undemanding, it requires a thorough understanding of two key ingredients—communication and culture. Just as the first requirement in constructing a house is to build a good foundation, the remaining sections in this essay will give you the background you need to comprehend the rest of the articles in this book more easily. We begin by examining communication and its various components. Then, culture is explained. Finally, we explore how these two concepts are fused into several components of intercultural communication.

## UNDERSTANDING COMMUNICATION

Communication is inescapable. It is something we have to do and something we enjoy doing, and in the digital age, we do a lot of it. Think about the many different ways that you engage in communication every day—by watching TV; listening to music; talking to friends; listening to a class lecture (well, at least pretending to); daydreaming; sending and receiving messages through e-mail, Facebook, and Twitter; searching for something new on YouTube; wearing a suit to an interview; and in many, many other ways.

These are but a few of the communication activities you participate in on a daily basis. If one is to function in today's data-rich society, one cannot avoid communicating. Moreover, we seem to have an innate need to associate with, and connect to, other people through communication. Thus, the motives for entering into any communicative interaction can be categorized under one of three broad classifications. When people communicate, regardless of the situation or context, they are trying to (1) persuade, (2) inform, or (3) entertain. In other words, when you communicate, you have a purpose, an objective.

## Explaining Communication

It should be intuitively evident that communication is fundamental to contemporary daily life. But what

> A knowledge of intercultural communication, and the ability to use it effectively, can help bridge cultural differences, mitigate problems, and assist in achieving more harmonious, productive relations.

exactly is communication? What happens when we communicate? In answering those questions, we will first define and then explain the phenomenon.

Communication has been defined variously, and each definition is usually a reflection of the author's objective or of a specific context. Often the definition is long and rather abstract, because the author is trying to incorporate as many aspects of communication as possible. In some instances, the definition is narrow and precise, designed to explain a specific type or instance of communication. When studying the union of culture and communication, however, a succinct, easily understandable definition is in everyone's best interest. Thus, for us, *communication is the management of messages with the objective of creating meaning* (Griffin, 2005). This definition is somewhat broad, yet is precise in specifying what occurs in every communicative episode. It does not attempt to establish what constitutes successful or unsuccessful communication, which is actually determined by the involved participants, can vary from one person to another, and is frequently scenario dependent. The only qualifiers we place on communication are intentionality and interaction. In other words, if communication is considered to be purposeful—to persuade, inform, or entertain—then we communicate with an intention, and we achieve our objective only by interacting with someone.

## The Framework of Communication

Employing the definition of communication provided above, let's now examine the eight major structural components used to manage messages and create meaning. The first and most obvious is the **sender**—the person or group originating the message. A sender is someone with a need or desire, be it social, work, or public service, to communicate with others. In completing this desire, the sender formulates and transmits the message via a channel to the receiver(s).

The **message** consists of the information the sender desires to have understood—the data used to create meaning. Messages, which can be verbal or nonverbal, are encoded and transmitted via a **channel** to the receiver. The channel is any means that provides a path for moving the message from the sender to the receiver. For example, an oral message may be sent directly when in the immediate presence of the receiver or mediated through a cell phone, a conference call, or a YouTube video. A visual, or nonverbal, message can be transmitted directly, such as by smiling to indicate pleasure, or mediated through a photograph or text. Today, websites such as YouTube, Facebook, and MySpace provide channels that offer senders a means to reach millions of receivers through mediated messages.

The **receiver(s)** is the intended recipient of the message and the location where meaning is created. Because the receiver interprets the message and assigns a meaning, which may or may not be what the receiver intended, communication is often characterized as *receiver based*. You may send a friend a text message, but for a variety of reasons, such as lack of nonverbal cues or insufficient context, the receiver may (mis)interpret the message and feel offended.

After interpreting the message and assigning a meaning, the receiver may prepare a **response**. This is any action taken by the receiver as a result of the meaning he or she assigns to the message. A response can be benign, such as simply ignoring a provocative remark, or, at the other extreme, a physically aggressive act of violence.

The **feedback** component of communication is related to, yet separate from, the response. Feedback helps us to evaluate the effectiveness of a message. Perhaps the receiver smiles, or frowns, after decoding your message. This offers a clue as to the meaning the receiver assigned to the message and helps you adjust to the developing situation. Depending on the feedback, you may rephrase or amplify the message to provide greater clarity, ask whether the message was understood, or perhaps even retract the statement.

Every communicative interaction takes place within a physical and contextual **environment**. The physical environment refers to the location where the communication occurs, such as a classroom, coffee shop, business office, or airplane cabin. The contextual, or social, environment is more abstract and exerts a strong influence on the style of communication employed. Think about the different styles of communication you use when participating in an interview, applying for a student loan, asking a stranger for directions, visiting your professor's office, or apologizing when late to meet a friend. We alter our communicative style in response to the occasion and the receiver—the contextual environment.

**Noise**, the last component of communication, concerns the different types of interference or distractions that plague every communication event. *Physical noise* is separate from the communication participants and can take many forms, such as two people talking in the back of the classroom during a lecture, someone talking loudly on the subway, the sounds of traffic coming through the window of an apartment, or static on your cell phone.

Noise that is inherent to the people participating in the communication episode can take a variety of forms. Suppose that during a Friday afternoon class you find yourself concentrating more on plans for a spring break trip than on the lecture. Perhaps you are in a funk after learning your car needs an expensive brake job, or are worried about a term paper due the next week. These are examples of *psychological noise* that can reduce your understanding of the classroom communication. *Physiological noise* relates to the physical well-being of the people engaged in the communication activity. Coming to class with too little sleep, dealing with a head cold, or simply feeling too hot or cold in the room will interfere with your ability to comprehend fully the classroom activity.

The final type of noise often occurs during intercultural communication and can easily produce misunderstandings. For effective communication in an intercultural interaction, participants must rely on a common language, which usually means that one or more individuals will not be using their native tongue. Native fluency in a second language is very difficult, especially when nonverbal behaviors are considered. People who use another language will often have an accent or might misuse a word or phrase, which can adversely influence the receiver's understanding of the message. This type of distraction, referred to as *semantic noise*, also encompasses jargon, slang, and specialized professional terminology (West & Turner, 2004).

Collectively, these eight components provide an overview of factors that can facilitate, shape, or hamper communication encounters. But there is also another influential factor that normally plays a role in communicative interactions. Our *culture* provides each of us with a set of standards that govern how, when, what,

and even why we communicate. However, you must first understand the concept of culture itself in order to appreciate how it influences communication.

## WHAT IS CULTURE?

*Culture* is an extremely popular and increasingly overused term in contemporary society. Expressions such as *cultural differences, cultural diversity, multiculturalism, corporate culture, cross-culture*, and other variations continually appear in the popular media. Culture has been linked to such fields as corporate management, health care, psychology, education, public relations, marketing, and advertising. We often hear about U.S. forces operating in Afghanistan with insufficient knowledge and understanding of the local culture. The pervasive use of the term *culture* attests to the increased awareness of the role it plays in our everyday activities. Seldom, however, are we given a definition of just what constitutes culture or exactly what culture does. This section will provide that information.

### Explaining Culture

As with communication, the term culture has been the subject of numerous and often complex, abstract definitions. What is frequently counted as one of the earliest and easily understandable definitions of culture, and one still used today, was written in 1871 by British anthropologist Sir Edward Burnett Tylor, who said culture is "that complex whole which includes knowledge, belief, art, morals, law, custom, and any other capabilities and habits acquired by man as a member of society" ("Sir Edward," 2010, para 1).

Ruth Benedict offered a more succinct definition when she wrote, "What really binds men together is their culture—the ideas and the standards they have in common" (1959, p.16). A more complex explanation was provided by Clifford Geertz, who said culture was "a historically transmitted pattern of meaning embodied in symbols, a system of inherited conceptions expressed in symbolic forms by means of which men communicate, perpetuate, and develop their knowledge about and attitudes toward life" (1973, p. 89). Contemporary definitions of culture commonly mention shared values, attitudes, beliefs, behaviors, norms, material objects, and symbolic resources (e.g., Gardiner & Kosmitzki, 2008; Jandt, 2009; Klyukanov, 2005; Lustig & Koester, 2009; Martin & Nakayama, 2010; Neuliep, 2008; Oetzel, 2008; Samovar, et al., 2009). Indeed, the many and varied definitions attest to the complexity of this social concept called culture.

We propose an applied and hopefully more simplified explanation of culture. Stop for a minute and think about the word *football*. What mental picture comes to mind? Most U.S. Americans will envision two teams of eleven men each in helmets and pads, but someone in Montréal, Canada, would imagine twelve men per team. A resident of Sidney, Australia, may think of two eighteen-man teams in shorts and jerseys competing to kick an oblong ball between two uprights, while a young woman in Sao Paulo, Brazil, would probably picture two opposing teams of eleven men, or women, attempting to kick a round ball into a net. In each case, the contest is referred to as "football," but the playing fields, equipment, and rules of each game are quite different.

Try to think about how you would react in the following situations. Following your successful job interview with a large Chinese company, you are invited to dinner. At the restaurant, you sit at a round table with other people, and plates of food are continually being placed on a turntable in the table's center. People are spinning the turntable, taking food from different dishes, talking with each other, and urging you to try items you are completely unfamiliar with. *How do you feel?* At a later date, one of your close friends, whose parents immigrated from Mumbai, India, invites you to his home for the first time. There, you are introduced to your friend's grandfather, who places his palms together in front of his chest as if praying, bows and says *namaste*. *What do you do?* In each of these examples, perhaps you felt unsure of what to do or say, yet in China and India, these behaviors are routine.

These examples illustrate our applied definition of culture. Simply stated, *culture is the rules for living and functioning in society*. In other words, culture provides the rules for playing the game of life (Gudykunst, 2004; Yamada, 1997). Because the rules differ from culture to culture, in order to function

and be effective in a particular culture, you need to know how to "play by the rules." We learn the rules of our own culture as a matter of course, beginning at birth and continuing throughout life. As a result, own culture rules are ingrained in the subconscious, enabling us to react to familiar situations without thinking. It is when you enter another culture, with different rules, that problems are encountered.

## What Culture Does

If we accept the idea that culture can be viewed as a set of societal rules, its purpose becomes self-evident. Cultural rules provide a framework that gives meaning to events, objects, and people. The rules enable us to make sense of our surroundings and reduce uncertainty about the social environment. Recall the first time you were introduced to someone you were attracted to. You probably felt some level of nervousness because you wanted to make a positive impression. During the interaction, you may have had a few thoughts about what to do and what not to do. Overall, you had a good idea of the proper courtesies, what to talk about, and generally how to behave. This is because you had learned the proper cultural rules of behavior by listening to and observing others. Now, take that same situation and imagine being introduced to a student from a different country, such as Jordan or Kenya. Would you know what to say and do? Would the cultural rules you had been learning since childhood be effective, or even appropriate, in this new social situation?

Culture also provides us with our identity, or sense of self. From childhood, we are inculcated with the idea of belonging to a variety of groups— family, community, church, sports teams, schools, and ethnicity—and these memberships form our different identities. Our cultural identity is derived from our "sense of belonging to a particular cultural or ethnic group" (Lustig & Koester, 2006, p. 3), which may be Chinese, Mexican American, African American, Greek, Egyptian, Jewish, or one or more of many, many other possibilities. Growing up, we learn the rules of social conduct appropriate to our specific cultural group, or groups in the case of multicultural families such as Vietnamese American, Italian

> *Culture provides the rules for playing the game of life.*

American, or Russian American. Cultural identity can become especially prominent during interactions between people from different cultural groups, such as a Pakistani Muslim and an Indian Hindu, who have been taught varied values, beliefs, and different sets of rules for social interaction. Thus, cultural identity can be a significant factor in the practice of intercultural communication.

## Culture's Components

While there are many explanations of what culture is and does, there is general agreement on what constitutes its major characteristics. An examination of these characteristics will provide increased understanding of the abstract, multifaceted concept and also offer insight into how communication is influenced by culture.

*Culture Is Learned.* At birth, we have no knowledge of the many societal rules needed to function effectively in our culture, but we quickly begin to internalize this information. Through interactions, observations, and imitation, the proper ways of thinking, feeling, and behaving are communicated to us. Being taught to eat with a fork, a pair of chopsticks or even one's fingers is learning cultural behavior. Attending a Catholic mass on Sunday or praying at a Jewish Synagogue on Saturday is learning cultural behaviors and values. Celebrating Christmas, Kwanzaa, Ramadan, or Yon Kippur is learning cultural traditions. Culture is also acquired from art, proverbs, folklore, history, religion, and a variety of other sources. This learning, often referred to as enculturation, is both conscious and subconscious, and has the objective of teaching us how to function properly within our cultural milieu.

*Culture Is Transmitted Intergenerationally.* Spanish philosopher George Santayana wrote, "Those who cannot remember the past are condemned to repeat it." He was certainly not referring to culture, which exists only if it is remembered and repeated by people. You learned your culture from family members, teachers, peers, books, personal observations, and a host of media sources. The appropriate way to act, what to say, and things to value were all communicated to the members of your generation by these many sources. You are also a source for passing these cultural expectations, usually with little or no variation, to succeeding generations. Culture represents our link to the past and, through future generations, hope for the future. The critical factor in this equation is communication.

*Culture Is Symbolic.* Words, gestures, and images are merely symbols used to convey meaning. It is our ability to use these symbols that allows us to engage in the many forms of social intercourse used to construct and convey culture. Our symbol-making ability facilitates learning and enables transmission of meaning from one person to another, group to group, and generation to generation. In addition to transmitting meaning, the portability of symbols creates the ability to store information, which allows cultures to preserve what is considered important and to create a history. The preservation of culture provides each new generation with a road map to follow and a reference library to consult when unknown situations are encountered. Succeeding generations may modify established behaviors or values, or construct new ones, but the accumulation of past traditions is what we know as culture.

*Culture Is Dynamic.* Despite its historical nature, culture is never static. Within a culture, new ideas, inventions, and exposure to other cultures create change. Discoveries such as the stirrup, gunpowder, the nautical compass, penicillin, and nuclear power are demonstrations of culture's susceptibility to innovation and new ideas. More recently, advances made by minority groups, the women's movement, and gay rights advocates have significantly altered the fabric of contemporary U.S. society. Invention of the computer chip and the Internet and the discovery of DNA have brought profound changes not only to U.S. culture but also to the rest of the world.

*Diffusion*, or cultural borrowing, is also a source of change. Think about how common pizza (Italian), sushi (Japanese), tacos (Mexican), and tandoori chicken and naan bread (India) now are in the U.S. American diet. The Internet has accelerated cultural diffusion by making new knowledge and insights easily accessible. Immigrants bring their own cultural practices, traditions, and artifacts, some of which become incorporated into the culture of their new homeland—for example, Vietnamese noodle shops in the United States, Indian restaurants in England, or Japanese foods in Brazil.

Cultural calamities, such as war, political upheaval, or large-scale natural disasters, can cause change. U.S. intervention in Afghanistan is bringing greater equality to the women of that nation. For better or worse, the invasion of Iraq raised the influence of Shia and Kurdish cultural practices and lessened those of the Sunni. International emergency relief workers responding to the earthquake in Haiti brought their own cultural practices to the situation, some of which have likely become intermingled with the cultural practices of the native Haitians.

Immigration is a major source of cultural diffusion. Many of the large U.S. urban centers now have areas unofficially, or sometimes officially, called Little Italy, Little Saigon, Little Tokyo, Korea Town, Chinatown, Little India, etc. These areas are usually home to restaurants, markets, and shops catering to a specific ethnic group. However, they also serve to introduce different cultural practices into other segments of the population.

Most of the changes affecting culture, especially readily visible changes, are often topical in nature, such as dress, food preference, modes of transportation, or housing. Values, ethics, morals, the importance of religion, or attitudes toward gender, age, and sexual orientation, which constitute the deep structures of culture, are far more resistant to major change and tend to endure from generation to generation.

*Culture Is Ethnocentric.* The strong sense of group identity, or attachment, produced by culture can also lead to *ethnocentrism*, the tendency to view one's own culture as superior to other cultures. Ethnocentrism can arise from one's enculturation. Being continually told that you live in the greatest country in the world, that America's way of life is better than those of other nations, or that your values are superior to those of other ethnic groups can lead to feelings of cultural superiority, especially among children. Ethnocentrism can also result from a lack of contact with other cultures. If you were exposed only to a U.S. cultural orientation, it is likely that you would develop the idea that your country is the center of the world, and you would tend to view the rest of the world from the perspective of U.S. culture.

An inability to understand or accept different ways and customs can also provoke feelings of ethnocentrism. It is quite natural to feel at ease with people who are like you and adhere to the same social norms and protocols. You know what to expect, and it is usually easy to communicate. It is also normal to feel uneasy when confronted with new and different social values, beliefs, and behaviors. You do not know what to expect, and communication is probably difficult. However, to view or evaluate those differences negatively simply because they vary from your expectations is a product of ethnocentrism, and an ethnocentric disposition is detrimental to effective intercultural communication.

## INTEGRATING COMMUNICATION AND CULTURE

By now you have probably realized that culture is an extremely complex, abstract concept that exerts a pervasive influence on every aspect of your life. A number of culture-related components are important to the study of intercultural communication. These include (1) perception, (2) patterns of cognition, (3) verbal behaviors, (4) nonverbal behaviors, and (5) the influence of context. Although we will discuss each of these components separately in this essay, you must keep in mind that in an intercultural setting, all become integrated and function at the same time.

## Perception

Every day we encounter an overwhelming amount of varied stimuli that we must cognitively process and assign a meaning to. This process of selecting, organizing, and evaluating stimuli is referred to as *perception*. The volume of environmental stimuli is far too large for us to pay attention to everything, so we select only what we consider relevant or interesting. After determining what we will attend to, the next step is to organize the selected stimuli for evaluation. Whether in this book or in the university library, media news outlets, or websites, information must be given a structure before it can be interpreted. The third step of perception thus becomes a process of evaluating and assigning meaning to the stimuli.

A common assumption is that people conduct their lives in accordance with how they perceive the world. These perceptions are strongly influenced by culture. In other words, we see, hear, feel, taste, and even smell the world through the criteria that culture has placed on our perceptions. Thus, one's idea of beauty, attitude toward the elderly, concept of self in relation to others—even one's perception of what tastes good or bad—are culturally influenced and can vary among social groups. For example, Vegemite is a yeast extract spread used on toast and sandwiches that is sometimes referred to as the "national food" of Australia. Yet, few people other than those from Australia or New Zealand like the taste, or even the smell, of this salty, dark paste.

As you would expect, perception is an important aspect of intercultural communication, because people from dissimilar cultures frequently perceive the world differently. Thus, it is important to be aware of the more relevant socio-cultural elements that have a significant and direct influence on the meanings we assign to stimuli. These elements represent our belief, value, and attitude systems and our worldview.

*Beliefs, Values, and Attitudes.* **Beliefs** can be defined as individually held subjective ideas about the nature of an object or event. These subjective ideas are, in large part, a product of culture, and they directly influence our behaviors. Bullfighting is thought to be cruel and inhumane by most people in the United States, but certainly not by the many people in Spain and Mexico who love the sport. A strict adherent of Judaism or Islam would probably find the thought of eating a ham sandwich repulsive. Regarding religion, many people believe that there is only one god but others pay homage to multiple deities.

**Values** represent those things we hold important in life, such as morality, ethics, and aesthetics. We use values to distinguish between the desirable and the undesirable. Each person has a set of unique, personal values and a set of shared, cultural values. The latter are a reflection of the rules a culture has established to reduce uncertainty, lessen the likelihood of conflict, help in decision making, and provide structure to social organization and interactions. Cultural values are a motivating force behind our behaviors. Someone from a culture that places a high value on harmonious social relations, such as Japan,

will likely employ an indirect communication style. In contrast, a U.S. American can be expected to use a more direct style, because frankness, honesty, and openness are valued.

Our beliefs and values push us to hold certain **attitudes**, which are learned tendencies to act or respond in a specific way to events, objects, people, or orientations. Culturally instilled beliefs and values exert a strong influence on our attitudes. Thus, people tend to embrace what is liked and avoid what is disliked. Someone from a culture that considers cows sacred will take a negative attitude toward your invitation to have a Big Mac for lunch.

*Worldview.* Although quite abstract, the concept of worldview is among the most important elements of the perceptual attributes influencing intercultural communication. Stated simply, worldview is what forms people's orientation toward such philosophical concepts as deities, the universe, nature, and the like. Normally, worldview is deeply imbedded in one's psyche and operates on a subconscious level. This can be problematic in an intercultural situation, where conflicting worldviews can come into play. As an example, many Asian and Native North American cultures hold a worldview that people should have a harmonious, symbiotic relationship with nature. In contrast, Euro-Americans are instilled with the concept that people must conquer and mold nature to conform to personal needs and desires. Individuals from nations possessing these two contrasting worldviews could well encounter difficulties when working to develop an international environmental protection plan. The concept of democracy, with everyone having an equal voice in government, is an integral part of the U.S. worldview. Contrast this with Afghanistan and parts of Africa, where worldviews hold that one's tribe takes precedence over the central government.

## Cognitive Patterns

Another important consideration in intercultural communication is the influence of culture on cognitive thinking patterns, which include reasoning and approaches to problem solving. Culture can often produce different ways of knowing and doing. Research by Nisbett (2003) has disclosed that Northeast Asians (Chinese, Japanese, and Koreans) employ a holistic thinking pattern, whereas Westerners use a linear cause-and-effect model that places considerable value on logical reasoning and rationality. Thus, problems can be best solved by a systematic, in-depth analysis of each component, progressing from the simple to the more difficult. Northeast Asians, however, see problems as much more complex and inter-related, requiring a greater understanding of, and emphasis on, the collective rather than a focus on individual parts.

Thought patterns common to a culture influence the way individuals communicate and interact with each other. However, what is common in one culture may be problematic in another culture. To illustrate the potential of this problem, in Japanese–U.S. business negotiations the Japanese have a tendency to reopen previously discussed issues that the U.S. side considers resolved. United States negotiators find this practice to be frustrating and time consuming, believing that once a point has been agreed upon, it is completed. From the Japanese perspective, however, new topics can have an influence on previously discussed points (McDaniel, 2000). This example demonstrates both the importance of understanding that different patterns of cognition exist, and the need to learn how to accommodate them in an intercultural communication encounter.

*Culture can often produce different ways of knowing and doing.*

## Verbal Behaviors

The role of language in intercultural communication is self-evident in that all of the participants must, to some degree, share a language, be it their first or second. What is not so self-evident is the symbiosis that exists between culture and language, because one cannot exist without the other. Without a common language, a group of people would not be able to establish and perpetuate a culture. They would be unable to share their beliefs, values, social norms, and worldview with one another or to transmit these cultural characteristics to succeeding generations. In turn, culture helps people to establish, evolve, and

preserve their language. Like culture, language must be shared in order to exist.

Language itself is merely a set of symbols that a cultural group has arbitrarily agreed upon to help them bring meaning to objects, events, emotions, experiences, places, and the like. Different cultures have, of course, decided to use different sets of symbols. The use of symbol systems to construct and express meaning, however, is an inexact process, because the meanings for words are open to a variety of translations by both individuals and cultures. The word *parallel* can be used to demonstrate how culture influences meaning and can lead to misunderstandings in intercultural exchanges. In the United States, telling someone they are on a "parallel" course implies agreement or similarity of views. In Japanese, however, "parallel" is used to indicate that the parties disagree, because parallel lines (*heik–o–sen*) never converge.

## Nonverbal Behavior

Another critical factor in intercultural communication is nonverbal behavior, which includes gestures, facial expressions, eye contact and gaze, posture and movement, touch, dress, silence, the use of space and time, objects and artifacts, and paralanguage. These nonverbal behaviors, which are inextricably intertwined with verbal behaviors, often communicate as much or more meaning than spoken words. Like language, culture also directly influences the use of, and meanings assigned to, nonverbal behavior. In intercultural communication, inappropriate or misused nonverbal behaviors can easily lead to misunderstandings and sometimes result in insults. A comprehensive examination of all nonverbal behaviors is beyond the scope of this chapter, but we will draw on a few culture specific examples to demonstrate their importance in intercultural communication exchanges.

Nonverbal greeting behaviors show remarkable variance across cultures. In the United States, a firm handshake among men is the norm, but in some Middle Eastern cultures, a gentle grip is used. In Mexico, acquaintances will often embrace (*abrazo*) each other after shaking hands. Longtime Russian male friends may engage in a bear hug and kiss each other on both cheeks. People from Japan and India traditionally bow to greet each other. Japanese men will place their hands at the side of the body and bow from the waist, with the lower-ranking person bowing first and dipping lower than the other person. Indians will perform the *namaste*, which entails holding the hands together in a prayer-like fashion at mid-chest while slightly bowing the head and shoulders.

Eye contact is another important culturally influenced nonverbal communication behavior. For U.S. Americans, direct eye contact is an important part of making a good impression during an interview. However, in some cultures, direct eye contact is considered rude or threatening. Among some Native Americans, children are taught to show adults respect by avoiding eye contact. When giving a presentation in Japan, it is common to see people in the audience with their eyes shut, because this is thought to facilitate listening. (Try it—you may be surprised.) How a person dresses also sends a strong nonverbal message. What are your thoughts when you see an elderly woman wearing a *hijab*, a Jewish boy with a *yarmulke*, or a young black man in a colorful *dashiki*?

Nonverbal facial and body expressions, like language, form a coding system for constructing and expressing meaning, and these expressions are culture bound. Through culture, we learn which nonverbal behavior is proper for different social interactions. But what is appropriate and polite in one culture may be disrespectful or even insulting in another culture. People engaging in intercultural communication, therefore, should try to maintain a continual awareness of how body behaviors may influence an interaction.

## Contextual Influences

We have defined culture as a set of rules established and used by a group of people to conduct social interaction. These rules determine what is considered correct communicative behavior, including both verbal and nonverbal elements, for both physical and social (situational) contexts. For example, you would not normally attend a funeral wearing shorts and tennis shoes or talk on your cell phone during the service. Your culture has taught you that these behaviors are contextually inappropriate (i.e., disrespectful).

Context is also an important consideration in intercultural communication interactions, where the rules for specific situations usually vary. What is appropriate in one culture is not necessarily correct in another. As an example, among most White U.S. Americans, church services are relatively serious occasions, but among African American congregations, services are traditionally more demonstrative, energetic gatherings. In a restaurant in Germany, the atmosphere is usually somewhat subdued, with customers engaging in quiet conversation. In Spain, however, the conversation is much louder and more animated. In U.S. universities, students are expected to interactively engage the instructor, but in Japan the expectation is that the instructor will simply lecture, with very little or no interaction.

In these examples, we see the importance of having an awareness of the cultural rules governing the context of an intercultural communication exchange. Unless all parties in the exchange are sensitive to how culture affects the contextual aspects of communication, difficulties will most certainly arise and could negate effective interaction.

## CONCLUSION

We began with a discussion of how globalization has harnessed the forces of contemporary geopolitics, technology, economics, immigration, and media to produce an ever-shrinking world community, making interaction among people from different cultures more and more common and necessary. We end with a reflection on the requirement and urgency for greater tolerance of cultural differences generated by this new multipolar world order.

The world's population, as well as U.S. domestic demographics, continues to move toward a pluralistic, multicultural society at a quickstep pace. The social forces behind this movement will not easily or soon subside. The resulting cultural mixing requires that we, both individually and as a society, become more tolerant of the varied beliefs, worldviews, values, and behaviors of people from other cultures. Acceptance or tolerance may not be appropriate in every situation, nor is universal, unquestioning acquiescence to every difference advocated. We do, however, have to be willing to "live and let live" on a broader scale. That we do not yet seem able or prepared to do this is demonstrated by ongoing international and domestic struggles.

The international community is beleaguered with sectarian violence arising from ideological, cultural, and ethnic differences. As we write this chapter, conflict between religious factions in Iraq appears to be resurging. In the Darfur region of Sudan, people continue to be killed and driven from their homes as a result of cultural and racial differences. The long-standing Israeli–Palestinian conflict remains unresolved, and there is little promise of a solution in the near future. The dispute between India and Pakistan continues over who should control the disputed region of Jammu and Kashmir in the Himalayas. The conflict between the Russian government and separatist movements in the Caucasus continues to ebb and flow. The indigenous Uygur ethnic minority in western China continues to exhibit animosity toward government policies favoring immigration into the region by other Chinese ethnic groups, especially the Han. Drought, famine, a burgeoning population, and ineffective governmental control continue to exacerbate ethnic and religious violence throughout the Horn of Africa. Maoist insurgents in eastern India, claiming that the government exploits poor rural peasants, have escalated their violence. The global war on terrorism, a product of variant ideological and cultural perspectives, continues with little prospect of a final solution. Disagreement over what constitutes human rights remains a source of tension among many nations.

Intolerance of differences is also a continuing issue within the United States, where we are divided over a seeming multitude of culturally based issues, many of which fall along a conservative vs. liberal ideological divide. The demands of coping with the diverse customs, values, views, and behaviors inherent in a multicultural society are producing increased levels of personal frustration, social stress, and often violence.

## Selected Societal Sources of U.S. Domestic Division

- Stem cell research
- Gay rights
- Affirmative action
- Right to life vs. freedom of choice
- School prayer
- Legalization of drugs
- Death penalty
- Assisted suicide
- Same-sex marriage
- Illegal immigration
- Government involvement in health care or health insurance
- School voucher program
- Sex education
- Gun control

As tides of immigrants and refugees continue to arrive in the United States and other developed nations, we will be confronted with increased cultural diversity. If we are to continue to assert that cultural diversity is a valuable, desirable asset and embrace the concept of a global village, we must quickly learn to accept and tolerate the resulting differences. Your authors do not profess to have the solution to these problems. However, as a means of better preparing you for life in the global village, which will require frequent interactions with people who experience the world differently from you, we do hope to stimulate thought and discussion about the advantages and difficulties of multiculturalism and the need for effective intercultural communication.

## References

And Is There Honey Still for Tea? (2009, November 21). *The Economist*, p. 59.

Belgian committee votes for full Islamic veil ban (2010, March 31). *BBC News*. Retrieved April 4, 2010 from http://news.bbc.co.uk/2/hi/europe/8597142.stm

Benedict, R. (1959). *Patterns of Culture* (Sentry Edition). Boston: Houghton Mifflin.

Crary, D. (2007, April 13). Interracial marriages surge across U.S. *The Washington Post*, para. 4. Retrieved April 5, 2010 from http://www.washingtonpost.com/wp-dyn/content/article/2007/04/13/AR2007041300423_pf.html

DISH Network (2010). *International packages*. Retrieved April 1, 2010 from http://www.dishnetwork.com/international/default.aspx

Economics focus. (2009, March 7). *The Economist*, p. 84.

Gardiner, H. W., & Kosmitzki, C. (2008). *Lives across cultures* (4th ed.). Boston: Pearson Education.

Geertz, C. (1973). *The interpretation of cultures*. New York: Basic Books.

Griffin, E. (2005). *A first look at communication theory* (6th ed.). Boston: McGraw-Hill.

Gudykunst, W. B. (2004). *Bridging differences* (4th ed.). Thousand Oaks, CA: Sage.

Jandt, F. E. (2009). *An introduction to intercultural communication* (6th ed). Thousand Oaks, CA: Sage.

The job search. (2009, November 23). *The San Diego Union Tribune*, p. B5.

Kramer, A. E. (2009 June 16). Emerging economies meet in Russia. *The New York Times*. Retrieved April 3, 2009 from http://www.nytimes.com/2009/06/17/world/europe/17bric.html

Klyukanov, I. E. (2005). *Principles of intercultural communication*. Boston: Allyn and Bacon.

Leagues apart. (2010, March 27). *The Economist*, p. 65.

Lustig, M. W., & Koester, J. (2006). The nature of cultural identity. In M. W. Lustig & J. Koester (Eds.), *Among us: Essays on identity, belonging, and intercultural competence* (2nd ed., pp. 3–8). New York: Longman.

Lustig, M. W. & Koester, J. (2009). Intercultural competence: Interpersonal communication across cultures (6th ed.). Boston: Allyn & Bacon.

Martin, J. N., & Nakayama, T. K. (2010). *Experiencing intercultural communication: An introduction* (4th ed.). Boston: McGraw-Hill.

McDaniel, E. R. (2000). *Japanese negotiation practices: Low-context communication in a high-context culture*. Unpublished doctoral dissertation, Arizona State University.

Moreno, J. (2009, April 30). Wal-Mart gives its Supermercado concept a tryout. *Houston Chronicle*. Retrieved April 4, 2010 from http://www.chron.com/disp/story.mpl/business/6400294.html

Neuliep, J. W. (2008). *Intercultural communication: A contextual approach* (4th ed.). Boston: Houghton Mifflin.

A new (under) class of travelers. (2009, June 27). *The Economist*, p. 67.

Nisbett, R. (2003). *The geography of thought*. New York: Free Press.

Oetzel, J. G. (2008). *Intercultural communication: A layered approach*. Boston: Allyn & Bacon.

Office of Travel and Tourism Industries. (2010 March). *International Visitation to the United States: A Statistical Summary of U.S. Arrivals* (2009). U.S. Department of Commerce: International Trade Administration. Retrieved March 31, 2010 from http://www.tinet.ita.doc.gov/outreachpages/download_data_table/2009_Visitation_Report.pdf

The others. (2009, December 19). *The Economist*, p. 107.

Passel, J. S., & Cohn, D. (2008). *U.S. Population Projections: 2005–2050*. Washington, D.C.: Pew Research Center. Retrieved April 4, 2010 from http://pewhispanic.org/files/reports/85.pdf

A Ponzi scheme that works. (2009 December 19). *The Economist*, p. 41.

Pulsipher, L. M., & Pulsipher, A. (2008). *World regional geography: Global patterns, local lives*. New York: W. H. Freeman.

Samovar, L. A., Porter, R. E., & McDaniel, E. R. (2009). *Communication between cultures* (7th ed.). Boston: Wadsworth Cengage.

Sir Edward Burnett Tylor. (2010). In *Encyclopædia Britannica*. Retrieved April 6, 2010, from Encyclopædia Britannica Online: http://www.britannica.com/EBchecked/topic/611503/Sir-Edward-Burnett-Tylor

Summary: Copenhagen Climate Summit. (2009). *Fifteenth Session of the Conference of the Parties to the United Nations Framework Convention on Climate Change and Fifth Session of the Meeting of the Parties to the Kyoto Protocol*. Pew Center on Global Climate Change. Retrieved April 3, 2009 from http://www.pewclimate.org/international/copenhagen-climate-summit-summary

Swiss Ban Minarets in National Referendum. (2009, November 30). *San Diego Union Tribune*, p. A3.

Taking the hill less climbed. (2009, October 31). *The Economist*, p. 76.

A treacherous path? (2009, August 29). *The Economist*, p. 72.

U.S. Army (2010). *Human terrain system*. Retrieved April 1, 2010 from http://humanterrainsystem.army.mil/default.htm

U.S. Census Bureau. (2010). *United States Census 2010*. Retrieved April 2, 2010 from http://2010.census.gov/2010census/index.php.

U.S. Census Bureau. (2008). *An older and more diverse nation by midcentury. U.S. Census Bureau News*. Washington, DC: Author. Retrieved April 2, 2010 from http://www.census.gov/Press-Release/www/releases/archives/population/012496.html

U.S. Marine Corps. (2010). *Center for advanced operational cultural learning*. Retrieved from http://www.tecom.usmc.mil/caocl/

Walmart Corporate. (2009, April 28). New Supermercado de Walmart opens in Houston. Retrieved April 4, 2010 from http://walmartstores.com/pressroom/news/9106.aspx

The war of French dressing. (2010, January 16). *The Economist*, p. 49.

Warner, K., Ehrhart, C., de Sherbinin, A., Adamo, S., & Chai-Onn, T. (2009). *In search of shelter: Mapping the effects of climate change on human migration and displacement.* NY: Care. Retrieved April 4, 2010 from http://www.ciesin.columbia.edu/documents/climmigr-report-june09_final.pdf

Water: Our Thirsty World. (2010 April). *National Geographic, 217*(4).

West, R., & Turner, L. H. (2004). *Introducing communication theory: Analysis and application* (2nd ed.). Boston: McGraw-Hill.

Yamada, H. (1997). *Different games, different rules: Why Americans and Japanese misunderstand each other.* New York: Oxford University Press.

## Concepts and Questions

1.  Do you believe that most people are prepared to engage in intercultural communication? Explain.

2.  How often do you find yourself in situations where an increased facility in intercultural communication would be useful? What are some of these occasions?

3.  How can knowledge of the basic principles of communication be useful in daily life?

4.  How do the authors define culture? Can you think of other definitions of culture that might help you to understand intercultural communication better?

5.  What is the purpose of culture?

6.  What do the authors mean by the statement, "culture is learned"?

7.  What are some instances in your life that demonstrate how culture is learned?

8.  What are cultural values? How do they relate to individual values?

9.  Distinguish several ways in which verbal behavior might differ between cultures.

10. What role does context play in communication? How does context affect intercultural communication?

11. Think of five different situations where an understanding of culture and communication behaviors would be beneficial.

# Dimensionalizing Cultures: The Hofstede Model in Context

GEERT HOFSTEDE

*A thorough understanding of the study of culture and intercultural communication must include the influential work of Geert Hofstede, a contemporary pioneer in using statistical methods to discern the cultural traits of social groups. Professor Hofstede begins his essay with a definition of culture and a description of the various disciplines of cultural research. He then provides a review of the efforts of earlier scholars to establish a system of categorization that can be used to classify cultures. Hofstede then explains the statistical methodology employed in his groundbreaking study of international employees in IBM subsidiaries in fifty countries. This is followed by an overview of his cultural dimensions model, which continues to be widely studied and applied in intercultural research. He contrasts the differences among five extensively used cultural dimensions: (1) small- and large-power distance cultures, (2) weak- and strong-uncertainty avoidance societies, (3) collectivistic and individualistic societies, (4) feminine and masculine societies, and (5) short- and long-term oriented societies.*

*Next, Hofstede explains how his research led to additional investigation by other scholars, who extended his findings and developed new investigative scales. This led to further refinement of Hofstede's theoretical concepts, including the development of additional cultural dimensions that could be used to characterize cultural groups. Use of the cultural dimensions in studying organizational culture is then discussed. Hofstede concludes his essay with an account of an envisioned model for the future study of culture.*

*The significance of Hofstede's work will become apparent as you read subsequent essays in this text, where his cultural dimensions model is referred to frequently.*

Online Readings in Psychology and Culture (Unit 2, Chapter 14), June 2009. Reprinted by permission of the author. Geert Hofstede is Professor Emeritus from the University of Maastricht and a Fellow of the Center for Economic Research at the University of Tilburg, both in the Netherlands.

# INTRODUCTION

Culture has been defined in many ways; this author's shorthand definition is, *"Culture is the collective programming of the mind that distinguishes the members of one group or category of people from others."* It is always a collective phenomenon, but it can be connected to different collectives. Within each collective there is a variety of individuals. If characteristics of individuals are imagined as varying according to some bell curve, the variation between cultures is the shift of the bell curve when one moves from one society to the other. Most commonly the term culture is used for tribes or ethnic groups (in anthropology), for nations (in political science, sociology and management), and for organizations (in sociology and management). A relatively unexplored field is the culture of occupations (for instance, of engineers versus accountants, or of academics from different disciplines). The term can also be applied to the genders, to generations, or to social classes. However, changing the level of aggregation studied changes the nature of the concept of "culture." Societal, national and gender cultures, which children acquire from their earliest youth onwards, are much more deeply rooted in the human mind than occupational cultures acquired at university, or than organizational cultures acquired on the job. The latter are exchangeable when people take a new job. Societal cultures reside in (often unconscious) values, in the sense of *broad tendencies to prefer certain states of affairs over others* (Hofstede, 2001:5). Organizational cultures reside rather in (visible and conscious) practices: the way people perceive what goes on in their organizational environment.

> *"Culture is the collective programming of the mind that distinguishes the members of one group or category of people from others".*

# CLASSIFYING CULTURES: CONCEPTUAL DIMENSIONS

In an article first published in 1952, U.S. anthropologist Clyde Kluckhohn argued that there should be universal categories of culture:

> In principle ... there is a generalized framework that underlies the more apparent and striking facts of cultural relativity. All cultures constitute so many somewhat distinct answers to essentially the same questions posed by human biology and by the generalities of the human situation.... Every society's patterns for living must provide approved and sanctioned ways for dealing with such universal circumstances as the existence of two sexes; the helplessness of infants; the need for satisfaction of the elementary biological requirements such as food, warmth, and sex; the presence of individuals of different ages and of differing physical and other capacities (Kluckhohn, 1962:317–18).

Many authors in the second half of the twentieth century have speculated about the nature of the basic problems of societies that would present distinct dimensions of culture (for a review see Hofstede, 2001, 29–31). The most common dimension used for ordering societies is their degree of economic evolution or modernity. A one-dimensional ordering of societies from traditional to modern fitted well with the nineteenth- and twentieth-century belief in progress. Economic evolution is bound to be reflected in people's collective mental programming, but there is no reason why economic and technological evolution should suppress other cultural variety. There must be dimensions of culture unrelated to economic evolution.

U.S. anthropologist Edward T. Hall (1976) divided cultures according to their ways of communicating, into high-context (much of the information is implicit) and low-context (nearly everything is explicit). In practice this distinction overlaps largely with the traditional versus modern distinction.

U.S. sociologists Talcott Parsons and Edward Shils (1951:77) suggested that all human action is determined by five *pattern variables*, choices between pairs of alternatives:

1. *Affectivity* (need gratification) versus *affective neutrality* (restraint of impulses);
2. *Self-orientation* versus *collectivity-orientation*;
3. *Universalism* (applying general standards) versus *particularism* (taking particular relationships into account);

4. *Ascription* (judging others by who they are) versus *achievement* (judging them by what they do);

5. *Specificity* (limiting relations to others to specific spheres) versus *diffuseness* (no prior limitations to nature of relations).

Parsons and Shils claimed that these choices are present at the individual (personality) level, at the social system (group or organization) level, and at the cultural (normative) level. They did not take into account that different variables could operate at different aggregation levels.

U.S. anthropologists Florence Kluckhohn and Fred Strodtbeck (1961:12) ran a field study in five geographically close, small communities in the Southwestern United States: Mormons, Spanish Americans, Texans, Navaho Indians, and Zuni Indians. They distinguished these communities on the following value orientations:

1. An evaluation of human nature (evil—mixed—good);

2. The relationship of man to the surrounding natural environment (subjugation—harmony mastery);

3. The orientation in time (toward past—present—future);

4. The orientation toward activity (being—being in becoming—doing); and

5. Relationships among people (lineality [that is, hierarchically ordered positions]—collaterality [that is, group relationships]—individualism).

Others have extrapolated Kluckhohn and Strodtbeck's classification to all kind of social comparisons, without concern for their geographic limitations, without considering the effect of levels of aggregation, and without empirical support.

British anthropologist Mary Douglas (1973) proposed a two-dimensional ordering of ways of looking at the world:

1. "*Group*" or inclusion—the claim of groups over members, and

2. "*Grid*" or classification—the degree to which interaction is subject to rules.

Douglas saw these as relating to a wide variety of beliefs and social actions: views of nature, traveling, spatial arrangements, gardening, cookery, medicine,

the meaning of time, age, history, sickness, and justice. She seemed to imply that these dimensions are applicable to any level of aggregation.

The one- or more-dimensional classifications above represent subjective reflective attempts to order a complex reality. Each of them is strongly colored by the subjective choices of its author(s). They show some overlap, but their lack of clarity about and mixing of levels of analysis (individual–group–culture) are severe methodological weaknesses.

These weaknesses were avoided in an extensive review article by U.S. sociologist Alex Inkeles and psychologist Daniel Levinson (1954). The authors limited themselves to culture at the level of nations, and they summarized all available sociological and anthropological studies dealing with what was then called *national character,* which they interpreted as a kind of modal (most common) personality type in a national society. What I have labeled *dimensions* they called *standard analytic issues.* They proposed

> To concentrate, for purposes of comparative analysis, on a limited number of psychological issues … that meet at least the following criteria. First, they should be found in adults universally, as a function both of maturational potentials common to man and of sociocultural characteristics common to human societies. Second, the manner in which they are handled should have functional significance for the individual personality as well as for the social system (1969:44).

From their survey of the literature Inkeles and Levinson distilled three standard analytic issues that met these criteria:

1. Relation to authority;

2. Conception of self, including the individual's concepts of masculinity and femininity; and

3. Primary dilemmas or conflicts, and ways of dealing with them, including the control of aggression and the expression versus inhibition of affect.

As will be shown below, Inkeles and Levinson's standard analytic issues were empirically supported in a study by this author more than 20 years later.

## EMPIRICAL APPROACHES AND THE HOFSTEDE DIMENSIONS

In 1949, U.S. psychologist Raymond Cattell published an application of the new statistical technique of factor analysis to the comparison of nations. Cattell had earlier used factor analysis for studying aspects of intelligence from test scores of individual students. This time he took a matrix of nation-level variables for a large number of countries, borrowing from geography, demographics, history, politics, economics, sociology, law, religion and medicine. The resulting factors were difficult to interpret, except for the important role of economic development. Replications of his method by others produced trivial results (for a review see Hofstede, 2001:32–33). More meaningful were applications to restricted facets of societies. U.S. political scientists Phillip Gregg and Arthur Banks (1965) studied aspects of political systems; U.S. economists Irma Adelman and Cynthia Taft Morris (1967) studied factors influencing the development of poor countries, and Irish psychologist Richard Lynn (1971; with S.L. Hampson, 1975) studied aspects of mental health.

In the 1970s this author more or less by accident got access to a large survey database about values and related sentiments of people in over fifty countries around the world (Hofstede, 1980). These people worked in the local subsidiaries of one large multinational corporation: IBM. Most parts of the organization had been surveyed twice over a four-year interval, and the database contained more than 100,000 questionnaires. Initial analyses of the database at the level of individual respondents proved confusing, but a breakthrough occurred when the focus was directed at correlations between mean scores of survey items at the level of countries. Patterns of correlation at the country level could be strikingly different from what was found at the individual level, and needed an entirely different interpretation. One of the weaknesses of much cross-cultural research is not being aware of the difference between analysis at the individual level and at the culture level. This leads to what I call a reverse ecological fallacy. In an impressive review of 180 studies using my work by Kirkman et al. (2006), more than half failed to distinguish individual level results from culture-level generalizations, which led to numerous errors of interpretation and application.

My hunch that the IBM data might have implications beyond this particular corporation was supported when I got the opportunity to administer a number of the same questions to nearly 400 management trainees from some 30 countries in an international program unrelated to IBM. Their mean scores by country correlated significantly with the country scores obtained from the IBM database. So it seemed that employees of this multinational—a very special kind of people—could serve for identifying differences in *national* value systems. The reason is that from one country to another they represented almost perfectly matched samples: they were similar in all respects except nationality, which made the effect of national differences in their answers stand out unusually clearly.

Encouraged by the results of the country-level correlation analysis I then tried country-level factor analysis. The latter was similar to the approach used earlier by Cattell and others, except that now the variables in the matrix were not indices for the country as a whole, but mean scores and sometimes percentages of survey answers collected from individuals in those countries. Analyses of data at higher levels of aggregation are sometimes called *ecological*. Ecological factor analysis differs from the factor analysis of individual scores in that a usual caution no longer applies: the number of cases does not need to be (much) larger than the numbers of variables. The stability of the results of an ecological factor analysis does not depend on the number of cases, but on the number of individuals whose scores were aggregated into these cases. One may even start from a matrix with fewer cases than variables.

Factor analyzing a matrix of 32 values questions for initially 40 countries, I found these values to cluster very differently from what was found at the individual level. The new factors revealed common problems with which IBM employees in all these societies had to cope, but for which their upbringing in their country presented its own profile of solutions. These problems were:

1. Dependence on superiors;
2. Need for rules and predictability, also associated with nervous stress;
3. The balance between individual goals and dependence on the company;

4. The balance between ego values (like the need for money and careers) and social values (like cooperation and a good living environment). The former were more frequently chosen by men, the latter by women, but there were also country differences.

These empirical results were strikingly similar to the *standard analytical* issues described in Inkeles and Levinson's 1954 article. Dependence on superiors relates to the first, need for predictability to the third, the balance between the individual and the company to the conception of self, and the balance between ego and social values to concepts of masculinity and femininity, which were also classified under the second standard analytic issue.

The four basic problem areas defined by Inkeles and Levinson and empirically supported in the IBM data represent dimensions of national cultures. A dimension is an aspect of a culture that can be measured relative to other cultures. Later, on the basis of research by Canadian psychologist Michael Harris Bond centered in the Far East (Hofstede and Bond, 1988), a fifth dimension was added. These dimensions were labeled (Hofstede, 1991, 2001):

1. *Power Distance*, related to the different solutions to the basic problem of human inequality;

2. *Uncertainty Avoidance*, related to the level of stress in a society in the face of an unknown future;

3. *Individualism* versus *Collectivism*, related to the integration of individuals into primary groups;

4. *Masculinity* versus *Femininity*, related to the division of emotional roles between women and men;

5. *Long Term* versus *Short Term Orientation*, related to the choice of focus for people's efforts: the future or the present and past.

Each country could be positioned relative to other countries through a score on each dimension. The dimensions were statistically distinct and occurred in all possible combinations, although some combinations were more frequent than others.

After the initial confirmation of the country differences in IBM in data from management trainees elsewhere, the IBM dimensions and country scores were validated through replications by others, using the same or similar questions with other cross-national populations. Between 1990 and 2002 six major replications (14 or more countries) used country elites, employees and managers of other corporations and organizations, airline pilots, consumers and civil servants; (see Hofstede and Hofstede, 2005, p. 26).

A breakthrough in the research occurred when country scores on the dimensions turned out to correlate significantly with conceptually related external data. Thus Power Distance scores correlated with a dimension from Gregg and Banks' analysis of political systems and also with a dimension from Adelman and Morris' study of economic development; Uncertainty Avoidance correlated with a dimension from Lynn and Hampson's study of mental health; Individualism correlated strongly with national wealth (Gross National Product per capita) and Femininity with the percentage of national income spent on development aid. These external validations are continued, and the second edition of *Culture's Consequences* (Hofstede, 2001:503–20) lists more than 400 significant correlations between the IBM-based scores and results of other studies. Recent validations show no loss of validity, indicating that the country differences these dimensions describe are, indeed, basic and long-term.

In correlating the dimensions with other data the influence of national wealth (Gross National Product per capita) should always be taken into account. Two of the dimensions, Individualism and small Power Distance, are significantly correlated with wealth. This means that all wealth-related phenomena tend also to correlate with these dimensions. Differences in national wealth can be considered a more parsimonious explanation of these other phenomena than differences in culture. In correlating with the culture dimensions, it is therefore advisable to always include the wealth variable. After controlling for wealth, correlations with culture may disappear. The shared correlation of Individualism and (small) Power Distance with national wealth implies that these dimensions tend to be intercorrelated. However, if national wealth is controlled for, this intercorrelation usually disappears.

Of particular interest is a link that was found between culture according to the Hofstede dimensions and personality dimensions according to the empirically based Big Five personality test (Costa and McCrae, 1992). This test has now been used in over 30 countries, and significant correlations were found between country norms on the personality dimensions (Neuroticism, Extraversion, Openness to experience, Agreeableness and Conscientiousness) and culture dimension scores. For example, 55% of country differences on Neuroticism can be explained by a combination of Uncertainty Avoidance and Masculinity, and 39% of country differences on Extraversion by Individualism alone (Hofstede and McCrae, 2002). So culture and personality are linked but the link is statistical, and should not be used for stereotyping individuals.

Validating the dimensions is of course not only and not even mainly a quantitative issue. Equally important is the qualitative interpretation of what differences on the dimensions mean for each of the societies studied, which calls for an emic approach to each society, linking it to the *etic* of the dimensional data.

# THE HOFSTEDE DIMENSIONS IN A NUTSHELL

In this section I will summarize the content of each dimension, opposing cultures with low and high scores. These oppositions are based on correlations with studies by others, and because the relationship is statistical, not every line applies equally strongly to every country.

*Power Distance* has been defined as the extent to which the less powerful members of organizations and institutions (like the family) accept and expect that power is distributed unequally. This represents inequality (more versus less), but defined from below, not from above. It suggests that a society's level of inequality is endorsed by the followers as much as by the leaders. Power and inequality, of course, are extremely fundamental facts of any society. All societies are unequal, but some are more unequal than others. Table 1.1 lists a selection of differences between national societies that validation research showed to be associated with the Power Distance dimension. For a more complete review the reader is referred to Hofstede, 2001 and/or Hofstede and Hofstede, 2005. The statements refer to extremes; actual situations may be found anywhere in between the extremes, and the association of a statement with a dimension is always statistical, never absolute.

Power distance index scores were higher for East European, Latin, Asian and African countries and lower for Germanic and English-speaking Western countries.

*Uncertainty Avoidance* is not the same as risk avoidance; it deals with a society's tolerance for

**TABLE 1.1** Ten Differences Between Small- and Large- Power Distance Societies

| Small Power Distance | Large Power Distance |
|---|---|
| Use of power should be legitimate and is subject to criteria of good and evil | Power is a basic fact of society antedating good or evil: its legitimacy is irrelevant |
| Parents treat children as equals | Parents teach children obedience |
| Older people are neither respected nor feared | Older people are both respected and feared |
| Student-centered education | Teacher-centered education |
| Hierarchy means inequality of roles, established for convenience | Hierarchy means existential inequality |
| Subordinates expect to be consulted | Subordinates expect to be told what to do |
| Pluralist governments based on majority vote and changed peacefully | Autocratic governments based on co-optation and changed by revolution |
| Corruption rare; scandals end political careers | Corruption frequent; scandals are covered up |
| Income distribution in society rather even | Income distribution in society very uneven |
| Religions stressing equality of believers | Religions with a hierarchy of priests |

ambiguity. It indicates to what extent a culture programs its members to feel either uncomfortable or comfortable in unstructured situations. Unstructured situations are novel, unknown, surprising, different from usual. Uncertainty avoiding cultures try to minimize the possibility of such situations by strict behavioral codes, laws and rules, disapproval of deviant opinions, and a belief in absolute Truth; "there can only be one Truth and we have it". Research has shown that people in uncertainty avoiding countries are also more emotional, and motivated by inner nervous energy. The opposite type, uncertainty accepting cultures, are more tolerant of opinions different from what they are used to; they try to have fewer rules, and on the philosophical and religious level they are relativist and allow different currents to flow side by side. People within these cultures are more phlegmatic and contemplative, and not expected by their environment to express emotions. Table 1.2 lists a selection of differences between societies that validation research showed to be associated with the Uncertainty Avoidance dimension.

Uncertainty avoidance scores are higher in East and Central European countries, in Latin countries, in Japan and in German speaking countries, lower in English speaking, Nordic and Chinese culture countries.

> *Masculinity versus its opposite, Femininity… refers to the distribution of values between the genders.*

*Individualism* on the one side versus its opposite, *Collectivism*, as a societal, not an individual, characteristic, is the degree to which people in a society are integrated into groups. On the individualist side we find cultures in which the ties between individuals are loose: everyone is expected to look after him/herself and his/her immediate family. On the collectivist side we find cultures in which people from birth onwards are integrated into strong, cohesive in-groups, often extended families (with uncles, aunts and grandparents) that continue protecting them in exchange for unquestioning loyalty. Again, the issue addressed by this dimension is an extremely fundamental one, regarding all societies in the world. Table 1.3 lists a selection of differences between societies that validation research showed to be associated with this dimension.

Individualism prevails in developed and Western countries, while collectivism prevails in less-developed and Eastern countries; Japan takes a middle position on this dimension.

*Masculinity* versus its opposite, *Femininity*, again as a national, not as an individual characteristic, refers

**TABLE 1.2** Ten Differences Between Weak- and Strong- Uncertainty Avoidance Societies

| Weak Uncertainty Avoidance | Strong Uncertainty Avoidance |
| --- | --- |
| The uncertainty inherent in life is accepted and each day is taken as it comes | The uncertainty inherent in life is felt as a continuous threat that must be fought |
| Ease, lower stress, self-control, low anxiety | Higher stress, emotionality, anxiety, neuroticism |
| Higher scores on subjective health and well-being | Lower scores on subjective health and well-being |
| Tolerance of deviant persons and ideas: what is different is curious | Intolerance of deviant persons and ideas: what is different is dangerous |
| Comfortable with ambiguity and chaos | Need for clarity and structure |
| Teachers may say 'I don't know' | Teachers supposed to have all the answers |
| Changing jobs no problem | Staying in jobs even if disliked |
| Dislike of rules—written or unwritten | Emotional need for rules—even if not obeyed |
| In politics, citizens feel and are seen as competent towards authorities | In politics, citizens feel and are seen as incompetent towards authorities |
| In religion, philosophy and science: relativism and empiricism | In religion, philosophy and science: belief in ultimate truths and grand theories |

**TABLE 1.3** Ten Differences Between Collectivist and Individualist Societies

| Individualism | Collectivism |
|---|---|
| Everyone is supposed to take care of him- or herself and his or her immediate family only | People are born into extended families or clans which protect them in exchange for loyalty |
| "I"—consciousness | "We"—consciousness |
| Right of privacy | Stress on belonging |
| Speaking one's mind is healthy | Harmony should always be maintained |
| Others classified as individuals | Others classified as in-group or out-group |
| Personal opinion expected: one person one vote | Opinions and votes predetermined by in-group |
| Transgression of norms leads to guilt feelings | Transgression of norms leads to shame feelings |
| Languages in which the word "I" is indispensable | Languages in which the word "I" is avoided |
| Purpose of education is learning how to learn | Purpose of education is learning how to do |
| Task prevails over relationship | Relationship prevails over task |

to the distribution of values between the genders, which is another fundamental issue for any society to which a range of solutions are found. The IBM studies revealed that (a) women's values differ less among societies than men's values; (b) men's values from one country to another contain a dimension from very assertive and competitive and maximally different from women's values on the one side, to modest and caring and similar to women's values on the other. The assertive pole has been called "masculine" and the modest, caring pole "feminine." The women in feminine countries have the same modest, caring values as the men; in the masculine countries they are somewhat assertive and competitive, but not as much as the men, so that these countries show a gap between men's values and women's values. In masculine cultures there is sometimes a taboo around this dimension (Hofstede et al., 1998). Taboos are based on deeply rooted values; this taboo shows that the Mas/Fem dimension in some societies touches basic and often unconscious values, too painful to be explicitly discussed. In fact, the taboo validates the importance of the dimension. Table 1.4 lists a selection of differences between societies that validation research showed to be associated with this dimension.

Masculinity is high in Japan, in German-speaking countries, and in some Latin countries like Italy and Mexico; it is moderately high in English speaking Western countries; it is low in Nordic countries and in the Netherlands and moderately low in some Latin and Asian countries like France, Spain, Portugal, Chile, Korea and Thailand.

*Long-Term* versus *Short-Term Orientation*: This fifth dimension was found in a study among students in 23 countries around the world, using a questionnaire designed by Chinese scholars (Hofstede and Bond, 1988). Values associated with Long Term Orientation are thrift and perseverance; values associated with Short Term Orientation are respect for tradition, fulfilling social obligations, and protecting one's "face." Both the positively and the negatively rated values of this dimension are found in the teachings of Confucius around 500 B.C. So it is not correct to equal Long-Term Orientation with Confucianism; it represents a focus on the future-oriented maxims of Confucianism, at the expense of the past-oriented ones. Also, the dimension applies equally well to countries without a Confucian heritage. Table 1.5 lists a selection of differences between societies that validation research showed to be associated with this dimension.

Long-term oriented are East Asian countries, in particular China, Hong Kong, Taiwan, Japan, and South Korea but to a lesser extent also India and Brazil. A medium term orientation is found in most

**TABLE 1.4** Ten Differences Between Feminine and Masculine Societies

| Femininity | Masculinity |
|---|---|
| Minimum emotional and social role differentiation between the genders | Maximum emotional and social role differentiation between the genders |
| Men and women should be modest and caring | Men should be and women may be assertive and ambitious |
| Balance between family and work | Work prevails over family |
| Sympathy for the weak | Admiration for the strong |
| Both fathers and mothers deal with facts and feelings | Fathers deal with facts, mothers with feelings |
| Both boys and girls may cry but neither should fight | Girls cry, boys don't; boys should fight back, girls shouldn't fight |
| Mothers decide on number of children | Fathers decide on family size |
| Many women in elected political positions | Few women in elected political positions |
| Religion focuses on fellow human beings | Religion focuses on God or gods |
| Matter-of-fact attitudes about sexuality; sex is a way of relating | Moralistic attitudes about sexuality; sex is a way of performing |

**TABLE 1.5** Ten Differences Between Short- and Long-Term-Oriented Societies

| Short-Term Orientation | Long-Term Orientation |
|---|---|
| Most important events in life occurred in the past or take place now | Most important events in life will occur in the future |
| Immediate need gratification expected | Need gratification deferred until later |
| There are universal guidelines about what is good and evil | What is good and evil depends upon the circumstances |
| Traditions are sacrosanct | Traditions are adaptable to changed circumstances |
| Family life guided by imperatives | Family life guided by shared tasks |
| What one thinks and says should be true | What one does should be virtuous |
| Children should learn tolerance and respect | Children should learn to be thrifty |
| Social spending and consumption | Saving, investing |
| Unstructured problem solving | Structured, mathematical problem solving |
| In business, stress on short-term profits | In business, stress on future market position |

European countries, but the United States and Britain are more short term oriented. A very short-term orientation is found in Africa and in a number of Islamic countries.

# OTHER APPLICATIONS OF THE DIMENSIONAL PARADIGM

When *Culture's Consequences* appeared in 1980, it represented a new paradigm in social science research:

analysing survey-based values data at the national level and quantifying differences between national cultures by positions on these dimensions. Like other new paradigms, it initially met with rejection, criticism and ridicule next to enthusiasm (Kuhn, 1970). By the 1990s the paradigm had been taken over by many others, and discussions shifted to the content and number of dimensions. The paradigm inspired a number of other studies into dimensions of national cultures.

Many studies further explored the dimension of individualism and collectivism (e.g. Kim et al., 1994; Triandis, 1995; Hofstede, 2001: Chapter 5). From all the Hofstede dimensions, this one met with the most positive reactions among psychologists, especially in the U.S.A., which happened to be the highest scoring country on it. Ind/Col scores were strongly correlated with national wealth, which led some people to the conclusion that promoting individualism in other cultures would contribute to their economic development. In fact, data show that the causality is most probably reversed: wealth tends to lead to individualism (Hofstede, 2001: 253). The individualism in U.S. culture also led people to studying it at the *individual* level (comparing one person to another), not at the level of societies. In this case it is no longer a dimension of culture but possibly a dimension of personality. Also, there is no more reason why individualism and collectivism need to be opposite; they should rather be considered separate aspects of personality. An extensive review of studies of individualism *at the individual level* was published by Oyserman, Coon and Kemmelmeier (2002). Comparing these studies across societies, they found a different ranking of countries from the Hofstede studies; but Schimmack, Oishi and Diener (2005) proved this was due to a methodological error: Oyserman et al. forgot to control for acquiescence (response set), and the acquiescence in their data was significantly negatively correlated with the object of their study which made their results random.

The cultural focus on the Individualism versus Collectivism dimension led Triandis (1995) to splitting it into horizontal and vertical individualism. This split overlooks the fact that the Hofstede dimension of large versus small Power Distance already covered the horizontal/vertical aspect quite satisfactorily.

From my point of view the horizontal/vertical distinction for Ind/Col as a dimension of culture is redundant. It may be useful at the individual level, but this is for others to decide.

Like individualism and collectivism, the terms masculinity and femininity have also been used for describing values at the individual level. Earlier studies by U.S. psychologist Sandra Bem (1974) showed already that in this case masculinity and femininity should again rather be treated as separate aspects than as opposite poles.

An important alternative application of the dimensional paradigm was developed by the Israeli psychologist Shalom Schwartz. From a survey of the literature, Schwartz composed a list of 56 values. Through a network of colleagues he collected scores from samples of elementary school teachers and of college students in over 50 countries. (Schwartz, 1994; Schwartz and Bardi, 2001). Respondents scored the importance of each value 'as a guiding principle in my life'. Schwartz at first assumed the same dimensions would apply to individuals and to countries, but his data showed he needed different classifications at different levels. At the country level he distinguished seven dimensions: Conservatism, Hierarchy, Mastery, Affective autonomy, Intellectual autonomy, Egalitarian commitment and Harmony. Country scores for teachers published by Schwartz in 1994 were significantly correlated with the IBM scores for Individualism, Masculinity and Uncertainty Avoidance (Hofstede, 2001, p. 265).

Another large scale application was the GLOBE (Global Leadership and Organizational Behavior Effectiveness) project, conceived by US management scholar Robert J. House in 1991. At first House focused on leadership, but soon the study branched out into other aspects of national and organizational cultures. In the period 1994–1997 some 170 voluntary collaborators collected data from about 17,000 managers in nearly 1,000 local (non-multinational) organizations belonging to one of three industries: food processing, financial services, and telecommunication services, in some 60 societies throughout the world. In the preface to the book describing the project (House et al., 2004), House writes "We have a very adequate dataset to replicate Hofstede's (1980) landmark study and extend that study to test hypotheses relevant to relationships among societal-level variables, organizational practices, and leader attributes and behavior".

For conceptual reasons GLOBE expanded the five Hofstede dimensions to nine. They maintained the labels Power Distance and Uncertainty Avoidance (but not necessarily their meaning). They split Collectivism into Institutional Collectivism and In-Group Collectivism, and Masculinity–Femininity into Assertiveness and Gender Egalitarianism. Long Term Orientation became Future Orientation. They added two more dimensions: Humane Orientation and Performance Orientation. The nine dimensions were covered by 78 survey questions, half of them asking respondents to describe their culture ("as is") and the other half to judge it ("should be"). GLOBE thus produced 9 × 2 = 18 culture scores for each country: nine dimensions "as is" and nine dimensions "should be."

In an evaluation of the GLOBE project (Hofstede, forthcoming), I re–factor analyzed the country scores on GLOBE's 18 dimensions. Five meta-factors emerged, of which the strongest, grouping seven of the 18 measures, was highly significantly correlated with GNP per capita and next with the Hofstede Power Distance dimension. Three more meta-factors were significantly correlated with, respectively, the Hofstede Uncertainty Avoidance, Individualism and Long Term Orientation dimensions. The GLOBE questionnaire contained very few items covering Masculinity in the Hofstede sense, but whatever there was belonged to the fifth meta-factor. The results show that in spite of a very different approach, the massive body of GLOBE data still reflected the structure of the original Hofstede model.

An author sometimes cited as having researched dimensions of national culture is the Dutch management consultant Fons Trompenaars (1993). He distinguished seven conceptual dimensions, the first five borrowed from Parsons and Shils (1951) and the last two from Kluckhohn and Strodtbeck (1961), which he applied to the level of nations (see earlier in this article). Trompenaars collected a database of survey items related to these dimensions, but in the only statistical analysis of his data published so far, applying Multidimensional Scaling to some 9,000 questionnaires, only two interpretable factors emerged,

both correlated with Hofstede's Individualism, one of these also with Power Distance (Smith, Trompenaars and Dugan, 1995; Smith, Dugan and Trompenaars, 1996). The only country scores that could be based on Trompenaars' data refer to these two flavors of individualism (Smith, Peterson and Schwartz, 2002). Trompenaars' claim to seven dimensions therefore lacks empirical support.

One large international survey effort that developed independently from the search for cultural dimensions is the World Values Survey led by U.S. political scientist Ronald Inglehart. A study of values via public opinion surveys was started in the early 1980s as the European Values Survey. In 1990 a second round was started, renamed the World Values Survey (WVS). It eventually covered some 60,000 respondents across 43 societies, representing about 70 percent of the world's population with a questionnaire including more than 360 forced-choice questions. Areas covered were ecology, economy, education, emotions, family, gender and sexuality, government and politics, health, happiness, leisure and friends, morality, religion, society and nation, and work (Inglehart, Basañez and Moreno, 1998; Inglehart et al., 2004). Although the search for dimensions was not a primary purpose of this study, Inglehart in an overall statistical analysis found two key country-level factors which he called: "Well-being versus survival" and "Secular-rational versus traditional authority" (Inglehart, 1997, p. 81–98). These were again significantly correlated with the Hofstede dimensions: Well-being versus survival correlated with a combination of Individualism and Masculinity; Secular-rational versus traditional authority negatively with Power Distance. Further analysis of the enormous WVS survey data bank may produce additional dimensions; one promising example follows.

## EXPANDING THE HOFSTEDE DIMENSIONAL MODEL WITH NEW DATA: MINKOV'S CONTRIBUTION

The first, 1980 edition of *Culture's Consequences* was inspired by my personal experiences as a psychologist on the international staff of IBM, and its research base was the data bank of employee attitude survey scores collected by the IBM World Trade Corporation across more than fifty national subsidiaries. At that time (the mid-1970s), the IBM database was very likely the largest cross-national collection of comparative value statements in the world.

Now, more than thirty years later, a number of new cross-national databases of value measurements have been created and made accessible to the researcher. If I had to start from scratch now, I would select the most relevant data from presently available sources like the World Values Survey. The second, 2001 edition of *Culture's Consequences* where possible correlates my IBM-based dimension scores with such new data. I considered a continuing search into the ever-expanding body of data highly desirable, but beyond my possibilities. Much to my pleasure, Professor Michael Minkov from Sofia, Bulgaria, who some ten years ago crossed my path, took up this challenge, as he proved with his 2007 book *What Makes Us Different and Similar*.

My cooperation with Minkov and two other colleagues led to a new, 2008 version of the Values Survey Module, a set of questions available to researchers who wish to replicate my research into national culture differences. Earlier versions were issued in 1982 (VSM82) and 1994 (VSM94). Next to the established five Hofstede dimensions, the VSM08 includes, on an experimental basis, two new dimensions from Minkov: Indulgence versus Restraint, and Monumentalism versus Self-Effacement (or Flexumility).

The Values Survey Module (VSM) can be downloaded from www.geerthofstede.nl. Aspiring users should carefully study the accompanying Manual before they decide to collect their own data. In most cases, the use of existing quality research is to be preferred above amateur replications.

## DIMENSIONS OF ORGANIZATIONAL CULTURES

The dimensional paradigm has also been applied at the level of organizations. A research project similar to the IBM studies but focusing on organization rather than national cultures was carried out by this author and a team of collaborators in the 1980s (Hofstede *et al.*, 1990). Qualitative and quantitative data were collected in twenty work organizations or parts of organizations in the Netherlands and Denmark. The units studied varied from a toy manufacturing company to two municipal police corps. This study found large differences among units in perceptions of daily practices but only modest differences in values, beyond those due to such basic facts as nationality, education, gender and age group.

Six independent dimensions are used to describe the larger part of the variety in organization practices. These six dimensions can be used as a framework to describe organization cultures, but their research base in twenty units from two countries is too narrow to consider them as universally valid and sufficient. For describing organization cultures in other countries and/or in other types of organizations, additional dimensions may be necessary or some of the six may be less useful. The six dimensions were:

> *The dimensional paradigm has also been applied at the level of organizations.*

1. *Process-oriented* versus *results-oriented*. Process-oriented cultures are dominated by technical and bureaucratic routines, results-oriented by a common concern for outcomes. This dimension was associated with the culture's degree of homogeneity: in results-oriented units, everybody perceived their practices in about the same way; in process-oriented units, there were vast differences in perception among different levels and parts of the unit. The degree of homogeneity of a culture is a measure of its 'strength': the study confirmed that strong cultures are more results-oriented than weak ones, and vice versa (Peters & Waterman, 1982).

2. *Job-oriented* versus *employee-oriented*. The former assume responsibility for the employees' job performance only, and nothing more; employee-oriented cultures assume a broad responsibility for their members' well-being. At the level of individual managers, the distinction between job orientation and employee orientation has been popularized by Blake and Mouton's Managerial Grid (1964). The Hofstede *et al.* study shows that job versus employee orientation is part of a culture and not (only) a choice for an individual

manager. A unit's position on this dimension seems to be largely the result of historical factors, like the philosophy of its founder(s) and the presence or absence in its recent history of economic crises with collective layoffs.

3. *Professional* versus *parochial*. In the former, the (usually highly educated) members identify primarily with their profession; in the latter, the members derive their identity from the organization for which they work. Sociology has long known this dimension as 'local' versus 'cosmopolitan', the contrast between an internal and an external frame of reference (Merton, 1949).

4. *Open systems* versus *closed systems*. This dimension refers to the common style of internal and external communication, and to the ease with which outsiders and newcomers are admitted. This is the only one of the six dimensions for which a systematic difference was found between Danish and Dutch units. It seems that organizational openness is a societal characteristic of Denmark more than of the Netherlands. This shows that organization cultures also contain elements from national culture differences.

5. *Tight* versus *loose control*. This dimension deals with the degree of formality and punctuality within the organization; it is partly a function of the unit's technology: banks and pharmaceutical companies can be expected to show tight control, research laboratories and advertising agencies loose control; but even with the same technology some units may still be tighter or looser than others.

6. *Pragmatic* versus *normative*. The last dimension describes the prevailing way (flexible or rigid) of dealing with the environment, in particular with customers. Units selling services are likely to be found towards the pragmatic (flexible) side, units involved in the application of laws and rules towards the normative (rigid) side. This dimension measures the degree of 'customer orientation', which is a highly popular topic in the management literature.

The research grounding of these dimensions is documented extensively in Hofstede et al. (1990). Applications and implications can be found in Hofstede and Hofstede (2005, Chapter 8).

## DIMENSIONALITY OF CULTURES IN THE FUTURE

The fact that the world around us is changing does not need to affect the usefulness of the dimensional paradigm; on the contrary, the paradigm can help us understand the internal logic and the implications of the changes.

Some critics suggest that the number of dimensions should be extended. Triandis (2004) has defended this position, and the GLOBE project actually tried to extend the five Hofstede dimensions to eighteen. But additional dimensions are only meaningful if they are both conceptually and statistically independent from those already available, and they should also be validated by significant correlations with conceptually related external measures. There is an epistemological reason why the number of meaningful dimensions will always be small. Dimensions should not be reified. They do not "exist" in a tangible sense. They are constructs: if they exist, it is in our minds. They should help us in understanding and handling the complex reality of our social world. But human minds have a limited capacity for processing information, and therefore dimensional models that are too complex will not be experienced as useful. In a famous little article, Miller (1956) argued that useful classifications should not have more than seven categories, plus or minus two. I would go for the minus rather than the plus.

Within the dimensional model cultures can of course change their position on a dimension. Critics argue that Hofstede country scores based on IBM subsidiaries around 1970 are obsolete. But studies correlating the old country scores with related variables available on a year-by-year basis find no weakening of the correlations. A good reason for this is that the country scores on the five dimensions do not provide *absolute* country positions, but only their positions *relative to the other countries* in the set. The relationship of the dimensions to basic problems of societies and the historical evidence of the continuity of national solutions to such problems suggest that even over much longer periods the measures obtained will retain their validity. Influences like those of new technologies tend to affect all countries without necessarily changing their relative position or ranking; if their cultures change, they change in formation. Only if on a dimension one country leapfrogs over others will the validity of the original scores be reduced. This is a relatively rare occurrence.

Some authors predict that new technologies will make societies more and more similar. Technological modernization is an important force toward culture change and it leads to partly similar developments in different societies, but there is not the slightest proof that it wipes out variety on other dimensions. It may even increase differences, as on the basis of pre-existing value systems societies cope with technological modernization in different ways.

Culture change basic enough to invalidate the country dimension index rankings, or even the relevance of the dimensional model, will need either a much longer period—say, 50 to 100 years—or extremely dramatic outside events. Many differences between national cultures at the end of the 20th century were already recognizable in the years 1900, 1800 and 1700 if not earlier. There is no reason why they should not play a role until 2100 or beyond.

# References

Adelman, I & Morris, C. T. (1967). *Society, Politics and Economic Development: A Quantitative Approach*. Baltimore: Johns Hopkins University Press.

Bem, S. L. (1994). The measurement of psychological androgyny. *Journal of Consulting and Clinical Psychology*, 42, 155–62.

Blake, R. R. & Mouton, J. S. (1964). *The Managerial Grid*. Houston TX: Gulf.

Cattell, R. B. (1949). The dimensions of culture patterns by factorization of national characters. *Journal of Abnormal and Social Psychology*, 44, 443–69.

Costa, P. T., Jr. & McCrae, R. R. (1992). *Revised NEO Personality Inventory (NEO-PI-R) and NEO Five-Factor Inventory (NEO-FFI) Professional Manual*. Odessa FL: Psychological Assessment Resources.

Douglas, M. (1973). *Natural Symbols: Explorations in Cosmology*. Harmondsworth U.K.: Penguin.

Gregg, P. M. & Banks, A. S. (1965). Dimensions of political systems: Factor analysis of a cross-polity survey. *American Political Science Review*, 59, 602–14.

Hall, E. T. (1976). *Beyond Culture*. Garden City NY: Anchor.

Hofstede, G. (1980). *Culture's Consequences: International Differences in Work-Related Values*. Beverly Hills CA: Sage.

Hofstede, G. (1991). *Cultures and Organizations: Software of the Mind*. London: McGraw-Hill U.K.

Hofstede, G. (2001). *Culture's Consequences: Comparing Values, Behaviors, Institutions and Organizations across Nations*. Thousand Oaks CA: Sage.

Hofstede, G. (2006). What did GLOBE really measure? Researchers' minds versus respondents' minds. *Journal of International Business Studies*.

Hofstede, G. & Bond, M. H. (1988). The Confucius connection: from cultural roots to economic growth. *Organizational Dynamics*, 16(4), 4–21.

Hofstede, G. & McCrae, R. R. (2004). Culture and personality revisited: Linking traits and dimensions of culture. *Cross-cultural Research*, 38(1), 52–88.

Hofstede, G. & Hofstede, G. J. (2005). *Cultures and Organizations: Software of the Mind*, Revised and expanded 2nd edition. New York: McGraw-Hill.

Hofstede, G., Neuijen, B., Ohayv, D. D. & Sanders, G. (1990). Measuring organizational cultures: A qualitative and quantitative study across twenty cases. *Administrative Science Quarterly*, 35, 286–316.

Hofstede, G. with Arrindell, W. A., Best, D. L., de Mooij, M. Hoppe, M. H., van de Vliert, E., van Rossum, J. H. A., Verweij, J., Vunderink, M. & Williams, J. E. (1998). *Masculinity and Femininity: The taboo dimension of national cultures*. Thousand Oaks CA: Sage.

House, R. J., Hanges, P. J., Javidan, M., Dorfman, P. W. & Gupta, V. (Eds.) (2004). *Culture, Leadership, and Organizations: The GLOBE Study of 62 Societies*. Thousand Oaks CA: Sage.

Inglehart, R. (1997). *Modernization and Postmodernization: Cultural, Economic, and Political Change in 43 Societies*. Princeton NJ: Princeton University Press.

Inglehart, R., Basañez, M. & Moreno, A. (1998). *Human Values and Beliefs: A Cross-Cultural Sourcebook. Political, Religious, Sexual, and Economic Norms in 43 Societies. Findings from the 1990-1993 World Values Survey*. Ann Arbor: The University of Michigan Press.

Inglehart, R., Basañez, M., Diez-Medrano J., Halman, L. & Luijkx, R. (2004). *Human Beliefs and Values*. Mexico City: Siglo XXI Editores.

Inkeles, A. & Levinson, D. J. (1969[1954]). National character: The study of modal personality and sociocultural systems. In G. Lindzey & E. Aronson (Eds.), *The Handbook of Social Psychology IV* (pp. 418–506). New York: McGraw-Hill.

Kim, U, Triandis, H. C., Kagitçibasi, C. Choi, S. C. & Yoon, G. (Eds., 1994), *Individualism and Collectivism: Theory, Method and Applications*. Thousand Oaks CA: Sage.

Kluckhohn, C. (1962[1952]). Universal categories of culture. In S. Tax (Ed.), *Anthropology Today: Selections* (pp. 304–20). Chicago: University of Chicago Press.

Kluckhohn, F. R. & Strodtbeck, F. L. (1961). *Variations in Value Orientations*. Westport CT: Greenwood Press.

Kuhn, T. S. (1970). *The Structure of Scientific Revolutions*, 2d. ed. Chicago: University of Chicago Press.

Lynn, R. (1971). *Personality and National Character*. Oxford: Pergamon Press.

Lynn, R. & S. L. Hampson (1975). National differences in extraversion and neuroticism. *British Journal of Social and Clinical Psychology, 14*, 223–40.

Merton, R. K. (1968[1949]). *Social Theory and Social Structure*. New York: Free Press.

Miller, G. A. (1956). The magical number seven, plus or minus two: Some limits on our capacity for processing information. *Psychological Review, 63*, 81–97.

Minkov, M. (2007). *What Makes Us Different and Similar: New Interpretation of the World Values Survey and Other Cross-Cultural Data*. Bulgaria: Klasika y Stil Publishing House.

Oyserman, D., Coon, H. M. & Kemmelmeier, M. (2002). Rethinking Individualism and Collectivism: Evaluation of Theoretical Assumptions and Meta-Analyses. *Psychological Bulletin, 128(1)*, 3–72.

Parsons, T. & Shils, E. A. (1951). *Toward a General Theory of Action*. Cambridge MA: Harvard University Press.

Peters, T. J. & Waterman, R. H., Jr. (1982). *In Search of Excellence: Lessons from America's Best-Run Companies*. New York: Harper & Row.

Schimmack, U., Oishi, S. & Diener, E. (2005). Individualism: A valid and important dimension of cultural differences between nations. *Personality and Social Psychology Review, 9*, 17–31.

Schwartz, S. H. (1994). Beyond individualism/collectivism: New cultural dimensions of values. In U. Kim, H. C. Triandis, C. Kagitçibasi, S. C. Choi & G. Yoon (Eds.), *Individualism and Collectivism: Theory, Method and Applications* (pp. 85–119). Thousand Oaks CA: Sage.

Schwartz, S. H. & Bardi, A. (2001). Value hierarchies across culture: Taking a similarities perspective. *Journal of Cross-Cultural Psychology, 32*, 268–90.

Smith, P. B., Trompenaars, F. & Dugan, S. (1995). The Rotter locus of control scale in 43 countries: A test of cultural relativity. *International Journal of Psychology, 30*, 377–400.

Smith, P. B., Dugan, S. & Trompenaars, F. (1996). National culture and the values of organizational employees: A dimensional analysis across 43 nations. *Journal of Cross-Cultural Psychology, 27*, 231–64.

Smith, P. B., Peterson, M. F. & Schwartz, S. H. (2002) Cultural values, sources of guidance, and their relevance to managerial behavior: a 47-nation study. *Journal of Cross-Cultural Psychology, [TX]*, 188–208.

Sondergaard, M. (2002). Values of local government CEOs in job motivation: How do CEOs see the ideal job? In *Social Bonds to City Hall*, P. Dahler-Larsen (Ed.), pp. 57–75. Odense, Denmark: Odense University Press.

Triandis, H. C. (1995). *Individualism and Collectivism*. Boulder CO: Westview.

Triandis, H. C. (2004). The many dimensions of culture. *Academy of Management Executive 18(1)*, 88–93.

Trompenaars, F. (1993). *Riding the Waves of Culture: Understanding Cultural Diversity in Business*. London: Economist Books.

van Nimwegen, T. (2002). *Global banking, global values: The in-house reception of the corporate values of ABN AMRO*. Ph.D. dissertation, Nyenrode University, Delft: Eburon.

## Concepts and Questions

1. Hofstede refers to culture as "a collective phenomenon." How would you explain this? Can you provide some examples?

2. What is the purpose of attempting to categorize or classify cultures through the use of "cultural dimensions"? How would you define a cultural dimension?

3. What are the strengths and weaknesses of the methodology Hofstede used to identify his set of cultural dimensions?

4. Why do you think power distance scores were lower in English-speaking Western countries?

5. Do you see yourself as a high- or low- uncertainty avoidance person? Why?

6. Some scholars contend that traditionally collectivistic-leaning nations are becoming more individualistic. What do you think might be some causes behind a movement from a group focus to an individual focus?

7. According to Hofstede's research, the United States scores moderately high in masculinity. Do you think immigrants to the Unites States will affect this score? In what way?

8. Looking at Hofstede's Short- and Long-Term dimension, what are some of the problems that a U.S. company doing business in China might encounter?

9. Do you think that Hofstede's cultural dimensions model can be a reliable measure of organizational culture? Why?

10. In your opinion, will new and emerging technologies make national cultures more or less similar? What is the basis for your opinion?

# Culture and Conflict

### HARRY C. TRIANDIS

*In the third essay, Harry C. Triandis introduces a different way of approaching intercultural communication. Triandis begins by underscoring one of the propositions of this book—that culture and communication are linked. However, he goes on to show that cultural differences often lead to miscommunication, which can and does cause conflict. This connection becomes evident when he speaks of culture as including "the knowledge that people need to have in order to function effectively in their social environment."*

*To assist you in identifying what "knowledge" is most useful when interacting with another culture, Triandis examines what he calls* cultural syndromes—*"a shared pattern of beliefs, attitudes, self-definitions, norms, and values organized around a theme." In his discussion, Triandis defines, explains, and relates nine different syndromes, and reports that miscommunication can occur when people are not aware of these syndromes. Because effective intercultural communication is dependent on mutual knowledge of contemporary social diversity, we ask you to learn about these syndromes as part of your intercultural communication training.*

A report that appeared in the *New York Times* claimed that on January 9, 1991, at a meeting where the Foreign Minister of Iraq, Tariq Aziz, met the Secretary of State of the United States, James Baker, they miscommunicated. According to the report, Baker was very clear that the United States would attack if Iraq did not leave Kuwait. But he said it calmly. The miscommunication occurred because next to Aziz was seated Saddam Hussein's brother, who paid attention only to how Baker talked, rather than to *what* he said. He reported back to Baghdad, "the Americans will not attack. They are weak. They are calm. They are not angry. They are only talking."

> *Cultural differences often lead to miscommunication, which can and does cause conflict.*

We do know that Western individualist cultures sample mostly the *content* of communications, whereas Eastern collectivist cultures sample mostly the context of communication (Gudykunst, 1993; Triandis, 1994). Thus, it is plausible that Hussein's brother, who had little exposure to the West, did not sample the conversation correctly. Also, Baker did not throw anything at Aziz to show that he was angry. He acted calmly. It is doubtful that Baker could have thrown anything. People cannot change their behavior that drastically, just because they are interacting with members of other cultures. We do not know what report Aziz gave to Hussein, but it is plausible that Hussein paid special attention to his brother's assessment, because trust in collectivist cultures is much greater within the intimate in-group than within the outer in-group. In any case, we do know that a war took place after that meeting. Cultural differences often cause miscommunications and conflict.

Conflict is greater when the two cultures are very different than when they are similar. Technically this difference is called "cultural distance" (Triandis, 1994).

## CULTURAL DISTANCE

Cultural distance is greater when people speak different languages. Even speaking languages that are related can be a problem. For example, the ancient Greek root of *sympathetic* is "to feel together." That is fairly close to the English meaning. But modern Greek, Italian, Spanish, and French use terms that are derived from that root yet mean "a nice, pleasant person." So, "I am sympathetic" does not translate correctly into "Je suis sympatique!"

From *The International Journal of Psychology.* Copyright © 2000, 35(2), 145–152, www.psypress.co.uk. Reprinted by permission of Taylor & Francis. Dr. Harry C. Triandis is Professor Emeritus in the Department of Psychology at the University of Illinois, Urbana-Champaign.

Triandis (1994) listed many funny examples of mistranslations. For instance, at the office of an Italian physician: "Specialist in women and other diseases." Of course, what happens when languages are members of the same language family (say, Indo-European) can be even more of a problem when the languages have very different structures (e.g., tonal or click languages).

Cultural distance is also greater when people have different social structures, such as family structures. Todd (1983) has identified eight types of family structure, and simple terms such as "aunt" may convey different meanings when the family structure is different.

Religion, of course, can be a great source of differences in points of view. Even when one knows that the other person believes something different, there is the problem that humans use themselves as the anchors for such judgments. The diplomat may not believe that it is possible for the other diplomat to have such "outlandish" beliefs. A well-established social psychological phenomenon is called the "false consensus" effect (Mullen et al., 1985). Even when people know about this bias, they cannot wipe it out (Krueger & Clement, 1994). The phenomenon is that if we agree with a particular position, we believe that most other people also agree with it; if we disagree with a particular position, we believe that most people disagree with it. The phenomenon is even stronger when we interact with people who are similar to us in dress, profession, and other characteristics.

Differences in standards of living can create cultural distance. When the cost of sending a letter is a substantial fraction of one's budget, one may not be as likely to send the letter as when the cost is trivial in relation to one's budget.

Values differ substantially between cultures (Schwartz, 1992, 1994). These values are related to the cultural syndromes that we will discuss here.

## MEANING OF CULTURE

Culture is a shared meaning system found among those who speak a particular language dialect, during a specific historic period, in a definable geographic region (Triandis, 1994). It functions to improve the adaptation of members of the culture to a particular ecology, and it includes the knowledge that people need to have in order to function effectively in their social environment.

Cultures differ drastically in the amount of aggression that is found both within and between them. For example, the Lepcha of the Indian Himalayas had one murder two centuries ago (Segall, Ember, & Ember, 1997). Homicide rates in some segments of U.S. society are extremely high. There is evidence that the absence of fathers during socialization is a factor in high rates (Segall et al.). There is some evidence that high between-cultures aggression is related to high within-culture aggression (Segall et al.). Warfare is associated with the unpredictability of resources and conflicts over territory; it is found most usually in societies where aggression within the family is permitted, where the media of communication portray aggression, where there are warlike sports, and where wrongdoing is severely punished (Segall et al.). There is evidence that democracies do not fight with each other (Ember, Ember, & Russett, 1992), so much so that some analysts have argued that it is "counterproductive to support any undemocratic regimes, even if they happen to be enemies of our enemies" (Ember & Ember, 1994).

*Western individualist cultures sample mostly the content of communications, whereas Eastern collectivist cultures sample mostly the context of communication.*

Shared patterns of elements of subjective culture constitute subjective cultural syndromes (Triandis, 1996). A cultural syndrome is a shared pattern of beliefs, attitudes, self-definitions, norms, roles, and values organized around a theme.

Cultural differences are best conceptualized as different patterns of sampling information found in the environment (Triandis, 1989). In collectivist cultures (most traditional cultures, most Asian and Latin American cultures), people are more likely (a) to sample the collective self (reflecting interdependence with others) and to think of themselves as interdependent with their groups (family, coworkers, tribe, coreligionists, country), rather than to sample the individual self (reflecting an independent self) and to see themselves as autonomous individuals who are independent of their groups

(Markus & Kitayama, 1991); (b) to give more priority to the goals of their in-group than to their personal goals (Triandis, 1995); (c) to use in-group norms to shape their behavior more than personal attitudes (Abrams, Ando, & Hinkle, 1998; Suh, Diener, Oishi, & Triandis, 1998); and (d) to conceive of social relationships as communal (Mills & Clark, 1982) rather than in ex-change theory terms (Triandis, 1995). That is, they pay attention to the needs of others and stay in relationships even when that is not maximally beneficial to them. There is evidence that these four aspects are interrelated (Triandis & Gelfand, 1998).

The sampling of collectivists focuses on groups, with people seen as appendages of groups; the sampling of individualists focuses on individuals. A recent example is the coverage of the Kosovo war: CNN and BBC cover the refugees (individuals) in great detail. The Russian and the Serbs present nothing about the refugees on their television. The *Times* of London (April 7, 1999) had a story about a member of the Russian Duma who was so upset that the Russian TV did not mention the refugees at all that he went on a hunger strike. Finally, 12 days into the war, an independent Russian station mentioned the refugees. We called a friend in Belgrade and asked her whether she knew why NATO was bombing her city. She did not! Of course, such control of information is part of the war effort, but when it is consistent with the culture, it is a natural bias.

Culture shapes us, so we pay more attention to individuals and to the internal processes of individuals (attitudes, beliefs) if we are raised in an individualist culture, and more attention to groups, roles, norms, duties, and intergroup relationships if we are raised in a collectivist culture. Collectivist cultures have languages that do not require the use of "I" and "you" (Kashima & Kashima, 1997, 1998). They also have many culture-specific relational terms that are not found in individualist cultures, such as *philo-limo* in Greek (Triandis, 1972), which is a positive attribute of an individual who does what the in-group expects; *amae* in Japanese, which reflects tolerance of deviation from norms by a dependent person (Yamaguchi, 1998); and *simpatia* among Latin

> *Cultural differences are best conceptualized as different patterns of sampling information found in the environment.*

Americans (Triandis, Marin, Lisansky, & Betancourt, 1984), which reflects the expectation that social relationships will include mostly positive and very few negative behaviors.

Collectivists use action verbs (e.g., he offered to help) rather than state verbs (e.g., he is helpful). This is because they prefer to use context in their communications. Zwier (1997), in four studies, obtained support for this cultural difference. Specifically, she found that the accounts of events given by Turkish and Dutch students show this difference. She content-analyzed the radio commentaries of Turkish and Dutch radio personalities and found the same difference. She asked Turkish and Dutch students to write a letter requesting a favor, and content-analyzed the letters. She examined the writing of Turkish/Dutch bilinguals when writing in the two languages, and found the same pattern.

The contrasting cultural pattern is individualism. Here people tend to (a) sample the individual self—this pattern is very common in North and Western Europe, North America (except Mexico), Australia, and New Zealand, where the self is conceived as independent of in-groups; (b) give priority to personal goals; (c) use attitudes much more than norms as determinants of their social behavior; and (d) pay attention only to their own needs and abandon interpersonal relationships that are not optimally beneficial to them. Individualist cultures have languages that require the use of "I" and "you" (Kashima & Kashima, 1997, 1998). English is a good example. It would be difficult to write a letter in English without using these words. Individualists are very positive about "me" and "we," whereas collectivists are sometimes ambivalent about "me" but very positive about "we."

## CULTURAL SYNDROMES
### Complexity

Some cultures (e.g., hunters and gatherers) are relatively simple, and other cultures (e.g., information societies) are relatively complex. The organizing theme of the syndrome is complexity. For example, in complex societies one finds subgroups with different beliefs and attitudes, whereas in simple societies individuals are in considerable agreement about their beliefs and attitudes. In fact, cultural uniformity and conformity are higher in simple than in complex societies. Simple cultures have few jobs; if we take into account specialties such as urologist and general practitioner, complex cultures have a quarter of a million different jobs (see Dictionary of Occupational Titles, 1977). The size of settlements is one of the best ways to index cultural complexity (Chick, 1997).

## Tightness

Tight cultures have many rules, norms, and ideas about what is correct behavior in each situation; loose cultures have fewer rules and norms. In tight cultures, people become quite upset when others do not follow the norms of the society, and may even kill those who do not behave as expected, whereas in loose cultures people are tolerant of many deviations from normative behaviors.

Thus, conformity is high in tight cultures. In Thailand, which is a loose culture, the expression *"mai bin rai"* (never mind) is used frequently. In Japan, which is a tight culture, people are sometimes criticized for minor deviations from norms, such as having too much suntan, or having curly hair (Kidder, 1992). Most Japanese live in fear that they will not act properly (Iwao, 1993).

> *Tight cultures have many rules, norms, and ideas about what is correct behavior in each situation; loose cultures have fewer rules and norms.*

Tightness is more likely when the culture is relatively isolated from other cultures, so that consensus about what is proper behavior can develop. It is also more likely that tightness will occur in situations where people are highly interdependent (when the other deviates from norms it hurts the relationship) and where there is a high population density (high density requires norms so that people will not hurt each other; also, when the other deviates one notices it).

When cultures are at the intersection of great cultures (e.g., Thailand is at the intersection of China and India), contradictory norms may be found, and people cannot be too strict in imposing norms. Also, when the population density is low, it may not even be known that a person who is miles away has behaved improperly. Cosmopolitan cities are loose, except when they have ethnic enclaves, which can be very tight, whereas small communities are relatively tight.

## Individualism and Collectivism

Triandis (1994) has suggested that individualism emerges in societies that are both complex and loose; collectivism, in societies that are both simple and tight. For example, theocracies or monasteries are both tight and relatively poor; Hollywood stars live in a culture that is both complex and loose. This speculation has not been tested rigorously, but the data seem to hang together reasonably well. It may be the case, for instance, that contemporary Japan, which is now quite complex, is less collectivist than the Japan of the 19th century. In fact, reports of 19th-century travelers to Japan (see Edgerton, 1985) mentioned hundreds of rules for how to laugh, sit, and so on, that apparently no longer operate in modern Japan.

Bond and Smith (1996) did a meta-analysis of studies of conformity that used the Asch paradigm, and found that collectivist cultures were higher in conformity than individualist cultures. This is what we would expect if tightness and collectivism were closely linked.

Kim and Markus (1998) showed that in the West people see "uniqueness" as desirable, whereas in East Asia it is often seen as "deviance"; in the West "conformity" is sometimes seen as undesirable, but in East Asia it is seen as "harmony." For example, content analyses of advertisements from the United States and Korea show different frequencies of uniqueness and conformity themes. Conformity themes were used by 95% of the Korean and 65% of the American advertisements; uniqueness themes were used by 89% of the American and 49% of the Korean advertisements.

## Vertical and Horizontal Cultures

Vertical cultures accept hierarchy as a given. People are different from each other. Hierarchy is a natural state. Those at the top "naturally" have more power and privileges than those at the bottom of the hierarchy. Horizontal cultures accept equality as a given. People are basically similar, and if one is to divide any resource it should be done equally (Triandis, 1995).

## Active–Passive Cultures

In active cultures, individuals try to change the environment to fit them; in passive cultures, people change themselves to fit into the environment (Diaz-Guerrero, 1979). The active cultures are more competitive and action oriented, and emphasize self-fulfillment; the passive ones are more cooperative, emphasize the experience of living, and are especially concerned with getting along with others. In general, individualist cultures are more active than collectivist cultures, though the relationship between the two cultural syndromes is not strong.

## Universalism–Particularism

In universalist cultures, people try to treat others on the basis of universal criteria (e.g., all competent persons, regardless of who they are in terms of sex, age, race, etc., are acceptable employees); in particularist cultures, people treat others on the basis of who the other person is (e.g., I know Joe Blow and he is a good person, so he will be a good employee; Parsons, 1968). In general, individualists are universalists and collectivists are particularists.

## Diffuse–Specific

Diffuse cultures respond to the environment in a holistic manner (e.g., I do not like your report means I do not like you). Specific cultures discriminate different aspects of the stimulus complex (e.g., I do not like your report says nothing about liking you; Foa & Chemers, 1967).

## Instrumental–Expressive

People may sample more heavily attributes that are instrumental (e.g., get the job done) or expressive (e.g., enjoy the social relationship). In general, individualists are more instrumental and collectivists are more expressive. When Latin Americans meet a friend in the street, they are likely to stop and chat, even when they are late for an appointment. The importance of the social relationship eclipses the importance of the instrumental relationship (Levine & Norenzayan, 1999).

## Emotional Expression or Suppression

People may express their emotions freely, no matter what the consequences, or they may control the expression of emotion. The free expression of negative emotions can disrupt relationships, so collectivists tend to control such emotions. Individualists are often high in emotional expression. For example, Stephan, Stephan, and de Vargas (1996) tested the hypothesis that people in collectivist cultures would feel less comfortable expressing negative emotions than people in individualist cultures, and found strong support for that hypothesis.

In addition, the instigation of emotion is often culture specific. Stipek, Weiner, and Li (1989) found that when Americans were asked to recall what made them angry, they remembered mostly events that happened to them personally; when Chinese were given that task, they remembered mostly events that occurred to other people. This self-focus versus other-focus is an important contrast between individualism and collectivism (Kagiteibasi, 1997).

## The Weights Given to Different Attributes in Social Perception

In addition to sampling different attributes, members of different cultures give different weights to the attributes that they sample. For example, in a conflict situation, an individual might sample the ethnicity of the other person, his profession, and his competence. Members of some cultures will give most of the weight to ethnicity and react to the other person on the basis of ethnicity; members of other cultures will give most of the weight to competence and profession, and disregard ethnicity. Triandis (1967) reviewed many cross-cultural studies showing differences in the weights used in social perception. In general, members of collectivist cultures tend to sample and weigh ascribed attributes more heavily, whereas members of individualist cultures sample and weigh achieved attributes more heavily. One can identify many more syndromes, such as those reflected in the Kluckhohn and Strodtbeck (1961) value orientations, the culture of honor (Nisbett &

Cohen, 1996), and others. This introduction is sufficient for our purposes.

## CULTURAL SYNDROMES AND THE SITUATION

Humans have a predisposition to respond that can be traced to culture, but their behavior depends very much more on the situation. For example, all humans have both collectivist and individualist cognitions, but they sample them with different probabilities depending on the situation. When the in-group is being attacked, for instance, most humans become collectivists.

The larger the in-group, the less effective it is likely to be in calling for individuals to do what the in-group authorities want done. A call to arms by a clan leader is more likely to be effective than a call to arms by a state, though penalties may make the latter effective in many countries.

Certain factors increase the probability that the collectivist cognitive system will be activated. This is most likely to happen when (a) the individual knows that most other people in the particular situation are collectivists, which makes the norm that one must act as a collectivist more salient; (b) the individual's membership in a collective is especially salient—for instance, the individual represents a country; (c) within an in-group, the situation emphasizes what people have in common—for instance, common goals; (d) within an in-group, the situation emphasizes that people are in the same collective—for instance, people wear the same uniforms; and (e) within an in-group, the task is cooperative.

Certain factors increase the probability that the individualistic cognitive system will be activated. This is most likely to happen when (a) others in the situation are and behave like individualists, which makes individualist norms more salient; (b) the situation makes the person focus on what makes him or her different from others (Trafimow, Triandis, & Goto, 1991)—for instance, the person is dressed very differently from the rest of the group; and (c) the task is competitive.

> *All humans have both collectivist and individualist cognitions, but they sample them with different probabilities depending on the situation.*

Culture is relevant for understanding conflict in at least two domains: how conflict starts and how conflict evolves. Problems of poor communication are the major causes of the first, and problems of the way members of different cultures treat outgroups are relevant for understanding the second of these domains.

## CULTURAL SYNDROMES AND COMMUNICATION

When people come into contact with members of other cultures, they are often not aware of their miscommunications, because they think that the others are more or less like they are. This is the stage of *unconscious incompetence*. After some interpersonal difficulties, people realize that they are miscommunicating, but they do not know exactly what is wrong. That is the stage of *conscious incompetence*. As they get to know more and more about the culture of the other, they begin communicating correctly, but they have to make an effort to communicate in a different way. That is the stage of *conscious competence*. Finally, after they develop habits of correct communication with members of the other culture, they reach the stage of *unconscious competence* where the communication is effortless and correct.

A very serious problem in communication is that people do not perceive the same "causes" of behavior (Miller, 1984; Morris & Peng, 1994). We call these *attributions*. When the actor thinks that a behavior is due to one cause and the observer thinks that the behavior is due to a different cause, they each give a different meaning to the behavior. For instance, a diplomat may invite another diplomat to dinner. The inviter may do so because he likes the other diplomat. The invitee, however, may use the cause "his boss told him to invite me." Obviously, the meaning of the invitation is different for the two diplomats.

There are training procedures called "culture assimilators" (Fiedler, Mitchell, & Triandis, 1971), which consist of 100 or so episodes involving interactions between members of the two relevant cultures, with each episode followed by four attributions. Usually three attributions are "incorrect" from the point of view of the culture the trainee is learning about, and one is "correct." The trainee selects one attribution, and gets feedback as to whether it is the correct one from the point of view of the culture the trainee is trying to learn about. People who go through this training gradually learn to make the correct attributions from the point of view of the other culture. This reduces miscommunications (Bhawuk, 1998).

There is a well-researched phenomenon regarding attributions. When two groups, A and B, are in conflict, if a member of group B does something "nice," members of group A attribute the behavior to external factors (e.g., he was forced to do it by the circumstances); when a member of group B does something "nasty," members of group A attribute it to internal factors (e.g., they are nasty "by nature"). The attributions that group B makes about the behavior of group A are exact mirror images; that is, when A does something nice it is due to external factors, and when A does something nasty it is due to internal factors. When a member of group A makes attributions about the actions of other members of group A, if the action is positive it is attributed to internal factors and if it is negative it is attributed to external factors.

In all cultures, when we ask actors why they did something, they report external causes, but observers of these actions tend to use causes internal to the actor. This is called the "fundamental attribution error." In short, people all over the world have a tendency to make attributions incorrectly. However, those from individualistic cultures are even worse in this bias than those from collectivist cultures.

Another factor in miscommunications is the tendency of collectivists to sample the context of communications more than individualists, which results in their paying more attention to gestures, eye contact, level of voice, the direction of the two bodies, touching, the distance between the bodies, and the like. There is a large opportunity for errors and misinterpretations in the way people interpret paralinguistic cues. Also, the way people use time can result in misunderstandings, because people from monochronic time cultures are used to carrying out one conversation at a time, whereas people who use polychronic time carry several conversations simultaneously, which confuses and frustrates the users of monochronic time.

The structure of messages can be another source of difficulties. Western people tend to organize their thoughts and messages in a linear fashion: fact 1, fact 2, and so on; generalization; and conclusion. In many other cultures, people start with the conclusion, then find facts that fit the conclusion, and permit deviations from a straight line. In some cases, the argument is like a spiral, starting from general ideological or mystical considerations and gradually zeroing to a conclusion (Triandis, 1994). The extent to which ideology versus pragmatic matters are sampled also varies with culture. Glenn (1981) gave an interesting example. At a UN conference, the Russians advocated the use of reinforced concrete structures (ideal for all), whereas the American delegates said that "it depends on what works best" (pragmatic). Delegates from the Third World interpreted the exchange in favor of the Russians. They thought that the Americans were saying that "we are not good enough to use what they are using."

When a universalist meets a particularist, there can be interpersonal difficulties. For example, when presenting a position, the universalist may expect that all the facts will "fit in" with the position, whereas the particularist may not consider this necessary. When such expectations are present, the particularist might need to start the presentation with a universalist position (e.g., "we are all in favor of peace") and then present the particularist view.

Another source of miscommunication is that in some cultures communication is "associative" and in others "abstractive." In the West, it is typically abstractive; that is, one abstracts the most important elements of the argument and organizes them for the presentation. An associative presentation can present anything that is vaguely related to the point, which can frustrate the Westerner (Szalay, 1993). For example, in 1932, the finance minister of Japan was assassinated after agreeing to a 17% revaluation of the yen. In 1971, the American Treasury Secretary Connally, oblivious to Japanese history, demanded a 17% revaluation of the yen. His Japanese counterpart rejected it without explanation. When Connally

> *The structure of messages can be another source of difficulties.*

suggested a 16.9% upward revaluation, the Japanese minister accepted it (Cohen, 1991).

Examples of associative communications abound. The *Los Angeles Times*, on February 12, 1977, published a conversation between two Egyptians. One was westernized, and the other was traditional. The communication of the traditional was not understood by the Westernized. Another example was the presentation of the Egyptian ambassador to the UN in 1967, in which he accused the Americans of actively helping the Israelis. The American ambassador asked for proof, but the Egyptian answered that no proof was needed because it was "obvious that the Americans had intervened. How else could one explain that three quarters of the Egyptian air force was destroyed in a few hours? Only a large, powerful country could do this."

In sum, cultural distance can result in miscommunications, which may lead to international conflict. We now turn to the way the conflict is carried out, and look at the role of cultural syndromes in this area.

## CULTURAL SYNDROMES AND CONFLICT

We need to distinguish conflict within the in-group from conflict between groups. Individualism is associated with conflict inside a culture, such as crime or divorce. Collectivism is associated with conflict between groups, such as ethnic cleansing or war.

Factors that have been found to increase aggression (see Triandis, 1994) include biological factors (e.g., high levels of testosterone), social structural factors (such as low family cohesion, few intimate relationships, low father involvement in the upbringing of sons, isolation from kin, and anonymity, all of which are associated with individualism), high levels of arousal (because of frustration, competition), hot weather, modeling (aggressive models, aggressive people receive more status in the society), gender marking (men and women are seen as very different), retaliation, economic inequality, few resources (associated with collectivism), social stress (e.g., high levels of inflation), ease of being aggressive (e.g., availability of weapons), and low costs (aggression does not lead to punishment). Clearly there are many factors, many of which do not have much to do with cultural patterns. Yet culture is important for many of these

factors (Segall et al., 1997). Some of the factors, such as weak families, are associated with individualism and lead to within-group aggression; others are associated with collectivism.

When interacting with in-group members, people from collectivist cultures tend to be unusually sensitive to the needs of the others, supportive, helpful, and even self-sacrificing. However, when interacting with out-group members, they are usually indifferent and, if the two groups have incompatible goals, even hostile.

Once the in-group has been called to action against an out-group by in-group authorities, vertical collectivists are especially likely to become aggressive. This pattern leads to especially high levels of hostility when a "culture of honor" is present. Such cultures are found in situations where there are no police (or other authorities that can resolve conflict), so that people have to protect themselves against intruders by means of their personal efforts (Nisbett & Cohen, 1996). To extrapolate to the international scene, conflict would be higher if international bodies such as the United Nations did not exist.

Certain combinations of cultural syndromes can lead to treating the out-group inhumanely. In simple cultures, the distinction between different kinds of "others" is unlikely to occur. In vertical cultures, there is likely to be a perception that "others" are very different, just as people at the top and bottom of a hierarchy are seen as very different. In active cultures, the elimination of out-groups (e.g., ethnic cleansing) is likely to be seen as an especially good way to change the sociopolitical environment. In universalist cultures, treating all out-group members the same fits the cultural pattern. If one enemy is to be killed, all should be killed. In diffuse cultures, making distinctions between different kinds of enemies is not likely, so that all out-group members are likely to be treated badly. Instrumental cultures may be particularly effective in eliminating their enemies. Thus, when a particular combination of cultural syndromes is found—namely active, universalistic, diffuse, instrumental, vertical collectivism—inhumane treatment of out-groups is likely to occur.

All humans are ethnocentric (Triandis, 1994). That means that they think of their in-group as the standard of what is good and proper, and of other groups as good only to the extent that they are similar to the in-group. Ethnocentrism also results in members of a culture seeing their own norms and behavior as "natural" and "correct" and those of members of other cultures as "unnatural" and "incorrect." Ethnocentrism leads people to see their norms as universally valid; to avoid questioning norms, role definitions, and values; and to help in-group members feel proud of the in-group and, simultaneously, to reject out-groups (Triandis, 1994).

The rejection of out-groups is especially likely to occur in collectivist cultures. In extreme collectivist cultures, out-groups are often seen as "not quite human" and "not deserving any rights." Although individualists are capable of dealing with out-groups in an inhuman way (e.g., the My Lai incident during the Vietnam War), collectivists are even more extreme in dealing with out-groups (e.g., the rape of Nanking, where an estimated 300,000 civilians were killed, Chang, 1997; the Holocaust). Fortunately, the particular combination of active, universalistic, diffuse, instrumental, vertical collectivism is rare, so that such incidents do not occur frequently.

Furthermore, as indicated earlier, typical collectivism is usually incompatible with the active, universalistic, and instrumental syndromes so that the above-mentioned combination is really rare. Nevertheless, in the twentieth century we have witnessed many cases of genocide and ethnic cleansing, so we cannot ignore the data.

One way to avoid these inhuman actions would be to monitor cultures that tend toward this undesirable combination of syndromes and to change them to reduce the probability of occurrence of the particular combination of syndromes. There is very little research about the factors that result in the various syndromes mentioned earlier, but we do know something about the occurrence of collectivism.

## PREVALENCE OF COLLECTIVISM

Collectivism is found in societies that are not affluent (Hofstede, 1980), especially where there is only one normative system—that is, a single culture that is not cosmopolitan. There is a fair amount of evidence about the attributes of collectivism and the causes of the development of this cultural pattern (Triandis, 1990).

Collectivism is also high among the lower social classes of any society (Kohn, 1969; Marshall, 1997), among those who have not traveled (Gerganov, Dilova, Petkova, & Paspalanova, 1996) or been socially mobile, and among those who have not been exposed to the modern mass media (McBride, 1998). When the major economic activity is based on agriculture, rather than on hunting, fishing, industry, or service, collectivism is often high.

Collectivism is thus found in societies that are relatively homogeneous (so that in-group norms can be widely accepted); where population density and job interdependence are high (because they require the development of and adherence to many rules of behavior); among members of the society who are relatively old (Noricks et al., 1987) and who are members of large families (because it is not possible for every member to do his or her own thing); and in groups that are quite religious (Triandis & Singelis, 1998). When the in-group is under pressure from the outside, collectivism increases. Thus, one consideration in international relations is whether the advantages of putting pressure on a country outbalance the disadvantages of increasing the collectivism of the country.

*All humans are ethnocentric.*

## CONCLUSION

We examined two major ways in which culture is related to conflict. One is that cultural distance increases the probability of miscommunication. There are training programs that can overcome this problem. The second is the way a combination of cultural syndromes results in the inhuman treatment of out-groups.

## References

Abrams, D., Ando, K., & Hinkle, S. (1998). Psychological attachment to groups: Cross-cultural differences in organizational identification and subjective norms as predictors of workers' turnover intentions. *Personality and Social Psychology Bulletin, 24,* 1027–1039.

Bhawuk, D. P. S. (1998). The role of culture theory in crosscultural training: A multimethod study of culture specific, culture general, and culture theory-based assimilators. *Journal of Cross-Cultural Psychology, 29,* 630–655.

Bond, R., & Smith, P. B. (1996). Culture and conformity: A meta-analysis of studies using Asch's (1952b, 1956) line judgement task. *Psychological Bulletin, 119,* 111–137.

Chang, I. (1997). *The rape of Nanking: The forgotten holocaust of World War II.* New York: Basic Books.

Chick, G. (1997). Cultural complexity: The concept and its measurement. *Cross-Cultural Research, 31,* 275–307.

Cohen, R. (1991). *Negotiating across cultures.* Washington, DC: United States Institute of Peace.

Diaz-Guerrero, R. (1979). The development of coping style. *Human Development, 22,* 320–331.

*Dictionary of Occupational Titles* (4th ed.). (1977). [Supplements in 1986]. Washington, DC: U.S. Government Publications Office.

Edgerton, R. B. (1985). *Rules, exceptions, and social order.* Berkeley: University of California Press.

Ember, M., & Ember, C. R. (1994). Prescriptions for peace: Policy implications of cross-cultural research on war and interpersonal violence. *Cross-Cultural Research, 28,* 343–350.

Ember, C. R., Ember, M., & Russett, B. (1992). Peace between participatory polities: A cross-cultural test of the "Democracies rarely fight each other" hypothesis. *World Politics, 44,* 573–599.

Fiedler, F. E., Mitchell, T., & Triandis, H. C. (1971). The culture assimilator: An approach to cross-cultural training. *Journal of Applied Psychology, 55,* 95–102.

Foa, U., & Chemers, M. M. (1967). The significance of role behaviour differentiation for cross- cultural interaction training. *International Journal of Psychology, 2,* 45–57.

Gerganov, E. N., Dilova, M. L., Petkova, K. G., & Paspalanova, E. P. (1996). Culture-specific approach to the study of individualism/collectivism. *European Journal of Social Psychology, 26,* 277–297.

Glenn, E. (1981). *Man and mankind: Conflicts and communication between cultures.* Norwood, NJ: Ablex.

Gudykunst, W. (Ed.). (1993). *Communication in Japan and the United States.* Albany: State University of New York Press.

Hofstede, G. (1980). *Culture's consequences.* Beverly Hills, CA: Sage.

Iwao, S. (1993). *The Japanese woman: Traditional image and changing reality.* New York: Free Press.

Kagiteibasi, C. (1997). Individualism and collectivism. In I. W. Berry, M. H. Segall, & C. Kagiteibasi (Eds.), *Handbook of cross-cultural psychology* (2nd ed., pp. 1–50). Boston: Allyn & Bacon.

Kashima, E. S., & Kashima, Y. (1997). Practice of the self in conversations: Pronoun drop, sentence co-production and contextualization of the self. In K. Leung, U. Kim, S. Yamaguchi, & Y. Kashima (Eds.), *Progress in Asian social psychology* (Vol. 1, pp. 165–180). Singapore: Wiley.

Kashima, E. S., & Kashima, Y. (1998). Culture and language: The case of cultural dimensions and personal pronoun use. *Journal of Cross-Cultural Psychology, 29,* 461–486.

Kidder, L. (1992). Requirements for being "Japanese": Stories of returnees. *International Journal of Intercultural Relations, 16,* 383–394.

Kim, H., & Markus, H. R. (1998). *Deviance or uniqueness, harmony or conformity? A cultural analysis.* Unpublished manuscript.

Kluckhohn, F., & Strodtbeck, F. (1961). *Variations in value orientation.* Evanston, IL: Row, Peterson.

Kohn, M. K. (1969). *Class and conformity.* Homewood, IL: Dorsey Press.

Krueger, I., & Clement, R. W. (1994). The truly false consensus effect: An ineradicable egocentric bias in social perception. *Journal of Personality and Social Psychology, 67,* 596–610.

Levine, R. V., & Norenzayan, A. (1999). The pace of life in 31 countries. *Journal of Cross-Cultural Psychology, 30,* 178–205.

Markus, H., & Kitayama, S. (1991). Culture and self: Implications for cognition, emotion and motivation. *Psychological Review, 98,* 224–253.

Marshall, R. (1997). Variances in levels of individualism across two cultures and three social classes. *Journal of Cross-Cultural Psychology, 28,* 490–495.

McBride, A. (1998). Television, individualism, and social capital. *Political Science and Politics 31,* 542–555.

Miller, J. G. (1984). Culture and the development of everyday social explanation. *Journal of Personality and Social Psychology, 46,* 961–978.

Mills, J., & Clark, M. S. (1982). Exchange and communal relationships. In L. Wheeler (Ed.), *Review of personality and social psychology* (Vol. 3, pp. 121–144). Beverly Hills, CA: Sage.

Morris, M. W., & Peng, K. (1994). Culture and cause: American and Chinese attributions for social and physical events. *Journal of Personality and Social Psychology, 67,* 949–971.

Mullen, B., Atkins, J. L., Champion, D. S., Edwards, C., Handy, D., Story, J. E., & Venderklok, M. (1985). The false consensus effect: A meta-analysis of 115 hypothesis tests. *Journal of Experimental Social Psychology, 21,* 262–283.

Nisbett, R. E., & Cohen, D. (1996). *Culture of honor*. Boulder, CO: Westview Press.

Noricks, J. S., Agler, L. H., Bartholomew, M., Howard-Smith, S., Martin, D., Pyles, S., & Shapiro, W. (1987). Age, abstract things and the American concept of person. *American Anthropologist, 89*, 667–675.

Parsons, T. (1968). *The structure of social action*. New York: Free Press.

Schwartz, S. H. (1992). Universals in the content and structure of values: Theoretical advances and empirical tests in 20 countries. In M. Zanna (Ed.), *Advances in experimental social psychology* (Vol. 25, pp. 1–166). New York: Academic Press.

Schwartz, S. H. (1994). Beyond individualism and collectivism: New cultural dimensions of value. In U. Kirn, H. C. Triandis, C. Kagiteibasi, S. C. Choi, & O. Yoon (Eds.), *Individualism and collectivism: Theory, method and applications* (pp. 85–122). Newbury Park, CA: Sage.

Segall, M. H., Ember, C. R., & Ember, M. (1997). Aggression, crime, and warfare. In J. W. Berry, M. H. Segall, & C. Kagiteibasi (Eds.), *Handbook of cross-cultural psychology* (2nd ed., Vol. 3, pp. 213–254). Boston: Allyn & Bacon.

Stephan, W. G., Stephan, C. W., & de Vargas, M. C. (1996). Emotional expression in Costa Rica and United States. *Journal of Cross-Cultural Psychology, 27*, 147–160.

Stipek, D., Weiner, B., & Li, K. (1989). Testing some attribution-emotion relations in the People's Republic of China. *Journal of Personality and Social Psychology, 56*, 109–116.

Suh, E., Diener, E., Oishi, S., & Triandis, H. C. (1998). The shifting basis of life satisfaction judgements across cultures: Emotions versus norms. *Journal of Personality and Social Psychology, 74*, 482–493.

Szalay, L. B. (1993). *The subjective worlds of Russians and Americans: A guide for mutual understanding*. Chevy Chase, MD: Institute of Comparative Social and Cultural Studies.

Todd, E. (1983). *La troisième planète*. Paris: Editions du Seuil.

Trafimow, D., Triandis, H. C., & Goto, S. (1991). Some tests of the distinction between private and collective self. *Journal of Personality and Social Psychology, 60*, 649–655.

Triandis, H. C. (1967). Toward an analysis of the components of interpersonal attitudes. In C. Sherif & M. Sherif (Eds.), *Attitudes, ego-involvement, and change* (pp. 227–270). New York: Wiley.

Triandis, H. C. (1972). *The analysis of subjective culture*. New York: Wiley.

Triandis, H. C. (1989). The self and social behaviour in differing cultural contexts. *Psychological Review, 96*, 506–520.

Triandis, H. C. (1990). Crosscultural studies of individualism and collectivism. In I. Berman (Ed.), *Nebraska Symposium on Motivation* (pp. 41–133). Lincoln: University of Nebraska Press.

Triandis, H. C. (1994). *Culture and social behaviour*. New York: McGraw-Hill.

Triandis, H. C. (1995). *Individualism and collectivism*. Boulder, CO: Westview Press.

Triandis, H. C. (1996). The psychological measurement of cultural syndromes. *American Psychologist, 51*, 407–415.

Triandis, H. C., & Gelfand, M. (1998). Converging measurement of horizontal and vertical individualism and collectivism. *Journal of Personality and Social Psychology, 74*, 118–28.

Triandis, H. C., Marin, G., Lisansky, J., & Betancourt, (1984). *Simpatia* as a cultural script of Hispanics. *Journal of Personality and Social Psychology, 47*, 1363–1374.

Triandis, H. C., & Singelis, T. M. (1998). Training to recognize individual differences in collectivism and individualism within culture. *International Journal of Intercultural Relations, 22*, 35–48.

Yamaguchi, S. (1998, August). The *meaning of amae*. Paper presented at the Congress of the International Association of Cross-Cultural Psychology, Bellingham, WA.

Zwier, S. (1997). *Patterns of language use in individualistic and collectivist cultures*. Unpublished doctoral dissertation, Free University of Amsterdam, The Netherlands.

## Concepts and Questions

1. Differentiate between message *content* and message *context*. How do different cultures react to content and context? How might cultural diversity in attending to content and context affect intercultural communication?

2. What does Triandis mean by cultural distance? How does language affect cultural distance?

3. What is Triandis referring to when he discusses different patterns of sampling information found in the environment? How might these differences affect intercultural communication between an individual from a collectivist culture and someone from an individualistic culture?

4. What differences may be found in the use of "I" and "you" in collectivistic and individualistic cultures?

5. What is cultural tightness? How might cultural diversity in tightness affect intercultural communication?

6. Differentiate between vertical and horizontal cultures.

7. How is culture relevant to understanding conflict?

8. Triandis holds that a very serious problem in communication is that people do not perceive the same "causes" of behavior. How does cultural diversity affect the perception of causes?

9. How does culture affect interpersonal aggression? What cultures do you believe would be least prone to violence?

# Intercultural Communication in a Globalized World

BERNARD SAINT-JACQUES

*Our next essay discusses the impact of globalization on the study of culture and intercultural communication. Professor Saint-Jacques first critiques pre–globalization era theoretical concepts of culture and proposes a new approach. He contends that events over the past several decades have changed the way we should consider culture because globalization has created a "mixture of cultures and people within each culture." As a result, earlier cultural concepts, such as Hofstede's model of individualism–collectivism, are dated and no longer reflect the contemporary societal setting. Saint-Jacques believes that any theory of culture in the globalized society must address "three basic facts: (1) Cultural Predestination!, (2) Individual Values, and (3) A Set of Dynamic Processes of Generation and Transformation." These three considerations are then integrated to form the basis for Saint-Jacques's proposed new theoretical approach to culture. Japan is used as a case study to illustrate how culture is being transformed by the shrinking global community.*

*The concept of identity and how it has been altered by globalization is also discussed in the essay. Saint-Jacques sees people in modern society as "living at the same time within particular cultural settings on the one hand, and between different cultural environments on the other one," which produces multiple identities. In the second part of his essay, Saint-Jacques proposes an approach to teaching intercultural communication (ICC) in the globalized society. His method involves viewing culture as "ways of thinking, beliefs, and values," and a greater incorporation of language into the teaching of ICC.*

*Our inclusion of this essay is intended to show you that there are many ways of viewing culture, but also that your views should not become static. Culture and communication are influenced by societal changes, and these changes need to be acknowledged, both in theory development and in classroom instructional methods.*

## A NEW APPROACH TO A THEORY OF CULTURE
### Introduction

Intercultural communication is based on intercultural understanding. Intercultural understanding cannot be realized without an objective and up-to-date understanding of the notion of culture. Globalization, however, has changed the notion of culture. Culture can no longer be described as the property of a single nation. Globalization has changed the concept of culture (Ogura, 2006:23). Globalization stands for the overlapping of global and local factors (Robertson, 1997). Human beings are living at the same time **within** particular settings on the one hand, and **between** different cultural environments on the other one. This is nothing new. One lives **between** one's home in a family on the one side, and also is situated in the daily life world—going to school, working in one's professional life on the other. This has been happening for thousands of years. In a culturally globalized world, **between-situations** are becoming essential for any understanding of culture. There were three stages in globalization. The first one was political, the founding of the United Nations in 1945. The second one was the economic globalization, the spread of free-market capitalism in virtually every country of the world since 1980. The third one is … cultural globalization, which has an essential function for the efficient working of the political and economic globalizations of the world. In fact, the economic and political globalizations have given rise to the problematic triangle "identity–culture–communication" in international relations (Wolton, 2005). As the technology for worldwide transmission of information continues to progress, attempts by some countries to restrict this transmission are becoming more and more ineffective (McPhail, 1989). The debates on globalization have focused on economic and political issues, but the powerful impact of globalization on culture has not been sufficiently analyzed and researched.

Globalization provides a good opportunity to reflect on the efficiency of the tools which the intercultural enterprise so far has developed to promote intercultural understanding (Kalscheuer, 2002). Thomas's (1996) definition of culture as a system that is valid for all members of a society or nation, as well as Hall's (1984) and Hofstede's (1980, 1991, 1997) "cultural dimensions", fixed sets of polar attributes (collectivism vs. individualism, monochromic vs. polychronic, high power distance vs. low power distance, high context culture vs. low context culture, etc …) obtained with questionnaires to very small groups of participants of a given society, are not any more adapted to research in intercultural understanding. Cultures are not homogeneous and stable entities. Recent cultural theory takes into account the increasing mixture of cultures and people within each culture, and emphasizes the hybrid nature of culture (Bhabba, 1994, Pieterse, 1994, Shweder & Sullivan, 1990). Welsh (1999) stresses the reciprocal influences of cultures.

> *The powerful impact of globalization on culture has not been sufficiently analyzed and researched.*

## Three Decades Have Passed

It is essential to recall that three decades have passed since Hofstede proposed his cultural dimensions and his classification of countries. During that time, there were many reviews of Hofstede's work expressing several important caveats in dimensionalising cultural values. A large number of questions remains as to how exactly these concepts work in real-life relationships. These concepts suffer from the same weakness as the concepts of culture in that they are too readily used to explain everything that occurs in a society (Kim, Triandis, Kagitcibasi, Choi, 1994). Concerning individualism versus collectivism, the multidimensional nature of these concepts has been frequently discussed. We can be both individualistic in some situations and collectivistic in others (Kim et al., 1996). In a recent paper, Chirkov, Linch, and Niwa (2005), examining the problems in the measurements of cultural dimensions and orientations, raised three basic questions: (1) "The operationalization of individualism/collectivism assumes a high degree of cultural homogeneity of the surveyed countries across geographical regions and across different life domains. This assumption however is far from reality, especially in multi-ethnic countries" (p. 472). (2) Moreover, this operationalization of cultural dimensions ignores the fact that different cultural values and practices may be internalized by people to different degrees, thus demonstrating high interpersonal variation in their endorsement (D'Andrade, 1992). (3) Measuring culture-related constructs to average individuals' scores on, for example, an individualism–collectivism self-report scale, across samples taken from different countries is wrong. "This does not make sense because culture is not an attribute of a person, nor is it the main value of some aggregate of individuals" (p. 473). Further, quoting Fisk (2002), Chirkov et. al. (2005) conclude that "taking the mean of a group of individual scores does not make such variables into measurements of culture" (p. 473). Moreover, the expressed cultural values of many intercultural surveys and questionnaires are not necessarily the same as behaviors. The sample and the participants used in intercultural surveys have often been criticized as not representative of the culture of a given country being studied. In many cases, the participants were college or university students, and sometimes surveyed outside of their country of origin, without taking into account the cultural influence of the country in which they had been international students for some years. Visser, Krosnick and Lavrakas (2000) have emphasized the non-probability and the non-representative sample of participants in most cross-cultural studies. These authors warned social and cross-cultural psychologists that "social psychological research attempting to generalize from a college student sample to a nation looks silly and damages the apparent credibility of our enterprise" (p. 237, quoted in Chirkov et al., 2005).

In Goodwin's book *Personal Relationships across Cultures* (1999), one can find interesting discussions of Hofstede's classification. In the introduction, Goodwin writes: "I will try to demonstrate how many of our cherished views of other cultures are becoming less relevant and less accurate—If, indeed, they were ever accurate at all" (1999, p. 1). What is also striking is that data from a reexamination of Hofstede's country classifications, conducted twenty-five years after the original research, suggests "significant shifts in value classifications in some countries" (Fernandez, et. al., 1997, p. 52). In an interview in Canada published in the *InterCultures Magazine*, Oct. 2006, when asked, "Between the time that you were first analyzing the IBC data and now, has your definition of culture changed at all?" Hofstede answered:

No, not really. Of course, you have to realize that culture is a construct. When I have intelligent students in my class, I tell them: "One thing we have to agree on: culture does not exist." Culture is a concept that we made up which helps us understand a complex world, but it is not something tangible like a table or a human being. What it is depends on the way in which we define it. So, let's not squabble with each other because we define culture slightly differently; that's fine.

From this interview, it is quite clear that Hofstede's "cultural dimensions" are not at all the rigid and universal fixed sets of polar attributes that several scholars are still using in their intercultural research.

For instance, in a recent paper by Sasaguwa, Toyada, and Sakano (2006, p. 337), I was astonished by their grouping Australia, Belgium, Canada, England, France, Germany, Italy, Scotland, Spain, and the United States as individualistic countries, and China, Columbia, Ecuador, Egypt, India, Indonesia, Hong Kong, Kazakhstan, Korea, Malaysia, Mexico, Saudi Arabia, Morocco, Singapore, Panama, Paraguay, Peru, Philippines Thailand, Turkey, United Arab Emirates, The Netherlands, South Africa, [and] Switzerland as collectivistic. The three Japanese authors of this paper must have regretted their allegiance to this rigid dichotomy "individualistic versus collectivistic", because their results show that "students returning from so-called collectivistic countries were more individualistic than returnees from so-called individualistic countries" (p. 340). Moreover, these 141 Japanese students had sojourned in 39 different countries, which as a sample per country means only 3.6 participants! One more example of this traditional approach to the study of culture and intercultural understanding can be found in a study by Merkin (2006) that reports data tending to confirm the following in Hofstede's hypotheses:

[H1]: Members of strong uncertainty-avoidance cultures are more likely to communicate ritualistically than members of weak uncertainty-avoidance cultures,

[H2]: Members of strong uncertainty-avoidance cultures are less likely to use harmonious facework strategies than members of weak uncertainty-avoidance cultures,

[H3]: Members of strong uncertainty-avoidance cultures will be more likely to respond to face-threatening acts with aggression than members of weak uncertainty-avoidance cultures. These confirmations are based on the following data: 658 college students (442 women and 216 men) representing the following six countries: Japan, Sweden, Israel, Hong Kong, Chile and the United States. The samples from each country were not equal, the United States having the largest number—241 students, and Hong Kong only 32. From this data, one can have serious doubts about the scientific value of these confirmations of the Hofstede hypotheses which read "Members of strong Uncertainty-Avoidance cultures ...", when in this paper "members" is restricted to college students who in 5 of the 6 countries represent a very small number of participants. As mentioned before, any social psychological research attempting to generalize from a college sample to a nation has no scientific basis.

Several other examples could be given. It is quite clear, however, that intercultural research based on the traditional cultural dimensions is certainly not the key for intercultural understanding. From now on, research dealing with cultures can no longer be satisfied with the approach which consists only in trying to apply to all cultures so-called universal "cultural dimensions" or fixed sets of polar attributes.

## Three Basic Facts for a Theory of Culture and Intercultural Understanding

Any theory of culture in this globalized world must address the following three basic facts: (1) Cultural Predestination!, (2) Individual Values, and (3) A Set of Dynamic Processes of Generation and Transformation. Some aspects of these facts are not new and have been discussed by scholars in the past; these basic facts, however, have often been disregarded by those doing research in intercultural communication, resulting in very dubious affirmations about the nature of various cultures and people living in

*Research dealing with cultures can no longer be satisfied with the approach which consists only in trying to apply to all cultures so-called universal "cultural dimensions" or fixed sets of polar attributes.*

these cultures. The pragmatic integration of these three facts in intercultural research represents the essential basis for the new approach to a theory of culture proposed in this paper.

## Cultural Predestination!

Cultural comparisons should avoid overstressing differences because it leads to overemphasizing the features of a given culture, as if it were a unique attribute. It is quite clear that in the past, in order to make comparisons more striking, people have been tempted to exaggerate differences, leading to a focus on a given country's distinctive features at the expense of those characteristics it shares with other societies. Yamazaki (2000, p. 3) writes:

"Human beings seem to like to give themselves a sense of security by forming simplistic notions about the culture of other countries." Stereotypes are then often created. It is essential to research distinctive features in the light of features which are common to other cultures. To put it in Yamazaki's words: "Commonalities are essential if comparisons are to be made" (Yamazaki, 2000. p. V). Cultures are not predestined to have some immutable distinctive characteristics. Yamazaki uses the expression "cultural predestination" (2000, p. 9) and Demorgon (2005, p. 170) emphasizes the same idea: "The absolute distinctiveness of cultures is a problematic notion." The reason for this is quite simple: cultures influence each other and often there is a process of fusion. How can one attribute at a given moment distinctive features to a culture which is in perpetual development and change? This point will be developed to a greater extent in the section dealing with the dynamism of cultures.

## Individual Values

A nation or an ethnic group cannot be considered as a single unit. Nations are not culturally homogeneous. Within the same nation, social classes, age, gender, education, religious affiliations and several other factors constitute the self-awareness and self-consciousness which become the markers of cultural identity, subcultures within a national culture. There are, within a nation, regional cultures, cultures of towns and villages, small group cultures, and family cultures which form cultural units. Renan's 1882 famous definition of nation, "L'essence d'une nation est que tous les individus aient beaucoup de choses en commun" [The essence of a nation is that the individuals of this nation have many things in common] has to be extended to the various groups which constitute cultural units in a nation. The members of these groups also have many things in common. Nations are not culturally homogeneous. Individuals within a given nation are not always identical and their cultural behavior might be different. Several studies, for instance, Kim (2005), and Kim, Hunter, Miyara, Horvath, Bresnahan and Yoon (1996) have emphasized this point. Very often, individual values rather than cultural values will be better predictors of behavior (Leung, 1989, Leung & Bond, 1989, Triandis, 1988). It is quite evident in the modern world that culture-level generalizations or national-culture generalizations are no longer adequate for intercultural research. It is sufficient to consider the vast number of countries in the world which are multicultural and multilingual and where there is considerable immigration. Canada, where you have English-Canadians and French-Canadians, First Nations, and another 35 percent of the population which is neither from British or French origin but coming from forty different countries, is only one example. It is also the case for the United States, all countries of the European Union, South American countries, most Asian and African countries. Here, one cannot resist quoting some passages of a very recent article by James B. Waldram (2009): "Anthropologists began to appreciate the artificial nature of their notion of 'cultures' as distinct, bounded units harbouring culturally identical citizens.... We began to appreciate 'culture' as a live experience of individuals in their local, social worlds" (p. 173). In addition, he adds: "Cross-cultural psychology has retained the broad generalizations and essentializations rejected by anthropology, to continue to assign research participants to groups as if there were no significant intra-cultural variability, and then engage in primarily quantitative comparisons" (p. 174).

It is now more than evident that serious cultural research cannot apply anymore the absolute and general dimensions of individualism versus collectivism, high-context versus low-context and other similar dimensions to most countries in the world.

## Culture Is a Set of Dynamic Processes of Generation and Transformation

The third fact which must be considered in intercultural research is that culture is not static, it is a dynamic process. In his recent book, Demorgon (2005) insists that cultures are not static phenomena; they change constantly and are indefinitely renewable. Yamazaki makes the same point: "Culture is by no means a fixed entity, but a set of dynamic processes of generation and transformation" (Yamazaki, 2000, p. 119). To affirm the singularity of culture is questionable, insists Demorgon (2005, p. 21), how indeed can one label a culture as unique and coherent when it is in constant development? Different cultures influence each other, occasionally fusing. It is necessary therefore to direct attention from narrowly defined culture theory and seek not for the attributes present in specific cultures, but for the fundamental principles that precede and give rise to all cultures. These pre-cultural principles are subliminally present in every culture. According to Yamazaki, cultural fusion, therefore, is not a matter of one culture assimilating features of another but something in the other culture stimulating the full flowering of aspects already present in the first. One of these pre-cultural principles is individuation. The tendency toward individuation represents the drive to preserve individual units of life. This principle is antecedent to culture. The concept of individuation relates to the modern notion of individualism but precedes it (Yamazaki, 2000, p. 13).

*Culture is not static, it is a dynamic process*

Following several authors, Waldram (2009) argues that the concept of acculturation has outlived whatever usefulness it may have had, and that scholars should focus on the process of enculturation, or culture learning. For Waldram, culture learning is "the process of learning to be cultural in a given real world context" (Waldram, 2009, p. 174). He concludes that a new paradigm for culture is needed: "one that is theoretically and conceptually driven, rather than methodologically driven".... This, of course, represents quite a shift in thinking from the classic emphases on contact involving "autonomous cultural systems" (Waldram, 2009, p. 175).

Moreover, it has to be strongly emphasized that globalization is not a factor of homogenization but of diversity. In a recent paper, Bhawuk (2008, p. 316) writes: "Creating new knowledge using concepts and ideas from indigenous cultures will help increase the diversity of theories and models which may be necessary for the global village.... Quality cross-cultural research demands that models and theories that question the contemporary values, beliefs, and models be welcomed.... Globalization is not about homogeneity but about diversity.... It is hoped that researchers will contribute to the differentiation of knowledge base rather than force homogeneity for defending mono-cultural theories."

## Individualism–Collectivism, the Case of Japan

In relation to the individualism-collectivism dimension, many scholars have disregarded the three facts mentioned above. A typical example is the Japanese culture. During the last 30 years, drastic changes have taken place in one aspect of Japanese culture: the group orientation. *Jiko tassei*, the promotion of the individual, is no longer a taboo subject. Individualization has been making strong inroads in the Japanese society. For the young generation, self, the individual, has become more important than the group. Recently, in a white paper, the Japanese government described these changes, giving examples. An example is the young salary man who refuses to work late at night or during weekends because he wants to relax or do things that he likes. Or again, the young salary man who refuses to be transferred to another city, thus giving up a promotion, because he wants to be with his family. The lifetime employment, which is the lifetime commitment between corporations and their employees, is also under siege (Abegglen, 2003). According to a survey by the Management and Coordination Agency, in the one-year period ending February 1989, about 2.5 million Japanese switched jobs. Seventy-three percent said they changed jobs to seek better working conditions for themselves. Gakusei Engokai in 1989 conducted a survey among young salary men aged between 20 and 30 in the Tokyo and Osaka areas: Seventy-four percent declared that their own personal work and happiness were more important than the company which employs them. Ninety percent of these same salary men also believe that in the future even more salary people will change jobs (Saint-Jacques, 2005). In a recent paper, Shigeyuki writes:

> Around the year 2000, personnel managers began talking about how the latest recruits had a whole new outlook. They said that the new employees were narrowly focused on their careers, interested only in themselves, and lacking loyalty to the company (2006, p. 20).

The seniority-based wage systems and promotion systems are giving way to performance-based systems, and companies are looking for talented individuals who would be an asset for the company from day one.

This new "individualism" tendency also influenced the most basic group underlying all other groups: the family. The rate of divorce has climbed to previously unknown heights. Japanese women marry later and have fewer children. Many women now decide not to marry. In the 2005 census, about 60 percent of women in their late twenties and 30 percent in their early thirties reported they were single. In comparison with the 1975 census, the first figure has roughly tripled and the second quintupled.

In his recent book, *The New Japan*, Matsumoto, quoting his own research and that of several other scholars, makes the statement that "there is no support for the claim that Japanese are less individualistic and more collectivistic than Americans" (2002, p. 41). He makes the distinction of two groups in Japan, the young generation being more individualistic and the older generation still attached to the importance of the group. He proposes the concept of "individual collectivism," that is, a society which can celebrate cultural diversity in thought and action, that is, individualism, while maintaining core values related to the importance of the group and hierarchy, that is, collectivism. Robert Christopher was more than prophetic when in 1983 he wrote: "To an extent unmatched by the inhabitants of any other nations, the Japanese succeeded in marrying the social discipline that is the chief virtue of a strong collective consciousness with individualism" (Christopher, 1983, p. 328). Moreover, it should be remembered, as Tanaka points out in his 2007 paper "Cultural Networks in Premodern Japan," that the Japanese of the Edo period were not nearly as group-oriented (collectivism) as most people are inclined to believe. The Japanese of the Edo period did not have the group mentality in the sense in which this concept is generally understood: that is, a strong tendency for the individual to conform to group norms in respect to education, values, skills, fashions and lifestyle (Tanaka, 2007). It is quite evident that Japan cannot simply be classified as a collectivistic culture.

## Identity

Closely related to the concept of culture are the notions of individual, social and national identities. Identity, particularly in the age of globalization, is never a fixed reality, a pre-given identification; it is a dynamic and evolving reality. "Cultural identity is a matter of becoming as well as being. It belongs to the future as much as to the past. It is not something which already exists, transcending places, time, history and culture. Cultural identities come from somewhere, they have histories. But like everything which is historical, they undergo constant transformation" (Hall, 1990, p. 225). "Identity is never *a priori*, not a finished product" (Bhabba, 1986, p. xvi). "Things fall apart, the centre cannot hold" ("Yeats"). This famous quotation from Yeats, which he wrote in the aftermath of the First World War, has often been used to highlight the current sense of cultural fragmentation and dislocation of the individual in the new world dominated by globalization. In this new world, individual identities, group identity, cultural and ethnic identity, as well as national identity are no longer clearly defined concepts to which individuals and groups can relate and find their own identification. Identity is no longer conceptualized as a given but rather as something which is constantly negotiated and struggled over (Saint-Jacques, 2002, p. 13). In this world, the individual's activity has been diversifying and group membership becomes more pluralistic; belonging to a number of groups means that the individual will have several identities or multiple identities. The case of immigrants is a good example. In a recent article, Van Oudenhoven, Ward and Masgoret write that immigrants may give up parts of their cultural heritage without giving up their cultural identity (2006, p. 647), Hybridity and multiple identities (whether affirmed or negated) are part of the human condition, and we should begin considering them as "normal" (Boyland, 2005). In their recent paper, Bhatia and Ram (2009) rightly make the point that acculturation and immigrant identity is not only an individual process: "We call for a shift from conceptualizing acculturation and immigrant identity as an individual process to a more broad, contextual, and political phenomenon" (p. 141). Their research shows clearly that the acculturation experiences of Indian immigrants living in the diaspora in the United States "are constructed through a dynamic, back-and-forth play concurrently between structure and self, being privileged and marginalized, caught in the web of socio-political and historical forces" (p. 147). Human beings are living at the same time within particular cultural settings on the one hand, and between different cultural environments on the other one. Bayart (2005) argues that identities are fluid, never homogenous and sometimes invented. Fixed cultural identities never exist.

> *Identity, particularly in the age of globalization … is a dynamic and evolving reality.*

Globalization can be a profoundly enriching process, opening minds to new ideas and experiences, and strengthening the finest values of humanity. "The homogenizing influences of globalization that are most often condemned by the new nationalists and by cultural romanticists are actually positive: globalization promotes integration and the removal not only of cultural barriers but of many of the negative dimensions of culture. Globalization is a vital step toward both a more stable world and better lives for the people in it" (Rothkopf, 1997). This new approach to intercultural understanding might help intercultural communication.

## HOW TO TEACH MULTICULTURAL COMMUNICATION

Multicultural or intercultural communication cannot be learned without intercultural understanding, which is based on the knowledge of culture. The word "culture" has four different meanings: (1) High culture, the achievements of a society in terms of the most esteemed forms of literature, art, music. (2) Culture as behavior, the ways people agree to behave, act, and respond. (3) Culture as ways of thinking: modes of perception, beliefs and values. (4) Culture as language, the close link between language and culture. The second meaning of culture, that is, culture as behavior, is related to clothing, food, architecture, transportation, appearance and so on, it is usually called "overt culture" or, in the "iceberg model of culture", what is above the waterline and therefore easily observable. Culture as behavior is subject to constant changes and is easily learned. The third meaning of culture, modes of perception, beliefs and values, [is] not easily observable and [is] often out of our own and others' awareness, it is called "covert culture" and, in the "iceberg model of culture," what is below the waterline. In our search of how to teach and learn intercultural understanding and communication, we shall be dealing with meanings three and four of culture.

## Culture as Ways of Thinking, Beliefs and Values

Culture is first of all perceptions concerning our system of values, our ways of thinking, our beliefs, our psychological orientations. Intercultural understanding is therefore the ability to understand the perceptions concerning one's own culture and the perceptions of the people who belong to another culture, and the capacity to negotiate between the two. The Greek philosopher Socrates had chosen for himself the following maxim: "*gnôthi seauton*," "Know Thyself." The same is true for intercultural understanding. The first step for intercultural understanding is to have a clear idea about one's own culture and about our personal perceptions of this culture. This is not an easy task, however. Perceptions about one's culture are mostly unconscious. When asked to describe one's culture, a person might have very vague answers or often provide certain social generalizations which are stereotypes about one's culture. There are two important facts concerning perceptions of one's culture: First, nations are not culturally homogeneous, individuals in a nation might have different perceptions about their culture. These perceptions will vary according to social class, age, education, gender, experiences in life and many other factors. Second, cultures are not static, they change constantly. These two facts are true for all cultures.

Does this mean that it is practically impossible to find out the perceptions a person has about her or his own culture or the perceptions a person of a different culture holds about her or his own culture? No, it is quite possible through questioning, debates, discussions, reflective writing **about one single cultural aspect**, thus allowing the person to reflect about her or his own perception about one cultural aspect, often linked to other aspects of the culture. Thus, the door to one's perception of one's culture has been opened. The types of questions and discussions in this approach will vary according to the age and background of students. Let's say that we are dealing with university students. If a student or a person of another culture is present, this is an ideal situation because that person can also answer the same question and then a lively discussion can take place. When it is not possible, however, answers for a question can be found in books dealing with a variety of cultures. Here are some examples of questions that students have to answer, and statements they have to qualify: strongly agree, agree, no opinion, disagree, or strongly disagree:

*Multicultural or intercultural communication cannot be learned without intercultural understanding which is based on the knowledge of culture.*

- Men in my country usually expect women to prepare and serve food.
- A married man should help around the house, doing cleaning, ironing and cooking.
- In my country, it is common for a man to give up his seat to a woman on public transport.
- In my country, it is not typical for women to speak their minds and contradict men.
- Do you think that both husband and wife should contribute to the household income?
- How normal is "going Dutch" (when each pays half of the costs) when a man and a woman go out?
- If a man and a woman are having dinner together, is it OK for the woman to pay the bill?
- Is it OK for a man to give a woman a pat on the backside to show he likes her?
- Is it proper for a man to hold a door open for a woman?

- Whenever a mixed group of people (male/female) come together the men always sit together.

- If you are a student at school and you received a mark that seemed not to reflect your knowledge, is it proper to talk to the teacher about it?

- If children do well at school, parents should reward them with a present or pocket money.

- Do students in your country treat what the teachers and textbooks teach as something final and unquestionable?

- Faithfulness is the most important factor for a successful marriage.

- In English, the terms stewardess (or steward for men) have been replaced with the gender-neutral term "flight attendant." Can you give examples of such changes in your language?

These are only a few examples. Statements and questions could be prepared dealing with all aspects of life, but only one cultural aspect at a given time. After discussions, students can be asked to do some reflective writing, for instance, describe what YOU think of marriage. It is quite possible that students of the same culture have different perceptions about several cultural aspects.

Pictures and videos showing daily life scenes of people (for instance, ways of greeting between two men, two women or between a man and a woman) from one's country and other countries are also excellent indirect ways to start fascinating discussions about differences in cultures and students' reactions about these differences. This approach is the first step to the understanding of one's perception about one's culture and absolutely essential for apprehending the perceptions of a person of another culture, that is, intercultural understanding and communication.

## Culture as Language: The Close Link Between Language and Culture

It is quite evident that the teaching and learning of a second language could be an excellent way to access another culture and therefore to improve intercultural understanding and communication. This, however, is possible only if this learning and teaching begin with the idea that language and culture learning are fundamentally interrelated and that this interrelationship

constitutes the centre of the teaching and learning processes. A language is a window into the culture of people speaking this language. For instance, the teaching of personal pronouns **I** and **You** in languages like French, German, Spanish, and Japanese is an excellent opportunity to enter various aspects of the cultures of these languages, such as the social relations between two persons talking together: How well do they know each other? Is one superior to the other because of age, sex, position, or the social group to which one belongs? In these languages, there are choices of personal pronouns which have to be selected according to the reference points mentioned earlier. In French, for **You, tu or vous**, in German, **du or Sie**, in Spanish, **tu or usted**. In Japanese, for **I**, (to mention only a few) **ore, boku, watakushi, watashi**, for **You, omae, kimi, anata** (Saint-Jacques, 1971). In the English language, the speaker does not have to worry about these various points of reference: the personal pronouns **I**, and **You** are the only pronouns. However, in these other languages, the teaching of these pronouns provides a unique opportunity to observe language as an essential and closely integrated element of social behavior. In these languages, the wrong choice of pronouns can have disastrous effects for the speaker. Recently, a German driver who was arrested for speeding was so mad that he forgot the basic rules of pronouns in his mother tongue: the pronoun **du** is not to be used with people who are not close friends. He was fined for using **du** to the officer who arrested him! Intercultural learning involves developing an understanding of one's own language and culture in relation to an additional language and culture (Liddicoat, Scarino, Papademetre & Kohler 2003, p. 43). Traditional language teaching and learning with the sole emphasis on phonetics and syntax cannot produce speakers who have acquired some understanding of one's own language and culture in relation to an additional language and culture— necessary conditions for intercultural understanding and communication.

Moreover, there is also another important reason to link the teaching and learning of a language together with the culture of the people speaking this language. To learn a language, whether it is a first or second language, two basic conditions are essential: motivation and the opportunity to use this language. These two facts are closely related to each other, if there is no opportunity to use a language, motivation also ceases to exist, that is, the learner's motivation to learn the language will become weaker and eventually disappear. The opportunity or necessity to use a language is a fundamental law of language learning. A language which is not used for frequent communication will slowly disappear, first on the active level, speaking and writing, and eventually on the passive level, listening and reading. Does it mean that the teaching and learning of a second language is a waste of time? The various benefits of second language learning usually identified in the defense of language education fall into two categories: (1) the practical and tangible benefits of being able to communicate in a second language, and (2) the broader benefits of expanding one's intellectual experience, the improvement of cross-cultural awareness and a better understanding of other cultures. A language is like a window to the world of another culture (Saint-Jacques, 2006). Even if a person loses the active and even the passive knowledge of a second language, the learning of this language is a very enriching and beneficial process. Sakuragi (2006), in a recent paper, gives the example of second language teaching in the United States: "While the practical benefits of language learning in the United States are sometimes questioned due to the increasing dominance of English in international communication, the argument that language study helps students develop a sense of being a 'world citizen' remains cogent" (p. 20). There are many second language learners who will never become fluent in their second language because of the lack of opportunity to use the language for communication. Even for them, in the cultural perspective, the study of languages is very beneficial. There are many countries in the world where a great majority of citizens does not have the necessity or opportunity to use another language for communication. The learning of languages, however, is part of the curriculum in schools and universities because it can provide students with a better understanding of other cultures as well as their own culture.

## Notes

1. Some of these questions were inspired by *Developing Intercultural Understanding: An Introduction for* *Teachers*, Australian Government Department of Education, 2005.

## References

Abegglen, J. (2003). Kaisha missionary. *International House of Japan Bulletin, 23*(2), 2.

Bayart, J. F. (2005). *The illusions of cultural identity*. Chicago: University of Chicago Press.

Bhabba, H. (1986). *The location of culture*. London: Routledge.

Bhatia, S., & Ram, A. (2009). Theorizing identity in transnational and diaspora cultures: A critical approach to acculturation. *International Journal of Intercultural Research, 33*(2), 140–149.

Bhawuk, D. (2008). Globalization and indigenous cultures: Homogenization or differentiation. *International Journal of Intercultural Research, 32*(4), 305–317.

Boyland, P. (2005). Keynote talk at the 6th annual IALIC conference, Brussels, Belgium, December 11, 2005.

Chirkov, V., Linch, M., & Niwa, S. (2005). Application of the scenario questionnaire of horizontal and vertical individualism and collectivism to the assessment of cultural distance and cultural fit. *International Journal of International Relations D.S. 29*(4), 469–490.

Christopher, R. C. (1983). *The Japanese mind: The goliath explained*. New York: Linden Press/Simon & Schuster.

D'Andrade, R. G. (1992). Schemas and motivation. In R. G. D'Andrade & C. Strauss (Eds.), *Human Motives and Cultural Models* (pp. 23–44). Cambridge: Cambridge University Press.

Demorgon, J. (2005). *Critique de l'interculturel*. Paris: Anthropos.

Fernandez, D. R., Carlson, D. S., Stepina, L. P. & Nicholson, J. D. (1997). Hofstede's country classification 25 years later. *The Journal of Social Psychology, 137*(1), 43–45.

Fiske, A. (2002). Using individualism and collectivism to compare cultures—a critique of the validity and measurement of the constructs. *Psychological Bulletin, 128*(1), 78–88.

Goodwin, R. (1999). *Personal relationships across cultures.* London: Routledge.

Hall, E. T. (1984). *The dance of life: The other dimension of time*. Garden City, NY: Anchor.

Hall, S. (1990). Cultural identity and diaspora. In J. Rutherford, (ed.) *Identity, community, culture, difference* (pp. 223–237). London: Lawrence & Wishart.

Hofstede, G. (1980). *Culture's consequences. International differences in work-related values.* Newbury Park, CA: Sage.

Hofstede, G. (1991). *Cultures and organizations: Software of the mind.* London: McGraw-Hill.

Hofstede, G. (1997). *Lokales Denken, globales Handeln. Kulturen, Zusammernarbeit und Management.* München: Beck.

Kalscheuer, B. (2002). *Ein Schritt vor und einer zurück: Über die neue Praxis der Kulturellen Grenzziehung in der Interkulturalitätsforschung.* Vortrag im Rahmen dem 6 internalionalen Kongress der Neuen Gesellschaft für Psychologie, Berlin, February.

Kim, M. S. (2005). Culture-based conversational constraints theory: Individual- and culture level analyses. In W. B. Gudykunst (Ed.) *Theorizing about intercultural communication* (pp. 93–117). Thousand Oaks: Sage Publications.

Kim, M. S., Triandis, H. C., Kagitcibasi, C., & Choi, S. C. (1994). *Individualism and collectivism: Theory, method and applications.* Thousand Oaks, CA: Sage.

Kim, M. S., Hunter, J. E., Miyahara, A., Bresnahan, M., & Yoon, H. J. (1996). Individual versus cultural level dimensions of individualism and collectivism: Effects on preferred conversational styles. *Communication Monographs, 63,* 29–49.

Leung, K. (1989). Cross-cultural differences: Individual-level versus cultural-level analyses. *International Journal of Psychology, 24,* 703–904.

Leung, K., & Bond, M. H. (1989). On the empirical identification of dimensions for cross-cultural comparisons. *Journal of Cross-Cultural Psychology, 20,* 133–151.

Liddicoat, A. J., Scarino. A., Papademetre, L., & Kohler, M. (2003). *Report on intercultural language learning.* Canberra: Commonwealth Department of Education, Science and Training.

Matsumoto, D. (2002). *The new Japan: Debunking cultural stereotypes.* Yarmouth (Maine): Intercultural Press.

McPhail, T. (1989). Inquiry in international communication. In K. A. Asante & E. Gudykunst (Eds.), *Handbook of international and intercultural communication* (pp. 47–66). London: Sage.

Merkin, R. (2006). Uncertainty avoidance and facework: A test of the Hofstede model. *International Journal of Intercultural Relations, 30*(2), 213–228.

Ogura, K. (2004). Japan's new cultural diplomacy. *International House of Japan Bulletin, 24*(2), 17–28.

Pieterse, J. N. (1994). Globalization as hybridization. *International Sociology, 9*(2), 161–184.

Renan, E. (1882). Qu'est-ce qu'une nation? In. H. Psichari (Ed.), *Oeuvres Complètes de Etrnst Renan. Paris: Calman-Lévy.*

Robertson, R. (1997). Glokalisierung, homogenität und heterogintät in raum und zeit. U. Beck (Hg.) *Perspektiven der Weltgesellschaft.* Frankfurt am Main: Suhrkamp, 87–124.

Rothkopf, D. (1997, Summer). In praise of cultural imperialism. *Foreign Policy, 107,* 38–53.

Saint-Jacques, B. (1971). *Structural analysis of modern Japanese.* Vancouver: University of British Columbia Press.

Saint-Jacques, B. (2002). Identity and communication. *Intercultural Communication Studies, 5,* 13–23.

Saint-Jacques, B. (2005). The new Japan: A model for other societies. In J. F. Kress & H. Lansdowne (Eds.). *Why Japan matters* (pp. 241–248). Victoria: University of Victoria Centre for Asia Pacific Initiatives.

Saint-Jacques, B. (2006). The paradox of English learning in Japan: Problems and policies. International Political Science Association Fukuoka Congress, July 9–12.

Sakuragi, T. (2006). The relationship between attitudes toward language study and cross-cultural attitudes. *International Journal of Intercultural Relations, 30*(1), 19–31.

Sasagawa, S., Toyoda, H., & Sakano, Y. (2006). The acquisition of cultural values in Japanese returnee students. *International Journal of Intercultural Relations, 30*(3), 333–343.

Shigeyuki, J. (2006). End of the road for the seniority system. *Japan Echo, 33*(5), 18–22.

Shweder, R, & Sullivan, M. (1990). The semiotic subject of cultural psychology. In L. A. Pervin (Ed.), *Handbook of Personality,* (pp. 399–416). New York: Guilford Press.

Tanaka, Y. (2007, April). Cultural networks in premodern Japan. *Japan Echo, 34*(2), retrieved from http://www.japanecho.co.jp/sum/2007/340217.html

Thomas, A. (1996) Analyse der Handlungswirksamkeit von Kulturstandards. In *Psychologie interkulturellen Handelns,* Göttingen, Germany: Hogrefe (pp. 107–135).

Triandis, H. C. (1988). Collectivism and individualism: A reconceptualization of a basic concept in cross-cultural psychology. In Verma & Bagley (Eds.), *Personality, Attitudes and Cognitions* (pp. 60–95). London: Macmillan.

Van Oudenhoven, J. P., Ward, C., & Masgoret, A. M. (2006). Patterns of relations between immigrants and host societies. *International Journal of Intercultural Relations, 30*(6), 637–652.

Visser, P. S., Krosnick, J. A. & Lavrakas, P. J. (2000). Survey research. In H. T. Reis & C. M. Judd (Eds.) *Handbook of Research Methods in Social and Personality Psychology* (223–252). Cambridge: Cambridge University Press.

Yamazaki M. (1994). *Individualism and the Japanese: An alternative approach to cultural comparison.* Trans. Barbara Sugihara, Trans. Tokyo: Japan Echo, Inc. (Originally published as M. Yamazaki, 1990, *Nihon bunka to kojinshugi,* Chuo Koron Sha.)

Waldram, J. B. (2009). Is there a future for "culture" in acculturation research? An anthropologist perspective. *International Journal of Intercultural Relations,* 33(2), 172–176.

Welsch, W. (1999). Transculturality: The puzzling form of cultures today. In M. Featherstone & S. Lash (Eds.), *Spaces of Cultures,* (pp. 194–213). London: Sage.

Wolton, D. (2005). *Il faut sauver la communication.* Paris: Flammarion.

Yeats, W. B. (1991). *Selected Poetry.* Harmondsworth: Penguin.

## Concepts and Questions

1. Saint-Jacques says we are living "*within* particular settings" and concurrently "*between* different cultural environments." Explain this assertion using examples from an international context.

2. How do you think that "identity–culture–communication" could be a problem in international relations for a globalized society?

3. Can you think of situations where you act in an individualistic manner and others where you take a more collectivistic approach? Explain.

4. Do you agree or disagree with Saint-Jacques's opinion that "research dealing with cultures can no longer be satisfied with the approach which consists only in trying to apply to all cultures so-called universal 'cultural dimensions' or fixed sets of polar attributes"? Why?

5. Explain the term "cultural predestination" as used in this essay.

6. According to Saint-Jacques, "nations are not culturally homogeneous." Explain this statement using the Unites States as your context.

7. Do you think globalization is making the world more homogeneous or more diverse? Why?

8. For Saint-Jacques, identity in the age of globalization "is never a fixed reality, a pre-given identification; it is a dynamic and evolving reality." Explain this statement. How does it apply to your identity?

9. Why is understanding one's own culture an important part of intercultural communication?

10. What do you think Saint-Jacques means when he writes, "language and culture learning are fundamentally interrelated"?

# Worldview in Intercultural Communication: A Religio-Cosmological Approach

SATOSHI ISHII • DONALD KLOPF • PEGGY COOKE

*We extend our understanding of culture with the essay "Worldview in Intercultural Communication: A Religio-Cosmological Approach," which uses the concept of worldview as a window for looking at culture. The authors, Satoshi Ishii, Donald Klopf, and Peggy Cooke, contend that worldview is a fundamental building block of culture that "permeates all other components of culture" and helps us to distinguish among cultures. A culture's worldview represents a collective description of how the cosmos and universe function and how each individual fits into that religious and philosophical scheme. Your personal worldview serves as a guide to answering questions related to pain, suffering, death, the meaning of life, and many more philosophical considerations. The authors' basic premise is that worldview shapes a culture's psyche and helps the members of that culture make sense of the world.*

This original essay appeared in print for the first time in the twelfth edition. All rights reserved. Permission to reprint must be obtained from the publisher and the authors. Dr. Satoshi Ishii is Professor Emeritus at Dokkyo University, Japan, Dr. Donald Klopf is Professor Emeritus at the University of Hawaii and West Virginia University, and Dr. Peggy Cooke is an intercultural communication consultant and manages a training program for the State of Washington.

*While worldview can take a variety of forms (scientific, metaphysical, and religious), it is generally agreed that religion exerts the greatest influence. Even a secular person is greatly affected by the writings, attitudes, beliefs, and ethics advanced by a culture's religious traditions. To help you appreciate the impact of religion on culture, this essay highlights the major dimensions of Eastern and Western religions, which collectively encompass some 80 percent of all people in the world. The authors also provide a discussion of some of the problems that might occur when Eastern and Western worldviews collide in the context of environmental communication. They conclude by recommending a "religio-cosmological approach" to investigating worldview, which can help to resolve and prevent intercultural communication problems.*

Today we live in a world in which we are inescapably connected to each other, yet separated by divergent points of view that make it increasingly difficult to reach each other. How can we achieve understanding across the gulf of worldviews that separate and threaten us? (*Spectra*, December 2006, p. 10)

Worldview forms some of the most fundamental portions of culture and serves to distinguish one culture from another. Its importance stems from the role it plays in defining reality and truth or explaining the purposes of human life. Worldview thus represents one of the most essential qualities of culture, impacting all aspects of how a culture perceives and recognizes the environment. Nurius (1994) reflects that the propensity for individuals to establish and sustain an image of a comprehensive, orderly, and predictable world fulfills one of the most fundamental human needs. Pennington (1985) proclaims that worldview must be given high, if not first, priority in the study of culture because it permeates all other components of culture. She further suggests that by understanding a culture's worldview, it is possible to attain reasonable accuracy in predicting behaviors and motivations in other dimensions. As such, worldview becomes a critical element of successful intercultural and environmental communication.

Under such scholarly circumstances, this study attempts to delineate major qualities, types, and religio-cosmological perspectives of worldview.

> *Worldview forms some of the most fundamental portions of culture.*

# WORLDVIEW DEFINED

Although the term *worldview* probably originated in German philosophy as *Weltanschauung*, literally *worldview*, it has come to represent a variety of approaches to help understand the underpinnings of cultural diversity. It consists of the most general and comprehensive concepts and unstated assumptions about human life.

Anthropologists Spradley and McCurdy (1980) define *worldview* as the way people characteristically look out on the universe. To communication educators Paige and Martin (1996), *worldview* is one of the lenses through which people view reality and the rest of the world. Sociologists Cosner, Nock, Steffan, and Rhea (1987) define it as a definition of reality. Psychologist Harriman (1947) relates the association of *worldview* with German *Weltanschauung* and considers it to be a total frame of reference.

Reflecting a religious perspective, Helve (1991) characterizes *worldview* as a systematized totality of beliefs about the world. In the same vein, Emerson (1996) conceives it as a set of assumptions about how the world is and ought to be organized. Nurius (1994), operating from a social work orientation, assumes a tack at odds with other worldview advocates. She uses the term *assumptive worlds* to describe clusters of fundamental assumptions that people hold about themselves and the world surrounding them. Samovar, Porter, and McDaniel (2007) report a more inclusive view: that *worldview* is culture's orientation to supernatural, human, and natural entities in the cosmological universe and other philosophical issues influencing how its members see the world.

Klopf and McCroskey (2007) also offer an inclusive perspective in their definition of *worldview*:

> Worldview is a set of interrelated assumptions and beliefs about the nature of reality, the organization of the universe, the purposes of human life, God, and other philosophical matters that are concerned with the concept of being. Worldview relates to a culture's orientations toward ontological matters or the nature of being and serves to explain how and why things got to be as they are and why they continue that way. (p. 97)

## ELEMENTS OF WORLDVIEW

What constitutes worldview? The definitions stated above include some of the essential elements of worldview. Other elements are to be added beginning with an anthropological analysis extended by Redfield (1953). He argues that the framework is the same for every culture's interpretation of worldview. His Cartesian-dualistic system includes twelve general conceptions of these elements:

1. The self or principal actor on humankind's stage
2. The others, those within the purview of the self
3. Other people—the unidentifiable mass
4. Differences between men and women
5. Distinctions between "we" (our own people) and "they" (other people)
6. Distinctions between what is human and what is not
7. Invisible beings, forces, and principles
8. Animals
9. Concepts of human nature
10. A spatial orientation
11. A temporal orientation
12. Ideas about birth and death

Pennington's (1985) cosmological conceptions of worldview elements appear in the form of ten statements. The salient characteristics of her statement list are:

1. The culture's dominant beliefs and attitudes about a human's place in nature and society
2. The general pattern of relationships between humans and nature
3. The relationship between humans and the culture's supreme being
4. The supreme being's power over life and events
5. Humans' competitive or cooperative nature
6. Humans' expressions of their beliefs
7. Humans' myths about the origins of people
8. Humans' beliefs in the supernatural
9. The living patterns as group practices
10. The ways a group uses rituals, prayers, and other ceremonies

Dodd (1987) categorizes worldview elements into nine groups, most of which tend to stereotypically contrast the East and the West.

**Shame vs. Guilt**. An Easterner bringing shame to a group is likely to be cast out of it. Westerners consider the individual more important than the group. Saving face is important in the East; not so in the West.

**Task vs. People**. The East accentuates people's relationships. The West stresses task accomplishment.

**Secular vs. Spiritual**. Eastern spiritual cultures rely on intuition and introspection. Secular Western cultures are analytical and logical.

**Dead vs. Living**. The East believes the dead can influence the living, bringing them luck or harm. The West is less prone to think that way.

**Human vs. Nature**. Humans are either subject to nature, in harmony with nature, or should control nature. The East favors harmony with nature; the West, control.

**Doing vs. Being**. The East prefers harmonious relations, being rather than doing.

**Linear vs. Cyclical**. In the East, life is birth, life, death, and rebirth. In the West, [it is] birth, life, and death.

**Fatalism vs. Control**. To the fatalist, what happens is beyond a person's control; this tends to be an Eastern view. In the control view, people are masters of their own destiny; this tends to be a Western view. Worldview is thus closely connected with religious attitudes, beliefs, values, and practices.

## FORMATION OF WORLDVIEWS

Worldview is implicit and symbolically implied but not explicitly expressed. Helve (1991) believes it is improbable that people would be aware of their latent worldview. How it is formed, therefore, is a significant matter of speculation.

Worldview evidently develops in early childhood. Helve (1991) determined through empirical research that its actual growth can be comprehended by applying one or all of the theories identified as *cognitive development, social learning*, or *socialization*. She concluded [that] each extended a sensible explanation.

Rubin and Peplau (1975) credit the child's parents, religious instruction, and education in the schools attended as contributors to worldview formation. Each child's maturation, his or her experiences in the physical environment, and his or her activities in the social environment contribute to the formation of worldview. Then each child draws conclusions about what the world is like from his or her experiences and activities in the physical and social environment. In this respect, each child is an active product of the environment, and his or her way of viewing the world is shaped by shared images and constructions of his or her social group or class.

Children and young people view and conceptualize the world in various ways at different stages in their growth according to their own physical and mental development. Infancy, childhood, and adolescence involve distinct stages in behaving, learning, and thinking. The shaping of their needs, desires, beliefs, and values vary from stage to stage and so too does their worldview undergo change as they grow and mature.

Emerson (1996) places stress on religion in the development of worldview. By outlining what ought to be and by creating and reinforcing social group norms through interaction, religion has a substantial influence on a person's worldview. Religion not only shapes reasoning but also provides the meaning, importance, and properness of different social arrangements and institutions. Religion thus infuses all of these with universal, if not transcendent, significance.

Religious beliefs and practices greatly differ, of course: that is why, as Emerson (1996) contends, people hold different worldviews. Those with conservative worldviews base their moral and ethical authority in the transcendent. Those holding more liberal worldviews participate in the religious and secular cultures that root their moral and ethical norms in humans. They generally stress reason and logical thinking.

Even though Emerson (1996) emphasizes religion's role in worldview development, he recognizes

*Worldview is implicit and symbolically implied but not explicitly expressed.*

a person's position in the social structure as significant. He perceives it, however, as only secondary. Reasonable people living in different cultures of the world are exposed to dissimilar realities in their everyday life. This dissimilar exposure leads them to arrive at distinct worldviews. Emerson's point is substantiated by Cooke (1992), who measured worldview among university students in Japan, Korea, Puerto Rico, and the United States. Her survey findings reveal significant differences among the four socio-cultural groups; each group arrived at different conceptions of worldview.

Although religion plays one of the most significant roles in the formation of worldview, it is inappropriate to constrain it to a purely religious dimension. Worldview stems from a variety of other sources.

## TYPES OF WORLDVIEW

Helve (1991) classifies worldview into three major types. In doing so, she appears to endorse the Chamberlain and Zika (1992) position. Helve's types are *scientific, metaphysical*, and *religious*.

The *scientific* worldview is based on the rules laid down by the exact sciences. It is open and self-correcting in accordance with new systematic and methodological findings. Helve (1991) found it to appear most clearly among scientific scholars. A quasi-scientific worldview results from television, newspaper, and magazine influences, she notes, and it is more "information based" as a worldview than scientific. Those with a scientific bent do not harbor this quasi-scientific worldview.

A *metaphysical* worldview tends to be based on abstract general reasoning without an empirical base. For example, the metaphysical worldview of young children may contain beliefs in imaginary beings such as Santa Claus, ghosts, monsters, witches, and fairies. Older children may include elements of magic and superstition. Teenagers might construct their worldview around horoscopes and behave in accordance with the advice they give. The metaphysical worldview is apt to consist of certain types of unnatural beings, their characteristics, and their relationships. These beings originate partly in religious traditions and partly in folklore, some of which is created by the mass media.

The third type of worldview is *religious*. For most people, religion serves as the foundation of their worldview. The content of their beliefs will vary from person to person depending upon their religious perspectives. A Catholic's worldview undoubtedly will differ from that of a Jew, a Protestant's from a Buddhist's, a Muslim's from a Hindu's, and a Confucianist's from a Shintoist's.

## THE RELIGIOUS PERSPECTIVE

Religion, as has been repeatedly stressed, is a deep and pervasive determinant of worldview. Even the most secular of people feel religion's influences. Those who reject religious faith still follow much of the religious heritage that influences their culture.

## Dimensions of Religion

Religion, Emerson (1996) attests, is multidimensional. He conceptualizes it along two representative dimensions, religiosity and orthodoxy, each with two subdivisions, public and private. Religiosity refers to the intensity and consistency of religious practices. Orthodoxy is the degree to which a person's beliefs center on a guiding authority, for example, the scriptures of the church.

> *Religion ... is a deep and pervasive determinant of worldview.*

Public religiosity describes the religious activities practiced with other people. It is manifest in frequent church attendance and participation in membership functions. Private religiosity is a person's personal and undisclosed religious practice. Examples include the frequency of prayer and holy scripture reading as well as a doubt-free faith.

Public orthodoxy refers to the sharing of religious beliefs in the company of others. Private orthodoxy is the held beliefs that rely on a transcendent authority, a god, or a supernatural being.

## EASTERN AND WESTERN RELIGIO-COSMOLOGICAL WORLDVIEWS

As a more manageable thinking about the world's diverse faiths, Smart (1988) groups them into two major divisions: Eastern and Western. Each division can help

increase an understanding of the impact that religion has on the content and development of a person's worldview. Eastern and Western religious traditions may account for some 80 percent of the world's population. The remaining 20 percent will consist of animists, atheists, shamanists, and the like.

## Religious Similarities

Although the two major divisions, Eastern and Western, have few common teachings, they do possess similarities typical of all religions. Samovar, Porter, and McDaniel (2007, p. 78) identify five such similarities, the most important being *sacred writings*. All of the world's major religions have sacred writings, such as the Holy Bible, the Qur'an, and Buddhist sutras, commonly revered by believers. These writings function as the means and vehicles for the propagation of the religion's knowledge and wisdom.

Another similarity is an *authority figure*. God, Allah, the Buddha, Jesus, and Muhammad are all representative authority figures who are believed to be far greater and more powerful than the religion's members.

*Rituals* are the third similarity. They are religious practices required of the membership or acts that are forbidden to the members. For example, believers must meditate regularly or be baptized. They must pray at special times and fast on designated days. They may not eat pork or beef. These acts embody humility, restraint, and behaviors of great religious significance.

*Speculation*, as another similarity, typifies all religions. Humans commonly seek answers to mysteries of life—what is life, death, suffering, or origins of the universe—and religions are believed to supply answers to such mysteries, speculative at best.

Religion also commonly includes *ethics*, a set of moral principles for the membership to observe. For most religions, the set contains moral items such as prohibiting killing, stealing, and lying, observing marital fidelity, paying honor to parents, and the like.

## Eastern Religio-Cosmological Worldview

Eastern (Chinese, Indian, Japanese, Korean, and other) cultures commonly embrace religious traditions that

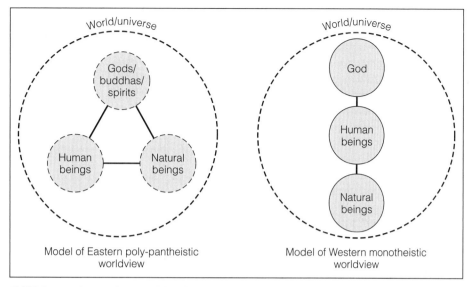

**FIGURE 1.1** Contrastive Models of Eastern Poly-Pantheistic and Western Monotheistic Worldviews

feature relational harmony as the ultimate good (Smart, 1988). Relational harmony has been consistently believed to be the major tenet recognized in Eastern religions such as Buddhism, Confucianism, Hinduism, Shintoism, and Taoism. Further, although these religions differ considerably, their theological foundations are similar in that gods and deities are in every place and in every form, rather than a single place or form.

In Figure 1.1, Ishii (2001) has developed Contrastive Models of Eastern Poly-Pantheistic and Western Monotheistic Worldviews from religio-cosmological perspectives to graphically illustrate the respective positions and correlations of supernatural beings, human beings, and natural beings. The outer broken circle of the left model of Eastern poly-pantheistic worldview signifies that the world/universe in which supernatural beings (e.g., buddhas, deities, gods, goddesses, spirits, etc.), human beings, and natural beings (e.g., animals, astronomical objects, mountains, plants, rivers, etc.) are believed to exist is a cosmologically open system, spatially and/or temporally limited or unlimited.

The three triangularly arranged broken circles, respectively, imply various supernatural beings' realm, human beings' realm, and natural beings' realm. Their triangular arrangement is not hierarchically predetermined and rigidly fixed but is

relative, dynamic, and interchangeable according to contextual and situational changes. The brokenness of each circle indicates that the sovereignty of each existential realm is not decisively predetermined and closed to [the others'] but is relative, flexibly open, and dynamically interchangeable.

These characteristics of Eastern religio-cosmological worldview have traditionally given extensive influences to Eastern people's cognitive, affective, and behavioral activities in not simply human-to-human but also human-to-supernatural and human-to-nature communication contexts.

## Western Religio-Cosmological Worldview

The Western capsulation of religion, and hence worldview, is in sharp contrast to the Eastern one. Western religions [as] represented by Judaism, Christianity, and Islam perceive the ultimate good as transformation and salvation, stressing that divine grace is the desired end, whether in this life or the next.

Differences among these religions are obvious, yet they have a common religio-cosmological foundation. The three religions are monotheistic, believing in one Almighty God, who is "out there"; everything else is here, with a great gulf in between.

Smart (1988) states that in the Western religions everything is ultimately headed to one end—to the Kingdom of God or to heaven. At the end of a person's life will be an accounting or payoff, either eternal death or resurrection of his or her body. Further, the things that belong to Almighty God are highly sacred, to be treated with special awe and reverence. What is of particular importance in the Western religions is felicity—happiness and bliss—beyond this earthly life.

In Figure 1.1, like the outer broken circle of the left model, the right model of Western monotheistic worldview is hypothetically believed to have an outer broken circle of the world/universe in which one Almighty God's realm, human beings' realm, and natural beings' realm exist. Their hierarchical positions and interrelations are absolute, rigidly predetermined, and unchangeable. Almighty God's realm is always placed at the top of the hierarchy, human beings' realm in the middle, and natural beings' realm at the bottom. The three solid circles respectively imply that the three realms are fixed and closed to each other, and not interchangeable.

In promoting the study of worldview in this age of interreligious conflicts, it is growingly essential to investigate the potential influences of Western monotheistic religious cosmology on Westerners' cognitive, affective, and behavioral activities in intercultural communication contexts.

## Contrastive Summary of Eastern and Western Worldviews

Psychologists Gilgen and Cho (1979) perceive religio-cosmological worldview in an East-West dichotomy—the East based on Eastern poly-pantheistic religions and the West on European and North American monotheistic beliefs. They are contrastively summarized as follows:

| Eastern Worldview | Western Worldview |
| --- | --- |
| Humans are one with nature and perceive the spiritual and personal physical as one. | Humans are separate from nature and overshadowed by a God. |
| Mind and body are one. | Humans consist of mind, body, and soul. |
| Humans should accept their basic oneness with nature rather than try to control it. | Humans have to manipulate and control nature to survive. |
| Humans are one with nature; they should feel comfortable with anyone. | Humans should reward actions competitive in spirit. |
| Science and technology create an illusion of progress. | Science and technology provide the good life. |
| Enlightenment causes differences to disappear and brings oneness with the universe, coming about through meditation. | No such belief. |

In order to improve interreligious issues repeatedly breaking out in the contemporary world, intercultural communication scholars and educators are widely urged to conduct systematic studies of different religio-cosmological worldviews from ethnocentrism-free perspectives.

## Colliding Worldviews and Environmental Communication

Unfortunately, fruitful intercultural encounters and relations are not always the norm even when highly educated men and women meet together. Misunderstandings, conflicts, and serious consequences occasionally result in their encounters and relations.

No less contentious are the frequent encounters and relations between developers and environmentalists, those who want to conquer and exploit nature and those who try to maintain that humans are one with nature and that destroying nature will lead to destroying humans. These conflicts and collisions are being fought at various levels: local, national, and international.

Clark (1998) warns us that environmental destruction is speedily accelerating in many parts of the world. At the local level, the loss of forests, soil erosion, and overdrafts of ground water are common occurrences.

At the national level, increased yields of timber and food crops are now unsustainable. At the international level, people worldwide are mining natural resources, particularly fossil fuels. Human-induced global warming, overgrazing, and deforestation are compounding large-scale droughts, famines, storms, and floods. Pollution issues are multiplying as waters are poisoned, as forests, rivers, and lakes are decimated by acid rain, and as cities worldwide suffer from foul air.

Dodd (1987) reminds us about the appropriateness of humans' relations with nature—either humans are subject to nature, in harmony with it, or should control it. Today's environmental state suggests that harmony is absent, control is not working, and consequently humans will soon be subject to total natural disaster. Worldviews are thus colliding as we communicate [more and more closely] about environmental issues with our fellow humans throughout the world.

Clark (1989) points a finger at the Western worldview, placing blame for contemporary environmental conditions directly on the West. Although major polluters, soil eroders, and deforesters are prevalent in the East as well, Clark believes it is the Western nature-controlling worldview that is destroying the environment. She suggests that the Western worldview lacks proper values and goals, and has grown obsolete. All worldviews, she claims, require adjustment if humans are to survive. However, the most in need of critically rethinking and redoing is that of ... Western civilization, whose enormous military, science-technological, and economic power and hegemony increasingly impinge upon the entire globe.

## Untying the Gordian Knot

Clark (1989) gives us a thread with which we might find our way out of the labyrinth created by colliding worldviews. Her way may help untie the Gordian knot in which disparate worldviews are enmeshed as they attempt to exist together in the twenty-first century.

In ages past, Clark (1989) argues, worldviews evolved gradually, often imperceptibly. With today's enormous powers unleashed by science and technology from the Western worldview creating excessive environmental change, humankind can no longer rely on the old, indiscernible thinking. Human goals need to be reordered.

All worldviews require some degree of adjustment if the species is to survive. Tracing the beliefs and assumptions underlying them is the first step in making social change possible. This first step is one that students of intercultural communication can undertake, learning to understand the differences in worldview globally, and to comprehend the beliefs and assumptions on which they are based.

Clark (1989) cautions that imposing a new worldview certainly will fail unless it comes from within the cultural context. People of a culture must actively participate in the change making. For a new worldview to evolve, everyone must participate in the change process.

In her 1998 article in *Zygon*, Clark (1998) expounds on her new worldview in detail. Her plan may appear too esoteric for students of intercultural communication to consider. Pennington (1985) believes, however, that reasonable preciseness can be reached in predicting behaviors and motivations in the social, economic, and political lives of cultures of the globe. As Smart (1988) prompts us, we tend to ignore at our peril the worldview dimensions of our communication across cultures.

## SUMMARY AND CONCLUSION

This study has attempted to define *worldview*, describe its conceptual elements and structure, illustrate its hypothetical connection with religious cosmology, and finally make possible suggestions to improve, if not solve, contemporary worldview and environmental conflicts emerging in various parts of the world. The religio-cosmological approach to the study of worldview will serve as a new groundbreaking signpost for intercultural communication scholars and educators by providing new imminent scholarly tasks from a variety of interdisciplinary perspectives.

Tehranian and Chappell (2002), scholars of interreligious and intercivilizational studies, contend

> The way to resolve these conflicts is not to pit one camp against another ... ; for the human race to survive, it is necessary to open up all channels of communication for dialogue, negotiation, and creation of values commensurate with the challenges of our own times. (p. xxix)

# References

Chamberlain, K., & Zika, S. (1992). Religiosity, meaning in life, and psychological well being. In J. F. Schumacher (Ed.), *Religion and mental health* (pp. 138–148). New York: Oxford University Press.

Clark, M. E. (1989). *Ariadne's thread: The search for new modes of thinking*. New York: St. Martin's Press.

Clark, M. E. (1998). Human nature: What we need to know about ourselves in the twenty-first century. *Zygon, 333*, 645–659.

Cooke, P. (1992). *The relationship between culture and worldview: A cross-cultural comparison of Japan, Korea, Puerto Rico, and the United States*. Unpublished master's thesis, West Virginia University, Morgantown, WV.

Cosner, L., Nock, S., Steffan, P., & Rhea, B. (1987). *Introduction to sociology* (2nd ed.). San Diego, CA: Harcourt Brace.

Dodd, C. H. (1987). *Dynamics of intercultural communication* (2nd ed.). Dubuque, IA: W. C. Brown.

Emerson, M. O. (1996). Through tinted glasses: Religion, worldviews, and abortion attitudes. *Journal for the Scientific Study of Religion, 35*, 41–55.

Gilgen, A., & Cho, J. (1979). Questionnaire to measure Eastern and Western thought. *Psychological Report, 44*.

Helve, H. (1991). The formation of religious attitudes and worldviews: A longitudinal study of young Finns. *Social Compass, 38*, 373–392.

Ishii, S. (2001). An emerging rationale for triworld communication studies from Buddhist perspectives, *Human Communication, 4*(1), 1–10.

Klopf, D. W., & McCroskey, J. C. (2007). *Intercultural communication encounters*. Boston: Pearson Education.

Nurius, P. S. (1994). Assumptive worlds, self-definition, and striving among women. *Basic and Applied Social Psychology, 15*, 311–327.

Paige, R. M., & Martin, J. N. (1996). Ethics in intercultural training. In D. Landis & R. S. Bhagat (Eds.), *Handbook of Intercultural Training* (2nd ed.). (pp. 35–60). Thousand Oaks, CA: Sage.

Pennington, U. L. (1985). Intercultural communication. In L. Samovar & R. E. Porter (Eds.), *Intercultural Communication: A Reader* (4th ed.). (pp. 30–39). Belmont, CA: Wadsworth.

Redfield, R. (1953). *The primitive world and its transformation*. Ithaca, NY: Cornell University Press.

Rubin, Z., & Peplau, L. A. (1975). Who believes in a just world? *Journal of Social Issues, 31* 65–89.

Samovar, L., Porter, R. E., & McDaniel, E. R. (2007). *Communication between cultures* (6th ed.). Belmont, CA: Wadsworth.

Smart, R. (1988). Religion-caused complications in intercultural communication. In L. Samovar & R. E. Porter (Eds.), *Intercultural communication: A Reader* (5th ed.). (pp. 62–76). Belmont, CA: Wadsworth.

*Spectra* (2006, December), *42*(12), p. 10.

Spradley, J. P., & McCurdy, U. W. (1980). *Anthropology: The cultural perspective* (2nd ed.). Prospect Heights, IL: Waveland.

Tehranian, M., & Chappell, D. W. (2002). Introduction: Civilization, terror, and dialogue. In M. Tehranian & D. W. Chappell (Eds.), *Dialogue of civilizations: A new agenda for a new millennium* (pp. xxi–xxxiv). London: I. B. Tauris.

## Concepts and Questions

1. According to Ishii, Klopf, and Cooke, how does worldview shape and represent culture?

2. What is the most significant aspect of worldview? How does cultural diversity lead to differing worldviews?

3. What are the major characteristics of *scientific, metaphysical*, and *religious* worldviews?

4. What are religiosity and orthodoxy? How do they contribute to shaping worldviews?

5. According to the essay, what are the five similarities typical of all religions?

6. How does worldview generally differ between Eastern polytheistic and Western monotheistic cultures?

7. What are the three types of human relationships with nature? How do they represent Eastern and Western worldviews?

8. According to one source cited in the essay, "the Western worldview lacks proper values and goals, and has grown obsolete." What does this imply? Do you agree or disagree? Why?

9. How would you differentiate between Eastern and Western perspectives regarding ethics?

10. What should be done to rectify, if not resolve, today's worldwide interreligious conflicts, particularly from the perspective of worldview?

# "Harmony without Uniformity": An Asiacentric Worldview and Its Communicative Implications

## YOSHITAKA MIIKE

*"Harmony without Uniformity': An Asiacentric World-view and Its Communicative Implications" continues our study of worldview but brings a different cultural perspective into consideration. Yoshitaka Miike proposes that conflict arises not from cultural difference itself but from the ignorance of that difference. Moreover, as global citizens, not only must we appreciate cultural diversity, we must learn from that diversity. According to Miike, all too often cultural difference is viewed through the lens of one's own worldview, but to understand and learn from another culture, "we must understand the worldview of the culture and its impact on the forms and functions of communication."*

*The essay contends that many intercultural studies have imposed a European worldview on other cultures, resulting in a critical examination rather than an investigation designed to gain "insight and inspiration." To begin the process of learning from, rather than merely about, other cultures, the author suggests that you need to (1) understand your own worldview, (2) understand other cultures' worldviews, and (3) understand how other cultures perceive your culture. This latter recommendation is particularly relevant on the stage of contemporary international relations.*

*In the second half of his essay, Miike discusses an "Asiacentric worldview and its communicative implications in local and global contexts." He proposes five Asiacentric communication propositions, which reflect his interpretation of the Asian worldview. These include (1) circularity, (2) harmony, (3) other-directedness, (4) reciprocity, and (5) relationality. Awareness and understanding of these propositions offers greater insight into Asian cultures and presents an alternative to the Eurocentric worldview. The essay concludes that the processes of*

*globalization have increased the requirement not just to learn about other cultures but also to find ways that promote and facilitate intercultural learning.*

We may speak of many civilizations in human history, some dead, others living. But human civilization should also be viewed as a grand old tree with many branches, flowers, and fruits, nurtured by the same earth, water, air, and human ingenuity. There is a clear unity in diversity.

**Majid Tehranian (2007, p. 46)**

In response to Samuel Huntington's (1993, 1996) proposition that the world would be divided by "the clash of civilizations," Tu Weiming (2006) tersely states, "Civilizations do not clash. Only ignorance does" (p. 12). Indeed, ignorance of cultural diversity, not cultural diversity itself, is a source of disharmony and conflict in the global village. To be sure, as Chesebro (1996) notes, "multiculturalism is a symbolic issue, a question of how we understand ourselves, how we understand our heritages, and how we understand our futures to be" (p. 13). Hence, it does sometimes radically challenge our basic sense of identity, community, and humanity. And yet, we must learn to appreciate all cultural traditions as valuable resources for humanity because diversity is vital to human survival and flourishing (Tu, 2001a). It is counterproductive to see difference as an obstacle to "progress" in the age of intercultural encounters. Our task as global citizens is not to "liberate" different people from their "primitive" and "uncivilized" traditions, but to learn from different people with their respective traditions about alternative visions of humanity and communication.

> *Conflict arises not from cultural difference itself but from the ignorance of that difference.*

---

In this essay, I will share my thoughts on the what and the how of culture learning to achieve mutual understanding and dialogue, and discuss, as an illustrative example, how Asians and non-Asians alike may be able to benefit from an Asiacentric worldview and its implications for communication. I will re-interpret Molefi Kete Asante's (1993) idea of "multiculturalism without hierarchy" (i.e., the co-existence of many cultures alongside) in the global context and apply the Confucian ideal of "harmony without uniformity" (i.e., the balanced integration of different elements) to the contemporary world. Wisdom is a precious gift to humanity. Every continent, every community, and every culture has accumulated indigenous wisdom, from which we can learn a great deal about how we should relate to one another, nature, and the sprits in the universe (Miike, 2004). It is my argument in the succeeding discussion, therefore, that, if we are to remain hopeful for a prosperous and peaceful world and to realize unity in diversity in the global society, we ought to reflect earnestly on the question of humanity and the way of communication from different local knowledges in different cultures.

*Cultures alongside is the form of cultural co-existence in which we see all cultures equal.*

## CULTURES IN HIERARCHY AND CULTURES ALONGSIDE

Asante (2003b) claims that difference alone does not create a problem, and that it is the assigning of hierarchical value to difference that creates a problem. His idea of "multiculturalism without hierarchy" thus pinpoints how cultures should relate to one another in the context of diversity. He implies that, if multiculturalism is defined as the co-existence of many cultures, there are two ways of cultural co-existence: (1) cultures in hierarchy and (2) cultures alongside. *Cultures in hierarchy* is the form of cultural co-existence in which we see one culture above others so that we learn a frame of reference from one culture and view others through the single cultural standpoint. *Cultures alongside* is the form of cultural co-existence in which we see all cultures equal so that we learn different outlooks from different cultures and view all cultures through their respective cultural lenses. Asante (1993) refers to the second form of cultural co-existence as pluralism without hierarchy and hegemony. He believes that, when we bring together local knowledges from all cultures,

we will have a truly global knowledge about people in the world and move toward a truly transcultural understanding of humanity, diversity, and communication. In this section, using Satoshi Ishii's (1997) conceptualization of culture, I will envision the ideal of culture learning that enhances "multiculturalism without hierarchy." My premise here is that, in order to appreciate any culture, we must understand the worldview of the culture and its impact on the forms and functions of communication.

## Worldview as the Mental Layer of Culture

Ishii (1997) proposes a three-layer-structure model of culture (see Figure 1.1). According to him, culture consists of three layers—material, behavioral, and mental. The most external, overt, and visible layer of culture is the material one, which is represented by various artifacts (e.g., food and clothing) produced, operated, and controlled by the behavioral layer. The semi-overt layer of culture is the behavioral one, which is [composed] of verbal and nonverbal behaviors as symbols (e.g., words and gestures) and reflects the mental layer. The most internal, covert, and invisible layer of culture is the mental one, which functions in the form of values, beliefs, and attitudes. Ishii (1997) is of the opinion that "understanding the mental layer is the most

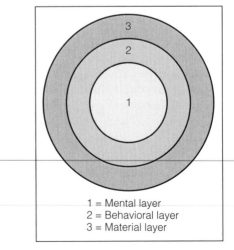

1 = Mental layer
2 = Behavioral layer
3 = Material layer

**FIGURE 1.1** Satoshi Ishii's Model of Culture

important in intercultural communication situations because it is the core of culture which operates and controls the two outer behavioral and material layers" (p. 321). The mental layer of a culture is, in a nutshell, a cultural worldview that answers ultimate questions about humanity and the universe—the triworld of humans, nature, and the supernatural (Ishii, 2001)—and their relationships (e.g., Who are we? Where have we been before birth? Where will we go after death? For what do we live? What should we do in this secular world? How should we relate to other humans, nature, and the spirits?)

Samovar, Porter, and McDaniel (2010) define a worldview as "a culture's orientation toward God, humanity, nature, the universe, life, death, sickness, and other philosophical issues concerning existence" (p. 150). A worldview should be regarded [as] neither completely static nor completely fluid. It is always evolving and transforming and yet maintains the contours of the culture. Different portions of the worldview are instilled in the minds of different members of the culture. Given that it is the deep structure of communication (i.e., the mental layer), we may or may not be aware of its profound impact on the surface structure of communication (i.e., the behavioral and material layers). Because the mental layer of a culture is the most internal and invisible, we can only guess what it is like by comprehensively interpreting the linguistic, religious, philosophical, and historical foundations of the culture. As Ishii, Klopf, and Cooke (2009) comment, a worldview is, more often than not, "implicit and symbolically implied but not explicitly expressed.... How it is formed, therefore, is a significant matter of speculation" (p. 30).

## Learning About and From Cultures

Learning *about* cultures is one thing. Learning *from* cultures is another. We can be very arrogant and ethnocentric, but we can still learn about other cultures. Learning from cultures, on the other hand, requires us to be humble and modest to understand and appreciate other cultures (Miike, 2008a). The former approach is an attempt to describe, interpret, and evaluate a different culture through the worldview that is *not* derived from the culture. In other words, we use the mental layer of our own culture to analyze the material, behavioral, and mental layers of other cultures. In this approach, cultural critique, rather than culture learning, is prone to take place because we tend to treat other cultures like texts for criticism and their members like objects for analysis. I call such an approach "centrism." For example, if we use the mental layer of European cultures to understand African cultures, our Eurocentrism (*not* Eurocentricity) will most likely distort the cultural realities of the African world from an outsider's point of view (see Figure 1.2). When we consciously or unconsciously presume that independence, individualism, and freedom are better than interdependence, communalism, and obligation without reference to the African worldview, we are tempted to view African and European cultures in hierarchy, not alongside, and fail to acknowledge the *ubuntu*-based humanity in the African context (see Kamwangamalu, 2008). Indeed, we relate only to African cultures in a *hierarchical* way.

The latter approach is an attempt to describe, interpret, and evaluate a different culture through the worldview that is derived from the culture. To

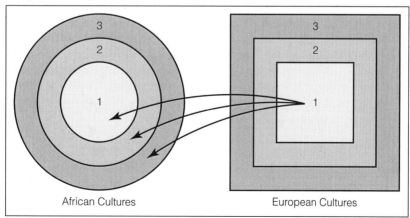

African Cultures                    European Cultures

**FIGURE 1.2** Eurocentrism

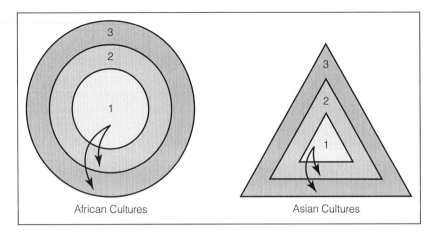

**FIGURE 1.3** Afrocentricity and Asiacentricity

put it in another way, we use the mental layer of the culture to understand its material and behavioral layers. In this approach, culture learning and cross-cultural self-reflection are likely to take place because we tend to view other cultures as resources for insight and inspiration, and their members as willful agents. I call such an approach "centricity." For instance, if we use the mental layers of African and Asian cultures to understand the material and behavioral layers of African and Asian cultures, our Afrocentricity and Asiacentricity (*not* Afrocentrism and Asiacentrism) will more accurately capture the cultural realities of the African and Asian worlds from an insider's point of view (see Figure 1.3). It goes without saying that it is often difficult but critically important for us to engage in learning from, not about, cultures if we wish to broaden and deepen the understanding of culture-specific thought and action, and to expand the notion of humanity in cultural context. This ideal form of culture learning undoubtedly helps us achieve multi-culturalism without hierarchy and facilitate dialogue among civilizations (Miike, 2008a).

## HUMANITY AS AN EXPRESSION OF EUROCENTRISM

What is problematic in many intercultural studies is that the mental layer of European cultures is frequently used to analyze the behavioral and material layers of non-European cultures, which de-contextualizes them and obscures their nexus with the mental layer of non-European cultures (Miike, 2003a, 2010b). Because it is the mental layer of culture that explains why these symbolic behaviors and material artifacts are of immense value, such analyses will not result in the deeper appreciation and better understanding of behavioral and material layers of non-European cultures. Consequently, those descriptions, interpretations, and evaluations present them as exoteric, irrational, and backward and, hence, ultimately create the image of "the Other." In other words, they impose the Eurocentric vision of humanity on other versions of humanity. I contend that we should begin to rethink the role of non-Western worldviews in comprehending non-Western behaviors and in redefining and reconceptualizing humanity and communication. I reiterate that we must see all cultures as central resources for humanistic insight and inspiration, not peripheral targets for ethnocentric analysis and critique.

The nature and ideal of humanity have often been delimited by the Eurocentric worldview. The Enlightenment mentality of the modern West is undoubtedly the most powerful ideology that dominates the Eurocentric worldview. Its core values are instrumental rationality, individual liberty, calculated self-interest, material progress, and rights consciousness (Tu, 2002, 2007). Although aggressive individualism, excessive scientism, and self-destructive anthropocentrism may result in the isolated self, the fragmented community, and the over-exploited earth, these values have served as Eurocentric criteria from which to scrutinize and judge non-European versions and visions of humanity. They have shaped false dichotomies such as the civilized and the primitive, the modern and the traditional, the progressive and the backward, the developed and the developing, and the humane and the inhumane.

## Rethinking Civilization and Development

Tehranian (2007) persuasively argues that, if civilization is defined not as modernization but as "the pursuit of peace with peaceful means," it is an "unfinished journey." All nations and regions are civilized in some ways and uncivilized in other respects. Tehranian (1990, 1999) also convincingly demonstrates that, if we rethink development not in terms of the living standard (e.g., economic growth) but in terms of the quality of life (e.g., human warmth), all societies and communities are both developed and underdeveloped. In his "communitarian" eyes, each country and every culture is struggling to achieve a sustainable balance among the contradictory themes of individual freedom, social equality, civil order, benevolent community, and sacred nature in the conflict-ridden waves of globalism, regionalism, nationalism, localism, and spiritualism (Tehranian, 1993). These themes are perennial concerns and yet intractable issues facing both the local community and the global society.

> *All nations and regions are civilized in some ways and uncivilized in other respects.*

The indigenous *Sarvodaya* movement in Sri Lanka, for instance, is based on this holistic philosophy and practice of development (see Dissanayake, 1984, 1991). According to Tu (2007), China's major challenge today is "to embrace the market economy without turning the whole country into a market society. It would be disastrous if academic institutions, mass media, city organizations and even families were eventually to be totally marketized" (p. 12). The painful realization of many well-informed citizens in materially over-developed environments is that modernization can liberate us from material poverty, but it can also enslave us to spiritual poverty. Without the bonds of fellowship and community, we can be easily driven to the world of psychological alienation, status anxiety, social envy, relentless acquisition, and conspicuous consumption (Tehranian, 1990, 1993).

In spite of criticisms of the aforementioned invalid binaries, Eurocentric constructions of humanity have led to Eurocentric critiques of other non-Western views of humanity. They have also made [us] oblivious to … the past and potential contributions of non-European cultures to human civilization. As Rogers (1976) cautions, therefore, it is very easy for us to "forget that India, China, Persia, and Egypt were old, old centers of civilization, that their rich cultures had in fact provided the basis for contemporary Western cultures" (p. 216). In retrospect, Rogers (1978) goes on to say that, "even if their family life displayed a warmer intimacy and their artistic triumphs were greater, *that* was not development. It could not be measured in dollars" (p. 65). Looking at the non-Western world only with a Eurocentric *critical* eye and looking at the West only with a Eurocentric *uncritical* eye, nonetheless, poses a serious problem in approximating and appreciating the fullest potentials of humanity, civilization, and communication. This is especially so when the Eurocentric vision of humanity, heavily influenced by the Enlightenment in the West, is undermining the human condition (Tu, 2002).

## Being a Teacher and Being a Student

Asante (1998) posits … "Any interpretation of African culture must begin at once to dispense with the notion that, in all things, Europe is teacher and Africa is pupil" (p. 71). There is a persistent and pervasive tendency to approach European cultures from a student's perspective and non-European cultures from a teacher's perspective in the study of culture and communication. As discussed earlier, much cross-cultural and intercultural research deals with non-European cultures as targets for analysis and critique, but not as resources for insight and inspiration. Therefore, it promotes a teacher's perspective on non-European cultures, which decenters and dislocates non-European people. It should be kept in mind, however, that we do not appreciate cultures when we always analyze and critique them. We appreciate cultures when we learn from them. We must be diligent students of non-Western learning and abandon the role of being teachers from the West all of the time. (Miike, 2006). Tu (2008), for example, duly insists on the value of seeing African cultures from a student's point of view:

> If we consider ethnic, cultural, linguistic, and religious diversity as a global asset, Africa should not be characterized by the HIV epidemic, poverty, unemployment and social disintegration alone. It should also be recognized as a rich reservoir for human spirituality and the wisdom of elders. The African Renaissance, symbolized by the geological and biological diversity of the tiny area around Capetown (said to be comparable in richness to the vast area of Canada) ought to be a source of inspiration for a changed mindset that addresses social development as a global joint venture. (p. 331)

## Three Steps to Cross-Cultural Dialogue

With "a global mindset by which we try to see things through the eyes of others and add their knowledge to our personal repertoires" (Chen & Starosta, 2000, p. 1), we can perhaps take three steps to cross-cultural dialogue. The first step is to understand the mental layer of our own culture and its impact on the behavioral and material layers. The second step is to understand the mental layer of other cultures and its impact on the behavioral and material layers. The third step is to listen to others' perspectives on our culture and share our perspectives on other cultures in order to reflect on what it means to be human in both local and global contexts and how humans should relate to one another, nature, and the spirits. In this step, we must engage in intercultural dialogue with Asante's (2006) spirit of mutual respect and learning: "As creators of our own societies, we have valuable experiences to share, not to impose, which might be examined and adapted in a spirit of sharing and dialogue. This is the real meaning of intercultural interaction" (p. 154). Tu (2008) echoes Asante's position by saying that "the celebration of cultural diversity, without falling into the trap of pernicious relativism, is profoundly meaningful for global stewardship" (p. 331).

Centricity in the first step of cross-cultural dialogue is the beginning and basis of equality and mutuality in intercultural communication (Miike, 2008a). It prevents our interactions with people from different countries and cultures from becoming a mere imposition-imitation encounter. This point should be well taken, especially by non-Westerners who wish to have sincere and serious conversations about intercultural cooperation and collaboration with Westerners on an equal footing. As Asante (2009) elucidates, centricity urges us, first and foremost, to inquire about our own identities, cultures, and histories as a way of contributing to the grand flow of the entire humanity without being imitators who blindly follow others. Paradoxically, in this soul-searching process, we may discover that the development of our own culture is, in fact, indebted to other cultures, and that the nature of human civilization is truly multicultural and synergic. In any case, imitation is not intercultural (Miike, 2008a).

# ASIACENTRIC WORLDVIEW AND COMMUNICATION

In this section, I will draw on my previous writings (Miike, 2003a, 2004, 2007) based on the principle of Asiacentricity (see Miike, 2006, 2008b, 2010a, 2010b) and outline an Asiacentric worldview and its communicative implications in local and global contexts. More specifically, I will discuss five Asiacentric propositions on human communication. They are *propositions, not truths*, in the sense that they reflect my interpretation of the *invisible* mental layer of Asian cultures and my intent to tap into Asian cultural wisdom both for an Asiacentric understanding of Asian communication and for dialogue among civilizations. Hence, they do not capture the whole profile of the Asian communicator and the entire picture of Asian communication. Every scholarly investigation must "make certain simplifying assumptions about complex realities that it studies" (Rogers, 1990, p. 261). The present inquiry of Asiacentricity is no exception in this regard. My discussion here is based on the five elements of an Asiacentric worldview that I have identified from the existing literature on the psychology and practices of Asian cultures and communication (e.g., Chen & Miike, 2003; Dissanayake, 1988; Kincaid, 1987; Miike, 2009a, 2009b; Miike & Chen, 2006, 2007; Nordstrom, 1983): (1) circularity, (2) harmony, (3) other-directedness, (4) reciprocity, and (5) relationality. These recurring themes collectively paint an Asiacentric picture of humanity and communication.

## Communication as a Reminder of Non-Separateness

The first Asiacentric proposition is that *communication is a process in which we remind ourselves of the interdependence and interrelatedness of the universe*. This proposition can complement the Western dominant thinking that communication is a process in which we demonstrate our independence and express our individuality. The two Asian themes of relationality and circularity have much to do with the ontological belief that the universe is a great whole in which everyone and everything are interrelated across space and time. No one and nothing in the universe exists in isolation (Chen, 2006; Jung, 2009; Miike, 2003a). Asian religions and philosophies illuminate the interpenetrated nature of the self, family, community, society, nation, world, and cosmos.

Confucius (551–479 BCE) remarks in the *Analects* (6: 30) that "if you wish to establish yourself, you have to help others to establish themselves; if you wish to complete yourself, you have to help others to complete themselves." Similarly, in the words of Suzuki (2006), Buddhism teaches: "So to save oneself we have to save others…. By helping others, I may be able to save myself. My salvation and others' salvation are so intimately involved, connected together, that we can never save ourselves just by ourselves. We must always be saved together" (p. 19). More interestingly, the Hindu notion of *Virat Purusha* [Cosmic Person] views each individual as the manifestation of the cosmos itself. The universe is "a single body where each element lives for all and all live for one … [T]he weal and woe of one individual affect another" (Saral, 1983, p. 54). It is the teaching of Hinduism that "the world of distinct and separate objects and processes is a manifestation of a more fundamental reality that is undivided and unconditioned" (Jain, 1991, p. 80).

The Asian worldview demands that we constantly communicate with fellow humans, nature, and the world of spirits in order to escape from the

*The Asian worldview demands that we constantly communicate with fellow humans, nature, and the world of spirits.*

illusion that we are independent individuals in a particular place at a particular time (Miike, 2007). For humans are prone to engage in a present-oriented and lifeworld-centered way of thinking. It comes as no surprise, then, that Asian patterns of small group and organizational communication correspond especially to this ideal of communication as a reminder of … non-separateness with a view to strengthening group or organizational unity, loyalty, and harmony. The Indonesian *musyawarah-mufakat* performance and the Japanese *nemawashi* practice, for instance, allow group members not only to exchange ideas but also to increase the sense of interdependence and interrelatedness (Saito, 1982).

The Asian worldview essentially defines communication as an endless process in which we continuously locate and relocate ourselves in an ever-expanding network of relationships across space and time. This ancient yet radical Eastern idea of communication must be taken seriously now that the global village has never been so divided by wealth, power, technology, and influence in world history, and [now] that we have polluted the air we breathe and poisoned the water we drink to the extent that we risk our own lives (Tu, 1998, 2002). Social disintegration is also becoming a worldwide phenomenon in modern societies. As Asante (2005) observes, "The lack of connectedness creates insensitivity to others, harshness, abrasiveness, and arrogance" (p. 135). Yum (2000) further points out that "[a]lthough individualism has its own strength as a value, individualism that is not accompanied by commitments to large entities eventually forces people into a state of isolation, where life itself becomes meaningless" (p. 71). We must learn about communication as a way to realize that our well-being is inextricably and inescapably intertwined with [the well-being] of other members of the human family, nature, and even the supernatural.

## Communication as Ego-Reduction and Self-Cultivation

The second Asiacentric proposition is that *communication is a process in which we reduce our selfishness and* egocentrism. This Eastern viewpoint makes a sharp contrast to the Western presumption that communication is a process in which we enhance our self-esteem and protect our self-interest (Yin, 2009; Yin & Miike, 2008). Dogen (1200–1253), the founder of the Soto Zen school in Japan, writes at the very beginning of his 13th-century book *Shobogenzo* [*Treasury of the Eye of the True Dharma*]: "To study the Way is to study the self. To study the self is to forget the self. To forget the self is to be enlightened by ten thousand things." What he meant was that removing all the divisions and distinctions of self and other renders it possible to form an ultimate unity with everything. According to Dogen, intrapersonal communication, in which we reduce selfishness and egocentrism, can lead to ultimate communication with the whole universe (Saito, 1970). Likewise, the Confucian way of learning to be human is to engage in ceaseless self-cultivation and creative self-transformation by crafting the self as *a center* of myriad relationships, not *the center* of all things. The point of departure in quest of our authentic identity is, paradoxically, to overcome selfishness and egocentrism (Tu, 2002). What is intriguing about Buddhist and Confucian epistemologies is that we need to reduce our selfishness and egocentrism through communication and then become better communicators as a result of self-discipline and self-cultivation.

It should not be misunderstood, however, that Asian traditions of thought discourage the values of autonomy and agency. Confucian thought, for example, enunciates the view that "the reciprocal interplay between self as center and self for others enables the self to become a center of relationships. As a center, personal dignity can never be marginalized and, as relationships, the spirit of consideration is never suppressed" (Tu, 2001b, p. 26). While they recognize the importance of individuality in collectivity and independence in interdependence, Asian religious-philosophers, especially Buddhist thinkers, are critically aware that humans are by nature self-centered and egocentric. Therefore, their teachings impel humans to discipline and cultivate themselves so that they can experience the oneness of the universe and harmoniously coexist with fellow humans, nature and the world of spirits. In the Asian worldview, communication is conceptualized as central to this process of self-discipline, self-cultivation, self-development, and self-realization. In such a line of thinking, the Asian way of knowing is grounded on the elimination of excessive and aggressive ego as a primary source of mental suffering and perceptual barriers (Ishii, 2004).

Asian daily experiences appear to concertedly indicate that interacting with other humans, nature, and the spirits facilitates the process of disciplining and cultivating ourselves. Asians may be truly touched and highly motivated to discipline themselves and work harder when they listen to, or simply observe, individuals who possess sophisticated skills through their years of practice or people who are struggling against all odds in their lives. Moreover, reducing selfishness and egocentrism means increasing connection and cooperation not only at the interpersonal level but also at other levels. From the perspective of Zen Buddhism, "An awareness of 'oneness' develops from emptying oneself and accepting the other" (Saito, 1970, p. 17). Encountering fellow humans, nature, and the spirits in a way that we reduce our selfishness and egocentrism enables us to rise above nepotism, parochialism, ethnocentrism, and anthropocentrism as well as egocentrism.

In such a sense, this second communicative proposition is, once again, in consonance with the two Asian themes of relationality and circularity. In this increasing ego-driven world, the time is right to turn our attention to the role of interpersonal communication as an ego-reduction and self-decentering practice. For, as Chen (2005) understands, in order for us to fully unfold our potential as co-creators of the whole universe with heaven and earth, our self must be "ceaselessly edified, constantly liberated, and perpetually purified" (p. 7) in intercultural encounters with the other.

## Communication as Sensing and Feeling

The third Asiacentric proposition is that *communication is a process in which we feel the joy and suffering of all sentient beings*. This proposition is linked particularly with the Asian theme of other-directedness. As the Chinese concept of *renqing*, the Japanese concept of *ninjo*, and the Korean concept of *jung* imply, emotional sensitivity, not instrumental rationality, occupies a central place in being and becoming fully human in the Asian worldview. To feel through sensitivity, rather than to analyze through rationality, is one of the "habits of the heart" in Asian communication (Chen & Starosta, 2003). Such a feature manifests in many trans-Asian premises and practices of communication. The Filipino *pahiwatig-pakikiramdam* dynamics (Maggay, 1999; Mansukhani, 2005; Mataragnon, 1988), the Japanese *enryo-sasshi* style (Ishii & Bruneau, 1994; Miike, 2003, 2010c), and the Korean *saryo-nunchi* anticipation (Choi & Choi, 1992; Robinson, 2003), for example, underscore and underline the importance of communicative sensitivity to the joy and suffering of fellow human beings. This preponderance toward affection instead of cognition does not mean that Asians are not rational and do not rely on reason (Chen, 2006), but feelings and emotions are equally, or even more, valued as essential qualities in the Asian version of humanity and communication.

Asian religions and philosophies also endorse this communicative proposition. Confucianism delimits the cardinal concept of *ren* [human-heartedness] in light of sympathy and empathy. Buddhism likewise emphasizes the development of compassion, which literally means "feelings in common." Tu (2001a) accounts for the centrality of emotional sensitivity in Buddhist and Confucian visions of humanity:

> [B]oth Confucianism and Buddhism maintain that sympathy, empathy and compassion are at the same time the minimum requirement and the maximum realization of the human way. According to Confucian and Buddhist modes of thinking, human beings are sentient beings. Sensitivity, rather than rationality, is the distinctive feature of humanity. We feel; therefore we are. Through feeling, we realize our own existence and the coexistence of other human beings, indeed birds, animals, plants and all the myriad things in the universe. Since this feeling of interconnectedness is not merely a private emotion but a sense of fellowship that is intersubjectively confirmable, it is a commonly shareable value. (pp. 83–84)

It is important to note that the Asian worldview does not encourage speaker-centered affective communication where individuals explicitly disclose their emotions to one another. According to the Asian experience, because "[r]elational emotions that bind and bond individuals together, not the private and narcissistic emotions, are emphasized" (Kim, 2001, p. 67), emotional convergence in communication is often possible when the ego-decentered and other-directed listener attempts to sense and read the speaker's emotional dynamics. Thus, to be communicatively active in the Asian sense is to be perceptive, receptive, and introspective to *feel together* with fellow humans, nature, and the spirits (Miike, 2007). The desirable profile of such a sensitive Asian communicator is close to what Gordon (2009) has in mind as an "attuned communicator": "To develop sensitivity to the importance of 'fine-turning' to the other, to sensing who they are, where they've been, what they believe and value, and feel what they need, what their style is, what their rhythms are, this is the work of an 'attuned' communicator" (p. 13).

Buddhist theories postulate that the development of compassion parallels the increased degrees of the awareness of interdependent interrelatedness and egoless altruism. As the first and second Asiacentric propositions suggest, then, communication can augment such an awareness and egolessness, which, in turn, helps us develop empathic sensitivity to communicate and feel togetherness and interdependence. This Asian portrait of communication may be pressed into service so as to extend the affective and altruistic aspect of humanity in the global community.

## Communication as Reciprocal Duty and Responsibility

The fourth Asiacentric proposition is that *communication is a process in which we receive and return our debts to all sentient beings*. Many Asian religious-philosophical teachings as well as everyday practices highlight the fact that our existence is dependent on all other beings. The Buddhist doctrine of *pratitya*

> *The Asian worldview does not encourage speaker-centered affective communication where individuals explicitly disclose their emotions to one another.*

*samutpada* [dependent co-arising] is a case in point (see Chang & Holt, 1991; Dissanayake, 1983; Ishii, 1998). It is the idea that "the existence of every being in the universe is made possible only by Buddhist *engi* or predetermined cooriginations and corelationships with all other beings" (Ishii, 2001, p. 7). Implicit in this Asian worldview is that we must be grateful to our fellow humans, natural environments, and ancestral spirits for our blessings and have ethical obligations to return something to them. We owe our debts of gratitude to our ancestors, parents, siblings, neighbors, teachers, friends, animals, oceans, rivers, mountains, and plants. Confucianism and Hinduism similarly accentuate the primacy of obligatory reciprocity in embodying supportive and cooperative interdependence and in nurturing loyal and long-term relationships (Chen & Chung, 2000; Saral, 1983; Yum, 2000). The Asian theme of reciprocity comes into play here.

Daisetsu Suzuki (1870-1966), perhaps the most renowned scholar of Zen Buddhism in the West, once advocated the importance of *shujo-no-on* [the debt of gratitude that we owe to the universe for our existence] for humanity (Sato, 1959). In traditional Japanese culture, people ought to feel obligated to remember and repay the *on* [debt of gratitude] that they had received from all contacts in the course of their life. In particular, four types of *on* were emphasized: *on* from parents as life givers, *on* from teachers and mentors, *on* from lords, and *shujo-no-on*. From a Buddhist viewpoint, *shujo-no-on* is the ultimate *on* of interdependence based on our awareness and appreciation of the support of the universe with which we are living on the earth. It is age-old wisdom similar to the emerging and evolving philosophy of "ecopiety" about the self-defeating humanity and the endangered earth (see Jung, 2009). Suzuki in Sato (1959) explicates this concept as follows:

> It rains and the ground becomes wet. It is the *on* of rain; it is the virtue of rain. The earth absorbs the rain, and sends it to the roots of trees and grasses, and then to their buds. This is the *on* of the great earth. They are helping each other, loving each other; it is *on*. I receive *on* from others, at the same time I extend *on* to others.... It is love and the action of love we feel as *on* for each other. To understand *shujo-no-on* means to get rid of the world of power-domination, to enter into the area of loving each other and

helping each other. "*Okage-sama*" means literally "appreciation of the protection of the tree under its shade," but the implication can be extended to our existence on the earth in the solar system, in this Universe. Indeed, true meaning of human existence lies in realizing this relationship. (p. 244)

Other Asian concepts in Asian languages such as the Filipino concept of *utang na loob* and the Thai concept of *bhunkun* also allude to communication as the process of reciprocating love and kindness. These cultural practices ideally enhance our deep affection and thoughtful consideration toward others. It is noteworthy that this communication process of receiving and returning debts of gratitude often goes beyond here-and-now reciprocity. As Ho (1993) attests, the Asian worldview stresses an extended and circular perspective on space and time in the need to repay our debt of gratitude. That is, if we are unable to pay in our present life, the debt may be passed on to the next and future generations. Or it may also be assumed in our next life. "In a sense," Yum (2000) writes, "a person is forever indebted to others, who in turn are constrained by other debts" (p. 66). Such an Asian perspective on communication as assuming responsibilities, not as asserting rights, may be perceived as a challenge to individual freedom, but it can project duty-centered character building and ethical intelligence in the age of global exploitation (Yin, 2009; Yin & Miike, 2008).

## Communication as Moralizing and Harmonizing

The fifth Asiacentric proposition is that *communication is a process in which we moralize and harmonize the universe*. This proposition concerns itself with the Asian axiological emphasis on the social order and, ultimately, the order of the universe. It is also pertinent to an Asian criterion by which to evaluate communicative conduct. In Asian cultures, generally speaking, communication is positively evaluated when it attempts to actualize the moral integrity and harmony of the universe, while it is negatively evaluated when it aims to pursue our own individual self-interest. Like the African worldview, "humaneness is characterized by how well people live in harmony with each other and nature. To be inhumane is to live poorly in relationship to your fellow human beings and nature" (Asante, 2005, p. 135). Hence, ethics and morality revolve around harmony from the intrapersonal level to the cosmological level. In the Asian worldview, harmony is the end rather than the means of communication (Chen, 2004, 2006). As Chen and Starosta (2003) clarify, harmony in Asian communication processes "represents a kind of ethical appeal that can induce a sense of duty for cooperation with the other party, not by the communicator's strategic words but by the sincere display of whole-hearted concern with the other" (p. 6).

The Asian de-emphasis on speech has been stereotypically exaggerated in the culture and communication literature to the extent that it gives the impression that Asians traditionally have not valued the act of speaking at all. But speaking for the benefit of others, not for the sake of self-interest, "is much cherished in Asian traditions of thought. Dissanayake (2003), for instance, explores the Buddhist teaching of *samma vaca* [right speech] and its moral implications in human communication. There are four primary guidelines for right speech: (1) right speech should be de-linked with falsehoods of any sort; (2) right speech discourages slander and calumny leading to friction and hostility among people; (3) right speech presupposes the absence of, and refraining from, harsh language; and (4) right speech encourages speakers to desist from frivolous and idle chatter and to embrace purposeful and productive speech. There is also much to learn from Confucius's teaching of "humble talk and moral action" (see Chang, 2008) and Gandhi's nonviolent philosophy of *Satyagraha* (see Pandikattu, 2001; Starosta & Shi, 2007) about moralizing and harmonizing styles and strategies of communication.

"An exemplary person seeks harmony but not uniformity," Confucius opines in the *Analects* (13:23). This ideal of "harmony without uniformity" can be an ultimate goal of communication both in Asian societies and in the global village. In Confucius's mind, a global citizen is a person who can fully recognize diversity as the basis for harmony and take the moral responsibility to make the best out of it. To such a citizen, intercultural communication is a means of integrating differences without creating the

sameness. Tu in UNESCO (2006) articulates the critical relationship between harmony and diversity:

> Harmony is predicated on diversity and difference. The opposite of harmony is sameness. The "great unity" is diametrically opposed to homogenized unity. The greatness of the "great unity" lies in its convergence, confluence, integration and harmonization of different colors, sounds, tastes and experiences. Harmony embraces difference. Without difference, harmony is impossible. If we do not mix spices, we cannot make tasty soup. Without different sounds, there is no music. Without different colors, there are no paintings. Geodiversity and biodiversity are preconditions for human survival, and linguistic and cultural diversity is congenial to human flourishing. (p. 181)

## Asiacentric Communication Ethics and Competence

Asia is diverse and dynamic. It is a region of cultural complexity, continuity, and change, although the term signifies a certain geographical location in the world, designates a common historical and political struggle against Western imperialism and colonialism, and implies shared religious-philosophical foundations and cultural heritage (Miike, 2003a). Asian nations are plural societies. They "have a dominant community and a number of minority communities divided on the basis of language, religion, caste, and ethnicity living together under a single polity" (Goonasekera, 2003, p. 368). Chen and Starosta (2003) vividly depict such a place of remarkable variety and vitality:

> Indonesia is largely Muslim, yet it contains a large Hindu enclave in Bali. Indians were also imported to parts of Malaysia, and Buddhism, started in India, [but] can hardly be found there now, except [as] a political reaction to casteism. Instead, it has taken root in China, Sri Lanka, and elsewhere. Shintoism thrives in Japan, but maybe nowhere else. Asia has some massive cities, but 80% of some Asian countries are rural. India and China have 800 language varieties or dialects. (p. 1)

Obviously, therefore, all Asian communicators do not subscribe to the above-discussed five propositions. These propositions do not necessarily reflect the way Asians actually communicate in real-life situations. Nevertheless, they serve as theoretical lenses from which to see an Asian version of humanity and to view Asian thought and action. They are designed to provide much food for thought in rethinking the nature and ideal of human communication in Asia and beyond from an alternative vantage point.

For example, the advent of the global village and the crisis of the human condition have made it compelling to ruminate on communication ethics and competence in intercultural contexts (Chen, 2005; Miike, 2009b; Tehranian, 2007). There have been extensive discussions on Eurocentric biases in the definitions and components of these key concepts (e.g., Chen & Starosta, 2008; Ishii, 2009; Shuter, 2003; Xiao & Chen, 2009). We can reexamine current conceptualizations of communication ethics and competence from the five Asiacentric propositions. They suggest that an ethical communicator can (1) remind herself or himself and others of interrelatedness and interdependence through communication, (2) discipline and cultivate herself or himself without being overly self-centered through communication, (3) develop her or his altruistic sensitivity to the sufferings of others, (4) feel her or his obligation to remember the debts that she or he has received and to try to return them in one way or another, and (5) speak up for greater harmony and morality.

Just like many proponents of Asian values who are often misunderstood by Western conservative intellectuals (Mahbubani, 2002), I am *not* asserting that these Asiacentric viewpoints on humans communicating are superior to Eurocentric ones, but I am protesting that they are not inferior to them. They are rooted in the Asian worldview and yet may be sharable along with those rooted in, say, the African worldview toward what Tu (2006, 2007) calls "a dialogical civilization" or what Sitaram (1998) calls "a higher humanity." In Sitaram's (1998)

> *The advent of the global village and the crisis of the human condition have made it compelling to ruminate on communication ethics and competence in intercultural contexts.*

view, such a truly human civilization "is not an extension of any one culture; rather it would be the essence of all cultures of the entire humanity" (p. 13). Hence, there is room for Asiacentric, as well as Afrocentric and other non-Western, contributions. As Asante (1993) avers, there is also "space for Eurocentricity in a multicultural enterprise so long as it does not parade as universal. No one wants to banish the Eurocentric view. It is a valid view of reality where it does not force its way" (p. 188).

## "CHERISHING THE OLD TO KNOW THE NEW"

It was my intention in this essay to argue that learning from, not about, cultures for self-reflexivity is a *sine qua non* for cross-cultural dialogue and to illustrate how Asians and non-Asians can benefit from an Asiacentric worldview and its implications for communication in local and global contexts. Tu (2001a) propounds two propositions on globalization. First, globalization can be hegemonic homogenization without cultural diversity and sensitivity, but through dialogue it may lead to a genuine sense of global community. Second, the search for identity can degenerate into extreme ethnocentrism and exclusion, but through dialogue it may lead to an authentic way of intercultural communication and to a real respect for diversity. It is then up to us whether we will further risk our lifeboat by imposing the ethnocentric version of humanity on others and dividing the world with the clash of ignorance, or we will engage in mutual dialogue with the principle of "multiculturalism without hierarchy" toward "harmony without uniformity." In either case, Mahatma Gandhi's statement that "this world has enough for all of us but not enough for the greed of a single person" (Tehranian, 1999, p. 191) now sounds soberer than ever before.

Asante (2003a) asseverates that innovation and tradition are key to humanizing the world. He contends that "The generation of the new, the novel, is basic to the advancement of cultural ideas but also is the maintenance of the traditional" (p. 78). His contention is in perfect resonance with the Confucian spirit of "cherishing the old to know the new" (*Analects*, 2: 11). It is indeed imperative for us to study and apply old wisdoms both locally and globally in order to respond to new situations in the changing world (Miike, 2004). Tu (1998) aptly describes where we stand in search of global ethics and humanistic values:

> The problematique of the viability of the human race ... is that having transformed ourselves into the most aggressive and self-destructive animal the evolutionary process has ever witnessed, we have now added ourselves to the long list of endangered species. This is the magnitude of the human dilemma today. We are urgently in need of a new way of perceiving, a new mode of thinking, even a new form of life, which is predicated on a radically transformed attitude and worldview. Paradoxically, our determined effort to move away from militarism, materialism, aggression, conflict, and destruction may be a new discovery, but it is also a return to the spiritual roots that have provided the ground for humans to survive and flourish for centuries. In this sense, our humanity is at a crossroads. (p. 3)

# References

Asante, M. K. (1993). Multiculturalism without hierarchy: An Afrocentric response to Diane Ravitch. In F. J. Beckwith & M. E. Bauman (Eds.), *Are you politically correct? Debating America's cultural standards* (pp. 185–193). Buffalo, NY: Prometheus Books.

Asante, M. K. (1998). *The Afrocentric idea* (Rev. ed.). Philadelphia: Temple University Press.

Asante, M. K. (2003a). *Afrocentricity: The theory of social change* (Rev. ed.). Chicago: African American Images.

Asante, M. K. (2003b). Education for liberation: On campus with a purpose. In V. L. Farmer (Ed.), *The Black student's guide to graduate and professional school success* (pp. 162–169). Westport, CT: Greenwood Press.

Asante, M. K. (2005). *Race, rhetoric, and identity: The architecton of soul*. Amherst, NY: Humanity Books.

Asante, M. K. (2006). The rhetoric of globalization: The Europeanization of human ideas. *Journal of Multicultural Discourses, 1*(2), 152–158.

Asante, M. K. (2009). *Erasing racism: The survival of the American nation* (2nd ed.). Amherst, NY: Prometheus Books.

Chang, H.-C. (2008). Language and words: Communication in the *Analects* of Confucius. In M. K. Asante, Y. Miike, & J. Yin (Eds.), *The global intercultural communication reader* (pp. 95–112). New York: Routledge.

Chang, H. -C., & Holt, G. R. (1991). The concept of *yuan* and Chinese interpersonal relationships. In S. Ting-Toomey & F. Korzenny (Eds.), *Cross-cultural interpersonal communication* (pp. 28–57). Newbury Park, CA: Sage.

Chen, G. -M. (2004). The two faces of Chinese communication. *Human Communication: A Journal of the Pacific and Asian Communication Association, 7*(1), 25–36.

Chen, G. -M. (2005). A model of global communication competence. *China Media Research, 1*(1), 3–11.

Chen, G. -M. (2006). Asian communication studies: What and where to now. *Review of Communication, 6*(4), 295–311.

Chen, G. -M., & Chung, J. (2000). The "Five Asian Dragons": Management behaviors and organizational communication. In L. A. Samovar & R. E. Porter (Eds.), *Intercultural communication: A reader* (9th ed., pp. 301–312). Belmont, CA: Wadsworth.

Chen, G. -M., & Miike, Y. (Eds.). (2003). Asian approaches to human communication [Special issue]. *Intercultural Communication Studies, 12*(4), 1–218.

Chen, G. -M., & Starosta, W. J. (2000). Communication and global society: An introduction. In G.-M. Chen & W. J. Starosta (Eds.), *Communication and global society* (pp. 1–16). New York: Peter Lang.

Chen, G. -M., & Starosta, W. J. (2003). Asian approaches to human communication: A dialogue. *Intercultural Communication Studies, 12*(4), 1–15.

Chen, G. -M., & Starosta, W. J. (2008). Intercultural communication competence: A synthesis. In M. K. Asante, Y. Miike, & J. Yin (Eds.), *The global intercultural communication reader* (pp. 215–237). New York: Routledge.

Chesebro, J. W. (1996, December). Unity in diversity: Multiculturalism, guilt/victimage, and a new scholarly orientation. *Spectra: Newsletter of the Speech Communication Association, 32*(12), 10–14.

Choi, S. -C., & Choi, S. -H. (1992). The conceptualization of Korean tact, *noon-chi*. In S. Iwawaki, Y. Kashima, & K. Leung. (Eds.), *Innovations in cross-cultural psychology* (pp. 49–61). Amsterdam: Swets & Zeitlinger.

Dissanayake, W. (1983). The communication significance of the Buddhist concept of dependent co-origination. *Communication, 8*(1), 29–45.

Dissanayake, W. (1984). A Buddhist approach to development: A Sri Lankan endeavor. In G. Wang & W. Dissanayake (Eds.), *Continuity and change in communication systems: An Asian perspective* (pp. 39–51). Norwood, NJ: Ablex.

Dissanayake, W. (Ed.). (1988). *Communication theory: The Asian perspective*. Singapore: Asian Mass Communication Research and Information Center.

Dissanayake, W. (1991). Ethics, development, and communication: A Buddhist approach. In F. L. Casmir (Ed.), *Communication in development* (pp. 319–337). Norwood, NJ: Ablex.

Dissanayake, W. (2003). Asian approaches to human communication: Retrospect and prospect. *Intercultural Communication Studies, 12*(4), 17–37.

Goonasekera, A. (2003). Communication studies in Asia: Theoretical and methodological issues. In A. Goonasekera, L. C. Wah, & S. Venkatraman (Eds.), *Asian communication handbook 2003* (pp. 358–369). Singapore: Asian Media Information and Communication Center.

Gordon, R. D. (2009). *On becoming an attuned communicator*. Bloomington, IN: iUniverse.

Ho, D. Y. F. (1993). Relational orientation in Asian social psychology. In U. Kim & J. W. Berry (Eds.), *Indigenous psychologies: Research and experience in cultural context* (pp. 240–259). Newbury Park, CA: Sage.

Huntington, S. P. (1993). The clash of civilizations? *Foreign Affairs, 72*(3), 22–49.

Huntington, S. P. (1996). *The clash of civilizations and the remaking of world order*. New York: Simon & Schuster.

Ishii, S. (1997). Tasks for intercultural communication researchers in the Asia-Pacific region in the 21st century. *Dokkyo International Review, 10*, 313–326.

Ishii, S. (1998). Developing a Buddhist *en*-based systems paradigm for the study of Japanese human relationships. *Japan Review, 10*, 109–122.

Ishii, S. (2001). An emerging rationale for triworld communication studies from Buddhist perspectives. *Human Communication: A Journal of the Pacific and Asian Communication Association, 4*(1), 1–10.

Ishii, S. (2004). Proposing a Buddhist consciousness-only epistemological model for intrapersonal communication research. *Journal of Intercultural Communication Research, 33*(2), 63–76.

Ishii, S. (2009). Conceptualizing Asian communication ethics: A Buddhist perspective. *Journal of Multicultural Discourses, 4*(1), 49–60.

Ishii, S., & Bruneau, T. (1994). Silence and silences in cross-cultural perspective: Japan and the United States. In L. A. Samovar & R. E. Porter (Eds.), *Intercultural communication: A reader* (7th ed., pp. 246–251). Belmont, CA: Wadsworth.

Ishii, S., & Klopf, D., & Cooke, P. (2009). Worldview in intercultural communication: A religio-cosmological approach. In L. A. Samovar, R. E. Porter, & E. R. McDaniel (Eds.), *Intercultural communication: A reader* (12th ed., pp. 28–36). Boston, MA: Wadsworth Cengage Learning.

Jain, N. C. (1991). Worldview and cultural patterns of India. In L. A. Samovar & R. E. Porter (Eds.), *Intercultural communication: A reader* (6th ed., pp. 78–87). Belmont, CA: Wadsworth.

Jung, H. Y. (2009). *The way of ecopiety: Essays in transversal geophilosophy*. New York: Global Scholarly Publications.

Kamwangamalu, N. M. (2008). *Ubuntu* in South Africa: A sociolinguistic perspective to a pan-African concept. In M. K. Asante, Y. Miike, & J. Yin (Eds.), *The global intercultural communication reader* (pp. 113–122). New York: Routledge.

Kim, U. (2001). Culture, science, and indigenous psychologies: An integrated analysis. In D. Matsumoto (Ed.), *Handbook of culture and psychology* (pp. 51–75). New York: Oxford University Press.

Kincaid, D. L. (Ed.). (1987). *Communication theory: Eastern and Western perspectives*. San Diego, CA: Academic Press.

Maggay, M. P. (1999). *Understanding ambiguity in Filipino communication patterns*. Quezon City, Philippines: Institute for Studies in Asian Church and Culture.

Mahbubani, K. (2002). *Can Asians think? Understanding the divide between East and West*. South Royalton, VT: Steerforth Press.

Mansukhani, R. (2005). *Pakikiramdam*: A critical analysis. In R. M. Gripaldo (Ed.), *Filipino cultural traits: Claro R. Ceniza Lectures* (pp. 185–202). Washington, DC: Council for Research in Values and Philosophy.

Mataragnon, R. H. (1988). *Pakikiramdam* in Filipino social interaction: A study of subtlety and sensitivity. In A. C. Paranjpe, D. Y. F. Ho, & R. W. Rieber (Eds.), *Asian contributions to psychology* (pp. 251–262). New York: Praeger.

Miike, Y. (2003a). Beyond Eurocentrism in the intercultural field: Searching for an Asiacentric paradigm. In W. J. Starosta & G. -M. Chen (Eds.), *Ferment in the intercultural field: Axiology/value/praxis* (pp. 243–276). Thousand Oaks, CA: Sage.

Miike, Y. (2003b). Japanese *enryo-sasshi* communication and the psychology of *amae*: Reconsideration and reconceptualization. *Keio Communication Review, 25*, 93–115.

Miike, Y. (2004). Rethinking humanity, culture, and communication: Asiacentric critiques and contributions. *Human Communication: A Journal of the Pacific and Asian Communication Association*, 7(1), 67–82.

Miike, Y. (2006). Non-Western theory in Western research? An Asiacentric agenda for Asian communication studies. *Review of Communication*, 6(1/2), 4–31.

Miike, Y. (2007). An Asiacentric reflection on Eurocentric bias in communication theory. *Communication Monographs*, 74(2), 272–278.

Miike, Y. (2008a). Advancing centricity for non-Western scholarship: Lessons from Molefi Kete Asante's legacy of Afrocentricity. In A. Mazama (Ed.), *Essays in honor of an intellectual warrior, Molefi Kete Asante* (pp. 287–327). Paris: Editions Menaibuc.

Miike, Y. (2008b). Toward an alternative metatheory of human communication: An Asiacentric vision. In M. K. Asante, Y. Miike, & J. Yin (Eds.), *The global intercultural communication reader* (pp. 57–72). New York: Routledge.

Miike, Y. (2009a). "Cherishing the old to know the new": A bibliography of Asian communication studies. *China Media Research*, 5(1), 95–103.

Miike, Y. (Ed.). (2009b). New frontiers in Asian communication theory [Special issue]. *Journal of Multicultural Discourses*, 4(1), 1–88.

Miike, Y. (2010a). An anatomy of Eurocentrism in communication scholarship: The role of Asiacentricity in de-Westernizing theory and research. *China Media Research*, 6(1), 1–11.

Miike, Y. (2010b). Culture as text and culture as theory: Asiacentricity and its *raison d'être* in intercultural communication research. In R. T. Halualani & T. K. Nakayama (Eds.), *The handbook of critical intercultural communication*. Oxford, UK: Wiley-Blackwell.

Miike, Y. (2010c). *Enryo-sasshi* theory. In R. L. Jackson (Ed.), *Encyclopedia of identity*. Thousand Oaks, CA: Sage.

Miike, Y., & Chen, G. -M. (2006). Perspectives on Asian cultures and communication: An updated bibliography. *China Media Research*, 2(1), 98–106.

Miike, Y., & Chen, G. -M. (Eds.). (2007). Asian contributions to communication theory [Special issue]. *China Media Research*, 3(4), 1–109.

Nordstrom, L. (Ed.). (1983). Communication—East and West [Special issue]. *Communication*, 8(1), 1–132.

Pandikattu, K. (Ed.). (2001). *Gandhi: The meaning of Mahatma for the millennium*. Washington, DC: Council for Research in Values and Philosophy.

Robinson, J. H. (2003). Communication in Korea: Playing things by eye. In L. A. Samovar & R. E. Porter (Eds.), *Intercultural communication: A reader* (10th ed., pp. 57–64). Belmont, CA: Wadsworth.

Rogers, E. M. (1976). Communication and development: The passing of the dominant paradigm. *Communication Research*, 3(2), 213–240.

Rogers, E. M. (1978). The rise and fall of the dominant paradigm. *Journal of Communication*, 28(1), 64–69.

Rogers, E. M. (1990). Communication and social change. In G. L. Dahnke & G. W. Clatterbuck (Eds.), *Human communication: Theory and research* (pp. 259–271). Belmont, CA: Wadsworth.

Saito, M. (1970). Learning to communicate. *General Semantics Bulletin*, 37, 14–18.

Saito, M. (1982). *Nemawashi*: A Japanese form of interpersonal communication. *ETC: A Review of General Semantics*, 39(3), 205–214.

Samovar, L. A., Porter, R. E., & McDaniel, E. R. (2010). *Communication between cultures* (7th ed.). Boston, MA: Wadsworth Cengage Learning.

Saral, T. B. (1983). Hindu philosophy of communication. *Communication*, 8(1), 47–58.

Sato, K. (1959). The concept of *on* in Ruth Benedict and D. T. Suzuki. *Psychologia: An International Journal of Psychology in the Orient*, 2(4), 243–245.

Shuter, R. (2003). Ethics, culture, and communication: An intercultural perspective. In L. A. Samovar & R. E. Porter (Eds.), *Intercultural communication: A reader* (10th ed., pp. 449–455). Belmont, CA: Wadsworth.

Sitaram, K. S. (1998). Introduction: Multiculturalism for a higher humanity. In K. S. Sitaram & M. H. Prosser (Eds.), *Civic discourse: Multiculturalism, cultural diversity, and global communication* (pp. 1–14). Stamford, CT: Ablex.

Starosta, W. J., & Shi, L. (2007). Alternate perspectives on Gandhian communication ethics. *China Media Research*, 3(4), 7–14.

Suzuki, D. (2006). *Daisetsu speaking on Zen: Three lectures in English that impressed the world* (in Japanese and in English, S. Shigematsu, Trans.). Tokyo: Art Days.

Tehranian, M. (1990). Communication, peace, and development: A communitarian perspective. In F. Korzenny & S. Ting-Toomey (Eds.), *Communicating for peace: Diplomacy and negotiation* (pp. 157–175). Newbury Park, CA: Sage.

Tehranian, M. (1993). Ethnic discourse and the new world dysorder: A communitarian perspective. In C. Roach (Ed.),

*Communication and culture in war and peace* (pp. 192–215). Newbury Park, CA: Sage.

Tehranian, M. (1999). *Global communication and world politics: Domination, development, and discourse.* Boulder, CO: Lynne Rienner Publishers.

Tehranian, M. (2007). *Rethinking civilization: Resolving conflict in the human family.* London: Routledge.

Tu, W. (1998). Mustering the conceptual resources to grasp a world in flux. In J. A. Kushigian (Ed.), *International studies in the next millennium: Meeting the challenge of globalization* (pp. 3–15). Westport, CT: Praeger.

Tu, W. (2001a). The context of dialogue: Globalization and diversity. In G. Picco (Ed.), *Crossing the divide: Dialogue among civilizations* (pp. 49–96). South Orange, NJ: School of Diplomacy and International Relations, Seton Hall University.

Tu, W. (2001b). The global significance of local knowledge: A new perspective on Confucian humanism. *Sungkyun Journal of East Asian Studies, 1*(1), 22–27.

Tu, W. (2002). Beyond the Enlightenment mentality. In H. Y. Jung (Ed.), *Comparative political culture in the age of globalization: An introductory anthology* (pp. 251–266). Lanham, MD: Lexington Books.

Tu, W. (2006). The Confucian ethic and the spirit of East Asian modernity. In UNESCO (Ed.), *Cultural diversity and transversal values: East-West dialogue on spiritual and secular dynamics* (pp. 7–13). Paris: UNESCO.

Tu, W. (2007). Toward a dialogical civilization: Identity, difference and harmony. In D. Zhao (Ed.), *Dialogue of philosophies, religions and civilizations in the era of globalization* (pp. 11–14). Washington, DC: Council for Research in Values and Philosophy.

Tu, W. (2008). Mutual learning as an agenda for social development. In M. K. Asante, Y. Miike, & J. Yin (Eds.), *The global intercultural communication reader* (pp. 329–333). New York: Routledge.

UNESCO. (Ed.). (2006). *The forum of reflexion: What UNESCO for the future?* Paris: UNESCO.

Xiao, X., & Chen, G.-M. (2009). Communication competence and moral competence: A Confucian perspective. *Journal of Multicultural Discourses, 4*(1), 61–74.

Yin, J. (2009). Negotiating the center: Towards an Asiacentric feminist communication theory. *Journal of Multicultural Discourses, 4*(1), 75–88.

Yin, J., & Miike, Y. (2008). A textual analysis of fortune cookie sayings: How Chinese are they? *Howard Journal of Communications, 19*(1), 18–43.

Yum, J. O. (2000). The impact of Confucianism on interpersonal relationships and communication patterns in East Asia. In L. A. Samovar & R. E. Porter (Eds.), *Intercultural communication: A reader* (9th ed., pp. 63–73). Belmont, CA: Wadsworth.

## Concepts and Questions

1. How does the essay describe worldview? In what ways is this different from or similar to the previous essay?

2. Differentiate between learning *about* other cultures and learning *from* other cultures.

3. What is meant by "cultures in hierarchy"? Is this considered a negative or positive perspective? Why? Is there a better way of viewing cultures?

4. Describe and provide examples of the core values underlying the Eurocentric worldview.

5. Are there any dangers to exploring other cultures from a strictly descriptive perspective? Will simply analyzing and critiquing another culture help or hinder intercultural understanding and communication?

6. Describe and discuss the three steps to cross-cultural dialogue.

7. Summarize, with examples, the five Asiacentric communication propositions.

8. According to the essay, "the Asian worldview stresses an extended, circular perspective on space and time…" How is this similar or different from the worldview structure discussed in the previous essay?

9. What are some ways that a culture's worldview could influence communication style? How could these create difficulties during an intercultural communication interaction?

10. Do you think there are any benefits that Westerners can obtain from the Asiacentric worldview? If not, why? If yes, what are they?

# 2  Identity: Issues of Belonging

*Identity would seem to be a garment with which one covers the nakedness of the self, in which case, it is best that the garment be loose, a little like the robes of the desert, through which one's nakedness can always be felt, and, sometimes, discerned.*  **James Baldwin**

*Identity is a concept of our age that should be used very carefully. All types of identities, ethnic, national, religious, sexual or whatever else, can become your prison after a while. The identity that you stand up for can enslave you and close you to the rest of the world.*

**Murathan Mungan**

We are living in an era of rapid social change, where the old is quickly swept away by the new. The processes of globalization continue to exert pressure on established geopolitical orders. The dynamic social environment evolving from these changes is exerting powerful influences on the construction and maintenance of people's identities. Behind the critiques frequently leveled against globalization is the concern that non-Western nations will ultimately become homogenized representations of Western capitalism and in the process forfeit the originality represented by their national and cultural identities. As a result, an understanding of the role of identity and how culture works in forming, communicating, and preserving your identity has assumed greater importance.

Identities are an integral part of your life. They play a central role in all your activities by serving as a source of self-definition. In other words, we organize meaning around our self-identity (Castells, 1997). In part, the origins of one's many identities provide a foundation for meaning because they stem from a variety of influences, such as geography, history, fantasies, religion, and many, many more. Identity also takes various time-and scenario-dependent forms, to include nation, state, region, religion, ethnic, gender, socioeconomic status, profession, and others. A major influence of identity formation and maintenance is culture. Your identity is socially constructed through a cultural lens, employing the medium of communication. For example, if you grow up constantly being told that you are important as an individual, that you need to stand up for yourself, that you can be the best in anything you do, then your identity will have a strong individualistic orientation. On the other hand, someone brought up to believe that the family, community, tribe, or another affiliation or organization is the central focus of life will have an identity strongly tied to, and dependent on, his or her in-group membership.

**Identities are an integral part of every person's life.**

Our ever-changing social environment is increasingly characterized by frequent and unavoidable multicultural interactions. Now, it is common for sojourners to live and work for extended periods in other cultures. The U.S. population is characterized by an overwhelming majority of people who came to this land from another country, and contemporary immigration continues to add to this patchwork quilt of ethnicities and cultures. As a result, the influence of culture on identity must be understood. For this reason, in this chapter we offer six essays dealing with various aspects of culture and identity. We begin with an essay that examines the influence of globalization and urges movement toward the development of an intercultural identity.

## REFERENCE

Castells, M. (1997). *The power of identity*. Malden, MA: Blackwell.

# Globalization and Intercultural Personhood

## YOUNG YUN KIM

*"Globalization and Intercultural Personhood: Issues of Belonging," by Young Yun Kim, is based on one of the central themes of this book—the idea that today's interconnected, rapidly evolving world community requires that you reexamine previously formed assumptions about your culture and your place within that culture. In viewing the dynamics of contemporary society, which Kim characterizes as "a world of clashing traditions and collective identities," she sees particularistic group identity being overemphasized to the detriment of "the larger identity of national and world citizenry." To ameliorate this evolution, Kim advances a philosophical orientation that she calls "intercultural personhood," which moves beyond the "largely static, monolithic, and value-laden" conditions of contemporary "cultural identity." Intercultural personhood is offered as a way of enhancing our adaptability to the mounting diversity of modern society.*

*One result of globalization is the erosion of the established social order, which ushered in an age of cultural dynamism. This has led to many questions concerning the merit of globalization as traditional forms of societal organization are altered and long-held ideals are subjected to critique and reassessment. According to Kim, contemporary society is presenting many people and organizations, both domestically and internationally, with an environment that calls for them to become "more open, flexible, and inclusive." She offers a way of achieving this through a process of acculturation and deculturation, and a model that includes stress, adaptation, and growth. The collective process leads to intercultural identity, described as an "identity that is open ended, adaptive, and transformative."*

> One of the results of globalization is the erosion of the established social order.

Four decades ago, Alvin Toffler (1970) presented in his seminal book, *Future Shock*, a vivid description of what would happen to people when overwhelmed by change. He detailed the revolutionary development in digital and communication technology and the scope and pace of change it spurred, both from the grand perspectives of history and from the vantage point of individuals who experience it. In particular, he pointed to the "fantastic intrusion of novelty, newness into our existence" (p. 34) as well as the dramatic increase in mobility, both of which would diminish, or throw into a state of confusion, the traditional sense and commitment to "place." Toffler cautioned that such historically unprecedented forces of change would lead to more transient relationships between the individual and the outer world, with potentially profound consequences of social upheaval and psychological "overstimulation" that would force them to operate above the adaptive range. Hence, the main proposition Toffler put forth calls for creative restructuring of the way individuals, as well as organizations and institutions, orient themselves to the world, in order to become "infinitely more adaptable and capable than ever before" (p. 35).

Today, Toffler's prescient insights remain as relevant and significant as ever. Such is particularly the case with respect to the blurring lines and dizzying interface of national, ethnic, cultural, linguistic, and religious traditions—the once-clear definitions of "us and them." This tightly knit system of communication and transportation has brought differing communities closer than ever before in a web of interdependence and a common fate. The business-as-usual ways of doing things are fast losing their

This essay appears here in print for the first time. All rights reserved. Permission to reprint must be obtained from the author and the publisher. An earlier version of this essay appeared in the *International Journal of Intercultural Relations, 32*(4), 359–368. Dr. Young Yun Kim is a Professor in the Department of Communication at the University of Oklahoma, Norman, Oklahoma.

relevance, as culture in its "pure" form has become more a nostalgic concept than a reality. Individuals are challenged to face one another's various differences and search for human similarities, so as to be able to move beyond their customary imagination in search of creative solutions to problems.

Ours is also a world of clashing traditions and collective identities. The very forces that diminish physical boundaries exacerbate ethnic and national rivalries, rendering alarming daily news headlines and a deeply unsettling political landscape. To many people around the world, the seemingly innocent banner of some kind of group identity is now a compelling sore spot galvanizing them into us-against-them posturing. Some of the most passionate domestic and international tension and disputes headlining the daily media involve differing identities, particularly along tribal, racial, and religious lines. From long-festering prejudices, discriminations, and hatreds to the more recent acts of violent rage and terror, people in all corners of the world are witnessing so many angry words, hurt, and destruction. The relatively simple civic consensus in the vision of a diverse yet peaceful and democratic society is being challenged by one that upholds a particular group identity in place of the larger identity of national and world citizenry. Often absent in the identity polemics are the main ideals of multiculturalism itself, that is, people with different roots can coexist, that they can learn from each other, and that they can, and should, look across and beyond the frontiers of traditional group boundaries with minimum prejudice or illusion, and learn to strive for a society and a world that celebrates diversity side by side with unifying cohesion.

Pragmatic concerns such as these underpin, and signify, the central aim of this essay, that is, to make a case for *intercultural personhood* as a way to answer Toffler's call for an adaptive response to the accelerating interface of cultures all around. The concept of intercultural personhood serves as a counterpoint to, and as an extension of, the commonly held conception of *cultural identity* that is largely static, monolithic, and value-laden. Intercultural personhood highlights the complex and evolving nature of human existence, one that represents the phenomenon of identity adaptation and transformation beyond the perimeters of the conventional cultural categories. As such, intercultural personhood is proposed as a constructive response to globalization—as a way of increasing our fitness in our increasingly diverse communities, both local and global, and as a way of relating to others that conjoins and integrates, rather than separates and divides.

## CULTURAL IDENTITY: A CRITIQUE

From the early years of the 20th century (e.g., Simmel, 1908/1950; Stonequist, 1937), and particularly for the past several decades, the notion of identity, in general, and cultural identity, in particular, has occupied a central place in social science research, most extensively in the United States. Systematic investigations of cultural identity can be traced back to psychologist Erikson's (1950) theoretical framework. Erikson described the process of identity development as one in which the two identities—of the individual (or the personal) and of the group (or the social collective)—are merged into one. Erikson thus placed cultural identity at the core of the individual and yet also in the core of his or her "common culture."

Erikson's identity conception has since been echoed in subsequent academic writings, but in a way that is increasingly idealized. For De Vos (1990), for example, cultural identity is rooted in "the emotionally profound self-awareness of parentage and a concomitant mythology of discrete origin," (p. 14) and provides "a sense of common origin, as well as common beliefs and values, or common values" and serves as the basis of "self-defining in-groups" (p. 204). For Giordano (1974), ethnic identity is a psychological foundation offering the individual a "ground on which to stand" that "no one can take away" (p. 16). Similarly, Yinger (1986) saw ethnic attachment as a "genuine culture" that formed the person's "basic identity" and offered "a sense of historical continuity and embeddedness and a larger existence in a collectivity of one's group" (p. 21), while Roosens (1989) saw cultural identity as "the psychosocial driving force of individual and collective ethnic self-affirmation" (p. 15).

> *Intercultural personhood highlights the complex and evolving nature of human existence.*

## The Pluralistic Turn

Idealized conceptions of cultural identity, such as the ones sampled above, parallel and mirror the ideological shift toward greater pluralism and multiculturalism, beginning with the "new ethnicity" movement prompted by the civil rights movement in the 1960s in the United States. In their early work, Glazer and Moynihan (1963) concluded a sociological analysis by stating that ethnicity pervades all spheres of life among ethnic minorities: "The point about the melting pot is that it did not happen" (p. 290). Novak (1971), in *The Rise of the Unmeltable Ethnics,* argued against assimilation and advocates "equal ethnicity for all." He described the feelings of alienation held by one large ethnic group, Poles, who had been drawn to "ethnic power" movements in the competition for jobs, respect, and attention.

The pluralistic turn in academic conceptions of cultural identity has capitalized on the inherent dilemma, that is, a contradiction arising from the inevitable gap between the classical liberal ideal of transcending group categories and the reality of everyday life, in which group categories continue to constrain ethnic minorities. In this movement, the primacy of individual identity has been challenged by contrary claims of *group identity* and the associated attempts to elevate group distinctiveness over an individual, or human, identity. Replacing the traditional "melting-pot" metaphor with newer ones such as "mosaic," "quilt," and "salad bowl," the pluralistic construction of personhood has elevated collective interests as a concern to the individual above their implications for personal self-interest. Cultural or ethnic identity, in effect, entails "a shift towards the perception of self as an interchangeable exemplar of some social category and away from the perception of self as a unique person" (Turner, Hog, Oakes, Reicher, & Wetherell, 1987, p. 50).

Along with the pluralistic turn in the United States and now around the world, we have seen an increasing trend of departure in research addressing issues of cultural identity from the traditional normative-representational stance of value neutrality to the stance of social advocacy and other forms of activism. This politicization of research is reflected in the increased number of traditional social scientists who are committed to the social causes of diversity and justice and who find the principally value-neutral stance of the traditional normal science approach less than satisfying (cf. Hammersley, 1995; Thornton, 1996). Academic arguments are made, for example, for a redistribution of power and resources to overcome inequalities in group status (e.g., Hacker, 1992) and for a greater diversity of the university curriculum by replacing it with one "that would focus on the achievements of marginalized peoples" (Traub, 1998, p. 25). Pressure is felt by many traditional researchers who find the field too politicized, so much so that a given theory, along with the credibility of the theorist, appears to be dismissed by some based on the implied question, "Whose side are you on?"

In the global context, the shift in emphasis from value-neutral theory to value-driven activism has been most evident in the works of scholars in "postmodern" schools such as "critical theory" and "cultural studies." Vigorous arguments have been mounted to gear research directly to "emancipator" political goals of eliminating "White racism" at home and countering Western/American "imperialism" abroad. Tsuda (1986), for instance, criticized the Western cultural domination, particularly the dominance of English language, as the genesis of "distorted intercultural communication" around the world. Likewise, Young (1996) presented his criticism of Western "cultural imperialism" by depicting today's global reality as one of power asymmetry between communicators rooted in "oppressive" and "imperialistic" Western cultural-institutional systems.

## Problematics in Pluralistic Conceptions

A close examination of the contemporary pluralistic academic writings on issues of cultural identity and intercultural relations, such as the ones cited above, reveals at least two main problematics: *positivity bias* and *oversimplification*. These two issues pertain to the implicit or explicitly stated common assumptions that misrepresent the reality of identity experiences at the level of individuals.

A *positivity bias* is reflected in the unconditional moral imperative commonly seen in various academic conceptions of cultural identity. Pluralistically inclined social scientists in general, and postmodern-critical scholars in particular, have been largely silent about the "dark side" of cultural identity—the tendencies of collective self-glorification and denigration of other groups. An insufficient amount of attention has been given to the fact that too strict an adherence to a cultural identity can raise even separatist sentiments, fear and distrust of other groups, and even the dangers of violence, cruelty, and political humiliation (Levy, 2000). Intended or not, some critical writings suggest a sense of "cultural identity at any cost." Cultural identity is not only to be recognized, respected, and preserved, but also to be a means to combat unjust practices of an out-group, real or imagined. Implicit in such a claim is the notion that cultural groups are deemed inherently equal in their original states, but that their original natures are seen as being distorted and corrupted in the process of interaction with others in society and through the development of sociocultural institutions (Tsuda, 1986, pp. 62–63).

The positivity bias is inseparably linked to the problem of *oversimplification*. There is a tendency in many pluralistic academic writings to portray cultural identity as an "all-or-none" or "either-or" entity that belongs exclusively to a particular category of people. A person is often viewed to belong to one, and only one, particular ethnic group. The monolithic and static conception of cultural identity is often reflected in statements that inflate uniformity among the individuals who are associated with a particular group category. Some researchers have tended to lump together all individuals ascribed to a particular group and portray them as if they were a homogeneous group with identical characteristics. In *Two Nations,* for example, Hacker (1992) described the contemporary Black as someone who was marginal, separate, and victimized in the White world, despite the many contrary statistics presented in the book.

Coupled together, positive bias and oversimplification clearly reflect the desire to offer an intellectual voice to the traditionally subordinated or oppressed people. At the same time, they tend to serve as the philosophical grounding for political arguments that lack evenhandedness and realism—such as the conspicuous silence among pluralistically inclined researchers in the face of human sufferings and systematic injustices instigated within non-Western countries. Relatedly, positive moral values categorically

assigned to cultural identity fails to acknowledge one of the basic tenets of intergroup theories such as the social identity theory (Tajfel, 1974, 1978; Tajfel & Turner, 1979). That is, individuals identify with a group in a manner that is self-serving. The way people experience cultural identity is essentially not a rational but an emotionally driven experience. When it comes to our relationships to an out-group in competition or conflict, we are less than likely to be fair and objective, and more likely to be irrational and defensive, favoring our in-group and discriminating against the out-group that threatens our in-group.

The positivity bias and oversimplification with respect to cultural identity is suggested in the approval in October 2005 by all members of … UNESCO, except the United States, of the convention on the "protection and promotion" of cultural diversity. The drafters worried that globalization represented a challenge for cultural diversity, namely, in view of risks of imbalance between rich and poor countries. The fear was that the values and images of Western mass culture, like some invasive weed, were threatening to choke out the world's native flora, so to speak. Yet, as Kwame Anthony Appiah (2006), the Ghana-born professor of philosophy at Princeton University, points out, this UNESCO convention offers a misplaced moral judgment.

> What's really important, then, cultures or people? … Many of globalization's cultural critics are aiming at the wrong targets.… Human variety matters … because people are entitled to options.… If we want to preserve a wide range of human conditions because it allows free people the best chance to make their own lives, we can't enforce diversity by trapping people within differences they long to escape… Cultural consumers are not dupes. They can adopt products to suit their own needs, and they can decide for themselves what they do and do not approve of. (pp. 32–35)

## INTERCULTURAL COMMUNICATION, ADAPTATION, AND TRANSFORMATION

Individual ability and freedom to choose flexibility in identity orientation is further addressed in a number of theoretical models that are designed to explain intercultural communication competence. Imahori and Cupach (2005) highlight the fact that individuals are able to manage their cultural identity when interacting with individuals of differing backgrounds, and that "facework" or the ability to handle each other's cultural identity flexibly is a key to being a competent intercultural communicator. A similarly nuanced identity conception underlies Ting-Toomey's (2005) theory that places "identity negotiation" at the center of "communicative resourcefulness" in intercultural encounters. In addition, Kim (2005b, 2009) identifies "identity inclusivity" and "identity security" as the key communicator characteristics that help explain the degree to which individuals tend to engage themselves more actively with ethnically dissimilar others.

Moving beyond flexibility and situational variations in identity orientation, the present author (Kim, 1988, 2001, 2005a) has theorized about, and documented empirical evidence for, the dynamic and evolving nature of identity. Grounded in the General Systems perspective (Bertalanffy, 1956), this theory argues that each person is an "open system" that exchanges information with the environment through communication, and co-evolves with the changing environment. As such, the theory characterizes a person's identity undergoing changes throughout life. Plasticity, the ability to learn and change through new experiences, is highlighted as one of the most profound characteristics of the human mind and as the very basis upon which individuals acquire an identity.

## Acculturation and Deculturation

This theory (Kim, 1988, 2001, 2005a) is intended primarily to explain the common adaptive experiences of individuals who are born and raised in one cultural or sub-cultural environment and have relocated to a new and different one for an extended period. Yet, the core concepts and the theoretical arguments are applicable to the broader context of the increasing intercultural communicative interface accompanying the process of globalization. One no longer has to leave home to experience acculturation.

Through mass media and other technological means of communication, people around the world are increasingly exposed to the images and sounds of once-distant cultures. In large urban centers, local people are routinely coming in contact with foreign-born individuals. In many ways, globalization presents individuals with numerous situations that deviate from the familiar original cultural script.

Extensive and prolonged experiences of intercultural communication constitute the essence of *acculturation,* that is, the acquisition of the new cultural practices in wide-ranging areas including the learning of a new language. Acculturation brings about a development of cognitive complexity, or [a] refinement in an individual's internal information-processing ability with respect to the target culture. An equally significant aspect of acculturation is the acquisition of new cultural aesthetic and emotional sensibilities, a new way of appreciating beauty, fun, joy, as well as of despair, anger, and the like. Acculturalitive learning does not occur randomly or automatically following intercultural contacts and exposures. New cultural elements are not simply added to prior internal conditions. Rather, it is a process over which each individual has a degree of freedom or control, based on his or her predispositions, pre-existing needs and interests. Such an ego-protective and egocentric psychological principle is demonstrated in Bognar's (2001) identification of an uneven development in gender role change between male and female immigrants, and in Chang's (2001) finding from a study of Asian immigrants in Singapore of relatively higher levels of acculturation in workplace-related and public norms and values compared to private realms and home life.

As new learning occurs, *deculturation,* or un-learning of at least some of the old cultural elements, has to occur, at least in the sense that new responses are adopted in situations that previously would have evoked old ones. "No construction without destruction," in the words of Burke (1974). The act of acquiring something new is the suspending and, over a prolonged period, even losing some of the old habits at least temporarily. This interplay of acculturation and deculturation underlies the psychological evolution individuals undergo—from changes in "surface"

> One no longer has to leave home to experience acculturation.

areas such as outwardly expressive behaviors, like choices of music, food, and dress, to deeper-level changes in social role-related behaviors and fundamental values.

## The Stress-Adaptation-Growth Dynamic

As the interplay of acculturation and deculturation continues, each experience of adaptive change inevitably accompanies *stress* in the individual psyche, a kind of identity conflict rooted in resistance to change, the desire to retain old customs in keeping with the original identity, on the one hand, and the desire to change behavior in seeking harmony with the new milieu, on the other. This conflict is essentially between the need for acculturation and the resistance to deculturation, that is, the "push" of the new culture and the "pull" of the old. The internal disequilibrium created by such conflicting forces can be manifested in intense emotional "lows" of uncertainty, confusion, and anxiety. Such intense situations can generate "crises" in which our mental and behavioral habits are brought into awareness and called into question.

Stress, indeed, is an expression of the instinctive human desire to restore homeostasis, that is, to hold constant a variety of variables in internal structure to achieve an integrated whole. Some people may attempt to avoid or minimize the anticipated or actual "pain" of disequilibrium by selective attention, denial, avoidance, and withdrawal, as well as by compulsively altruistic behavior, cynicism, and hostility toward the new external reality. Others may seek to regress to an earlier state of existence in the familiar "home" culture, a state in which there is no feeling of isolation, no feeling of separation. From this open systems perspective, then, Toffler's (1970) notion of "future shock" as well as the phenomenon commonly referred to as "culture shock" (e.g., Ward, Bochner, & Funiham, 2001), are essentially manifestations of the generic process that occurs whenever an individual's internal capabilities are not adequate to the demands of the changing or changed environment.

Even in the form of anguish and tribulations, however, stress presents us with an opportunity to search deep inside ourselves for new possibilities to recreate ourselves. Over time, such conflicts, in turn, make us susceptible to external influence and compel individuals to learn new cultural elements. For most people, internal changes take hold as they embrace environmental challenges and strive to stabilize themselves by overcoming the predicament and partake in the act of *adaptation*. As such, adaptation encompasses the entirety of *the phenomenon in which individuals who, through direct and indirect contacts with an unfamiliar environment, strive to establish and maintain a relatively stable, reciprocal, and functional relationship with the environment.* At the core of this conception is the goal of achieving an overall person–environment "fit," a congruence between their internal conditions and the conditions of the environment. Adaptation, thus, is an activity that is "almost always a compromise, a vector in the internal structure of culture and the external pressure of environment" (Sahlins, 1964, p. 136).

What follows a successful, long-term management of the stress-adaptation disequilibrium is a subtle and often imperceptible psychological *growth* in the sense of an increased complexity in an individual's internal system. Periods of stress pass as an individual works out new ways of handling problems, owing to the creative forces of self-reflexivity of human mentation. Together, the concepts of stress, adaptation, and growth constitute three-pronged experiences of the *stress-adaptation-growth dynamic* of psychological movement in the forward and upward direction of increased chances of success in a changing or changed environment. Stress, in this regard, is intrinsic to complex living systems and essential in their adaptation process—one that allows for self-(re)organization and self-renewal. The stress-adaptation-growth dynamic does not play out in a smooth, steady, and linear progression, but in a dialectic, cyclic, and continual "draw-back-to-leap" pattern. Each stressful experience is responded to with a "draw back," which, in turn, activates adaptive energy to help individuals reorganize themselves and "leap forward." As growth of some units always occurs at the expense of others, the adaptation process follows a pattern that juxtaposes integration and disintegration, progression and regression, and novelty and confirmation. This systems-theoretic explanation echoes Dubos' (1965) view of human adaptation as "a dialectic between permanence and change" (p. 2).

The stress-adaptation-growth process continues as long as there are new environmental challenges,

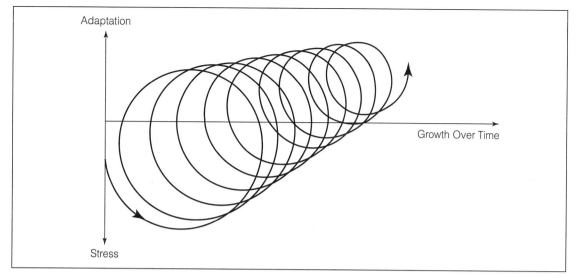

**FIGURE 2.1** The stress-adaptation-growth dynamic
*Source:* Kim, 2001, p. 59.

with the overall forward and upward movement in the direction of greater adaptation and growth. In this process, large and sudden changes are more likely to occur during the initial phase of exposure to a new or changing cultural milieu. Such drastic changes are themselves indicative of the severity of difficulties and disruptions. Over a prolonged period of undergoing internal change, the diminishing fluctuations of stress and adaptation become less intense or severe, leading to an overall "calming" of our internal condition, as depicted in Figure 2.1.

## Identity Transformation: Individuation and Universalization

Emerging from the experiences of acculturation, deculturation, and the stress-adaptation-growth dynamic is an emergence of *intercultural identity*. The concept *intercultural identity* depicts identity that is open-ended, adaptive, and transformative. As such, it needs to be differentiated from other similar terms that represent various forms of additions and subtractions of specific cultural components such as "bicultural," "multicultural," "multiethnic," or even "hybrid" identity. Instead, intercultural identity highlights one of the

> *Intercultural identity depicts identity that is open-ended, adaptive, and transformative.*

well-known central maxims for all living systems: "The whole is greater than the sum of its parts." Existing terms closest to intercultural identity include "meta-identity," "cosmopolitan" or "transcultural" identity, all of which indicate less dualistic and more meta-contextual conceptions of self and others rather than rigid boundedness vis-à-vis conventional social categories such as ethnicity or culture.

One of the two key elements of intercultural identity development is *individuation*, which involves a clear self-definition and definition of the other as a singular individual rather than a member of a conventional social category. With this capacity, one is better able to see oneself and others on the basis of unique individual qualities rather than categorical stereotypes. Individuation, thus, fosters an outlook on people that exhibits greater differentiation and less stereotyping (Oddou & Mendenhall, 1984). Accompanying individuation is *universalization,* a parallel development of a synergistic cognition "of a new consciousness. Universalization is born out of an awareness of the relative nature of values and of the universal aspect of *human* nature" (Yoshikawa, 1978, p. 220; Italics added for emphasis). As people advance in their identity transformation process, they are better able to see the common humanity among different cultures and ethnicities, and locate the points of consent and complementarity beyond the parochial points of difference and contention.

## DATA AND ILLUSTRATIONS

A broad array of research data offers empirical support for the above theoretical accounts of acculturation and deculturation, and of the interrelationship of stress and subsequent adaptation and growth leading to a gradual identity transformation toward an increasingly intercultural personhood. Additional empirical evidence can be obtained from a variety of publicly available personal accounts told in biographical stories that provide illuminating anecdotes on intercultural identity transformation. (See Kim, 2001, for a more extensive documentation of empirical studies as well as case illustrations.)

### Research Evidence

Direct and indirect research evidence for the acculturation- deculturation process and the stress-adaptation-growth dynamic comes largely from more than half a century of social scientific studies of immigrants and of temporary sojourners conducted in the United States and many other parts of the world. Eaton and Lasry (1978), for example, reported that the stress level of more upwardly mobile immigrants was greater than those who were less upwardly mobile. Among Japanese-Americans (Marmot & Syme, 1976) and Mexican-American women (Miranda & Castro, 1977), the better-adapted immigrants had initially experienced a somewhat greater frequency of stress-related symptoms (such as anxiety and a need for psychotherapy) than the less adapted group. Similar patterns of relationship between stress, adaptation, and growth have been shown in studies of temporary sojourners. Findings from Ruben and Kealey's (1979) study of Canadian technical advisors in Nigeria, for example, suggested that those who were the most effective in their new environment underwent the most intense culture shock during the initial transition period.

More recently, based on a study among college students from the United States in Japan and a number of other countries, Milstein (2005) concluded that the sojourn experience resulted in increased levels of "self-efficacy." Employing the above-described theoretical account of the stress-adaptation-growth dynamic, Milstein showed further that the increase in self-efficacy was linked positively to the level of challenge the students reported to have experienced and to the eventual perceived success of their sojourn. In another study employing a 15-month ethnographic fieldwork among American exchange students studying in a college in France, Pitts (2009) documented in detail how, at various stages of the sojourn, the stress-adaptation-growth dynamic plays out in the college students' intercultural experiences and in their own verbal accounts thereof.

With respect to long-term, cumulative acculturation-deculturation and intercultural transformation, Suro (1998) reported that Hispanics in the United States showed diminished Hispanic "cultural scripts" in their judgments and increased social interactions with non-Hispanics. Similarly, Murphy-Shigematsu (1987) reported that Amerasians with first-generation Japanese mothers and White American fathers struggled with their mixed racial and cultural conditions and were successful in forming their authentic identity in society. Another study by Dasgupta (1983) indicated that Asian-Indian immigrants were able to resolve the conflict between their traditional value of holism and ascription and the American cultural values of individualism, achievement, and competition by dichotomizing and attaining a healthy balance between primary in-group relationships and achievement in their occupational lives in the larger society.

Similar patterns of intercultural identity development and emergence of intercultural personhood have been observed by Shearer (2003) in native-born "mainstream" individuals, as well. Using a biographical case study method, Shearer examined two white Australians' intercultural experiences over the years. Through an in-depth interpretive analysis, Shearer reported that the cases of two mainstream Australians show some evidence of intercultural personhood and make identity claims comparable with minority ethnic individuals.

### Case Illustrations

Along with systematic research data such as those described above, information gleaned from publicly available first-hand personal accounts of individuals whose life stories bear witness to concrete realities of intercultural persons. Such accounts have appeared in case studies, memoirs, biographical stories, and essays of self-reflection. Many of these accounts, including the three presented below as case illustrations, provide compelling empirical support for the present theoretical articulation of intercultural identity and intercultural personhood.

One of the most succinct testimonials to the present theoretical formulation of intercultural personhood was offered by Muneo Yoshikawa (1978), a native of Japan and currently a professor emeritus as Kauai Community College, University of Hawaii. As someone who had lived in Japan and in the United States, Yoshikawa offered the following insight into his own psychological development—an insight that captures what it means to be an intercultural person.

I am now able to look at both cultures with objectivity as well as subjectivity; I am able to move in both cultures, back and forth without any apparent conflict…. I think that something *beyond the sum of each [cultural] identification* took place, and that it became something akin to the concept of *"synergy"—when* one adds 1 and 1, one gets 3, or a little more. This something extra is *not culture-specific* but something unique of its own, probably the *emergence of a new attribute or a new self-awareness,* born out of an awareness of the relative nature of values and of the *universal aspect of human nature….* I really am not concerned whether others take me as a Japanese or an American; I can accept myself as I am. I feel I am much *freer* than ever before, not only in the cognitive domain (perception, thoughts, etc.), but also in the affective (feeling, attitudes, etc.) and behavioral domains. (Italics added for emphasis; p. 220)

Transcendence of cultural categories through the individuation and universalization of identity orientation is further reflected in the many-faceted career of cellist *Yo-Yo Ma.* His life story and his philosophy offer a testament to a continual search for intercultural learning and synthesis. Born to Chinese parents living in Paris, he began to study the cello with his father at age 4 and soon came with his family to New York, where he spent most of his formative years and received his musical education at the Juilliard School.

He draws inspiration from a wide circle of collaborators, and has explored music as a means of intercultural communication and as a vehicle for the migrations of ideas across a range of cultures throughout the world. In his own words posted on his website (www.yo-yoma.com), Ma explains his intercultural journey as follows.

In my musical journey I have had the opportunity to *learn from a wealth of different musical voices—* from the immense compassion and grace of Bach's cello suites, to the ancient Celtic fiddle traditions alive in Appalachia, to the soulful strains of the bandoneon of Argentina's tango cafes. Throughout my travels I have thought about the culture, religions and ideas that have been influential for centuries along the historic land and sea routes that comprised the Silk Road, and *have wondered how these complex interconnections occurred and how new musical voices were formed from the diversity of these traditions….* In 1998, I founded the Silk Road Project to study the ebb and flow of ideas among different cultures along the Silk Road, illuminating the heritages of its countries and identifying the voices that represent these traditions today. Through this journey of discovery, the *Silk Road Project* hopes to *plant the seeds of new artistic and cultural growth,* and to celebrate living traditions and musical voices throughout the world. (Italics added for emphasis)

The insight into human conditions rooted in the life of intercultural personhood appears to have been also the driving passion for the 2006 winner of the Nobel Prize in Literature, the Turkish novelist *Orhan Pamuk.* Pamuk is recognized for having captured in his writings new symbols for the interlacing of cultures. In an interview aired on National Public Radio following the Nobel Prize announcement (National Public Radio, October 12, 2006), Pamuk was reminded by the interviewer that he had talked previously about "coming from one of those countries … on the periphery of the Western world where the art was developed, and being one of those writers who is grabbing that art from the center to the periphery and then *producing something new* to show the world" (Italics added for emphasis). Pamuk reaffirmed this intercultural focus in his work and explained his inclusive intercultural identity as follows.

My whole book, my whole life, is a testimony to the fact that East and West actually *combine, come together gracefully and produce something new.* That is what I have been trying to do all my life.... I don't believe in clashes of civilization. I think that was a fanciful idea which, unfortunately, is sometimes coming to be true. But no, I think that East and West meet. I think that my whole work is a testimony to the fact that *we should find ways of looking, combining East and West without any clash, but with harmony, with grace, and produce something new for humanity.* (Italics added for emphasis)

## TOWARD INTERCULTURAL PERSONHOOD

There is a great deal of uncertainty and stress in our rapidly globalizing world. With the advent of electronic communication and globalization, distance no longer dictates the extent of intercultural communication. Whether at home or in a foreign soil, numerous people the world over are being challenged to undergo at least some degree of acculturation, deculturation, and the experience of the stress-adaptation-growth dynamic. To the individuals, social organizations, communities, and nations that are nostalgic for the age of certainty, permanence, and a fixed and unitary cultural identity, this changing global reality can represent a particularly unsettling discontinuity and malaise. One may refuse to admit this reality, but only at the cost of the immense effort of spending one's life resisting or denying it. Such a psychological posture may help one to "feel better," at least temporarily, about oneself and one's group. Yet it is also likely to engender a further refusal to adapt.

The theoretical account and case illustrations presented in this essay offer a viable alternative vision of being oriented to oneself and to the world that is more open, flexible, and inclusive. It speaks to the process a uniquely human plasticity, "our relative freedom from programmed reflexive patterns ... the very capacity to use culture to construct our identities" (Slavin & Kriegman, 1992, p. 6). It projects a special kind of mindset in which cross-borrowing of identities is not an act of "surrendering" one's personal and cultural integrity, but an act of respect for cultural differences that leaves neither the lender nor the borrower deprived. The dynamic and evolutionary concept of intercultural personhood is no less genuine than the familiar ways of being and relating. It projects a way of relating to oneself and to fellow human beings with greater realism and evenhandedness. It shows a way of being engaged in the world by seeking a constructive way to embrace complexities of our changing world without losing ourselves.

It is, in the end, up to each person to decide for himself or herself as to how one wishes to relate to changing global cultural environment. The intercultural outlooks on self, others, and the world are represented by the integrative thoughts of Muneo Yoshikawa, Yo-Yo Ma, and Orhan Pamuk. It is individuals such as these in which the viability of the present model of intercultural personhood rests. They bear witness to the remarkable human spirit and capacity for self-renewal. Their individuated and universalized identity orientations defy the simplistic and conventional categorizations of people. Instead, their intercultural identity orientations can help to hold together and elevate diverse cultural traditions, to help fellow citizens see their collective "blind spots," and to discourage excessive glorification of cultural identity based on nostalgia and false pride. Their personal insights show a way of being in the world that nurtures the primacy of individual freedom and creativity in meeting one of the singular challenges of our time, that is, the necessity of what Toffler (1980) called the "personality of transcendence":

> [The individual] must reach out in totally new ways to anchor himself, for all the old groups—religion, nation, community, family or profession—are now shaking under the hurricane impact of the accelerative thrust of change ... each time we link up with some particular subcultural group or groups, we make some change in our self image. (pp. 121–123)

## References

Appiah, K. A. (2006, January 1). The case for contamination. *The New York Times Magazine*, 30–37, 52.

Bertalanffy, L. (1956). General systems theory. *General Systems, 1*, 1–2.

Bognar, N. (2001, April). *Cross-cultural adjustment and gender-related norms: A study of Eastern Europeans in* the United States. Paper presented at the 2nd biennial congress of the International Academy for Intercultural Research, Oxford, MS.

Burke, K. (1974). Communication and the human condition. *Communication, 1* (December 1974): 135–52. UK.: Gordon and Breach Science Publishers, 135–52.

Chang, W. C. (2001, April). *A model of situation-specific multiculturalism of Asian immigrants in Singapore.* Paper presented at the 2nd biennial congress of the International Academy for Intercultural Research, Oxford, MS.

Dasgupta, S. (1983). *Indian immigrants: The evolution of an ethnic group.* Unpublished doctoral dissertation, University of Delaware, Newark, DE.

De Vos, G. (1990). Conflict and accommodation in ethnic interactions. In G. A. De Vos & M. Suarez-Orozco, *Status inequality: The self in culture* (pp. 204–245). Newbury Park, CA: Sage.

Dubos, R. (1965). *Man adapting.* New Haven, CT: Yale University Press.

Eaton, W., & Lasry, J. (1978). Mental health and occupational mobility in a group of immigrants. *Science and Medicine, 12,* 53–58.

Erikson, E. (1950). *Childhood and society.* New York: W. W. Norton.

Giordano, J. (1974). *Ethnicity and mental health: Research and recommendations.* New York: Institute on Pluralism and Group Identity.

Glazer, N., & Moynihan, D. (1963). *Beyond the melting pot.* Cambridge, MA: MIT Press.

Hacker, A. (1992). *Two nations: Black and White, separate, hostile, unequal.* New York: Scribner's.

Hammersley, M. (1995). *The politics of social research.* London: Sage.

Imahori, T., & Cupach, W. (2005). Identity management theory: Facework in intercultural relationships. In W.Gudykunst (Ed.), *Theorizing about intercultural communication* (pp. 195–210). Thousand Oaks, CA: Sage.

Kim, Y. Y. (1988). *Communication and cross-cultural adaptation: An integrative theory.* Clevedon, United Kingdom: Multilingual Matters.

Kim, Y. Y. (2001). *Becoming intercultural: An integrative theory of communication and cross-cultural adaptation.* Thousand Oaks, CA: Sage.

Kim, Y. Y. (2005a). Adapting to a new culture: An integrative communication theory. In W. Gudykunst (Ed.), *Theorizing about intercultural communication* (pp. 375–400). Thousand Oaks, CA: Sage.

Kim, Y. Y. (2005b). Association and dissociation: A contextual theory of interethnic communication. In W. Gudykunst (Ed.), *Theorizing about intercultural communication* (pp. 323–349). Thousand Oaks, CA: Sage.

Kim, Y. (2008). Intercultural personhood: Globalization and a way of being. In Y. Kim & D. Bhawuk (Eds.), *Globalization and diversity: Theoretical and applied perspectives [Special Issue]. International Journal of Intercultural Relations, 32*(4), 359–368.

Kim, Y. (2009). The identity factor in intercultural competence. In D. K. Deardorff, (Ed.), *The Sage Handbook of Intercultural Competence* (pp. 53–65). Thousand Oaks, CA: Sage.

Levy, J. (2000). *The multiculturalism of fear.* New York: Oxford University Press.

Marmot, M., & Syme, S. (1976). Acculturation and coronary heart disease in Japanese-Americans. *American Journal of Epidemiology, 104*(3), 225–247.

Milstein, T. J. (2005, March). Transformation abroad: Sojourning and the perceived enhancement of self-efficacy. *International Journal of Intercultural Relations, 29,* 217–238.

Miranda, M., & Castro, F. (1977). Culture distance and success in psychotherapy with Spanish speaking clients. In J. Martinez, Jr. (Ed.), *Chicano Psychology* (pp. 249–262). New York: Academic Press.

Murphy-Shigematsu, S. (1987). The voices of Amerasians: Ethnicity, identity, and empowerment in interracial Japanese Americans (Doctoral dissertation, Harvard University, 1987). *Dissertation Abstracts International, 48*(04), 1143B.

National Public Radio (October 12, 2006). Once resented, Pamuk takes solace in Nobel. Interview transcript from All Things Considered. http://www.npr.org/templates/story/story.php?storyId=6256030

Novak, M. (1971). *The rise of the unmeltable ethnics.* New York: Macmillan.

Oddou, G., & Mendenhall, M. (1984). Person perception in cross-cultural settings. International *Journal of Intercultural Relations, 8*(1), 77–96.

Pitts, M. J. (2007, May). Identity and the role of expectations, stress, and talk in short-term student sojourner adjustment: An application of the integrative theory of communication and cross-cultural adaptation. *International Journal of Intercultural Relations, 33*(6), 450–462.

Roosens, E. (1989). *Creating ethnicity: The process of ethnogenesis.* Newbury Park, CA: Sage.

Ruben, B., & Kealey, D. (1979). Behavioral assessment of communication competency and the prediction of cross-cultural adaptation. *International Journal of Intercultural Relations, 3*(1), 15–27.

Sahlins, M. (1964). Culture and environment: The study of cultural ecology. In S. Tax (Ed.), *Horizons of anthropology* (pp. 132–147). Chicago: Aldine.

Shearer, H. E. (2003, December). *Intercultural personhood: A "mainstream" Australian biographical case study.* Unpublished doctoral dissertation, Griffith University, Mt Gravatt, Queensland, Australia.

Simmel, G. (1908/1950). The stranger. In K. H. Wolff (Ed. and Trans.), *The sociology of Georg Simmel.* New York: The Free Press.

Slavin, M., & Kriegman, D. (1992). *The adaptive design of the human psyche.* New York: Guilford.

Stonequist, E. (1937). *The marginal man.* New York: Scribner's.

Suro, R. (1998). *Strangers among us: How Latino immigration is transforming America.* New York: Alfred A. Knopf.

Tajfel, H. (1974). Social identity and intergroup behavior. *Social Science Information, 223*(2), 96–102.

Tajfel, H. (1978). Social categorization, social identity and social comparison. In H. Tajfel (Ed.), *Differentiation between social groups* (pp. 61–76). New York: Academic Press.

Tajfell, H., & Turner, J. (1979). An integrative theory of intergroup conflict. In W. Austin & S. Worchel (Eds.), *The social psychology of intergroup relations* (pp. 33–47). Monterey, CA: Brooks/Cole.

Thornton, M. (1996). Hidden agendas, identity theories, and multiracial people. In M. Root (Ed.), *The multiracial experience: Racial borders as the new frontiers* (pp. 101–120). Thousand Oaks, CA: Sage.

Ting-Toomey, S. (2005). Identity negotiation theory: Crossing cultural boundaries. In W. B. Gudykunst (Ed.), *Theorizing about intercultural communication* (pp. 211–233). Thousand Oaks, CA: Sage.

Toffler, A. (1970). *Future shock.* New York: Bantam Books.

Toffler, A. (1980). *The third wave.* New York: Bantam Books.

Traub, J. (1998, June 28). Nathan Glazer changes his mind, again. *The New York Times Magazine,* 22–25.

Tsuda, Y. (1986). *Language inequality and distortion in intercultural communication: A critical theory approach.* Amsterdam: John Benjamins.

Turner, J., Hogg, M., Oakes, P., Reicher, S., & Wetherell, M. (1987). *Rediscovering the social group: A self-categorization theory.* Oxford, UK: Basil Blackwell.

Ward, C., Bochner, S., & Furnham, A. (2001). *The psychology of culture shock* (2nd ed.). Philadelphia: Routledge.

Yinger, J. (1986). Intersection strands in the theorization of race and ethnic relations. In J. Rex & D. Mason (Eds.), *Theories of race and ethnic relations* (pp. 20–41). New York: Cambridge University Press.

Yoshikawa, M. (1978). Some Japanese and American cultural characteristics. In M. Prosser, *The cultural dialogue: An introduction to intercultural communication* (pp. 220–239). Boston: Houghton Mifflin.

Young, R. (1996). *Intercultural communication: Pragmatics, genealogy, deconstruction.* Philadelphia: Multilingual Matters.

## Concepts and Questions

1. Think of several different social conditions or events that have arisen from globalization. How are they viewed by people from older generations?

2. What is meant by the term *intercultural personhood?*

3. Describe cultural identity.

4. What are acculturation and deculturation? Provide some examples from your community.

5. Apply Kim's stress–adaptation–growth dynamic model to your first college semester.

6. How would you define intercultural identity?

7. In your opinion, how does a person become competent in a culture other than his/her own?

8. Do you think that Eastern and Western civilizations are currently clashing, or are integrating to create something new? Explain your position.

9. What conditions are required for the emergence of intercultural personhood?

10. List and discuss what you would do to achieve intercultural personhood.

# An Alternative View of Identity

## GUO-MING CHEN

*The essay by Guo-Ming Chen, "An Alternative View of Identity," contains an insightful overview of contemporary approaches to the study of identity and then offers you an alternative to those approaches. First, the article provides an explanation of that abstract concept called "identity." Second, the essay offers a comprehensive, yet succinct, interdisciplinary overview of the principal theories grounding contemporary identity study. Third, readers are exposed to four major Eastern religious and philosophical doctrines. Lastly, Chen suggests an alternative to the Western view of identity by presenting an Eastern perspective.*

*Chen begins with a historical review and critique of several identity theories and then provides a thorough discussion of identity theory and social identity theory. Chin then moves to the field of communication, where the study of identity has been largely the province of intercultural communication scholars. He explains that the bulk of this work has arisen from four approaches: (1) intergroup, (2) cultural, (3) critical cultural, and (4) postcolonial. Following a brief explanation of each approach, Chen puts forward an alternative for considering self and identity by suggesting an Eastern perspective.*

*In explicating his proposal, Chen examines the foundational Eastern religions and philosophies of Confucianism, Hinduism, Buddhism, and Taoism. This is followed by a more comprehensive discussion of Taoism and how it offers an alternative to the Western perspective on identity and the self. Chen concludes the essay by pointing out that identity in the West focuses on the individual, but in an era of increasing multiculturalism, this attitude could facilitate misunderstanding by highlighting differences rather than bringing out similarities among people(s). Taoism, on the other hand, "advocates the importance of attending to the self and the other*

*simultaneously by fitting in and being harmoniously interdependent with each other."*

The impact of globalization has led scholars from different disciplines to study the concept of identity from various aspects and encourage people to find, maintain, and negotiate their identity. Unfortunately, abundant research seems to mystify the concept further. Worse, the aggressive advocate of the importance of establishing, authenticating, maintaining, or negotiating one's own or group identity may motivate people to tightly hold their own ego. Like a cocoon, the problem has a tendency to weave a stronghold preventing a person from penetrating the identity of others. Facing this dilemma, this paper attempts to first offer a critical overview of this line of research, and then to propose a different view on the nature of the self and identity from an Asian perspective.

> *Identity has become a significant concept among social science scholars.*

## AN OVERVIEW OF IDENTITY RESEARCH
### Disciplines of Anthropology, Psychology, and Sociology

Identity has become a significant concept among social science scholars since the 1960s. Identity theory and social identity theory represent the two main perspectives in this line of research. As Hogg, Terry, and White (1995) indicated, identity theory, which was originated in sociology, "deals with the structure and function of people's identity as related to the behavioral roles they play in society"; and social identity theory, which was originated in psychology, "deals with the structure and function of identity as related to people's membership in groups" (p. 265).

This original essay appears here in print for the first time. All rights reserved. Permission to reprint must be obtained from the author and the publisher. An earlier version of this paper first appeared in *China Media Research*, 5(4), 2009, pp. 109–118. Dr. Guo-Ming Chen is a Professor in the Department of Communication Studies at the University of Rhode Island, Kingston, Rhode Island.

Identity theory mainly views the social nature of self from the role positions a person occupies, and the role identities vary with respect to their salience (e.g., Stets, 2006; Stryker, 1987). The theory treats society as a differentiated but an organized system rather than as an undifferentiated whole, thus the self is a multifaceted and an organized social construct emerging from one's roles in society, and the variation in self-concepts depends on the diverse role identities. It is the self-defining role identities that provide meaning for self, though meanings acquired by role identities are originated from social interaction.

Social identity theory was rooted in Tajfel's (1963) studies on social and cultural factors in perception, cognition and beliefs. The theory concentrates on subjects of social self, group processes and intergroup relations. It stipulates that the social category with which a person identifies defines who the person is (Hogg, 2003). Social identity theory was integrated with self-categorization theory, developed in the 1980s (Turner, 1985), which indicates that one's social identity is dictated by how the self and others are categorized into an in-group or an out-group. As a theory of social group, social identity theory does not construct group process from an interpersonal perspective, but is closely intertwined with intergroup relations. It incorporates role identities in group context and opens up studies on a range of group behaviors, such as conformity, discrimination, ethnocentrism, stereotyping and prejudice (e.g., Hogg, 2006).

Although some scholars believed it was not possible to reconcile the differences of the two theories, more and more scholars felt the need to establish a general theory that could integrate the two theories to avoid the redundancies of studies on the different aspects of the self and identity. For example, Stets and Burke (2000) argued that the differences between identity theory and social identity theory have more to do with emphasis rather than kind; thus the two theories can be linked to establish a more complete picture of understanding the self, which in turn will lead to a stronger social psychology.

Stets and Burke further pointed out that an integrated theory needs to consider not only the role and the group, but also the person, as the basis of identity, because the person can provide stability across groups, situations and roles. According to Stets (1995), personal identities represent a set of meanings that make the self an individual. These meanings may overlap the meanings of role identities, because different identities are from different sources. In addition, some aspects of social identities may be based on personal feelings and values, thus personal identities can become part of social identities characteristics (Deaux, 1992). Hence, role identities and social identities are always closely related to personal identities.

The study of identity in psychology and sociology is even more entangled if we look at it from traditional approaches. As Cote and Levine (2002) pointed out, identity formation and identity maintenance are the two major traditions in the study of self and identity in psychology. The two traditions were founded in Erikson's (1968) works on the three concepts of ego identity, personal identity and social identity. These concepts represent the three forms of continuity, which include the sense of identification of the self with itself, the relationship between the self and the other, and the integration between the self and the other.

Research on identity formation was further elaborated by Marcia's (1966, 1993) identity status paradigm. Research on identity maintenance or self-psychology, which stemmed from the works of Colley (1902), James (1948), and Mead (1934), was further developed by Gergen (1991) from a postmodern perspective. Gergen identified the romantic, modern, and postmodern as the three periods scholars in the West used to study the self. Unfortunately, the progress of the research on the self and identity from the psychological perspective continues to suffer from [two] problems … being unable to fully appreciate Erikson's classification of the three different identities (i.e., ego, personal and social) and to adequately theorize the concept of "social" (Cote & Levine, 2002).

Sociological approaches to the study of identity, according to Weigert, Teitge, and Teitge (2007), were also inspired by Erikson's early works on identity. Five distinct sociological traditions were developed: (1) the Chicago School of symbolic interactionism focuses on the emergent and procedural nature of social reality (e.g., Blumer, 1969; Goffman, 1959; Hewitt, 2006; Strauss, 1959); (2) the Iowa School of symbolic interactionism emphasizes the structural and fixed nature of social reality (e.g., Kuhn & McPartland, 1954; Stryker, 1968; Tajfel, 1981); (3) the sociology of interpretive knowledge emphasizes that the social reality embedded in cultural and historical circumstances and directly influences the well-being and survival of human beings (e.g., Berger & Luckmann, 1966); (4) the structural-functionalist perspective stipulates that social order and continuity are maintained by the interdependent subsystems of the society, thus social identity is embedded in the society's institutional structure (e.g., Kurkeim, 1964; Parsons, 1968); and (5) the critical theory of identity indicates that identity is grounded in the relationship between individual and social development; the interactive-communicative, the cognitive-affective, and the social-structural represent the three levels of analysis in the study of identity (e.g., Habermas, 1974).

The sociological tradition demonstrates its theoretical richness in the study of identity. However, this theoretical richness also reflects the lack of empirical association in many of its theoretical claims (Cote & Levine, 2002). This lack of empirical evidence inevitably leads to difficulty in reaching a consensus among scholars in the study of identity. In order to understand better the process of identity formation and maintenance, Cote and Levine (2002) also advocated for the convergence between psychological and sociological approaches to the study of the self and identity, especially through the examination of the relevance of "structure" and "agency" and the extent of "inner" versus "outer" origin when conceptualizing identity.

In the discipline of anthropology, identity is embedded in the concept of culture and other dimensions such as boundary, space, place, authenticity, and ethnicity (e.g., Barth, 1969a; Cohen, 1985). According to Cohen (2000b), the formation, expression, management and stability of collective identities are discriminated based on the cultural boundary. Cultural differences usually create a boundary that distinguishes people on both sides not only by degree, but also by kind. Thus, identity within the boundary is construed as being authentic and absolute by people in the group.

The authenticity of the social or cultural identity can be enhanced by the presence of the other. However, the identity may be contingent and fluid through the cross-boundary interaction. In other words, what seems peripheral to the center of a culture may not be noticed across the boundary line and therefore becomes the center in the peripheral area. Hence, the ascription of a group or cultural identity is possibly subjected to the cross-boundary struggle for control. This indicates the cross-boundary interaction may challenge the collective identity within the group itself.

Identity is therefore encapsulated by the boundary which marks the beginning and the end of a group or community. The cultural experience of the group is a bounded symbolic whole covered with a range of meanings for the development of norms and values that in turn provide a collective sense of identity (Cohen, 1985). The sustainment and maintenance of a coherent collective identity must occur through time, such as a collective memory and lived and shared traditions, and [through] space, such as a mapping of territory and the principle of inclusion and exclusion (Morley, 1995).

Barth (1969b) further pointed out that ethnic boundaries exist despite the interaction of people between two different communities. Geographic and social isolation are not the critical factors in sustaining cultural differences, though the bounded ethnic group and the management of ethnic identity are influenced by the presence of significant others and subject to the ongoing negotiations of boundaries between groups of people. Moreover, Barth (2000) argued that boundaries provide a template in which distinct categories of the mind are separated. When dealing and interacting with boundary relations, it is important to understand members' experiences and cognitive categories. Therefore, ethnic identities are interdependent. They are the product of a continuous process of ascribing and self-ascribing and are maintained through a relational process of inclusion and exclusion.

In the study of identity, the emphasis on the concept of culture diverts anthropologists' attention from the aspect of self and individual (Sokefeld, 1999). It is ironic that, given the importance of the concept of culture in anthropology, scholars are unable to give a more focused view on the cultural perception of the self or person and how it affects the emergence of identity. Furthermore, many questions regarding the study of identity from anthropology are still left unanswered. For example, if identity is fluid and changes over time and is reshaped by interactions with members of different ethnic groups, could we say that a group really possesses an identity and this chameleon-like identity can be considered as being authentic (Cohen, 2000)?

# The Discipline of Communication Studies

The study of identity in communication is mainly conducted from the intercultural communication perspective, which extends the line of research from the traditions of Tajfel's social identity and Barth's ethnic identity. Intercultural communication scholars agree that identity is socially constructed, interactive, negotiated, relational, multifaceted, and space claimed (e.g., Collier, 1997; Jackson, 2002). They investigate how identity is constructed through and affects interaction, and how it is influenced by dominance and power from the aspects of intergroup approach, cultural approach, critical cultural approach and postcolonial approach (Shin & Jackson, 2003).

The intergroup approach applies social identity theories to explain the role social identity plays in the process of inter-ethnic communication from the perspectives of uncertainty reduction and ethnolinguistics (e.g., Giles & Johnson, 1987; Gudykunst & Lim, 1986; Kim, 1986). The cultural approach treats communication competence as a culturally and ethnically specific variable. Identity in this approach is considered a cultural product and is formed through culture embedded in group members' interaction. Thus ethnic or cultural identity, as the feeling of belonging to an ethnic culture, is defined by competently using the cultural symbols and affirming the beliefs, norms and values in that specific cultural context (e.g., Carbaugh, 1996; Philipsen, 1975).

The critical cultural approach is grounded in the sociological perspective of critical theory and expanded on by Hall (1990) through his studies on media presentation of race, identity, culture and ethnicity. This approach views identity as an ideological construct and representation of power structure, which mirrors the political inequality and oppression towards class, gender and race (hooks, 1984, 1992; van Dijk, 1991). Employing the critical cultural approach, intercultural communication scholars have tried to deconstruct the discursive formation of identity and to demystify the structural oppression of marginal groups in the United States (e.g., V. Chen, 1997; Mendoza, 2002). The approach was also extended to study the ethnic identity of Asian-Indian immigrants (Hedge, 1998), gender identity (e.g., Houston, 1992), and the dominance of whiteness (e.g., Nakayama & Martin, 1999). The challenge of Eurocentrism from Afrocentric and Asiacentric paradigms as well is embedded in this approach (e.g., Asante, 1980; Chen, 2006; Chen & Miike, 2006; Dissanayake, 1988; Gunaratne, 1991; Miike, 2003).

Finally, the postcolonial approach can be treated as an extension of the critical cultural approach. As an alternative to the Eurocentric or white-centric perspective, the approach is based on the works of Bhabha (1983) and Spivk (1986). The basic assumption of the self and identity is that "the *other* identity is imposed and inscribed by power structures (or colonizers) in a hegemonic way that needs to be *de*-scribed toward reconstruction of a self" (Shin & Jackson, 2003, p. 224). This postcolonial approach argues that the forgotten or erased true self should be recovered through cultural discourse. The cultural differences of class, culture, gender, race, and skin color can be recognized and deconstructed through the process of rejecting the other. The formation of cultural identity is then based on an authentic, unique and indigenous self, where a cultural space is claimed and the collective selfhood can be interplayed with in-group and out-group elements.

*The concept of the self or identity is still confined or dominated by the Western thinking and practice.*

The integration of research from various disciplines gives communication scholars an advantage in perceiving the identity from interactive and relational aspects and seeing the tension between the self and the other. However, the cross-cultural advantage did not give communication scholars advantages in conceiving the foundation of identity, i.e., the self, from an angle that is different from traditional social sciences. In other words, the concept of the self or identity is still confined or dominated by … Western thinking and practice. In order to remedy this problem, the following section provides an alternative view on the study of the self and identity.

## AN ALTERNATIVE VIEW OF THE SELF AND IDENTITY

As Geertz (1979) indicated, individual identity is established in Western culture as a dynamic center of awareness, emotion and action. As a unique and bound universe, the self has a clear sense of direction, purpose and volition, and through the realization of the true self, identity is established. The self from the Western perspective is characterized as autonomous and egocentric; it is then important to attend to the self, to assert the self, and to emphasize one's difference from others (Markus & Kitayama, 1991). This Western individualistic self is treated as the center of the universe through which the world is perceived; thus to develop a sense of personal control becomes essential for building and holding the centrality and sovereignty of the self.

The Western conceptualization of the self and identity has been facing challenges from cross-cultural studies, feminism, social constructivism, systems theory, critical theory and deconstructionism (Sampson, 1989). The cross-cultural research has provided alternative views on self and identity from different cultural traditions. Feminists propose distinct views of person through the reconceptualization of the patriarchal way of perceiving human life. The social constructionists assert that the self and identity are socially and historically constructed rather than occurring naturally. Systems theory sees the self and identity as being relational rather than independent entities. The critical theory argues that self and identity are created for ideological purposes. Lastly, deconstructionists challenge the centrality and sovereignty of the self and its relationship with the society. These views [of] the study of self and identity open up a venue for exploring the subject from different points of view. This section provides a different view from Asian cultural traditions by focusing on the Taoist perspective.

Buddhism, Confucianism, Hinduism and Taoism form the foundation of Asian philosophical and religious thought, and each of the four traditions provides a specific view on the self and identity. As the dominant paradigm of social life in Far Eastern areas, Confucianism postulates an ethic guideline based on *wu lun* (the Five Codes of Ethics), which governs the five basic human relationships of ruler and subject, father and son, husband and wife, older brother and younger brother, and between friends. The structure of these relationships is particularistic, hierarchical, reciprocal,

*Buddhism, Confucianism, Hinduism and Taoism form the foundation of Asian philosophical and religious thoughts.*

interrelated, formal, and in-group\out-group distinct (Chen & Chung, 1994).

The self is demonstrated through the role one plays in this relationship network. Ho (1995) indicated that the Confucian self is a relational self, which emerges only in the social presence of others. The Confucian identity is then a relational identity defined by one's social relationships. The self in Confucianism is a subdued self. The ultimate goal of life is to realize the self through self-cultivation in a harmonious relationship. This relation-centered perception of the self dictates that the meaning of a person's life can only be completed in the presence of the other. The absence of another's presence will lead to the loss of one's identity.

Hinduism considers the self an illusion originated from ignorance; thus an individual identity has no way to exist. If there is a true self, it will be identical with the ultimate Brahman. To Hinduism, the realization of the true self, or Atman, means the total loss of individual identity or a surrender of the self to the absolute, ineffable and ubiquitous Brahman (Ho, 1995).

Similar to Hinduism's deconstruction of the ego, Buddhism holds a view of non-duality on the distinction of the subject and the object and the self-other demarcation must be negated. The Buddhist further claims that the realization of self cannot be sought, because the self does not exist.

The non-self view denies the very existence of the self and therefore the individual identity. The universe is in constant flux; there can be no permanent entity. In other words, the Buddhist thought of *anicca* (impermanence) dictates that everything that comes into existence will also cease to exist at a certain point in time. The temporary existence of things is subject to the law of *paticcasamupada* (causes and conditions): when the causes change, so the things will change too. Although these causes come together and dependently originate or conditionally co-produce (*paticcasamupada*) the transient existence, the interrelatedness causes of all things. This leads Buddhism to advocate that people should liberate themselves through meditation to reach the state of nirvana, in which there is the total detachment from or no more transmigration of the impermanent self or identity (Watts, 1957).

## Taoist View on the Self and Identity

Taoists take a different route to deal with the self and identity, compared to the views of Confucianism, Hinduism, and Buddhism. Unlike Buddhism and Hinduism, Taoism recognizes the existence of the self and identity, which is different from the Confucian relational self. The Confucian self is an extension of or defined by social relationships. Instead, the self is but a manifestation of the Tao; it is identical with and equally co-produces with the universe. To the Taoist, the duality of subject and object and the demarcation of the self and the other are negated in the oneness of the Tao. This negation of the duality does not imply the undifferentiating between the self and others, but refers to no fixed ideas of the self or to selflessness by giving total freedom to individual identity. It allows the interpenetration and interfusion between the two polarities (Starosta & Chen, 2003). This is different from Hinduism, because after being identical with the Tao, the self or the individual identity will not be lost.

Transcending one's egocentricity results in freedom from partiality and partisanship and achieving equalitarianism among the co-existences. In order to reach this co-existing state within the Tao, the self needs to acquire the ability of great empathy (Chen & Starosta, 2004). Great empathy completely rejects the distinction between subject and object through the process of *wang wo* (forgetting myself), which leads to the transformation of all things, as Chuang Tzu indicated in the chapter of *Qi Wu Lun*:

> Once I, Chuang Chou, dreamt that I was a butterfly and was happy as a butterfly. I was conscious that I was quite pleased with myself, but I did not know that I was Chou. Suddenly I awoke, and there I was, visibly Chou. I do not know whether it was Chou dreaming that he was a butterfly or the butterfly dreaming that it was Chou. Between Chou and the butterfly there must be some distinction. [But one may be the other.] This is called the transformation of things. (Chan, 1963, p. 190)

Through the process of transformation, "The universe and I exist together, and all things and I

> *Unlike Buddhism and Hinduism, Taoism recognizes the existence of the self and identity.*

are one" (p. 186). In other words, things are identical rather than relative, for "this" and "that" produce each other, imply each other, and are identical with each other. As Chuang Tzu further stated:

> There is nothing that is not the "that" and there is nothing that is not the "this"... Therefore I say that the "that" is produced by the "this" and the "this" is also caused by the "that." This is the theory of mutual production.... The "this" is also the "that." The "that" is also the "this."... When "this" and "that" have no opposites, there is the very axis of Tao. (pp. 182–183)

The key to releasing the tension between the self and the other or between two individual identities is being aware of the identification and interpenetration of opposites or polarities. It forms the realm of *da tong* (grand interfusion), mirroring a picture of the wholeness of parts that shows the unity of dualities, the reconciliation of opposites, and a unity in multiplicity. Thus, the Taoist teaching of cultivating egoless selfhood aims to free a person from the four great hindrances of preconceptions, predeterminations, obduracy and egoism, which were stipulated by Confucius, in order to bring out what is hidden within the self to activate the process of concrescence or unity within multiplicity (Chang, 1963).

According to Chen and Starosta (2004), the state of grand interfusion is achieved through great empathy, which is embedded in two human abilities: creativity and sensitivity. Creativity is the basis of egolessness. It refers to being free from the entanglements of time and space, while at the same time it identifies with all those that are temporal and spatial with common essence. The interaction between the detachment from and identification with the self and the other therefore produces abundant potentialities and possibilities within the realm of Tao. More specifically, creativity is moving from one to many by expanding the unity to diversity, and engenders the manifold diversities of existence.

Sensitivity, on the other hand, contracts the diversity into unity by moving from many to one through the process of differentiation and discrimination. Sensitivity promotes creativity, which can produce and reproduce potentiality and possibilities.

Through sensitivity an individual is able to obtain "shared communication symbols and project the self into another person's mind by thinking the same thoughts and feeling the same emotions as the person" (Chen & Starosta, 2000, p. 13). Hence, the contraction and expansion between sensitivity and creativity manifests the infinite interfusion and interpenetration of diversities in unity and the potentiality of unity in diversity (Chang, 1963).

It is here that we see the potential contribution of Taoist thinking in presenting an alternative view on the self and identity that is different from the Western practice and other Asian philosophical and religious thoughts. The free movement between subject and object or between the self and the other demonstrates the ability to release the stronghold of the ego, penetrating the cocoon, overcoming the boundary, and diminishing the wall between different identities.

## CONCLUSION

The increasing intercultural interaction due to globalization has impacted the meaning of the self and identity. The dominant Western value of individualism indicates that an individual should strive for independence from others by attending to the self and asserting one's unique personal attributes. The emphasis on differences between the self and the other is likely to deepen the misunderstanding in the dynamic process of intercultural interaction if both parties lack the abilities of empathy or sensitivity. In order to project a distinct identity, a person may be subdued to hold oneself as a castle or cocoon by building a wall or an impenetrable boundary to exclude the other.

In contrast, the Taoist advocates the importance of attending to the self and the other simultaneously by fitting in and being harmoniously interdependent with each other. The authenticity of each other's identity is held, and then both identities are integrated into one within the Tao through the process of interpenetration and interfusion with the abilities of creativity and sensitivity. The Taoist method of treating the self and identity avoids the pitfalls of Western individualism and overemphasis of the self and individual identity. It is also free from the potential oppression of the self in Confucian teachings and from the annihilation view of the self and identity advocated by Buddhism and Hinduism.

## References

Asante, M. K. (1980). Intercultural communication: An inquiry into research directions. In D. Nimmo (Ed.), *Communication Yearbook 4* (pp. 401–411). New Brunswick, NJ: Transaction.

Barth, F. (Ed.) (1969a). *Ethnic groups and boundaries: The social organization of culture difference*. Boston, MA: Little, Brown and Company.

Barth, F. (1969b). Introduction. In F. Barth (Ed.), *Ethnic groups and boundaries: The social organization of culture difference* (pp. 9–38). Boston, MA: Little, Brown and Company.

Barth, F. (2000). Boundaries and connections. In A. P. Cohen (Ed.), *Signifying identities: Anthropological perspectives on boundaries and contested values* (pp. 17–36). New York: Routledge.

Berger, P. L., & Luckmann, T. (1966). *The social construction of reality*. Garden City, NY: Doubleday.

Bhabha, H. (1983). Difference, discrimination, and the discourse of colonialism. In F. Barker, et al. (Eds.), *The politics of theory* pp. 71–87. Colchester, UK: University of Essex.

Blumer, H. (1969). *Symbolic interactionism: Perspective and method*. Englewood Cliffs, NJ: Prentice-Hall.

Carbaugh, D. (1996). *Situating selves: The communication of social identities in American scenes*. Albany, NY: State University of New York Press.

Chan, W-t (1963). *A source book in Chinese philosophy*. Princeton, NJ: Princeton University Press.

Chang, C-y (1963). *Creativity and Taoism: A study of Chinese philosophy, art, and poetry*. New York: Harper & Row.

Chen, G. M. (2006). Asian communication studies: What and where to now. *The Review of Communication, 6*(4), 295–311.

Chen, G. M., & Chung, J. (1994). The impact of Confucianism on organizational communication. *Communication Quarterly, 42*, 93–105.

Chen. G. M., & Miike, Y. (2006). The ferment and future of communication studies in Asia: Chinese and Japanese perspectives. *China Media Research, 2*(1), 1–12.

Chen, G. M., & Starosta, W. J. (2004). Communication among cultural diversities: A dialogue. *International and Intercultural Communication Annual, 27*, 3–16.

Chen, G. M., & Starosta, W. J. (2000). The development and validation of the intercultural sensitivity scale. *Human Communication, 3*, 1–15.

Chen, V. (1997). (De)hyphenated identity: The double voice in *The Woman Warrior*. In A. Gonzalez,

M. Houston, & V. Chen (Eds.), *Our voices: Essays in culture, ethnicity, and communication* (pp. 3–11). Los Angeles, CA: Roxbury.

Cohen, A. P. (1985). *The symbolic construction of community.* New York: Routledge.

Cohen, A. P. (2000b). Introduction: Discriminating relations: Identity, boundary and authenticity. In A. P. Cohen (Ed.), *Signifying identities: Anthropological perspectives on boundaries and contested values* (pp. 1–13). New York: Routledge.

Colley, C. H. (1902). *Human nature and the social order.* New York: Scribner's.

Collier, M. (1997). Cultural identity and intercultural communication. In L. Samovar & R. Porter (Eds.), *Intercultural communication* (pp. 36–44). Belmont, CA: Wadsworth.

Cote, J. E., & Levine, C. G. (2002). *Identity formation, agency, and culture: A social psychological synthesis.* Mahwah, NJ: Lawrence Erlbaum.

Deaux, K. (1992). Personalizing identity and socializing self. In G. M. Blackwell (Ed.), *Social psychology of identity and the self-concept* (pp. 9–33). London: Surrey University Press.

Dissanayake, W. (Ed.). (1988). *Communication theory: The Asian perspective.* Singapore: Asian Mass Communication Research and Information Center.

Durkheim, E. (1964). *The division of labor in society.* New York: Free Press.

Erikson, E. H. (1968). *Identity: Youth and crisis.* New York: Norton.

Geertz, C. (1979). From the native's point of view: On the nature of anthropological understanding. In P. Rabinow & W. M. Sullivan (Eds.), *Interpretive social science* (pp. 225–241). Berkeley, CA: University of California Press.

Gergen, K. J. (1991). *The saturated self: Dilemmas of identity in contemporary life.* New York: Basic Books.

Giles, H., & Johnson, P. (1987). Ethnolinguistic identity theory: A social psychological approach to language maintenance. *International Journal of the Sociology of Language, 68,* 66–99.

Goffman, E. (1959). *The presentation of self in everyday life.* Garden City, NY: Doubleday.

Gudykunst, W., & Lim, T. S. (1986). A perspective for the study of intergroup communication. In W. Gudykunst (Ed.), *Intergroup communication* (pp. 1–10). London: Edward Arnold.

Gunaratne, S. A. (1991). Asian approaches to communication theory. *Media Development, 38*(1), 53–55.

Habermas, J. (1974). On social identity. *Telos, 19,* 91–103.

Hall, S. (1990). Cultural identity and diaspora. In J. Rutherford (Ed.), *Identity, community, culture, and differences* (pp. 222–237). London: Lawrence & Wishart.

Hedge, R. S. (1998). Swinging the trapeze: The negotiation of identity among Asian Indian immigrant women in the United States. In D. V. Tanno & A. Gonzalez (Eds.), *Communication and identity across cultures (International and Intercultural Communication Annual,* Vol. 21, pp. 34–55). Thousand Oaks, CA: Sage.

Hewitt, J. P. (2006). *Self and society: A symbolic interactionist social psychology.* Boston: Allyn & Bacon.

Ho, D. Y. F. (1995). Selfhood and identity in Confucianism, Taoism, Buddhism, and Hinduism: Contrasts with the West. *Journal for the Theory of Social Behaviour, 25*(2), 115–139.

Hogg, M. A. (2003). Social identity. In M. R. Leary & J. P. Tangney (Eds.), *Handbook of self and identity* (pp. 462–479). New York: The Guilford.

Hogg, M. A. (2006). Social identity theory. In P. Burke (Ed.), *Contemporary social psychological theories* (pp. 111–136). Stanford, CA: Stanford Social Sciences.

Hogg, M. A., Terry, D. J., & White, K. M. (1995). A tale of two theories: A critical comparison of identity theory with social identity theory. *Social Psychology Quarterly, 58*(4), 255–269.

hooks, b. (1984). *Feminist theory from margin to center.* Boston, MA: South End.

hooks, b. (1992). *Black looks: Race and representation.* Boston, MA: South End.

Houston, M. (1992). The politics of differences: Race, class, and women's communication. In L. Rakow (Ed.), *Women making meaning* (pp. 45–49). New York: Routledge.

Jackson, R. (2002). Cultural contracts theory: Toward an understanding of identity negotiation. *Communication Quarterly, 50*(3/4), 359–367.

James, W. (1948). *Psychology.* Cleveland, OH: World Publishing.

Kim, Y. Y. (Ed.) (1986). *Interethnic communication: Current research (International and Intercultural Communication Annual,* Vol. 10). Beverly Hills, CA: Sage.

Kuhn, M. H., & McPartland, T. S. (1954). An empirical investigation of self-attitude. *American Sociological Review, 19,* 68–76.

Marcia, J. E. (1966). Development and validation of ego identity status. *Journal of Personality and Social Psychology, 3,* 551–558.

Marcia, J. E. (1993). The ego identity status approach to ego identity. In J. E. Marcia, A. S. Waterman, D. R. Matteson, S. L. Archer, & J. L. Orlofsky (Eds.),

*Ego identity: A handbook for psychosocial research* (pp. 3–41). New York: Springer-Verlag.

Markus, H. R., & Kitayama, S. (1991). Culture and the self: Implications for cognition, emotion, and motivation. *Psychological Review, 98*(2), 224–253.

Mead, G. (1934). *Mind, self, and society: From the standpoint of a social behaviorist.* Chicago, IL: University of Chicago Press.

Mendoza, S. L. (2002). *Between the homeland and the Diaspora: The politics of theorizing Filipino and Filipino American identities.* New York: Routledge.

Miike, Y. (2003). Beyond Eurocentrism in the intercultural field: Searching for an Asiacentric paradigm. In W. J. Starosta & G. M. Chen (Eds.), *Ferment in the intercultural field: Axiology/value/praxis* (pp. 243–276). Thousand Oaks, CA: Sage.

Morley, D. (1995). *Spaces of identity: Global media, electronic landscape and cultural boundaries.* New York: Routledge.

Nakayama, T., & Martin, J. (1999). Introduction: Whiteness as the communication of social identity. In T. Nakayama & J. Martin (Eds.), *Whiteness: The communication of social identity* (pp. vii–xiv). Thousand Oaks, CA: Sage.

Parsons, T. (1968). The position of identity in the general theory of action. In C. Gordon & K. J. Gergen (Eds.), *The self in social interaction* (pp. 11–23). New York: Wiley.

Philipsen, G. (1975). Speaking "like a man" in Teamsterville: Culture patterns of role enactment in an urban neighborhood. *Quarterly Journal of Speech, 61,* 13–22.

Sampson, E. E. (1989). The deconstruction of the self. In J. Shotter & K. J. Gergen (Eds.), *Texts of identity* (pp. 1–19). Newbury Park, CA: Sage.

Shin, C. I., & Jackson, R. L. (2003). A review of identity research in communication theory. In W. J. Starosta & G. M. Chen (Eds.), *Ferment in the intercultural field* (*International and Intercultural Communication Annual,* Vol. *26*, pp. 211–240). Thousand Oaks, CA: Sage.

Sokefeld, M. (1999). Debating self, identity, and culture in anthropology. *Current Anthropology, 40*(4), 417–447.

Spivak, G. C. (1986). Imperialism and sexual difference. *Oxford Literacy Review, 8,* 1–2.

Starosta, W. J., & Chen, G. M. (2003). "Ferment," an ethic of caring, and the corrective power of dialogue. *International and Intercultural Communication Annual, 26,* 3–23.

Stets, J. (1995). Role identities and person identities: Gender identity, mastery identity, and controlling one's partner. *Sociological Perspectives, 38,* 129–150.

Stets, J., & Burke, P. J. (2000). Identity theory and social identity theory. *Social Psychological Quarterly, 63*(3), 224–237.

Strauss, A. L. (1959). *Mirrors and masks: The search for identity.* Glencoe, IL: The Free Press.

Stryker, S. (1968). Identity salience and role performance: The importance of symbolic interaction theory for family research. *Journal of Marriage and the Family, 30,* 558–564.

Stryker, S. (1987). Identity theory: Developments and extensions. In K. Yardley & Honess, T. (Eds.), *Self and identity* (pp. 89–104). New York: Wiley.

Tajfel, H. (1963). Social identity and intergroup behavior. *Social Science Information, 13,* 65–93.

Tajfel, H. (1981). *Human groups and social categories: Studies in social psychology.* Cambridge: Cambridge University Press.

Turner, J. C. (1985). Social categorization and the self-concept: A social cognitive theory of group behavior. In E. J. Lawler (Ed.), *Advances in group processes: Theory and research* (pp. 77–122). Greenwich, CT: JAI.

van Dijk, T. A. (1991). *Race and press: Critical studies in racism and migration.* New York: Routledge.

Watts, A. W. (1957). *The way of Zen.* New York: Pantheon.

Weigert, A. J., Teitge, J. S., & Teitge, D. W. (2007). *Society and identity: Toward a sociological psychology.* Cambridge: Cambridge University Press.

## Concepts and Questions

1. What is Chen's reason and purpose in proposing a new approach to viewing identity?

2. After reading how anthropology, psychology, and sociology approach the study of identity, which approach do you find is more closely aligned with your personal concept of what identity is and does?

3. What does "identity" mean to you? How do you manifest your different identities?

4. Explain the cultural approach to studying identity. Do you agree with this perspective? Why or why not?

5. Explain the critical approach to studying identity. Do you agree with this perspective? Why or why not?

6. In your opinion, which of the following is a religion and which is a philosophy? Explain your reasoning.

   a. Confucianism
   b. Buddhism
   c. Hinduism
   d. Taoism

7. What makes Taoism different from Confucianism, Hinduism, and Buddhism?

8. Can you think of any weaknesses in Chen's Taoist approach to identity? What are they?

# Living Within Whiteness: A Project Aimed at Undermining Racism

JOHN T. WARREN

*In our third essay, John Warren looks at the issue of "whiteness" in the United States, which he casts as both a form of identity and a social structure. The author begins by explaining four broad categories used by communication scholars to examine whiteness. These are (1) whiteness as an anti-racist practice; (2) how whiteness is promoted in scholarship, film, TV, and other forms of text; (3) how whiteness influences our communicative behaviors; and (4) how whiteness is performed.*

*Warren sees identity as a product of communicative behaviors in their entirety, arising from daily social interactions. Using an ordinary personal anecdote, he demonstrates how whiteness is both an identity and a social structure, completely intertwined and mutually supportive. The essay concludes with a forecast on future whiteness scholarship and a suggestion for a constructive approach.*

## INTRODUCTION

In 1995, I took a feminist theory course at my undergraduate university. It was the final requirement in my women's studies minor, a set of courses I took primarily because as a man in this society I desired a more full understanding of how my gender worked to privilege me, even in ways not immediately apparent to me. In that course, I was introduced to Ruth Frankenberg's (1993) impressive book *White Women, Race Matters: The Social Construction of Whiteness*. While I found much of interest in that book for my study of feminism and my own male privilege, I discovered a question—a project—that would serve as the site for the first part of my research career (Warren, 2003). The idea of whiteness, much like the idea of my maleness, would force me to ask about how privilege worked in and through my body, even in ways that I couldn't readily see or imagine.

In this brief essay, I want to reflect on the whiteness project—to ask how this research frames white identity and white people's responsibility within conversations and debates on racism in the United States (and, as Raka Shome, 1999 reminds us, the majority of the Westernized world). Further, I want to highlight some major contributions communication scholars have contributed to this project. This will provide an opportunity to examine the central question whiteness scholars are asking today: how do we keep in tension questions of the individual actor in culture and the cultural systems that constitute the individual actor? This system-individual has been a major issue since Peggy McIntosh (1997) demanded we talk about it in her early essay "White Privilege, Male Privilege." Thus, the final portion of this essay asks about the future of the whiteness project and where students of intercultural communication might take this research in the future.

## THE WHITENESS PROJECT: IDENTITY OR SOCIAL STRUCTURE

In the intercultural communication course I teach, I often begin class conversations with structure, asking students to see how communication functions to create structures that frame, and in some ways determine, how we live our lives. One need only look to grammar as a system to see how structures determine how we move through the world—random words without grammatical structure are nonsensical; they do not help us as we do our daily activities. Grammar is but one structure that rules, much like the subject-verb-object rules of grammar itself, our daily interactions. But grammar is not the only structure that rules our communication with others. Indeed, we live with and under all sorts of cultural and social rules. From how to talk to a professor to how one interacts with people who are different from us, we come to see communication as a rule-bound structure, taught to us from birth. Early on in my own childhood, I was carefully taught how to be a good person, how to be a man, and as I have come to understand, I was taught how to enact race, even if those rules were never stated as such. But I was taught how to walk down the street, understand my worth, and how to understand my relationship to others in a way that was highly marked and coded by race. My whiteness, my white skin in a world that privileges such things, was taught to me in very careful ways.

Yet, as I remind my students, to blame social structure alone—those multiple sites in which I was learning my whiteness—is to forget how social structure gets there in the first place. Indeed, it is in the minor moments (a comment from my mother, a television show, a news story, a novel in my English class) in which these structures are built. Like grains of sand, these moments build on top of one another and with pressure and time come to take on the appearance of rock. Looking at a rock outside of historical context, one sees only smooth surfaces, feels the hard textures, and senses the weight; however, seen in

> *Whiteness is both an identity and a social structure.*

historical context, sedimentary rock is only the grains of sand under pressure over time. The rock is only what the individual grains generated. And so is my whiteness, generated through my ancestors and repeated over time, an outcome of social norms and social practices. The acts themselves, the moments of entering a mall and not getting followed as an elementary example, build on top of those other grains and produce the rock of race, the appearance of something that somehow exists outside of everyday actions.

But making this case in class can be tough—race is both social structure and individual actions. It is both—and that is what makes talking about whiteness so hard, so difficult. As a teacher, my first response is to do two seemingly opposite things: tell people to change their everyday actions and at the same time tell them to understand that their individual actions are not the cause or end of racism in this country. It feels like a trap. And this is what makes whiteness—the idea of racial privilege—so hard to

discuss. Whiteness, like any racial category, is slippery (Johnson, 2003). It shifts as soon as you think you have a grasp of what it can do.

Simply put: Whiteness is both an identity and a social structure—it is both who I am (or who I have been constituted as, in those moments of learning during my lifetime) and the structure of power which privileges me, makes me the benefactor of power in unseen (to me) ways. To talk about whiteness as only structure or only identity is to forget the complicated nature of how race works in the United States. The work on whiteness has a long history, chronicled at least in part by Roediger's (1998) collection *Black on White,* and can be traced to early conversations about skin politics and cultural power. White scholars, however, have recently taken up charges by bell hooks (1990) and others to investigate how whiteness marks our lives. Indeed, since that time, hundreds of articles, books, conference papers, and videos have been generated to tackle this thing called whiteness. By way of a brief summary, I will return to a logic of organizing the literature that I created some time ago as I think it still offers a heuristic way of imagining the work being done in this field (Warren, 1999).

First, several scholars have engaged in what I call Whiteness as Anti-Racist Practice. In this set of writings, scholars seek to deconstruct whiteness, to see its logic and power, in an effort to undermine it. For instance, in Frankenberg's (1993) *White Women, Race Matters* we see an effort to locate in women's everyday talk the logics of racism, the ways people understand their whiteness. Also, in Peggy McIntosh's (1997) early work, she offered a listing of privileges that she receives as a result of her race. In Christine Sleeter's (1996) work in education studies, she offers a way of thinking about multicultural education that works against white supremacy and dominance in the classroom. Each of these complicated and important studies offers a peek at how whiteness functions with the sole purpose of undermining it, of calling it out, of asking readers to pause and reconsider our actions as implicated people in the world. While not necessarily citing Freire's (1992) oft-quoted "Changing our language is part of the process of changing the world" (p. 74), this work asks us to understand how racism is perpetuated, while also providing the possibility and hope for change.

Second, multiple scholars have looked to various texts (film, television, and other textual sites like scholarship) to see how, in our own writing and in our cultural/historical texts, we have perpetuated whiteness. Harris (1998), in a very powerful analysis of U.S. legal history, analyzes how whiteness was conceived in early U.S. law as property, as something a person could count on as a form of currency. Toni Morrison's (1992) *Playing in the Dark* is a masterful piece on the role of whiteness metaphors in literature. In her work, she reveals how major novels like *Moby Dick* have generated decades of cumulative power in the racial imagination, affecting how people even understand the terms "white" and "black." This was built on by Richard Dyer's (1988) work "White," which examines film texts and uncovers how metaphors of color have been played out in film. In all of these studies, the authors allow access to how race is repeated within these texts to recreate whiteness.

Third, rhetorical scholars have busily worked to establish an impressive body of literature examining whiteness as a rhetorical location. Here, the focus on discursive constructions of whiteness has generated a powerful way of seeing whiteness in and through our everyday talk. Most notable is Nakayama and Krizek's (1995) essay "Whiteness: A Strategic Rhetoric," in which the authors extract the major identifier labels white students use to describe themselves. In this work, they can see how the use of "majority" or "American" works to recreate whiteness as a privileged location. From this work, Crenshaw (1997) and Shome (1996) each produced essays that worked with these ideas of racial privilege embedded in everyday talk. Nakayama and Martin's (1999) *Whiteness: The Communication of a Racial Identity* brought together multiple rhetoricians on the topic. In other fields, scholars like Staub (1997) and Chambers (1997) have added to this body of literature.

The fourth and final general trend in the literature is Whiteness as a Performative Accomplishment, seeking to uncover how whiteness is produced through discourse over time in ways that produce bodies—that is, asking how our communicative norms produce the rules and practices that govern how bodies are reproduced. This is where I have spent the majority of my time (Warren, 2001a, 2001b, 2003). In my work, I have tried to understand how race is not located in the body (in my white body)—but rather, my white body stands as a result of multiple racist practices. That is, the social norms that have produced my body were determined by the norms that produced my grandparents' and my parents' bodies. Those norms also produced the body of my son, who is now implicated in a system he did not design but will nonetheless benefit from. Others in this area of study are Butler (1993), Cooks (2003), and several others who are featured in a new book on whiteness and performance (Cooks & Simpson, in press).

## WHITENESS: MAJOR CONTRIBUTIONS FROM COMMUNICATION

It is probably best to ask someone who is not a communication scholar what communication truly offers to the study of whiteness. Perhaps, I and others in the field of intercultural communication might be biased when we (or I) say that communication research has changed the conversation in whiteness studies. We have done so by forcing a more complicated relationship between identity and bodies, between communication and the institutionalized nature of racial power in the United States. A good example of this is the debate between those who desire to divorce the discursive power of whiteness (norms of talk, language structures, and interaction styles) from white bodies (individuals who may or may not participate in racism). The principal author in this debate, for me, is Annlouise Keating (1995), who works diligently to separate whiteness from white people: "The fact that a person is born with 'white' skin does not necessarily mean that s/he will think, act, and write in the 'white' ways" (p. 907). Keating is, in many ways, correct—the structure of power in which her and my [bodies] live is not the same as our everyday practices. Certainly, I can look at my body of work and my interactions with students and friends and strangers and say that I've tried not to repeat the racism I know to be so embedded in me. I can do my best, knowing that I may not be aware of the many ways I do whiteness without knowing it. But conflating the two does not help our understanding of racism and power. In this way, Keating is correct.

Yet, one must never imagine the picture (clean divisions between systems of race and those who benefit from them) is so easy. In a powerful response, Dreama Moon (1999), a communication scholar, reminds us that while whiteness and white people are not the same, they are not so easily distinguishable either. Indeed, they are woven together in powerful ways:

> While I agree that it is important not to conflate [whiteness and white people], I would argue that it is politically unwise to pretend that white *people* somehow are not implicated in the everyday production and reproduction of 'whiteness.' (p. 179)

With Moon's correction, we have just a glance of how intercultural communication scholars have made a difference in this conversation.

In another important dialogue on whiteness, education and social activist authors have sought to create an abolitionist project for whiteness, calling on everyday (white) people to enact treason to whiteness, to deny those privileges that whiteness grants (see Ignatiev & Garvey, 1996; McLaren, 1999). These so-called "race traitors" advocate turning one's back to whiteness in solidarity with people of color who do not receive the same advantages. They call upon notions of performance, asking people to "do brownness" in an effort to reject the power of whiteness (McLaren, 1999). Communication scholars have retorted, reminding us that we must be much more careful with such terms, for the logic of abolitionist projects is loaded (Moon & Flores, 2000) and the use of performance is often offered without careful application and understanding of the term and its history (Warren, 2001b).

These are just two ways that communication scholars are working to contribute to the field. But the central addition to advancing debates on whiteness and anti-racism, I would argue, is the careful analysis and study of communication in everyday contexts. In so much of the literature on whiteness, the discussion reads as if one's identity (that is, their whiteness) is a given; they fail to see the major corrective that intercultural communication insists upon. That is, many scholars fail to note how identity is created in the first place. This is where communication scholars shine the brightest, for it is within the logic of communication—the idea that one's self is a product of their (and others') communication over time—where we even begin to understand how identity is formed. By analyzing communication (between people, over time, via multiple formats and venues), we are able to see the messages that form decisions that produce identity.

An example: consider the movie *Crash*, the blockbuster film set in Los Angeles that discusses prejudice and the effect of racism on the lives of a series of individuals. In this movie, Sandra Bullock, when faced with the presence of two black men on an open street, pulls her purse to her chest, probably unconsciously, to protect it. In this moment, one can see how communication constitutes identity—hers, as a possible victim, and the black men, as possible victimizers. Yet, that act alone is not sufficient to produce identity. Sandra Bullock's character did not invent this moment, for it is widely available in a multitude of contexts. In media and everyday contexts, this moment is repeated, re-done, re-said through nonverbals (looks, expressions, movements, and adjustments of space). And in this moment, this remaking of potential victim and potential victimizer, race is recreated, for race (and racialized gender) is exactly the message that is produced, not only for the characters, but [also for] the millions of audience members who bought their tickets to see *Crash*. So this moment, if not examined in communication terms, can seem like an act of racism, these identities playing out their script. However, with communication as the center, we see that it is the script (and the repeating of the script) that makes the identities possible. For how can we understand race without the communicative cues that mark Sandra Bullock a white woman in need of protection and the two black men as raced figures in need of being protected against?

Communication, as shown previously, allows you to see how identities come to be and not [to] take their status for granted. That is, within a communicative frame one sees that identity is produced through communication, made possible within our everyday interactions. The consideration of

> One's self is a product of their (and others') communication over time.

interaction as productive is not entirely new (we often note in communication classes that when we talk or when we gesture that meaning is made); what is new is that we often consider the self to be the maker of that communication and of that meaning. The radical shift that innovative communication theory allows for is that it is the communicators that are created in these moments.

## WHITENESS: IDENTITY AND SOCIAL STRUCTURE

I began this essay by asking whether whiteness was an identity or social structure. I suggested that it is both—indeed, here I want to take that issue up to a larger extent. In this section, I want to draw greater connections between whiteness as an identity and whiteness as a social structure that guides and directs one's actions. My hope here is to explain how and in what ways they co-construct each other—that is, the way identity and structure occur and are made at the same time. In order to do so, I will examine a moment of my own life and try to unpack how whiteness was produced. To be clear, this moment is not an extreme example, though the analytical process would likely be the same if it were. Rather, I use a more mundane, everyday moment to show how communication need not be extraordinary to make a big difference.

The moment: I was in my office talking with a colleague and, like so many other professors have before, we covered the major things we always talk about: our latest faculty meeting, the new memo from the Dean's office, and, of course, our students. In our talk of our students, we begin talking about a favorite student of mine—a young black student of ours, a good student with a kind of dedication we both enjoy. He is in both of our classes and doing well, but we both note a weakness in his writing, a kind of failure to understand the basic principles of constructing traditional argument. His form is off, as he struggles to get the principles of APA citation correct or build a traditional argument, or write the clear literature review we desire. We both note this and comment that we hope he finds his footing before the ground swallows him. After my fellow professor leaves my office I turn to the stack of papers on my desk and while I have to read them before class, I'm distracted, thinking of this student, his brilliant ideas, and my concerns about his writing. I also begin to wonder why I never find myself this distracted by my students who know the form and continue to repeat the same story over and over again. That is, here is this amazing student with these amazing ideas and I'm obsessed with the structure of his ideas, not the ideas themselves. And like so many of my students who turn in the most beautiful prose that says nothing in particular, I (many times) fail to wonder about the absence of ideas in light of easily readable writing.

This moment is not spectacular—it fails to capture the attention and does not really suggest the kind of drama that burning crosses and riots might create. This moment is more likely to be the kind of thing anyone can foster in his or her memory. It happens in multiple contexts, differently to be sure, but the script is repeated: questions about person X, a person of color (most often black) followed by questions of form over structure. They are often coded in the seemingly complimentary beginning ("she is so articulate") but closely followed by the hitch ("you'd never guess..."). So here is this moment—what does it say about the relationship between whiteness and the identity/structure conversation at hand?

I begin by noting that my colleague and I are both white—that is, we both identify as white people and our skin is marked by so many privileges. We both have enjoyed the invisibility of white skin, never having to account for race since it never mattered to us. Of course, this is juxtaposed to our student's body, which is not white and has never "enjoyed" the luxury of invisibility (most assuredly within this predominantly white university). During this conversation, in which we are basking in our institutional privilege that allows us to critique and discuss this student of color, we carefully work (with the best of intentions) to individualize this student—it is his inabilities we are noting, not (1) our own; (2) the institution's; or (3) the norms that have created the standards we are so vigorously trying to protect. That is, it is significant that our critique falls upon this student without any questions of the origins of the critique. Our position is clear—we are professors and we knowingly evaluate others.

He, the student, is the one who fails or succeeds in meeting our expectations. This movement is not only about diverting attention away from us and our own location within social structures, but is really about individualizing this student, ripping him from this academic context. That is, he stands on his own. This is significant because it is quite powerful to remove a person from context. His writing, in this way, is not about failing to meet our expectations and assumptions about what writing should be like, but about failing to meet the institutional norms my colleague and I protect. It is complicated, this moment. We both want him to succeed, even as we hold up the norms that make his success questionable.

What does this say about whiteness? In this moment, whiteness can be seen as social structure. That is, whiteness serves as the overarching structure under which both my colleague and I operate, as well as the system of power this student understands he must negotiate. Whiteness guides my understandings of proper writing, undergirds my evaluative comments, and allows me to see this student outside any context and/or cultural tradition he might treasure. Whiteness structures the educational system that we all function within, even if our skin is not white. Whiteness is coded in the language choices we use and the academic language we use to try to communicate, even across our differences. Whiteness structures the larger world, the larger picture of government, entertainment, and education generally. Whiteness has created who I am, who I will become, and how I will see myself. It is the water that surrounds the fish, the air that surrounds the nose; whiteness serves as the social rules that permeate the way I move down the hallway or across the street. Whiteness is the structure.

Yet, whiteness is not a rulebook or an essential characteristic that we all "just have," regardless of how much it might seem like it. Rather, whiteness exists in the small repeated ways we do our lives, complete our speech, and live our lives. Whiteness is recreated as we move down the hallways or the street—the doing of it remakes the idea of whiteness. It makes the identity of whiteness possible.

> *Whiteness structures the larger world, the larger picture of government, entertainment, and education generally.*

We make ourselves, each of us, in the acts of our everyday interactions. In this way, whiteness is an identity—one created and recreated many times without our direct knowledge or consent. In the example earlier, it is not my colleague and I who invent whiteness—but we remake it in our talk, in our evaluation, and in our unreflective support of the system of whiteness. Whiteness is not ours alone, but we have done our part.

And so, whiteness is both. It is a structure, but one recreated through each of our everyday actions; on the other hand, whiteness is an identity recreated through each of our everyday actions. And because it is both, it makes it hard to pinpoint with any ease or reliability.

## WHITENESS: THE FUTURE OF A QUESTION

I end here with a brief note on the future of the whiteness question. I'm often asked, "Where is this area of research going and how will communication lead the way?" I offer here three directions that I suspect will become the eventual outcomes of this work.

First, research in whiteness and cultural power will continue. Simply said, the studies that have been done thus far in the field of communication (as well as education, sociology, and cultural studies, to name a few) have only suggested the depth of the problem. We have yet to really grasp what is at stake in the whiteness research, much less really construct any coherent response to it. Like so many areas of research, whiteness research suffers from too much research too soon, leaving the field with too much scholarship on the topic—too much doing very similar work. However, this early period of writing is about trying to understand it, getting the basic idea of it, and trying to create a language for talking about it. We are not done with this work—much remains to be said. I think the next great movement in this research is probably going to be inspired (as the initial project was) by scholars of color, pushing white researchers to do better work on the topic. I have faith that when pushed, the research will advance. Second, privilege research will continue to grow. One might locate whiteness research within the growing literature that examines privilege. Certainly, Peggy McIntosh's (1997) leading research article on white privilege was sparked by her work in women's studies, which has been asking about male privilege for decades. As research grows analyzing issues of class and sexuality, one can see a whole new growth in research from varying perspectives. This is good for us as both a discipline and a culture for, as bell hooks (1990) might ask us to do, we need to radically change how we understand issues of power and oppression. For too long we have allowed these questions to be about those who suffer the pains of oppression and have left the ones who benefit from systems of power unchallenged. By engaging in privilege studies, we might better understand the depths to which whiteness (and heterosexuality, class privilege, etc.) has inscribed how we live our lives.

Third, a critical approach to the changing nature of power will result in/through this research. That is, as we become more comfortable in asking questions about privilege, we will need to account for that comfort. This is to say, we will need to ask questions that go to the heart of our research, questioning the taken-for-granted in our research, and talk about privilege. For instance, in a recent article I co-wrote with Kathy Hytten (Warren & Hytten, 2004), we talk about various positions that individuals take up when faced with research and critical analyses of whiteness. We identified four problematic "faces" or relations to whiteness: The *Torpified* is a position characterized by guilt and fear, leaving the privileged individual paralyzed to act and imagine new ways of moving forward in the world. The *Missionary* is an individual who acts without the proper focus, believing that in his or her own privilege he or she is the one who knows how to "fix" the problem of racism. The *Cynic* is the person who, when faced with the question of racism, fails to see beyond the problem, denying any possibility for change. The final position we found was the *Intellectual*, that figure who turns questions of racism and the problem of privilege into an intellectual game that never allows the work to affect his or her own actions. Each of these shares a number of problems, even as they vary in how they get applied. At the heart of each is an effort to individualize problems of racism, never putting their own complicity

and/or participation with racism on the line. Further, each position keeps whiteness and racism stable—even as these positions are *in relation to* whiteness research, they nevertheless remain quite distanced from allowing that research to affect their actions in ways that are dialogic and progressive.

I end here in much the same way that Kathy and I do in the essay described above—I call for what we named the "Critical Democrat," a position that is reflexive (that is, deeply committed to understanding how racism has marked their lives) and critical (that is, dedicated to a balanced and careful examination that places one's actions and understandings next to the voices and understandings of others). Here, one never assumes their own vision of the world is correct or the only way to understand issues of racism, but rather a position that acknowledges that our understandings are cultural products and therefore always already tainted by our own lived histories and circumstances. To do this, we must understand that whiteness (like any privileged position) is both an identity—who we are (or may be)—as well as a social system that levies power and produces those/our identities. To understand power and privilege within this matrix is to see it as an active process imbued with history and embedded with subjective cultural knowledge.

# References

Butler, J. (1993). *Bodies that matter: On the discursive limits of "sex."* NY: Routledge.

Chambers, R. (1997). The unexamined. In M. Hill (Ed.), *Whiteness: A critical reader*, (pp. 187–203). New York: New York University Press.

Cooks, L. (2003). Pedagogy, performance, and positionality: Teaching about whiteness in interracial communication. *Communication Education*, 52, 245–57.

Cooks, L., & Simpson, J. (Eds.) (2007). *Whiteness, pedagogy and performance: Displacing race.* Lanham, MD: Lexington.

Crenshaw, C. (1997). Resisting whiteness' rhetorical silence. *Western Journal of Communication*, 61, 253–78.

Dyer, R. (1997). *White.* London: Routledge.

Frankenberg, R. (1993). *White women, race matters: The social construction of whiteness.* Minneapolis: University of Minnesota Press.

Freire, P. (1992). *Pedagogy of hope: Reliving pedagogy of the oppressed.* New York: Continuum.

Harris, C. (1998). Whiteness as property. In D. Roediger (Ed.), *Black on white: Black writers on what it means to be white* (pp. 103–118). New York: Schocken Books.

hooks, b. (1990). *Yearning: Race, gender, and cultural politics*. Boston: South End Press.

hooks, b. (1990). *Yearning: Race, gender, and cultural politics*. New York: Routledge.

Ignatiev, N., & Garvey, J. (1996). Abolish the white race: By any means necessary. In N. Ignatiev & Garvey, J. (Eds.), *Race traitor* (pp. 9–14). New York: Routledge.

Johnson, E. P. (2003). *Appropriating Blackness: Performance and the politics of authenticity*. Durham: Duke University Press.

Keating, A. (1995). Interrogating "whiteness," (de)constructing "race." *College English, 57*, 901–18.

McIntosh, P. (1997). White privilege and male privilege: A personal account of coming to see correspondences through work in women's studies. In R. Delgado & J. Stepfanic (Eds.), *Critical white studies: Looking behind the mirror* (pp. 291–99). Philadelphia: Temple University Press.

McLaren, P. (1999). Unthinking whiteness, rethinking democracy: Critical citizenship in gringolandia. In C. Clark & J. O'Donnell (Eds.), *Becoming and unbecoming white: Owning and disowning a racial identity* (pp. 10–55). Westport, CT: Bergin & Garvey.

Moon, D. (1999) White enculturation and bourgeois ideology: The discursive production of good (white) girls." In T. K. Nakayama & J. Martin (Eds.), *Whiteness: The communication of social identity* (pp. 177–97). Thousand Oaks, CA: Sage.

Moon, D., & Flores, L. A. (2000). Antiracism and the abolition of whiteness: Rhetorical strategies of domination among "race traitors." *Communication Studies, 5*, 97–115.

Morrison, T. (1992). *Playing in the dark: Whiteness and the literary imagination*. New York: Vintage.

Nakayama, T. K., & Krizek, R. L. (1995). Whiteness: A strategic rhetoric. *Quarterly Journal of Speech, 81*, 291–309.

Nakayama, T. K., & Martin, J. N. (Eds.) (1999). *Whiteness: The communication of social identity* (pp. 107–28). Thousand Oaks, CA: Sage.

Roediger, D. (1998). *Black on white: Black writers on what it means to be white*. New York: Schocken Books.

Shome, R. (1999). Whiteness and the politics of location: Postcolonial reflections. In T. K. Nakayama & J. N. Martin (Eds.), *Whiteness: The communication of social identity* (pp. 107–28). Thousand Oaks, CA: Sage.

Shome, Raka (1996). Race and popular cinema: The rhetorical strategies of whiteness in "City of Joy." *Communication Quarterly, 44*, 502–18.

Sleeter, C. (1996). *Multicultural education as activism*. Albany, NY: SUNY Press.

Staub, M. E. (1977). The whitest I: On reading the Hill-Thomas transcripts. In M. Hill (Ed.), *Whiteness: A critical reader* (pp. 47–62). New York: New York University Press.

Warren, J. T., & Hytten, K. (2004). The faces of whiteness: Pitfalls and the critical democrat. *Communication Education, 53*, 321–339.

Warren, J. T. (1999). Whiteness and cultural theory: Perspectives on research and education. *The Urban Review, 31*, 185–203.

Warren, J. T. (2003). *Performing purity: Whiteness, pedagogy, and the reconstitution of power*. New York: Peter Lang.

Warren, J. T. (2001a). Doing whiteness: On the performative dimensions of race in the classroom. *Communication Education, 50*, 91–108.

Warren, J. T. (2001b). Performing whiteness differently: Rethinking the abolitionist project. *Educational Theory, 51*, 451–67.

## Concepts and Questions

1. Do you agree with the author's statement that he is privileged as a result of his gender? Why?

2. What are some of the cultural and social "rules" that influence your daily life? Do they facilitate or hinder your daily activities? How?

3. What does the author mean when he says he considers his whiteness as "generated through my ancestors and repeated over time, an outcome of social norms and social practices"?

4. As discussed in this essay, how are white skin and the concept of whiteness different?

5. Warren provides an example of whiteness being enacted in the movie *Crash*. Can you think of some examples that you have seen or enacted?

6. How does communication work to produce, sustain, and even change identity?

7. Warren considers whiteness to be both an identity and a social structure. Explain this idea.

8. How does whiteness structure the "larger world, the larger picture of government, entertainment, and education generally"?

# American Indian Identity: Communicating *Indian-ness*

STEVEN B. PRATT • MERRY C. PRATT • LYNDA D. DIXON

*In their essay, Steven Pratt and his co-authors explore the concept of identity among America's indigenous population by focusing on three topics: (1) how American Indians are defined, (2) problems related to researching American Indian issues, and (3) contemporary identity issues of American Indians. They first highlight that American Indians are often asked to "prove" their ethnic heritage in one way or another, whereas most other U.S. groups need only state their cultural identity. The authors indicate that while manifestations of identity are not an overt requirement for members of the majority culture, this becomes an explicit part of daily life among American Indians. Furthermore, in the United States, American Indians need a federally issued Certificate of Degree of Indian Blood to prove they are Indian. Other ethnic groups, however, usually need only voice their cultural affiliation.*

*The essay also discusses how American Indians' traditional connection to their tribe has been eroded by modernity. This has brought about a lessening of tribal-ness and a movement toward increased Indian-ness. The authors then provide a discussion of the media's influence on the formation and transmission of the image most people hold of American Indians, pointing out that these images are often based upon misinformation, characterized by stereotypes, and tend to aggregate all Indians into a single, homogeneous grouping.*

*Although the American Indian has been the subject of study across many academic disciplines, the authors point out that little research has been devoted to Indian communication practices. The essay also explains the difficulties related to researching this topic due to issues of discerning what constitutes cultural competency and an inability to generalize cultural traits across all American Indians. Pratt and his cohorts advocate an approach to studying Indian communicative behaviors that breaks away from the theories and approaches used to examine communication among European Americans.*

An American Indian student, assisting with the administration of a survey on which I was working, asked me a striking question: "Do you want me to administer this questionnaire to only traditional Indians or to 'apples' also?" Asked what he meant by "traditional Indians" or "apples," the Indian student responded, "You know, do you want me to use only real Indians or those who claim to be Indian?" This dialogue between the Indian student and me suggests the significance, recurrence, and unavoidable character of the question for American Indians that occurs in the context of their everyday lives: What exactly constitutes a "real" Indian? A counterpart to that question is How do real Indians know other real Indians, and how do they make themselves known as real Indians to other real Indians? (Pratt, 1985, p. 29)

> American Indians are often asked to "prove" their ethnic heritage.

## AMERICAN INDIAN IDENTITY: COMMUNICATING *INDIAN-NESS*

This essay investigates several areas of what Pratt (1985) identifies as "*Indian-ness*," such as what is an Indian (how is one defined), what is problematic in researching Indians, and what are some contemporary issues of American Indian identity. We attempt to illuminate some pervasive questions for discussion when studying Indians as a cultural group. Although Indians are researched, there are still many misconceptions as to identifying, researching, and

This original essay appears here in print for the first time. All rights reserved. Permission to reprint must be obtained from the lead author and the publisher. Dr. Seven B. Pratt is a Professor in the Department of Communication at the University of Central Oklahoma. He was born and raised on the Osage Indian reservation. Dr. Merry C. Pratt is an Associate Professor of Interpersonal Communication at the University of Central Oklahoma. Dr. Lynda D. Dixon is a Professor in the Department of Interpersonal Communication, School of Communication Studies at Bowling Green State University.

understanding Indian identity. Our purpose here is to shed some light on these concerns and to provide you with a better understanding of some issues that are specific to studying the communicative behaviors of the American Indian.

When it comes to American Indians, they are often still misrepresented as to *who* is Indian. In other words, other cultural groups generally do not have [to face] the questions associated with being an Indian, such as "How much (blood) Indian are you?" or "Are you a real Indian?" Few other groups of people are visible representations of a race, but constantly asked about or assessed as to their degree of cultural authenticity. Because of these inconsistencies, we present this paper as a means to address some of these anomalies and answer some questions about what it means to … "be Indian." McDaniel, Samovar, and Porter (2009) note that communication and culture are intertwined and "exert a pervasive influence on every aspect of our lives" (p. 13). Thus, in discussing American Indian identity, we emphasize the communicative acts and contexts specific to the American Indian experience.

## DEFINING *INDIAN-NESS*

How often are you asked to "prove" who you are in regard to your cultural identity? Most likely, not very often. Let us consider, for example, an Irish American. An Irish American's "Irish-ness" is not often called into question; neither is the Irish American person constantly asked if he or she "has been back to the old country" nor told by the interlocutor that his or her ancestry includes an Irish princess. These statements are routinely encountered by Indians. Although, in the case of Indians, one may have a specific blood quantum, this does not necessarily establish this person as a real Indian. Being Indian consists of more than just possessing a certain amount of Indian blood. Simply because a person may *look* Indian, it does not mean that he or she is really Indian, that is, regarded by other Indians as a full-fledged bona fide culturally competent member. Being Indian includes appropriately enacting the communicative behaviors that constitute *Indian-ness*. In other words, an Indian must comport himself or herself as an Indian, while enacting appropriate behaviors, i.e., communicating in a way that is truly Indian. However, these "appropriate communicative behaviors" are not often recognizable. Just as culture cannot be taught by using a checklist, one cannot pinpoint a "real" Indian by using the obvious cues such as skin color, facial features, or hair color and texture. Within this paper, we address some of the patterns of communication specific to *Indian-ness*.

Most European Americans have not had the opportunity to spend time socializing with a typical American Indian family in their traditional milieu. They have not been able to observe how the Indian family engages in the maintenance of daily life: to see how Indians love to engage each other in their unique humor, to hear elders tell stories of their past and be able to recognize that in each story lies the lineage and history of their family and tribe, or to be intrinsically involved in "putting on" (i.e., planning and preparing) and participating in a tribal ceremony. The typical European American probably hasn't had the privilege of being a guest on an Indian reservation or in a predominantly Indian community with the opportunity to actually observe and be a part of contemporary American Indian life.

Culturally competent Indians, or those Indians who express their identities through communicative patterns, can attest to how Indian people tacitly define themselves in their everyday interactions, thus communicating their *Indian-ness*. They notice that whoever is encountered is always greeted as a relative. They recognize how everyone seems to know everyone. They are able to ascertain when it is appropriate to ask questions. They know not only when to interrupt, but also when it is okay just to sit in silence. They understand when it is appropriate to not look at a speaker; they know not to show discomfort when someone orates or prays too long.

The aims of our essay are to focus on American Indian identity: to formulate and articulate the problem of what it means to … identify identity and, more importantly, to begin the discussion of what constitutes Indian identity. We know that identity is socially constructed (Berger & Luckmann, 1966) and manifested through communication. Therefore, our

> *Being Indian consists of more than just possessing a certain amount of Indian blood.*

identity, the very essence of *who we are,* is a process bound and defined by our communicative acts. We begin by providing an overview of the problematic nature of identity and being identified.

To begin this journey into Indian life, we focus on American Indian identity in terms of identity negotiation, as well as what it means to be Indian in contemporary American society—with *Indian-ness* as our keystone. Although each American Indian tribe is divergent (e.g., geographically, linguistically), the existence and overlap of communicative commonalities create a unified, indigenous worldview that we refer to as *Indian-ness.*

## You're Not a Full Blood, Are You?

Perhaps the most perplexing issue for many people (particularly those in the majority culture) is to understand the nature of tribal or Indian identity. Seldom is one ever asked, "How much white are you?" or "How much white blood do you have?" Like so many things implicit in our lives that do not get our attention until something *makes* us look further, identity is only examined when it is called into question. For example, whites do not often have to explain their whiteness or "verify" how they are part of the European American group. It is absolutely taken for granted. Therefore, for many of those in the majority culture, establishing, expressing, and maintaining identity is not an explicit part of their daily existence, topic of conversation, or object of direct questioning like it is for many American Indians.

This is not true among Indians. A constant for Indians, particularly among each other, is the endless process of establishing, confirming, and attesting to what is termed *Indian-ness* (Pratt, 1995). The question of identity is a question that is literally asked of all Indian people regardless of tribal affiliation. These questions—whether posed in a social context by other Indians ("What tribe are you?", "Do you sing around the big drum?", "Do you pow-wow?"); or by non-Indians ("How much Indian are you?" "You're not a full-blood, are you?"); or by federal and tribal agencies ("Do you have a CDIB [Certificate of Degree of Indian Blood] or a tribal membership card?"); or simply "Are

> *For Indian people, there are a variety of ways to identify—e.g., blood quantum or socio-linguistic type.*

you really an Indian? You don't look like an Indian"—are questions of identity that most Indians face on a daily basis. For Indian people, the question of identity is not restricted to identification for tribal and federal social services but also for purposes of determining the cultural competency or *Indian-ness* of one who self-identifies as an American Indian.

Racial, cultural, and [gender] identity for most Americans is neither a quantifiable nor a federally documented point of concern. If one chooses to be a member of a racial, cultural, or gendered group all one simply has to do is self-identify, comport one's self in a culturally competent manner, be identified by other group members, or be identified by out-group members as a member of a particular group.

Yet, for the indigenous people of this country, the American Indian, this governmental documentation of blood quantum is a requirement for membership and subsequent federal identification. Members of American Indian tribes must provide this documentation in order to enjoy the constitutionally protected rights that are granted to all citizens except the American Indian. Constitutional privileges such as the right to worship in a culturally sanctioned manner, access to health care, voting in tribal elections, management of personal monies, choices of housing, and opportunities for employment hinge upon governmental certification.

## DEFINING THE CONTEMPORARY INDIAN EXPERIENCE

The definition of an Indian, or who an Indian is, is a question in flux. For Indian people, there are a variety of ways to identify—e.g., blood quantum or socio-linguistic type. Interestingly, most lay people are unaware of the difference between *Indian-ness* and *tribal-ness* (Pratt, 1998). These two terms are often intertwined and used synonymously, yet they mean very different things. The cultural decline and/or transformation of many American Indian tribes is due to such influencing factors as language loss, intermarriage, death of elders, and relocation. These factors have contributed to tribes moving away from their basic nature of cultural competency. Although many tribes have attempted to preserve their culture, they are working against incredible shifts in thought and time. For centuries, Indians centered their lives on tribal-ness, which eventually gave way to *Indian-ness* as the most recognized mode of social identity. Therefore, when we refer to the communicative practices and study of Indians, we are generally more focused on their *Indian-ness* as opposed to their tribal-ness.

What is important to note is that although tribal members attempted to hold on to a traditional lifestyle, the tribal way of life began to deteriorate. Change was inevitable. Forced assimilation began to have its effect, with many tribal members moving away from the reservation and not returning. Concomitantly, tribes began experiencing the loss of elders and other culturally competent members, who had traditionally been responsible for teaching cultural behaviors, and loss of tribal languages. As a result of the relocation of tribal members to urban or non-reservation areas and loss of culturally competent members, the concept of a tribal identity or "tribal-ness" was gradually replaced with a general Indian or *Indian-ness* identity. Thus, *Indian-ness*, replaced "tribal-ness" as a lifestyle or form of social identity.

## INDIAN-NESS AND TRIBAL IDENTITY

Pratt's (1996) discussion of the uses of humor as a form of identification among Indians notes that Indian identity is not the same as tribal identity, although belonging to a tribe is a constituent of being an Indian. Tribal identity is derived from an adherence to and acceptance of a unique rather than a generalized lifestyle. "All tribes have differing languages and customs, but under the rubric of Indian, it is a generalization of a combination of various tribal life ways. Thus, it is this 'generalizability' that creates *Indian-ness*" (Pratt, 1995, p. 239).

There are many ways in which *Indian-ness* can be interpreted. For example, a non-Indian may consider anyone who stereotypically resembles an Indian as having been socialized in a traditional Indian environment and being cognizant of tribal or Indian ways. However, physical appearance is not the sole indicator of cultural competency for "*Indian-ness* to Indian people is a concept that espouses the eclectic lifestyles of indigenous people which serves to unify

the various tribal groups under one rubric" (Pratt, 1995, p. 239).

Let us consider the role of *Indian-ness* with regard to tribalism. For example, it is possible to be an Indian and an Osage; that is, a person who has been socialized in Osage culture and is accepted as an Osage by other Osages and also maintains an identity with members of other tribes. He or she enacts appropriate communicative behaviors that enable acceptance by other Indians. Moreover, one can be an Indian but not be Osage. This person has been socialized in an urban or Indian environment, is accepted by other Indians, but has not been socialized into the Osage tribe and is not accepted by other Osages. Finally, it is possible to be an Osage but not be an Indian. This individual has been socialized into the Osage culture, has limited contact with members of other tribes, and primarily views his or her world from the cultural template created by Osage life ways.

## NEGOTIATING AMERICAN INDIAN IDENTITY

The popularity of films such as *Dances with Wolves*, *Geronimo*, *Bury My Heart at Wounded Knee*, *Pocahontas*, and *Last of the Mohicans*, has created renewed interest in the indigenous people of this country. As a result of these somewhat historical (albeit romanticized versions) and animated renditions of Indian figures from the 1800s, most people have a pre-conceived notion of the lifestyle and history of the American Indian. Generally, this notion is based upon information gleaned from sources such as school, personal experience, experiences of others, and primarily, the media. For many, this preconceived image of the contemporary Indian is similar to that of the homogenous picture depicted in chapters and movies of the "Old West"—an image created by Hollywood in which the "Native American (is) devoid of tribal characteristics or regional differences" (Bataille & Silet, 1980, p. xxiii).

This "Old West" image is one in which all Indians possess the same cultural characteristics reflective of the Plains Indian culture and are perceived to be living the cinematic *Dances with Wolves* version of life. In a review of current communication text chapters, which focus upon intercultural communication, we found this overgeneralized, stereotypical image almost always portrayed. Indians are portrayed as living an idyllic, romanticized lifestyle in which they dwell in harmony with nature, are childlike, oblivious to pain, are promiscuous, and willingly engage in forms of self-torture. According to prevalent stereotypes, Indians worship such forces of nature as the wind, water, sun, lightning, thunder, and fire. Indians are often thought to believe in many gods or spirits—typically including a reference to the "Great Spirit." Ganje (2003) contends that Indian stereotypes are propagated through false images of Indians as either spirit guides or noble savages. Another common misconception about Indians concerns tribal religious practices. Although most non-Indians recognize the terms "shaman" and "sweat lodge" as synonymous with Indian religion, few have any idea what they mean or which Indians actually use them (Lustig & Koester, 2006).

Seldom is any evidence provided for their claims, nor do they make distinctions among tribal groups. Not all Indians worship inanimate objects such as rocks or thunder; however, most do have a respect for environmental elements stemming from an indigenous world-view. Many Indians are Christians and do not believe in multiple gods or spirits and are not able to withstand pain any better than their non-Indian counterparts. Moreover, the medicine wheel and sweat lodge are only utilized by some tribes in the northern plains and are not a part of all Plains Indian culture. Further, not all Indians live in a tipi or hogan; they do not all use dream catchers. That is, these cultural elements are not standard components of all tribal cultures. The few sentences about differing cultural behaviors provide no supporting data and in some cases, cite novels as reference sources.

## ISSUES IN RESEARCHING INDIANS

The center of this essay on American Indian identity also poses the most easily identifiable problem for researchers who choose to study American Indian communication. For starters, who is the one that decides who is a real or competent Indian? Is the presence of a Certificate of Degree of Indian Blood (CDIB) proof of *Indian-ness*? If a person simply looks Indian, does that automatically qualify him or her for the study? What if

*Unlike any other cultural group, American Indian identity is called into question even when making themselves available to be studied.*

the individual merely self-identifies as an Indian, or claims to be a member of a particular tribe? Should a researcher ask for "proof" of cultural competency (i.e., request to see a CDIB card)? In this way, you can see that the researcher who studies American Indians encounters identity issues from the start. Unlike any other cultural group, American Indian identity is called into question even when Indians make themselves available to be studied.

The American Indian, whether as a racial group or tribal group, has been the focus of study for disciplines such as anthropology, sociology, linguistics, semantics, and socio-linguistics. Various aspects of Indian culture—from how Indians operate on "Indian time" to religious practices—have been studied. However, little research is devoted to identifying or describing Indian communicative behavior such as tribal forms of public oratory, humor, listening, singing, and uses of hedging. Most importantly for those conducting research among the indigenous people, seldom has the notion of cultural competency or the knowledge and day-to-day enactment of cultural ways been taken into account. When working with minorities, particularly American Indians, researchers are inclined to afford complete cultural competency to anyone who is identified or self-identifies as an Indian. Many American Indian researchers consider any person who identifies as an Indian as being culturally competent. However, many tribal members are socialized in an urban or non-Indian environment and possess scant knowledge of their tribal background. Think of the implications of this for data collection and research findings.

When conducting research, the question of whether or not someone is a culturally competent member, and what type of Indian identity they exhibit, is not readily addressed. Instead, their cultural expertise is taken for granted, particularly [by investigators] conducting qualitative research. Social scientists should be concerned with whether or not they are actually testing and identifying Indian or tribal communicative behavior. In addition, they should be concerned with identifying and delineating what Indian or tribal behavior is.

Interestingly, the communicative behavior of the American Indian has primarily been studied from an *a priori* perspective. Rather than attempting to identify specific cultural speech behaviors, (e.g., compliance gaining, listening), contemporary research has glossed over or categorized observable cultural communicative acts into European American behavior equivalents.

Contributing further to this difficulty is … that there is neither one common type of Indian identity nor a standard set of behaviors that can be generalized to all Indians. [C]ontemporary Indians may have very little knowledge of tribal background or they may be very well versed in their tribal beliefs and activities; they may have not been socialized in a traditional environment [so] the behaviors they exhibit are more akin to [those of] European Americans; or they have been socialized in a traditional environment and exhibit behaviors reflective of their tribal culture. For Real Indians, a traditional environment is one in which the tribal language is spoken and tribal behaviors are enacted on a daily basis with full understanding of the significance of tribal acts. However, recent ethnographic research has begun identifying and explicating Indian speech acts and communicative behaviors (Carbaugh, 2005; Modaff, 2004; Modaff, Modaff, Pratt, & Buchanan, 2008; Pratt & Buchanan, 2004; Pratt, Pratt, & Miller, in press).

## CULTURAL COMPETENCY OR *INDIAN-NESS*

Personal and social identity goes beyond simply checking an appropriate box or self- proclamation. Wieder and Pratt (1990) note that being an Indian or culturally competent tribal member "is not something one can simply be, but is something one becomes and/or is, in and as the doing of being and becoming a real Indian" (p. 50). They contend that "doing, being, and becoming" a competent member requires the participation of other culturally competent members, for a person must not only know how to "do" being and becoming a culturally competent member, but one must continue to practice what one knows, that is, comport oneself as an Indian.

## Current Issues in American Indian Identity

Like so many other patterns of human communicative behaviors, identity is not a concern until it is called into question. Writers, scholars, and researchers focus abundant works on African American identity, Asian American identity, and Hispanic American identity. However, extant research is almost devoid of identity research when it comes to the American Indian experience.

## CONCLUSION

So what does it mean to "be Indian?" *Indian-ness* is implicit. *Indian-ness* is identifiable to the informed observer. *Indian-ness* is not skin color. *Indian-ness* is a tacit privilege. True or "real Indians" can identify each other with accuracy, just as they can identify the "wanna-be Indians" or, in current vernacular, "posers." Real Indians can describe what it means to be Indian, although they are not often called to do so—therein lies the paradox of American Indian identity research and identity negotiation. Real Indians are hard pressed to come up with a "list" of what it means to be a real Indian. Real Indians don't make a practice of "doing" Indian, they practice "being" Indian.

This essay emphasizes a communicative approach to understanding American Indian identity. This perspective allows us to illustrate how *Indianness* is created by the manner in which Indian people speak to others and how others speak to them. Communication is the medium through which identity is expressed. Our focus is to explore not only American Indian identity but also to open discussion on what it means to be a Real Indian. Specifically, we are interested in how Indians communicate their *Indian-ness*. Culture, identity, and in-group membership are interlaced with the threads of interpretation and social discourse.

In particular, American Indian communication research must wrestle free from the culture-bound approaches to European American communication research and theories. Kim (2002) calls for a shift from the Anglo-centered forms of human communication research, suggesting that "alternative cultural perspectives will reveal how cultural frameworks powerfully structure both everyday and scientific understandings" (pp. 4–5). We believe that this essay is a first step in exploring the study of American Indian identity as we begin with the questions of what comprises identity, *Indian-ness*, and the intersects with contemporary communication.

# References

Bataille, G. M., & Silet, C. L. P. (1980). *The pretend Indians: Images of Native Americans in the movies*. Ames, IA: Iowa State University Press.

Berger, P. L., & Luckmann, T. (1966). *The social construction of reality*. Garden City, NY: Anchor Books.

Carbaugh, D. (2005). *Cultures in conversation*. Mahwah, NJ: Lawrence Erlbaum.

Ganje, L. A. (2003). Native American stereotypes. In P. M. Lester & S. D. Ross (Eds.), Images that injure: Pictorial stereotypes in the media (2nd ed.). Westport, CT: Praeger.

Kim, M. S. (2002). *Non-western perspectives on human communication*. Thousand Oaks, CA: Sage.

Lustig, M. W., & Koester, J. (2006). *Intercultural competence: Interpersonal communication across cultures (5th ed.)*. Boston: Allyn & Bacon.

McDaniel, E. R., Samovar, L. A., & Porter, R. E. (2009). Understanding intercultural communication: The working principles. In L. A. Samovar, R. E. Porter, & R. E. McDaniel (Eds.), *Intercultural communication: A reader* (12th ed., pp. 6–17). Boston, MA: Wadsworth Cengage Learning.

Modaff, D. P. (2004). Native virtues: Applying traditional Sioux philosophy to the contemporary basic communication course. *Basic Communication Course Annual, 16*, 261–278.

Modaff, D. P., Modaff, J. A. B., Pratt, S. B., & Buchanan, M. C. (2008). *UnCONVENTIONal Balance: Marriage, Family, and Research on the Rez*. Panel presentation to the 94th annual National Communication Association Convention. San Diego, CA.

Pratt, S. B. (1985). *Being an Indian among Indians*. Unpublished doctoral dissertation, University of Oklahoma.

Pratt, S. B. (1998). Razzing: Ritualized uses of humor as a form of identification among American Indians. In D. V. Tanno & A. Gonzalez (Eds.), *Communication and identity across cultures* (pp. 56–69). Thousand Oaks, CA: Sage.

Pratt, S. B., & Buchanan, M. C. (2004). "I want you to talk for me": An ethnography of communication of the Osage Indian. In M. Fong & R. Chuang (Eds.) Communicating ethnic and cultural identity (pp. 261–273). Lanham, MD: Rowman and Littlefield.

Pratt, S. B., Pratt, M. C., & Miller, R. (in press). Osage naming ritual: Communicating cultural identity. In A. Gonzalez, M. Houston, & V. Chen (Eds.), Our voices: *Essays in culture, ethnicity, and communication* (5th ed.). London: Oxford University Press.

Wieder, D. L., & Pratt, S. (1990). On being a recognizable Indian among Indians. In D. Carbaugh (Ed.), *Cultural communication and intercultural contact* (pp. 45–64). Hillsdale, NJ: Lawrence Erlbaum.

## Concepts and Questions

1. The essay states that identity is "socially constructed and manifested through communication." Explain this statement and provide an example.

2. What do the authors mean by the term *Indian-ness*?

3. What is the purpose of the Certificate of Degree of Indian Blood (CDIB)?

4. What are some of the factors leading to the decline of cultural competency among American Indians?

5. Contrast "tribal identity" and "Indian identity" as discussed in the essay. Why has one become more prevalent than the other?

6. What sources do most non-Indians draw on to construct their image of American Indians? Do these sources present a valid representation? Why?

7. What are some of the difficulties scholars encounter when researching American Indians?

8. How does one become a culturally competent tribal member?

9. What is meant by the phrase "identities are negotiated"?

# We Don't Talk Right. You Ask Him

JOAN WYNNE

Our next essay demonstrates the synergy between culture and language, each forming the other and each perpetuating the other. Additionally, it illustrates how language can project an image of our identity to others. In "We don't talk right. You ask him," Wynne begins by relating her experience with a group of African American high school students who are hesitant to speak out at a meeting dominated by Whites because they consider their own English incorrect. She offers additional examples to show that the dominant culture often negatively stereotypes minority groups based on their language usage. This can create "language biases" that actually suppress the creativity and self-esteem of the non–dominant group members. Conversely, these biases deny members of the dominant culture an awareness and understanding of the diversity that surrounds them.

> Language can project an image of our identity to others.

To illustrate the concept of linguistic superiority, Wynne draws on people's contrasting perception of, and attitude toward, the use of Ebonics and Standard English. She then explicates the contradiction in these perceptions by pointing out the frequent usage of terms from the African American dialect by media celebrities and in advertising. To negate cultural stigmas, Wynne advocates instilling young people, from both dominant and non-dominant groups, with an appreciation for the validity and beauty of language diversity. This will lead to enhanced intercultural understanding and greater acceptance of cultural diversity, part of the requirement for successful participation in the globalized society.

The world is richer than it is possible to express in any single language.

**Ilye Priggogine**

## INTRODUCTION

It was over twenty years ago, but it could have happened yesterday. I had taken a group of African American high school newspaper staff to a university journalism workshop and awards ceremony. There were about eight students with me that day to learn more about print journalism, and, more importantly, to receive an award for one of the ten best high school newspapers in the metropolitan area.

We were sitting together, in a sea of White faces, listening to one of the media experts talk about ways to improve school newspapers. After he had spoken, he opened the session to questions. My students had several they wanted to ask in their effort to discover new ways of writing creatively for their peers back at school. One of my editors leaned over to me and whispered, "Here is a list of questions we want you to ask him."

I said, "No, you ask him," surprised that my student and his cohort were suddenly shy.

"We don't talk right. You ask him."

No amount of encouragement from me would prompt them to speak. What I now know is that until that moment, I did not understand how psychologically damaging language biases are. I watched eight students, who happened to be some of the brightest young people I have ever taught, shrink from their brilliance. Here they sat, knowing they had competed with other journalism staffs for the best newspaper— and won—yet, at the same time, they felt inferior. They were silenced by language biases born of racism, biases that crippled their inquisitive natures. Their typical bold acts of discovery became impotent in the midst of a White majority. And the majority lost

From *The Skin That We Speak: Thoughts on Language and Culture in the Classroom,* edited by Lisa Delpit and Joanne Kilgour Dowdy. The New York Press, 2002, pp. 205–219. Reprinted by permission.

a golden opportunity to hear my students' thoughts and learn from their brilliance.

Looking back now, I recognize the full measure of my own miseducation. My schooling had not prepared me, as an English major, to understand the depth and breadth of language oppression. No one had taught me that the language I had grown up loving was used to bludgeon others into submission and feelings of inferiority. But, even worse, none of my teachers had ever encouraged me to assist these youngsters in creating a psychological sanctuary so they didn't succumb to unfounded language bias when exposed to the dominant culture. In the absence of that instruction, I had made those adolescents vulnerable to the prejudices of the majority, reflected in their own internalized notions of being linguistically inadequate. Nothing had prepared my students or me for that moment of defeat, a moment when they should have been reveling in victorious celebration.

Many years later, during a trip to South Africa, I was once more made aware of the contradictions in perceptions of language between a dominant culture and the "other." While helping to build houses in Alexandria, a black township outside of Johannesburg, I consistently heard from White South Africans how deficient Black South Africans were in their use of language, how they were slow in thinking, and how much "like children" they were. In fact, almost every complaint reminded me of the remarks describing American Blacks that I had heard while growing up in the South. Again, though, those remarks were in conflict with the reality that presented itself to me as I worked in Alexandria. I was often surrounded by young children attempting to help in our construction efforts. Their warmth and friendliness always charmed me, but it was their language facility that totally disarmed me. Those small children, four, five, six, and seven years old, easily moved from speaking Swahili to Xhosa to English to Afrikaans to Zulu, and several other languages that I can't even remember the names of now. In that small two-mile radius of a township, where over two million people from many different cultures were herded together by the rules of apartheid, Black children had quickly learned to communicate across the cultural divides. Amazingly, though, despite that gift of language facility, the same insidious myths about language superiority ran rampant. And the myths are destructive. They lie about people's ability to think, and, perhaps, equally as tragic, they prevent the dominant culture from learning from the gifts of "the other."

Sometimes, the lie seems to take on a life of its own. At Morehouse College, the United States' premier African American male college, where I taught for fourteen years, I observed intelligent, sophisticated students misled by those myths. There, young men parroted what they had heard mainstream English teachers, like myself, proclaim for years, that the use of standard English was "talking right." In Morehouse classrooms, the students and I would often struggle through discussions on the speech patterns of the children who lived in the housing projects surrounding the college and who were mentored by the Morehouse students. My college students often would argue with me about my contention that the language of those children was as valid as theirs. Because the Morehouse students had fallen prey to invalidated linguistic assumptions of the mainstream culture, they had no tolerance for the speech of these children. The mentors assumed that the children's speech indicated not only linguistic but cognitive deficit. Of course, if we want these children to be socially and economically mobile in mainstream culture, we must teach them standard English; yet, if we reject them by rejecting the language they grew up with, we alienate them from the very places where they could learn the standard dialect. And by teaching children that their language is inferior, we teach a lie.

The lasting impact of that lie became clear again only last week at a town meeting of parents in a small Southern school district where approximately three to four hundred middle- and upper-middle-class mainstream parents and working-class African American parents met to discuss possible changes in their elementary schools. Out of the twenty or so parents who spoke at the microphone, only one was an African American parent. After the meeting I was told by several of the African American mothers that while they felt very strongly about the issues at stake, they could not and would not speak to the whole group because they felt uncomfortable about their

> *No one had taught me that the language I had grown up loving was used to bludgeon others into submission and feelings of inferiority.*

speech in front of those mainstream parents. They had no trouble articulating their ideas to me, but only after I had approached them asking why they had chosen to remain silent. Like my former journalism staff, those parents harbored the mistaken notion that their speech was not good enough to air in front of a majority White audience. Yes, the distortions we teach in schools last a long time. In those places we begin to hush the voices that might lead the way out of the labyrinth of our educational malpractices. That silencing "like a cancer grows" (Simon and Garfunkel, 1966).

## TEACHING LANGUAGE SUPREMACY DISTORTS REALITY FOR MAINSTREAM CHILDREN

I believe that the abuses of linguistic oppression toward the children of color are horrendous; the consequences are severe; and the damage to the self-esteem of youths is unconscionable. But I also believe that there is another dark side to this issue—the severe consequences of notions of language supremacy for the children of the dominant culture.

By neglecting to teach about the beauty and richness of the language of Black America, we also damage White children. If we believe, [like] James Baldwin, that all languages define, articulate, and reveal individual realities ("Black English," 1997), then by not recognizing Ebonics, we keep white children trapped in myopic visions of world realities. We give them one more reason to bolster their mistaken notions of supremacy and privilege. If we believe, too, as Baldwin suggests, that Black English "is rooted in American history," then, by discounting Ebonics, we keep White children oblivious to significant slices of their own country's history. We deny them the opportunity to look at their own ancestors and history in a way that might help them recognize their collective responsibility for injustices, as well as their collective potential for redemption.

In a nation that is home to a multitude of cultures, and in a world that, through technology, has become a global village, cross-cultural respect and understanding are imperative. Yet if our mainstream children think that their language is superior to others, how can they expect anyone else to believe that they, the privileged, value other people's

*All languages define, articulate, and reveal individual realities.*

cultures? With such notions, how will our children ever work collaboratively across cultures to build those bridges of understanding that will allow people to cross the racial divide that separates us as a nation, a world, and a species?

We have learned that prejudice of any kind can stifle our children's growth in critical thinking. In *The Open and Closed Mind* (1960), M. Rokeach found that

> Persons who are high in ethnic prejudice and/or authoritarianism, as compared with persons who are low, are more rigid in their problem-solving behavior, more concrete in their thinking, and more narrow in their grasp of a particular subject; they also have a greater tendency to premature closure in their perceptual processes and to distortions in memory, and a greater tendency to be intolerant of ambiguity (p. 16).

As Rokeach suggests, by fostering prejudice such as language biases, we stifle all students' cognitive development. Thinking their language is a superior language, which is, after all, what too many teachers teach and too many in society believe, White children may become incapable of really hearing other cultures and, thus, learning from them (Allport, 1958; Hall, 1989). For as long as mainstream students think that another's language is inferior to theirs, they will probably not bother to understand it, and therefore, there will be much about the other that they will always fail to understand. Not only will this further widen the cultural divide, but it will prevent the group in power from accessing the knowledge base—and, subsequently, potential solutions to a myriad of world problems—of those deemed "other" by virtue of language form.

Several weeks ago one of my university colleagues explained to me that she had recently tried to listen to a noted African American historian who, during a television interview, continuously referred to every Black person he spoke about as "Brother" or "Sister." This cultural tradition seemed excessive to my associate, annoying her to the point that she felt forced to switch the channel. The seemingly intrusive nature of this different linguistic ritual kept her from hearing the message of a nationally respected scholar of history. For her, and I think for too many of us, our obsession with the familiar form can obliterate the significance of the content. I have found in my thirty years of experience in the education profession that this kind of unconscious intolerance of difference cuts us off from learning from one another.

My colleague was so uncomfortable with a cultural pattern of speech that it forced her to "tune out" a speaker whom she knew to be a reputable scholar. Might her reaction suggest the serious intellectual consequences of intolerance, cited earlier in Rokeach's study—that if cultural intolerance is strong, it is more difficult to take in new information? Except for those with telepathic gifts, language is the closest way humans know of getting inside another person's head. If our tolerance of language diversity is so fragile that we turn away from those persons who exhibit cultural linguistic patterns different from ours, how can we ever expect to begin to understand each other and, thereby, build a community of learners? If the tolerance is that fragile, how can those of us who are responsible for educating the next generation of teachers adequately teach them to be sensitive to the language differences of the children they teach or of other faculty members with whom they work?

## LANGUAGE SUPREMACY AND THE EDUCATION OF TEACHERS

Recently, I gave a short questionnaire to fifteen pre-service teachers at a university asking them their opinions about Ebonics and Standard English. These students are in their last months of their undergraduate program. Because they were not new to the university or to teacher training, I was surprised at some of their responses. Most of the students responded to the question, "How would you describe 'Standard English'?" with the answer, "Correct English," or "Proper English." When answering questions about the description and use of Ebonics, one intern said, "To me, Ebonics is the use of incorrect English... I do not think that allowing children to speak 'Ebonics' in the classroom does them a service. I think that 'standard English' is the grammatically correct form of the English language." His response typified the answers of the others in the group.

One student response, however, seemed more emotional and dogmatic than the others. "Ebonics," she said, "should not be allowed in the classroom. Our education system should not cater to lower standards of language." She and a few of the other soon-to-be teachers were unknowingly expressing one of the basic tenets of linguistics: that languages are defined politically, not scientifically—and that a "language is a dialect with an army and a navy" (Dorsett, 1997, O'Neil, 1997). The responses of the pre-service teachers reflected no awareness that each dialect and language has an internal integrity unto itself; that one language clearly is not scientifically better than the other, but that one is politically more acceptable than the other—for one dialect belongs to the power structure (Dorsett, 1997; Fillmore 1998; Perry and Delpit, 1998).

As I continued to read the comments of these university students, I wondered why, when language is the major medium of instruction, would we in schools of education give so little time, effort, and attention to teaching our pre-service teachers about the basic assumptions of the realities of language diversity? Why would we choose to ignore the significance of instructing all of our interns, whether they are to teach mathematics, science, language arts, or shop, that language is a political decision and a group experience of a lived reality, not a manifestation of intellectual prowess or language superiority?

In the same semester, in another course of thirty-four graduate students, most of whom are practicing teachers, I listened to a class discussion about African American children's language. This very heated debate emerged from discussing the question, "What is excellence in urban education?" During the discussion, none of the students addressed the political nature of selecting one dialect as the "standard dialect." The one thing that all participants seemed to agree upon was that all students needed to know "proper" or "correct" English. Many insisted that any time a student used Ebonics in the classroom, she should be corrected. How is it that we might forget to inform every pre-service and in-service student that all teachers are obliged to honor the many languages we speak? As James Baldwin, Toni Morrison, and many others suggest, language is who we are. If any of us refuse to respect the other's language, it becomes too easy, consciously or unconsciously, to then disrespect the person.

Later, I gave a language attitude questionnaire to five teachers, who were asked to give them to their individual faculties. With very few exceptions, the teachers' responses reflected the same assumptions about Ebonics and "Standard English" as the university pre-service and graduate students. One teacher answered that Ebonics should never be spoken in the classroom because "it sounds ridiculous and illiterate." Without an apparent understanding of multilingualism in any form, another teacher said all children should speak "Standard English" because "We are a part of the Human Race and Standard English is the common denominator," adding that Standard English was a "neutral and universal language." Even those teachers who voiced some respect for Ebonics speakers agreed that children should not speak Ebonics in the classroom. With the research that is now available about the importance of schools accepting a child's home language while still teaching them the standard dialect, too many teachers are astoundingly ignorant of the basic truths about language. The lack of knowledge about language development amongst many of our teachers spoke to a gap in the professional development of these teachers; and, to me, it suggests as well how insignificant many colleges of education may assume that kind of knowledge is.

But such neglect by colleges to include in their curriculum the politics of language is no small matter. Growing up in a segregated South, I saw "up close and personal" the impact of that neglect on the psyches of children. The ignorance of teachers, myself included, about the role of institutional power in deciding whose language is "standard" played a part in making many African American children feel inferior about their home language when they were in school. Moreover, all children—as well as teachers who are never given a forum to examine the oppressive assumption that one language is better than another— become vulnerable to other acts of oppression. It is an egregious failure for colleges to cavalierly omit from teacher education any discussions of the political ramifications of language use and acceptance. Teachers without this knowledge will limit the worlds of White children and make children of other ethnicities vulnerable to the negative views held by educators and society in general regarding their cognitive competence.

> *We in the dominant culture do not seem to recognize the contradictions in our attitudes about the language Black people use.*

Again, none of this discussion is to suggest that the Standard Dialect is not to be taught to our students from kindergarten through college—It is, after all, the language, of power, the chosen form of communication of those who own the missiles, the tanks, the banks, the bombs, and the government. But its importance as a *dialect* must be put in a context that produces less damage to ourselves and our students. Glorifying Standard English as a superior mode of expression is intellectually limiting.

## WHAT SHOULD HAPPEN IN THE CLASSROOMS?

Nothing short of a revolution in our language instruction will suffice. Mainstream children and children of color suffer from their linguistic "miseducation." Ironically, we in the dominant culture do not seem to recognize the contradictions in our attitudes about the language Black people use. We are fascinated with the cleverness of Ebonics, as shown by our incorporation of many of its idioms into our everyday speech. For example, mainstream television personalities such as the *Today* show's Katie Couric and Matt Lauer have consistently used such phrases as "Don't 'diss' me like that" and "my bad" during their morning banter. Mainstream advertisers, too, often use expressions and rhythms from rap music to sell their products. Yet at the same time, most of our media and educational institutions insist that the language is somehow inferior to the Standard Dialect. Perhaps, we might share those kinds of contradictions with our students as a way to begin our conversations about the political nature of language choice.

The brilliant writing of Nobel Prize–winning author Toni Morrison might be a great starting place for yeasty discussions on the merits of diverse languages and dialects, of issues of racism, and of the power of storytelling to connect us to our individual and collective history. We can use her words to teach African American children the majesty of their home languages, and White children the beauty and validity of other languages. Morrison explains that language "is the thing that black people love so much—the saying of words, holding them on the tongue, experimenting with them, playing with them. It's a love, a passion." By saying this she suggests a very different relationship between her people and their language from that portrayed anywhere in the mainstream culture. It's a perspective that pre-service and in-service teachers might explore to counteract the erroneous messages that academia, the media, and other institutions send us about the inferior "dialect" of African Americans.

Linguist Charles Fillmore, in a speech delivered at UC Berkeley, suggested that educators might "offer serious units in dialect in middle school and high school classes throughout the country as a general part of language education" for all children (Fillmore 1998). Walt Wolfram, another noted linguistic scholar, suggested that activities in such units make it possible for children to "discover generalizations and systematicities in their own speech and in the speech of others" (Fillmore 1998).

Recently, hearing "the speech of others" caused a visceral reawakening in me of the power of language diversity. While attending Al Sharpton's "Shadow Inauguration" rally in Washington, D.C., I heard a dozen or more African American speakers give testimony to the part they, their parents, or their grandparents had played in turning a nation around. They spoke of shattering notions of segregated equality; of dismantling unfair voting laws; and of surviving as a people killings, lynching, attacks by dogs and by police wielding billy clubs and water hoses. While listening to these stories, I thought about the Southern Freedom movement and of its impact on freedom movements in China, in South Africa, and other parts of the globe (Harding, 1999). I remembered that representatives of only 13 percent of the population of the United States forever changed the South, the nation, and the world. That day I stood in the midst of throngs of descendants of Africans as they chanted "No Justice, No Peace"; as they sang "Ain't gonna' let nobody turn me 'round"; and "a walkin'… a talkin'… Marching up to freedom land." The power of the words, of the rhythm, of the cadences of the slogans moved me as we marched in the rain toward the Supreme Court Building to register our disapproval of its justices' most recent decision against voting rights.

I came home with those chants, those testimonies, ringing in my ears. And I couldn't help but wonder…. How dare we patronize as an inferior dialect the language of such heroes and sheroes? Those now grown-up activists who created the sit-ins of the '60s, in the marches, who survived the jails, have told me about the power of the chants, the songs, the language to keep them alive, committed, and unified in a struggle that no one thought they could win (Conversations, 1988, 2000, 2001; Reagon, 1998; King, 1987). That language and those stories belong in our children's classrooms.

Joseph Campbell, in *The Hero with a Thousand Faces (1968)*, tells us that a hero must assimilate his opposite, must put aside his pride, and in the end must realize "that he and his opposite are not of differing species, but one flesh." We have to educate our White children to understand that we are, indeed, "one flesh." That we are "the other." Then, what a gift to teach them that they are connected to the heroism of those African American students who engaged in sit-ins and marches; who against all odds survived arrests and beatings; and who created "a dazzling moment of clarity" for the South and the nation (Curry 2000). To be taught that they belong not only to the history of the oppressor but also to the history of those who so bravely fought and won those battles for justice is a lesson all children deserve to hear.

What a breath of fresh air it would be for our young people to read about other young people who nonviolently took on a violent and corrupt government and won. To use their language and their stories in the classroom might be one of the greatest lessons of empowerment we could give all of America's children. Telling our students of the audacity of ordinary young people like themselves, who dared to think they had the right to shape the world around them, might do more toward creating critical thinkers in our classrooms than any of the other pedagogical tricks that we have up our sleeves.

Alice Walker, in *The Same River Twice: Honoring the Difficult* (1996), says that "even to attempt to respectfully encounter 'the other' is a sacred act, and leads to and through the labyrinth. To the river. Possibly to healing. A 'special effect' of the soul." Encountering the other is difficult, for all humans, whether it be in language or in ritual; yet, for me, it sometimes seems the only way we will ever make this democracy work. If we in schools of education stay silent while others proclaim language superiority, how do we help our students "respectfully encounter 'the other'"? Shouldn't we, who teach teachers, create spaces in our classrooms to explore the political nature of language choices? Shouldn't we in our courses facilitate discussions about the need to value diverse languages, especially in these rocky political times? That we are sending into public school classrooms teachers whose limited knowledge about language caused them to respond so dismally to a questionnaire about Ebonics suggests that we are failing our teachers' intellectual development, failing their future students' language growth, and failing our troubled democracy. Helping students, in a fragmented modern society, make connections to each other and to a larger world is a respectable outcome (Delpit 1997; Hilliard 1997; Palmer 1998; 'Wilson 1998) that many scholars believe can be advanced through the study of diverse dialects and languages. Learning the skills of reading, writing, and mathematics, as well as every other discipline, can happen within that context of making connections.

As they learn those skills, our students need a time and space to discover that the interdependence of all of humanity and of all species is a concept that poets and mystics have proclaimed for thousands of years, and is now one that physicists are validating through their study of the universe, from the subatomic level to the formation of the galaxies. Our students need to understand that scientists are continuously discovering the complex interconnectedness of all life, matter, and energy. And all students need to learn that notions of supremacy, whether they come in the shape of superior races or superior languages, do not fit into that grand scheme of things (Bogardus 1960). Finally, all of us need to remind ourselves of what Ilya Prigogine's quotation at the head of this essay seems to suggest—that the worship of a single language limits our ability to know and to express that interconnectedness, that "full richness of the world."

# References

Allport, G. W. (1958). *The Nature of Prejudice*. Garden City, NY: Doubleday.

Baldwin, James (1997). If Black English Isn't a Language, Then Tell Me, What Is? *Rethinking Schools*, *12*(1).

Bogardus, E. S. (1960). *The Development Of Social Thought*. New York: Longmans, Green.

Campbell, J. (1968). 2nd ed. *Hero with a Thousand Faces*. Princeton: Princeton University Press.

Conversations with Joan Browning, February 2001.

Conversations with Connie Curry, January 1988; February 2000; February 2001.

Conservations with Charlie Cobb, Zaharah Simmons, April 2000.

Curry, Browning, et al. (2000). *Deep in Our Hearts: Nine White Women in the Freedom Movement*. Athens, GA: University of Georgia Press.

Delpit, Lisa (1997). "Ten Factors for Teaching Excellence in Urban Schools." Speech at Urban Atlanta Coalition Compact Town Meeting, September, Atlanta, GA.

Dorsett, C. (1997). *Ebonics—21st Century Racism?* Website: http:j'members.tripod.com/~cdorsett/ebonics.htm

Fillmore, C. (1998). Speech at UC Berkeley, http://www.cal.org/ebonics/fillmore.html

Hall, E. (1989). *Beyond Culture*. New York: Doubleday Dell, Anchor Books edition.

Hilliard, A. G. III (1997). *SEA: The Reawakening of the African Mind*. Gainesville, Fla.: Makare Publishing Co.

King, Mary (1987). *Freedom Song: A Personal Story of the 1960s Civil Rights Movement*. New York: Morrow.

Linguistic Society of America (1997). "Resolution on the Oakland 'Ebonics' Issue," http://www.lsadc.org/ebonics.html

O'Neil, Wayne (1997). If Ebonics isn't a language, then tell me, what is? *Rethinking Schools*, *12*(1).

Palmer, P. (1998). *The Courage to Teach*. United States: Jossey-Bass.

Perry, T., and L. Delpit (1998). *Rethinking Schools*. Boston: Beacon.

Reagan, B. J. (1998). "Oh Freedom": Music of the Movement, *A Circle of Trust: Remembering SNCC*. Greenberg, G., ed. New Brunswick: Rutgers University Press.

Rokeach, M. (1960). *The Open and Closed Mind*. New York: Basic Books.

Simon and Garfunkel (1966). "The Sounds of Silence." On *Sounds of Silence*. Columbia 9269.

Skutnabb-Kangas, T. (2000). *Linguistic Genocide in Education—or Worldwide Diversity and Human Rights*. Mahwah, NJ: L. Erlbaum Associates.

Smith, Ernie A. (1976). *A Case for Bilingual and Bicultural Education for United States Slave Descendants of African Origin*. Fullerton: Department of Linguistics Seminar Series, California State University, Fullerton.

Smitherman, Geneva (1997). Black English/Ebonics: What It Be Like? *Rethinking Schools*, *12*(1).

_____ (1977). _Talkin and Testifyin: The Language of Black America_. Boston: Houghton Mifflin.

Walker, Alice (1996). _The Same River Twice: Honoring the Difficult_. New York: Scribner.

Wilson, Amos (1998). _Blueprint for Black Power: A Moral, Political and Economic Imperative for the Twenty-first Century_. New York: Afrikan World InfoSystems.

## Concepts and Questions

1. How would you explain the term "language oppression"? Provide an example.

2. What are some consequences of language oppression for non-dominant and dominant culture members?

3. When you hear someone speaking incorrectly or using heavily accented English, what is your first impression of that person?

4. What do you think is meant by the statement "languages are defined politically, not scientifically"? Do you agree or disagree? Why?

5. Drawing on James Baldwin's writings, the essay states, "all languages define, articulate, and reveal individual realities." What does the statement mean to you?

6. Give some examples of speech usage or patterns from another culture that are considered negatively by U.S. mainstream culture.

7. Do linguistic habits influence one's identity? How?

8. What are some of the benefits of teaching children to respect the dialects and accents of other people?

# International Marriages in Japan: Cultural Conflict and Harmony

STEVEN E. QUASHA • FUMIKO TSUKADA

_Our final essay, "International Marriage in Japan: Conflict and Harmony" by Steve Quasha and Fumiko Tsukada, examines some of the numerous cultural factors that influence marriages between Euro-Americans and Japanese, with identity being only one of many. They begin by telling us that while cross-cultural marriages are not new in Japan, the era of globalization had resulted in a quantum increase in such unions. A brief look at contemporary Japanese demographics and immigration trends provides an introduction to some of the reasons behind this growing trend. Of concern to the authors is the disproportionate number of divorces between Japanese and non-Japanese spouses. This led Quasha and Tsukada to interview international married couples living in central Japan._

_Following some general background information about the couples, an overview of the theoretical concepts informing Quasha and Tsukada's work is provided. This includes such topics as conflict management, identity or facework, group orientation, high and low context communication, hierarchy, and the uniquely Japanese cultural characteristics of tatemae, honne, wa, and gaman. The authors then move to the interviews with the four couples. The first couple, "The Divorcees," comprises two Euro-Americans, each of whom had previously been in an international marriage with Japanese spouses but finally decided that divorce was the best way to achieve happiness. During the interviews, they relate the many cultural differences which ultimately drove them to that decision._

_Interviews with the husband and wife of the "Seeking Common Ground" couple revealed the dangers of entering into an international marriage without sufficient cultural knowledge and language skills. This couple is struggling to keep the marriage together. Interviews with the "Par for the Course" couple provide you an_

> Globalization has resulted in a quantum increase of cross-cultural marriages.

This original essay appears here in print for the first time. All rights reserved. Permission to reprint must be obtained from the authors and the publisher. Steven E. Quasha and Dr. Fumiko Tsukada are both Associate Professors in the Department of Modern Management at Sugiyama Jogakuen University, Nagoya, Japan.

*overview of what the authors consider a typical marriage between a Japanese and a Euro-American living in Japan. This couple has learned to manage most of the cultural differences that affect their relationship but do not seem to appreciate some of the more subtle, long-term aspects needed to become truly culturally competent. "The In-Step Duo" offers an excellent example of how to achieve success in an international marriage. Both Alex and Yuri have made dedicated efforts to learn each other's language and achieve intercultural competence. While Yuri does not understand her husband's passion for the Christmas season, she is willing to participate in his aim of establishing a family tradition centering on the holiday.*

*After each set of interviews, the authors provide a discussion on the cultural issues involved in that couple's marriage. The essay concludes with an overview of several general lessons learned from the interview data.*

International marriage has existed for thousands of years as humankind migrated across borders to trade goods, escape persecution, wage war, or simply seek out a better life for themselves and their families. Typically, these early cases involved men that married local women and started a new life in a foreign land. However, globalization and migration have changed this landscape and we now live in a much smaller world, where affordable air travel and online dating have accelerated opportunities for people from different cultures to meet, interact, and establish relationships. Yoon (2009) found that international migrants—both skilled and unskilled labor—accounted for 2.9 percent of the world population in 2005, amounting to between 90 million and 95 million people. Additionally, there are at least 1.8 million international students pursuing higher education outside their home countries. The reality is that some of these migrants and students will end up marrying people from another country. As a result, the world is experiencing a significant rise in international marriages.

In Japan's case, interethnic marriage dates back to the seventh century, when Chinese and Korean immigrants began intermarrying with the local population. In the latter sixteenth century, some 50,000 Koreans were forcibly brought to Japan, where they intermarried with the local population. In the early part of the seventeenth century, around 58,000 Japanese travelled abroad, and many of these men intermarried with local women in Southeast Asia (Leupp, 2003). Shortly thereafter Japan enacted a self-imposed period (1641–1853) of national isolation (*Sakoku*) (Tanaka & Ishi, 2009). As a result, legitimate contact with the outside world was restricted to *Dejima*, a small island off Nagasaki used by Dutch and Chinese traders. The only Japanese women permitted to visit the island were prostitutes. Kamoto (2001) noted that this de facto system of ethnic purification stayed intact until the modernizing Meiji era (1868–1912) forced Japan to adopt more internationally accepted policies. During the American occupation of Japan (1945–1954), international marriage between American servicemen and Japanese women became quite prevalent (Nitta, 1988), but the majority of those war brides immigrated to the United States, and the number of international-marriage couples residing in Japan remained rather low. Over the past few decades, however, that number has changed dramatically, as demonstrated in the following section.

## CONTEMPORARY JAPAN

An examination of Japan's current demographic trends reveals some disturbing prospects for the nation's current and future societal structure. Statistically, Japan's population will become the world's oldest by the year 2020 (Colmas, 2007). This gentrification is because the majority of Japanese are marrying much later in life or, for a growing number, not at all (Hisane, 2006). This is resulting in a sharply decreasing birthrate and a falling population. At the current rate, the working-age population of Japan will decline over 11 percent by 2020. One possible solution to offset this demographic shift is increased immigration, which will help maintain the labor force and provide contributions to the tax base supporting social programs for the elderly,

Indeed, immigration to Japan has been increasing over the past several decades, and the immigrant population nearly doubled between 1990 and 2007, when it reached 2.15 million (Daimon, 2009). Over half are Chinese and Korean, along with a large group of low-wage workers of Japanese ancestry from Brazil and Peru. Japan has also initiated a program that brings a limited number of health care workers from Indonesia and the Philippines. The Japan

Exchange Teaching Program (JET), established in the 1980s, has brought more than 50,000 teachers from over 50 countries to Japan (JET, 2009). Foreign business representatives and students also form part of Japan's international community. Many of these men and women have taken up long-term or permanent residence throughout the Japanese archipelago and have intermarried with Japanese nationals.

According to Ministry of Health, Labour, and Welfare (2009a) data, international marriage in Japan increased almost 70 percent between 1995 and 2005. In 2007 marriage between a Japanese citizen and a non-Japanese accounted for more than 5 percent of all marriages. This is rather surprising considering Japan still has the lowest percentage of immigrants and expatriate workers (1.37 percent in 2008) of any industrialized country (Suzuki, 2010).

The majority of these international marriages involved a Japanese man marrying a non-Japanese. The agricultural sector, for instance, publicly supports importing foreign brides, because young Japanese women are reluctant to become farmers' wives. For many twenty-first century educated Japanese women, the intense labor demands of a rural life are unappealing. This has given rise to a brisk business in mail order brides and overseas tours to find foreign wives, mostly Asian, for Japanese farmers (Asakura, 2002; French, 2002).

> *Approximately 45% of intercultural marriages in Japan fail.*

Taken collectively, these international marriages have increased the level of multiculturalism in Japan's relatively homogenous society. However, they have in turn produced a compelling social problem. Recent government statistics reveal an unusually high divorce rate among international couples, who accounted for over 7 percent of all Japanese divorces in 2007 (Ministry of Health, Labour and Welfare, 2009b). With approximately 45 percent of the intercultural marriages failing, this alarming trend raises several questions: What is going wrong? Are language and cultural gaps the main cause for ending the relationship? How do international couples foster cross-cultural understanding and remain together? The purpose of the series of interviews reported in this essay was to seek answers to those questions by examining the issues facing international couples and the ways they resolve them.

## APPROACH

Anecdotally, the authors have many friends married to Japanese spouses and nearly all have voiced concerns about the difficulties of their married life and the endless array of cultural nuances. A common refrain is "My spouse can speak my language to a certain degree but doesn't really understand my cultural background." To gain a more in-depth understanding of how cultural differences impact international marriage in Japan, we interviewed four couples, representing five international marriages, living in central Japan.

One couple was interviewed at a local restaurant while the other interviews were conducted by telephone. All of the participants' names were changed to protect their privacy. The couples, all volunteers, represent a wide range of ages and period of residency in Japan. Two of the older participants are American citizens that divorced their Japanese spouses after approximately 20 years of marriage and are now involved in a relationship with each another. Both had raised their families in Japan and offered insight into the perceptions and realities of international marriage. The other three couples are all in the 30-to-over-40 age range, with two of the men from the United States and one from Canada. The spouses of these three men are all native Japanese women; none had studied English abroad, and one could not speak any English when she first met her eventual husband.

We should point out that this interview study has several limitations since it included a mere eight participants representing five international marriages, of which only one is a foreign female. We do not expect readers to commit the fallacy of multiplication and interpret these cases as representative of all international marriages in Japan. Rather, the participants' experiences represent a snapshot that offers a glimpse of some of the difficulties that can arise in intercultural relationships. Readers should also realize that some of the marital difficulties disclosed in the interviews may be the result of factors other than cultural differences. For instance, socioeconomic difficulties and personality differences no doubt play a role in some conflicts. For illustrative purposes, we have surmised the problems to be culturally based. Future research should expand the number of participants and increase the number of women married to Japanese men. Additionally, we made a conscious decision to limit the interviews to Japanese and Euro-American couples, as they were the most readily available population for us.

There are a number of cultural themes that informed preparations for the interviews and subsequent analysis of the data. For instance, Japan is characterized as a vertical, hierarchical, group-oriented society (Hendry, 2003; Nakane, 1970), in contrast to Western society, which values individualism and egalitarianism. We wondered how Japan's highly defined gender roles and social hierarchy would join with the Western emphasis on equality. Related to this are Triandis' (2002) findings on the relationship of individualism and collectivism to personality. Would this bring about a compensatory response from Japanese spouses married to foreigners? In other words, did these spouses willingly give up some aspects of their own culture to help foster their marriage?

Face-negotiation theory (Ting-Toomey, 2005) and identity management theory (Imahori & Cupach, 2005) were seen as offering important insight into distinguishing and understanding problems that could arise in an international marriage. In managing interpersonal conflict, Ting-Toomey (2005) holds that individualistic cultures—such as the United States and Canada—generally favor dominating/competing conflict styles, but collectivistic cultures, like Japan, prefer conflict avoidance/obliging styles. On the question of identity in an intercultural relationship, Imahori and Cupach (2005) concluded that situations or actions which threatened a person's face were also detrimental to their identity. The Japanese cultural motivation to avoid conflict, coupled with the importance of face, is essentially in opposition to the Western acceptance of conflict as a natural part of interpersonal relations and the much lower emphasis on face concerns. These contrasting cultural values clearly heighten the likelihood of misunderstanding and disagreement in a marriage between a Japanese and a Euro-American.

The varying communication styles used in the United States/Canada and Japan was another area seen as holding considerable potential for difficulties.

According to Hall (1976), Japan is considered a high-context culture, and meaning from communicative interactions often has to be discerned from *how* something is said. Being able to understand what is really being said by reading between the lines and being attuned to nonverbal communication cues becomes a requirement. Use of implicit communication (*hara-gei*) and silence (*chinmoku*) are also considered necessary communication skills in Japanese society (Davies & Ikeno, 2002). In contrast, for low-context cultures, like the United States and Canada, *what* is said carries the greatest importance, and a more direct, often confrontational, communication style is the norm (Ohbuchi, Fukushima, & Tedeschi, 1999).

The cultural traits known as *tatemae* and *honne* are often used to help explain the Japanese communication style. The former is what is said for public consumption, and the latter is used to express genuine, personal opinions (Hendry, 2003). In other words, the Japanese will often use *tatemae* in an effort to avoid confrontation, maintain relational harmony (*wa*), and save face for the individual and the group. This is counter to the Western ideal of open, direct communication that calls for the person to "speak their mind."

Social obligations or reciprocity (*giri*) is also a cultural concept that needs to be addressed when examining interpersonal relations in Japan (Davis & Ikeno, 2002; Lebra, 1976). The Japanese culture stresses public cooperation or group consciousness, and there is a strong sense of obligation to the family, community, and society as a whole. Not surprisingly, individuals that tilt toward a self-reliant existence are often frowned upon or even ostracized.

Yet another concept unique to Japanese society is the notion of *gaman*. In simple terms, it means enduring, with dignity and grace, what seems unbearable (De Mente, 1997), but it can also mean persistence and determination in the face of adversity and failure (Sugimoto, 2003). Japanese people portray *gaman* as an integral part of a value system that teaches a person the necessary patience and humility to assimilate and prosper within society. Thus, in a situation where a Euro-American may consider the best option would be to cut one's losses and move on, a Japanese may feel compelled to continue the struggle, regardless of personal hardship or self-sacrifice.

## THE COUPLES

The cultural concepts outlined here paint a picture of Japanese and Euro-Americans coming from vastly different cultural backgrounds. Our interviews sought to determine if and how the couples' varied cultural values and behaviors affected their marriage, and how the differences were managed.

### The Divorcees

Jim and Becky are both American expatriates divorced from Japanese spouses and have raised children in Japan. Although now in a relationship with each other, they were interviewed separately, and we elected to tell their stories separately.

*Jim's story.* Fifty-eight-year-old Jim teaches English at a Japanese university, was married to Hanako for over 20 years, is the father of three children, and had lived in Japan for a few years before settling down with Hanako. During the interview, a number of difficulties were raised that related to the cultural differences present in their international marriage. In particular, Hanako's aversion to discuss issues that Jim saw as the cause of serious friction in their relationship was one of the main reasons for the divorce. Many times he asked Hanako to sit down and talk things through, only to be given the cold shoulder or told that she was not ready to discuss the issue. This scenario continued for a number of years and seemed to only exacerbate the situation.

Both English and Japanese were used throughout their courtship and married life, and Jim recalled that one of their first family agreements was to raise the children bilingually. However, since the children spent so much more time with their mother, their primary language soon became Japanese, and English eventually became an afterthought. Even though Jim

made an effort to speak to the kids in English, they always replied in Japanese. And although his Japanese language ability is at the Professional Working/Full Professional level,[1] Jim did express feelings of being shut out because the family conversations usually reverted back to native-level Japanese that he had difficulty keeping up with.

Initially, they shared common interests in music and cooking, and Jim spent weekends with the family. He also enjoyed an amicable relation with Hanako's parents, who were not entirely opposed to her marrying a foreigner since she was already in her late twenties and, by Japanese standards, was considered past her prime for finding a suitable spouse. Other than some minor language issues, Jim did not mind visiting with his in-laws and felt they treated him much better after the grandchildren began to arrive.

In the area of family finances, Jim bucked the trend of the typical Japanese husband. His monthly paycheck was sent to the bank via direct deposit, and Jim then gave Hanako money to pay their living expenses. In a typical Japanese household, the wife—even though she may be a stay-at-home mother—manages the money. It is traditionally the wife's responsibility to pay bills and educational costs and budget all household expenses. She will dole out a small monthly discretionary allowance to her husband (Vogel, 1991), which relieves him of the burden of running the family finances and allows him to concentrate on work. The responsibility for managing the family's financial accounts is considered one of the major roles of a Japanese housewife. In Jim's case, he did not feel comfortable relinquishing control of the money. In response, he initiated a culturally inverted arrangement where he handed an allowance to his wife to use for household costs. This topic proved to be a major source of discussion with all of our interviewees, and it raised some

---

[1]We have tried to use the Interagency Language Roundtable (ILR) scale to assign a level of Japanese-language proficiency to the Euro-American participants. Our assessment is subjective, based on personal perception.
The ILR scale is as follows:
- Elementary proficiency (S-1)
- Limited Working proficiency (S-2)
- Professional Working proficiency (S-3)
- Full Professional proficiency (S-4)
- Native or Bilingual proficiency (S-5)

A full description of each level is available at http://www.sil.org/lingualinks/languagelearning/mangngyrlngglrnngprgrm/theilrfsi proficiencyscale.htm

important points concerning identity and family role models within Japanese culture.

Jim indicated that soon after the children were born, he began to feel that he and Hanako were growing apart. Fully aware that Japanese husbands typically defer to their wives to raise the children and manage the household, Jim vowed to be different. After the kids were born, he got up at sunrise to cook breakfast for the entire family and also helped change diapers. In his eyes, he was determined to be an integral part of his kids' lives and did not want to shirk his perceived responsibilities. However, as his job became more demanding, Jim found that he was no longer able to help out in the kitchen and with housework.

When asked about contention in the marriage, Jim expressed that money, budgeting, talking about sex, negotiation through difficult times, and interpersonal issues created an impasse in their lives. Jim believes that Hanako's inability to express her emotions was one of the most common sources of their arguments. From his perspective, the repression of her feelings exacerbated their troubles and nothing was ever solved. After an argument, when he attempted to broach a subject, his wife often ignored him. Her silence or avoidance indicated that she was not ready to talk.

As the years passed, the lack of physical and emotional attraction between Jim and his wife left him feeling isolated and lonely. With the last of their children nearly finished with high school, Jim felt his obligation to hold the family together was drawing to a close. Now in his late fifties, Jim met Becky—who was in a similar relational situation—and decided to file for divorce, because he saw no point in spending the rest of his life in a loveless marriage. Being an individualist, Jim sought a release from his dilemma.

When informed of Jim's decision, Hanako was shocked and went through a long period of denial. Many times Jim tried discussing their problems, but she refused and—according to Jim—considered it merely a temporary burst of anger exhibited by her American husband. Although his wife seemed to have resigned herself to their so-called marital arrangement, Jim speculated that his wife's outlook was that their marriage represented another situation where Japanese people are expected to display *gaman*—or persevere through trouble.

*Becky's story.* Originally from the United States, 43-year-old Becky teaches English at a university and has her own language school. Her transpacific odyssey of marital life offers a unique glimpse into migrating cultural relationships. She was married to her Japanese husband, Hiro, for 19 years, and they have two children. Although they met in Japan, English was their dominant language, because Hiro was a musical performer and enjoyed learning the language. After living in Japan for a few years, they moved with their two young sons to the United States, where Hiro became a sushi chef and enjoyed the laid-back lifestyle of southern California. Becky, however, had difficulty finding a suitable teaching position, so after five years the family returned to Japan. Hiro was reluctant about returning, but sided with his wife's decision.

Language was never too much trouble for the couple, as they both seemed to maintain a functional spoken level of both English and Japanese. When discussing areas of contention, Becky mentioned that her husband was always rather quiet so it was not particularly easy to communicate about things in either language. One source of friction in the relationship proved to be the division of household labor and budgeting. Upon returning to Japan, Becky became the primary wage earner, and Hiro took care of the children, becoming a stay-at-home dad. However, his impression of cleanliness diverged from Becky's and grew into a continuing problem for the couple. To make matters worse, even though Hiro was in charge of family finances, in Becky's opinion he continuously failed to budget properly, which left her feeling disappointed and angry.

However, the biggest chasm in the relationship was their respective beliefs concerning child rearing. For instance, once the children turned three to four years old, Hiro refused to hug them anymore. He reasoned that hugging was for babies, and his sons needed to recognize they had passed that stage in their lives. Becky disagreed with him and continued nurturing the children. Also, although Becky was a huge proponent of reading to the children, Hiro did not agree with that approach. He believed their sons should try to read on their own and become independent learners without the need for supervision. According to Becky, Hiro developed a series of criteria or milestones for the children to accomplish by certain ages throughout their childhood. Becky, on the other hand, was admittedly more laid back and went with the flow. She did not foresee her children developing problems in life if they had not mastered potty training by a certain age. Furthermore, she found it disconcerting that her husband seemed overly eager to set these pre-determined milestones. It all seemed too rigid and militaristic compared to her preferred role as a loving and nurturing mother.

Overall, Hiro insisted on a more authoritarian approach—often used by Japanese parents—which he justified by saying it would help prepare the children to better assimilate into Japanese society. Becky added that he often said to them, "You should not ask for a reason why; just do it." Additionally, Becky recalled that minor mistakes made by the children at the dinner table, such as the misplacement of utensils or the way the kids held their chopsticks, seemed to aggravate her husband. Hiro often resorted to raising his voice at the table, which created an atmosphere of apprehension for Becky and the children.

Ironically, none of her husband's personality traits surfaced while they lived in the United States. Becky stated that after returning to Japan, Hiro increasingly morphed into another person. He constantly reminded her that as the father of the family it was his obligation to be a stern disciplinarian. He reasoned that was his role within the family and dismissed her lackadaisical California attitude. Becky did not agree and wanted to promote a more loving and nurturing family environment. In Becky's opinion, after the family returned to Japan, Hiro placed too much emphasis on conforming. When they resided in California, Hiro did not seem to pay attention to what other people thought about him and the family. Conversely, in Japan he often went out of his way to perform duties that she perceived were trivial—like cutting only slightly overgrown grass or washing the car—because he worried what the neighbors would think. From Hiro's perspective, this was an important part of Japanese culture, and he was eager to fulfill his role in the home and in society. In hindsight, Becky wondered whether it was the social pressure associated with the way others would view them that motivated Hiro?

Similar to Jim, Becky preferred to resolve arguments by talking things through, but Hiro insisted on waiting a week or two in order to let their emotions abate. This frustrated Becky as she felt time did not heal all wounds—Hiro's perspective—and their marital problems actually worsened. For Becky, it became clear that their marriage had become something solely for the sake of the children. On numerous occasions, she asked Hiro to make quality time for them as a couple, but her suggestions fell on deaf ears. Becky inquired about setting a date night each week or taking a dance class together; however, this would have represented an anomaly for couples in Japan. For example, the concept of baby-sitting as practiced in the United States does not exist in Japan, and if couples want time alone most have to ask their parents or in-laws to look after the children. Since Hiro was not close with his family, creating quality time opportunities was virtually impossible.

Becky also indicated that she slowly came to loathe the concept of *giri*, frequently translated as a sense of duty or social obligation. Much too often Hiro seemed preoccupied with helping friends move and performing other tasks after they returned to Japan. To a puzzled Becky, he remarked that it was *giri* and an integral part of Japanese culture. When queried further, Hiro responded that he must help his friends so they would do the same for him someday. Becky contemplated whether such actions came from the heart or were merely a chance to be owed a favor. Much to her chagrin, when it came time for them to move, her husband was too proud to ask his friends for any help and none ever seemed to come their way.

Finally, Becky started to think about the formidable process of divorce in Japan. People around her constantly said that she would never be able to raise a family on her own, and Becky realized that single mothers in Japan are frequently treated as social pariahs. There remains scant government and legal support for divorcing a Japanese spouse and working through this complicated process made Becky feel isolated. To compound matters, many of her Japanese "so-called" friends that had promised they would be there for her seemed to avoid Becky after she went through with the divorce. She attributes their actions as examples of *tatemae*—tokenism or lip service—all of which seemed rather dishonest to Becky. It became apparent that her Japanese friends' *hone*—real intentions—were that they likely chose to remain friends with her ex-husband and could not directly explain this to Becky.

*Cultural insights.* There were significant cultural factors contributing to the failure of these two international marriages. Both Jim and Becky came from an individualistic, low-context background, where forthright communication is valued. For them, openly confronting issues in an effort to work out an amicable solution was common sense. However, for someone from Japan, this approach to conflict resolution runs the risk of disturbing the relational harmony and carries a potential loss of face. For the two Japanese spouses, the norm was to avoid the topic of interpersonal difficulties or remain silent. These behaviors were high-context communication messages signaling discomfort with the directness of the western approach to resolving disagreements.

Identity issues were also apparent in both marriages. Perhaps quite unknowingly, Jim's insistence on being the family financial manager created multiple cultural contradictions for his wife. This was counter to the traditional Japanese gender role model, and affected Hanako's identity, perhaps creating a loss of face, especially among family and friends. In Becky's case, as a product of Japan's highly male–dominated society (Sugimoto, 2003), Hiro saw himself in the traditional Japanese role of being the family's authority figure. As such, it was his responsibility to instill the children with discipline and teach the social skills they would need to "fit in" Japan's collective society. Hiro's concern for what the neighbors might think was another manifestation of the need to "fit in" and not lose face.

Both Jim and Becky disclosed that the romance before marriage was wonderful, but their spouses' seemingly complete transformation into a mother or father role was disheartening. The love they showered on the children seemed to replace what they had once shared for each other. This social-role change can be explained by the varied values of individualism and collectivism. For members of a group-oriented culture, proscribed behaviors are the norm (Brett & Gelfand, 2005). In a much older work, Smith (1983) found that individuals in Japan are constrained by a common social order organized around principles of hierarchy, reciprocity, formality, and harmony. Thus, after the children were born, the two Japanese spouses adjusted to the social role model of parent as prescribed by Japanese culture.

Differing cultural values appear to have also played a role in the decisions to end the two marriages. Similar to Jim's reasons, Becky chose to divorce her Japanese spouse because she could not foresee living a life full of compromises. This course of action is characteristic of individualism, where personal fulfillment can take precedence over relationships. From the collective perspective, this is a reflection of selfishness, placing personal interests over the benefit of the group. In Japan, couples may not get along, yet may adhere to the cultural belief of *gaman*, or perseverance. They endure self-sacrifice to sustain the continuity of the family group. Despite all the difficulties between them, Jim's wife, Hanako, would have preferred to persevere (*gaman*) in the marriage, no doubt motivated, at least in part, by the traditional model of the Japanese mother-child relationship representing the core of the family (Okubo, 2010).

The failure of Becky to grasp the influence of *giri* on her husband's behavior or distinguish the use of *tatamae* and *honne* are examples of how cultural differences can create miscommunication and conflict in an international marriage. Some cultural issues can be extremely difficult to discern or accept by an outsider. As Hendry (2003) points out, the *tatamae/honne* dichotomy is considered one of the more bewildering cultural concepts for non-Japanese to comprehend.

> Jim's insistence on being the family financial manager created multiple cultural contradictions for his wife.

## Seeking Common Ground

Rick, a 42-year old American, and his Japanese wife, Kyoko, have been together for six years, and the marriage represents his second foray into matrimony. His first wife was an American and they had one son. Rick and Kyoko initially met in an online chat room and began dating by visiting each other approximately twice a year. The couple now resides in central Japan, where Rick works as a private English tutor and sells hand-made crafts online.

*Rick's story.* Initially, the couple's common language was English, but since moving to Japan about five years ago, Rick has developed a limited working proficiency in spoken Japanese. Kyoko's English is about the same level, and they typically communicate in both languages at home. Yet, there are numerous times that Kyoto will speak Japanese too fast for Rick to follow. Prior to meeting Kyoko, Rick had never been outside the United States. Because he has only a high school education, Rick has been faced with limited job opportunities in Japan. His current income is insufficient to meet the family's needs, and they have had to borrow money. While they are not in poverty, their earnings fall far below the national income average for a couple of their age bracket. Kyoko is very unhappy with their present condition and frequently voices her discontent.

These days they hardly ever spend time together. Rick says he would like to have more activities as a family, but his wife usually takes their daughter out alone. Additionally, Kyoko's family seems to have run out of patience with Rick's inability to provide for his family. It is obvious that finances have placed a burden on their relationship, but Rick thinks his wife places too much emphasis on money in general and on keeping up with the Suzukis (i.e., the Joneses). Rick has his own bank account but allows Kyoko to manage the household finances. To increase their family income, Kyoko has taken on a part-time job.

When it comes to discussing issues, he feels Kyoko simply ignores everything he says. Arguments tend to revert back to Kyoko retorting that he does not understand because he is not Japanese. After hearing this rationale so often, he has developed a somewhat negative view of Japanese culture. Although Kyoko speaks English and acts like she wants to learn about his culture, he thinks it is merely *tatemae*. He believes that she views him as her foreign trophy husband, because in front of her friends, Kyoko tends to boast about his uniqueness, yet in private she is always critical. Disagreements are never resolved as the couple just avoids each other until things eventually cool down. Rick says that he just tunes out Kyoko's constant nagging even though he recognizes this must annoy her even more.

Interestingly, Rick was very opinionated about perceptions he held prior to living in Japan. He thought the Japanese had stronger morals and a sense of honor, but now, Rick feels that they often lie to cover their mistakes, something he had not expected. Further, Rick mentioned that it seems as though the Japanese people follow a premise that a sin is not a sin if nobody sees it. Morally, he has found his experience of living in Japan challenging. Also, Rick initially thought children would be better raised in Japan, but he has not found that to be the case regarding behavior and discipline. He feels his daughter is spoiled and too pampered by her doting grandparents.

Rick explained that his wife is a mere shell of the vibrant person he met six years ago. Since becoming a mother, she no longer makes time for him, and their romantic life is non-existent. He wishes they could find time to be with each other, but Kyoko doesn't seem to show any interest. When asked if this had to do with his lack of providing a stable income, Rick deliberated and thought that it may, but then concluded that Kyoko had too many other personal problems.

When asked for advice to offer someone that may decide to marry a Japanese and live in Japan, a dejected Rick just shook his head. He believes it is impossible to make the marriage work unless you give up your identity, and perhaps even then it will not be enough since you are not Japanese. He loathes the notion of people performing a task in Japan so they will get something in return (*giri*). It all seems much too calculating and cunning to Rick.

Although the interview was supposed to last 20 to 30 minutes, it continued for nearly two hours, during which time Rick disclosed how he ended up living in Japan. Even though Kyoko promised that she would reside in the United States after marriage, something far different occurred. After having the baby and living in a small U.S. city for nearly one year, Kyoko became emotionally depressed and returned to Japan. Upon arrival, she sent a short text message requesting Rick to forget about her and their daughter. The message went on to say that their lives were now separate. Rick was distraught and angered by his wife's actions, and after checking his legal rights, he realized that he would need to go to Japan and reconcile with Kyoko or risk never seeing his daughter again.[2]

***Kyoko's story.*** Rick's wife, Kyoko, is 10 years his junior. In a separate interview, conducted in Japanese, she related that after meeting online they exchanged trans-Pacific visits until deciding to get married when she became pregnant. Kyoko revealed that living in Rick's small U.S. hometown was the first time she had lived abroad, other than as a tourist. After awhile, she came to feel increasingly isolated and finally decided to return to Japan. The couple uses both English and Japanese for daily communication. She considers her English ability to be at approximately the same level as Rick's Japanese but feels he lacks cultural awareness.

The most important thing that Kyoko and Rick have in common is an appreciation for music and handicrafts. They delight in seeing each other's works, and Kyoko enjoys this creative aspect of their lives. Kyoko said that among her family, Rick has a reputation as a know-it-all and as a person who does not make the effort to find a decent job to support his family. As a result, they have little respect for Rick, so it is sometimes rather difficult for them to socialize together.

For Kyoko, the biggest concern about the marriage is Rick's lack of a steady job. This situation leaves her feeling insecure and creates tremendous stress, as she constantly worries about finding money to pay the rent and meet living expenses. Kyoko grew up in a middle-class household and attended both a fairly prestigious private high school and university. Thus, her present socio-economic level is well below what she experienced before marriage. On numerous occasions, she has had to borrow money from her family and feels embarrassed about asking for handouts. Initially, she thought her husband would be able to teach English in Japan, but without a university degree, coupled with heightened competition in that field, Rick's options proved to be quite limited for teaching positions.

Regarding personality, Kyoko feels that Rick is too self-assertive or opinionated, traits which are viewed negatively in Japan. Kyoko explained that when an argument occurs, Rick is reluctant to admit that sometimes he may be at fault. Kyoko believes that both sides must acknowledge a certain degree of fault when they have a disagreement. Yet, she feels Rick seems to always transfer the blame onto her. Based on her responses, it seems that Kyoko wants to take responsibility for improving their life as a couple, but she thinks that Rick seems unwilling to cooperate and remains very rigid in his thinking. Rick's actions and unwillingness to admit any fault for their current situation has left Kyoko feeling extremely frustrated.

Another area of disagreement in the marriage is the couple's different perspectives on child rearing. Rick and Kyoko appear to perceive their daughter's upbringing through vastly different prisms. While Kyoko regards learning American culture as appropriate, she believes that Japanese must be their daughter's dominant culture because Japan is their home. Thus, while Rick tries to instill some of his own cultural values into his daughter's life, the reality is that the young girl spends far more time with her mother and has become more acculturated to Japanese mores.

> *Many of their problems could have been ameliorated by each having greater insight into the other's culture.*

[2]Japan is not a signatory to the 1996 Hague Convention on international child abduction. One of the main reasons Japan has yet to become a signatory to the pact is that in the eyes of Japanese law, the child is to remain with its mother in times of domestic strife ("Japan-where," 2010). Although there are cases of Japanese fathers gaining full custody of their children, it remains a cultural anomaly. The language barrier, myriad of legal details, and the fact that most Japanese spouses have a supportive family in country to help raise the children of divorced couples usually eliminates foreign fathers from receiving custody. As a result of Kyoko fleeing the United States, Rick was forced to give up a stable job and move to Japan in his late 30s without any language skills, cultural knowledge, or job prospects. To this day, he still blames Kyoko for this, but grudgingly resides in Japan in order to be a part of his daughter's upbringing.

When asked for advice to give a foreigner about to marry a Japanese, Kyoko replied that being able to speak Japanese and understand its culture is very important if the couple plans to live in Japan. She felt those skills could help eliminate some major frustrations, decrease arguments, and create more autonomy for the non-native spouse.

*Cultural insights.* The interviews with Rick and Kyoko brought out several areas of cultural conflict in their marriage. Many of their problems could have been ameliorated by each having greater insight into the other's culture. Adapting to life in a different culture is normally quite stressful and can be lonely. It involves, along with other things, learning and accepting new norms, developing a new identity, finding and making new friends, and using a new language (Kim, 2001). Moving from Japan and learning to live in a small U.S. town, removed from friends, family, and other support systems, no doubt created considerable psychological stress for Kyoko. Going to Japan and trying to find employment with little appreciation for the culture or linguistic ability was a guaranteed source of anxiety for Rick. The demands of cultural adaption add a considerable layer of stress to an international marriage and require the two people to be accepting and non-judgmental of values and behaviors different from their own.

As in the case of the first two couples, the styles of conflict management used by Rick and Kyoko were at variance. Rick's Euro-American cultural grounding had instilled him with the value of being assertive and taking care of his own face. This, of course, clashed with Kyoko's cultural perception of the need to avoid open conflict. Indeed, her feeling that both sides needed to assume some of the fault in an argument is an example of mutual-facework, which is prevalent in collectivistic cultures (Ting-Toomey, 2005). Moreover, Domenici and Littlejohn (2006) point out that mutual-facework can help maintain or improve a relationship by constructing a sense of shared identity. Thus, Rick viewed their marital differences from an individualistic perspective and sought to protect his own face—a win-lose approach. This is counter to Kyoko's collectivistic method, designed to help maintain both Rick's and her own face—a win-win approach.

Rick's disdain for *giri* was also a manifestation of his individualistic cultural values. Japan's group orientation and desire for social harmony is strongly supported by a sense of mutual obligation (*giri*). In essence, if you do something for me, I *must* do something in return, which helps mitigate one-sided relationships. Additionally, if asked by a friend to do something, a collectivist will more likely be reluctant to say no for fear of disrupting the social balance. However, people from individualistic cultures, like Rick, normally do something because *they want* to do it, and they are not hesitant to say no to a request.

The couple's varied cultural understanding was also evident in their attitudes toward child rearing. The birth of their daughter meant Kyoko had to shed her carefree attitudes and assume the more serious, culturally defined role of a Japanese mother. For someone raised in an individualistic culture, where the birth of a child has far less impact on the mother's identity, this change can be rather dramatic, and even unsettling.

The need to know how to properly enact Japanese social roles was the reason Kyoko gave priority to teaching their daughter the Japanese language and culture. To be successful in Japan, their daughter must know the socially prescribed skills and behaviors required to "fit in." The individualistic cultural norms that Rick adhered to would be of minimal value to their daughter and in some cases could even prove detrimental.

## Par for the Course?

Phil and his wife, Yuko, have been together for approximately 10 years and represent a rather typical international marriage between a Japanese and a Euro-American residing in Japan. Phil has a limited working proficiency in Japanese, but Yuko speaks a higher level of English than Phil's Japanese, so English is the dominant language in their relationship. However, more Japanese than English is spoken to him by their six-year-old daughter. Prior to meeting Yuko, Phil had been living in Japan teaching at an English conversation school for approximately two years. He now works as an adjunct English lecturer at several universities in the area.

*Phil's story.* Phil indicated that he and Yuko share a passion for movies and still find time to go to the cinema on date nights. They try to spend their free time together, but seem to always be busy, even on the weekends, because Phil has part-time work. According to Phil, they generally enjoy visiting each other's families. However, on a recent trip to the United States, Phil explained that Yuko became very uncomfortable dealing with the countless child-rearing suggestions offered by his mother. Although Yuko disagreed with most of her mother-in-law's advice, she found it difficult to voice her own opinion.

Phil indicated that he controls the family finances. He realizes it is customary in Japan for the wife to hold the family purse strings, but he simply does not feel comfortable with that arrangement. Therefore, he provides his wife with the necessary living expenses and an allowance. Although the couple purchased a house in Japan, Phil periodically envisions the family returning to California and living near his parents. Even though Yuko has expressed an interest in moving to the United States, he thinks this would create serious problems with her family.

A key difference Phil noted between his relationship with his wife and with former long-term American girlfriends is that his marriage lacks a sense of spontaneity. Everything in their home life—including meal times and foods—seems a bit too regimented, and he often wonders if his existence is far too predictable. Phil wishes that he and Yuko could escape for an occasional weekend together, but realizes that Japanese society does not seem to foster romantic get-aways for married couples. Also, Phil finds it frustrating that Yuko does not display much interest in politics. He would like to be able to discuss world events and political affairs, but she seems to have an aversion to these topics.

A cultural practice that Phil finds troubling is Yuko's habit of leaving their front door unlocked during the day. This habit is likely a product of the *mura-shakai*—village society—mind-set, the foundation for Japanese family life, which places less value on the individual's privacy (Bestor, 1989; Nakane, 1970). Unfortunately, with crime on the rise, it is no longer prudent to leave doors unlocked. Yet, Yuko sometimes forgets and leaves the door open. This allows salespeople to occasionally open the door and shout out a polite greeting to gain the attention of the residents. Phil is highly resentful of this aspect of Japanese life, which he considers an invasion of his privacy.

Phil, now 47 years old, had lived in Japan prior to meeting Yuko, and was rather familiar with the Japanese lifestyle. Thus, he harbored no preconceived ideas about marriage to a Japanese. When asked about advice for someone planning to marry a Japanese, Phil recommended that they discuss where they would like to live in the future so neither person ends up resentful or disappointed. Phil had discussions with other foreigners wed to Japanese before he married Yuko, but based on his personal experience, he thinks every situation is different and anecdotal advice can be good or bad, depending on the couple.

*Yuko's story.* Phil's wife Yuko, in her early forties, was interviewed in Japanese and seemed to agree with many of the things voiced by her husband. She had never lived outside Japan before meeting Phil, but had previously dated another foreigner. Prior to becoming a full-time housewife, Yuko worked as a piano teacher. She considers her English skills to be at a functional level as well as her husband's Japanese, but English clearly remains their dominant language. Yuko indicated she wished Phil possessed enough Japanese-language ability to communicate fluently with her family, because she is forced to translate most of the time, a requirement she finds can become mentally and physically draining. Additionally, Phil struggles with reading Japanese, and this limits his ability to help out with household chores like grocery shopping.

Yuko reported that Phil controls the bank account and provides her with money to pay the mortgage and monthly household bills. Going into the marriage, she knew this situation was unavoidable. When queried for further explanation, she replied that because Phil was an American and not the type of person to let someone else manage his finances, she was willing to endure this arrangement. She would prefer to be in control of family finances and be relied upon to make key decisions, but she understands Phil's need for individuality and independence.

Counter to her husband's claim, Yuko finds visiting each other's families quite stressful. As previously mentioned, having to translate for Phil when visiting her family can become taxing, and she feels overwhelmed functioning in English 24/7 during trips to the United States. More importantly, Yuko does not appreciate it when Phil goes out with old friends for the entire evening. This situation always leaves her alone to try and make small talk with her in-laws.

Complaints aside, Yuko is happy with her marriage and appreciates Phil's kindness. She does however, wish he would accept certain elements of Japanese culture and stop comparing things to his own cultural background. She believes Phil remains too confrontational with Japanese people and fails to recognize many of the subtle messages that serve as a common form of Japanese discourse. Yuko acknowledges that this non-verbal language can be difficult to understand; however, Phil's life would be easier if he learned to recognize these cues.

The two primary sources of friction in their relationship, according to Yuko, are money and Phil's occasional late-night soirees at sports bars. Not controlling the family purse strings is something that Yuko still finds almost unnatural in her role as a Japanese housewife. As their daughter is about to begin school, she is thinking about returning to her job as a piano teacher. Yuko hopes this will help with family finances and provide her with a life outside the role of mother.

*The value of social relations and harmony among the Japanese was evident in Yuko's reluctance to discuss politics or world affairs.*

When asked about advice for someone contemplating an international marriage in Japan, Yuko chuckled and said that the ideal person should be fluent in Japanese. She reflected that such a condition would make life much easier and cause less stress within the relationship. Initially, she had preconceived notions that a foreign husband would be more of a gentleman than a Japanese spouse. While she has not found that to be completely the case, she does believe Phil exhibits more sympathy than the Japanese husbands of her friends. Overall, Yuko thinks that if a couple loves each other, even with communication difficulties, they will find a way to be happy in their lives together.

*Cultural insights.* Rick and Yuko appear to be able to work around their cultural dissimilarities, or at least accept the differences, in most situations. Their interviews did, however, bring out some culturally based issues that each considered troublesome. For instance, Yuko found visiting Phil's family in the United States to be stressful, and part of that stress came from being unable to respond to her mother-in-law's constant suggestions on child raising. Culturally conditioned to avoid conflict and respect older family members, Yuko chose to endure the situation in order to maintain a harmonious relationship.

Rick's comment about the predictability of his family life offers an example of how deep uncertainty avoidance runs in the Japanese culture. The value placed on social harmony, strong interpersonal relations, and face creates an environment where unpredictability is cast in a negative light. By knowing what to expect in almost any social situation, the Japanese can behave and speak in the proper way (*shikata*) and avoid actions that others may consider inappropriate or offensive (De Mente, 2005). This is quite in contrast with the Euro-American attitude that embraces and promotes change and is characterized by the adage "variety is the spice of life."

The value of social relations and harmony among the Japanese was evident in Yuko's reluctance to discuss politics or world affairs. Euro-Americans, raised in a culture that encourages political banter, find pleasure in discussing and debating opposing opinions. But for the Japanese, this type of social interaction carries the potential for conflict, which could lead to a loss of face and threaten the relationship. Therefore, among most Japanese, politics is not a common conversation topic (Hendry, 2003).

A particularly salient aspect of the marriage that demonstrated the couple's cultural difference was the management of family finances. As with the other couples, Rick's strong sense of individualism appeared to be behind his desire to retain control of the money. This situation was clearly a problem for Yuko. Not only did it erode her social identity in Japan's gender-specific society, it deprived her of an important means of contributing to the family effort, of participating equally to sustain the feeling of mutual dependence. Yet, despite this condition, she persevered (*gaman*).

Yuko also highlighted the significance of being sensitive to Japan's high-context communication style. Not only is this an important asset when dealing with the Japanese in general, it is a particularly valuable skill when married to a Japanese. Knowing when yes really means no, or when to apologize for an action, not only demonstrates cultural sensitivity but also contributes to creating a close, caring relationship.

## The In-Step Duo

Alex, a 37-year-old Canadian, has been married to Yuri for 10 years. A one-year high school exchange program introduced Alex to the Japanese language and culture at a relatively young age. Thus, he has never really suffered from many of the language and cultural complexities that often confront his expatriate friends with Japanese spouses. Employed as a high school English teacher, Alex is extremely dedicated to his profession and has obtained a Japanese teaching certificate, a rare accomplishment for a foreign teacher. This permits Alex to teach his own classes, rather than being relegated to team-teaching, the more common occupation for native English–speaking teachers at the K-12 level in Japan.

Alex and Yuri met in Japan and dated for a few years before marrying and now have two small children. Although Alex has achieved a full professional or higher level of Japanese, he and Yuri make a dedicated effort to use English with the children in their home. In fact, Alex rarely speaks Japanese with his two children.

*Alex's story.* During the interview, Alex revealed that a sense of humor and taste in music are two things he shares with his wife. Due to his busy teaching schedule, which includes coaching the high school volleyball team on weekends, Alex is seldom able to accompany Yuri and the children when they visit her parents twice a month. However, when possible, Alex does enjoy visiting with his wife's family and her siblings.

Unlike the other couples we interviewed, Alex allows his wife to receive his salary and gives her complete control of family finances. He feels this arrangement makes his life much less complicated and is one less thing to worry about. The question of providing financial assistance to or taking care of Yuri's parents, should they need it in the future, is something that Alex is willing to discuss. Although it is more probable they would go to live with Yuri's older brother, Alex believes that such a situation would be discussed among all immediate family members and agreed upon without incident.

One cultural point that Alex feels Yuri does not recognize is the importance he places on family during the Christmas holiday season.[3] However, Alex excitedly mentioned that Yuri has come to support him more and more in celebrating the holiday, including giving presents to the kids and eating traditional holiday food. He is quite happy that the event has become a family tradition.

Alex offered a few helpful suggestions regarding international marriages. First, he believes couples must accept their differences. Japan and North America are distinctly opposite cultures so couples can often have diverging opinions. Second, some Euro-American men have a tendency to try and force their wives to become more Canadian or American. Yet, it is usually the husband that has chosen to live in Japan. Alex counseled that people should refrain from implementing an agenda of cultural imperialism within the relationship.

*Yuri's story.* Speaking in Japanese, 36-year-old Yuri indicated she is quite satisfied with her international marriage. Prior to meeting Alex, she was a factory worker in rural Japan. Although Yuri enjoyed the work and the friendships she made there, after becoming pregnant she quit to become a full-time mother and homemaker. However, she expressed an interest in finding part-time work, or even a full-time job, when the children are older.

Prior to meeting Alex, Yuri had never ventured outside Japan. Now, she enjoys visiting Alex's family in Canada and even looks forward to possibly taking trips abroad as a family. Although she had no interest in speaking English prior to meeting Alex, Yuri

---

[3]The primary religions in Japan are Shintoism and Buddhism, with Christians constituting approximately 2 percent of the population. As a result, the meaning and celebration of Christmas in the United States/Canada and in Japan are quite different. Christmas is not a national holiday in Japan, and Christmas Eve is unofficially designated as one of the year's most romantic nights for young couples. Japanese families celebrate by eating eat grilled chicken—a banner night for Colonel Sander's KFC outlets—and Christmas cake. Exchanging presents is not a part of the local tradition.

decided to learn the language so she could communicate with her in-laws, and also thought it would be ideal to raise their children in a bilingual home. To achieve this, she made a concerted effort to learn English on her own and with the help of Alex. Now, Yuri is very pleased with her ability to communicate with Alex's friends and family in English.

One of the most important things that she feels proud of is the fact that Alex is socially accepted by his colleagues and students. In her eyes, he has worked hard to earn their respect. She also mentioned that Alex's cultural adjustment into their residential area has been successful. Oftentimes, this can cause some stress for non-Japanese because most neighborhoods have associations that typically ask inhabitants to participate in occasional cleanup duty, evening crime watch patrol, and other cooperative endeavors.

Financially, Yuri is content with their situation and seems happy that her husband can earn enough money to provide a comfortable life for the family. The couple built a new home together shortly after getting married, and she believes this has helped them grow as a family. Yuri is also quite happy that Alex is able to maintain a good relationship with her relatives. Another positive aspect of the relationship is the consideration Alex exhibits for their children. Yuri has a great deal of respect for Alex's caring way of communicating with their two young children and with those around him. This has made her realize that her husband is a very patient and caring person.

However, one thing that Yuri is unable to comprehend is why Alex holds Christmas Day in such high regard. Having never lived abroad and only experiencing Christmas in Japan, Yuri finds it difficult to understand the reason Alex makes an endless list of Christmas preparations and then showers the children with an abundance of presents. Her view is that the western concept of Christmas is an unrealistic representation of the modern family. She thinks that giving the children so many presents runs the risk of spoiling them and perhaps creating a false sense of wealth.

Yuri derives a great deal of fulfillment from the supportive role she has in the marriage. Throughout their relationship, she has contributed to Alex's success. Whenever he needs any language support, she is always there to encourage and provide assistance. For example, she helped Alex complete his handwritten Japanese application forms to gain his position as a teacher. Speaking with Yuri, one gets the feeling that she and her husband have a symbiotic relationship and recognize their respective roles. Yuri's only advice for someone marrying a person from another culture is that a couple should try to learn and respect each other's language and culture.

*Cultural insights.* Of all the couples interviewed, Alex and Yuri appeared to have the strongest relationship, as well as the most respect for each other's culture. Allowing Yuri to handle finances enabled her normative Japanese social identity and a feeling of contributing to the family's well-being. Alex demonstrated an awareness of the collectivistic emphasis on relationships through his use of sensitive, caring communication and the acceptance that one day he may have to help care for his wife's parents. Yuri's determination to learn English displayed her willingness to make personal sacrifices (*gaman*) for the marriage. By participating in Alex's Christmas celebrations, even though not completely in agreement, Yuri demonstrated a high level of ethnorelativism. Opportunities to help Alex with various aspects of his teaching profession have also made Yuri aware that her marriage is based on mutual obligation. Overall, the success of their marriage appears to be, at least in part, a result of the ability of Alex and Yuri to move beyond the confines of their respective culture. Indeed, Alex's skill in moving seamlessly and successfully between the Japanese and Euro-American expatriate communities suggests he has achieved biculturalism and acquired bicultural communication competence (Kim, 2002).

> *Allowing Yuri to handle finances enabled her normative Japanese social identity.*

## AFTER THOUGHTS

Although limited in number, the interviewed couples offer examples of dysfunctional, stable, and highly synergistic international marriages in Japan. Taken collectively, the interview data offer several culturally informative lessons. The most noteworthy finding is that those foreign spouses who take a dedicated interest in their partner's language and culture are much more likely to enjoy a successful union. By ignoring or minimizing those factors, however, an international couple risks confusion and disillusionment in their relationship.

Another key finding that emerged from the interviews was the importance of competent intercultural communication between spouses in an international marriage. The linguistic reality is that communication in Japan is often high context, with the message being more nonverbal than verbal. This is a difficult process for a non-Japanese to grasp and carries the potential to increase misunderstanding and confusion for an international couple. After conducting these interviews and hearing a host of intercultural communication problems, it made us recall the phrase *anmoku no ryoukai*, which equates to tacit understanding. In English, this would amount to "reading between the lines," or more like a form of mind reading. While we assume this ability for tacit understanding is common among Japanese couples, it would be worthwhile to explore what role a Japanese spouse expects this form of communication to play in an international marriage.

The interviews also brought out the adverse affect that can result from a spouse being deprived of their normative social identity while living in their own culture. This can be attributed, in part, to the Japanese perception that life occurs in distinct stages, with each phase being characterized by gender-specific, highly defined social protocols. For example, after marriage, spouses are expected to take on new roles or adjust their identities as they move from being newlyweds, to parenthood, into middle age, and eventually into their silver years. This progression was noted by Tanaka (1998), who explained that the Japanese magazine publishing industry targets women at various stages in their lives and this has a tremendous impact on consumer goods, lifestyles, and family planning.

Japanese wives and husbands are expected to adhere to the social models characterizing these stages without questioning how this will impact their personal relationship. The maintenance of social stability by being a compliant member of the group is a paramount consideration. As a result, it seems that Japanese spouses are strongly influenced by socially defined roles regarding matrimonial life. Additional research to support this notion is needed to gain further understanding.

Mutual respect is another area that requires additional inquiry since Japanese women seem to expect their husband to adequately provide for the family's needs. Any husband that fails to fulfill this aspect of the marriage contract, like Rick for instance, tends to alter the normative social model, which can adversely affect the relationship. Japanese women enter into married life with certain definitive expectations. Husbands are supposed to provide the economic resources and allow their wives to fulfill their role as manager of the household. Through this dialectic relationship, they complement each other in a relationship that favors success for the family unit (i.e., group) over the pursuit of individual happiness. Altering this role can be acceptable, as we found with Phil and Yuko, but completely disrupting it can produce negative repercussions for the international couple's well-being. The expectation that the Japanese husband will provide a comfortable living is probably no different from that of brides anywhere, but in Japan, it appears to be more acute and carries considerable face concerns.

Finally, there is the delicate subject of intimacy or lack thereof for married couples. Recent surveys in Japan reveal that sexless marriages among Japanese couples are much more prevalent than believed (*Kekkon sannenme*, 2010). The research noted that in many cases husbands and wives seem to consider their marriage as more reminiscent of a deep friendship or brother-sister type relationship. While this may be acceptable for Japanese nationals, the situation can become problematic if this arrangement is erroneously applied to foreign brides and grooms, who have quite different expectations about emotional and physical fulfillment. Again, we can surmise that the doctrine and meaning of marriage can vary between people from different cultures.

As the world becomes smaller, international marriages will continue to rise in Japan. Unfortunately, cultural nuances and unrealistic expectations will coincide with this phenomenon. It is our hope that international couples will make the effort to learn more about each other's language and cultural background and avoid becoming a divorce statistic. By exerting a willingness to compromise and acknowledging that an international spouse comes from a distinctly varied background, marriage partners can help avoid a life full of misunderstandings, argument, and regrets.

# References

Asakura, T. (2002, Jan 8). Bachelors looked abroad after eligible local girls fled village life for city. *The Japan Times Online*. Retrieved 22 April 2010 from http://search.japantimes.co.jp/cgi-bin/nn20020108b9.html.

Bestor, T. (1989). *Neighborhood Tokyo*. Palo Alto: Stanford University Press.

Brett, J., & Gelfand, J. (2006). A cultural analysis of the underlying assumptions of negotiation theory. In L. Thompson (Ed.) *Negotiation theory and research—frontiers of social psychology* (pp. 173–201). Oxford: Psychology Press.

Colmas, F. (2007). *Population decline and ageing in Japan—The social consequences*. London: Routledge.

Daimon, S. (2009, April 30). Opening the door to foreigners. *The Japan Times Online*. Retrieved 22 April 2010 from http://search.japantimes.co.jp/cgi-bin/nn20090430f1.html.

De Mente, B. L. (2005). *Japan unmasked*. Rutland, VT: Tuttle.

Domenici, K., & Littlejohn, S.W. (2006). *Facework: Bridging theory and practice*. Thousand Oaks, CA: Sage.

Davies, R., & Ikeno, O. (2002). *The Japanese mind: Understanding contemporary Japanese culture*. Tokyo: Tuttle.

De Mente, B.L. (1997). *The Japanese have a word for it: The complete guide to Japanese thought and culture*. New York: McGraw Hill.

French, H. (2002, July 31). For more Japanese, love is a multiethnic thing. *The New York Times*. Retrieved 7 July 2010 from http://www.nytimes.com/2002/07/31/world/for-more-japanese-love-is-a-multiethnic-thing.html?pagewanted=1.

Hall, E.T. (1976). *Beyond culture*. New York: Doubleday.

Hendry, J. (2003). *Understanding Japanese society*. London: Routledge.

Hisane, M. (2006). Japan stares into a demographic abyss. *Asia Times Online*. Retrieved 7 July 2010 from http://www.atimes.com/atimes/Japan/HE09Dh04.html.

Imahori, T. T., & Cupach, W. R. (2005). Identity management theory. In W.B. Gudykunst (Ed.), *Theorizing About Intercultural Communication* (pp. 195–210). Thousand Oaks, CA: Sage.

Japan—where some parents never see their kids (2010, February 5). *The Daily Yomiuri*, pp. 1–2.

JET Programme. (2009). *History of the JET programme. The Japan exchange and teaching programme*. Retrieved 22 April 2010 from http://www.jetprogramme.org/e/introduction/history.html.

Kamoto, I. (2001). *Kokusai kekkon no tanjou: Bunmeikoku Nihon e no michi*. [The birth of the international marriage: The path to a culturally enlightened Japan]. Tokyo: Shinyosha.

*Kekkon sannenme no risou to zetsubou*. [The ideals and despair after three years of marriage]. (2010, April 5). *AERA*, pp. 36–41.

Kim, Y.Y. (2001). *Becoming intercultural*. Thousand Oaks, CA: Sage.

Kim, M-S. (2002). *Non-Western perspectives on human communication*. Thousand Oaks, CA: Sage.

Kurman, J. (2003). Why is self-enhancement low in certain collectivist cultures? *Journal of Cross-Cultural Psychology, 34*, 5, 496–510.

Lebra, T. (1976). *Japanese patterns of behavior*. Honolulu: University of Hawaii Press.

Leupp, G. (2003). *Interracial intimacy in Japan*. New York: Continuum International Publishing Group.

Ministry of Health, Labour, and Welfare. (2009a). *Vital statistics annual report: Marriage: Table 2: Annual number and percentages of marriages by nationality of husband and wife*. Tokyo, Japan. Retrieved 21 April 2010 from http://www.mhlw.go.jp/toukei/saikin/hw/jinkou/suii07/marr2.html.

Ministry of Health, Labour and Welfare. (2009b). *Vital statistics annual report: Divorce: Table 2: Annual number and percentages of divorces by nationality of husband and wife*. Retrieved 21 April from http://www.mhlw.go.jp/toukei/saikin/hw/jinkou/suii07/marr2.html.

Nakane, C. (1970). *Japanese society*. Berkeley: University of California Press.

Niita, F. (1988). Kokusai kekkon: Trends in intercultural marriage in Japan. *International Journal of Intercultural Relations, 12*, 205–232.

Ohbuchi, K., Fukushima, O., & Tedeschi, J. (1999). Cultural values in conflict management. *Journal of Cross-Cultural Psychology, 30*(1), 51–71.

Okubo, T. (2010, February 8). Family sleeping arrangements as culture. *Daily Yomiuri Online*. Retrieved from http://www.yomiuri.co.jp/adv/wol/dy/opinion/culture_100208.htm.

Smith, R. (1983). *Japanese society: Tradition, self, and the social order*. London: Cambridge University Press.

Sugimoto, Y. (2003). *An introduction to Japanese society* (2nd ed.). NY: Cambridge University Press.

Suzuki, T. (2010). The latest development in population of Japan: The 2008 revision. *The Japanese Journal of Population, 8*, 1, 95–98. Retrieved 7 July 2010 from http://www.ipss.go.jp/webj-ad/WebJournal.files/population/2010_Vol.8/Web%20Journal_Vol.8_04.pdf

Tanaka, Keiko (1998) "Japanese Women's Magazines: The Language of Aspiration" in Martinez, D.P. (ed.) *The Worlds of Japanese Popular Culture: Gender, Shifting Boundaries and Global Cultures* (pp. 110–132), Cambridge: Cambridge University Press.

Tanaka, T., & Ishi, M. (2009). *Taigai kankei jiten*. [A Dictionary of International Relations] Tokyo: Yoshikawa Kobunkan.

Ting-Toomey, S. (1991). Intimacy expression in three cultures: France, Japan, and the United States. *International Journal of Intercultural Relations, 15*, 29–46.

Ting-Toomey, S. (2005) The Matrix of Face: An Updated Face-Negotiation Theory. In W.B. Gudykunst (Ed.), *Theorizing About Intercultural Communication* (pp. 71–92). Thousand Oaks, CA: Sage.

Triandis, H. (2002). Individualism-collectivism and personality. *Journal of Personality 69*, 6, 907–924.

Vogel, E. (1991). *Japan's new middle class: The salaryman and his family in a Tokyo suburb.* Berkeley: University of California Press.

Yoon, I. (2009, August 6). *Asia on the Move: International migration and social transformations in Asia.* Presentation given to the 2009 Summer Institute of Waseda University. Retrieved 23 April 2010 from: http://www.wasedagiari.jp/sysimg/imgs/200908_si_ppt_yoon.pdf.

## Concepts and Questions

1. What are some reasons behind the increased number of international marriages in Japan specifically and the world more generally?

2. In the case of Jim and Hanako, why did Jim's decision to handle the family financial matters create a problem?

3. What are some of the reasons people from a group-oriented society may want to avoid open confrontation?

4. Are there any culturally based motivations that would explain Hiro's different behaviors in Japan and in the United States?

5. Explain the concept of *giri*. Is there anything similar in the United States?

6. What are some cultural reasons behind Hiro's concern for what his neighbors might think?

7. Why does the concept of "harmony" (*wa*) play a larger, more important role in Japan than in the United States?

8. Why does social identity seem to be more important in Japan than the United States?

9. Based on findings by Quasha and Tsukada, it appears that social roles are much more defined and rigid in Japan than in the United States. What might be some of the cultural reasons for this?

10. The essay suggests that the Japanese are less willing to discuss their feelings than people from the United States. What are some cultural reasons for this?

# 3 International Cultures: Understanding Diversity

*It is not the language but the speaker that we want to understand.*      **Indian Saying**

*Our distrust is very expensive.*      **Ralph Waldo Emerson**

One fundamental truism regarding human behavior is that your past experiences affect your current actions in both subtle and manifest ways. This maxim is so transparent that we fear people often overlook its impact on personal patterns of social perception and interaction. Think for a moment about some of those situations in which you and some of your friends shared what you believed to be the *same experience*, yet later when you talked about the event you soon discovered there were differences in your perceptions of that experience. We offer a simple example to make our point. If you and your friends were walking through a park and a large dog came bounding up to you, that event could be perceived quite differently by each person depending upon his or her *prior experiences* with dogs. You might have had a pet dog as a child and, therefore, perceived the dog as friendly and bent down to pet it. As a child, however, one of your friends might have been bitten by a dog and, therefore, had a very different perception of the event. He or she might have reacted to the dog by moving away or even running. Although this example may seem naive and rather basic, nevertheless, it focuses your attention on the fundamental idea that the stimuli you received from the environment were the same, yet because everyone has a unique personality and background, each of you experienced a unique set of feelings, sensations, and responses.

When you add the element of culture to the perceptual process, individual histories take on added significance. For, as we have stressed throughout this book, you are not only a creation of your individual experiences, you are also a product of your culture.

As we have already discussed, culture affects your ways of perceiving and acting. Culture has instilled in you the accepted societal behaviors and values that have been passed from generation to generation. Yet, because these behaviors are so much a part of your persona, you might forget that behaviors are culturally engendered and vary across cultures. This is why someone from Japan, for example, might remain silent if disturbed by another's actions, whereas an Israeli or an Italian would more likely vigorously verbalize their displeasure. Whatever the culture, you can better understand your behavior and the reactions of others during an interaction if you realize that what you are hearing and seeing is a reflection of the other's culture. As you might predict, cultural understanding comes more easily when your cultural experiences are similar to those of the people with whom you are interacting. Conversely, when different and diverse backgrounds are brought to a communication encounter, it is often difficult to share internal states and feelings. In this chapter we will focus on these difficulties by examining some of the experiences and perceptual backgrounds found among a sampling of international cultures.

> **You are not only a creation of your individual experiences, you are also a product of your culture.**

We begin with this question: How do you learn to interact with and understand people who come from very different areas of the global village? This answer is not simple, yet it is at the core of this book. The need for such understanding is obvious. If you look around the world at any particular moment, you will find people from diverse cultures in constant interaction with one another. The nightly news makes it abundantly clear that all cultures, including those that are quite different from yours, are linked in the global community. Events that happen in one part of the world can and do influence events all over the world. Whether its people are concerned about the global economy, food, water, energy, global warming, or major differences in sociopolitical philosophies, no culture can remain completely isolated from nor unaffected by the rest of the world.

Two things are crucial if you are to relate effectively to people from diverse international cultures: (1) you must be knowledgeable about the diversity of people from other cultures; and (2) you must respect their diversity. This chapter presents six essays that will assist you with both of these assignments. Through these essays you will explore the rich diversity found in several international cultures. Although they represent only a small portion of the countless cultures found throughout the world, they are somewhat representative and should help you discover how people in other cultures develop their views of the world. To a very great extent a culture's worldview determines how its members perceive themselves, each other, and their place in the universe; it serves as an underlying pattern for interaction within a culture.

# The Spirituality of "Being" Grace, Tao, and Awaken in Intercultural Communication

MARY FONG

Mary Fong opens this chapter with an innovative approach to understanding intercultural communication. In an essay titled "The Evolving Spirit in 'Being' Grace, Tao and Awaken in Intercultural Interactions," it is Fong's contention that while communication researchers have studied intercultural communication from a host of perspectives, "little has been written on the spirituality of intercultural communication." Fong believes that recognizing the dimensions of spirituality can help you extend yourself to others and, of course, influences how you perceive the world. Moreover, like so many other dimensions of personality, spirituality has its roots in culture.

Fong begins with a discussion of two spiritual concepts and their related key components to assist you in developing a wider, deeper, and richer understanding of your intercultural counterparts. The first perspective is grace. Found in Christianity, grace is considered a significant attribute of God that promotes kindness without regard to worth or merit of the individual to whom it is directed. In her explanation, Fong traces the historical roots of grace as found in the teachings of Jesus. Ideally, one receives grace by incorporating it into everyday life and extending the act of grace to others in daily interactions.

The second perspective is the notion of the Tao, which originated in China during the fourth and third centuries B.C.E. Taoists pursued individual perfection, deeper understanding of the life-force workings of nature, and a union with the cosmic principle they believed existed in all entities. To this end Taoists were opposed to man-made institutions, elaborate ceremonies, social conventions, and rules of behavior they believed formed a cover for hypocrisy and self-seeking, scheming, reaching for power, enslavement of peasants, and wasteful, destructive wars.

Fong traces the development of Taoist teachings through the writings of Chuang-tzu and Lao-Tzu. Taoist philosophy was derived through a profound contemplation of nature and the variety of human experiences and conditions. Taoism believes that the only freedom worth pursuing and preserving is perfect harmony with the power or principle that is embodied in the heart of all that is, which is the Tao, or the Way. From this point of view, "all things are in process and intertwined and interdependent."

Continuing her dialogue, Fong introduces you to the concepts of yin and yang forces, which are the dynamic, dualistic interaction that creates all of reality. She also discusses the principle of Te, which is the power, effect, or vital force of the Tao. Te is seen as an inner quality of the individual that is effective in influencing people and events without conscious effort. After she outlines the basic characteristics of grace and the Tao, Fong presents a comparison of the two perspectives, revealing some of their major differences. For example, Christians have a personal relationship with their God. On the other hand, Chuang-tzu held that people have no closer relationship to the ultimate principle of the universe than an ant or a rock. Thus, from the Taoist perspective, all things are of equal worth. She continues by pointing out how the Christian and Taoist approaches lead to differences in spiritual worldviews that can influence intercultural communication. These differences then lead Fong into a discussion of the practice of spiritual ways in which she outlines some ideas from both Taoism and Christianity and how they are put into practice.

> How the Christian and Taoist approaches lead to differences in spiritual worldviews can influence intercultural communication.

*Before she concludes her essay, Fong offers an interesting commentary on what she calls "our human and spiritual existence in the Universe." Specifically, she develops the idea that "everything is energy and everyone reincarnates many lives." Fong ends her essay with an illustration of intercultural communication differences by presenting two scenarios where varied spiritual worldviews led to differences in the interpretation of events. Fong relates how the situations developed and how they might be handled from a perspective of grace and from a perspective of Tao.*

## THE EVOLVING SPIRIT OF "BEING" GRACE, TAO, AND AWAKEN IN INTERCULTURAL INTERACTIONS

Darwin has proposed a perspective on the biological evolution of human beings. Science and Technology have evolved over the centuries from the spark of two sticks rubbed together to flickering candles to Thomas Edison's electric light bulb to energy-saving luminescent lighting. Virtually every physical form has evolved from primitive times to old-fashioned days to modern times to contemporary trends and into the future.

Can we also observe and sense the evolution of the formless within our lives? Appreciating the beauty of a flower's soft delicate petals, the sparkling rainbow prism of a crystal, or a bird that takes flight so effortlessly as it soars—all provide moments of sensing liberation and tranquility that radiates within our inner spiritual being. Symbolic are the jewel in the lotus flower that is central in Buddhism and the white dove representing the Holy Spirit in Christianity. Tolle (2005), a spiritual teacher, says that Buddha, Jesus, and others were messengers and humanity's early flowers who were precursors, rare and precious beings. He believes that the seeds of spirituality were planted in "preparing the ground for a more profound shift in planetary consciousness that is destined to take place in the human species." (p. 5). Tolle also believes there is a spiritual awakening that we are beginning to witness now, as he sets forth in his book, *A New Earth*.

Communication researchers have studied various aspects of intercultural communication such as adaptation (Adler, 1975; Furnham, 1987; Furnham and Bochner, 1982; Hammer, Gudykunst, and Wiseman, 1978; Kim, 1988), intercultural communication competence (Bennett, 1986; Chen, 1989; Gudykunst & Hammer, 1987), relationship development (Chen, 1995; Nakanishi, 1987; Ogawa, 1979; Casmir & Asuncion-Lande, 1989), differences across cultures in terms of values (Kluckhohn & Strodbeck, 1961), language (Hoijer, 1994), nonverbal communication (Andersen, 1994; Ricard, 1993), conflict management (Ting-Toomey, 1988), and so forth. Little attention has been given to the spirituality of intercultural communication.

When intercultural differences and conflicts arise because of culturally diverse ways of communicating, intercultural interactants may or may not always have knowledge of the differing meanings and intent behind the cultural acts. I believe that our practice of spirituality can be a way to extend ourselves to one another to facilitate understanding and strengthen intercultural relationships. With this in mind, I believe our spiritual practices can help promote humanistic insights and adaptations that can transcend our cultural differences because we are simply human beings who share common emotions, desires, hopes, and dreams.

In this essay, I introduce two spiritual perspectives and selected key concepts that may be edifying to people who encounter differences and conflicts in their intercultural communications. I will begin by discussing the concept of grace, as commonly known in the Christian faith. Next, I will introduce *Tao* (pronounced as Dao), a central precept in the Eastern spirituality of Taoism. In understanding some aspects of Taoism, some discussion of *yin* and *yang, te*, and *wu wei* will be unraveled. Thereafter, the fruits of the spirit in Christianity are explained. Finally, I contextualize people and their spiritual faiths within the Universe.

## TWO SPIRITUAL WAYS OF "BEING"
### Grace

Grace is a significant attribute of God in the Christian faith. God in one respect is described in the Bible as merciful, gracious, long-suffering, and abounding in goodness and truth (New International Version, Exodus 34:6). The term *grace* is defined as "favor or kindness shown without regard to the worth or merit of the one who receives it and in spite of what that person deserves" (Youngblood, 1995, p. 522). Terms such as mercy, love, compassion, and patience are almost always related to the concept of grace. In the Christian faith, the grace of God is manifested in Jesus Christ's teachings, His act of salvation for human beings, the gift of the Holy Spirit, and spiritual blessings (Youngblood, 1995).

The Christian faith believes that Jesus Christ is the incarnation of God into human form come to earth to spread truth and love to people; and to help them to realize the fallible aspects of their lives, to have them turn away from weak living, and to receive God's grace. Jesus Christ's act of salvation for human beings involved His persecution and dying on the cross to save humankind by laying down His life, an ultimate act of love, in order to triumph over Satan. Jesus Christ died on the cross and did not give into temptation and hatred toward His persecutors, but rather asked for His Heavenly Father to forgive His persecutors for their wrongful acts. Jesus Christ died, but rose from the dead by revealing His Holy Spirit to witnesses. Rather than succumbing to the power of Satan, Jesus through his act of salvation, showed God's love and power over Satan. Days prior to Jesus' death, he said,

> *Grace is a significant attribute of God in the Christian faith.*

… I will ask the Father, and he will give you another Counselor to be with you forever—the Spirit of truth. The world cannot accept him (heavenly God), because it neither sees him nor knows him. But you know him, for he lives with you and will be in you. I will not leave you as orphans; I will come to you. Before long, the world will not see me anymore, but you will see me. Because I live, you also will live. On that day you will realize that I am in my Father, and you are in me, and I am in you (NIV, John 14:16-20, p. 1625) … All this I have spoken while still with you. But the Counselor, the Holy Spirit, whom the Father will send in my name, will teach you all things and will remind you of everything I have said to you. Peace I leave with you; my peace I give you. I do not give to you as the world gives. Do not let your hearts be troubled and do not be afraid (NIV, John 14:25-27, p. 1626).

When a person receives God's grace, he or she comes to experience and acknowledge this phenomenon of grace in his or her everyday life. There is the act of giving and receiving grace to one another. Do you recall a time when someone did a kind or generous act toward you, and you felt you did nothing to deserve it? For instance, when I was researching for this essay, I spent hours in a Christian bookstore reading and typing notes from books on this topic. As I was reading, I kept thinking that I want to experience the sense of God's grace so that I would have a better grasp of this concept in my life. The sun had just set and I packed my belongings.

As I approached my car in the parking lot, I saw a dime on the ground next to the driver's door. I smiled and happily picked up the coin, tucking it in my jeans pocket, knowing that for more than 20 years, I have repeatedly experienced this path of God's grace in my life. Virtually every time I have come across a coin on the floor, I am typically thinking about something important at the time. I get this sense of validation of my thoughts and also that I am moving in the right direction. I was joyful about receiving the coin because I felt my efforts working on this essay and wanting to sense this concept of grace were being validated.

In my car, I buckled up, turned the ignition key, and my entire dashboard lit up, flickered, and died along with my motor, which refused to turn over. I was shocked and tried the ignition key again. No luck, my car battery was dead. I was stuck, some twenty-five miles from home. "Oh, no, what should I do?" I thought to myself. I was not a "Triple A" member.

I got out of the car, walked back to the bookstore, and asked several women and men if they had jumper cables. Finally, a man had a set, and I followed him to his SUV, which was parked next to mine. We both were hoping that it was just my car battery, since my relatively new car was just over two years old. He connected the jumper cables to both of our car batteries. I turned my ignition key, and my car started! I was so pleased and relieved that I could drive home. I thanked the man and said, "You're a life saver!" He smiled and said, "Drive safely."

As I was driving on the freeway, I realized that I just had experienced God's grace. A kind stranger gave me grace through giving of his time, efforts, and sharing his jumper cables to help start my car when I did nothing to deserve or earn his assistance. He received nothing from me in return, and I was someone who took time away from his family who was visiting the Christian bookstore. He did it cheerfully and graciously.

With this stranger, I had to take a leap of faith to trust his character and that he would help my car get started. With a similar thought, people take a leap of faith to trust and to receive grace from a total stranger, that is, a heavenly God, Jesus Christ's teachings and His act of salvation for human beings to bring goodness in their lives. This concept of receiving grace from God extends to the act of people giving grace to others in our everyday communications, and for the purposes of this essay, in our intercultural interactions. This leads us to the Taoist spiritual perspective, discussing the *tao*.

## Tao

Taoism flourished in China in the period identified as the Warring States during the fourth and third centuries B.C. (401-221 B.C.). During this era, there was much political and social unrest and great intellectual developments. Confucians were primarily concerned with creating an acceptable political and social system. The Taoists pursued individual perfection, a deeper understanding into the life force and workings of nature, and union with the cosmic principle that they believed exists in all entities (Smith, 1980).

The Taoists were against artificialities of man-made institutions, elaborate ceremonial and moral social conventions, detailed rules of behavior that formed a cover for hypocrisy and self-seeking, scheming, positioning for power, enslavement of peasantry, and wasteful destructive wars. Instead, the Taoists believed that people ought to learn to conform to spontaneous and natural processes of natural phenomena such as birth, growth, decay, and death. Freedom, peace, and happiness for all human beings can only be attained by conformity to the natural cosmic laws, and not man-made laws (Smith, 1980).

The Taoist teachings of Chuang-tzu and the famous Chinese anthology classic attributed to Lao-Tzu

*Tao seeks to avoid extremes, and maintain viewpoints that are free of prejudicial tendencies.*

called the *Tao-Te-Ching* are often referred to in understanding Taoism. Chuang-tzu, a famous Taoist philosopher, profoundly contemplated nature and the variety of human experience and conditions. The Taoists expounded on two fundamental precepts: the Way (Tao) and its efficacy (Te). Chuang-tzu's Taoist teachings were predicated on the fundamental principle that a person's life and one's spiritual integrity are to be most valued. Further, the only freedom worth pursuing and preserving is the perfect harmony with the power or principle which is embodied in the heart of all that is, which is the *tao* (Smith, 1980).

Ni (1997) describes the Tao as integral truth, a truth that does not emphasize any point of view and that is neutral, like zero. Tao seeks to avoid extremes, and maintain viewpoints that are free of prejudicial tendencies. This zero doctrine means returning to stillness, purity, nothing, or zero in order to be at a point of clarity. If a person holds a doctrine, one does not have a mind that is open and flexible because one is fixed on that doctrine.

Based on an analysis of some of the passages in *Tao Te Ching*, the *tao* is creative, giving rise to a world of rich diversity and also maintaining its comprehensive harmony (Cheng, 2004). "The natural constant Way (Tao) gives birth to beings but does not possess them, it produces evolution but does not rule it. All beings are born depending on it, yet none know to thank it, all die because of it, yet none can resent it" (Clearly, 1991, p. 4). The constancy of *tao*, for example is "not enriched by storage and accumulation, nor is it impoverished by disbursement and enjoyment" (Clearly, 1991, p. 4). This constant *tao*, when discussed, is only a reference, and can only be internally experienced and focused on in indirect ways that involve subtle observation and prudent focus of the mind, not explicitly and easily expressible in language. … The famous Taoist philosopher, Lao-Tzu … describes the constant *tao* as non-spoken, something independent of any finite or definite object or event, and beyond our phenomenal world of things. Tao as ultimate truth cannot be defined because language has its limitations and truth is defined by one's viewpoint (Ni, 1997). Language, however, can be used to express the human experience and the perception of the *tao* (Cheng, 2004).

Lao-Tzu stated, "One needs a mind of emptiness in order to see the subtleties of the [*tao*]; one needs a mind of distinctions to see the boundaries of the [*tao*]." (Cheng, 2004, p. 146). To "be with the Tao," or to be on the wavelength of the natural workings of the cosmic universe, involves a person moving with the rhythm of the oneness and the many interacting components as smoothly as water flowing down a stream (Combs, 2004). Everything is in a state of constant change and transition. All things are in process and are intertwined and interdependent. The true Way consists of right conduct, to strive to act as heaven had ordained for humankind.

*Yin and Yang.* Two opposite modalities, *yin* and *yang*, represent the dynamic, dualistic interaction that creates all of reality. These two equal and opposite forces work together in a harmonious perpetual transformation that occurs within everything. The *yin* force has characteristics such as passive, female, receptive, night, cold, soft, wet, winter, shadow, and negative. The *yang* force has characteristics such as active, male, creative, day, heat, hard, dry, summer, sun, and positive. For the Taoist, yin and yang are the opposite, but equal complementary forces that are independent of any concept of morality. These forces sustain an evolving process in everything in the universe where completion and unity exist in the Tao (Smith, 1980; Wing, 1979). In the center of the white and black fields of the Yin and Yang are dots that represent the seeds of change as polar reversals (Wing, 1979) such as [that] the sun reaches its peak at noon (yang); thereafter, the sun slowly begins to wane and the day increasingly becomes darker as the sun sets (yin) and becomes night, evolving slowly to the break of the day. There are myriad differences as the Tao fosters life: it harmonizes dark and light, regulates the four seasons, and tunes the forces of nature (Clearly, 1991).

> *Two opposite modalities,* yin *and* yang, *represent the dynamic, dualistic interaction that creates all of reality.*

*Te.* The power, effect, or vital force of the Tao is *te*. It is also described to be the form, character of an entity and its potentiality to become. *Te* is an inner quality of character of a person that is powerfully effective in influencing people and shaping events without conscious effort. The Taoists believe that *te* is the spontaneous unfolding of the *tao* of their own nature and a person can exercise one's *te* by being his true self. A person who has kingly *te* is one who is able to see light in total darkness, can penetrate to the spiritual essence of entities, and takes care of the needs of all who seek his help (Smith, 1980).

*Wu Wei.* The concept of *wu wei* refers to the avoidance of action or nonaction that is hostile or aggressive in nature. To treat a person in an inferior way is the essence of aggression. Aggressive action may be direct or indirect in nature. Verbal insults, lying, hatred, harmful actions with malicious intent, and violence are direct aggressive action. Indirect aggressive action may come in the form of ignoring, sneers, excluding others intentionally, passive-aggressive behaviors, and so on. By practicing *wu wei*, a person avoids starting new vicious cycles of indirect aggressive behaviors and direct aggressive behaviors (e.g. lying, hatred, and violence) and thus interrupts the cycles. Instead, a person returns to the roots of one's nature, that is, being natural and spontaneous (Welch, 1966). Moreover, doing nonaction that is not aggressive is simply letting the nature of Tao take its own course and there is no subject to claim action, whether effortless or effortful (Cheng, 2004).

# CHRISTIANITY AND TAOSIM
## Some Differences

The Christian and Taoist approaches have areas of marked contrast. Followers of the Christian faith believe in a personal, creative, and redemptive God. In contrast, Taoist followers believe there is no God, but that Tao is represented as being devoid of action, thought, feeling, and desire. It is nonpurposive (Smith, 1980).

Christians have a personal relationship with God. Christians see themselves as children of God and through their faith they receive the promise of the Holy Spirit (NIV, Galatians 4:7). In Taoism, however, Chuang-tzu believed that people hold no closer relation to the ultimate principle of the universe than does a lowly insect, such as the ant or an inanimate object. From the standpoint of Tao, all things are of equal worth. To attain human form is a source of joy. However, a person's life on earth is only a passing moment in an eternal process of transformation through reincarnation in which there are myriad forms equally good (Smith, 1980).

In Christianity, there is a realization that there are conflicting powers of good and evil, truth and lies, spiritual light and darkness that are opposed to one another with the intent to destroy the other (Smith, 1980). Believers of Christ believe that in all things, both good and bad, God works for the good of those who love Him (NIV, Romans 8:28). In Taoism, *yin* and *yang* are not conceived as good or bad. Rather, *yin* and *yang* are seen as two opposing and equally complementary forces, which work together in harmony, and are in constant transformation within the Tao. In the next section, we delve deeper into practicing spiritual ways.

## PRACTICING SPIRITUAL WAYS

Although both spiritual approaches have differing perspectives and ways, they have the commonality of pursuing the truth, freedom from unhealthy binds, development of one's spirituality and having the right conduct. All of these commonalities bring positive energy of attitude, intent, values, and the striving for goodness that can transcend differences and conflicts that might arise in intercultural interactions where differing patterns of communication exist. I will briefly present some ideas and spiritual teachings in both Taoism and Christianity related to developing people's spirituality and what is considered healthy conduct in communicating with people.

## Tao

The original meaning of the Chinese character 道, *tao*, is a road, a path, a way. Extending the concept of *tao*, it came to mean the Way in which a person acts, the method one uses, the principle that directs what a person does in relationships and situations. This Way is of the Heaven or Nature in which people handle themselves with right conduct to bring peace, happiness, and welfare to themselves and to others (Smith, 1980).

Mo Tzu's school of Ancient Taoism taught that all people return to the faith of impartial Heaven by following the Heavenly Way. This Heavenly Way is a good spiritual life, listening to one's own spiritual wisdom or internal energy awareness or conscience. Mo Tzu emphasized that one should treat everyone fairly in every circumstance and avoid favoritism and biases (Ni, 1997).

Chuang-tzu taught that wise people seek harmony in relationships. In order to accomplish this, one needs to make a conscious and persistent effort to pursue the Tao or Way. Following the sages of olden times in their pursuit of the Tao in their lives, they practiced four virtues: love, righteousness, propriety, and wisdom. Chuang-tzu taught that goodness is not something external from oneself that one must pursue to attain. In the lives of humans, just as in the natural world, there are no absolute norms of virtue, justice or happiness that function at all times and in all situations. Chuang-tzu also taught that people can attune themselves to the rhythm of life. People ought to relinquish their anxieties, fretfulness, and conscious striving for power, glory, wealth or fame. Chuang-tzu believed that there is an eternal principle that is contained within and beyond all that exists (Smith, 1980).

The book *Wen-Tzu: Understanding the Mysteries* is filled with Lao-Tzu's teachings. He said,

> Virtue is in what you give, not in what you get. Therefore when sages want to be valued by others, first they value others, when they want to be respected by others, first they respect others. When they want to overcome others, first they overcome themselves, when they want to humble others, first they humble themselves. So they are both noble and lowly, using the Way to adjust and control this. (Clearly, 1991, p. 59)

Lao-Tzu said: "Great people are peaceful and have no longings, they are calm and have no worries" (Clearly, 1991 p. 4). "... sages cultivate the basis within and do not adorn themselves outwardly with superficialities. They activate their vital spirit and lay to rest their learned opinions. Therefore, they are open and uncontrived, yet there is nothing they do not do, they have no rule, yet there is no unruliness" (Clearly, 1991, p. 5).

Lao-Tzu said, "Those who serve life adapt to changes as they act. Changes arise from the times, those who know the times do not behave in fixed ways. Therefore, I say, "Ways can be guides, but not fixed paths, names can be designated, but not fixed labels" (Clearly, 1991, p. 8). Sages do "what is appropriate without scheming, they are trusted without speaking. They succeed without thinking about it, achieve without contriving to do so." (Clearly, 1991, p. 9). They just "be."

Lao-Tzu also spoke of the Way as "empty and unreified, even and easy, clear and calm, flexible and yielding, unadulterated and pure, plain and simple. These are concrete images of the Way." (Clearly, 1991, p. 5.) Moreover, a person who achieves the state of emptiness means there is no burden within. Evenness refers to the state of a person's mind as unrestrained. When desires do not burden a person, this is the consummation of emptiness. When a person has no likes or dislikes, this is the consummation of evenness. When a person is unified and unchanging, this is the consummation of calmness. When a person is not mixed up in things, this is the consummation of purity. When a person neither grieves nor delights, this is the consummation of virtue (Clearly, 1991). Real people embody the *tao* through "open emptiness, even easiness, clear cleanness, flexible yielding, unadulterated purity, and plain simplicity, not getting mixed up in things" (Clearly, 1991, p. 7).

Lao-Tzu and the Classic Taoists move in a state of emptiness, meander in the great nothingness. They go beyond convention and are not constrained or bound by society. Lao-Tzu further said, "When people are caught up in social customs, they are inevitably bound physically and drained mentally, therefore they cannot avoid being burdened. Those who allow themselves to be tied down are always those whose lives are directed from outside" (Clearly, 1991, pp. 24–25).

"Clear serenity is the consummation of virtue. Flexible yielding is the function of the Way. Empty calm is the ancestor of all beings. When these three are put into practice, you enter into formlessness. Formlessness is a term for oneness, oneness means mindlessly merging with the world" (Clearly, 1991, p. 11) … "Spiritual light is attainment of the inward. When people attain the inward, their internal organs are calm, their thoughts are even, their eyes and ears are clear, and their sinews and bones are strong. They are masterful but not contentious, firm and strong yet never exhausted. They are not too excessive in anything, nor are they inadequate in anything" (Clearly, 1991, p. 12).

Lao-Tzu said, "When the disposition is harmonious, one sacrifices oneself to serve others" (Clearly, 1991, p. 60). Moreover, Lao-Tzu said, "Virtue is in what you give, not in what you get. Therefore, when sages want to be valued by others, first they value others, when they want to be respected by others, first they respect others. When they want to overcome others, first they overcome themselves, when they want to humble others, first they humble themselves. So they are both noble and lowly, using the Way to adjust and control this" (Clearly, 1991, p. 59).

Taoist followers are encouraged to practice meditation, yoga, and fasting in order to purify the mind and body. The purpose of these practices is to help the follower develop calmness, stillness, and emptiness within as a way to relinquish desires, constraints, and burdens of one's life in order to return to one's true self and achieve clarity.

## Fruit of the Spirit

In the Christian faith, believers are taught to develop and strive for qualities known as the fruit of the spirit for the purpose of developing one's spiritual character as well as learning how we ought to conduct ourselves and treat others. "Let your conversation be always full of grace …," said Apostle Paul (NIV, Colossians 4:6, p. 1817). The Christian faith teaches that people ought to manifest the fruit of the Spirit in giving grace to others in our conversations and behavior. The "fruit of the Spirit is love, joy, peace, patience, kindness, goodness, faithfulness, gentleness and self-control" (NIV, Galatians 5:22, p. 1787). "Joy is love enjoying, peace (or longsuffering) is love waiting … faithfulness is love keeping its word…." (Stanley, 1996, p. 377).

As defined in the Bible,

> Love is patient, love is kind. It does not envy, it does not boast, it is not proud. It is not rude, it is not self-seeking, it is not easily angered, and it keeps no record of wrongs. Love does not delight in evil but rejoices with the truth. It always protects, always trusts, always hopes, always perseveres. Love never fails. (NIV, 1 Corinthians 13:1-8, p. 1752).

Joy is referred to as a positive attitude or pleasant emotion or a feeling of delight. There are many levels of joy that are referred to in the Bible, including gladness, contentment, and cheerfulness. The highest joy is one that is holy and pure. This kind of joy rises above circumstances and focuses on the very character of God. For instance, the psalmist rejoices over God's righteousness (NIV, Psalm, 71:14-16), salvation (NIV, Psalm, 21:1; 71:23), mercy (NIV, Psalms, 31:7), creation (NIV, Psalms, 148:5), word (NIV, Psalm, 199:14, 162), and faithfulness (NIV, Psalm, 33:1-6). Christians rejoice because of God's characteristics and His acts (Youngblood, 1995). This joy is required of the righteous person (NIV, Psalm 150; NIV, Philippians 4:4) that is produced by the Spirit of God (NIV, Galatians 5:22). This kind of joy is possible even in the midst of sorrow (NIV, 1 Corinthians 12:26; 2 Corinthians 6:10; 7:4), looking to our sovereign God, who works out all good and bad things for our ultimate good to achieve the character of Christ (NIV, Romans 8:28-30).

Peace, patience, and kindness are also fruit of the Spirit. Jesus Christ spoke of peace involving inner tranquility, hope, trust, faith, and quietness in the mind and soul of a person through a relationship with God. Peace sometimes had a physical meaning, suggesting security (NIV, Psalm 4:8), contentment (NIV, Isaiah 26:3), prosperity (NIV, Psalm 122:6–7) and the absence of war (NIV, 1Samuel 7:14). Patience is defined as a Christlike quality that a person is encouraged to have by having "forbearance under suffering and endurance in the face of adversity" (Youngblood, 1995, p. 950). In the New Testament of the Bible, the Greek word translated as "grace" best represents the idea of God's kindness or loving kindness. That is, God's graciousness toward believers, in turn, encourages people to treat all with kindness or grace (NIV, Luke 6:35).

The final fruits are goodness, gentleness, and self-control. Goodness has the quality of praiseworthy character, of moral excellence. God's goodness consists of righteousness, holiness, justice, kindness, grace, mercy, and love (NIV, Exodus 33:19; NIV, Romans 2:4). Faithfulness refers to dependability, loyalty, and stability, particularly as it describes God in His relationship to human believers. And it is expected of Christians to develop this quality in their lives and how they conduct themselves. Gentleness is defined in *Nelson's New Illustrated Bible Dictionary*

(Youngblood, 1995) as "kindness, consideration, a spirit of fairness, and compassion" (p. 488). Apostle Paul declared that Christians should have a spirit of gentleness toward all people (NIV, Philippians 4:5; 2 Corinthians 10:1). Self-control involves the control of one's actions and emotions by human will, which is governed by the Holy Spirit within oneself.

There are other spiritual qualities and proper conduct that Christians are encouraged to develop. In the Bible, the Apostle Paul spoke of clothing,

> … clothing yourselves with compassion, kindness, humility, gentleness and patience. Bear with each other and forgive whatever grievances you may have against one another. Forgive as the Lord forgave you. And over all these virtues put on love, which binds the all together in perfect unity. Let the peace of Christ rule in your hearts, since as members of one body you were called to peace. (NIV, Colossians 3:12-15, p. 1816)

Humility and compassion are two more important spiritual qualities that are encouraged in the Bible that are worthy of discussion. Humility is a "freedom from arrogance that grows out of the recognition that all we have and are comes from God … True humility does not produce pride but gratitude" (Youngblood, 1995, p. 586). We have infinite worth and dignity because of our relationship with God (1 Corinthians 4:6-7; 1 Peter 1:18-19).

Nouwen, McNeill, and Morrison (1982) discuss the compassion act of "self-emptying for others," which involves the process of paying

> … attention to others with the desire to make them the center and to make their interests our own…. When someone listens to us with real concentration and expresses sincere care for our struggles and our pains, we feel that something very deep is happening to us. Slowly, fears melt away, tensions dissolve, anxieties retreat, and we discover that we carry within us something we can trust and offer as a gift to others. The simple experience of being valuable and important to someone else has a tremendous re-creative power. (p. 81)

As Nouwen, McNeill, and Morrison (1982) have said, compassion is not just a feeling, it is an act of doing something for another who is in need. The Bible teaches doing good to all (NIV, Galatians 6:10), love for both your neighbors and enemies (NIV, Matthew 5:43), showing respect to everyone (NIV, 1 Peter 2:17), brotherly kindness (NIV, 2 Peter 1:5-7), considerate .... impartial and sincere (NIV, James 3:17).

Fisher (2005) states, "Jesus plants a seed in our hearts for a desire to really know the Holy Spirit. What we do with this challenge is totally up to us" (p. 64). Moreover, Fisher (2005), a theologian, explains if we are open to receiving His messages of ideas and learning from the Holy Spirit, it would require being a good listener.

The Apostle Paul said, "But now you must rid yourselves of all such things as these: anger, rage, malice, slander, and filthy language from your lips. Do not lie to each other, since you have taken off your old self with its practices and have put on the new self, which is being renewed in knowledge in the image of its Creator" (Colossians 3: 8-10, p. 1816). Elsewhere in the Bible, the Apostle Paul said, "... whatever is true, whatever is noble, whatever is right, whatever is pure, whatever is lovely, whatever is admirable—if anything is excellent or praiseworthy—think about such things. Whatever you have learned or received or heard from me, or seen in me—put it into practice. And the God of peace will be with you" (Philippians 4: 8-9, p. 1809).

In developing their spirituality and learning proper conduct, Christian believers learn by attending church, fellowship groups, prayers to God, reading the Bible, and from their experiences and interactions with people. All of these practices are done for the purpose of learning more about God's character, spiritual wisdom, and development of one's spirituality and Godly conduct towards people.

## Some Similarities between Christianity and Taoism

Although the Christian faith and Taoism differ in their respective ways, I will only mention some similarities between them. Both spiritual approaches believe that their followers ought to have liberation. Chuang-tzu taught the need to be free and unfettered. He taught that the only freedom worth obtaining is the freedom that is aligned in perfect harmony with the power or principle which lies at the center of all, which he refers to as the Tao (Smith, 1980). For Christians, liberation comes through the act of praying to and receiving Jesus Christ as their Savior and God who saved them from the bondage of evil and sin. Jesus said, "If you hold to my teaching, you are really my disciples. Then you will know the truth, and the truth will set you free (NIV, John 8:32, p. 1613).

Another commonality that both spiritual approaches have is the belief that God and Tao have a constant or unchanging quality about them. Both are believed to have supreme or absolute goodness inherent, and this goodness can be found in believers who follow and practice the Tao (Cheng, 2004) or follow Jesus Christ's teachings, the Holy Spirit within believers, and/or God. Both spiritual approaches encourage people to develop their spiritual qualities of peace, kindness, harmony, compassion, patience, love, humility; practice moral conduct; and so on. In the next section let's take a look at two intercultural interactions and see how both spiritual approaches are displayed.

> *Both spiritual approaches believe that their followers ought to have liberation.*

## YOU AND THE UNIVERSE

To better understand our spiritual "being" in light of these concepts from Christianity and Taoism, it is necessary to connect these aspects of "being" to their places in the Universe. In appreciating our human and spiritual existence in the Universe, two significant aspects warrant our consideration in order to contextualize our "being": (1) Everything is energy. (2) Everyone reincarnates many lives. The field of physics supports the scientific fact that every animate and inanimate entity in the Universe is all energy (Weiss, 2000). All entities consist of atoms, which are the basic units of matter. Atoms contain smaller elements known as neutrons, protons, and a nucleus. Science has also discovered that there are even smaller particles called quarks, gluons and neutrinos. However, because they are too tiny, move at tremendous speeds, and tend to decay rapidly there is no current technology that permits direct observations of these smaller particles. Scientists have only observed the tracks of these tiny bits as they zip or vibrate at an extremely high velocity, which creates an illusion that matter is solid (Capra, 1977). The invisible space we see all round us, along with all animate and inanimate entities, are all parts of the Universe that make up this vast energy field. Wei (1996) has explained the philosophy of the Universe in terms of an interactive energy field:

> The creation of matter from energy is the desire of the Universe to manifest itself—to manifest itself in all its myriad forms. And we? We are the Universe experiencing itself. We, and all else that has been manifested from the energy field, are how the Universe experiences itself.... Once we perceive that our Universe is alive, a living, pulsating organism that has awareness and intelligence, vast intelligence, we come to know that the Universe and everything in it reacts to stimulation—our stimulation (p. 36–37).

He further explains that human thoughts, feelings, and actions stimulate and influence the energy field of the Universe. Physics has also discovered the scientific fact that energy cannot be destroyed. If energy cannot be destroyed, and living and concrete entities are all energy, then as human beings we do die, but our soul or spirit continues to live. Under these premises, we are thus immortal. Although contemporary Christian churches teach the fundamental belief that adherents live one earthly life and will die and continue to live in eternity in heaven, researchers (Cerminara, 1978; Dunlap, 2007) argue that there is evidence that Jesus Christ indirectly spoke of the existence of reincarnation in the Bible. Reincarnation refers to the rebirth of the soul and living many lives. The researchers explain that Christ has taught many things to his disciples that He did not teach to the multitudes. The original records of Jesus' teachings have gone through many interpretations of what was said and translations into other languages through the centuries. There are clues within the Bible that suggest that reincarnation exists. One example was when Jesus told his disciples that John the Baptist was Elijah. Jesus said, "But I tell you, Elijah has already come, and they did not recognize him, but have done to him everything they wished. In the same way the Son of Man is going to suffer at their hands" (NIV Matthew 17:12). The disciples understood that he was talking to them about John the Baptist (NIV, Matthew 17:13).

Historically, reincarnation was written about in the New Testament until the time of Constantine, when the Romans censored it; Buddhists and Hindus have accumulated past life cases for thousands of years; and it was standard teaching until the early 19th century in some sects of Jewish mysticism (Weiss, 2004). Socrates (480 or 469 B.C.) and his protégé, Plato (427 B.C.–347 B.C.) were proponents of reincarnation (Dunlap, 2007). Over the past three decades, mounting empirical clinical research on thousands of cases of patients who had past life sessions or regressive hypnosis that have been validated (Weiss, 2004). "There is considerable historical and clinical evidence that reincarnation is a reality," said Weiss, (2000, p. 2), a medical doctor and chair of the department of psychiatry at Mount Sinai Medical Center in Miami Beach, Florida, who has published 40 scientific papers and book chapters and achieved international recognition in psychopharmacology and brain chemistry. Over the past 20 years, Weiss claims to have regressed more than 2,000 patients to past-life memories. Newton (2009), another previous-life investigator, explained that once his patients were regressed into their soul state they displayed a significant consistency in responding to questions about the spirit world. He further said that his patients used the same words and graphic descriptions when discussing their lives as souls. Stevenson, who was a psychiatrist and former director of the Department of Psychiatry and the Division of Personality Studies at the University of Virginia, conducted over 40 years of ethnographic research on reincarnation and past life work (Dunlap, 2007). His evidence for reincarnation is based on past life memory recall of 2,000 case studies of children who between the ages of two and five years of age were less susceptible to giving fraudulent accounts, and their memories of their previous life are considered "fresh." Each case study involved an interview; detailed records were transcribed, and to verify the details, medical or autopsy records were used to cross-check data (Stevenson, 1974, 1997, 2003). Stevenson's research found a significant degree of accuracy, about 90 percent, in the data (Albrecht, 1982). Even critics and skeptics of reincarnation, along with academic peers, have stated that Stevenson's extensive research on past lives is well-documented and offers strong evidence for the existence of reincarnation (Haraldsson, 1995; Keil, 1996, Mills, 2000; Tucker, 2005).

If we are able to accept these two premises: (1) everything is energy and (2) everyone reincarnates through many lifetimes, we have, consequently, taken a significant conscious shift in how we view ourselves and our "being" in this universe.

## "Being" and Awaken in Intercultural Interactions

Extending our understanding of our "being" in this Universe, Tolle (2005) writes about experiencing the presence, being one with what you are doing in the now, the stillness and the deeper self of consciousness in the act of "awakening." Being engaged in an awakening also involves being aware in the now moment as an observer of one's stream of thoughts, memories, behaviors, others' behaviors and conditions. Being aware in the present enables the person to observe if one's ego intrudes in one's own thinking and behavior and is able to recognize it in others. Having awareness enables the person to diminish one's egoic tendency in thinking and behaving. Tolle (2005) writes extensively about recognizing egoic thinking and behavior that separate people and hurt self and others.

> Whatever behavior the ego manifests, the hidden motivating force is always the same: the need to stand out, be special, be in control; the need for power, for attention, for more. And, of course, the need to feel a sense of separation, that is to say, the need for opposition, enemies. (p. 79–80)

Moreover, he writes that the egoic layers have covered up the sense of the profound joy of connectedness with the higher consciousness, Being, the Source, God. Tolle (2005), a spiritual teacher, makes clear that a person's ego is not who that person is; rather, differing degrees of egoic layers cover that person's true essence, which are the qualities of God in which everyone originates and consist of within their inner being. Each of us must be awake, aware, conscious of all that is, and spiritually evolve by diminishing the egoic tendencies, to allow our true essence to radiate in all that we do. Our awareness, our consciousness, our awakening enables us to diminish our egoic tendencies because both entities cannot exist simultaneously. Being involved in this awakening entails your true essence and your inner purpose of life where your inner being and God merge, and in which you bring this power forward into this world. Tolle (2008) participating on a webcast show with Oprah Winfrey, said,

> You are allowing the spirit of God to flow through you and to become. You're connecting yourself to the bigger source—creativity, when you let that source come within you. A new way of looking at something. The spirit of God you allow to guide you along your path. The consciousness is rising, there's a shift occurring. We are transforming into a new species—a conscious species that is waking up. Let God flow through us.

Tolle (2005, 2008) states that we humans are evolving an awareness or consciousness of who we are in our origination and in our purpose in life. This involves knowing that our consciousness is connected to a higher consciousness or God in which all people share. Drawing on empirical research on reincarnation, Weiss (2004) articulates further about this consciousness:

> I call it another dimension, a higher level of consciousness or higher state of consciousness. The soul certainly exists outside of the physical body, and it makes connections not only to the other lifetimes of the person it just departed but to all other souls. We die physically, but this part of us is indestructible and immortal. The soul is timeless (p. 11).

Weiss (2004) further asserts, "I think that at the highest level all souls are connected. It is our illusion or grand delusion that we are individuated, separate

... [In the] Higher realm there is nothing physical, only pure consciousness" (pp. 1213).

If we accept the premise that humans originate from the same higher consciousness, Semkiw (2003), a reincarnation researcher, reasons how people ought to not harm each other. He said, "If we all realize that we may return to this world as a person of the opposite sex, belong to another religion, country, race, we would realize we are all one and not persecute each other."

The Christian and Taoist approaches, along with other spiritual faiths, ethnic, and cultural groups, have some differences in terms of spiritual worldviews and ways of communicating. As human beings socialized in our faiths and cultural communities, we have learned principles of life and rules of what are considered appropriate and inappropriate communications. Someone once said, "We are not human beings having a spiritual experience. We are spiritual beings having a human experience." In the mist of cultural differences, such as if our social expectations are not met, or when we perceive inappropriate behavior from our own cultural standards, or where there are differences in communication styles based on our spiritual and cultural systems, we respond in either a functional or a dysfunctional manner. A person who uses dysfunctional behaviors is negative or hostile with an attitude of suspicion, fear, prejudice, or ethnocentrism. Dysfunctional strategies such as criticizing, withdrawing, and ignoring are most likely to result in alienation, isolation, and chaos in intercultural interactions (Fong, 2004). Tolle (2005, 2008) cautions us, as human beings, that we are prone to egoic thinking and behaviors, which comes from our human nature, rather than our spiritual being. Part of the egoic thinking and behavior is to feel superior over others, and when we feel threatened we become negative in terms of judging, criticizing, showing I'm right and you're wrong, and other strategies.

How do we bring forth our spiritual being in the form of a human being as we engage and manage our intercultural interactions? We can begin practicing our communication skills of functional behavior, which are positive and nurturing with an attitude of openness, acceptance, trust, and respect, while choosing adaptive communication strategies such as explaining, observing, listening, and inquiring. All of these are likely to result in building rapport, understanding, and harmony in our intercultural relations (Fong, 2004). Tolle (2005) writes in detail of the nature and functions of egoic thinking and behavior; and how we need to awaken ourselves to dissolve this negative behavior that separates our spiritual oneness from that of others. By not feeding negativity to your ego and those of others, awareness or presence of observing this behavior helps in dissolving the ego. Tolle (2005) further writes,

> Nonreaction to the ego in others is one of the most effective ways, not only of going beyond the ego in yourself, but also of dissolving the collective human ego. But you can only be in a state of nonreaction if you can recognize someone's behavior as coming from the ego, as being an expression of the collective human dysfunction. When you realize it's not personal, there is no longer a compulsion to react as if it were (p. 62).

The more we are aware and conscious that patterns of thoughts and behaviors are developed and conditioned from our past experiences and culture, the more we become awaken. Tolle (2008) sees spirituality in how a person thinks and behaves toward others in situations. We can enhance and foster our intercultural relations and our communications toward one another by looking beyond our differences and conflicts, by looking beyond our immediate judgments of the other, and by looking beyond ourselves to have a spiritual disposition that is receptive, flexible, and consciously aware of ourselves in this universe. To have a desire to talk and listen to understanding another's perspective and intentions, rather than argue a point of view in order to be right; and a desire to be open to differences, rather than to rigidly adhere to cultural rules and expectations for self and others, will enable intercultural interactants to receive and appreciate one another's way of communicating and who others are as people. Being aware that we originate from the same higher consciousness and tapping into our spirituality and nonreactive stillness within us, we are likely to foster satisfying intercultural interactions that bridge differences. In the next section let us take a look at two intercultural interactions and see how spirituality can enhance relationships.

## Intercultural Communication Differences

Both scenarios come from my personal intercultural interactions. The first scenario was with a former housemate and student from Mainland China. One day she was in the kitchen and I was elsewhere in the house. Suddenly I heard this tremendous scream, "Oh, my goodness! Aauugghh! Aaugghh!" I ran to the kitchen and saw her in a terrible panic, and asked urgently, "What's the matter?" I saw her hands on her face, trembling, and pointing over at the counter. I said, "Oh ants. We can just clean it up." She shook her head frantically and said that she could not kill ants. She said that she could not kill anything because of her beliefs. I said, "O.K., then I'll just clean it up." She saw me cleaning up the ants, and she would scream now and then. From the Taoist approach, all living beings are of equal existence. From the Christian view, there is no saying that we cannot kill ants. From my Christian view, I did not judge her for her beliefs. I only was concerned about cleaning up the ants. I was a bit surprised that she was so hysterical—screaming, covering her face, and trembling. Otherwise, I just accepted the situation and communicated with a spirit of patience, kindness, gentleness, and self-control.

The second scenario involved having some people over at my home one evening at 6 p.m. to work on a campus-community project. A Caucasian American 25-year-old male graduate student had arrived five to ten minutes early. I had come out of the shower just a few minutes prior to 6 p.m. What made matters worse was that my bathroom electrical outlet had blown a fuse and I could not blow-dry my hair. So I quickly went to the hallway to blow-dry my hair. I heard pounding on my front door and someone ringing my doorbell several times—back and forth, pound, pound, pound, ding-dong, ding-dong. I dried my hair a bit more and ran downstairs to open the door. My student walked in my home upset and said, "You are always late!" I said, "Oh, how long were you waiting?" He said, "I was waiting some five minutes. You're always late!" I said, "I'm sorry about that." I told him that he was the first to arrive, and I only

arrived home shortly from running errands. I changed the subject and asked him if he could connect my VCR to my television. As he was working on that, I noticed the time on the cable box on the television and asked the student to read the time. He said, "6:03." I said, "Alex, it's 6:03, what do you mean I'm late?" Alex was culturally brought up to either arrive early or be on time. I figured for a small group meeting, it was very appropriate to be fashionably late since people were getting off work and had to fight traffic. The other group members trickled in 10 to 15 minutes after six, since they were coming from work.

The point of this illustration is to show that Alex handled the cultural differences of time in a dysfunctional manner. Alex chose to react in a demanding and rude manner by pounding the door and ringing the doorbell several times when his expectations were not met. He lacked self-control, gentleness, and patience, amongst other spiritual qualities. A Taoist would have also observed that Alex lacked humbleness and self-constraint. "A person who is humble, always has others' interests in mind, and practices self-emptying and self-constraint would be like a nourishing and soothing water and thus can be said to embody the *dao* and be considered a good person" (Cheng, 2004, p. 171).

A Taoist might offer Alex the saying from Chapter 8 of Lao-Tzu's classic book, *Tao-Te-Ching*, which reads:

The highest good is like water.

Water gives life to the ten thousand things and does not strive.

It flows in places men reject and so is like the Tao.

In dwelling, be close to the land.

In meditation, go deep in the heart.

In dealing with others, be gentle and kind.

In speech, be true.

In ruling, be just.

In business, be competent.

In action, watch the timing.

No fight: No blame.

# References

Adler, P. S. (1975). The transitional experience: An alternative view of culture shock. *Journal of Humanistic Psychology, 15*, 13–23.

Andersen, P. A. (1994). Explaining intercultural differences in nonverbal communication. In L. A. Samovar & R. E. Porter (Eds.), *Intercultural communication: A reader* (7th ed., pp. 229–239). Belmont, CA: Wadsworth.

Barker, K. (1985). *The NIV study bible*. Grand Rapids, MI: Zondervan.

Bennett, M. J. (1986). A developmental approach to training for intercultural sensitivity. *International Journal of Intercultural Relations, 10*, 179–196.

Capra, F. (1975). *The tao of physics*. Boulder, CO: Shambhala.

Casmir, F. L., & Asuncion-Lande, N. (1989). Intercultural communication revisited: Conceptualization, paradigm building, and methodological approaches. *Communication Yearbook, 12*, 278–309.

Cerminara, G. (1978). *Many mansions: The Edgar Cayce story on reincarnation*. New York: New American Library.

Chen, G. M. (1989). Relationships of the dimensions of intercultural communication competence. *Communication Quarterly, 37*, 118–133.

Chen, G. M. (1995). Differences in self-disclosure patterns among Americans versus Chinese: A comparative study. *Journal of Cross-Cultural Psychology, 26*, 84–91.

Cheng, C. Y. (2004). Dimensions of the dao and onto-ethics in light of the DDJ. *Journal of Chinese Philosophy, 31*(2), 143–182.

Clearly, T. (1991). *Wen-Tzu: Understanding the mysteries: Further teachings of Lao-Tzu*. Boston, MA: Shambhala.

Combs, S. C. (2004). The useless-/usefulness of argumentation: The dao of disputation. *Argumentation and Advocacy, 41*, 58–70.

Dunlap, J. W. (2007). Reincarnation and survival of life after death: "Is there evidence that past life memories suggest reincarnation?" *Academy of Spirituality and Paranormal Studies, Inc. Annual Conference Proceedings.*

Feng, G-F., & English, J. (1972). *Tao Te Ching: Lao Tsu*. New York: Vintage.

Fisher, E. (2005). *Embraced by the Holy Spirit*. Sheppensburg, PA: Destiny Image.

Fong, M. (2004). Identity and the speech community. In M. Fong and R. Chuang (Eds.), *Communicating ethnic and cultural identity* (pp. 3–18). Lanham, MD: Rowman & Littlefield.

Furnham (1987). The adjustment of sojourners. In Y. Y. Kim and W. Gudykunst (Eds.), *Cross-cultural adaptation: Current approaches* (pp. 42–61). Beverly Hills, CA: Sage.

Furnham, A., & Bochner, S. (1982). Social difficulty in a foreign culture: An empiric analysis of culture shock. In S. Bochner (Eds.), *Culture in contact: Studies in cross-cultural interaction* (pp. 161–198). New York: Pergamon.

Furnham, A., & Bochner, S. (1986). Culture shock: Psychological reactions to unfamiliar environments. London: Methuen.

Gudykunst, W. B., & Hammer, M. R. (1987). Strangers and hosts: An uncertainty reduction based theory of intercultural adaptation. In Y. Y. Kim & W. B. Gudykunst (Eds.), *Cross-cultural adaptation: Current approaches* (pp. 106–139). Newbury Park, CA: Sage.

Hammer, M. R., Gudykunst, W. B., & Wiseman, R. L. (1978). Dimensions of intercultural effectiveness: An exploratory study. *International Journal of Intercultural Relations, 2*, 382–392.

Haraldsson, E. (1995). Personality and abilities of children claiming previous-life memories. Journal of Nervous and Mental Disease, 183, 445–451.

Hoijer, H. (1994). The Sapir–Whorf hypothesis. In L. A. Samovar & R. E. Porter (Eds.), *Intercultural communication: A reader* (7th ed., pp. 194–200). Belmont, CA: Wadsworth.

Keil, H. H. J. (1996). Cases of the reincarnation type: An evaluation of some indirect evidence, with examples of silence cases. *Journal of Scientific Exploration, 10*, 467–485.

Kim, Y. Y. (1988). *Communication and cross-cultural adaptation: An integrative theory*. Philadelphia: Multilingual Matter.

Kluckhohn, C., & Strodbeck, F. (1961). *Variations in value orientations*. Evanston, IL: Row, Peterson.

Mills, A. (2000). Past-life experiences. In E. Cardena & S. J. Krippner (Eds). *Varieties of anomalous experience: Examining the scientific evidence* (pp. 283–313). Washington DC: American Psychological Association.

Nakanishi, M. (1987). Perceptions of self-disclosure in initial interaction: A Japanese sample. *Human Communication Research, 13*, 305–318.

Newton, M. (2009). *Destiny of Souls*. Woodbury, MN: Llewellyn.

Ni, Hua-Ching (1997). *Entering the Tao*. Boston: Shambhala.

Nouwen, H. J. M., McNeill, D. P., & Morrison, D. A. (1966). *Compassion: A reflection on the Christian life*. New York: Image Books Doubleday.

Ogawa, D. (1979). Communication characteristics of Asian Americans in urban settings: The case of Honolulu Japanese. In M. K. Asante, E. Newmark, & C. A. Blake (Eds.), *Handbook of intercultural communication* (pp. 321–339). Beverly Hills, CA: Sage.

Ricard, V. B. (1993). *Developing intercultural communication skills.* Malabar, FL: Krieger.

Semkiw (2003). *Return of the Revolutionaries.* Charlottesville, VA: Hampton Roads.

Smith, D. H. (1980). *The wisdom of the Taoists.* New York: New Directions.

Stanley, C. (1996). *Charles Stanley's handbook for Christian living.* Nashville, TN: Thomas.

Stevenson, I. (1974). *Twenty cases suggestive of reincarnation.* (2nd rev. ed.) Charlottesville, VA: University Press of Virginia.

Stevenson, I. (1997). *Reincarnation and biology: A contribution to the etiology of birthmarks and birth defects.* Westport, CT: Praeger.

Stevenson, I. (2003). *European cases of the reincarnation type.* Jefferson, NC: McFarland.

Tolle, E. (2005). *A New Earth* New York: Penguin Group.

Tolle, E. (2008). *A New Earth.* Webcast with Oprah Winfrey. Retrieved February 2010 from http://www.Oprah.com/podcasts/anewearth.xml

Ting-Toomey, S. (1988). Intercultural conflict styles: A face-negotiation theory. In R. Wiseman (Ed.), *Intercultural communication theory* (pp. 115–147). Thousand Oaks, CA: Sage.

Tucker, J. B. (2005). *Life Before life: A scientific investigation of children's memories of previous lives.* New York: St. Martin's Press.

Wei, W. (1996). *I Ching life.* Los Angeles: Power Press.

Weiss, B. (2000). *Messages from the Masters.* New York: Grand Central.

Weiss, (2004). *Same Soul, Many Bodies.* New York: Free Press.

Welch, Holmes (1966). *Taoism: The parting of the way.* Boston: Beacon Press.

Wing, R. L. (1979). *The I Ching workbook.* Garden City, New York: Doubleday.

Youngblood, R. F. (Ed.). (1995). *Nelson's new illustrated Bible dictionary* Nashville, TN: Thomas Nelson.

## Concepts and Questions

1. How may understanding the spirituality prevalent in another culture facilitate intercultural communication between you and a member of that culture?

2. Compare and contrast the Christian concept of grace with the Taoist concept of Tao.

3. What are the sources of grace and of Tao? How do these sources differ?

4. How does the concept of harmony between being and nature compare to the concept of grace?

5. In what ways does the Tao act as a guide to proper conduct?

6. In what ways do the Taoist forces of *yin* and *yang* relate to the Christian force of grace?

7. How can the Christian and Taoist spiritual worldviews affect intercultural communication?

8. In what ways are the spiritual approaches of Christianity and Taoism similar? How do they differ?

# Chimerica: U.S.–China Communication for the Twenty-first Century

WENSHAN JIA • DEXIN TIAN • XUANZI B. JIA

The first essay in this chapter compared aspects of China and the United States on a somewhat spiritual level. The second essay, while still concentrating on China and the United States, is far more practical. In an essay titled "Chimerica: United States–China Communication for the 21st Century," Wenshen Jia, Dexin Tian, and Xuanzi B. Jia advance the thesis that events during the last thirty years have created a new dynamic in the relationship between the United States and China. The authors stress that more than ever and for a host of reasons, the people of the United States and China are now interacting out of design and necessity. Because of this major shift in geopolitics, the authors maintain it behooves the citizens of both cultures to learn to work together more harmoniously. Using the impact of globalization as a backdrop, the authors insist that the two countries are interdependent. Jia, Tian and Jia, drawing on the work of Ferguson and Schularick (2007), use the word "Chimerica" to describe the coming together of these two superpowers. More specifically, the term Chimerica is used to refer to "the sum of China, the world's most rapidly growing emerging market, and America, the world's most financially advanced developed economy." The authors argue that the interdependence goes well beyond economic concerns. For example, the authors contend that the interdependence includes such issues as fighting terrorism, nuclear proliferation, global warming, reducing worldwide poverty, and battling world hunger.

Early in their essay, the authors place the United States and China's relationship into a historical context. Throughout this historical review, which includes both past successes and failures, the authors stress that it is in the best interests of both countries to work together. They suggest that some of the contact points could be mutual visits, meetings, correspondence, the employment of intermediaries, educational exchange programs, and the like. The authors praise the efforts of numerous student and academic exchange programs. They point out that over 300,000 Chinese students have studied in the United States and then returned to China with an increased awareness of American history and culture. The authors estimate that in 2010 the number of American students who will have studied in China will reach 200,000. Jia, Tian, and Jia also mention a large number of other contact points that they believe will "increase positive bilateral communication." Among these are the United States–China Friendship Association, the National Committee on United States–China Relations, and the John King Fairbank Center for China Studies.

Toward the end of their paper, the authors construct a profile of what an efficient and functional Chimerican would be like. In general, this would be a person who was comfortable in both the American and Chinese cultures. He or she would be able to communicate in both English and Chinese and be knowledgeable "about the geography, history, economy, politics, culture, media, and so on of both countries." We concur with the sound advice offered by Jia, Tian, and Jia, since the first step toward improved intercultural understanding is an awareness of the cultural background of the person you will be interacting with. The authors remind you that those backgrounds and experiences are composed of a host of interrelated variables. This essay seeks to expose you to many of those variables.

> Events during the last thirty years have created a new dynamic in the relationship between the United States and China.

Dr. Wenshan Jia is an associate professor in the Department of Communication at Chapman University, Orange, California. Dr. Dexin Tian is an assistant professor in the Department of Arts, English, and Humanities at Louisiana State University, Alexandria, Louisiana. Xuanzi B. Jia is studying in the Departments of Political Science and Asian Studies at Smith College, Northampton, Massachusetts.

With the collapse of the Berlin Wall in 1989 and the dissolution of the former Soviet Union in 1991, the United States found itself the only superpower in the world at the start of the twenty-first century. Meanwhile, China, characterized by Napoleon as "a sleeping giant," has been making big strides as a rising economic superpower since the launch of its market-oriented policies in 1979. While the United States and China's bilateral relationship has become increasingly interdependent in a variety of aspects within the context of globalization, the two countries have been examining each other closely and cautiously from the opposite sides of the Pacific Ocean. By globalization, we are referring to the transformative process of global integration in terms of the transnational flow of people, trade, finance, technologies, ideas, and communication (Shome & Hegde, 2002). In our globalized world, Koh (2004) remarked, "The United States cannot succeed by acting as a Lone Ranger" due to the paradoxical situation where it "has never been so powerful and, at the same time, so dependent on the rest of the world" (p. 35). Similarly, Fenby (2008) noted, "In the 30 years since Deng Xiaoping launched China on the path to the free market, no country has benefited more from globalization" than China. However, "to maintain its economic growth and development, China must continue to borrow from, sell to, and learn from the US" (pp. 1–2).

> *Chemeria is a term used to describe the integration process of the North American and Chinese economies.*

To describe the integration process of the North American and Chinese economies, Ferguson and Schularick (2007) coined the term "Chimerica" to refer to "the sum of China, the world's most rapidly growing emerging market, and America, the world's most financially advanced developed economy" (p. 1). Specifically, Chimerica accounts for 13 percent of the world's land surface, one-fourth of the world's population, a third of its gross domestic product (GDP), and over half of the global economic growth over the past six years. This symbiotic relationship between the United States as the big spender and China as the big saver is likened to "a marriage made in heaven" and regarded as "the defining feature of the current world economy" (p. 1). To a great extent, Ferguson and Schularick (2007) are correct because, as different as they are, the United States and the People's Republic of China are not only economically complementary but also co-dependent in their concerted efforts to aid programs in the pursuit of agendas to find solutions to problems such as anti-terrorism and non-proliferation, global warming and poverty reduction, transnational crime and HIV/AIDS; mitigation of energy shortages; and cultural exchanges, just to name a few.

As the two countries are brought closer through intensified contacts and broadened exchanges due to their economic complementariness and potential areas of cooperation, we find it worthwhile to explore the prospects of communication between the United States and China in the twenty-first century. To this end, we will begin this essay with the description of the current situation in the interdependence between the United States and China. Then, we will provide a discussion about ways to deepen and broaden the understanding between the two nations. What follows is an introduction to some of the existing programs and approaches implemented in both the United States and China, and an evaluation of them from the intercultural communication perspective in light of pragmatism or social constructionism. Finally, we will end with suggestions on how to improve United States-China intercultural communication so as to maximize mutual benefit, and to ensure increased global peace and harmony.

## THE CURRENT INTERDEPENDENCE BETWEEN THE UNITED STATES AND CHINA

There are three things that are worth mentioning before we embark on our discussions about the interdependence and mutual understanding between the United States and China. First, from a historical point of view, the United States and China were allies during World War II, and, President Roosevelt had hoped that Sino-American cooperation would continue, as the United States had intended to transform China into one of the largest democratic countries in Asia (Kissinger, 1994). However, what followed was a three-decade absence of communication—a result of the severance of the diplomatic relations between the two countries due to the takeover of power in China by the Chinese Communist Party in 1949. But the circumstances before the breakup can still serve as a foundational basis or reference for our present discussion. Second, by "current," we refer to the time period from the end of the Cold War in 1991 till the present. It is from this point on that the United States has begun reconsidering the strategic role of China as a rising power rather than China's instrumental function as a chess pawn against the former Soviet Union. Finally, and most importantly, we need to clarify the grand strategies of the two countries because they are the determining factors for the nature, scope, and degree of the United States-China interdependent relationship.

Since the end of the Cold War, the position of China with respect to the United States has been rotating between a strategic partner and a strategic competitor, depending on the changing focus of the United States' grand strategy. Historically, both liberals and conservatives have strongly believed that the United States is a revolutionary country, founded on the principles of freedom, equality, and progress, which have universal applicability. After emerging as the only winner from the Cold War bipolarity, and having experienced a short period of post-Cold War multi-polarity, the United States has become what the French Foreign Minister Hubert Védrine referred to as a "hyper-power" (Ikenberry, 2001, p. 1). As a hyper-power, the United States considers it a predestined duty to guard American interests worldwide. As a result, the China policies established by all U.S. post-Cold War administrations have been shifting from either "countenance[ing] China's emergence as a peer competitor" or to "give[ing] China the opportunity to integrate itself into the American-led international order on Washington's terms" (Layne & Thayer, 2007, p. 70). Seeing China as a rising power in East Asia and a strategic competitor, the George W. Bush administration, in its early period, adopted the containment policy towards China as an alternative to engagement and strategic partnership, as was advocated in the second term of the Clinton administration. Since the containment policy dramatically increased tensions between United States and China, and due to the war on terror, the Bush Administration had to shift to the policy of "congagement" (Khalilzad, 1999), consisting of both containment and engagement

towards China. Some realist pessimists, who argued that rising powers tended to be troublemakers in history, even compared rising China to Germany and Japan during the two world wars. However, there have been signs today that the Obama administration wants to emphasize the United States' commitment to, if not a strategic partnership yet, a stronger cooperative relationship with China. For example, when they met at the G-20 summit in London on April 1, 2009, Chinese President Hu Jintao and U.S. President Barack Obama "agreed to work together to build a positive, cooperative, and comprehensive relationship in the twenty-first century" (Xinhua, 2009, p. 1). Thus, the realist-pessimistic voice for United States containment of China is gradually drowned by the liberal-optimistic voice for United States engagement and cooperation with China—perhaps a manifestation of the Obama administration's smart-power model of strategic thinking.

What is China's grand strategy, then? With an average annual economic growth rate of 9 percent over the past decades, China has been emerging, or reemerging, as a rising financial power in Asia. The velocity and impact of the growth of China's comprehensive national capability, and lack of knowledge about the direction of her development and future intentions, caused China's neighboring countries and other great powers such as the United States to view Chinese intentions with caution, suspicion, and even fear. China announced that she had been pursuing a goal of "peaceful rise." As one Chinese government–affiliated think tank researcher noted, "China aims to grow and advance without upsetting existing orders, and we are trying to rise in a way that benefits our neighbors" (Funabashi, 2003, p. 2). While taking a series of confidence-building measures to offset the regional concerns, Beijing even officially adjusted the description of China's emergence from "peaceful rise" to "peaceful development" (Gries, 2007, p. 46). This line of thought has directly come from the development targets of the Chinese leadership. Former Chinese leader Deng Xiaoping's target was to "increase China's per capita GDP fourfold by 2020 to attain a state of relatively comfortable livelihood," and President Hu Jintao's "'big idea' is to create a 'harmonious and prosperous society' via 'peaceful development'" (Dorn, 2008, p. 13). As for its relationship with the United States, China has been faithfully following

Deng's maxim to never act haughtily towards the United States while "hiding our capacities and biding our time" (Gompert, et al. 2005, p. 36). Thus, China has been concentrating on her domestic construction and refraining from demonstrating her power externally. On one hand, China intends to learn a lesson from the collapse of the Soviet Union and avoid confronting the United States, so as to maintain security and stability for a prosperous state and a harmonious society. On the other hand, China will not jump on the bandwagon and accept the U.S. version of the universal value system without considering the degree of that system's compatibility with the Chinese cultural heritage.

Having explained the grand strategies of the two countries, we find it easier to understand and describe the complex and multi-faceted United States-China relationship and the interdependence between the two countries. As was reported in the meeting between the two presidents at the G-20 London Summit, the United States and China share common interests in tackling the global financial crisis, striving to recover global economic growth, dealing with international and regional issues, and safeguarding world peace and security. Viewing each other in a positive perspective, the two countries expect to deepen exchanges and cooperation with regards to the world issues dealing with the economy, counterterrorism, non-proliferation, law enforcement, energy, climate change, science and technology, education, culture, health care, and military affairs. More importantly, both presidents recognize that a positive relationship between the United States and China extends far beyond the interests and benefits of the two countries. For instance, President Hu said, "Good relations with the United States are not only in the interests of the two peoples, but also beneficial to peace, stability and prosperity of the Asia-Pacific region, and the world at large" (Xinhua, 2009, p. 2). Similarly, President Obama reiterated, "I said publicly that our relations are not only important for citizens of the two countries, but also help set the stage for how the world deals with a host of challenges" (Xinhua, 2009, p. 2). To calculate roughly, the two presidents agree that the United States and China share common interests in four main fields and

that they look forward to expanding exchanges and cooperation in twelve major areas. This suggests that the two countries are interdependent in at least a dozen different areas.

According to Ching (2009), when U.S. President-elect Barack Obama was asked about his foreign priorities, he listed nuclear proliferation, climate change and global poverty, Iraq, Afghanistan, Iran, the trans-Atlantic alliance, Russia, the Israeli-Palestinian conflict, and managing the United States' relationship with China and the entire Pacific Rim, with the latter added as a seeming afterthought. Although the afterthought reflects a relatively calm state of relationship, with no crisis that needs immediate attention, Ching (2009) emphasized that China "is not just a relationship to be managed—but perhaps the key relationship that the United States sustains if Obama is to achieve success in virtually all of his other foreign policy priority areas" (p. 1).

> A good United States-China relationship not only benefits the American and Chinese people but will also bring about world peace and prosperity.

## WAYS TO DEEPEN AND BROADEN THE UNDERSTANDING BETWEEN THE TWO NATIONS

As you can see from the above discussion, a good United States-China relationship not only benefits the American and Chinese people but will also bring about world peace and prosperity. It is now important for both the United States and China to readjust their foreign policies toward a "more positive and constructive" relationship, and for the two to implement the "positive, cooperative, and comprehensive" programs of exchanges and cooperation (Xinhua, 2009, p. 2). To meet these goals, first of all, the decision makers of the two countries should be so well informed via regular and smooth communication that they will neither misjudge each other's development intentions nor overestimate their own strength. By starting with their joint efforts in tackling the global financial crisis and striving to spur global economic growth, the United States and China can then gradually deepen and broaden their understanding and appreciation of each other's sincerity, and contributions to their cooperation projects and exchange programs, one after another. The significance of regular and smooth communication can never be emphasized enough, especially in the management of a crisis. According to Yang Jiechi (Yang, 2009), Chinese foreign minister, the leaders of the two countries have maintained close communication on major issues concerning bilateral relations, "through mutual visits, meetings, telephone calls, and correspondence," which "have given a strong boost to the sustained, sound, and steady growth of our relations" (p. 4). Yet, Lampton (2004) listed three examples of deficient communication cases in U.S.-China relations in recent years. First, on the tragic Tiananmen Square incident of June 4, 1989, Chinese leader Deng Xiaoping repeatedly refused to pick up the telephone when U.S. President George Herbert Walker Bush called. In return, the U.S. Congress suspended all minister-level exchanges between the two countries for a considerable period of time during 1989 and 1990. Second, in 1999, after the Chinese Embassy in Belgrade was bombed, it took President Jiang Zemin a long time to respond to President Clinton's initiatives to talk, and the Chinese military curtailed bilateral exchanges. Third, immediately after a U.S. Navy patrol aircraft and a Chinese F-8 fighter collided over the South China Sea on April 1, 2001, the U.S. ambassador to China could not make contact with any member of the Chinese government to talk about the incident. Moreover, the U.S. Department of Defense curtailed military-to-military exchanges with China. According to Professor David Lampton, Director of China Studies at Johns Hopkins-SAIS and the Nixon Center, "…when we are angry at each other our reflex has been to cut communication at the highest levels and between our militaries. This is the wrong impulse!" (p. 6).

Beijing must have drawn lessons from the above when it took a series of confidence-building measures to offset the concerns of the neighboring countries regarding her rising power. For instance, she strengthened bilateral security dialogues with Australia, India, Japan, Mongolia, and South Korea and invited some of them to observe and participate in joint military exercises. Meanwhile, China actively participated in the Association of South East Asian Nations (ASEAN) Regional Forum with the intention to establish a regional cooperative security community (Shambaugh, 2005). In contrast, the United States took the risk of creating an impression of being "a dangerous trigger-happy military power interested only in its own safety by elevating the concept of

'preemption'" after 9/11 (Kim, 2004, pp. 18–19). To many people in Asia, the causes of terrorism are multiple and complex, and the U.S. policy of trying to eradicate it through the use of force alone is ineffective.

According to Suettinger (2003), American and Chinese policy makers have made many mistakes about each other such as factual inaccuracies, poor intelligence, errors of judgment, sins of commission and omission, misperceptions, mistranslations, overestimates of knowledge, under-estimates of sensitivity, misplaced confidence, misread intentions, unintended consequences, unfulfilled rewards, missed signals, ineffective bluffs, and violations of confidence. In many ways, the above mistakes are attributable to groupthink, pervasive among the decision-making groups of both countries, a phenomenon characterized by over-estimation of their own power or moral superiority, closed-mindedness toward the out-group, and pressure for in-group uniformity. Thus, to minimize such mistakes, we see the necessity and urgency to not only ensure that the United States-China communication channels are open and smooth, but also to improve the quality of communication through periodic top-level contacts and regular exchanges in as many aspects and on as many levels as possible.

Both the United States and China have been serious in their commitment to tackling the global financial crisis through intensified cooperation and exchanges. For example, during her recent visit to Beijing, U. S. Secretary of State Hillary Rodham Clinton (2009) remarked that, facing the global economic crisis that hit both the United States and China, "we have to look inward for solutions, but we must also look to each other to take a leadership role in designing and implementing a coordinated global response to stabilize the world's economy, and begin recovery" (p. 2). Actually, Neil Ferguson (2008), a professor of history at Harvard University and one of the inventors of the term "Chimerica," noted that at the heart of this financial crisis is the considerable imbalance between the United States with her current account deficit of more than 1 percent of the world GDP, and the surplus countries that finance her such as the oil exporting nations, Japan, and other emerging Asian countries. Of course, "the relationship between China and America has become the crucial one," and "an alternative for the Chinese is to turn inward to increase its domestic consumption" (p. A19). One point that needs clarification here is "[t]he reality that the growth in U.S. government spending and borrowing, not the trade deficit with China, is the key reason for concern" (Dorn, 2008, p. 153).

Although China "only accounts for about twenty-five percent of the U.S. overall current account deficit of around $800 billion" (Dorn, 2008, p. 153), the Chinese government made it her top priority to combat the financial crisis in 2009. In his speech entitled "Broaden China-United States Cooperation in the Twenty-first Century," Chinese Foreign Minister Yang Jiechi (2009) reported that, while closely following the measures taken by the U.S. government to stabilize financial markets and stimulate economic recovery, the Chinese government launched a four trillion Renminbi (Chinese currency equivalent to 585 billion dollars) investment program to jump-start growth by boosting domestic demand, reinvigorating industries, developing science and technology, and improving the social safety net. Yang remarked, "Some of the measures have already produced initial results, as evidenced by the recent signs of economic recovery" (p. 4). Besides, the Chinese government has also applied conventional tools, such as large interest-rate cuts and a massive fiscal stimulus plan of $588 billion for 2009 and 2010. To restore consumer confidence, local governments in China have issued various consumption coupons as a response to the recent call of Premier Wen Jiabao, who stated, "Confidence is more valuable than gold" (Xu, 2009, p. 3). Although it is still too early to know the United States' comments on the Chinese efforts, we strongly believe that timely and responsible commitment to the areas of mutual and global interests is key to the success of collaborations between the two countries.

To sum up, any deepened or broadened understanding between the United States and China results from regular correspondence and smooth communication at various levels and in a variety of ways. The showcase of China's serious commitment

> *Any deepened or broadened understanding between the United States and China results from regular correspondence and smooth communication at various levels and in a variety of ways.*

to the most acute and immediate area of collaboration—tackling bilateral trade imbalance and global financial crisis—definitely invites more confidence and greater success in other areas of mutual and global interests like clean energy and climate change, safeguarding world peace and security, as well as counter-terrorism and nuclear non-proliferation. However, there are two caveats here. First, genuine cooperation between the United States and China can result only from quality communication between the two countries, each with a different culture, a different social system, and a different ideology. Thus, quality communication will have to be based on mutual understanding, mutual adjustment, and mutual respect, seeking harmony amid differences, and cooperation for win-win results.

Second, in the globalized world situation, true understanding between the two nations needs to take such new elements as economic globalization, domestic politics, and geopolitical strategy into consideration. Economic globalization makes the United States-China relationship go beyond national boundaries with a network of dynamic relations. Due to the difference in the distribution of profit from the interdependence between the United States and China, different interest groups will exert their influence and pressure on the national policies of their respective countries. In terms of geopolitical strategies, the United States needs China's cooperation in regional and global affairs while China needs the support of the United States to sustain a stable global environment for her peaceful development.

## INSTITUTIONALIZED EFFORTS PROMOTING UNITED STATES-CHINA COMMUNICATION

Since the President Nixon–Chairman Mao summit in the early 1970s, various institutionalized efforts have been made by both the Chinese and U.S. governments, as well as business, educational institutions, and NGOs (non-governmental organizations). While

China created a United States-China Friendship Association, the United States established her own counterpart. In addition, some leading American scholars of China studies, such as Lucian Pye, Robert Scalapino, and others founded the National Committee on United States-China Relations, which aims to promote Track II diplomacy.[1] The East-West Center, founded and funded by the State Department of the United States in the early 1960s, has also been playing a vital intellectual role in promoting intercultural understanding between the West and the East, particularly between the United States and China. The Institute of Culture and Communication of the East-West Center, which has unfortunately been closed, was created to address specifically the issues of intercultural miscommunication. Similarly, the John King Fairbank Center for China Studies, the Harvard-Yenching Institute, and the Asia Center, all at Harvard University, have been instrumental in deepening an intellectual understanding between China and the United States. Moreover, the Committee of 100 (Bai-Ren-Hui) is an NGO founded by the elite of the Chinese-American community, such as I. M. Pei, at the beginning of the 1990s when the relationship between China and the United States was virtually at a new dead end after the 1989 Tiananmen Student Demonstration was put down. With a mission to build new bridges between the United States and China, it consists of distinguished members such as the world-renowned cellist Yo-Yo Ma and Steven Chen, co-founder and chief technology officer of YouTube.

Since China's economic rise in the beginning of the twenty-first century, many American educational institutions have been investing more and more in Chinese language and cultural education venues. Some eighty Confucian academies funded by the Chinese government have already been established in the United States, with the co-sponsorship of American universities such as University of Maryland at College Park and University of California at Los Angeles. The College Board has recently included Chinese as an Advanced Placement subject in American high schools. Multiple elementary schools and middle schools on the East and West Coasts of the United States have begun to provide Chinese language classes to their students. The growth of East Asian Studies, American and China Studies, and Asian Studies programs has been explosive, due in large part to the growing demand to learn everything about China. New centers of China studies have been mushrooming and exchange programs between American and Chinese universities have been multiplying. For example, the Institute for International Education of Students, headquartered in Chicago, which was founded in 1950, has recently expanded into China with the addition of two centers.

Compared with the United States, China seems to have studied the United States on a larger scale. Since Deng Xiaoping's visit to the United States in 1978, China has been conducting massive campaigns of English language learning on the campuses of Chinese universities, as well as on many high school and even elementary school campuses. Today, about 300 million Chinese are fluent English speakers with considerable knowledge of the United States and American culture. These Chinese, especially China's newly emerging youth, are ferociously consuming American culture, news, and consumer goods in English. Furthermore, one million Chinese have studied overseas since 1978; almost half of them have studied or are currently studying in the United States. More than 300,000 Chinese students have already returned to China after studying abroad in various countries around the world. Some of them, especially returnees from the United States, are assuming leadership positions in the Chinese government. Zhili Chen, who was a visiting scholar at Pennsylvania State University at University Park in the 1980s, was Minister of Education, and now is the Vice-Chairwoman of China's People's Congress. Both the current Chinese Communist Party Secretary, Weifang Ming, and President of Peking University Fengqi Zhou received their Ph.D. degrees in the United States in the 1980s. In addition, selected members of the younger generation of Chinese government leaders have received or are receiving training from the Kennedy School of Government, Harvard University. Yale University has been offering training to multiple groups of Chinese university presidents. Yuanchao Li, Director of Department of Personnel of the Chinese Communist Party, was one of the first groups of China's young leaders to receive training at Harvard University in 1998.

Even though so much has been done to promote mutual understanding by the respective countries, neither side thinks that it is enough. Both sides feel the need to do more United States-China exchanges. On the American side, in November 2009, during President Obama's state visit to China, the Obama administration announced that it planned to increase the number of American students who study in China fivefold in the next few years. This means that in a few years, the number of American students who study in China each year will reach approximately 200,000. On the Chinese side, in March of 2010, the Chinese Ministry of Education announced that it plans to have every principal in the K-12 education system in China receive training in the United States and/or European countries during the next few years. The United States has also become one of the hottest destinations for Chinese tourists. Even while the United States and China were exchanging hostile words with each other over the White House's decision to sell arms to Taiwan, New Yorkers continued to welcome the arrival of 1000 Chinese tourists in New York City on February 19, 2010. In the meantime, Hong Kong welcomed the port call of the American aircraft carrier Nimitz on the eve of the Chinese Spring Festival on February 17, 2010.

Such frequent educational, cultural and military exchanges between the two countries are occurring simultaneously with frequent high-level intergovernmental visits and dialogues; obviously these concerted efforts are exerting a positive impact on United States-Chinese relations. Collectively, they are personalizing the impersonal and contentious trade relations between the United States and China and expanding Ferguson's economic concept of Chimerica into an intercultural one. As a result, Chimerica not only means economic interdependence between the United States and China, but also is increasingly characterized by an intercultural identity drawing upon, and emerging from, the deepened interaction between the American and Chinese cultures, which are unique in their own ways and are complementary in nature. This is because such persistent and prolonged communicative efforts, from the perspective of pragmatism (i.e., Jia, 2005), and America's home-grown philosophy, contribute to the creation of more shared knowledge,

> *Whether you are a Chinese or an American, whether you like it or not, you are being drawn into a transnational entity called Chimerica and becoming a willing or unwilling member of Chimerica.*

more shared experiences, more common ground, and ultimately a shared destiny and a shared identity between the American and Chinese cultures.

## BECOMING A FUNCTIONAL CHIMERICAN

As we have shown above, Chimerica is a new phenomenon created by globalization in the second half of the twentieth century. It challenges the traditional concept of nation-state and it is redefining the economic, cultural and economic contour of the human race in the twenty-first century. As an individual, whether you are a Chinese or an American, whether you like it or not, you are being drawn into a transnational entity called Chimerica and becoming a willing or unwilling member of Chimerica. A functional Chimerican would be someone who is proficient in both English and Chinese, competent in communicating between Chinese and Americans. A functional Chimerican should also have a working knowledge of the geography, history, economy, politics, culture, media, etc. of both countries and an understanding of the history of the relationship between the two nations and two cultures, as well as an understanding of the current status and future prospect of Chimerica.

If you are not from Chimerica, this does not mean that you do not have to know about Chimerica or need not learn how to communicate with Chimericans. Since Chimerica is the marriage of the world's most advanced country with the world's largest developing country, this marriage will only continue to make an undeniably large impact on the future global community. To learn to get along with Chimerica and Chimericans means to grasp the meanings, functions and global implications of an intricate and complex system of hybridized worldviews, mixed political models, diversified cultures and synergized economies called Chimerica. While Chimericans are responsible for improving Chimerica in an effort to increase peace, unity and harmony between the United States and China internally and externally, non-Chimericans are advised to check against the ethics of Chimerica's global behavior externally to ensure balance and a diversity of opinions. Such conjoint internal and external efforts are expected to sustain Chimerica along a positive path and prevent Chimerica from deteriorating into Chimera—a fire-breathing monster with no harmony on the inside and posing a threat to harmony on the outside. But in order to ensure this monster does not emerge, let's start to do our own homework today.

## Note

1. Track II diplomacy is diplomatic action taken by individuals or agencies other than politicians and government representatives. For example, U.S. academic or business representatives engaging in discussions with their Chinese counterparts on how to resolve U.S.-China trade imbalances would be conducting Track II diplomacy.

## References

Ching, F. (2009, Jan. 3). China: Key to U.S. foreign policy success. *The Japan Times*, 1–3.

Clinton, H. R. (2009, Feb. 21). Toward a deeper and broader relationship with China: Remarks with Chinese Foreign Minister Yang Jiechi. Retrieved April 2, 2009, from http://www.state.gov/secretary/rm/2009a/02/119432.htm

Dorn, J. A. (2008, June 13). The danger of economic nationalism. *Beijing Review*, 13–14.

Dorn, J. A. (2008). The debt threat: A risk to US-China relationships? *The Brown Journal of World Affairs*, 14 (2), 151–164.

Fenby, J. (2008, July 24). China's rumble with globalization, Part II. *YaleGlobal*, 1–4.

Ferguson, N. (2008, Nov. 17). Team 'Chimerica." *The Washington Post*, A19.

Ferguson, N., & Schularick, M. (2007, Feb. 5). Chimerical? Think again. *The Wall Street Journal*, 1–4.

Funabashi, Y. (2003, Dec. 19). China's "peaceful ascendancy." *YaleGlobal*, 1–4.

Gompert, D. C., Godement, F., Medeiros, E. S., & Mulvenon, J. D. (2005). *China on the Move*. RAND: National Defense Research Institute, Santa Monica, CA. Retrieved 22 March 2010 from http://www.rand.org/pubs/conf_proceedings/2005/RAND_CF199.pdf

Ikenberry, G. J. (2001). Getting hegemony right. *The National Interest*, 63, 1–2.

Jia, W. S. (2005). The Deweyan pragmatism: Its implications for the study of intercultural communication. *Heisey Festchrift* (special issue) *Intercultural Communication Studies, XIV* (1), 101–107.

Khalilzad, Z. M. (1999). *Congage China*. Santa Monica, CA: Rand/IP-187.

Kim, K. (2004). Northeast Asia. In K. Kim, T. Koh & F. Sobhan (Eds.), *America's role in Asia: Asian views*. San Francisco: The Asian Foundation.

Kissinger, H. (1994). *Diplomacy*. New York: Simon & Schuster.

Koh, T. (2004). Southeast Asia. In K. Kim, T. Koh & F. Sobhan, (Eds.), *America's role in Asia: Asian views*. San Francisco: The Asian Foundation.

Lampton, D. M. (2004). The United States and China: Competitors, partners, or both? Speech delivered at the US Foreign Policy Colloquium, George Washington University. Retrieved April 2, 2009, from http://www.nixoncenter.org/publications/ElliotSchoolSpeech.pdf

Layne, C., & Thayer, B. A. (2007). *American empire: A debate*. New York: Routledge.

Shambaugh, D. (2005, April 20). Rising dragon and the American eagle, Part I. *YaleGlobal*, 1–4.

Shome, R., & Hedge, R. S. (2002). Culture, communication, and the challenge of globalization. *Critical Studies in Media Communication*, 19(2), 172–189.

Suettinger, R. L. (2003). *Beyond Tiananmen: The politics of US-China relations 1989-2000*. Washington, D.C.: Brookings Institution Press.

Xinhua. (2009). China, U.S. to build positive, cooperative and comprehensive relationship in 21st century. Retrieved April 5, 2009, from http://china-embassy.org/eng/zmgx/t555667.htm

Xu, S. T. (2009, Jan. 30). US and China: Grappling over economic rescue, Part I. *YaleGlobal*, 1–4.

Yang, J. C. (2009, March 12). Broaden China-US cooperation in the 21st century: Remarks by Foreign Minister Yang Jiechi at the Center for Strategic and International Studies, Washington, D.C. Retrieved April 12, 2009, from http://www.china-embassy.org/eng/zmgx/t542231.htm

Zhang, C. (2007). Harmony, hegemony, & US-China relations. *World Literature Today*, 45–47.

## Concepts and Questions

1. What are Jia, Tian, and Jia implying when they write, "The United States cannot succeed by acting as a Lone Ranger"?

2. What is globalization? Why is globalization of interest to students of intercultural communication?

3. How do you define Jia, Tian, and Jia's use of the word "Chimerica"?

4. In what ways are the United States and China interdependent? Is this interdependence good for both countries?

5. How does an awareness of the historical link between the United States and China help explain the current relationship between the two countries?

6. What do Jia, Tian, and Jia mean when they refer to "the grand strategies" of China and the United States?

7. What are some methods the United States and China have employed to maintain open communication channels?

8. Why do you believe it is beneficial for the United States and China to continue to communicate as "friends" instead of adversaries?

9. What do Jia, Tian, and Jia mean when they write about "institutionalized efforts for promoting U.S.-China communication"?

10. According to Jia, Jia, and Tian, what are some traits that should be developed if one seeks to become a "functional Chimerican"?

# Communicating with Indians

RAJESH KUMAR • ANAND KUMAR SETHI

Having presented two views of Chinese culture, we now move to India. Like China, the nation of India has a population of over one billion. The impact of globalization has led Americans and Indians into greater contact with one another, resulting in an ever-increasing need for effective intercultural communication. Due to the outsourcing of manufacturing and service elements by American businesses to India and the need to conduct serious international negotiations, each country now must learn about the perceptions and communication styles of the other. Rajesh Kumar and Anand Kumar Sethi, in their article "Communicating with Indians," are concerned with how Western managers dealing with their counterparts from India might respond to behaviors that are very different from those found in their own culture. Although the authors focus on the business setting, their assumptions and suggestions apply to any interaction involving India and the West.

To understand better how these interactions might take place, Kumar and Sethi begin with a detailed analysis of four general communication dimensions: (1) high context versus low context, (2) ideological versus pragmatism, (3) associative versus abstractive, and (4) verbal versus nonverbal communication. Once these dimensions are explained the authors compare how these characteristics are revealed differently in India and the West. Using the four communication dimensions as a template, the authors offer some concrete steps that "Western expatriates can undertake to enhance effective communication with Indians." Specifically, they believe your chances for successful communication with Indians increase if you are aware of Indian communication styles and learn to control your initial emotional response. Controlling that response by avoiding negative feelings and avoiding ideological debates can aid you in developing a positive attitude toward Indian culture. As noted earlier, even though their examples are drawn from the business context, their four suggestions can be applied to any face-to-face interaction involving Indians and Westerners.

> Your chances for successful communication with Indians increase if you are aware of Indian communication styles.

Human beings draw close to one another by their common nature, but habits and customs keep them apart. **Confucian Saying**

From *Doing Business in India: A Guide for Western Managers* (New York: Palgrave Macmillan, 2005, pp. 103, 107–114, 150–152.) Reprinted by permission.

Now it is not good for the Christian's health to hustle the Asian brown, for the Christian riles and the Aryan smiles and he weareth the Christian down; At the end of the fight is a tombstone white with the name of the late deceased and the epitaph drear: "**A fool lies here who tried to hustle the East**."     **Rudyard Kipling**

What kind of a bird are you, if you can't sing?" chirped the bird "What kind of a bird are you, if you can't swim?" quacked the duck.

**Prokofiev in "Peter and the Wolf"**

The great common door through which most forms of negativity enter is premature expectation.... All expectations are a judgment.

Communication is a fundamental aspect of human interaction in that individuals cannot but not communicate.[1] One may be effective or ineffective in accurately conveying what one wishes to say to the other party, but without question whenever we interact with another individual one does convey some message, whether or not we intended to convey that message to the other party. Above all, communication is a goal-driven activity in which one is either conveying some information to the other party to get them to do something or is trying to extract information from another person to further one's own objectives. Whether it is setting up a business meeting, or making an offer to buy or sell a particular commodity, communication serves as the medium to help accomplish these goals.

Even within the confines of a particular culture communication is not necessarily problem free. Individual differences in personality, age, gender, social skills, and socioeconomic background are all likely contributors to communicative difficulties.[2] That said, communicative difficulties increase when one crosses cultural boundaries. As the cultural distance increases, so do the *assumptions* on the basis of which individuals communicate. Individuals socializing in different cultures communicate on the basis of *radically different assumptions* without necessarily being acutely aware of the assumptions that are shaping their behavior.[3]

The aim here is to assess the causes and the consequences of the communicative difficulties between the Indians and the Western expatriate manager. We will begin with a discussion of the communicative style common to India and then outline ways by which the Western expatriate manager might handle these challenges both efficiently as well as effectively.

## THE INDIAN COMMUNICATIVE STYLE

The communicative style of a particular cultural group can be analyzed on the basis of different dimensions.[3a] The four dimensions that have garnered a lot of attention in the literature are: (a) high context versus low context; (b) ideologism versus pragmatism; (c) associative versus abstractive communication; and (d) verbal versus nonverbal communication.[4] We outline the salient characteristics of each of them and then indicate how the Indian culture maps on to them.

## High-Context versus Low-Context Communicative Patterns

This is one of the most influential characterizations of different types of communicative styles and it draws attention to the fact that members of different cultural groups are more or less sensitive to the context of the message.[5] As Hall and Hall note, "*Context* is the information that surrounds an event; it is inextricably bound up with the meaning of that event. The elements that combine to produce a given meaning—events and contexts—are in different proportions depending on the culture."[6] *Context* has a powerful impact on how people choose to convey information, and in particular, it influences the communication mode that people choose to employ. Scholars have drawn a distinction between indirect versus direct, succinct versus elaborate, contextual versus personal, and affective versus instrumental modes of communicating.[7] In an indirect communicative mode, messages are conveyed implicitly rather than directly whereas in a direct communicative mode people state their intentions as clearly as they possibly can.

The distinction between a succinct and an elaborate communicative mode rests on the fact that in the former, people rely less on words and more on nonverbal nuances whereas in the elaborative mode, verbal expression is clearly prized. A contextual style is accommodative of the relationship among the parties whereas in a personal style people try to lessen the barriers among themselves. The affective mode of communication is more concerned with the "how" of communication whereas the instrumental mode of communication is intimately related to the issue of goal attainment. In high context cultures, communication is more often than not likely to be indirect, often elaborate, contextual, and affective rather than instrumental.[8]

In practical terms what this means is that in these cultures people will not overtly express their wishes and/or express rejection of any terms/conditions regarding a proposal. It also has the implication that in these cultures individuals may state the same thing in so many different ways. Likewise, the communicative tone and the content of the message will be heavily dependent on the hierarchical quality of the relationship among the parties. Finally, the communicative patterns in this context are not likely to be intimately related to the issue of goal attainment.

Many have pointed out that the Indian communicative style is indirect in nature.[9] The Indians often do not like to say "no" directly to the other party for fear of offending. As Girish Paranjpe, President (Finance) of Wipro Technologies states, "Indians do not speak up in meetings and do not like confronting the client, which sometimes leads to awkward situations like project delays and cost overruns."[10] Similar comments have been made by others as well.

Wendell Jones, Vice President Worldwide Service Delivery at DEC, who managed the outsourcing relationship between NASDAQ and Tata Consultancy Services, noted that communicative difficulties stemming from differences in cultures was one of the major problems that he had to deal with.[11] Commenting on the interactions between the Germans and the Indians, Sujata Banerjee notes, "Well, it is difficult for Germans when an Indian says 'no problem' as the German *suspects* that the real *challenges* are not being admitted. For the Indian, 'no problem' simply means, 'I know there will be problems, but I am doing the best I can *at my end.*'"[12]

The Indian communicative style is also characterized by elaborateness rather than succinctness. The Indians like to talk and express their viewpoint in multiple ways. This behavioral tendency is most likely reinforced by the fact that Indians are context sensitive. Context sensitivity has the implication that all possible contingencies must be outlined and their implications clearly delineated. As Araoz points out, "The Indian engineer is often unaware that verbosity is very hard on Americans, who generally like co-workers to be succinct and logical in their business communication."[13]

The Indian communicative style is also very contextual, in that what individuals communicate and how they communicate is shaped by the nature of the relationship between the individuals. For example, the Indian culture is hierarchical and this affects the pattern of communication between employees at different organizational levels. The Indian employee may adopt a very deferential attitude toward his superior and for this reason may be reluctant to initiate communication, much less convey information that may not be palatable to his or her superior.

As an Indian manager working in the subsidiary of a Danish company noted, "We Indians cannot say 'no' to our boss. The boss will get angry."[14] The director of British American Corporation, a company studied by Sinha, noted, "Indians wasted their time talking too much. They rarely stick to the agenda in a meeting. There is a wide gap between what Indians professed and what they actually did. They were more concerned about what other people would say than what was the 'right' thing to do."[15]

Finally, it would be fair to say that the Indian communicative style is more affective rather than instrumental. This is a style that "requires the listener to carefully note what is being said and to observe how the sender is presenting the message…. The part of the message that is being left out may be just as important as the part that is being included."[16] A good example of this may be gleaned in the interactions between the U.S. Ambassador Allen and India's first Prime Minister, Jawaharlal Nehru. When the United States decided to give military aid to Pakistan in 1954, President Eisenhower instructed the American ambassador in India to meet Nehru and convey the message that this action was not directed against India. During the meeting Nehru was calm and

> *Many have pointed out that the Indian communicative style is indirect in nature.*

restrained, leading the American ambassador, Allen, to conclude that Nehru was not offended by this action. However, as Cohen points out, this represented complete misjudgment by the American ambassador. He failed to understand the real meaning behind Nehru's reaction.[17]

## Ideological versus Pragmatic Communicative Style

An ideological communicative style utilizes the dominant ideology extant in that culture at a particular point in time to structure communication, and as Triandis has pointed out this "assumes that the other person has the same view."[18] By contrast, a pragmatic communicative style utilizes a mode of communication that achieves the intended goal. The Indian communicative style is often ideological, shaped as it is both by an idealistic mode of thinking, and more recently by a resurgence in Indian nationalism. Indeed as Perry points out, "Washington D.C.–based Pew Research Center's 2003 Global Attitude Survey found India was the most nationalistic place on earth with 74% of the respondents 'completely agreeing' that Indian culture is superior."[19] An ideological mode of communication uses one particular point of view to look at all types of problems. This has the implication that "When the universalistic person communicates with a particularistic, pragmatic opponent, the universalistic is likely to see the pragmatist as dealing with trivialities and as not having great thoughts, while the pragmatist is likely to see the 'universalists' as theoretical, fuzzy thinking, and dealing with generalities."[20] A related problem is that it may be hard to find common ground between the ideologist and the pragmatist, given that they are operating on the basis of radically different philosophies.

Historically, the ideological mode of thinking was dominant in India, and especially insofar as multinational firms were concerned. Even with the onset of liberalization in 1991, foreign investors, at least initially, were greeted with some degree of skepticism. The high-profile disputes involving many independent power producers and the likes of Cargill are a testimony to this fact. However … the rapid rise of India's software industry, and the recognition that international firms have played a positive role in its development, is, to be sure, altering the way in which foreign investors are being viewed in India. That said, there is without question an upsurge in Indian nationalism, with a strong desire for India to be recognized and accorded its due status in the world as a major power. This, of course, has the implication that all communication has to be viewed from the prism of Indian pride and greatness.

## Associative versus Abstractive Communication Style

Scholars have also drawn a distinction between an associative and an abstractive communication style.[21] An associative style of communication does not engage in sharp differentiations between who the person is and what the person does. By contrast, an abstractive communication style makes such differentiations. This difference has important implications for the way messages are transmitted and how they are decoded in different cultures. If, for example, there is no sharp differentiation between who the person is and what the person does, it may be difficult to give negative feedback to the other person without offending him or her.

It may also make it difficult to discuss the merits or demerits of any policy action in the abstract without assessing its implications for the individual or individuals concerned. It would be fair to say that while the Indian culture comprises both the associative as well as an abstract mode of communication, the associative style may be somewhat more dominant. This follows from the fact that the Indians are highly sensitive to criticism and may find it hard to follow the well-known precept of Fisher and Ury to "separate the people from the problem."[22] Although the issue of saving face may be less important in India compared to the Confucian cultures of China, Korea, Taiwan, and Japan, there is no question that face-related concerns are important. When one considers the fact that status, caste, age, and hierarchy are important, it is inevitable that issues of face become important. Communication designed to give feedback, elicit task-related compliance, and motivate employees must therefore be sensitive to these concerns.

A good example is that of Tata Steel, a company that was actively trying to reshape its corporate culture. As Sinha points out, many senior managers resisted the change to an alternative system that was more egalitarian. He cites the comments of a young officer who noted, "There are senior managers who are power hungry; I mean those who are brought up in the old culture. For them this change is erroneous and obnoxious. They feel they should be informed, their consent should be solicited, and all the files must be routed through them."[23] The interpretation of their behavior is that the senior Indian managers would have lost face as a consequence of the alternative system, even though the system may have increased the efficiency of the organization.

## Nonverbal Communication

Scholars are often at pains to point out that while individuals often pay attention to words, much of the most important communication often occurs nonverbally.[24] As Copeland and Griggs note, "On a very unconscious level many of us abroad can turn people off even when we are on good behavior."[25] This may occur for a number of different reasons such as making inappropriate gestures, or maintaining an inappropriate personal distance with the other party. Likewise, eye contact may make individuals in some cultures uncomfortable just as touching or informality may make others unhappy. Nonverbal behavior has four main components to which managers must pay attention. These are the issues of (a) distance, (b) touching, (c) eye contact, and (d) body movement.[26]

The North American or western European expatriate manager may find that the typical Indian manager or employee may have a very different style of nonverbal communication than what he or she might be used to doing. One such example is provided by Gesteland who, when working in India, was taken out for lunch by his Indian business partner. As they went for lunch, the Indian held the hand of Gesteland, and at least initially, it made him a trifle uncomfortable. In the European or American environment handholding is clearly indicative of sexual interest, but in the Indian environment, it only signifies friendship. Fortunately, Gesteland was "able to recognize this aspect of the Indian culture soon enough, and this prevented any behavior on his part that may have been considered to be a cultural faux pas."[27]

The personal space or distance among individuals is dependent on the status of the individual one is interacting with. In general, this distance increases when one is talking with one's superior or when one is relating to someone who comes from a lower rung of the hierarchy. It has also been pointed out that while in the past Indians preferred to maintain eye contact only with a person of equal status, it is no longer true in contemporary India. As a manual prepared by the Canadian International Development Agency notes, "As middle to high ranking women employees in the public and private sectors look directly at a person while addressing them, they expect the same from their male colleagues."[28] Practitioners have also pointed out differences in the use of gestures, with the reference often being made to the fact that Indians often say "yes" by shaking their heads sideways, a gesture that would signify a "no" in the Western cultural tradition.

It is important to point out that nonverbal communication is unconscious and for that reason not very easy to control. That said, it makes it even more important that European and American managers pay attention to it, for otherwise they will end up communicating a message which they never intended. This can lead to an unsuccessful negotiation, demotivation of an employee, or an overall climate in which people fail to communicate effectively and in a timely way.

> *The typical Indian manager or employee may have a very different style of nonverbal communication than what he or she might be used to do.*

## COMMUNICATING WITH INDIANS: IMPLICATIONS FOR WESTERN MANAGERS

What can Western managers do to enhance their effectiveness in communicating with the Indians? At the outset, it should be stated that there is no magical solution that will help Western managers improve the effectiveness of their communication with Indians overnight. It is also important to point out that Indian companies have now increasingly become cognizant of the cultural gap and are instituting training programs to enhance the cross-cultural skills of their employees in interacting with their European and North American counterparts.[29]

For example, the Bangalore-based company Wipro Technologies is training their Indian employees to interact more effectively with the Americans. They have brought in American trainers and have hired consultants from companies such as McKinsey & Co. to provide training both in India as well as overseas. Infosys Technologies is also reportedly developing a program of change management for its employees.[30] One can reasonably surmise that one of its likely consequences would be a decrease in communication barriers over time. It is also important to point out that Indian professionals find it easier to communicate and work in the North American context vis-à-vis the European context for a wide variety of reasons, ranging from country-specific differences in language and culture in Europe, to a greater sense of conservatism in the European environment.[31]

That said, what concrete steps can the Western expatriate undertake to enhance his effectiveness in communication with the Indians? The Western expatriate needs to (a) have a better awareness about Indian communicative patterns, (b) be able to deal with his or her emotions more effectively, (c) avoid ideological debates, (d) be able to create the perception of an individual who enjoys working in the Indian subcultural milieu. The following paragraphs elaborate these steps.

## Better Awareness about Indian Communicative Style

This is a truism but that does not lessen its importance. If Western managers lack an appreciation of how Indians communicate, they may find themselves in all sorts of difficulties and may lose their motivation to effectively conclude their assignment. Although this recommendation has a commonsensical quality to it, it is extremely important for a number of different reasons. First, and foremost, heightened awareness has the implication that the Western manager is likely to have more realistic or accurate expectations about his interactions with the Indian counterpart.

When expectations are realistic and accurate, the manager may learn to recognize, for example, that the unwillingness on part of the Indians to say "no" does not imply that the Indian is in perfect agreement on the specific issue or subject under discussion. He or she may have to probe further to get the answer he or she is looking for. In other words, a heightened sense of awareness will minimize misunderstandings or miscommunication. Similarly, when expectations are accurate, the manager is unlikely to experience negative emotions like frustration, anger, or anxiety, and this is surely beneficial for the interaction at hand. Not only are the manager's attentions not diverted from the task at hand; he or she is also unlikely to act in ways that may jeopardize future interaction. Accurate expectations may also convey to the Indian counterpart that the Western manager is truly interested in India, in that he or she has taken the time to learn about the local culture. This can only have positive effects on the interaction among the parties.

*Indian companies have now increasingly become cognizant of the cultural gap and are instituting training programs to enhance the cross-cultural skills of their employees.*

## Better Equipped to Deal with Negative Emotions

Negative emotions are often inevitable in intercultural interactions. As mentioned earlier, these emotions are a product of conflicting expectations. Although heightened awareness of another culture does limit the emergence and the intensity of these emotions, it cannot prevent them entirely for a variety of reasons. First, the expectations of Western managers doing business in India are not going to change overnight. It takes a while before managers can both fully appreciate an alternative way by which people live, and most importantly, internalize these new expectations in their daily interactions with the Indian colleagues. Second, even with the best of preparation, no Western manager can hope to fully or completely grasp the Indian cultural nuances, with the implication that sometimes they may experience these emotions notwithstanding their prior preparation or understanding about the Indian culture.

How, then, can the Western manager hope to deal with these emotions effectively? It must be said at the outset that in managing emotions there are important personality differences, with some individuals being more capable of handling these emotions well. That said, the Western manager can clearly take steps that will minimize their occurrence. One of the things that may help the manager deal with these emotions in a positive way may come from the recognition that *he or she is not alone*. In other words, he or she must consider the possibility that there may be other Western expatriates who may be experiencing the same emotions. This recognition may not only bolster his or her self-confidence but may also induce him or her to network with other expatriates in the area. Most importantly, this will lead him or her to the invaluable insight that he or she has not been dealt with in a unique way by the Indians. This, in turn, is likely to prevent him or her from developing a negative attitude about the Indians and that can surely be considered to be a positive development.

Second, even if the expatriate experiences negative emotions, he or she must resist the urge to express them. As Ambrose Bierce once remarked, "Speak when you are angry and you will make the best speech you will ever regret."[32] Emotions like anger, if expressed openly, will damage the relationship and make it that much harder to put the relationship back on track. This does not imply that the expatriate should not express his or her concerns about any issue or issues over which he or she has reservation; the argument is only that these concerns should be expressed in a culturally sensitive way. The Western manager may express his concerns calmly, may seek to revisit the issue later, or use the services of a key informant who may serve as a culturally adept mediator.

Third, the Western expatriate manager could seek to reframe the situation. He or she may want to look for the positive in an admittedly negative situation. This is not easy, but that is not to say that one should not attempt it. Maybe there is something in what the Indians have said, that at the very least, may be worth thinking about. This does not by any means exhaust all that the Western manager could do, but it does provide a broad overview of the strategies that the expatriate managers may use in bridging the cultural divide with their Indian counterpart.

## Avoid Ideological Debates

It is very easy to fall into this trap, and exiting from it is likely to be difficult. The Indian mind-set is both nationalistic and idealistic, and while the latter may be changing as India integrates itself in the world economy, nationalism is unlikely to disappear any time soon. The Western mind-set is for the most part pragmatic (although there may well be differences across countries) and this sets the stage for a clash of conflicting ideologies. In a business-related context, ideological debates on the rapidity of the economic reform process in India, and how open India should be to the transnational corporation, have emerged.

These debates have also carried over to the issue or issues of protecting intellectual property, privatization, and the role of the government in the economy. Ideological debates brook no room for compromise, and if anything, may harden the position of the parties further. They may also detract from effective problem solving and may be counterproductive in the extreme. What is interesting about India is that ideological conflicts notwithstanding, transnational corporations can function effectively and profitably in the Indian context (though the energy sector may be an exception).

## Creating the Perception of a Positive Attitude Toward India

It is important that Western expatriates demonstrate a positive attitude toward India. This is a proposition that would be equally true for any culture one wishes to operate in, but this is likely to have a particular resonance in the Indian cultural context. The Indian mind-set has, fortunately or unfortunately, been deeply shaped by the colonial experience, and this has the implication that there is, at least initially, a certain degree of suspicion toward the foreign investor.

Clearly this suspicion may not be equally targeted toward all foreign investors, but it does mean that the foreign investor has to create a certain sense of reassurance in the Indian mind. This reassurance is best demonstrated by creating the perception that the expatriate has a positive view about India. A good example is provided in a study of the BAC Corporation in India conducted by Sinha. Mr. Wilson, a British national, who was the Managing Director of the company, had adapted and felt comfortable with the Indian mores. As Sinha notes, "He freely mixed with employees, often took lunch with them, attended their marriage ceremonies, spoke broken Hindi and Punjabi, and seemed to love the Indian curry. Employees found in him a great listener."[33] This may indeed be one of the reasons as to why the Indian employees had positive views of British expatriates.

Communicating cross-culturally is neither easy nor predictable. Each party seeks to communicate on the basis of its own sets of assumptions and this is without a doubt the starting point of any conflict. This essay has attempted to outline the cultural divide separating the Western manager from his or her Indian counterpart. In years to come, this divide may be lessened, but in the interim some suggestions as to how best this divide can be mediated have been provided.

> *Communicating cross-culturally is neither easy nor predictable.*

## References

The epigraphs in this essay are drawn from W. B. Gudykunst and Y. Y: Kim (1992), *Communicating with strangers: An approach to intercultural communication* (pp. 41, 89); C. Storti (1990), *The art of crossing cultures*, Yarmouth, ME: Intercultural Press; and D. C. Thomas (2002), *Essentials of international management: A cross-cultural perspective*, Thousand Oaks, CA: Sage.

## Notes

1. Cited in W. B. Gudykunst and Y. Y. Kim (1992). *Communicating with strangers: An approach to intercultural communication*. New York: McGraw Hill (p. 41).

2. M. Guirdham (1999). *Communicating across cultures.* Hampshire, UK: Palgrave Macmillan.

3. H. W Lane, J. J. DiStefano, & M. L. Maznevski (1998). *International management behavior*. Oxford, UK: Blackwell.

3a. H. C. Triandis (1995). *Culture and social behavior*. New York: McGraw Hill.

4. Ibid.

5. E. T. Hall & M. R. Hall (1995). *Understanding cultural differences: Germans, French, and Americans*. Yarmouth, ME: Intercultural Press.

6. Ibid., p. 6.

7. R. M. Hodgetts & F. Luthans (2000). *International management: Culture, strategy, and behavior*. New York: McGraw Hill.

8. A. M. Francesco & B. A. Gold (1998). *International organizational behavior*. Upper Saddle River, NJ: Prentice Hall.

9. Canadian International Development Agency (1994). *Working with an Indian partner: A cross cultural guide for effective working relationships*, [city, province]: Author; P. Hobbs (2002). "The Complexity of India," *New Zealand Business*, November, pp. 12–13; R. Gopalakrishnan (2002). "If only India knew what Indians know." Retrieved from www.tara.com/rata_sons/articles/20020426_palkrishnan_2.htm

10. M. Jayashankar. "Building outsourcing bridges: Change management teams help US clients and Indian firms understand how to work together." Retrieved from www.businessworldindia.corn/june21st,2004./indepth02.asp

11. Kramer, R. M., & Messick, D. M. (1998). Getting by with a little help from our enemies: Collective paranoia and its role in intergroup relations. In C. Sedikides, J. Schopler, and C. Insko (Eds.), Intergroup cognition and intergroup behavior, pp. 233–255. Hillsdale, NJ: Lawrence Erlbaum.

12. R. Gibson. "Intercultural Communication: A Passage to India." Interview with Sujara Bannerjee. Retrieved from www.business-spodight.de/dodI3053?PHPSESSID, May 2003

13. Araoz. "When Cultures Collide." Cited in J. B. P. Sinha (2003). *Multinationals in India: Managing the interface of cultures*. New Delhi: Sage.

14. Cited in J. B. P. Sinha (2003). *Multinationals in India: Managing the interface of cultures*. New Delhi: Sage.

15. Cited ibid., p. 144.

16. Hodgetts & Luthans.

17. R. Cohen (1997). *Negotiating across cultures: Communication obstacles in international diplomacy*. Washington, DC: United States Institute of Peace.

18. H. C. Triandis (1995). *Culture and social behavior* (p. 193). New York: McGraw Hill.

19. A. Perry. "An Eternally Faltering Flame: Despite Its Billion-Plus Population, India is Always an Also-Ran at the Olympics." Retrieved from www.time.com/asia/magazine/article/0,13673,501040823-682346,00.html, February 9, 2004.

20. Triandis. *Culture and Social Behavior*.

21. Ibid.

22. R. Fisher & W. Ury (1991). *Getting to Yes*. Boston: Houghton Mifflin.

23. Cited in J. B. P. Sinha (2003). *Tata Steel: Becoming world class*. New Delhi: Sri Ram Center for Industrial Relations and Human Resources.

24. L. Beamer & I. Varner (2001). *Intercultural communication in the workplace*. New York: McGraw Hill.

25. L. Copeland & L. Griggs (1985). *Going international: How to make friends and deal effectively in the global marketplace*. New York: Random House.

26. R. R. Gesteland (1999). *Cross cultural business behavior: Marketing, negotiating, and managing across cultures*. Copenhagen, Denmark: Copenhagen Business School Press.

27. Ibid. (p. 71).

28. Canadian International Development Agency (1994). "Working with an Indian partner: A cross cultural guide for effective working relationships" (p. 16).

29. A. Viswanathan. "Indian Companies are Adding Western Flavour." Retrieved from www.wipro.com/newsroomn/newsitem/newstory288.htm, July 28, 2004.

30. Jayashankar. "Building Outsourcing Bridges."

31. P. Jasrotia. "IT Pros Find it Harder to Work in Europe." Retrieved from www.expressitpeople.com/20011029/cover1.htm, October 29, 2001.

32. Cited in A. Ben Ze-'ev (2000). The subtlety of emotions. Cambridge, MA: MIT Press.

33. Sinha. *Multinationals in India*, p. 139.

## Concepts and Questions

1. Why do Kumar and Sethi assert that communication problems increase in difficulty when you include the dimension of cross-cultural differences? Can you think of three or four examples in your life when those differences created problems?

2. How would you compare high-context communication patterns to low-context communication patterns as they apply to India and the United States? How might these differences be reflected when these two cultures interact?

3. What are the differences between ideological and pragmatic communication styles as they pertain to India and the United States?

4. How would you compare associative and abstractive communication styles as they relate to India and the United States?

5. What are some differences in nonverbal communication between India and the United States?

6. What advice do Kumar and Sethi offer to Western managers attempting to improve the manner in which they do business with members of Indian culture?

# When Face-to-Face Won't Work: Use of Informal Intermediaries to Communicate Interpersonally in Sub-Saharan Africa

ANN NEVILLE MILLER

*The next essay in this chapter is titled "When Face-to-Face Won't Work: Use of Informal Intermediaries to Communicate Interpersonally in Sub-Saharan Africa." This essay is noteworthy on two counts. First, it looks at a region of the world that is unfamiliar to most Westerners. Although nearly 400 million people live in this part of Africa, the people of this area remain a mystery to most of us. Second, Miller looks at a type of interpersonal communication that employs informal intermediaries—a practice that is not very common in the United States. Yet, as Miller points out, "using third parties to communicate certain interpersonal messages is a phenomenon that appears with regularity in a variety of cultures."*

*Intermediaries are most often used to mediate disputes or to convey sensitive information. Usually, this third person is not directly involved with the dispute in question. The subjects "carried" by the intermediary from person to person frequently deal with issues related to conflicts with supervisors or co-workers, sensitive situations between friends and family, or marital and financial problems. Another common use of the personal "conduit" is the transmission of bad news. Information concerning terminal illness and death is a frequent inter-mediated topic.*

*To explain her analysis Miller uses two theoretical constructs that apply to collective cultures—face negotiation theory and politeness theory. Both theories emphasize minimal face-to-face conflict as part of the cultural value system. If, for example, someone has an "outsider" carry negative, poignant, or emotional messages, they can avoid the trauma often associated with delivering such messages while at the same time maintaining group harmony. This process helps keep the*

> *Miller looks at a type of interpersonal communication that employs informal intermediaries.*

*originator of the message from suffering a loss of face. And, when unequal social relationships are involved, it also permits intermediaries to help the parties "keep their distance." Maintaining one's relational position is an important component of politeness theory.*

*By reading Miller's discussion of intermediaries you should be better able to appreciate that not all cultures solve problems or deal with interpersonal discord in the same manner. Cultures may develop very different processes for resolving social problems and interpersonal conflicts. Lacking an appreciation of how these processes are carried out could lead you into a difficult interpersonal situation if you violate or fail to use appropriate third-party intermediaries.*

## INTRODUCTION

The young suitor doesn't wake up one fine day and walk up to his future father-in-law to tell him he intends to marry the daughter. Even facing the father-in-law alone is considered disrespectful. So he has to send a male relative of his father-in-law's age who will present the request by saying, "There is a cow in this home we are interested in buying." That puts the message across politely and if they are agreeable then the negotiations start (Sang, 2006, p. 1).

The use of go-betweens, both formal vs. informal, was mentioned as a cultural trait early in the history of the field of intercultural communication (Condon & Yousef, 1975), but the idea has attracted little attention in communication literature in the three decades since. Scattered evidence does exist that the use of third parties to communicate certain interpersonal messages is a phenomenon that appears with regularity in a variety of cultures (e.g. Kenen,

Arden-Jones, & Eeles, 2004; Muira, 2000; Ting-Toomey & Kurogi, 1998). Marriage brokering, for example, is not uncommon in many parts of the world, especially south Asia. The broker may be entrusted not only with locating the prospective mate, but also with "testing the waters" to ensure that a family will not be embarrassed by undertaking an unsuccessful suit (Jaimon, 2005). The concept of third party disclosure of information has also been raised occasionally in U.S.-based health communication research, but almost always with reference to the violation of an individual's privacy through unauthorized leaking of a diagnosis by a confidante (see Greene, Derlega, Yep, & Petronio, 2003). Aside from these tidbits, a would-be sojourner culling communication literature for advice on the circumstances in which to expect this sort of interaction would not find much in the way of guidance. The informal use of uninvolved persons to mediate disputes or to convey information—what this essay will term "intermediated communication"—is distinctly understudied.

In many sub-Saharan African cultures, on the other hand, intermediaries are used frequently and intentionally to accomplish a range of relational tasks. Conflicts with supervisors or co-workers, requests by children to parents or elders, sensitive situations between friends, marital problems, all may at times be more gracefully handled by bringing in a third party to assist with communication. Bad news such as terminal illness as well as death and bereavement may also be communicated in an intermediated fashion.

In some of these circumstances use of an intermediary is just one among several options legitimately available to a communicator. Siblings might discuss how to inform their mother about the serious road accident in which their brother had been involved; neighbors might strategize how to reveal concerns about the behavior of an errant child. In other situations third party communication is almost or fully institutionalized. During marriage negotiations, for example, the groom-to-be is often accompanied to his prospective bride's home by his uncles and clan elders, or family friends. These people speak in his behalf as the bride-price is agreed upon, while the young man himself and even his parents are expected to remain silent. In years past, intermediation could begin even earlier in the courtship process as uncles, aunts, or other relatives were called upon to arrange an initial meeting between a young man and the young woman who had caught his eye. A similarly intermediated system of introduction has recently been described in neighboring Uganda, in which younger siblings or friends assist with the arrangement of adolescent sexual liaisons. (Morrow, Sweat, & Morrow, 2004.)

Intermediaries can be relatives, friends, pastors, or co-workers, and the appropriate intermediary for one issue might not be selected to assist with another. But in all cases such individuals are chosen to carry an interpersonal message that for any of a number of reasons would not be possible or comfortable for the initiator to deliver in person. This chapter explores intermediated communication in one sub-Saharan context, describing patterns of third party communication in various cultural groups in Kenya. First, however, I will briefly discuss two possible theoretical frameworks for consideration of use of intermediaries in interpersonal communication.

> *In many sub-Saharan African cultures, on the other hand, intermediaries are used frequently and intentionally to accomplish a range of relational tasks.*

## FACE NEGOTIATION THEORY AND POLITENESS THEORY APPLIED TO INTERMEDIATED COMMUNICATION

Although there is a paucity of material that specifically addresses intermediated communication, the practice is undoubtedly connected to a number of more regularly researched cultural and communicative constructs. Two models that claim to be valid across cultural groups—face negotiation theory and politeness theory—offer schemes by which this type of communication might be analyzed. Both give a central role to the concept of "face," or the sense of social self-image claimed by an individual in his or her relational network (see Domenici & Littlejohn, 2006). Both propose variables that should predict the type of "facework" that is likely to be used in a given situation, that is, the communicative behavior that individuals use to manage their own face and to uphold or threaten the face of others.

Ting-Toomey's (1988) face negotiation theory identifies individualism-collectivism and high-low power distance as the primary value orientations explaining understandings of face across cultures. Collectivism is defined as "the broad value tendencies of a culture in emphasizing the importance of the 'we' identity over the 'I' identity, in-group interests over individual interests, and mutual-face concerns over self-face concerns" (Ting-Toomey & Kurogi, 1998, p. 189). Individualism, on the other hand, stresses self-interest over other-interest; the "I" of personal identity over the "we." Both individualism and collectivism are assumed to exist to some degree in every culture, and for that matter in every individual, but one or the other tends to predominate in a given society. Most of sub-Saharan Africa is classified as collectivist in orientation (Gudykunst, 1998; Gyekye, 1997; Hofstede, 1991; Triandis, 1995).

Although the constructs of individualism and collectivism lack certain nuances needed for emic understandings of group-oriented thinking and values in some cultures, they are still important heuristics for at least beginning explorations of cultural contrasts. For instance, numerous studies have indicated that members of collectivist cultures (or individuals with interdependent self-construals; Markus & Kitayama, 1991) are more inclined than persons from more individualistic societies (or individuals with independent self-construals) to make use of indirect means of communication (e.g. Gudykunst, Matsumoto, Ting-Toomey, Nishida, Kim, et al., 1996; Holtgraves, 1997; Singelis & Brown, 1995; Triandis, 1995).

Collectivism has also, though much less commonly, been connected with intermediated communication. In a comparative study of conflict styles among four cultures, Ting-Toomey and associates (1999) found that Latinos and Asian Americans were more likely to use avoiding and third party conflict styles than were European Americans. Third party intermediaries tended to be of high status, possessed a credible reputation, and had a good relationship with both parties. Chinese participants in Leung's (1987) study preferred use of third parties

for bargaining and mediation as a means of resolving conflict because it was deemed to be more likely to reduce animosity. In contrast, Americans preferred adversary adjudication, viewing it as more objective and fair. Leung also cited the status of the intermediary and his/her relationship to disputants as factors affecting preference for intermediated communication. African collectivism has been connected to intermediated communication by Moemeka (1996), who observed, "If what a person has to say is not in the best interest of the community, the person would be bound by custom to 'swallow his (or her) words.' Of course, the affected individual may whisper complaints into the ears of those who may be able to help in such other ways that would not conflict with community interest" (pp. 202–203).

Face negotiation theory further claims that the value dimension of power distance is also associated with cultural patterns of face negotiation. Hofstede (1991) defined power distance as the view that differences in status among community members are natural and desirable. This vertical power orientation is manifest in hierarchical roles, asymmetrical relationships, and rewards and punishments on the basis of rank, status, and sometimes age and gender. Individuals in high power distance cultures are concerned with maximizing the distance between high- and lower-power parties as a means of displaying deference. Thus conflict, the major communicative goal with which the theory is concerned, is often managed in such cultures with avoidance, indirectness, or curtailing of emotional expression (Blankston, 2008). It may also be negotiated by informal third party mediation. Moemeka (1996) described the implication of this orientation for African communication:

*In Africa, vertical communication follows the hierarchical sociopolitical ranks within the community.*

In Africa, vertical communication follows the hierarchical sociopolitical ranks within the community. What a person says is as important as who he or she is. In other words, social statuses within the community carry with them certain cultural limitations as to what to say, to whom to say it, how to say it, and when to say it. On the other hand, horizontal communication is relatively open and usually occurs among people of the same age (sometimes, only of the same sex), those who work together, live in proximity, or belong to the same ethnic group. (pp. 200-201).

In comparison to face negotiation theory, politeness theory has a narrower scope of concern and has not, to the author's knowledge, been specifically applied to intermediated communication. Brown and Levinson's well-known model (1978, 1987) cites a close relative of intermediated communication—conversational indirectness—as the major sociolinguistic feature indicative of tending to matters of face. It suggests that culturally appropriate levels of indirectness can be predicted by the relational variables of power and social distance, plus the situational variable of magnitude of interpersonal imposition. All other factors being equal, the closer the relationship between two persons, the less the power differential between them, and the smaller the magnitude of imposition, the less likely it is that they will employ conversational indirectness. Although the weights of these factors in determining levels of indirectness in different cultures might vary (Song, 2008), once those weights are taken into account a speaker's social cognitions may be revealed through how he or she chooses to communicate the same information to different individuals (Goldsmith, 2008; Gonzales, Manning, & Haugen, 1992; Holtgraves & Yang, 1992).

Most investigations of politeness theory have been limited to the speech acts of requesting, inviting, or complimenting (Craig, Tracy, & Spissak, 1986; Goldsmith, 2008; Johnson, 2007; Pan, 2000; Wilson, Kim, & Meischke, 1991), but a model in the tradition of politeness theory that addresses politeness phenomena across interaction types is available in Scollon and Scollon's (1995) analysis of Athabaskan communication. The authors locate three overarching politeness systems: solidarity (used among persons who see themselves as equal in power and close in social relations and therefore comprising direct communication with one another), deference (used when persons are equal in power but want to emphasize differences using indirectness) and hierarchical (used in asymmetrical relationships where persons on the top use direct communication and subordinates use indirect). The appropriateness of this framework to African contexts cannot, of course, be assumed (in fact, Gough, 1995, raised questions about the applicability of aspects of politeness theory to some African cultures). It does, however, raise the possibility that

indirectness may operate across speech acts within certain relational systems, and it is at least feasible to consider that factors posited by the theory as determining levels of indirectness might also impact the choice to engage in intermediated communication.

## APPLICATION TO INTERMEDIATED COMMUNICATION IN KENYA

These theories suggest that a major impetus for incorporating third parties into communication of interpersonal information might be concern over loss of face for one or the other party. Face negotiation theory proposes that third parties are more likely to be called in to assist with conflict resolution in collectivistic as opposed to individualistic cultures, and in high power distance as compared with low power distance societies. Politeness theory suggests that within those environments indirect communication, and by extension intermediated communication, is most likely when magnitude of imposition and power differential between parties are large and when the level of relational closeness is low.

Using these last three factors to structure the discussion, I now turn to a description of everyday use of intermediated communication in Kenyan society. Or, more accurately, Kenyan societies. Kenya has not one, but somewhere between 40 and 50 distinct indigenous cultural and linguistic groups, each with its own rules, values, and traditions. To complicate matters further, many of these cultures are in a state of rapid but uneven westernization. Traditional practices in some cultures have scarcely changed for decades, especially in the rural areas. Other cultural patterns, especially in urban settings, have undergone massive metamorphosis. Although common themes run across ethnic groups and span the rural-urban divide, any comments made about Kenyan use of intermediated communication must be recognized as generalizations about a vastly diverse cultural landscape.

## Magnitude of Threat to Face

Based on politeness theory we might anticipate that a high degree of threat to the face of either the communicator or the other party could prompt persons to engage in intermediated communication. Indeed, in the Kenyan environment disastrous family news such as the pregnancy of an unwed daughter can be communicated via an intermediary, particularly to the father. The girl's mother, or perhaps an aunt, would traditionally be the bearer of the bad tidings, and in such cases intermediation might be combined with indirectness. A father who was thus informed that one of the family cows had broken its leg would recognize from the metaphorical reference to incapacitation of a valued animal that the forthcoming news would be severe, and that an attempt was being made to soften its impact.

Communication about marital difficulties by nature also involves loss of face to various parties. Because harmony in marriage is one of the chief cornerstones on which harmony throughout Kenyan society in general is built, any conflict that arises between husband and wife must be handled carefully. Traditionally, if a couple had serious disagreements to the point that the wife left and returned to her birth family, the husband could not expect to be reconciled to her unless he went to her family's home accompanied by his uncles and the clan elders. These intermediaries would make apologies to the family of the woman on behalf of her husband and often present a gift by way of appeasement for any wrongs she had suffered.

> *The sense that serious marital issues cannot and should not be addressed by the couple alone remains very current in Kenyan society.*

In the contemporary urban environment the role of the uncles and clan elders is often reassigned to the "best couple" or even a pastor. A participant in Miller and associates' (2009) study of couples communication among the Kamba ethnic group described how the best couple might become involved. "The best couple in our wedding is very close friends of ours. My wife can tell her all the problems. Then the best maid would tell the husband who would come and tell me what my wife is complaining about. If I have a problem I will explain to my best man who will tell the wife who in turn will tell my wife" (p. 20).

Whatever the identity of the intermediary, the sense that serious marital issues cannot and should not be addressed by the couple alone remains very current in Kenyan society. For example, a couple with whom I am acquainted had an argument that resulted in the wife's storming out and spending the night at the house of a relative. Because he felt that something very disturbing had happened in their marriage, something that had hurt him badly, the husband was shocked when his wife returned alone to their home the next day. It was only after two other couples were brought into the situation as intermediaries that he was able to believe that she was sincere in seeking reconciliation.

## Power Differential Between Parties

Politeness theory suggests that power differential within relationships plays a major role in determining the degree to which communication in a given situation is indirect. Use of intermediated communication in the Kenyan context also seems to be heavily influenced by power concerns. The societal structure of many Kenyan ethnic groups has traditionally been composed of nested hierarchies of relationships, with authority and submission based on age, marital status, wealth, and gender. In the millennial generation the hierarchy has to some degree been redefined, with education gaining importance as a sign of social status in certain communities such as the Luo, and wealth trumping other qualifications in some communities such as the Kikuyu. Nevertheless, the centrality of respect for, and proper submission to, authority as a cultural value remains to a great extent intact.

Power hierarchy in the family, too, was clearly delineated in past years. Although the position of father as supreme and unquestioned authority has eroded among some groups, even urban children still understand for the most part that interaction with their fathers must display a certain respectful deference. As a result of the outworking of this system, mothers may play an intermediary role between children and fathers. It has already been noted that in traditionally oriented families, if a daughter becomes pregnant out of wedlock, responsibility to make the father aware of the situation and to absorb some of his wrath on behalf of the child may fall to the mother or to an aunt. Intermediation may also be undertaken by mothers for children in more mundane matters. As one of my students recalled, "When I grew up and especially during my primary and secondary school, I never used to ask my father to buy me new school uniforms or inform him when I was sick. For the uniform, I could tell my mother who would in turn report to my father." Even when they are adults, children may have difficulty addressing their fathers directly until they themselves have attained a certain status either by virtue of being married and having children or because they have begun to display recognizable leadership qualities within the extended family circle.

Gender-based power differential is a defining component in the husband-wife relationship. Spousal power may have equalized to some degree in recent years, but many wives still find they must on occasion add to the credibility of their own status by bringing in a third party to carry messages to their husbands. When it comes to selecting an intermediary from within the family it is more common for women to approach their husband's family than their own for assistance (Miller et al., 2009). This is in part because a man's family may be assumed to know him well, but it is also because in many Kenyan kinship systems, once a woman marries she is no longer considered to be a member of her own family but is presumed to have transferred her membership to the family of her husband (see Ndeti, 1972). In polygamous families mothers may even use children to mediate communication with their husbands, anticipating that requests carried by such charming envoys will be difficult to resist. A child might be asked to carry a meal the mother had cooked over to the father in his hut, delivering the mother's message along with the food.

It is also common for women to enlist friends to enact intermediated communication with their husbands. A personal anecdote may serve as an example. Some time ago during a gathering that my husband and I attended, a Kenyan wife jokingly told a group of friends that she was trying to convince her husband to have another child, but without much success. "Yes, I keep telling him he needs a daughter to spoil!" she teased. The wife was, in fact, indirectly appealing to the men in the group to undertake intermediated communication for her. Her husband was fully aware

> *Even when they are adults, children may have difficulty addressing their fathers directly until they themselves have attained a certain status.*

of her strategy, and when two or three of the men present picked up the thread of conversation and encouraged him to have a third child he took notice. A year later, cradling his new daughter in his arms, he traced his change of mind explicitly to that conversation, "I thought, if these *wazee* [older men] are telling me to do this, I need to reconsider." My husband, who in true American style had viewed the entire conversation as good-natured ribbing of a friend, was surprised to be singled out among the *wazee* for the effectiveness of his (unwitting) part in the persuasive effort.

Because of their more powerful relational position men engage in intermediated communication less frequently than women. However, exceptions to this rule do occur. Research on disclosure of HIV positivity within couples has indicated that men are less likely than women to reveal their diagnosis directly to their spouse or partner (Miller & Rubin, 2007). It appears that when they discover they are HIV positive a substantial number of men persuade their wives that both should be tested for the virus and thereafter sit together to receive their test results. By withholding from their wives the fact that they already know their own diagnosis, husbands and boyfriends are able to maneuver clinic personnel into the position of intermediaries. A possible explanation of this finding may be that being HIV positive dramatically lowers men's relational status. Because they have a stigmatized condition that they might very well have contracted through the socially unacceptable behavior of marital unfaithfulness, they may find themselves in the sort of low-power position normally occupied by their wives. To make matters worse, the message they know they need to convey is of the most sensitive and negative sort imaginable. As a result they turn, uncharacteristically, to intermediated communication.

## Social Distance Between Interactants

The level of indirectness in a specific conversational exchange is also predicted in politeness theory by the relational closeness of the individuals involved. In unequal relationships, social distance as a determining factor for intermediated communication is likely to be eclipsed by the effect of discrepancies in power. Even so, and especially within horizontal relationships, having a close relationship can render intermediated communication less necessary. Close friends can often speak frankly about sensitive issues.

Relational closeness is also a key to the special place that grandparents often hold in family conflict resolution. Among the Kikuyu, for example, it is traditional to name each succeeding child after a specified grandparent. Grandparents maintain a singular relationship with their namesakes, and with the namesakes of their spouses, to the extent that a grandmother may refer to the grandson who is named after her spouse as "my husband," and a grandfather may similarly refer to a granddaughter as "my wife." By virtue of this close relationship grandparents may play a key intermediary role in conflicts between parents and children.

The following incident, related to me by an urban Kenyan woman, illustrates the interaction of all three predictive factors described above and gives something of a sense of the careful attention required for effecting intermediation in a sensitive situation. Carole, a young urban resident in an ethnically mixed marriage, came to her friend Jane for advice on what to do about increasingly severe marital problems. The two had known one another for many years so Carole felt free to be completely honest and open with Jane about her situation. After a long discussion they agreed that Carole needed to let her mother know what was happening. They also determined that the best means of doing so would be for Carole to send Jane as an emissary to Carole's mother's younger sister. The aunt, although of the same generation as Carole's mother, was closer age-wise to Carole and Jane, and could serve as a bridge between mother and daughter.

Carole knew her aunt was at the moment getting her hair done just minutes from downtown Nairobi where she and Jane were talking, so she contacted her aunt via cell phone to tell her that Jane wanted to drop by to say hi. This tactic was intended to alert the aunt that there was an issue that needed to be discussed, which it did. Jane then went alone to see the aunt on behalf of her friend.

> *Grandparents may play a key intermediary role in conflicts between parents and children.*

Upon arrival at the beauty parlor Jane spent some minutes discussing a wide range of generalities until the aunt finally asked pointedly, "So, how is Carole's husband these days?" Having received the expected cue, Jane then unfolded the entire story. The conversation closed with Jane and the aunt's agreeing in principle that Carole's mother ought to know about her daughter's difficulties. Even though it was not explicitly stated, Carole's aunt correctly inferred from that comment that she herself was being requested to broach the subject with her sister.

This story presents a fascinating combination of direct, indirect, face-to-face (f2f) and intermediated communication. Four different combinations are evident: (1) f2f-direct communication (Carole tells Jane that she is having marital problems); (2) f2f-indirect communication (at the beauty parlor Jane hints to Carole's aunt that there is an important issue she needs to discuss with her); (3) intermediated-direct communication (Carole directly requests Jane to talk to her aunt about the problem); and (4) intermediated-indirect communication (Jane hints to Carole's aunt that Carole's mother needs to know about the situation and the aunt understands this to be a request for her to serve as intermediary).

The direct and face-to-face communication in the incident occurred primarily between Jane and Carole, whose close relationship made it unnecessary for them to use intermediated communication even when the issue was extremely sensitive and embarrassing. At the same time intermediated communication was the method of choice for approaching Carole's mother, despite the fact that there is no indication in the story (or in real life) that their relationship was not a close one. Their difference in generational status, in combination with the sensitive and face-threatening nature of the information, were apparently determining factors in that decision. The aunt was an appropriate choice for intermediary because she had a foot in both generations and she and Carole were emotionally close. Nevertheless, due to the face-threatening nature of the information she herself was initially approached in an intermediated manner. Carole's selection of the best means of accomplishing her communicative and relational goals, therefore, was a result of the relational factors of social distance and power, in combination with the situational factor of the nature of the information.

## INTERMEDIATION BEYOND FACEWORK

Politeness theory and face negotiation theory privilege the concept of face as an explanation of certain types of communication, but defense against shame and management of face-threat are not the only motivations for sending messages via third parties in the Kenyan context. Another critical determining factor in the decision to seek an intermediary appears to be the degree to which the message contains distressing or negative news. For example, instead of communicating news of death directly to close kin of the deceased, concerned friends may request an intermediary, often an elderly or respected relative, to bear the ill tidings. It is assumed that because of this person's age and experience he or she will know how to gently or gradually break the news and afterward how best to comfort the individual. During the time I was writing the original version of this chapter, one of my Kenyan students came to excuse herself from class, explaining that a relative had called her and told her that she needed to go home immediately. After giving her permission to miss class I said that I hoped nothing bad had happened. "So do I," she responded. The intermediary had purposefully given her just enough information for her to infer that the problem might be serious, but apparently had judged it best to let her find out the specifics upon arrival so that she would not be upset while she was traveling home.

There is a sense in which the distance achieved through intermediated and indirect communication expresses respectful appreciation. The explanation by one of my students of traditional Luo wedding negotiations is revealing in that regard:

During negotiations, the young man would be accompanied by clan elders and uncles to the lady's home and these people would talk on his behalf since he wasn't meant to talk, out of respect for his future in-laws. The young lady's uncles and aunties would also receive them on behalf of her parents who were not meant to take part verbally in negotiations to maintain respect between the two parties.

Directness, in traditional environments at least, can be rude. This is perhaps not surprising when considered in conjunction with the requirements in many Kenyan cultures for keeping not only figurative but also physical distance within certain relationships. A man or woman who saw his or her parents-in-law—or among some groups, any elderly person—approaching on a path would step aside to give them a wide space in which to pass. Even now in the city some spatial prohibitions designed to show respect are still in force. For example, when visiting a friend in the hospital recently I ran into a male colleague who was seated on a bench outside the entrance waiting for his wife to emerge. He explained that she was visiting a female relative whose relationship to him made it culturally inappropriate for him as a man to enter the hospital room. From such a perspective the American penchant for talkativeness and direct expression can be unappealing and, when employed with authority figures, disrespectful (see Hastings, 2000). A full explanation of the use of intermediated communication would have to make provision not only for embarrassing or face-threatening situations but also for non–face-related instances like these.

## Closing Thoughts

This brings me to several concluding thoughts. First, it must be mentioned that there is a downside to intermediated communication. If the practice serves to reinforce values of hierarchy within society (see Piot, 1993) then it is to be expected that persons on the lower rungs of the ladder might at times feel that the requirement that authority figures be approached through third parties serves to petrify inefficient or even unjust systems. Creative but frustrated lower- and middle-level employees can be heard bemoaning the fact that no mechanism exists for them to give constructive input into corporate or institutional policies. Within the family, too, the expectation of intermediated communication between husbands and wives can perpetuate an inequitable relational power balance. In years past the distance between spousal statuses was so dramatic that within some cultural groups, such as the Baganda in neighboring Uganda, women could not even inform their husbands face-to-face that they were pregnant. Such extreme examples are few nowadays, but the fact remains that in a majority of African marriages wives are still the lower power partner, and the practice of intermediated communication by spouses is a confirmation of, if not a contributor to, that reality.

Second, intermediated interpersonal communication is not confined to sub-Saharan societies. As evidence, I urge North American readers to recall a time in elementary or middle school when they sent or were sent by friends to inquire of a pre-adolescent heartthrob, "So-and-so likes you. Do you like her?" Intermediated communication is present in American life as well, and it does not entirely stop when we cross the threshold into high school. In fact, United States history contains one of the most famous instances of intermediation for purposes of courtship, that of Miles Standish, whose intermediary turned out to be singularly ill suited for the communicative task with which Standish entrusted him. Thus although this chapter has focused on describing distinctively Kenyan approaches to intermediated communication, the recognition that third party communication plays a pivotal role in some African cultures should also motivate Western scholars to examine the role of informal intermediaries in their own backyards.

Third, Westerners must take care not to project their own (or Miles Standish's) cultural experiences onto the Kenyan situation and to assume that careful orchestration of third party involvement means that persons who engage in this type of communication suffer from chronic communication apprehension or lack of assertive communication skills (see Hara & Kim, 2004). Kenyans are as capable of being as direct and face-to-face in their communications as are Americans or Europeans. Stating a message indirectly and using intermediaries are more often signs of strength, self-control, and communicative sophistication than indications of lack of competence.

Intermediated communication as practiced in Kenyan interpersonal relationships, then, involves intricate, subtly choreographed interpersonal maneuvering, and provides a fascinating topic for observation. Unfortunately, like African communication patterns in general (Miller, 2005), it has been infrequently engaged in scholarly work. Yet from a practical standpoint, any sojourner in much of sub-Saharan Africa who hopes to be culturally alert, any aid worker who intends to be culturally effective, must on occasion be either the sender or recipient of such third party communication. In the age of AIDS, when a fuller understanding of interpersonal communication in the sub-Sahara has become critical, it is to be hoped that future scholarship will take up the challenge.

# References

Blankson, H. (2008). Curtailing Emotional Expression: The Role of Power-Distance. *Conference Papers—National Communication Association*, 1.

Brown, P., & Levinson, S. (1978). Universals in language usage: Politeness phenomena. In Goody, E. (Ed.), *Questions and politeness* (pp. 56–389). London: Cambridge University Press.

Brown, P., & Levinson, S. (1987). *Politeness: Some universals in language usage*. Cambridge, England: Cambridge University Press.

Condon, J., & Yousef, F. S. (1975). *An introduction to intercultural communication*. Indianapolis: Bobbs-Merrill.

Craig, R. T., Tracy, K., & Spissak, F. (1986). The discourse of requests: Assessment of a politeness approach. *Human Communication Research*, *12*, 437–268.

Domenici, K., & Littlejohn, S. W. (2006). *Facework: Bridging Theory and Practice*. Thousand Oaks, CA: Sage.

Goldsmith, D. (2008). Politeness theory. *Engaging theories in interpersonal communication: Multiple perspectives* (pp. 255–267). Thousand Oaks, CA: Sage.

Gonzales, M. H., Manning, D. J., & Haugen, J. A. (1992). Explaining our sins: Factors influencing offender accounts and anticipated victim responses. *Journal of Personality and Social Psychology*, *62*, 958–971.

Gough, D. H. (1995). Some problems for politeness theory: Deference and directness in Xhosa performative requests. *South African Journal of African Languages*, *15*, 123–125.

Greene, K., Derlega, V. J., Yep, G. A., & Petronio, S. (2003). *Privacy and disclosure of HIV in interpersonal relationships: A sourcebook for researchers and practitioners*. Mahwah, NJ: Lawrence Erlbaum.

Gudykunst, W. (1998). Individualistic and collectivistic perspectives on communication: An introduction. *International Journal of Intercultural Relations*, *22*, 107–134.

Gudykunst, W. B., Matsumoto, Y., Ting-Toomey, S., Nishida, T., Kim, K., & Heyman, S. (1996). The influence of cultural individualism-collectivism, self-construals, and individual values on communication styles across cultures. *Human Communication Research*, *22*, 510–543.

Gyekye, K. (1997). *Tradition and modernity: Philosophical reflections on the African experience*. New York: Doubleday.

Hara, K., & Kim, M.-S. (2004). The effect of self-construals on conversational indirectness. *International Journal of Intercultural Relations, 28*, 1–18.

Hastings, S. (2000). Asian Indian "self-suppression" and self-disclosure: Enactment and adaptation of cultural identity. *Journal of Language and Social Psychology, 19*, 85–109.

Hofstede, G. (1991). *Cultures and organizations: Software of the mind*. London: McGraw-Hill.

Holtgraves, T. (1997). Styles of language use: Individual and cultural variability in conversational indirectness. *Journal of Personality and Social Psychology, 78*, 624–647.

Holtgraves, T., & Yang, J.-N. (1992). Interpersonal underpinnings of request strategies: Principles and differences due to culture and gender. *Journal of Personality and Social Psychology, 62*, 246–256.

Jaimon, R. S. (2005, May 7). The case of the vanishing matchmaker. *The Hindu: Online edition of India's National Newspaper*. Accessed May 16, 2007 at http://www.hinuonnet.com/thehindu/mp/2005/05/07/stories.htm.

Johnson, D. (2007). Politeness theory and conversational refusals: Associations between various types of face threat and perceived competence. *Western Journal of Communication, 71*(3), 196–215.

Kenen, R., Arden-Jones, A., & Eeles, R. (2004). We are talking but are they listening? Communication patterns in families with a history of breast/ovarian cancer. *Psycho-oncology, 13*, 335–345.

Leung, K. (1987). Some determinants of reactions to procedural models for conflict resolution: A cross-national study. *Journal of Personality and Social Psychology, 53*, 898–908.

Markus, H., & Kitayama, S. (1991). Culture and the self: Implications for cognition, emotion, and motivation. *Psychological Review, 98*, 224–253.

Miller, A. N. (2005). Keeping up with cartography: A call to study African communication. *International and intercultural communication annual, 28*, 214–236. Washington DC: NCA.

Miller, A. N., Golding, L., Ngula, K., Wambua, M. A., Kizito, M. N., Mutua, E., Odondi, C., Booker, N. A., Mwithia, J. K., & Rubin, D. L. (2009). Couples communication on sexual and relational issue in Machakos District, Kenya. *African Journal of AIDS Research, 8*, 51–60.

Miller, A. N., & Rubin, D. L. (2007). Motivations and methods for self-disclosure of HIV seropositivity in Nairobi, Kenya. *AIDS and Behavior, 11*, 687–697.

Moemeka, A. (1996). Interpersonal communication in communalistic societies in Africa. In W. B. Gudykunst, S. Ting-Toomey, & T. Nishida (Eds.), *Communication in personal relationships across cultures* (pp. 217–236). Thousand Oaks, CA: Sage.

Morrow, O. I., Sweat, M. D., & Morrow, R. H. (2004). The *matalisi*: Pathway to early sexual initiation among the youth of Mpigi, Uganda. *AIDS and Behavior, 8*, 365–378.

Muira, S. (2000). The mediation of conflict in the traditional Hawaiian family: A collectivist approach. *Qualitative Research Reports in Communication, 1*, 19–25.

Ndeti, K. (1972). *Elements of Akamba life*. Nairobi: East African Publishing.

Pan, Y. (2000). *Politeness in Chinese face-to-face interaction*. Stamford, CT: Ablex.

Piot, C. D. (1993). Secrecy, ambiguity, and the everyday in Kabre culture. *American Anthropologist, 95*, 353–370.

Sang, N. (2006). *Reflections on politeness theory*. Unpublished paper.

Scollon, R., & Scollon, S. B. KI. (1995). *Intercultural communication: A discourse approach*. Cambridge: Blackwell.

Singelis, T. M. & Brown, W. J. (1995). Culture, self, and collectivist communication: Linking culture to individual behavior. *Human Communication Research, 21*, 354–389.

Song, S. (2008). The role of culture in expressing politeness through speech act in a second language. *Dissertation Abstracts International Section A, 69*, 2250.

Ting-Toomey, S. (1988). Intercultural conflict styles: A face-negotiation theory. In Y. Y. Kim & W. Gudykunst (Eds.), *Theories in intercultural communication*. Newbury Park, CA: Sage.

Ting-Toomey, S., & Kurogi, A. (1998). Facework competence in intercultural conflict: An updated face-negotiation theory. *International Journal of Intercultural Relations, 22*, 187–225.

Ting-Toomey, S., Yee-Jung, K., Shapiro, R., Garcia, W., Wright, T., & Oetzel, J. (2000). Ethnic/cultural identify salience and conflict styles in four U.S. ethnic groups. *International Journal of Intercultural Relations, 24*, 47–81.

Triandis, H. C. (1995). *Individualism and collectivism*. Boulder, CO: Westview.

Wilson, S. R., Kim, M.-S., Meischke, H. (1991). Evaluating Brown and Levinson's politeness theory: A revised analysis of directives and face. *Research on Language and Social Interaction*, 25, 215–252.

Acknowledgement: The author expresses appreciation to Daystar University M.A. students and faculty as well as numerous friends for sharing their thoughts on this topic with her.

## Concepts and Questions

1. In parts of sub-Saharan Africa, what are some of the communicative tasks intermediaries are asked to perform. Do you think there is a need for such tasks to be carried out in North America? Why or why not?

2. Why is the concept of "saving face" used more in other countries than in the United States?

3. Do you see "saving face" as a communication value you would like to employ in your interpersonal relationships? Why or why not?

4. Why do collective cultures employ intermediaries with greater regularity than do individualistic cultures? What do those differences tell you about the values imbedded in each of these orientations?

5. Why is "politeness theory" related to the concept of intermediaries? Is "politeness theory" a notion that is popular in the United States?

6. In what situations in your life would you have found it useful to have had an intermediary at your disposal?

7. What is Miller referring to when she writes about conversational indirectness and intermediaries?

8. Why do certain power hierarchy relationships lend themselves to intermediaries? Have you ever been involved in one of those types of relationships?

9. What are some of the shortcomings to use of intermediaries that Miller discusses in her essay? Can you think of any other limitations in the use of intermediaries?

# Russian Cultural Values and Workplace Communication Patterns

MIRA BERGELSON

*It is only fitting that we have included an essay on Russian culture in this new edition: Russia, with a population of nearly 150 million people, is one of the world's major superpowers. Mira Bergelson helps you understand this multinational culture in an essay titled "Russian Cultural Values and Workplace Communication Patterns." Like so many of the essays in this book, Bergelson's contribution begins with a reminder of the importance of intercultural communication in today's world. She notes, "Cross-cultural communication issues, and their potential for creating obstacles to effective, successful and professional interactions, have become a critical aspect of the movement toward a globalized society." To keep many of these damaging and destructive issues from impeding communication between Russians and Americans, Bergelson offers a number of insights into Russian culture. She begins*

*by looking at four key Russian values that reflect the Russian worldview. These values are emotionality (expressing the way one feels), judgmental attitudes (passing moral judgments on other people), fatalism (the Russian belief that they "have no control over the world"), and irrationality (the belief that the world is an irrational place).*

*Bergelson also offers useful information about Russian culture when she discusses how discrepancies and variances exist between "Russian traditional and Soviet-era cultures." These differences often create inconsistencies in how the world is viewed from these orientations. In addition to a discussion of the differences in these two historical perspectives, Bergelson offers a detailed evaluation of the communication patterns that exist in both Russia and the United States. According to Bergelson,*

This original essay appears here in print for the first time. All rights reserved. Permission to reprint must be obtained from the author and the publisher. Dr. Mira Bergelson is a professor in the Intercultural Communication Program, Department of Foreign Languages at Moscow State University. She has also served as the Cultural Assistant in the American Embassy in Moscow.

these differences can "bring about misunderstandings or create conflict." She is primarily concerned with differences in politeness patterns as they relate to Russians and Americans. After examining six of these differences, she concludes that "taken collectively, Russians are more insistent on expressing and reviving solidarity politeness." A communication style, Bergelson believes, at least for Americans, "lacks expression of deferential politeness."

Bergelson concludes her analysis by presenting a grid that looks at ten communication and cultural variables found in Western culture, the former Soviet-style culture, and traditional Russian cultures. The ten dimensions she compares are the I/We orientation, human relationships, activity orientation, time orientation, relation to nature, form and substance, progress, history, freedom and discipline, and age.

## CULTURAL SENSITIVITY AND CULTURAL KNOWLEDGE

Cross-cultural communication issues, and their potential for creating obstacles to effective, successful organizational and professional interactions, have become a critical aspect of the movement toward a globalized society. Competent communication, a central instrument for an organization to create a sustainable competitive advantage, is further complicated when cultural differences must be managed (Persikova, 2002). To overcome these communication difficulties and lessen misunderstandings, individuals and professional organizations have instituted cross-cultural training programs, one of which is discussed in the final section of this essay.

In addition to general intercultural sensitivity training, corporate managers need to acquire culture-specific knowledge before embarking on an overseas assignment. This requirement is made difficult by the amount of available cultural information and the need to determine what is beneficial and what is useless. For instance, noting that characters in Russian films always seem to be quarrelling (while, in fact, they are not) can be confusing. Just observing this activity as a behavioral display will only produce negative opinions (a reason why Soviet—and now Russian—films never enjoyed commercial success in the U.S.). But spending time and effort to analyze what the behavior

> Bergelson offers a detailed evaluation of the communication patterns that exist in both Russia and the United States.

may denote, and how it relates to other facets of Russian culture, can often provide insight into problems of cross-cultural organizational communication and group dynamics.

In this paper, I examine some of the seemingly unrelated and isolated pieces of Russian cultural information in a systematic way. Specifically, I look at *surface representations* of certain *basic cultural values*, which will enable you to draw correct *cultural inferences*. For instance, in the example from the Russian movie, we have a surface (behavioral) representation— loud and intense pronunciation. This activity may be considered as "too loud, too emotional" and evaluated negatively by an outsider who unconsciously compares it to similar situations in his or her own culture ("people speak loudly and emotionally when they quarrel"). However, the communicative behavior displayed in the movie can be used to gain knowledge of the basic, invisible cultural values underpinning the activity (e.g., *demonstrating attitudes* and *directness of communication* are acceptable and normative).

This illustration demonstrates the limitations of relying on surface representations of behavioral traits to understand a culture. The enlightened outsider will be able to assign a cultural value to the observable behaviors, and use that knowledge to effectively manage cultural differences. Culturally mindful communications will arise from the process of making cultural inferences only after surface representations have been attributed to basic cultural values. Therefore, in order to fully understand Russian communicative behaviors one must have an appreciation of the basic cultural values which form the Russian worldview.

## RUSSIAN CULTURAL VALUES REFLECTING BASIC WORLDVIEW

Linguistic research of cross-culture communication and related cultural anthropology topics is generally in agreement that basic cultural values, which indicate a culture's worldview, are often reflected in certain "key words" or "key concepts" (Shmeljov, 2002). Wierzbicka's (1992) influential book on cross-cultural pragmatics provides generalizations about the basic values and features of Russian culture.

## Emotionality

For Russians, expressing the way you feel (both good and bad) and attention to what other people say about their feelings are favorably considered in a wide variety of contexts. From this, it is clear that for Russians relationships are more important than the contextual reality.

This cultural feature can be observed in language strategies such as heavy use of "culturally loaded words" like *dusha*—"soul", which signals the importance of the inner world. Also, the abundant use and great variety of active emotional verbs (as if emotions emerge on their own and are not just experienced)—*volnovat'sja, pechalit'sja, udivljat'sja, radovat'sja*—as compared to the English terms for emotional states—*be worried, be surprised, be happy*. In the realm of proper names, Russia is famous for having lots of nicknames (expressive derivation), not only towards children as in English (e.g., *Teddy, Tommy*) but towards adults without distinction of age or gender. These are used in a variety of contexts to express the extremely important role of closeness and intimacy and to communicate the minute aspects of feelings between individuals and the subtle shades of their relations—in other words, the ability to express *solidarity politeness* by minimizing social distance.

> For Russians, expressing the way you feel (both good and bad) and attention to what other people say about their feelings are favorably considered in a wide variety of contexts.

## Judgmental Attitudes

Russians have an inclination toward judgmental attitudes, with a tendency for ethical evaluation. Among Russians, one can expect to be morally judged and it is considered appropriate to treat others the same way. Russians are eager to voice their opinions, and people expect, and sometime require from others, moral evaluations of mutual loyalty, respect, and sincerity. This cultural value is reflected in the Russian language by the abundance (as compared to English) of nouns—both positive and negative—expressing absolute moral judgment. This is quite different from using adjectives, which describe only a feature of a person, because nouns classify a person as a certain type.

## Fatalism

Many Russians possess an attitude of "having no control over the world". The realm of the uncontrollable, and thus unconceivable, is quite broad. This is directly opposite to Americans' pragmatism when assessing and dealing with difficulties.

## Irrationality

The world is considered an irrational place, and a Russian may behave and think as if unable to always rely on objective methods of analysis and logic. This is in opposition to American positivism.

These Russian cultural values give rise to the following behavioral attitudes, which can create difficulties when interacting with Westerners in an organizational context:

- Relationships are more important than results.
- Intrapersonal reality can often become external.
- The realm of the uncontrollable and, thus, unconceivable is broader than in the West.
- Things can go wrong or get worse at any moment.
- One cannot completely rely on objective methods of analysis and causality.
- Ethical evaluations are important and there is a tendency toward them.

There are, of course, many more cultural obstacles than those mentioned above. For example, problems can arise due to the variation between Russian traditional and Soviet-era cultures. Modern Russia is a huge conglomerate of significantly contradictory cultural patterns. What makes it different from, say, the multiculturalism of the United States is the lack of a legacy: neither historically nor *de jure* was multiculturalism acclaimed in the national context. Still, there are some recent positive trends in public opinion about the real values of multiculturalism, a position often advocated by top Russian authorities, and it is proclaimed as one of the pillars of the modern Russian state. Yet, Russia in all its ethnic and regional variations is one nation with one rather diverse culture. And the main divisions in that culture are along slightly different lines: between traditional Russian (TR), inherited from the Soviet system (S), and Westernized (W) cultural models. Therefore, one of the main cross-cultural communication problems for an outsider is deciding which cultural pattern (T, S, or W) one is dealing with at any given moment with any given individual. Some of the more easily detectable cultural patterns of the traditional and Soviet co-cultures include:

- A deep mistrust between the authorities and the people.
- General pessimism.
- Lack of critical thinking and negotiation skills.
- No, or little, respect for laws and rules.
- A deep-rooted practice of deceiving higher authorities, coloring the truth, and using roundabout ways.
- Mistrust of commercial activities (Jacobs, 1992).

From a western perspective, these patterns of behavior may seem contradictory, but Russians consider them to be the focus, the central line, of their history. Thus, Russians often feel sensitive, vulnerable, and angry towards what they consider to be "Western cultural imperialism". Partially, this attitude is a result of what Westerners consider "The End of the Cold War", but what Russians consider as "Transformations"—changes on a scale that no country has ever experienced before (Holden, Cooper, & Carr, 1998). These transformations embraced all aspects of public and private life—transformation of the political system, transition from a command to a market economy, new federal relations, new foreign policies, etc.

None of these changes went well, and most Russians believe that things should have been done differently and cannot agree on what exactly went wrong. They do agree, however, that the world paid insufficient attention to the enormity of what was done and to the suffering people experienced in transitioning from the Soviet era. As a result, the very idea of *changes* can be a problem in Russian organizations when western managers attempt to introduce and implement new management techniques of constant

*Russia in all its ethnic and regional variations is one nation with one rather diverse culture.*

change. Changes are generally viewed in Russian culture, especially in its more traditional layers, as a threat, and people want to avoid them.

## CULTURALLY INFLUENCED COMMUNICATION PATTERNS

It is one thing to recognize that values vary between cultures, but it is of perhaps greater importance to understand how those values influence culture-specific behavioral patterns, especially communication patterns. These communication patterns have been described in Hymes's (1974) model of SPEAKING. Gumperz (2001) posits that certain linguistic structures serve as clues to interpretation of meaning and inferences based on cultural assumptions of the participants.

I will now discuss the variant communication patterns that can bring about misunderstandings or create conflict during Russian-U.S. communicative interactions. My observations are informed by Kasper's (1996) discussion of Politeness Theory. The focus is on those Russian communication patterns that can lead to communicative failures both during the interaction and subsequent to the interaction by eroding a participant's perception of the other.

## Western (Anglo-American) and Russian Politeness Strategies and Communication Patterns

It is clear that culturally different communication practices can lead to failures in a cross-cultural organizational context—be it in the workplace, at the negotiation table, or choosing management strategies. A situation can be aggravated by the fact that language capabilities—even more so, fluency—do not necessarily help mitigate these failures. This is because while "pure" language mistakes (e.g., grammar, wrong lexical choices, pronunciation, etc.) are easily recognized as such, clumsy handling of politeness strategies or speech acts usage can be taken as personality traits (Kniffka, 1995). Thus, a person acting out his culture's politeness and other discourse strategies may seem to a representative of another culture as rude and imposing, or insecure and indirect, leading to a perception of the person as an unreliable partner or a pushy employee (Thomas, 1984).

## Politeness Related Problems

Research conducted by Ratmayr (1998) and Wierzbicka (1992), as well as others, have demonstrated that the following oppositions are generally valid for interpersonal communication between Russians and Americans.

| Russians | Americans |
| --- | --- |
| Value solidarity politeness more than deferential politeness | Pay more attention to negative politeness |
| Express more emotive data | More conventionally indirect in requests |
| Invest more effort into supporting requests by using justifications | Preface corrections with positive remarks more than Russians |
| Directness with familiars is associated with sincerity | Directness with familiars is associated with imposition on their freedom |
| There is a vast selection of Russian words and expressions used to show warmth and inoffensive closeness with familiars and intimates, thus amplifying positive politeness | When translated into English, these Russian words and expressions are typically rendered into expressions of patronizing attitudes, thus becoming offensive |
| Friends normally considered intimates | Friends normally considered familiars |
| Express more politeness to friends | Express more politeness to strangers |

Taken collectively, Russians are more insistent on expressing and reviving solidarity politeness. It normally means a smaller distance between equals. But, from a Western point of view, this style lacks expression of deferential politeness, which can create problems for teamwork. Leontovich (2002) provides an extensive treatment of cross-cultural communication between Russians and Americans.

## Information Processing Related Problems

In a cross-cultural communication setting, an extremely important factor is how one's messages and behaviors are interpreted by the other person. Specifically, as relates to this case, how a U.S. business representative processes the Russian representative's communicative acts will influence the assigned meaning. Without an understanding of Russian culturally influenced communication practices, a U.S. businessperson may well assign negative or incorrect meaning. The following are examples of normative Russian communicative behaviors that can become pitfalls in a cross-cultural environment.

- *Communication style is not targeted at reaching a consensus.* At least that is how it may be judged by Western participants at a business meeting with Russians. In normal conversational turn taking, Russians will often start with "no!" (*njet!*)

- *Offering wrong or no answers to your questions, or "knowing better what you need".* This means that judgments, or "good advice", are a common Russian response to information seeking behaviors. For example, asking a Russian colleague for a name of a potential partner (X) for an activity (Y) in town (Z) may lead to the answer "Person (M) in town (N) will better suit your activity (Y)". This does not imply rudeness or an unwillingness to cooperate, but just the opposite—friendliness and a desire to cooperate and help. This type of exchange is especially common between equals in an informal context—e.g., "Why do you use this chair? It is bad for your back!"

- *Addressee's responsibility for information.* In Russia, a person interested in getting information has to ask for it, and those who possess the information—especially intuitions—do not feel compelled to provide it without additional urging (i.e., you need this train schedule—you find a way to get it). And even when provided, the information can be inexplicit and incomplete. This Russian communication characteristic is extremely different from the U.S. style, where providing full, explicit, comprehensive information to the public is a primary duty of an organization. An example of how a U.S. businessperson could become frustrated by this Russian practice can come from a simple request for a phone number. When using the provided number, the U.S. representative may find it does not work as given but requires an additional code. The American may well ask the Russian provider, "Why didn't you tell me this before?" The Russian would reply, "You did not ask!" This communicative trait is drastically opposite to the demands of the modern communications age and has been changing rapidly—at least in the "new economy" spheres like Internet commerce.

- *Potential mistrust of "objective truths".* This culturally based feature can be especially disconcerting to U.S. partners when dealing with organizational issues. Imagine introducing new software to Russian colleagues and getting surprised looks and annoyed objections—"Why should we change anything? The old one works pretty well." In a cross-cultural exchange, this communicative trait may be perceived as irrational or argumentative. The U.S. member may feel mystified by the need to discuss things that seem self-evident.

- *Parallel processing of information.* This is what Hall (1959) calls polychronous, as opposed to monochronous, culture. The Russian multi-focus time orientation can easily lead to misinterpretations of behaviors by single-focus U.S. businesspersons.

## Culture and Business: Applied Communication Patterns

The West has historically considered Russia to be enigmatic (e.g., "a riddle, wrapped in a mystery, inside an enigma" was coined by Winston Churchill). However, the Western perception of Russia being difficult to understand has been heightened by the societal changes the country has experienced over the past two decades. For Russian business, the problems arising from the globalization process have been exacerbated by the dramatic changes wrought by the collapse of the former Soviet Union. Basically,

Russians must now confront the issues associated with the emergence of a new culture, a new national identity, and an absolutely new business culture. These enormous, dramatic changes, plus the embedded basic values of the traditional Russian culture, are coalescing to shape the business culture of modern Russia.

> *Russians must now confront the issues associated with the emergence of a new culture, a new national identity, and an absolutely new business culture.*

Research, anecdotal evidence, and personal impressions confirm that in organizational settings expectation gaps between Westerns and Russians (e.g., managers, entrepreneurs, professionals, staff, etc.) form one of the main obstacles to conducting business, creating successful partnerships, and organizing efficient work teams. Below are some of the widely supported statements from both parties that can strain relations between Russians and Westerners (Holden, Cooper, & Carr, 1998).

| Western Attitude | Russian Attitude |
|---|---|
| Russians don't know how to work hard. | Westerners have no appreciation of recent societal changes. |
| Business problems are simple in Russia. | Westerners don't know HOW to teach and how to transfer skills to Russians. |
| Change is impossible in Russia. | The West has failed to manage effective relationships with Russian partners. |
| Russians lack experience and know-how. | Westerners have no interest in the 'Russian mentality'. |
| Russians must follow the Western consultant's advice. | Relationship management must be based on equivalence. |
| Russians rely too much on an intuitive approach. | Russian staff feels undervalued, underutilized, and discriminated against. |

# APPLICATION

From the proceeding paragraphs, it is evident that Russian-U.S. cross-cultural communication in a business setting can be laden with challenging difficulties arising from culturally varied communicative styles and behaviors. The question then becomes, how does one successfully navigate around these potential problem areas? Knowledge is, of course, the answer. Each party, both Russian and American, has an obligation to be generally aware that culture shapes one's worldview in the form of beliefs and values which, in turn, influence communication styles, and all of this becomes manifest in the workplace. But when people of different cultures interact in the workplace, a broad appreciation of cultural influences will likely prove insufficient in preventing misunderstandings and miscommunications. Indeed, when working toward a common goal, such as in a cross-cultural business endeavor, more specific cultural knowledge relating to the other business partner is required.

In the field of cross-cultural communication, role-playing games have proven to be an effective means of instilling culture-specific information, developing cultural sensitivity, and internalizing cross-cultural business skills. One example of such a game was created by the author and titled "Let's get to know each other". Modeled after "The Emperor's Pot," by Batchelder (1996), the game stresses the important issues of Russian-Western professional communication, bringing out such concerns as the unpredictability of a cross-culture partner and multiple factors that may influence that partner's behavior. The role-play has varying levels of complexity and can be used in different formats depending on the types of expertise needed or available. Appendix I provides examples of some of the information that participants in the role game may use (see also Batchelder, 1996, p. 99).

It must be noted, however, that role-playing games represent only one means of acquiring culture-specific information. There is, of course, a growing body of literature on how to do business in specific cultures. There are also many books and journal articles devoted to the role of culture in international business, and there is an increasing number of websites that provide both culture-general and culture-specific information. Regardless of the source, the first step is to recognize the important role that culture plays when representatives of different nations interact.

## APPENDIX I Russian Culture Models

| Cultural Model | W-culture (Western oriented) | S-culture (Soviet style) | TR-culture (Traditional Russian) |
|---|---|---|---|
| I/We Orientation | Individual | Group | Group |
| Human Relationships | Individual | Ranked | Mutual |
| Activity Orientation | Doing | Pretending to be doing | Being |
| Time Orientation | Future | Future/Past | Present/Past |
| Relation to Nature | Control | Control/Abuse | Yielding, conforming |
| Form and Substance | Style is important | Outward form is of major importance | Inner substance is important, outward appearance is deceiving; one needs to look into one's soul |
| Progress | Progress is good | Technical progress is good; social changes are bad | Technical progress is dangerous because it leads to social changes that are bad |

*(Continued)*

| Cultural Model | W-culture (Western oriented) | S-culture (Soviet style) | TR-culture (Traditional Russian) |
|---|---|---|---|
| History | History is a linear progression, a development for good | Ideology shapes history | History is a cyclical and controversial phenomenon |
| Freedom/ Discipline, Authority | Rules/laws must be obeyed even if you don't like it. The less authority interferes with people the better | Caution and formal obedience to official authority. No consideration for individual rights. Vertically organized hierarchy regarded as most orderly and effective | Strong suspicion of authority |
| Age | Age means higher position in the official ranks; youth cannot be trusted, for they have no experience | It is not fashionable and convenient to be old, for old people still live in the Soviet past | There is a big gap between generations; old people must be supported for what they have done for each of us and because they suffered through all the Soviet times |
| Money | Brings you everything you want; Money is easy to earn today, but one needs a lot of it to have a decent life style; spending a lot is good; price is regarded as an index of quality | People got spoiled by easy money-making, and those who worked all their life don't have enough to support their families; those who have money are all criminals | Too bad there is such a dire need for money; the pursuit of money usually spoils |
| Work | Workaholics are not very popular in Russia. Still, they report a very high level of work-related stress in the new economy | Work is not even considered a means to an end | A means to an end rather than an end in itself; has no value in itself |
| Education | Education is very important, but it must be oriented toward getting a well-paying profession, not just knowledge. It is also important that the degree be from a prestigious university | Enjoys respect as a source of discipline and a means to an end, especially to, attain skill, money status; affects family prestige | Has even greater spiritual value as one's true activity. Being educated means being cultured. |
| Moral Superiority | There is nothing special about Russians except that they had to survive under hard conditions physically, politically and economically, so they now try to catch up with the West | A moral smugness stemming from a conviction that Russian people possess a set of cultural values and conditions that have made them unique | |

# References

Batchelder, D. (1996). The emperor's pot. Experiential activities for intercultural learning. In H. N. Seelye (Ed.), *Experiential Activities for Intercultural Learning* (pp. 85–99). Yarmouth ME: Intercultural Press.

Gumperz, J. J. (2001). Interactional sociolinguistics: A personal perspective. In D. Schiffrin, D. Tannen, & H. E. Hamilton (Eds.), *Handbook of Discourse Analysis*. Malden, MA: Blackwell.

Hall, E. T. (1959). *The Silent Language*. New York: Doubleday.

Holden, N., Cooper, C., & Carr, J. (1998). *Management cultures in collision: Dealing with New Russia*. New York: Wiley.

Hymes, D. (1974). *Foundations in sociolinguistics: An ethnographic approach*. Philadelphia: University of Pennsylvania Press.

Jacobs, J. (1992). *Systems of Survival*. New York: Random House. Retrieved from http://en.wikipedia.org/wiki/Systems_of_Survival

Kasper, G. (1996). *Politeness. Handbook of pragmatics*. Amsterdam: Verschueren.

Kniffka, H. (1995). *Elemente einer kulturkontrastiven Linguistik*. Frankfurt am Main: Lang.

Leontovich, O. (2002). *Russkie i amerikantsy: Paradoksy mezhkul'turnogo obschenija*. Volgograd, Russia: Peremena.

Persikova, T. (2002). *Mezhkul'turnaja kommunikatsija i korporativnaja kul'tura*. Moskva, Russia: Logos.

Ratmayr, R. (1998). *Hoeflichkeit als kulturspezifisches Konzept: Russisch im Vergleich*. (pp. 174–182).

Shmeliov, A. (2002). *Russkaja jazykovaja model' mira: Materialy k slovarju*. Moskva, Russia: jazyki slavjanskoj kul'tury.

Thomas, J. (1984). Cross-cultural discourse as 'unequal encounter': Towards a pragmatic analysis. *Applied Linguistics* 5(3): 227–235.

Wierzbicka, A. (1992). *Semantics, culture, and cognition: universal human concepts in culture-specific configurations*. New York: Oxford University Press.

## Concepts and Questions

1. What idea is Bergelson trying to convey when she discusses Russian films?

2. What does Bergelson mean when she speaks of *surface representations*?

3. How would you explain the Russian values of emotionality, judgmental attitudes, fatalism, and irrationality? Do you see the same four values being reflected in the United States?

4. How would you explain Bergelson's observation that "Modern Russia is a huge conglomerate of significantly contradictory cultural patterns"? Does the same generalization apply to the United States?

5. Why do Russians "feel sensitive, vulnerable, and angry toward what they consider to be Western cultural imperialism"? Should they feel this way?

6. What are some differences between politeness patterns in Russia and the United States?

7. What are some examples of normative Russian communicative behaviors that "become pitfalls in a cross-cultural environment"?

8. Bergelson asserts that "It is evident that Russian-U.S. cross-cultural communication in a business setting can be laden with challenging difficulties arising from culturally varied communicative styles and behaviors." What do you believe to be some of the difficulties?

9. Using Appendix I as a guide, compare and contrast the Western orientations with those of traditional Russians on some of the following dimensions: (1) I/We Orientation, (2) Human Relationships, (3) Activity Orientation, (4) Time Orientation, (5) Relation to Nature, (6) Progress, (7) History, and (8) Age.

# Ladylike Men and Guyland: Cross-Cultural Accomplishments of Masculinities

JUSTIN CHARLEBOIS

*Our last essay in this chapter, "Ladylike Men and Guyland: Cross-Cultural Accomplishments of Masculinities," explores how culture influences the perception and communication of gender manifestation, specifically masculinity. Beginning with a discussion of gender, Justin Charlebois examines "how masculinities are multiple, actively constructed, defined by hierarchical and hegemonic relationships, and dynamic." Using Japan and the United States as comparative models, the essay explores the role of culture in the development of masculinity in the two countries. Charlebois argues that while it is strongly influenced by culture, there do seem to be some universal aspects to the manifestation of masculinity, and he calls for a "broader conceptualization of masculinities and femininities."*

*Gender, as explained in the essay, is not a static concept based solely on one's biological sex. Rather, it is dynamic, multifaceted, and influenced by such factors as age, sexuality, culture, and more. Charlebois, however, contends that beyond these changes, contemporary masculinity continues to have the objective of maintaining and perpetuating "patriarchal privilege." He illustrates this through a discussion of the emerging concepts of masculinity in Japan and the United States, referred to as ojomen and "guyland," respectively. This cross-cultural comparison brings out differences as well as similarities in the two nations' emerging concepts of masculinity. This leads to the supposition that displays of masculinity are in fact competition with other males. The essay concludes with a call for greater tolerance and acceptance of an expanded concept of masculinity.*

> *Masculinities are multiple, actively constructed, defined by hierarchical and hegemonic relationships, and dynamic.*

## INTRODUCTION

A surge of popular psychology books has contributed to constructing and sustaining an urban legend that men and women are somehow inherently different (Gray, 1992; Tannen, 1990). These books help foster and perpetuate myths that men are inarticulate, poor caregivers, and naturally promiscuous, while women are skilled communicators, "natural" caregivers, and sexually loyal (Cameron, 2007; Connell, 2002). The significance of these myths is that they attribute women's subordinated social status to fixed, biologically based differences, effectively justifying social inequalities such as women's vast underrepresentation in corporate management, government, and the military; an unequal distribution of domestic labor and child-care responsibilities; and disparate salaries, and excuse sexual violence on the basis of men's "uncontrollable" sex drive (Connell, 1995, 2002; Hochschild & Machung, 2003). The "gender differences" perspective is unsupported by empirical research, overemphasizes and distorts sexual differences, diverts attention away from biological similarities, and accordingly can be seen as essentialist (Connell, 1987, 2002; Cameron, 2007; Thorne, 1993).

There may be a similar temptation to focus on differences and ignore similarities when comparing masculinities across cultures. For example, reserved, slender Japanese men appear feminine when compared with their rowdy, muscular American counterparts. When we delve beyond surface-level differences, however, and analyze the social norms which constitute masculinity in each culture, we see some striking commonalities which transcend culture.

The focus of this essay is on masculinities. After discussing the frequently misunderstood concept of *gender*, I will shift and maintain a focus on masculinities. Specifically, I will discuss how masculinities are multiple, actively constructed, defined by hierarchical and hegemonic relationships, and dynamic. The remainder of the essay conducts a comparative analysis of masculinities in the United States and Japan, which illustrates culture's influence on the construction of masculinities. My analysis will demonstrate that although there are culturally based differences between masculinities, there are also universal aspects of masculinities which appear to transcend culture. Based on the insights gained from this analysis, the final section of the chapter argues for a broader conceptualization of masculinities and femininities.

## GENDER

Research over the past couple of decades has demonstrated that gender is neither something we are born with nor acquire solely through socialization, but is a continuous, dynamic social accomplishment which intersects with age, race, and sexuality. Gender is actively accomplished through accepting, resisting, or reformulating normative behaviors which constitute masculinities and femininities in specific times and places. (Connell, 2002; Messerschmidt, 2004; Fenstermaker & West, 1995; West & Zimmerman, 1987). In contemporary American society, gender can be seen as the social significance constructed from reproductive differences between men and women (Connell, 1987, 2002). Since women have a unique capacity to bear children, a cultural assumption exists that women are also "natural" caregivers. As a result, a social division of labor has emerged where masculinity is associated with the public world of work and femininity with the private realm of the home. The significance of this division of labor is that domestic work is unpaid and that characteristics associated with femininity are undervalued by society, while paid labor and characteristics associated with masculinity are overvalued.

> *Gender is neither something we are born with nor acquire solely through socialization, but is a continuous, dynamic social accomplishment.*

Therefore, feminine characteristics are only advantageous in certain underpaid, "pastoral" professions such as nursing and elementary school teaching, while masculine characteristics are seen as desirable in more socially prestigious and higher-paid professions such as law and medicine. Despite the overall privileged position of masculinity in relation to femininity, masculinities are heterogeneous, not homogeneous; therefore, some are celebrated and acclaimed while others are disparaged and marginalized.

## MASCULINITIES

Masculinities can be defined as the forms of dress, patterns of consumption, and social actions that we ascribe to men and boys and thus delimit as not feminine. In contemporary American society, embodying masculinity could encompass a wide range of activities such as having an interest in cars and sports, consuming excessive amounts of alcohol, weight lifting, aggressively pursuing women, and disavowing femininity. These styles of dress, patterns of consumption, and behaviors can be seen as contextually available *masculine resources* (Messerschmidt, 2000) which can be drawn on to accomplish masculinity. Although masculinities vary by culture and social milieu, there are some commonalities which transcend specific socio-cultural contexts. A plethora of research has indicated that masculinities are multiple, actively constructed, defined by hierarchical and hegemonic relationships, and dynamic (Connell, 1995, 2000; Messerschmidt, 2000, 2004; Pascoe, 2007; Schippers, 2007).

Due to the existence of more than one masculinity in any given culture or social setting, it is now common to refer to "masculinities" in lieu of "masculinity" (Connell, 2000; Messerschmidt, 2004). This is perhaps most strikingly evident in culturally based variation; however, differences between masculinities can also emerge within a given social setting or culture. For example, within a secondary school there could be divisions between "jocks", "nerds", "preppies", and "burnouts". Even these categories are provisional at best because gender is accomplished differently within specific social settings (West &

Zimmerman, 1987; Fenstermaker & West, 1995). Therefore, a jock may display verbal bravado in front of his male friends, but emotional sensitivity when interacting with females.

Reflecting my earlier discussion of gender, masculinities are neither innate nor stable, but fluid and actively constructed within specific social contexts (Connell, 2000; Messerschmidt, 2004). Although social norms provide us with a script which defines normative gender performances, these norms in no way determine, but may exert an influence on, our situated accomplishments of gender. Hence, individuals possess agency to accept, contest, or modify this script and in the process construct their own masculine identity. However, as West and Zimmerman (1987) insightfully point out, "to 'do' gender is not always to live up to normative conceptions of femininity or masculinity; it is to engage in behavior *at the risk of gender assessment*" (p. 136). Individuals, therefore, may negatively assess and punish gender transgression, which demonstrates that masculinities are unequally valued.

Research has also demonstrated that masculinities form hierarchical and hegemonic relationships of dominance and subordination in two interrelated senses (Connell, 2000; Messerschmidt, 2004). First, masculinity is dominant in relation to femininity, which implies that masculinity is constructed from an ideology of male supremacy (Connell, 1995, 2000; Schippers, 2007). Second, relations between masculinities are hierarchically organized, which means that some masculinities are valorized and exalted while others are disparaged and stigmatized (Connell, 1987, 1995, 2000; Messerschmidt, 2004; Pascoe, 2007; Schippers, 2007). Connell (1987, 1995) succinctly demonstrates this point by distinguishing between *hegemonic* and *subordinated* masculinities. *Hegemonic masculinity* refers to an idealized form of masculinity in a particular historical and cultural context. In contemporary American society, we might associate hegemonic masculinity with characteristics such as aggressiveness, competitive individualism, a lean muscular body, athletic ability, and promiscuous heterosexuality (Messerschmidt, 2000). Professional athletes, local sports heroes, bodybuilders, and movie stars exemplify

> *Masculinities are neither innate nor stable, but fluid and actively constructed within specific social contexts.*

hegemonic masculinities. Hegemonic masculinities are ascendant in relation to *subordinated masculinities*, homosexual and effeminate heterosexual men, who are mercilessly ridiculed with disparaging monikers such as "sissy" or "fag" for their gender nonconformity (Connell, 1995; Pascoe, 2007; Thorne, 1993). Subordinated masculinities are also referred to as *male femininities* (Schippers, 2007) in order to capture the stigma toward embodied male femininity. Crucially, Connell's model demonstrates that femininity, whether embodied by men or women, occupies a subordinate position vis-à-vis masculinity.

Finally, masculinities are not static, but dynamic, which means they are subject to change over time (Connell, 2000; Messerschmidt, 2004). The media, changes in the economy, and the passage of gender equality legislation are all factors which can serve as catalysts for changing constructions of masculinities. Whereas the media presented hypermasculine images such as Arnold Schwarzenegger and Sylvester Stallone during the 1980s, contemporary representations of hegemonic masculinity such as Zac Efron appear softer and less macho. It needs to be stated, however, that seemingly subversive forms of masculinity are not necessarily less repressive than their "macho" counterparts. In fact, hegemonic masculinity sustains its ascendant position through the ability to reconfigure over time (Connell, 1987, 1995). As my analysis will demonstrate, contemporary American and Japanese masculinities are still built upon core values associated with hegemonic masculinity such as competitiveness, narcissistic body-management practices, and the sexual objectification of women. Significantly, these contemporary masculinities are not redefining masculinity but instead reinstating hegemonic masculinity in order to maintain patriarchal privilege.

## *Ojoman* and *Guyland* Masculinities

The ubiquitous *salaryman* is a definitive image of *hegemonic masculinity* in post-World War II Japan (Dasgupta, 2000; Roberson & Suzuki, 2003). Salarymen are white-collar workers who typically spend their entire careers in one organization and consequently are rewarded with a seniority-based wage system, regular promotions, health insurance, and other perks such as housing subsidies and low-interest loans. The metaphor "company as family" is often applied to describe this employer-employee relationship. Men loyally devote themselves to the organization and in return the corporation takes care of their material and social needs. In addition to the benefits described above, companies also organize annual trips and after-hours socializing in upscale clubs as part of this total care mentality (Allison, 1994). The costs incurred from reaping the benefits of a salaryman lifestyle include inhumane working hours, frequent transfers, work-induced health problems, estrangement from one's family, and feelings of isolation after retirement (Allison, 1994; Sugimoto, 2003; Taga, 2006). Notably, embodying hegemonic masculinity does not only entail benefits such as material wealth and social prestige but also incurs costs such as feelings of social and psychological isolation.

A long-term economic recession is rendering the total care traditionally provided by organizations obsolete (Sugimoto, 2003; Roberson & Suzuki, 2003). As in the United States, restructuring and downsizing are not simply buzzwords but the devastating reality facing many individuals. Consequently, a younger generation of Japanese men is no longer willing to single-mindedly devote themselves to an organization without the guarantee of lifetime employment. Instead, new masculinities are emerging which are not defined exclusively through work. Ojomen (ladylike men) are one example of an emergent masculinity.

*Ojomen* (Ushikubo, 2008) refers to men between the ages of twenty and thirty-four who have a weakness for sweets, an interest in shopping, an apathy toward dating and sex, but fervently consume pornography, and are uncompetitive at work. Despite the close association between shopping and femininity, many elements of ojoman masculinity are built upon traditional masculine tropes.

In tandem with the emergence of ojoman masculinity in Japan, a new form of masculinity is materializing in the United States. Sociologist Michael Kimmel (2008) uses the term *guyland* in reference to white, middle-class American men between the ages of sixteen and twenty-six who regularly purchase computer technology, video games, and pornography, pursue short-term heterosexual relationships, and delay the pursuit of a career.

Guyland and ojoman masculinity are comparable because they encompass men of roughly the same age and socioeconomic class. Although culture does exert an influence on guyland and ojoman masculinities, there are areas of overlap which transcend culture. Comparative analysis of masculinities, therefore, should not focus solely on identifying differences and interpreting their significance but also on analyzing the socio-culturally specific as well as universal aspects of masculinity. Devoting attention to similarities and differences between cultural constructions of masculinity is one way to prevent the formation and dispersion of cultural stereotypes.

Ojoman and guyland masculinity are both defined by consumption, not production. Whereas participation in the economic marketplace has been the *sine qua non* of hegemonic masculinity in Japan and the United States (Connell, 2002; Taga, 2006), ojomen and American guys resist this norm and instead define themselves as consumers. Ojomen buy brand-name clothes, cosmetics, cell phones, computer technology, and pornographic media, while American guys purchase computer technology, video games, and pornography. Most American men would consider an interest in fashion and using cosmetics as "feminizing" behavior and consequently avoid these practices. Despite this cultural difference regarding the types of products being purchased, masculinity is being redefined from production to consumption-based in both cultures, which superficially represents a departure from hegemonic masculinity.

In both Japanese and American cultures, work is apparently no longer central to the construction of masculinity as it was in previous generations. This change, however, may be attributable to an unstable economy where lifetime employment in one organization is not always a contextually available masculine resource. Men in both cultures, however, are drawing on consumption as a masculine resource and in the process redefining masculinity from work- to consumption-based. Importantly, this shift does not

> *New masculinities are emerging which are not defined exclusively through work.*

necessarily represent resistance toward hegemonic masculinity, but instead a reformulation of masculinity using contextually available resources.

Body-management practices are contextually available masculine resources central to the construction of both ojoman and guyland masculinities. In line with findings from previous research, the lived body is a central site through which individuals construct masculinity (Connell, 2000, 2002; Messerschmidt, 2004). For instance, a physically strong boy can use his body as a resource to assault other boys or girls and simultaneously embody masculinity. Similarly, ojomen engage in body-management practices such as dieting, getting facials, styling their hair, and donning brand-name apparel. Conversely, diet and exercise regimes designed to increase body mass constitute body-management practices in guyland. Similar to consumption habits, these different body-management practices reflect cultural norms concerning masculinity. Ojomen grew up in an era populated by fashionable male celebrities and thus masculinity came to encompass aesthetic appeal (Miller, 2003; Ushikubo, 2008). Consequently, male beautification rituals such as facials and body hair removal sessions are legitimized masculine social practices and not stigmatized as they would be in the United States, where a lean muscular body epitomizes hegemonic masculinity (Coles, 2007).

The divergent body-management practices of guyland and ojoman masculinity converge in that they are done for the common purpose of building self-confidence and competing with other men, which are characteristics associated with hegemonic masculinity (Messerschmidt, 2000). In an era where an unstable economy ensures that work is not a readily available masculine resource, men are drawing on their bodies as contextually available masculine resources as they attempt to compete with and dominate other men. Japanese men compete with each other by displaying their knowledge of the latest fashion trends, while American men use their muscular bodies as outward indicators of their power, coupled with verbal bravado about their alleged physical strength as they attempt to embody masculinity.

*In both Japanese and American cultures, work is apparently no longer central to the construction of masculinity as it was in previous generations.*

Both ojoman and guyland masculinity are constructed by the sexual objectification of women, which materializes as "hooking up," pornographic media, and video games. As previously discussed, masculinity is partly constructed through an erroneous ideology of male superiority and female inferiority. As a result, the sexual objectification of women is a primary conduit through which to mobilize this sexist belief. In Guyland, women are objectified through the prevalent practice of "hooking up" or "any type of sexual activity with someone you are not in a relationship with" (Kimmel, 2008, p. 195). Hooking up involves the key elements of "the appearance of spontaneity, the nearly inevitable use of alcohol, and the absence of any expectation of a relationship" (Kimmel, 2008, p. 198). The noxious effects of alcohol simultaneously function to make men feel empowered as well as blur any memories of their sexual insecurities or inadequacies. The absence of any expectation of a further relationship frees men from worrying about their partners' feelings or sexual satisfaction prior to, during, or following the encounter. Importantly, accounts of these alleged hookups become an invaluable masculine resource guys mobilize as evidence of their sexual virility and popularity among girls, which enables them to compete with other guys.

Although hooking up is specific to guyland, both Japanese and American men read pornographic magazines, view erotic websites, and play salacious video games. Notably, even more so than they do by hooking up, men presumably feel empowered by the dominant male sexuality and submissive female sexuality presented by these media. Like stories about hooking up, virtual media are a contextually available masculine resource men can use to denigrate women by viewing lecherous images and making misogynist comments, which together increase their status among other guys.

The similarity between hooking up and virtual media is that these sexual encounters do not involve mutual satisfaction but are completely devoted to appeasing men's sexual fantasies, and thus are far removed from the open communication and intimacy necessary to sustain a healthy relationship. Women may desire more committed relationships; however, hooking up is apparently the only option available to them (Kimmel, 2008). Unfortunately, since much of women's social status still depends upon forming heterosexual relationships, many attempt to conform to the unrealistic standards of "beauty" set by popular culture and submit to the demeaning hook-up culture in order to attract guys' attention and elevate their status (Kimmel, 2008; Pascoe, 2007). Given the relative ease with which American men can hook up and Japanese and American men can access lascivious media, it is no wonder that younger men are not choosing to form long-term romantic commitments. In contrast to one-night stands and pornographic media, actual relationships are simply "too much work" (Kimmel, 2008, p. 205). The unfortunate consequence of this situation is that men are not obtaining the necessary skills required to sustain a committed relationship prior to marriage but instead are engaging in self-indulgent sexual encounters which lack responsibility.

## DISCUSSION AND IMPLICATIONS

My analysis of ojoman and guyland masculinity has demonstrated that embodying masculinity is a primarily homosocial endeavor (Kimmel, 2001, 2008; Pascoe, 2007). As Kimmel (2001) states, "Masculinity is a *homosocial* enactment. We test ourselves, perform heroic feats, take enormous risks, all because we want other men to grant us our manhood" (p. 275). The homosocial component of masculinity was indicated by my discussion of narcissistic body-management practices and the sexual objectification of women, which are done for the purpose of competing with other men. As Kimmel (2008) points out, "hooking up may have less to do with guys' relationships with women and more to do with guys' relationships with other guys" (Kimmel, 2008, p. 206). Narratives about alleged sexual encounters become a masculine resource through which men can attempt to raise their status with other guys (Kimmel, 2008; Pascoe, 2007). Similarly, *ojomen* attempt to increase their position in relation to other men by displaying self-discipline through the maintenance of a slender physique, which they adorn with the latest fashions.

*In contrast to one-night stands and pornographic media, actual relationships are simply "too much work."*

American guys demonstrate their physical power and self-discipline by sculpting a lean muscular body and displays of verbal bravado about how much they can bench press. As these examples indicate, embodying masculinity is less about proving one's strength, power, and authority to women and more about displaying these characteristics to other men.

The predominantly homosocial environment where masculinity is constructed could promulgate a fear that one is homosexual, which is indisputably the antithesis of masculinity (Connel, 1995; Kimmel, 2001, 2007; Pascoe, 2007). This fear does not appear to be so widespread in Japan, where both men and women engage in beautification regimes and consequently the line between masculinity and femininity is blurry. In the United States, by contrast, homophobia, "the fear that people might misperceive you as gay" (Kimmel, 2008, p. 50), remains rampant and is "a central mechanism in the making of contemporary American adolescent masculinity" (Pascoe, 2007, p. 53). Therefore, guys use physical and verbal bullying of effete boys as contextually available masculine resources to concomitantly affirm their masculinity while eradicating others'. The derogatory "fag" epithet is an example of a masculine resource boys use to simultaneously punish and stigmatize boys who fail to conform to the rigid confines of masculinity and self-protect against being labeled "gay."

Homophobia also relates back to my earlier point that masculinity is partly constructed from an ideology of male superiority and female inferiority. Although the term "fag" can refer to a homosexual, it has more to do with "failing at the masculine tasks of competence, heterosexual prowess, and strength or in any way revealing weakness or femininity as it does with a sexual identity" (Pascoe, 2007, p. 54). Thus, the term is applied to boys who are unathletic, bookish, or sensitive. The significance of homophobia is that it represents a deep fear of being seen as weak, which is equated with femininity. Therefore, men who are striving to embody masculinity incessantly demonstrate their distance from and superiority over femininity. Homophobia reflects firm resistance toward any blurring of the boundary between masculinity and femininity in contemporary American culture.

# CONCLUSION

This essay has meant to demonstrate that while culturally based differences are relevant to the study of masculinities, there are also components of masculinity which are shared across cultures. Therefore, a focus on superficial differences between masculinities fails to capture the complex and nuanced nature of masculinities and can result in the formation of stereotypes. It cannot be overstated that masculinities are fluid, multiple, and intersect with age, race, social class, and sexuality. In reflection of this, more sophisticated comparative analysis of masculinities will not only encompass culturally attributable differences, but also age, race, and sexuality-based differences and similarities.

Despite the similarities between Japanese and American masculinities, there is a salient cultural difference which requires further discussion and has important implications for American college students. My discussion of *ojomen* indicated that the border between masculinity and femininity is weaker in Japan than in the United States. This is not to suggest that ojomen are staunch supporters of feminism, because they are not. As I discussed, ojoman masculinity is still built upon traditional masculine tropes of competitiveness, narcissist body-management practices, and sexually objectifying women, and therefore is not transgressive. Nevertheless, the point remains that Japanese society appears to have greater tolerance for a wider range of masculinities, while masculinity is rigidly and narrowly defined in American society.

In the United States, masculinity is not only a social accomplishment but also a "constant test—always up for grabs, always needing to be proved" (Kimmel, 2008, p. 51). Therefore, dangerous risk-taking behavior, heterosexual prowess, and incessant gay bashing are all masculine resources guys use to demonstrate their manliness to other guys. Guys who fail to conform to the rigid confines of masculinity and consequently fail to prove their masculinity are continuously reminded of their gender deviance by relentless bullying and cultural marginalization.

In conclusion, it is my hope that this essay will induce greater tolerance for a wider range of masculinities and a higher regard for femininity. The root of homophobia is the fear of being labeled feminine, which sadly reflects the overall subordinated status of femininity in American society. So-called feminine characteristics such as cooperation, empathy, nurturance, and the ability to experience and express emotion should not be seen as inferior characteristics but become part of our cultural definitions of masculinity and femininity. In this way, we can degender "masculinity" and "femininity" and move toward greater gender equality. If this degendering occurs, then masculinity and femininity will not exist as polarized opposites, but as complementary resources which men and women draw on and simultaneously construct a whole range of gendered identities.

# References

Allison, A. (1994). *Nightwork: Sexuality, pleasure, and corporate masculinity in a Tokyo hostess club.* Chicago: University of Chicago Press.

Cameron, D. (2007). *The myth of Mars and Venus: Do men and women really speak different languages?* Oxford, England: Oxford University Press.

Coles, T. (2007). Negotiating the field of masculinity: The production and reproduction of multiple dominant masculinities. *Men and Masculinities,* doi 10.1177/1097184X07309502.

Connell, R. W. (1987). *Gender and power.* Cambridge, England: Polity Press.

Connell, R. W. (1995). *Masculinities.* Cambridge, England: Polity Press.

Connell, R. W. (2000). *The men and the boys.* Cambridge, England: Polity Press.

Connell, R. W. (2002). *Gender.* Cambridge, England: Polity Press

Dasgupta, R. (2000). Performing masculinities? The 'salaryman' at work and play. *Japanese Studies, 20*(2), 189–200.

Fenstermaker, S. & West, D. (1995). Doing difference. *Gender & Society, 9*(1), 8–37.

Gray, J. (1992). *Men are from Mars, women are from Venus.* New York: HarperCollins.

Hochschild, A., & Machung, A. (2003). *The second shift.* New York: Penguin.

Kimmel, M. (2001). Masculinity as homophobia: Fear, shame, and silence in the construction of gender identity. In S. Whitehead & F. Barret (Eds.), *The masculinities reader* (pp. 266–287). Cambridge, England: Polity Press.

Kimmel, M. (2008). *Guyland: The perilous world where boys become men.* New York: HarperCollins

Messerschmidt, J. W. (2000). *Nine lives: Adolescent masculinities, the body, and violence.* Boulder, CO: Westview Press.

Messerschmidt, J. W. (2004). *Flesh and blood: Adolescent gender diversity and violence.* Lanham, MD: Rowman and Littlefield.

Miller, L. (2003). Male beauty work in Japan. In J. E. Roberson & N. Suzuki (Eds.), *Men and masculinities in contemporary Japan: Dislocating the salaryman doxa* (pp. 37–58). New York: Routledge.

Pascoe, C. J. (2007). *Dude, you're a fag: Masculinity and sexuality in high school.* Berkeley: University of California Press.

Roberson, J. E. & Suzuki, N. (Eds.) (2003). *Men and masculinities in contemporary Japan: Dislocating the salaryman doxa.* New York: Routledge.

Schippers, M. (2007). Recovering the feminine other: masculinity, femininity, and gender hegemony. *Theory and Society, 36,* 85–102.

Sugimoto, Y. (2003). *An introduction to Japanese society.* Cambridge, England: Cambridge University Press.

Taga, F. (2006). *Otokorashisa no Shakaigaku [The Sociology of Masculinity].* Kyoto, Japan: Sekaishiso.

Tannen, D. (1990). *You just don't understand: Women and men in conversation.* New York: Morrow.

Thorne, B. (1993). *Gender play: Girls and boys in school.* New Brunswick, NJ: Rutgers University Press.

Ushikubo, M. (2008). *Soushokukei danshi "ojoman" ga Nihon wo kaeru [The Herbivorous "ladylike" men are changing Japan].* Tokyo, Japan: Kodansha.

West, C. & Zimmerman, D. (1987). Doing gender. *Gender & Society, 1*(2), 125–151.

## Concepts and Questions

1. Based on Charlebois's essay, how would you define gender?

2. From your perspective, is masculinity portrayed differently or similarly on the two television channels Lifetime and Spike? Explain.

3. Give several examples of how someone may display their masculinity (or femininity) differently due to the situation.

4. Explain the difference between *hegemonic* and *subordinated* masculinities. Give some examples other than those provided in the essay.

5. What are some of the factors behind the creation of the Japanese *ojomen* masculinity?

6. Do you agree with Charlebois claim that both Japanese and U.S. men are using consumption to redefine "masculinity from work to consumption-based"? Why?

7. How does "body management" differ in the new Japanese and U.S. approaches to masculinity? How does this "body management" communicate masculinity?

8. According to the essay, what role does pornography play in the formation of the *ojoman* and guyland concepts of masculinity? Do you agree or disagree? Why?

9. How are *ojoman* and guyland masculinities similar? Different?

10. What does Charlebois consider the greatest difference between Japanese and U.S. concepts of masculinity?

# 4 Co-cultures: Living in a Multicultural Society

*We become not a melting pot but a beautiful mosaic. Different people, different beliefs, different yearnings, different hopes, different dreams.*                                        **Jimmy Carter**

*Whenever you find yourself on the side of the majority, it's time to pause and reflect.*

**Mark Twain**

In the previous chapter, we looked primarily at international cultures—those located outside U.S. borders—and generally focused on single cultural groups. In this chapter, we turn to the United States, where multiculturalism is commonly recognized as an important part of our history and future. Therefore, we now examine the dynamics of domestic multiculturalism by investigating some *co-cultures*—those diverse cultural groups that reside inside the United States. Co-cultures often have many of the defining characteristics found in any culture—a specialized language system, shared values, a collective worldview, common communication patterns, and often a common history. Also, members of a co-culture usually share a number of similar characteristics, such as religion, economic status, ethnic background, age, gender, or sexual preference. And with increasing frequency, many people residing in the United States hold dual or even multiple co-cultural memberships. A gay African American man would be considered a member of two co-cultures. The son of a Brazilian woman who emigrated to the U.S. and married a man who had emigrated from India would be a member of multiple co-cultural groups.

These diverse co-cultures bring new experiences and ways of interacting to an intercultural encounter. Their unique communicative behaviors may sometimes be confusing and baffling to members of the dominant culture. This diversity can become prominent when, for instance, members of a collectivistic co-culture, such as Asian Americans, interact with someone from the highly individualistic Euro-American dom-

> **Co-cultures often have many of the defining characteristics found in any culture—a specialized language system, shared values, a collective worldview, common communication patterns, and often a common history.**

inant culture. For example, a Vietnamese American, with strong extended family ties, might feel it important to ask for time off from work to help celebrate his uncle's 60th birthday. But a Euro-American, more focused on the nuclear family, may view such a request as an inappropriate excuse for a day off.

The United States is a pluralistic, multicultural society, with minority groups representing 34 percent of the total population ("Census," 2009). This creates a vital need for competent communication between the dominant culture and the numerous co-cultures, as well as among the co-cultures themselves. You cannot communicate effectively with a member of a co-culture until you learn to appreciate the unique, rich opportunity offered by that co-culture. Insufficient knowledge, stereotypes, and prejudice often lead to incorrect, harmful, and even insulting assumptions about people from co-cultures. An appreciation for the unique experiences of these co-culture members will help overcome many communication problems.

The rich cultural diversity and complexity of U.S. society flows from an almost overwhelming number of co-cultures. As a result, we are obviously unable to examine each co-culture in this chapter. Thus, our selections are based on three considerations: (1) we need to make ef-

> **The rich cultural diversity and complexity of U.S. society flows from an almost overwhelming number of co-cultures.**

ficient use of limited space; (2) we want to include some social groups that are often at odds with the dominant culture; and (3) we want to emphasize the range of different co-cultures. To this end, we selected essays representing the major co-cultures as well as those less often encountered. You will also learn about additional co-cultures in subsequent chapters.

# Unum and Pluribus: Ideological Underpinnings of Interethnic Communication in the United States

YOUNG YUN KIM

We begin this chapter with an essay that presents an ideological position informing intercultural communication among co-cultures. According to the author, Young Yun Kim, the theme of individualism is central to this ideology. In "Unum and Pluribus: Ideological Underpinnings of Interethnic Communication in the United States," Kim examines the historical development of American social institutions that were based on such liberal themes as equal rights and equal opportunity, constructs which form the cornerstone of the Declaration of Independence, the Constitution, and the Bill of Rights.

Even with the historical tradition of equality, Kim quickly points out, "Americans today are far from being of a same mind about various social issues" such as interethnic and interracial relations. She notes that in recent years "the traditional primacy of the individual has been increasingly challenged" as minorities have increased in number and power. This is a dilemma that has become a sore spot "at times galvanizing Americans into 'us-against-them' posturing in the form of 'identity politics.'"

After providing an overview of the current U.S. domestic social dilemma, Kim uses the issues of race, ethnicity, and interethnic relations to examine interethnic communication. She then offers an in-depth discussion of four types of interethnic messages—assimilation, pluralism, reconciliation, and extremism—that we frequently hear in the media. Kim follows this discussion with a synthesis of the messages and concludes that interethnic relations remain salient in U.S. society, but the future remains unclear as Americans continue to "struggle with competing visions of Unum and Pluribus … and what it means to be Americans." She concludes with a note of optimism: "the very fact that interethnic issues continue to engage American passion is itself an affirmation, and a hallmark, of the American liberal tradition. This tradition contributes to the stability of the American democracy."

The United States was founded as a construction organized by the ideology of classical liberalism in the Enlightenment tradition—a tradition rooted in the theories of European and Anglo-American philosophers such as John Locke, Adam Smith, and John Dewey. Central to this ideology is the theme of *individualism*, "the social priority of the individual vis-à-vis the State, the established Church, social classes … or other social groups" (Abercrombie, 1980, p. 56). While recognizing the existence of infinite individual differences, classical liberalism also stresses *universalism*, which sees human nature presupposing and transcending social group categories such as ethnicity and race. As Michael Billig and associates (1988) have noted: "The assertions 'we are all human' and 'We are all individuals' are both equally and self-evidently 'true'" (p. 124). The classical-liberal themes of individualism and universalism are further linked to the theme of *procedural equality*, that is, "equal rights" and "equal opportunities" afforded to all individuals in the form of "human rights"—the basic requisite of a free and democratic society. Enshrined in the Declaration of Independence, the Constitution, the Bill of Rights, and democratic and capitalistic institutions, these and related principles constitute the core of the American cultural ethos, projecting a vision of American society that seeks to transcend a monolithic tribal ancestral and territorial condition. Essayist

> Classical liberalism also stresses universalism, which sees human nature presupposing and transcending social group categories such as ethnicity and race.

Henry Grunwald (1976) captured this liberal tradition in a bicentennial essay:

> The U.S. was not born in a tribal conflict, like so many other nations, but in conflict over principles. Those principles were thought to be universal, which was part of the reason for the unprecedented policy of throwing the new country open to all comers. (p. 35)

Given these traditional ideals, however, Americans today are far from being of the same mind about various social issues. In fact, the opposite is true when it comes to "interethnic" (or "interracial") relations. Ever since the Reconstruction era of the late 19th century, when "civil rights" debates began (Wilson, 1998), American society has experienced an extraordinary degree of unease, conflict, self-criticism, and mutual criticism as it struggled to reconcile the ideals of individualism, universalism, and procedural equality with the reality of inequality, real or perceived, along particular ethnic/racial group lines. In recent decades, the traditional primacy of the individual has been increasingly challenged by the claims of the primacy of ethnic group identity over individual identity, particularistic group grievances that are historically and institutionally rooted, and the necessity to redress such grievances so as to achieve equality in group status.

This American dilemma continues to be a sore spot in the American consciousness. Even as ethnic minorities gain status in both the public and private sector, issues of ethnicity and race often stir heated public debates, at times galvanizing Americans into "us-against-them" posturing in the form of "identity politics." Essayist Russell Baker (1994) laments this situation in an essay entitled "Gone with the Unum":

> I have always been an "*E Pluribus Unum*" person myself, but the future does not look bright for an "*E Pluribus Unum*" America. The melting pot in which the Pluribus were to be combined into the Unum was not the success its advertisers had promised.... What is new these days is the passion with which we now pursue our tribal identities... O, Unum, what misery we courted when we forsook thee for Pluribus. (p. A15)

## ANALYSIS

This author has sought to better understand the often-contentious landscape of interethnic communication in the contemporary United States (Kim, 1999, 2005, 2007). To this end, the present analysis scrutinizes differing views and opinions of American people in order to identify multiple ways in which the tradition of classical liberalism plays out in the contemporary American interethnic communication messages. The term "ideology" is employed here in terms of what Billig (1991) refers to as "lived ideology" and "a latent consciousness or philosophy" (pp. 27–29). In this sense, ideology refers to a set of social forces that stimulate, substantiate, and constrain the intellectual beliefs and expressions of thinking individuals. Individuals formulate and express their opinions by invoking socially shared beliefs *as their own*, rather than passively following the dictates of the mental schema within a given ideological tradition. Even in making remarks that are self-serving or even contradictory, they tend to consider their argument reasonable or even persuasive in the eyes of a rational audience. Communication messages are, thus, more than mere expressions of a communicator's own independent thoughts. That is, to say something is very often to "fight"— in the sense that messages serve as strategy and tactics for advocating a given communicator's own version of what he or she believes to be "common sense." In Billig's (1991) words:

> To maximize their chances of being persuasive, speakers should make appeal to the *sensus comunis*, which they share with their audience. Particularly useful were commonplaces, or the sort of moral maxims which are laden with clichéd appeals to values. Thus, orators' discourse, which seeks to create new movements of opinion towards a position not commonly shared, will rehearse old commonly shared stereotypes. (p. 21)

Based on this social-psychological conception of ideology, a variety of data have been analyzed including messages communicated by political and civic leaders, activists, academicians, and ordinary citizens. Almost all of the data utilized in this analysis have been found in sources available since 1990. The data types range from trade books written for general readers to newsmagazine articles, articles in national and local newspapers, and transcripts of interviews and talk shows broadcast on radio and television. Some of these data are captured in naturally occurring events, whereas others are expressed in the form of personal reflections and testimonials. The data have been analyzed through a qualitative-interpretive exercise to surface the ideological themes underlying the publicly communicated messages pertaining to issues of ethnicity, race, and interethnic relations. This method of analysis shares features with other qualitative investigations, such as discourse (or rhetorical) analysis, designed to elucidate social-psychological processes through understanding spoken and unspoken messages (e.g., Billig et al., 1988; Billig, 1991; Van Dijk, 1997). In addition, systematic data from recent public opinion polls based on representative samples are utilized to complement the primarily episodic data.

The analysis has revealed four types of interethnic communication messages: (1) assimilationism, (2) pluralism, (3) reconciliation, and (4) extremism. Each of these message types is described in the following discussion. Commonly rooted in the ideology of classical liberalism, these message types capture the differing sets of beliefs and moral visions being voiced by Americans today. Together, they represent a full spectrum of ongoing debates and arguments about what American society is, should be, and should be doing with respect to issues of ethnicity, race, and interethnic relations.

> *Three core principles of classical liberalism-individualism, universalism, and procedural equality continue to directly and powerfully underpin the mainstream thinking of Americans about interethnic relations.*

## MESSAGES OF ASSIMILATIONISM

Three core principles of classical liberalism-individualism, universalism, and procedural equality continue to directly and powerfully underpin the mainstream thinking of Americans about interethnic relations. These liberal ideals shape the arguments commonly referred to as *assimilationism*. Employing such metaphors as "melting pot" and "color-blind society," assimilationist messages project a societal vision in which immigrants and indigenous ethnic minorities are mainstreamed into the normative culture and institutions. In this vision, the government is responsible for universally applying societal rules to all its citizens irrespective of skin color and religious creed. Immigrants and ethnic minorities, in turn, are expected to assimilate themselves socially and culturally, so as to become fully functional in the American society.

Assimilationist messages celebrate personal achievement and self-reliance. These messages place individual identity over and above group identity and question the validity and morality of categorical thought. Although each person is unique, all humans are also endowed with the same set of universal human needs, rights, and responsibilities. Prejudice directed for or against individuals simply based on group membership is morally wrong, not only because it is irrational but also because its focus on social categories contravenes the intellectual or moral prescription to value the unique qualities of every individual. The primacy of the individual over the group hinges on the value of equality as it pertains to the premise of common human nature and basic human rights that calls for equal applications of laws and rules to all people regardless of their group categories. A fair society is one in which all individuals, regardless of their backgrounds, are granted equal rights and equal opportunity. Equality in this view means "fair play"—a notion rooted in a biopsychological (or naturalistic) worldview and the notions of *equity* and *meritocracy*. This view accepts and appreciates differential individual merits in the allocation of resources and status based on the presumption that "there is a natural distribution of human talent, ranging from the few individuals of genius and talent to the defective and delinquent" (Rossides, 1976, p. 9).

As columnist David Brooks (2007) puts it, "when achievement and equality clash in America, achievement wins." Each person, and each person alone, is seen as ultimately responsible for his or her own achievement of status. Everyone is expected to "play by the rules." Insistence on group-based policies such as affirmative action in college admissions and employment practices is "un-American"—one that endangers the larger fraternity of all Americans and obscures differential individual merits that must be *earned* individually. Emphasis on group identity over individual identity is deemed wrong because it renders itself to what essayist Pico Iyer (1990) calls "state-sponsored favoritism," which mandates racial or ethnic "preferences" or "quotas" and "reverse discrimination." Iyer, himself an Indian-born immigrant and world traveler, expresses his objection to such practices as follows:

> As an alien from India, I choose to live in America precisely because it is a place where aliens from India are, in principle, treated no better (and no worse) than anyone else.... The problem with people who keep raising the cry of "racism" is that they would have us see everything in terms of race. They treat minorities as emblems, and everyone as typecast.... As an Asian minority myself, I know of nothing more demeaning than being chosen for a job, or even a role, on the basis of my race. Nor is the accompanying assumption—that I need a helping hand because my ancestors were born outside Europe—very comforting... Are we, in fact, to cling to a state of childlike dependency? (p. 86)

The assimilationist emphasis on individualism, universalism, and procedural equality has been repeatedly promoted in presidential inauguration addresses. Presidents, regardless of their party affiliations, have exalted the assimilationist values as the very heart of the American identity—a common identity constituted through individual identities, and one that transcends category-based distinctions. Former President William Jefferson Clinton, for example, spoke of American citizens' "primary allegiance to the values America stands for and values we really live by" and stated, "Long before we were so diverse, our nation's motto was *E Pluribus Unum*—out of many, we are one. We must be one—as neighbors; as fellow citizens; not separate camps, but family" (*Weekly Compilation of Presidential Documents, 31*, October 23, 1996, p. 851). The universal principles of individual identity and procedural equality are amply echoed in remarks of many other Americans. A newspaper reader wrote to the editor of *The New York Times Magazine* (April 29, 1992), objecting to an

earlier article "Cultural Baggage," on the significance of ethnic group identity:

> I've been fighting ethnic labels since I was 12 or 13, and decided that only I had a right to define myself.... I am not almost WASP. I am African-American. I'm also part Cherokee from both sides of my family. But so what? ... I've taken risks with my life that only I am responsible for, and I have reaped substantial rewards for daring to be myself and not just different. (p. 10)

Stanley Crouch, an African American essayist, speaks to the common humanity of all races in arguing against racial politics in his book, *Always in Pursuit* (1998): "We ... observe ourselves functioning in almost every capacity and exhibiting every inclination from the grand to the gaudy, from the idealistic to the shallow ethnic con" (p. 268). Likewise, Richard Lacayo, in an essay entitled "Whose peers?" in a special issue of *Time* magazine (1993), disagreed with those who have argued for a guarantee of minority representation in jury composition in courtroom trials:

> [Some] advocates argue that just such a guarantee of minority representation should be part of the law.... If that is so, is the only solution an outright racial-quota system? And how finely would the jury need to be divided? Could Latinos in general judge other Latinos? Or would Cuban Americans be needed for the trial of Cuban Americans, Mexican Americans for other Mexican Americans, and so on? If the goal is better justice and greater legitimacy, American juries certainly need to be more representative. But in a just society, the process of creating a true assembly of peers need not be reduced to a systematic gathering of the tribes. (p. 61)

Perhaps one of the most compelling articulations of the traditional liberal ideals and of disapproval of identity politics was offered by Glenn C. Loury (1993), an economic theorist and a public intellectual. In the following excerpt from one of his earlier writings, Loury reflects on his own social identity as an African American and his individual identity as a human being as follows:

> The most important challenges and opportunities that confront me derive not from my racial

condition, but rather from my human condition. I am a husband, a father, a son, a teacher, an intellectual, a Christian, a citizen. In none of these roles is my race irrelevant, but neither can racial identity alone provide much guidance for my quest to adequately discharge these responsibilities… The expression of my individual personality is to be found in the blueprint that I employ to guide this project of construction. The problem of devising such a plan for one's life is a universal problem, which confronts all people, whatever their race, class, or ethnicity. (pp. 7–10)

## MESSAGES OF PLURALISM

Directly challenging the aforementioned assimilationist messages are the messages of *pluralism*. Prominent in pluralist messages is the idea of the sanctity of the group. This notion is traceable to the experiences of unequal treatment, perceived or real, of certain individuals along ethnic lines. To varying degrees, pluralist messages replace the old "melting pot" metaphor with newer ones such as "mosaic," "quilt," and "salad bowl" that emphasize the distinctiveness of ethnic groups. As such, pluralist messages uphold *group identity* as a vital, if not primary, construct of personhood, highlighting a

> *Pluralist messages uphold group identity as a vital, if not primary, construct of personhood, highlighting a fact of life that we are different "types" of persons defined by social categories such as race, ethnicity, language, culture, and national origin.*

fact of life that we are different "types" of persons defined by social categories such as race, ethnicity, language, culture, and national origin. Rooted in the worldview of *relativism* that classifies humanity into categories of distinct qualities, pluralist messages emphasize in-group sameness and point to the existence of a "natural attitude" (cf. Garfinkel, 1967) for their moral and intellectual claims for group distinctiveness.

Pluralist messages are predicated on the persistent reality of racial and ethnic prejudice—a reality in which the old liberal ideal of procedural equality is seen as not working well when it comes to serving the needs of certain minority groups. The sense of systematic mistreatment along ethnic and racial lines has given way to a movement calling for a new politics of interethnic relations. Instead of defining equality

procedurally in terms of fairness of rules, pluralist messages advocate the contrary belief in *status equality* (in place of procedural equality), a demand for equal results in the interest of "emancipation" of specific groups that are historically oppressed or presently in need of institutional support through remedial laws and public policies. This outcome-based conception of equality is opposed to the procedure-based, universalistic view of equality, in that it allows for differential procedural treatments relative to different groups. Along this line, arguments have been made for a redistribution of power and resources to overcome racial inequalities (e.g., Hacker, 1992). Some pluralists advocate such an action as a remedy for status inequalities between and among ethnic and racial groups.

This pluralist position rejects the biopsychological explanation of inequality and replaces it with a sociocultural (or structural) explanation. That is, human beings are inherently equal in their original states, but their original natures become distorted and corrupted in the process of interaction with others in society and through the development of institutions such as language, culture, property, law, and social stratification among people (Tsuda, 1986). The traditional liberal notion of individual identity, universalistic application of laws, rules, rights, and responsibilities to everyone, and procedural equality without respect to equal outcomes is deemed a false ideology in that it serves only the end of legitimizing the capitalist system of "winners" and "losers" in society. In seeking group identity, relativism, and status equality, pluralist messages present race and ethnicity not merely as a basis for claiming cultural and social distinctiveness, but also as a central rallying point, a focal means to combat unjust practices such as "institutional racism." Prominent in these messages, accordingly, are terms such as ethnic "victimhood," "empowerment," "pride," "dignity," and "justice," as well as claims of personal "entitlement" based on one's ethnic identity (Major, 1994). Debunking the important classical-liberal values of American life such as intellectual freedom and "free speech," pluralist messages demand suppression of "hate speech," loosely defined as words that a minority group finds offensive.

Specifically, schools and universities have sought to bring about a greater diversity of the university curriculum by replacing it with one "that would focus on the achievements of marginalized peoples and on the sins of the nation's founders" (Traub, 1998, p. 25). In San Francisco, for instance, the school board was reported to be developing a plan to require every high school student in the district to read works by authors of color (*The New York Times*, March 11, 1998, p. A21). Many university campuses have rejected the idea of an immutable canon of indispensable Western classics in favor of recognizing the reality of ethnic diversity in the United States. Curriculum changes like these have become commonplace, reflecting the emergence of pluralism in national consciousness at the end of the 1980s advocating the normative rights of minority groups. Some advocates of pluralism even have attempted to extend the pluralist messages to arguing for a guarantee of minority representation as part of the law. Believing that race influences not only prominent cases such as the Rodney King trial but also most cases involving minority defendants, Sheri Lynn Johnson, a law professor, believes defendants should be guaranteed 3 members of their own racial group in a 12-member jury (cited in Lacayo, 1993, p. 61).

A similar pluralist view is expressed in the following reaction to the court decision ending the practice of race-based affirmative action programs in admission decisions at the University of Michigan (*The New York Times*, Editorials/Letters, March 30, 2001):

> Even with affirmative action in place, law school classes here at the University of Michigan are overwhelmingly dominated by white men. The compelling interest in maintaining such programs applies not just to minority students, but to all students who will now see even fewer nonwhite faces and even fewer nonwhite faces as law school classes become even more homogeneous. Our legal system has produced yet another significantly disappointing decision, and many of us here fear that America is on the verge of taking one giant leap backward. (p. A22)

Molefi K. Asante, a prominent scholar of African-American studies, offers an eloquent argument against the assimilationist ideals. In its place, Asante advocates the pluralist counter-ideals of group identity and status equality based on a particularistic view of human nature. In an essay entitled "Racism, Consciousness, and Afrocentricity," Asante (1993) reflects on his experience of growing up in a racist society and explains how he came to reject W. E. B. Du Bois's notion of "double consciousness" as a tragic outcome inescapable in the "Eurocentric" society. Asante, thus, proposes "Afrocentricity" as an alternative intellectual model based on which African Americans can claim an equal identity and status as a distinct people:

> The feeling that you are in quicksand is inescapable in the quagmire of a racist society. You think that you can make progress in the interpretation of what's happening now only to discover that every step you take sinks the possibility of escaping. You are a victim despite your best efforts to educate those around you to the obvious intellectual mud stuck in their minds.... Even from my young adult years I thought a precondition of my fullness, a necessary and natural part of my maturity, was the commitment to be who I am, to be Afrocentric.... Afrocentricity is the active centering of the African in subject place in our historical landscape. This has always been my search; it has been a quest for sanity (pp. 142–143).

The pluralistic insistence on a distinct group identity has drawn critical reactions from many for fostering division, "political correctness," and "self-segregation," and for eroding societal cohesion and common American identity. In *The Disuniting of America* (1992), for example, historian Arthur M. Schlesinger, Jr. warned that pressing ethnic awareness too far would pose the danger of the "disintegration of the national community, apartheid, Balkanization, tribalization" (p. 118). Charles J. Sykes (1992), in *A Nation of Victims,* revealed a society that was tribalizing, where individuals and groups defined themselves not by shared culture, but by their status as victims. Likewise, sociologist Todd Gitlin, in *The Twilight of Common Dreams* (1995), and political scientist Samuel P. Huntington, in *Who Are We* (2004), have offered that America would be lost unless its obsession with cultural differences could be transcended in the name of the common good. More recently, Orland Patterson (2006), an African American sociologist at

Harvard University, has characterized the phenomenon of self-segregation "the last major race problem" in the United States. Patterson finds it paradoxical that voluntary segregation on the part of ethnic minorities has been rising precisely as the decades of civil rights have struggled to tear down racial barriers. Acknowledging that African Americans mention ethnic pride and white hostility as their main reasons for not moving to white neighborhoods, Patterson argues that "the disadvantages [of self-segregation], especially for youth, far outweigh the psychic gains" (p. A19).

## MESSAGES OF RECONCILIATION

Straddled between the aforementioned ideological poles of assimilationism and pluralism are the voices of ideological reconciliation. These voices are what sociologist Alan Wolfe, in *One Nation, After All* (1998), asserts as occupying "the vital center"—the "middle" America. Based on 200 in-depth interviews conducted in Boston, Atlanta, Tulsa, and San Diego metropolitan areas, Wolfe found "little support for the notion that middle-class Americans are engaged in bitter cultural conflict with one another" (p. 278). Instead, according to Wolfe, they are "struggling to find ways in which their core beliefs can be reconciled with experiences that seem to contradict them" (p. 281), while insisting on a set of values "capacious enough to be inclusive but demanding enough to uphold standards of personal responsibility" (p. 322).

> *Messages of reconciliation reflect the struggle of many Americans seeking moderation, tolerance, accommodation, integration, and balance.*

The messages of reconciliation reflect the struggle of many Americans seeking moderation, tolerance, accommodation, integration, and balance. They are expressions of both hopes and difficulties in doing so. As such, reconciliation messages indicate a great deal of ambivalence, and even contradiction in the way many Americans think about the issues of race, ethnicity, and interethnic relations. They may, for example, support bilingual programs, but only if they are short-lived and not used as a political goal or instrument of power demanded by every group for its own separate slice of the political pie. They may support multiculturalism, but only to the extent that

ethnic identity is subsumed under the common "American identity" that emphasizes individualism. They may support affirmative action programs based on group identity, but consider "quota" systems as unfair, divisive, and ultimately counterproductive. Or they may accept and even appreciate *Hanukkahs* and *Kwanzaas*, but they may also find that some people have gone too far when insisting on avoiding traditional phrases such as "Merry Christmas" in favor of ethnicity-neutral phrases such as "Happy Holidays." In a newspaper opinion column, William A. Donohue (2006), then President of the Catholic League for Religious and Civil Rights, made just such a case as follows in a newspaper opinion column.

> The United States is 85 percent Christian, which means we are more Christian than India is Hindu and Israel is Jewish. Moreover, 96 percent of Americans celebrate Christmas. So why do we have to tippy-toe around the religious meaning of Christmas every December? There is something sick about Friendship Trees, Winter Solstice Concerts, Holiday Parades and Holly Day Festivals … Diversity means respect for the traditions and heritages of all groups, not just those which have been cherry-picked by the multicultural gurus.… To be excluded is normal. Mother's Day, Father' Day, Veteran's Day, Black History Month, Gay Pride Parades—they all exclude someone.… By celebrating Christmas we are celebrating diversity (p. A23).

An attempt at ideological reconciliation was voiced in a remark former President Clinton made during a roundtable discussion on race televised on PBS (Public Broadcasting System) on July 9, 1998: "I believe there is an independent value to having young people learn in an environment where they're with people of many different racial and ethnic backgrounds. And the question is, How can you balance that with our devotion to merit?" (*The New York Times*, July 9, 1998, p. A21.) A similar stance of reconciliation was taken in the late former President Gerald Ford's Op-Ed article in 1999 titled "Inclusive America, Under Attack," according to columnist

Jeffrey Toobin (2006). Toobin explained that Ford had written this article in support of affirmative action at the University of Michigan to argue that a pair of pending lawsuits would prohibit Michigan and other universities "from even considering race as one of many factors weighed by admission counselors," and that such a move would "condemn future college students to suffer the cultural and social impoverishment that afflicted my generation."

Reconciliatory views have been voiced by leaders of ethnic minorities, as well. Hugh Price, in his keynote address as the President of the National Urban League at the League's 1998 annual conference, shared his belief that the current conditions in the United States offer blacks the "best shot we have ever had to shove ourselves the rest of the way into the American mainstream" (*The New York Times*, August 13, 1998, p. A23). Racial discrimination still exists, Price pointed out, but African American parents must take greater responsibility for the education of their children:

> With unemployment so low, employers are gobbling up almost every willing and able worker with a pulse. Shame on us if we don't seize this historic opening in the economy... I think we are moving rapidly toward the day when if you've got something to put on the table, employers aren't going to care what color you are. (p. A23)

Likewise, on Columbus Day in 1992, Niles Bird Runningwater, then president of the Indian student association at the University of Oklahoma, communicated a message of reconciliation:

> We don't choose to protest this fallacy of American history, but rather to celebrate the survival and continuance of Indian peoples.... By doing this we can fully acknowledge 500 years of coexistence of Indian and non-Indian peoples in America.... We're trying to do our part in togetherness and participation by eliciting communication and excitement concerning the respect of others' cultures (*The Oklahoma Daily*, March 24, 1992, p, 3).

Messages of reconciliation such as these can be traced to the mainstream, integrationist civil rights movement led by Martin Luther King, Jr. The traditional liberal ideals of individualism, universalism, and procedural equality have been largely upheld in the struggle to eliminate systematic discrimination against African Americans as a group. In an address titled "A Realistic Look at Race Relations," delivered on May 17, 1956, in New York City at the second anniversary of the National Association for the Advancement of Colored People, King stated, "We honor our country and ourselves by being here. Contrary to all we have been hearing about the wisdom of our being here, we know that we are here in the noblest tradition of our Judeo-Christian tradition and our democratic heritage" ("Draft," 1963) In the widely quoted "I Have a Dream" speech delivered before the Lincoln Memorial on August 28, 1963, King challenged all Americans to uphold the classical liberal ideals of individualism, universalism, and procedural equality:

> So I say to you, my friends, that even though we must face the difficulties of today and tomorrow, I still have a dream. It is a dream deeply rooted in the American dream that one day this nation will rise up and live out the true meaning of its creed—we hold these truths to be self-evident, that all men are created equal.... I have a dream my four little children will one day live in a nation where they will not be judged by the color of their skin but by the content of their character. I have a dream today. (C. S. King, 1993, p. 101)

Voices of ideological reconciliation and ethnic integration often escape media attention or get lost in the midst of loud and conspicuous voices of committed ideologues from the left and the right. Yet messages of reconciliation are all around us when we look for them. In his autobiography *Walking with the Wind* (1998), John Lewis, a leader of the civil rights movement since the 1960s and currently a Democratic congressman from Georgia, articulated his abiding faith in the "Beloved Community," a vision of what society could become were people of all classes and ethnic backgrounds to reach across the barriers that divide them. In a political manifesto, *Achieving Our Country* (1998), Richard Rorty, a philosopher, argued for ideological moderation and objects to intransigent "leftists" and "conservatives." Tamar Jacoby, an outspoken advocate for liberalization of immigration laws, professed her faith in interethnic integration in *Someone Else's House* (1998), calling for realism in appreciating the real progress between blacks and whites that had taken place in American society and insisting on the need for both blacks and whites to stay the long and slow course of integration. Jacoby subsequently edited an anthology, *Reinventing the Melting Pot: The New Immigrants and What It Means to Be American* (2004), in which a diverse array of authors challenge the traditional notion of the American melting pot and, at the same time, advocate some form of absorption and assimilation of recent immigrants. With respect to higher education, Gerald Graff in *Beyond the Culture Wars* (1992) and Alan Ryan in *Liberal Anxieties and Liberal Education* (1998) insisted that category-based ideas of cultural diversity in the academe must be moderated and put in dialogue with traditional courses to avoid continuation of a disconnected curriculum and mutual resentment.

Economist Glenn Loury, whose words were quoted earlier in this essay as an expression of assimilationism, has moved away from his earlier stance toward a more balanced position of reconciliation. In *The Anatomy of Racial Inequality* (2003), Loury argues that what keeps African Americans from achieving their goals is not simply racial discrimination ("discrimination in contract"), but the more complex reality of "racial stigma" (or "discrimination in contact"). Loury agrees with some of the pluralist views on racial inequality and points out the moral and logical limitations of "color-blind" liberal individualism. At the same time, he critiques the intellectual complacency of the conventional pluralists who would explain any and all problems with the dated cry of racism and racial discrimination.

## MESSAGES OF EXTREMISM

The full spectrum of American public discourse on interethnic relations further includes the marginal voices of separatism, often characterized as "extremist" views. Whereas the aforementioned messages of assimilationism, pluralism, and reconciliation commonly adhere to the societal goal of interethnic integration (while disagreeing on specific visions as to how to achieve this goal), extremist messages often express a preference for a maximum in-group and out-group *separation.* Some of the most unambiguous separatist messages come from those identified with "extreme right" groups including the Ku Klux Klan, Neo-Nazis, Skinheads, and the Patriot movement. According to recent issues of *Intelligence Report*, the quarterly magazine of the Southern Poverty Law Center, such extremist groups are known for their commitment to racial purism, the supremacy of the white race, and, in some cases, even arms training and preparation for a race war. George Bundi (a.k.a. Eric Hawthorne), who reportedly has worked to revitalize the neo-Nazi movement through a powerful network on the Internet, states his separatist view toward blacks: "To put black men and women in American society, which is traditionally and essentially established on European traditions, and to say, 'Here you go, you're an equal, now compete,' is just as ridiculous as assuming that you could move white people to the Congo and have them effectively compete" (*The New York Times Magazine*, February 25, 1996, pp. 40–41). Separatist messages also come from the "extreme left," including contemporary ethnic nationalist groups such as the New Black Panthers and the Nation of Islam. Among such messages are Leonard Jefferies' description of white Americans as "ice people" and Louis Farrakhan's call for black nationalism and economic reparations, his widely reported assertion of black racial superiority and his condemnation of Jews as "bloodsuckers" (e.g., *Time*, February 28, 1994, pp. 21–25).

Separatist messages of the extreme left also come from lesser-known groups such as the black supremacist wing of the Hebrew Israelite movement. Its doctrine asserts that African Americans are God's true chosen people because they are the real descendants of the Hebrews of the Bible. According to the Southern Poverty Law Center (2008), this belief system is "the reversed-color mirror image of the Christian Identity theology embraced by many white supremacists" (p. 48).

Thus, *the extremes meet.* As much as separatist messages of the extreme right and the extreme left

> *Extremist messages often express a preference for a maximum in-group and out-group separation.*

differ dramatically in specific claims, they converge in rigid in-group–out-group distinction, characterization of the in-group as "victims," full-blown confrontational rhetorical posturing, and fortification of mutually intransigent moral claims. Separatist messages of both kinds violate the rationality and civility normally expected by most Americans in public discourse. As Billig et al. (1988) observe, "the extreme bigot is free to play consistently and unambiguously in an area which is beyond reality but which taunts reality. There is no need to hedge and qualify statements in order not to pass a seemingly unreasonable judgment" (p. 118).

Extreme separatist messages are sometimes voiced by those who are unaffiliated with a recognized extremist group. Although not always explicit, separatist views can be inferred from the inflammatory rhetorical devices employed to condemn or scapegoat an out-group or position the in-group as "victims." Patrick Buchanan, for example, used the term "culture war" in a speech he delivered during the 1992 Republican convention. In his book, *State of Emergency: The Third World Invasion and Conquest of America* (2006), Buchanan's messages connoted an unmistakable line drawn to "defend" what is believed to be the authentic American culture. Robert Kimball (1990) similarly characterized black studies in universities as "this war against Western culture" (p. xi); minority student protesters at Stanford University chanting "Down with racism, Western culture's got to go" (*The New York Times*, October 25, 1995, pp. AI, B8); a black student leader at Northwestern University insisting that no black people could be racists "because racism is a function of power" (*The New York Times*, October 25, 1995, p. B8); and a group of Hispanic students at Cornell University occupying a building to demand separate Hispanic housing (*The New York Times*, April 20, 1994, p. B8). Also, the wave of Latino immigration that began in the 1990s and continues today has sparked a nativist backlash that is largely responsible for a more-than-50% increase in the number of extremist groups operating in the United States since 2000 (Potok, 2009).

Separatist arguments, however, tend not to resonate with the American public at large. Although mainstream Americans diverge in their views on the *locus* of American life (individual vs. group identity);

the nature, rights, and responsibilities of humans (universalism vs. relativism); and the meaning of equality (procedural equality vs. status equality), they join in their objection to the separatist vision of the United States and in their shared condemnation of "hate" messages as fundamentally un-American. Exemplifying such common rejections of separatist messages are the responses of several readers to a *Time* magazine cover story featuring Farrakhan, entitled "Pride and Prejudice" (February 28, 1994, pp. 21–34). Their letters to the magazine editor characterize Farrakhan in such unflattering terms as "a wild, hate-mongering preacher," "the Minister of Rage," and "a streetwise hipster who shrewdly plays to the emotions of the most miserable and hopeless of his own people." One reader admonishes the editor for even featuring the story in the magazine: "As an African American, I find it very upsetting that every time Farrakhan speaks the media give him a microphone and an amplifier.... We should stop pointing fingers and making excuses that seem to confuse and anger more than unite our community. We can't continue at this level."

Others have responded to Farrakhan's separatist messages by warning against putting group identity over individual identity. Shelby Steel, an African American professor at San Jose State University, points to the danger of excessive claims of group identity in an opinion column in *The New York Times* (March 13, 1994, p. EI7):

> Louis Farrakhan personifies a specific territory in the collective imagination of black America. (Only this place in the imagination explains the vast disparity between his prominence and his rather small following.) It is the territory where the group ceases to be a mere identity or culture and becomes a value in itself. Here the group becomes synonymous with truth, and no longer needs approval from others.... It is precisely their break from universal truths—tolerance, brotherhood, fair-mindedness—that enables them to assert the supremacy of their group.

## IDEOLOGICAL CIRCLE: A SYNTHESIS

The present analysis has revealed varied renditions of the liberal ideological tradition. Classical liberalism is reproduced by individual Americans not so much in terms of a set of universally commonsensical values, as in the form of often dilemmatic and sometimes embattled conflicting values. Communication messages addressing issues of race, ethnicity, and interethnic relations do not automatically mirror the traditional liberal themes of individualism, universalism, and procedural equality. Rather, they are dynamically challenged by the contrary themes of group identity, relativism, and equal group status.

This ideological dialectic undergirds messages of assimilationism and pluralism, along with messages of reconciliation and separatism. These themes and counter-themes of classical liberalism broadly help us understand the full spectrum of messages we hear today. The traditional individualistic and universalistic ideals and the principle of procedural equality are most closely aligned with messages of assimilationism, generally identified as the position of the mainstream political right. On the other hand, messages of pluralism, often associated with the mainstream political left, advocate the primacy of group identity, and the application of laws and public policies relative to historical and institutional conditions particular to a group, so as to close the existing unequal status between groups. Struggling between these two ideological views are the moderating, balancing, integrating, and often-conflicted messages of reconciliation representing Middle America. In contrast, messages of extremism are commonly identified with the views of the extreme right and the extreme left—messages that emphasize in-group victimhood and moral superiority and maximum in-group–out-group separation.

Together, these four ideological positions constitute an *ideological circle,* described in Figure 4.1. In this circle, the four positions are differentiated based on two bipolar dimensions: (1) the horizontal dimension of classical liberal and contrary themes, and (2) the vertical dimension of integrationist and separatist

*Communication messages addressing issues of race, ethnicity, and interethnic relations do not automatically mirror the traditional liberal themes of individualism, universalism, and procedural equality. Rather, they are dynamically challenged by the contrary themes of group identity, relativism, and equal group status.*

visions for the American society. The oppositional relationship between the assimilationist messages of liberal themes and the pluralist messages of counter-themes is indicated by their respective positions of three o'clock and nine o'clock. Linking these two types of message are the integrationist messages of reconciliation placed at the twelve o'clock position. The separatist messages of extremism (from both the extreme political right and the extreme political left) are merged into the six o'clock position, opposite to the position of the integrationist messages of reconciliation.

Even while being rigorously challenged by the voices advocating pluralism and extremism, the classical liberal ideals continue to occupy the mainstay of American consciousness on interethnic relations in the form of assimilationism and reconciliation (or integration). The classical liberal tradition contains its own contrary themes, unresolved tensions, and dialectic—an ideological push-and-pull that often gives rise to heated debates and, in some cases, even acts of violence. These debates are not confined to the level of intellectual analysis; both themes and counter-themes have arisen from, and passed into, the everyday consciousness of Americans who reflect on, and speak to, various issues of ethnicity and race. Indeed, we do not blindly follow the dictates of classical liberalism. Rather, we exercise a degree of freedom in making our own individual interpretations and judgments within the constraints of the liberal tradition.

This conclusion is largely supported by findings from public opinion polls. In a 1997 Time/CNN poll of more than 1,100 Americans, 96% of the respondents agreed with the assimilationist statement, "It should be the duty of all immigrants to learn English if they plan to stay in this country." In response to the question, "Which comes closest to your view on bilingual education in public schools?" only 11% agreed with the pluralist view that that "children of immigrants should be taught in their native language

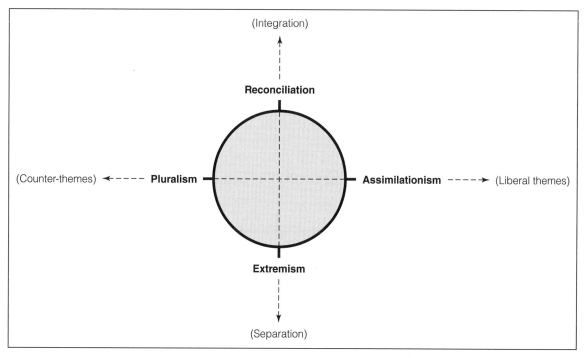

**FIGURE 4.1** Ideological circle linking four types of interethnic communication messages
Kim, 1999, p. 606

indefinitely." This is in sharp contrast with the 48% of the respondents who indicated, "children of immigrants should be taught in their native language only until they know enough English to join regular classes," and with the remaining 40%, who said, "all children should be taught in English" (Gray, 1998, p. 70). Similar sentiments underlie the decisive passage of "Proposition 227" in 1998 by California voters, thereby eliminating all bilingual education programs and replacing them with intensive English language instruction.

When "Ebonics" ("Black English") was endorsed by the Oakland Unified School District Board of Education at the end of 1996 as a legitimate language program, many public leaders who often diverge ideologically with respect to interethnic relations converged in denouncing and rejecting it as an "extremist," "dangerous," and "divisive" idea. From the camp commonly known as the "political right," then–Republican Senator Lauch Faircloth of North Carolina persisted in stating what had become the common view: "But I think Ebonics is absurd. This is a political correctness that has simply gone out of control." Similar voices were heard from the "political

left" as well. Jesse Jackson stated: "I understand the attempt to reach out to these children, but this is an unacceptable surrender, bordering on disgrace" (cited in Lewis, 1998). Senior *Wall Street Journal* editor Joseph N. Boyce was even more indignant: "As a black person and father of four, I find such notions insulting and, yes, racist" (cited in Palmeri, 1997). Poet Maya Angelou was also quoted to have been "incensed" by the plan, while Oakland writer Ishmael Reed labeled it a "travesty" (cited in Palmeri, 1997).

Despite, or perhaps even because of, the often passionate disputes, the United States has worked harder and gone farther than any nation in building a cohesive society of multitudes of ethnicities. Through it all, assimilative–integrative messages continue to serve as the nation's mainstream ideological base. The results of Gallup polls taken since the 1970s through mid-1990s showed a dramatic increase from 35% to 93% in the percentage of white Americans who are willing to vote for a black candidate (*USA Today,* August 8, 1995, p. A11). According to a USA Today/Gallup poll reported in early 2007, 95% of the participants reported that they themselves would consider voting for a black presidential candidate (Page, 2007) Indeed, in November 2008 Americans elected as their president Barack Obama, the son of a white American mother from Kansas and a black father from Kenya.

Many other indications point to the continuing efficacy of classical liberal ideals blurring and transcending ethnic categories in the United States. The percentage of Americans who approve of marriage between blacks and whites increased from 25% in 1972 to 61% in 1995 (*USA Today*, August 8, 1995, p. A11). In terms of actual intermarriages in the United States, the number has escalated roughly from 310,000 in the 1960s to more than 1.1 million in the 1990s. In addition, the incidence of births of mixed-race babies has multiplied 26 times as fast as that of any other group. As of the early 1990s, 52% of Jewish Americans, 65% of Japanese Americans, and 70% of Native Americans are reported to have married out of their faith, race, or ethnic heritage (Smolowe, 1993, pp. 64–65). In 2005, more than 7% of America's 59 million married couples were reported to be interracial, compared to less than 2% in 1970, factoring in all racial combinations (Crary, 2007). Furthermore, a recent study reports that education, not ethnicity, is the primary factor in shaping the individual status and authority at workplace over time (Mintz & Krymkowski, 2010). A poll by the Pew Research Center for the People and the Press reveals that 70% of white Americans and 60% of black Americans believe that blacks and whites have become more similar in the past decade (Williams, 2010). Interviews with American Muslims have shown that their satisfaction with their lives was similar to that of all Americans and much better than the Muslims in many other countries (Goodstein, 2009).

Exactly how the nature of American interethnic relations and the underlying forces of differing ideological perspectives will unfold remains to be seen. Some observers (e.g., Ramos, 2004; Suarez-Orozco & Paez, 2002) foresee a pluralistic trend in light of the rapidly increasing numbers of Hispanic Americans who tend to maintain a strong allegiance to their countries of origin. Undoubtedly, debates will continue as Americans struggle with competing visions of *Unum* and *Pluribus*—visions of "We the People" and what it means to be Americans. Free and public debates, indeed, are essential for American society to guard itself against stagnation, disintegration, and entropy. The very fact that interethnic issues continue to engage American passion is itself an affirmation, and a hallmark, of the American liberal tradition. This tradition contributes to the stability of the American democracy, one that most Americans recognize, cherish, and celebrate. In the essayist Grunwald's (1976) words:

> So one must love America, most of all and most deeply for its constant, difficult, confused, gallant and never finished struggle to make freedom possible. One loves America for its accomplishments as well as for its unfinished business—and especially for its knowledge that its business is indeed unfinished… One ultimately loves America for not what it is, or what it does, but for what it promises… we must deeply believe, and we must prove, that after 200 years the American promise is still only in its beginning. (p. 36)

*Exactly how the nature of American interethnic relations and the underlying forces of differing ideological perspectives will unfold remains to be seen.*

## References

Abercrombie, N. (1980). *Class, structure and knowledge*. Oxford: Basil Blackwell.

Asante, M. (1993). Racism, consciousness, and Afrocentricity. In G. Early (Ed.), *Lure and loathing: Essays on race, identity, and the ambivalence of assimilation* (pp. 127–148). New York: Penguin.

Baker, R. (1994, May 5). Gone with the Unum. *The New York Times*, p. A15.

Billig, M. (1991). *Ideology and opinions: Studies in rhetorical psychology*. London: Sage.

Billig, M., Condor, S., Edwards, D., Gane, M., Middleton, D., & Radley, A. (1988). *Ideological dilemmas: A social psychology of everyday thinking*. London: Sage.

Brooks, D. (2007, January 14). The American way of equality. *The New York Times*, Op-Ed Section, p. 12.

Buchanan, P. (2006). *State of emergency: The Third World invasion and conquest of America*. New York: Thomas Dunne Books.

Crary, D. (2007, April 12). Interracial marriages surge across U.S. *USA Today*. Retrieved 17 July 2010 from http://www.usatoday.com/news/health/2007-04-12-interracial-marriage_N.htm

Crouch, S. (1998). *Always in pursuit: Fresh American perspective*, 1995–1997. New York: Pantheon Books.

"Draft of Dr. Martin Luther King JR Address" (1963). Retrieved 18 June 2007 from http://i.a.cnn.net/cnn/SPECIALS/2007/king.papers/images/dream.draft.pdf

Donohue, W. A. (2006, November 28). Celebrate diversity: Celebrate Christmas. *The New York Times*, Op-Ed Section, p. A23.

Garfinkel, H. (1967). *Studies in ethnomethodology*. Englewood Cliffs, NJ: Prentice-Hall.

Gitlin, T. (1995). *The twilight of common dreams: Why America is wracked by culture wars*. New York: Metropolitan Books.

Goodstein, L. (2009, March 2). Poll finds U.S. Muslims thriving, but not content, *New York Times*, A-11.

Graff, G. (1992). *Beyond the culture wars: How teaching the conflicts can revitalize American education*. New York:

Norton Gray, P. (1998). Teach your children well. *Time*, 69–71.

Grunwald, H. (1976, July 5). Loving America. *Time*, 35–36.

Hacker, A. (1992). *Two nations: Black and White, separate, hostile, unequal*. New York: Charles Scribner's Sons.

Huntington, S. P. (2004). *Who are we? The challenges to America's national identity*. New York: Simon & Schuster.

Iyer, P. (1990, September 3). The masks of minority terrorism. *Time*, 86.

Jacoby, T. (1998). *Someone else's house: America's unfinished struggle for integration*. New York: The Free Press.

Jacoby, T. (Ed.). (2004). *Reinventing the melting pot: The new immigrants and what it means to be American*. New York: Basic Books.

Kim, Y. Y. (1999). *Unum* and *Pluribus*: Ideological underpinnings of interethnic communication in the United States. *International Journal of Intercultural Relations*, 23(4), 591–611.

Kim, Y. Y. (2005). Association and dissociation: A contextual theory of interethnic communication. In W. Gudykunst (Ed.), *Theorizing about intercultural communication* (pp. 323–349). Thousand Oaks, CA: Sage.

Kim, Y. (2007, December). Ideology, identity, and intercultural communication: An analysis of differing academic conceptions of cultural identity. *Journal of Intercultural Communication Research*, 36(3), 237–253.

Kimball, R. (1990). *Tenured radicals: How politics has corrupted higher education*. New York: Harper & Row.

King, C. S. (1993). *The Martin Luther King, Jr. companion: Quotations from the speeches, essays, and books of Martin Luther King, Jr.* (selected by Coretta Scott King). New York: St. Martin.

Lacayo, R. (1993, Fall). Whose peers? *The New Faces of America* [Special Issue]. *Time*. 60–61.

Lewis, J. (1998). *Walking with the wind: A memoir of the movement*. New York: Simon & Shuster.

Loury, G. (1993). Free at last? A personal perspective on race and identity in America. In G. Early (Ed.), *Lure and loathing: Essays on race, identity, and the ambivalence of assimilation* (pp. 1–12). New York: Allen Lane/Penguin.

Loury, G. (2003). *The anatomy of racial inequality*. Cambridge, MA: Harvard University Press.

Major, B. (1994). From social inequality to personal entitlement: The role of social comparisons, legitimacy appraisals, and group membership. *Advances in Experimental Social Psychology*, 26, 293–355.

Mintz, B., & Krymkowski, D. (2010). The ethnic, race, and gender gaps in workplace authority: Changes over time in the United States. *Sociological Quarterly*, 51(1), 20–45.

Page, S. (2007, Feb 2) Poll shows Clinton, Giuliani pull ahead as campaigns kick off. *USA Today*. Retrieved 18 July 2010 from http://www.usatoday.com/news/Washington/2007-02-13-2008-campaign-poll_x.htm

Palmeri, A. (1997, October). *Ebonics and politics: A Burkian analysis*. Paper presented at the annual meeting of the National Communication Association, Chicago.

Patterson, O. (2006, December 30). The last race problem. *The New York Times*, Op-Ed Section, p. A19.

Potok, M. (2009, Spring). Diversity and its discontents. *Intelligence Report*, 133, p. 1.

Ramos, J. (2004). *The Latino wave: How Hispanics will elect the next American president*. New York: Rayo.

Rorty, R. (1998). *Achieving our country: Leftist thought in twentieth-century America*. Cambridge, MA: Harvard University Press.

Rossides, D. (1976). *The American class system: An introduction to social stratification*. Washington, DC: University Press of America.

Ryan, A. (1998). *Liberal anxieties and liberal education*. New York: Hill & Wang.

Schlesinger, A. M. Jr. (1992). *The disuniting of America: Reflections on a multicultural society*. New York: W. W. Norton.

Smolowe, J. (1993, Fall). Intermarried ... with children. *The New Faces of America* [Special Issue]. *Time*, 64–65.

Southern Poverty Law Center (2008, Fall). Ready for war. *Intelligence Report*, 131, 46–54.

Suarez-Orozco, M., & Paez, M. (Eds.). (2002). *Latinos: Re-making America.* Berkeley, CA: University of California Press.

Sykes, C. (1992). *A nation of victims: The decay of the American character.* New York: St. Martin's Press.

Toobin, J. (2006, December 30). Gerald Ford's affirmative action. *The New York Times,* Op-Ed Section, p. A19.

Traub, J. (1998, June 28). Nathan Glazer changes his mind, again. *The New York Times Magazine,* 22–25.

Tsuda, Y. (1986). *Language inequality and distortion.* Philadelphia: John Benjamin.

Van Dijk, T. A. (Ed.). (1997). *Discourse as social interaction.* Thousand Oaks, CA: Sage.

Wilson, K. (1998, May). The contested space of prudence in the 1874-1875 civil rights debate. *Quarterly Journal of Speech, 84*(2), 131–149.

Wolfe, A. (1998). *One nation, after all.* New York: Viking.

## Concepts and Questions

1. Why has the *E Pluribus Unum* concept of a "melting pot" society failed to materialize in contemporary American society?

2. How do "tribal identities" contribute to interethnic conflict?

3. What characterizes messages of assimilation? From whom are messages of assimilation most likely to emerge?

4. Can or do messages of assimilation lend themselves to improved interethnic communication? How?

5. Give an example of a message of pluralism. How do messages of pluralism differ from messages of assimilation?

6. What are messages of reconciliation? How do they relate to messages of assimilation and of pluralism?

7. From whom are messages of reconciliation most likely to emanate?

8. What are messages of extremism? Which groups of American society are most likely to promulgate messages of extremism? Why?

9. How can an understanding of the philosophical underpinnings of the messages of assimilation, plurality, reconciliation, and extremism lead to better interethnic communication?

10. How can the American struggle between *Unum* and *Pluribus* be resolved?

# Action-Oriented Interfaith Dialogue with Muslim Communities

POLLY A. BEGLEY

*Our next essay begins with this assertion: "Islamophobia, hatred or fear directed toward Muslims, has increased in America and worldwide." It is Polly Begley's thesis, advanced in an essay titled "Beyond Tolerance: Action-Oriented Interfaith Dialogue with Muslim Communities," that a lack of knowledge about Islam is at the heart of the hostile perceptions and negative feelings directed at this religion—a religion that can lay claim to over a billion and half followers. In an attempt to clarify some of these false and dangerous images, Begley explores the origins, values, beliefs, and tenets of Islam. She also recommends a series of intercultural conversations and exchanges that might enable individuals to become more tolerant toward people who follow the Islamic faith. Begley calls these exchanges "action-oriented interfaith dialogues." She maintains that these dialogues can take place through educational campaigns, community outreach programs, media literacy, music, mass media, and the Internet. While*

This original essay appears here in print for the first time. All rights reserved. Permission to reprint must be obtained from the author and the publisher. Ms. Polly A. Begley teaches in the Department of Communication Arts at Fresno City College, Fresno, California.

*granting that there are extremists and "fringe fanatics" who are often the "face of Islam" in the West, Begley maintains that by linking an increased fund of knowledge about Islam with active interaction with members of the Islamic faith, many misconceptions about Islam can be dispelled.*

I love you when you bow in your mosque, kneel in your temple, pray in your church.
For you and I are sons of one religion, and it is the spirit.
**Khalil Gibran**

> *A lack of knowledge about Islam is at the heart of the hostile perceptions and negative feelings directed at this religion—a religion that can lay claim to over a billion and half followers.*

# INTRODUCTION

Islamophobia, hatred or fear directed towards Muslims, has increased in America and worldwide following 9/11. Ali-Karamali (2008) maintains,

> Islam is not encapsulated in the grim, glaring *Newsweek* photograph of Osama bin Laden. Islam is not epitomized by the deeply angry, bearded face of Ayatollah Khomeini. Islam is not apotheosized by the suicide bomber who detonates civilians. Islam *is* one of many American faiths. Muslims are ordinary people who share the same monotheistic traditions as Jews and Christians. We struggle with the same daily conflicts and challenges as our non-Muslim neighbors" (p. 2).

Imam Seyed Ali Ghazvini, Spiritual Leader of the Islamic Cultural Center of Fresno, California, thinks there needs to be discussion in America regarding how people are treated and regarded in everyday life. Would a non-Muslim student "be willing to work on a project with a girl who wears a *hijab* [scarf]? Would you accept her as a friend? Would you be willing to walk with her at the mall?" (personal communication, September 13, 2009) Americans and citizens around the globe witnessed violent images and stories of terrorism splashed across every newspaper, television, and computer since 9/11. Meanwhile, the vast majority of the *umma*, the Muslim world, have worked diligently to promote interfaith understanding and peaceful cooperation.

Thirty-eight percent of Americans, according to a study conducted by The Pew Forum on Religion and Public Life, thought, "Islam does encourage violence more than other faiths do" (2009, p. 2). This statistic may be discouraging for those hoping to dispel misconceptions and disassociate terrorism from Islam and Muslims. But the study also revealed that those who are personally acquainted with a Muslim and have some comprehension of Islam are less likely to see it as a religion encouraging violence.

Thus, in pursuit of enhanced knowledge, the focus of this essay will be to move beyond misunderstandings and mere tolerance to religious pluralism by exploring Islamic origins, values, beliefs, and tenets for living. Intellectual exploration further becomes a means to engage in action-oriented interfaith dialogue through educational campaigns, community outreach, media literacy, music, mass media, and the Internet. The rich diversity of Muslim communities worldwide prevents any brief essay such as this from being considered a comprehensive guide, but the following may provide an introductory glimpse into the lives of the followers of the Prophet and advance peaceful cooperation among faiths.

# ORIGINS AND CURRENT DEMOGRAPHICS

Islam began with Muhammad, who was the last of God's prophets. God spoke to him through the angel Gabriel about 609 A.D., and the messages were recorded in the Qur'an. The Qur'an, the book of Islam, is the miracle claimed by the Prophet and considered to be the exact words of God. This holy book contains 114 chapters (or *suras*) and outlines the will of God for the loyal followers of Islam (Waines, 1993). Ali-Karamali (2008) states that "Although Muslims revere Muhammad as the embodiment of goodness and human perfection, we have always resisted deifying him or attributing to him any superhuman characteristics" (p. 34). This respect is reflected when Muslims say the Prophet's name, they say immediately afterwards, *sallallahu 'alaihi wa sallam*, peace be upon him.

The Prophet received the divine revelations of God in the city of Mecca, located in what is now known as Saudi Arabia, but he had a great impact on all of Arabia. Historically, the Middle East was turbulent. Vast areas, harsh deserts, warring tribes, and a precarious value placed on human life contributed to turmoil in the region. A number of leaders attempted to create a consolidated empire, but it was Muhammad and his followers who united all of Arabia under their control. Islam's appeal to Muslims worldwide may lie in its pure simplicity and the ability to find "peace that comes when one's life is surrendered to God" (Smith, 1991, p. 222). Essentially, Islamic beliefs dominate every moment from birth to death and beyond.

Currently, Islam is one of the youngest and fastest growing major religions in the world. The Pew Forum on Religion and Public Life conducted a comprehensive demographic study in October 2009 and found that nearly one in four people, or approximately 1.57 billion worldwide, are Muslim. Sixty percent live in Asia, 20 percent in the Middle East and North Africa, fifteen percent in sub-Saharan Africa, less than 2 1/2 percent in Europe, and less than 1 percent in the Americas. The study further estimated that 10 to 13 percent are Shia Muslims and 87 to 90 percent are Sunni Muslims, but as the senior researcher on the Pew Forum project pointed out, these numbers are less reliable because this is a "very sensitive question. If asked, large numbers will say I am just a Muslim—not that they don't know, but it is a sensitive question in many places" (Greene, 2009, October 12). The Shia/Sunni split stemmed from disputes in the decades after the death of the Prophet regarding the question of rightful succession.

The Pew Study presented a demographic map of the global Muslim population and further revealed how this faith, its followers, and its influence have extended beyond Islam's Middle Eastern origins. Reza Aslan, the Iranian-American author of "No God but God," stated after the Pew study results were made public, "If the goal is to create better understanding between the United States and the Muslim world, our focus should be on south and southeast Asia, not the Middle East" (Greene, 2009, October 12). One of

*Interfaith dialogue becomes an indispensable strategy for promoting positive changes and cooperation while dispelling misconceptions within diverse communities.*

the challenges of interfaith interactions is for all participants to comprehend the vast diversity within every religious group. Liyakatali Takim says, "An exposition of how diverse Islam really is will challenge the myth of a homogenous and static Muslim world and will demonstrate the 'rainbow nature' of Islam" (2004, July, p. 350). Thus, comprehending the origins of Islam remains an important pursuit, but the ever-changing and dynamic nature of any faith must also be acknowledged.

## UNDERSTANDING ISLAM THROUGH ACTION-ORIENTED DIALOGUE

Interfaith dialogue becomes an indispensable strategy for promoting positive changes and cooperation while dispelling misconceptions within diverse communities. Ali-Karamali believes, "We in the United States have been bombarded with daily, unchecked, untrue, public denigration of Islam to an irresponsibly defamatory degree" (2008, p. 2). Gülen (2004), remarked, "How unfortunate it is that Islam, which is based on this understanding and spirit, is shown by some circles to be synonymous with terrorism. This is a great historical mistake; wrapping a system based on safety and trust in a veil of terrorism just shows the spirit of Islam remains unknown" (p. 58). In light of this denigration and association, Muslims have come to realize that they have to engage in dialogue with non-Muslims in order to defuse stereotypes. Historically, mosques and centers in America were closed to non-Muslims. But after the terrorist attacks of September 11, Muslim leaders reevaluated this closed-door policy. Imam Ghazvini said, "After 9/11, we thought, we have two options: We can create walls around us and separate ourselves from others or we can build bridges of understanding of others" (Orozco, 2007, May 26). There are extremists in every religion, and those fringe fanatics should not be allowed to speak or represent the majority of peaceful followers.

But multi-faith conversations should extend beyond experts and community leaders talking about peace at a conference or meeting. Takim (2004, July) argues that dialogue "must also confront the realities of hate, discrimination, and violence in society. Collaborative actions have become more important as Muslims realize that conversations with their non-Muslim friends ought to lead to shared commitment so as to address humanitarian issues that concern both communities" (p. 352). After the terrorist attacks of September 11, Muslims, especially Muslim women wearing headscarves, were victims of violence and harassment in greater numbers. Communities all over the United States came together to show support for their Muslim neighbors by guarding Mosques from and escorting women to prayer or shopping, and some non-Muslim women expressed solidarity by donning headscarves. A documentary film entitled, "A Lot to Share," directed by Karen Shopsowitz, was another example of interfaith interaction that transformed into social action. The film spotlighted a shared parking lot between a synagogue and mosque that eventually inspired shared humanitarian efforts, such as homeless intervention, youth and senior citizen outreach, and graffiti removal (National Film Board of Canada, 2009, May 26). Dialogue begins with education, but action-oriented dialogue moves beyond just understanding and dispelling myths about a particular religion to creating ways to enhance everyone's lives and communities.

> The everyday practices of Islam, such as praying five times daily or modest dress for women and men, mean it is not a religion that is easily kept secret.

## Dialogue Through Education

Should the sight of a group praying in an airport provoke suspicion and fear among bystanders? An airline agent reported seeing a group of men "praying very loud" in Arabic near a boarding gate in November 2006, at the Minneapolis-St. Paul International Airport. Several other passengers and flight attendants expressed alarm regarding their praying, behavior, and alleged political conversation. Ultimately, the men were ordered off the plane and questioned by the U.S. Marshals Service, the FBI, the Secret Service, and the Transportation Security Administration. The men were a group of six *imams*, or religious leaders, returning home from a North American Imams Federation conference. One of the men commented later, "We were never bothering anyone, not saying anything loudly. We were prostrating ourselves, the normal way we pray" (Von Sternberg & Miller, 2006). Terrorist

attacks in the United States and other countries have led to stricter airport security measures, but many questioned whether the airline employees had valid reasons for removing these men from the plane.

Perhaps the problem was that those observing the *imams'* behavior were not familiar with normal Muslim prayer routines. "Islam is a religion of orthopraxy, practice oriented rather than doctrine oriented" (Ali-Karamali, 2008, p. 6). The everyday practices of Islam, such as praying five times daily or modest dress for women and men, mean it is not a religion that is easily kept secret. Fadel Soliman, recently appointed National Chaplain of the World Assembly of Muslim Youth in North and Central America and the founder of the Bridges Foundation, commented that "Many Westerners view Muslims as creatures from outer space … worshipping a different God named Allah." Soliman, through the Bridges Foundation, specializes in introducing Islam to non-Muslims and also trains Muslims on how to present their faith to others. He explained that Allah is the same God worshipped by Christians and Jews and that "We give different attributes to the same God" (Shahine, 2006). The previous incident might not have occurred if more people understood the tenets and pillars of the Islam faith. Four tenets are central to understanding Islam: (1) It is a monotheistic religion. (2) God created the world. (3) Humans are fundamentally good from birth because they are God's creations and without "original sin." Muslims believe in the innate goodness of humanity, but contemporary societies "forget" their divine origins. (4) For each Muslim there will be a day of judgment when God decides whether each person will go to heaven or be condemned to hell (Smith, 1991).

Islam outlines five pillars for Muslims. First, *shahada*, creed, is the confession of faith: "*La illaha il-Allah Muhammad ur Rasulullah*. This means, 'There is no god but God and Muhammad is the messenger of God'" (Ali-Karamali, 2008, p. 36). Second, *salat*, prayer, is an important part of everyday life. Muslims are required to stop for prayer five times a day (*fajr, dhuhr, asr, maghrib, isha 'a*—dawn, after midday, afternoon, sunset, and nighttime) facing in the direction of the holy city of Mecca (Smith, 1991, p. 244).

Beattie (2005) described the call for the faithful to prayer: "'God is great,' the muezzins call: 'Allahu Akbar... At sundown, in particular the amplified sound of dozens of muezzins sounding simultaneously is a distinctive and ethereal reminder that Cairo is first and foremost an Islamic city" (p. 91). Third, zakat, giving alms, to the poor is expected of each person. Fourth, sawm, fasting, during the month of Ramadan is required. This fast prompts Muslims to be disciplined and reminds them to be more charitable to the hungry and the poor within their societies. Finally, the hajj, pilgrimage, to Mecca is a requisite trip for those who are able to make the journey (Nigosian, 1987). Islam does not require complicated rituals or sacrifices. If one repeats the shahada creed, then he or she is a Muslim. Good Muslims follow the five pillars.

Another reminder to non-Muslims that a person is a follower of the Prophet relates to styles of dress. In fact, Muslim males and females both have a responsibility to dress modestly, but the veil has been a source of stereotypes and misunderstandings regarding the roles of women in Islam. Farazi (2006) wrote about faith and fashion for Al Jazeera.net and reported that female religious garments may be a matter of convenience, a way to avoid male stares, or to assert that a woman's clothing choices are only one part of her identity.

> The head veil, or hijab, which literally means 'curtain,' is essentially a headscarf. The khimar, a step up in the veiling process, is a headscarf that covers the hair completely and extends down to the waist, fully disguising the breasts. And the niqab, usually a black wrap that resembles a cape, extending from the head to the floor and covering everything except the eyes, is the final stage. The hijab is considered by many Islamists to be obligatory for Muslim women, while those who wear or advocate the niqab tend to exist outside mainstream Egyptian society (p. 143).

In fact, the Qu'ran does not specify the shape or color of women's coverings and does not ask women to cover their faces. The hijab remains one of the most conspicuous signs of Islamic intent to embrace spiritual above secular values. The tension between spiritual and secular perspectives inspired an Egyptian website, hamasna.com, which launched in 2006. The web site was developed in response to Egyptian television's sexually explicit music videos and programming to encourage modesty through "The International Campaign for Defending Hijab." The site also "offers female singers and actresses alternative jobs should they decide to quit show biz and take the veil" (El-Jesri & Awad, 2006, August).

Other Muslim women embraced the spotlight while still maintaining their spiritual focus. Muneera Rashid and Sukina Abdul Noor, the members of the musical duo Poetic Pilgrimage, wear hijab and break down stereotypes of women in Islam through Sukina's lyrics in the song "Definition of a Pilgrim" (personal communication, February 8, 2007):

*evoking the name of Allah before I start roaming*
*desperately seeking something*
*cloaked in garments flowing*
*memorizing sacred hymns now my soul's glowing*
*I write these hip-hop poems*
*in praise of the All Knowing*

Muneera and Sukina say, "We try to make hijab appear the coolest thing in the world to our young fans .... We tell them in our music that hijab is cool and they should not be ashamed of it" (Mumisa, 2006).

Discussions about veiling often uncover a host of other stereotypes about Muslim women being repressed or mistreated, as they are commonly represented in mass media. Ali-Karamali (2008) contends, "If we peruse history, we find that Muslim women have been queens, heads of states, and rulers for centuries" (p. 118). Furthermore, female engineers and medical doctors were common and accepted in the Middle East and other predominantly Muslim countries before they were in Western countries. Ali-Karamali related, "Our parents' circle of friends always included many Muslim, Indian-Pakistani—American women doctors. These women had not become doctors only after immigrating to America. They had arrived as doctors." Lila Abu-Lughod more aptly said, "We must take care not to reduce the diverse situations and attitudes of millions of Muslim women to a single item of clothing. Perhaps it is time to give up the Western obsession with the veil and focus on some serious issues with which feminists and others should indeed be concerned" (2002, September, p. 786). In addition, most issues important to women of any faith are also of concern to larger communities.

## Dialogue through Community Outreach

Outreach campaigns serve to educate and connect groups of people. Americans who knew how Muslims refer to God and the name of Islam's sacred text expressed more positive perceptions of Muslims and were able to acknowledge similarities between Islam and other monotheistic religions (The Pew Forum on Religion and Public Life, 2009). Liyakatali Takim (2004, July) refers to community outreach by defining the "multi-faceted dimensions of dialogue. Increasingly, dialogue takes place not only in conferences but also in schools, workplaces, and even in the neighborhood" (p. 348). Imam Ghazvini recognized the importance of personal relations as he stated, "Personal friendships create a lot of impact.... I would tell my community to be available everywhere, encounter people, meet new people all the time, the chance is that people get to know you and see you, then this will change a lot of their misconceptions about the faith. The friendship itself will break a wall" (personal communication, September 13, 2009). The Islamic Cultural Center of Fresno, California, provides seminars to local law enforcement agencies, healthcare providers, and community members as well as inviting local citizens, political leaders, and religious leaders to experience Islamic celebrations, such as the traditional *Iftar* dinner (evening meal after *maghrib*, sunset, that breaks the Ramadan fast).

Community outreach should not be seen as evangelization. Fadel Soliman, who has addressed audiences regarding Islam, including members of the U.S. Congress and Pentagon officials, says that "Daawa [advocacy] is not about converting people to Islam, the way many people assume it is. Allah said to Prophet Mohammad that his only mission is to deliver the message perfectly and that it is up to people to believe or not to believe" (Shahine, 2006, September 7–13). Mohamed El-Moctar El-Shinqiti (2006) pointed out that historically Muslims

*Community outreach should not be seen as evangelization.*

subjugated populations for empire building as did other conquerors, but religious writings do not advocate conversion to Islam. In fact, he references religious tolerance in Islam: "Let there be no compulsion in religion ... (Al-Baqarah 2:256) ... Moreover, Prophet Mohammed (peace be upon him) is told in the Qur'an that his mission is to teach and preach, not to impose or compel" (Playing the Empire Game of El-Shinqiti (2006).section, para. 3).

But the media continues to attribute the concept of compulsion and, more specifically, "holy war" to Islam. *Jihad* is an Arabic word from the Qur'an that has often been mistranslated as "holy war." The mere mention of an Islamic *jihad* has been depicted within Western literature and media as religious fanatics on a killing rampage. In contrast, Muslims remember "holy war" in terms of the crusades of the 12th and 13th centuries when Christian soldiers, sanctioned by the Pope, led military campaigns in the Holy Land. The literal meaning of *jihad* in Arabic is "'Utmost effort' in promotion and defense of Islam" (Lippman, 1995, p. 113). In fact, El-Shinqiti (2006) states that the term "holy war" does not appear in the Qur'an. Even the terms of "defense of Islam" are limited, as it is said, "Fight in the way of Allah against those who fight against you, but begin not hostilities. Lo! Allah loves not aggressors (Al-Baqarah 2:190)" Most importantly, enhanced understanding of diverse faiths does not threaten one's own beliefs. Liyakatali Takim, noted that students in comparative religion classes, "often remarked that their faith and commitment to their own religious tradition has been strengthened by learning about other religions" (2004, p. 346).

## Dialogue through Media Literacy

Moderate Muslims, the majority of the followers of the Prophet, espouse nonviolent change. Unfortunately, the terms and labels utilized by some media and political or religious leaders contribute to misconceptions and fan the fires of hatred against the followers of Islam. Renee Hobbs, Professor of Communication at Babson College and a founding member of the board of directors of the Alliance for a Media Literate America, emphasized the importance of media literacy skills and courageous teachers who feel "responsible for helping students develop the skills to be citizens in an information age" (2001, p. 411). These citizens have to be able to ask critical questions about what they see, hear, and read every day.

"Fundamentalism" is a term once used for Protestant Christians who sought to reestablish religious values in secular society. Recently, the term "fundamentalist" has been "used indiscriminately in the popular press and in Western political discourse to refer to any Islamist, no matter whether his aim is violent revolution or peaceful transformation.... Its current usage to describe activist Muslims is almost always pejorative and obscures their thoroughly modern views on society and religion" (Abdo, 2000, p. 11). Other terms implying the innate violent nature of Islam are "Islamic terrorism," "Islamic fascism," or "Islamic radicals" (United Nations, 2006, p. 13). The use of such terms creates the impression that Islamic activism leads to militancy and violent confrontation. Redefining words such as "fundamentalist" may help to change perceptions about Islam. Consequently, some scholars prefer the term "Islamists," which refers to Muslim activists who wish to peacefully reestablish Islamic values in society, but does not carry the negativity of other group labels (Abdo, 2000).

The media also perpetuates confusion about "God" and "Allah." A previous section mentioned the *shahada*, creed, or confession of faith, *La illaha il-Allah Muhammad ur Rasulullah*. The wording and capitalization of the translation, 'There is no god but God' conveys the Islamic belief in the one and only God. Unfortunately, the *shahada* has also been translated in popular media as "There is no god but Allah." Ali-Karamali (2008) explained that "Newspapers and television reports often use 'Allah' instead of 'God' when speaking of Islam, as if Allah were an entirely different being, or as if no English equivalent existed for Allah.... But the Muslim God is the God of Moses and Jesus and Abraham and is called Allah because Muhammad, the Prophet of Islam, happened to speak Arabic" (p. 36). These incorrect or half translations used in the media exacerbate the perception of insurmountable differences among the world's major religions.

> In contrast to television and newspaper reports, music may represent one type of media that becomes a bridge of understanding and bonding across perceptual differences.

## Dialogue through Hip-Hop Music

In contrast to television and newspaper reports, music may represent one type of media that becomes a bridge of understanding and bonding across perceptual differences. Islamic beliefs and Muslim artists have influenced hip-hop from its very origins within African American communities. Afrika Bambaataa was a founding member of the Muslim-influenced youth music organization Zulu Nation in the United States during the 1970s. Bambaataa has since been described as the grandfather or godfather of hip-hop. The influence of Islam in contemporary American music is still apparent. Hip-hop artist and devout Muslim Mos Def recites *Bismallah Al-Rahman Al-Rahim*, "In the name of God, most Gracious, and most Compassionate," at the beginning of his albums (Abdel-Alim, 2005).

Many hip-hop artists see similarities between the rhythm and flow of rap with the linguistic style of the Qur'an. The Qur'an was revealed to the Prophet orally and in rhymed prose. The rhyming and oral nature of the Qur'an makes it easier for followers of the Prophet to become *hafiz*, a person who memorizes the entire Qur'an. Mos Def stated, "Like, there's a rhyme scheme in all of it [the Qur'an]. You see what I'm saying? And it holds fast to your memory. And then you start to have a deeper relationship with it on recitation" (Abdel-Alim, 2005). Likewise, hip-hop lyrics also serve to stick in one's memory and transmit more information in less time.

The hip-hop scene may have started in the United States, but has spread worldwide, connecting people to a global community of music. Muneera said, "Hip Hop can be seen as an American export, but it has now touched the globe, made babies, and has full-grown children in every part of the world" ("Ten Questions with Poetic Pilgrimage," 2009). Abdel-Alim called it the "'Transglobal hip hop *umma*' within a borderless Islamic nation." And this *umma* is creating lyrics in every language for and against every imaginable cause. Abdel-Alim (2005) contends that

Researchers are needed to study the trilingual (Arabic, Hebrew and English) rappers in Palestine as they rail against what they perceive to be the tyranny of the Israeli state, to explore the struggles of Muslim rappers in Algeria as they wage war on what they believe are corrupt regimes (rappers with African American–inspired names like Ole Dirty Shame, MC Ghosto and Killa Dox), and to examine how Muslim artists in South Africa are critiquing what they perceive as the hypocrisy of their nation's "new democracy."

Muslim rappers, similar to any other hip-hop artists, attempt to highlight problems within their communities. Muneera and Sukina of Poetic Pilgrimage, a popular U.K. hip-hop group, include references to societal issues in Muneera's verse from "Definition of a Pilgrim" (personal communication, February 8, 2007):

To get away from painted street scenes of crack and cocaine but everyday remains the same of the same

Time to fix up readjust my frames life's just a spectacle

Looking at life from a more metaphysical

As I adhere to the call of my Lord on all fours

I arise as a Pilgrim Samurai with thumping sound systems in my headphones

Muneera explains, "With all the harassment that we face in this harsh Islamophobic environment there is a need to express. Some of this tension is being let loose in the form of Hip Hop." She continues, "We try to speak for those who have no voice. Those whose stories may get missed or simply misrepresented. We make music from our heart" ("Ten Questions with Poetic Pilgrimage," 2009).

While lyricists in the U.K. express themselves freely, others such as Salome, an Iranian rapper, described herself as being "underground" and talked about what that means to her and other musicians in Iran (personal communication, February 8, 2009):

They [musicians in Iran] name themselves underground, not because they don't want to be 'on the ground,' but because they can't get the chance. But to me, I see being underground as an ideology itself, standing against mainstream and refusing to obey what popular culture wants, what society wants or what government wants. So even if I could sign a contract with a big time

music company or get all the permissions in the world to make my art popular, I won't. Because that would lead to accepting what capitalism wants, what the company wants, etc. If I do want to do things my way, I must be independent, so I got to be underground.

Salome writes in Farsi and Turkish and said her music may be categorized, "but my style can't." She tells people to listen to her songs and figure it out for themselves (personal communication, July 11, 2009):

Democracy doesn't have a name in there, it is not defined but it exists

They all are united saying: "love and joy." There is no elections to do fraud

A black liquid, a transparent stone, is not the base of economy

Bring apple and take fig, there is no computer

Nobody heard of capitalism, worker, employee and employer

I will do anything just for your smile, I will sacrifice myself

There is no global warming, the ices don't melt, the races doesn't extinct

The nature keeps going as it is supposed to go, the sequence of season won't foul

Of course, the reach of underground hip-hop artists has extended with the Internet. The transglobal hip-hop *umma* and Salome fans may find her on myspace.com and see her videos on youtube.com if they want to figure out her style or listen to her lyrics. Salome says, "My goal in my music is just to express myself, express my pain, this 'pain' is not something gloomy and dark, but something that gives strength I am not trying to get somewhere, or be a preacher. It is really satisfying when I meet even one person who understands" (Reshad, 2006, August 6). Artists of any creed may be searching for the one person or people who understand and connect with their messages.

## Dialogue through Mass Media and the Internet

Musicians are not the only ones who are able to extend their audience impact through the Internet and other mass media. M. Fethullah Gülen (2004) describes the "ideal human" as a person who stays "in touch and communicates with people's minds, hearts, and feelings, these new men and women will use the mass media and try to establish a new power balance of justice, love, respect, and equality among people. They will make might subservient to right, and never discriminate on grounds of color or race" (p. 82). Islamic Cultural Centers in major cities across the United States and worldwide utilize the mass media to send positive messages. Ali-Karamali (2008) pointed out that "Muslims all over the world *did* denounce the terrorists and specifically condemn the September 11th attacks. Many offered explanations of Islam and how terrorism violated Islamic principles" (p. 220). Unfortunately, these positive messages made the headlines much less often than the negative. Islamic Centers and organizations reach out to non-Muslims by posting news releases and information on their own Internet websites.

Technological advances have changed the way we communicate, educate, and persuade. Groups fixated on promoting violence have been cognizant of the power of the Internet to persuade target audiences for quite some time. Kepel (2004) contended that "the war for Muslim minds entered the global jungle of the internet" as graphic pictures of torture, beheadings, and wartime atrocities were made available online (p. 7). Fortunately, the *umma* have also begun to utilize the power of the Internet to counter information sent out by violent factions. Their messages focus on peace and invitations for discussions between Muslims and non-Muslims. For example, the Internet site IslamOnline.net was launched in early 2006 after cartoons with offensive depictions of the Prophet, considered blasphemous by Muslims, were published in Denmark's Jyllands-Posten. IslamOnline was designed to dispel misconceptions and educate about the Prophet and Islam. The United Nations publication (2006), "Alliance of civilizations: Report of the high-level group," also referenced MuslimHeritage.com and Beliefnet.com as being effective sources for increasing *ilm* (knowledge) about Islam and other faiths. Soliya.net is another online site for university students from the United States and Arab and Muslim countries to meet and discuss global issues.

## CONCLUSION

On April 4, 1968, after Martin Luther King, Jr. was assassinated, New York Senator Robert F. Kennedy spoke before an angry crowd in Indianapolis, Indiana: "What we need in the United States is not division; what we need in the United States is not hatred; what we need in the United States is not violence or lawlessness." Kennedy pled for "love," "wisdom," "compassion," and "justice" ("John F. Kennedy," 1968). These sentiments still apply today as global communities struggle to understand diversity in faiths and engage in action-oriented dialogue to advance human understanding of each other and ourselves.

This chapter encourages community efforts to move beyond misconceptions and mere tolerance through an exploration of Islamic origins, values, beliefs, and tenets for living. Such an investigation engages Muslims and non-Muslims in action-oriented interfaith dialogue through education, community outreach, media literacy, music, mass media, and the Internet. Kennedy spoke of "hatred" in the United States in 1968 and President Obama referred to that same emotion is his inaugural speech more than forty years later on January 20, 2009 (Associated Press):

> We are a nation of Christians and Muslims, Jews and Hindus—and non-believers. We are shaped by every language and culture, drawn from every end of this Earth; and because we have tasted the bitter swill of civil war and segregation, and emerged from that dark chapter stronger and more united, we cannot help but believe that the old hatreds shall someday pass; that the lines of tribe shall soon dissolve; that as the world grows smaller, our common humanity shall reveal itself; and that America must play its role in ushering in a new era of peace.

Do people of one faith community still view those of another religion with suspicion or fear? Would the daughters and sons of non-Muslim and Muslim neighbors play together freely? And would those same daughters and sons feel comfortable walking in public together or committing themselves to feeding the homeless or removing racist graffiti from local mosques, temples, or churches? Gülen (2004) used the analogy of human physical oneness (p. 7):

As we are all limbs of the same body, we should cease this duality that violates our very union. We should clear the way to unite people; this is one of the greatest ways in which God grants people success in this world, and how He transforms this world into a Paradise. It is in this way that the doors of Heaven will be opened wide in order to give us a warm welcome. Hence, we should remove all ideas and feelings that pull us apart, and run to embrace one another.

The pursuit of greater understanding of our neighbors and ourselves help us to go beyond stereotypes, misconceptions, and mere tolerance. And only with this understanding will we be able to solve the immense social ills that every community faces.

# References

Abdel-Alim, H. (2005, July 7-13). Hip hop Islam. *Al-Ahram Weekly On-Line*, 750. Retrieved December 27, 2009 from http://weekly.ahram.org.eg/2005/750/feature.htm

Abdo, G. (2000). *No God but God: Egypt and the triumph of Islam*. New York: Oxford University Press.

Abu-Lughod, L. (2002, September). Do Muslim women really need saving? Anthropological reflections on cultural relativism and its others. *American Anthropologist, 104* (3): 783–790.

Ali-Karamali, S. (2008). *The Muslim next door: The Qur'an, the media, and that veil thing*. Ashland, Oregon: White Cloud Press.

Associated Press. (2009, January 20). *'Time has come to reaffirm our enduring spirit:' Text of Obama's speech for his inauguration as 44th president*. Retrieved from MSNBC.com website: http://www.msnbc.msn.com/id/28751183/ns/politics-inauguration/page/2/

Beattie, A. (2005). *Cityscapes: Cairo*. New York: Oxford University Press.

El-Jesri, M., & Awad, S. (2006, August). *Culture 101: The latest in news and gossip from cultural circles*. Retrieved August 25, 2006, from Egypt Today website: http://www.egypttoday.com/article.aspx?ArticleID=6866

El-Shinqiti, M. E. (2006, September 3). *From holy war to holy peace*. Retrieved December 16, 2006, from IslamOnline.net website: http://www.islamonline.net/English/Living_Shariah/ContemporaryIssues/Interfaith/2006/08/01.shtml

Farazi, I. (2006, March 29). *Following faith and fashion*. Aljazeera.net. Retrieved August 25, 2006, from Aljazeera.net website: http://english.aljazeera.net/NR/exeres/CC89DE2B-E038-48E9-8178-F23181008CB4.htm

Greene, R. (2009, October 12). *Nearly 1 in 4 people worldwide is Muslim, report says*. Retrieved November 18, 2009, from CNN.com/Asia website: http://edition.cnn.com/2009/WORLD/asiapcf/10/07/muslim.world.population/index.html

Gülen, M. (2004). *Toward a global civilization of love & tolerance*. New Jersey: The Light Incorporated.

Hobbs, R. (2001). Media literacy skills: Interpreting tragedy. *Social Education, 65*(7), 406–411.

John F. Kennedy Presidential Library & Museum. (1968, April 4). *Statement on the assassination of Martin Luther King*. Retrieved December 27, 2009 from http://www.jfklibrary.org/Historical+Resources/Archives/Reference+Desk/Speeches/RFK/Statement+on+the+Assassination+of+Martin+Luther+King.htm

Kepel, G. (2004). *The war for Muslim minds: Islam and the West*. Cambridge, MA: The Belknap Press of Harvard University Press.

Lippman, T. W. (1995). *Understanding Islam: An introduction to the Muslim world* (2nd ed.). New York: Meridian.

Mumisa, M. (2006, August 17-23). Sacred tunes. *Al-Ahram Weekly On-Line*, 808. Retrieved August 25, 2006, from http://weekly.ahram.org.eg/2006/808/feature.htm

National Film Board of Canada. (2009, May 26). *NFB Profiles: Shopsowitz Karen*. Retrieved December 27, 2009, from http://www.onf-nfb.gc.ca/eng/portraits/karen_shopsowitz/

Nigosian, S. (1987). *Islam: The way of submission*. Great Britain: Crucible.

Orozco, R. (2007, May 26). Islamic cultural center opens its doors to create more dialogue with other members of the community. *The Fresno Bee*. Retrieved from http://www.icfresno.org/multimedia/04l.htm

Reshad, K. (2006, August 6). *Iranian underground art media and basement*. Retrieved August 23, 2009, from Kohah Studio website: http://www.kolahstudio.com/Underground/?p=192

Shahine, G. (2006, September 7-13). Fadel Soliman: Faces of Islam. *Al-Ahram Weekly On-Line*, 811. Retrieved December 16, 2006, from http://weekly.ahram.org.eg/2006/811/profile.htm

Smith, H. (1991). *The world's religions: Our great wisdom traditions*. San Francisco: Harper Collins.

Takim, L. (2004, July). From conversion to conversation: Interfaith dialogue in post 9–11 America. *The Muslim World, 94*, 343–355.

*Ten Questions with Poetic Pilgrimage.* (2009, March 10). Retrieved August 23, 2009 from Trinity International Hip-Hop Festival website: http://trinityhiphop.org/2009/03/10-questions-with-poetic-pilgrimage/

The Pew Forum on Religion & Public Life. (2009). *Views of religious similarities and differences: Muslims widely seen as facing discrimination.* Retrieved November 18, 2009 from http://pewforum.org/newassets/images/reports/summer09/survey0909.pdf

United Nations. (2006, November 13). *Alliance of civilizations: Report of the high-level group.* Retrieved January 19, 2007, from http://www.unaoc.org/repository/HLG_Report.pdf

Von Sternberg, B. & Miller, P. (2006, November 21). Uproar follows imams' detention. *Star Tribune.* Retrieved January 31, 2007, from http://www.startribune.com/462/story/826056.html

Waines, D. (1995). *An introduction to Islam.* Great Britain: Cambridge University Press.

## Concepts and Questions

1. Have you ever observed any signs of Islamophobia in your community? If yes, what form did this behavior take?

2. Why does Begley believe that "comprehending the origins of Islam remains an important pursuit"?

3. What have been your major sources of information about Islam? Do you believe the information you gathered has been fair and accurate?

4. Why is the Qur'an an important book for Muslims?

5. What is Begley referring to when she speaks of "interfaith dialogues"? Do you believe that such dialogues can be useful? If so, why?

6. What are action-oriented dialogues? Have you ever participated in such a dialogue?

7. What are the four tenets that Begley maintains are central to understanding Islam?

8. What does Begley mean when she writes, "The *hijab* remains one of the most conspicuous signs of Islamic intent to embrace spiritual above secular values"?

9. Have you ever been involved in any community outreach programs that were intended to promote understanding and harmony between two groups of people from diverse backgrounds? If yes, what techniques were employed to accomplish this purpose?

10. What does Begley mean when she writes, "The media perpetuates confusion about 'God' and 'Allah'"?

# America in Black and Brown: Exploring Sources of Intercultural Tensions between Blacks and Latinos in the United States

PETER OGOM NWOSU

*Conflict is an inescapable part of any relationship, and if managed improperly can lead to irreparable breakdowns —alienation at the interpersonal level or war in the international arena. As you might suspect, how conflict is viewed, managed, and resolved within a society is a function of cultural values. For the dominant U.S. culture, differences are considered inevitable, healthy, and valuable. Thus, conflict is viewed as a natural part of social intercourse and resolution is usually accomplished through a dialectical process. In other cultures, particularly those with a group orientation, conflict represents a threat to social-order stability and is something to be avoided. As a result, cultures, including U.S. co-cultures, often have dissimilar means of managing and resolving conflicts.*

This original essay appears here in print for the first time. All rights reserved. Permission to reprint must be obtained from the author and publisher. Dr. Peter Ogom Nwosu is chair and a professor in the Department of Communication Studies, and Director, Center for Human Relations at California State University, Northridge.

With this in mind, *conflict is a central theme in our next essay, "America in Black and Brown: Exploring Sources of Intercultural Tensions between Blacks and Latinos in the United States," which looks at existing tensions between two U.S. co-cultures. Peter Ogom Nwosu examines the often-contentious relationship between Blacks and Latinos in the United States from historical, cultural, and political perspectives. Arguing that neither group has a good understanding of the other, he provides a comprehensive comparison of their different historical experiences. The essay then uses these varied historical backgrounds as a foundation to explain how and why the psychological, cultural, and political perspectives of each group differ. Nwosu contends that although Latinos are generally aware of the Black experience, there is little understanding of Black culture. Equally problematic is the lack of awareness among Blacks about Latino culture. A particularly salient problem that tends to exacerbate the schism is the culturally based, contrasting communication styles employed by Blacks and Latinos. The essay concludes with a call for greater understanding and cooperation between the two co-cultures and for the need to value efforts to gain greater representation and opportunity, not as an ethnic struggle, but as one for human rights for everyone.*

> *Conflict is an inescapable part of any relationship, and if managed improperly can lead to irreparable breakdowns— alienation at the interpersonal level or war in the international arena.*

## INTRODUCTION

More than fifteen years ago, in a 1990 issue of *Time* magazine, William Henry III, a staff writer with *Time,* commented about the uneasiness among American Blacks regarding the rising Latino population in the United States.[1] Black uneasiness, according to Henry, stemmed from three factors: first, Blacks believe they have waited the longest and endured the most in the fight for equality and justice, and the presence of Latinos weakens their prospects for more Black access to resources in a nation that has not treated them fairly; second, Blacks fear being supplanted by Latinos as the nation's most influential minority group; and third, Blacks fear being outstripped in wealth, and consequently in status by, in their view, this new group to America.

The last few years have witnessed a significant rise in the Latino population, thus making it the nation's largest and fastest growing minority population, exacerbating Black fears as identified above, and consequently increasing the tension in Black–Latino relations. Indeed, if ever there was any doubt about the fragile, albeit competitive nature of Black–Latino relations, it can be seen in the racial skirmishes between students from both groups in our nation's public schools, in the shifting alliances among both groups in the direction of where there is the largest gain for each group, and in voting booths across the nation. The 2001 mayoral election in Los Angeles, for example, revealed, to some degree, the nature of the fragile and competitive relationship between both groups. The election—a contest between the former speaker of the State Assembly, Antonio Villaraigosa, a Latino, and White city attorney James Hahn, both Democrats—ended in defeat for the once-powerful speaker. Villaraigosa lost to an unusual amalgam of Whites and Blacks. In fact, 80 percent of the Black vote went to Hahn, who also won 59 percent of the White vote. Villaraigosa secured 82 percent of the Latino vote, and as much as 54 percent of the Jewish vote, not enough to install him as the first Latino mayor of Los Angeles in over a century. In 2005, Villaraigosa ran again, this time with support of the Black community. He defeated Hahn in a run-off election to become the first Latino to govern Angelinos in more than 100 years. Villaraigosa won nearly 60 percent of the Black votes, a huge contrast to the less than 20 percent of the Black electorate that voted for him four years earlier. Political scientist Raphael Sonenshein has noted that the really interesting question is "what happens to relations between Latinos and Blacks now." Sonenshein's question is worth exploring in full because Black support for a Latino candidate is by no means "the sign of a full-scale coalition," given the fragile and purely competitive relationships between the two groups.[2]

This essay examines the nature of the fragile and competitive relationship between both groups from a historical, cultural, and political perspective. First, we begin with an examination of the history of both the African American and Latino experiences in the United States. Second, we examine both communities' perceptions of each other, focusing on psychological, cultural, and political factors that shape these perceptions. Third, we explore some consequences for both groups of a strain in Black–Latino relations, and fourth, we offer suggestions for moving beyond the politics and the narrow vision of ethnicity that threatens to widen the relational chasm between both ethnic groups.

## BLACK–LATINO RELATIONS: TWO HISTORIES

Any attempt to understand the growing tension in Black–Latino relations must begin first with a discussion of the historical experiences of both groups in the United States. Much is well known about the African American experience in the United States. Much has been written about slavery and the quest for free labor as the driving engine of the Black presence in America. Nearly 400 years since the first set of Africans arrived on the shores of Jamestown, Virginia, much continues to be written about the institution of slavery and state–church complicity in the denial of basic rights that officially defined the nature of Black–White relations in America. Even today, nearly 200 years after slavery was abolished, more than 140 years after the Emancipation Proclamation, and more than 40 years after the historic Civil Rights Act of 1964 and the momentous Voting Rights Act of 1965, Blacks' freedom struggle remains fundamental to the existence of Black America.

> *Any attempt to understand the growing tension in Black–Latino relations must begin first with a discussion of the historical experiences of both groups in the United States.*

However, because American Blacks have been consumed by their long personal and collective struggles for freedom, few have paid attention to the historical struggles for those same rights reflected in the Latino experience in America. Moreover, the paucity of research on the Hispanic experience in the United States further complicates any knowledge or understanding among American Blacks regarding the Latino freedom struggle. Most Americans, including Blacks, as reflected in Black fears noted earlier, tend to associate Latino history with immigration, and believe that most Spanish speakers are immigrants. This is not the case. Most Americans, including Blacks, in fact are unaware that Americans of Hispanic heritage have a varied history and a complicated ancestry that dates back more than 400 years. Americans of Hispanic origin are from birth "the result of the encounter of diverse people such as the Spaniards and the Portuguese with the diverse Indian nations of the Americas such as the Incas, Aztecs, Quechuas, Mayas, Tainos, Siboneyes, and others."[3] Americans of Hispanic origin are also the result of encounters with African peoples who were brought as slaves by force to the Americas. From these encounters emerged the different Latino peoples of Peru, Bolivia, Colombia, El Salvador, Mexico, Cuba, Puerto Rico, the Dominican Republic, Brazil, and other Latin American countries.[4]

Indeed contrary to popular opinion, "there are Spanish-speaking Californians, New Mexicans, and Texans whose ancestors lived in the Southwest long before their respective states became part of the United States."[5] In their authoritative account titled *The Hispanics in the United States: A History,* Stanford University scholars L.H. Gann and Peter Duignan note that Hispanics, like the vast majority of other Americans, trace their original homes to different countries including Mexico, Puerto Rico, Cuba, Nicaragua, El Salvador, Honduras, Spain, and Argentina.

Some of them are proficient in Spanish, although others have lost the use of their ancestral tongue. Some are indifferent to their cultural inheritance and regard themselves as un-hyphenated Americans; others have a strong commitment to their Hispanic legacy. Some are rich and some are poor; some are conservative and some are radical; some are fair-skinned and some are swarthy or black.[6]

## LATINOS AND SLAVERY

What is also significant in the context of Black–Latino relations is that few Blacks recognize the historic opposition to slavery by Latinos in the 1800s. The emerging historical account suggests that it was the opposition to American engagement in slavery that aroused a bitter debate in the United States over war with Mexico. L.H. Gann and Peter Duignan write that those who were the principal advocates of war with Mexico were Southerners who wanted to safeguard slavery as an institution within the United States through the creation of a new (possibly several) slave state(s). This desire became the imperative that shaped the discourse between those who were for war and those who were against war. The anti-war movement, already opposed to slavery, believed that the annexation of Texas was a conspiracy led by slave owners to essentially undermine American freedom and basic human rights. Given the charged atmosphere, James Polk, U.S. president at the time, decided on what seemed to be a middle-course solution to "satisfy both the slave states and the 'free soil' states: he would acquire not only Texas but also Oregon and California, thus extending America's boundaries to the Pacific ocean."[7] President Polk not only made good on his quest by acquiring Texas and California, but he also acquired New Mexico and purchased Oregon from the British. Indeed, all of the western and southwestern states of the United States—California, New Mexico, Arizona, Nevada, Utah, Colorado, Wyoming, and Texas— were Mexican territories until 1848, when the Mexican–American war ended.

> *What is also significant in the context of Black–Latino relations is that few Blacks recognize the historic opposition to slavery by Latinos in the 1800s.*

## The Story of Texas

The story of Texas is particularly unique because the immediate cause for the Mexican-American war that began in 1846 derived from disputes over the territory and what behaviors were permissible within it. As English and German settlers from the United States flooded the province to engage in plantation agriculture with the aid of slave labor, the Mexican government began to insist that the newcomers abide by Mexican laws. One such law outlawed slavery. The position of the Mexican government incensed the newcomers, most of them from the American south, who argued that Mexican laws undermined their inalienable rights and their professed notion of "manifest destiny." In 1836, the newcomers, taking advantage of the weaknesses in the Mexican leadership, declared Texas an independent sovereign state. The Mexican government under President Antonio López de Santa Anna tried to crush the rebellion, but failed due to the political problems Santa Anna was facing at home.

The next ten years saw strong political debates in the United States on whether the country should go to war to acquire Texas, and the rich territories of California and New Mexico, also at the time belonging to Mexico. The British, who were no friends of the Americans at the time, also had interests in these territories. While Mexico was willing to let Texas remain an independent sovereign state, and was being pressured by the British to recognize it as such, the Mexican government feared that the annexation of Texas by the United States might lead to the loss of other Mexican territories. The United States, on its own, feared that any failure to act might give advantage over these vast territories and the Pacific to the British, who already had a controlling presence in Australia and New Zealand. In 1846, following months of wrangling, finger pointing, counter-accusations, and the admission of Texas as the 28th state, Mexico and the United States went to war, with the United States defeating the Mexican army, forcing Mexico to sign a peace treaty with the Americans on February 2, 1848. The treaty signed at Guadalupe Hidalgo, near Mexico City, surrendered control of California and New Mexico to the United States.

Although Mexico lost the war, the Treaty of Guadalupe Hidalgo provided guarantees that while these territories no longer belonged to Mexico, the U.S. government would respect the property, religious, and cultural rights (including language rights) of citizens of the conquered territories. In fact, as part of the treaty and to prevent any future claims, the U.S. government paid Mexico 15 million dollars in cash in exchange for the territories, and another 3.25 million dollars for claims made by American citizens on the Mexican government as a result of the war.

The propensity to expand the American frontier through the acquisition of land held by Latinos (especially Mexicans) in the heydays of the American experiment has been a defining fissure in Latino–Anglo relations. Each conquered territory resulted in the subjugation of Latinos into second-class citizens. Hispanic struggles for justice have thus been with respect to these rights. The Treaty of Guadalupe

Hidalgo provides the basis for these struggles and is therefore seen by many Latinos as the most important document for American Hispanics.

## The Latino Population

While the Latino community in the United States has been around for well over 400 years, the rapid growth in its population began in the late 1960s as a result of refugee movements, immigration reform, and illegal immigration from several Latin American countries. By 1970, the U.S. government coined the term "Hispanic" to refer to people who were born in any of the Spanish-speaking countries of the Americas or people who could trace their ancestry to Spain or former colonial territories of Spain. Few Latinos, however, refer to themselves as Hispanics.

By 1980, Americans witnessed large Latino migrant populations settling in such places as Washington, DC, New York, Trenton, Newark, Buffalo, and Providence in the Northeast; Miami, Houston, and Atlanta in the South; Las Vegas, Sacramento, San Jose, Santa Rosa, Anaheim, San Diego, and Los Angeles in the West; and Chicago and Lake County, Illinois, in the Midwest. In the last two decades, in some of the areas mentioned, Latinos have become a part of fully multi-ethnic neighborhoods, while in other areas ethnic Latino enclaves have emerged.

> The differing historical experiences of American Blacks and American Hispanics provide an important framework for examining the differing perceptions of each other in both communities.

The latest Bureau of the Census numbers show that across the country, Latinos are now the nation's largest minority group, numbering about 37 million, compared with approximately 36.2 million Blacks. These numbers represent a 4.7 percent rise in the Latino population since April 2000, compared with a 1.5 percent rise in the Black population; and a 0.8 percent increase for Americans of European background, whose population currently stands at 196 million. The current surge in Latino population, which has made American Blacks uncomfortable, is due essentially to higher birthrates and a huge wave of immigration, including illegal immigration. By the end of the 1990s, more than 50 percent of new immigrants who came to the United States came from Latin America, compared to 1970 when only 19 percent of new immigrants came from the region.[8] Given current trends, demographers project that by 2050, the U.S. population will be 52.8 percent European American, 24.5 percent Latino, 13.6 percent African American, 8.2 percent Asian American, and 1.0 percent Native American.[9] These numbers are important in assessing how each group jockeys for a fair share of the national cake.

## DIFFERENT HISTORIES, DIFFERENT PERCEPTIONS

The differing historical experiences of American Blacks and American Hispanics provide an important framework for examining the differing perceptions of each other in both communities. Such examination must draw from three explanations: *a psychological explanation, a cultural explanation, and a political explanation.* The psychological explanation is crucial because it provides a prism to understanding the *how* and the *why* of the fragile nature of Black–Latino relations in America. The cultural explanation offers a window for understanding the nature and the consequences of the culture gap between the two ethnic minorities, and the political explanation provides a framework for exploring the basis for the emerging political divide between Hispanic America and Black America.

## A Psychological Explanation

Communication scholars, whose discipline has been informed a great deal by psychology, make the case that human interactions are motivated by certain needs and desires. When people affiliate with others, they do so because such affiliation satisfies a particular need. Black–Latino relations can be likened to the sort of relations developed by two battered women who experience a low point in their lives because of abuse from their spouses or friends. The parallel experience of both women, an experience grounded in victimization, is precisely the basis or the reason for the *functional* relationship. Thus they become friends only because they have something in common. They see themselves as victims. They perform the mutually satisfying function of comforting each other. But once they get past the psychological feeling of pain and helplessness, they see no more need for the function.

One of the major crises of meaning in Black–Latino relations in America lies in this type of functional relationship. Black America and Hispanic America see each other as victims of an oppressive regime. The common enemy is White America. They come together to share a common feeling or attitude toward a perceived enemy, in this case, a negative attitude. Once the attitude is gone, the temporary friendship is gone. The friendship, after all, is based on the psychological need to find succor in others who share common problems. Without appearing simplistic, what binds the two groups together is the common enemy—nothing substantive, and nothing tangible. Here is a typical conversation overheard between two angry members of both ethnic groups over their failure to secure admission into a university graduate program:

BLACK MALE: Man, I can't believe they wouldn't let me into the program....

LATINO MALE: Me too, that sucks.

BLACK MALE: That department is so racist.

LATINO MALE: I was so qualified. I have been trying to get in since last year. And I hear there are no Mexicans in that program.

BLACK MALE: You know, that's right, you're right, I never thought about that.

LATINO MALE: I'm tired of being put down by White people. Those racist m—f—!

BLACK MALE: Yeah, me too. I have had enough of being put down.

As you might guess, these two men both walked out together bonded by their common experience—a shared history of victimization, so to speak—without knowing anything about each other. What brings them together is that they are victims, and the relationship ends there—at the contact stage. The tragedy in the type of dialogue reflected by the two gentlemen is that the reliance on a common set of negative feelings toward a problem does nothing to enhance the relationship between both

individuals. If Black–Latino relations are to improve, the relations must move beyond this type of casual contact. What is needed is a new kind of involvement and social bonding between both groups, where a sense of mutuality and of being connected is present, and both groups learn more about each other and make a commitment to further each other's purpose. Real friendships and alliances begin with the desire to build lasting and sustained friendships.

## A Cultural Explanation

Real friendships do not grow and flourish in an environment where participants do not know one another. The cultural explanation for the differing perceptions between American Blacks and Latinos draws fundamentally from this lack of knowledge about each other. Indeed, a culture gap does exist between Hispanic America and Black America. Both ethnic groups understand little of each other. The negative cultural stereotypes and the subterranean current of animosity between both groups further exemplify this gap. In truth, most Latinos are aware of *the Black experience,* but few understand *Black culture.* The distinction between the *Black experience* and *Black culture* is important here, because the former reflects the African American experience with slavery and its legacy of racism (of which most Latinos are aware), while the latter speaks to African American cultural patterns and communication style (which few Latinos understand).

Few Latinos recognize that the majority of Blacks who came to the United States brought with them a strong cultural heritage, which later became grounded in the spirituality of the Baptist faith. Under the weight of European oppression and exploitation, however, American Blacks lost a great deal of their true cultural and ethnic identities. This is why Alex Haley's compelling book *Roots,* and its subsequent dramatization as a series on national television, provided a spiritual lift to the cultural psyche of American Blacks. *Roots* also transformed Blacks in terms of their self-esteem, and spurred a new movement that placed Africa as central in the cultural lives of American Blacks.

While accounts of Africanisms or African cultural retentions in America have been provided in the numerous volumes on African history stored in various libraries across America, it is clear that not one major African language of the more than 250 languages spoken by Blacks brought in chains to the Americas survived the onslaught. What we know today as Black language in America is a patchwork of West African languages and English that most linguists and scholars now refer to as *Ebonics*. Ebonics has its own structure, syntax, and pragmatics, and various dialects of the language are spoken by Black people in many parts of the United States, especially in the South. A much more original strand of this language is used by the Gullah, Black people who inhabit parts of Georgia, South Carolina, Florida, and the Sea Islands off the coast of those three states. Although Ebonics is looked down upon as incorrect English (which it is not), most educated and middle-class Blacks clearly identify with it. They find great comfort and pleasure in the use of this language, and have developed the capacity to alternate between their native tongue and Standard American English—to code switch. What governs a person's desire to switch linguistic codes are the subject of conversation, the context of the conversation, and the gender of conversational partners. While Spanish is the *lingua franca* of many Latinos in the United States, a new language, *Spanglish*—a patchwork of Spanish and English—is emerging as the third most important language for Latinos. Like most Blacks, many Latinos are also able to alternate between these languages depending on the subject, the context, and the gender of conversational partners. But as Richard Rodriguez notes, Español (or Spanish) is "my family's language....

> A family member would say something to me (in Español) and I would feel myself specially recognized. My parents would say something to me and I would feel embraced by the sounds of their words. Those sounds said: I am speaking with ease in Spanish. I am addressing you in words I never use with los gringos (Europeans). I recognize you as someone special, close, like no one outside. You belong to us. In the family.[10]

In a sense, the use of these languages in both Black and Hispanic America suggest a particular comfort level and a strong feeling of belonging that one does not necessary have when one uses a language outside of one's cultural experience. Language therefore is an important instrument for maintaining group identity.

Black cultural patterns and communication styles are also a patchwork of Africanisms and some (not all) European American ways. The European ways present in African American cultural patterns and communication styles reflect the historical experience of American Blacks in the context of slavery. For example, inherent in Ebonics or Black English is a communication style that values animation or excitement, is loud, colorful, very direct, overt, and very straightforward. This approach to communication, which draws from both African (animation, loud, and colorful) and European ways (direct, overt, and straightforward), flies in the face of what is considered appropriate communication style among Hispanics. In comparison to that of American Blacks, Latino communication style is less animated, less direct, and has a much greater focus on face-saving. Since few Latinos understand Black communication style, most of them generally perceive Blacks as rude and disrespectful.

An almost similar cultural ignorance about Latinos is equally present in Black America, where many Blacks are both unaware of the Latino struggle for justice in America, but more importantly, do not understand Latino cultural patterns and communication styles. Latinos, for example, place a great deal of emphasis on respect for the elderly, and this respect is reflected in how language is used. There is also a relationship between one's status or hierarchy and the level of respect one receives from subordinates. Furthermore, there is a strong religious faith in Latino culture shaped by a Catholic tradition. The common phrase *Uno nunca se olvida de Dios,* "One should never forget about God," guides how one relates to self and to others. The loud, outspoken person, and the one who talks about his or her accomplishments and how good the individual looks, is looked down upon in Latino culture. Modesty, then, is the *soul* of communication in Latino culture. Few Blacks recognize and understand this fundamental cultural pattern and communication style of Latinos, and sometimes view Latinos as too cagey to be trusted.

## Misconceptions and Stereotypes

Under the present dispensation, ethnic misconceptions and negative stereotypes about each group have found expression and welcome in candid conversations in both communities. Anti-Black and anti-Latino sentiments and prejudices, including the use of racial slurs, now abound on both sides of the ethnic divide. It is not uncommon in the Latino community (especially in California) to hear such racial slurs as *mayate* (the Spanish term for the *n* word) hurled around in reference to the Black community. The racial skirmishes in our nation's public schools among young Blacks and Latinos reflect the increasing level of distrust in both communities. And while most Blacks supported Villaraigosa in his 2005 mayoral election, such support for a Latino candidate is by no means "the sign of a full-scale coalition," given the purely competitive relationship between the two groups.[11] At the hub of the growing pain in Black-Latino relations is the political explanation.

## A Political Explanation

In the last two decades, Blacks have perceived the tremendous growth in Latino population as a threat to Black political power. This may explain why many Blacks voted against Villaraigosa in 2001. Even more startling was Black opposition to unchecked or un-regulated immigration when many Blacks in California voted for the famous Proposition 187. Exit polls showed that 56 percent of African Americans and 64 percent of Whites voted in favor of Proposition 187. About 31 percent of Latinos, according to exit polls, also voted, surprisingly, for the proposition. Proposition 187 barred illegal immigrants from receiving public support throughout California's public education system, and required public educational institutions to verify the legal status of both immigrant students and their parents. Proposition 187 also required all providers of publicly funded, non-emergency health care services to verify the legal status of persons seeking services in order to be reimbursed by the state. In addition, Proposition 187 made the production and use of false documents a state felony, and required all service providers to report suspected illegal immigrants to law enforcement authorities and to the Immigration and Naturalization Service (INS).

Proposition 187 was based on the simple premise that denying public services to illegal immigrants would discourage them from coming to the United States. We know that most of the illegal immigrants to California that were to be affected by Proposition 187 were Latinos. Most came from Mexico, and many of them worked as migrants in farms and garment shops. That many Blacks ironically voted for Proposition 187 was not so much because they were, in principle, opposed to the goals of the proposition—(that illegal immigrants were draining state resources needed for other areas of governance), but they voted for Proposition 187 merely because of anti-Latino feelings on what was perceived as the emerging threat to Black political strength posed by a growing Latino population in California. The feelings are the same in several southern and midwestern states where there is a growing Latino population. Thus the politics of numbers have outweighed any serious effort at controlling or managing the complexities of illegal immigration in the country.

As we have seen since the passage of Proposition 187 in California, denying public services to illegal or undocumented immigrants has not been an easy proposition. Many public agencies refused to comply with its verification requirements, fearing that Proposition 187 affected innocent people. How does one, for example, deal with the U.S.-born child, children, or family members, all U.S. citizens by law, of a so-called illegal immigrant now living in the United States? While Proposition 187 was presented as an honest attempt to address a serious federal problem, the motivations became muddied in accusations that the proposition was racially or ethnically tainted.

There is a deep-seated feeling in Black America today that Hispanics (and other groups) have benefited too much from the spoils of the freedom struggle without making any substantive contribution to the struggle. While Blacks have fought hard, more than any other group in America, for affirmative action, public housing, and desegregation in public schools, they worry that groups whose history and experience do not compare to the Black experience are now benefiting at the same level from the gains won in these areas. Any growth in Latino population is therefore viewed in the context of what it means to the Black share of the national cake.

Syndicated columnist Julianne Malveaux, an African American, captured this feeling well in a series of questions she posed in her analysis of the election of Assemblyman Cruz Bustamante as the Lieutenant Governor of California, the first Latino to hold this position in more than a hundred years. "What happens," she asked, "when demographic shifts suggest that gains African Americans fought hard for must now be shared? Are we interested in offering the same affirmative action for which we have long fought? Or will we emulate Whites in forcing our Latino brothers and sisters to wrest gains from us?"[12] There is an undercurrent of feeling in Black America that these gains cannot be shared. There is also a perception in Black America that Latinos think that they are next to White because of their fair skin. Related to this perception is the politics of race in America that had historically (rightly or wrongly) classified Latinos as White because of their skin color. The consequence of this is the emergence of the feeling in Black America that Latino light skin has provided certain White-skin privileges to American Hispanics that have been denied to Blacks. But this argument is illogical because it ignores the fact that light-skinned Blacks have also benefited from certain White-skin privileges, and they have not been denied access to the gains of the freedom struggle.

The root of some of the anti-Black sentiments in the Latino community can be found in this sad state of affairs. Writes Malveaux:

> I'll never forget sitting on a panel with a Latino brother who excoriated African American leadership for taking all of the political spoils and leaving 'crumbs' for Latinos. Strident and angry, the man went down a list of our best and brightest, pronouncing them all insensitive and corrupt. 'Wait until we get our turn,' he spat.[13]

## CONCLUSION: COMMON PROBLEMS, COMMON SOLUTIONS

Black America and Hispanic America cannot afford to wait until each gets its turn to hurt the other. Black and Latino historical struggles for freedom and justice are so intertwined that separation and divorce cannot be the most genuine pathway for progress in America and for creating a new vision of community in America. First, both groups must transcend the narrow vision about their common historical struggle. The vision of a common feeling about "the enemy," without anything substantive for sustained and lasting friendship, must end. Second, both communities must begin to build a culture of respect for each other. Building a culture of respect begins with closing the culture gap between both groups and removing long-standing negative cultural stereotypes that have become the perceptual lens through which each community has filtered the other for years. Third, genuine cooperation and partnership must guide Black–Latino relations.

In point of fact, there have been a few examples in which both groups have come together over common problems. In 1988, for example, when Cesar Chavez, the charismatic labor leader, went on a 36-day fast to fight for migrant farm workers' rights, the Reverend Jesse Jackson and several activists came on board to participate. But the struggles for justice in both communities are often narrowly perceived in ethnic terms, rather than in terms of a broad-based coalition for change. The sentiment present but often not expressed is that "It's not really my problem, I'm only here to help you." In this context, the farm workers' struggle for justice is seen solely as a Latino struggle. The struggle for civil rights is seen solely as a Black struggle. Sadly, when Blacks or Latinos or other groups become involved in these causes, they do so because they simply want to help. There is not a feeling of *ownership* in the involvement.

The fact of the matter is that a farm worker's right is not just a Latino struggle, and civil rights should not be seen as a Black struggle either. The origins of the struggles are certainly ethnic. But ethnic claims to ownership for these causes do serious damage to the struggles for justice. These struggles are purely struggles for human rights. We must cease to view them with ethnic lenses.

*Black and Latino historical struggles for freedom and justice are so intertwined that separation and divorce cannot be the most genuine pathway for progress in America and for creating a new vision of community in America.*

## Notes

1. Henry, W. III (1990, April 9). Beyond the melting pot. *Time*. Retrieved 17 July 2010 from http://www.time.com/time/magazine/article/0,9171,969770,00.html

2. Finnegan, M. & Baraback, M. (2005, May 19). Villaraigosa's support goes beyond Latinos. *Los Angeles Times*. Retrieved 17 July 2010 from http://articles.latimes.com/2005/may/19/local/me-exit19

3. Aldarondo, E. (2003, January 29). Hispanics have a long and rich history in the United States. *The Standard-Times*, New Bedford, MA, p. A13.

4. Ibid.

5. Gann, L. H. & Duignan, P. J. (1986). *The Hispanics in the United States: A history*. Boulder, CO: Westview Press, p. xi.

6. Ibid.

7. Ibid., p. 16.

8. U.S. Census Bureau. (1999). *Coming to America: A profile of the nation's foreign-born*. Washington, DC: Author.

9. U.S. Census Bureau. (1996). *Statistical Abstract of the United States* (16th ed.). Washington, DC: Author.

10. Rodriguez, R. (1982). *Hunger of memory: The education of Richard Rodriguez*. Toronto, Canada: Bantam Books.

11. Finnegan & Baraback, (2005).

12. Malveaux, J. (1998, November 26). Black and brown people: Coalition or competition? *Black Issues in Higher Education*, 15(20), 42.

13. Ibid.

## Concepts and Questions

1. What are some of the reasons behind the rise in the U.S. Latino population? Why has this rise created tensions with Black Americans?

2. What does the term "Hispanic" mean to you? Do you think this term generalizes or specifies people's cultural origins?

3. How can different historical experiences create different worldviews? What is the American historical experience of your ethnic group, and how has it shaped your worldview?

4. What do you see as the major differences and the major similarities between the Black American and Latino American historical experiences?

5. Do you agree or disagree with Nwosu's assertion that one's native language can provide a feeling of comfort and belonging? Why?

6. How does language serve as a means of maintaining group identity?

7. Discuss and contrast the communication styles of Black Americans, Latinos, and European Americans. What areas carry the greatest potential to create misunderstanding and produce conflict?

8. What measures can you think of to alleviate the concerns of many Black Americans that the gains they have made in civil rights cannot be shared with other minorities?

9. Nwosu suggests that one way to lessen tensions between Blacks and Latinos is to "close the culture gap." What does he mean by this? Can you think of other "culture gaps"?

# "Which Is My Good Leg?": Cultural Communication of Persons with Disabilities

DAWN O. BRAITHWAITE • CHARLES A. BRAITHWAITE

*The next co-cultural group we consider is the disabled community. For many people, persons with disabilities are not recognized as a distinct co-culture. According to the U.S. Census Bureau, however, there are more than 41 million Americans over five who suffer from various types of disabilities—sensory, physical, mental, and self-care*

This original article first appeared in the eleventh edition. All rights reserved. Permission to reprint must be obtained from the authors and the publisher. Dr. Dawn O. Braithwaite is Willa Cather Professor and Professor of Communication Studies at the University of Nebraska—Lincoln and a past president of the National Communication Association. Dr. Charles A. Braithwaite is Director of International Studies at the University of Nebraska-Lincoln.

(Brault, 2008). Many Americans with disabilities are injured veterans from the Iran and Afghanistan wars, as well as earlier conflicts. These veterans can suffer not only from physical wounds that may have resulted in lost limbs, paralysis, blindness, or dementia, but also from posttraumatic distress disorder (PTSD) which frequently can be a disabling, dysfunctional emotional condition.

Individuals with disabilities, including war veterans, often find themselves misunderstood, marginalized, or even cut off from the dominant nondisabled culture. Dawn O. and Charles A. Braithwaite look at some of the reasons for this isolation in "'Which Is My Good Leg?': Cultural Communication of Persons with Disabilities." They specifically examine how persons with disabilities view their communicative relationships with nondisabled persons. Reviewing research consisting of more than 100 in-depth interviews with adults with disabilities, the Braithwaites discovered that these people go through a process of redefinition involving three steps: (1) redefining the self as a part of the "new" culture, (2) redefining disability, and (3) redefining disability for the dominant culture. Being familiar with these steps will help you improve your ability to interact and communicate effectively with members of the disabled co-culture.

## UNDERSTANDING COMMUNICATION OF PERSONS WITH DISABILITIES AS CULTURAL COMMUNICATION

Jonathan is an articulate, intelligent, 35-year-old professional man who has used a wheelchair since he became paraplegic when he was 20 years old. He recalls inviting a nondisabled woman out to dinner at a nice restaurant. When the waitperson came to take their order, she looked only at his date and asked, in a condescending tone, "And what would he like to eat for dinner?" At the end of the meal the waitperson presented Jonathan's date with the check and thanked her for her patronage.[1]

Kim describes her recent experience at the airport: "A lot of people always come up and ask can they push my wheelchair. And I can do it myself.

They were invading my space, concentration, doing what I wanted to do, which I enjoy doing; doing what I was doing *on my own*.... And each time I said, 'No, I'm doing fine!' People looked at me like I was strange, you know, crazy or something. One person started pushing my chair anyway. I said [in an angry tone], 'Don't touch the wheelchair.' And then she just looked at me like I'd slapped her in the face."

Jeff, a nondisabled student, was working on a group project for class that included Helen, who uses a wheelchair. He related an incident that really embarrassed him. "I wasn't thinking and I said to the group, 'Let's run over to the student union and get some coffee.' I was mortified when I looked over at Helen and remembered that she can't walk. I felt like a real jerk." Helen later described the incident with Jeff, recalling,

At yesterday's meeting, Jeff said, "Let's run over to the union" and then he looked over at me and I thought he would die. It didn't bother me at all; in fact, I use that phrase myself. I felt bad that Jeff was so embarrassed, but I didn't know what to say. Later in the group meeting I made it a point to say, "I've got to be running along now." I hope that Jeff noticed and felt OK about what he said."

Although it may seem hard for some of us to believe, these scenarios represent common experiences for many people with physical disabilities and are indicative of what often happens when people with disabilities and nondisabled others communicate.

The passage of the Americans with Disabilities Act of 1990 (ADA), a "bill of rights" for persons with disabilities, highlighted the fact that they are now a large, vocal, and dynamic group within the United States (Braithwaite & Labrecque, 1994; Braithwaite & Thompson, 2000). People with disabilities constitute a large segment of the American population that has increased over the years; estimates of how many people in the United States have

> Individuals with disabilities, including war veterans, often find themselves misunderstood, marginalized, or even cut off from the dominant nondisabled culture.

disabilities run as high as one in five (Cunningham & Coombs, 1997; Pardek, 1998).

There are two reasons for increases in the numbers of persons with disabilities. First, as the American population ages and has a longer life expectancy, more people will live long enough to develop disabilities, some of them related to age. Second, advances in medical technologies now allow persons with disabilities to survive life-threatening illnesses and injuries where survival was not possible in earlier times. For example, when actor Christopher Reeve became quadriplegic after a horse-riding accident in May 1995, advances in medical technology allowed him to survive his injuries and to live with a severe disability.

In the past, most people with disabilities were sheltered, and many spent their lives at home or living in institutions; today, they are very much a part of the American mainstream. Each of us will have contact with people who have disabilities within our families, among our friends, or in the workplace. Some of us will develop disabilities ourselves. Marie, a college student who was paralyzed after diving into a swimming pool, remarked:

> I knew there were disabled people around, but I never thought this would happen to me. I never even *knew* a disabled person before *I* became one. If before this happened, I saw a person in a wheelchair, I would have been uncomfortable and not known what to say.

Marie's comment highlights the fact that many nondisabled people feel uncomfortable, some extremely so, interacting with people who are disabled. As people with disabilities continue to live, work, and study in American culture, there is a need for people with and without disabilities to know how to communicate effectively.

## DISABILITY AND CULTURAL COMMUNICATION

Our goal in this essay is to focus on communication between nondisabled persons and persons with disabilities as *intercultural communication* (Carbaugh,

*People with disabilities use a distinctive speech code that implies specific models of personhood, society, and strategic action that differ from those of nondisabled people.*

1990). People with disabilities use a distinctive speech code that implies specific models of personhood, society, and strategic action that differ from those of nondisabled people. People with disabilities develop distinctive meanings, rules, and ways of speaking that act as a powerful resource for creating and reinforcing perceptions of cultural differences between people with and without disabilities. The distinctive verbal and nonverbal communication used by people with disabilities creates a sense of cultural identity that constitutes a unique social reality.

Several researchers have described the communication of disabled and nondisabled persons as intercultural communication (Braithwaite, 1990, 1996; Emry & Wiseman, 1987; Fox, Giles, Orbe, & Bourhis, 2000; Padden & Humphries, 1988). That is, we recognize that people with disabilities develop certain unique communicative characteristics that are not shared by the majority of nondisabled individuals. In fact, except for individuals who are born with disabilities, becoming disabled is similar to assimilating from being a member of the nondisabled majority to being a member of a minority culture (Braithwaite, 1990, 1996). The onset of a physical disability requires learning new ways of thinking and talking about oneself, and developing new ways of communicating with others.

Adopting a cultural view of disability in this chapter, we start by introducing communication problems that can arise between persons in the nondisabled culture and those in the disabled culture. Second, we discuss some of the weaknesses of the earlier approaches researchers used to understand communication between nondisabled and disabled persons. Third, we discuss research findings from interviews with people who have physical disabilities that show them engaged in a process of redefinition; that is, they critique the prevailing stereotypes about disability, and they communicate in order to redefine what it means to be part of the disabled culture. Last, we talk about important contributions both scholars and students of intercultural communication can make to improve relations between people with and without disabilities.

## Challenges for Communicators Who Are Disabled

As we adopt a cultural view and attempt to understand the communicative challenges faced by people with disabilities, it is useful to understand what a disability is. We start by distinguishing between "disability" and "handicap." Even though people often use these two terms interchangeably in everyday conversation, their meanings are quite different. The two terms imply different relationships between persons with disabilities and the larger society. The term *disability* describes those limitations that a person can overcome or compensate for by some means. Crewe and Athelstan (1985) identify five "key life functions" that may be affected by disability: (a) mobility, (b) employment, (c) self-care, (d) social relationships, and (e) communication. Many individuals are able to compensate for physical challenges associated with the first three key life functions through assistive devices (e.g., using a wheelchair or cane or using hand controls to drive a car); through training (e.g., physical therapy or training on how to take care of one's personal needs); through assistance (e.g., hiring a personal care assistant); or through occupational therapy to find suitable employment.

A disability becomes a *handicap* when the physical or social environment interacts with it to impede a person in some aspect of his or her life (Crewe & Athelstan, 1985). For example, a disabled individual with paraplegia can function well in the physical environment using a wheelchair, ramps, and curb cuts, but he or she is handicapped when buildings and/or public transportation are not accessible to wheelchair users. When a society is willing and/or able to create adaptations, people with disabilities are able to lead increasingly independent lives, which is very important to their self-esteem and health (Braithwaite & Harter, 2000; DeLoach & Greer, 1981). For people with disabilities, personal control and independence are vitally important, and "maintenance of identity and self-worth are tied to the perceived ability to control the illness, minimize its intrusiveness, and be independent" (Lyons, Sullivan, Ritvo, & Coyne, 1995, p. 134). This does not mean that people with disabilities deny their physical condition, but rather that they find ways to manage it, to obtain whatever help they need, and to lead their lives (Braithwaite & Eckstein, 2003).

It is important to realize that the practical and technological accommodations that are made to adapt the physical environment for people with disabilities are useful for nondisabled people as well. Most of us are unaware of just how handicapped we would be without these physical adaptations. For example, the authors' offices are located on the upper floors of our respective office buildings, and we often get to our office via elevator. We know that stairs take up a significant amount of space in a building. Space used for the stairwell on each level takes the place of at least one office per floor. The most space-efficient way to get people to the second floor would be a climbing rope, which would necessitate only a relatively small opening on each floor. However, how many of us could climb a rope to reach our offices? Clearly, we would be handicapped without stairs or elevators. When a student is walking with a heavy load of library books, automatic door openers, ramps, curb cuts, elevators, and larger doorways become important environmental adaptations that everyone can use and appreciate. Physical limitations become handicaps for all of us when the physical environment cannot be adapted to meet our shortcomings.

## Challenges to Relationships of People with Disabilities

Although it is possible to identify and find accommodations for physical challenges associated with mobility, self-care, and employment, the two key life functions of social relationships and communication often present much more formidable challenges. It is often less difficult to detect and correct physical barriers than it is to deal with the insidious social barriers facing people with disabilities. Coleman and DePaulo (1991) label these social barriers as "psychological disabling," which is common in Western culture where "much value is placed on physical bodies and physical attractiveness" (p. 64).

When people with disabilities begin relationships with nondisabled people, the challenges associated with forming any new relationship are often greater. For nondisabled people, this may be due to lack of experience interacting with people who are disabled, which leads to high uncertainty about how to interact with a person who is disabled (Braithwaite & Labrecque, 1994). Nondisabled persons may be uncertain about what to say or how to act. They are afraid of saying or doing the wrong thing or of hurting the feelings of the person with the disability, much as Jeff was with his group member, Helen, in the example at the beginning of this essay. As a result, nondisabled persons may feel overly self-conscious, and their actions may be constrained, self-controlled, and rigid because they feel uncomfortable and uncertain (Belgrave & Mills, 1981; Braithwaite 1990; Dahnke, 1983; Higgins, 1992). Their behaviors, in turn, will appear uninterested or unaccepting to the person who is disabled. The nondisabled person will need to figure out how to communicate appropriately. Higgins (1992) pointed out that sometimes these communication attempts are not successful: "Wishing to act in a way acceptable to those with disabilities, they may unknowingly act offensively, patronizing disabled people with unwanted sympathy" (Higgins, 1992, p. 105).

High levels of uncertainty can negatively affect interaction and relationship development between people. It becomes easier to avoid that person rather than deal with not knowing what to do or say. Interestingly, researchers have found that the type of disability a person possesses does not change the way nondisabled persons react to them (Fichten, Robillard, Tagalakis, & Amsel, 1991). Although uncertainty reduction theory can be overly simplistic, especially when applied to ongoing relationships, this theory is useful in understanding some of the initial discomfort nondisabled people may feel when interacting with a stranger or early acquaintance who is disabled. Understanding the effects of uncertainty, people with disabilities work to devise ways to help nondisabled others reduce their discomfort (Braithwaite, 1990, 1996; Braithwaite & Labrecque, 1994).

Even when a nondisabled person tries to "say the right thing" and wants to communicate acceptance to the person with the disability, his or her nonverbal behavior may communicate rejection and avoidance instead (Thompson, 1982). For example, people with disabilities have observed that many nondisabled persons may keep a greater physical distance, avoid eye contact, avoid mentioning the disability, or cut the conversation short (Braithwaite, 1990, 1991, 1996). These nondisabled persons may be doing their best not to show their discomfort or not crowd the person with the disability. However, the outcome may be that the person with the disability perceives they do not want to interact. In this case, a person's disability becomes a handicap in the social environment as it can block the development of a relationship with a nondisabled person, who finds the interaction too uncomfortable.

> *When people with disabilities begin relationships with nondisabled people, the challenges associated with forming any new relationship are often greater.*

Complicating matters, many nondisabled people hold stereotypes of people from the disabled culture. Coleman and DePaulo (1991) discuss some of these stereotypes concerning disabled people:

> For example, they often perceive them as dependent, socially introverted, emotionally unstable, depressed, hypersensitive, and easily offended, especially with regard to their disability. In addition, disabled people are often presumed to differ from nondisabled people in moral character, social skills, and political orientation. (p. 69)

Stereotypes like these do nothing but raise the level of uncertainty and discomfort the nondisabled person is experiencing.

When nondisabled persons make the effort to overcome discomfort and stereotypes to interact with people from the disabled culture, they often find themselves with conflicting expectations. On the one hand, Americans are taught to "help the handicapped." At the same time, Americans conceptualize persons as "individuals" who "have rights" and "make their own choices" (Carbaugh, 1988) and thus are taught to treat all people equally. However, when nondisabled persons encounter a person with a disability, this model of personhood creates a real dilemma. How can you both help a person and treat that person equally? For example, should you help a person with a disability open a door or try to help him up if he falls? If you are working with a blind person, should you help her find a doorway or get her lunch at the cafeteria? These dilemmas often result in high uncertainty for nondisabled people, who often end up trying to give more help than people with disabilities want or need (Braithwaite &

Eckstein, 2003). In the end, it may simply seem easier to avoid situations in which you might have to interact with a disabled person rather than face feelings of discomfort and uncertainty (this is how many people react to communicating with people from other cultures). However, avoidance is not a very good solution in the end, especially if this person is to be a member of your work group or family, for example.

It should not be surprising to learn that most people with disabilities are well aware of the feelings and fears many nondisabled persons have. In fact, in research interviews, people with disabilities tell us they believe they "can just tell" who is uncomfortable around them or not. They are able to provide a great amount of detail on both the verbal and nonverbal signals of discomfort and avoidance of nondisabled persons (Braithwaite, 1990, 1996; Braithwaite & Eckstein, 2003), and they develop communication strategies to help them interact in these situations. For example, people with disabilities tell us that when they meet nondisabled persons, they will communicate in ways designed to get the discomfort "out of the way." They want the nondisabled person to treat them as a "person like anyone else," rather than focus solely on their disability (Braithwaite, 1991, 1996). For example, they may talk about topics they believe they have in common with the nondisabled person, such as cooking, sports, or music.

People with disabilities develop strategies to help them handle situations in which they may need help from nondisabled others in order to help reduce the uncertainty and discomfort of the nondisabled person (Braithwaite & Eckstein, 2003). For example, two men who are wheelchair users who need help getting out of their van in parking lots described how they plan ahead to get the help they need:

> Well, I have a mobile phone.... I will call into the store and let the store manager or whoever know, "Hey, we're in a white minivan and if you look out your window, you can see us! We're two guys in wheelchairs; can you come out and help us get out of the van?"

These men plan ahead in order to avoid having to ask others for help, which may place nondisabled strangers in potentially uncomfortable communication situations. Other people described situations in which they might accept help that they did not need

because they understood that refusing help might increase the discomfort and uncertainty of the nondisabled person.

## CHANGING THE FOCUS OF RESEARCHERS

When we first began looking at the research on communication between nondisabled and disabled persons, three problems came clearly to the forefront (for a recent summary, see Thompson, 2000). First, very little was known about the communication behavior of disabled people. Although a few researchers have studied disabled persons' communication, most of them have studied nondisabled persons' *reactions* to disabled others. These studies on "attitudes toward disabled persons" are analogous to the many studies that look at majority members' attitudes toward other "minority groups." A look at the intercultural communication literature as a whole reveals few studies from the perspective of persons representing minority groups. Although there has been some improvement over the years, there is still relatively little information on communication from the perspective of people with disabilities.

A second, related problem is that many researchers talk *about* people with disabilities, not *with* them. People with disabilities have rarely been represented in survey data. Most often these studies consist of nondisabled people reporting their impressions of disabled people. In experimental studies, the disabled person is most often "played" by a nondisabled person using a wheelchair (and not surprisingly, most people can tell that this is not a disabled person!). There are still too few studies that give us a sense of how people with and without disabilities communicate in actual conversations.

Third, and most significant, the research has most often taken the perspective of the nondisabled person; that is, researchers tend to focus on what people with disabilities should do to make nondisabled others feel more comfortable. Coming from this perspective, researchers do not consider the effects of communication on the person with the disability. For example, several studies have found that nondisabled persons are more comfortable when people with disabilities disclose about their disability, so the researchers suggest that disabled people should self-disclose to make nondisabled others more comfortable. Braithwaite (1991) points out that these researchers have forgotten to look at how self-disclosing might affect people who are disabled. Therefore, what we see coming from much of the nondisabled-oriented research is an *ethnocentric bias* that ignores the perspective of people from the disabled culture. Although there has been more research from the perspective of disabled interactants in recent years, there are still too few empirical studies, and we are left with a very incomplete picture of the communication of people who are disabled.

In the remainder of this essay, we will present selected findings from ongoing studies, conducted from the perspective of people with disabilities, which help us understand the communication of people with and without disabilities from a cultural perspective. These research findings come from more than 100 in-depth interviews completed by the first author with adults who are physically disabled. All of these people have disabilities that are visible to an observer, and none of them has significant communication-related disabilities (e.g., blindness, deafness, speech impairments). The goal of the research has been to describe communication with nondisabled people from the frame of reference of people who are disabled. Doing research by talking *with* people who are disabled helps to bring out information important to them and allows people with disabilities to describe experiences from their own cultural framework.

## PROCESS OF REDEFINITION

A central theme emerging from the interviews is what we call *redefinition;* that is, people who are disabled critique the prevailing stereotypes about being disabled, they create new ways of perceiving themselves and their disability, and they develop ways of communicating as a result. We were able to see three types of redefinition: (a) redefining the self as part of a "new" culture, (b) redefining the concept of disability, and (c) redefining disability for the dominant culture.

## Redefining the Self as Part of the Disabled Culture

In research interviews, many people with disabilities talk about themselves as part of a minority group or a culture. For some of the interviewees, this definition crosses disability lines; that is, their definition of "disabled" includes all those who have disabilities. For others, the definition is not as broad; when they think of disability, they are thinking about others with the same type of disability they have. For example, some of the people with mobility-related disabilities also included blind and deaf people with the discussed disability, and others talked only about other wheelchair users. However narrowly or broadly they define it, many do see themselves as part of a minority culture. For example, one of the interviewees said that being disabled "is like *West Side Story.* Tony and Maria; White and Puerto Rican. They were afraid of each other; ignorant of each other's cultures. People are people." Another man explained his view:

> First of all, I belong to a subculture [of disability] because of the way I have to deal with things, being in the medical system, welfare. There is the subculture… I keep one foot in the nondisabled culture and one foot in my own culture. One of the reasons I do that is so that I don't go nuts.

This man's description of the "balancing act" between cultures demonstrates that membership in the disabled culture has several similarities to the experiences of other American cultural groups. Many of the interviewees have likened their own experiences to those of other cultural groups, particularly to the experiences of American people of color. Interviewees describe the loss of status and power that comes from being disabled, and they perceive that many people are uncomfortable with them simply because they are different.

When taking a cultural view, it is important to recognize that not everyone comes to the culture the same way. Some people are born with disabilities, and others acquire them later. For those people who are not born with a disability, membership in the culture is a process that emerges over time. For some, the process is an incremental one, as in the case of a person with a degenerative disease such as multiple sclerosis that develops over many years. For a person who has a sudden-onset disability, such as breaking one's neck in an accident and "waking up a quadriplegic," moving from the majority (a "normal" person) to the minority (a person who is disabled) may happen in a matter of seconds. This sudden transition into the disabled culture presents many significant challenges of redefinition and readjustment in all facets of an individual's life (Braithwaite, 1990, 1996; Goffman, 1963).

If disability is a culture, when does one become part of that culture? Even though a person is physically disabled, how one redefines oneself, from "normal" or nondisabled to disabled, is a process that develops over time. It is important to understand that becoming physically disabled does not mean one immediately has an awareness of being part of the disabled culture (Braithwaite, 1990, 1996). In fact, for most people, adjusting to disability happens in a series of stages or phases (Braithwaite, 1990; DeLoach & Greer, 1981; Padden & Humphries, 1988). DeLoach and Greer (1981) describe three phases of an individual's adjustment to disability: (1) stigma isolation, (2) stigma recognition, and (3) stigma incorporation. Their model helps us understand what is occurring in the process of adjustment to disability as acculturation. During this process, persons with disabilities progress from the onset of their disability to membership in the disabled culture.

Imagine the experience of Mark, a college student majoring in physical education who has a car accident and wakes up to find he is paralyzed. Mark enters the first phase, *stigma isolation,* upon becoming disabled. At this point, he is focusing on rehabilitation and all of the physical changes and challenges he is experiencing. It is likely that Mark has not yet noticed the changes in his social relationships and communication with nondisabled others.

The second phase, *stigma recognition,* begins when Mark realizes that his life and relationships have changed dramatically and he will need to find ways to minimize the effects of his disability as much as possible. Mark may try to return to normal routines and old relationships; for example, he may return to college. This can be a frustrating phase, because often things have changed more than the person at first realizes. Mark may try to reestablish his old relationships, only to find that his friends are no longer comfortable with him or that they can no longer share activities they had in common. For example, Mark may find it hard to maintain relationships with his friends from his

> *Even though a person is physically disabled, how one redefines oneself, from "normal" or nondisabled to disabled, is a process that develops over time.*

softball team. Mark's friends, who were visiting him around the clock in the hospital, may not know what to do or say around him and may even start to avoid him. It is at this point that individuals who are disabled start to become aware that they are now interacting as members of a different culture than they were before, and they begin to assimilate the new culture into their identity and behavior (Braithwaite, 1990, 1996). Mark may notice how his friends are treating him, and he may not enjoy their company much at this point either.

This begins the third phase, what DeLoach and Greer (1981) call *stigma incorporation.* At this point, persons with a disability begin to integrate being disabled into their identity, their definition of self. The person begins to understand both the positive and negative aspects of being disabled and begins to develop ways to overcome and cope with the negative aspects of disability (DeLoach & Greer, 1981). In this stage of adjustment, people with disabilities develop ways of behaving and communicating so that they are able to function successfully in the nondisabled culture (Braithwaite, 1990, 1996). For example, after all he has experienced, Mark may find he now has an interest in psychology and sees more career opportunities there. When he switches his major, he finds he has a knack for statistics that he never knew he had, organizes a study group for his statistics class, and starts to make new friends.

Braithwaite (1996) argues that stigma incorporation represents what Morse and Johnson (1991) have labeled "regaining wellness," which occurs when individuals begin to take back control of their own lives and relationships, live as independently as possible, and adapt to new ways of doing things in their lives. Individuals develop ways of communicating with nondisabled others that help them live successfully as part of the disabled and nondisabled cultures simultaneously (Braithwaite, 1990, 1991, 1996; Braithwaite & Labrecque, 1994; Emry & Wiseman, 1987). This is what researchers call interability, intergroup communication (see Fox et al., 2000).

In this third phase, then, the person incorporates the role of disability into his or her identity and into his or her life. One man said, "You're the same person you were. You just don't do the same things you did before." Another put it this way: "If anyone refers to me as an amputee, that is guaranteed to get me madder than hell! I don't deny the leg amputation, but I am *me*. I am a whole person. *One*." It is during this phase that people can come to terms with both the negative and positive changes in their lives. One woman expressed it this way:

> I find myself telling people that this has been the worst thing that has happened to me. It has also been one of the best things. It forced me to examine what I felt about myself ... my confidence is grounded in me, not in other people. As a woman, I am not as dependent on clothes, measurements, but what's inside me.

The late actor Christopher Reeve demonstrated the concept of stigma incorporation in an interview with Barbara Walters, four months after his devastating accident:

> You also gradually discover, as I'm discovering, that your body is not you. The mind and the spirit must take over. And that's the challenge as you move from obsessing about "Why me?" and "It's not fair" and move into "Well, what is the potential?" And, now, four months down the line I see opportunities and potential I wasn't capable of seeing back in Virginia in June ... genuine joy and being alive means more. Every moment is more intense than it ever was.

One implication of this example is that stigma incorporation, becoming part of the disabled culture, is a process that develops over time.

## Redefining Disability

A second type of redefinition discussed by interviewees is redefining the concept of disability. For example, one interviewee explained, "People will say, 'Thank God I'm not handicapped.' And I'll say, 'Let's see, how tall are you? Tell me how you get something off that shelf up there!'" His goal in this interchange is to force others to see disability as one of many *characteristics* of a person. From this perspective, everyone is handicapped in one way or another by our height, weight, sex, ethnicity, or physical attributes, and people must work to overcome those

characteristics that are handicapping. Short people may need a stool to reach something on a high shelf, and people who are very tall may be stared at and certainly will not be able to drive small, economy-size cars. Most middle-aged professors cannot climb a rope to their office and need the accommodation of stairs. Similarly, people with disabilities must adapt to the physical and social challenges presented to them. One interviewee, who conducts workshops on disability awareness, talked about how he helps nondisabled people redefine disability:

> I will say to people, "How many of you made the clothes that you're wearing?" "How many of you grew the food that you ate yesterday?" "How many of you built the house that you live in?" Nobody raises their hand. Then after maybe five of those, I'll say, "And I bet you think you're independent." And I'll say, "I'll bet you, if we could measure how independent you feel in your life versus how independent I feel in mine, then I would rate just as high as you do. And yet here I am 'depending' on people to get me dressed, undressed, on and off the john, etc. It's all in our heads, folks. Nobody is really independent." I can see them kind of go "Yeah, I never thought of it that way." And they begin to understand how it is that somebody living with this situation can feel independent. That independence really is a feeling and an attitude. It's not a physical reality.

It is also important to remember that, like any characteristic that we have, disability is context specific. For example, a blind person will function better in a dark room than sighted persons, who will find themselves handicapped in that environment. The first author of this chapter spent several days at Gallaudet University in Washington, DC. At Gallaudet, where most students are deaf, it was the *author* who was disabled, as she needed interpreters to talk with the students there. At Gallaudet, people talk about being part of Deaf culture, but not about being disabled.

Redefining disability can also be reflected through changing the language we use to talk about disability. One interviewee objected to the label "handicapped person," preferring the label "persons with a handicapping condition." He explained why: "You emphasize that person's identity and then you do something about the condition." The goal is to speak in ways that emphasize the *person,* rather than the disability. One interviewee, who had polio as a child, rejected the term "polio victim" and preferred to label herself as "a person whose arms and legs do not function very well." Talking with disability activists around the nation, we find many different approaches to language and labels about disability. One way we have found to accentuate the person is to talk about "*people* with disabilities" rather than "disabled people." The goal is to emphasize the person first, before introducing the disability, much like using the label "people of color." These are all forms of strategic action that help to create and maintain a sense of unique cultural identity among persons with disabilities (Braithwaite, 1996; Braithwaite & Thompson, 2000).

Redefining disability is also reflected in sensitizing oneself to commonly used labels for being disabled, such as being a "polio victim" or an "arthritis sufferer," or being "confined to a wheelchair" or "wheelchair bound." When trying to redefine disability as a characteristic of the person, one can change these phrases to a "person with polio," a "person who has arthritis," or a "wheelchair user." Some researchers suggest that we avoid talking about the communication of disabled and nondisabled people and instead use the phrase "interability communication" (see Fox et al., 2000). At first glance, it may be tempting to think this is no more than an attempt at political correctness, but those who understand language and culture know how strongly the words we use influence our perception of others, and theirs of us. The way people with disabilities are labeled will affect how they are seen by others and how they perceive themselves.

One of the more humorous and, at the same time, powerful examples of language regarding disability is the use of "TABs" to refer to nondisabled people. "TAB" is short for "temporarily able-bodied." One interviewee joked, "Everyone is a TAB…. I just got mine earlier than you!" Being called a TAB serves to remind nondisabled persons that no one is immune from disability. From this perspective, everyone is becoming disabled! It certainly does challenge our perspective to think about that. To end our discussion of disability and language, whatever labels we choose to use, it is clear that the language both creates and reflects the view of people with disabilities and disabled culture.

In addition to redefining disability, the interviewees also redefined "assisting devices" such as wheelchairs or canes. For example, one man told the following story about redefining his prosthetic leg:

> Now there were two girls about eight playing and I was in my shorts. And I'll play games with them and say "Which is my good leg?" And that gets them to thinking. Well, this one [he pats his artificial leg] is not nearly as old as the other one!

Another interviewee redefined assisting devices this way: "Do you know what a cane is? It's a portable railing! The essence of a wheelchair is a seat and wheels. Now, I don't know that a tricycle is not doing the exact same thing." Redefining assisting devices helps us see how they might mean different things to disabled and nondisabled persons. For example, several interviewees expressed frustration with people who played with their wheelchairs. One interviewee exclaimed, "This chair is not a toy, it is *part of me.* When you touch my chair, you are touching *me.*" Another woman, a business executive, expanded on this by saying, "I don't know why people who push my chair feel compelled to make car sounds as they do it." In these examples, then, the problem is not the disability or the assisting device, but how one perceives the person using them.

## Redefining Disability within Nondisabled Culture

Last, as people with disabilities redefine themselves as members of a culture, they also define what it means to have a disabling condition. Our experience is that people with disabilities are concerned with changing the view of disability within the larger culture (Braithwaite, 1990, 1996). Most people with disabilities we have encountered view themselves as public educators on disability issues. People told stories about taking the time to educate children and adults on what it means to be disabled. They are actively working to change the view of themselves as helpless, as victims, or as ill, and the ensuing treatment such a view brings. One wheelchair user said:

> People do not consider you, they consider the chair first. I was in a store with my purchases on

my lap and money on my lap. The clerk looked at my companion and not at me and said, "Cash or charge?"

This incident with the clerk represents a story we heard from *every* person in some form or another, just as it happened to Jonathan and his date at the beginning of this chapter. One woman, who has multiple sclerosis and uses a wheelchair, told of shopping for lingerie with her husband accompanying her. When they were in front of the lingerie counter, the clerk repeatedly talked only to her husband, saying, "And what size does she want?" The woman told her the size, and the clerk looked at the husband and said, "And what color does she want?"

Persons with disabilities recognize that nondisabled persons often see them as disabled first and as a person second (if at all). The most common theme expressed by people with disabilities in all of the interviews is that they want to be *seen and treated as a person first.* One man explained what he thought was important to remember: "A lot of people think that handicapped people are 'less than' and I find that it's not true at all… Abling people, giving them their power back, empowering them." The interviewees rejected those situations or behaviors that would not lead them to be seen. A man with muscular dystrophy talked about the popular Labor Day telethon:

> I do not believe in those god-damned telethons … they're horrible, absolutely horrible. They get into the self-pity, you know, and disabled folk do not need that. Hit people in terms of their attitudes then try to deal with and process their feelings. And the telethons just go for the heart and leave it there.

One man suggested what he thought was a more useful approach:

> What I am concerned with is anything that can do away with the "us" versus "them" distinction. Well, you and I are anatomically different, but we're two human beings! And at the point, we can sit down and communicate eyeball to eyeball; the quicker you do that, the better!

> *People with disabilities do recognize themselves as part of a culture, and understanding communication and relationships from this perspective sheds new light on the communication challenges that exist.*

Individually and collectively, people with disabilities do identify themselves as part of a culture. They are involved in a process of redefinition of themselves, and of disability. They desire to help nondisabled people understand and internalize a redefinition of people of the disabled culture as "persons first."

## CONCLUSION

The research we have discussed highlights the usefulness of viewing disability from a cultural perspective. People with disabilities do recognize themselves as part of a culture, and understanding communication and relationships from this perspective sheds new light on the communication challenges that exist. Some time ago, Emry and Wiseman (1987) first argued for the usefulness of intercultural training about disability issues. They called for unfreezing old attitudes about disability and refreezing new ones. Our experience indicates that people with disabilities would agree with this goal.

We have asked people with disabilities whether they had training in communication during or after their rehabilitation. We anticipated that they would have received information and training to prepare them for changes in their communication and relationships after becoming disabled. We speculated that this education would be especially critical for those who experience sudden-onset disabilities because their self-concepts and all of their relationships would undergo such radical changes. Surprisingly, we found that less than 30 percent of the interviewees received disability-related communication training.

We believe intercultural communication scholars can help design research and training that could help make the transition from majority to minority an easier one (Braithwaite, 1990; Emry & Wiseman, 1987). We are encouraged by some advances that are taking place in educational and organizational settings (e.g., Colvert & Smith, 2000; Herold, 2000; Worley, 2000). We also see the need for research that expands to different types of disabilities—for example, for those with invisible disabilities (e.g., emphysema, diabetes) and socially stigmatized disabilities such as HIV. Overall, we see important contributions for communication scholars to make. When Braithwaite and Thompson (2000) published their *Handbook of Communication and People with Disabilities,* they were struck by how many researchers in communication studies are now studying disability communication and how many of these scholars are disabled. Clearly, the future does look brighter than when we began our work in disability and communication some years back. However, we still have a long way to go.

We do believe that students of intercultural communication should have an advantage in being able to better understand the perspective of people with disabilities, as presented in this chapter. We hope that you will be able to adapt and apply intercultural communication concepts and skills to interactions with persons in the disabled culture. We believe that people with disabilities themselves will better understand their own experience if they study intercultural communication and come to understand the cultural aspects of disability.

In closing, taking an intercultural perspective on communication and disability culture leads us to suggest the following practical proscriptions and prescriptions.

DON'T:

- *Avoid* communication with people who are disabled simply because you are uncomfortable or unsure.

- *Assume* that people with disabilities cannot speak for themselves or do things for themselves.

- *Force* your help on people with disabilities.

- *Use* terms such as "handicapped," "physically challenged," "crippled," "victim," and the like, unless requested to do so by people with disabilities.

- *Assume* that a disability defines who a person is.

DO:

- *Remember* that people with disabilities have experienced others' discomfort before and likely understand how you might be feeling.

- *Assume* that people with disabilities can do something unless they communicate otherwise.

- *Let people with disabilities tell you* if they want something, what they want, and when they want it. If a person with a disability refuses your help, don't go ahead and help anyway.

- *Use terms* such as "*people* with disabilities" rather than "disabled people." The goal is to stress the *person first,* before the disability.

- *Treat* people with disabilities as *persons first,* recognizing that you are not dealing with a disabled person but with a *person* who *has* a disability. This means actively seeking the humanity of the person with whom you are speaking, and focusing on individual characteristics instead of superficial physical appearance. Without diminishing the significance of a person's physical disability, make a real effort to focus on all the many other aspects of that person as you communicate.

## Note

1. The quotes and anecdotes in this chapter come from in-depth interviews with people who have visible physical disabilities. The names of the participants in these interviews have been changed to protect their privacy.

## References

Belgrave, F. Z., & Mills, J. (1981). Effect upon desire for social interaction with a physically disabled person of mentioning the disability in different contexts. *Journal of Applied Social Psychology, 11,* 44–57.

Braithwaite, D. O. (1990). From majority to minority: An analysis of cultural change from nondisabled to disabled. *International Journal of Intercultural Relations, 14,* 465–483.

Braithwaite, D. O. (1991). "Just how much did that wheelchair cost?": Management of privacy boundaries by persons with disabilities. *Western Journal of Speech Communication, 55,* 254–274.

Braithwaite, D. O. (1996). "Persons first": Expanding communicative choices by persons with disabilities. In E. B. Ray (Ed.), *Communication and disenfranchisement: Social health issues and implications* (pp. 449–464). Mahwah, NJ: Erlbaum.

Braithwaite, D. O., & Eckstein, N. (2003). Reconceptualizing supportive interactions: How persons with disabilities communicatively manage assistance. *Journal of Applied Communication Research, 31,* 1–26.

Braithwaite, D. O., & Harter, L. (2000). Communication and the management of dialectical tensions in the personal relationships of people with disabilities. In D. O. Braithwaite & T. L. Thompson (Eds.), *Handbook of communication and people with disabilities: Research and application* (pp. 17–36). Mahwah, NJ: Erlbaum.

Braithwaite, D. O., & Labrecque, D. (1994). Responding to the Americans with Disabilities Act: Contributions of interpersonal communication research and training. *Journal of Applied Communication Research, 22,* 287–294.

Braithwaite, D. O., & Thompson, T. L. (Eds.). (2000). *Handbook of communication and people with disabilities: Research and application.* Mahwah, NJ: Erlbaum.

Carbaugh, D. (1988). *Talking American.* Norwood, NJ: Ablex.

Carbaugh, D. (Ed.). (1990). *Cultural communication and intercultural contact.* Hillsdale, NJ: Erlbaum.

Coleman, L. M., & DePaulo, B. M. (1991). Uncovering the human spirit: Moving beyond disability and "missed" communications. In N. Coupland, H. Giles, & J. M. Wiemann (Eds.), *Miscommunication and problematic talk* (pp. 61–84). Newbury Park, CA: Sage.

Covert, A. L., & Smith, J. W. (2000). What is reasonable: Workplace communication and people who are disabled. In D. O. Braithwaite & T. L. Thompson (Eds.), *Handbook of communication and people with disabilities: Research and application* (pp. 141–158). Mahwah, NJ: Erlbaum.

Crewe, N., & Athelstan, G. (1985). *Social and psychological aspects of physical disability.* Minneapolis: University of Minnesota, Department of Independent Study and University Resources.

Cunningham, C., & Coombs, N. (1997). *Information access and adaptive technology.* Phoenix, AZ: Oryx Press.

Dahnke, G. L. (1983). Communication and handicapped and nonhandicapped persons: Toward a deductive theory. In M. Burgoon (Ed.), *Communication yearbook 6* (pp. 92–135). Beverly Hills, CA: Sage.

DeLoach, C., & Greer, B. G. (1981). *Adjustment to severe physical disability: A metamorphosis.* New York: McGraw-Hill.

Emry, R., & Wiseman, R. L. (1987). An intercultural understanding of nondisabled and disabled persons' communication. *International Journal of Intercultural Relations, 11,* 7–27.

Fichten, C. S., Robillard, K., Tagalakis, V., & Amsel, R. (1991). Casual interaction between college students with various disabilities and their nondisabled peers: The internal dialogue. *Rehabilitation Psychology, 36,* 3–20.

Fox, S. A., Giles, H., Orbe, M., & Bourhis, R. (2000). Interability communication: Theoretical perspectives. In D. O. Braithwaite & T. L. Thompson (Eds.), *Handbook of communication and people with disabilities: Research and application* (pp. 193–222). Mahwah, NJ: Erlbaum.

Goffman, E. (1963). *Stigma: Notes on the management of spoiled identity.* New York: Simon & Schuster.

Herold, K. P. (2000). Communication strategies in employment interviews for applicants with disabilities. In D. O. Braithwaite & T. L. Thompson (Eds.), *Handbook of communication and people with disabilities: Research and application* (pp. 159–175). Mahwah, NJ: Erlbaum.

Higgins, P. C. (1992). *Making disability: Exploring the social transformation of human variation.* Springfield, IL: Charles C. Thomas.

Lyons, R. F., Sullivan, M. J. L., Ritvo, P. G., & Coyne, J. C. (1995). *Relationships in chronic illness and disability.* Thousand Oaks, CA: Sage.

Morse, J. M., & Johnson, J. L. (1991). *The illness experience: Dimensions of suffering.* Newbury Park, CA: Sage.

Padden, C., & Humphries, T. (1988). *Deaf in America: Voices from a culture.* Cambridge, MA: Harvard University Press.

Pardeck, J. T. (1998). *Social work after the Americans with Disabilities Act: New challenges and opportunities for social service professionals.* Westport, CT: Auburn House.

Thompson, T. L. (1982). Disclosure as a disability management strategy: A review and conclusions. *Communication Quarterly, 30,* 196–202.

Thompson, T. L. (2000). A history of communication and disability research: The way we were. In D. O. Braithwaite & T. L. Thompson (Eds.), *Handbook of communication and people with disabilities: Research and application* (pp. 1–14). Mahwah, NJ: Erlbaum.

Worley, D. W. (2000). Communication and students with disabilities on college campuses. In D. O. Braithwaite & T. L. Thompson (Eds.), *Handbook of communication and people with disabilities: Research and application* (pp. 125–139). Mahwah, NJ: Erlbaum.

## Concepts and Questions

1. How does becoming disabled lead to changes in a person's communication patterns?

2. What are some of the cultural problems inherent in communication between persons with and without disabilities?

3. Why do Braithwaite and Braithwaite believe you should learn about the communication patterns of

persons with disabilities? What purpose will be served by your knowing this information?

4. Give examples of what the Braithwaites mean when they say that "the distinctive verbal and nonverbal communication used by persons with disabilities create a sense of cultural identity that constitutes a unique social reality"?

5. How would you distinguish between *disability* and *handicap*?

6. Why is nonverbal communication a factor when persons with and without disabilities engage in communication?

7. Enumerate the problems Braithwaite and Braithwaite describe relating to the current research being conducted on persons with disabilities.

8. What is meant by the term *redefinition* as used in this essay?

9. How would you answer the following question: If disability is a culture, then when does one become part of that culture?

# In Plain Sight: Gay and Lesbian Communication and Culture

WILLIAM F. EADIE

*The next essay introduces you to the communicative behaviors and dynamics associated with the gay and lesbian co-culture. In his article, "In Plain Sight: Gay and Lesbian Communication and Culture," William F. Eadie acknowledges that there is a disparity of views, ranging from hostility to acceptance, regarding the gay and lesbian community. As a means of diminishing this antagonism, he challenges you to become acquainted with the cultural characteristics and communication style of the gay and lesbian members of our society.*

*Eadie specifies three general statements about lesbian and gay culture: (1) being open about sexual orientation is a political statement; (2) lesbian and gay culture must deal with tensions relating to how open one should be about his or her sexuality; and (3) although lesbian and gay culture is generally characterized as being about sexual attraction and desire, being lesbian or gay is about much, much more than just sex. The essay also provides insight into lesbian and gay communication behaviors and how sexual attraction and intimacy are negotiated. Eadie's essay offers first-hand insight into the lesbian and gay community and provides you with a much greater understanding of this co-culture.*

Just the idea of unique gay and lesbian communication patterns that create culture is a controversial one. Some may dismiss it as part of a "gay agenda" to promote acceptance where there can be none. An extreme case of this position could be found in the African country of Uganda, where at the time this essay was written a law was pending that could have mandated execution for anyone showing same-sex affection.

If there is a gay agenda in the U.S., however, it is diverse enough to consist of many different viewpoints. In this essay, I'll present some of those viewpoints on communication and culture in the lesbian and gay community. I use the term "viewpoints" because there is no precise way to define, measure, and track developments in lesbian and gay culture, so we have to rely on observers to analyze and present what they see. Many of those viewpoints will be backed by data collected through systematic research, but some will reflect general observations of societal trends.

My experience as a gay man has helped me to see that a major issue facing lesbians and gays in contemporary U.S. society is that it is easy to hide.

This original essay appears here in type for the first time. All rights reserved. Permission to reprint must be obtained from the author and the publisher. Earlier versions of this essay have appeared in previous editions. Dr. William F. Eadie is a professor of journalism and media studies at San Diego State University, San Diego, California.

Defying societal pressures and choosing to live openly as a lesbian or gay man is thus a political act, one that has ramifications, both positive and negative, for many of our everyday interactions. And, it is from those everyday interactions that cultural differences are created.

Below, I'll elaborate how this personal information becomes political. I'll include material on the "outsider" status that lesbians and gay men feel in society, the media's role in creating and perpetuating stereotypes, and the processes by which those stereotypes have been changing. I'll discuss the coming-out process, the role of communication in that process, and how gay men and lesbians eventually are able to achieve intimacy and find themselves a community. I'll provide examples of how people manage the tensions of displaying their sexuality to others, how public spaces are made safe for communication, how same-sex partners negotiate sexual attraction, and the problems entailed in achieving and maintaining intimacy in same-sex relationships.

## WHEN THE PERSONAL IS POLITICAL
### The Not-So-Hidden Outsiders

> More than other non-majority groups, lesbians and gay men have a better chance of living undetected by individuals within mainstream society.

More than other non-majority groups, lesbians and gay men have a better chance of living undetected by individuals within mainstream society. While ethnicity and national origin are relatively easy to discern merely by looking at an individual, sexual orientation is not readily apparent.

Of course, there are plenty of people who think that they can tell otherwise. When I was in high school, students called Thursday "Queersday" and passed around the story that those who wore green on Thursday would be saying to all that they were queer (a term that had a negative meaning in those days).

Why would students focus on clothing as an indicator that a classmate was gay? Perhaps it is because children from an early age are made very aware of differences between them and others, and by adolescence there is tremendous pressure to conform. A person who dresses differently enough to be beyond the boundaries of conformity communicates "outsider" status.

And, lesbian, gay, bisexual, transgendered, and questioning youth feel their outsider status intensely. One of the most eloquently written descriptions of these feelings comes from Paul Monette's (1992) award-winning memoir, *Becoming a Man*:

> Everyone else had a childhood, for one thing—where they were coaxed and coached and taught all the shorthand … And every year they leaped further ahead, leaving me in the dust with all my doors closed… Until I was twenty-five, I was the only man I knew who had no story at all… That's how the closet feels, once you've made your nest in it and learned to call it home. Self-pity becomes your oxygen. (p. 1)

Of course, what is in fashion changes rapidly and probably isn't a good indicator of sexuality over time. In urban areas, one can easily find straight and gay men and women who dress alike.

If clothing is becoming less and less of a giveaway, then what clues do people use to judge sexuality? Rieger, Linsenmeier, Gygax, Garcia, and Bailey (2010) attempted to answer that question by having homosexual and heterosexual men and women guess the sexuality of similarly aged men and women who had been recorded answering informal questions about their interests. Rieger, et al., asked their raters to base their judgments on appearance (by viewing a photo only), reading a transcript of the person's description of their interests, listening to an audio recording of the response, watching a video that revealed the person's movement pattern only, or watching and listening to a video of the individual giving the response. Results indicated that the raters were over 80% accurate in guessing the sexuality of the people they rated, regardless of whether the rater was heterosexual or homosexual. Raters were most accurate when viewing the video with all of the potential cues available and the least accurate when viewing the movement only.

A second study by the same research team asked a different set of raters to indicate the degree to which the people being rated seemed to be masculine or feminine. Raters attributed more feminine qualities to the gay men and more masculine qualities to the lesbian women, while reversing the pattern for the heterosexual men and women they saw.

This study debunks to some degree the idea that lesbians and gay men have a special ability to recognize each other (a phenomenon called "gaydar"). The raters who were lesbian or gay had no overall ability to recognize other lesbian and gay individuals, and both groups were quite accurate in identifying sexuality from 6- to 10-second video clips. Contrast this finding with research on deception that indicates that raters seeing similar-length clips have no better than a 50/50 chance of guessing whether someone is lying or telling the truth (Levine, 2009), and an over 80% accuracy rate is quite impressive.

The second study by Rieger, et al. (2010) confirmed that if men seem to act "feminine" or women act "masculine" they are likely to be assumed to be gay. But the results could also be confirming stereotypes. If young people can accurately judge the sexuality of 80% of their peers in less than 10 seconds, they might have done so and then assumed that the men acted more feminine and the women more masculine and rated accordingly.

And, what about the 20% whose sexuality was not judged accurately? Accuracy might be improved with time. For example, Kitzinger (2005) found that if individuals do not talk about their heterosexual relationships, or if they are vague in the pronouns or labels used to describe the relationships they do have, they may be assumed to be gay. And, vocal tone that sounds stereotypically gay will evoke negative judgments, even if individuals are told that the speaker is heterosexual (Gowen & Britt, 2006). Gay men and lesbians may, through experience, become better at sorting out these more subtle clues, but their first impressions of sexuality are likely to be no more accurate than those of heterosexuals.

Indeed, some gay men and lesbians may incorporate aspects of opposite-gender behavior in order to be noticed by other gay men and lesbians. But the adoption of these behaviors doesn't necessarily mean that the individual would rather *be* the opposite gender. Most lesbians and gay men are happy being women or men; they are simply emotionally and sexually attracted to members of the same gender.

> *Most lesbians and gay men are happy being women or men; they are simply emotionally and sexually attracted to members of the same gender.*

## Media and Stereotypes

Media portrayals of lesbians and gays have helped both to perpetuate stereotypes and, more recently, to promote tolerance and acceptance. According to Fejes and Petrich (1993), who reviewed a large number of studies on how lesbians and gays had been portrayed in films, on television, and in the news, gay characters in entertainment were often cast as farcical, weak, or menacing.

Smyth (2004) identified four classic stereotypes of gay men: (1) gay males are effeminate, (2) gay males are "sick" or mentally ill, (3) gay males are sexual predators, and (4) gay males are "violent, libido-driven monsters." Smyth studied stories that appeared in *Time* and *Newsweek* between 1946 and 2002, and he found that there were three distinct periods reflecting differences in how these periodicals covered gays.

From 1946 to 1969, the newsmagazines portrayed gay men almost exclusively from a dark point of view, as sexually deviant, predatory, and sick. From 1969, following the Stonewall Riots, to 1980, coverage focused mostly on the emerging Gay Liberation movement, and reactions to that movement, mostly from religious or quasi-religious groups. While the articles themselves often focused on an emerging gay male identity and political agenda, there were still mentions of the old stereotypes in many of the articles. It was also during this period that the American Psychiatric Association removed homosexuality from its list of mental illnesses. From 1980 to 2002, the number of articles about gays surged dramatically. Portrayals of gay men as effeminate dropped sharply, though the news magazines still were interested in gay serial killers and unusual sexual practices. The prevalence of HIV and AIDS among gay men helped to perpetuate the "sick" stereotype, and coverage of the spread of AIDS perpetuated the stereotype of the sexual predator.

Similarly, Branchik (2007) analyzed representations of gay men in print advertising from 1917 to 2004 and found that these representations passed through four stages that were roughly equivalent to changes in societal views of gay men. These stages were (a) recognizing the men as being homosexual,

(b) ridiculing them, (c) accepting them as "cutting edge," and (d) portraying them with respect.

Streitmatter (2009) also traced mainstream media portrayals of gay men. He believed that these portrayals moved away from ridicule in 1977, with the debut of *Soap,* the first television series to feature a recurring openly gay character. He thought that Branchik's (2007) "respect" stage began in 1993 with the debut of the film, *Philadelphia,* which starred Tom Hanks as a gay attorney who had AIDS (it would be years before an openly gay actor would portray a gay character in film or television—or that an openly gay actor such as Neil Patrick Harris would prove to be popular playing heterosexual roles).

Streitmatter (2009) believed that the next stage of acceptance would be showing male–male or female–female lovemaking on network television. Indeed, in December 2009, the ABC soap opera, *One Life to Live,* broke this new ground by featuring the show's recurring gay character making love with another man.

Even though stereotypes have been dissipating in media coverage, they persist in many people's thinking. And, like all stereotypes, they have some basis in fact. Some scholars would characterize these stereotypes as being products of *heterosexism.* That is, they arise from an assumption that behavior of heterosexual individuals is "normal" and behavior of homosexual individuals is "deviant," as opposed to merely "different." In fact, there are probably more heterosexual men who are effeminate, sick, predatory, or prone to sex-related criminal acts than there are gay men, because same-sex orientation is statistically still very much the exception (independent estimates range anywhere from 2–10% of the population).

Of course, I have been discussing 21st century ideas about same-sex orientation. It has not always been thus, and in fact there is considerable historical evidence that sexuality with others of the same gender has in the past been honored instead of looked on with suspicion (see, for example, Boswell, 1994; Crompton, 2003; Greenberg, 1988).

## Overcoming Stereotypes

One way that many people seem to have of letting go of their stereotypes is to meet someone who doesn't fit them. A 2009 Gallup Poll (Morales, 2009) indicated that knowing even one gay person affected the degree to which one felt positively about same-sex relationships. Those who knew at least one lesbian or gay person also reported less discomfort about interacting with lesbian or gay individuals generally. Those with liberal political and social views were more likely to say that they knew someone who was gay than were those who held moderate or conservative views.

Media viewing can also affect individuals, even if they do not know anyone who is gay. A study of viewers of the television show *Will and Grace,* which featured gay characters in leading roles, found that they held more positive attitudes toward lesbians and gays than did people who did not watch the show (Schiappa, Gregg, & Hewes, 2006). While one might expect that people seek out television programming that fits with their attitudes, positive attitudes toward lesbians and gays persisted even among those viewers who did not claim to have lesbian or gay friends.

Though these numbers indicate that attitudes are changing, there is still danger associated with being openly lesbian or gay. In particular, this danger seems to affect people under 21 to the greatest degree. For example, Huebner, Rebchook, and Kegeles (2004) reported on a survey of 1248 gay and bisexual men aged 18–27. Overall five percent of those surveyed reported that they had been the victims of anti-gay violence, while eleven percent indicated that they had been discriminated against because they were gay. But, of those under 21, the numbers jumped to 10 percent as having experienced anti-gay violence, while half reported that they had been discriminated against because they were gay. Horn (2006) found that adolescents aged 14–16 are most likely to exhibit hostility toward lesbian and gay peers, and that open displays of hostility decline as adolescents age into young adulthood. Nevertheless, the possibility of being reviled for being open about one's sexuality remains throughout one's life.

These data bring us back to the point that being openly lesbian or gay is a political statement. When the odds are not strong that others will have a favorable attitude toward you as a lesbian or gay man, and when the odds are even greater that your openness at a young age may result in negative, even violent, consequences, no wonder many non-heterosexual individuals keep that information to themselves. They may date members of the opposite sex and may also marry and have families. Men in this situation may seek anonymous same-sex encounters outside of marriage, because the means for having such encounters are often readily (though, not always legally) available. These men may also deny that they have any same-sex attraction. Public health workers call these individuals MSMs, or "Men who have Sex with Men." People in the African American and Latino communities call this practice being "on the down low" (Wolitski et al., 2006).

## The Process of Coming Out

Despite the potential for negative consequences, it is healthier for people to be open about their same-sex attraction. But getting to that point is not always easy. D'Augelli (1994) theorized what he called "six interactive stages that non-heterosexual" individuals pass through as they develop an identity. The stages are:

1. Recognizing that one's attractions and feelings are not heterosexual, as well as telling others that one is not heterosexual

2. Summarizing self-concepts, emotions, and desires into a personal identity as gay/lesbian/bisexual

3. Developing a non-heterosexual social identity

4. Disclosing one's identity to parents and redefining familial relationships afterward

5. Developing capabilities to have intimate gay/lesbian/bisexual relationships

6. Becoming a member of a gay/lesbian/bisexual community.

It is possible that these stages can be passed through quickly, but it is equally as likely that these stages will progress slowly if at all (indeed, individuals may work on multiple stages at once or may double-back to previous stages). Each stage requires some degree of change to how one talks and each stage requires the ability to share with others what heretofore one considered to be private information. As people search for new ways of talking and for what they might consider to be the "right words" to say, they look to the examples of others. This process of learning to communicate differently helps lesbian and gay individuals to assimilate into the lesbian/gay/bisexual community.

The fact that disclosure of information about one's sexuality may evoke responses ranging from delight to spews of hateful words makes such disclosure a political one. "Political" communication, in this case, is constituted by messages that have the potential for promoting controversy. "Political" also means that such a disclosure tends to carry with it an assumption that the speaker holds a set of attitudes and beliefs that may be at odds with those of the listener. Such assumptions may not be correct ones.

## Communication and Identity Formation

D'Augelli's (1994) stages of identity formation are called "interactive" because they rely on communication with others to occur. As same-sex attraction is controversial information, lesbians and gays beginning on D'Augelli's stages need to find strategies for disclosing this information. These initial disclosures will usually be tentative and told to a confidant, often a trusted friend or an adult who is not a parent. The initial messages may not be in the form of "I am lesbian," but may be more general statements such as "I'm having trouble with starting to date. My friends are dating, but I'm not," or even a statement such as "I'm not sure that people like me; I don't fit in very well." The realization that one is attracted to members of the same sex may be present, but the individual may be choosing to hide that information behind what is often legitimate confusion. Depending on the response, the individual may finally say that they think they are more attracted to members of the same sex than to members of the opposite sex, or they may label themselves lesbian, gay, or bisexual. In many cases, the first formulation of sexual identity might be "I'm bisexual," because the speaker may believe that this statement is more socially acceptable than "I'm gay" (Rust, 2002).

Once some form of admission that "I am different" is made, the gay or lesbian person will begin to look for information that will help him or her to figure out what is going on. Sometimes this information search is confined to books, magazines, or informational web sites. Other times the information may come from pornography or erotica or from seeking out places where gays or lesbians gather, including online (Gray, 2009).

Sometimes, these places will be ones where anonymous sex might be had. Males in particular may try to experiment with gay sex to see if they find it to be exciting. The fact that sex in public places is usually against the law may add to the thrill of the experience.

As the lesbian or gay individual has contact with other lesbians and gays and compares themselves favorably to those other individuals, the idea that "I am different" should eventually become, "I am lesbian," or "I am gay." At that point, the dilemma becomes whether and if so how to let others know of one's sexual identity.

## Coming Out as Event

The process of "coming out of the closet" is actually described by all of D'Augelli's (1994) stages, taken collectively. The moments when the lesbian or gay individual actually tells the people closest to them of their sexual identity should ideally be (1) when that individual is ready and prepared to make the disclosure, and (2) when the other members are ready to hear what this individual has to say. In many cases, however, these scenes are not nearly so clean and well planned. Parents may learn about their child's sexuality, for example, by catching them with same-sex pornography, by reading their diaries, or by discovering them with a same-sex partner. Or, initial sexual experimentation may lead to trouble with the law or with delinquency. Or, the individual may burst out with the information at an emotional, but unplanned, moment.

Reactions to this information will be varied. The ideal reaction, from the lesbian or gay person's point of view, is described in advice available on the website of the support organization, Parents and Friends of Lesbians and Gays (PFLAG) (Human Rights Campaign & Parents and Friends of Lesbians and Gays, n.d.):

- Ask respectful questions to show you are interested.

- Be honest. If you feel awkward, say so. Ask the "dumb" questions.

- Laugh a little, but do it gently and respectfully. Don't use slang terms that could be considered to be derogatory.

- Send gentle signals that it's all right to continue to talk with you about being lesbian or gay.[1]

Still, there are many families where parents and siblings do not process this news in nearly as supportive a manner. Some family members may immediately cut off contact with the lesbian or gay member. Some families may try to persuade the lesbian or gay person that "this is a phase" or that "you can change."

No wonder that individuals who are questioning their sexuality are reluctant to talk to others about it until they are sure of a lesbian or gay identity. And no wonder that some people stay in the closet for years. Many lesbian and gay individuals feel tensions in their relationships with family, work, and social and religious institutions (e.g., Calzo & Ward, 2009; Gortmaker & Brown, 2006; McDermott, 2006). Lesbians and gays may resolve these tensions in a variety of ways. They may decide to create alternative support institutions, such as "families of choice," as opposed to "families of origin." They may strive to achieve at work or in an arena where they can gain recognition. They may become part of alternative social and religious structures. They may also become politically active, seeking to root out and eliminate discrimination wherever they find it. If they join political groups, these groups may employ tactics ranging from traditional lobbying to attention-grabbing demonstrations where same-sex couples deliberately engage in public displays of affection. (For an analysis of the political dimensions of two men kissing in public, see Morris & Sloop, 2006.)

> *Fear of being discovered, fear of what others will think, or fear of losing one's job can keep people in hiding and afraid of their own sexuality.*

## Achieving Intimacy

It is usually difficult for a lesbian or gay person to progress to D'Augelli's (1994) fifth stage, learning how to develop intimate same-sex relationships, without having completed at least some of the fourth stage, allowing the people who matter to them to know them as sexual beings. Intimacy, by its very nature, demands a degree of honesty that is usually suppressed by the need to hide a major portion of one's self. In addition, fear of being discovered, fear of what others will think, or fear of losing one's job can keep people in hiding and afraid of their own sexuality. However, sometimes finding another person to trust and love can help an individual to be more open about same-sex attraction. Of course, intimate relationships can and do happen between people who can't be open with others. Sometimes, these relationships are described to others as "roommates" or "friends," which is how a neighbor of mine described his living arrangement with his partner of 17 years when I first met him. As soon as he realized that I was sympathetic, however, he began talking to me in much more open terms. The ability to be openly a part of an intimate relationship in the community at large is a test of not only how accepting people have become of their own sexuality but how interactions with the community can create a climate where the couple are accepted and included by those around them.

## Building Community

D'Augelli's (1994) final stage entails becoming a part of a lesbian/gay/bisexual community. This stage, too, does not necessarily wait for the other stages to finish, but can occur even while completing the earliest stages of the process. High school gay–straight alliance clubs can provide a supportive place to be different in an environment that puts a high premium on conformity. Universities may provide a means for "out" lesbians and gays to gather but also often provide private groups, typically run by a professional staff member, where questioning students can explore their sexuality. Lesbian and gay community centers also provide "coming out" workshops and other social services designed to assist people to find a community and to feel as though they belong there.

Being in a community typically involves having a concentration of like-minded people with whom to interact on a daily basis. The 2000 U.S. Census was the first to allow individuals to identify themselves as same-sex couples, and Gates and Ost (2004) compiled census data to learn about lesbian and gay living patterns. They found that gay male and lesbian women couples tend to live on the East or West Coasts of the United States, though not necessarily in the same locales. The 10 most popular spots for gay male couples to live were San Francisco, CA; Fort Lauderdale, FL; Santa Rosa, CA; Seattle-Bellevue-Everett, WA; New York, NY; Jersey City, NJ; Los Angeles-Long Beach, CA, Santa Fe, NM; Oakland, CA; and Miami, FL. Gay male couples tended to live in places that had higher concentrations of other gay couples, and they tended to live in more urban areas. For lesbian couples, the most popular places were often in college towns: Santa Rosa, CA; Santa Cruz-Watsonville, CA; Santa Fe, NM; San Francisco, CA; Oakland, CA; Burlington, VT; Portland, ME; Springfield, MA; Corvallis, OR; and Madison, WI. Gates and Ost also reported that 99% of U.S. counties had at least one same-sex couple living there.[2]

In an update based on 2008 data, Gates (2009) refined his results to distinguish between same-sex spouses (people who specifically designated themselves in that manner) and same-sex unmarried partners. In terms of places of residence, the patterns were similar to those reported earlier; in particular, same-sex spouses tended to live in states where their partnership could be recognized legally. Gates's analysis also revealed some demographic characteristics of same-sex spouses: they were more likely to be women who were raising children, and they tended to have lower incomes and higher levels of unemployment than did same-sex unmarried partners. Despite the lower incomes, they were more likely to be homeowners, however.

Gates (2009) also found that same-sex spouses and opposite-sex spouses were more alike than different. They were similar in average age, income, rate of home ownership, education levels, and degree to which both partners were of the same or different ethnicities. The only differences Gates found were that same-sex spouses were less likely to be raising children and that it was less likely for both partners to be employed than were different-sex spouses.

Once in a community, gays and lesbians will often become involved in social organizations, such as square dancing or choral singing, business and networking groups such as a lesbian and gay Chamber of Commerce, and causes that benefit the community as a whole. There have even begun to be retirement communities created for lesbians and gays (Neville, 2007).

Over time, gay men have been involved in prevention of HIV/AIDS transmission and in raising funds for research on this disease, which began in the gay community but now affects far more heterosexual people worldwide. Lesbians have actively been involved in raising awareness about breast cancer and in funding breast cancer research. Both groups have campaigned against laws that allow discrimination in hiring and housing or that criminalize private and consensual sexual practices commonly engaged in by lesbian and gay couples. These campaigns culminated in the U.S. Supreme Court's 2003 decision in *Lawrence v. Texas*, where Justice Anthony Kennedy, writing for the Court majority, declared that two gay men could engage in consensual sexual activity in the privacy of one's home and "still retain their dignity as free persons."

Most recently, the lesbian and gay community has been galvanized by a drive to legalize marriage for same-sex couples. This drive created a great amount of national debate, as well as spawning decisions to allow same-sex marriages and legal attempts to restrict the term "marriage" to recognizing relationships among opposite-sex couples. But the *New York Times'* decision to print announcements of the unions of same-sex couples in its wedding announcements pages did much for increasing the social acceptability of those relationships.

## COMMUNICATION AND THE TENSIONS OF BEING GAY

In U.S. culture, gays and lesbians needed to remain hidden yet visible for so long that they developed ways of signaling their sexual orientation to likeminded people that would remain oblique to society as a whole. Alternatively, they choose to be so flamboyant that their sexuality could not be ignored.

The author and playwright Oscar Wilde proved to be a masterful practitioner of hiding a gay subtext in his stories and plays, work that was acclaimed by mainstream critics and audiences alike. For example, in his novella *The Picture of Dorian Gray*, Wilde concocted a tale about a man who finds the secret to staying eternally beautiful and youthful. The secret is a portrait of himself that he has hidden in his attic. The portrait, not the man, is the one that ages. Ultimately, the story ends in horror, and the man receives his comeuppance, but its central fantasy appealed to the soul of every gay man who read it. Wilde himself was married to a woman but had many dalliances with young men, including at least one long-term lover. Tried in court for being a homosexual, a crime in Victorian England, Wilde defended himself by claiming that he merely enjoyed the company and

energy of younger men. Wilde was convicted and jailed, however, and the experience left him sick and defeated, unable to produce the kind of tales that had once made him the toast of London.

## Camp as Gay Sensibility

Wilde has been credited not only as being the person around which our modern ideas about same-sex love were conceived but also as being the first practitioner of "camp." Camp has evolved into a central concept in understanding gay culture. In her famous 1964 essay, "Notes on 'Camp'," critic Susan Sontag defined camp as a "sensibility," as opposed to an idea or a thing. Sensibilities, according to Sontag, are difficult to describe, but she argued that camp is a sensibility that requires aesthetic appreciation, because it is a style or taste. Since styles and tastes change frequently, however, one must be nimble and not given to set ways of seeing the world. Indeed, camp often turns the world on its ear, relying on exaggeration and a tendency to see double meaning in words and acts. Camp is theatrical, an attempt to be and do extraordinary things. Camp is "fabulous" (Sontag, 1964).

In a later essay, Meyer (1994) extended Sontag's analysis to argue that camp encompasses how lesbians and gays perform their lives in front of others. Camp is the embodiment of how gay individuals manage the tensions of being open about their sexuality in a society that brands them as deviant. Rather than hide one's difference, camp helps the gay or lesbian person to find an alternative way of being in the world, a "queer" reality that doesn't have to rely on the norms of mainstream society, a reality that, in fact, often mocks those norms.

A good example of this alternate reality is the concept of drag. Drag not only bends the idea of gender by allowing men to dress up as women and women as men, but it requires that the "drag queen" or "drag king" play with the character in some way.

Perhaps a good way of explaining drag would be to compare it to female impersonation. Let's say that both a drag queen and a female impersonator are portraying actress and pop star Madonna. The female impersonator will attempt to look and sound as much like Madonna as possible, to create the illusion of Madonna as a tribute to her talent. The drag queen, on the other hand, will portray an exaggerated version of Madonna, playing with her persona to distort it in humorous or ironic ways.

Drag also allows an individual to be "someone else," at least for a while. One acquaintance of mine confided to me, "When I go to a bar in drag, all of the cute boys want to talk to me. I have a quick mouth, and they love my comebacks. But out of drag I'm a large, older man, and if I went into the same bar as that person those boys wouldn't have anything to do with me. In drag, I'm fun and safe, but out of drag I'm someone to be avoided."

While camp originated as an integral part of gay life, Whitney (2006) has argued that it has been co-opted by the heterosexual world and as such may become a subtle means of oppressing the gay community while disguising itself as a liberating experience for all. Time and experience will tell whether this argument, while provocative, turns out to be valid.

## It's About Sex, but Not Only About Sex

Of course, the point of same-sex attraction is that gays and lesbians want to find someone of the same gender with whom to be physically, emotionally, and spiritually intimate. Recall, however, that while D'Augelli's (1994) stages of developing a non-heterosexual identity included the capacity to form and maintain intimate same-sex relationships, D'Augelli placed this capacity down his list, after coming out to family and friends. Clearly, a lot of developing a lesbian and gay identity involves exploring one's same-sex attraction and learning to flirt with and meet people who might be candidates for intimate relationships. And many, if not most, lesbians and gays do not wait until they have found their "soul mate" before having sex. Gay men often talk about finding Mr. Right, as opposed to finding Mr. Right-Now. But as you might imagine, the latter is much easier to locate.

## Making Public Communication Safe

Meeting other lesbian and gay people face to face and in public is not an easy task, however. If one is in a "safe" space, where everyone there is gay or accepting of same-sex attraction, then conversing openly is not a problem. Bars have traditionally filled this role,

though to a greater extent for men than for women. Coffee houses and some community-based restaurants have also emerged as bar alternatives, especially for gay and lesbian youth who are not of legal drinking age, and for those who may want a less pressured atmosphere. Social and volunteer organizations also serve as safe spaces for lesbians and gays to meet.

Meeting someone outside of these spaces can be tricky, especially if one isn't sure that the other person shares one's same-sex attraction. In public places, contact is usually established by exchanging gazes, typically more than once. Holding another's gaze is generally interpreted as a sign that the other person might be interested. A conversation will often ensue, and an early task in that conversation will be to say something socially acceptable but that the other person can identify as a gay reference. Leap (1996), who has studied how gay men talk, both in the United States, and internationally, provided an example of a conversation between a clothing sales clerk and a customer:

**C:** What are you asking for these? *[Points to one set of gray sweatshirts]*

**S:** Oh, I'm afraid they're not on sale today. But that colored shirt would look nice on you. *[Points to a pile of lavender sweatshirts, which are on sale]*

**C:** Yeah, I know. I own a few of them already. *[Grins]*

**S:** *[Grins back, no verbal comment]* (1996, p. 13)

Undoubtedly, these men walked away from this conversation with the knowledge that they were both gay. They understood that fact by (a) the reference to "lavender," a color generally associated with being gay; (b) the exaggerated response to the suggestion that the lavender shirt would look good on the customer; and (c) the fact that both men had exchanged mutual glances prior to beginning the conversation and they both grinned at the end of it. The conversational space was thus "safe," though still public, and if the two had been interested in pursuing each other's company further they could have exchanged contact information.

Online environments have burgeoned as purportedly safe places for gay men and lesbians to interact and meet others. Various dating sites have sprung up and offered services to people seeking same-sex dates, as well as to those seeking opposite-sex dates, though one of the most popular, EHarmony, did so only under court order (Colker, 2009). In fact, EHarmony created a separate site for same-sex clients, called "Compatible Partners," but placed a disclaimer on the site's front page that the company's compatibility questionnaire was developed using married heterosexual couples, implying that it might not work for same-sex relationships.

## Negotiating Sexual Attraction

The above example involved two men who might have been interested in each other as potential friends or potential dates. When gay men are looking for sex partners, however, they will tend to use mostly nonverbal signals to do so. What gay men call "cruising" typically starts with making eye contact with someone as the two pass each other. If one is interested, that person will typically slow down and look back. If the other person also looks back, one person may begin to follow the other person. The two might stop and begin a conversation, or they might silently look for a place to have sex (there is a classic set of photographs that illustrates this sequence online at http://phillips depury.liveauctioneers.com/lot2509621.html).

Generally, when men engage in an anonymous sexual encounter, the less they know about the other person the better. Many choose to avoid the danger of sex in public by going to any of several Internet sites that feature ads from gays or lesbians looking for a "hook-up" in a particular geographical area (Ashford, 2006). Of course, cruising isn't limited to gay men, and using the Internet to find partners for dating or sex is a pervasive activity for people of all sexualities. Moreover, like a lot of relational communication activity, interaction patterns on the Internet don't seem to be terribly different whether one is straight or gay.

One common feature of gay Internet sex sites is postings by men who say that they are bisexual. Gay men often scoff at the notion of bisexuality, saying that men who claim to be bisexual are really gay and in denial. Empirical support for this claim comes from research (Rieger, Chivers, & Bailey, 2005) on arousal patterns of men who claimed to be straight, gay, and bisexual. Gay men were aroused more by erotic pictures of men, while straight men were aroused by erotic pictures of women, as might be expected. Men who claimed to be bisexual, however, tended to show arousal patterns that resembled those of gay men. When questioned, however, those men claimed that they were aroused about equally by the erotic images of both men and women.

This study reminds us that people define their own sexuality and choose the label that they believe fits them best, including being "asexual" (for details of this emerging movement, see http://www.asexuality.org). There is no definitive test that demonstrates one's sexual orientation, and sexual orientation is probably determined by a number of factors, including both biological and social influences. Many people experience sexual orientation as something about which they had no choice, however (American Psychological Association, 2008), and most claim that their sexual orientation is something they cannot change. In fact, the American Psychological Association has reported that there is no scientific evidence that therapy designed to change one's sexual orientation is either safe or effective.

Nevertheless, it is clear that a number of individuals exhibit attraction to both men and women, and Rust (2002, 2009), in reviewing the scholarly literature on bisexuality, has argued that we may be more upset by not being able to put a person into either the heterosexual or homosexual camp than anything else. Bisexuality seems to be more acceptable in women than in men, and, in fact, some scholars are currently investigating whether women demonstrate a more fluid sexuality than do men (Bergner, 2009; Wade, 2007).

## Negotiating Intimacy

Most lesbians and gay men put a high premium on dating and forming intimate relationships. Their courtship communication patterns in many ways resemble those of their heterosexual counterparts in similar age groups. Only a couple of differences have been found so far. One is that both lesbians and gay men are more likely to remain in touch with their former partners after the relationship ends (Peplau & Fingerhut, 2007). A second is that lesbian couples are quite adept at managing conflict in their relationships (Roisman et al., 2008).

Lesbian and gay couples do have unique issues to negotiate on their way to achieving intimacy at all of the physical, emotional, and spiritual (Tan, 2005) levels, however. For one thing, the issue of "who does what" in the relationship has to be worked out bit by bit. In heterosexual relationships, societal expectations for the roles that men and women play can either be followed or they can be reversed by the couple's decision. In lesbian and gay relationships, couples generally reject the notion that one of them plays the "man" and the other plays the "woman." So, each physical or emotional task has to be worked out, either consciously, or by one person taking on that task and having it become part of who that person is in the relationship. Many lesbians and gay men also reject that their relationships should have to conform to the normative expectations of the heterosexual community (Slagle, 2006). These issues often revolve around setting rules for how much physical, emotional, or spiritual attraction is allowed to each member of the couple outside of the relationship: lesbian and gay couples may not conform to heterosexual definitions of "cheating" in their relationships.

Studies of gay male couples in San Francisco (Hoff & Beougher, in press; Hoff, Beougher, Chakravarty, Darbes, & Neilands, in press; Hoff, Chakravarty, Beougher, Darbes, Dadasovich, & Neilands, 2009) have provided details on negotiation processes regarding sexual practices. These studies were based on surveys and interviews regarding whether couples had agreements regarding sex outside of the relationship, how those agreements functioned, whether they had been broken, and how the breaks had been handled.

Couples often reported that they had agreements about sexual matters, particularly the degree to which monogamy was expected, but that those agreements were not always explicit (and, in a few cases, the researchers found that each of the pair had a different understanding of the agreement). The agreements were generally unique to the relationship but could be classified as varying by how exclusive the relationship was expected to be, sexually, and if sex with others was allowed with whom (e.g., no ex-boyfriends) and under what circumstances (e.g., only with one's partner present). Breaks were handled depending on how long the agreement was in place. Breaks early on prompted being more specific or renegotiating the conditions, but a break after the agreement had been in place and stable for a while might call for a reexamination of the relationship itself. While couples with all sorts of agreements reported being satisfied with this aspect of their relationships, monogamous couples as a group tended to report that they felt more invested in their agreements, more satisfied with their relationships, and greater intimacy, trust, and equality in the relationship.

And there are certainly differences in the sexual area. Storkey (2001) contended that men typically have difficulty achieving emotional closeness and that sex is often seen as the route to shedding inhibitions and achieving intimacy. For women, however, emotional warmth is typically an end in itself and those feelings need to be present before women commit to the relationship in a sexual manner. According to this analysis, it would not be surprising to find that most gay men look for sexual attraction and compatibility before working on emotional commitment, while most lesbian couples work on emotional connection first before committing to sex.

This negotiation work is hard, and if it becomes too hard or leads to major conflict before the couple has committed to each other there will be a tendency to break off the relationship, rather than to work through the conflicts.

The fact that same-sex couples have no legal standing in many parts of the United States also means that couples either have to keep their finances and other matters separate, or have legal documents drafted spelling out their agreements, all the while knowing that the validity of those documents might be challenged successfully, perhaps by members of one individual's family, at some future date.

## SOME CLOSING THOUGHTS

In writing this essay, the readers I was keeping in mind were traditionally aged university sophomores and juniors. Accordingly, I tried to select and emphasize material that I thought might be most relevant to both the intellectual and emotional journeys of 19- or 20-year-olds. Clearly, not every second- or third-year college student is 19 or 20 years old, and if you fall into that category my examples may not fit where you are in your life so well.

I also tried to emphasize material that might be common to both lesbians and gay men. Because there has been much more research on the communication and relationship patterns of gay men than on lesbians, and because I am a gay man, this choice probably means that readers interested in lesbians as a group may feel disappointed in what they learned from this essay. For example, research indicating that lesbians are less likely to be "out" at work (McDermott, 2006) is interesting but beyond the scope of what I wanted to cover. If you'd like to understand more about the psychology of lesbians and gay men, I'd refer you to book-length works such as Coyle & Kitzinger (2002).

I have also ignored the "T," or transgender, part of the "LGBT" formulation. Earlier in this essay, I wrote that exhibiting the behavior of the other gender doesn't necessarily identify one as a lesbian woman or gay man, and I commented that many, if not most, of us were quite happy being men or women. Transgendered individuals, on the other hand, do sense that they ought to be the opposite gender from what they are, physically. Much of the research on transgendered individuals is still quite new (see Papoulias, 2006, for a summary) and is related to a burgeoning body of scholarship on gender identity (see, for example, Factor & Rothblum, 2008). Some transgendered individuals identify as being lesbian or gay, while others do not. The American Psychological Association has a good publication with answers to questions about gender identity available online at http://www.apa.org/topics/sexuality/transgender.aspx.

Finally, I have not written about many of the issues about which many lesbians and gay men care deeply, as well as about several of the tensions that exist within the lesbian and gay community. These tensions include poverty and homelessness among lesbians and gays, particularly youth; racism and sexism; concerns about how to foster healthy communication among lesbians and gay men of different ages (Hajek & Giles, 2002) or between gays and straights (Hajek & Giles, 2005); and worries that lesbian and gay culture is becoming too mainstream, resulting in the possible loss of the community's identity (Hattersley, 2004; McNamara, 2004).

Despite these shortcomings, I hope that I have provided you with some insight about communication among gay men and lesbians and how that communication manifests itself in the U.S. as a "culture." It used to be said that the members of the lesbian and gay community were "hiding in plain sight." Now that so many are no longer hiding, I hope that this information will help you to understand the ways in which members of this community may be different from others and the ways we are the same.

## Notes

1. Brault, M. (2008). *Disability Status and the Characteristics of People in Group Quarters*. U.S. Census Bureau: Disability. Retrieved 15 April 2010 from http://www.census.gov/hhes/www/disability/GQdisability.pdf

2. Census Bureau Estimates Nearly Half of Children Under Age 5 are Minorities. (2009). U.S. Census Bureau News: Department of Commerce. Retrieved 15 April 2010 from http://www.census.gov/Press-Release/www/releases/archives/population/013733.html

## References

American Psychological Association. (2008). Answers to your questions: For a better understanding of sexual orientation and homosexuality. Washington, DC: Author. Retrieved from www.apa.org/topics/sorientation.pdf

Ashford, C. (2006). The only gay in the village: Sexuality and the net. *Information & Communications Technology Law, 15*, 275–289.

Bergner, D. (2009, January 25). What do women want? *New York Times Magazine*, 26–33, 46, 51–52.

Boswell, J. (1994). *Same-sex unions in premodern Europe*. New York: Villard.

Branchik, B. J. (2007). Pansies to parents: Gay male images in American print advertising. *Journal of Macromarketing, 27*, 38–50.

Calzo, J. P., & Ward, L. M. (2009). Contributions of parents, peers, and media to attitudes toward homosexuality: Investigating sex and ethnic differences. *Journal of Homosexuality, 56*, 1101–1116.

Colker, D. (2009, March 31). EHarmony launches gay matchmaking service. *Los Angeles Times*. Retrieved from http://articles.latimes.com/2009/mar/31/business/fi-eharmony31

Coyle, A., & Kitzinger, C., Eds. (2002). *Lesbian and gay psychology: New perspectives*. Oxford: Blackwell.

Crompton, L. (2003). *Homosexuality and civilization*. Cambridge, MA: Harvard University Press.

D'Augelli, A. R. (1994). Identity development and sexual orientation: Toward a model of lesbian, gay, and bisexual development. In E. J. Trickett, R. J. Watts, & D. Birmans (Eds.), *Human diversity: Perspectives on people in context* (pp. 312–333). New York: Oxford University Press.

Factor, R., & Rothblum, E. (2008). Exploring gender identity and community among three groups of transgender individuals in the United States: MTFs, FTMs, and genderqueers. *Health Sociology Review, 17,* 235–253.

Gates, G. J. (2009). *Same-sex spouses and unmarried partners in the American community survey, 2008.* Los Angeles: The Williams Institute, UCLA. Retrieved from http://www.law.ucla.edu/WilliamsInstitute/pdf/ACS2008_Final(2).pdf

Gates, G. J., & Ost, J. (2004). *The gay and lesbian atlas.* Washington, DC: The Urban Institute Press.

Gortmaker, V. J., & Brown, R. D. (2006). Out of the college closet: Differences in perceptions and experiences among out and closeted lesbian and gay students. *College Student Journal, 40,* 606–619.

Gowen, C. W., & Britt, T. W. (2006). The interactive effects of homosexual speech and sexual orientation on the stigmatization of men. *Journal of Language & Social Psychology, 25,* 437–456.

Gray, M. L. (2009). Negotiating identities/queering desires: Coming out online and the remediation of the coming-out story. *Journal of Computer-Mediated Communication 14,* 1162–1189.

Greenberg, D. (1988). *The construction of homosexuality.* Chicago: University of Chicago Press.

Hajek, C. & Giles, H. (2002). The old man out: An intergroup analysis of intergenerational communication among gay men. *Journal of Communication, 30,* 698–714.

Hajek, C. & Giles, H. (2005). Intergroup communication schemas: Cognitive representations of talk with gay men. *Language & Communication 25,* 161–181.

Hattersley, M. (2004, January-February). Will success spoil gay culture? *Gay and Lesbian Review Worldwide, 11,* 33–34.

Herek, G.M. (2002). Heterosexuals' attitudes toward bisexual men and women in the United States. *Journal of Sex Research, 39,* 264–274.

Hoff, C. C., & Beougher, S. C. (2010). Sexual agreements among gay male couples. *Archives of Sexual Behavior, 39* (3), 774–778.

Hoff, C. C., Beougher, S. C., Chakravarty, D., Darbes, L. A., & Neilands, T. B. (2010). Relationship characteristics and motivations behind agreements among gay male couples: Differences by agreement type and couple serostatus. *AIDS Care, 22* (7), 827–835.

Hoff, C. C., Chakravarty, D., Beougher, S. C., Darbes, L. A., Dadasovich, R., & Neilands, T. B. (2009). Serostatus differences and agreements about sex with outside partners among gay male couples. *AIDS Education and Prevention, 21,* 25–38.

Horn, S. S. (2006). Heterosexual adolescents' and young adults' beliefs and attitudes about homosexuality and gay and lesbian peers. *Cognitive Development, 21,* 420–440.

Huebner, D. M., Rebchook, G. M., & Kegeles, S. M. (2004). Experiences of harassment, discrimination, and physical violence among young gay and bisexual men. *American Journal of Public Health, 94,* 1200–1203.

Human Rights Watch & Parents and Friends of Lesbians and Gays (n.d.). A straight guide to GLBT Americans. Retrieved April 12, 2007 from http://www.pflag.org/fileadmin/user_upload/Support/straightguideWEB.pdf

Kitzinger, C. (2005). "Speaking as a heterosexual": (How) does sexuality matter for talk-in-interaction? *Research on Language and Social Interaction, 38,* 221–265.

Leap, W. L. (1996). *Word's out: Gay men's English.* Minneapolis: University of Minnesota Press.

Levine, T. R. (2009). Deception. In Eadie, W. F. (Ed.), *21st century communication: A reference handbook* (pp. 471–478). Thousand Oaks, CA: Sage Publications.

McDermott, E. (2006). Surviving in dangerous places: Lesbian identity performances in the workplace, social class, and psychological health. *Feminism & Psychology, 16,* 193–211.

McNamara, M. (2004, April 25). When gay lost its outré. *Los Angeles Times.* Retrieved from http://www.latimes.com/features/lifestyle/la-ca-mcnamara25apr25,1,6298374.story

Meyer, M., Ed. (1994). *The politics and poetics of camp.* London: Routledge.

Monette, P. (1992). *Becoming a man: Half a life story.* New York: Harcourt Brace Jovanovich.

Morales, L. (2009, May 29). Knowing someone gay/lesbian affects views of gay issues. Retrieved from http://www.gallup.com/poll/118931/knowing-someone-gay-lesbian-affects-views-gay-issues.aspx

Morris, C. E., & Sloop, J. M. (2006). "What lips these lips have kissed": Refiguring the politics of queer public kissing. *Communication & Critical/Cultural Studies, 3,* 1–26.

Neville, T. (2007, April 6). Birds of a feather. *New York Times.* Retrieved from http://www.nytimes.com/2007/04/06/travel/escapes/06retire.html?ex=1334116800&en=5c1bf7a5b0bf7bbb&ei=5124&partner=permalink&exprod=permalink

Papoulias, C. (2006). Transgender. *Theory, Culture & Society*, *23*, 231–233.

Peplau, L. A., & Fingerhut, A.W. (2007). The close relationships of lesbians and gay men. *Annual Review of Psychology*, *58*, 405–424.

Rieger, G., Chivers, M., & Bailey, J. (2005). Sexual Arousal Patterns of Bisexual Men. *Psychological Science*, *16*, 579–584. doi: 10.1111/j.1467-9280.2005.01578.x.

Rieger, G., Linsenmeier, J. A. W., Gygax, L., Garcia, S., & Bailey, J. M. (2010). Dissecting "gaydar": Accuracy and the role of masculinity–femininity. *Archives of Sexual Behavior*, *39*, 124–140. doi: 10.1007/s10508-008-9405-2.

Roisman, G., Clausell, E., Holland, A., Fortuna, K., & Elieff, C. (2008). Adult romantic relationships as contexts of human development: A multimethod comparison of same-sex couples with opposite-sex dating, engaged, and married dyads. *Developmental Psychology*, *44*, 91–101. doi: 10.1037/0012-1649.44.1.91

Rust, P. (2002). Bisexuality: The state of the union. *Annual Review of Sex Research*, *13*, 180–240.

Rust, P. C. R. (2009). Bisexuality in a house of mirrors: Multiple reflections, multiple identities. In P. L. Hammack & B. J. Cohler (Eds.), *The story of sexual identity: Narrative perspectives on the gay and lesbian life course* (pp. 107–130). New York: Oxford University Press.

Schiappa, E., Gregg, P., & Hewes, D. (2006). Can one TV show make a difference? *Will & Grace* and the Parasocial Contact Hypothesis. *Journal of Homosexuality*, *51*, 15–38.

Slagle, R. (2006). Ferment in LGBT studies and queer theory: Personal ruminations on contested terrain. *Journal of Homosexuality*, *52*, 309–328.

Smyth, M. (2004, May). (Mis-)Shaping gay, lesbian, and bisexual representations in popular discourse: historical analyses. Paper presented to the International Communication Association, New Orleans.

Sontag, S. (1964, Autumn). On "Camp." *The Partisan Review*, *30*.

Storkey, E. (2001). *Origins of difference: The gender debate revisited*. Grand Rapids, MI: Baker Academic.

Streitmatter, R. (2009). *From 'perverts' to 'fab five': The media's changing depiction of gay men and lesbians*. New York: Routledge.

Tan, P. P. (2005). The importance of spirituality among gay and lesbian individuals. *Journal of Homosexuality*, *49*, 135–144.

Wade, N. (2007, April 10). Pas de deux of sexuality is written in the genes. *New York Times*. Retrieved from http://www.nytimes.com/2007/04/10/health/10gene. html?ex=1333857600&en=87d00a870b9db178& ei= 5124&partner=permalink&exprod=permalink

Whitney, E. (2006). Capitalizing on camp: Greed and the queer marketplace. *Text & Performance Quarterly*, *26*, 36–46.

Wolitski, R. J., Jones, K. T., Wasserman, J. L., & Smith, J. C. (2006). Self-identification as "Down Low" among men who have sex with men (MSM) from 12 US cities. *AIDS Behavior*, *10*, 519–529.

## Concepts and Questions

1. Why would some readers be eager to read Eadie's article while other would prefer to avoid it?

2. Does Eadie's personal history affect your attitudes toward the lesbian and gay culture? How?

3. How does revealing one's lesbian or gay sexuality become a political statement? What specific behaviors might be interpreted as a political statement?

4. How do media portrayals of lesbians and gays perpetuate stereotypes? And how do the media foster positive images toward gays and lesbians?

5. What are the six interactive stages through which non-heterosexual individuals pass as they develop their identity?

6. How does Eadie describe the process by which gays and lesbians deal with the tensions associated with being open about sexuality?

7. What is the role of "camp" in the lesbian and gay culture? How would you explain "camp"?

8. What does Eadie mean when he refers to being in a "safe" space when meeting other lesbian and gay people?

9. What are some of the unique gay communication patterns Eadie describes? How do these forms of communication serve the gay culture?

10. What are some of the "societal expectations" that men and women are expected to adhere to in the "straight" community?

11. What are some of the benefits that lesbians and gays would gain by legalized gay and lesbian relationships?

# 5 Intercultural Messages: Verbal and Nonverbal Communication

*Great things can best be said in silence.*            **Polish Proverb**

*You are as many a person as languages you know.*            **Armenian Proverb**

Our most distinguishing feature as a species is our ability to create symbols to represent reality. This rare gift has allowed humans to evolve and develop an extensive and highly complex language system. Part of this system allows you to receive, store, retrieve, manipulate, and generate symbols that stand for something else. By merely making certain sounds or marks on paper, hitting the keys on a keyboard, or producing movements of the body, you can relate to and interact with others. You can show them and tell them how you are feeling, what you are thinking, and what you want to know. At first blush, verbal and nonverbal language appear rather simple—you create an action (linguistic—saying "hello" or non-linguistic—smiling) and other people respond to what you have done. Yet, as you know from personal experience, accurately sharing your ideas and feelings is not a trouble-free affair. As we pointed out in Chapter 1, communication is a complex activity that is subject to a host of variables. The series of readings in this chapter seeks to explain some of those complexities—especially as they apply to the symbols you exchange in the intercultural setting.

This chapter contends that a culture's use of verbal and nonverbal symbols takes place on both a conscious and an unconscious level. It involves forms of reasoning, how discourse is performed, specialized linguistic devices such as analogies and idioms, the use of time and space, unique ways of moving, and behaviors that display emotions. Hence, understanding the verbal and nonverbal language of any culture implies viewing language from this larger perspective. This eclectic outlook toward verbal and nonverbal symbol sharing will help you recognize and appreciate the interaction patterns of cultures and co-cultures that are different from your own.

All of the selections in this chapter are predicated on two truisms: First, *verbal and nonverbal meanings are learned as part of a person's cultural affiliation*. Second, these meanings reside within the individual. For each culture, there is a very elaborate set of verbal and nonverbal symbols to which people within that culture have learned to attach meaning. Although we consider verbal and nonverbal forms of symbolic interaction separately for convenience, we hasten to point out they are interrelated. Both involve very elaborate symbol systems where writing, speaking, or some other action are used to express an idea or feeling

**This eclectic outlook toward verbal and nonverbal language will help you recognize and appreciate the interaction patterns of cultures and co-cultures that are different from your own.**

contained inside the person. They are also interrelated because nonverbal behavior usually accompanies verbal behavior. Verbal messages often rely on their nonverbal accompaniment for cues that aid the receiver in decoding the verbal symbols. Nonverbal behaviors not only function to amplify and clarify verbal messages but can also serve as forms of symbolic interaction without verbal counterparts.

When you communicate with other members of your own culture, you do so with relative ease. Your experiential backgrounds are similar enough that you share *approximately* the same meanings for most of the words and actions used in everyday living. Notice we used the word "approximately" in the last sentence. For, even within a culture, people often disagree about the meanings of many of the verbal and nonverbal symbols being employed. As words and actions move further from the reality of sensory data and become more abstract, there is far less agreement about appropriate meanings. In the use of words, for example, what do highly abstract words such as *worship, freedom, mental illness, "The Tea Party," equal opportunity, social equality, terrorism*, and *civil liberties* mean to you? Do they mean the same things to everyone? If you are in doubt, ask some friends; take a poll. You will find that people have dissimilar notions of these concepts and consequently attach distinctive meanings to these words. Their experiences have been different, and they hold different beliefs, attitudes, values, concepts, and expectations. Yet most, or perhaps all, of these people can be from the same culture. In nearly all instances, educational backgrounds, experiences, and concepts of the universe are somewhat uniform.

The same ambiguity that we just mentioned can be applied to nonverbal messages. You notice two people talking and one has a clenched fist. You need to decide if they are agreeing, are about to get into a fight, or are expressing exhilaration and enthusiasm over what just transpired. Even perceiving someone in tears can produce a variety of responses. Are these tears of joy or sorrow? Remember, in all of our examples to this point we refer to people from the *same* culture. When cultural diversity is introduced to the process of decoding words and actions, much larger discrepancies in meanings and usage are found. A very simple yet vivid example can be seen in the unadorned word *dog*. To Americans, the word usually represents a furry, friendly, domesticated pet—a pet that is often treated like a member of the family. Yet, in some Asian cultures the meaning is very different. The "pet" often ends up on the dinner plate instead of on the family couch. What is true of

> **Reflect for a moment about all the potential meanings for the word *Jihad*. Does it mean a holy war or a war within oneself (i.e., an internal struggle)?**

the often-ambiguous nature of words can also be seen in your nonverbal actions, particularly as when applied to culture. First, culture tends to determine the specific nonverbal behaviors that represent specific thoughts, feelings, or states of the communicator. Thus, what might be a sign of greeting in one culture might very well be an obscene gesture in another; or, what is considered a symbol of affirmation in one culture could be meaningless or even signify negation in another. Second, culture determines when it is appropriate to display or communicate various thoughts, feelings, or internal states; this is particularly evident in the display of emotions. Although there seems to be little cross-cultural difference in the nonverbal behaviors that express emotional states, there can be significant cultural differences in the specification of *which* emotions should be displayed, the degree to which they may be displayed, who may display them, and when or where they may be displayed. Think for a moment of all the different interpretations that can be attached to touch, gaze, attire, movement, space, and the like when you send and receive messages. Successful intercultural communication therefore requires that you recognize and understand culture's influence on both verbal and nonverbal interaction. It is the purpose of this chapter to assist you in that understanding. Reflect for a moment about all the potential meanings for the word *Jihad*. Does it mean a holy war or a war within oneself (i.e., an internal struggle)?

# The Nexus of Language, Communication, and Culture

MARY FONG

*The first essay in this chapter begins with an examination of a basic principle that we have already discussed— language and culture are inseparable. Mary Fong, in a selection titled "The Nexus of Language, Communication, and Culture," echoes that same fundamental proposition when she writes, "Language, communication, and culture are intricately intertwined with one another." The reason for her assertion is that the words you utilize reflect your feelings, attitudes, values, and view of the world—a view which, to a great extent, has been cultivated by your cultural experiences. To better explain her position concerning language, Fong turns to the Sapir–Whorf hypothesis. This is a hypothesis "which proposed linguistic relativity and was one of the first modern observations of the relationship between language and culture." After explaining the Sapir– Whorf hypothesis, Fong traces and describes current approaches to language and culture by examining three additional methodologies—the developmental, the interactional, and the psychological. Once this analysis is completed, Fong applies these three techniques to the Chinese language. Part of her discussion demonstrates the rich linguistic practices embedded in Chinese culture.*

T hroughout the centuries, scholars around the world have been interested in both oral and written languages and the role they serve in contributing to cultural societies. Confucius observed that proper human conduct maintains a civil society, and cautioned, "If language not be in accordance with the truth of things, affairs cannot be carried on to success." Saint-Exupery's comment that "to grasp the meaning of the world of today we use a language

> *The words you utilize reflect your feelings, attitudes, values, and view of the world—a view which, to a great extent, has been cultivated by your cultural experiences.*

created to express the world of yesterday," and the biblical injunction "may the words of my mouth and the meditation of my heart be acceptable in thy sight, oh Lord" also reflect this concern. In the current era, anthropologists, linguists, psychologists, philosophers, and communication scholars continue to try to fathom the role of language and communication in human activity and its nexus with culture.

In this essay, I first define language, communication, and culture. Then, I examine briefly some basic perspectives about the relationship between language, communication, and culture. In the course of this analysis, I begin with a description of the Sapir– Whorf hypothesis and then review the more current directions of language, communication, and culture research. Finally, in order to demonstrate some of the relationships between language, communication, and culture using qualitative methodologies, I draw from research on the Chinese culture to demonstrate the nexus of language, communication, and culture in examples from both cultural and intercultural interactions.

## INTERRELATIONSHIP OF LANGUAGE, COMMUNICATION, AND CULTURE

Language, communication, and culture are intricately intertwined with one another. Language is a symbolic system in which meaning is shared among people who identify with one another. Both verbal and nonverbal aspects of language exist. In the study of language and culture, the verbal aspect of both written and spoken communications has been the predominant focus of research.

---

Spoken language is a vehicle for people to communicate in social interaction by expressing their experience and creating experience. Words reflect the sender's attitude, beliefs, and points of view. Language expresses, symbolizes, and embodies cultural reality (Kramsch, 1998). Communication cannot exist without language, and language needs the process of communication to engage people in social interaction.

Both language and communication reflect culture. For Sherzer (1987), culture is the organization of individuals who share rules for production and interpretation of behavior. Language and communication represent an individual's symbolic organization of the world. Language is a medium that reflects and expresses an individual's group membership and relationships with others. Both written and oral languages are shaped by culture, and in turn, these languages shape culture. As Kramsch points out:

> Culture both liberates and constrains. It liberates by investing the randomness of nature with meaning, order, and rationality and by providing safeguards against chaos; it constrains by imposing a structure on nature and by limiting the range of possible meanings created by the individual. (1998, p. 10)

With this same tenor, language and communication both liberate and constrain. Language and communication enable people to express themselves, while simultaneously constraining them to conform to shared cultural standards. Culture is a social system in which members share common standards of communication, behaving, and evaluating in everyday life.

## PERSPECTIVES ON LANGUAGE AND CULTURE

A major assertion of linguistic relativity and one of the first modern observations of the relationship between language and culture is the Sapir–Whorf hypothesis. This notion proposes a deterministic view that language structure is necessary in order to produce thought. In other words, language and its categories—grammar, syntax, and vocabulary—are the only categories by which we can experience the world. Simply stated, language influences and shapes how people perceive their world, their culture. This vision dominated scholarly thinking as a point of discussion, research, and controversy for more than five decades.

The Sapir–Whorf hypothesis also holds that language and thought covary. That is, diversity in language categories and structure lead to cultural differences in thought and perceptions of the world. This position is known as *linguistic relativity*. Sapir (1951) believed that the "real world" is largely built on the unconscious language habits of the group. Benjamin Whorf was a student of Edward Sapir at Yale University from 1931 (Carroll, 1992). Initial publications of Whorf's (1956) views about language and culture were printed in a series of articles in 1940-1941. He writes:

> We cut nature up, organize it into concepts, and ascribe significances as we do, largely because we are parties to an agreement to organize it in this way—an agreement that holds throughout our speech community and is codified in the patterns of our language. (p. 213)

Sapir and Whorf's ideas have been understood to mean that people who speak different languages segment their world differently. Thus, any language such as Russian, Chinese, or German structures a "Russian," "Chinese," or "German" reality by framing and screening what these cultural members pay attention to. If there is a word for "it" in their language, then cultural members know that "it" exists, and if not, "it" is nonexistent to them.

For instance, when I was five years old, I remember my mother asked me to stick out my tongue so that she could look at it. She looked at it briefly and said in Chinese Cantonese, "*Ni yao yi hay,*" meaning "You have heat." My mother observed the texture, color, and coating of my tongue and lips. In the Chinese culture, it is common knowledge than an aspect of our physical health is viewed in terms of *yi hay* (heat) or *leung* (cool), which are extreme conditions that may be balanced through various types of foods

> *Language, communication, and culture are intricately intertwined with one another.*

and herbs. It is not the actual temperature of the food, but rather the *nature* of the food that produces a cool or warm effect on your body. If a person eats too many fried and baked foods and not enough cool foods such as particular fruits, vegetables, and liquids, then the person will eventually have a condition of too much heat in the body. If a person has a cool condition, one way to increase the heat in one's body is to lessen the consumption of cool foods and to increase one's diet of warm nature foods. This is one way that the Chinese strive to maintain a healthy physical balance.

*People will label an object, an idea, a process, and so forth based on the importance and utilization it has for them.*

This is an example of a "Chinese" reality of framing and screening what these cultural members pay attention to. On the other hand, the "American" reality promotes eating a well-balanced diet from the four main food groups: fruits and vegetables, meat and poultry, breads and grains, and dairy products. The American reality does not typically categorize food as warm or cold in nature in understanding and maintaining a balanced diet to increase one's health.

The system of labeling food, drink, medicines, herbs, illnesses, and medical procedures as either cold or hot is based on a system originating with the ancient Greeks and spreading to Central Asia (Dresser, 1996). For instance, as perceived in many Asian cultures, after a major surgery or childbirth, the body loses blood, energy, and heat. Therefore, the heat must be replenished, and avoidance of drinking cold water, eating cool foods, or taking showers is recommended. Middle Eastern and Latin American peoples also have a system of classifying foods, medicines, and procedures, but all cultural groups may differ in varying degrees depending on their principles (Dresser, 1996).

The situation of my mother observing my physical condition and the examples of foods, medicines, and procedures provide instances of how people in various cultures segment their world and reality in varying ways. Furthermore, this natural cultural process of thinking and perceiving influences how members may communicate by accepting or rejecting particular foods, medicines, and procedures in certain circumstances. A person who is not familiar with another person's cultural ways will be likely to misinterpret the person's actions.

Another scholar, Brown (1958), in part disagreed with the Sapir–Whorf hypothesis and argued that a person's worldview is not determined by language. He held, rather, that people categorize their world by attaching labels to what is out there. People use language to do what they need it to do. According to Brown, people will label an object, an idea, a process, and so forth based on the importance and utilization it has for them. For example, CDs, DVDs, cell phones, and the Internet are relatively new inventions that need labeling through language so that people can communicate their ideas about them. Because antiquated technology such as a record player, a rotary phone, or a slide rule is no longer important or used by people, the once-common labels for these objects are now archived in museums and hardly referred to in conversation. Brown's position, however, supports the idea of linguistic relativity because the perceptual categories that are frequently used receive labels, whereas unused or insignificant categories may not be labeled.

Several research studies on color terms and color perception tested the Sapir–Whorf hypothesis (Berlin & Kay, 1967; Bruner, Oliver, & Greenfield, 1966; Greenfield & Bruner, 1966; Kay & Kempton, 1984). Eastman (1990) reviewed these studies that supported the idea of linguistic relativity and stated, "It appears to be the case that world view is a matter more of linguistic relativity than linguistic determinism" (p. 109).

Other researchers have found it difficult to test how strongly the structure of a language influences the worldview of people because reliable methods for assessing the worldview of a person independently of the language he or she speaks are needed (Brown, 1976; Carroll, 1967; Kay & Kempton, 1984). The deterministic view of the Sapir–Whorf hypothesis is not taken seriously (Kramsch, 1998). Carroll (1992) believes that researchers and theorists generally regard the Sapir–Whorf hypothesis as either unconfirmable or incorrect because the evidence offered in its support is viewed as being flawed. He further contends that if the hypothesis can be sustained, it would only suggest a weak influence of language structure on thought.

The linguistic-relativity focus of the Sapir–Whorf hypothesis has been important because it does contribute to an understanding of the relationship between language and culture. Thus, when two speakers come from other cultures, Sapir–Whorf suggests they are operating under different language and communication systems that influence their perceptions and interpretation of an event. As Kramsch (1998) suggests, speakers from different cultures define reality or categorize experience in different ways. Achieving understanding across languages is dependent on common conceptual systems rather than on structural equivalences. They may differ in terms of the meaning and value of a concept.

## CURRENT RESEARCH TRENDS AND DIRECTIONS

In 1974, Hymes described the development of linguistic research in the first half of the 20th century, which was distinguished by a drive for the autonomy of language as an object of study and a focus on description of [grammatical] structure, and in the second half of the century, which was distinguished by a concern for the integration of language in sociocultural context and a focus on the analysis of function (p. 208).

Hymes's description was accurate because the second half of the 20th century was marked by several research methods, such as discourse analysis, pragmatics, ethnography of communication, rhetorical analysis, and quantitative analysis, as ways to investigate the linkages among language, communication, and culture. Examples of themes of interest to researchers are the relationship between language and context, the relationship between language and identities (i.e., personal identity, social role identity, and cultural ethnolinguistic identity), and multiple functions and meanings of language and communication in relationship to culture (Ting-Toomey, 1989).

Current approaches to the study of language, communication, and culture are developmental, interactional, and social psychological. The *developmental* approach focuses on language acquisition and cultural communication practices simultaneously in the language development stages of a child. Developmental theorists are interested in understanding the connection between language and cognitive processing in a culture (Ting-Toomey, 1989). The *interactional* approach investigates what people are doing with speech as they interact face to face in a particular interactional context. Interactional theorists are interested in identifying appropriate communication styles and norms in various cultures (Ting-Toomey, 1989). The *social psychological* approach explores the underlying factors that influence language choices in multilingual communication contexts. For example, group comparison factors, identity salience factors, and attitudinal and motivational factors have significant association to the language accommodations process in intergroup communication situations. Social psychological theorists are interested in delineating specific social psychological conditions that account for first-language or second-language usage in majority and minority groups in cultural communities globally (Ting-Toomey, 1989).

For some researchers, the controversy over whether language determines or reflects thought or thought determines or reflects language is not the primary concern. According to Sherzer (1987), what is at issue is the analysis of discourse as the "embodiment of the essence of culture and as constitutive of what language and culture relationship is all about." Sherzer (1987) also views discourse as the intersection where language and culture interrelate: "It is discourse that creates, recreates, focuses, modifies, and transmits both culture and language and their intersection" (p. 295).

For Sherzer (1987), culture is the organization of individuals who share rules for production and interpretation of behavior. Language represents an individual's symbolic organization of the world. Language is a medium that reflects and expresses an individual's group membership and relationships with others. Discourse analysis derives from pragmatics and speech act theory (Saville-Troike, 1989). *Pragmatics* or *speech act theory* refers to the study of the connotative (inner) and denotative (outer) meanings of "expressions when used in a conversation or a written work" (Paul, 1987, p. 101). According to Silverstein (1976), pragmatics is "the study of the meaning of linguistic signs relative to their communicative functions" (p. 20). Pragmatics also entails cultural members applying their knowledge of the world to the interpretation of what is said and done in interaction (Fromkin & Rodman, 1983; Gumperz, 1982).

The ethnography of communication provides the researcher with a framework of observation and interviewing techniques to facilitate capturing the interlocutors' meanings in various communicative acts both culturally and interculturally. The ethnographer endeavors to describe the communicative choices that interlocutors make. This involves describing and accounting for the interpretive systems and practices through which members construct actions and deal with behaviors.

Hymes (1962), the originator of the ethnography of communication, states that the "study of speech as a factor in cognitive and expressive behavior leads to concern with the ethnographic patterning of the uses of speech in a community" (p. 102). Investigating language, communication, and culture is discovering not only linguistic structural regularities, but also regularities of usage that have motives, emotions, desires, knowledge, attitudes, and values attached to them. An essential aim of studies on language, communication, and culture using the ethnography of communication approach is to make implicit cultural beliefs, attitudes, values, norms of interpretation, rules of speaking, norms of interaction, and so forth explicit in order to understand and to practice communication competence within a particular culture, and eventually in intercultural interactions.

## LANGUAGE STUDIES

Some of the sample findings in the cultural and intercultural studies that follow are illustrations of language and culture analysis. The qualitative methods—discourse analysis, pragmatics, and ethnography of communication—jointly provide tools and perspectives to make possible an in-depth examination of the communicative phenomena.

## A Cultural Study

An ethnographic study of the Chinese New Year celebration in Hong Kong (Fong, 2000) provides one instance of the manner in which the Chinese employ

language to reverse bad luck. By examining a speaking pattern that is used when someone makes a negative comment during the Chinese New Year, it is possible to understand how Chinese people are prepared to avoid arguments and negative talk during the Chinese New Year. It is also possible to understand how Chinese are prepared to handle a rule violation committed.

Chinese people engage in positive talk and try to avoid arguments and negative talk during the Chinese New Year. Spoken words are carefully watched to avoid saying words that signify death, sickness, poverty, or anything else unlucky. All of the participants in this cultural study agreed with the same ideas as the following participant, who explains why negative comments during the New Year celebrations are avoided:

> Of course you don't say unlucky things. Always be positive. Chinese New Year is supposed to be a happy occasion. Try not to say something unlucky, like mentioning death or misfortune. Say it after the New Year. Perhaps some people may even think that saying those things during Chinese New Year will bring bad luck in the coming year. Those things may happen.

If someone accidentally talks about something unfortunate or utters a negative comment during this holiday, the rule of positive speaking is violated in this context. The hearer of the message may say:

/tou³ hæu² sæy² dzɔi³ gɔŋ² gwə³/*
("Spit out your saliva; speak once more.")

Another expression that participants in the study reported is:

/tsɔi¹/ or /tsɔu¹, dai⁶ gæt⁷ lei⁶ si⁶/
("lucky" or "very lucky, auspicious")

These expressions are said in order to reverse the bad luck that has been invited into good luck.

To understand what linguistic devices the Chinese employ, it is necessary to understand a few rules of behavior and speaking. Shimanoff (1980) proposes an "If ... then ..." method of concisely stating a rule of behavior. To develop Shimanoff's method of stating behavioral rules, I will add a "because ... meaning ..." sequence in order to add a meaning component to a formulation of a communication rule.

In this situation, the sequential rule statement begins with the initial linguistic "If ..." slot that provides information on the particular context, condition, or situation, such as a speech event, speech act, or genre. It is followed by the "then ..." slot, which refers to the speaking and/or behavioral interaction pattern discovered from the researcher's ethnographic data analysis.

The third linguistic device, the "because ..." slot, provides a concise rationale for why people of a particular culture behave the way they do. Here, an underlying belief, value system, or cultural principle may be revealed to provide an explanation for a people's way of communicating. The final linguistic device, the "meaning ..." slot, serves the same function as Hymes's component norm of interpretation of a symbol, the speaking and/or behavioral interaction pattern, a particular speech act, speech event, scene, and so forth.

These sequential rules statement provide the following formula:

*If* ... (context, condition, or situation, such as a speech event, speech act, or genre),

*then* ... (speaking and/or interaction pattern),

*because* ... (belief, value system, or cultural principle),

*meaning* ... (norm of interpretation of a symbol, speaking pattern, interaction pattern, a particular speech act, speech event, scent, etc.).

Applying these sequential rules to the Chinese custom of reversing the negative comments can be expressed in a concise rule statement using the following formula:

*If* a person makes a negative comment on Chinese New Year Day,

*then* a Hong Kong Chinese person who hears it should say:

/tsɔi¹/ or /tsɔi¹, dai⁶ gæt⁷ lei⁶ si⁶/

("lucky" or "very lucky, auspicious")

/tou³ hæu² sæy² dzɔi³ gŋ² gwɔ³/

("Spit out your saliva; speak once more.")

*because* this is believed to counteract the bad luck and create good luck,

*meaning* that the negative comments will not come true in the coming new year.

## An Intercultural Study

An intercultural study on compliment interactions between Chinese immigrants and European Americans from the perspective of Chinese immigrants (Fong, 1998) found that the two cultural groups have differing ways of speaking in compliment interactions (Chen, 1993; Chiang & Pochtrager, 1993; Fong, 1998). European Americans on the West Coast and in the Midwest generally accept a compliment (Chen, 1993; Chiang & Pochtrager, 1993; Fong, 1998).

On the other hand, the literature reports that Chinese have the tendency to deny compliments in order to give an impression of modesty (Chen, 1993; Chiang & Pochtrager, 1993; Gao, 1984; Zhang, 1988). In one study (Fong, 1998), an informant from Mainland China explained the primary difference and the internal similarity between two cultural groups:

> On the surface I say "no, no, no." ... But inside I accept it. I feel really excited. In western culture, they say "yes" means accept the compliment. But in China, people say "no," but really, really accept the compliment. Different [speaking] way, but the feeling is the same. (p. 257)

Four adaptations by Chinese immigrant participants (CIPs) to European American compliments were found. An orientation is a state or condition that is changeable from one interaction to another depending on one's adaptation to intercultural communication differences. Four orientations in which the CIP can be located are (1) intercultural shock state, (2) intercultural resistance state, (3) intercultural accommodation state, and (4) bicultural competence state. For the purpose of this essay, we will capture a glimpse of one of the orientations, the intercultural shock state, in order to have a sense of Chinese immigrants' thinking and speaking patterns.

Affectively, CIPs reported feeling uncomfortable, unnatural, uneasy, nervous, stressed, embarrassed, surprised, shocked, or afraid when a European American complimented them. The situational outcome of the intercultural compliment interaction for CIPs, however, was an appreciation in receiving praise because they felt accepted, liked, and welcomed by European Americans. CIPs reported that compliments helped them reduce some of their stress as a newcomer to the United States.

Cognitively, CIPs in the intercultural shock state have minimum knowledge of the intercultural communication differences in compliment interactions with European Americans. Before coming to the United States, CIPs reported that they were not familiar with the European Americans' generosity in giving (1) compliments, (2) compliments containing strong positive adjectives, (3) compliments intended to encourage a person after an unsatisfactory performance, and (4) compliments on a wide variety of topics, and they were unfamiliar with (5) accepting compliments and (6) face-to-face compliments in all types of relationships.

Behaviorally, five speaking patterns were found; two examples are provided here. One type of compliment response that Chinese immigrants used was the Direct Denial + Verbal Corrective/Prescriptive response. Following is a reported intercultural compliment interaction:

(AMERICAN) BOYFRIEND: You're the most beautiful person that I've seen.

(HONG KONG) GIRLFRIEND: Oh gaaa. Oohh. Please don't say that.

Because Chinese immigrants value indirectness and modesty, the compliment was interpreted as being direct (e.g., face-to-face, expressing openly with positive adjectives on the complimentee's appearance), which is contrary to the reported Chinese way of compliment interactions. The response was made to avoid self-praise and to suggest to the complimenter not to make such a direct compliment.

CIPs who were in the intercultural shock state were also found to use the silence response. The following intercultural compliment interaction is reported to have occurred at work:

(AMERICAN FEMALE) BOSS: I want to thank you for doing a wonderful job. You're very, very nice.

(CHINESE FEMALE) WORKER: [silence]

Chinese immigrant interlocutors value modesty highly, but they are also aware of one of the American values of directly accepting and appreciating compliments. The compliment was interpreted as direct (i.e., face-to-face, expressing openly their positive thoughts with positive adjectives), which is contrary to the reported Chinese way of compliment interactions. The response was made because Chinese immigrant recipients reported that they felt ambivalent about which cultural response to use; thus the Chinese immigrant recipient remained silent.

## CONCLUSION

The excerpt from the cultural study (Fong, 2000) illustrates the Chinese way of thinking and speaking. When a negative comment is made during the Chinese New Year holiday, the Chinese way of thinking is to interpret the incident as forthcoming bad luck in the coming new year. Through speech, however, the perceived bad luck is reversed to good luck.

The intercultural compliment interaction study (Fong, 1994) sheds light on the way Chinese immigrants in the intercultural shock state reveal patterns of thinking and speaking. The denial response is a pattern of speaking that is commonly used in the intercultural shock state. CIPs in this orientation essentially perceive European Americans as being generous in giving compliments with relatively strong positive adjectives, and in accepting compliments.

Current ethnographic methods hold that the best way to capture a view of language, communication, and culture is to observe the communicative phenomenon in a naturalistic setting and to have the speakers identify and classify the interaction or event as being culturally significant. The crossroads of language, communication, and culture is found in the culturally shared meaning of ideas and behaviors that are voiced as symbolic utterances, expressions, dialogue, and conversations in such various contexts as interpersonal and group interactions, research interviews, and public speaking forums.

In the two qualitative studies described in this essay, the ways of speaking and thinking were the two primary interrelated foci that reveal and reflect the outer and inner shared substances of communications that primarily make up a speech community. To examine a speech community's patterns of speaking without also discovering the norms of interpretation or the shared sociocultural knowledge of that community's members is to silence their cultural humanness as a speech community. To study only the shared sociocultural knowledge of a cultural group and not attend to how it is relevant to their way of speaking is to lose an opportunity to understand more about different cultural communication styles. In accomplishing this goal, potential sources at borderlines and intersections of cultural differences are able to richly understand and resolve intercultural conflicts.

Both examples of findings from the mentioned qualitative studies illuminate, in part, what Hymes (1974) has suggested:

> It has often been said that language is an index to or reflection of culture. But language is not simply passive or automatic in its relation to culture … Speaking is itself a form of cultural behavior, and language, like any other part of culture, partly shapes the whole; and its expression of the rest of culture is partial, selective. That selective relation, indeed, is what should be interesting to us. Why do some features of a community's life come to be named—overtly expressible in discourse— while others are not? (p. 127)

## Note

*The International Phonetic System was used in transcribing this and other Chinese dialogue.

## References

Berlin, B., & Kay, P. (1967). *Universality and evolution of basic color terms*. Working Paper #1, Laboratory for Language Behavior Research, University of California, Berkeley.

Brown, R. (1958). *Words and things*. New York: Free Press.

Brown, R. (1976). In Memorial Tribute to Eric Lennenberg. *Cognition, 4*, 125–153.

Bruner, J., Oliver, R. R., & Greenfield, P. M. (1966). *Studies in cognitive growth*. New York: Wiley.

Carroll, J. B. (1967). Bibliography of the Southwest Project in Comparative Psycholinguistics. In D. Hymes (Ed.), *Studies in southwestern ethnolinguistics* (pp. 452–454). The Hague: Mouton.

Carroll, J. B. (1992). Anthropological linguistics: An overview. In W. Bright (Ed.), *International encyclopedia of linguistics*. New York: Oxford University Press.

Chen, R. (1993). Responding to compliments: A contrastive study of politeness strategies between American English and Chinese speakers. *Journal of Pragmatics, 20*, 49–75.

Chiang, F., & Pochtrager, B. (1993). A pilot study of compliment responses of American-born English speakers and Chinese-born English speakers. (Available in Microfiche only, ED 356649)

Dresser, N. (1996). *Multicultural manners*. New York: Wiley.

Eastman, C. M. (1990). *Aspects of language and culture* (2nd ed.). Novato, CA: Chandler & Sharp.

Fong, M. (1994). Patterns of occurrence of compliment response types. In *Chinese immigrants' interpretations of their intercultural compliment interactions with European-Americans*. Unpublished doctoral dissertation, University of Washington, Seattle.

Fong, M. (1998). Chinese immigrants' perceptions of semantic dimensions of direct/indirect communication in intercultural compliment interactions with North Americans. *Howard Journal of Communications, 9*(3), 245–262.

Fong, M. (2000). "Luck talk" in celebrating the Chinese New Year. *Journal of Pragmatics, 32*, 219–237.

Fromkin, V., & Rodman, R. (1983). *An introduction to language* (3rd ed.). New York: CBS Publishing and Holt, Rinehart, & Winston.

Gao, W. (1984). Compliment and its reaction in Chinese and English cultures. *Working papers in discourse in English and Chinese* (pp. 32–37). Canberra, Australia: Canberra College of Advanced Education.

Greenfield, P. M., & Bruner, J. S. (1966). Culture and cognitive growth. *International Journal of Psychology, 1,* 89–107.

Gumperz, J. J. (1982). *Discourse strategies.* New York: Cambridge University Press.

Hymes, D. (1962). The ethnography of speaking. In T. Gladwin & W. Sturtevant (Eds.), *Anthropology and human behavior* (pp. 99–137). Washington, DC: Anthropological Society of Washington.

Hymes, D. (1964). Toward ethnographies of communication: The analysis of communicative events. *American Anthropologist, 66,* 21–41.

Hymes, D. (1974). *Foundations in sociolinguistics: An ethnographic approach.* Philadelphia: University of Pennsylvania Press.

Kay, P., & Kempton, W. (1984). What is the Sapir–Whorf Hypothesis? *American Anthropologist, 86,* 65–79.

Kramsch, C. (1998). *Language and culture.* London: Oxford University Press.

Paul, A. (1987, July 15). Review of Joseph H. Greenberg, *Language in the Americas. Chronicle of Higher Education,* 6.

Sapir, E. (1951). The status of linguistics as a science. In D. Mandelbaum (Ed.), *Selected writings.* Berkeley: University of California Press, 160–166.

Saville-Troike, M. (1989). *The ethnography of communication* (2nd ed.). New York: Basil Blackwell.

Sherzer, J. (1987). A discourse-centered approach to language and culture. *American Anthropologist, 89,* 295–309.

Shimanoff, S. B. (1980). *Communication rules: Theory and research.* Beverly Hills, CA: Sage.

Silverstein, M. (1976). Shifters, linguistics categories, and cultural description. In K. H. Basso & H. A. Selby (Eds.), *Meaning in anthropology* (pp. 11–56). Albuquerque: University of New Mexico Press.

Ting-Toomey, S. (1989). Language, communication, and culture. In S. Ting-Toomey & F. Korzenny (Eds.), *Language, communication, and culture* (pp. 9–15). Newbury Park, CA: Sage.

Whorf, B. L. (1956). *Language, thought, and reality: Selected writings of Benjamin Lee Whorf* (J. B. Carroll, Ed.). Cambridge, MA: MIT Press. (Original work published 1940)

Zhang, Z. (1988). A discussion of communicative culture. *Journal of Chinese Language Teacher Association, 23,* 107–112.

## Concepts and Questions

1. What does Fong mean when she writes, "Language and thought vary with one other"? Do you agree?

2. Can you think of some specific examples that illustrate the link between culture and language?

3. How would you explain Fong's assertion that language influences and shapes how people perceive their world?

4. What is meant by the following phrase: "People who speak different languages segment their world differently"?

5. How do Chinese immigrants and Euro-Americans differ in their ways of interaction regarding compliments?

6. When referring to anthropologist Sherzer, what does Fong mean when she writes, "Culture is the organization of individuals who share rules for production and interpretation of behavior"?

7. How do the Chinese use language to reverse bad luck?

8. In what ways do Chinese and Euro-Americans express themselves differently?

# Dialogue, Argument, and Cultural Communication Codes between Israeli-Jews and Palestinians

DONALD G. ELLIS • IFAT MAOZ

*Clashes, both verbal and physical, in the Middle East between Israeli Jews and Palestinians have a lengthy, sad, and bloody history. Antecedents of today's conflicts extend over thousands of years. Traditional discord notwithstanding, there might be ways in which the negative stereotypes, mutual distrust, and severe miscommunication that highlight today's relationships, could be managed through an understanding of what Donald G. Ellis and Ifat Maoz call "transformative dialogues." In their essay titled "Dialogue, Argument, and Cultural Communication Codes between Israeli-Jews and Palestinians," the authors posit that the Israeli-Jewish and Arabic cultures, because of the special circumstances of their histories, have developed unique speech codes that reflect their nearly polar-opposite cultural differences. Ellis and Maoz suggest that the Arabic language employs speech codes that seek to "accommodate" or "go along with," which orients speakers toward harmonious relationships. On the other hand, they assert that the Israeli-Jewish speech code is direct, pragmatic, assertive, explicit, and clear. These speech code differences are essentially the opposites of one another and, according to Ellis and Maoz, are partially responsible for the failure of dialogue to resolve the conflict between the two cultures. The authors believe that by studying these speech codes you can gain some insight into the linguistic bases of cultural conflict and be better prepared to help mediate that conflict.*

## INTRODUCTION

The conflict between Palestinians and Israeli-Jews fills newspapers and television programs with images of violence and conflict. The origins of the conflict between Israeli-Jews and Palestinian-Arabs can be traced to the end of the nineteenth century with the appearance of political Zionism and the resulting waves of Jewish immigration to Palestine. Zionism sought to establish a Jewish state in Palestine. However, on the same land lived Arabs with a Palestinian national identity. This resulted in a clash between the Jewish and Palestinian communities over the ownership of the land, the right for self-determination, and statehood. Violence between the two communities first erupted in the 1920s, and has pervaded the relationship in various forms and with varying degrees of intensity ever since (Kelman, 1997; Rouhana & Bar-Tal, 1998).

The communal clash that characterized the first decades of the twentieth century escalated into a war that involved the neighboring Arab states. This war erupted after the United Nations (UN) declared in November 1947 the partition of Palestine into two states—one Arab and one Jewish. The Palestinians rejected the UN partition plan and an independent Jewish state was established in 1948. Israel won the war, and the vast majority of Palestinians who lived in the portion of Palestine on which Israel was now established were dispersed to the neighboring Arab countries, partly having fled war zones and partly having been expelled by Israeli forces (Maoz, 1999).

Other historical turning points in the relationship between Israelis and Palestinians include the 1967 war between Israel on one side, and Egypt, Jordan, and Syria on the other, which brought the remainder of Palestine under Israeli control. The first intifada (1987–1993) was an uprising of the Palestinians in the West Bank and Gaza Strip territories, expressing resistance to the Israeli occupation of these lands. (Rouhana & Bar-Tal, 1998).

The original version of this essay first appeared in the 10th edition. This updated version appears here in print for the first time. All rights reserved. Permission to reprint must be obtained from the authors and the publisher. Dr. Donald G. Ellis teaches in the School of Communication at the University of Hartford, West Hartford, Connecticut. Dr. Ifat Maoz teaches in the Department of Communication at The Hebrew University, Mt. Scopus Campus, Jerusalem, Israel.

In 1993, peace accords were signed in Oslo, Norway, and this signaled a breakthrough in the relations between Israelis and Palestinians. This dramatic agreement included an exchange of letters of mutual recognition between representatives of the two peoples, which was followed by a declaration of principles that stipulated the establishment of a Palestinian authority in Gaza and Jericho as a first step in Palestinian self-rule (Kelman, 1997). At this time—which was indeed historic—prospects for the success of the peace process seemed exceptionally good. There was hope that the peace accords would end violence and lead to reconciliation. However, a few years after signing the accords it became clear that this optimism was premature. A chain of violent incidents began in November 1995 with the assassination of the then–Israeli prime minister and continued with a number of terrorist attacks in the first half of 1996. These events signaled a slowdown in the Israeli-Palestinian peace process. Increasingly, the adversaries presented obstacles and impediments to the peace process, posed problems for the implementation of the different stages of the agreements, and violated the agreements. In October 2000 the al-Aqsa intifada broke out and the relationship between the Israelis and the Palestinians again took a violent turn.

> The political and cultural differences between Israeli-Jews and Palestinians involve negative stereotypes, mutual delegitimization, and severe miscommunication.

Yet, political leaders from both sides continue to try to return to peace making and peace building. Although the conflict centers on the issue of land, and who has legitimate rights to the land, an issue that has strong historical, religious, and emotional significance, it is also a cultural conflict, a conflict over identities and recognition. The political and cultural differences between Israeli-Jews and Palestinians involve negative stereotypes, mutual delegitimization, and severe miscommunication. Dialogue and group encounters are one way to cope with these difficult problems. Dialogue sessions between Israeli-Jews and Palestinians involve

a process of transformative communication aimed at improving the relations between the sides (Maoz, 2000a).

## TRANSFORMATIVE COMMUNICATION BETWEEN GROUPS IN CONFLICT

Intergroup dialogues are useful venues for growth, change, and conflict management. Transformative dialogue between cultural groups in conflict helps reduce prejudice and hostility and foster mutual understanding (Gergen, 1999). Such dialogue experiences have been successful at helping groups cope with conflict in Northern Ireland, South Africa, and the Middle East (Ellis, 2006).

The notion of transformative contact or dialogue, when used in the context of intergroup conflict, draws heavily from the contact hypothesis in social psychology. This theory was first presented by Allport (1954) and has been the subject of numerous studies since then (Amir, 1976; Pettigrew, 1998). The contact hypothesis states that under certain conditions contact between groups in conflict reduces prejudice and changes negative intergroup attitudes. The contact hypothesis is optimal under certain conditions. First, the two groups should be of equal status, at least within the contact situation. Contacts of unequal status, where the traditional status imbalance is maintained, can act to perpetuate existing negative stereotypes. Second, successful contact should involve personal and sustained communication between individuals from the two groups. Third, effective contact requires cooperative interdependence, where members of the two groups engage in cooperative activities and depend on one another in order to achieve mutual goals. The fourth condition of the contact hypothesis states that social norms favoring equality must be the consensus among the relevant authorities.

> The contact hypothesis states that under certain conditions contact between groups in conflict reduces prejudice and changes negative intergroup attitudes.

## TRANSFORMATIVE DIALOGUES BETWEEN ISRAELIS AND PALESTINIANS

The first attempts to address the dispute between Israelis and Palestinians by means of structured communication events were in interactive problem-solving workshops developed by Herbert Kelman from Harvard University in the early 1970s and have been conducted since then by him and his colleagues (Kelman, 1997). These workshops brought together politically active and influential Israelis and Palestinians for private direct communication facilitated by unofficial third-party mediators (Kelman, 1995, 1997). Since the Oslo peace agreements in 1993, numerous Israeli-Palestinian dialogue events are conducted each year that are targeted at grassroots populations from both sides (Adwan & Bar-On, 2000). These dialogue events typically last two to three days and are aimed at building peace and reconciliation through processes of constructive communication (Maoz, 2000b). The dialogues are facilitated by both Israelis and Palestinians. In some sessions all of the participants meet, and in others they are divided into smaller groups. There are also several uninational meetings where participants meet only with members of their own group. Dialogues are conducted either in English, or in Hebrew and Arabic that is translated.

The concept of "dialogue" as discussed by scholars such as Martin Buber, Carl Rogers, and Mikhail Bakhtin is the general guiding principle of these groups. That is, the goal of the communication is to avoid "monologue," or the pressure of a single authoritative voice, and strive instead for "dialogue," which emphasizes the interplay of different perspectives where something new and unique emerges. At its best, dialogue is a search for deep differences and shared concerns. It asks participants to inquire genuinely about the other person and avoid premature judgment, debate, and questions designed to expose flaws.

The process of change and transformation during dialogue is difficult, complex, and slow. There are many issues that enter the mix of politics, psychology, culture, and communication. In our work we have found that the communication process remains central. There is simply no possibility for reconciliation and peace without sustained interaction. For this reason we direct our attention to the issues in culture and communication that characterize these groups. The remainder of this essay is devoted to explaining the cultural communication codes that typify interactions between Israeli-Jews and Palestinians, and an explanation of how these speech codes are expressed in actual dialogues when Israeli-Jews and Palestinians are arguing.

## SPEECH CODES

Whenever a group of people live in a culture they have certain characteristics and behaviors in common. We know, for example, that people in cultures dress similarly, share tastes in food preparation, and have many common attitudes. But they also share orientations toward communication. Members of cultural communities share principles of language use and interpretation. This simply means that your use of language (word choice, slang, accents, syntax) and your tendencies to interpret and understand this language in a certain way are dependent on your cultural membership. For example, assume you overheard the conversation below (Ellis, 1992).

> *Your use of language (word choice, slang, accents, syntax) and your tendencies to interpret and understand this language in a certain way are dependent on your cultural membership.*

**JESSE**: Yea, I'm thinkin' bout getting some new ink.

**GENE**: Really, where you gonna put it?

**JESSE**: Oh, I don' know. I've still got some clean spots.

For the moment, this conversation is probably pretty confusing and odd. What does it mean to "get new ink?" Why is Gene concerned about where to put it? What do "clean spots" refer to? Who are these people and what cultural functions is this conversation serving? Is Jesse thinking about buying a new bottle of ink for his fountain pen and Gene does not think there will be room for it on his messy desk?

This is a conversation between two tattoo enthusiasts who live and work among others in a tattoo culture that has developed norms of speaking. If you were a member of the culture and understood the "speech code," then you could participate in this conversation easily and competently. You would know that "new ink" refers to a "new tattoo" and that "clean spots" were places on the body that had no tattoos. You would understand the personal identity satisfaction that members of this culture gain from their unique code of communication.

Jesse and Gene are speaking in a cultural code, and you can only understand and participate in the conversation if you understand the code. The concept of speech codes has been studied by Bernstein (1971), Ellis (1992, 1994), and Philipsen (1997). Philipsen's treatment is most thorough in communication and it is the perspective we rely on here. But first we describe two cultural communication codes termed *dugri* and *musayra* known to characterize Israeli-Jews and Arabs, respectively. This will be followed by an elaboration of the concept of speech codes and an explanation of their role in intercultural communication dialogues for peace.

Israeli-Jewish and Arab cultures have emerged from the special circumstances of their history, and different norms of communication emerge from this history. These contrasting speech codes can make for difficult and uncoordinated communication. Several researchers have described an Arab communication code called *musayra* (e.g., Feghali, 1997; Katriel, 1986). *Musayra* means "to accommodate" or "go along with." It is a way of communicating that orients the speaker toward a harmonious relationship with the other person. *Musayra* emerges from the core values of Arab culture, which have to do with honor, hospitality, and collectivism. An Arab speaker who is engaging in the code of *musayra* is being polite, indirect, courteous, and non-confrontive to the other member of a conversation.

More specifically, *musayra* is composed of four communication features. The first is **repetition**, in which the communication is characterized by repetitive statements that are formulaic in nature. Repetition is used primarily for complimenting and praising others, which is an important communication activity when you are trying to be gracious and accommodating. Repetition is also used as an argumentative style

where repeated phrases are used to influence beliefs rather than Western-style logic. **Indirectness** is a second feature of the *musayra* code. This is a communication strategy that reflects the cultural tendency to be interpersonally cautious and responsive to context. By being indirect, one can shift positions easier to accommodate the other person. Indirectness also facilitates politeness and face saving. **Elaboration** is a third feature and it pertains to an expressive and encompassing style. It leads to a deeper connection between speakers and affirms relationships. The final characteristic is **affectiveness**, or an intuitive and emotional style. Again, this allows for identification with the other person and the maintenance of an engaged relationship.

The speech code of Israeli-Jews is a sharp contrast to *musayra*. The Israeli-Jews employ a direct, pragmatic, and assertive style. This style has been termed *dugri* by Katriel (1986). *Dugri* means "straight talk" and is a well-documented code used by Israeli-Jews. *Dugri* is the opposite of *musayra*. It is direct, explicit, and clear. *Dugri* speech is "to the point" with the communication of understanding and information as the most important communicative goals. Emotional appeals and personal niceties are of secondary importance. In *musayra* it is important to maintain the face or positive image of the other speaker. In *dugri* speech the speaker is more concerned with maintaining his or her own image of clarity and directness.

*Dugri* and *musayra* are excellent examples of speech codes. Philipsen (1997) describes five main ideas that characterize cultural speech codes. We can see how these are powerfully ingrained in the communication of cultural members and are often responsible for misunderstanding and problems in intercultural communication. We further elaborate on *dugri* and *musayra* by explaining them within the context of the five principles of speech codes.

## Speech Codes Are Culturally Distinctive

Speech codes are identified with a specific people in a specific place. When you first listen to someone speak you often ask or wonder, "where are they from?" Language is always identified with locations such as countries (e.g., American English, British

English, or Australian English), regions (e.g., the South or the East), or neighborhoods. Israeli *dugri* speech is associated with native-born Israelis of Jewish heritage in the land of Israel. The code is unique to Jews primarily of European heritage, and became crystallized in the pre-state period of the 1930s and 1940s (Katriel, 1986). *Musayra* is culturally distinct for speakers of Arabic and members of Arabic cultures. However, its geographic location is more complex than *dugri* because Arabic cultures are more geographically diverse. In both cases, however, when speakers of a code change geographical locations they modify their code use.

> *Speech codes are identified with a specific people in a specific place.*

## Speech Codes Result from a Psychology and Sociology Unique to the Culture

Speech codes are intimately connected to the psychological qualities of a culture; they are related to how people see themselves. In other words, certain attitudes, values, and states of mind are more descriptive of one culture than another. For example, an Arab using a *musayra* code is maintaining consistency with his culture's expectations of honor. Honor is a controlling psychological value that legitimates a modesty code and the hospitality that one bestows. To use a *musayra* code—to be indirect, affective, and polite—is to maintain honor and express a distinct psychology of Arabs. Israeli-Jews, on the other hand, use *dugri* to express their strong native identity. This identity is rooted in the pride and strength they feel with respect to the state of Israel. Historically, Jews had been a dislocated and oppressed people but the establishment of the state of Israel altered this historical condition. *Dugri* speech is a communicative expression of this pride.

## The Meaning and Significance of Messages Are Fundamentally Dependent on Codes

You may be familiar with the maxim that "meanings are in people, not words." This means that a true understanding of communication is dependent on the people speaking and the code they use. When people communicate, they are performing some type of action and that action is interpreted by others. The interpretation relies on the speech code. When an Arab speaker deploys a *musayra* code and is polite, indirect, and courteous, a non–code user might interpret this as being weak, obsequious, or manipulative. This can lead to communication problems. Israeli-Jews have a reputation for being rude and aggressive. The *dugri* code contains a directness of style that includes bluntness and forthrightness. It is not uncommon to hear Israeli-Jews in a meeting say things like "you are wrong" or "not true." This kind of directness is considered rude by many, but not if you understand the code. A listener who "speaks" the *dugri* code will not come to any hasty conclusions about the dispositions of the other because they use the same code to define the communicative act. In other words, bold utterances such as "you are wrong" are understood as normal ways of speaking rather than a rude way of speaking.

## Speech Codes Are Located in the Language and Communication of Native Speakers

This simply means that speech codes are on display in the language of others. These codes are not inside the heads of others or contained in the generalities about culture. They are empirically observable in the communication of cultural members. Thus, when a native Israeli speaks directly and bluntly the *dugri* code is very apparent. Speech codes are also found in the ritualized functions of communication. These are the known and repeated ways of organizing interaction, and they have code-specific symbolic forms. A greeting ritual is an example. An African American will greet another African American differently than he would a White person. They might use certain vocabulary and body movements to signal a bond or friendship. The same is true for *dugri* and *musayra*. Both have symbolic forms that project and affirm an identity. By studying these symbolic forms and communication patterns we can discover how the cultural world is orderly rather than chaotic.

## Speech Codes Can Be Used to Understand, Predict, and Control Communication

The artful understanding and use of speech codes can be used to improve communication. People do not communicate like machines. Even if they are steeped in cultural codes, they often think reflectively about the code and alter typical patterns. This means there is potential for change and opportunities to avoid the more troublesome aspects of codes. An Israeli who is being very *dugri* can learn to recognize how he is perceived by others and perhaps alter certain patterns of communication. Moreover, situations can alter speech codes. In the following section of this essay we explain how codes are influenced by particular communication situations.

## ARGUMENT BETWEEN ISRAELI-JEWS AND PALESTINIANS

Argument is a persistent characteristic of the relationship between Israeli-Jews and Palestinians. In fact, argument is very important to these groups because it is an acceptable mechanism of conflict resolution. We prefer that these two groups argue with one another rather than shoot at each other. We might expect from the previous discussion that *dugri* speech would be characteristic of Israeli-Jews and the mode of speech preferred by them during argument since Israeli-Jews have a speech code that includes an argumentative style. And, *musayra* is not argument oriented at all. Interestingly, the little research that exists on Arab argument patterns is consistent with *musayra*. Hatim (1991), in a study devoted to this issue, found that argumentation in modern Arabic is related to politeness and saving face. Group status is one of the problems for groups in dialogue situations. When cultural groups are very different in status, the arguments produced by the high status groups can carry more weight. Israeli-Jews, given their military and economic advantages, carry considerably more status into dialogues. Their speech codes, moreover, are more conducive to argument. But dialogue groups that work to promote open discussion and equal relations can help lessen status differences. They become a context that levels differences. Even though Arabs come from a cultural background where argument is considered disrespectful, there are situations where this difference can be diminished.

In our studies (Maoz & Ellis, 2001, 2002; Ellis & Maoz, 2002; Ellis & Maoz, 2007), we found that the arguments during political dialogues between Israeli-Jews and Palestinians were not necessarily consistent with expectations from cultural speech codes. In other words, the Israeli-Jews do not necessarily use more-assertive arguments and the Arabs are not necessarily less overtly aggressive. It appears that the dialogue context of communication does alter speech codes and provides an environment for more equal status discussion. Palestinians are more assertive during these dialogues than speech code theory would suggest. They speak more and engage in more reasoning and elaboration. This means that they do state propositions and then support them with evidence in the classic tradition of argument.

> *It appears that the dialogue context of communication does alter speech codes and provides an environment for more equal status discussion.*

The Israeli-Jews are somewhat consistent with the *dugri* code because they are quick to object to allegations and challenge assertions made by the Palestinians. Their experience with the *dugri* code makes it easy for them to sharply deny charges and demand justifications. But these dialogues do provide an environment for transformative communication because they afford the Palestinians an opportunity to accuse the Israeli-Jews of historical injustices. This is why the Israeli-Jews are typically on the defensive with objections and challenges to various statements. But, interestingly, the Israeli-Jews are also more hesitant and submissive in these dialogues. They do things such as qualify their arguments, backtrack, and provide context. Again, they are being challenged and responding in an accommodating and yielding manner rather than in a style associated with *dugri*. It is the dialogue context, and its transformative qualities, that is probably responsible for these changes since typical roles are altered.

This dialogue context may also strengthen the sense of unity for groups with minority status. And the communication patterns reflect this. The

Palestinians argue in such a way that they elaborate and provide evidence for arguments in a manner much more akin to *dugri* than their own *musayra*. They clearly use the context to transform themselves into a power coalition. The Palestinians engage in a form of "tag team" argument (Brashers & Meyers, 1989). This is where one's own group is in a repetitive elaboration of a point to produce the perception of unity. Following is an example of a tag-team argument. The Palestinians are expressing their anger about being prevented from entering Jerusalem. The Israelis say it is because of security but the Palestinians "gang up" on the Israelis saying that the security measures—which are checkpoints that the Palestinians pass through and that are monitored by the Israeli military—do not work and it is just harassment.

PAL: If we go into Jerusalem, not through the *Machsom* (Hebrew word for "checkpoint"), I can go in. They see me and they don't care. It is that they want to make it difficult for me.

PAL: There are three ways to go from Bethlehem to Jerusalem.

PAL: If I want to go to Jerusalem, I am there in five minutes.

PAL: 60,000 Palestinians every day go to Israel without permission, every day. 40,000 with permission. So it's not security, its politics. This is the information. I am not saying this to support.

The Palestinians are emboldened. The dialogue context helps transform the indigenous code of each group. This is an important matter with respect to the power relationship between each group. It suggests that the speech codes are pliant and that situations and activities can be found that reduce the cultural strength of these codes and make change and growth more possible. Moreover, these communication experiences balance the relationship between hostile and unequal groups in such a way as to promote egalitarianism and make future interactions more productive. In some new research using Internet groups we have found that these relations remain true (Ellis & Maoz, in press).

In this essay we have explained and illustrated cultural communication patterns between Israeli-Jews and Palestinians. These two groups are in bitter conflict, experiencing tremendous pressures and tensions for reconciliation and change. Clearly, national leaders and negotiators for peace need to solve the legal and legislative issues with respect to land, sovereignty, and other legal obligations. But true peace and prosperity "on the ground" will only come when these two groups learn to work together and improve communication. We have shown in this essay that each national group has evolved a different code and orientation to communication. These codes can be bridges or barriers to communication. Although communication codes are relatively firm, they are not unyielding. We have shown that there are contexts and situations where codes do not predict communication behavior. But, more importantly, a thorough understanding of codes is necessary for dialogue and negotiation. Even words that are translated the same from different languages carry additional cultural baggage that is lost in the translation. Words are not neutral. They acquire their meaning from a culturally charged set of symbols that make up a speech code. The task for the future is to continually explore the nature of speech codes and their role in dialogue and conflict management.

# References

Adwan, S., & Bar-On, D. (2000). *The role of non-governmental organizations in peacebuilding between Palestinians and Israelis*. Jerusalem: PRIME (Peace Research Institute in the Middle East), with the support of the World Bank.

Allport, G. (1954). *The Nature of Prejudice*. Reading, MA: Addison-Wesley.

Amir, Y. (1976). The role of intergroup contacts in change of prejudice and ethnic relations. In. P. Kats, (Ed.), *Toward the elimination of racism* (pp. 245–308). New York: Pergamon.

Bernstein, B. (1971). *Class, codes and control*. (Vol. 1). London: Routledge & Kegan Paul.

Brashers, D. E., & Meyers, R. A. (1989). Tag-team argument and group decision making: A preliminary investigation. In B. E. Graonbeck (Ed.), *Spheres of argument: Proceedings of the sixth SCA/AFA Conference on Argumentation*. (pp. 542–550). Annandale, VA: Speech Communication Association.

Ellis, D. G. (1992). Syntactic and pragmatic codes in communication, *Communication Theory*, 2 1–23.

Ellis, D. G. (1994). Codes and pragmatic comprehension. In S. A. Deetz (Ed.), *Communication Yearbook 17* (pp. 333–343). Thousand Oaks, CA: Sage.

Ellis, D. G. (2006). *Transforming conflict: Communication and ethnopolitical conflict.* Boulder, CO: Rowman and Littlefield.

Ellis, D. G. & Maoz, I. (2002). "Cross-cultural argument interactions between Israeli-Jews and Palestinians. *Journal of Applied Communication Research, 30,* 181–194.

Ellis, D., & Maoz, I. (2007). Online argument between Israeli- Jews and Palestinians. *Human Communication Research.*

Feghali, E. (1997). Arab cultural communication patterns. *International Journal of Intercultural Relations, 21,* 345–378.

Hatim, B. (1991). The pragmatics of argumentation in Arabic: The rise and fall of text type. *Text, 11,* 189–199.

Gergen, K. (1999, May 27–31). *Toward transformative dialogue.* A paper presented to the 49th Annual Conference of the International Communication Association, San Francisco, CA.

Katriel, T. (1986). *Talking straight: Dugri speech in Israeli Sabra culture.* Cambridge, MA: Cambridge University Press.

Kelman, H. (1995). Contributions of an unofficial conflict resolution effort to the Israeli-Palestinian breakthrough. *Negotiation Journal, 11,* 19–27.

Kelman, H. (1997). Group processes in the resolution of international conflicts: Experiences From the Israeli-Palestinian case. *American Psychologist, 52,* 212–220.

Maoz, I. (2000a). Multiple conflicts and competing agendas: A framework for conceptualizing structured encounters between groups in conflict—the case of a coexistence project between Jews and Palestinians in Israel." *Journal of Peace Psychology, 6,* 135–156.

Maoz, I. (2000b). An experiment in peace: Processes and effects in reconciliation aimed workshops of Israeli and Palestinian youth. *Journal of Peace Research, 37,* 721–736.

Maoz, I. (1999). From conflict to peace? Israel's relations with Syria and the Palestinians. *Middle East Journal, 53,* 393–416.

Maoz, I., & Ellis, D. G. (2001). Going to ground: Argument in Israeli-Jewish and Palestinian encounter groups." *Research on Language and Social Interaction, 34,* 399–419.

Philipsen, G. (1997). A theory of speech codes. In G. Philipsen & T. L. Albrecht (Eds.), *Developing communication theories* (pp. 119–156). Albany: State University of New York Press.

Pettigrew, T. (1998). Intergroup contact theory. *Annual Review of Psychology, 49,* 65–85.

Rouhana, N., & Bar-Tal, D. (1998). Psychological dynamics of intractable ethnonational conflicts: The Israeli-Palestinian case. *American Psychologist, 53,* 761–770.

## Concepts and Questions

1. What roles do land rights, religion, and cultural conflict play in defining the communication dynamics of Israeli Jews and Palestinian Arabs?

2. What do Ellis and Maoz imply when they refer to "transformative communication"?

3. How does transformative communication help improve communication between groups that are experiencing a degree of conflict?

4. According to Ellis and Maoz, what conditions should be met if the two groups in conflict are to employ the contact hypothesis to help reduce prejudice and negative intergroup attitudes?

5. How does the concept of "dialogue," as discussed by Buber, Rogers, and Bakhtin, provide some guiding principles for transformative dialogue?

6. How do cultural differences in speech codes affect communication between Israeli Jews and Palestinian Arabs? Provide some examples of differences in speech codes for each of these groups.

# Mexican *Dichos:* Lessons Through Language

CAROLYN ROY

*Possibly one of the most important areas of U.S. intercultural communication, be it international or domestic, is between U.S. Americans and Mexicans. Not only does Mexico share a common border with the United States, but it is also a major trading partner and continues to be the largest source of new immigrants entering the United States—both legally and illegally. The fusion of the two cultures was highlighted in a special issue of* Time *magazine that detailed the unique culture developing along both sides of the United States–Mexican border. The new culture evolving is a combination of Euro-American, native Mexican, and Spanish-influenced Mexican backgrounds. To help you better understand the nature of this culture and the Mexican values that contribute to it, our next essay, "Mexican Dichos: Lessons Through Language," by Carolyn Roy, explores Mexican values as expressed by* dichos. Dichos *are popular proverbs, adages, and sayings that pass on many of the values that are important to Mexicans. The proverbs and adages shine a light on what the particular culture deems essential for daily living. For example, Roy discusses how key values such as the cheerful acceptance of the "will of God," the need to place trust in others with great care, the significance of appearances, the necessity to guard one's privacy and not breach the privacy of others, prescribed gender roles, a communal spirit, and the imperative of family life are expressed and reinforced through use of Mexican* dichos. *Through concrete examples Roy is suggesting that an awareness of* dichos *can offer you a window into Mexican culture.*

> *Possibly one of the most important areas of U.S. intercultural communication, be it international or domestic, is between U.S. Americans and Mexicans.*

## MEXICAN CULTURE AND ITS REFLECTED IMAGES

The late Octavio Paz, one of Mexico's most renowned writers, asserts in his classic *The Labyrinth of Solitude:* *Life and Thought in Mexico* that the Mexican's "face is a mask" (Paz, 1961, p. 29). Paz thereby implies that knowing *the* Mexican national character might be impossible. Carlos Fuentes, another of Mexico's most esteemed men of letters, employs the imagery of dark, ancient Aztec polished hematite mirrors reflecting the soul of Mexico when he writes "Is not the mirror both a reflection of reality and a projection of the imagination?" (Fuentes, 1992, p. 11). Despite the self-confessed inscrutable nature of Mexican national character, *dichos*—popular sayings including, but not limited to, *proverbios*/proverbs, *adagios*/adages, and *refranes*/refrains—open an avenue for exploring the attributes most esteemed and salient in Mexican popular culture. Using Fuentes' metaphor, however, our understanding of Mexican culture remains a darkly reflected image. Our understanding is further obscured by the difficulty of precise idiomatic translation of the complex Mexican language that hybridizes the Spanish brought from Europe with the intricately nuanced indigenous languages, predominantly Nahuatl, of Mexico's native peoples. Nevertheless, popular sayings heard from the northern reaches of the Chihuahuan desert to the highlands of southern Chiapas do provide insight into some commonly held values in Mexican culture.

Such popular sayings transmit "what a culture deems significant" (Samovar, Porter, & McDaniel, 2010, p. 29). Examination of these orally transmitted traditional values offers an excellent means of learning about another culture because these oft-repeated sayings fuse past, present, and future. These sayings focus our attention on basic principles accepted within the culture. The premise of this present exercise is that we can learn much about Mexican values through scrutiny of these distilled lessons of life transmitted through their language.

Although some of these popular sayings are uniquely Mexican, many more of them were brought to Mexico by Spaniards after 1519; therefore, they reflect the fusion of cultures, especially Castilian and Muslim, found in recently "reconquered" and unified early–sixteenth-century Spain. Because many values are universally human, similar sayings may be found just as often in cultures around the globe. For example, most cultures attribute some responsibility for a child's character or nature to the parents; hence, in the United States one might hear "like father, like son" or "a chip off the old block," while in Mexico the close approximation is *de tal palo, tal astilla* (from such a stick, such a splinter). But the proverb *Al nopal nomás lo van a ver cuando tiene tunas* (One only goes to see the cactus when it has prickly pear fruit) derives specifically from the Mexican milieu. However, one might readily overhear a parent in the United States complaining to an adult child, "You only come to see me when you want something." So the principle of the saying is universal, but the expression relates uniquely to its culture. Although some sayings are culturally unique, and others universal, our purpose here is to focus on specific Mexican sayings that reflect some of the values of that culture.

> *Examination of these orally transmitted traditional values offers an excellent means of learning about another culture because these oft-repeated sayings fuse past, present, and future.*

## MEXICAN DICHOS

Popular sayings—*dichos*—reflect many of the basic values of contemporary Mexican society, although the roots of these expressions of popular culture extend far back into both European and pre-Columbian Native American civilizations. Although many of these expressions demonstrate the universality of proverbs generally, many uniquely mirror Mexican reality. Yolanda Nava writes about Latin American culture in general, but her observation applies equally well to Mexican sayings in particular. She notes, "*Dichos* feel good on the tongue … they are, after all, a verbal shorthand which … elders used countless times to remind [one] … to behave wisely" (2000, p. 35). *Dichos* may be pithy condensations of wisdom gained through centuries of experience. They are one form of transmitting folk wisdom. The sayings selected here might be heard in any Mexican household.

Many of the proverbs in the following sections may be readily consulted in Sellers (1994), but caution must be exercised in reviewing Sellers' interpretations of these *dichos*. One must always maintain cognizance of the cultural context. Although a Mexican might playfully jest, saying *No hagas hoy lo que puedas hacer mañana* (Don't do today what you can put off until tomorrow), such should not be taken literally (as Sellers apparently does, p. 26). This inverted *dicho* merely jocularly reminds the listener that one should *No dejar para mañana lo que se puede hacer hoy* (Not put off until tomorrow what can be done today), a well-known adage in many cultures.

The Mexican tradition of playfulness with words, as in the previous example, or the use of double meaning (*doble sentido*, often with obscured sexual undertones—most frequently heard with such apparently innocuous words as *huevos*/eggs, *aguacates*/avocados, and so on, used as anatomical designations), or using a word for its exact opposite, has ancient roots in pre-Columbian Mexican linguistic practices. Among the Aztecs, it was proper practice to refer to an older person as "my dear young one," much as a Mexican mother today may call her toddler "my dear father" (*mi papito*). Those expressions chosen for discussion here reflect some of the values central to Mexican popular culture. These values include cheerful acceptance of the "will of God," the need to place trust with great care, the significance of appearances, the necessity to guard one's privacy and not breach that of others, prescribed gender roles, a communal spirit, and the importance of family.

## Acceptance of "God's Will"

*No hay mal que por bien no venga.* (There is no bad that good does not accompany.) Mexicans have often been characterized as fatalistic, but their nature seems more than merely accepting of the inevitable. Much of Mexican folk wisdom relates to acceptance of poverty and even laughing at it. Mexican folk seem to relish the challenge of finding happiness in the face of adversity.

Some of the most frequently heard proverbs reflect that optimism. This proverb might be equated to "It's an ill wind that brings nobody good," but that does not carry the same positive outlook that the Spanish phrase indicates. Closer to the Mexican concept might be "Every cloud has a silver lining."

*Mejor reír que llorar.* (Better to laugh than to cry.) If one laughs at adversity, whether a simple upset of plans or that which is most inevitable—death—then there is nothing that can disturb one's happiness. Much of Mexican art reflects the duality of life and death, as can be seen in art from pre-Columbian times to the present. The very popular woodcuts of José Guadalupe Posada, depicting skeletons in scenes that range from the mundane to the hilariously outrageous, clearly demonstrate the Mexican's friendly attitude toward death. If one can laugh, then there is no need for lament.

*El hombre propone y Dios dispone.* (Man proposes and God disposes.) Few Mexican women would dare to make plans, whether it be meeting for lunch tomorrow or making plans for a child's future, without adding before concluding those plans, *Si Dios quiere* (If God wills). It would be presuming much to think that one could control the future, which is viewed as in God's hands alone. In the South of the United States, one hears a similar expression made popular by Southern folklorists: "If the Lord's willing and the creek don't rise," but this seems less an attitude of fatalistic acceptance than an almost humorous excuse in the event of inclement weather in the backwoods. Whereas *Si Dios quiere* is an expression used almost exclusively by Mexican women, "If the Lord's willing" may be used by males or females.

*No por mucho madrugar amanece más temprano.* (No matter how early one rises, the sun will not come up any sooner.) One must simply accept what one cannot change. Nothing is accomplished by unnecessary effort. Only the foolish will attempt to defy the forces of nature.

*Cuando el pobre tiene para carne sea vigilia.* (When the poor have [money] to buy meat, it must be Lent.)

> *The very popular woodcuts of José Guadalupe Posada, depicting skeletons in scenes that range from the mundane to the hilariously outrageous, clearly demonstrate the Mexican's friendly attitude toward death.*

The poor must accept that when they have the good fortune to have money, then it will be a time of fasting (not eating meat). The poor must accept that they will not have good luck. This is an instance of making fun of—of laughing at—adversity. If I am poor, I should expect to eat beans and tortillas, not meat.

*Quien canta su mal espanta.* (He who sings frightens away his grief.) By singing, the individual can dispel sadness and drive away gloom. Singing and other forms of music accompany most private Mexican gatherings, but can also be heard in the Metro stations and on street corners of metropolitan centers.

## Sparing Bestowal of Trust

*En confianza está el peligro.* (There is danger in trust.) For the Mexican to place trust in another, particularly anyone who is not a blood relative, indicates that person is held in very high esteem. But when one does bestow trust, then the greatest harm possible would be to betray that trust. It is a great risk to have faith in another; therefore, trust must never be granted lightly.

*La confianza también mata.* (Trust also kills.) Betrayal of trust kills the spirit as surely as a bullet might kill the body. And the betrayal of trust would be the gravest ill that one friend could commit against another. Another *dicho* conveys the gravity of betrayal of trust: *Ni te fíes de amigo reconciliado, ni de manjar dos veces guisado.* (Do not trust a reconciled friend nor a dish twice cooked.) If a trust has been betrayed, the lost trust can never be recovered.

*Del dicho al hecho hay mucho trecho.* (From said to done, there is a great gap.) One should not trust that promises will be fulfilled. Even with the best of intentions, circumstances intervene; thus, one should always be prepared to accept less than is promised, thereby avoiding disappointment.

*Músico pagado toca mal son.* (The musician who has been paid plays bad music.) The most foolish act that an employer could commit would be to pay the worker before the task is completed. Such an employer would not be viewed as kind or generous, merely foolish. If a worker is paid in advance, then the foolish employer deserves to be treated with contempt. One of the first lessons to be learned when interacting within Mexican culture is that easy trust is not valued. Trust/*confianza* must be given sparingly and only after being earned. Reserving payment until the work is completed is viewed as prudent. The lesson of the saying is that paying for a job before it is completed produces bad results.

## THE IMPORTANCE OF APPEARANCES

*Dime con quien andas y te diré quien eres.* (Tell me with whom you associate [walk, travel], and I will tell you who you are.) Whom you choose as your companions and associates reflects your quality. If you associate with "common people," then you will be judged common. It follows that one always seeks to associate with people of higher status in order to improve on one's station in life. In English one hears "Birds of a feather flock together," but that does not fully convey the idea that one can rise in status by associating with a better class of people.

*Quien anda con lobos a aullar se aprenda.* (One who goes around with wolves learns to howl.) In this same vein is the biblical principle in English "Evil companions corrupt good morals." If you run with the wolves, you will learn their wild ways; therefore, one should avoid such savages and associate with cultured society. One must choose associates with great care. They not only reflect one's position, but also influence one's character.

*El que es buen gallo dondequiera canta.* (A good rooster can crow anywhere.) Despite the previous admonitions, quality is quality no matter the circumstance. A person of true character will show that character in all circumstances, but a person of poor character will not be able to measure up in difficult circumstances.

### Respect for Privacy

*Agua que no has de beber, déjala correr.* (Water that you do not have to drink, leave it to flow.) Aranda (1977) translates this as "Don't meddle in others' affairs; don't start trouble." If you stir up the water, then it will be undrinkable for anyone. So let everyone tend to their own problems and thus avoid spreading them to others.

*Bueno aconsejar, mejor remediar.* (It is good to give advice, but it is better to solve the problem.) When there is a problem, it is good to give advice when it is sought, but it would be better to solve the problem. If you cannot solve the problem, then refrain from giving advice. And there are even times when the truth is better left unsaid, as attested by the proverb *Si dices la verdad no pecas, pero no sabes los males que suscitas* (If you tell the truth you do not sin, but you don't know the troubles you cause, so keep your own counsel).

*En boca cerrada no entran moscas.* (Flies do not enter a closed mouth.) If you keep your mouth shut, then you will not have to worry about "putting your foot in it." Be careful of what you say, because *Un resbalón de lengua es peor que el de los pies* (A slip of the tongue is worse than a slip of the foot). The foot will heal, but damage done by words will not. Also, *Rezarle solo a su santo* (Pray only to your saint); that is, only someone who can help you should know of your problems.

*Mejor quedarse para vestir los santos que tener que desvestir un borracho.* (It is better to remain single than to have to undress a drunk.) Women who do not marry are often said to "dress the saints"; that is, they spend their lives caring for the images of saints, which often involves making new garments for the images or painting and refurbishing them. Thus, single women often justify their unmarried state by suggesting that they prefer dressing the saints' images to having to undress a drunken husband.

*Más vale solo que mal acompañado.* (It is better to remain single than to be disagreeably accompanied.) In a society in which women are viewed as weak and vulnerable, single women must justify their unmarried state, so that women most often cite the refrain that it is better to be single than to be married to an unbearable spouse.

*A la mujer ni todo el amor ni todo el dinero.* (To a woman neither all your love nor all your money.) A real Mexican male must maintain control of himself and his money. Men make a certain portion of their income available to women for maintaining the household, but the rest of their earnings belong to them. One of the great enigmas of Mexican culture is the *machismo* (strong, dominant male) versus *marianismo* (longsuffering, submissive female). This concept is most readily seen in the fact that *cantinas*/bars are exclusively for males (and women of ill repute).

*Triste está la casa donde la gallina canta y el gallo calla.* (Sad is the house where the chicken crows and the rooster is quiet.) The proper role for a man is as the master of his house, and the woman should be silent. It is a reversal of proper roles for the Mexican woman to make the decisions and the man to allow her to do so. In English a similar refrain is, "A whistling girl and a crowing hen always come to some sad end." Women are assigned their proper roles and men theirs. A sad state results when these roles are reversed.

## Communalism

*Mucha ayuda, poco trabajo.* (Much help, little work.) When many work together, it is little work for any of them. When work is shared, it goes quickly and is not much effort for anyone. The tradition of communal work precedes European contact with the New World. Among the Aztecs, taking turns at doing community service was widely practiced.

*Vida sin amigos, muerte sin testigos.* (Life without friends; death without witnesses. Life without friends, no mourners when it ends.) If one does not live so as to have many friends, then death will come with no one there to mourn that death. In Mexican culture, it is extremely important that there be mourners to accompany the deceased. It has long been common practice to pay mourners so that the dead will be accompanied to the cemetery. Again, this reflects the importance of one's public persona, one's appearance to the rest of the world, even in death.

## Family

*¿A dónde vas que valgas más?* (Where are you going that you are worth more?) Where would you be valued more than at home? The Mexican family is extended, but still very close. When an individual needs help, the family is expected to supply it. The understanding is that you are always better off at home.

*Amor de padre o madre, lo demás es aire.* (The love of mother or father, everything else is air.)

Compared to a mother or father's love, there is nothing else of importance. Father and mother will love their children when everyone and everything else fails. It is not unusual to encounter adult children living in the home of their parents and even rearing their own children in that same home. At times this is done out of economic necessity, but just as often it is the choice of the extended family. Grandparents become the caregivers for the offspring and take a hand in their upbringing.

## SUMMARY

Popular sayings reflect basic cultural values. They do not even require literacy because they transmit the values orally to all who hear them. They metaphorically condense timeless lessons into readily recalled phrases. Through *dichos* we are reminded that our experiences are not unique; others have experienced the same things in other times and other places and left messages to guide us. By reviewing a selection of Mexican *dichos*, one readily perceives some of that culture's more significant values: cheerful acceptance of one's lot in life, the need to exercise caution, the importance of appearances, the sanctity of privacy, proper gender roles, communalism, and family.

> *By reviewing a selection of Mexican* dichos, *one readily perceives some of that culture's more significant values: cheerful acceptance of one's lot in life, the need to exercise caution, the importance of appearances, the sanctity of privacy, proper gender roles, communalism, and family.*

## References

Aranda, C. (1977). *Dichos: Proverbs and sayings from the Spanish.* Santa Fe, NM: Swanstone Press.

Fuentes, C. (1992). *The buried mirror: Reflections on Spain and the New World.* New York: Houghton Mifflin.

Nava, Y. (2000). *It's all in the frijoles: 100 famous Latinos share real-life stories, time-tested dichos, favorite folktales, and inspiring words of wisdom.* New York: Fireside.

Paz, O. (1961). *The labyrinth of solitude: Life and thought in Mexico.* New York: Grove Press.

Samovar, L. A., Porter, R. E., & McDaniel, E. R. (2010). *Communication Between Cultures* (7th ed.). Boston: Wadsworth/Cengage Learning.

Sellers, I. M. (1994). *Folk wisdom of Mexico.* San Francisco: Chronicle Books.

## Concepts and Questions

1. In what ways does the study of a culture's most familiar proverbs and sayings offer insights into some of the important values of that culture?

2. Which Mexican sayings discussed by Roy are used in some other cultures?

3. Can you think of some sayings from your own culture that are learned so they can be used to "teach" a specific value?

4. What sayings in the United States stress the value of individualism?

5. What sayings in Mexican culture reflect the underlying religious worldview of that culture?

# The Basis of Cultural Differences in Nonverbal Communication

PETER A. ANDERSEN

*At the core of our next essay is the supposition that nonverbal communication is an omnipresent and commanding form of human communication. The nonverbal cues people exchange help signal personal and cultural identities while also sending messages about how one feels toward the situation one is confronted with. These messages allow people to express their feelings, emotions, and attitudes by body movements, facial expressions, voice, and the like. And while, as Peter Andersen points out, many of these nonverbal actions are universal and demonstrate very few cultural variations, "most nonverbal behaviors show a considerable imprint of culture." That "imprint" serves as the major thesis of Andersen's essay, titled "The Basis of Cultural Differences in Nonverbal Communication." Throughout the essay Andersen reaffirms the position that "Culture shapes the display rules of when, how, what, and with whom certain nonverbal expressions should be revealed or suppressed and dictates which displays are appropriate in which specific situations." To help us appreciate and understand these codes, Andersen begins by offering a synopsis of nonverbal communication and its relevance to culture. This summary is followed by a brief discussion of the eight basic codes of nonverbal communication:*

> The nonverbal cues people exchange help signal personal and cultural identities while also sending messages about how one feels toward the situation one is confronted with.

*physical appearance (attire), proxemics (space and distance), chronemics (time), kinesics (facial expressions, movements, gestures), haptics (touch), oculesics (eye contact and gaze), vocalics (paralanguage), and olfactics (smell). After a description of the eight codes, Andersen moves to an analysis of how these codes can differ from one culture to another. He does this by means of a comparative study of the essential intercultural dimensions found in the seminal works of Edward T. Hall and Geert Hofstede. These dimensions include (a) high and low context—the degree to which communication is explicit and verbal or implicit and nonverbal; (b) identity—a culture's degree of individualism versus collectivism; (c) power distance—the degree to which power, prestige, and wealth are unequally distributed in a culture; (d) gender—the degree of traditional gender role achievement, control, and power; (e) uncertainty—the degree to which a culture values risk and ambiguity; (f) future orientation—the degree to which people in a culture have a long-term or short-term orientation; and (g) immediacy—the degree of closeness, intimacy, and availability for communication. During his explanation of these seven dimensions Andersen offer numerous examples of culturally diverse nonverbal behavior.*

This original essay appears here in print for the first time. All rights reserved. Permission to reprint must be obtained from the author and the publisher. Dr. Peter A. Andersen is a professor emeritus in the School of Communications at San Diego State University, San Diego, California.

# INTRODUCTION

Humans are noteworthy among living things because they use language. Yet most messages lie beyond language in a communication system popularly called body language or, more correctly, nonverbal communication (Andersen, 2004, 2007). Compared to verbal communication, nonverbal messages are both more powerful and more ambiguous because they are signaled and interpreted through multiple channels such as facial expressions, bodily language, tones of voice, spatial relationships, and the environment. Though nonverbal communication is both intentional and unintentional, it operates at a lower level of awareness and is more spontaneous and mindless than language (Andersen, 2004, 2007; Buck & Van Lear, 2002). Overall, nonverbal communication is a pervasive and powerful form of human behavior, which involves a subtle, nonlinguistic, multidimensional, spontaneous process (Andersen, 1999a).

Although, some nonverbal behaviors are universal and show little or no cultural variation (Brown, 1991), most show a considerable imprint of culture. Culture is "a shared system of socially transmitted behavior that describes, defines, and guides people's ways of life, communicated from one generation to the next" (Matsumoto, 2006, p.220). At one time, each culture was located in a particular geographic area or country. This is still the case to some degree, but cultures today may be based as much on the cultural identification and connection among its members as through geographic separation. Culture is mainly an unspoken, nonverbal phenomenon because most aspects of one's culture are learned through observation and imitation rather than by explicit verbal instruction or expression. The primary level of culture is communicated implicitly, without awareness, and chiefly by nonverbal means (Andersen, 1999a; Hall, 1984). Our cultural behaviors and attitudes are so deeply ingrained that people think that behaviors enacted by their own culture are the *only* ways that humans should behave. Speaking of nonverbal communication, Sapir (1928) long ago stated:

> We respond to gestures with an extreme alertness, and one might say, in accordance with an elaborate and secret code that is written nowhere, known to none, and understood by all (p. 556).

Andersen (1997) stated, "Indeed, culture is so basic, learned at such a tender age, and so taken-for-granted that it is often confused with human nature itself (p.244). Of course, culture is not human nature, but it is called "second nature" because it is nearly as deep within us as the fact that we are members of the human species. The belief that culture is part of human nature has a dark side. In many cultures, it is believed that people with different attire, religious customs, special behavior and many other aspects of nonverbal communication are subhuman or at least deficient humans because their behavior is viewed as subhuman or at least a less refined, righteous, or proper way for humans to behave. Only through the experience of cultural differences via education or travel can cultural variations in nonverbal behavior be understood and appreciated.

Nonverbal communication is composed of both biologically determined and cultural-specific components. Some factors that are innate and genetic produce cross-cultural similarities in nonverbal behavior (Brown, 1991; Ekman, 1972), but abundant cross-cultural differences exist in nonverbal behavior also and create intercultural miscommunication, friction, and confusion.

With dramatically increasing numbers of people pursuing higher education, traveling for business and pleasure, and immigrating to other countries, the probability of communicating with people from other cultures is greater than ever before. Despite a one-year downturn in international tourism due to the global economic crisis, generally international tourism has steadily increased for decades (United Nations, 2009). Likewise, inexpensive electronic communication via email, Skype, or social networking sites makes international communication more likely.

*Culture is mainly an unspoken, nonverbal phenomenon because most aspects of one's culture are learned through observation and imitation rather than by explicit verbal instruction or expression.*

Understanding intercultural communication, particularly nonverbal communication for which there is no dictionary, is more important than ever before.

Nonverbal messages serve a variety of functions in intercultural communication (Ting-Toomey, 1999). People rely on nonverbal cues to signal their identity (Burgoon, Guerrero & Floyd, 2010) and receivers rely on perceived judgments based upon those cues. From artifacts such as clothing, jewelry, cosmetics, and accessories to use of vocalic cues such as pitch, volume, articulation, and tempo, individuals in different cultures present, enhance, and/or assert a sense of self via various nonverbal behaviors (Ting-Toomey, 1999). Not only do nonverbal messages reflect strong personal identity, they also carry and infer powerful feelings, emotions, and attitudes typically through facial, bodily, and gestural movement and use of voice (Ting-Toomey, 1999). Culture shapes the display rules of when, how, what, and with whom certain nonverbal expressions should be revealed or suppressed (Ekman & Friesen, 1975; Ekman & Oster, 1979) and dictates which displays are appropriate in which specific situations.

> *Culture shapes the display rules of when, how, what, and with whom certain nonverbal expressions should be revealed or suppressed.*

Prior research on intercultural communication in general, and cultural difference in nonverbal communication in particular, has provided many useful and interesting anecdotes about intercultural differences. This essay attempts to connect these fragmented accounts and proposes a theoretical perspective that helps to explain thousands of differences in nonverbal communication across culture with a unified perspective. The article will first briefly review research in cross-cultural differences that lie along eight nonverbal codes, *physical appearance, proxemics, chronemics, kinesics, haptics, oculesics, vocalics,* and *olfactics,* and then focus on seven primary dimensions of cultural variation in nonverbal behavior based on the seminal work of Hall (1966a, 1976, 1984) and Hofstede (1984, 1991, 1998, 2001, 2003) in cultural dimensions, and many follow-up scholarly efforts in the field (Albert & Ah Ha, 2004; Andersen, 1988, 2000; Andersen, Hecht, Hoobler & Smallwood, 2002; Fernandez, Carlson, Stepina & Nicholson, 1997; Gudykunst & Nishida, 1986; Merritt, 2000; Shackleton & Ali, 1990). The seven dimensions of intercultural nonverbal communication include *context, identity, power distance, gender, uncertainty, future orientation,* and *immediacy.*

## NONVERBAL CODES

Nonverbal messages communicate what verbal messages cannot express and usually generate more trust than verbal messages (Andersen, 1999a; Ting-Toomey, 1999). A smile, a wink, a scowl, a squeaky voice, prolonged eye contact, fingers drumming on a tabletop—all these expressions reveal feelings, thoughts, and subtle messages. Nonverbal communication runs the gamut from easily readable facial expression and gestures to attitudes expressed by body posture or vocal tones hidden beneath the surface of spoken words. Most discussions of cultural differences in nonverbal communication are anecdotal and atheoretical, offering numerous examples of intercultural differences for each nonverbal code without providing a theoretical frame for the basis of such differences. Following a discussion of the codes of nonverbal communication, this essay provides a conceptual framework for understanding the underlying basis of cultural difference in nonverbal communication.

*Physical appearance* is the most externally obvious nonverbal code and covers relatively stable physical features of human beings such as gender, height, weight, skin color, and body shape, as well as the strategic use of artifacts associated with one's physical appearance like clothing, jewelry, make-up, hairstyles, and accessories. All of these elements play an important role during initial encounters. Hairstyles vary greatly across cultures and even across time; in America and Europe body hair has become less and less stylish across the last 50 years (Andersen, 2007). Cultural attire is obvious and leads to ethnic stereotypes. During a field study conducted at an international airport, the author witnessed Tongans in multicultural ceremonial gowns, Sikhs in white turbans, Hasidic Jews in blue yarmulkes and Africans in white dashikis—all alongside Californians in running shorts and halter tops (Andersen, 1999a). Blue jeans and business suits have become increasingly accepted attire internationally, but local attire still abounds. Little formal research has been conducted on the impact of physical appearance on intercultural communication. Discussions of intercultural differences in appearance are provided by Scheflen (1974) and Samovar, Porter, & McDaniel (2010). Cultural cues of physical appearance are often very subtle; for example, the level of a woman's veil in rural north India indicates her sexual or romantic interest or disinterest (Lambert & Wood, 2005), a burka or a yarmulke may signal one's culture and religion, and a business suit may signal formality or an occupation. Preoccupation with physical appearance is hardly a new phenomenon. Since the dawn of culture, humans from the upper Paleolithic period (40,000 years ago) to the present have adorned their bodies in varied ways (Samovar et al., 2010).

A number of studies have shown that race and culture have an effect on the recognition of faces (Meisner & Brigham, 2001; Sporer, 2001a, 2001b). We have all heard people say about people of other races: "They all look alike!" The failure to distinguish between different people of an ethnic group other than one's own, called the cross-race effect, can be the cause of embarrassing interactions where you think you recognize another person when in fact you have never seen the person before. More seriously, it can even result in misidentifying a defendant in a criminal trial. The primary reason for such an effect is a lack of quality and quantity of contact with members of other ethnic groups and the human psychological tendency to stereotype, a cognitive shortcut. Increased intercultural contact appears to reduce the effect. But it is more than mere contact; people who have qualitatively richer intercultural interactions and spend time communicating with people of other races and ethnicities show less sign of the cross-race effect (Sporer, 2001a).

*Proxemics* examines nonverbal communication differences via a culture's most fundamental elements—space and distance. Research has documented that cultures differ substantially in their use of personal space, their regard for territory, and the meanings they assign to proxemic behavior (Albert & Ah Ha, 2004; Gudykunst & Kim, 1992; Hall, 1959, 1966a, 1966b, 1976; Scheflen, 1974). For example, people from Mediterranean and Latin cultures maintain close distances, whereas people from Northern European and Northeast Asian cultures maintain greater distances (Hall, 1966b; Beaulieu, 2004; Neulip, 2002; Ozdemir, 2008). But this behavior is highly contextual. At rush hour in Tokyo, the normally respectful, distant Japanese are literally jammed into subways and trains.

*Chronemics*—or the study of meanings, usage, and communication of time—is probably the most discussed and well-researched nonverbal code in the intercultural literature (Bruneau, 1979; Gudykunst & Kim, 1992; Hall, 1959, 1976, 1984). Indeed, time orientation may be one of the fundamental foundations of culture itself (Albert & Ah Ha, 2004; Hofstede, 2001). Some cultures follow monochronic time schedules and use time in linear ways, whereas people in polychronic cultures tend to engage in multiple activities simultaneously (Hall & Hall, 1987). Perceptions of time vary dramatically from culture to culture. In the United States, time is viewed as a commodity that can be wasted, spent, saved, and used wisely (Andersen, 1999a). In the Middle East and Latin American cultures, bringing in a historical time perspective is very important before addressing a current issue (Cushner & Brislin, 1996). To many Asians, time is more of a relational issue rather than a clock time issue (Tung, 1994). And in some less-developed countries, life moves to the rhythms of nature, the day, the seasons, the year. Such human inventions as seconds, minutes, hours, and weeks have no real meaning. As we will discuss later, future orientation is a fundamental basis of culture (Hofstede, 2001).

*Kinesic* behavior is communication of the body in motion and includes aspects of people's facial expressions, body movements, gestures, and conversational regulators (Gudykunst & Kim, 1992; Hall, 1976; Scheflen, 1974). Research on subtle differences in the appearance of facial expressions of emotion across cultures reveal that these facial expressions contain nonverbal "accents" that identify the expresser's nationality or culture (Elfenbein & Ambady, 2003; Jack, Blais, Scheepers, Schyns, & Caldera, 2009; Marsh, Elfenbein, & Ambady, 2003; Wickline, Bailey, & Nowicki, 2009) making them more recognizable to people from one's own culture (Dovidio,

> *Perceptions of time vary dramatically from culture to culture.*

Hebl, Richeson, & Shelton, 2006; Mandal & Ambady, 2004). Nonetheless, there is little support for unique cultural facial expressions of emotion; emotional expressions are generally recognizable across culture (Beaupre & Hess, 2005; Matsumoto, 2002, 2006), just at lower levels of accuracy. Display rules for facial expressions of emotion are mostly learned from one's culture. A study of 11-month-old babies revealed that Chinese babies are less expressive than either Japanese or European-American babies (Camras et al., 1998). While hereditary differences cannot be ruled out, the fact that Japanese babies behaved more like European-American babies than like Chinese babies suggests this is likely a difference due to socialization and enculturation. Likewise, an intercultural study of three-year-olds by Camras, Chen, Bakeman, Norris, and Cain (2006) found that the native Chinese children were less expressive than Chinese children adopted by American families, and the adopted children were less expressive than European American children. Some research suggests that Asians and other collectivistic people are less likely to recognize facial expressions, particularly negative ones, due to learned cultural display rules (Beaupre & Hess, 2005). Research also shows that cross-cultural training can improve the recognition of subtle differences in facial expression across culture (Elfenbein, 2006).

Likewise, kinesic conversational behaviors differ across culture. One study showed that Japanese interactants are much more likely to use kinesic listener responses or backchannel behaviors, particularly head nods, than British interactants (Cutrone, 2005). This is attributed to the greater supportiveness and collectivism of Asian versus European communicators, discussed in detail later in this essay.

Gestures differ dramatically across cultures in meaning, extensiveness, and intensity. Stories abound in the intercultural literature of gestures that signal endearment or warmth in one culture but may be obscene or insulting in another. Scholars specifically focusing on spontaneous gestures accompanying speech claim that both the types and timing of gestures can vary with the language spoken (Goldin-Meadow, 2003). Gestures with symbolic dictionary meanings, called emblems, are most likely to vary across culture. One study shows that recognition of such cultural gestures is highest by people from the same culture and is recognized more accurately by people with more exposure to the culture and by people with greater intercultural communication competence (Molinsky, Krabbenhoft, Ambady, & Choi, 2005).

*Haptics*, or tactile communication, also shows considerable intercultural variation (Jourard, 1966; Andersen & Leibowitz, 1978; Ford & Graves, 1977; McDaniel & Andersen, 1998; Samovar et al., 1998). Research has shown vast differences in international and intercultural touch in amount, location, type, and public or private manifestation (Jones, 1994; McDaniel & Andersen, 2010). Italians, Greeks, Hispanics, and other people with Mediterranean origins touch more and are more comfortable with touch than the English, French, Dutch, U.S. Americans, and other cultures that originated in Northern Europe (DiBiase & Gunnoe, 2004; Shuter, 1976, 1977). A recent study showed hugs and kisses were deemed more appropriate by therapists in Brazil than in the United States (Miller, Commons & Guthiel, 2006), which is consistent with the equatorial location and Mediterranean origins of Brazilian culture. Touching is less common and more embarrassing and discomforting among Chinese and Japanese (McDaniel & Andersen, 1998). And to touch an Arab Muslim with the left hand, which is reserved for toilet use, is considered a social insult (Samovar & Mills, 1998).

*Oculesics*—the study of messages sent by the eyes, including eye contact, blinks, eye movements, and pupil dilation—is an important code of nonverbal communication that has attracted considerably less intercultural research (Gudykunst & Kim, 1992; Samovar et al., 2010). Because eye contact has been called an "invitation to communicate," its variation cross-culturally is an important communication topic. In North America and Western Europe direct eye contact communicates interest and respect, while Japanese people may look away from another's eyes almost completely to be polite (Samovar & Mills, 1998).

*Vocalics*, or *paralanguage*, includes all the nonverbal elements of the voice. Not surprisingly, culture affects vocalics (Gudykunst & Kim, 1992; LaBarre, 1985; Samovar et al., 2010; Scheflen, 1974); members of cultures with strong oral traditions, such as African Americans and Jews, tend to speak with more passion; Italians and Greeks talk more and talk louder than Asians, who appreciate silence as a way of showing politeness (Samovar & Mills, 1998). However, music and singing, universal forms of aesthetic communication, have been almost completely overlooked in intercultural research, except for an excellent series of studies (Lomax, 1968) that identified several groups of worldwide cultures through differences and similarities in their folk songs. Despite the considerable differences in vocalics across cultures, recent research shows that basic human emotions are recognizable in the voice at levels exceeding chance even when they occur in a language the receiver does not understand (Pell, Monetta, Paulmann, & Katz, 2009).

*Olfactics*, interpersonal communication via smell, has been virtually ignored in intercultural research despite its importance (Samovar et al., 2010). Americans are the most smell-aversive culture in the world (Andersen, 1998). While most of the world's people emit natural body smells, cultures in the most developed parts of the world use an array of cosmetics to eliminate body odor or to replace it with artificial smells.

## DIMENSIONS OF INTERCULTURAL NONVERBAL COMMUNICATION

Research has shown that cultures can be located along behavioral dimensions that help explain why people act in different ways in various cultures. Most cultural differences in nonverbal behavior are a result of variations along the seven dimensions discussed in the following section (See Table 5.1).

**TABLE 5.1** Dimensions of Intercultural Nonverbal Communication

| Dimension | One Extreme | The Other Extreme |
|---|---|---|
| Context | Low Context | High Context |
| Identity | Individualism | Collectivism |
| Power | Low Power Distance | High Power Distance |
| Gender | Femininity | Masculinity |
| Uncertainty | Uncertainty Avoidance | Uncertainty Tolerance |
| Time | Long Term | Short Term |
| Immediacy | Low Contact | High Contact |

## Context

The first cultural dimension of communication, proposed decades ago, is *context*—the degree to which communication is explicit and verbal versus implicit and nonverbal. Hall (1976, 1984) has described high-context cultures in considerable detail: "A high-context (HC) communication or message is one in which most of the information is either in the physical context or internalized in the person, while very little is in the coded, explicit, transmitted parts of the message" (Hall, 1976, p. 91). "In a high-context culture such as that of Japan, meanings are internalized and there is a large emphasis on nonverbal codes" (Lustig & Koester, 2003. p. 112). Married couples or old friends skillfully use HC or implicit messages that are nearly impossible for others to understand. The situation, a smile, or a glance provides implicit meaning that needs no articulation. In HC cultures, information is integrated from the environment, context, situation, and subtle nonverbal cues that give messages meaning not available in explicit verbal utterances.

Low-context (LC) messages are the opposite; most are communicated through explicit codes and usually via verbal communication (Andersen, 1999a; Hall, 1976). LC messages must be detailed, unmistakable, and specific. Unlike personal relationships, which are high-context message systems, institutions such as courts of law and formal systems such as mathematics and computer languages require explicit LC systems because nothing can be taken for granted (Hall, 1984).

Huge cultural variations exist in the degree of context used in communication. Research suggests that the lowest-context cultures are Swiss, German, North American, and Scandinavian (Gudykunst & Kim, 1992; Hall, 1976, 1984). LC cultures are logical, analytical, linear, and action-oriented, and people tend to stress clearly articulated spoken or written messages (Hall, 1984). Cultures with characteristics of both HC and LC systems include the French, English, and Italian (Gudykunst & Kim, 1992).

Most HC cultures are found in Asia, especially China, Japan, and Korea (Elliott et al., 1982; Hall, 1976, 1984; Lustig and Koester, 2003). Although most languages are explicit LC communication systems, in China even the language is an implicit, high-context system. To use a Chinese dictionary, one must understand thousands of characters that change meaning in combination with other characters along with the context. Buddhism, a major influence in Japan and China, places a high value on silence, lack of emotional expression, and the unspoken, nonverbal parts of communication (McDaniel & Andersen, 1998). Recent research reports that in China apologies are much more likely to be implicit and nonverbal, whereas in America apologies tend to be explicit and verbal (Park & Guan, 2009). Americans often complain that the Japanese never "get to the point," but they fail to recognize that HC culture must provide a context and setting and let the point evolve (Hall, 1984). In research on airport farewell episodes, McDaniel and Andersen (1998) found Asians to be the least tactile of any cultural group studied. American Indian cultures with ancestral migratory roots in East Asia are remarkably like contemporary Asian cultures in several ways, especially in their need for high-context communication (Hall, 1984). Latin American cultures—a fusion of Iberian (Portuguese–Spanish) and Asian traditions—are also high-context cultures. Likewise, people from the southern and eastern Mediterranean, such as Greeks and Turks, and people from the Persian Gulf region, including Persians and Arabs, are also high context.

Communication is used rather differently in HC and LC cultures. Andersen, Hecht, Hoobler, and Smallwood (2002) suggest that these differences between HC and LC communication can be explained by four principles.

1. *Verbal communication and other explicit codes are more prevalent in low-context cultures such as the United States and Northern Europe.* People from LC cultures are often perceived as excessively talkative, belaboring of the obvious, and redundant. People from HC cultures may be perceived as nondisclosive, sneaky, and mysterious. Recent research shows that U.S. Americans are more likely to use explicit verbal strategies when apologizing; Chinese interactants are more likely to employ nonverbal, implicit apology strategies (Park & Guan, 2009).

2. *HC cultures do not value verbal communication the same way that LC cultures do.* Elliot et al. (1982) found that more-verbal people were perceived as more attractive in the United States, but less-verbal people were perceived as more attractive in Korea, which is an HC culture.

3. *HC cultures are more reliant on and tuned in to nonverbal communication.* In LC cultures, most people, particularly men, fail to perceive as much nonverbal communication as do members of HC cultures. Nonverbal communication provides the context for all communication (Watzlawick, Beavin, & Jackson, 1967), but people from HC cultures are particularly affected by these contextual cues. Thus, facial expressions, tensions, movements, speed of interaction, location of the interaction, and other subtle forms of nonverbal communication are likely to be more easily perceived by and have more meaning for people from HC cultures.

4. *In HC cultures, interactants expect more than in LC cultures* (Hall, 1976). People in HC cultures anticipate that communicators will understand unspoken feelings, implicit gestures, and environmental clues that people from LC cultures do not process. Given that both cultural extremes fail to recognize these basic communication differences, intercultural attributions about the meaning of behavior are often incorrect.

In conclusion, HC cultures rely more on nonverbal communication and less on verbal communication (See Table 5.2). Generally, HC cultures are also

**TABLE 5.2** Summary of Context Dimension

| Dimension 1. Context | One Extreme | The Other Extreme |
| --- | --- | --- |
| The degree to which communication is explicit and verbal or implicit and nonverbal. | Low Context | High Context |
| **Core Values** | Freedom of speech, directness | Silence, indirectness |
| **Nonverbal Traits** | Literal meaning, specific details, and precise time schedules | Information in the physical context, or internalized in the person |
| **Typical Cultures** | Switzerland, Germany, North America | China, Japan, Korea |

somewhat more collectivistic and less individualistic than LC cultures (Gudykunst et al., 1996; Andersen et al., 2002). Given this fact, it is appropriate that the next dimension of culture to be examined is cultural identity—individualism/collectivism.

## Individualism/Collectivism

A culture's individualism versus collectivism is one of the most widely researched dimensions of culture. Individualistic cultures emphasize I-identity and value personal rights and freedom whereas collectivistic cultures advocate we-identity and are more group oriented. Individualism/collectivism determines how people live together: alone, in families, or in tribes (Hofstede, 2001; Nisbett, Peng, Choi, & Norenzayan, 2001); their values; and how they communicate. Americans are extreme individualists, take individualism for granted, and are blind to its impact until travel brings them into contact with less individualistic, more collectivistic cultures.

Individualism has been applauded as a blessing and has been elevated to the status of a national religion in the United States. The best and worst in our culture can be attributed to individualism. Individualism is arguably the basis of liberty, democracy, freedom, and economic incentive and serves as protection against tyranny. Conversely, individualism may be the basis of loneliness, selfishness, pollution, and narcissism. Indeed, Hall (1976) has claimed that as an extreme individualist, "Western man has created chaos by denying that part of his self that integrates while enshrining the part that fragments experience" (p. 9). There can be little doubt that individualism is a fundamental dimension that distinguishes cultures. Western culture is individualistic, so people rely on personal judgments to a greater degree than they do on group decisions (Andersen et al., 2001). People in western cultures are more likely to perceive more individual, dispositional causes of behavior than people from eastern cultures (Patterson & Montepare, 2007) who are more likely to perceive situational causes for behavior. Eastern cultures emphasize harmony among people and between people and nature, and value collective judgments. Tomkins (1984) argued that even an individual's psychological makeup is the result of this cultural dimension. Western civilization has tended toward self-celebration, positive or negative. In contrast, Asian cultures generally reflect cooperation among people and harmony with nature.

In a landmark intercultural study of individualism in 40 noncommunist countries, Hofstede (1980) reported that the 10 most individualistic nations (starting with the most) were the United States, Australia, Great Britain, Canada, the Netherlands, New Zealand, Italy, Belgium, Denmark, and Sweden, all of which primarily derive from European cultures. The least individualistic nations (starting with the least) were Venezuela, Colombia, Pakistan, Peru, Taiwan, Thailand, Singapore, Chile, and Hong Kong, all of which are Asian or South American cultures. Likewise, Sitaram and Codgell (1976) reported that individuality is a primary value in Western cultures, of secondary importance in African cultures, and of little importance in Eastern and Muslim cultures.

Even though the United States is the most individualistic country on earth (Andersen, 1999a; Hofstede, 1982), some of its regions and ethnic groups diverge in their degree of individualism. Elazar (1972) found that the central Midwest and the Mid-Atlantic states have the most individualistic political culture, whereas the Southeast is the most traditional and least individualistic; however, this relationship is relative and, by world standards, even South Carolina is an individualistic culture. As Bellah and colleagues (1985) stated, "Individualism lies at the very core of American culture.... Anything that would violate our right to think for ourselves, judge for ourselves, make our own decisions, live our lives as we see fit, is not only morally wrong, it is sacrilegious" (p. 142). Likewise, different ethnic groups may vary within a culture. African Americans, for example, emphasize individualism (Hecht, Collier, & Ribeau, 1983), whereas Mexican Americans emphasize group and relational solidarity (Albert & Ah Ha, 2004). American's extreme individualism makes intercultural communication difficult. America is unique; all other cultures are less individualistic. As Condon and Yousef (1983) stated: "The fusion of individualism and equality is so valued and so basic that many Americans find it most difficult to relate to contrasting values in other cultures where interdependence greatly determines a person's sense of self" (p. 65).

Every aspect of nonverbal communication is affected by the degree of individualism or collectivism of a culture (See Table 5.3). Collectivistic cultures are

**TABLE 5.3** Summary of Identity Dimension

| Dimension 2. Individualism/Collectivism | One Extreme | The Other Extreme |
|---|---|---|
| The degree to which the society reinforces individual or collective achievement and interpersonal relationships. | Individualism | Collectivism |
| **Core Value** | Individual freedom | Group harmony |
| **Nonverbal Traits** | Proximally distant, different schedules, expressive of emotions | Proximally close, coordinated facial expressions and body movements |
| **Typical Cultures** | United States, Australia, Great Britain | Venezuela, China, Pakistan |

interdependent; members work, play, live, and sleep in proximity to one another. One study reports that people in individualistic cultures are more distant proximally than collectivists (Gudykunst et al., 1996). Hofstede (2001) suggests that as hunters and gatherers people lived apart in individualistic, nuclear families or small groups. When humans became agricultural, interdependent families began living in proximity in large families or tribal units. Urban–industrial societies returned to a norm of individualism, nuclear families, and a lack of proximity to one's neighbors, friends, and co-workers.

Culture also sets up the way people use time. In a study of doing business with Japanese, researchers discovered that the Japanese are slow to reach a decision whereas Americans prefer to take immediate actions (Hall & Hall, 1987). The greatest distinction between the two cultures lies in the Japanese's strong dependence on groups. They base their individual identities on the groups they belong to and seek dependent relationships from larger entities, especially employers. However, such dependency would be considered a negative trait in the United States since Americans value independence and individual initiative. A study comparing Anglo/European New Zealanders to Asians in New Zealand found that the Asians exhibited much more other-oriented, sociocentric communication, whereas Anglos exhibited far more ideocentric, task-oriented communication; this is consistent with the harmony

*Every aspect of nonverbal communication is affected by the degree of individualism or collectivism of a culture.*

and collectivistic scripts so characteristic of Asian communicators (Pekerti & Thomas, 2003).

Kinesic behavior tends to be more coordinated in collectivistic cultures where people match one another's facial expressions, and body movements are in sync. Where families work collectively, movements, schedules, and actions need to be highly coordinated (Argyle, 1975). Individualists are responsible for their relationships and their own happiness, whereas collectively oriented people regard compliance with norms as a primary value and personal or interpersonal happiness as a secondary value (Andersen, 1999a). Matsumoto (1991) reports, "collective cultures will foster emotional displays of their members that maintain and facilitate group cohesion, harmony, or cooperation, to a greater degree than individualistic cultures" (p. 132). Studies show that Asians are more likely to employ supportive back-channeling behaviors, particularly nodding, during conversation (Cutrone, 2005). Several scholars indicate that people in individualistic cultures display emotions more freely and diversely, particularly to out-groups, than do collectivists, who are discouraged from showing a range of positive and/or negative emotions outside of the immediate in-group (Matsumoto, 2006; Porter & Samovar, 2010). Similarly, children in collectivistic Chinese families displayed less facial emotion than Chinese children adopted by European American parents. These adopted children displayed less facial emotion than European American children, suggesting that facial expressivity is a learned behavior encouraged in individualistic cultures and discouraged in collectivistic ones.

Lustig and Koester (2003) maintain that "people from individualistic cultures are more likely than those from collectivistic cultures to use confrontational strategies when dealing with interpersonal problems; those with a collectivist orientation are likely to use avoidance, third-party intermediaries, or other face-saving techniques" (p. 127). In collectivistic cultures, people suppress both positive and negative emotional displays that are contrary to the mood of the group, because maintaining the group is a primary value (Andersen, 1999a). Recent research has shown that during apologies Chinese interactants use a more sincere tone of voice when apologizing to an outgroup member than an in-group member, consistent with the collectivistic nature of Chinese culture (Park & Guan, 2009). Bond (1993) found the Chinese culture to be lower in frequency, intensity, and duration of emotional expression than other cultures. Bond asserts, "The expression of emotion is carefully regulated out of a concern for its capacity to disrupt group harmony and status hierarchies" (p. 245).

> *People in individualistic cultures are encouraged to express emotions because individual freedom is a paramount value.*

People in individualistic cultures are encouraged to express emotions because individual freedom is a paramount value. Research suggests that people in individualistic cultures are more nonverbally affiliative. Wong, Bond, & Mosquera (2008) report that the emotion of joy is most likely to be displayed in autonomous, individualistic cultures. Individualistic cultures do not require affiliation or expression, so why are affiliativeness and positive emotional expression higher in individualistic cultures? Hofstede (1982) explained:

> In less individualistic countries where traditional social ties, like those with extended family members, continue to exist, people have less of a need to make specific friendships. One's friends are predetermined by the social relationships into which one is born. In the more individualistic countries, however, affective relationships are not socially predetermined but must be acquired by each individual personally (p. 163).

In individualistic countries such as the United States, affiliativeness, dating, flirting, small talk, smiling, and initial acquaintance are more important than in collectivistic countries where the social network is more fixed and less reliant on individual initiative.

Bellah et al. (1985) maintain that for centuries in the individualistic and mobile North American society, people could meet more easily, and their communication was more open; however, their relationships were usually more casual and transient than those found in more collectivistic cultures.

## Power Distance

Another basic dimension of intercultural communication is *power distance*—the degree to which power, prestige, and wealth are unequally distributed in a culture. (See Table 5.4.) Power distance has been

**TABLE 5.4** Summary of Power Distance Dimension

| Dimension 3. Power Distance | One Extreme | The Other Extreme |
| --- | --- | --- |
| The degree of equality or inequality between people in the country or society. | Low Power Distance | High Power Distance |
| **Core Value** | People's equality | Respect for status |
| **Nonverbal Traits** | Located at high latitudes, more tactile, relaxing and clear vocalic cues | Located near the equator, untouchable, regulated nonverbal displays |
| **Typical Cultures** | Austria, Israel, Denmark | Philippines, Mexico, Venezuela |

measured in many cultures using Hofstede's (2001) Power Distance Index (PDI) and Schwartz's (2004) hierarchy dimension. Like individualism, power distance varies greatly among cultures. Cultures with high PDI scores have power concentrated in the hands of a few rather than more equally distributed throughout the population. Condon and Yousef (1983) distinguish among three cultural patterns: democratic, authority centered, and authoritarian.

High PDI countries, from highest to lowest, are the Philippines, Mexico, Venezuela, India, Singapore, Brazil, Hong Kong, France, and Colombia (Hofstede, 1982), all of which, except France, are southern countries located near the equator. Gudykunst and Kim (1992) report that African and Asian cultures generally maintain hierarchical relationships characteristic of high power distance. Asian students are expected to be modest and deferent nonverbally to their instructors. Likewise, Vietnamese people consider employers to be their mentors and will not question orders.

The lowest PDI countries are, respectively, Austria, Israel, Denmark, New Zealand, Ireland, Sweden, Norway, Finland, Switzerland, and Great Britain (Hofstede, 2001), all of which are Northern European or of Northern European origin, middle-class, democratic, and located at high latitudes. The United States is slightly lower than the median in power distance, indicating smaller status differentials than in many other countries. Cultures differ in terms of how status is acquired. In many countries, such as India, class or caste determines one's status. In the United States, power and status are typically determined by money and conspicuous material displays (Andersen, 2008).

It is obvious that power distance would affect a culture's nonverbal behavior (See Table 5.4). In high PDI cultures, such as India, where a caste system severely limited interactions, traditionally any contact with the "untouchables" by members of other castes was forbidden and considered "polluting." Certainly, tactile communication among people of different castes is greatly curtailed in Indian culture. High PDI countries with less rigid stratification than India may still prohibit free interclass dating, marriage, and contact, all of which are taken for granted in low PDI countries. A study of status-related behavior showed that although a similar gap was found between perceptions of nonverbal behavior of lower- and higher-status people in Japan and the United States, greater differences were discovered in the hierarchical Japanese culture than in the more egalitarian American culture (Kowner & Wiseman, 2003).

Social systems with large power discrepancies produce unique kinesic behavior. Cultures with high power distance encourage emotional expressions that reveal status differences. For example, in hierarchical, high–power-distance cultures, people are expected to show only positive emotions to high-status others and only negative emotions to low-status others (Matsumoto, 1991). One recent study found that negative emotions such as shame, guilt, and fear are constrained in hierarchical cultures where order is paramount and individual violations of the social order are inappropriate (Wong et al., 2008). Nonverbal behaviors of subordinate classes display less power by lowering one's body, employing inconvenience displays, and not asserting authority. According to Andersen (2008), subordinates' bodily tension is obvious in power-discrepant relationships. Andersen (2008) reports that in such circumstances, subordinates smile more in an effort to appease superiors and to appear polite. The seemingly continuous smiles of many Asians are a culturally inculcated effort to appease superiors and smooth social relations—behaviors that are appropriate to a high PDI culture.

The power distance of a culture also affects vocalic and paralinguistic cues. Members of low PDI cultures are often unaware that their vocal volume may be offensive to others. American vocal tones are perceived as noisy, exaggerated, and childlike (Condon & Yousef, 1983). Lomax (1968) showed that in countries with centralized political authority, the voice box and singing voices are tighter and more closed, whereas societies that are more permissive produce more relaxed, open, and clear sounds.

## Gender

Perhaps the most researched issue in social science during recent decades is gender. Nations and cultures, like humans, can be viewed as more or less masculine; no cultures are really feminine or matriarchal in nature. The gender orientation of culture has an impact on many aspects of nonverbal behavior (See Table 5.5). This includes the nonverbal

**TABLE 5.5** Summary of Gender Dimension

| Dimension 4. Gender | One Extreme | The Other Extreme |
| --- | --- | --- |
| The degree of traditional gender roles of achievement, control, and power. | Femininity | Masculinity |
| **Core Value** | Caring for others | Material success |
| **Nonverbal Traits** | Relaxed and coordinated vocal patterns, nurturing | High level of stress, loud, aggressive |
| **Typical Cultures** | Sweden, Norway, the Netherlands | Japan, Austria, Venezuela |

expressions permitted by each sex, occupational status, nonverbal aspects of power, the ability to interact with strangers or acquaintances of the opposite sex, and all aspects of interpersonal relationships between men and women. *Gender*, as discussed in this article, refers to the rigidity of gender rules. In masculine cultures, gender rules are more rigid and traits such as strength, assertiveness, competitiveness, and ambitiousness are valued. In more feminine or androgynous cultures, attributes such as affection, compassion, nurturance, and emotionality are valued (Bem, 1974; Hofstede, 2001). In less gender-rigid cultures, both men and women can express more diverse, less stereotyped sex-role behaviors.

Cross-cultural research shows that girls are expected to be more nurturing than boys, although there is considerable variation from country to country (Hall, 1984). Hofstede (2001) has measured the degree to which people of both sexes in a culture endorse masculine or feminine goals. Masculine cultures regard competition and assertiveness as important, whereas feminine cultures place more importance on nurturance and compassion. Not surprisingly, the masculinity of a culture is negatively correlated with the percentage of women in technical and professional jobs and total women in the work force, whereas it is positively correlated with segregation of the sexes in higher education (Hofstede, 2001).

Countries with the 10 highest masculinity index scores, according to Hofstede (2001), are Japan, Austria, Venezuela, Italy, Switzerland, Mexico, Ireland, Great Britain, Germany, and the Philippines. The 10 countries with the lowest masculinity scores are Sweden, Norway, the Netherlands, Denmark, Costa Rica, Finland, Chile, Portugal, Thailand, and

Peru. Not surprisingly, high-masculinity countries have fewer women in the labor force, have only recently afforded voting privileges to women, and are less likely to consider wife rape a crime than are low masculinity countries (Seager & Olson, 1986).

The Scandinavian countries, with their long history of equal rights for women, are the most feminine countries. But why would South American cultures be less masculine and not manifest the Latin pattern of machismo? Iberian countries like Spain and Portugal have relatively feminine cultures, as do their South American cultural descendants like Chile and Peru. Hofstede (2001) suggests that machismo is more present in the Caribbean region than South America. In fact, South America, compared to Central America, has a much higher percentage of working women, higher school attendance by girls, and more women in higher education (Seager & Olson, 1986).

Considerable research shows that androgynous behavior (both feminine and masculine) results in higher self-esteem, social competence, success, and intellectual development for both males and females (Andersen, 2007). Nonverbal styles where men and women can express both masculine traits (such as dominance and anger) and feminine traits (such as warmth and emotionality) are likely to be both healthier and more effective. Buck (1984) has demonstrated that males may harm their health by internalizing emotions rather than externalizing them as women usually do. Internalized emotions that are not expressed result in more stress and higher blood pressure. Not surprisingly, cultures that are more masculine show higher stress levels (Hofstede, 2001).

Research has also demonstrated significant vocal differences between egalitarian and nonegalitarian countries. Countries in which women are economically important and where sexual standards for women are permissive show more relaxed vocal patterns than do other countries (Lomax, 1968). Moreover, egalitarian countries show less tension between the sexes, more vocal solidarity and coordination in their songs, and more synchrony in their movement (Lomax, 1968).

The United States tends to be a masculine country, according to Hofstede (2001), although it is not among the most masculine. Intercultural communicators should keep in mind that other countries may be either more or less sexually egalitarian than the United States. Most countries are more feminine than the United States (that is, nurturing and compassionate), so Americans of both sexes seem loud and aggressive by world standards. By demeanor, history, and current foreign policy the United States and its citizens are likely to be perceived as aggressive and even belligerent, even though our self-perceived ethos is peace loving and kind. Likewise, Americans' attitude toward women may seem sexist in high feminine locations such as Scandinavia.

Most importantly, in relatively more feminine countries, both men and women can engage in either masculine or feminine nonverbal behaviors. In masculine countries, the nonverbal behavior of men and women is carefully prescribed and adheres to narrower sexual scripts. So, in feminine countries like Sweden and Norway, women can engage in more powerful speaking styles, wear masculine clothing, be more vocally assertive, and choose to have children whether married or not. Similarly, men in feminine countries can show emotions like sadness or fear and engage in nurturing and nondominant behavior. In feminine countries, men more commonly take parental leave to do child care.

## Uncertainty

Some cultures value stability and certainty; other cultures value change and ambiguity. Uncertainty tolerance is a cultural predisposition to value risk and ambiguity (Andersen et al., 2002; Hofstede, 2001) over certainty and stability. At the individual level, this is called tolerance for ambiguity (Martin & Westie, 1959). People with intolerance of ambiguity have high levels of uncertainty avoidance, seek clear,

black-and-white answers, and prefer societies where the rules are clear and individual decision making is limited. People with tolerance of ambiguity have lower uncertainty avoidance and are more tolerant, accept ambiguous answers, and see shades of gray.

Countries vary greatly in their tolerance for uncertainty. In some cultures, freedom leads to uncertainty, which leads to stress and anxiety. Hofstede (2001) held that intolerance of ambiguity and dogmatism is primarily a function of the uncertainty-avoidance dimension rather than the power-distance dimension. The 10 countries with the highest levels of uncertainty avoidance are Greece, Portugal, Belgium, Japan, Perú, France, Chile, Spain, Argentina, and Turkey (Hofstede, 2001), countries whose culture originated in the Mediterranean region. The 10 countries lowest in uncertainty avoidance and highest in tolerance are Singapore, Denmark, Sweden, Hong Kong, Ireland, Great Britain, India, the Philippines, the United States and Canada. This list is dominated by Northern European nations and includes three Asian countries that were previously under the rule of Britain or the United States. Not surprisingly, these low-uncertainty avoidance countries have a long history of democratic rule that is likely to be both the cause and an effect of uncertainty avoidance. Catholic and Islamic countries are higher in uncertainty avoidance, whereas Protestant, Hindu, and Buddhist countries tend to be more accepting of uncertainty (Hofstede, 2001). Eastern religions and Protestantism tend to be less "absolute," whereas Catholicism and Islam are more "absolute" and "certain" religions. In their study of regional cultures in the United States, Andersen, Lustig, and Andersen (1990) report that intolerance for ambiguity is much higher in Southern states than in the Northern states, tending to reflect the international pattern of latitude and tolerance.

Few studies have examined nonverbal behavior associated with uncertainty. Hofstede (2001) maintains that countries high in uncertainty avoidance tend to display emotions more than do countries that are low in uncertainty avoidance.

An exception to this is Japan and Korea, where their polite collectivism trumps that normal pattern of expressiveness found in high–uncertainty avoidance countries. Furthermore, Hofstede (2001) reports that the emotional displays of young people are tolerated less in countries with high uncertainty

**TABLE 5.6** Summary of Uncertainty Dimension

| Dimension 5. Uncertainty | One Extreme | The Other Extreme |
|---|---|---|
| The degree of avoidance or tolerance for uncertainty and ambiguity within the society | Uncertainty avoidance | Uncertainty tolerance |
| **Core Value** | Certainty; what is different is dangerous | Exploration; what is different causes curiosity |
| **Nonverbal Traits** | More emotional displays; higher level of anxiety | More positive and friendly to strangers |
| **Typical Cultures** | Greece, Portugal, Belgium | Singapore, Denmark, Sweden |

avoidance. Certainly, disagreement and nonconformity are not appreciated if uncertainty avoidance is high. Nonverbal behavior is more likely to be codified and rule-governed in countries with high uncertainty avoidance. This seems to fit a country such as Japan, but the hypothesis remains to be tested. Hofstede (2001) found that nations high in uncertainty avoidance report more stylized and ritual behavior, so we should expect that nonverbal behavior is more prescribed in these cultures. When people from the United States communicate with people from a country such as Japan or France (both high in uncertainty avoidance), the Americans may seem unruly and unconventional, whereas their Japanese or French counterparts might seem too controlled and rigid to the Americans (Lustig & Koester, 2003). People from cultures that embrace uncertainty are much more likely to treat strangers with positive nonverbal behaviors such as smiles and other indications of immediacy and warmth (See Table 5.6).

## Future Orientation

Some societies have a future orientation that consists of relatively more focus on long-term orientation than short-term orientation (Hofstede, 2001). Cultures with a long-term orientation believe in continuity, persistence, work orientation, thrift, investments in real estate, and a more relative view of morality. Long-term cultures believe that ego and face-saving are vices, that personal adaptability is important, and that relationships are significant, but ordered by status.

Cultures with a short-term orientation, by contrast, value instant gratification, quick results, short-range profits, and importance of the bottom line.

Short-term cultures value leisure time, saving face is important, good and evil are absolute values, and status is not particularly important in personal relationships.

These deep culture values are manifested in a number of differences in nonverbal communication. Short-term cultures show less deference to status, whereas in long-term cultures people defer to high-status individuals including elders, corporate executives, professors, and government officials. A prototypic manifestation of the reverence for status in long-term cultures is the extremely deep bows to prominent people in many Asian countries. In short-term cultures status is elastic and may change quickly over time, or even across context. Elders are not particularly revered and nonverbal deference and attention are more likely to focus on the young and beautiful, rather than the wisdom and longevity. Nonverbal communication is more ritualized and prescribed in long-term cultures; nonverbal communication is informal and liberated in the short-term culture. In long-term cultures etiquette and modesty are important, and reciprocity is essential. As a result, long-term cultures reciprocate emotions, facial expression and gift giving.

The countries with the most short-term orientation are Pakistan, Nigeria, the Philippines, Canada, Zimbabwe, Great Britain, and the United States. Countries with the most long-term orientation are China, Hong Kong, Taiwan, Japan, South Korea, Brazil, and India—all Asian countries except Brazil. Research suggests that a major origin of long-term orientation is Confucianism, the Asian philosophy that emphasizes thrift, persistence and decorum (Hofstede, 2001).

# Immediacy

Immediacy behaviors and displays of interpersonal warmth are actions that signal closeness, intimacy, and availability for communication rather than avoidance and greater psychological distance (Andersen, 1985, 1998). Examples of immediacy behaviors are smiling, touching, eye contact, closer distances, and more vocal animation. Some scholars have labeled these behaviors as "expressive" (Patterson, 1983). Cultures that display considerable interpersonal closeness or immediacy have been labeled "contact cultures" because people in these countries stand closer together and touch more (Hall, 1966). People in low-contact cultures tend to stand apart and touch less. According to Patterson (1983):

> These habitual patterns of relating to the world permeate all aspects of everyday life, but their effects on social behavior define the manner in which people relate to one another. In the case of contact cultures, this general tendency is manifested in closer approaches so that tactile and olfactory information may be gained easily. (p. 145)

High-contact cultures are generally located in warmer countries with more sunlight, nearer the equator, and low-contact cultures are found in cooler climates father from the equator. Explanations for these latitudinal variations have included energy level, climate, and metabolism (Hofstede, 2001; Andersen, Lustig, & Andersen, 1990). Evidently, cultures in cooler climates tend to be more task-oriented and interpersonally "cool," whereas cultures in warmer climates tend to be more interpersonally oriented and interpersonally "warm." Even within the United States, the warmer latitudes tend to be higher-contact cultures. Andersen, Lustig, and Andersen (1990) reported that students at universities located in the so-called Sunbelt are more touch-oriented. Pennebaker, Rimé, and Sproul (1994) found a correlation between latitude and expressiveness within dozens of countries. Northerners are more expressive than southerners, according to their data, in Belgium, Croatia, France,

Germany, Italy, Japan, Serbia, Spain, Switzerland, and the United States, with an overall difference within the entire Northern Hemisphere. Pennebaker et al. (1994) conclude,

> Logically, climate must profoundly affect social processes. People living in cold climates devote more time to dressing, to providing warmth, to planning ahead for food provisions during the winter months.... In warm climates, people are more likely to see, hear, and interact with neighbors year around. Emotional expressiveness then would be more of a requirement. (pp. 15–16)

Similarly, Andersen, Lustig, and Andersen (1990) conclude,

> In Northern latitudes societies must be more structured, more ordered, more constrained, and more organized if the individuals are to survive harsh weather forces.... In contrast, Southern latitudes may attract or produce a culture characterized by social extravagance and flamboyance that has no strong inclination to constrain or order their world. (p. 307)

Research has shown that high-contact cultures comprise most Arab countries, including North Africa; the Mediterranean region, including France, Greece, Italy, Morocco, Portugal, and Spain; Jews from both Europe and the Middle East; Eastern Europeans and Russians; and virtually all of Latin America (Condon & Yousef, 1983; Jones, 1994; Jones & Remland, 1982; Mehrabian, 1971; Miller et al., 2006; Neuliep, 2002; Patterson, 1983; Samovar, Porter, & Jain, 1981; Scheflen, 1972). Australians are moderate in cultural contact level, as are North Americans (Patterson, 1983). Research shows that low-contact cultures comprise Northern Europe, including Scandinavia, Germany, and England; British Americans; white Anglo-Saxons (the primary culture of the United States); and virtually every Asian country, including Burma, China, Indonesia, Japan, Korea, the Philippines, Thailand, and Vietnam (Andersen, Andersen, & Lustig, 1987; Heslin & Alper, 1983;

*Cultures that display considerable interpersonal closeness or immediacy have been labeled "contact cultures" because people in these countries stand closer together and touch more.*

Jones, 1994; Jones & Remland, 1982; McDaniel & Andersen, 1998; Mehrabian, 1971; Patterson, 1983; Remland, 2000; Samovar, Porter, & Jain, 1981; Scheflen, 1972). Research reported by Remland (2000) indicates that people touch significantly more in southern Europe than in northern Europe.

Other studies suggest that the biggest differences in immediacy are not between North America and Europe, both of which are probably moderate-to high-contact cultures. Compared to the rest of the world, Northeast Asian cultures are extremely non-contact (McDaniel & Andersen, 1998; Remland et al., 1991). Another study shows that, contrary to Hall's hypothesis, strangers sit closer to, not farther from, one another in the United States than in Spain or Morocco (Mazur, 1977). These three studies question whether Hall's (1966) original designation of some cultures as "low contact" is an oversimplification. Whether a generational shift or internationalization may have produced this change is unclear, but much of the Western world, including the United States, appears to be a contact culture. Indeed, McDaniel and Andersen's (1998) study of public touch suggests that the biggest difference is between Asians, who rarely touch in public, and virtually every other culture, which all manifest higher degrees of public touching. These findings are consistent with other research suggesting that China and Japan are distinctly nontactile cultures (Barnland, 1978; Jones, 1994).

Without a doubt, cultures differ in their immediacy (See Table 5.7). Generally, people living in northern countries, northern parts of individual countries, in traditional cultures, and in Northeast Asia are the least immediate and expressive. Conversely, people living in the south, modern countries, and non-Asian cultures are the most expressive and immediate. Obviously, these findings are painted with a fairly broad brush and will await a more detailed cultural portrait.

## CONCLUSIONS

These seven dimensions of intercultural nonverbal communication aim at providing a theoretical framework that helps move studies on nonverbal communication across cultures from detailed descriptions to the realm of meanings, functions, outcomes, and relationships behind the screen. This list is neither exhaustive nor discrete. However, scholars and cultural training practitioners have increasingly utilized the conceptual scaffold outlined in this chapter to better understand and further explain the underlying basis of thousands of cultural differences in nonverbal behavior.

Although studying these six dimensions cannot ensure competence in intercultural communication, combining cognitive knowledge from intercultural readings and courses with actual encounters with people from other cultures will definitely help boost one's intercultural communication competence. More importantly, these six dimensions of cultural variation in nonverbal communication have pointed out directions for future studies. As Andersen, Hecht, Hoobler, and Smallwood (2002) suggested, the rich interplay among the six dimensions, the interactions among people who differ along the same dimensions, the phenomenon that some members of a society do

**TABLE 5.7** Summary of Immediacy Dimension

| Dimension 6. Immediacy | One Extreme | The Other Extreme |
|---|---|---|
| The degree of closeness, intimacy, and availability for communication | Low Contact | High Contact |
| **Core Value** | Certainty; what is different is dangerous | Exploration; what is different causes curiosity |
| **Nonverbal Traits** | Located in cooler climates, stand apart and touch less, stay "cool" | Located in warmer countries nearer the equator, stand closer together and touch more, expressive |
| **Typical Cultures** | Japan, China, Korea | North Africa, France, Brazil |

not seem to fully manifest the general tendencies of a particular culture, and group behavior investigated in well-situated cultural context are of great research value and potential.

# References

Albert, R. D. & Ah Ha, I. (2004). Latino/Anglo-American differences in attributions to situations involving touch and silence. *International Journal of Intercultural Relations, 28*, 353–280.

Andersen, J. F., Andersen, P. A., & Lustig, M. W. (1987). Opposite-sex touch avoidance: A national replication and extension. *Journal of Nonverbal Behavior, 11*, 89–109.

Andersen, P. A. (1985). Nonverbal immediacy in interpersonal communication. In A. W. Siegman & S. Feldstein (Eds.), *Multichannel integrations of nonverbal behavior* (pp. 1–36). Hillsdale, NJ: Lawrence Erlbaum.

Andersen, P. A. (1987). The trait debate: A critical examination of the individual differences paradigm in intercultural communication. In B. Dervin & M. J. Voigt (Eds.), *Progress in communication sciences, Vol. VIII* (pp. 47–82). Norwood, NJ: Ablex.

Andersen, P. A. (1988). Explaining intercultural differences in nonverbal communication. In L. A. Samovar & R. E. Porter (Eds.), *Intercultural communication: A reader* (5th ed., pp. 272–282). Belmont, CA: Wadsworth.

Andersen, P. A. (1997). Cues of Culture: The basis of intercultural differences in nonverbal communication. In L. A. Samovar & R. Porter (Eds.), *Intercultural Communication: A Reader* (8th ed., pp. 244–256). Belmont, CA: Wadsworth.

Andersen, P. A. (1998). The cognitive valence theory of intimate communication. In M. T. Palmer & G. A. Barnett (Eds.), *Progress in communication sciences, Volume XIV: Mutual influence in interpersonal communication: Theory and research in cognition, affect, and behavior.* (pp. 39–72). Stamford, CT: Ablex.

Andersen, P. A. (1999a). *Nonverbal communication: Forms and functions.* Mountain View, CA: Mayfield.

Andersen, P. A. (1999b). 1999 WSCA Presidential address. *Western Journal of Communication, 63*, 339–543.

Andersen, P. A. (2000). Explaining intercultural differences in nonverbal communication. In L. A. Samovar & R. E. Porter (Eds.), *Intercultural communication: A reader* (9th ed., pp. 258–279). Belmont, CA: Wadsworth.

Andersen, P. A. (2004). *The complete idiot's guide to body language.* Indianapolis, IN: Alpha Books.

Andersen, P. A. (2007). *Nonverbal communication: Forms and functions.* Long Grove, IL: Waveland Press.

Andersen, P. A. (2008). Positions of power: Status and dominance in organizational communication. In L. K. Guerrero & M. L. Hecht (Eds.), *The nonverbal communication reader* (pp. 350–467). Long Grove, IL: Waveland Press.

Andersen, P. A., Hecht, M. L., Hoobler, G. D., & Smallwood, M. (2002). Nonverbal communication across culture. In B. Gudykunst and B. Mody (Eds.), *Handbook of international and intercultural communication,* (pp. 89–106). Thousand Oaks, CA: Sage.

Andersen, P. A., & Leibowitz, K. (1978). The development and nature of the construct touch avoidance. *Environmental Psychology and Nonverbal Behavior, 3*, 89–106.

Andersen, P. A., Lustig, M. W., & Andersen, J. F. (1986). *Communication patterns among cultural regions of the United States: A theoretical perspective.* Paper presented at the annual convention of the International Communication Association, Chicago.

Andersen, P. A., Lustig, R., & Andersen, J. F. (1990). Changes in latitude, changes in attitude: The relationship between climate and interpersonal communication predispositions. *Communication Quarterly, 38*, 291–311.

Argyle, M. (1975). *Bodily communication.* New York: International Universities Press.

Barnland, D. C. (1978). Communication styles in two cultures: Japan and the United States. In A. Kendon, R. M. Harris, & M. R. Key (Eds.), *Organization of behavior in face-to-face interaction* (pp. 427–456). The Hague, the Netherlands: Mouton.

Beaulieu, C. M. (2004). Intercultural study of personal space: A case study. *Journal of Applied Social Psychology, 34*, 794–805.

Beaupre, M. & Hess, U. (2005). Cross-cultural emotion recognition among Canadian ethnic groups. *Journal of Cross-Cultural Psychology, 36*, 355–370.

Bellah, R. N., Madsen, R., Sullivan, W. M., Swidler, A., & Tipton, S. (1985). *Habits of the heart: Individualism and commitment in American life.* New York: Harper & Row.

Bem, S. L. (1974). The measurement of psychological androgyny. *Journal of Consulting and Clinical Psychology, 42*, 155–162.

Bond, M. H. (1993). Emotions and their expression in Chinese culture. *Journal of Nonverbal Behavior, 17*, 245–262.

Brown, D. E. (1991). *Human universals.* Philadelphia: Temple University Press.

Bruneau, T. (1979). The time dimension in intercultural communication. In D. Nimmo (Ed.), *Communication yearbook 3* (pp. 423–433). New Brunswick, NJ: Transaction Books.

Buck, R. (1984). *The communication of emotion.* New York: Guilford Press.

Buck, R. & Van Lear, C. A. (2002). Verbal and nonverbal communication: Distinguishing symbolic, spontaneous, and pseudo-spontaneous communication. *Journal of Communication, 52,* 522–541.

Burgoon, J. K., Guerrero, L. K., & Floyd, K. (2010). *Nonverbal Communication.* Boston: Allyn and Bacon.

Camras, L. A., Chen, Y., Bakeman, R., Norris, K., & Cain, T. R. (2006). Culture, ethnicity, and children's facial expressions: A study of European American, Mainland Chinese, Chinese American and adopted Chinese girls. *Emotion, 6,* 103–114.

Camras, L. A. Oster, H., Campos, J., Campos, R., Ujiie, T., Miyake, K., Wang, L., & Meng, Z. (1998). Production of emotional facial expressions in European American, Japanese, and Chinese infants. *Developmental Psychology, 34,* 616–628.

Condon, J. C., & Yousef, F. (1983). *An introduction to intercultural communication.* Indianapolis, IN: Bobbs-Merrill.

Cushner, K., & Brislin, R. (1996). *Intercultural interactions: A practical guide* (2nd ed.). Thousand Oaks, CA: Sage.

Cutrone, P. (2005). A case study examining backchannels in conversations between Japanese-British dyads. *Multilingua, 24,* 237–274.

DiBiase, R. & Gunnoe, J. (2004). Gender and culture differences in touching behavior. *Journal of Social Psychology, 144,* 49–62.

Dovidio, J. F., Hebl, M., Richeson, J. A., & Shelton, J. N. (2006). Nonverbal communication, race, and intergroup interaction. In V. Manusov & M. L. Patterson (Eds.), *The Sage Handbook of Nonverbal Communication,* (pp. 481–500). Thousand Oaks, CA: Sage.

Elazar, D. J. (1972). *American federalism: A view from the states.* New York: Thomas P. Crowell.

Elfenbein, H. A. (2006). Learning in emotion judgements: Training and the cross-cultural understanding of facial expression. *Journal of Nonverbal Behavior, 30,* 21–36.

Elfenbein, H. A. & Ambady, N. (2003). When familiarity breeds accuracy: Cultural exposure and facial expression recognition. *Journal of Personality and Social Psychology, 85,* 276–290.

Elliot, S., Scott, M. D., Jensen, A. D., & McDonough, M. (1982). Perceptions of reticence: A cross-cultural investigation. In M. Burgoon (Ed.), *Communication yearbook 5* (pp. 591–602). New Brunswick, NJ: Transaction Books.

Ekman, P. (1972). Universal and cultural difference in the facial expression of emotion. In J. R. Cole (Ed.), *Nebraska symposium on motivation* (pp. 207–283). Lincoln, NE: University of Nebraska Press.

Ekman, P., & Friesen, W. (1975). *Unmasking the face.* Englewood Cliffs, NJ: Prentice-Hall.

Ekman, P., & Oster, H. (1979). Facial expression of emotion. *Annual Review of Psychology, 30,* 527–554.

Fernandez, D. R., Carlson, D. S., Stepina, L. P., & Nicholson, J. D. (1997). Hofstede's country classification 25 years later. *Journal of Social Psychology, 137,* 43–54.

Ford, J. G., & Graves, J. R. (1977). Differences between Mexican-American and white children in interpersonal distance and social touching. *Perceptual and Motor Skills, 45,* 779–785.

Geertz, C. (1973). *The interpretation of cultures.* New York: Basic Books.

Goldin-Meadow, S. (2003). *Hearing gestures.* Cambridge, MA: The Belknap Press of Harvard University Press.

Gudykunst, W. B., & Kim, Y. Y. (1992). *Communicating with strangers: An approach to intercultural communication.* New York: Random House.

Gudykunst, W. B., Matsumoto, Y., Ting-Toomey, S., Nishida, T., Kim, K., & Heyman, S. (1996). Influence of cultural individualism–collectivism, self-construals, and individual values on communication styles across cultures. *Human Communication Research, 22,* 510–543.

Gudykunst, W. B., & Nishida, T. (1986). Attributional confidence in low- and high-context cultures. *Communication Research, 12,* 525–549.

Hall, E. T. (1959). *The silent language.* New York: Doubleday.

Hall, E. T. (1966a). A system of the notation of proxemic behavior. *American Anthropologist, 65,* 1003–1026.

Hall, E. T. (1966b). *The hidden dimension* (2nd ed.). Garden City, NY: Anchor/Doubleday.

Hall, E. T. (1976). *Beyond culture.* Garden City, NY: Anchor.

Hall, E. T. (1984). *The dance of life: The other dimension of time.* Garden City, NY: Anchor.

Hall, E. T., & Hall, M. (1987). *Hidden differences: Doing business with the Japanese.* Garden City, NY: Anchor Press/Doubleday.

Hecht, M. L., Collier, M. J., & Ribeau, S. A. (1993). *African-American communication: Ethnic identity and cultural interpretation.* Newbury Park, CA. Sage.

Heslin, R., & Alper, T. (1983). Touch: A bonding gesture. In J. M. Wiemann & R. Harrison (Eds.), *Non-verbal Interaction* (pp. 47–75). Beverly Hills, CA: Sage.

Hofstede, G. (1984). *Culture's consequences*. Beverly Hills, CA: Sage.

Hofstede, G. (1991). *Cultures and organizations: Software of the mind*. London: McGraw-Hill.

Hofstede, G. (1998). Masculinity/femininity as a dimension of culture. In G. Hofstede (Ed.), *Masculinity and femininity: The taboo dimension of national cultures* (pp. 3–28). Thousand Oaks, CA: Sage.

Hofstede, G. (2001). Culture's consequences (2nd ed.). Beverly Hills, CA: Sage.

Hofstede, G. J., Pedersen, P. B., & Hofstede G. (2003). *Exploring culture: Exercises, stories and synthetic cultures*. Yarmouth, ME: Intercultural Press.

Jack, R. E. Blais, C., Scheepers, C., Schyns, P. G. & Caldera, R. (2009). Cultural confusions show that facial expressions are not universal. *Current Biology, 19*, 1543–1548.

Jones, S. E. (1994). *The right touch: Understanding and using the language of physical contact*. Cresshill, NJ: Hampton Press.

Jones, T. S., & Remland, M. S. (1982, May). *Cross-cultural differences in self-reported touch avoidance*. Paper presented at the annual convention of the Eastern Communication Association, Hartford, CT.

Jourard, S. M. (1966). An exploratory study of body-accessibility. *British Journal of Social and Clinical Psychology, 5*, 221–231.

Kowner, R., & Wiseman, R. (2003). Culture and status-related behavior: Japanese and American perceptions of interaction in asymmetric dyads. *Cross-Cultural Research, 37*, 178–201.

LaBarre, W. (1985). Paralinguistics, kinesics, and cultural anthropology. In L. A. Samovar & R. E. Porter (Eds.), *Intercultural communication: A reader* (4th ed., pp. 272–279). Belmont, CA: Wadsworth.

Lambert, H. & Wood, K. (2005). A comparative analysis of communication about sex, health and sexual health in India and South Africa: Implications for HIV prevention, *Culture, Health & Sexuality, 7*, 527–541.

Lomax, A. (1968). *Folk song style and culture*. New Brunswick, NJ: Transaction Books.

Lustig, M. L., & Koester, J. (2003). *Intercultural competence: Interpersonal communication across culture*. (4th ed.). New York: HarperCollins.

Mandal, M. K. & Ambady, N. (2004). Laterality of facial expressions of emotion: Universal and culture specific influences. *Behavioral Neurology, 15*, 23–34.

Marsh, A. A., Elfenbein, H. A., & Ambady, N. (2003). *Psychological Science, 14*, 373–376.

Martin, J. G., & Westie, F. R. (1959). The intolerant personality. *American Sociological Review, 24*, 521–528.

Matsumoto, D. (1991). Cultural influences on facial expressions of emotion. *Southern Communication Journal, 56*, 128–137.

Matsumoto, D. (2006). Culture and nonverbal behavior. In V. Manusov & M. L. Patterson (Eds.). *The Sage Handbook of Nonverbal Communication*, (pp. 219–235). Thousand Oaks, CA: Sage.

Matsumoto, D. (2002). Methodological requirements to test a possible in-group advantage in judging emotions across cultures: Comment on Elfenbein and Ambady (2002) and evidence. *Psychological Bulletin, 128*, 236–242.

Matsumoto, D. (2006). Culture and nonverbal behavior. In V. Manusov & M. L. Patterson (Eds.), *The Sage Handbook of Nonverbal Communication*, (pp. 219–235). Thousand Oaks, CA: Sage.

McDaniel, E. R., & Andersen, P. A. (1998). Intercultural variations in tactile communication. *Journal of Nonverbal Communication, 22*, 59–75.

Mehrabian, A. (1971). *Silent Messages*. Belmont, CA: Wadsworth.

Meissner, C. A, & Brigham, J. C. (2001). Thirty years of investigating the own-race bias memory for faces: A meta-analytic review. Psychology, *Public Policy, and Law, 7*, 3–35.

Merritt, A. (2000). Culture in the cockpit: Do Hofstede's dimensions replicate? *Journal of Cross-Cultural Psychology, 31*, 283–301.

Molinsky, A. L., Krabbenhoft, M. A., Ambady, N., & Choi, Y. S. (2005). Cracking the nonverbal code. Intercultural competence and gesture recognition across cultures. *Journal of Cross-Cultural Psychology, 36*, 380–395.

Nisbett, R. E., Peng, K., Choi, I., & Norenzayan, A. (2001). Culture and systems of thought: Holistic vs. analytic cognition. *Psychological Review, 108*, 291–310.

Ozdemir, A. (2008). Shopping malls. Measuring interpersonal distance under changing conditions across cultures. *Field Methods, 20*, 226–248.

Park, H. S. & Guan, X. (2009). Cross-cultural comparisons of verbal and nonverbal strategies of apologizing. *Journal of International and Intercultural Communication, 2*, 66–87.

Pell, M., Monetta, L., Paulmann, S. & Katz, S. A. (2009). Recognizing emotions in a foreign language. *Journal of Nonverbal Behavior, 33*, 107–120.

Patterson, M. L. (1983). *Nonverbal behavior: A functional perspective*. New York: Springer-Verlag.

Patterson, M. L. (2007). Nonverbal behavior in a global context: Dialogue, questions and responses. *Journal of Nonverbal Behavior, 31*, 167n168.

Pekerti, A. A. & Thomas, D. C. (2003). Communication in intercultural interaction: An empirical investigation of ideocentric and sociocentric communication styles. *Journal of Cross-Cultural Psychology, 34*, 139–154.

Pennebaker, J. W., Rimé, B., & Sproul, G. (1994). *Stereotype of emotional expressiveness of Northerners and Southerners: A cross-cultural test of Montesquieu's hypotheses*. Unpublished paper, Southern Methodist University, Dallas, TX.

Porter, R. E., & Samovar, L. A. (1998). Cultural influences on emotional expression: Implications for intercultural communication. In P. A. Andersen & L. K. Guerrero (Eds.) *Handbook of communication and emotion: Research theory, applications and contexts* (pp. 451–472). San Diego, CA: Academic Press.

Remland, M. S., Jones, T. S., & Brinkman, H. (1991). Proxemic and haptic behavior in three European countries. *Journal of Nonverbal Behavior, 15*, 215–232.

Remland, M. S. (2000). *Nonverbal communication in everyday life*. Boston, MA: Houghton Mifflin.

Samovar, L. A., Porter, R. E., & Jain, N. C. (1981). *Understanding intercultural communication*. Belmont, CA: Wadsworth.

Samovar, L. A., Porter, R. E., & McDaniel, E. R. (2010). *Communication between cultures*. (7th ed.). Boston: Wadsworth/Cengage Learning.

Sapir, E. (1928). The unconscious patterning of behavior in society. In E. S. Drummer (Ed.), *The unconscious* (pp. 114–142). New York: Knopf.

Scheflen, A. E. (1972). *Body language and the social order*. Englewood Cliffs, NJ: Prentice-Hall.

Scheflen, A. E. (1974). *How behavior means*. Garden City, NY: Anchor.

Schwartz, S. H, (2004). Mapping and interpreting cultural differences around the world. In V. Vinken, J. Soeters, & P. Ester (Eds.), *Comparing cultures: Dimensions of culture in a comparative perspective* (pp 43–73). Leiden: the Netherlands, Brill.

Seager, J., & Olson, A. (1986). *Women in the world atlas*. New York: Simon & Schuster.

Shackleton, V. J., & Ali, A. H. (1990). Work-related values of managers: A test of the Hofstede model. *Journal of Cross-Cultural Psychology, 21*, 109–118.

Shuter, R. (1976). Proxemics and tactility in Latin America. *Journal of Communication, 26*(3), 46–52.

Shuter, R. (1977). A field study of nonverbal communication in Germany, Italy and the United States. *Communication Monographs, 4*, 298–305.

Sitaram, K. S., & Codgell, R. T. (1976). *Foundations of intercultural communication*. Columbus, OH: Charles E. Merrill.

Sporer, S. L. (2001a). Recognizing the faces of other ethnic groups: An integration of theories. *Psychology, Public Policy, and Law, 7*, 36–97.

Sporer, S. L. (2001b). The cross-race effect: Beyond recognition of faces in the laboratory. *Psychology, Public Policy, and Law, 7*, 170–200.

Ting-Toomey, S. (1999). *Communicating across cultures*. New York: The Guilford Press.

Tomkins, S. S. (1984). Affect theory. In K. R. Scherer & P. Ekman (Eds.), *Approaches to emotion* (pp. 163–195). Hillsdale, NJ: Lawrence Erlbaum.

Tung, R. (1994). Strategic management thought in East Asia. *Organizational Dynamics, 22*, 55–65.

United Nation World Tourism Organizations (2009), http://www.unwto.org/facts/eng/pdf/barometer/UNWTO_Barom09_2_en_excerpt.pdf Retrieved February 5, 2010.

Watzlawick, P., Beavin, J. H., & Jackson, D. D. (1967). *Pragmatics of human communication*. New York: W. W. Norton.

Wong, S. Bond, M. H. (2008). The influence of cultural value orientations on self-reported emotional expression across cultures. *Journal of Cross-Cultural Psychology, 39*, 224–229.

Wickline, V. B., Bailey, W., & Nowicki, S. (2009). Cultural in-group advantage: Emotional recognition in African American and European American faces and voices. *Journal of Genetic Psychology, 1*, 5–28.

## Concepts and Questions

1. Explain what you believe Andersen is suggesting when he writes the following: "Although some nonverbal behaviors are universal and show little or no cultural variations, most nonverbal behaviors show a considerable imprint of culture."

2. Why does Andersen assert that cross-cultural differences in nonverbal behavior create intercultural miscommunication, friction, and confusion?

3. Can you think of some ways that people rely on nonverbal cues to signal their identity?

4. Besides reflecting a person's personal and cultural identity, why does nonverbal behavior also carry "powerful feelings, emotions, and attitudes"?

5. From your personal experiences, can you think of some diverse ways that people from various cultures greet, show emotion, and beckon?

6. What is kinesic behavior? How does it vary from culture to culture?

7. What type of nonverbal communication does the word *haptics* refer to?

8. How is the degree of individualism within a culture manifested in nonverbal communication?

# Monochronic and Polychronic Time

EDWARD T. HALL

While Andersen looked at a large series of nonverbal components, our next essay scrutinizes a single nonverbal element—time. Anthropologist Edward T. Hall discusses what he describes as polychronic (P-time) and monochronic (M-time). Specifically, Hall examines the conscious and unconscious ways people, because of their cultural backgrounds, perceive and employ these two orientations toward time. We should note at the outset that these two points of reference (M-time and P-time) should not be viewed as either/or categories, but rather as representing the ends of a continuum that allows for cultural variations and placements along the continuum.

Individuals from P-time cultures, such as those found bordering the Mediterranean and in Africa and South America, operate near the P-time end of the continuum. As the term polychronic suggests, they do many things simultaneously, are more concerned with people and the present moment than with schedules, and believe that they are in command of time rather than being controlled by it. Cultures that operate near the M-time end of the time scale, such as those found in North America and Northern Europe, reflect traits that are monochronic. These cultures organize their lives around time by relying heavily on time-keeping instruments like clocks, calendars, computers, and cell-phone reminders. They emphasize schedules,

> Hall examines the conscious and unconscious ways people, because of their cultural backgrounds, perceive and employ these two orientations toward time.

the segmentation of time, and promptness. It is easy to imagine the potential for misunderstanding when people from these two contrasting orientations attempt to interact. Hall's essay helps you avoid communication problems by introducing you to the many forms and manifestations these two interaction patterns may take.

Lorenzo Hubbell, trader to the Navajo and the Hopi, was three-quarters Spanish and one-quarter New Englander, but culturally he was Spanish to the core. Seeing him for the first time on government business transactions relating to my work in the 1930s, I felt embarrassed and a little shy because he didn't have a regular office where people could talk in private. Instead, there was a large corner room—part of his house adjoining the trading post—in which business took place. Business covered everything from visits with officials and friends, conferences with Indians who had come to see him, who also most often needed to borrow money or make sheep deals, as well as a hundred or more routine transactions with store clerks and Indians who had not come to see Lorenzo specifically but only to trade. There were long-distance telephone calls to his warehouse in Winslow, Arizona, with cattle buyers, and to his brother, Roman, at Ganado, Arizona—all this and more (some of it quite personal) carried on in public, in front of our small world for all to see and hear. If you wanted to learn about the life of an Indian trader or the ins and outs of running a small trading empire (Lorenzo had a dozen posts scattered throughout northern Arizona), all you had to do was to sit in Lorenzo's office for a month or so and take note of what was going on. Eventually all the different parts of the pattern would unfold before your eyes, as eventually they did before mine, as I lived and worked on that reservation over a five-year period.

I was prepared for the fact that the Indians do things differently from [Anglo-European] (AE) cultures because I had spent part of my childhood on the Upper Rio Grande River with the Pueblo Indians as friends. Such differences were taken for granted. But this public, everything-at-once, mélange way of conducting business made an impression on me. There was no escaping it, here was another world, but in this instance, although both Spanish and Anglos had their roots firmly planted in European soil, each handled time in radically different ways.

It didn't take long for me to accustom myself to Lorenzo's business ambiance. There was so much going on that I could hardly tear myself away. My own work schedule won out, of course, but I did find that the Hubbell store had a pull like a strong magnet, and I never missed an opportunity to visit with Lorenzo. After driving through Oraibi, I would pull up next to his store, park my pickup, and go through the side door to the office. These visits were absolutely necessary because without news of what was going on, life could become precarious. Lorenzo's desert "salon" was better than a newspaper, which, incidentally, we lacked.

Having been initiated to Lorenzo's way of doing business, I later began to notice similar mutual involvement in events among the New Mexico Spanish. I also observed the same patterns in Latin America, as well as in the Arab world. Watching my countrymen's reactions to this "many things at a time" system, I noted how deeply it affected the channeling and flow of information, the shape and form of the networks connecting people, and a host of other important social and cultural features of the society.

> *For polychronic people, time is seldom experienced as "wasted," and is apt to be considered a point rather than a ribbon or a road, but that point is often sacred.*

I realized that there was more to this culture pattern than one might at first suppose.

Years of exposure to other cultures demonstrated that complex societies organize time in at least two different ways: events scheduled as separate items—one thing at a time—as in North Europe, or following the Mediterranean model of involvement in several things at once. The two systems are logically and empirically distinct. Like oil and water, they don't mix. Each has its strengths and its weaknesses. I have termed doing many things at once: Polychronic, P-time. The North European system—doing one thing at a time—is Monochronic, M-time. P-time stresses involvement of people and completion of transactions rather than adherence to preset schedules. Appointments are not taken as seriously and, as a consequence, are frequently broken. P-time is treated as less tangible than M-time. For polychronic people, time is seldom experienced as "wasted," and is apt to be considered a point rather than a ribbon or a road, but that point is often sacred. An Arab will say, "I will see you before one hour," or "I will see you after two days." What he means in the first instance is that it will not be longer than an hour before he sees you, and in the second instance, it will be at least two days. These commitments are taken quite seriously as long as one remains in the P-time pattern.

Once, in the early 1960s, when I was in Patras, Greece, which is in the middle of the P-time belt, my own time system was thrown in my face under rather ridiculous but still amusing circumstances. An impatient Greek hotel clerk, anxious to get me and my ménage settled in some quarters that were far from first class, was pushing me to make a commitment so he could continue with his siesta. 1 couldn't decide whether to accept this rather forlorn "bird in the hand" or take a chance on another hotel that looked, if possible, even less inviting. Out of the blue, the clerk blurted, "Make up your mind. After all, time is money!" How would you reply to that at a time of day when literally nothing was happening? 1 couldn't help but laugh at the incongruity of it all. If there ever was a case of time not being money, it was in Patras during siesta in the summer.

Although M-time cultures tend to make a fetish out of management, there are points at which M-time doesn't make as much sense as it might. Life in general is at times unpredictable; and who can tell exactly how long a particular client, patient, or set of transactions will take? These are imponderables in the chemistry of human transactions. What can be accomplished one day in 10 minutes may take 20 minutes on the next. Some days people will be rushed and can't finish; on others, there is time to spare, so they "waste" the remaining time.

In Latin America and the Middle East, North Americans are often psychologically stressed. Immersed in a polychronic environment in the markets, stores, and souks of Mediterranean and Arab countries, one is surrounded by other customers all vying for the attention of a single clerk who is trying to wait on everyone at once. There is no recognized order as to who is to be served next, no queue or numbers to indicate who has been waiting the longest. To the North European or American, it appears that confusion and clamor abound. In a different context, the same patterns can be seen operating in the governmental bureaucracies of Mediterranean countries: A typical office layout for important officials usually includes a large reception area (an ornate version of Lorenzo Hubbell's office) outside the private suite, where small groups of people can wait and be visited by the minister or his aides. These functionaries do most of their business outside in this semipublic setting, moving from group to group conferring with each in turn. The semiprivate transactions take less time and give others the feeling that they are in the presence of the minister and other important people with whom they may also want to confer. Once one is used to this pattern, it is clear that there are advantages, which often outweigh the disadvantages of a series of private meetings in the inner office.

Particularly distressing to Americans is the way in which polychronic people handle appointments. Being on time simply doesn't mean the same thing as it does in the United States. Matters in a polychronic culture seem in a constant state of flux. Nothing is solid or firm, particularly plans for the future; even important plans may be changed right up to the minute of execution.

In contrast, people in the Western world find little in life exempt from the iron hand of M-time. Time is so thoroughly woven into the fabric of existence that we are hardly aware of the degree to which it determines and coordinates everything we do, including the molding of relations with others in many subtle ways. In fact, social and business life, even one's sex life, is commonly schedule-dominated. By scheduling, we compartmentalize; this makes it possible to concentrate on one thing at a time, but it also reduces the context. Since scheduling by its very nature selects what will and will not be perceived and attended, and permits only a limited number of events within a given period, what gets scheduled constitutes a system for setting priorities for both people and functions. Important things are taken up first and allotted the most time; unimportant things are left until last or omitted if time runs out.

M-time is also tangible; we speak of it as being saved, spent, wasted, lost, made up, crawling, killed, and running out. These metaphors must be taken seriously. M-time scheduling is used as a classification system that orders life. The rules apply to everything except birth and death. It should be mentioned that without schedules or something similar to the M-time system, it is doubtful that our industrial civilization could have developed as it has, but there are other consequences. Monochronic time seals off one or two people from the group and intensifies relationships with one other person or, at most, two or three people. M-time in this sense is like a room with a closed door ensuring privacy. The only problem is that you must vacate the "room" at the end of the allotted 15 minutes or an hour, a day, or a week, depending on the schedule, and make way for the next person in line. Failure to make way by intruding on the time of the next person is not only a sign of extreme egocentrism and narcissism, but also just plain bad manners.

Monochronic time is arbitrary and imposed, that is, learned. Because it is so thoroughly learned and so thoroughly integrated into our culture, it is treated as though it were the only natural and logical way of

> *By scheduling, we compartmentalize; this makes it possible to concentrate on one thing at a time, but it also reduces the context.*

organizing life. Yet, it is not inherent in man's biological rhythms or his creative drives, nor is it existential in nature.

Schedules can and often do cut things short just when they are beginning to go well. For example, research funds run out just as the results are beginning to be achieved. How often have you had the experience of realizing that you are pleasurably immersed in some creative activity, totally unaware of time, solely conscious of the job at hand, only to be brought back to "reality" with the rude shock of realizing that other, often inconsequential previous commitments are bearing down on you?

Some Americans associate schedules with reality, but M-time can alienate us from ourselves and from others by reducing context. It subtly influences how we think and perceive the world in segmented compartments. This is convenient in linear operations but disastrous in its effect on nonlinear creative tasks. Latino peoples are an example of the opposite. In Latin America, the intelligentsia and the academicians commonly participate in several fields at once—fields that the average North American academician, business, or professional person thinks of as antithetical. Business, philosophy, medicine, and poetry, for example, are common, well-respected combinations.

Polychronic people, such as the Arabs and Turks, who are almost never alone, even in the home, make very different uses of "screening" than Europeans do. They interact with several people at once and are continually involved with each other. Tight scheduling is therefore difficult, if not impossible.

Theoretically, when considering social organization, P-time systems should demand a much greater centralization of control and be characterized by a rather shallow or simple structure. This is because the leader deals continually with many people, most of whom stay informed as to what is happening. The Arab fellah can always see his sheik. There are no intermediaries between man and sheik or between man and God. The flow of information, as well as people's need to stay informed, complement each other. Polychronic people are so deeply immersed in each other's business that, they feel a compulsion to keep in touch. Any stray scrap of a story is gathered in and stored away. Their knowledge of each other is truly extraordinary. Their involvement in people is the core of their existence, but this approach has bureaucratic implications. For example, delegation of authority and a buildup in bureaucratic levels are not required to handle high volumes of business. The principal shortcoming of P-type bureaucracies is that as functions increase, there is a proliferation of small bureaucracies that really are not set up to handle the problems of outsiders. In fact, outsiders traveling or residing in Latin American or Mediterranean countries find the bureaucracies unusually cumbersome and unresponsive. In polychronic countries, one has to be an insider or have a "friend" who can make things happen. All bureaucracies are oriented inward, but P-type bureaucracies are especially so.

There are also interesting points to be made concerning the act of administration as it is conceived in these two settings. Administration and control of polychronic peoples in the Middle East and Latin America is a matter of job analysis. Administration consists of taking each subordinate's job and identifying the activities that contribute to make up the job. These are then labeled and indicated on the elaborate charts with checks to make it possible for the administrator to be sure that each function has been performed. In this way, it is believed that absolute control is maintained over the individual. Yet scheduling how and when each activity is actually performed is left up to the employee. For an employer to schedule a subordinate's work for him would be considered a tyrannical violation of his individuality—an invasion of the self.

In contrast, M-time people schedule the activity and leave the analysis of the activities of the job to the individual. A P-type analysis, even though technical by its nature, keeps reminding the subordinate that his or her job is not only a system but also part of a larger system. M-type people, on the other hand, by virtue of compartmentalization, are less likely to see their activities in context as part of the larger whole. This does not mean that they are unaware of the "organization"—far from it—only that the job itself or even the goals of the organization are seldom seen as a whole.

Giving the organization a higher priority than the functions it performs is common in our culture. This is epitomized in television, where we allow the TV commercials, the "special message," to break the continuity of even the most important communication. There is a message all right, and the message is that art gives way to commerce—polychronic advertising agencies impose their values on a monochronic population. In monochronic North European countries, where patterns are more homogeneous, commercial interruptions of this sort are not tolerated. There is a strict limit regarding the number as well as the times when commercials can be shown. The average American TV program has been allotted one or two hours, for which people have set aside time, and is conceived, written, directed, acted, and played as a unity. Interjecting commercials throughout the body of the program breaks that continuity and flies in the face of one of the core systems of the culture. The polychronic Spanish treat the main feature as a close friend or relative who should not be disturbed and let the commercials mill around in the antechamber outside. My point is not that one system is superior to another; it's just that the two don't mix. The effect is disruptive and reminiscent of what the English are going through today, now that the old monochronic queuing patterns have broken down as a consequence of a large infusion of polychronic peoples from the colonies.

Both M-time and P-time systems have strengths as well as weaknesses. There is a limit to the speed with which jobs can be analyzed, although once analyzed, proper reporting can enable a P-time administrator to handle a surprising number of subordinates. Nevertheless, organizations run on the polychronic model are limited in size; they depend on having gifted people at the top; and they are slow and cumbersome when dealing with anything that is new or different. Without gifted people, a P-type bureaucracy can be a disaster. M-type organizations go in the opposite direction. They can and do grow much larger than the P-type model; however, they combine bureaucracies instead of proliferating them (e.g., with consolidated schools, the business conglomerate, and the new superdepartments we are developing in government).

The blindness of the monochronic organization is to the humanity of its members. The weakness of the polychronic type lies in its extreme dependence on the leader to handle contingencies and stay on top of things. M-type bureaucracies, as they grow larger, turn inward; oblivious to their own structure, they grow rigid and are apt to lose sight of their original purpose. Prime examples are the Army Corps of Engineers and the Bureau of Reclamation, which wreak havoc on our environment in their dedicated efforts to stay in business by building dams or aiding the flow of rivers to the sea.

At the beginning of this chapter, I stated that "American time is monochronic." On the surface, this is true, but in a deeper sense, American (AE) time is both polychronic and monochronic. M-time dominates the official worlds of business, government, the professions, entertainment, and sports; however, in the home—particularly the more traditional home in which women are the core around which everything revolves—one finds that P-time takes over. How else can one raise several children at once, run a household, hold a job, and be a wife, mother, nurse, tutor, chauffeur, and general fixer-upper? Nevertheless, most of us automatically equate P-time with informal activities and with the multiple tasks and responsibilities and ties of women to networks of people. At the preconscious level, M-time is male time and P-time is female time, and the ramifications of this difference are considerable.

In the conclusion of an important book, *Unfinished Business*, Maggie Scarf vividly illustrates this point. Scarf addresses the question of why depression (the hidden illness of our age) is three to six times more prevalent in women than it is in men. How does time equate with depression in women? It so happens that the time system of the dominant culture adds another source of trauma and alienation to the already overburdened psyches of many American women. According to Scarf, depression comes about in part as a consequence of breaking significant ties that make up most women's worlds. In our culture, men as a group tend to be more task oriented, whereas women's lives center on networks of people and their relations with people. Traditionally, a woman's world is a world of human emotions, of love, attachment, envy, anxiety, and hate. This concept is a little difficult for twenty-first-century people to accept because it implies basic differences between men and women that are not fashionable at the moment. Nevertheless, for most cultures around the world, the feminine mystique is intimately identified with the development of the human relations side of the personality rather than the technical, cortical left-brain occupational side. In the United States, AE women live in a world of people and relationships, and their egos become spread out among those who are closest to them by a process we call identification. When the relationships are threatened or broken or something happens to those to whom one is close, there are worries and anxieties, and depression is a natural result.

Polychronic cultures are by their nature oriented to people. Any human being who is naturally drawn to other human beings and who lives in a world dominated by human relationships will be either pushed or pulled toward the polychronic end of the time spectrum. If you value people, you must hear them out and cannot cut them off simply because of a schedule.

M-time, on the other hand, is oriented to tasks, schedules, and procedures. As anyone who has had experience with our bureaucracies knows, schedules and procedures take on a life all their own without reference to either logic or human needs. And this set of written and unwritten rules—and the consequences of these rules—is at least partially responsible for the reputation of American business being cut off from human beings and unwilling to recognize the importance of employee morale. Morale may well be the deciding factor in whether a given company makes a profit or not. Admittedly, American management is slowly, very slowly, getting the message. The problem is that modern management has accentuated the monochronic side at the expense of the less manageable, and less predictable, polychronic side. Virtually everything in our culture works for and rewards a mono chronic view of the world. But the antihuman aspect of M-time is alienating, especially to women. Unfortunately, too many women have "bought into" the M-time world, not realizing that unconscious sexism is part of it. The pattern of an entire system of time is too large, too diffuse, and too ubiquitous for most to identify its patterns. Women sense there is something alien about the way in which modern organizations handle time, beginning with how the workday, the week, and the year are set up. Such changes

> *Polychronic cultures are by their nature oriented to people.*

> *There are many instances where culture patterns are on a collision course, and there can be no resolution until the point of conflict is identified.*

as flextime do not alter the fact that as soon as one enters the door of the office, one becomes immediately locked into a monochronic, monolithic structure that is virtually impossible to change.

There are other sources of tension between people who have internalized these two systems. Keep in mind that polychrome individuals are oriented toward people, human relationships, and the family, which is the core of their existence. Family takes precedence over everything else. Close friends come next. In the absence of schedules, when there is a crisis the family always comes first. If a monochronic woman has a polychronic hairdresser, there will inevitably be problems, even if she has a regular appointment and is scheduled at the same time each week. In circumstances like these, the hairdresser (following his or her own pattern) will inevitably feel compelled to "squeeze people in." As a consequence, the regular customer, who has scheduled her time very carefully (which is why she has a standing appointment in the first place), is kept waiting and feels put down, angry, and frustrated. The hairdresser is also in a bind because if he does not accommodate his relative or friend regardless of the schedule, the result is endless repercussions within his family circle. Not only must he give preferential treatment to relatives, but the degree of accommodation and who is pushed aside or what is pushed aside is itself a communication!

The more important the customer or business that is disrupted, the more reassured the hairdresser's polychronic Aunt Nell will feel. The way to ensure the message that one is accepted or loved is to call up at the last minute and expect everyone to rearrange everything. If they don't, it can be taken as a clear signal that they don't care enough. The M-time individual caught in this P-time pattern has the feeling either that he is being pressured or that he simply doesn't count. There are many instances where culture patterns are on a collision course, and there can be no resolution until the point of conflict is identified. One side or the other literally gives up. In the instance cited above, the hairdresser usually loses a good customer. Patterns of this variety are what maintain ethnicity. Neither pattern is right, only different, and it is important to remember that they do not mix.

Not all M-times and P-times are the same. There are tight and loose versions of each. The Japanese, for example, in the official business side of their lives where people do not meet on a highly personalized basis, provide us an excellent example of tight M-time. When an American professor, businessperson, technical expert, or consultant visits Japan, he may find that his time is like a carefully packed trunk—so tightly packed, in fact, that it is impossible to squeeze one more thing into the container. On a recent trip to Japan, I was contacted by a well-known colleague who had translated one of my earlier books. He wanted to see me and asked if he could pick me up at my hotel at twelve-fifteen so we could have lunch together. I had situated myself in the lobby a few minutes early because the Japanese are almost always prompt. At twelve-seventeen, I could see his tense figure darting through the crowd of arriving businesspeople and politicians who had collected near the door. Following greetings, he ushered me outside to the ubiquitous black limousine with chauffeur, with white doilies covering the arms and headrests. The door of the car had hardly closed when he started outlining our schedule for the lunch period by saying that he had an appointment at three o'clock to do a TV broadcast. That set the time limit and established the basic parameters in which everyone knew where he would be at any given part of the agenda. He stated these limits—a little over two hours—taking travel time into account.

My colleague next explained that not only were we to have lunch, but he wanted to tape an interview for a magazine. That meant lunch and an interview, which would last thirty to forty minutes. What else? Ah, yes. He hoped I wouldn't mind spending time with Mr. X, who had published one of my earlier books in Japanese, because Mr. X was very anxious to pin down a commitment on my part to allow him to publish my next book. He was particularly eager to see me because he missed out on publishing the last two books, even though he had written me in the United States. Yes, I did remember that he had written, but his letter arrived after my agent had made the decision on the Japanese publisher. That, incidentally,

was the very reason why he wanted to see me personally. Three down and how many more to go? Oh, yes, there would be some photographers there, and he hoped I wouldn't mind if pictures were taken? The pictures were to be both formal group shots, which were posed, and informal, candid shots during the interview, as well as pictures taken with Mr. X. As it turned out, there were at least two sets of photographers as well as a sound man, and while it wasn't "60 Minutes," there was quite a lot of confusion (the two sets of photographers each required precious seconds to straighten things out). I had to hand it to everyone—they were not only extraordinarily skilled and well organized, but also polite and considerate. Then, he hoped I wouldn't mind, but there was a young man who was studying communication who had scored over 600 on an examination, which I was told put him 200 points above the average. This young man would be joining us for lunch. I didn't see how we were going to eat anything, much less discuss issues of mutual interest. In situations such as these, one soon learns to sit back, relax, and let the individual in charge orchestrate everything. The lunch was excellent, as I knew it would be–hardly leisurely, but still very good.

All the interviews and the conversation with the student went off as scheduled. The difficulties came when I had to explain to the Japanese publisher that I had no control over my own book—that once I had written a book and handed it in to my publisher, the book was marketed by either my publisher or my agent. Simply being first in line did not guarantee anything. I had to try to make it clear that I was tied into an already existing set of relationships with attached obligations and that other people made these decisions. This required some explaining, and I then spent considerable time trying to work out a method for the publisher to get a hearing with my agent. This is sometimes virtually impossible because each publisher and each agent in the United States has its own representative in Japan. Thus an author is in their hands, too.

We did finish on time—pretty much to everyone's satisfaction, I believe. My friend departed on schedule as the cameramen were putting away their equipment and the sound man was rolling up his wires and disconnecting his microphones. The student drove me back to my hotel on schedule, a little after 3 p.m.

The pattern is not too different from schedules for authors in the United States. The difference is that in Japan the tightly scheduled monochronic pattern is applied to foreigners who are not well enough integrated into the Japanese system to be able to do things in a more leisurely manner, and where emphasis is on developing a good working relationship.

All cultures with high technologies seem to incorporate both polychronic and monochronic functions. The point is that each does it in its own way. The Japanese are polychronic when looking and working inward, toward themselves. When dealing with the outside world, they have adopted the dominant time system, which characterizes that world. That is, they shift to the monochronic mode and, characteristically, since these are technical matters, they outshine us.

## Concepts and Questions

1. Have you ever observed Hall's conception of M-time or P-time being acted out in your culture? If so, how?

2. What difficulties might an M-time–oriented person experience when interacting with someone who follows a P-time orientation?

3. What does Hall imply by the statement, "there are points at which M-time doesn't make as much sense as it might seem"?

4. How does an M-time orientation affect perception?

5. Which of the two time orientations are most common in your culture? In what ways have you seen yourself reflecting the orientation found in your culture?

6. How is "administrative scheduling" affected by M-time and P-time orientations?

7. What does Hall mean by his statement that "European-American (EA) time is both polychronic and monochronic"?

8. In what ways have you seen cultural differences in time conceptualization lead to intercultural communication problems? Try to be specific.

# Mexicans and Americans: A Different Sense of Space

NED CROUCH

*We conclude this chapter by turning to an examination of nonverbal behavior that is unique to a particular culture— the Mexican culture. Specifically, Ned Crouch, in his essay titled "Mexicans and Americans: A Different Sense of Space," examines how Mexicans employ space in a manner that can be quite dissimilar to how space is employed in most Western cultures. The use of space, like other aspects of human behavior, is deeply embedded in the core of a culture. For example, Crouch links the notion of personal space to Mexican values related to collectivism versus individualism. In Mexico, with its group orientation, people feel comfortable and are not threatened when they share their space with others. In the West, as Crouch points out, most people "carry a protective shell around them." Crouch observes that you can even observe this "protective shell" in how homes are arranged. In the United States people speak of "my room" and "my privacy." This is not the case in Mexico. Employing numerous examples, Crouch shows how Mexicans share their space with others. He ties that "sharing of space" to a variety of Mexican perceptions and ideals. At the conclusion of his essay Crouch offers some excellent examples of how Americans can adapt their views of space to the Mexican business setting.*

From Ned Crouch, *Mexicans and Americans: Cracking the Culture Code*, (2004), pp. 45–54. Used by permission of Intercultural Press, A Nicholas Brealey Publishing Company.

It's Sunday morning. You're up extra early so you can beat the crowds, get down to the beach, commune with nature. You want to recharge your batteries so you'll be your usual go-getter self come Monday. What could be better? The sound of the surf, a cup o' hot coffee, not a living soul in sight—nobody, that is, until a Mexican plunks down right beside you.

Crossing five hundred feet of unoccupied sand, he greets you with a polite, *"Buenos dias!"* Then he shouts excitedly to his whole family, motioning for the nursemaids and the dog to come join you.

You say, *"Buenos dias"* rather politely, but your body language betrays your displeasure. You wait a few moments so that your next action isn't too obvious. Then—knowing you're going to come off as a tight-assed gringo, but not caring—you pick up your cup and towel and head back to the hotel. You're thinking, "A half mile of beach in either direction, and they have to pick on me! What's with these people? Can't they see they're invading my personal space?"

The answer is no. No they can't. This isn't how they see it at all. Mexicans have a different sense of space. They sit down beside you because "that's where the people are." It doesn't occur to them that this is objectionable or impolite. On the contrary, it's the natural, friendly, obvious thing to do. Unlike Americans, who prefer to spread out, Mexicans tend to congregate. If another gringo had come along, he would have settled about halfway toward the horizon to the south. Intuitively he would understand that both you and he want space and tranquility. If a third gringo had arrived, he would have gone halfway toward the northern horizon. According to our sense of space, we tend to seek the maximum convenient distance between one another before the inevitable crowd arrives. We draw a circle around ourselves—a circle as big as circumstance will allow. It shrinks as conditions dictate, until we feel agitated and claustrophobic. The Mexicans look disappointed as you leave, and quietly, very quietly, the señora asks papa what happened. "I don't know. I must have done something wrong. I can't imagine what it is. Or perhaps he does not like Mexicans." Mexicans are quick to pick up on any show of irritation or impatience and assume that they

have caused the displeasure. But they are also aware that some of us don't like them. They hear us complain about illegal immigrants, the oil slicks in the Gulf of Mexico, losing jobs, drugs. We blame it all on them. They have seen our police beating them on TV: They know that we can be prejudiced and they're thinking, "Maybe it's our brown skin." Somehow a moment of solitude on the beach has turned into an international racial incident. You're feeling violated; they're feeling discriminated against. While you're asking why they are so intrusive, they're wondering what it is about them that you don't like. But the real issue is not lack of manners or skin color. It's space.

## BUMPER TO BUMPER

I pull into the parking lot of the Hispanic Center in Michigan with my brand-new car. Wanting to avoid dings in my doors, I deliberately park three rows away from the building in an area sixty feet from any other car and ninety feet farther from the front door than the closest available parking slot. As I am getting out of my car, a woman swings through the entrance, around the median, and parks right next to me. How do I know she's not an Anglo? Could it be that she parked next to me because that's where the people are parking now?

*Unlike Americans, who prefer to spread out, Mexicans tend to congregate.*

In keeping with their sense of space, Mexicans tolerate a high compression factor. An American manager sent to Mexico was concerned because his wife had invited about thirty couples to their small apartment in Monterrey. When the guests started showing up with their children, there was hardly room to breathe. Much to his surprise, no one seemed to mind. In fact, he noted that as the rooms became more crowded, his guests seemed to relax and have more fun. This is the Mexican's sense of space in action.

## SOCIAL ORIENTATION

Our sense of space is directly tied to how we perceive our connection to other people. Whereas we Americans draw circles around the individual, Mexicans draw circles around the group. Most of the world is closer to the Mexicans in this regard. We—plus some western and *most* northern Europeans—are the exceptions. People from Latin America, the Middle East, Africa, and Asia tend to be more group-oriented and are less sensitive to individual space needs.

Differences in our sense of space undoubtedly contribute to the impression held by most Mexicans that Americans are somewhat cold and distant. Space becomes a big issue on trains, on planes, and in cars. Travel is definitely more uncomfortable for those of us in cultures where the sense of personal space is tighter. Our natural instinct is to feel stress when we are crowded onto a small commuter plane in Mexico, where passengers carry on a year's worth of luggage and cram themselves into smaller seats.

We Americans will always be more comfortable being separated; Mexicans will always be more comfortable being part of a group. We will always resist being crowded; they will always want to get closer. It's not personal. It's not prejudice. They don't know it, but on that Sunday morning at the beach, you would have gotten up and left if another gringo had sat next to you—only faster.

Because the Mexican and American notions of space are so deeply embedded, it is unrealistic to think that either is going to change. Nor should we expect change. Both senses of space are natural and not insensitive.

> *Mexicans draw a circle around the group, they are constantly looking inward toward that group.*

When we draw circles around ourselves, we are inside the circle looking out. Since Mexicans draw a circle around the group, they are constantly looking inward toward that group. Figuratively speaking, the Mexican family surrounded by the walls of their house look inward toward one another. We, on the other hand, are inside the house looking out through the biggest picture window we can afford, hoping that nobody will build within sight of us—a markedly different social orientation.

In the United States, our sense of space begins to develop from the moment we are brought home from the hospital in a bassinet. From that moment on, the American child develops an expectation of privacy. He or she begins referring to "my room" and "my toys." The walls are going up. Children begin to feel more comfortable with a private space that they can crawl off to for insulation against pressure. This is quite different from the Mexican experience. We Americans become territorial about our half of the dorm room at college. We set up separate shelves in the community refrigerator. We want a den in our dream house where we can put our feet up and think about what we should have said today and mentally project what we will do tomorrow—all without interruption from the family. Not so in Mexico.

Mexicans' closer sense of space is related to the way they have been raised—living much closer together in the home and looking inward to each other for support and nurturing. Physical closeness goes along with closer families and less sibling rivalry. Each child does not get his own room. Boys and girls are not necessarily divided until a more advanced age, and then only if resources allow. There's nothing inherently better or worse about either the American or Mexican approach—although Mexican children sure do get along well, both among themselves and with others. When passing playgrounds in Mexico, I'm always struck with the pleasant sounds. No taunting, teasing, or squabbling.

There is a story about a Mexican worker who came to the United States for training. His supervisor asked a coworker to take Javier home to show him how Americans live. The American coworker took him through his house. "This is the entry hall where we take off our snowshoes. Here's the living room, but we spend more time in the den over there where the TV is. This is the dinette next to the kitchen. Here's Bertha's and my room. Here's the boys' room. Here's where little Martha sleeps, except when Grandma and Grandpa visit and she sleeps in the den." Javier was delighted with the tour and said, "You know, it's exactly the same in Mexico—except for the walls." This story is not intended to be derogatory in any way. It is instructive.

## DON'T FENCE ME IN

Although Mexicans are less concerned than Americans about defining individual space, they are generally more concerned with sharply demarcating one family's living space from another family's. This usually means having a wall between houses. When

Mexicans visit the United States, they often marvel at the open lawns between homes. The Mexican wonders, "How do they know where their property stops and their neighbor's begins?" Americans know. We know exactly where to mow, don't we? To construct walls between houses seems to run counter to something in the American spirit. "Something there is that doesn't love a wall," wrote Robert Frost in his quintessentially American poem, "Mending Wall." The Mexican's feelings run just as deep on the other side. For them it is important to define family space. This is because the family and its space are a final refuge from the chaos and uncertainty of life outside their walls. The home is the one place where, with all the gods playing their ungodly tricks, they can finally feel in control. Protecting the group space is paramount.

When we Americans observe Mexicans, we see them piled onto a train with families, chickens, goats, and a whole menagerie. We wonder how they can fit so many on a bus. We observe clusters of family members moving around Sears in unison. We make jokes about crowding into a pickup truck. But we are observing only the top ten percent of a cultural phenomenon that rises above the surface. What is going on underneath the surface is a clash in our opposing sense of space.

There is a strong correlation between sense of space and behavior. We Americans have a definite sense of individual space and we carry a protective shell around our individuality. Our sense of individuality goes with us wherever we go. We act independently, whereas Mexicans see themselves as part of a group. They act as a group, looking to each other for direction, approbation, and survival. When they are in their group space, they behave according to what that space is dedicated to. If they are in the receiving hall outside the mayor's office, they wait for the mayor like dutiful citizens. If they are in the polishing department, they see themselves as polishers. When they are in the home, they act like a family. As Americans, we too adjust our behavior and shift gears depending on what is required of us. We cooperate with the team and blend into the choir, but we don't shed the circle

around ourselves. Typically, we see ourselves as discrete individuals operating within the group, whereas Mexicans are *the group*.

Whether working in the United States or in Mexico, Mexicans working on the factory floor of a large manufacturing entity perceive the walls of their department as enveloping their circle. In this setting, they have their backs to the wall and relate to the group. By contrast, when Americans visualize the overall operation of a plant, we see a continuous production line cutting through all departments. We draw little boxes for machines and little circles for operators performing specific tasks. Mexican workers, on the other hand, relate primarily to the inner circle of their department and secondarily to the larger space where the entire company team works together.

Another difference in our respective senses of space is that Americans feel threatened if our personal space is invaded, whereas Mexicans are alarmed if their group space is invaded. We feel as though our person is being violated. They feel that their group identity is being threatened.

> *Another difference in our respective senses of space is that Americans feel threatened if our personal space is invaded, whereas Mexicans are alarmed if their group space is invaded.*

## HERE'S LOOKING AT YOU

What happens when you enter their space? Both Mexicans and Americans have rituals for approaching another person or group's space. But our respective rituals are very different.

In her novel *Stones for Ibarra* (1984), Harriet Doerr writes about a local man visiting the house where the author and her husband were living in a remote Mexican village. The local was looking for work. He didn't want to disturb the American couple needlessly, so, rather than knock on the door, he went around the house, window to window, looking in to see if they were there and if they were busy. Had they been in the kitchen sipping coffee, he would have gone to the back door and announced himself. Had they been in bed, he would have left quietly to return the next day. Within the context of his peasant Mexican culture, he was behaving perfectly properly in the way he approached the author's space. He was being polite. It was jarring to the writer, however.

What if Harriet and her husband were in an intimate embrace? What if they were naked? How can someone just come up to your window and look in?

From the Mexican peasant's perspective, his actions were innocent and nonthreatening. (This may be one reason Mexican city dwellers put walls all the way around their houses.) Had he seen anything of a personal nature, he would have averted his eyes and returned later. As for the nakedness, well, it is as natural as can be and nothing to get excited about. He would have been confused if the gringos had come out screaming and shooing him off. It would not have computed. He would not have understood why the gringos were so hostile.

## BACKING OFF

You probably don't recognize that Americans routinely behave ritualistically, but we do. Imagine that you want to borrow a rake from your neighbor. First, you knock on his screen door and then quickly back up. If nobody comes, you knock again, this time yelling to the upstairs window. Did you peer in through the screen? No. Did you walk around the house looking for the rake? No. Somewhere along the line we picked up cultural cues about personal space that tell us how to approach the neighbor's house. We have learned that there is an acceptable, nonthreatening way to get the attention of a neighbor whom we consider vulnerable because his doors and windows are open.

Ritualistic practices also help us cope with confined spaces, such as crowded elevators. As we get on, we lower our eyes, turn toward the buttons, and press our floor. We face front and say nothing. If we must, we say, "Out please." or "Excuse me," with our Yankee penchant for economy of words. It's different in Mexico. They get on an elevator and say, "Buenas tardes," to everybody. It is not unusual to hear chatter among the strangers. They ask permission to get off—"Con permiso." The others respond, "Propio" (of course). Or they may insist that you go first.

There is a different ritual in Mexico for entering shopping spaces. We Americans go into a store and immediately put up our defense shields. If forced to speak, we say, "Just looking around." Mexicans go to a store and, recognizing that they have entered the shopkeeper's space, immediately proffer a "Buenas

tardes" to the owner and staff. There is nothing more out of place than the woman in Bermuda shorts and Rockports who says, "Nada mas mirando"—a lame translation of "just looking," which to the Mexican means absolutely nothing. In Mexico the clerk will follow you around the store quietly—not uttering a word. We feel crowded by her presence. Is she checking up on us? No. She's there, close to you, in case you have any questions. Be aware that we think we're shopping, whereas they think we have come for a visit. This is their space, and we will get better service, when the time comes, if we act as though we are invitees rather than dispassionate purchasing agents.

## CORRECT DISTANCE

Americans' individual space is quite well defined, though most of us don't realize it. The correct face-to-face distance between American men is one arm's length, less the hand. The distance woman-to-woman is a bit closer than man-to-man. If you are a man, the next time you're at a cocktail party or convention, try moving one-half step closer to the man you're talking to. You will see him avert his eyes, shift his feet, turn sideways, and finally take a half step back. He won't be conscious of his own actions. You then take another half step closer. He will repeat his backward shuffle. Keep it up, and you could waltz him around the room and out the door.

Understanding the different boundaries of personal space is important when doing business. In the United States, if a woman were to move a little closer to a man, he may interpret the narrowing of space as an invitation to flirt, which would be taboo in the workplace. If a Mexican woman stands closer to an American male, however, it is not a come-on. In fact, it means nothing of the sort. Her circle of personal space is simply smaller, or less acutely felt than his. Men and women generally stand closer in Mexico. If you are showing a Mexican woman something on your computer screen, she will get much closer to you than an American woman would. She may stand with her legs right next to your arm or lean over your shoulder. American males should note that this is not a come-on.

In the States, the personal space between individuals remains the same, irrespective of status—whether speaking to the president of the company or the guy who sets up our AV equipment. In Mexico's more hierarchical society, there is a need to establish greater separation between the workers and the *jefe*, or "big man." The workers tend to operate together more closely than in the United States, but the president maintains more distance between himself and his accounting clerk. The Mexican boss will have an exaggeratedly large office and desk to emphasize the hierarchical distance between himself and his minions. This is his "power distance."

As an American operating with Mexicans, you want to be sensitive to the greater zone that surrounds the president of a company. But in the course of your dealings, when the president takes a step closer, puts his arms around you, and gives you an *abrazo*, or hug, he is indicating that he means to accept you as an equal. If you are a woman, the parallel behavior might be a pat on the arm and an "air kiss" (touching cheeks and smacking the void next to the woman's head), which acknowledges trust and confers respect. Whatever you do, don't pull back and blow it. In this context, the gesture signals that you have crossed into the Mexican president's circle and are trusted to work within his group. You must now maintain that relationship and build on it. I explained the *abrazo* practice to middle management at Chrysler Motors. "Hold on a minute," one man interjected. "In sensitivity training, we were told never to touch *anybody*." I'm not suggesting you go hugging anyone unless you feel comfortable getting that close. On the other hand, be aware that men will hug men in Mexico, and it means nothing beyond friendship and acceptance.

> The Mexican boss will have an exaggeratedly large office and desk to emphasize the hierarchical distance between himself and his minions. This is his "power distance."

Americans and Mexicans have been living next to each other for many years and have learned to appreciate each other's customs: I have a friend in McAllen, Texas, named Mike Heap. (There is no more Anglo-Saxon name than Mike Heap.) Mike is a laconic Texan, a cowboy, and a former bronco-buster who is now on the rodeo circuit as a clown. He loves Mexicans, his girlfriend is Mexican, and like most Anglos in the Rio Grande Valley, he speaks Spanish. When he goes to Mexico, he gives his men friends *abrazos*. I, too, give and receive *abrazos* when I go to Mexico. But Mike and I would never hug each other.

According to street lore, the *abrazo* came into being as a means of "patting down" the person you greet to make sure he's not armed. But today it means "Welcome to my space."

## GROUP SPACE

How should Americans adapt our usual business practices in response to the Mexicans' sense of space? Since Mexicans draw a circle around their group and focus inward, as previously mentioned, anyone entering their space makes a big impact. So in the business setting, how you enter a Mexican group's space is important. A proper greeting, avoiding flamboyant gestures, not shouting, and general circumspection are appreciated.

Most how-to books tell you how to greet and what to wear. But remember that in addition to proper manners, violating Mexicans' group space may be perceived as a threat to how they live and work. If we go into their group space and disrupt the harmony of the group, we are signaling to the group that we do not care about them. They may assume that they are the next to be transferred, fired, or shot.

When a gringo walks into a native cantina in a remote village, suddenly everything goes quiet. When they realize you are just there to throw down tequila, they relax and start talking again. We are clearly outsiders. But once we enter the group and behave, they accept us. If we buy one of them a drink and tell a good joke, the atmosphere turns to jubilation.

In the workplace, Mexicans can favor us with cooperation and the rewards of group effort if we are sensitive to the effect we are having on their space. By minimizing disruption when we enter their space, we indicate respect for their group and earn their support. The unfortunate corollary for us is that often once we leave their space, we may no longer exist to them. We have to be in their space to get the best results. Once in their group space, we have to spend time building relationships or else we will be "out of sight, out of mind."

## Concepts and Questions

1. How does Crouch link Mexican use of space to their value toward collectivism?

2. Why does Crouch conclude that North Americans prefer to "spread out"?

3. In what ways does North Americans use of space reflect their attitude toward privacy?

4. What does Crouch mean when he writes of "ritualistic practices"? How do these practices relate to the use of space?

5. Why is it important to know a particular culture's boundaries in the use of space? Have you ever been in a situation where a "violation" of those boundaries caused a problem?

6. How is the use of space related to notions of power?

7. Crouch asks the following question: "How should Americans adapt their use of space to the Mexican sense of space in the business setting?" How would you answer this question?

8. What specific "tips" does Crouch advance at the conclusion of his essay that might help you modify your use of space when doing business in Mexico?

# 6 Cultural Contexts: The Influence of the Setting

*Where my reason, imagination or interest were not engaged, I would not or I could not learn.*
**Winston Churchill**

*The new reality of diversity in the workplace is that each individual is his unique, diverse story.*
**Deepika Bajaj**

Helping you develop the ability to communicate effectively with people from diverse cultures and co-cultures is the primary goal of this book. We have, therefore, presented you with essays that (1) introduced the ideas of intercultural communication, (2) helped you understand the importance of cultural identity, (3) revealed the diversity found between both international cultures and domestic co-cultures, and (4) shown you how cultural diversity in both verbal and nonverbal behavior impacts the communication process.

There is, however, another communication dimension you must understand: *Human interaction takes place within a specific social and physical environment*. We call this environment the *social context*. When you are communicating, you must be aware of the specific context and adapt your communicative behavior so that it is appropriate to the particular situation. Consideration of the social context is important because the setting is never neutral; it always exerts an influence on how communication participants behave. Think for a moment about the following social contexts: football game, nightclub, physician's office, business meeting, place of worship. These social environments contain many physical and social elements that influence how

> The impact and influence of context on communication is rooted in three interrelated assumptions: *(1) Communication is rule governed; (2) The setting helps you define what "regulations" are in operation; (3) Most of the communication rules you follow have been learned as part of your cultural experiences.*

you and your communication partners will produce and respond to messages. What you wear, what you talk about, to whom you talk, and even the volume of your voice are in many ways governed by the context in which you find yourself. You have learned proper patterns of communicative behavior for the various social contexts in which you find yourself within your own culture. But, as with other aspects of intercultural communication, the appropriate patterns of behavior in various social contexts are culturally diverse. When you find yourself in an unfamiliar social context without an internalized set of rules to act as a guide, you can encounter communication problems you may not recognize or understand.

The impact and influence of context on communication is rooted in three interrelated assumptions:

1. *Communication is rule governed* (each encounter has implicit and explicit rules that regulate your conduct). These rules tell you everything from what is appropriate attire to what topics may be discussed.

2. *The setting helps you define what "regulations" are in operation.* Reflect for a moment on your own communication behavior as you move to and from the following arenas: classroom, courtroom, church, hospital, basketball game, and movie theater. Visualize how your behavior changes as you move from one place to another.

3. *Most of the communication rules you follow have been learned as part of your cultural experiences.* Although cultures might share the same general settings, their specific notions of proper behavior for each context reflect the values and attitudes of that culture. For instance, turn-taking, the use of time, space and language, appropriate manners, displays of nonverbal behavior, the appropriateness of silence, and the control of the communication flow are primarily extensions of culture.

In this chapter, we offer essays that discuss the interrelationships among context, culture, and communication. What emerges from these essays is a realization that to communicate effectively with members of another culture you must know and respect the contextual rules that govern that culture's communicative behavior. Although intercultural communication occurs in a wide variety of contexts, we have selected three social environments where you are likely to find yourself interacting with people from diverse cultures: *business, health care,* and *education.* To assist you in developing comprehensive intercultural competence when you communicate in any of these contexts, we have selected essays that focus on both international and domestic settings.

The growth of international businesses has been astonishing. Business that involved overseas transactions and generated millions of dollars annually just a few decades ago are now multibillion-dollar operations. Many former national companies have transformed themselves into global, transnational entities with offices, employees, production, and service facilities located around the world. This trend toward multinational companies has evolved for several reasons. One is the creation of national regulations requiring some product manufacturing to be done within a country where the product is to be marketed. This requirement, for instance, applies to such companies as Toyota Motors, which manufactures parts and assembles automobiles in the United States so that their cars may be sold there. A second cause has been mergers and acquisitions, in which one company may buy or merge with another across national boundaries. A third impetus for this trend is a recognition that business productivity increases when work occurs locally. And, finally, you can see changes that have occurred within the United States. In many geographic areas of the country, immigration has created a pluralistic, multicultural society. The result is that a multicultural workforce is now present in most companies, whether they are local, regional, national, or international businesses.

Because of this worldwide economic growth and the internationalization of many businesses, people no longer have the comfort of working exclusively with others who possess the same cultural background and experiences. One's associates, clients, subordinates, and even supervisors are often from different cultures and even from different countries. Many aspects of business life, such as negotiation, decision making, policy formulation, socializing, gender relationships, marketing techniques, management structure, human resource management, gift giving, and patterns of communication, are now affected by cultural diversity.

The presence of global and multicultural populations also has major implications for health care providers. This cultural context is important for a number of reasons. First, the promotion of health and the prevention of disease is an urgent priority for any civilized culture. Second, some diseases are highly contagious and can be easily transmitted into a host culture. Third, and from a cultural perspective most important, is cultural diversity in perceptions about the causes, treatment, and prevention of illness. And, finally, members of dissimilar cultures may utilize different communication patterns and styles when they interact in the health care setting. Members of one culture, for instance, may talk openly and freely to a health care provider about their medical situation, whereas members of another culture may be reluctant to talk or to reveal personal information.

What is true about the importance of intercultural business communication and health care communication also applies to the education setting. That is to say, the forces of globalization, immigration, and population change have caused large numbers of classrooms in the United States and elsewhere to become new multicultural/multinational communities. In the United States alone, nearly one in three students now identifies him- or herself as African American, Latino, Asian, Pacific Islander, Arab, or American Indian. According to the Pew Research Center, in 2007 nationwide 59 percent of students were White, 20 percent Hispanic, 15 percent African American, and 6 percent Asian. Moreover, among the U.S. student population, some 10 million come from homes where

English is not the primary language, and over 49 million students are classified as having limited English proficiency (LEP).

Because of the cultural experiences of these groups, schools must accommodate widely diverse learning styles, interaction patterns, preferences for competition or cooperation, and diversity in the use and meaning of silence, as well as the status and role of the teacher.

As we have just highlighted, your understanding of how communication operates in the multicultural business setting, the health care setting, and the educational environment becomes more important as cultural diversity increases. In order to help you communicate successfully in these arenas, we offer the following seven essays.

## THE BUSINESS CONTEXT

The first three essays focus on the business context. These selections demonstrate how cultural diversity touches many aspects of business activity. All business actions involve some form of communication. However, the styles of communication patterns found in the conduct of business are frequently culturally unique.

Decision making is an essential element of any business organization. Both day-to-day operations and long-range planning require decisions. These can range from whether to hire additional employees to making changes in product design or production practices to determining whether the company should merge with or acquire a competitor. Decision making can range from informal decisions at low levels of the organizational structure to high-level decisions that must be made or accepted by the highest authority in the business. The process by which decisions are made is a dynamic of the culture of the business organization. But this business culture is strongly influenced by the deep structure of the culture of the society in which the business resides. Thus, the processes by which decisions are reached and accepted are culturally diverse and can be very different.

# Japanese Style of Decision Making in Business Organizations

KAZUO NISHIYAMA

*You have already been introduced to some of the cultural differences that exist between Eastern and Western societies. One difference was the collectivistic or group-oriented nature of Eastern cultures. Collectivism strongly influences the processes by which decisions are made in Eastern culture. To give you a glimpse of the differences in decision-making process between Western and Eastern cultures, we have selected an essay by Professor Kazuo Nishiyama titled "Japanese Style of Decision Making in Business Organizations." From this essay you will (1) understand how collectivism plays a large part in Japanese decision making, (2) become familiar with the concept of* ringi, *which is a Japanese decision-making protocol, (3) gain an understanding of the vital role informal face-to-face discussions play in reaching consensus on a decision, and (4) receive advice about how Western businesspeople should proceed when engaged in business negotiations or discussions with Japanese counterparts.*

*Professor Nishiyama provides you with an enlightening description of how decisions are reached in Japanese business organizations. To help you fully appreciate this process, Nishiyama begins with a background discussion about the corporate culture in Japan and how it fosters a strong group orientation. This process begins in April of each year, when Japanese companies hire new recruits selected from high school and university graduates. The new recruits receive their company orientation together at the company's training center. This process helps build close bonds and interpersonal relationships that tend to last a lifetime. These close bonds and interpersonal relationships provide the foundation for the Japanese decision-making style.*

*Nishiyama discusses how Japanese decision making follows a* ringi, *or group decision-making protocol. This style of decision making is rooted in the Japanese traditions of interpersonal harmony, cooperation, and consensus. Plans are initiated by lower- or middle-ranking managers who are charged with drafting a proposal.*

*Before the proposal is even written and distributed, the initiator will discuss the general idea informally with key personnel. When positive reactions are obtained from the appropriate people, the proposal is written, along with a request for a decision. The proposal then goes through many face-to-face, informal, behind-the-scene discussions by the people who will be involved in implementing a decision. Not until informal consensus has been gained among those involved is the proposal circulated through the management hierarchy. Only then is the document hand-delivered to the company president for his approval.*

*Kaigi, or a face-to-face conference, is the key to Japanese decision making. This consultation proceeds quite differently from a typical business meeting in most Western organizations. Nishiyama points out that in most Western business meetings, proposals will be debated until a decision is reached. In the Japanese system, "the Japanese business meeting is an occasion to formally confirm what has been already decided informally through intensive* nemawashi [or informal discussions]."

*Nishiyama concludes his essay with detailed advice for Western businesspeople who are involved in negotiations or decision making with Japanese counterparts. He suggests that Westerners maintain close personal contacts, do not rush their Japanese counterparts, and do not consider* ringi *as a negative, slow process. In addition, he suggests that Westerners bring gifts for their Japanese counterparts, that they acquire a good understanding of Japanese culture and social customs, that they do not talk too much, that they be patient, and, finally, that they try to provide visual aids in Japanese.*

Western scholars and businesspeople are still very critical of Japanese decision-making processes as being intuitive and irrational. They are often frustrated and even dismayed that seemingly ultra-modern Japanese business organizations have not adopted more objective and rational approaches

---

to decision making as expected. The Japanese organizations may all claim that they have modernized decision-making processes with extensive use of Web sites for dissemination and e-mails for exchanges of in-house information. Except for nontraditional IT-related companies, however, almost all other companies still continue to use the traditional *ringi-seido* (group decision making) and *kaigi* (face-to-face conference). The obvious reason for this continuation is that these traditional methods of communication are not only acceptable but also feasible in the context of Japanese corporate culture. Therefore, it is important to examine specific aspects of Japanese culture that instill and perpetuate the particular type of interpersonal relationships and decision-making practices in Japanese business organizations.

## EMPLOYMENT SYSTEM IN JAPAN

Japanese companies are still group-oriented organizations despite the fact that the younger Japanese generation is becoming more individualistic. The major reasons for perpetuation of group orientation among Japanese salaried workers are how they are recruited and how they are trained and indoctrinated into their workplace (Nishiyama, 1995). The following are the most common personnel recruitment practices used in Japan today:

> *Japanese companies are still group-oriented organizations despite the fact that the younger Japanese generation is becoming more individualistic.*

1. Japanese companies usually recruit new employees from among new graduates of high schools and universities during the month of April. The new recruits go through induction training together at the company's training center. This training will last two or more weeks. They all live together and engage in group-oriented activities in addition to listening to lectures by senior members of the company. This "bonding" among the new recruits is considered a very important aspect of their entire career with the company. When talking about comradeship, they often say, *onaji kama no meshi wo tabeta nakama* (comrades who eat rice from the same rice cooker).

2. Japanese companies are still reluctant to hire workers who have had previous work experience with other companies. They fear that the experienced workers, called *chuuto saiyoo sha* (mid-career recruits), may disrupt interpersonal harmony among those who have been hired directly into the company upon completion of their education. There are, however, many exceptions today in recruitment policies. For example, IT-related companies need experienced workers who can bring with them specific, advanced skills and technical knowledge. These companies even recruit computer programmers from China, Singapore, and India because they have no time to train programmers from among new Japanese recruits, and the foreign programmers are comparatively cheaper to hire.

3. All Japanese companies use different classifications of employees in order to retain good and loyal workers and to differentiate them from other, less desirable workers. There are *honyatoi* (regular employee), *rinjiyatoi* (temporary employee), *paato* (part-time employee), *keiyaku shain* (contract employee), *haken shain* (dispatched employee), etc. Those workers who are employed as regular employees usually have good educational backgrounds and personal qualifications. They comprise a group of "elite workers" who can look forward to becoming members of management and receiving lifetime employment, plus annual advancement. Temporary employees (*rinjiyatoi*) are hired when the company needs to augment its workforce for a specific period of time. They will never be given lifetime employment, no matter how long and how hard they work for the organization. They may receive only a few basic fringe benefits, and are the first ones to be fired whenever the workload is reduced. Part-time workers (*paato*) are given hourly wages without fringe benefits. Contract employees are hired for a certain period of months or years. Computer programmers from China, for example, are contract employees hired for one or two

years. Dispatched employees (*haken shain*) are recruited by a *jinji haken kaisha* (personnel dispatch company) and assigned to client companies. Many English teachers working for multinational Japanese corporations are dispatched employees. They receive their wages and fringe benefits from their personnel dispatch company, not from the corporations they work for as English teachers. Still another classification is called *friitaa* or *frii arubaitaa* (casual workers). They are young Japanese men or women who do not have any career plans or ambitions to succeed in their professions. They work whenever or wherever they decide to work as temporary workers.

Among these groups of workers, only the regular employees are bona fide employees of the company they work for. There is a distinct separation between and among these differently classified employees. These groups of employees do not interact with each other on the same level of comradeship and interpersonal trust. In fact, the regular employees sometimes discriminate against other groups and cooperate with them only with a certain amount of suspicion.

## BUILDING UP INTERPERSONAL RELATIONSHIPS

The above discussion clearly shows that establishing close relationships and a group-oriented mentality is reserved for regular employees. This process begins with the induction training when they are first hired and the elaborate *nyushashiki* (entering company ceremony). During the induction training, all new employees are required to learn the "President's Teachings" (corporate missions and mottos), the "Company Song," the corporate history and philosophy, etc. All learning takes place through group activities. Those who attend the same induction training sessions become *doohai* (same-year comrades) and they will continue to associate with each other as such (Nishiyama, 2000).

This entering company ceremony is a major annual event just like a commencement ceremony. The president, top executives, managers, senior employees, and some parents attend the ceremony. The president welcomes the new recruits and also challenges them in his inspirational speech to work hard for the corporate goals. In response, a representative of the new recruits answers his challenge. In fact, every recruit becomes a new member of the corporate family and pledges his alliance and loyalty to the company (Rohlen, 1974). New generations of Japanese workers do not particularly like this type of induction, but they are often forced to accept these traditional practices.

Even though a Japanese company tries to establish one unified work group, it is also true that there are *habatsu*, or factions, within the company. The factions are often based on *gakubatsu*, or school cliques, *senpaikoohai kankei* (senior-junior relationships), and city or state of birth. The managers who graduated from a certain university will give personal favors to the new recruits from the same university in exchange for the latter's loyalty. If, for example, University A's graduates hold powerful executive positions in a company, the graduates of the same university will be treated better than University B's graduates. Naturally, the senior members who took good care of the new recruits will make the latter feel obligated to them, creating a mutual dependency relationship. Obviously, relationships among these factions can become troublesome at times because of intense interfaction rivalries and conflict.

## *RINGI* OR GROUP DECISION MAKING

The *ringi* style of decision making is deeply rooted in Japanese culture, which emphasizes interpersonal harmony, cooperation, and consensus. Today, it is often said that modern Japanese organizations have been streamlining or rationalizing this outdated process due to wide use of in-house Web sites and e-mail networks (McDaniel, 2003). It is still true, however, that the *ringi* system, even in its modified form, is being used to satisfy a number of important sociocultural demands among the members of most Japanese business organizations. It is almost impossible for the Japanese to abandon this process and adopt a Western decision-making style where individuals at the top management level make decisions.

Unlike their counterparts in Western business organizations, Japanese executives and managers are not really independent decision makers. A Japanese company president, for example, cannot make a quick and independent decision on his own, unless he is the founder and the majority owner of the company. And if he does so too frequently, he will be accused of being a *wanman shahoo* (dictator president). Japanese companies may use the title "Chief Executive Officer," but the Japanese C.E.O. does not have the same decision-making authority as his counterpart in Western business organizations. The position of president is oftentimes honorary, given to someone before his retirement or promotion to the position of chairman. He will never, therefore, risk making any unpopular decisions on his own. His decisions are usually based on group consensus. Actually, the person in charge of decision making is the *senmu torishimari yaku* (managing director), who actually runs the daily affairs of his company. But he still needs the president's seal of approval on any decisions that he may make. In addition, he still needs other executives and managers' concurrence and support.

## Process of *Ringi* Decision Making

The *ringi* process begins with a *kiansha* (plan initiator), usually a lower- or middle-ranking manager (supervisor or section chief), who is in charge of drafting a *ringisho* (proposal). Before drafting this document, he discusses the general idea informally with key executives, managers, and supervisors. Only after getting fairly positive initial reactions from them will he draft the proposal document. This document includes the request for a decision, supporting data and information, detailed explanations, and justifications. This informal discussion is called *nemawashi,* which literally means "twisting the tree roots around." In practice, *nemawashi* refers to holding many face-to-face, informal, behind-the-scenes discussions about a proposal among all the people who would be involved in implementing any decision to be made later.

The act of *nemawashi* is analogous to twisting a planted tree around to cut off bothersome roots or "objections" so that it can be uprooted easily. The *nemawashi* process is a sounding board for unofficially testing the responses to a proposed idea without any risk of unnecessarily causing loss of face for any one individual or group. In this process, no one individual or group can claim all the credit if it is

successful, and at the same time, no one will be blamed should it fail.

Once a *ringi* proposal is completed, the initiator circulates it to every executive and manager who will be asked to approve it after careful review. The circulation is executed in reverse order of each individual's hierarchical position, beginning with the lowest-ranked supervisor, to middle management, top management, and finally to the president. The cover sheet of the proposal has many small boxes for *han* (seal of approval) to be affixed by all those who will review and approve it. The proper order of circulation is strictly adhered to because skipping any person on the hierarchical ladder will cause serious procedural and interpersonal problems. If any of the managers or executives have questions or objections, the initiator will have to answer them in person. The decision can be delayed indefinitely until the person who is objecting receives convincing justification based on new data and information. When all the seals of approval have been obtained, the document will be hand delivered to the president for his approval. This final approval from the president, called *kessai* (final approval), is the last step in the *ringi* decision-making process.

Suppose, for example, that a Japanese faculty member wants to invite an American professor to a Japanese private university as a visiting professor. The Japanese professor will begin *nemawashi* (informal consultation) among his colleagues. He needs to find out whether or not any professor in his department objects to inviting this particular U.S. professor. If he is a junior assistant professor, he will have to gain the approvals of senior professors, who may have more power. Only then can he ask his department chairperson to request that the personnel department begin the necessary paperwork for employing this foreign professor. Unlike an American university, this Japanese university chairperson needs to obtain the approval of his dean and the university president. Naturally, he has to prepare a lengthy *ringi* document and go through the process as explained above.

If one of the professors objects for any reason, the assistant professor needs to tactfully persuade this objecting professor. His reason for objection could be that he feels threatened by the visiting professor, maybe because the visitor is very famous in the same field of study. Or perhaps he received a rather negative review of his conference paper from the visitor in the past. In this case, the junior professor is required to mediate the situation. If the objecting professor grudgingly agrees to go along, he will make sure that he will receive *kashi* (credit) from the junior professor. This means that the latter owes a favor to the former, and he will have to repay this *kari* (debt) later on. During the process of *nemawashi, kashi-kari kankei* (an obligatory relationship) is established quite frequently within any Japanese organization (Nishiyama, 2000).

## Kaigi, or Face-to-Face Conference

*Kaigi* in Japanese business organizations outwardly appears to be similar to a business meeting or conference in Western business organizations. However, it is quite different from a typical Western-style meeting in purpose, procedure, content of discussion, and participation of attendees. Generally speaking, the purpose of a Western-style business meeting is to facilitate decision making in face-to-face situations. In contrast, the Japanese business meeting is an occasion to formally confirm what has been already decided informally through intensive *nemawashi*. In many instances, Japanese participants go through the ritual of asking questions and debating certain points. But, in fact, they are merely saying what has been discussed and agreed upon beforehand. In addition, they do not want surprise questions or strong objections from any one of the participants during the actual meeting.

*In the Japanese cultural context, however, such changing of one's mind is a serious social infraction and betrayal of interpersonal trust.*

In the Western cultural context, it is acceptable to change one's mind about what has been informally agreed upon prior to the meeting, if a much better idea or new compelling evidence is presented. In the Japanese cultural context, however, such changing of one's mind is a serious social infraction and betrayal of interpersonal trust. Any agreement that has been reached during informal consultations is considered a firm commitment. It is different from the tentative commitment or personal opinion that Western businesspeople usually try to obtain when going through the process of "touching the bases."

The role of each Japanese participant is different from that of his Western counterpart. The Japanese chairperson's main role is not to aggressively take direct control over the decision-making process, but to mediate the consensus-building process among all participants. In fact, the second-ranking person (usually *buchoo*, or department head) will do most of the talking and direct other participants to contribute to the ongoing discussion in a predetermined order. Each of the junior-ranking participants presents a brief report prepared in advance and seeks everyone's approval. The participants seldom disagree with others during face-to-face meetings because they have probably talked about their reports informally and obtained everyone's concurrence beforehand. There may be a few questions for clarification but open arguments or heated discussions will not be permitted. In some instances when important decisions are being made, the president or the top executive may show up at the conference just for a few minutes to give the participants moral support. However, he would never stay long and participate in the actual decision-making process. *Kao wo dasu* (showing one's face) has a significant meaning in this context.

If a junior participant wishes to voice his opinion, he will preface his remarks by saying, "I may be making this comment based on my limited experience and I may be wrong, but …" or he may also say, "Please tell me if you think I am wrong, but …." He needs to take a tentative approach and also show humility in order not to cause loss of face among any of the participants. Other participants will also hesitate to voice frank opinions or disagreement, because they fear even their constructive criticisms could be taken as personal attacks or insults. They all tend to look for subtle verbal or nonverbal cues and try to understand how the other participants feel about what is being discussed.

The above discussion seems to indicate that Japanese businesspeople would never exchange their frank, honest opinions or comments. They do so, however, by intentionally creating informal opportunities outside the conference rooms. They frequently go out together for drinking and dining, where they exchange their true feelings. An unhappy participant may even complain bitterly, pretending that he has had too much to drink, but he is allowed to do so because this is one of the ways to appease the dissatisfied member. The Japanese call this method of communicating while drinking alcohol *"nomini-cation"* (drink and communicate). Even in this *nomini-cation* context, it is important for all the participants to remember their position in the organizational hierarchy. A so-called "drunk person" is expected to apologize to his senior members on the following morning for his misbehavior. He might say, "I am sorry I was so drunk last night. I don't remember what I said," even if he remembers clearly what he complained about.

Unlike the Japanese counterpart, an American chairperson controls the discussion of a conference and encourages active participation from the participants. He might even challenge every participant to voice his or her own opinions and comments openly. And the participants feel free to exchange constructive criticisms and objections based on their knowledge and experience without fear of being ostracized or alienated.

Westerners, particularly Americans, are often frustrated when they attend a so-called "decision-making conference" in Japan. They are often dismayed because they expect that the Japanese participants across the conference table will act the same way as they do. They usually find it difficult to read subtle verbal and nonverbal cues offered by the Japanese participants. For example, the Japanese would say "yes, yes" and nod their head in agreement, this is called *aizuchi* (nodding in agreement), but these verbal and nonverbal cues do not mean they are agreeing at all in most instances. They may mean, "I hear what you are saying," "Please explain more," or "I will pretend I agree with you for now, but I still have objections." Another problem is that in the Japanese language, they can say, "Yes, I don't agree with you, which literally means, "Yes, you are right. I don't agree with you" (Nishiyama, 2000).

In order to accurately assess what the Japanese counterparts mean by what they say, it is often necessary for the Americans to go out drinking and dining with a few of their Japanese counterparts. Perhaps one of the Japanese participants may help them "interpret" what has transpired during the conference. He may divulge certain important information *ofureko* (off the record) during after-hours *nomini-cation*.

## ADVICE ON OVERCOMING COMMUNICATION DIFFICULTIES

1. *Maintain close personal contacts.*

   It is extremely important to cultivate and maintain close interpersonal relationships with those who are in charge, because decisions are often made on personal preference, not merely on objective facts and data. For example, an American who makes a good impression on the initiator of a *ringi* proposal can win the latter's friendship. The Japanese representative will keep the American informed as to the progress of the decision making by the involved top executives. Sending direct e-mail reminders will not work in this context.

2. *Do not rush Japanese counterparts.*

   Western businesspeople are always working by setting deadlines for actions, because "time is of the essence" in their culture. They must understand that Japanese deadlines are more flexible, especially when the Japanese side is the buyer in a business deal. In Japan, "A customer is king," and they expect that a seller, who has a lower status, will abide by his customer's deadline.

3. *Do not consider ringi negative because it is slow and cumbersome.*

   The *ringi* process is indeed slow and cumbersome, but implementation of the decision is swift once it is made. For example, the visiting professor in the above example does not have to worry about acquainting himself with his new Japanese colleagues, because everyone in the department will already know who he is and what he has written. They may even know about his wife, children, and other personal matters. Indeed, the "welcome mat" will be laid out upon his arrival.

4. *Bring gifts for Japanese counterparts.*

   Gift giving is still an important custom in establishing amicable interpersonal relationships. A gift does not have to be an expensive one, but it should be a token of friendship. For example, an American businessperson may give a bottle of Johnnie Walker whiskey or a carton of American cigarettes when visiting a Japanese counterpart for the first time. This small gift is not considered as a bribe in Japan, as it is a common practice among Japanese businesspeople. And the Japanese side will usually give the American an *okaeshi* (return gift) when he is leaving Japan.

5. *Good understanding of Japanese culture and social customs is necessary for successful participation in decision-making conference.*

Seating should be arranged strictly according to each participant's status, not by work group or area of specialization. The order of speaking and of asking questions should also be based on the relative status of the Japanese participants. Seniority and ranking are important. For example, a junior manager cannot speak up before his senior manager speaks. Moreover, he must wait for a subtle signal, verbal or nonverbal, from the senior before he can speak.

6. *Do not talk too much and do not dominate discussions.*

Western businesspeople have a tendency to dominate verbal exchanges when participating in a business conference with the Japanese. They believe that winning arguments or using logical persuasion will bring about good results. On the contrary, Japanese participants may be offended by an aggressive and argumentative presentation from their Western counterparts. They may win the argument, but they will lose the deal. When English is used as a medium of communication, the Japanese participants feel handicapped. They may need more time to think in Japanese first and translate their thoughts into English. During meetings and official functions, U.S. business representatives should never help a Japanese counterpart with English by trying to put words into the speaker's mouth.

7. *Be patient and disregard the "Western time orientation."*

Westerners are generally "clock oriented," whereas the Japanese are "people oriented." This means that Japanese people are more inclined to adjust the handling of time based on who is speaking. For example, each participant could be asked to make his or her comment within five minutes, but a senior Japanese participant might take more than ten minutes and ramble along in broken English. Nevertheless, it would be extremely rude to stop him before he finishes what he wants to say. In this situation, who is speaking is more important than what the time restraint is.

8. *It is a good strategy to prepare visual aids in Japanese.*

In order to facilitate accurate communication, visual aids such as charts, graphs, figures, or slides should be used. The Japanese usually want to have written documents that cover important data and information. This strategy will help them better understand what is being explained in English.

> *Japanese participants may be offended by an aggressive and argumentative presentation from their Western counterparts. They may win the argument, but they will lose the deal.*

## CONCLUSION

Despite the fact that many Japanese companies claim that they are revamping the traditional decision-making practices, it seems that they are not able to make drastic changes. Clearly, they must change their personnel recruitment and training system first if they wish to create a new corporate culture amenable to more efficient digital communication. To remove the fear among managers of not knowing what is going on, the Japanese companies still continue to provide information to every level of management by the use of the *ringi* decision-making system. And in order to have amicable interpersonal relationships, Japanese managers still want to hold face-to-face conferences, even though they sometimes find it unnecessary to participate in time-consuming meetings.

During the economic boom years, prior to the burst of Japan's "Bubble Economy" in the early 1990s, there were some innovative measures to change the traditional personnel management system by doing away with permanent employment and seniority-based compensation. The subsequent recession, however, forced many Japanese companies to restructure or scale down their operations. This situation, in turn, created the fear of losing jobs among all levels of managers, and many corporations again went back to the more comfortable and nonthreatening methods of decision making that they had been used to. Those companies that claim that they streamlined decision-making practices still use *ringi* and *kaigi* in making important decisions. These traditional, culturally based methods of decision making, however modified, will continue to be used as long as Japan's corporate culture requires them.

## Index of Japanese Terms

| | |
|---|---|
| *aizuchi* | nodding in agreement |
| *buchoo* | department head |
| *chuuto saiyoo sha* | mid-career recruit |
| *doohai* | same-year comrade |
| *gakubatsu* | school clique |
| *friitaa, frii arubaitaa* | casual worker |
| *habatsu* | faction |
| *haken shain* | dispatched employee |
| *han* | seal |
| *honyatoi* | regular employee |
| *jinji haken kaisha* | employee dispatch company |
| *kaigi* | face-to-face conference |
| *kao wo dasu* | showing one's face |
| *kari* | debt |
| *kashi* | credit |
| *kashi-kari kankei* | obligatory relationship |
| *keiyaku shain* | contract employee |
| *kessai* | final approval |
| *kiansha* | initiator |
| *nemawashi* | informal consultation |
| *nyushashiki* | company entering ceremony |
| *nomini-cation* | drink and communicate |
| *ofureko* | off-the-record |
| *okaeshi* | return gift |
| *onaji kama no meshi wo tabeta nakama* | comrades who ate rice from the same cooker |
| *paato* | part-time worker |
| *ringi* | group decision making |
| *ringisho* | proposal for decision |
| *rinjiyatoi* | temporary worker |
| *senmu torishimari yaku* | managing director |
| *senpai-koohai kankei* | senior-junior relationship |
| *wanman shahoo* | dictator president |

## References

McDaniel, E. R. (2004). Changing Japanese organizational communication patterns: The impact of information technology. *San Diego State University Center for International Business Education and Research* (CIBER). *Working Paper Services C04-015.*

Nishiyama, K. (1995). *Japan–U.S. Business Communication.* Dubuque, IA: Kendall/Hunt.

Nishiyama, K. (2000) *Doing business with Japan: Successful strategies for intercultural communication.* Honolulu: University of Hawaii.

Rohlen, T. (1974). *For harmony and strength: Japanese white-collar organization in anthropological perspective.* Berkeley, CA: University of California.

## Suggested Readings

Castells, M. (2000). End of millennium (2nd ed.). Malden, MA: Blackwell.

Gudykunst, W. B., & Nishida, T. (1994). Bridging Japanese/North America differences. Thousand Oaks, CA: Sage.

Hall, I. (1998). *Cartels of the mind: Japan's intellectual closed shop.* New York: Norton.

Japan External Trade Organization (1992). *Japanese corporate decision-making.* Tokyo: Author.

March, R. M. (1980). *The Japanese negotiator: Subtlety and strategy beyond Western logic.* Tokyo: Kodansha International.

Quasha, S., & McDaniel, E. R. (2003). Reinterpreting Japanese business communication in the information age. In L. Samovar & R. Porter (Eds.), *Intercultural communication: A reader* (10th ed., pp. 283–292). Belmont, CA: Wadsworth.

Yoshida, S. (2002). Globalization and issues of intercultural communications: Doing successful business in Asia. *Vital Speeches of the Day,* 68(22), 708–771.

Yoshimura, N., & Anderson, P. (1997). *Inside the Kaisha: Demystifying Japanese business behavior.* Boston: Harvard Business School Press.

## Concepts and Questions

1. Why is a group-oriented mentality important in Japanese business organizations?

2. How does the Japanese employment system foster group orientation?

3. Why are Japanese employers reluctant to hire employees who have worked for other companies?

4. Nishiyama has indicated that although companies try to establish one unified work group, there may be factions within the company. What are the bases for these factions? How do these factions fit in with the idea of a group-oriented workforce?

5. How does the position of chief executive officer in Japanese companies differ from that position in Western business organizations?

6. What are the cultural significances of the Japanese *ringi* decision-making process?

7. How does the *ringi* process differ from decision-making processes in Western organizations?

8. Why is it important for a Western businessperson to understand the *kaigi* process?

9. In what ways do face-to-face conferences in Japanese business organizations differ from those in Western business organizations?

10. In group-oriented Japanese business organizations where harmonious relationships are important, how do Japanese business people exchange and express frank and honest opinions?

# Comparing and Contrasting German and American Business Cultures

MICHAEL B. HINNER

*Although the diversity found between Eastern and Western cultures looms the largest, there are important differences between U.S. American and European business cultures that can also lead to confusion and misunderstanding. Michael Hinner next presents his analysis of German and American business cultures. From this analysis you will (1) gain insight into the similarities between the German and American business cultures, (2) recognize how European geography plays a role in the development of German cultural values, (3) see how the German tendency toward uncertainty avoidance influences their cultural behaviors, (4) gain some insight into the German legal system and its influence on the conduct of business, (5) learn about the differences between German and American corporate organizations, and (6) see some of the major differences between German and American methods of doing business.*

*Hinner begins by relating that the German and American economies are similar because they are capital based and market driven. He points out, however, that "a closer look at German and American business cultures also reveals differences." He also shows how Germany's position*

*in the heart of Europe, which has placed it in the center of wars and conflicts going back to antiquity, has influenced the development of many German cultural values. High uncertainty avoidance (the extent to which a member of a culture is fearful of the unknown) is a major characteristic found within the German culture. Hinner points out how this has led the Germans to create many rules and regulations that help minimize risks in advance and promote the successful accomplishment of any task at hand. Hinner also points out that Germany has a long history of regional autonomy, giving the country a very different tradition than is found in the United States.*

*As a background for further understanding German culture, Hinner describes the German legal system and how it differs from that of the United States. The major difference is that German law is code based while American law is case based. In Germany, the law seeks to anticipate illegal actions, which must be listed expressly in the legal code to be deemed illegal. Law in the United States applies the principle of analogy and is able to extend existing law to cover new circumstances.*

This original essay appears here in print for the first time. An earlier version of this essay appeared in the twelfth edition. All rights reserved. Permission to reprint must be obtained from the author and the publisher. Dr. Michael B. Hinner teaches Business English, Business Communication, and Intercultural Communication at the TU Bergakademie, Freiberg, Germany, and Dresden International University in Dresden, Germany.

*Hinner continues his essay with a description of the differences between German and American corporate organization. German companies are controlled by two different boards: a management board and a supervisory board. The management board runs the company, while the supervisory board is charged with the task of seeing that management policies and operations are always in the best interest of shareholders. By German law, in corporations of over 500 employees, one-third of the supervisory board members must be employees. This provision is consistent with the German principles of consensus and parity. By describing the organization of American corporations and the role of their boards and CEOs, Hinner shows just how different business organizations are in Germany and the United States.*

*Hinner concludes his essay with a discussion of communication problems that can arise during business negotiations between Americans and their German counterparts. He explains how diversity in some cultural values influences the interactions. For instance, while both Americans and Germans tend to be monochronic in their work routines, Germans are more rigid and believe small talk to be a waste of time; meetings should commence immediately with the business at hand. Also, the German need for order and organization requires that in any business meeting the Germans will want to have an initial and comprehensive understanding of all aspects of a problem before attempting to solve it.*

At first glance, German and American business cultures seem very similar. After all, both economies are capital based and market driven. Shares of large German and American corporations are traded in both countries. In fact, numerous German corporations have been active on the American market for many decades now, such as Bayer, BMW, Braun, T-Mobile, and Volkswagen, as have been many American corporations on the German market, for example, Coca-Cola, Ford, IBM, McDonald's, and Microsoft. The list of such companies could easily be extended. But a closer look at German and American business cultures also reveals differences—differences that emerge slowly and only after a longer period of contact, cooperation, or interaction. If and when such differences do emerge, their root cause—cultural differences—is often not identified as a reason for these differences; instead, other readily perceivable factors are used to provide an explanation for these differences and difficulties, e.g., differences in the distribution network, personality characteristics, financial resources, etc. (Harris & Moran, 1996; Hofstede & Hofstede, 2005; Trompenaars & Hampden-Turner, 1998). One need only recall the failed Daimler Chrysler merger to realize the scope of the potential difficulties (Edmunds Auto Observer, 2007, May 17). While some cultural problems might arise prior to establishing close business relationships, most tend to surface later during the day-to-day business routine after a relationship is in place (Harris & Moran, 1996; Hofstede & Hofstede, 2005; Trompenaars & Hampden-Turner, 1998). If one is not sensitized to culture, then one will not consider it as a factor in the analysis of business phenomena and instead consider other explanations (Hinner, 2005).

## CULTURE

Most people do not consider culture to be an issue if the participants appear to be fairly similar to one another (Chen & Starosta, 1998; Gudykunst & Kim, 1997; Samovar et al., 2010). It seems that people need to associate culture with something tangible and visible to realize that differences do exist between the interactors. It is usually only when someone speaks a different language, wears different clothes, and works in an entirely different work environment that most people perceive a difference (Gudykunst & Kim, 1997; Klopf, 1998; Samovar et al., 2010). In today's global economy, many international business partners are fluent in English, wear similar business clothes, and often work in similar office environments so that "surface" differences tend to blend into a similar appearance (Harris & Moran, 1996; Hofstede & Hofstede, 2005; Samovar et al., 2010; Trompenaars & Hampden-Turner, 1998). But culture is more than external appearance (artifacts). Culture also includes social organization and interaction (sociofacts), and cognitive patterns, (mentifacts), which are not always readily apparent to the observer but are expressed by the actions and behavior of people as well as in the thinking and decision-making process (Chen & Starosta, 1998; Gudykunst & Kim, 1997; Klopf, 1998; Martin & Nakayama, 1997; Samovar et al., 2010). These "hidden" differences, though, often emerge and cause problems in the day-to-day routine of human interaction (Hofstede & Hofstede, 2005; Klopf, 1998; Samovar et al., 2010).

If, however, the external differences are striking, then the participants of an intercultural encounter will probably expect to encounter difficulties since these differences are perceivable as such (Chen & Starosta, 1998; Gudykunst & Kim, 1997; Klopf, 1998; Martin & Nakayama, 1997; Samovar et al., 2010). But one does not expect to encounter difficulties if there are few external differences and/or the actors appear to exhibit similar behavior.[1] All the more surprising, then, if differences are encountered when least expected. Because these differences are not anticipated, they become all the more surprising due to their *unexpectedness*. And this is the crux of culture: People tend to associate cultural differences with exotic differences, and few expect culture to play any role in modern international business relationships (De Mooij, 2007; Harris & Moran, 1996; Hofstede & Hofstede, 2005; Trompenaars & Hampden-Turner, 1998), especially if two Western cultures are involved in an international business transaction, as is, for example, the case with Germans and Americans, who share a long tradition of contact and interaction.

## German and American Similarities

German and American cultures have many similarities because they share, to some extent, a common European heritage. In fact, many Americans trace their family roots back to German immigrants (German American, 2007). Conversely, the majority of Germans have been exposed to and influenced by American culture since the end of World War II (*Facts about Germany*, 1998; Jankuhn et al., 1983; Zentner, 1980). This close relationship of both cultures is also illustrated by the many German loan-words in American English and the many English loanwords in German. Examples include *kindergarten, kaffeeklatsch,* and *sauerkraut* in American English,[2] and *Designerbaby, Evergreen,* and *Preshave* in German.[3] Likewise, many German products have become icons in the United States—the Volkswagen Beetle and Bayer aspirin, as have U.S. products in Germany, such as Levi's jeans and Coca-Cola. The list of similarities and parallels could be extended easily.

## German and American Differences

But the transfer and exchange of products and cultural artifacts between Germany and the United States is not always identical because adjustments also must be made to local tastes. In Germany, the *Frankfurter Würstchen* can be served with mustard and possibly a roll or even a serving of *sauerkraut*; in the United States, franks are served on a bun with a topping of *sauerkraut*, mustard, and/or ketchup and called "hot dogs." McDonald's, for example, includes beer in its program of beverages in Germany, something it is just starting to offer to its customers in the United States. And Coca-Cola adapted the taste of its soft drinks, in particular, Fanta and Cherry Coke, to German taste buds (Hinner, 1998). The average Bayer aspirin tablet sold in Germany has a higher dosage than those sold in the U.S.A., which explains why aspirin is usually only sold in pharmacies in Germany (Hinner & Rülke, 2002). And while the Volkswagen Jetta is a very popular car among young drivers in the United States, many young Germans consider it to be a car for senior citizens because the Jetta has a trunk, a symbol of stodginess, and not a hatchback, a sign of being hip.[4]

> *German and American cultures have many similarities because they share, to some extent, a common European heritage.*

---

[1]It should also be remembered that most business partners seek contact with potential partners because each side hopes to benefit in some form from this relationship. This beneficial end goal also tends to have an impact on the interpretation and evaluation of the communicated messages by both sides, i.e., it tends to make the initial interpretation positive as long as you assume that you are not being cheated. In fact, this positive association is usually applied to the general transactional relationship that is in the process of being established.

[2]These American English words were taken from *Webster's New World College Dictionary* (2001), 4th edition.

[3]These German words were taken from *Duden* (2006), 6th edition.

[4]VW even tried to improve the lagging sales by changing the car's name in Germany from Jetta, initially to Vento and later to Bora, but without success. In the United States, VW kept the name for all Jetta generations.

## Culture and Consumers

The Volkswagen Jetta example illustrates how the same product can have different associations among consumers in different cultures. It thus quickly becomes apparent that classic market segmentation is insufficient in an intercultural context (De Mooij, 2007; Sandhusen, 1997). This may be illustrated by the following example. Single, female secretaries aged twenty to twenty-five years who live in the suburbs and commute to work in the city, listen to the same music, pursue the same hobbies, and have a similar disposable income might be classified as one and the same market segment (Homburg & Krohmer, 2003; Meffert, 2000) even though they live and work in Germany and the United States. Marketing considers these perceivable factors to be helpful in developing marketing campaigns directed at this consumer group. Yet despite all these surface similarities, differences do exist which can translate into missed business opportunities. These differences, though, are not found in classic segmentation categories because these differences rest in cultural differences (De Mooij, 1007; Hinner, 1998; Hinner, 2004; Hinner & Rülke, 2002). If culture is not a criterion in the segmentation, it will not be considered by marketers. So if a German shoe manufacturer were to target this particular market segment, the company would probably assume that American secretaries wear footwear similar to German secretaries. Company representatives might actually have encountered American secretaries while visiting the United State on a business trip and noticed that American secretaries wear high heels in the office. But the Germans might not have noticed that many American secretaries also wear sneakers during the commute to work and only change to high heels in the office. German secretaries, in contrast, tend to wear the same shoes during the commute and in the office. Without any knowledge of this slight but relevant difference in behavior, the German shoe manufacturer would miss out on an important bit of information that could also have consequences for the business. But probably no one would deliberately point out these differences, because everyone would assume that all secretaries exhibit similar behavior in a similar context regardless of whether it is Germany or the United States. From this example, though, it should be apparent that direct comparisons based on classic market segmentation can miss out on important consumer behavior if cultural differences are not considered (De Mooij, 2007). This case also illustrates how people perceive, interpret, and evaluate the behavior of others on the basis of their own past experiences in similar situations instead of attempting to discover the real reason for the observed behavior (Adler & Rodman, 2003).

*Business people are also members of a society at large and its culture and, thus, affected by the same cultural factors that influence all other members of that society.*

## Characteristics of Culture

That is why this essay looks at how a country's culture influences and, to some degree, determines the business culture of that country. After all, business people are also members of a society at large and its culture and, thus, affected by the same cultural factors that influence all other members of that society. Germany shall serve as an example for comparison with American culture to demonstrate how two relatively closely related cultures are actually quite different from one another in how their businesses are organized, how their business people interact with one another, and how they solve problems. The examination of German culture will reveal many particulars of German culture and, thus, help explain the artifacts, sociofacts, and mentifacts of German business culture, and why they are in some instances similar to, and in other instances quite different from, American business culture.[5]

"The how and why behind a culture's collective action can be traced to its (1) world view (religion),

---

[5]It will be assumed that the reader is somewhat familiar with American culture, but not German culture. In fact, Samovar et al.'s *Communication between Cultures* makes numerous references to and includes many examples taken from American history. That is why the focus will be on German culture, which will, though, be compared to and contrasted with American culture to illustrate the differences in both.

(2) family structure, and (3) history and government. Working together, these three social forces create, transmit, maintain, and reinforce the basic elements found in all cultures" (Samovar et al., 2010, p. 88). The worldview is essential in explaining how the universe functions and the role people play in it. From this core belief system, a society develops its values. Values are standards of behavior and, thus, essential for human interaction and for forming personal attitudes which reflect what one thinks of these standards. These core beliefs and values are transmitted by society at large and the family. After all, culture is learned and passed down from one generation to the next (Samovar et al., 2010). So in many ways, the recounting of the past and the lessons learned (or not) play an important role in the instruction of the subsequent generation(s). History, whether it is family or national history, helps create identity in that it tells people who they are and where they come from (Lustig & Koester, 2006; Oetzel, 2009; Samovar et al., 2010).

> ... when we refer to history as one of the deep structures of a culture, we are also talking about a culture's formal and informal government, its sense of community, its political system, its key historical "heroes," and even its geography. All of these, working in combination, provide the members of every culture with their identity, values, goals, and expectations (Samovar et al., 2010, p. 123).

And, finally, the environment needs to be added as a fourth element because the environment can determine, for example, what food people eat and what houses are built with what materials. Sometimes a similar environment can produce a similar solution. For example, houses built in regions with a lot of snow have steep roofs that to allow the snow to slide off easily, thus reducing the likelihood of the roof collapsing due to the weight of the accumulated snow. In contrast, houses in hot and dry regions tend to have flat roofs since they do not have to worry about too much precipitation accumulating on the roof. The same applies to the business environment. If the environmental factors are similar, then similar artifacts may be produced and/or used. That is why a factory equipped with similar assembly technology will look fairly similar in many parts of the world. But how it is organized, how people interact and communicate with one another, and how they reach decisions will vary from one culture to another (Hofstede, 2005). In other words, artifacts can be similar if the environment is similar, but the sociofacts and mentifacts can be quite different.

## General Disposition and Individual Diversity

It should, though, be kept in mind that the discussion of "typical" behavioral norms refers to generalities and that individual behavior can and will vary, even deviate considerably, from these cultural "standards." Sometimes, a specific microculture will exhibit radically different behavior from other microcultures within the same macroculture (Chen & Starosta, 1998; Klopf, 1998; Lustig & Koester, 2006; Oetzel, 2009; Samovar et al., 1998), e.g., teenagers vs. senior citizens, bankers vs. construction workers, atheists vs. fundamentalists. Nonetheless, active members of a particular culture will have had to have learned when and where what behavioral standards and norms are expected. Otherwise, a person will not be able to interact successfully in a particular cultural environment (Chen & Starosta, 1998; Klopf, 1998; Lustig & Koester, 2006; Oetzel, 2009; Samovar et al., 2010). This demonstrates that certain standards and norms can be identified and that people can learn these standards and norms if they wish to.

## GERMAN CULTURE

As Samovar et al. (2010) point out, culture is rooted in and influenced by history and geography. Germany's location in the heart of Europe has placed it in the center of conflict for a very long time (Herrmann, 1988; Jankuhn et al., 1983; Zentner, 1980). The conflicts go back to classical antiquity and only stopped recently with the fall of the Berlin Wall in 1989 (*Facts about Germany*, 1998). These ceaseless wars and the resultant chaos are often cited as a reason for the great desire to avoid uncertainty, provide a degree of predictability, establish order, and maintain stability (Lord, 1998). Consequently, many rules and regulations were created in Germany in order to reduce uncertainty as much as possible (Hofstede & Hofstede, 2005). It is generally assumed in Germany that these rules and regulations have proven their worth because they help minimize risks in advance, which, in turn, results in the successful accomplishment of the task at hand and the creation of future stability (Schroll-Machl, 2002).

## A History of Political Disunion

Germany has also a long history of regional autonomy (*Facts about Germany*, 1998; Herrmann, 1988; Jankuhn et al., 1983; Zentner, 1980). In fact, a unified country did not exist until 1871, and it was divided again into two separate states for slightly more than 40 years after World War II (*Facts about Germany*, 1998; Herrmann, 1988). In other words, Germany has only been unified politically as country for less than a century. With such political disunion, Germany has a very different tradition than neighboring countries like France or Denmark, for example (Zentner, 1980). Over time, this strong regional diversity led to many regions being associated with specific characteristics. For example, Swabians, who live in southwestern Germany, are said to be frugal; Bavarians, who live in southeastern Germany, are said to be jovial; and northern Germans are said to be taciturn. This regional division is also reflected in the German constitution, which guarantees the federal states a number of privileges and rights which set Germany apart from many neighboring countries like France, Italy, or Denmark (*Facts about Germany*, 1998). The long history of political disunion also helps explain why to this day German companies have fairly autonomous departments and business units with little or no communication between the various organizational compartments of a company (Opitz, 2003).

## Linguistic Diversity

The traditional division of Germany is also expressed in linguistic differences. The German language has three principal dialect groups, namely Low German in the north, Middle German in the center, and High German in the south (König, 1989; Waterman, 1976). The primary difference between the principal dialects is expressed by the consonant shift of *p, t, k* to *f, s, ch*, so that Low German *peper, water, maken* become High German *Pfeffer, Wasser, machen* (König, 1989; Waterman, 1976). The dialect difference is actually more complex and includes many regionally unique words and phrases and grammatical differences which make mutual understanding very difficult (König, 1989; Waterman, 1976). For example, the word *butcher* can be *Fleischer, Fleischhacker, Metzger*, or *Schlachter* depending on where one lives and works in Germany (König, 1989). And the grammatical gender of the noun *Cola* can be feminine—*die Cola*—or neuter—*das Cola* (Duden, 2006). In fact, it is often easier for a person from Northern Germany to understand a native of the Netherlands than a fellow German from Southern Germany. Since language is a symbolic expression of culture and classified as a cultural artifact (Klopf, 1998; Samovar et al., 1998), this linguistic variety of Germany clearly expresses the degree of regional cultural diversity in Germany.

Companies seeking to enter the German market need to take this linguistic diversity into consideration, especially when product names could result in misunderstandings, confusion, or even rejection. For example, the *potato* is called *Kartoffel* in Standard German as well as some parts of Northern Germany, but it is called *Grumbeere* in some parts of Western Germany, *Erdäpfel* in Southeastern Germany, and *Nudel* in parts of Northeastern Germany, to name only some variations, because there are many others (König, 1989). One can well imagine what the consequences would be for a distributor of potatoes in Germany, because the regional names are often unknown outside the respective regions. In fact, *Nudel* will result in a misunderstanding because in Standard German *Nudel* is a *noodle* and not a potato.

## Religious Division

In addition to linguistic variety, German regional differences are also expressed by traditional religious differences. Germany has been divided roughly into a Protestant north and a Catholic south and west since the Reformation in the 16th century (Herrmann, 1988; Jankuhn et al., 1983; Zentner, 1980). And with German reunification, an atheistic east must be added —legacy of 40 years of communism (*Facts about Germany*, 1998). While most children in West Germany celebrate either communion or confirmation, which are Christian ceremonies, most East German children celebrate the *Jugendweihe*, a secularized ceremony to admit adolescents into adult society. This regional difference in religion results in different public holidays throughout Germany because the majority of legal holidays in Germany are religious holidays. Consequently, a predominantly Protestant state will be closed for business on different days throughout the year than a Catholic state in Germany. In the predominantly Catholic Rhineland, for example, virtually all businesses shut down during the *Karneval* (Mardi Gras) season, which lasts for about a week. And the dichotomy of the German work ethic—working very hard on the job but also having six weeks of paid vacation per year and strictly separating work from pleasure—may also be explained by the broad mix of the Protestant work ethic and the Catholic *joie de vivre* found within Germany.

## East and West Germany

East Germany looks back on 40 years of communism preceded by 12 years of Nazi dictatorship; this means that three generations of East Germans lived under totalitarianism. In West Germany, the 12 years of Hitler and the Holocaust were followed by 60 years of democracy and early integration into Western alliances such as NATO and the European Community (*Facts about Germany*, 1998). It is, therefore, not surprising that new regional differences evolved after World War II as well. While East Germans also point to differences among Saxons and Brandenburgers, there is also a transcending issue of East vs. West Germans, referred to as *Ossis* and *Wessis*.[6] This difference between East and West is reflected in a number of opinion polls and election results. The former communist party of East Germany, now called *Die Linke* (The Left), still racks up around a quarter to a third of all the votes in East Germany, while in West Germany the same party gets only 1 vote in 10. During the last federal elections in 2009, for example, the Left party got 26.4 percent of the votes in East Germany and only 8.3 percent of the votes in West Germany, which translates into 11.9 percent for all of Germany (ARD.de, 2009) since the population in West Germany is more than three times

larger than that in East Germany. While in West Germany the Left party only reached fifth place among the five major German political parties, they gained second place in East Germany—only 3 percent behind Chancellor Merkel's Christian Democrats[7] (CDU) and well ahead of the other three major political parties. The Left party actually ended up winning the most votes in two East German states, namely Brandenburg and Saxony Anhalt, and reached second place in the remaining three East German states: Mecklenburg, Western Pomerania, Saxony, and Thuringia (ARD.de, 2009). These figures clearly speak volumes of the political division in East and West Germany. An interesting twist of the East–West division has recently emerged in the Left party, where there was talk of an intraparty divide between members from West and East Germany (Welt Online, 2010, January 19).[8] Twenty years after German reunification, the majority of East Germans still do not identify themselves with the Federal Republic of Germany, while the majority of West Germans do, according to a recent survey (Siemon, 2007, March 22).

This political division has also created a different approach to work and what role the government should assume. While most West Germans would not work on Sundays or public, (historically, religious) holidays, East Germans typically do work on those days without such reservations. Compared to East Germans, most West Germans would be willing to take more risks, which explains the greater proportion of entrepreneurship in West Germany. On the other hand, the many years of scarcity in East Germany resulted in more improvisation among East Germans than among West Germans (*Facts about Germany*, 1998). But 40 years of communism still seems to have left its legacy. A 2008 poll taken before the economic crisis showed that 61 percent of East Germans felt the government did not provide enough guarantees to protect their jobs, 69 percent thought the government should do more about medical care, and 79 percent believed that the government needed to augment the state retirement program. In contrast

---

[6]Interestingly, some of the stereotypes associated with *Wessis* parallel those associated with Yankee carpetbaggers during Reconstruction in the American South.

[7]It will be recalled that Chancellor Merkel is herself a native of East Germany.

[8]This is actually a bit ironic because the Communist Party wants to transcend class and national barriers; after all, their party anthem is *The Internationale*.

to East Germans, West Germans did not expect the government to assume such a significant role in these matters, believing that some private initiative is also needed (*Sächsische Zeitung*, 2008, March 26). In fact, most East Germans feel that social and welfare programs are more important than individual freedom, an opinion that is not shared by West Germans (Schuler, 2010, February 19).

## Consensus and Parity

These strong regional differences probably also contributed to the use of so many rules and regulations in Germany because otherwise it would not have been possible to reach any consensus. In fact, Standard German can be considered an artificial dialect that combines a number of aspects from the principal dialects to achieve some degree of mutual comprehension (König, 1989; Waterman, 1976). But it also helps explain why consensus is so important to German culture, because it helped establish a unified national identity. The concept of consensus and parity is even anchored in the German constitution, the *Grundgesetz* (the Basic Law [*Facts about Germany*, 1998]). After World War II, when the Basic Law was written in West Germany, the notion of shared fiscal revenues was applied to the principle of *Länderausgleich* (state parity). This constitutional provision specifies that the rich federal states have to allocate a certain portion of their revenues to poorer states in order to assist the poorer states. This redistribution of wealth was designed to create economic parity among all the federal states so that no inhabitant would be forced to live in a state that offers fewer amenities than the other states (*Facts about Germany*, 1998).[9]

Not surprisingly, East Germany under communism went a step further and implemented a rigorous program of identical services and products throughout the entire country. Hence, regardless of regional traditions, a centralized system of uniformity was introduced and enforced in East Germany, and the social class system was officially abolished (*Facts about Germany*, 1998; Herrmann, 1988). After German reunification, the principle of parity was extended to the new federal states in East Germany with the introduction of the Solidarity Pact, which includes a special tax to help finance the enormous costs of German reunification so that the East German infrastructure is raised to West German standards, in addition to the usual *Länderausgleich* (*Facts about Germany*, 1998). Consensus and parity are so ensconced in German thinking that they are also present in many aspects of German business culture, including corporate policy and governance, as will be shown below.

## Government System

Germany is a federal republic, and regional differences play an important role in the German governmental system. The nationally elected parliament is called the *Bundestag*, and the party or parties having a parliamentary majority head the federal government under the leadership of the Federal Chancellor (*Facts about Germany*, 1998). The Chancellor, thus, automatically has a parliamentary majority in the *Bundestag*. All federal bills must be passed by a majority vote in the *Bundestag* (*Facts about Germany*, 1998). All legislation affecting the interests of the states must additionally be approved by the *Bundesrat*, the other legislative body, which represents the interests of the states (*Facts about Germany*, 1998). Unlike the United States Senate, the German *Bundesrat* "does not consist of elected representatives of the people but of members of the state governments or their representatives" (*Facts about Germany*, 1998, p. 174). After a bill has passed the appropriate legislative chamber(s), it must be signed by the Federal President to become a law (*Facts about Germany*, 1998). The Federal President heads the German nation but not the federal government, which is headed by the Federal Chancellor as noted above (*Facts about Germany*, 1998). Germany has, thus, two separate and distinct executive offices: one for matters of state, and another for matters of government. The United States, in contrast, unites both executive positions in the office of the President. This division of the executive office into two separate offices with distinct duties and responsibilities is a feature that is repeated in many other German administrative organizations

---

[9]This principle of economic parity reaches down all the way to local municipalities in counties where richer communities have to help finance poorer communities (*Sächsische Zeitung*, March 27, 2007).

such as schools and universities as well as corporations; this is not the case in the United States.

## Legal System

Not surprisingly, German and American laws are based on different legal principles. Traditionally, German law is code based while American law is case based (*Facts about Germany*, 1998; Howard, 1965).[10] German law seeks to anticipate illegal actions, which have to be listed expressly in the legal code to be deemed illegal. If an action has not been anticipated and, thus, is not included in the legal code, it is not considered to be illegal.[11] The German legal code, therefore, has to be constantly amended in order to keep abreast of changes in society or technology. This is different from law in the United States, which applies the principle of analogy (Howard, 1965). Thus, for example, legal provisions regulating horse-drawn carriages were interpreted in the United States to also include automobiles when cars first appeared on America's roads, since horse-drawn carriages and "horseless carriages" are both road vehicles designed to transport people. In Germany, the traffic law had to be amended expressly to also include automobiles. Something similar occurred with copyright regulations and the introduction of new technologies such as photocopiers, computers, and MP3 players. In each instance, the German legal code had to be amended; in some cases the amendments got amended. German

*German law seeks to anticipate illegal actions, which have to be listed expressly in the legal code to be deemed illegal. If an action has not been anticipated and, thus, is not included in the legal code, it is not considered to be illegal.*

law, therefore, seeks great precision, which usually results in very comprehensive (and cumbersome) legal codes. Hence, the German legal principle conforms to the general concept prevalent in Germany of attempting to break everything down to the most precise subcategory possible, which is designed to reduce uncertainty. By breaking everything down to the smallest possible category, it is assumed that the size of the problem is also reduced, thus making the problem more manageable.

## Educational System

Education is important in shaping and transmitting culture (Chen & Starosta, 1998; Gudykunst & Kim, 1997; Klopf, 1998; Samovar et al., 2010). Not surprisingly, the German educational system reflects the regional differences of Germany as well because education is a matter of the individual states as specified by the Basic Law (*Facts about Germany*, 1998).[12] At the same time, there are also a number of similarities among all German states that are, to some degree, quite unique to Germany. Most

*Most German states decide during the fourth grade, i.e., when children are nine or ten years old, which type of secondary school a child is to attend.*

German states decide during the fourth grade, when children are nine or ten years old, which type of secondary school a child is to attend. There are typically three types of secondary school in Germany: the *Hauptschule*, which is to prepare students for vocational careers; the *Realschule*, which is to prepare students for clerical positions; and the *Gymnasium*, which is to prepare students for university studies (*Facts about*

---

[10]A legal code comprises laws, statutes, and regulations that have been enacted and are "codified" in books, whereas legal cases are court cases that establish a legal precedent and tradition on which the law of the land is based. (Typically, these cases also are recorded in books.)

[11]This can create a dilemma, as a recent case of cannibalism illustrates. The German criminal code does not expressly forbid cannibalism since no one had thought this would happen in modern Germany. Consequently, when a person actually did commit an act of cannibalism recently, it was not possible to convict the person of cannibalism since it had not been declared illegal. The criminal court could only rule on manslaughter.

[12]This regional difference is particularly noticeable at the secondary level since the states have different curricula. Consequently, it is difficult for children to overcome this gap, which is why most German parents are wary of moving their families to a different state.

Germany, 1998). Theoretically, it is possible for students of both the *Hauptschule* and *Realschule* also to attend universities (*Facts about Germany*, 1998), but in practice it does not happen very often. This effectively bars the majority of students from university studies, which is one reason why the United Nations criticized the German secondary education system a few years ago (*Sächsische Zeitung*, 2007, March 22). This educational segmentation is also continued in the apprenticeship and trainee programs in which adolescents are trained for a very specific, albeit highly qualified vocation (*Facts about Germany*, 1998). Even the university education is typically based on narrowly focused degrees which revolve around curricula that only contain courses on the subject in question. So if someone majors in mathematics, that person will typically only need to take math courses. As a consequence, the German educational system—at the primary, secondary, vocational, and college level—produces highly specialized professionals while essentially shunning a general, broader, interdisciplinary education.[13]

## Labor Market

Because German employees have typically been trained in very narrowly defined vocations and professions, it is often difficult to switch job fields since the employees do not have comparable skills and training in another occupation. In fact, German employers look for job candidates who fit precisely the job description contained in the want ads because these descriptions are created based on the standardized occupational qualification. This is very different from the United States where it is generally assumed that not all applicants will be able to meet all specifications. Instead, it is frequently assumed that candidates will be able to acquire the necessary skills in due time while learning on the job. This, in part, explains why some unemployed in Germany have become chronic unemployed: these people had originally been trained in vocations

for which there are no longer sufficient jobs available, since these occupations have been superseded by new technology and/or outsourced to countries with lower wages. At the same time, Germany lacks skilled employees in other job fields—typically in newly created high-tech vocations for which the educational system has not been able to generate sufficient graduates yet.

## GERMAN BUSINESS CULTURE

The above excursion into German culture provides an explanation and understanding of German business culture since both are intimately entwined with one another. It is, thus, not surprising that most German businesses tend to have a fairly strict division of staff into blue- and white-collar employees, and also between white-collar clerical positions and management posts (Hofstede & Hofstede, 2005). Trompenaars and Hampden-Turner (1998), therefore, classify German corporations as bureaucratic organizations in which personal relations play a minor role because the focus is on the tasks at hand. According to Trompenaars and Hampden-Turner (1998), German corporate careers are based on professional qualifications. "Manpower planning, assessment centers, appraisal systems, training schemes and job rotation all have the function of helping to classify and produce resources to fit known roles" (Trompenaars & Hampden-Turner, 1998, p. 174). Since one of the tasks of education is to provide the right training of potential employees for the job market, it becomes clear why the German educational system pursues a highly segmented educational approach: so that these specific occupations can be filled with employees meeting precisely those specified qualifications.

## Problem Solving

The problem-solving methods conveyed in German schools focus not so much on finding a solution; instead, emphasis is placed on outlining and

---

[13]This is also expressed in the application documents. German application documents are very different from typical American application documents. A German resume contains detailed personal information including a photograph of the candidate, the date of birth and place of birth, and marital status, as well as the occupation of the applicant's parents, and even the religion of the applicant. The education section describes in detail all school types starting with the primary school, while the employment section only mentions the dates of employment, the place of employment, and the occupation. A detailed job description, so typical of American resumes, is not needed because the job title suffices since German employers will know exactly what qualifications and skills that job entails. In addition to the resume and cover letter, German applications need to also include certified copies of any and all relevant documents, certificates, degrees, letters of reference, etc.

following the proper steps to a solution. Thus, the actual solution to a math problem, for example, will be awarded with only a small percentage of the points for the right answer while the majority of the points will go to the application of the right steps.[14] This explains why, in a business context, so much emphasis is put on finding the right steps to a solution. Americans tend to get irritated because Germans take considerable time for deliberations and reaching decisions. But Germans feel that it is necessary to consider and discuss at length all variables before reaching any decision. After all, most Germans are interested in finding long-term solutions. Americans, in contrast, tend to be more interested in getting short-term results, which explains why American corporations publish quarterly results and German companies, traditionally, annual results.[15] And if a plan does not work, it is quickly replaced by a new one. This may be best illustrated by the approach to house building. While many houses in the United States are built with frame construction, drywall, and asphalt roof shingles in a relatively short period of time, most German houses are built with reinforced concrete, bricks, and cement roof tiles. Consequently, house construction typically takes much longer in Germany than in the United States. In Germany, most people still feel that a house has to be built to last for a long time so that future generations can continue to live in it as well. From a German perspective, this makes sense since the marked regional differences traditionally led many people to stay close to their home because it is where people speak the same dialect and practice the same religion. While this has been changing, most Germans would still prefer to stay in their home region if given a choice.[16]

## Business Organizations

German corporations, not surprisingly, have a different organizational structure than U.S. corporations. Traditionally, stock markets played a minor role in the acquisition of capital in Germany. Consequently, only a small proportion of businesses in Germany are organized as corporations (Wentges, 2002). Other reasons for the relatively small percentage of corporations in Germany include the many corporate regulations, the partial loss of control, tax disadvantages, and considerable codetermination of employees in Germany (Nassauer, 2000). Most of the capital for German businesses is provided by banks (Emmons & Schmid, 1998). It was actually the German banks which provided the capital to the growing industrial enterprises in the nineteenth century when German industrialization began. Since private citizens did not have the capital, and well-developed stock markets did not yet exist, banks were the only source of capital in Germany at that time (Nassauer, 2000). Consequently, banks often have direct influence on German companies that goes well beyond the typical American creditor–company relationship. That is why it is not surprising for banks to be represented in virtually all of the large German corporations (Emmons & Schmid, 1998).

## German Corporations

German corporations are controlled by two boards, the *Vorstand* (management board), which is responsible for managing the company, and the *Aufsichtsrat*, (supervisory board), which exercises control over the management. According to German corporate law, management and control of a company must be exercised separately in companies having more than 500 employees (*Facts about Germany*, 1998; Nassauer, 2000). The assumption is that management does not necessarily pursue the interests of shareholders and, therefore, requires an independent board which acts as a counterbalance to management's power (*Facts about Germany*, 1998; Nassauer, 2000), thus applying the principle of parity.

The *Vorstand* is empowered to run the business and, thus, formulates and implements the business strategies. It also represents the company externally

---

[14]This information is based on what the author was told in a number of conversations with German students.

[15]German corporations listed, for example, on the New York Stock Exchange have to, of course, conform to American law when it comes to financial statements and their publication.

[16]This information is based on information ascertained from a number of conversations with Germans in various regions. All expressed a strong attachment to their home region, in part due to linguistic and religious reasons as well as due to close ties to family and friends.

(Conyon & Schwalbach, 1999; *Facts about Germany*, 1998; Wentges, 2002). The *Vorstand* can consist of one or more executives. Generally, all members of the *Vorstand* are jointly responsible for decisions or actions of a corporation. In practice, though, each member of the *Vorstand* has special duties and competencies in specific business sectors (Wentges, 2002), which conforms to the German desire to segment everything according to areas of expertise. The members of the *Vorstand* are appointed by the *Aufsichtsrat* for a maximum term of five years (Conyon & Schwalbach, 1999; Emmons & Schmid, 1998). Reappointments are possible (Emmons & Schmid, 1998). Once a year, the *Vorstand* has to report to the *Aufsichtsrat* on the current state and the intended business policy (Conyon & Schwalbach, 1999).

The *Aufsichtsrat* monitors the activities of the *Vorstand*. In order to meet the requirement of separating the decision-making process and control, the *Aufsichtsrat* is not empowered to run a business (*Facts about Germany*, 1998; Wentges, 2002). Nevertheless, some activities by the management do require approval of the *Aufsichtsrat*. The *Aufsichtsrat* consists of 3 to 21 members, depending on the size of the corporation (*Facts about Germany*, 1998; Nassauer, 2000). While the members of the *Aufsichtsrat* are classified as non-executives, former CEOs of the company usually chair the *Aufsichtsrat* (Emmons & Schmid, 1998).

The *Mitbestimmungsgesetz* (codetermination act) of 1976 introduced the requirement to have employees in the *Aufsichtsrat*. In corporations of more than 500 employees, one-third of the *Aufsichtsrat* have to be employees; in corporations of more than 2,000 employees, that number increases to half (Conyon & Schwalbach, 1999; *Facts about Germany*, 1998; Nassauer, 2000).[17] The remaining members of the *Aufsichtsrat* are elected by the shareholders at the annual shareholders' meeting. This principle of including employees in corporate governance conforms, once again, to the German principles of consensus and parity. The main duties of the *Aufsichtsrat* are the nomination and discharge of the members of the *Vorstand* and the appointment of the corporate auditor (Wentges, 2002). The *Aufsichtsrat* has considerable rights to receive information in order to effectively monitor the *Vorstand's* activities, and fixes the compensation of the corporate executives (Nassauer, 2000).

In contrast, American corporations do not have a two-tier board system in which corporate management and control are separated; instead, a single board of directors is responsible for running the company (Wentges, 2002). Corporations make up about 20 percent of all businesses in the United States, which is a much higher proportion than in Germany (Nassauer, 2000). This is primarily due to the fact that no minimum capital is needed to found a corporation in the USA (Nassauer, 2000). In addition, it is quite common for private individuals to risk investing in businesses or even business ideas in the United States. Consequently, banks play a smaller role for—and in—U.S. American corporations than they do in Germany (Nassauer, 2000).

In the United States, the board of directors is responsible for running a corporation. The board is responsible for both the management of the company and control of the management; it typically consists of eleven to thirteen members (Nassaue, 2000). The board is elected at the annual shareholders' meeting, but it is an independent entity that can reach decisions without following the instructions of the shareholders (Wentges, 2002). The board is responsible for setting the corporation's strategies, controlling the executive officers, nominating the chief executive officer (CEO), and determining executive compensation (Wentges, 2002). The management team of a U.S. corporation is headed by the chief executive officer (CEO) who is superior to all the other managers and usually chairs the board (Witt, 2002). The CEO is usually also the center of public attention since the CEO is typically identified with the corporation (Witt, 2002). Thus, the CEO has a very powerful and encompassing position when compared to the head of a German corporation.

## Wages and Salaries

Wages and salaries of German employees are typically fixed by so-called collective tariff agreements which

---

[17]In fact, all German companies need to have works councils, i.e., *Betriebsrat*, which are a permanent fixture in the companies. These work councils have to approve "all matters concerning personnel, such as hiring, job classifications, departmental restructuring and transfers" (*Facts about Germany*, 1998, p. 393).

are negotiated between trade union representatives and the representatives of the employers' association of a particular industrial and/or service branch; for example, the metal industry, which includes the automobile industry (*Facts about Germany*, 1998). These agreements regulate, for example, the wages and salaries, the working hours, holidays, minimum notice, and overtime rates, and applies them to all enterprises of that particular branch in that particular region of Germany (*Facts about Germany*, 1998), thus establishing parity among all employees in the same sector. This system essentially serves to keep employees tied to a particular employer since it would make little sense to switch employers because one would continue to earn the same pay for the same occupation elsewhere. And since German employees are typically qualified for a specific job field, it is not easy to switch to another job field without proper qualifications, as noted above. Likewise, the tariff system reduces the need for strikes, which helps reduce uncertainty for both sides. Compared to other European countries, Germany has relatively few strikes. This is usually ascribed to the collective tariff system and the principle of co-determination, i.e., consensus (*Facts about Germany*, 1998).

> *Germans do not like to make mistakes, because they are expected to be experts in their field of specialization.*

Thus, it is not surprising that German business culture reflects many aspects of German culture. Indeed, national culture often serves as a model for corporate culture. This is reflected in the fact that German corporations are headed by two distinct governing bodies, which mirrors the division of power in the German executive branch, while U.S. American corporations only have one governing body, which reflects the single executive branch. And it is also not surprising that the notions of parity and consensus are incorporated into German corporate governance via the representation of the employees in the *Aufsichtsrat*, since it is a fundamental principle of the German Basic Law.

## THE INTERRELATIONSHIP OF CULTURE AND BUSINESS CONDUCT

While some people might notice some differences in corporate structure and organization, few would assume that work routines and thinking processes differ across cultures—after all, business is business no matter where it is conducted on the globe. Yet, it is precisely these subtle differences that lead to misunderstandings, frustration, and even anger in many international business alliances (Harris & Moran, 1996; Hofstede & Hofstede, 2005; Trompenaars & Hampden-Turner, 1998).

## Task Oriented

Germans, like U.S. Americans, are very task oriented. But, in Germany, as noted above, the specific expertise of individuals is also considered to be very important because it is assumed that such expertise leads to the best possible results. Consequently, Germans will usually argue and try to convince others with facts and data (Schroll-Machl, 2002). This explains why German presentations (and applications) will contain as many facts and as much data as possible, because the more facts and data one presents, the more convincing one will be. Germans do not like to make mistakes, because they are expected to be experts in their field of specialization. Should, therefore, someone present the wrong facts and figures, that person will lose respect because that person occupies a position for which he or she does not have sufficient expertise. Consequently, most Germans do not like to admit to having made a mistake (Lord, 1998) because mistakes result in uncertainty—something most Germans would like to avoid. While Americans will also use facts and figures, they will appeal to people's ideals and emotions as well; especially if they are attempting to motivate others (Lewis, 2000). Germans, in contrast, consider emotions to be unprofessional in a business context because emotions are neither tangible nor objective and, thus, distort the facts.

## Relationships

Germans tend to strictly separate business relationships from private relationships. A friendly atmosphere at work and getting along with others in a business context is considered to be a nice side effect, but it is not really essential for a successful interaction in Germany (Schroll-Machl, 2002). Indeed, it is not uncommon for German colleagues to use the formal *Sie* and the last name with title when addressing and conversing with one another even though they may have worked together for many years. The use of titles is another expression of uncertainty avoidance and also of a larger power distance. If someone has a title or titles, then that person will be addressed by that/those title(s). Titles appear on bank cards, driver's licenses, and ID cards, etc. Titles identify a person's status and background, thus identifying a person's qualifications, competence, and rank within a corporate and social hierarchy at a glance.

## Time Management

Germans are very punctual and tend to be very monochronic in their work routine. In business appointments, most Germans would expect an apology if the visitor was more than a minute late.[18] That is why most Germans will make an effort to actually arrive ahead of the appointed time. Time is considered to be very important, like in the United States, but it also leads most Germans to consider small talk to be a waste of time in a business context since it has nothing to do directly with the task at hand. Presentations and meetings, consequently, will commence immediately with the business at hand (Lewis, 2000). When Germans make appointments, they do not reconfirm them—even if the appointment is made half a year in advance; this reinforces reliability and avoids uncertainty. One usually only contacts the other party if one needs to cancel or postpone the appointed meeting. Germans tend to completely finish a particular task or assignment before starting another undertaking (Lewis, 2000). This tenacious approach is often also found in product development, which translates into product improvement in Germany. The aim is to achieve absolute perfection and precision in any product or product family. This, in part, explains the excellent reputation German precision products and engineering have in many parts of the world.

## Information Flow

Another typical German characteristic is the monopolization of information. Consequently, there is little free flow of information between departments of a company (horizontal communication), and between the various hierarchical levels (vertical communication).[19] German companies are traditionally very compartmentalized and often closed to outsiders. This might also explain why office doors are usually closed in German companies, unlike in American companies where employees walk down the hall to exchange information with their colleagues (Lewis, 2000). In fact, this different "door policy" illustrates how cultural patterns influence people's thinking and behavior. When, for example, American visitors enter a typical German office building and encounter closed doors, the Americans might assume that the office doors have been closed because no one is to overhear the conversations inside the offices, as is often the case in the United States. If those American visitors came to the German company to negotiate a deal, the visitors may think that the Germans are deliberately trying to hide something from them. Consequently, the Americans may assume that the negotiations will be difficult, troublesome, and tricky. During the subsequent meeting, this negative predisposition of the Americans could result in a negative interpretation of everything the Germans say (or seem to say) and do even though that is not the intention of the Germans. Hence, this makes for a difficult meeting because the Americans will be wary and suspicious while the Germans will be wondering why the Americans are behaving so strangely. This could, in turn, make the Germans wary and suspicious of the Americans' intentions, thus, creating a detrimental chain reaction.

## Business Meetings and Negotiations

As noted above, Germans like to be well prepared for a meeting, which often, though, translates into a lack of spontaneity. Not surprisingly, brainstorming sessions are quite rare in Germany (LeMont Schmidt, 2001).

---

[18]This maximum of one minute was confirmed in many conversations with German executives.

[19]Proudfoot Consulting calculated lost productivity due to improper or lack of communication in German corporations at $223.1 billion in 2001, which translates into 14.9 percent of the German GDP (see Optiz, 2003, for details). The figures are similar even today.

Because Germans have researched a subject and prepared themselves in great detail for a meeting, they are often inflexible in responding to unanticipated questions. When, for example, it comes to negotiating the price, most Germans are only willing to consider a divergence of 10 percent from the asking price, since they will have considered all aspects and determined precisely the exact price of an item in advance and, thus, see no reason to continue haggling over the price (Otte, 1996; Hill, 1998). This reduces the uncertainty of a bargaining session and saves precious time.

## German and American Group Work

The following example describes the different approaches typically employed by Germans and Americans when they work together in a group. Germans like to have an initial and comprehensive understanding of all aspects associated with a problem. This means that any and all details, including potential possibilities and possible unintended consequences, are considered. Hence, existing approaches and solutions play an important role, while new ideas are considered and evaluated critically. This evaluation process is carried out within a group. When it is assumed that all aspects have been considered and discussed, then tasks will be assigned to the group members according to their field of expertise and experience. This ends the planning phase (Schroll-Machl, 1995). Next follows the execution phase during which everyone works alone with little or no exchange of information. There is little or no need to meet and talk because everything has been discussed during the initial planning phase, including anticipated possibilities. Therefore, repetition would be a waste of valuable time. And since everyone is a specialist in his or her own field, there is little need to talk with others because the others would not be able to make a valuable contribution as they lack expertise outside their field of specialization. Subsequent meetings are, thus, only necessary if an intermediate meeting had been scheduled previously, or if there is an unanticipated problem. But alterations to any previously fixed details are rarely done and not liked, since it indicates that the

initial planning had been insufficient and, therefore, inexpert (Schroll-Machl, 1995; Gibson, 2000).

Americans, in contrast, like to focus on the goal after having been assigned a task. This is usually done in form of brainstorming, in which the group members present their thoughts and ideas. Once the goal has been determined, the group decides on a plan of action to solve the problem at hand. The group leader assigns the various tasks to the group members, which ends the planning phase. The execution of the plan begins when every group member creates a detailed work plan. The experiences of the group members are applied in solving the problem. The group members often consult with one another on how to best solve the problem. This results in very active communication and a lively exchange of information among all group members, while there is constant feedback on whether or not a solution leads to the desired goal. The exchange of information occurs also with one's superiors. The initial plan of action can be changed any time if it proves to be necessary and the goal becomes untenable (Schroll-Machl, 1995; Gibson, 2000).

The above example clearly illustrates that Germans and Americans use different approaches in tackling problems despite the fact that they are actually much closer to each other culturally than to Chinese or Japanese culture, for example. The brainstorming session would probably cause difficulties for German group members since it is not typically applied in Germany, while the detailed discussion of possible and anticipated problems would seem to be too detailed for American group members. This attitude would be frowned upon by the German group members, who would consider Americans to be too superficial and imprecise. The isolated work environment with little or no contact to other group members and virtually no feedback from one's supervisors would seem problematic to Americans because information exchange and communication are of paramount importance in solving any problem. To the Germans, this need for communication and feedback would simply signify that either the initial planning was faulty and superficial, or that the American colleagues are not as expert as they claim to be; otherwise, they should have

> *Because Germans have researched a subject and prepared themselves in great detail for a meeting, they are often inflexible in responding to unanticipated questions.*

been able to solve the problem at hand. Consequently, both Germans and Americans would be frustrated because the group work did not lead to any concrete results. But the reasons for these feelings would be different, as indicated above.

## CONCLUDING REMARKS

The more one studies German and American business cultures, the more one will notice differences that become apparent not only in the artifacts of both business cultures, but also in their respective sociofacts and mentifacts. That is why one needs to be aware of these subtle but decisive cultural differences. If, however, someone lacks this awareness, it can result in frustration because that person does not know why the others are behaving and/or communicating the way they are. Viewed and evaluated from one's own cultural perspective, the behavior of the others can be seen as inefficient and ineffective, even wrong. So awareness can foster understanding. Understanding, though, is only possible if one is aware of the fact that cultural differences exist also in the world of business, and that these cultural differences influence the way people conduct their business. With proper understanding, though, it is possible to overcome these differences and to foster mutually profitable business relationships across diverse cultures.

## References

Adler, R. B., & Rodman, G. (2003). *Understanding human communication*, 8th ed. New York: Oxford University Press.

ARD.de (2009). Die Ergebnisse der Bundeswahl im Überblick. Retrieved February 18, 2010 from www.tagesschau.de/wahl

Chen, G-M., & Starosta, W. J. (1998). *Foundations of intercultural communication*. Boston: Allyn and Bacon.

Conyon, M. J., & Schalbach, J. (1999). Corporate governance, executive pay and performance in Europe. In J. Carpenter & D. Yermack (Eds.), *Executive compensation and shareholder value: Theory and evidence* (pp. 13–33). Dordrecht: Kluwer Academic Publishers.

De Mooij, M. (2007). The reflection of culture in a global business and marketing strategy. In M. B. Hinner (Ed.), *The influence of culture in the world of business* (pp. 343–356). Frankfurt am Main: Peter Lang.

*Duden*. (2006). Mannheim: Dudenverlag.

Edmunds Auto Observer. (2007, May 17). Daimler-Chrysler: Why the marriage failed. Retrieved August 18, 2008 from www.autoobserver.com/2007/05/daimler-chrysler-why-the-marriage-failed.html

Emmons, W. R., & Schmid, F. A. (1998). Universal banking, control rights, and corporate finance in Germany. *Federal Reserve Bank of St. Louis Review 80*, 19–42.

*Facts about Germany*. (1998). Frankfurt am Main: Societäts Ver.

Gibson, R. (2000). *Intercultural business communication*. Berlin: Cornelsen & Oxford University Press.

Gudykunst, W. B., & Kim, Y. Y. (1997). *Communicating with strangers: An approach to intercultural communication*, 3rd ed. Boston: McGraw Hill.

Harris, P. R., & Moran, R. T. (1996). *Managing cultural differences: Leadership strategies for a new world of business*, 4th ed. Houston: Gulf Publishing Company.

Herrmann, J. (Ed.) (1988). *Deutsche Geschichte in 10 Kapiteln*. Berlin: Akademie-Verlag.

Hill, R. (1998). *EuroManagers & Martians*. Brussels: Europublic.

Hinner, M. B. (1998). The importance of intercultural communication in a globalized world. *Freiberger Arbeitspapiere der Fakultät für Wirtschaftswissenschaften 06*.

Hinner, M. B. (2004). Culture and product integration. *German American Trade 15 (7)*, pp. 19–21.

Hinner, M. B., & Rülke, T. (2002). Intercultural communication in business ventures illustrated by two case studies. *Freiberger Arbeitspapiere der Fakultät für Wirtschaftswissenschaften 03*.

Hinner, M. B. (2005). Can quality communication improve business relationships? In M. B. Hinner (Ed.). *Introduction to business communication* (pp. 15–40). Frankfurt am Main: Peter Lang.

Hofstede, G. (2005). The universal and the specific in 21st century management. In M. B. Hinner (Ed.), *Introduction to business communication* (pp. 273–286). Frankfurt am Main: Peter Lang.

Hofstede, G., & Hofstede, J. G. (2005). *Cultures and organizations: Software of the mind*. New York: McGraw Hill.

Howard, L. B. (1965). *Business law: An introduction*. Woodbury, NY: Barron's Educational Series, Inc.

Jankuhn, H., Boockmann, H., & Treue, W. (Eds.) (1983). *Deutsche Geschichte in Bildern von der Urzeit bis zur Gegenwart*. Wiesbaden: Verlag für Wissenschaft und Forschung—AULA.

Klopf, D. W. (1998). *Intercultural encounters: The fundamentals of intercultural communication*, 4th ed. Englewood, NJ: Morton.

König, W. (1989). *Dtv-Atlas zur deutschen Sprache*, 7th ed. Munich: Deutscher Taschenbuch Verlag.

LeMont Schmidt, P. (2001). *Die amerikanische und die deutsche Wirtschaftskultur im Vergleich: Ein Praxisbuch für Manager*, 3rd ed. Göttingen: Hainholz Verlag.

Lewis, R. D. (2000). *Handbuch internationale Kompetenz: Mehr Erfolg durch den richtigen Umgang mit Geschäftspartnern weltweit*. Frankfurt am Main: Campus Verlag.

Lord, R. (1998). *Culture shock! Germany: Guide to customs and etiquette*. Portland: Graphic Arts Center Publishing Company.

Lustig, M. W., & Koester, J. (2006). *Intercultural competence: Interpersonal communication across cultures*, 5th ed. Boston: Pearson Education, Inc.

Martin, J. N., & Nakayama, T. K. (1997). *Intercultural communication in contexts*. Mountain View, CA: Mayfield.

Nassauer, F. (2000). *Corporate Governance und die Internationalisierung von Unternehmungen*. Frankfurt am Main: Peter Lang.

Oetzel, J. G. (2009. *Intercultural communication: A layered approach*. New York: Pearson Education.

Opitz, I. (2003). Good internal communication increases productivity. *Freiberger Arbeitspapiere der Fakultät für Wirtschaftswissenschaften 07*.

Otte, M. (1996). *Amerika für Geschäftsleute: Das Einmaleins der ungeschriebenen Regeln* Frankfurt am Main: Campus Verlag.

*Sächsische Zeitung*. (2007, March 22). Uno kritisiert das deutsche Schulsystem, pp. 1 + 4.

*Sächsische Zeitung*. (2007, March 27). Firmen zahlen kräftig Steuern, p. 13.

*Sächsische Zeitung*. (2008, March 26). Im Osten ist die Hälfte unzufrieden, p. 2.

Samovar, L. A., Porter, R. E., & McDaniel, E. R. (2010). *Communication between cultures*, 7th ed. Belmont, CA: Wadsworth.

Schroll-Machl, S. (1995). Die Zusammenarbeit in internationalen Teams—Eine interkulturelle Herausforderung dargestellt am Beispiel USA–Deutschland. In J. M. Scholz (Ed.), *Internationales Change-Management: Internationale Praxiserfahrungen bei der Veränderung von Untenehmen und Humanressourcen* (pp. 201–222). Stuttgart: Schäffer-Poeschel Verlag.

Schroll-Machl, S. (2002). *Die Deutschen – Wir Deutsche: Fremdwahrnehmung und Selbstsicht im Berufsleben*. Göttingen: Vandenhoeck & Ruprecht.

Schuler, R. (2010, February 19). Wie geschmacklos ist der Osten? *Sächsische Zeitung*, p. 5.

Siemon, P. (2007, March 22). Langzeitstudie in Sachsen: Nostalgische Rückkehr zu sozialistischen Idealen. In *Dresdener Morgenpost*. Retrieved March 26, 2007 from www.wiedervereinigung.de/sls/PDF/mopo220307.pdf

Trompenaars, F., & Hampden-Turner, C. (1998). *Riding the waves of culture: Understanding diversity in global business*, 2nd ed. New York: McGraw Hill.

Waterman, J. T. (1976). *A history of the German language*. Revised ed. Seattle: University of Washington Press.

Welt Online. (2010, January 19). Ost-West-Debatte: Lafontaine warnt vor Spaltung der Linken. Retrieved February 18, 2010 from www.welt.de/politik/Deutschland/artikel5911997/Lafontaine-warnt-vor-Spaltung-der-Linken.html

Wentges, P. (2002). *Corporate Governance und Stakeholder Ansatz: Implikationen für die betriebliche Finanzierung*. Wiesbaden: Deutscher Universitätsverlag.

Zentner, C. (1980). *Geschichtsführer in Farbe: Weltgeschichte in Bildern, Daten, Fakten*. München: Delphin Verlag GmbH.

## Concepts and Questions

1. How might the similarities between American and German business cultures affect intercultural communication?

2. What does Hinner mean when he writes about external and hidden cultural differences? How can these differences affect product marketing?

3. How does the history of Germany influence the culture of German business organizations?

4. In what ways does the tradition of regional autonomy influence German business culture?

5. How do the bases of American and German law compare? How do these differences contribute to the distinct business cultures found in each country?

6. In what ways does the German educational system differ from that of the United States? How does the German education system support German business?

7. Describe how the German culture's emphasis on order and hierarchy is displayed in the division of employees in business organizations.

8. What are the differences between German and American corporate organization? How do these differences affect communication within and between German and American businesses?

9. List the advantages and disadvantages of the German corporate system of simultaneously operating under two different boards of directors. Would such a system be effective in the United States?

# The Problem of Globalization: Jamaican Managers at the Intersection of Past and Present Cultural Challenges

MAURICE L. HALL

*We have alluded to the extent that globalization has affected worldwide business. But globalization presents unique problems in some cultures that are not found in others. A case in point is the business culture of Jamaica. Maurice Hall in his essay "The Problems of Globalization: Jamaican Managers at the Intersection of Past and Present Cultural Challenges" provides you with an understanding of how the past colonial history of a country can influence its development of a business culture in the contemporary world. From this essay you will learn (1) how the influence of U.S. and other Western business professionals has led to the emergence of hybridized world cultures and the assumption that U.S. and Western European knowledge and procedures are automatically relevant in other nations (2) that for countries that face economic survival, cultural and tribal conflict; and geopolitical dependency, Western management strategies may not be appropriate; (3) about the conflicts that Jamaican managers face in operating at the nexus of old cultural values and the development of modern business organizations; (4) the tensions faced by managers faced with developing business ideas appropriate to indigenous organizational concerns and yet participating in the universe of more highly developed industrial nations; and (5) how communication plays an important role in reducing the cultural tensions faced by Jamaican managers.*

*Hall begins with a discussion of the Jamaican cultural context reflecting on how the former British colony had only gained its political independence in 1962. He tells of how the pervasive racism, directed largely at people of African descent, in Jamaica and the legacies of slavery and protracted colonial rule has led to a deep sense of national cultural racial inferiority that influences the way in which Jamaican managers relate to the larger international community. He then moves into a protracted description of Jamaican managers' aspirations toward being competitive in the international business arena. This is followed by a discussion of the impact of the local cultural context on managers' attempts to meet these aspirations. Finally, Hall ends his essay with a discussion of communication and management practices in Jamaica.*

## GLOBALIZATION AND DEVELOPING COUNTRIES

The concept of the Global Village has been widely hailed and celebrated in popular culture. Globalization heralds the transnational flow of cultural products and education. It also suggests that the influence of U.S. popular culture, as well as the influence of large numbers of U.S.-trained professionals around the world, have led to the development of hybridized world cultures (Kraidy, 2002). But there is a darker side to this phenomenon; the problem is that the transnational cultural flow is often one way, and knowledge produced in the United States and Western Europe is assumed to be automatically relevant in other national contexts, but not vice versa (Bhabha, 1994; Kraidy, 2002).

This one-way flow of influence has problematic consequences for many managers from small, developing countries, who look to developed countries such as the United States for the educational, economic, and cultural resources that will help improve the status and functioning of the organizations they lead (Nkomo, 2006). In their often-uncritical appropriation of U.S. models of leadership education and training, these managers have sought to implement strategies that sometimes cannot be easily sustained in a developing country nor are intended for these specific socio-political contexts. The question of how the politics of globalization impacts the managing of organizations in developing countries is an important one. Postcolonial scholar Bill Ashcroft (2001) sets the stage for thinking about globalization as a modern synonym for a form of imperialism. Ashcroft sees imperialism and globalization as similar systems, both grounded in systems of domination.

## THE POLITICS OF GLOBALIZATION

Since much of what we know about leadership is taken from studies conducted in North America and Europe (Nkomo, 2006; Blunt & Jones, 1997), understanding the leadership styles and practices of many non-Western managers requires an interpretive perspective that envisions leadership and culture as existing in emergent, sometimes contested, and often highly contextual relationships. The work of Hofstede (2001) and House, Hanges, Javidan, Gorfman, & Gupta (2004) offer groundbreaking approaches to studying leadership in multicultural contexts representing several regions of the world. However, many of these studies have a tendency to treat large collectivities of cultures by using oversimplified or overly generalized classification schemes. Culture, in these studies, is often conceptualized as fixed within very specific dimensions. Communication scholars who study developing countries, particularly those that are former colonies of Western European nations, have long realized that culture must be conceptualized as a complex negotiation of power, discourse and communication (see, for example, the work, of Drzewiecka & Halualani, 2002; Shome & Hegde, 2002).

Small, developing countries, particularly those that have experienced colonial domination, are unique cultural contexts, and the problems they face involve economic survival, institutional viability, cultural and tribal conflict, and geopolitical dependency. These issues are frequently not relevant to the practice of management strategies in Western

industrialized nations (Blunt & Jones, 1997; Nkomo, 2006). Often, as these managers have sought to develop managerial models that are unique to developing-country contexts, they have focused on external resources. However, what they have found has not always worked effectively. In terms of the struggle for re-negotiating a national identity among smaller, less-developed nation-states, many scholars believe that the one-way flow of North American cultural products actually reinforces Western cultural hegemony (Nkomo, 2006; Bolden & Kirk, 2005).

## GLOBALIZATION AND JAMAICA

In this essay, I will use the island of Jamaica as a means of examining some of the challenges facing the managers of this country as they communicate and interact in a globalized world. While I am only looking at one culture, I believe the problems faced by Jamaican managers are representative of other developing countries. I present data from an interpretive study I conducted among Jamaican managers, analyzing the tensions facing these managers as they seek to manage and develop new organizations in a global environment. The Jamaican managers in this study, like many of their international counterparts, are having to confront complex issues of culture and modern organizations. More specifically, this essay aims to explore the ways in which developing countries exist in vulnerable cultural spaces as concerns "modernization" and "development."

*Small, developing countries, particularly those that have experienced colonial domination, are unique cultural contexts, and the problems they face involve economic survival, institutional viability, cultural and tribal conflict, and geopolitical dependency.*

## THE JAMAICAN CULTURAL CONTEXT

Jamaica, an island of 2.5 million people and a former British colony, became politically independent in August 1962. Caribbean scholar and cultural anthropologist Deborah Thomas (2004) provides a detailed ethnographic account of the extent to which there was pervasive racism, directed largely at people of African, descent in Jamaica. The legacies of slavery and protracted colonial rule resulted in a deep sense of national cultural and racial inferiority, and a widespread distrust of the viability of indigenous cultural and social innovations. In addition, there was a continued, dogged Eurocentric mindset among the black Jamaican middle classes and other cultural elites (Thomas, 2004). While the inhabitants of Jamaica are mostly black, the interests that own the economic resources in Jamaica have always been white Anglo-American/Western Europeans, or a white local planter class (Robotham 1998). White and brown people are generally the property owners, with a relatively small professional black and brown middle class and a significant black underclass (Robotham 1998; Patterson 1995). The owners of property and the means of production have shifted location, but the positions are still the same: black bodies mark the peasant class, the workers, not the owners. The black population provided the small farmers and field workers who harvested the sugar cane and bananas to be sold as exports.

In the 1970s and 80s, therefore, the government of Jamaica embarked on a quest to use various political, social, and cultural institutions to help Jamaica craft a national identity that valorized the African roots of Jamaica's cultural heritage (Thomas, 2004). The crafting of a more indigenous national identity resulted in many organizations creating a structure and organizational culture that reflected the reality of modern-day politically independent Jamaica. But the persistence of Eurocentric perspectives among the Jamaican professional and cultural elite, the influence of large international lending institutions that fund Jamaica's economy (including the major world banks such as the International Monetary Fund), and large-scale North American investors who create and/or fund Jamaican organizations that are parent companies of or are run by North American businesses, set the parameters for how much the structure, functioning, and performance of many important Jamaican organizations can deviate from what is seen in the United States and much of Western Europe as recognized practices of management. The dominance of the Western European organizational form in a developing country such as Jamaica

> *The legacies of slavery and protracted colonial rule resulted in a deep sense of national cultural and racial inferiority, and a widespread distrust of the viability of indigenous cultural and social innovations.*

is often reinforced, then, by the interactions with the financial actors that fund the country's survival.

Jamaica, as do most developing countries, exists in the context of "larger (and unequal) histories and geographies of global power and culture" (Shome & Hegde, 2002, p. 253). This is further complicated by the effects of policies associated with the North American Free Trade Agreement (NAFTA), and the fallout from shifting market conditions related to globalization, which have forced the islands in the Caribbean into a hopeless competition with larger developing countries in Latin America that have more access to larger, more diversified natural resources (Louisy, 2001).

Without strong natural resources that provide the country with a competitive leg up in the global economic market, Jamaica is forced to depend on creating well-functioning public and private national institutions in order to create sustainable economic development. Since many of the political, cultural and educational institutions in Jamaica were initially set up as political and cultural derivations of British institutions and systems, the managers and business professionals interviewed for the study are dealing with the challenge of building viable organizations and institutions in the context of a history that has imposed a European organizational bureaucratic form while simultaneously marginalizing the value and viability of indigenous cultural organizational innovations. Jamaican managers must also lead in the context of fierce global economic competition among developing countries and in the context of the relentless cultural and economic domination of Western democracies such as the United States, its closest developed neighbor (Thomas, 2004).

## METHODOLOGY

Data for this study were collected as part of a larger study using in-depth individual interviews. A total of 21 managers were recruited for the study using a snowball technique. All of the interviews were conducted in Kingston, the capital city of Jamaica, and almost all of the interviews took place in the offices of the participants. Almost all of the managers interviewed represented industries in Jamaica's service sector. The industries represented were shipping, airlines, secondary and tertiary education, corporate training and development, banking, investment management, the police force, the civil service (government-run organizations), trade unions, human resource management, and management consulting, all of which represent most of the largest and most prominent organizations in Jamaica. Most of the interviews were conducted as face-to-face interviews; one participant, a vice president, who was abroad on travel, was interviewed over the telephone. The interviews ranged between 30 minutes and two hours.

## JAMAICAN MANAGERS' ASPIRATIONS TOWARDS BEING INTERNATIONALLY COMPETIVE

For a small, developing country, there is, perhaps, always a tension between the need to originate business ideas and solutions that are relevant to and address indigenous organizational concerns and participating in the wider universe of knowledge that represents the advances of more industrialized nations. That tension between the global and the local, the so-called "traditional" and "modern," can be overstated, but there was clearly a sense of unease, even urgency, in the comments of many of the managers as they reflected on the extent to which their ability to manage effectively was dependent on factors they perceived to be inherent in an increasingly transnational economy. Almost every one of the managers interviewed, whether the organization they represented was government run or a private, for-profit organization, offered lengthy, detailed comments concerning globalization. None of the questions posed specifically referenced globalization as a topic, and so it was noteworthy that the focus on globalization nevertheless dominated much of the conversation with the managers.

Many of the managers in this study defined globalization as the importance of being competitive in a global context by emulating American organizations and almost exclusively using American multinational organizations as the standard against which the performance of the local organization is measured. The responses of the managers interviewed suggest that most of them prefer to think of themselves as competing with and even emulating organizations that are in the United States rather than organizations that are located in Jamaica or in the wider Caribbean.

For example, the manager of a mid-sized banking organization commented on the importance of globalization for her organization:

> We recognize, too, that for organizations to remain viable and competitive in this global economy then we have to compete on a platform which … might be alien to us … the Ritz-Carlton taught us a number of things about customer service … what we try to do, we try to emulate the activities and the strategies that we see working for others. We have to make sure that we don't think narrow.

The result of the awareness of the impact of globalization for this manager is the decision to pursue a strategy to 'emulate' the activity and the strategy of the Ritz Carlton Hotel, a high-end North American hotel chain that has gained a widespread reputation for its customer service. The focus on emulating the Ritz-Carlton business strategy suggests that, for this manager, there are no local or regional alternatives worth imitating.

For a senior executive from the country's largest shipping organization, his leadership strategies focused almost entirely on the international implications of operating his business:

> I mean, shipping is a globalized business and a lot of the people that we do business with on a day-to-day level are non-Jamaicans … both living in Jamaica and working here as well as living abroad. And we have to communicate with them. But we are also largely homegrown. And as I explained that a lot of what we do evolved out of our own experience.

In order to underscore his point, this participant emphasized that the organization was founded in Jamaica and evolved within the context of the Jamaican experience. He presented a detailed overview of his business that emphasized the fact that the operating standard was organizations located in the United States and Latin America:

A vessel is leaving Miami going to Panama … and Kingston is its first stop. So that vessel is loading at an American port, loading, discharging at Kingston and then going on to Panama. It has a crew, which comprises of course a captain from Germany, a first mate from Sweden. It has a crew, which largely would be Filipinos or, as now exists, a lot of Eastern Europeans. And it's coming to Kingston and spending twelve hours using a shipping association work force along with terminal handling, equipment handling, staff, and supervisors from the port. That vessel, among other things, is gauging … efficiency of the loading and discharge operation, at Kingston, at Miami, and at … Panama. It is expecting very little, if any, variations in the operation. So it doesn't take a great mind to recognize that you have to work together to insure that the standards … met and kept at Kingston are at least comparable to those in those two other ports. And that is the kind of context in which we find ourselves. That's the kind of context in which our workers have to operate.

His emphasis here is the extent to which his business is inextricably linked to factors and considerations that are international and not just local in nature. From his standpoint, the work practices, standards and expectations required of him as a manager, and of his workforce, are uniform with what is expected in Miami and Panama. What is implied is the significant competitive pressure on a shipping organization founded in a small, developing country to compete on an even keel with shipping organizations in one of the world's most industrialized countries, the United States. His comment that the standards that have to be met in Kingston have to be "at least comparable" to those in Miami and Panama underscores the sense that the benchmarking for his organization is linked almost exclusively to the standards of highly industrialized economies.

In a similar vein, one of the country's most prominent senior airline executives framed his responsibilities for managing the national airline in the context of the geopolitical implications of Jamaica's "positioning" in the Caribbean and the

implications for competing with airlines in the United States that fly to the Caribbean. He framed Jamaica as the logical midpoint between flight destinations in Latin America, such as Venezuela and Colombia, and destinations in North America, such as Miami:

… It's a fabulous opportunity to make Jamaica a hub within the Caribbean. It's not just because of its geographic positioning, but also it's geopolitical positioning. And as you know, Jamaica gets along with everybody, including people who don't get along with each other.

There is, in this manager's comments once again, the sense that a Jamaican industry needs to be positioned to compete on an equal footing with countries that are much larger and more developed. The managers with whom I spoke did not conceive of international competition as occurring between and among the other islands in the Caribbean; rather, the reference points were almost consistently Europe, North America and Latin America. More than anything else, the prevalence of the references by the Jamaican managers to the interconnections of Jamaican organizations with international ones certainly speaks to the extent to which these managers are continually conscious of managing in an interconnected, international environment, and the extent to which they perceive institutions in the United States as the most relevant source of competition.

Many of the managers interviewed lead airline, banking and shipping organizations that must meet international standards of practice to remain viable. But when their talk about being competitive is juxtaposed against the reality of the economic conditions under which they must operate, it becomes clear that, at the very least, they are not operating on a level playing field with the work conditions in industrialized countries. This has put many of these managers in a situation of intense conflict with the local unions, which see themselves as leading a struggle for social justice against a managerial class that will not meet their demands.

## THE DEMANDS ON THE JAMAICAN MANAGERS OF THE LOCAL CULTURAL CONTEXT

At the time of these interviews, even as many of these managers spoke of needing to meet the challenges of globalization, there were stark reminders of the constraints imposed by the fragile economy of a developing country and a workforce that is struggling with pervasive economic hardship. The trade unions, the government of Jamaica and many public and private organizations were struggling to find a compromise in the context of worsening economic conditions on the island. The various parties eventually developed a Memorandum of Understanding, as explained by the Board Chair of the shipping organization:

> The government had a couple of years ago a memorandum of understanding where they fixed a cap on the salaries of government employees at 3%, while inflation was moving out of kilter at 13% to 20%. Now when you have a situation [like] that you have to find a mechanism how to get your work force … because they have to buy things that are on the shelf at higher prices. And they have to feed their families.

The references by many of the managers to globalization were matched only by the numerous references, such as the one above, to the constraints imposed by the trade unions on their decision-making strategies. Again, without specific prompting from the interviewer's questions, discussion of the impact of the trade unions was as predominant as the discussion of globalization.

Generally speaking, the trade unions in Jamaica have operated in a unique role in the country. The trade unions were among the first organized efforts on the part of the majority of poor and working-class black Jamaicans to resist the most egregious economic disparities that were part of the resulting aftermath of British colonialism. One of the senior banking executives whom I interviewed discussed the role of the trade unions in the context of the aftermath of colonialism:

> But I think … management in Jamaica … is informed by our history. It's informed by the trade union history, which we have. Trade unions in Jamaica, unlike a lot of places, actually gave birth to political parties. So, a lot of our legislature today that helps to determine how we do Human Resources [were] driven by Prime Ministers who used to be heads of unions, and employers.

The interrelationship of the trade unions with the political and organizational leadership of Jamaica is integral to understanding the connections between Jamaica's struggle for political and economic independence in the aftermath of British colonial rule, and the evolution of indigenous organizations. One senior manager of the shipping organization with whom I spoke more specifically linked the history of the trade unions to Jamaica's colonial history and the history of how management practices evolved in many local organizations:

> In 1939, three organizations came into being: People's National Party, the Trade Unions, and Shipping Association of Jamaica. These three organizations came out of exactly the same struggle: the struggle for self-determination, the struggle for independence, but also the struggle for improved conditions of work for the masses of Jamaica, starting in particular with the port workers and the sugar industry employees.

The important emphasis in this manager's retelling of the trade union history is the link between the trade unions and the early struggles to ensure that the largest number of people ("the masses of Jamaica") had conditions that significantly improved upon the problems and issues that existed in the aftermath of British colonial rule. The situation underscores the extent to which Jamaican managers are constantly grappling with issues that are part of the legacy of negotiating the aftermath of colonialism, and also the competitive demands they see being imposed on them by the demands of the new global economy. The board chairman of the shipping organization captured that sense of existing in the intersection between the past and the present, the legacy of colonialism and the demands of globalization. As managers who exist in the context of a small island nation caught in the currents of a changing and unsettling world, his comments encapsulate the real tightrope the managers must consistently walk:

> … In 1998 … we had our negotiations [with the trade unions] started in October. And when we saw that there was [sic] unusually large demands coming from the unions, we said to them, look, gentlemen, the business that we're in, the largest part of that business is

transshipment business ... we spent six months collecting, brought in experts from all over the world to give their insight as to what is happening in our region, what is happening in the world, because of the globalization I spoke about, and where Jamaica can fit in the scheme of things if we don't make certain adjustments.... If we don't do it, we're going to end up with our Kingston terminal as a white elephant. So we need your help, really, to get where we want to be.

These comments by this manager illustrate the extent to which many of these managers saw themselves as existing in the intersection between the local and the global, the past and the present.

While many Jamaican organizations are reasonably successful by local standards, the talk of being internationally competitive is undercut by the significant restraints inherent in the fragile economy of a developing country. Specifically, for managers in government-affiliated organizations, there was a stiff challenge in providing for the needs of employees. A senior executive who worked for an organization affiliated with the police force outlined some of the challenges he constantly faces:

> ... [as] a public sector organization, we're strapped for resources. That's our biggest challenge, that we have a resource constraint, a serious resource constraint ... [the] attrition rate is high, very, very high.

This manager underscored the seriousness of the situation by explaining that even though this was a government-affiliated organization, it was dependent on funding from external sources:

RESEARCH PARTICIPANT: And so it's ... (kind of) got the support of the U.S. government and the British government. I think that's how we really survive.

RESEARCHER: Really?

RESEARCH PARTICIPANT: ... I'm paid, my job is paid for by the British government ... the British government. That's how we're doing the recruitment.

RESEARCHER: Right.

RESEARCH PARTICIPANT: The British government funds the director.

Many of the public-sector managers argued that the economic constraints had implications, for example, for the extent to which they could discipline employees for absenteeism or lateness since the reality is that heavy rainfall may mean employees cannot get to work for a day or two, and turbulent personal finances may make it hard for employees not to miss work sometimes.

## COMMUNICATION AND MANAGEMENT PRACTICES OF JAMAICAN MANAGERS

When senior leaders in privately owned organizations were asked about the strategies they used to manage and motivate employees, a very positive picture emerged, one in which communication and collaboration assumed centrality and importance. Many of the managers I interviewed pointed to examples of distinctive practices in their organizations that seemed to promote inclusive, collaborative cultures based on open, healthy communication strategies.

### Openness and Collaboration

One study participant who expressed the most forceful sentiments about the importance of collaboration was the chief executive officer of a major airline operating out of Jamaica. He was an example of the extent to which North American and Jamaican managerial cultures were intertwined: he was a white American who had founded and managed a successful airline in the United States for several years. He had been recruited from the United States some eight months earlier to run this Caribbean airline, which also had offices in the United States. He viewed achieving effective collaboration and communication with the employees as a consequence of removing barriers to creativity and providing reasonable job security. He used, as an example, the fact that he made it mandatory that all paperwork concerning candidates for job termination had to be reviewed by him before any employee could be fired. He spoke at length about the need to avoid micro-managing employees, arguing that more freedom encouraged initiative taking:

> If you create an open environment where the penalty for failure is not death, now you've got

ideas that are coming forth that you've never had before. And then that way the whole pot moves forward based on everybody's intellectual contribution, and not just the person at the top.

In de-linking employee initiative from harsh consequences for risk taking, he sought to prioritize employees responding to the organization as stakeholders rather than merely as peripheral social actors. Similar sentiments were expressed by a female manager of a small financial organization, reflecting on the extent to which she perceived that the increased educational savvy of the workforce had an impact on how one behaved as a manager:

> So we recognize that times change, things change. And the top-down culture works very well when you employ people at the bottom.... now, when you take a decision to employ professionals, then the top-down culture don't [sic] work...so you can't employ at this level and expect them to keep quiet and take what you give them. So we employ and get them to participate and to come up with suggestions…

## Authoritarianism

Despite these very positive accounts of communication and collaboration, however, one area of historic social practice that was a colonial legacy outlined by participants in the study was the perpetuation of an autocratic style of managerial interaction with workers that ensured that significant social distance was maintained between managers and workers, mimicking the social distance between whites and blacks during colonial rule. The General Manager of Jamaica's largest teachers' union discussed some of the problematics of this colonial legacy in terms of managerial practice:

PARTICIPANT: … and, you know we must confess that, you know as a postcolonial society a lot of our initial [organizational] socialization was from our … that colonial historical context.

RESEARCHER: Right. The legacy of British education.

PARTICIPANT: Right. British. And you also know that in terms of management as a science and management as a science that involves human communication, it is [for us] a fairly new fact.

RESEARCHER: Right.

PARTICIPANT: So, I just want to put that on the table … even the research that was done in Jamaica by our own local researcher… pointed out to us sufficient weakness in how management interacts and communicates with the average worker. Because this whole top dog approach …

RESEARCHER: Right.

PARTICIPANT: … in fact … one of the major, major issues for workers was the lack of respect by management of the workers at the bottom. And so we have evolved out of a culture of top dog.

In the exchange with this participant, he underscores a few important issues. First, he links the colonial history of the country with a managerial practice that he characterizes as autocratic and authoritarian. His repeated use of the vernacular phrase "top dog" refers to the sense of hierarchy inherent in the interactions managers have with their employees. He implicates the role played by social class in this phenomenon by clarifying that this type of authoritarianism is directed at "workers at the bottom," underscoring the extent to which those with the least education and training are the most vulnerable.

## Managerial Social Distance

A lot of the complaints were coming from employees who worked in public sector organizations, such as public utility organizations or those organizations that were part of the government bureaucracy that was most directly a legacy of previous British colonial governmental structures. Study participants who worked in public sector organizations cited a litany of issues that exacerbated the problems between the managers and employees, but prominent among them were the pervasive issues of social class and education. One study participant was the Director of Human resources for one of the country's largest public utility organizations. She spoke of the continual struggle she faced to intervene in the structural and bureaucratic issues that defined her organization. On the one hand, she faced a group of managers who interpreted their status as one that needed constant reinforcement through artifacts that reflected their privilege:

> There are some persons, especially at the management level, and I start at the management because this is where the problem is, who has

[sic] a bit what I call [a] status problem. They must get a ... check ... with their name on it. They must get a business card whenever they go to meet any customer or any businessperson. They must get a newspaper. And these little things ... And what I have been trying to do is to show them that these things are fluff, and it doesn't really add any value to what we do, right? I was told once by somebody that you know a newspaper will—it motivates, they said. I said show me how it motivates.

Her anecdotes reflect a frustration with managers who become fixated on the importance of performances of social distance as the defining feature of their status as managers in the organization. On the other hand, she found that even implementing basic policies in the organization inadvertently marginalized whole categories of employees:

> ... we have a very broad spectrum of persons, from persons with [a] doctorate to persons who cannot read ... illiterate. So, if we all need to get communication, we have to do quite a bit more at certain levels. So we have done that. We also used the intranet ... post information on the intranet. Because there are people who can't read and write, persons who have access to a PC will be able to access all that information on the intranet. So we have ... to assist ... we encourage all managers to have staff meetings.

The significant differences in education and social class that was discussed by the Director of the Teachers Union earlier in this paper, itself a public organization, was also reflected in these comments by this participant. Participants indicate that these differences allow for several employees to be vulnerable to a destructive hierarchical culture in many organizations, reflected at its most extreme in public organizations such as this one. These differences also allow for the continual reinforcement of class, social, and bureaucratic hierarchical structures that were seen by these participants as featuring a stifling organizational culture that mitigated against collaboration and innovation.

## DISCUSSION

The participants in this study report managerial practices that are collaborative as well as authoritarian.

Some of that is influenced by the particular organizational context within which each manager works (for example, public vs. private organizations), but there also exists an ongoing tension between more democratic vs. less democratic managerial styles. This tension emerges from some of the difficult issues that the managers in this study report having to deal with. The destructive hierarchical managerial practices that were being discussed by the participants reflects, therefore, rules and resources used by organizational actors that draw on these rigid hierarchies of status linked to color, class, gender and education; moreover, the systems of education and training were not initially set up to educate for the purposes of independence, but to educate for the purposes of being good workers within the colonial structure. For example, the managers in this study reference the extent to which they and others draw on rules and resources, and act within a social system of practices that produce and reproduce organizational cultures that seem to replicate aspects of the colonial cultural heritage and history of the island. These managers also lead organizations that exist in a country with an African cultural heritage, but are primarily White and Western in form and design. Social class and race are the social identities that both constituted and continually reinforce this tension between the culture within the organization and its structure and hierarchy.

But these managers must also provide leadership in the context of a rapidly expanding global economy where standards of practice are becoming more homogenized and where intense competition is inherent in the job. Despite its lingering influence, much about the colonial structure has changed; the development of indigenous systems of education and training are now in competition with the lure of American education and training. Participants have also spoken of the reliance on American consultant expertise in crucial industries. This has produced differing kinds of cultural effects for the managers. On the one hand, many of the more collaborative practices reported by participants in the study reflected modern international practices of business that emphasize workplace participation and democracy. On the other hand, the competitive pressures inherent in modern business practice may exacerbate the tendency in the culture towards social distance based on class and hierarchy, thus laying a foundation for more destructive managerial practices. These managers are caught in the binary tensions of the local vs. the global management context by virtue of the cultural legacy of Jamaica's colonial history and its almost immediate transition to modern dependence on international lending institutions.

There is no easy, immediate solution to this issue. Many of these managers from this small, developing country look to developed countries such as the United States for educational, economic, and cultural resources that will help improve the status and functioning of the organizations they lead. Specifically, many of the managers in this study have been trained in the United States, look to U.S. organizations as peer organizations against which they benchmark themselves, and creatively adapt leadership models and strategies developed in the U.S. for implementation in Jamaican organizations. Yet, through their educational preparation and their focus on preparing for globalization, these managers may have created the very situation they tried to avoid. They perceive that doing well economically depends on performing effectively in the international arena, but performing well in the international arena depends on developing a motivated workforce with acceptable conditions of work and compensation. The focus on using or emulating American business models and leadership training has produced, as discussed above, positive results as well as intractable tensions that have had some crippling effects on the country.

## CONCLUSION

Jamaica has had to struggle to find its place in the world in the aftermath of its independence. The problematics of both the history and modern culture of Jamaica have a tremendous impact on how these managers make decisions or deploy strategies because the country exists at the intersection of past and present social and economic vulnerabilities. The comments of these managers reveal part of the broader struggle of Jamaicans for national identity. Yet, as Deborah Thomas (2004) observes, issues such as those discussed in this essay mark the struggle of a culture that is marginalized from the global centers of power, yet is integral to the creation and maintenance of that culture's dominance.

## References

Ashcroft, B. (2001). *Post-colonial transformation*. New York, NY: Routledge.

Bhabha, H. K. (1994). *The location of culture*. New York, NY: Routledge.

Blunt, P., & Jones, M. L. (1997). Exploring the limits of Western leadership theory in East Asia and Africa. *Personnel Review, 26(1/2)*, 6–23.

Bolden, R., & Kirk, P. (2005). *Leadership in Africa: Meanings, impacts and identities*. Unpublished manuscript.

Drzewiecka, J., & Halualani, R. (2002). The Structural–Cultural Dialectic of Diasporic Politics. *Communication Theory 12*, 340–366.

Hofstede, G. (2001). *Culture's consequences*. Thousand Oaks, CA: Sage.

House, R. J., Hanges, P. J., Javidan, M., Gorfman, P., & Gupta, V. (Eds.). (2004). *Leadership, culture, and organizations: the Globe study of 62 societies*. Thousand Oaks, CA: Sage.

Kraidy, M. (2002). Hybridity in cultural globalization. *Communication Theory, 12*, 316–339.

Louisy, P. (2001). Globalisation and comparative education: a Caribbean perspective. *Comparative Education, 37*, 425–438.

Nkomo, S. (2006). *Images of African leadership and management in organizational studies: Tensions, contradictions and re-visions*. Unpublished manuscript.

Patterson, O. (1995). The Culture of caution. *New Republic, 213(22)*, 22–26.

Robotham, D. (1998). Transnationalism in the Caribbean: Formal and informal. *American Ethnologist 25(2)*, 307–321.

Shome, R., & Hegde, R. (2002). Postcolonial approaches to communication: Charting the terrain, engaging the intersections. *Communication Theory 12*, 249–270.

Thomas, D. (2004). *Modern Blackness: Nationalism, globalization, and the politics of culture in Jamaica*. Durham, NC: Duke University Press.

## Concepts and Questions

1. How does the one-way flow of Western business knowledge affect Jamaican managers?

2. What kinds of problems are faced by small former colonial cultures in the development of their business practices?

3. How has globalization influenced business practices in Jamaica?

4. How does traditional Jamaican culture pose problems for the "modernization" of business practices?

5. How might the presence of Eurocentric perspectives among the Jamaican professional and cultural elite influence communication between Jamaican business organizations and business organizations from highly industrialized countries?

6. How can Jamaican managers best communicate their need to develop indigenous business ideas and solutions to other nations with whom they wish to do business?

7. How did many of the managers interviewed by Hall define globalization? How do they see it affecting their organizations?

8. How do foreign expectations of efficiency standards influence business in Jamaica?

9. In what way do the Jamaican trade unions influence the development of management practices in Jamaica?

10. What are some of the major characteristics of management communication within Jamaican business organizations?

11. How do differences of education and social class influence communication within Jamaican business organizations?

*We devoted three essays to the business context because we believe that international business and the proper utilization of a multicultural workforce in the United States are areas where competent intercultural communication skills are very important. However, we do not want to leave you with the idea that business is the only important context. In the next essay, we will deal with diverse cultural issues found in the health care context.*

## THE HEALTH CARE CONTEXT

# Health Journeys: Intersections Between Ancient Healing and Modern Medicine

POLLY A. BEGLEY • DEBBIE A. OCKEY

*The United States is a multicultural society. The health care context, thus, is of major importance because health care providers must be able to communicate effectively with patients who may have widely divergent ideas about the causes, prevention, and treatment of illness, have limited English proficiency, do not understand treatment protocols, and have culturally different ways of communicating with health care providers.*

*This next essay will give you an overview of how cultures differ in their approaches to the diagnosis, treatment, and prevention of illness. In their essay "Health*

*Journeys: Intersections between Ancient Healing and Modern Medicine," Polly A. Begley and Debbie A. Ockey indicate that alternative beliefs about standard American medical practice can lead to major intercultural communication difficulties. From this essay you will come to understand (1) the differences between Western biomedicine and traditional approaches that have been practiced since the fifth century B.C.; (2) several major medical approaches involving integrative medicine, whole medical systems, mind–body interventions, and shamanism, as well as biologically based practices; (3) the practice of*

This original essay appears here in print for the first time. All rights reserved. Permission to reprint must be obtained from the authors and the publisher. Ms. Polly A. Begley teaches in the Department of Communication Arts at Fresno City College, Fresno, California. Ms. Debbie A. Ockey teaches English as a Second Language at Fresno City College, Fresno California.

*cultural competency in health care settings; (4) the need for linguistically appropriate health care; (5) the need for cross-cultural dialogues in health care; and (6) ways in which innovative programs can improve health care in a culturally diverse society.*

*The authors begin with a discussion about the cultural collisions that can occur when those who embrace traditional healing are faced with the biomedical culture that abounds in contemporary American medicine. They then discuss how changing global populations bring about a need for health care providers to understand diverse medical approaches.*

*Next, the authors relate the various belief systems connected to health care by describing the biomedical belief system that is predominant in the United States and the supernatural belief system, which is a traditional system that views illness as a punishment for evil deeds, an outside possession of the body, an evil spell, or a wounded soul. They also describe the holistic belief system, which requires that in order for people to be well they must remain in harmony with natural laws and be able to adjust to changes in the environment. Finally, they describe alternative medical approaches that include chiropractors, massage therapists, homeopaths, and naturopaths.*

*Based upon the foundation they have established, Begley and Ockey discuss the challenges to providing health care that is culturally and linguistically appropriate for a diverse population. They believe that culturally appropriate medical care includes being able to effectively treat a patient with different beliefs about the origins of illness and disease. This includes developing medical plans and recommendations that are consistent with the patient's and family's beliefs and expectations.*

*After discussing the issues of health literacy and the linguistic challenges inherent in a multicultural health care system, the authors provide several models for success that involve solutions and innovative programs. They call for increased knowledge and understanding of diverse health care beliefs and increasing the diversity of health care professionals. Included in their discussion are a series of questions that should be asked by health care providers to ensure that cultural diversity is taken into consideration in the development of treatment plans.*

The highly developed physician, however, is able to detect illness in its infancy; he or she detects the tracks of the illness.... He or she knows how to carefully 'watch the door and the window in order to catch the thief.' The mediocre doctor, however, waits until the illness has taken hold to apply treatment.

### The Yellow Emperor's Canon of Internal Medicine, 2500 B.C.

One person chooses herbs and plants, another prays, someone else consults a shaman, others take prescription drugs prescribed by a physician. Each person chooses remedies or treatments she or he believes will allow them to enjoy better health. But how do we decide upon the "best" course when there are so many medical theories and methods? As societies developed biomedical practices, a false dichotomy emerged pitting the scientific approach against traditional folk remedies and cures. Practitioners of modern integrative medicine recognize the great value of medical science while understanding and even capitalizing on the benefits of diverse medical viewpoints. The truth is that neither biomedicine, which is prevalent in American hospitals and clinics, nor any other medical philosophy has all the solutions for every patient. Plotkin (1993), an ethnobotanist, has stated, "The fact is that no one system has all the answers, but a melding of the two might bring us closer to that goal. We need to learn from the medicine man ways to treat our incurable illnesses much as he needs to learn from our physicians how to treat introduced diseases like measles and whooping cough" (p. 237). Diverse medical approaches reveal glimpses into cultural backgrounds, personal values, beliefs, and attitudes. Understanding intersections between ancient and modern medicine also give health providers and patients a better opportunity to direct their journeys to health and healing.

Present-day patients are increasingly choosing from a variety of different medical practices for whatever proves to be the most useful and available cure or treatment. In this essay we will examine influential aspects of communication including complementary/ alternative (CAM), or integrative, and biomedical/allopathic practitioners involving patients from diverse cultural and linguistic backgrounds and healing traditions. The first section concentrates on understanding major medical philosophies from a historical perspective. Secondly, significant issues related to practicing culturally and linguistically appropriate integrative health care will be discussed. Finally, we will review patient-centered models of care and strategies to improve communication competence between health care providers and patients. It is with no small degree of trepidation that we narrowed down the topics for this chapter as we sorted through the myriad of ancient healing and modern medical approaches. Our caveat here is that this is far from an extensive inventory, but merely a peek at a number of potential journeys that may be undertaken for enhanced health and healing.

## BIOMEDICAL OR ALLOPATHIC MEDICINE

This is the dominant medical system found in American hospitals and clinics and other regions of the world. Historically, some biomedical beliefs may be traced back to the fifth century B.C. and the Hippocratic doctors. These doctors began by elevating themselves above root-gatherers, diviners, and others whom they dismissed as "ignoramuses and quacks" and established a code of physician conduct and a scientific approach that still influence modern medicine today (Porter, 2002, p. 25).

This scientific approach used in biomedical or allopathic medicine contributed greatly to people living longer and better lives across the globe. According to the 2008 World Health Report, "People are healthier, wealthier, and live longer than 30 years ago" (p. xii). Medical organizations and caregivers the world over responded to the challenges of contemporary life by making such improvements as sanitation, antenatal care, health literacy, access to clean water, and intensified exchanges among countries in the face of shared health threats.

Countries that invested in the health and well-being of citizens expanded their populations' access to biomedical health care. For example, mortality rates have fallen to less than one-fifth of what they were thirty years ago in Chile, Malaysia, Portugal, and Thailand. Another dramatic example comes from The Sultanate of Oman, which invested in the health sector over the last several decades and saw an average fourteen-year increase in lifespan among residents and an amazing 94 percent drop in mortality rates for children below

the age of five. The World Health Organization (2008) points to the worldwide trend of people living longer and healthier lives and estimated that 18,329 children are being saved daily in comparison to 1978 rates because of improved access to health care (p. 2).

Although world health statistics represent good news for global societies, lingering health disparities still exist across the globe. The World Health Organization (2008) points to disappointing variations in life expectancy rates, child mortality, vaccination coverage, and health literacy among many countries, regions, and groups. Furthermore, these health disparities have been associated with "the unmistakable relation between health and wealth" (p. 4). Sub-Saharan Africa remains a dramatic and often repeated illustration of the correlation between health and wealth, but the extent of inequalities goes further. "Most Swedish citizens, for example, were probably unaware that the difference in life expectancy between 20-year-old men from the highest and lowest socioeconomic groups was 3.97 years in 1997" (Burstrôm, Johannesson, & Didericksen as cited in World Health Report, 2008, p. 15). This research and other studies conclude that those without adequate access to health care suffer the consequences of ill health. Some may choose complementary and alternative medicine as a less expensive or more accessible treatment option. But another societal development in the United States is that many patients who have adequate access to clinics and hospitals still seek out additional routes to health and well-being.

## UNDERSTANDING MAJOR MEDICAL APPROACHES
### Complementary and Alternative Medicine (CAM) and Integrative Medicine

Alternative medicine is typically used *instead* of biomedicine, while complementary medicine is used *with* biomedicine. Generations of poorer families throughout the United States utilized backyard herb gardens, home remedies, and non-licensed community healers in lieu of expensive visits to clinics or hospitals. But recent studies discovered another trend in those who seek out complementary and alternative medicine.

Those individuals were increasingly female, had a higher level of education, had a higher socioeconomic status, lived in western regions of the United States, and had a health complaint (Nahin, et al., 2007). This trend may indicate a level of dissatisfaction with complete reliance on biomedicine or allopathic medicine. According to a government-sponsored survey in December 2008, about 38 percent of U.S. adults used some type of complementary alternative medical therapy. The number increases to 62 percent when prayer is considered a medical remedy (Barnes, Bloom, & Nahin, 2008, December 20).

The term *alternative* was frequently used to describe any medical practice that is not validated or utilized in biomedical practices. Chiropractors, massage therapists, hypnotists, herbal therapists, homeopaths, and naturopaths were all examples of what have been considered alternative medical practitioners. Norton, of the Chiropractic Wellness Center in Central California, points out that less-invasive medical approaches and preventive care ought to be the norm, while drugs and surgery should be considered *alternative* (personal interview, March 23, 2006). Dr. David Simon prefers to define his practice as *integrative* rather than alternative medicine. This approach allows for the use of "external intervention, be that pharmacology, surgery, or radiation therapy" and the use of "practices that are more about awakening the person's internal healing system" (Collie, 2007, p. 81). Dr. Brent Bauer, Director of the Department of Internal Medicine's Complementary and Integrative Medicine Program at the Mayo Clinic in Rochester, Minnesota, also states that "even the name 'alternative'—used to describe therapies outside the scope of traditional medicine—can be misleading now.... As more health-care providers offer such services, it makes sense to refer to the therapies as complementary or integrative" (Oleck, 2007, p. E2).

The terms *CAM* and *integrative* have been used interchangeably, but more experts now agree that *integrative medicine* or *integrative health care* should replace the more divisive labels *alternative* and *complementary*.

> *Modern integrative medicine attempts to balance ancient and modern techniques by returning focus to the patient and utilizing extensive observation and provider-patient interactions as a basis for diagnosis and creating customized treatment plans.*

Integrative medicine describes evolving health care practices in which previously considered alternative therapies already proven effective in scientific studies are now being integrated with biomedicine (Mayo Clinic Book of Alternative Medicine, 2007). The American Association of Integrative Medicine (AAIM, 2009) recognizes a multi-disciplinary approach for which the patient is "the most important member of the medical team and applies all safe and effective therapies without subservience to any one school of medical thought." Integrative medicine reunites mind, body, and spirit through a focus on patient-centered care without ignoring the importance of evidence-based medical science.

Modern integrative medicine attempts to balance ancient and modern techniques by returning focus to the patient and utilizing extensive observation and provider-patient interactions as a basis for diagnosis and creating customized treatment plans. The stereotype of the family doctor who spends a few minutes with the patient and then says, "Take two of these pills and *don't* call me in the morning" has been replaced with an integrative physician. This physician may sit down and talk with the patient at eye level, and with an interpreter if needed, to discover the source of the pain and then work with the patient to analyze and co-create an individualized treatment plan. Essentially, integrative medicine redefines the accepted culture of biomedicine and the expert-patient relationship while it capitalizes on the benefits of biomedical or allopathic medicine as well as CAM. It relies on a much more holistic view of the human body and the importance of the mind–body connection. The deficit model of disease underpinning biomedicine, which defines a condition as an impairment or dysfunction, is rejected by an integrative practitioner; instead, he or she treats the whole patient, thus restoring balance to the body (Shenk, 1999).

## Whole Medical Systems

These systems embody a complete collection of knowledge and practice. Examples are Ayurveda and

Traditional Chinese Medicine (TCM), originating in Asia, and naturopathic medicine, which was developed in western cultures. Three commonalities exist among these whole medical systems. First, most of the knowledge base, particularly for Ayurveda and TCM, stems from oral or written medical texts that are thousands of years old. Secondly, there is a general reliance on non-invasive (non-surgical) techniques such as observation and extensive interactions for diagnosis and treatment. Finally, each treatment plan is designed specifically for the patient (no one-size-fits-all drugs or procedures).

Ayurveda is a whole medical system from South Asia. "Ayurvedic physicians attempt to determine the patient's constitution … through careful observation and questioning. They seek a detailed history of the patient's health, emotional state, diet, and social environment" (Baer, 2004, p. 74). This medical system, like many other holistic medical approaches, seeks to restore balance or equilibrium among mind, body, and spirit as a way to promote health and wellness. Treatment could also include massage, yoga, herbs, or joining a laughing club in order to alleviate stress. Reeves (2009) gave an account of Ashok Aswani, an Ayurvedic physician in India, who gives patients complaining of depression DVDs of Charlie Chaplin. Dr. Aswani says, "This makes them feel better." Dr. Aswani's approach may not be very different from the use of clowns, reportedly used as a way to reduce anxiety and speed healing among children and geriatric patients (Schor, 2010).

TCM is a whole medical system from China, which developed over thousands of years. A quintessential classic tome of TCM is the Yellow Emperor's Classic of Medicine, or the *Neijing*, believed to have been written during the third millennium BCE. One passage from the *Neijing* maintains that "Health and well-being can be achieved only by remaining centered in spirit, guarding against the squandering of energy, promoting the constant flow of *qi* and blood, maintaining the harmonious balance of *yin* and *yang*, adapting to the changing seasonal and yearly macrocosmic influences, and nourishing one's self preventively. This is seen as the way to a long and healthy life" (Maoshing, 1995, p. xiii). According to Lixin Huang, the president of the American College of Traditional Chinese Medicine (ACTCM) in San Francisco, California, almost every hospital in her region of the country has hired a licensed TCM acupuncturist working under the aegis of "pain management" (personal communication, October 3, 2008). Megan Haungs, dean of the master's degree program at the ACTCM, points out that TCM may be used to treat pain, but practitioners ultimately will look for the root cause of the pain. She stresses with her students the value of getting a patient's whole history and lifestyle details in order to encourage the patient to discover her or his own path to enhanced health. Dr. Haungs gave an account of collective work in the early 1980s in the South Bronx, New York, where there was a movement to see if acupuncture could help drug addicts. One female heroin addict, during an acupuncture session, said, "Wow! I feel great. What's in those needles?" The TCM practitioner responded, "It's you. We've tapped into you!" In other words, TCM helped this patient find her own "innate [healing] potential" (personal communication, October 3, 2008).

Initial appointments at the ACTCM are two hours long and subsequent appointments last for an hour. Just listening to a patient's pulse could take three minutes to half an hour. The five pillars of TCM taught at the college focus on acupuncture, massage, diet, herbs (a concentrated form of diet), and qigong (movement and breathing). Ultimately, this whole medical system relies significantly on careful observation and extensive conversations between practitioners and patients for successful diagnosis and treatment.

Naturopathic medicine is a whole medical system developed in western cultures during the eighteenth and nineteenth centuries. The popular acceptance of surgery and drugs in the mid-twentieth century turned people away from naturopathic and other natural healing modalities, but interest in natural methods returned as patients in recent decades became disillusioned with the side effects of drugs and surgical complications. The American Association of Naturopathic Physicians (2009) affirms that contemporary naturopathic doctors (N.D.s) "blend the best of modern medical science and traditional natural medical approaches to not only treat disease, but to also restore health." In a case reported by Ehrlich (2002), Mahlee, who suffered from malignant hypertension, consulted an N.D. and an M.D. because she struggled with multiple side effects stemming from high doses of beta-blockers. The N.D. kept in close contact with her cardiologist and through these interactions a regimen was designed that "included diet, exercise, and creative expression" (p. 96). Mahlee's medical team reduced her reliance on prescription and over-the-counter medication and eliminated drug side effects. N.D.s may evaluate the patient's emotional state as well as their physical state. N.D. and author Jacob Schor (2010) reported on various studies analyzing the influence of emotions, specifically laughter, upon various health complaints. Some studies detailed by Schor revealed that watching humorous videos could lessen allergic responses. Schor acknowledges that "Although the practice of medicine is a serious task, we should keep in mind that humor is a potentially useful therapeutic tool" (p. 3). Naturopathic medicine, much like Ayurveda and TCM, depends upon a close and interactive relationship between patient and health provider.

## Mind-Body Interventions

The seventeenth-century philosopher René Descartes contended that mind and body were separate from each other. This mind-body dichotomy influenced Western medical practitioners to deemphasize psychological, emotional, or spiritual factors as sources of illness and instead concentrate on "physiological disturbances such as genetic disorders, biochemical imbalances, and infectious organisms" as the origins of disease (Luckman, 2000, p. 44). In contrast to early Western medicine, ancient and modern mind-body interventions recognized a person as a whole and included, "meditation, prayer, and therapies that use creative outlets" as well as other spiritual and religious practices (Zahourek, 2008, p. 34). Ancient mind-body interventions are still widely practiced around the world and as populations become more diverse, many of these early medical traditions have been incorporated into the biomedical system.

One example of mind-body interventions is shamanism, which recognizes all the sources of disease that may "result from any number of causes, including the breaking of a taboo, the casting of a magic spell, the anger of the gods, or disharmony between the physical and spiritual worlds" (Plotkin, 1993, p. 203). According to Amazonian shamans, "all negative thoughts… are dark spirits speaking to us, trying to scare us into reacting; the spirits then feed on our reactivity, growing stronger and more formidable until they finally rule over us" (Salak, 2006, p. 4). A Taoist shamanistic ritual known as *shoujing* reclaims people's frightened souls and is practiced in Taipei's Hsingtien Temple. "The believers will tell you there is no need to list your symptoms, because the *shoujing* ritual is a catch-all—'It cures if you're ill, and blesses if you're not'" (Hwang, 2004, pp. 12–13). Chang Hsun, a researcher at the Academia Sinica's Institute of Ethnology, says there is a tendency in Taiwan for the less educated to seek spiritual healing at the first sign of illness; the highly educated will wait longer, but ultimately, "both will go to the temple" (Hwang 2004, p. 15). Most Taiwanese combine *shoujing* rituals with biomedicine. Chang says, "Pills take care of physical symptoms, but people also feel that they need something for their souls, if they want to heal completely" (Hwang 2004, p. 17). Shamans may communicate with the spirit world and conduct sacred rituals, but many also have a thorough understanding of how to heal everyday diseases of this world with local plants and trees, relaxation and visualization techniques, massage, hypnosis, and dietary analysis.

Shamanism is also commonly practiced within the Southeast Asian Hmong-American communities living primarily in California, Minnesota, and Wisconsin. In the highly publicized case of Lia Lee in the early 1980's, Fadiman (1997) reported hearing "doctors at the Merced Community Medical Center complain that the Hmong seemed to care less than Americans did whether their sick children got better, since they spurned the hospital's free medical care" (p. 111). As a matter of fact, Lia's family invested vast amounts of time, energy, and money into restoring the child's health through traditional approaches such as "amulets filled with sacred healing herbs from Thailand," cupping, pinching, herbs, animal sacrifices, and taking Lia to a well known *tvix neeb*, shaman (p. 111). Lia's doctors observed that her parents failed to give her medication during a vital period of time, but never asked what other healing methodologies they were using for her. The vast differences between the medical team's proposed treatment plan and the family's beliefs and traditional remedies led to inevitable misunderstandings and an ultimately tragic outcome. Lia Lee's story, poignantly documented by Fadiman (1997), is now commonly required reading at leading medical schools across the United States.

## Biologically Based Practices

According to the National Center for Complementary and Alternative Medicine (2007), this practice "includes, but is not limited to, botanicals, animal-derived extracts, vitamins, minerals, fatty acids, amino acids, proteins, prebiotics, and probiotics, whole diets, and functional foods." As noted previously, biologically based treatments are also incorporated within many other CAM philosophies.

This knowledge has been used and practiced for centuries in ancient cultures including the Aztec civilization, which also had a comprehensive understanding of medicine and herbs. Elena Avila recounts her route to becoming a *curandera*, a traditional folk healer, in her book "Woman Who Glows in the Dark." She points out that during the Spanish conquest of Mexico, the conquistadors marveled at the advanced medical knowledge of the Aztecs, which contributed to contemporary *curanderismo*. (Avila and Parker, 1999, p. 29). "Curanderismo's strength comes from its practice of always incorporating whatever is useful and available into its treatment, in an intuitive and creative way" (p. 17).

Dr. Rosita Arvigo, an American doctor of naprapathy, a manipulative therapy, chose another course that took her to the rainforest of Belize, where she apprenticed for ten years with a famous traditional healer named Don Elijio Panti. She learned to heal with prayers, roots, vines, barks and massage. Don Elijio Panti's healing medicine and knowledge came from the Mayan spirits and from years of experience and observation of nature (Arvigo, Epstein, & Yaquinto, 1994). Biologically based knowledge permeates many natural medical philosophies and treatment plans and has also increasingly become a standard feature of modern integrative medicine.

## Manipulative and Body-Based Practices

Chiropractors, osteopathic physicians, and massage therapists are all examples of practitioners who heal by manipulating one or more body parts. Dr. M.

Norton, with the Norton Chiropractic Wellness Center in Central California, uses the Torque Release Technique, a gentle method of spinal/nervous system care. Dr. Norton maintains that "by design, these bodies are made to work perfectly," and as a chiropractor, describes his role as "facilitat[ing] a self-healing system." His treatment plans help people to return to "wholeness" without having to resort to drugs that mask the true cause of illness (personal interview, March 23, 2006). Studies show that chiropractors may be used more than any other alternative provider. The most common form of chiropractic is spinal manipulation, which, according to the American Chiropractic Association (2009), seeks to "restore joint mobility by manually applying a controlled force into joints that have become… restricted in their movement—as a result of tissue injury." Chiropractors are also trained to provide nutritional, dietary, and lifestyle counseling. Manipulative and body-based practitioners, similar to other holistic health providers, provide patients with additional health options beyond drugs and surgery, but also refer more serious cases to biomedical physicians if needed.

> *Health care providers today must understand some of the beliefs and customs that influence a patient's approach to health and illness. For treatment to be successful, it has to be accepted by the patient.*

## PRACTICING CULTURAL COMPETENCY IN HEALTH SETTINGS

Health care providers today must understand some of the beliefs and customs that influence a patient's approach to health and illness. For treatment to be successful, it has to be accepted by the patient. Understanding and valuing patients' diverse cultures is essential in order to eliminate health care disparities, improve access to services and provide quality health care to all patients. As health care teams strive to achieve cultural competency, studies show that health outcomes improve due to better communication, understanding and greater patient compliance with treatment plans. Cultural competency for health care organizations is a journey that includes provider training, coordination with traditional healers, involvement of family members or community leaders, and organizational accommodations (Salas-Lopez, 2007).

Cultural competency "is a process in which healthcare providers learn from and about different cultures, and with this knowledge, they are able to modify their healthcare practices to accommodate and share in the culture of their patients" (Maddalena, 2009, p. 153). The Association of American Medical Colleges (2005) outlines the goals of culturally competent care as attaining cultural awareness, cultural knowledge, and cultural skills, and increasing cultural encounters. Culturally competent communication in a health care setting relates positively to higher levels of patient satisfaction, cost efficiency, and improved health outcomes. Increasing cultural knowledge and understanding includes being aware of the unique needs of particular patient populations. Anthony Yamamoto explained that people in the Central Valley of California are very spiritually and culturally diverse, but some patients lack "medical sophistication." In some cases, they are unaware of medical practices or anatomy. Their perspectives about the cause of an illness may include phenomenon such as lunar eclipses or cultural beliefs about "soul loss." In addition, lack of educational literacy can cause complications with medical directions or follow-up care. He described one parent who came into the Children's Hospital of Central California unable to read numbers or tell time. "Her child required routine dosages at consistent times. If the child is not given the appropriate dosage on time, the treatment is not effective and may contribute to other complications or health consequences" (Yamamoto, 2005). To enable providers to better serve diverse patient populations, the U.S. Department of Health and Human Services, Office of Minority Health, developed online training for physicians which includes a message of appreciation for the healing practices of a variety of cultures and teaches cross-cultural skills including history taking, problem solving, and promoting patient compliance. Physicians review actual clinical encounters within Cultural Competence Curriculum Modules and assess how they would handle the situations. One case involved a Native American patient with diabetes and a previous amputation who was refusing more treatment because she believed that being in the hospital would kill her. Many Native Americans believe that mentioning an illness or medical consequence will cause it to occur. The patient did not want to "die in some teeny room that smells of sickness." The doctor had to show respect for her traditions and allow her to continue using herbs and prayer, while negotiating a plan to continue medication and testing. In another case, an Ethiopian immigrant felt unwelcome in his local clinic and believed, "This place has nothing for me here." Traditional Ethiopian beliefs are rooted in the concept that health results from equilibrium between the body and the outside world, and illness comes from lack of that balance. The doctor in this case had to develop a better understanding of the local Ethiopian community and reach out to the community leaders to make the clinic a safe and welcoming place for them. The clinic eventually incorporated the services of a doula, a traditional midwife, to work with the Ethiopian patients (Office of Minority Health, U.S. Department of Health and Human Services). "How patients feel about their care is an important factor in compliance with treatment. Allopathic physicians lose patients to CAM providers if the patients feel the physician is not listening to their concerns. This can be devastating if the patient truly needs allopathic care" (Roe, 2002, pp. 2–3). Increasingly, physicians and the health care industry in America have realized the correlation between successful treatment of illness and health promotion with an enhanced understanding and integration of diverse approaches to health and healing. whether they are interventions stemming from TCM, the mind-body connection, substances found in nature, physical manipulation, energy evaluations, or biomedicine.

> *Many Native Americans believe that mentioning an illness or medical consequence will cause it to occur.*

## CULTURALLY AND LINGUISTICALLY APPROPRIATE HEALTH CARE
### Culturally Appropriate Health Care Delivery: Issues and Solutions

The potential for a conflict of values or misunderstandings is great when health care providers and patients come from different cultural, linguistic, or social groups. Such differences embody not just different opinions or beliefs, but different ways of everyday living and different systems of meaning. Many

Spanish speakers will expect to be treated with *personalismo* (formal friendliness) which could be as simple as asking about the patient's family or life at each visit. In addition, showing *respecto* (respect) to the parents or oldest members of the family, including using the respectful titles of *señor or señora*, will make patients feel that the doctor values their concerns. Finally, demonstrating simple politeness and courtesy will ensure that patients feel the physician is *simpatico* (likeable or congenial). When the caregiver does not recognize and give service to these cultural values, the patient may perceive a lack of respect and believe that the physician does not really care about him or her (Flores, Rabke-Verani, Pine, & Sabharwal, 2002). One Cultural Competence Curriculum Module illustrates the need for cultural competency in health care delivery by reviewing the case of Arturo, a teenage patient being treated for depression who was brought in after a possible suicide attempt. The doctor believed the boy had overdosed intentionally, but the social worker disagreed. After further investigation, it was revealed that the boy's mother spoke very little English and had misunderstood the dosing instructions. The doctor knew her English was poor, but he felt he had been very clear and had even written down the instructions, "once a day." The social worker had to explain to the doctor that "once" in Spanish means "eleven." She also pointedly asked the doctor, "Why would you think she could *read* English any better than she could speak it?" (Office of Minority Health, U.S. Department of Health and Human Services, n.d.). Trained interpreters, who are also familiar with cultural nuances, are essential and can educate the health care team to eliminate the types of misunderstandings that occurred in Arturo's case.

The federal government mandates culturally competent training for all health organizations receiving federal funds as part of the national CLAS (Culturally and Linguistically Appropriate Services) standards. One standard states that patients must receive care in a manner that is compatible with their cultural beliefs and practices and in their preferred language (Office of Minority Health and Research Center, April 12, 2007).

> *Understanding the important cultural values that facilitate communication in a particular language is essential for culturally competent care.*

Understanding the important cultural values that facilitate communication in a particular language is essential for culturally competent care. In situations where interpreters are needed, they must be able to comprehend diverse beliefs and healing practices in order to understand their clients and their needs. McDonough (2009) has pointed out, "One recipe will not be useful for every culture." She explained that interpreters at her hospital are trained by using "real life case scenarios." An example of the key role an interpreter can play was in evidence in the true story of a young Guatemalan woman who was screaming hysterically in the maternity ward after delivery. An interpreter was called and quickly discovered the reason for her distress. In her native village, the cultural belief is that if a baby's hair is brushed to one side, it will be mute. The interpreter was able to bridge the cultural gap and calm the mother while helping the nurses understand that combing the baby's hair was not necessary in this case. In another situation, a young Hispanic woman who went to a breast center for an ultrasound because of a suspicious growth became very upset and agitated when her husband was not allowed in the room. The doctor was impatient, but the interpreter was able to explain that in the Hispanic culture the presence and opinion of family members in such a serious situation was very important. The husband was allowed in and the patient relaxed. At the follow-up visit, the doctor thanked the interpreter for helping her understand an important part of the culture (*Hablamos Juntos*, n.d.).

## Linguistically Appropriate Health Care Delivery: Issues and Solutions

As the health care industry treats an increasingly diverse patient population, the need for culturally and linguistically appropriate services has increased. A provider's experience and knowledge represent competence only if they can be effectively communicated to the patient. Misunderstandings often occur between a patient and a health care provider when they both speak English as their first language, but the potential for miscommunication increases when the patient's first language is not English. In research conducted at the Medical College of Wisconsin, Flores (2006) found that 26 percent of the patients stated that language barriers were the major reason they did not seek treatment or deferred follow-up visits.

Interpreter-mediated communication between doctors and patients has become a common clinical situation. However, bilingualism alone does not guarantee the ability to interpret effectively. The Massachusetts Medical Interpreter Association states, "An interpreter must be able to convert messages uttered in one language into the appropriate sociolinguistic framework of another language" (Anderson, 2002). McDonough (2009) has described one case she was familiar with where an "untranslatable" word, a word with no linguistic equivalent, caused a communication breakdown, and impeded the health care provider from imparting essential information. The physician, assisted by an interpreter, was having a meeting with the parents of a Cambodian child admitted to the pediatric ICU and told them their daughter had a serious blood infection. The interpreter asked, "Doctor, what kind of infection? In my culture, we only know about a skin infection from a cut or wound. Could you explain this in a different way?" In order to grasp the meaning, the Cambodian interpreter had to ask for clarification of the concept of "infection." To get this concept across to the family, she needed to work with the provider to find a way to transmit the essential information underlying this concept. To create trust and rapport and ensure the best possible outcomes, the interpreter needed to make sure the patient and family fully comprehended all the information.

As noted previously, misunderstandings may occur even when providers and patients are speaking the same language. Doctors may be using medical terms that do not have an equivalent in another language, or are too complex for the patients to understand, making them feel confused and frustrated. This lack of understanding may lead to noncompliance with the doctor's instructions for treatment. Bower and Taylor (2003) found that the customary use of medical jargon contributed to widespread inability to understand over-the-counter drug instructions. Regulations regarding the use of "plain language," such as replacing "indications," "abdominal," "pulmonary," and "persists" with "uses," "stomach," "lung," and "does not go away" were first instituted in 1999 (p. 146).

Dr. Ruth Parker of Emory University points out that there is general confusion surrounding how to take drugs. She compares all the colored labels attached to pill bottles to "Christmas trees." Patients often don't know what to pay attention to and the wording is often confusing even when it appears very simple. Dr. Parker was involved in research to test patients' understanding of the instructions "Take two tablets twice daily." A third of the patients surveyed, who were all literate, were confused as to whether that meant a total of two or four pills. A clearer way to explain that would be to instruct the patient to "take two tablets in the morning and two at night" (cited in Neergaard, 2009). Today, many health care organizations are following guidelines for disseminating clear information in plain language, which include writing drug instructions at a fifth-grade reading level, using simple visuals, and sending patients to the Internet for detailed information about follow-up care (The Institute for Healthcare Advancement, 2008).

## Cross-Cultural Dialogues: Getting the Whole Story

In order to make sure nothing gets lost in translation, health care teams need to be aware of patient communication styles, both verbal and nonverbal, and their implications. Patients from some cultures might appear passive to the physician, but their behavior may be part of a non-confrontational communication style. The "nodding syndrome" described by medical providers describes a nod that doesn't mean a "yes" answer. Nodding could mean the patient does not understand at all, but out of respect for the authority figure, he or she does not disclose that and keeps nodding affirmatively. Likewise, silence does not always reflect agreement, but it could indicate only politeness and/or the need to discuss health issues and decisions with the family (McDonough, 2009). Although regional, educational, and class differences make it impossible to generalize about any ethnic group, some Spanish speakers use a communication style more like storytelling. Their narrative tends to be rich in detail and shows a circular, non-linear mode of thinking. Their answers are often much more detailed than a simple "yes/no" answer. Kolenda (2008) has described Spanish-speaking patients who prefer to tell the entire story, and if they are interrupted, then they start over at the beginning. A case illustrating the "storytelling" style occurred when a physician at the University of Massachusetts Memorial Medical Center asked a patient about previous surgeries. The physician specifically wanted information about a breast surgery, but the patient provided many more details. "It was in '66, when I came from Puerto Rico and I lost my baby and I had my appendix removed and they removed the baby; then the milk settled in my breast and some 'glandulitis' (little nodules) developed" (McDonough, 2009). Without an understanding of the patient's communication style, the physician may become frustrated and miss important details that are buried in the narrative discourse. This encounter illustrates the need for cultural sensitivity and patience on the part of the health care team in order to facilitate effective communication between the provider and the patient.

## Building Meaningful Relationships

The most important communication skill for health care professionals is the ability to relate to patients. Regenstein (2007) believes, "Making care more patient centered means many things to many people, but at its most fundamental level, patient centered care rises or falls on the quality of communications." In order to build meaningful relationships, providers need to respect patients' values and attitudes, accommodate their beliefs and identify their needs and expectations. One model of care, developed by Ruth Hansten, is the Relationship and Results Oriented Health Care Program (RROHC), which focuses on improved patient satisfaction and outcomes obtained through individualized relationships between care providers and the patient. Many hospitals discovered, when they started tracking patient satisfaction while using RROHC, that some basic aspects of care had been missing from their protocols. Patient satisfaction ratings started going up as they instituted "bedside work." One RROHC practice that goes back to basics has nurses communicating with patients at eye level while sitting beside them, rather than towering over them. Nursing staff are also taught to practice focused listening skills and maintain eye contact, clearly

> *The most important communication skill for health care professionals is the ability to relate to patients.*

communicating the treatment plan and the health care team's roles while using touch and body language (Pullins, 2009). "It's all about… bringing that personal touch back to the bedside" (Lopez, 2009).

## INNOVATIVE PROGRAMS AND APPROACHES IN HEALTH CARE
### Latino Community Outreach Program

In the United States, 21 million people speak English "less than well" and are classified as limited-English proficient (LEP) (U.S. Bureau of the Census, 2000). For these groups, access to health care is an ongoing challenge. In addition, LEP individuals are less likely to have a primary care physician and receive fewer preventive health services (Regenstein, 2007). Language barriers can also affect the quality and delivery of health care. In order to provide culturally and linguistically appropriate services to diverse populations, many clinics and hospitals have developed innovative, multi-faceted programs. Vista Community Clinic in San Diego County in California began Project MAACHO to reach out to male Latino migrant workers. The goal was to provide preventative care to a population that historically had very little access to health care due to linguistic barriers and a lack of understanding of how to navigate the health care system. In order to reach this population, bilingual staff posted fliers, visited the workers' campsites and provided free transportation to the clinic from designated stops. A full physical is provided free of charge with trained interpreters available to assist the physicians. The patients are provided with assistance in filling out paperwork, scheduling follow-up visits, obtaining medications and determining if they qualify for any government programs. According to Palomo-Zerfas (2009), the response to this creative program has been very positive. Vista Community Clinic is able to deliver essential services, while compliance, adherence to medication, and patient satisfaction have all increased.

### Partners in Healing Program

Nationwide, many hospitals are also trying to accommodate the cultural, religious and spiritual beliefs of their patient populations. In the Central Valley of California, one ethnic group which has a long history of using shamanism as part of their healing practices is the Hmong. Originally from the highlands of Laos, more than 55,000 Hmong have settled in the Central Valley since the Vietnam War. Calling on a traditional healer is an essential part of the recovery process for the Hmong. In 2000, health professionals and Hmong community leaders recognized the need to bridge the cultural gap. Healthy House within a MATCH (Multidisciplinary Approach to Cross-Cultural Health) Coalition developed a forty-hour certificate program called "Partners in Healing" for Hmong shamans, which is an entire curriculum, including safety protocols, infection control and hospital practices. Wilkerson (2009) is proud of the fact that eighty-nine shamans have received certificates which enable them to perform healing ceremonies in the hospital. The shamans are also invited to quarterly follow-up meetings where they tour various specialized units such as the cancer center and watch videos of actual surgeries. This allows them to reassure their patients that surgeries are safe and necessary. As a result of the success of this collaboration, Mercy Medical Center has developed a unique program, the first in the country, which guarantees in writing that Hmong shamans will be allowed to work with the doctors to provide the optimum chance for healing. Other hospitals may allow some healing ceremonies, but Mercy's written policy is unusual. Jacqueline Voigt-Dieball, cultural-competency manager at the University of Michigan's Health System, believes the policy is "quite amazing." Marilyn Mochel, clinical director at Healthy House within a MATCH Coalition, points out that a written policy "recognizes the value of this complementary healing service" (Anderson, 2009, p. A6). The shaman are allowed to perform a variety of healing ceremonies, including tying strings around the wrist to maintain a soul, or using soft chanting to keep the body safe or call the soul back to the body. The hospital has taken the unusual step of allowing the ceremonies not just in the patients' rooms, but also in the emergency room and surgery preparation areas. Physicians at the hospital are very supportive of the program, as it allows them to learn from the shaman, and they see it as being in the best interests of their patients. They understand that the shaman is someone Hmong patients fully trust and believe in for healing. The blending of ancient and modern medical practices is exemplified by the fact that one of the shamans can be contacted at any time by pager (Wilkerson, 2009). Other hospitals are looking at Mercy's policy to determine how it could be adapted to meet their needs. Susan Vang, coordinator of the Hmong Health Collaborative in Fresno, California, explained, "We are hoping that by creating a space and place…to work together and heal, additional doors will open for other ethnic groups to do the same" (Anderson, 2009, p. A7). Since the hospital began this policy, they have had inquiries about how it works from around the country and as far away as Malaysia.

## Health Immersion Approach at Duke University

As part of the movement in biomedicine towards treating and respecting the whole patient, the philosophy and practice of patient-centered care have emerged. Today health care providers are increasingly allowing patients to be partners in their own health care. This includes developing integrative health care programs. Duke University (2009) was one of the founders of the Consortium of Academic Health Centers of Integrative Medicine in 1991. Today, there are more than thirty-eight such centers at major universities. The primary mission of the Duke Integrative Center is to heal the whole person, mind, body, spirit and community, to provide optimal health and healing. Dr. Tracy Gaudet, executive director of the center, explained that biomedical doctors are "trained to first diagnose the disease, to treat the disease and to cure the disease. That's important, but it leaves out how do you actually improve health?" Integrative medical centers like the one at Duke University offer a number of innovative therapeutic services and are based on the philosophy of partnering with the patient to make behavior and lifestyle changes. For example, the Health Immersion Experience at The Duke University Integrative Center is a multiple-day retreat that begins with an eighty-minute evaluation by the physician. The patient is taken care of by an entire team, which includes a health coach. The coach helps facilitate behavior and lifestyle changes in a supportive partnership. They continue to have monthly conversations with patients by telephone even after discharge. John Munce, a cancer patient at the center, was grateful to find that "The healing goes on a long time after the cure" (Duke University Integrative Medicine Center, 2009). Increasingly, medical education is being modified to include nonallopathic approaches. The first Integrative Medicine fellowship for physicians was developed by The University of Arizona College of Medicine in 2001 (Humphrey, 2001). One study found that 83 percent of medical schools in the U.S. offer at least one complementary medicine course (Owen & Lewith, 2004).

## UCSF Osher Center Integrative Medicine Approach

The integration of modern medicine and ancient healing was visibly demonstrated when the Shaolin monks from Songshan, China, visited the UCSF (University of California, San Francisco) Osher Center for Integrative Medicine in March 2009. The monks wanted to learn more about how the center integrates Traditional Chinese Medicine and meditation into modern practice. Yongxin, principal Abbot at the monastery, explained, "We see Chinese medicine as part of science." A fundamental principle of the Osher Center is that the healing power of Integrative Medicine is based on the whole-person approach. Susan Folkman, director of the Osher Center, explained, "Our team…works to address whole-person healing, not just the treating of isolated ailments,"… "Integrative medicine combines modern medicine with established practices from around the world. Through these combined practices, our practitioners help relieve suffering, reduce stress and maintain the well-being of the patients" (Shipra, 2009). The Osher Center philosophy exemplifies how ancient and modern may be balanced within integrative healing.

## CONCLUSION

This essay examined influential aspects of communication including complementary/alternative medicine (CAM), integrative medicine, and biomedical/allopathic practitioners and involving patients from diverse cultural and linguistic backgrounds and healing traditions. American hospitals, clinics, medical schools, and physicians have taken notice of increasing patient interest in healing methods and practices outside of biomedicine. Dr. Alan Waxman,

professor of obstetrics and gynecology at the University of New Mexico in Albuquerque, explained, "Patients have been using them [complementary and alternative methods] for years. Doctors are just catching up." Integrative physicians recognize the need to treat the whole person, and to learn about natural and less-invasive methods of improving health as a way to meet patients' needs and expectations. There is no doubt that modern science has advanced life-saving treatments and deepened our understanding of human physiology. "Now, however, it is time to move into a new climate of collaboration and a respect for new models" (Lawson, 2002, p. 16). The journey to health and healing has become a true alliance between patient and provider. Modern medicine has moved toward a more pluralist view with a variety of ancient approaches to healing working in tandem with modern biomedicine on an equal basis.

## References

American Association of Integrative Medicine. (2009). *About.* Retrieved from http://www.aaimedicine.com/about/

American Chiropractic Association. (2009). *What is chiropractic?* Retrieved December 16, 2009, from http://www.acatoday.org/level2_css.cfm?T1ID=13&T2ID=61

Anderson, B. (2009, October 11). Hospital Healers. *The Fresno Bee*, pp. A1, A6.

Anderson, C. C. (2002, June). *Linguistically appropriate access and services; an evaluation and review for healthcare organizations.* Retrieved August 7, 2009, from http://www.ncihc.org/mc/page.do?sitePageId=57022&orgId=ncihc

Arvigo, R., Epstein, N., & Yaquinto (1994). *Sastun: My apprenticeship with a Maya healer.* San Francisco: HarperCollins.

Association of American Medical Colleges (2005). *Cultural competence education.* Retrieved from http://www.aamc.org/meded/tacct/culturalcomped.pdf

Avila, E., & Parker, J. (1999). *Woman who glows in the dark: A curandera reveals traditional Aztec secrets of physical and spiritual health.* New York: Penguin.

Baer, H. (2004). *Toward an integrative medicine: Merging alternative therapies with biomedicine.* Walnut Creek, CA: Rowman & Littlefield Publishers.

Barnes, P. M., Bloom, B., & Nahin, R., (2008, December 20). *Complementary and alternative medicine use among* adults and children: United States, 2007. CDC National Health Statistics Report #12. Retrieved December 20, 2009 from http://nccam.nih.gov/news/camstats/2007/

Bower, A. B., & Taylor, V. A. (2003, March–April). Increasing intention to comply with pharmaceutical product instructions: An exploratory study investigating the roles of frame and plain language. *Journal of Health Communication: International Perspectives*, 8(2), 145–156.

Collie, A. J. (2007, January). A western doctor faces east. *Hemispheres*, 78–83.

Duke University Integrative Medicine Center. (2009). *Health packages and membership: The health immersion experience.* Retrieved May 22, 2009 from http://www.dukeintegrativemedicine.org/index.php/2009011921/health-packages-memberships/the-health-immersion-experience.html

Ehrlich, S. (2002). Naturopathy. In M. A. Herring & M. M. Roberts (Eds.), *Blackwell complementary and alternative medicine: Fast facts for medical practice* (pp. 91–96). Malden, MA: Blackwell Publishing.

Fadiman, A. (1997). *The spirit catches you and you fall down: A Hmong child, her American doctors, and the collision of two cultures.* New York: Farrar, Straus and Giroux.

Flores, G. (2006, April 27). Lost in translation: Language barriers, interpreters, communication and quality in health care. Lecture delivered at Children's Hospital, Fresno, CA.

Flores, G., Rabke-Verani, J., Pine, W., & Sabharwal, A. (2002). The importance of cultural and linguistic issues in the emergency care of children. *Pediatric Emergency Care*, 18(4), 271–284.

Hablamos Juntos: Language Policy and Practice in Health. (n.d.). *Mission: Why language barriers? Why Latinos?* Retrieved May 22, 2009 from http://www.hablamosjuntos.org/mission/default.mission.asp

Hablamos Juntos: Language Policy and Practice in Health. (n.d.). *True stories.* Retrieved May 22, 2009 from http://www.hablamosjuntos.org/mediacenter/default.true_stories.asp#susalud1

Humphrey, G. (2001, February 7). *Program in integrative medicine accepts physicians to its integrative medicine fellowship.* Retrieved September 6, 2009, from University of Arizona UA News website: http://uanews.org/node/4349

Hwang, J. (2004, August). Body and soul. *Taiwan Review*, pp. 12–17.

Lawson, K. (2002). Political and economic issues in CAM. In M. A. Herring & M. M. Roberts (Eds.), *Blackwell complementary and alternative medicine: Fast facts for medical practice* (pp. 14–19). Malden, MA: Blackwell Publishing.

Lopez, D. (2009). *Relationships and results oriented health care revisited* [webinar 07222009]. Retrieved July 22, 2009 from http://www.rrohc.com

Luckman, J. (2000). *Transcultural communication in health care.* Albany, NY: Delmar/Thomson Learning.

Maddalena, V. (2009, May/June). Cultural competence and holistic practice: Implications for nursing education, practice, and research. *Holistic Nursing Practice*, 153–157.

Maoshing, N. (1995). *The Yellow Emperor's classic of medicine.* Boston, MA: Shambhala Publications.

*Mayo clinic book of alternative medicine: The new approach to using the best of natural therapies and conventional medicine.* (2007). New York: Time Incorporated.

McDonough, E. (2009), Coordinator of Education and Training Interpreter Services at the University of Massachusetts Memorial Medical Center, personal correspondence, August 3.

Nahin, R. L., Dahlhamer, J. M., Taylor, B. L., Barnes, P. M., Stussman, B. J. Simile, C. M., Blackman, M. R., Chesney, M. A., Jackson, M., Miller, H., & McFann, K. K. (2007, August 27). Health behaviors and risk factors in those who use complementary and alternative medicine. *BMC Public Health*, 7, 217. Retrieved from http://www.biomedcentral.com/1471-2458/7/217

National Center for Complementary and Alternative Medicine (2007, February). *What is CAM?* Retrieved September 6, 2009, from http://nccam.nih.gov/health/whatiscam/overview.htm

Neergaard, L. (2009, July 31). New: A chronic problem. *The Fresno Bee*, pp. A1, A10.

Office of Minority Health and Research Center. (2007, April 12). *National standards on culturally and linguistically appropriate services (CLAS).* Retrieved May 22, 2009 from http://hhs.state.ne.us/minorityhealth.docs/CLAS-Brochure.pdf

Office of Minority Health, U.S. Department of Health and Human Services. (n.d.). *Project overview for physicians.* Retrieved June 5, 2009, from https://www.thinkculturalhealth.org/cccm/

Office of Minority Health, U.S. Department of Health and Human Services. (n.d.). *Cultural competence curriculum modules CCCM- video vignettes.* Retrieved June 5, 2009 from https://cccm.thinkculturalhealth.org/videos/index.htm

Oleck, C. (2007, February 17). Cutting-edge care. *The Fresno Bee*, pp. E1–E2.

Owen, D. & Lewith, G. (2004, January 30). Teaching integrated care: CAM familiarization courses. *The Medical Journal of Australia*, 181 (5), 276–278. Retrieved December 15, 2009 from http://www.mja.com.au/public/issues/181_05_060904/owe10062_fm.html

Palomo-Zerfas, A. (2009), Program Director, Vista Community Clinic, San Diego County, California, personal communication, December 14.

Plotkin, M. J. (1993). *Tales of a shaman's apprentice: An ethnobotanist searches for new medicines in the Amazon rain forest*. London, England: Penguin Books.

Porter, R. (2002). *Blood and guts: A short history of medicine*. New York: W.W. Norton & Company.

Pullins, L. (2009), personal communication, July 30.

Reeves, P. (2009, September 24). *An Indian doctor's cure-all: Charlie Chaplin*. Retrieved December 16, 2009, from NPR National Public Radio website: http://www.npr.org/templates/story/story.php?storyId=113029425

Regenstein, M. (2007, November 22). Measuring and improving the quality of hospital language services: Insights from the Speaking Together Collaborative. *Journal of General Internal Medicine*, (Supp. 2), published online 2007 Oct 24 doi: 10.1007/s11606-007-0358-2, 356–359. Retrieved June 5, 2009, from http://www.pubmedcentral.nih.gov/articlerender.fcqi?article=2078553

Roe, S. (2002). Significance of CAM in healthcare. In M. A. Herring & M. M. Roberts (Eds.), *Blackwell complementary and alternative medicine: Fast facts for medical practice* (pp. 1–8). Malden, MA: Blackwell Publishing.

Salak, K. (2006, March). Peru: Hell and back. *National Geographic Adventure*. 55.

Salas-Lopez, D. (2007, May). *Cross-cultural patient-centered care: The rationale, the case, and the policy*. Lecture delivered at University of California, San Francisco, Fresno Center for Medical Education and Research, Fresno, CA.

Schor, J. (2010, January). Emotions and health: Laughter really is good medicine. *Natural Medicine Journal*, 2 (1), 1–4. Retrieved from http://naturalmedicinejournal.com/pdf/NMJ_JAN10_LR.pdf

Shenk, J. W. (1999, May 1). America's altered states: When does legal relief of pain become illegal pursuit of pleasure? *Harper's*. Retrieved from http://www.shenk.net/altered.htm

Shipra, S. (2009, April 7). *Shaolin monks visit UCSF's Osher Center for Integrative Medicine*. Retrieved April 17, 2009, from University of California, San Francisco, Osher Center for Integrative Medicine website: http://today.ucsf.edu/stories/shaolin-monks-visit-ucsfs-osher-center-for-integrative-medicine/

The American Association of Naturopathic Physicians. (2009). *What is naturopathic medicine?* Retrieved December 16, 2009 from http://www.naturopathic.org/content.asp?pl=16&sl=59&contentid=59

The Institute for Healthcare Advancement (2008). *10 common errors medical professionals make when communicating with their patients*. Retrieved from http://www.citihealth.com/print_article.php?art=1368

U.S. Bureau of the Census (2000). *Population briefs*. Retrieved July 25, 2009, from http://www.census.gov/population/sss/cen2000/briefs/phc-t20/tables

Whorton, J. C. (2002). *Nature Cures: The history of alternative medicine in America*. New York: Oxford University Press.

Wilkerson, J. (2009). Director of Mission Integration at Mercy Medical Center in Merced, California, personal communication, December 15.

World Health Organization (2008). *The world health report 2008: Primary health care now more than ever*. Retrieved September 5, 2009 from http://www.who.int/whr/2008/whr08_en.pdf

Yamamoto, A. (2005), Director of Social Work Services at Children's Hospital Central California, personal correspondence, October 3.

Zahourek, R. P. (2008, November 10). Integrative holism in psychiatric-mental health nursing. *Journal of Psychosocial Nursing, 46*, 31–37.

## Concepts and Questions

1. What are the differences between biomedical medicine and alternative medicine? What assumptions underlie these systems?

2. What do Begley and Ockey mean when they refer to "whole medical systems"?

3. What are the characteristics of culturally and linguistically appropriate health care?

4. How do cultural values affect belief systems about illness and healing?

5. Why is it important for biomedical caregivers to understand and respect traditional and holistic medical processes?

6. How does patient health literacy relate to effective medical treatment?

7. What are some of the language-related problems that can arise when treating patients who do not speak or have limited English proficiency?

8. Why do Begley and Ockey believe it is necessary to increase the cultural diversity of health care professionals?

9. In what ways might a health care provider's cultural background influence his or her interactions with patients from other cultures?

# Culture and Communication in the Classroom

GENEVA GAY

*The final context we will examine is education. This is a setting that continues to grow more culturally diverse. Worldwide, the children of immigrants are being educated in their new homelands. The faces of the people in these schools, and the languages they speak, are as diverse as those found in the business and health care settings. Because educational practices at any level in a multicultural society are affected by the cultural diversity of the classroom, we believe that educators must be proficient in intercultural communication. Traditional approaches to education and the use of a single communication strategy are inadequate in a multicultural context. Cultural diversity affects thinking habits, learning strategies, communication patterns and styles, prejudice and stereotyping, educational expectations, and classroom behavior.*

*In her classic essay "Culture and Communication in the Classroom," Geneva Gay introduces the semiotic relationship that exists among communication, culture, teaching, and learning. From this essay you will (1) learn to recognize some of the critical features and pedagogical potentials for different ethnic groups of color; (2) develop an awareness of some key assertions about culture and communication in teaching and learning in general; (3) understand some of the major characteristics of the communicative modes of African Americans, Native Americans, Asian Americans, and European Americans; (4) learn about how culture influences classroom participation in communication; (5) become aware of the conditions under which they will participate; and (6) see how student classroom participation patterns are governed by culture.*

A semiotic relationship exists among communication, culture, teaching, and learning, and it has profound implications for implementing culturally responsive teaching. This is so because "what we talk about; how we talk about it; what we see, attend to, or ignore; how we think; and what we think about are influenced by our culture ... [and] help to shape, define, and perpetuate our culture" (Porter & Samovar, 1991, p. 21). Making essentially the same argument, Bruner (1996) states that "learning and thinking are always situated in a cultural setting and always dependent upon the utilization of cultural resources" (p. 4). Culture provides the tools to pursue the search for meaning and to convey our understanding to others. Consequently, communication cannot exist without culture, culture cannot be known without communication, and teaching and learning cannot occur without communication or culture.

## INTRODUCTION

The discussions in this article explicate some of the critical features and pedagogical potentials of the culture—communication semiotics for different ethnic groups of color. The ideas and examples presented are composites of group members who strongly identify and affiliate with their ethnic group's cultural traditions. They are not intended to be descriptors of specific individuals within ethnic groups, or their behaviors in all circumstances. If, how, and when these cultural characteristics are expressed in actual behavior, and by whom, are influenced by many different factors. Therefore, the ethnic interactional and communication styles described in this article should be seen as general and traditional referents of group dynamics rather than static attributes of particular individuals.

Students of color who are most traditional in their communication styles and other aspects of culture and ethnicity are likely to encounter more obstacles to school achievement than those who think, behave, and express themselves in ways that approximate school and mainstream cultural norms. This is the case for many highly culturally and ethnically affiliated African Americans. In making this point, Dandy (1991) proposes that the language many African Americans speak "is all too often degraded or simply dismissed by individuals both inside and outside the racial group as being uneducated, illiterate, undignified or simply non-standard" (p. 2). Other groups of color are "at least given credit for having a legitimate language heritage, even if they are denied full access to American life" (p. 2). Much of educators' decision making on the potential and realized achievement of students of color is dependent on communication abilities (their own and the students'). If students are not very proficient in school communication and teachers do not understand or accept the students' cultural communication styles, then their academic performance may be misdiagnosed or trapped in communicative mismatches. Students may know much more than they are able to communicate, or they may be communicating much more than their teachers are able to discern. As Boggs (1985, p. 301) explains, "The attitudes and behavior patterns that have the most important effect upon children... [are] those involved in communication." This communication is multidimensional and multipurposed, including verbal and nonverbal, direct and tacit, literal and symbolic, formal and informal, grammatical and discourse components.

The discussions of culture and communication in classrooms in this article are organized into two parts. The first outlines some key assertions about culture and communication in teaching and learning in general. These help to anchor communication within culturally responsive teaching. In the second part of the article, some of the major characteristics of the communication modes of African, Native, Latino, Asian, and European Americans are presented. The focus throughout these discussions is on discourse dynamics—that is, who participates in communicative interactions and under what conditions, how these participation patterns are affected by cultural socialization, and how they influence teaching and learning in classrooms.

> *Students of color who are most traditional in their communication styles and other aspects of culture and ethnicity are likely to encounter more obstacles to school achievement than those who think, behave, and express themselves in ways that approximate school and mainstream cultural norms.*

## RELATIONSHIP AMONG CULTURE, COMMUNICATION, AND EDUCATION

In analyzing the routine tasks teachers perform, Smith (1971) declares that "teaching is, above all, a linguistic activity" and "language is at the heart of teaching" (p. 24). Whether making assignments, giving directions, explaining events, interpreting words and expressions, proving positions, justifying decisions and actions, making promises, dispensing praise and criticism, or assessing capability, teachers must use language. And the quality of the performance of these tasks is a direct reflection of how well teachers can communicate with their students. Smith admonishes educators for not being more conscientious in recognizing the importance of language in the performance and effectiveness of their duties. He says, "It could be that when we have analyzed the language of teaching and investigated the effects of its various formulations, the art of teaching will show marked advancement" (p. 24). Dandy (1991) likewise places great faith in the power of communication in the classroom, declaring that "teachers have the power to shape the future, if they communicate with their students, but those who cannot communicate are powerless" (p. 10). These effects of communication skills are especially significant to improving the performance of underachieving, ethnically different students.

Porter and Samovar's (1991) study of the nature of culture and communication, the tenacious reciprocity that exists between the two, and the importance of these aspects to intercultural interactions provides valuable information for culturally responsive teaching. They describe communication as "an intricate matrix of interacting social acts that occur in a complex social environment that reflects the way people live and how they come to interact with and get along in their world. This social environment is culture, and if we are to truly understand communication, we must also understand culture" (p. 10). Communication is dynamic, interactive, irreversible, and invariably contextual. As such, it is a continuous, ever-changing activity that takes place between people who are trying to influence each other; its effects are irretrievable once it has occurred, despite efforts to modify or counteract them.

Communication is also governed by the rules of the social and physical contexts in which it occurs (Porter & Samovar, 1991). Culture is the rule-governing system that defines the forms, functions, and content of communication. It is largely responsible for the construction of our "individual repertoires of communicative behaviors and meanings" (p. 10). Understanding connections between culture and communication is critical to improving intercultural interactions. This is so because "as cultures differ from one another, the communication practices and behaviors of individuals reared in those cultures will also be different," and "the degree of influence culture has on intercultural communication is a function of the dissimilarity between the cultures" (p. 12).

Communication entails much more than the content and structure of written and spoken language, and it serves greater purposes than the mere transmission of information. Sociocultural context and nuances, discourse logic and dynamics, delivery styles, social functions, role expectations, norms of interaction, and nonverbal features are as important as (if not more so than) vocabulary, grammar, lexicon, pronunciation, and other linguistic or structural dimensions of communication. This is so because the "form of exchange between child and adult and the conditions in which it occurs will affect not only what is said, but how involved the child will become" (Boggs, 1985, p. 301). Communication is the quintessential way in which humans make meaningful connections with each other, whether in caring, sharing, loving, teaching, or learning. Montague and Matson (1979, p. vii) suggest that it is "the ground of [human] meeting and the foundation of [human] community."

Communication is also indispensable to facilitating knowing and accessing knowledge. This is the central idea of the Sapir–Whorf hypothesis about the relationship among language, thought, and behavior. It says that, far from being simply a means for reporting experience, language is a way of defining experience, thinking, and knowing. In this sense, language is the semantic system of meanings and modes of conveyance that people habitually use to code, analyze, categorize, and interpret experience (Carroll, 1956; Hoijer, 1991; Mandelbaum, 1968). In characterizing this relationship, Sapir (1968) explains that "language is a guide to 'social reality'... [and] a symbolic guide to culture.... It powerfully conditions all of our thinking about social problems and processes" (p. 162). People do not live alone in an "objectified world" or negotiate social realities without the use of language. Nor is language simply a "mechanical" instrumental tool for transmitting information. Instead, human beings are "very much at the mercy of the particular language which has become the medium of expression for their society" (p. 162). The languages used in different cultural systems strongly influence how people think, know, feel, and do.

Whorf (1952, 1956; Carroll, 1956), a student of Sapir, makes a similar argument that is represented by the "principle of linguistic relativity." It contends that the structures of various languages reflect different cultural patterns and values, and, in turn, affect how people understand and respond to social phenomena. In developing these ideas further, Whorf (1952) explains that "a language is not merely a reproducing instrument for voicing ideas but rather is itself the shaper of ideas, the program and guide for the individual's mental activity, for his analysis of impressions, for his synthesis of his mental stock in trade" (p. 5). Vygotsky (1962) also recognizes the reciprocal relationship among language, culture, and thought. He declares, as "indisputable fact," that "thought development is determined by language... and the sociocultural experience of the child" (p. 51).

Moreover, the development of logic is affected by a person's socialized speech, and intellectual growth is contingent on the mastery of social means of thought, or language. According to Byers and Byers (1985), "the organization of the processes of human communication in any culture is a template for the organization of knowledge or information in that culture" (p. 28). This line of argument is applied specifically to different ethnic groups by theorists, researchers, and school practitioners from a variety of disciplinary perspectives, including social and developmental psychology, sociolinguistics, ethnography, and multiculturalism. For example, Ascher (1992) applied this reasoning to language influences on how mathematical relationships are viewed in general. Giamati and Weiland (1997) connected it to Navajo students' learning of mathematics, concluding that the performance difficulties they encounter are "a result of cultural influences on perceptions rather than a lack of ability" (p. 27). This happens because of the reciprocal interactions among language, culture, and perceptions. Consistently, when these scholars refer to "language" or "communication," they are talking more about discourse dynamics than structural forms of speaking and writing.

Thus, languages and communication styles are systems of cultural notations and the means through which thoughts and ideas are expressively embodied. Embedded within them are cultural values and ways of knowing that strongly influence how students engage with learning tasks and demonstrate mastery of them. The absence of shared communicative frames of reference, procedural protocols, rules of etiquette, and discourse systems makes it difficult for culturally diverse students and teachers to genuinely understand each other and for students to fully convey their intellectual abilities. Teachers who do not know or value these realities will not be able to fully access, facilitate, and assess most of what these students know and can do. Communication must be understood to be more than a linguistic system.

> *Thus, languages and communication styles are systems of cultural notations and the means through which thoughts and ideas are expressively embodied. Embedded within them are cultural values and ways of knowing that strongly influence how students engage with learning tasks and demonstrate mastery of them.*

talking. Individual students gain the right to participate in the conversation by permission of the teacher. The verbal discourse is accompanied by nonverbal attending behaviors and speech-delivery mechanisms that require maintaining eye contact with the speaker and using little or no physical movement. Thus, students are expected to be silent and look at teachers when they are talking and wait to be acknowledged before they take their turn at talking. Once permission is granted, they should follow established rules of decorum, such as one person speaking at a time, being brief and to the point, and keeping emotional nuances to a minimum (Kochman, 1981; Philips, 1983).

These structural protocols governing discourse are expressed in other classroom practices as well. Among them are expecting students always to speak in complete sentences that include logical development of thought, precise information, appropriate vocabulary, and careful attention to grammatical features such as appropriate use of vocabulary and noun-verb agreement. Student participation in classroom interactions is often elicited by teachers asking questions that are directed to specific individuals and require a narrow range of information-giving, descriptive responses. It is important for individuals to distinguish themselves in the conversations, for student responses to be restricted to only the specific demands of questions asked, and for the role of speaker and audience to be clearly separated.

## CULTURALLY DIFFERENT DISCOURSE STRUCTURES

In conventional classroom discourse, students are expected to assume what Kochman (1985) calls a *passive-receptive* posture. They are told to listen quietly while the teacher talks. Once the teacher finishes, then the students can respond in some prearranged, stylized way—by asking or answering questions; validating or approving what was said; or taking individual, teacher-regulated turns at

In contrast to the passive-receptive character of conventional classroom discourse, some ethnic groups have communication styles that Kochman (1985) describes as *participatory-interactive*. Speakers expect listeners to engage them actively through vocalized, motion, and movement responses *as they are speaking*. Speakers and listeners are action-provoking partners in the construction of the discourse. These communicative styles have been observed among African Americans, Latinos, and Native Hawaiians. As is the case with other cultural behaviors, they are likely to be more pronounced among individuals who strongly identify and affiliate with their ethnic groups and cultural heritages. For example, low-income and minimally educated members of ethnic groups are likely to manifest group cultural behaviors more thoroughly than those who are middle class and educated. This is so because they have fewer opportunities to interact with people different from themselves and to be affected by the cultural exchanges and adaptations that result from the intermingling of a wide variety of people from diverse ethnic groups and varied experiential backgrounds.

## ETHNIC VARIATIONS IN COMMUNICATION STYLES

Among African Americans, the participatory-interactive style of communicating is sometimes referred to as *call-response* (Asante, 1998; Baber, 1987; Kochman, 1972, 1981, 1985; Smitherman, 1977). It involves listeners' giving encouragement, commentary, compliments, and even criticism to speakers *as they are talking*. The speaker's responsibility is to issue the "calls" (making statements), and the listeners' obligation is to respond in some expressive, and often auditory, way (smiling, vocalizing, looking about, moving around, "amening," and so on) (Dandy, 1991; Smitherman, 1977). When a speaker says something that triggers a response in them (whether positive or negative; affective or cognitive), African American listeners are likely to "talk back." This may involve a vocal or motion response, or both, sent directly to the speaker or shared with neighbors in the audience. Longstreet (1978) and Shade (1994) describe the practice as "breaking in and talking over." This mechanism is used to signal to speakers that their purposes have been accomplished or that it is time to change the direction or leadership of the conversation. Either way, there is no need for the speaker to pursue the particular discourse topic or technique further.

African Americans "gain the floor" or get participatory entry into conversations through personal

> *Among African Americans, the participatory-interactive style of communicating is sometimes referred to as* call-response. *It involves listeners' giving encouragement, commentary, compliments, and even criticism to speakers as they are talking.*

assertiveness, the strength of the impulse to be involved, and the persuasive power of the point they wish to make, rather than waiting for an "authority" to grant permission. They tend to invest their participation with personality power, actions, and emotions. Consequently, African Americans are often described as verbal performers whose speech behaviors are fueled by personal advocacy, emotionalism, fluidity, and creative variety (Abrahams, 1970; Baber, 1987). These communication facilities have been attributed to the oral/aural nature of African American cultural and communal value orientations (Pasteur & Toldson, 1982; Smitherman, 1977). Many teachers view these behaviors negatively, as "rude," "inconsiderate," "disruptive," and "speaking out of turn," and they penalize students for them.

Native Hawaiian students who maintain their traditional cultural practices use a participatory-interactive communicative style similar to the call-response of African Americans. Called "talk-story" or "co-narrative," it involves several students working collaboratively, or talking together, to create an idea, tell a story, or complete a learning task (Au, 1980, 1993; Au & Kawakami, 1985, 1991, 1994; Au & Mason, 1981; Boggs, Watson-Gegeo, & McMillen, 1985). After observing these behaviors among elementary students, Au (1993) concluded that "what seems important to Hawaiian children in talk-story is not individual... but group performance in speaking" (p. 114). These communication preferences are consistent with the importance Native Hawaiian culture places on individuals' contributing to the well-being of family and friends instead of working only for their own betterment (Gallimore, Boggs, & Jordon, 1974; Tharp & Gallimore, 1988).

A communicative practice that has some of the same traits of call-response and talk-story has been observed among European American females. Tannen (1990) calls it "cooperative overlapping" and describes it as women "talking along with speakers to show participation and support" (p. 208). It occurs most often in situations where talk is casual and friendly. This rapport-talk is used to create community. It is complemented by other traditional women's ways of communicating, such as the following:

- Being "audience" more often than "speaker" in that they are recipients of information provided by males
- Deemphasizing expertise and the competitiveness it generates
- Focusing on individuals in establishing friendships, networks, intimacy, and relationships more than exhibiting power, accomplishment, or control
- Negotiating closeness in order to give and receive confirmation, support, and consensus
- Avoiding conflict and confrontation (Belensky, Clinchy, Goldberger, & Tarule, 1986; Klein, 1982; Maltz & Borker, 1983; Tannen, 1990)

While these habits of "communal communication and interaction" are normal to the users, they can be problematic to classroom teachers. On first encounter, they may be perceived as "indistinguishable noise and chaos" or unwholesome dependency. Even after the shock of the initial encounter passes, teachers may still consider these forms of communication socially deviant, not conducive to constructive intellectual engagement, rude, and insulting. They see them as obstructing individual initiative and preempting the right of each student to have a fair chance to participate in instructional discourse. These assessments can prompt attempts to rid students of the habits and replace them with the rules of individualistic, passive-receptive, and controlling communication styles predominant in classrooms.

Teachers may not realize that by doing this they could be causing irreversible damage to students' abilities or inclinations to engage fully in the instructional process. Hymes (1985) made this point when he suggested that rejecting ethnically different students' communication styles might be perceived by them as rejection of their personhood. Whether intentional or not, casting these kinds of aspersions on the identity and personal worth of students of color does not bode well for their academic achievement.

## Problem Solving and Task Engagement

Many African American, Latino, Native American, and Asian American students use styles of inquiry and responding that are different from those employed most often in classrooms. The most common practice among teachers is to ask convergent (single-answer) questions and use deductive approaches to solving problems. Emphasis is given to details, to building the whole from the parts, to moving from the specific to the general. Discourse tends to be didactic, involving one student with the teacher at a time (Goodlad, 1984). In comparison, students of color who are strongly affiliated with their traditional cultures tend to be more inductive, interactive, and communal in task performance. The preference for inductive problem solving is expressed as reasoning from the whole to parts, from the general to the specific. The focus is on the "big picture," the pattern, the principle (Boggs et al., 1985; Philips, 1983; Ramirez & Castañeda, 1974; Shade 1989).

Although these general patterns of task engagement prevail across ethnic groups, variations do exist. Some teachers use inductive modes of teaching, and some students within each ethnic group of color learn deductively. Many Asian American students seem to prefer questions that require specific answers but are proposed to the class as a whole. Many Latino students may be inclined toward learning in group contexts, but specific individuals may find these settings distracting and obstructive to their task mastery.

In traditional African American and Latino cultures, problem solving is highly contextual. One significant feature of this contextuality is creating a "stage" or "setting" prior to the performance of a task. The stage setting is invariably social in nature. It involves establishing personal connections with others who will participate as a prelude to addressing the task. In making these connections, individuals are readying themselves for "work" by cultivating a social context. They are, in effect, activating their cultural

*Many African American, Latino, Native American, and Asian American students use styles of inquiry and responding that are different from those employed most often in classrooms.*

socialization concept that an individual functions better within the context of a group. Without the group as an anchor, referent, and catalyst, the individual is set adrift, having to function alone.

These cultural inclinations may be operating when Latino adults begin their task interactions with colleagues by inquiring about the families of other participants and their own personal well-being or when African American speakers inform the audience about their present psychoemotional disposition and declare the ideology, values, and assumptions underlying the positions they will be taking in the presentation (i.e., "where they are coming from"). This "preambling" is a way for the speakers to prime the audience and themselves for the subsequent performance. Students of color may be setting the stage for their engagement with learning tasks in classrooms (such as writing an essay, doing seatwork, or taking a test) when they seem to be spending unnecessary time arranging their tests, sharpening pencils, shifting their body postures (stretching, flexing their hands, arms, and legs, etc.), or socializing with peers rather than attending to the assigned task. "Preparation before performance" for these students serves a similar purpose in learning as a theater performer doing yoga exercises before taking the stage. Both are techniques the "actors" use to focus, to get themselves in the mood and mode to perform.

Those Asian Americans who prefer to learn within the context of groups use a process of *collaborative and negotiated problem solving*. Regardless of how minor or significant an issue is, they seek out opinions and proposed solutions from all members of the constituted group. Each individual's ideas are presented and critiqued. Their merits are weighed against those suggested by every other member of the group. Discussions are animated and expansive so that all parties participate and understand the various elements of the negotiations. Eventually, a solution is reached that is a compromise of several possibilities. Then more discussions follow to ensure that everyone is in agreement with the solution and understands who is responsible for what aspects of its implementation. These discussions proceed in a context of congeniality and *consensus building* among the many, not with animosity, domination, and the imposition of the will of a few.

A compelling illustration of the positive effects of this process on student achievement occurred in Treisman's (1985; Fullilove & Treisman, 1990) Mathematics Workshop Program at the University of California, Berkeley. He observed the study habits of Chinese Americans to determine why they performed so well in high-level mathematics classes and if he could use their model with Latinos and African Americans. He found what others have observed more informally—the Chinese American students always studied in groups, and they routinely explained to each other their understanding of the problems and how they arrived at solutions to them. Treisman attributed their high achievement to the time they devoted to studying and to talking through their solutions with peers. When he simulated this process with African Americans and Latinos, their achievement improved radically. Treisman was convinced that "group study" made the difference. Given other evidence that compatibility between cultural habits and teaching/learning styles improves student performance, this is probably what occurred. Communal problem solving and the communicative impulse were evoked, thus producing the desired results.

These are powerful but challenging pedagogical lessons for all educators to learn and emulate in teaching students of color. Collective and situated performance styles require a distribution of resources (timing, collective efforts, procedures, attitudes) that can collide with school norms; for instance, much of how student achievement is assessed occurs in tightly scheduled arrangements, which do not accommodate stage setting or collective performance. Students of color have to learn different styles of performing, as well as the substantive content, to demonstrate their achievement. This places them in potential double jeopardy—that is, failing at the level of both procedure and substance. Pedagogical reform must be cognizant of these dual needs and attend simultaneously to the content of learning and the processes for demonstrating mastery. It also must be bidirectional— that is, changing instructional practices to make them more culturally responsive to ethnic and cultural diversity while teaching students of color how to better negotiate mainstream educational structures.

## Organizing Ideas in Discourse

In addition to mode, the actual process of discourse engagement is influenced by culture and, in turn, influences the performance of students in schools. Several elements of the dynamics of discourse are discussed here to illustrate this point: organizing ideas, taking positions, conveying imagery and affect through language, and gender variations in conversational styles. How ideas and thoughts are organized in written and spoken expression can be very problematic to student achievement. Two techniques are commonly identified—*topic-centered* and *topic-associative*, or *topic-chaining*, techniques. European Americans seem to prefer the first while Latinos, African Americans, Native Americans, and Native Hawaiians (Au, 1993; Heath, 1983) are inclined toward the second.

In *topic-centered* discourse, speakers focus on one issue at a time; arrange facts and ideas in logical, linear order; and make explicit relationships between facts and ideas. In this process, cognitive processing moves deductively from discrete parts to a cumulative whole with a discernible closure. Quality is determined by clarity of descriptive details, absence of unnecessary or flowery elaboration, and how well explanations remain focused on the essential features of the issue being analyzed. The structure, content, and delivery of this discourse style closely parallel the expository, descriptive writing and speaking commonly used in schools. A classic example of topic-centered discourse is journalistic writing, which concentrates on giving information about who, what, when, where, why, and how as quickly as possible. Its purpose is to convey information and to keep this separate from other speech functions, such as persuasion, commentary, and critique. Another illustration is the thinking and writing associated with empirical inquiry, or critical problem solving. Again, there is a hierarchical progression in the communication sequence—identifying the problem, collecting data, identifying alternative solutions and related consequences, and selecting and defending a solution. There is a clear attempt to separate facts from opinions, information from emotions.

A *topic-associative style* of talking and writing is episodic, anecdotal, thematic, and integrative. More than one issue is addressed at once. Related explanations unfold in overlapping, intersecting loops, with one emerging out of and building on others. Relationships among segments of the discourse are assumed or inferred rather than explicitly established (Cazden, 1988; Lee & Slaughter-Defoe, 1995). Thinking and speaking appear to be circular and seamless rather than linear and clearly demarcated. For one who is unfamiliar with it, this communication style sounds rambling, disjointed, and as if the speaker never ends a thought before going to something else.

Goodwin (1990) observed topic-chaining discourse at work in a mixed-age (4- to 14-year-olds) group of African Americans in a Philadelphia neighborhood as they told stories, shared gossip, settled arguments, and negotiated relationships. She noted the ease and finesse with which a child could switch from a contested verbal exchange to an engaging story and dramatically reshape dyadic interactions into multiparty ones. Using a single utterance, the children could evoke a broad history of events, a complex web of identities and relationships that all participants understood without having elaborate details on any of the separate segments. The talk-story discourse style among Native Hawaiians operates in a similar fashion, which explains why Au (1993) characterizes it as a "joint performance, or the cooperative production of responses by two or more speakers" (p. 113).

Two other commonplace examples are indicative of a topic-chaining or associative discourse style. One is used by many African Americans, who literarily try to attach or connect the sentences in a paragraph to each through the prolific use of conjunctive words and phrases—for example, frequently beginning sentences with "consequently," "therefore," "however," "thus," "moreover," "additionally," and "likewise." These sentences are in close proximity to each other—sometimes as often as four of every five or six.

The second example illuminates the storytelling aspect of topic-chaining discourse. African Americans (Kochman, 1981, 1985; Smitherman, 1977) and Native Hawaiians (Boggs, 1985) have been described as not responding directly to questions asked. Instead, they give narratives, or tell stories. This involves setting up and describing a series of events (and the participants) loosely connected to the questions asked. It is as if ideas and thoughts, like individuals, do not function or find meaning in isolation from context. A host of other actors and events are evoked to assist in constructing the "stage" upon which the individuals eventually interject their own performance (i.e., answer the question). This narrative-response style is also signaled by the attention given to "introductions" and preludes in writing. They are extensive enough to prompt such comments from teachers as "Get to the point" or "Is this relevant?" or "More focus needed" or "Too much extraneous stuff" or "Stick to the topic." The students simply think that these preludes are necessary to setting the stage for the substantive elements of the discourse.

## Storytelling as Topic-Chaining Discourse

Speaking about the purposes and pervasiveness of storytelling among African Americans, Smitherman (1977) surmises that they allow many different things to be accomplished at once. These include relating information, persuading others to support the speaker's point of view, networking, countering opposition, exercising power, and demonstrating one's own verbal aestheticism. She elaborates further:

> An ordinary inquiry [to African American cultural speakers] is likely to elicit an extended narrative response where the abstract point or general message will be couched in concrete story form. The reporting of events is never simply objectively reported, but dramatically acted out and narrated. The Black English speaker thus simultaneously conveys the facts and his or her personal sociopsychological perspective on the facts.... This meandering away from the "point" takes the listener on episodic journeys and over tributary rhetorical routes, but like the flow of nature's rivers and streams, stories all eventually lead back to the source. Though highly applauded by Blacks, this narrative linguistic style is exasperating to Whites who wish you'd be direct and hurry up and get to the point. (pp. 148, 161)

It takes African American topic-chaining speakers a while to get to the point—to orchestrate the cast of contributors to the action. The less time they have to develop their storylines, the more difficult it is for them to get to the substantive heart of the matter. Frequently in schools, the time allocated to learning experiences lapses while African Americans are still setting up the backdrop for "the drama"—their expected task performance—and they never get to

demonstrate what they know or can do on the proposed academic task.

Posed to an African American student who routinely uses a topic-chaining discourse style, a simple, apparently straightforward question such as "What did you do during summer vacation?" might prompt a response such as the following:

> Sometimes, especially on holidays, you know, like July 4, or maybe when a friend was celebrating a birthday, we go to the amusement park. It's a long ways from where I live. And, that is always a big thing, because we have to get together and form car caravans. Jamie and Kelly are the best drivers, but I preferred to ride with Aisha because her dad's van is loaded, and we be just riding along, chilling, and listening to tapes and stuff. Going to the amusement park was a kick 'cause we had to drive a long way, and when we got there people would stare at us like we were weird or something. And we would just stare right back at them. All but Dion. He would start to act crazy, saying things like "What you lookin' at me for? I ain't no animal in no zoo. I got as much right to be here as you do." You see, Dion gets hyped real quick about this racist thing. And we be telling him, "Man, cool it. Don't start no stuff. We too far from home for that." Then, we just go on into the park and have us a good time. We try to get all the rides before everything closes down for the night. Then, there's the trip home. Everybody be tired but happy. We do this three or four times in the summer. Different people go each time. But, you know something—we always run into some kind of funny stuff, like people expecting us to make trouble. Why is that so? All we doing is out for a good time. Dion, of course, would say it's a racist thing.

The narrator does eventually answer the question, but it is embedded in a lot of other details. In fact, there are stories within stories within stories (celebration rituals, friendships, drivers, the drive, racism, risk taking, activities at the amusement park, similarities and differences, continuity and change, etc.). These elaborate details are needed to convey the full meaning of the narrator's answer to the initial question. But to culturally uninitiated listeners or readers, such as many classroom teachers, the account sounds like rambling and unnecessarily convoluted information, or Smitherman's (1977) notion of "belabored verbosity" (p. 161).

Teachers seeking to improve the academic performance of students of color who use topic-associative discourse styles need to incorporate a storytelling motif into their instructional behaviors. This can be done without losing any of the substantive quality of academic discourses. Gee (1989) believes topic-associative talking is inherently more complex, literary, and enriching than topic-centered speech. The assertions are verified by the success of the Kamehameha Early Elementary Program, which produced remarkable improvement in the literacy achievement of Hawaiian students by employing their cultural and communication styles in classroom instruction. Boggs (1985) found that the performance of Native Hawaiian students on the reading readiness tests correlated positively with narrative abilities. The children who told longer narratives more correctly identified the picture prompts than those who responded to individually directed questions from adults.

Yet topic-associative discourse is troubling to many conventional teachers. Michaels and Cazden's (1986) research explains why. The European American teachers who participated in their study found this discourse style difficult to understand and placed little value on it. African American teachers gave equal positive value to topic-centered and topic-associative discourse. We should not assume that this will always be the case. Some African American teachers are as troubled by topic-chaining discourse among students as teachers from other ethnic groups. The ethnicity of teachers is not the most compelling factor in culturally responsive teaching for ethnically diverse students. Rather, it is teachers' knowledge base and positive attitudes about cultural diversity, and their recognition of diverse cultural contributions, experiences, and perspectives, which enhance their ability to teach ethnically diverse students effectively.

> *Teachers seeking to improve the academic performance of students of color who use topic-associative discourse styles need to incorporate a storytelling motif into their instructional behaviors.*

## Taking Positions and Presenting Self

In addition to significant differences in the *organization* of thinking, writing, and talking, many ethnically diverse students *relate* differently to the materials, issues, and topic discussed or analyzed. Most of the information available on these patterns deals with African and European Americans. Not much research has been done on the discourse dynamics of Latinos and Native Americans. Deyhle and Swisher (1997) concluded their historical view of research conducted on Native Americans with a strong conviction that there are fundamental and significant linkages among culture, communication, and cognition that should help shape classroom instruction for ethnically diverse students. But they do not provide any descriptions of the discourse dynamics of various Native American groups. Fox (1994) examined the thinking, writing, and speaking behavior of international students from different countries in Africa, Asia, Latin America, and the Middle East studying in U.S. colleges and universities. She found that their cultural traditions valued indirect and holistic communication, wisdom of the past, and the importance of the group. Their cultural socialization profoundly affects how these students interact with professors and classmates, reading materials, problem solving, and writing assignments. How they write is especially important to their academic performance because, according to Fox (1994), "writing touches the heart of a student's identity, drawing its voice and strength and meaning from the way the student understands the world" (p. xiii).

## Personalizing or Objectifying Communications

Kochman (1972, 1981, 1985), Dandy (1991), and Smitherman (1977) point out that African Americans (especially those most strongly affiliated with the ethnic identity and cultural heritage) tend to take positions of advocacy and express personal points of view in discussions. Facts, opinions, emotions, and reason are combined in presenting one's case. The worth of a particular line of reasoning is established by challenging the validity of oppositional ideas and by the level of personal ownership of the individuals making the presentations. Declaring one's personal position on issues, and demanding the same of others, is also a way of recognizing "the person" as a valid data source (Kochman, 1981). Publication is not enough to certify the authority of ideas and explanations, or the expertise of the people who author them. They must stand the test of critical scrutiny and the depth of personal endorsement.

Consequently, Kochman (1981) proposes that African Americans are more likely to challenge authority and expertise than students from other ethnic groups. He suggests the following reason for this:

> Blacks … consider debate to be as much a contest between individuals as a test of opposing ideas. Because it is a contest, attention is also paid to performance, for winning the contest requires that one outperform one's opponents; outthink, outtalk, and outstyle. It means being concerned with art as well as argument.… [B]lacks consider it essential for individuals to have personal positions on issues and assume full responsibility for arguing their validity. Otherwise, they feel that individuals would not care enough about truth or their own ideas to want to struggle for them. And without such struggle, the value of ideas cannot be ascertained. (pp. 24–25)

According to Kochman (1981), the discourse dynamics of European Americans are almost the opposite of African Americans. He says they relate to issues and materials as spokespersons, not advocates, and consider the truth or merits of an idea to be intrinsic, especially if the person presenting it has been certified as an authority or expert. How deeply individuals personally care about the idea is irrelevant. Their responsibility is to present the facts as accurately as possible. They believe that emotions interfere with one's capacity to reason and quality of reasoning. Thus, European Americans try to avoid or minimize opposition in dialogue (especially when members of ethnic minority groups are involved) because they assume it will be confrontational, divisive, and lead to intransigence or the further entrenchment of opposing viewpoints. They aim to control impulse and emotions, to be open-minded and flexible, and to engage a multiplicity of ideas. Since no person is privy to all the answers, the best way to cull the variety of possibilities is to ensure congeniality, not confrontation, in conversation. As a result of these beliefs and desires, the European American style of intellectual and discourse engagement "weakens or eliminates those aspects of character or posture that they believe keep people's minds closed and make them otherwise unyielding" (Kochman, 1981, p. 20).

## Playing With and On Words

African American cultural discourse uses repetition for emphasis and to create a cadence in speech delivery that approximates other aspects of cultural expressiveness such as dramatic flair, powerful imagery, persuasive effect, and polyrhythmic patterns (Baber, 1987; Kochman, 1981; Smitherman, 1977). Some individuals are very adept at "playing on" and "playing with" words, thereby creating a "polyrhythmic character" to their speaking. It is conveyed through the use of nonparallel structures, juxtaposition of complementary opposites, inclusion of a multiplicity of "voices," manipulation of word meanings, poetic tonality, creative use of word patterns, and an overall playfulness in language usage. Although decontextualized, this statement written by a graduate student illustrates some of these tendencies: "The use of culturally consistent communicative competencies entails teachers being able to recognize the multitude of distinct methods of communication that African American students bring to the classroom." Another example of these discourse habits is the frequent use of verb pairs. Following are some samples selected from the writings of students:

*The discourse dynamics of European Americans are almost the opposite of African Americans.*

- A number of public issues to be explored and represented
- Numerous factors have impacted and influenced
- Make an attempt to analyze and interpret
- No model is available to interpret and clarify
- Many ways of explaining and understanding

- A framework that will enable and facilitate
- Validity was verified and confirmed
- He will describe and give account

Two other examples are helpful in illustrating the dramatic flair and poetic flavor of playing with words that characterize African American cultural discourse. One comes from Smart-Grosvenor (1982), who describes African American cultural communication as "a metaphorical configuration of verbal nouns, exaggerated adjectives, and double descriptives" (p. 138).

She adds (and in the process demonstrates that which she explains) that "ours is an exciting, practical, elegant, dramatic, ironic, mysterious, surrealistic, sanctified, outrageous, and creative form of verbal expression. It is a true treasure trove of vitality, profundity, rhythm—and, yes, style" (p. 138). Smitherman (1972) provides a second example of African American discourse style and aestheticism. She writes:

> The power of the word lies in its enabling us to translate vague feelings and fleeting experiences into forms that give unity, coherence, and expression to the inexpressible. The process of composing becomes a mechanism for discovery wherein we may generate illuminating revelations about a particular idea or event. (p. 91)

## Ambivalence and Distancing in Communication

Classroom experiences and personal conversations with Asian international and Asian American college students and professional colleagues reveal some recurrent communication features. These individuals tend not to declare either definitive advocacy or adversarial positions in either oral or written discourse. They take moderate stances, seek out compromise positions, and look for ways to accommodate opposites. They are rather hesitant to analyze and critique but will provide factually rich descriptions of issues and events. They also use a great number of "hedges" and conciliatory markers in conversations—that is, "starts and stops," affiliative words, and apologetic nuances interspersed in speech, such as "I'm not sure," "maybe ...," "I don't know, but ...," "I may be wrong, but...." These behaviors give the appearance of tentative, unfinished thinking, even though the individuals using them are very intellectually capable and thoroughly prepared academically. And many Asian and Asian American students are virtually silent in classroom discussions.

I have observed Asian and Asian American students frequently interjecting laughter into conversations with me about their academic performance. This happens in instructional and advising situations in which students are having difficulty understanding a learning task that is being explained by the teacher. Rather than reveal the full extent of their confusion, or lack of understanding, students will interject laughter into the conversations. It functions to defuse the intensity of their confusion and give the impression that the problem is not as serious as it really is. Teachers who are unaware of what is going on may interpret these behaviors to mean the students are not taking their feedback or advice seriously. Or they may assume that the students understand the issue so completely that they have reached a point in their intellectual processing where they can relax and break the mental focus (signaled by laughter). When queried about this practice, students invariably say, "It's cultural" and often add an explanation for it that invokes some rule of social etiquette or interpersonal interaction that is taught in their ethnic communities. Interestingly, Japanese, Chinese, Korean, Taiwanese, and Cambodians offer similar explanations about the motivation behind and meaning of this shared behavior. These students explain that "ritualized laughter" is a means of maintaining harmonious relationships and avoiding challenging the authority or disrespecting the status of the teacher.

These communication behaviors among students of Asian origin are consistent with those reported by Fox (1994). Hers were gleaned from observations, interviews, and working with students from non-Western cultures and countries (Fox refers to them as "world majority students") on their analytical writing skills in basic writing courses at the Center for International Education at the University of Massachusetts. Data were collected over three years. Sixteen graduate students from several different disciplines participated in the formal interviews. They represented twelve countries: Korea, Japan, the People's Republic of China, Nepal, Indonesia, Brazil, India, Chile, Sri Lanka, Cote d'Ivoire, Somalia, and Cape Verde.

Faculty members who worked closely with these students were also interviewed. Additional information was derived from informal conversations and interactions with other students; analysis of writing samples; the teacher's notes about how she and the students worked through writing difficulties; and students' explanations about what they were trying to say in their writing, why assignments were misunderstood, and connections among language, culture, and writing.

Among these students from different countries, several common writing habits emerged that conflict with formal writing styles of academe, known variously as academic argument, analytical or critical writing, and scholarly discourse (Fox, 1994). The characteristics and concerns included:

- Much background information and imprecise commentary

- Exaggeration for effect

- Prolific use of transitional markers, such as "moreover," "nevertheless," and "here again"

- Preference for contemplative instead of action words

- Much meandering around and digressions from the primary topic of discussion

- Emphasis on surrounding context rather than the subject itself

- Being suggestive and trying to convey feelings instead of being direct and concise and providing proof or specific illustrations, as is the expectation of academic writing in the United States

- Tendency to communicate through subtle implications

- Great detail and conversational tonality

- Elaborate and lengthy introductions

- Reticence to speak out, to declare personal positions, and to make one's own ideas prominent in writing

Although all the students shared these communication tendencies, according to Fox's (1994) study, how they were expressed in actual behaviors varied widely. Culturally different meanings of "conversational tone" illustrate this point. Fox notes:

> In Spanish or Portuguese ... speakers and writers may be verbose, rambling, digressive, holistic, full of factual details, full of feeling, sometimes repetitious, sometimes contradictory, without much concern for literal meanings. In many Asian and African languages and cultures, metaphor, euphemism, innuendo, hints, insinuation, and all sorts of subtle nonverbal strategies—even silence—are used both to spare the listeners possible embarrassment or rejection, and to convey meanings that they are expected to grasp. (p. 22)

These descriptions of Asian American and non-Western student discourse are based on observations and conversations with a small number of people, in college classes and professional settings. How widespread they are across other educational settings, ethnic groups, generations of immigrants, and social circumstances is yet to be determined. Much more description and substantiation of these communicative inclinations are needed.

The explanation of Asian students that their discourse styles are cultural is elaborated by Chan (1991), Kitano and Daniels (1995), and Nakanishi (1994). They point to traditional values and socialization that emphasize collectivism, saving face, maintaining harmony, filial piety, interdependence, modesty in self-presentation, and restraint in taking oppositional points of view. Leung (1998) suggests some ways these values translate to behavior in learning situations, which underscore the observations made by Fox. Students socialized in this way are less likely to express individual thoughts, broadcast their individual accomplishments, and challenge or disagree with people in positions of authority, especially in public arenas. These interpretations echo the connections between Asian American culture and communicative styles provided by Kim (1978). She suggests that one of their major functions is to promote social harmony and build community. Consequently, many Asian American students may avoid confrontations as well as the expression of negative feelings or opinions in classroom discourse.

## GENDER VARIATIONS IN DISCOURSE STYLES

Most of the detailed information on gender variations in classroom communication involves European Americans. Some inferences can be made about probable gender discourse styles among African, Latino, Native, and Asian Americans from their cultural values and gender socialization, since culture and communication are closely interrelated.

## Females Communicate Differently from Males

Lakoff (1975) was among the first to suggest that different lexical, syntactical, pragmatic, and discourse features existed for females and males. She identified nine speech traits prolific among females that are summarized by L. Crawford (1993) as specialized vocabulary for homemaking and caregiving, mild forms of expletives, adjectives that convey emotional reactions but no substantive information, tag comments that are midway between questions and statements, exaggerated expressiveness, super polite forms, hedges or qualifiers, hypercorrect grammar, and little use of humor.

Other research indicates that European American females use more affiliating, accommodating, and socially bonding language mechanisms, while males are more directive, managing, controlling, task focused, and action oriented in their discourse styles. Girls speak more politely and tentatively, use less forceful words, are less confrontational, and are less intrusive when they enter into conversations. By comparison, boys interrupt more; use more commands, threats, and boast of authority; and give information more often (Austin, Salem, & Leffler, 1987; M. Crawford, 1995; Grossman & Grossman, 1994; Hoyenga & Hoyenga, 1979; Maccoby, 1988; Simkins-Bullock & Wildman, 1991; Tannen, 1994). Because of these gender patterns, Maccoby (1988) concludes that "speech serves more egotistic functions among boys and more socially binding functions among girls" (p. 758).

These general trends were substantiated by Johnstone (1993) in a study of spontaneous conversational storytelling of men and women friends. The women's stories tended to be about groups of people (women and men) engaged in supportive relationships and the importance of community building. The men's stories were more about conquests (physical, social, nature) in which individuals acted alone. Invariably, the characters were nameless men who did little talking but engaged in some kind of physical action. More details were given about places, times, and things than about people. Based on these findings, Johnstone suggests that women are empowered through cooperation, interdependence, collaboration, and community. For men, power comes from individuals "conquering" and acting in opposition to others.

Research by Gray-Schlegel and Gray-Schlegel (1995–1996) on the creative writing of third- and sixth-grade students produced similar results. They examined 170 creative writing samples of eighty-seven students to determine if differences existed in how control, outcomes, relationships, and violence were used. Clear gender patterns emerged. Both boys and girls placed male characters in active roles more often than females, but this tendency increased with age only for the males. Females were more optimistic about the fate of their characters, while males were inclined to be cynical. Boys usually had their protagonists acting alone, while girls had them acting in conjunction with others. Regardless of age or the gender of the story character, boys included more crime and violence in their narratives.

## Gender Communication Patterns Established Early in Life

These kinds of gender-related discourse patterns are established well before third grade, as research by Nicolopoulou, Scales, and Weintraub (1994) revealed. They examined the symbolic imagination of four-year-olds as expressed in the kinds of stories they told. The girls' stories included more order and social realism. These concepts were conveyed through the use of coherent plots with stable characters, continuous plot lines, and social and familial relationships as the primary topics of and contexts for problem solving. Their stories emphasized cyclical patterns of everyday domestic life, along with romantic and fairy tale images of kings and queens, princesses and princes. They were carefully constructed, centered, and coherent, with elaborate character and theme development, and were invariably directed toward harmonious conflict resolution.

Whenever threatening disruptive situations occurred, the girls were careful to reestablish order before concluding their stories. The boys' stories contained much more disorder and a picaresque, surrealistic aesthetic style. These traits were apparent in the absence of stable, clearly defined characters, relationships, and plots; large, powerful, and frightening characters; violence, disruption, and conflict; and a series of loosely associated dramatic images, actions, and events.

The boys were not concerned with resolving conflicts before their stories ended. Instead, action, novelty, excess, defiance, destruction, and often escalating and startling imagery drove their plots.

In summarizing differences between how boys and girls construct stories, Nicolopoulou and associates (1994) made some revealing observations that should inform instructional practices. They noted that the stories produced by girls focused on "creating, maintaining, and elaborating structure." In comparison, the stories boys told emphasized "action and excitement" and involved a restless energy that is often difficult for them to manage (p. 110). Furthermore, the boys and girls dealt with danger, disorder, and conflict very differently. The girls' strategy was *implicit avoidance* while the boys' technique was *direct confrontation*.

Another fascinating verification of theorized gender differences in communication is provided by Otnes, Kim, and Kim (1994). They analyzed 344 letters written to Santa Claus (165 from boys and 179 from girls). Although the age of the authors was not specified, they were probably eight years old or younger, since children stop believing in Santa Claus at about this time. The content of the letters was analyzed to determine the use of six kinds of semantic units, or meaning phrases: (1) polite or socially accepted forms of ingratiation, (2) context-oriented references, (3) direct requests, (4) requests accompanied by qualifiers, (5) affectionate appeals, and (6) altruistic requests of gifts for someone other than self. For the most part, results of the study confirmed the hypothesized expectations. Girls wrote longer letters, made more specific references to Christmas, were more polite, used more indirect requests, and included more

> *Early gender patterns of communication may transfer to other kinds of social and educational interactions. They also can entrench disadvantages that will have long-term negative effects on student achievement.*

expressions of affection. By comparison, boys made more direct requests. There were no differences between boys and girls in the number of toys requested or the altruistic appeals made. Findings such as these provide evidence about the extent and persistence of patterns of culturally socialized communicative behaviors.

Early gender patterns of communication may transfer to other kinds of social and educational interactions. They also can entrench disadvantages that will have long-term negative effects on student achievement. Interventions to achieve more comparable communications skills for male and female students should begin early and continue throughout the school years. Efforts should also be undertaken in both research and classroom situations to determine if or how communicative styles are differentiated by gender in ethnic groups other than European Americans. Undoubtedly some differences do exist, since discourse styles are influenced by cultural socialization, and males and females are socialized to communicate differently in various ethnic groups.

## Problems with Gendered Communication Styles

The "gendered" style of communication may be more problematic than the gender of the person involved in the communication. If this is so, then a female who is adept at using discourse techniques typically associated with males will not be disadvantaged in mainstream social interactions. Conversely, males who communicate in ways usually ascribed to females will lose their privileged status. Hoyenga and Hoyenga (1979) offer some support for this premise. In their review of research on gender and communication, they report that "feminine communication styles" are associated with less intelligence, passivity, and submissiveness, while "masculine styles" evoke notions of power, authority, confidence, and leadership.

However, M. Crawford (1995) suggests that some of the claims about female–male communication differences need to be reconsidered. For example, indirectness and equivocation in communication are not inherently strategies of female subordination or dominance. They can be tools of power or powerlessness as well. Interpretations of speech behaviors may depend more on the setting, the speaker's status and communicative ability, and the relationship to listeners rather than the person's gender per se (Tannen, 1994). Sadker and Sadker (1994) propose that males may be at greater *emotional risk* than females because of their role socialization. Girls are encouraged to be caring and emotionally expressive, but boys are taught to deny their feelings and to be overly cautious about demonstrating how deeply they care. Thus, male advantages in conventional conceptions of academic discourse may be countered somewhat by the psychoemotional and social advantages that females have in interpersonal relations.

## CONCLUSION

Communication is strongly culturally influenced, experientially situated, and functionally strategic. It is a dynamic set of skills and performing arts whose rich nuances and delivery styles are open to many interpretations and instructional possibilities. Ethnic discourse patterns are continually negotiated because people talk in many different ways for many different reasons. Sometimes the purpose of talking and writing is simply to convey information. It is also used to persuade and entertain; to demonstrate sharing, caring, and connections; to express contentment and discontentment; to empower and subjugate; to teach and learn; and to convey reflections and declare personal preferences. In imagining and implementing culturally responsive pedagogical reform, teachers should not merely make girls talk more like boys, or boys talk more like girls, or all individuals within and across ethnic groups talk like each other. Nor should they assume that all gender differences in communication styles are subsumed by ethnicity or think that gender, social class, and education obliterate all ethnic nuances. Instead, we must be mindful that communication styles are multidimensional and multimodal, shaped by many different influences. Although culture is paramount among these, other critical influences include ethnic affiliation, gender, social class, personality, individuality, and experiential context.

The information in this essay has described some of the patterns, dynamics, and polemics of the discourse styles of different ethnicities and groups. Since communication is essential to both teaching and learning, it is imperative that it be a central part of instructional reforms designed to improve the school performance of underachieving African, Native, Asian, and European American students. The more teachers know about the discourse styles of ethnically diverse students, the better they will be able to improve academic achievement. Change efforts should attend especially to discourse dynamics as opposed to linguistic structures. The reforms should be directed toward creating better agreement between the communication patterns of underachieving ethnically diverse students and those considered "normal" in schools.

Knowledge about general communication patterns among ethnic groups is helpful, but it alone is not enough. Teachers need to translate it to their own particular instructional situations. This contextualization might begin with some self-study exercises in which teachers examine their preferred discourse modes and dynamics, and determine how students from different ethnic groups respond to them. They should also learn to recognize the discourse habits of students from different ethnic groups. The purposes of these analyses are to identify (1) habitual discourse features of ethnically diverse students; (2) conflictual and complementary points among these discourse styles; (3) how, or if, conflictual points are negotiated by students; and (4) features of the students' discourse patterns that are problematic for the teacher. The results can be used to pinpoint and prioritize specific places to begin interventions for change.

Whether conceived narrowly or broadly, and expressed formally or informally, communication is the quintessential medium of teaching and learning. It is also inextricably linked to culture and cognition. Therefore, if teachers are to better serve the school achievement needs of ethnically diverse students by implementing culturally responsive teaching, they must learn how to communicate differently with them. To the extent they succeed in doing this, achievement problems could be reduced significantly.

# References

Abrahams, R. D. (1970). *Positively Black*. Englewood Cliffs, NJ: Prentice-Hall.

Asante, M. K. (1998). *The afrocentric idea* (Rev. and exp. ed.). Philadelphia: Temple University Press.

Ascher, M. (1992). *Ethnomathematics*. New York: Freeman.

Au, K. R. (1980). Participation structures in a reading lesson with Hawaiian children: Analysis of a culturally appropriate instructional event. *Anthropology and Education Quarterly, 11*, 91–115.

Au, K. R. (1993). *Literacy instruction in multicultural settings*. New York: Harcourt Brace.

Au, K. R., & Kawakami, A. J. (1985). Research currents: Talk story and learning to read. *Language Arts, 62*, 406–411.

Au, K. R., & Kawakami, A. J. (1991). Culture and ownership: Schooling of minority students. *Childhood Education, 67*, 280–284.

Au, K. R., & Kawakami, A. J. (1994). Cultural congruence in instruction. In E. R. Rolling, J. E. King, & W. C. Hayman (Eds.), *Teaching diverse populations: Formulating a knowledge base* (pp. 5–23). Albany: State University of New York Press.

Au, K. P., & Mason, I. M. (1981). Social organizational factors in learning to read: The balance of rights hypothesis. *Reading Research Quarterly, 17*, 115–152.

Austin, A. M. B., Salem, M., & Leffler, A. (1987). Gender and developmental differences in children's conversations. *Sex Roles, 16*, 497–510.

Baber, C. R. (1987). The artistry and artifice of Black communication. In G. Gay & W. L. Baber (Eds.), *Expressively Black: The cultural basis of ethnic identity* (pp. 75–108). New York: Praeger.

Belensky, M. F., Clinchy, B. M., Goldberger, N. R., & Tarule, I. M. (1986). *Women's ways of knowing: The development of self, voice, and mind*. New York: Basic Books

Boggs, S. T. (1985). The meaning of questions and narratives to Hawaiian children. In C. B. Cazden, V. H. John, & D. Hymes (Eds.), *Functions of language in the classroom* (pp. 299–327). Prospect Heights, IL: Waveland.

Boggs, S. T., Watson-Gegeo, K., & McMillen, G. (1985). *Speaking, relating, and learning: A Study of Hawaiian children at home and at school*. Norwood, NJ: Ablex.

Bruner, I. (1996). *The culture of education*. Cambridge, MA: Harvard University Press.

Byers, P., & Byers, H. (1985). Nonverbal communication and the education of children. In C. B. Cazden, V. P. John, & D. Hymes (Eds.), *Functions of language in the classroom* (pp. 3–31). Prospect Heights, IL: Waveland.

Carroll, J. B. (Ed.). (1956). *Language, thought, and reality: Selected writings of Benjamin Lee Whorf*. Cambridge, MA: MIT Press.

Cazden, C. B. (1988). *Classroom discourse: The language of teaching and learning*. Portsmouth, NH: Heinemann.

Chan, S. (Ed.). (1991). *Asian Americans: An interpretative history*. Boston: Twayne.

Crawford, L. W. (1993). *Language and literacy learning in multicultural classrooms*. Boston: Allyn & Bacon.

Crawford, M. (1995). *Talking difference: On gender and language*. Thousand Oaks, CA: Sage.

Dandy, E. B. (1991). *Black communications: Breaking down the barriers*. Chicago: African American Images.

Deyhle, D., & Swisher, K. (1997). Research in American Indian and Alaska native education: From assimilation to self-determinations. In M. W. Apple (Ed.), *Review of research in education* (Vol. 22, pp. 113–194). Washington, DC: American Educational Research Association.

Fox, H. (1994). *Listening to the world: Cultural issues in academic writing*. Urbana, IL: National Council of Teachers of English.

Fullilove, R. E., & Treisman, P. U. (1990). Mathematics achievement among African Americans undergraduates at the University of California, Berkeley: An evaluation of the Mathematics Workshop Program. *Journal of Negro Education, 59*, 463–478.

Gallimore, R., Boggs, J. W., & Jordon, C. (1974). *Culture, behavior and education: A study of Hawaiian Americans*. Beverly Hills, CA: Sage.

Gee, J. P. (1989). What is literacy? *Journal of Education, 171*, 18–25.

Giamati, C., & Weiland, M. (1997). An exploration of American Indian students' perceptions of patterning, symmetry, and geometry. *Journal of American Indian Education, 36*, 27–48.

Goodlad, J. I. (1984). *A place called school: Prospects for the future*. New York: McGraw-Hill.

Goodwin, M. H. (1990). *He-said she-said: Talk as social organization among Black children*. Bloomington: Indiana University Press.

Gray-Schlegel, M. A., & Gray-Schlegel, T. (1995–1996). An investigation of gender stereotypes as revealed through children's creative writing. *Reading Research and Instruction, 35*, 160–170.

Grossman, H., & Grossman, S. H. (1994). *Gender issues in education*. Boston: Allyn & Bacon.

Heath, S. B. (1983). *Ways with words: Language, life, and work in communities and classrooms*. Cambridge, England: Cambridge University Press.

Hoijer, H. (1991). The Sapir–Whorf hypothesis. In L. A. Samovar & R. E. Porter (Eds.), *Intercultural communication: A reader* (6th ed., pp. 244–251). Belmont, CA: Wadsworth.

Hoyenga, K. B., & Hoyenga, K. T. (1979). *The question of sex differences: Psychological, Cultural, and biological issues*. Boston: Little Brown.

Hymes, D. (1985). Introduction. In C. B. Cazden, V. P. John, & D. Hymes (Eds.), *Functions of language in the classroom* (pp. xi–xvii). Prospect Heights, IL: Waveland.

Johnstone, B. (1993). Community and contest: Midwestern men and women creating their worlds in conversational storytelling. In D. Tannen (Ed.), *Gender and conversational interaction* (pp. 62–80). New York: Oxford University Press.

Kim, B. L. (1978). *The Asian Americans: Changing patterns, changing needs*. Montclair, NJ: Association for Korean Christian Scholars of North America.

Kitano, H., & Daniels, R. (1995). *Asian Americans: Emerging minorities* (2nd ed.). Englewood Cliffs, NJ: Prentice-Hall.

Klein, S. S. (Ed.). (1982). *Handbook for achieving sex equity through education*. Baltimore: Johns Hopkins University Press.

Kochman, T. (Ed.). (1972). *Rappin' and stylin' out: Communication in urban Black America*. Urbana: University of Illinois Press.

Kochman, T. (1981). *Black and White styles in conflict*. Chicago: University of Chicago Press.

Kochman, T. (1985). Black American speech events and a language program for the classroom. In C. B. Cazden, V. P. John, & D. Hymes (Eds.), *Functions of language in the classroom* (pp. 211–261). Prospect Heights, IL: Waveland.

Lakoff, R. (1975). *Language and women's place*. New York: Harper & Row.

Lee, C. D., & Slaughter-Defoe, D. T. (1995). Historical and sociocultural influences on African American education. In J. A. Banks & C. A. M. Banks (Eds.), *Handbook of research on multicultural education* (pp. 348–371). New York: Macmillan.

Leung, B. P. (1998). Who are Chinese American, Japanese American, and Korean American children? In V. O. Pang & L-R. L. Cheng (Eds.), *Struggling to be heard: The unmet needs of Asian Pacific American children* (pp. 11–26). Albany: State University of New York Press.

Longstreet, W. (1978). *Aspects of ethnicity: Understanding differences in pluralistic classrooms*. New York: Teachers College Press.

Maccoby, E. E. (1988). Gender as a social category. *Developmental Psychology, 24*, 755–765.

Maltz, D. N., & Borker, R. A. (1983). A cultural approach to male-female miscommunication. In J. J. Gumperz (Ed.), *Communication, language, and social identity* (pp. 196–216). Cambridge, England: Cambridge University Press.

Mandelbaum, D. G. (Ed.). (1968). *Selected writings of Edward Sapir in language, culture and personality*. Berkeley: University of California Press.

Michaels, S., & Cazden, C. B. (1986). Teacher/child collaboration as oral preparation for literacy. In B. B. Schietfelin & P. Gilmore (Eds.), *The acquisition of literacy: Ethnographic perspectives* (pp. 132–154). Norwood, NJ: Ablex.

Montague, A., & Matson, F. (1979). *The human connection*. New York: McGraw-Hill.

Nakanishi, D. (1994). *Asian American educational experience*. New York: Routledge.

Nicolopoulou, A., Scales, B., & Weintraub, J. (1994). Gender differences and symbolic imagination in the stories of four-year-olds. In A. H. Dyson & C. Genishi (Eds.), *The need for story: cultural diversity in classroom and community* (pp. 102–123). Urbana, IL: National Council of Teachers of English.

Otnes, C., Kim, K., & Kim, Y. C. (1994). Yes, Virginia, there is a gender difference: Analyzing children's requests to Santa Claus. *Journal of Popular Culture, 28*, 17–29.

Pasteur, A. B., & Toldson, I. L. (1982). *Roots of soul: The psychology of Black expressiveness*. Garden City, NY: Anchor Press/Doubleday.

Philips, S. U. (1983). *The invisible culture: Communication in classroom and community on the Warm Springs Indian Reservation*. Prospect Heights, IL: Waveland.

Porter, R. E., & Samovar, L. A. (1991). Basic principles of intercultural communication. In L. A. Samovar & R. E. Porter (Eds.), *Intercultural communication: A reader* (6th ed., pp. 5–22). Belmont, CA: Wadsworth.

Ramirez, M., III, & Castañeda, A. (1974). *Cultural democracy, bicognitive development and education*. New York: Academic Press.

Sadker, M., & Sadker, D. (1994). *Failing at fairness: How our schools cheat girls*. New York: Touchstone.

Sapir, E. (1968). The status of linguistics as a science. In D. G. Mandelbaum (Ed.), *Selected writings of Edward Sapir in language, culture and personality* (pp. 160–166). Berkeley: University of California Press.

Shade, B. J. (Ed.). (1989). *Culture, style, and the educative process.* Springfield, IL: Thomas.

Shade, B. J. (1994). Understanding the African American learner. In E. R. Hollins, J. E. King, & W. C. Hayman (Eds.), *Teaching diverse populations* (pp. 175–189). Albany: State University of New York Press.

Simkins-Bullock, J. A., & Wildman, B. G. (1991). An investigation into the relationship between gender and language. *Sex Roles, 24,* 149–160.

Smart-Grosvenor, V. (1982). We got a way with words. *Essence, 13,* 138.

Smith, B. O. (1971). On the anatomy of teaching. In R. T. Hyman (Ed.), *Contemporary thought on teaching* (pp. 20–27). Englewood Cliffs, NJ: Prentice-Hall.

Smitherman, G. (1972). Black power is Black language. In G. M. Simmons, H. D. Hutchinson, & H. E. Summons (Eds.), *Black culture: Reading and writing Black* (pp. 85–91). New York: Holt, Rinehart & Winston.

Smitherman, G. (1977). *Talkin' and testifyin': The language of Black America.* Boston: Houghton Mifflin.

Tannen, D. (1990). *You just don't understand: Women and men in conversation.* New York: Morrow.

Tannen, D. (1994). *Gender and discourse.* New York: Oxford University Press.

Tharp, R. G., & Gallimore, R. (1988). *Rousing minds to life: Teaching, learning, and schooling in social context.* Cambridge, England: Cambridge University Press.

Treisman, P. U. (1985). *A study of the mathematics achievement of Black students at the University of California, Berkeley.* Unpublished doctoral dissertation, University of California, Berkeley.

Vygotsky, L. S. (1962). *Thought and language.* Cambridge, MA: MIT Press.

Whorf, B. L. (1952). *Collected papers on metalinguistics.* Washington, DC: Department of State, Foreign Service Institute.

Whorf, B. L. (1956). Language, mind, and reality. In J. B. Carroll (Ed.), *Language, thought and reality: Selected writings of Benjamin Lee Whorf* (pp. 246–270). Cambridge, MA: MIT Press.

## Concepts and Questions

1. How do students' communication abilities affect teachers' perceptions of students?

2. Beyond the transmission of information, what other purposes does Gay suggest that language serves?

3. What does Gay mean when she says, "languages and communication styles are systems of cultural notations and the means through which thoughts and ideas are expressively embodied"?

4. What does Gay mean when she uses the term "discourse structures"?

5. Distinguish between *passive-receptive* and *participatory-interactive* styles of discourse.

6. Describe the methods employed by many African American students to gain entry into conversations. How does this style differ from the communication styles of Native Hawaiian students?

7. Describe differences in problem-solving styles among African Americans, Latinos, Native Americans, and Asian American students.

8. Distinguish between *topic-centered, topic-associative,* and *topic-chaining* techniques in organizing ideas in discourse. Which methods are associated with which cultural groupings of students?

9. How does the African American storytelling style function as topic-chaining discourse?

10. Distinguish between female and male communication styles.

# Enculturation of Values in the Educational Setting: Japanese Group Orientation

EDWIN R. MCDANIEL • ERIKO KATSUMATA

*Geneva Gay's essay dealt primarily with classrooms in the United States, but what about education in other cultures? Is it different? How different? How do cultural values affect the classroom? How is the interaction between student and teacher different from culture to culture? To what extent do the structural elements of other educational systems differ from those of the United States?*

*This essay addresses some of these questions by describing how Japanese schools enculturate values through their educational practices. In their essay "Enculturation of Values in the Educational Setting: Japanese Group Orientation," authors Edwin R. McDaniel and Eriko Katsumata describe and analyze the educational system prevalent in Japan and reveal how the values of the Japanese culture are not only taught in the schools but also affect the very structure of the educational system. In reading this essay you will (1) learn that in Japan a quality education is widely recognized as necessary for success in life; (2) be introduced to the preschool/kindergarten educational system, which is the beginning of an arduous education as well as the fostering of a collectivistic orientation; (3) explore the elementary school system and see how group affiliation takes on saliency through the educational experience; (4) be exposed to the Japanese middle school and high school educational system where students enter an even stronger group-oriented environment; (5) explore the Japanese university education, where group affiliation is strongly promoted; and (6) review Japanese corporate life, where the role and importance of groups is paramount.*

*McDaniel and Katsumata begin with a peek inside Japanese schools. They describe in detail the preschool/kindergarten, elementary school, middle school, and high school programs as well as the university system. By reading these descriptions, you will immediately see major differences from the educational system in the United States. Throughout their detailed description you will find the common thread of collectivism that pervades the educational system. All educational experiences seem to foster the importance of the group over that of the individual. As the authors point out, "observations suggest that the Japanese educational system continues to explicitly and implicitly communicate the role of group affiliation, which remains an important aspect of Japanese social organization."*

*McDaniel and Katsumata conclude their article by refuting some current arguments that Japan is moving away from its collective nature. Perhaps, they suggest, change will occur; but it will come neither easily nor quickly because the value of collective effort and identity continues to be passed on to generations through the existing educational system.*

> When I was a student, especially a junior high school student, I was always taught that everyone should place importance on harmony of their group. Therefore all students had the same [school] bag, socks, shoes of the same color, and so on. And, for example, if one student skip a club activity or chat during a club activity, our teacher scold not only the student but also all the team members. We have collective responsibility. Even if only one student make a mistake, teacher scold all the team members with responsible for the team. Like this, Japanese always value group harmony more than individual.
>
> Uchi[1]

## INTRODUCTION

An often touted perception is that "globalization" is rapidly eroding traditional cultures and moving societies toward a "global village," modeled after Western values centering on individualism and materialism. Part of the basis for this argument arises from international exposure to Western ideals as a result of increased tourism, international economic exchanges, environmental and health issues, and the ever-expanding presence of Western media throughout the world.

One aspect of this view of globalization's influence on cultural values is that Japan is moving away from its "collectivistic" traditions toward a more "individualistic" society. Some of the more well-known arguments advocating this view have been presented by Matsumoto et al. (1996, 1997) and Takano and Osaka (1999). In what is perhaps the most widely recognized work, *The New Japan: Debunking Seven Cultural Stereotypes*, Matsumoto (2002) argues that traditional collectivism is declining among Japan's younger generations and contends that his research demonstrates "not only is the stereotype concerning Japanese collectivism not supported, but in fact the opposite may be true—the Japanese may actually be less collectivistic, that is, more individualistic than are Americans" (p. 41). These reports are used as rationale to argue that cultural changes fostered by technology, diffusion, and a basic societal reordering (i.e., globalization) are instilling younger Japanese with a stronger, growing sense of individualism.

As scholars, we were keenly aware of these reports, but as first hand observers and teachers in Japan,[2] personal experiences push us toward quite different conclusions. Our classroom experiences, interaction with faculty, cohorts and students, and observations of day-to-day activities raised a reasonable doubt as to the premise of a rapidly declining group orientation at any level of Japanese society. Instead of growing individualism, we were continually confronted with demonstrations of group belonging and the importance attached to group identity. From our perspective as participant-observers, we have concluded that although Japan may not be as "collectivistic" as portrayed in previous academic reports, group affiliation remains a salient component of modern Japan's social structure.

To support this view, this essay first examines literature on the role of education in communicating normative societal values and forming cultural role expectations among children. Next, we argue that every level of the current Japanese educational system continues to instill group affiliation as a cultural value. In arguing the continuing importance of group orientation in Japanese society, we offer interpretations gained from personal observations, recurring interaction with Japanese university students, discussions with fellow faculty members, and visits to secondary schools, complemented by contemporary studies of the Japanese educational system.

## RELEVANT LITERATURE

Numerous factors, such as the established social order, identity needs, and the educational system, play an important role in shaping one's cultural orientation. For example, Miller and Kanazawa (2000) contend that "social order" exerts a considerable influence on day-to-day life in Japan and is sustained through group affiliation. They define social order as:

> the degree to which people follow explicit and implicit rules of behavior. That is, a society where the great majority of citizens obey laws and conform to social norms can be described as having a high degree of social order. Japan is such a society. (p. 3)

According to their argument, the structure of Japanese society directs individuals toward group membership, which offers in return security and identity.

Acceptance of the idea that social structures and the need for identity can influence personal choices allows us to move away from the broad canvas of culture generalized and consider how societal structures can influence and govern individual attitudes and behaviors. More specifically, this essay will illustrate how daily routines in Japan's educational system implicitly and explicitly communicate the value of group perspective, thereby perpetuating a collectivistic orientation.

The role of education in the communicative transmission of cultural values and normative societal deportment cannot be overstated. According to Samovar, Porter, and McDaniel, "The formal education process prevalent in a culture is tied directly to the values and characteristics of that culture" (2010, p. 331). Miller and Kanazawa (2000) echo this view when they state that the "socialization of children in any society is done with the explicit purpose of preparing children for entry into society" (p. 25). According to Patai (2002), national character, or a society's "modal personality," is a product of people being raised in a common environment, and he reports that teachers are a primary source of children's internalization of "the moral imperatives" of their social environment (p. 18). This idea is succinctly summarized by the Chinese philosopher Tehyi Hsei, who observed, "The schools of the country are its future in miniature."

These statements aside, it is somewhat intuitive that a child's school years exert a very formative influence, one that instills values and ideals carried throughout life. As stated by Samovar, Porter, and McDaniel, education "offers every child a set of guidelines and values for living a proper life" (2010, p. 327). Drawing on this premise, we explore each major level of the Japanese educational system, beginning with preschool and concluding with entry into the labor force. The objective is to demonstrate that enculturation of the group affiliation in Japan begins at an early age and continues throughout the school years. Personal observations and interpretations are melded with information from other reports.

*Two brightly colored mini-busses stop at the entrance of the small municipal park and began ejecting a seemingly endless stream of chattering kindergarten toddlers. All wear identical bright yellow hats, with sun flaps folded down over the ears and the back of the neck. With their hair hidden, it is hard to distinguish the boys from the girls. Only on closer observation do gender distinctions become apparent. The girls are dressed in identical red shorts and a white T-shirt with red lettering. The boys sport matching dark blue shorts and blue lettering on their white T-shirts. These small distinctions in color are the only outward appearances that differentiate this large group of children.*

> *The role of education in the communicative transmission of cultural values and normative societal deportment cannot be overstated.*

> *In Japan, education is a requisite key to the door of success. In an effort to unlock this entryway, a Japanese child's student days begin early in life.*

## INSIDE JAPANESE SCHOOLS
### Preschool/Kindergarten

In Japan, education is a requisite key to the door of success. In an effort to unlock this entryway, a Japanese child's student days begin early in life. Although not compulsory, pre-school is widely attended (Nemoto, 1999), and many parents spend considerable sums on tuition. The objective is to gain every possible advantage to help their child gain entrance to primary and secondary schools of ever-increasing reputation, culminating in admission to a prestigious university.

The above observations of how kindergarten students were dressed similarly for a school outing provide an illustration of early socialization to group orientation. These outward manifestations of group are a reflection of ideals imparted in preschool classrooms. In a study of twenty-seven Japanese preschools, Holloway (2000) found that teaching the value of group orientation was a common objective. The director of one pre-school explained it this way:

> Our basic principle is group education. The teacher does not raise individual children. Instead children learn from the group. Therefore it is essential to create a good group, and from the good group good individuals grow. (p. 68)

In summarizing her findings, Holloway reported that "the existence of individuality was not itself contested, but the opinion was strongly held that cultivation of that individuality at school was unnecessary and even harmful until the basic attributes shared by all could be firmly established" (2000, p. 110). The importance of inculcating group values in Japanese pre-schools and kindergartens is further exemplified by a 1998 Ministry of Education report which stated that an objective of kindergarten was "To encourage children to have self-realization through group activities" (Curriculum Council, 1998). The purpose of this group focus is, according to Tobin (1992), to prepare "children for the group life they will encounter in elementary school, junior high, and beyond" (p. 32).

*Each weekday morning small groups of elementary school students assemble near their homes and set out for their schoolhouse in classic military platoon formation. An older student leads the way, followed by one or two loosely arranged columns of younger students. A second older student follows at the rear. The younger children usually wear hats identical in color and shape. They also carry the ubiquitous backpack (randoseru), identifiable throughout Japan in shape and size and differing significantly in only the color—predominately red and black, but occasionally another color. The backpacks mark the wearers as elementary students and the hats denote the school attended.*

## Elementary School

The weekday ritual of gathering elementary students at neighborhood assembly points and walking to school under the supervision of one or two older students, usually fifth or sixth graders, provides the children a safety net against untoward actions, such as abduction attempts (Nemoto, 1999). Concomitantly, however, the young students are instilled with a sense of belonging to a particular group and a respect for hierarchy by being under the supervision of an older student, who is learning about group leadership and responsibility.

The practice of transiting from home to school as a group is quite in contrast to practices in the United States. There, parents usually accompany their children to a school bus stop or actually drive them to school each morning and pick them up in the afternoon.

Group affiliation takes on even greater saliency inside the Japanese elementary school classroom, where students are commonly divided into *han* groups (Cave, 2007; Nemoto, 1999; Sato, 2004; Tsuneyoshi, 2001). This organization is described by Benjamin (1997), who spent a year as a participant-observer at an elementary school near Tokyo.

*Han* means a platoon, a squad, a working group. It has implication for being the smallest operational group in a joint endeavor and of being a group that operates with little or no hierarchy. In Japanese classrooms, each *han* includes five to eight children, depending on the size of the class, and in order to be an efficient teaching and social environment, each class should have

six to eight of these groups. Both social and academic activities are carried out with *han* groups as the basic working unit. (p. 53)

Sato (2004) offers a similar picture of the elementary classroom:

Elementary students are organized into *han*, which are groups of 4-6 students. The composition of the groups may change for different activities, such as serving lunch, cleaning the classroom, or study groups for different topics. Indeed the composition of the *han* may be subject to periodic change by the classroom teacher. However, these groupings form the basic organizational pattern for all elementary school activities. (p. 82)

Both Benjamin (1997) and Sato (2004) reported that teachers would often address the *han*, rather than a specific student, praising or admonishing the entire group instead of individuals. Student groups (*han*) assigned to serve lunch will typically wear white caps and gowns while working, which provides a form of group identity. Moreover, working in these continually changing groups helps the children develop an ability to engage in cooperative endeavors, regardless of the personnel involved. Unlike in U.S. schools, where personal relationships become primary, the Japanese student learns that group affiliation and cooperation is the import aspect of relationships.

Japanese primary and secondary schools also hold a variety of nonacademic events that strengthen group identity and communicate the benefits of collective effort. These frequently include an annual school-wide sports day or cultural fair, where students may perform large group dances or drill formations which require considerable cooperation. Most athletic contests pit one class, or group, against another. Individual based contests such as races are conducted, but individual winners are seldom singled out for recognition. While attending sports day at one elementary school, races among all the boys of the same year grade were observed. Each race consisted of five or six students and as one group finished, the next group started. This continued until everyone had run. There was no effort to decide an ultimate winner by holding runoff races, and all of the participants were given a small gift at the end of their race. For these boys, participation in the race was the reward; individual ability was a secondary consideration, if at all. Benjamin (1997) and Feiler (2004) report similar observations of school sports day events emphasizing group participation and cooperation.

> *You see them everywhere! In the subway stations, waiting at bus stops, riding bicycles, or walking in twos or threes. Weekdays, weekends, and holidays! Even during the spring and summer school breaks. All of them, boys and girls alike, wear dark colored uniforms. The boys are dressed in dark trousers and white shirt—some with a tie and jacket and others with a tight fitting, high collar military style tunic. The girls wear dark—solid or plaid—pleated skirts, white blouse, and frequently a dark jumper with a sailor motif. Outwardly, each uniform carries enough variation to indicate a specific school, but overall they mark the wearer as a middle or high school student.*

## Middle School and High School

Junior high school brings Japanese students into an even stronger group-oriented environment. As illustrated above, beginning with the seventh grade and continuing through high school, all students are required to wear uniforms, whether attending public or private schools. These uniforms outwardly associate the individual with a broad age group and a specific institution. Students are keenly aware that they visibly represent their school and that improper activities will reflect on the reputation of their school. In some cases, students wear small lapel pins which designate their year group, and occasionally they may be seen wearing pins that indicate their specific class (*kumi*).[3] Another means of year group designation is the use of colored neckties and "room shoes."[4] Some schools will assign different-colored ties or shoes to each year group. In other schools, clothes worn during athletic activities ("sports wear") are color coded to the student's class. These different procedures provide a nonverbal means of group identity.

*Students are keenly aware that they visibly represent their school and that improper activities will reflect on the reputation of their school.*

Most schools place restrictions on female students wearing makeup or jewelry, and some schools go so far as designating the permissible style and length of hair (Feiler, 2004). In addition to the school dress code, which casts students into groups, the students themselves take measures to differentiate their class year. Feiler (2004), who taught at a Japanese junior high school northeast of Tokyo, reported that ninth-grade students devised unwritten rules dictating how junior classes had to wear their socks, button the top button of their shirt, and similar subtleties.

The physical organization of middle and high school classroom buildings also demonstrate the Japanese group and hierarchy orientations. Must classroom buildings consist of three stories, with junior year classes on the lower floor and senior students on the top, although in some instances this order may be reversed. Grouping same-year students on the same floor further strengthens feelings of group belonging, and separating the class years abets the feelings of hierarchy.

In general, middle and high school students will change classmates and homerooms at the beginning of the school year. In some schools, however, students may stay with the same classmates throughout the three years of middle and high school, respectively. Unlike their U.S. counterparts, who commonly change classrooms and classmates for different subjects, Japanese students remain together and leave their homeroom only when the topic requires a laboratory or for sports activities. Usually, Japanese students even eat lunch together in their homeroom. In his study of a Japanese middle school, Dawson (2008) observed that "the homeroom was the central unit of student grouping. Students spent the vast majority of their time with their classmates in the same homeroom" (p. 48).

Junior and senior high school classroom pedagogy continues to focus on small group work. Use of the *han* organization continues in middle school classes, but is less common in high school, except for cleaning groups.

Stand near the entrance of almost any U.S. high school when classes are over for the day, and you will see a steady stream of students, many driving their own cars, leaving the campus heading for home, the closest shopping mall, the nearest fast food outlet, or some other gathering place. If you stand near the entrance of a Japanese school when classes are over, you will likely see only a trickle of students departing, and certainly none will be driving an automobile.[5]

At the conclusion of classes, around 4:30 p.m., Japanese middle and high school students will spend fifteen to twenty minutes working in groups to clean their classroom, the hallways, and perhaps even removing litter from the campus. After janitorial chores, students usually adjourn to their school-sponsored clubs (*bukatsudou*), which can be classified into two categories—sports or culture. Generally, students may belong to only one club, but some schools allow the students to belong to two—one of each type. Clubs may meet one or two hours on school days, with activities frequently held on the weekends and throughout the summer and winter breaks. In middle school, Dawson (2008) found that a majority of the students also belonged to one of the numerous Student Government Activities committees with regularly scheduled monthly meeting.

Within the sports clubs, the students' class year also forms a group and there is typically a strict relationship between the different grades. Younger students are expected to obey the older students and perform menial tasks. This hierarchal relationship is particularly strict in sports clubs, where the entering students attend to a variety of chores, such as picking up sports gear at the conclusion of practice. Collective responsibility is assigned for these tasks, and, for example, if one or two freshmen fail to complete their part of the job, all of sport club's freshmen will be punished. This clearly demonstrates the value placed on intragroup dependency and hierarchy. It also reinforces the Japanese mentality of "I have to do my best, because I don't want to create trouble for others."

It is quite common to see high school students, still in uniform, boarding buses near their school or at subway stations as late as 5:30–6:00 p.m. on weekday evenings. Many of them are en route to a cram school (*juku*), which they attend 2–3 times a week, for a few additional hours of classroom work. These institutions provide instruction and text-taking practice, targeted primarily at passing high school entrance exams (Roesgaard, 2006) but also for private school and university admittance. When done, the student will return home to study, watch TV, listen to music, or relax in some way. Little time is available for casual interaction with people outside the student's school groups. Indeed, Johnson and Johnson (1996) reported that Japanese students enjoyed "less than half an hour in social relations with peers outside of school" (p. 4). This limited opportunity to interact with others can create a strong sense of identity with one's class and school.

Although becoming somewhat rare, a few Japanese private high schools still hold classes on Saturday. In one instance, a university freshman related that her school held classes six days a week from 8:30 in the morning until 6:00 in the evening and clubs were not allowed. When asked what she did on Sundays, the student looked briefly incredulous before replying, "Why study, of course!" Her opportunities to interact with peers other than classmates were virtually nonexistent.

While somewhat limited, Japanese junior and senior high school students are not completely restricted to their own school classmates for social interactions. They do have the opportunity to meet people outside their schools during music and sports club competitions, class outings to cultural sites, or at *juku* classes.

*Some women come to class in stylish dresses and high heels, often complemented by a strand of pearls and a coiffure. Others wear fashionable jeans or whatever casual clothes are currently in vogue. Make up and brand name accessories are common. The men are consistently dressed in a very relaxed, casual manner. After their freshmen and sophomore years, however, the dress becomes quite casual for both men and women, with one exception. Fourth year students are often seen wearing a black suit during the Winter Semester. The men complement their white shirt with a conservative tie, and the women always wear a white blouse. These university students, in their "recruit suits," are conducting job interviews, engaged in student teaching, or otherwise attempting to find an employer.*

## University

Entering university is a dramatic departure from the regimented, highly structured environment of Japan's primary and secondary schools. For most, graduation from high school represents the first real opportunity to openly explore and display their personal identity. This is often achieved in such small ways as having to decide for themselves what to wear each day. The opportunity for self-expression manifests itself in many forms and is clearly evident among freshmen the first few weeks of their first term.

While completion of high school provides greater personal freedom, it concurrently removes the graduate from the social support of preselected group affiliations, which have been a constant theme since preschool days. Entering college freshman, however, soon find that university life is replete with measures designed to help them form new social groups.

One such event involves a trip, modeled after a "retreat," designed to help entering students form new relationships. The "retreat" usually takes place the week before first-term classes begin and involves a department's entire freshman class going on an overnight field trip. The incoming students, accompanied by faculty, staff members, and a few upper-class students, travel to a hotel, sometimes at a hot springs spa, stopping en route at scenic, historical places, or interesting places. At the hotel, students listen to self-introductions by faculty members, engage in group activities, and have informal interaction with faculty members, upper-class students, and their new classmates.

On the surface, everything appears somewhat impromptu but outward appearances belie an underlying, purposeful organizational schema. At one university in central Japan, seating assignments on the bus and room assignments at the hotel were made sequentially using the students' university ID numbers. Freshmen were also enrolled in selected first- and second-term classes according to their ID number. Thus, students sitting next to each other on the bus, and sharing a hotel room, later found themselves in several of the same classes. These procedures assisted the incoming first-year students from different high schools and geographical locations to begin making new friends (i.e., forming groups).[6]

Another mechanism promoting group affiliation at the university level is the general absence of advanced placement classes.[7] Freshmen take only first-year level classes, regardless of ability or prior experience. For example, a student that has studied English abroad will usually have greater interaction than someone that has not been overseas. Both students, however, will be placed in the same class without consideration for ability. Even students that have earned credits in universities in other countries will have to begin as freshmen—there is usually no advance placement. Each year group advances together, as a whole, toward graduation.[8]

Another common academic practice among Japanese universities is the *zemi* (a seminar fashioned after the German model). Toward the end of their freshman or sophomore year, students will decide on a seminar topic that interests them. They may also choose a particular *zemi* to be with their friends. The outward objective of the *zemi* is to undertake an in-depth study of a particular topic for two to three years, under the guidance of a professor who is an expert on the subject, and culminate in a senior thesis. But another important aim is to help students develop interpersonal skills and relationships that can last a lifetime. According to one Japanese professor, the *zemi* is designed to help students "develop social skills and enhance interpersonal abilities… develop closer relationships than is possible in regular classes." To achieve this, *zemi* classmates often engage in group social events, such as dining out or sports activities; some classes even travel as a group to locations in Japan or take trips abroad.

University sports clubs provide another chance for students to join a group. Some schools host teams that engage in league competition, but often the clubs are more recreational in nature. The team members will practice before or after classes as well as on the weekend and go on outings together. Sports clubs involve demanding practice sessions and, normally, very strict rules for relations between the different class year groups. Thus, the sports club becomes both a social outlet and an important source of identity.

The importance attached to identifying with a group was discovered by an expatriate coach at a Japanese university. Finding he had enough players to form more than two complete teams, each with the necessary number of substitutes, the coach began contacting other area universities to see if a "B" team game could be arranged. But the other schools' teams reported that due to injuries they did not have enough players for a "B" game. The expatriate coach was then informed that injuries to his own players precluded a "B" team contest. Only later did he learn that players preferred to be seen as "substitutes" for the "A" team rather than as members of a "B" team!

Not only does this illustrate how university sports teams become a source of group identity, it also demonstrates the significance placed on membership in the *right* hierarchical group. For the Japanese players, it was more important to be identified as part of the "A" team group than to actually play the game. In the United States, the attitude would more likely be to use the "B" team game as an opportunity to demonstrate skills that would allow the individual to stand out and vie for a promotion to the "A" team.

Hierarchy continues to play a pronounced role at the university. In the sports clubs, students in the lower classes must defer to those higher than them, and freshmen are expected to perform all the menial jobs associated with their club. Heirarchy is also evinced in terms of reference, with underclass students referring to those above them with the honorific term *senpai*.

While university brings a degree of relief from the constraints of the rigid group organization encountered in primary and secondary schools, other collectivistic structures influence student life, as previously discussed. Even the selection of which university to attend carries a lifelong association with a group. This is because in Japan, "many companies judge and hire newcomers according to the university from which they graduate" (Nemoto, 1999, p. 189). An individual's university (group) can determine their future employer (group) and, ultimately, their socio-economic level (group).

*An evening TV news program airs a brief segment showing young men and women, all wearing dark suits, assembled in a large auditorium. They listen passively as corporate executives expound on organizational treatises. After a few moments, the scene switches to one of uniforms being issued to the new crop of employees. The men and women then retire to locker rooms to change. When the picture returns, all are wearing identical uniforms that mark them as an employee of the company.*

## Corporate Life

There is abundant literature on the role and importance of groups within Japanese corporate and governmental organizations. However, since the focus of this essay is on the educational setting, only three sources will be mentioned. Yoshimura and Anderson (1997) provide a comprehensive overview of the role of "reference groups" (p. 57) in Japanese business organizations and how they become a source of identity. Working in a Japanese industrial company between 1996 and 1999, Mehri (2005) found that groups were commonplace and often competed with each other for information and power. More recently, Abegglen (2006) argued that Japanese corporations continue to rely on a collective orientation.

> Over the past half-century of dramatic, economic, and technological change, has Japan's employment system changed? Basically, it has not. The underlying values on which it was built—the concept of community in which all fully and fairly participate as one does in family, village, and neighborhood—remain the foundation. Key practices—an emphasis on continuity, on group integrity, and on egalitarianism—remain in effect. (p. 89)

The continuation of group affiliation is exemplified by the induction ceremony, described above, acted out every year in early April, as companies, large and small, welcome their new employees. This opening ritual (*nyushashiki*) will be followed by weeks, or in some cases months, of classes designed to train the employees in their new responsibilities and concomitantly inculcate them with the corporate culture—into their work "group." In some cases, the corporate training can be somewhat rigorous. For example, one graduate reported that all members of her corporate entry group (*douki*) had been sent to a rural area to plant rice by hand, an extremely labor-intensive activity demanding considerable cooperative effort. This part of the training was intended to forge the members into an effective workgroup and demonstrate the benefits of collective effort.

## Community Activities

Beyond corporate organization, group orientation plays a significant role in community life. For example, neighborhood and city groups are active in numerous yearly festivals. These events bring community members together to both prepare for and participate in the festivities. Participants span all generations, with elders passing down the history and tradition of the occasion to the youth. These events not only instill participants with a feeling of local area pride, the co-operative effort enculturates a group-based sense of identity. Such group participation is considered beneficial and enjoyable, as was noted by Booth's observation of a community festival where some of the people "clearly derived the main part of the pride and enjoyment they found in participation from being members of a properly organized group, not from acting spontaneously" (1995, p. 329).

Japan's group perspective can also influence such mundane activities as taking out the garbage. In Japan, each apartment complex has a specific area where garbage is placed for pickup. As discovered by the first author, while living in Nagoya, it is unwise for a person to place garbage in any area other than that designated for his/her house/apartment building. When leaving his apartment on a garbage pickup morning, he simply dropped off the bag at the closest collection area, which was for an apartment complex across the street. A resident of the other building saw him and insisted the bag be moved to the author's own collection point. Despite the author's protestations that all garbage would be collected that morning, the woman remained insistent. The confrontation was resolved only when he took the bag to his apartment's collection point. Related to this, your second author lives in Tokyo and is part of a sixteen-family group that take turns cleaning up their trash collection point each week.

> *Japanese people will do things for friends [group members] even when they don't want to. They want to keep wa [harmony] and not embarrass others. In class, I don't speak English as well as I can. I don't want others to consider me "snooty."*
> Soto[9]

## WHAT DOES IT ALL MEAN?

Viewed collectively, the foregoing observations suggest that the Japanese educational system continues to explicitly and implicitly communicate the role of group affiliation and hierarchy, which remain important aspects of Japanese social organization. As early as preschool, children begin learning the value of group cooperation. This instruction continues throughout primary and secondary education as students become aware of their membership in an increasing number of groups (family, school, clubs, neighborhood, city, region, nation), many of which play an important role throughout life.

In the United States, group orientation or collectivism, terms often used interchangeably, is frequently interpreted as an overt desire to belong to groups and an affinity for other reference group members. But in the Japanese educational system, as we have seen, group membership is not a personal elective. Elementary and middle school students, for example, have little choice about being assigned to a *han* or even to which *han* they belong, nor can they elect to opt out and work alone if they disagree with another group member(s). Thus, from an early age, Japanese children are taught that cooperative endeavors are the norm and personal feelings must not impede collective achievement. Additionally, the process of being assigned to an in-group lessens the necessity for an individual to develop social skills for spontaneously engaging out-group members. This may, in part, help explain the shyness often displayed by many Japanese when encountering a new social environment.

Group efforts are common in every culture as people join together to accomplish collectively what cannot be achieved individually. Even in the United States, work groups, or teams, are often formed to solve a problem or complete a project. In Japan, however, groups take on a different complexion. In relation to work groups, these differences are described by Miller and Kanazawa (2000):

> Although Japanese often work in groups, those groups have certain characteristics. They tend to be fixed and long-term, where all members share a high dependency on the group, and

> *Viewed collectively, the foregoing observations suggest that the Japanese educational system continues to explicitly and implicitly communicate the role of group affiliation and hierarchy, which remain important aspects of Japanese social organization.*

high visibility allows for constant monitoring and sanctioning of inappropriate behavior. Japanese are not accustomed to forming *temporary groups* composed of strangers or loose acquaintances, whose behavior cannot be controlled by the group. (p. 107)

Additionally, the Japanese practice of assigning punishment and rewards collectively, rather than individually, strengthens group cohesion and provides a means of social control as the members develop feelings of mutual obligation. This sense of obligation, coupled with the group's longevity, creates interpersonal dependencies that tend to reduce nonconformity and the frequency of "free riders." For the Japanese, group membership provides fiscal, social, and emotional support, as well as identity (Miller & Kanazawa, 2000). Moreover, the difficulty in changing groups further discourages aberrant behaviors. In Japan, job hopping, for example, is still uncommon; it is much better to remain with one organization.[10]

This is not to say that a visitor to Japan will never see displays of individuality or deviations from the norm. Small personal trinkets are usually seen dangling from the backpack of an elementary school student or even the cell phone of an adult. Junior and senior high school students find small, often imperceptible, ways to wear or modify their uniforms (Feiler, 2004). It is not unusual to see Japanese teens and young adults dressed in a manner that sets them apart from the majority of their contemporaries. However, if you encounter one person dressed strangely, you will likely see several dressed similarly—a strangely dressed *group*. Any Sunday visit to Tokyo's Harajuku Park will reveal many groups of non-conformists, but the various groups will dress and behave similarly in displaying their nonconformity. Moreover, those assertions of nonconformity will likely be set aside on Monday, when it is time to return to their respective work groups.

Those individuals who do not wish, or cannot, conform to Japan's group-oriented social structure are left with few options. Some take residence in other countries, but this requires considerable capital or a particular skill that will gain them employment. A few even withdraw from all social life and become reclusive. Others seek employment in Japan-based foreign corporations,[11] which are not usually organized around group structures. Many simply endure the strictures of group life in order to earn income but find outlet in individual-oriented activities such as reading, music, photography, or travel. The overwhelming majority, however, learn to successfully balance group life and personal individuality. For most Japanese, the benefits and pleasures acquired through adherence to the social structures that promote group affiliation and cooperative effort are a normal, and valued, part of social life.

> *To us visitors, Japan seemed a nation where the collective good is the collective goal. This was shocking and nearly incomprehensible to those of us accustomed to the U.S. focus on the individual… The schools were filled with students whose collaborative sensibility and sense of responsibility stunned us.*
> Marla Muntner[12]

## PROGNOSIS

The foregoing observations of contemporary Japanese social order do not support Matsumoto's (2002) claim that Japan is becoming less group oriented. Japan's educational system inculcates group orientation and cooperation beginning in pre-school and continuing into university, ensuring that future generations will be imbued with a group perspective. Unless dramatic changes occur, these future generations will enter a workforce that is also structured to promote collective effort.

But, what about the social changes discussed by Matsumoto (2002) and others? There is no question that Japanese society is changing. Globalization is exposing almost every nation to varying beliefs and values, and Japan is no exception. Social changes in Japan range from a rising divorce rate to the institution of a new court system, incorporating peer juries, and erosion of the once sacrosanct lifetime employment. There are also indications that some Japanese corporations are redefining their management practices, including basing promotion on merit rather than on seniority (Fukukawa, 2001; McDaniel, 2004). Foreign managers are becoming commonplace among Japanese professional sports teams, and foreign participants in the ancient

Japanese sport of *sumo* are quite popular. Many of the social changes currently underway will no doubt influence how group affiliation is approached and viewed in the future. Abegglen (2006), however, suggests that in the workplace, new innovations are actually "adaptation to changing conditions whilst leaving intact the values and practices that have characterized Japanese management and that are the key source of the system's continuing strength" (pp. 89–90). Complementing this outlook, De Mente (2005) doubts that Japanese corporations will be able to adopt the merit system on a wide-scale basis "in the next decade or so, if ever, because the concept of seniority, combined with groupism and the obsession for harmony remains such a powerful part of Japanese culture" (p. 154).

There are, moreover, signs that suggest a reinforcement of the group perspective. For example, a 2001 survey suggested that "many Japanese still think a corporation exists for consumers and its employees rather than shareholders" (Fukukawa, 2001, p. 6). This indicates that some corporate employees continue to view their organization from a group affiliation perspective. More recently, Suzuki reported that corporate sports days were again becoming popular. Many organizations discontinued the practice in the early 1990s, when the bubble economy collapsed. Now companies, however, are "recognizing anew the beneficial effect" of bringing employees together, and one survey disclosed that among younger employees the desire to participate in "intracompany events" rose from 71 percent in 1999 to 83 percent in 2006 (Suzuki, 2006, p. 3).

The Japanese recognize the need to restructure the educational system to "emphasize individualism and entrepreneurship" (De Mente, 2005, p. 119), and efforts are being made to effect this change. In 2002, the Ministry of Education initiated reforms with one objective being to "stimulate students to be independent and self-directed learners" (Ellington, 2005, p. 2). Soon after his election in late 2006, then Prime Minister Abe announced educational reform as a top priority and formed a panel to "re-examine education from the ground up" (Nakamura, 2006, Oct 19, p. 2). But envisioned changes remain unclearly defined and there is no certainty that the pervasive emphasis on collective effort will be a part of any change. In fact, a former Minister of Education announced that

> We want to establish a constitution of education that encourages schools and communities to teach (children) Japanese traditional social norms… [the] Japanese are losing certain social norms, including the notion that relying too much on others is shameful. (Nakamura, 2006, Oct 3, p. 3)

These examples from the business and education context indicate that significant change in Japan will come neither easily nor quickly. Group orientation is a form of social organization that permeates all levels of Japanese society. The value of collective effort and identity acquired through group affiliation continues to be passed on to succeeding generations through the educational process. The dilemma was summed up by the mother of two elementary school students, "The schools teach that it is OK to be different, but we don't know how to be different."

Despite exposure of Japan's youth to Western ideals of individualism, the existing social structure and institutional forces will inevitably channel them toward group affiliation. For the Japanese, the forces of group orientation are just as compelling, valid, beneficial, and fulfilling as individual self-promotion is in the United States. Group affiliation offers the Japanese an enduring source of identity, a high degree of certainty, and social stability, all of which are as valued as much as individuality, personal freedom, and change are in the United States.

There is, however, one factor that has not been included in the equation of cultural change. Japan's population is declining! Some 20 percent of the nation's people are over sixty-five, and in 2005 the birth rate fell to a new low of 1.25 (2.1 is needed to maintain parity). Thus, Japan's population "has the world's highest proportion of elderly people and the lowest proportion of young people" ("20% of Japan," 2006, p. 1). According to the Ministry of Health, Labor and Welfare, if these conditions continue, Japan's population could decline from its present approximate 127 million to "less than 90 million by 2055" ("Japan's population," 2006, p. 1). These circumstances will obviously have an influence on cultural change in Japan, but the type of change cannot now be determined.

## CAVEAT

Throughout this essay, the concept of group orientation has been addressed from a one-dimensional perspective. This, unfortunately, may convey a misleading perception that in Japanese society group orientation works as a singular cultural force. Just as in every culture, however, in daily life the Japanese must deal with a multiplicity of cultural factors, which change as people move from one social context to another. Hierarchy, mutual obligation, and harmony have been mentioned briefly, but there is a host of other cultural dynamics that influence Japanese social life and communicative behaviors. These include such considerations as uncertainty avoidance, high-context communication, formality, face concerns, and many uniquely Japanese cultural factors like *gaman, honne/ tatemae, soto/uchi, giri/on, uchi/soto,* and others. Depending on the context and the individuals involved, these various cultural forces will exert their influence in concert, not singularly.

## Notes

1. *Uchi* is a pseudonym for a third-year Japanese university student. These comments were taken verbatim from a seminar assignment report. The examples presented in italics preceding section headings were given by students or taken from personal observations and discussions with colleagues.

2. From 2005 to 2009, Dr. McDaniel taught in a Japanese university in central Japan.

3. In urban areas, Japanese junior and senior high schools are quite large and usually have several "home rooms" for each class year. For example, one high school that was visited was originally built to contain twelve classes for each of the three-year groups. Students are normally assigned to a "homeroom" for at least one year, but in some cases it may be for their entire three years.

4. When entering primary and secondary schools, students change their "street" or outside shoes for shoes or slippers worn only inside the school.

5. To obtain a driver's license in Japan, one must be 18 years of age and have completed driving school. Most of the students do not get their license until their first year in college.

6. The activities described in these two paragraphs are based on observations at a single Japanese university. Other schools use different procedures. Additionally, these trips are more common in universities that focus on the humanities. At research-oriented universities, the advanced undergraduate students are assigned to a laboratory, where they work with a professor and a small group of student cohorts.

7. Not all Japanese universities adhere to this policy. In some schools, for example, if an entering freshman scores high enough on the English placement exam, he or she does not have to take the first-year English course.

8. There are a couple of exceptions. One is when a student decides to spend a year abroad, typically to study a foreign language. These students will return to graduate one or two terms behind their peers. The second is with students who transfer after completing junior college. These students enter as third-year students, but may be required to make up a few selected classes (e.g., *zemi*).

9. *Soto* is a pseudonym for a first-year Japanese university student. During high school, she spent a year abroad and acquired excellent English conversation skills. In class, however, she often spoke well below the level she used in private conversation with English instructors. Her stated objective was to ensure she did not stand out from her classmates and disrupt class harmony.

10. There is, however, growing usage of temporary workers (*haken shain*) in Japanese organizations. These individuals are assigned to a company and may work for a few months or a couple of years. How they are integrated with the full-time workers is currently unresearched.

11. There are a number of other reasons why Japanese seek employment in Western subsidiary companies, not the least is higher wages than can be earned in a Japanese corporation.

12. Muntner (2003) is a U.S. elementary school teacher who, as a participant in the 2001 Japanese Fulbright Memorial Fund Teacher Program, visited elementary, junior, and senior high schools, as well as Japanese homes.

## References

20% of Japan now age 65 or older. (2006, November 1). *The Japan Times.* 1.

Abegglen, J. C. (2006). *21st-century Japanese management.* NY: Palgrave-Macmillan.

Allik, J., & Realo, A. (1996). The hierarchical nature of individualism-collectivism: Comments on Matsumoto et al. (1996). *Culture and Psychology, 2,* 109–117.

Benjamin, G. R. (1997). *Japanese lessons*. NY: New York University.

Booth, A. (1995). *Looking for the lost: Journeys through a vanishing Japan*. NY: Kodansha.

Cave, P. (2007). *Primary School in Japan*. NY: Routledge.

The Curriculum Council. (1998, July). *National curriculum standards reform for kindergarten, elementary school, lower and upper secondary school and schools for the visually disabled, the hearing impaired and the otherwise disabled*. Ministry of Education, Culture, Sports, Science and Technology (MEXT). Retrieved March 26, 2010, from http://www.mext.go.jp/english/news/1998/07/980712.htm

De Mente, B. L. (2005). *Japan unmasked*. Tokyo: Tuttle.

Ellington, L. (2005). Japanese education. *Japan Digest*. National Clearing House for U.S.-Japan Studies. Retrieved March 10, 2007, from http://www.indiana.edu/~japan/digest5.html

Feiler, B. S. (2004). *Learning to bow*. NY: Perennial. Originally published in 1991.

Fukukawa, S. (2001, May 28). Sea change in Japan's values: Globalization, IT age prompt social diversification. *The Japan Times-on line*. Retrieved October 4, 2006, from http://search.japantimes.co.jp/print/nb20010528a2.html

Hofstede, G. (2001). *Culture's consequences* (2nd ed.). Thousand Oaks, CA: Sage. Originally published in 1980.

Holloway, S. D. (2000). *Contested childhood: Diversity and change in Japanese preschools*. NY: Routledge.

"Japan's population to fall 30% by 2055, study finds." (2006, 21 Dec). *The Japan Times*. Retrieved March 27, 2010, from http://search.japantimes.co.jp/cgi-bin/nn20061221a1.html

Johnson, M. L., & Johnson, J. R. (1996, October). Daily life in Japanese high schools. *Japan Digest*. Retrieved October 14, 2006, from http://www.indiana.edu/~japan/digest9.pdf

Matsumoto, D., Kudoh, T., & Takeuchi, S. (1996). Changing patterns of individualism and collectivism in the United States and Japan. *Culture and Psychology, 2*, 77–107.

Matsumoto, D., Weissman, M. D., Preston, K., Brown, B. R., & Kupperbush, C. (1997). Context-specific measurement of individualism-collectivism on the individual level: The individualism-collectivism interpersonal assessment inventory. *Journal of Cross-Cultural Psychology, 28*(6), 743–767.

Matsumoto, D. (2002). *The new Japan: Debunking seven cultural stereotypes*. Yarmouth, ME: Intercultural Press.

McDaniel, E. R. (2004). Changing Japanese organizational communication patterns: The impact of information technology. *San Diego State University Center for International Business Education and Research* (CIBER). *Working Paper Series C-04-015*.

Mehri, D. (2005). *Notes from Toyota-land: An American engineer in Japan*. Ithaca, NY: Cornell University.

Miller, A. S., & Kanazawa, S. (2000). *Order by accident: The origins and consequence of conformity in contemporary Japan*. Boulder, CO: Westview.

Muntner, M. (2003). Lessons learned: A glimpse into Japanese schools and life. *Multicultural Review 12*(4), 36–38.

Nakamura, A. (2006, Oct 19). Abe, education panel get to work on reforms. *Japan Times*, p. 2.

Nakamura, A. (2006, Oct 3). Education chief wants traditional values restored. *Japan Times*, p. 3.

Nemoto, Y. (1999). *The Japanese education system*. Parkland, FL: Universal.

Patai, R. (2002). *The Arab mind* (rev. ed.). NY: Hatherleigh Press. Originally published in 1976.

Rosegaard, M. H. (2006). *Japanese education and the cram school business*. Copenhagen: NIAS Press.

Samovar, L. A., Porter, R. E., & McDaniel, E. R. (2010). *Communication between cultures*. (7th ed). Boston: Wadsworth-Cengage Learning.

Sato, N. E. (2004). *Inside Japanese classrooms: The heart of education*. New York: RoutledgeFalmer.

Suzuki, J. (2006, Oct. 17). Corporate Japan once again embraces sports days. *The Japan Times-online*. Retrieved March 27, 2010, from http://search.japantimes.co.jp/cgi-bin/nn20061017f2.html

Takano, Y., & Osaka, E. (1999). An unsupported common view: Comparing Japan and the U.S. on individualism/collectivism. *Asian Journal of Social Psychology, 2*, 311–341.

Tobin, J. (1992). Japanese preschools and the pedagogy of selfhood. In N. R. Rosenberger (Ed.), *Japanese sense of self* (pp. 21–30). New York: Cambridge University.

Tsuneyoshi, R. (2001). *The Japanese model of schooling: Comparisons with the United States*. New York: RoutledgeFalmer.

Yoshimura, N., & Anderson, P. (1997). *Inside the Kaisha: Demystifying Japanese business behavior*. Boston: Harvard Business School.

## Concepts and Questions

1. In their article, McDaniel and Katsumata took you on a tour of the Japanese educational system. What are the differences between preschool/kindergarten education in Japan and that in the United States?

2. In what ways does the Japanese preschool/kindergarten experience promote group orientation?

3. Describe how Japanese elementary students are organized in order to promote group harmony. What role does the *han* play in this process?

4. How does the fact that teachers often address the *han* rather than individual students promote group orientation?

5. What differences in purpose are there in the wearing of uniforms by Japanese students and the wearing of uniforms by students in American schools?

6. How does the organization and duration of the Japanese middle school or high school student's day differ from that of U.S. students?

7. How do students who have graduated from high school establish new group affiliations to replace the group support they had from preselected groups in their school years?

8. What conclusions can you draw about the importance of sports clubs in promoting group orientations?

9. How does the introduction of college students to corporate life in Japan differ from how it occurs in the United States?

10. Although using work groups to accomplish what cannot be done by individuals is common in all cultures, what characteristics make Japanese groups different from other groups?

# Intercultural Communication and the Global Classroom

## CHARLES A. BRAITHWAITE[1]

*In intercultural communication classes, a vital component is the opportunity to engage in dialogue with students from diverse cultures. In many classes this is possible if there are students from diverse cultures. Even so, many of the international culturally diverse students may have been in the country long enough to have become somewhat enculturated and, thus, are not truly representative of an interaction between members of diverse cultures. Charles Braithwaite at the University of Nebraska-Lincoln had developed a program whereby intercultural communication is taught in a global classroom through the use of Internet technology that gives students an opportunity to engage in real-time, face-to-face intercultural communication. His program so far involves universities in Pakistan, Yemen, Russia, and Turkey whose students participate in a "global classroom" where they may interact "face-to-face" with other students in*

*several countries directly from their own physical classrooms.*

*From reading this essay you will (1) learn about the felt need to change the way in which intercultural classes are taught; (2) understand how existing Internet technology made this approach to teaching relatively easy and very low cost; (3) become aware of the dynamics of the "global classroom;" (4) examine the characteristics of the global classroom model; (5) become aware of the simultaneous active engagement between students from the United States, Russia, Turkey, Pakistan, and Yemen; and (6) wonder why your intercultural communication class was not taught using this technology.*

One joy of teaching in the communication studies field is that students can easily recognize that we are providing practical skills they will use throughout

This original essay appears here in print for the first time. All rights reserved. Permission to reprint must be obtained from the author and the publisher. Dr. Charles A. Braithwaite is a research professor in the Center for Plains Studies at the University of Nebraska-Lincoln, Lincoln, Nebraska.

life. Courses such as public speaking, interviewing, and small-group communication provide invaluable learning experiences that students can get from no other discipline. What can make these classes so meaningful is the experiential dimension that most of these classes provide. Students in public speaking classes actually give speeches; interviewing classes provide opportunities to do actual interviews; small-group communication courses can provide experience in working with real groups. This combination of theory and practice makes for outstanding learning environments. Unfortunately, courses that focus on intercultural communication rarely can claim to provide the same real-world experiences for students as the other "practical" communication courses. That is not to say we do not provide essential knowledge and background that will help students interact successfully in intercultural settings outside of the classroom. The discipline of intercultural communication produces very useful tools that give students almost everything they need to eventually become competent intercultural communicators (c.f. McDaniel, Samovar, and Porter, 2007). However, what the majority of intercultural communication courses cannot provide, and was essentially unavailable until recently, is real face-to-face intercultural experiences in the classroom. In a public speaking class, students can experience what it is like to stand up in front of a large group of people and attempt to deliver a competent speech. However, in an intercultural communication class, an instructor would never bring in a person from a foreign land, stand him or her up in front of the class, and expect students to interact as if that was a *real* intercultural context. And when we engage in simulations and games in a class meant to illustrate cultural differences, instructors never imply that this takes the place of actually being in an intercultural encounter. Intercultural communication courses do provide opportunities to learn about many cultures, develop an understanding of one's own culture, gain knowledge of important communicative principles which apply to intercultural contexts, and, occasionally, get out of the class and interact one-on-one with people from different ethnicities and backgrounds. But to have hours and hours of face-to-face intercultural interaction with people from the other side of the world is not something we ever could provide in the past. That is no longer the case.

New Internet technology now gives students an opportunity to engage in real-time, face-to-face intercultural communication in ways never before possible (Huntington & Sudbery, 2005; West, 2010). The Department of Communication Studies at the University of Nebraska-Lincoln teaches intercultural communication courses which include live, synchronous, video and audio connections with universities in Pakistan, Yemen, Russia, and Turkey. Using regular commercial Internet connections, at no cost to the schools and needing only a laptop, an inexpensive web-camera, and a computer projector, students have real-time interaction through the use of large-screen video projections that create a "virtual classroom" where students talk face-to-face. The life size projections and instantaneous video and audio allows students at the University of Nebraska to have class discussions with faculty and students at Fatima Jinnah Women University in Islamabad, Pakistan; Yeditepe University in Istanbul, Turkey; Ataturk University in Ezrurum, Turkey; The University of Science & Technology, Saan'a City, Yemen; Voronezh State Agricultural University, Russia; Tyumen State Agrarian Academy, Tyumen State University (located in the western Siberian province of Tyumen, Russia), with other countries and classes being added all the time.

For the past five years, and involving over 300 students from the USA and over 600 students from countries around the world, we have taught multiple sections of our "Global Classroom." Students now have the opportunity to share aspects of their respective cultures, as well as address current events and concerns relevant to the countries we are talking with, which provides an experiential dimension to intercultural communication classes never before available, changing the way we approach the teaching of this important set of skills to communicate interculturally.

In this essay I will outline the "Global Classroom" method for teaching intercultural communication and discuss the important learning outcomes for students. It is important to note that presenting this new model is not intended as a critique of other pedagogical strategies for introducing students to the complex field of intercultural communication. Rather, my intent is to provide an alternative model which might serve as a jumping off point for those who want to begin incorporating some additional experiential material into their existing courses.

## BACKGROUND

Until five years ago, I taught intercultural communication courses in what must be a familiar fashion to faculty and students in the discipline. We read essays on intercultural communication theory, analyzed many case studies of real instances of cultural and intercultural contact, conducted classroom exercises and out-of-class activities designed to highlight selected intercultural communicative phenomena, and had students complete individual or group assignments on contemporary and relevant intercultural issues (c.f., Carbaugh, 1990). However, I was frustrated that I could not create the kind of intercultural and international environments I knew my students would encounter when they left the classroom. Even the presence of many students from around the world both in and out of the class did not create the reality I desired, because these students were now living and interacting in a new world and, to be successful, had to adapt to the new communicative norms, which necessarily resulted in their behavior being less similar to the conduct they would display in their country of origin. So the question remained: how to create an intercultural space in the classroom where students could interact in much the same way they would when they travel abroad?

The answer to this question came when I received an invitation from the Office of the Under Secretary for Public Diplomacy and Public Affairs, U.S. State Department, to participate in what they called "The Virtual Classroom Project." If I agreed to teach a course to U.S. students and include live Internet video conferencing with students from universities in other parts of the world, the U.S. State Department would provide the training, equipment, and travel funds to set up such a course. The idea for the Virtual Classroom came from Drs. Rosina Chia and Elmer Poe at East Carolina University (Chia & Poe, 2004). Chia and Poe wanted to create a model that was inexpensive and adaptable to many different learning environments around the world. The development in 1996 of the "H.323" protocols for providing audiovisual communication across the Internet meant that there was now an easy way to connect classrooms from anywhere the Internet was available. The new cameras and software using this H.323 standard connection required very little bandwidth, an important concern with developing countries, and were very simple to operate. Starting in 2003 with a video conference between East Carolina University and Soochow University in China, East Carolina now has classes across the curriculum with counterparts at twenty-three institutions in seventeen different countries (Chia, R., Smith, K., Hansen, M., and Hall, C., 2005).

With training provided by Chia and Poe, equipment provided by the U.S. State Department, and support from my university to try this new model of teaching, we set about finding international partners. I first teamed with a senior technology person on my campus who has been my partner in traveling to host countries and for setting up the technical connections. Contacts developed by our Office of International Affairs led us to our first partner—Voronezh State Agricultural University, located about 400 kilometers south of Moscow, in what is often referred to as the "Black Earth" region of Russia. VSAU's administrators invited us to visit their campus and explain the new project. Although met with much initial skepticism, and encountering many technical problems (not the least of which was the language barrier), we finally set up a demonstration connecting VSAU with the University of Nebraska-Lincoln. When the Rector of VSAU saw the clarity of communication, and the ease at which his faculty and technicians could achieve this connection, he declared that when we started classes in the coming fall semester there would be an "October Revolution" in higher education.

Bolstered by this success, we were able to continue to create partnerships with any university that had the minimum technical requirements and were willing to commit the faculty, staff, and students to this new model. So, for the next several years, we visited schools in Yemen, Pakistan, Turkey, and Spain where we set up equipment and trained faculty and technicians in what we now called "The Global Classroom." I recommended dropping the term "virtual" because that implied that the connection was somehow not real or less than what happens in a "real" classroom. However, once we started our video connections, this notion of being inferior to a regular class was quickly dispelled.

We structure the sections of this introduction to intercultural communication course to have two international partners each semester. For example, a class that meets twice a week will have one international partner connect on a Tuesday, and the other partner will connect on a Thursday. Since most universities outside the United States begin their semesters five to six weeks after school begins here, this allows us to provide an extensive orientation to important intercultural communication principles through readings and lectures, as well as an understanding of the technology and dynamics of video conferencing, prior to beginning the video links. And it means once the video connections begin, we can then concentrate solely on those interactions for the remaining weeks of the semester. On average, each Global Classroom experience involves twenty-five hours of face-to-face interaction each semester.

## INTERACTION IN THE GLOBAL CLASSROOM

It is difficult to describe the sensation which occurs each semester when we have our first video link with an international partner. The class meets at 0800 (8 A.M.) because we are often dealing with time-zone differences of seven, eight, or even thirteen hours. The U.S. American students sleepily take their seats and sip coffee or close their eyes as we wait for the connection to begin. A few seconds or minutes after eight, we hear three short beeps, and then the screen is filled with faces from the other side of the globe. The students looking at us have usually just finished their classes for the day and always seem very excited to see us. The U.S. students now start to see that their relatively small town in the middle of the United States is actually linked up with Siberia, or eastern Turkey, or an Islamic capital city they heard about on last night's news report. The look on their faces is something I never forget, and something none of them forget if we are to believe the evaluations they write at the end of the semester.

Several important characteristics of the Global Classroom must be introduced to help explain the strengths and limitations of using this new technology in the classroom. First, and this is both an advantage and disadvantage, almost all of the classroom interaction uses the English language. All of our international partners like having their students participate in the video links with a U.S. American university because it is a way to improve English language proficiency. That is not to say this is an ESL course, but, rather, it is a course where students who need to be skilled in English can interact in an environment where they get to speak as they might be doing in their chosen profession. For the U.S. students, it means they do not have to learn a new language in order to participate, making this much like what they will encounter as they travel the world to places where they know little if any of the native tongue. U.S. students make a point of learning a few words from the language of our international partners, and during class discussions, our partners often spend considerable time talking among themselves in their own language. So, while this focus on English may appear to be somewhat hegemonic, both partners gain significant advantages from this characteristic.

A second characteristic of the Global Classroom model is that the technology does not allow for much in the way of simultaneous speech. The microphones give precedence over who is speaking, so it is difficult to interrupt a speaker. You can do so, but it garbles the communication of all speakers. What this leads to is longer turns at talk and a slower pace of conversation. Again, this can be seen as a constraint of interaction, but it also acts to create a communicative climate that gives speakers more control over their speech, which is important to U.S. and foreign students alike.

A third characteristic related to the technology is the use of "life-size" video projections of the classrooms. By using computer projectors to display entire classes, the sense of being in the same room is heightened. It is similar to having a classroom divided by a glass wall with a curtain. Once that curtain is pulled back, students are for all intent and purpose in the same building, but prevented from stepping into the rooms with their classmates "next door." This effect is so pronounced that we observe occasions when someone on the screen steps out of the peripheral range of the camera, a student from the other side

> *It is difficult to describe the sensation which occurs each semester when we have our first video link with an international partner.*

will try to look at the screen and then turn their head to angle their vision as if to see where the other person went. Of course, this is not possible, but the fact that students act as if someone could still be seen if they move off camera demonstrates the how real the Global Classroom can become.

A fourth characteristic for interaction in the Global Classroom is the need to remember that the camera, and not the image on the screen, is the "eye" of the person you are speaking with. I come from a cultural background where eye contact during talk is the preferred form of interaction. Therefore, it is difficult to not look at speakers and listeners on the screen even though that means our partners will see me looking somewhat away from them. We position the camera as close to the projector screen as possible, but there is still going to be the perception that we are looking somewhat askance. This creates a need for the instructor to give the students an occasional reminder to look at the camera as much as possible. However, in all of the course assessments over the years, no one has commented that they found this distracting or problematic for interaction.

## ACTIVE ENGAGEMENT IN THE GLOBAL CLASSROOM

What is it like to have a class where twenty U.S. students are speaking face-to-face with twenty students from Russia or Pakistan or Turkey? For the purpose of introducing students to intercultural communication, the focus is primarily on learning about each other's respective cultures. The content of the Global Classroom interaction is student driven in that topics for presentations and discussions come from suggestions generated through talking about what we want to learn about each other. This means that no boundaries are set by the instructors in either country on what students can or cannot talk about. It is often the students themselves who assume a topic would be inappropriate for a given international partner, which leads to a discussion of where that stereotype originated. For example, U.S. American students during one semester initially

assumed that asking questions about homosexuality with our partners in Pakistan would be inappropriate. My response was "why don't we ask the Pakistani students?" Although there was some initial hesitation to bring this up, it soon became clear that our partners in Islamabad were more than happy to talk about this topic. In fact, it led to a long discussion about the role of Pakistan's minority "hijra" (transgendered males) and the new civil rights they were recently awarded by the courts. This discussion not only taught my students something important about culture in Pakistan; they also learned how their preconceived notions about Pakistanis could sometimes get in the way of communication. Of course, they had read in their textbooks about the impact of stereotyping, but only through this Global Classroom interaction did they see how it gets played out in actual intercultural interaction.

This student-driven content means the responsibility for what we will learn about other cultures rests with the class. As an instructor I give up a great deal of control over course content, but it is not a decision I have ever regretted. I may raise some general topics for discussion, such as the family, religious differences, and education. However, the students from both classes are the ones who generate the real creativity. For example, recent classes with Russian students led to discussions on the collaboration between the two countries regarding space exploration, how both countries are addressing the global economic crisis, and how cell phones have changed dating and relationships. Topics that were brainstormed between Turkish and U.S. American students included the roles of aunts and uncles, the role of the Ottoman Empire in supporting the Protestant Reformation, and how American television humor translates on Turkish television. By bringing together two groups of students from different cultural backgrounds, we are able to generate innumerable topics for learning that never appear in our textbooks or from the instructor. This becomes a bonus lesson in international collaboration.

Discussion on these and most topics begins in class with a PowerPoint™ presentation created by the

> *By bringing together two groups of students from different cultural backgrounds, we are able to generate innumerable topics for learning that never appear in our textbooks or from the instructor. This becomes a bonus lesson in international collaboration.*

students which was uploaded the day before using a course management system such as Blackboard™. While an individual or a group in one class is going through the presentation, the international partner is following along on another screen or with handouts of the PowerPoint™ slides. This allows for partners to both see and hear the content, as well as giving a common point of reference for discussion. The slides also help when the English language proficiency of students may be limited. As we know, students learning English often initially can write the language better than they can speak the language. For example, a student from Russia described how he spent a holiday, and it included "going to the liquor store, where I buy beer, vodka, and shampoo." The last item seemed puzzling to the U.S. American students until they saw his slide had the word "champagne" and not shampoo. There was a few seconds' pause as the Russian students realized what happened and started to laugh. They clued in the students in my class about the mistake and all of us shared a good-natured laugh. It is "mistakes" like this in our intercultural conversations which break any tension students might experience in this new learning environment and opens everyone up to the enjoyment one can have when encountering new cultures and people.

*What used to be a vague notion of a "foreign people" now has become a personal connection to a classmate.*

Once a presentation is complete, there is a discussion period where some of the most important learning experiences about intercultural communication take place. Again, we place no restrictions on interaction beyond general guidelines related to respect and tolerance. Slowly students start to raise their hands. It is an interesting moment when my students realize that the international partners raising their hands expect us to point at them so they can start to speak. Either by using a unidirectional or a hand-held microphone, questions start going back and forth regarding the content of what was just introduced, the methods for getting the information, how the presenters themselves respond to the content, or something that might not even be related to the topic at hand (as is all too common in our "regular" classes). Questions are sometimes asked to be repeated, as well as answers, because there may be difficulty deciphering the words being used, overcoming the accent

spoken, relating the comments to the content, or a host of other reasons we end up having to replay conversations that occur in face-to-face intercultural communication. Students on both sides see these communication difficulties as interesting problems to solve, and the only frustration they exhibit is when we run out of class time. I don't know what it says about me as a teacher, but the Global Classroom is the first occasion where I have had students complain that the class periods are too short.

## EVALUATING THE GLOBAL CLASSROOM EXPERIENCE

There are at least four learning outcomes for students and faculty, both U.S. American ones and our international partners, which emerge from using this new model for teaching intercultural communication. First, by having as much as twenty-five hours of face-to-face interaction with people in lands around the world, the concept of "culture" is no longer an abstraction. That is, because of the relatively close contact we have with our partners every week for so many weeks, we don't talk about them as "Turks," or Yemenis," or "Pakistanis," but instead speak of Mera, Basak, Saadia, Dimitry, Hassan, Hakan, etc. What used to be a vague notion of a "foreign people" now has become a personal connection to a classmate. For example, when a major earthquake struck Pakistan a few years ago, I received eleven e-mails from former students asking about how the students and faculty we encountered in the class were affected by the disaster and whether there was anything we could do to help. To students who went through the Global Classroom experience, culture is now composed of an amalgam of colleagues with some similarities and some differences.

At the same time, a second outcome of being exposed to twenty or more people from one country during the course of a semester, and hearing them all talk about similar topics, is that the personal responses from one place invariably reveal communicative patterns that are shared and meaningful to that group. For example, after hearing students from Turkey talk about their home towns, the U.S. American students noticed now every Turkish student used the word "love" to describe their city: "I love Basra," "I love Erzurum," and "I really, really love Istanbul!" We discussed how this was a concept never used by students from Russia or U.S. America. Noticing this pattern led to writing short analysis papers as to why this phenomenon might occur; the paper involved doing interviews with Turkish students via email and/or Skype™ outside of class, reading about Ottoman and Turkish history, and speculating about the impact of traditional family structure on young people living in a modern democracy. Hearing from multiple students over ten or more weeks has a similar effect on our international partners. At the end of the semester, we all talk about what we learned from the class and what more we still want to learn. Time and again our international partners reveal the patterns they saw about their U.S. American colleagues, e.g., "you all work so hard," "every student really likes to ask questions," "you don't talk about ethnic conflict we hear so much about from the USA," "all of you are quick to laugh." My favorite example is when a student from Russia, not long after the U.S. American students had talked about all of their part-time jobs and volunteer activities, said, "before this class I thought all Americans were fat and lazy. Now I see you are not lazy."

A third learning outcome, which has already been alluded to, concerns how intercultural communication concepts, which we had read about and discussed prior to the video connections, really come to life while engaging in face-to-face interaction. It is important to have knowledge about the impact of stereotyping and ethnocentrism and how they might impact intercultural communication. However, these notions begin to take on a different reality when U.S. American students watch a young woman in Islamabad, wearing a "salwar kameez" (traditional dress for women in Pakistan) and a head covering that only exposes a small portion of the face, talking about how her favorite musician is Tupac Shakur, how much she loves "gangsta rap," and how often she plays the CD "Thug Life, Vol. 1." Whatever preconceived thoughts the U.S. American students had about life for women in Pakistan have to be very carefully reexamined. And the readings the students and I do related to living multicultural lives take on new meaning when the U.S. American students hear of how a modern Turkish public relations student,

someone who has visited the United States many times and drives a new American automobile, describes how she won't tell her father she has a boyfriend because he would then demand they get married. As many stories as I may be able to tell in a class about various cultures and my own international experiences as illustrations of these concepts, they simply pale beside the face-to-face accounts from our international partners.

Finally, the learning outcome that takes many weeks to work on, but seems to make the biggest difference, concerns developing communicative strategies for increasing comprehension in intercultural settings. All too often our intercultural communication instruction focuses on the larger questions related to intercultural contact such as what is culture, what paradigms influence our interaction, how to mediate intercultural conflict, etc. All of these are important and need to be addressed. However, I've discovered since teaching in the Global Classroom that most of the students need to learn and want to learn some straightforward communication techniques that will improve their conversation with people from different cultures. The following are ones that seem to make the most difference to the intercultural dialogue in the Global Classroom:

*Slow down our speaking rate:*

The number-one complaint our international partners have about talking with U.S. American students is the speed of talk. Most U.S. American students speak around 150-175 words per minute, and that is often too fast to be adequately understood by people who have English as a second language and do not get to practice speaking and hearing English on a daily basis. U.S. American students do not need to talk to our international partners as if they were talking to a child, but the rate needs to be slower than in a "normal" classroom.

*Ask one question at a time:*

Again, when speaking to people who are still learning a new language, asking multiple questions at a time means the hearer is still translating the first question while the speaker moves on to the other questions. We need to learn to avoid double-barreled, triple-barreled, and quadruple-barreled questions. Too often we ask things like "Where do you want to work when you graduate from college? Do you want to live in Moscow? Do you want to work in the US?" This needs to be reduced to simply asking, "Where do you want to work when you graduate?" The rule should be to ask one question and then stop! You can always ask a follow-up question later.

*Keep your questions short:*

The same is true for questions that are too wordy. Don't say "I was just wondering, maybe you can answer for me a question I had about people in Turkey, I was wondering how often you go to and attend and pray at a mosque." Instead, simply ask "How often do you go to a mosque?"

*Try to avoid "fillers" before your question:*

Too often U.S. American students add what we might call a pre-elocutionary phrases before they ask their questions, i.e., phrases such as "I was just wondering…." or "I have a question I want to ask…" Although it might seem to be polite, it is more effective to ask the question without including these "introductions" to the question.

*When you don't understand or hear an answer, please don't be afraid to say so:*

Because there might be some reluctance to admit to not comprehending an answer, or to try and protect the feelings of the international partner when the language they used was not understood, it is certainly acceptable to ask a colleague to repeat an answer. It is also acceptable to ask others in the class if they might have understood the answer even if you did not. That is the great advantage of working as a group of speakers interacting with the international partners rather than being on your own.

## CONCLUSION

Incorporating new technology is commonplace in communication studies classrooms, and it certainly has been an important tool in teaching intercultural communication. As early as 1989 there were intercultural communication teachers and researchers using an early form of electronic communication known as "BITNET" to set up communication links around the world. Many intercultural communication courses encourage students to create electronic "pen pals" using e-mail and/or social networking sites like Facebook™ to enhance learning about other cultures. Skype™, a free software program which allows people to make both voice and video calls from computer to computer, has been incorporated into classroom lectures and exercises in order to bring new voices to the intercultural conversation. Any technology or strategy to expand opportunities for communication among diverse and dispersed audiences is only going to benefit our discipline.

What is unique about the Global Classroom model is that it makes face-to-face interaction an expected and regular part of the educational experience. Although we never become blasé about the ability to have free and open communication to classrooms around the world, students, faculty and technicians working in the Global Classroom eventually develop a taken-for-granted assumption about our video connections. The very rare moments when a technical difficulty arises, and we are unable to connect for a class period, are treated the same way as if we found the classroom door locked. Once the video links begin we just assume this is the normal way an intercultural class should occur: having different people from different lands "drop in" to the classroom to talk.

Based on the consistently positive evaluations that emerge each semester, we know the Global Classroom experience makes a difference in the lives of students. Students from all participating countries express increased desire to study and travel abroad, and U.S. American students are now exploring other countries they more than likely never would have considered before this experience. Faculty and technicians who participate now have opportunities to engage in more collaborative research ventures, and new resources become available to all campuses in terms of guest lectures, international colloquia, and symposiums.

I vividly remember the first time I realized just how powerful this new intercultural communication pedagogy could be. It was during a session with a women's college in Pakistan. During my visit to

Islamabad I had purchased some pashmina scarves for my wife, and I brought the items to class to show native Pakistani crafts to my students. When a Pakistani student saw the items, she asked if my wife knew how to properly wear a scarf. She then proceeded to instruct my teaching assistant how to drape the fabric around her shoulders and head. At one point in the demonstration, my assistant placed the scarf over her right shoulder after the Pakistani woman had said to move it to the left. When that happened, the woman in Islamabad actually reached toward the screen as if to attempt to move the scarf. She caught herself as this happened, pulled her hand back, and expressed her embarrassment. However, I was almost in tears, having realized that because of our Global Classroom technology, this woman forgot for a split second that she was over 13,000 kilometers away.

## References

Carbaugh, D. (Ed.) (1990). *Cultural communication and intercultural contact*. Hillsdale, NJ: Lawrence Erlbaum.

Chia, R. C., & Poe, E. (2004). Innovations in international education. *International Psychology Reporter*, Spring, 7–12.

Chia, R. C., Smith, K., Hansen, M., & Hall, C. (2005). Using virtual communication technology to enhance international experience. *National Social Science Journal*, 25 (2), 16–25.

Fischer, K. (2009, May 7). East Carolina U. uses simple technology to link its students with peers overseas. *The Chronicle of Higher Education*. Retrieved from http://chronicle.com/article/East-Carolina-U-Uses-Simpl/44302/

Huntington, A., & Sudbery, J. (2005). Virtual classrooms: Experiences of European collaborative teaching and learning. *Social Work Education*, 24(3), 217–228.

McDaniel, E., Samovar, L., and Porter, R. (2003). Understanding intercultural communication: The working principles. In L. A. Samovar and R. E. Porter, and E. R. McDaniel (Eds.). *Intercultural Communication: A Reader*, (12th ed., pp. 6–17). Boston: Wadsworth Cengage Learning.

West, C. (2010). Borderless via technology. *International Educator*, 19(2), 24–33.

## Note

1. The author must thank the following partners in the Global Classroom who make this experience possible: Rabia Akhtar, Fatima Jinnah Women University, Pakistan; Elena Cernighina and Artak Kamalyan, Voronezh State Agricultural University, Russia; Andrei Tolstikov, Tyumen State Agrarian Academy, Russia; Ayseli Usluata, Yeditepe University, Turkey; and M.Basak Uysal, Ataturk University, Turkey. The Global Classroom at the University of Nebraska-Lincoln would not continue without the support of the following: Bruce Sandhorst, Academic Services Coordinator; William Seiler, Chair, Department of Communication Studies; Harriet Turner, Director, Office of International Affairs; John Gilliam, Distance Classroom Technology Associate, and Dawn Braithwaite, Willa Cather Professor of Communication and the 2010 President of the National Communication Association.

## Concepts and Questions

1. What are the advantages of teaching intercultural communication in a Global Classroom setting?

2. How do virtual face-to-face interactions between students from diverse cultures improve the experiences of intercultural communication students?

3. In what ways could face-to-face interactions between students from different cultures help reduce stereotypes, prejudice, and religious intolerance.

4. As a student in a Global Classroom, what topics would you want included in the course curriculum?

5. If you were interacting with students from a different culture, what topics do you believe would be of benefit to improving your intercultural communication abilities?

6. What disadvantages do you see in utilizing a Global Classroom?

7. In what ways do you see the interaction between students in the Global Classroom fostering understanding and respect for each other's cultures?

8. Other than language, what would be the largest difficulty for you in interacting with a student from another culture?

# 7 Communicating Interculturally: Becoming Competent

*The fish only knows that it lives in the water after it is already on the riverbank. Without our awareness of another world out there, it would never occur to us to change.*

**Unknown**

*The obstacles to cross-cultural understanding may be conceptualized as differences in cultural assumptions and values.*

**Edward C. Stewart**

The two opening quotations to this chapter serve as a fitting introduction to the entire chapter. For this is a chapter whose goal is to increase your fund of knowledge about intercultural communication. It is our contention that this expanded knowledge base is essential if you are to become a more effective communicator, especially when interacting with people of cultures different from your own. You will notice that the two quotations speak of "change" and "obstacles." The idea of *change* should remind you that becoming a competent communicator necessitates that you examine your communication behaviors and be willing to change some of those behaviors. Second, there are numerous *obstacles* built into the intercultural setting, since your communication partners might perceive the world in a manner that is very different from the way you see it. We should also add as part of this introduction that while this particular chapter uses the term "Becoming Competent" in its title, in a sense this entire book has been concerned with helping you become a competent intercultural communicator.

Each of the preceding chapters introduced you to diverse cultures and settings to demonstrate how people from a variety of cultures view the world and communicate as participants in that world. It is our conviction that by observing these cultural differences you have collected a fund of knowledge that will assist you in understanding people from a variety of cultures. However, our examination to this point has been more theoretical than practical. Knowing about other cultures and people is only the first step in attempting to understand how intercultural communication operates in the real world. Taking part in intercultural communication requires reciprocal and complementary participation by you and your communication partner(s). This means that intercultural communication becomes *an activity* in which participants must make simultaneous inference.

> **It is our belief that communication is something people do—*a shared activity that involves action.***

ences not only about their own roles, but also about the roles of the other(s) in the interaction. This act of mutual role taking must exist before people can achieve a level of communication that results in shared understanding. In intercultural communication this means that you must recognize your own culture and the culture of the other person(s) as well.

It is our belief that communication is something people do—*a shared activity that involves action*. Regardless of how much you may understand another culture or person on an intellectual level, even if you have a clear picture of them in your head, in the final analysis *communication means interaction*. This generalization implies that you are part of a behavioral exchange and must be prepared to adjust your communicative behaviors to the specific situation. The series of readings in this chapter are intended to improve the way you connect to others by providing some of the information needed to develop and improve your intercultural communication competence.

There are two common threads that link all the selections in this chapter together. First, they all speak of potential communication problems (obstacles). Second, they also suggest some possible solutions to those problems (change). It is our contention that being alert to potential problems, and knowing how to solve them, are major steps toward achieving intercultural communication competence. In short, once problems have been identified it is easier to seek out possible solutions to those problems.

# Axioms for a Theory of Intercultural Communication Competence

BRIAN H. SPITZBERG

*In this introductory essay Brian H. Spitzberg initiates a discussion intended to alert you to the added problems facing you when the component of culture is part of a communication event. He writes,*

> *The challenge of identifying the nature of communication competence is challenging enough when interactants share common cultural assumptions and orientations. When the complexity of divergent underlying cultural perspectives is taken into account, the prospect of formulating a valid theory or assessment of intercultural communication competence seems far more challenging.*

*To meet that challenge Spitzberg undertakes two major assignments. First, he inventories and explains the current state of research regarding intercultural communication competence. Second, using this summary of the status quo as a backdrop, Spitzberg offers some guidance for future study and research.*

*Spitzberg begins his analysis with a general definition of communication competence: "Communication competence is defined as social behavior that is perceived as relatively appropriate and effective for a given context." Employing this definition as a starting point, he then moves to a detailed survey of a number of intercultural communication competency and relational models: (1) compositional, (2) co-orientational, (3) developmental, (4) adaptational, (5) causal, and (6) relational. Once he has explicated these models the author offers seven axioms that serve to explain nearly all of the basic components of intercultural competency. While these axioms are somewhat definitional, when viewed as a whole these proposed truisms serve to clarify what Spitzberg calls a basic model: a model that helps describe the workings of competency. Spitzberg also suggests these truisms can be used for "future theory development." The seven axioms of intercultural communication competency developed by Spitzberg are*

1. *People are more similar across cultures than they are different.*
2. *Judgments of competence are subject to several systemic conditions.*
3. *Competence is a judgment.*
4. *Competence is evaluated most universally in terms of "quality."*
5. *Competence judgments are related to skills.*
6. *Competence judgments are related to motivation and knowledge.*
7. *People–not cultures–interact.*

## INTRODUCTION

Near the turn of the last century, psychologists began to explore scientifically the possibility that humans possess a common underlying intelligence and that this capability could be measurable. The yardstick of an intelligence quotient (IQ) was hypothesized, and it was not long before similar conceptions of "social intelligence" were suggested (Thorndike, 1920). By the 1960s, interest in social intelligence was reconceptualized in terms of interpersonal and communication competence. The prospect of a common human metric of social skillfulness retained its scientific attraction, but after almost a century of scholarly effort at identifying the existence or precise nature of this common metric, the goal continues to be elusive.

There are few places where the promise and performance of academic models of social skills has been so important, yet frustrating, as in the intercultural context. The challenge of identifying the nature of communication competence is challenging enough when interactants share common cultural assumptions and orientations. When the complexity of

This original essay appears here in print for the first time. All rights reserved. Permission to reprint must be obtained from the author and the publisher. Dr. Brian H. Spitzberg is a professor in the School of Communication at San Diego State University, San Diego, California.

divergent underlying cultural perspectives is taken into account, the prospect of formulating a valid theory or assessment of intercultural communication competence seems far more challenging.

Progress in pursuing a viable theory of intercultural communication competence (ICC) depends first on mapping the current conceptual territory by identifying and distinguishing among existing models of ICC. A second step will involve the formulation of a clear set of guideposts for future inquiry and research. This essay attempts these steps, with an eye toward developing a philosophical foundation for subsequent scholarly conceptualizations of ICC. This analysis draws from an accumulated consideration of the research and theory regarding communication competence (e.g., Spitzberg, 1983, 1987, 1989, 1993, 1994, 2000, 2007; Spitzberg & Brunner, 1991; Spitzberg & Chagnon, 2009; Spitzberg & Cupach, 1984, 1989, 2002).

## ORIENTING TO THE PHENOMENON

*Communication competence* is defined as social behavior that is perceived as relatively appropriate and effective for a given context. This is a working definition that recognizes that to qualify as communication, behavior must have a potential *social* audience and context in mind, and that to qualify as competent, this behavior must achieve some acceptable functional level of appropriateness and effectiveness in a given context. The *context* of any communication can be understood at numerous levels, including cultural, chronological, relational, physical or environmental, and functional (Spitzberg, 2000). *Culture* can be understood here as a relatively elemental theoretical term, consisting of the "enduring yet evolving intergenerational attitudes, values, beliefs, rituals/customs, and behavioral patterns into which people are born but that is structurationally created and maintained by people's ongoing actions" (Spitzberg & Chagnon,

> *There are few places where the promise and performance of academic models of social skills has been so important, yet frustrating, as in the intercultural context.*

> Communication competence *is defined as social behavior that is perceived as relatively appropriate and effective for a given context.*

2009, pp. 6–7). Culture is most commonly marked by such common designations as nationality, ethnicity, race, tribe, religion, or region. Thus, when interaction occurs among people from different cultures, it can be understood as involving intercultural communication competence. There have been dozens, if not hundreds, of attempts to develop models of intercultural communication competence, and sorting through these conceptual trees is a necessary first step in seeing the theoretical forest.

## THE STRUCTURE OF ICC MODELS

As part of a project to survey the landscape of current theoretical efforts, Spitzberg and Chagnon (2009) examined prominent models of ICC. The resulting summary analysis identified five basic types of ICC models: compositional, co-orientational, developmental, adaptational, and causal. To this typology will be added relational models.

*Compositional* models represent the conceptual or empirical components of intercultural communication competence. These models do not specify the nature of the interrelationships among these components, at least not in a manner that could be directly falsified. For example, Howard Hamilton (1998) proposes three basic components: attitudes, knowledge, and skills. Attitudes that promote ICC include awareness of cultural values, understanding and devaluing ethnocentrism or discrimination, and appreciation of the value of risk taking and cross-cultural interaction. Knowledge includes an awareness of self, an understanding of oppressions, and an appreciation of the nature of social change and the effects of cultural differences on communication. Skills include an ability to engage in self-reflection, identify differences, take multiple perspectives in multiple contexts, and challenge discriminatory acts. These components collectively comprise ICC, but their specific relationships to one another or to other types of processes, functions or outcomes are less articulated. Other typical models that fit the compositional category include facework (Ting-Toomey & Kurogi, 1998), pyramid (Deardorff, 2006), and global (Hunter, White, & Godbey, 2006) competence models.

*Co-orientational* models of ICC focus on the achievement of overlap in symbolic meanings across interactants. These models presume that a product of the process of ICC is greater commonality of meaning, understanding, accuracy, or mental content. Such models often value clarity, directness, feedback processes, or facilitators of overlap in symbolic meanings. For example, Fantini (1995) proposes that as two communicators interact, their use of pragmatic actions in a given sociocultural context link with symbol and form systems such as verbal and nonverbal messages, and also with semantic principles of meaning attribution. These links of pragmatics, symbol systems and semantics, when engaged in ongoing interaction, allow two distinct worldviews to achieve increasing correspondence in reference to a "cosmovision" of common reference and orientation. Other exemplars of co-orientational models include Byram's (1997) intercultural competence model, Rathje's (2007) coherence-cohesion model, and Kupka's (2008) intercultural competence model for strategic human resource management.

*Developmental* models are distinguished by their emphasis on a chronological process of change or evolution. Developmental models tend to identify phases, stages, or timelines along which certain changes are likely to be marked in the process of adapting to another culture. For example, Bennet (1986) hypothesized the two broad stages of ethnocentric processes and ethnorelative processes. When a communicator first experiences another culture, there is some denial of its value, then some defense or reversal of this view, and then some

> *Knowledge includes an awareness of self, an understanding of oppressions, and an appreciation of the nature of social change and the effects of cultural differences on communication.*

> *When a communicator first experiences another culture, there is some denial of its value, then some defense or reversal of this view, and then some minimization of the relevance or importance of differences between the native and new cultures.*

minimization of the relevance or importance of differences between the native and new cultures. The communicator is expected eventually to experience a shift into more ethnorelative stages, in which acceptance of the new culture in its uniqueness occurs, followed by adaptation and then integration. Other prototypes of developmental models include King and Baxter Magolda's (2005) intercultural maturity model and Lysgaard's (1955; see also Gullahorn & Gullahorn, 1962) well-known U-curve model.

*Adaptational* models are generally similar to compositional models, but are extended from a relatively individual perspective to a dyadic or group perspective. Adaptational models also tend to focus on a process of one communicator adjusting behavior to the host or other interactant's culture. Berry, Kim, Power, Young, and Bujaki (1989), for example, anticipate that there are four basic styles of attitude acculturation, defined by the answers to two questions: is maintenance of relationships with other groups valued, and is maintenance of cultural identity and characteristics valued? A communicator who values neither maintenance of relationships nor identity will engage in a marginalizing style of communication. A communicator who values identity but not relationship maintenance will lean toward a segregationist or separatist style of interaction. A communicator who values the maintenance of relationships but not self-identity will be inclined to assimilate, whereas a communicator who values both identity and relationship maintenance will pursue a style of communicative integration with the culture. Other prototypes of adaptational models include Kim's (1988) ICC model, Gallois, Franklin-Stokes, Giles, and Coupland's (1988) accommodation model, and Navas et al.'s (2005) relative acculturation model.

*Causal* models are typically designed specifically for a quantitative test of specific relationships among proposed ICC components. These models tend to predict particular concepts as they relate to one another and collectively predict an outcome for the intercultural system or relationship. Hammer, Wiseman, Rasmussen, and Bruschke (1998), for example, hypothesized four clusters of initial predictors: interpersonal saliencies (i.e., intimacy attraction); intergroup saliencies (i.e., cultural identity, knowledge of host cultural similarity); message exchange (i.e., passive strategies, interactive strategies, self-disclosure, language proficiency); and host contact conditions (i.e., host attitudes, favorable contacts). These concepts are expected to predict satisfaction with the interaction and relationship, but this influence is expected to occur through processes of attributional confidence and anxiety reduction. That is, favorable conditions for an intercultural relationship to be satisfying depend on the confidence of the communicator in the other culture, and the ability to manage the experience of anxiety about the other culture. Other causal path models include studies by Arasaratnam (2008), Griffith and Harvey (2000), and Ting-Toomey (1999). Deardorff (2006) also proposes a model that, although circular in visualization, proposes a particular outcome (i.e., effective and appropriate intercultural communication) at the end of a path of individual (i.e., attitudes and knowledge) and interaction (i.e. adaptability, flexibility, empathy, ethnorelative views) processes.

*Relational* models take on many of the features of adaptational, developmental and causal models, but explicitly focus their outcomes on relationship formation and development. Such models emphasize that communication is at some level what a relationship consists of, and it is the competence of that communication that is likely to determine the progression of that relationship. Typical of this category is a model by Imahori and Lanigan (1989), which hypothesizes that a sojourner's motivation, knowledge, skills, experiences and goals will interact with a host national's motivation, knowledge, skills, experiences and goals to predict a variety of relational outcomes. The relational outcomes include intercultural effectiveness, communication effectiveness, relational validation, intimacy, relational satisfaction, relational commitment, relational stability and uncertainty reduction.

There is clearly no shortage of approaches to conceptualizing intercultural communication competence.

While there may be intellectual value in diversity of approach, there are also drawbacks. First, one of the hallmarks of scientific credibility is the development of common terms, axioms, and common working paradigms through which "normal science" can be conducted (Kuhn, 1970). Second, the practical tasks of developing educational curricula, organizational training, counseling approaches, and the measures (i.e. "social intelligence tests") these imply, all presume a valid framework within which common objectives can be coordinated. Third, even if a common paradigm cannot be established, it is important to articulate what distinguishes one paradigm from another so that intellectual choices can be made on a more reasoned basis. In an attempt to resolve some of these challenges, an axiomatic framework is developed to facilitate theoretical and empirical progress in conceptualizing and measuring ICC.

## AN AXIOMATIC APPROACH TO ICC

Formal axiomatic theory is intended to formulate $x = fy$ types of statements (e.g., adaptability [$x$] is positively related [$f$] to intercultural communication competence [$y$]) that can then be deductively related and expanded. The axioms developed here are somewhat more definitional in nature (i.e., $x = y$), but nevertheless are intended to form a relatively coherent and useful system. They are also intended to constitute a basic model from which future theory development can proceed. The model will be best prefaced by a somewhat unexpected argument in a book about intercultural communication:

1. *People are far, far, far, far, more similar across cultures than they are different.*

   We evolved from a common set of genetic ancestors on this planet only a few thousand generations ago. As biological beings, we share very common needs—food, shelter, security, some degree of predictability of environment, curiosity, attachment, mating, and group relations such as cooperation and competition (Bugental, 2000). We are all hard-wired to learn language, have relatively accurate ways of perceiving the world around us (Osgood, 1969), and appear to have even evolved sets of relatively universal values (Schwartz et al., 2001). We are, in many ways, a universal people (Brown, 1991; Heine & Buchtel, 2009; Lonner, 1980). The importance of starting with this axiom is to indicate that a single theoretical model of ICC is not only plausible, but perhaps a necessary result of such speculation.

2. *Judgments of competence are subject to several systemic conditions.*

   Competence is commonly assumed to be a synonym for ability, and this is indeed a proper denotative meaning. In the context of actual human interaction, however, it seems clear that the determination of a communicator's actual ability is limited by a number of realizations about the nature of making such attributions. That is, in social contexts, actual ability is less important than what people think about the ability.

   2.1—*Equifinality.* Equifinality describes a characteristic of systems in which many possible paths may lead to the same endpoint, or more precisely, "the same final state can be reached from different initial conditions and in different ways" (von Bertalanffy, 1968, p. 79). Different behaviors (e.g., facial expression vs. questions) can produce the same outcome in the same context (e.g., a job interview). A potential lover may enact a smoothly practiced script of courtship and flirtation to get a date, whereas another may accidentally engage in self-deprecating or embarrassing slips of the tongue to get a date, and yet, both may succeed.

   2.2—*Multifinality.* Multifinality is a conceptual partner to equifinality. It describes the character of systems in which a given path might lead to multiple possible endpoints (Ramaprasad, 1983). The same behavior (e.g., smiling) may produce different outcomes in different contexts (e.g., a prayer service vs. a party). A roommate may yell one time at another roommate for not doing a fair share of the chores, and ask politely the next time, and both may produce similar compliance.

   Equifinality represents a type of "many-to-one" relationships, or a system property of "convergence," whereas multifinality represents a type of "one-to-many" relationships, or a system property of divergence (Wilden, 1972, p. 492). Both reflect the essential complexity and unpredictability of any given interaction or relationship based only upon knowledge of initial conditions. As such, these properties indicate the fundamentally creative potential that communication introduces to any encounter or relationship.

   2.3—*Locus.* Attribution theory proposes that there is a self-serving bias of perception, i.e., that people are inclined generally to view self in favorable ways compared to the views of others (Kelley & Michela, 1980; Miller & Ross, 1975). Research indicates that people generally perceive themselves as more competent than the average person (see, e.g., Dunning, Heath, & Suls, 2004; Kruger, 1999; Williams & Gilovich, 2008). Whether it is due to perceptual focus, activity salience or self-enhancing motivations, it is clear that different perceivers perceive a given performance or interactant differently. In any given episode of interaction, there may be several perspectives of perception, including self, fellow interactant(s), bystanders, and potentially, if the interaction is recorded and evaluated by teachers or researchers, observers. Each of these perspectives permit, and may systematically imply, divergent types of competence evaluations (Cupach & Spitzberg, 1983).

3. *Therefore, competence is a judgment.*

   3.1—*Competence is not inherent to behavior.* If any given behavior may produce different ends, and different behaviors can produce the same end, and if different perceivers perceive and evaluate a given behavior differently, it follows that competence is not *in* the behavior, but in people's *interpretations* of the behavior. At least since Korzybski (1994), it has been widely understood that the word is not the thing it refers to, and that therefore, meanings are in people and not the words themselves. Thus, competence, as an evaluative inference about a person's communication behavior, exists not in the performance itself but in the social evaluation of behavior by a given perceiver in a given context. Therefore,

3.2—*Competence is an impression or evaluative inference.* Competence is a judgment made about a given behavior or set of behaviors, and made in reference to socially negotiated criteria of relevance to the context in which behavior is performed and evaluated. A person may engage in highly polished and interesting flirtation behavior (a joke and a smile), but if it is in the context of a job interview or in the receipt of tragic news, such behavior is unlikely to be evaluated as competent. Thus, competence is not an ability or set of skills or behaviors per se, but a judgment about the adequacy or value of that behavior in context.

4. *Competence is evaluated most universally in terms of "quality."*

In any given particular context, there may be any number of relevant criteria of adequacy or value to infer about communication behavior. Many criteria for gauging the competence of behavior have been suggested, including clarity, content knowledge, understanding, satisfaction, efficiency, attractiveness, attraction, intimacy, and so forth. All of these criteria, however, seem subordinate to a general concept of quality. Communication of higher quality, however this may be defined, is generally preferable to communication of lower quality. Quality, in essence, takes into account the variations and complexities of a particular communication context, and still asks: what is the best thing to be done here? It follows that quality, in turn, is likely to be a function of two primary dimensions of evaluation: appropriateness and effectiveness.

4.1—*Appropriateness.* Appropriateness refers to the legitimacy or fit of behavior to a given context. It is often equated with normative behavior, or behavior that avoids violating expectancies or rules of the situation. A problem with this view, however, is that an action may be extremely creative or novel, and yet competent, and therefore not normative or expected. The ordinary rules or expectations of a first date, for example, may be to meet at a social place where food and drink and music are likely. In contrast, a person might instead invite another out to view an art auction or exhibit, feed parrots at an exotic bird rehabilitation site, or walk a path through a park as a first date. Such activities do not fit the typical societal expectancies for college student dating, but might have the benefit of distinguishing the person's creativity and difference from the norm. Furthermore, the best communicator may be the person who faces a difficult situation and finds a way of renegotiating the rules of the situation—redefining the very nature of the situation (Pearce & Cronen, 1980). Research indicates that many college students at some point or another renegotiate a relationship that was considered a (platonic) friendship into a romantic (sexual) relationship, or a romantic relationship that has ended into a friendship, and sometimes back again (as with "friends-with-benefits"), suggesting that competence sometimes exists in the ability to renegotiate the rules of a context (Bisson & Levine, 2009; Dailey, Pfiester, Jin, Beck, & Clark, 2009; Schneider & Kenny, 2000).

4.2—*Effectiveness.* Effectiveness refers to the ability to achieve relatively rewarding outcomes in a given context. Effectiveness is often inappropriately equated with achieving satisfying or desired outcomes. A problem with this equation is that there are contexts in which any action may produce undesired or dissatisfying outcomes. Breaking up with a person or delivering bad news may inevitably produce

> *Appropriateness refers to the legitimacy or fit of behavior to a given context.*

unpleasant outcomes, but there are more and less competent ways of delivering such news. Therefore, effectiveness refers to the achievement of outcomes that are preferable *relative to* the possibilities the context permits, even if this means the best way of minimizing losses or costs.

To a large extent, the self is the best judge of effectiveness, whereas others are the best judge of the self's appropriateness. Nevertheless, people make judgments of appropriateness and effectiveness about both their own behavior and the behavior of others. A person who is capable of communicating in a way that is perceived as effective at achieving preferable outcomes, and doing so in a way that preserves the collective sense of appropriateness in the context, is likely to have performed in a manner that is competent, moral, ethical, ideal, and high in quality (Spitzberg & Cupach, 2002). Such a universal claim, however, is not without some theoretical conditions.

4.3—*Probability conjecture*. Given that competence is not inherent in the behavior, and is instead in the inferences and judgments made of such behaviors, it follows that no algorithm can guarantee such inferences or judgments. Assuming the existence of at least a modicum of free will in the nature of human experience, the optimal conjectures and predictions that can be made are probabilistic in nature. No behavior or behavioral script guarantees competence—only a probability of competence.

4.4—*Expectancy conjecture*. One of the factors that is likely to affect the probability of competence impressions is the valence of expectancies. People enter social contexts with expectancies, either based on prior experiences or based on analogue contexts cognitively matched to the anticipated encounter. Consistent with enormous amounts of research into the evaluation-potency-

activity (E-P-A)dimensions of perception (Heise, 1979; Osgood, May & Miron, 1975), such expectations will be valenced. It follows that generally perceivers will evaluate communication more positively to the extent that it fulfills positively valenced expectancies, or appropriately violates negative expectancies. In contrast, communication will likely be viewed as more incompetent to the extent it fulfills negatively valenced expectancies or violates positively valenced expectancies.

4.5—*Continuum conjecture*. There may be social contexts that are purely dichotomous in relevant judgments of competence, but it seems likely that even these may be illusions of dichotomy. A job interviewee may not get a particular job, but there may be potential for that same interviewer to hire the candidate at a later date for a different job, or to refer the candidate to another employer. A divorce may seem final, but there are many paths and many ends to the various possible relationships the two people may negotiate subsequently. If competence is a function of appropriateness and effectiveness, it seems reasonable to conjecture that there are always *degrees* of competence to be evaluated. Judgments of quality are likely arrayed along a continuum, from lower to higher.

4.6—*Curvilinearity conjecture*. Any behavior or action can be performed to excess. The same behavior (e.g., eye contact) that is competent in any given context is likely to be perceived as incompetent if performed to excess (e.g., 50 percent eye contact vs. 100 percent eye contact). Research in a variety of areas suggests a curvilinear relationship between the amount of a behavior and its positive evaluation, including the relationships of (a) verbal output to behavioral receptivity and evaluation (Brown, 1980; Hayes & Meltzer, 1972; Street & Brady, 1982; Wheeless, Frymier, & Thompson, 1992); (b) self-disclosure and evaluations (Brewer & Mittelman, 1980; Cozby, 1972; Davis, Frye, & Joure, 1975); (c) cognitive or content complexity and verbal fluency (Berger, Karol, & Jordan, 1989; Schachter, Christenfeld, Ravina, & Bilous, 1991); (d) interactional proximity and positive impressions (Patterson & Sechrest, 1970); (e) nonverbal immediacy and learning (Comstock, Rowell, & Bowers, 1995); (f) desired intimacy and relationship quality (Harper & Elliott, 1988); and (g) behavioral accommodation and relationship quality (Fletcher, Thomas, & Durrant, 1999).

5. *Competence judgments are related to skills.*

Just because competence is not in the behavior does not diminish the importance of behavior to a theory of communication competence. The behavior is the communication, and as such, is expected to reveal systematic relationships to judgments of competence. That is, equifinality and multifinality do not prevent prediction—they just prevent *perfect* prediction. Certain skills are more likely than others to predict impressions of competence across context types, and research in a variety of domains has demonstrated across decades of research that certain types of behavior are more likely than others to be perceived as competent, attractive, efficient, or satisfying (see, e.g., Dillard & Spitzberg, 1984; Spitzberg & Chagnon, 2009; Spitzberg & Cupach, 1984, 2002). The objective of any theoretical or assessment program of instruction, intervention, or investigation is to identify the skills that are most *likely* to be perceived as competent, and identify ways in which understandings and performances of these skills can be optimally matched to relevant contexts.

This axiom ultimately provides a more ethical basis upon which curricula can be predicated. Instead of claiming that learning a behavior *makes* a person competent, which it cannot because competence does not inhere in the behavior, the claim is that learning a set of behaviors and their relationship to competence evaluations increases the student's *likelihood* of being competent. Such an approach is more likely to accord with students' everyday experiences and with the results of scientific research seeking to predict human behavior and perceptions.

6. *Competence judgments are related to motivation and knowledge.*

The probability of linkage between behavior and competence judgments has been conjectured as a broader complex than just skills. Skills do not emerge *ex nihilo*, but from a conative ontology of human action encompassing the components of motivation, knowledge and skills. Kantian and Cartesian influences have no doubt simplified the distinctions between the affective, the cognitive and the behavioral (Bloom, 1956; Havighurst, 1957). This tripartite distinction nevertheless has considerable heuristic value in formulating conceptions of competent interaction.

Of the over 20 models of intercultural communication competence reviewed by Spitzberg and Chagnon (2009), by far the most common constitutive components were motivation, knowledge, and skills, although not always labeled precisely with these terms. *Motivation* refers to the many positive and negative valences that move a communicator toward, against, or away from a particular path of activity. *Knowledge* represents the possession and understanding of resources that inform the enactment of skills in a given context, including the ability to acquire informational resources, whether by questions, observation, cognitive modeling, or creative introspection. *Skills* are repeatable goal-directed behavioral sequences producing some level of goal achievement. In general, it is conjectured that the more *motivated*, *knowledgeable*, and *skilled* a communicator is, the more likely it is the communicator will achieve the *outcome* of being perceived, by self and other(s), as competent in any given *context*. It is also conjectured that any theoretical model that excludes any of these core components (i.e., motivation, knowledge, skills, context, outcomes) is incomplete, and will be benefitted by including the missing components, in one form or another.

*7. People interact—not cultures.*

To some degree, the term "intercultural communication" is a misnomer. Communication does not occur *between cultures* so much as *between communicators who to some degree or another are differentially influenced by their cultural perspectives* (Spitzberg, 1989). The term intercultural communication is often applied in a presumptive manner—presuming that people who come from different nations, ethnicities, races, religions, and so forth are by definition engaging in intercultural communication. If competence is indeed an impression, and if there are many paths to the same end and many ends to a given path, it follows that culture does not *necessarily* alter the outcome of a given communicative encounter. A person seeking directions from a native may not share the language, perspective, or values of the host, and yet these interactants may be able to negotiate directions successfully. Interethnic romantic relationships and marriages may present more potential problems than intraethnic relationships, *ceteris paribus*, but this is quite different than presupposing that culture is a dominant factor influencing their negotiation of the relationship. The complexities of maintaining any relationship may vastly overshadow the role of culture in the relationship's outcomes.

The most immediate implication of this axiom is that a theory of intercultural communication competence is necessarily a subset of a theory of interpersonal communication competence. Excluding "interactions" such as diplomacy or interorganizational relations through document transfer, it is people who interact with one another, not cultures (Spitzberg, 1989). In any given context, culture may well be so deeply submerged into the background that it makes little difference to the foreground of competent interaction. Thus, the first priority to understanding intercultural communication competence is to develop a framework for understanding ICC, and then incorporate the theoretical conditions in which culture is likely to influence the interaction under investigation.

> *Most contexts of communication involve extensions of the motivation, knowledge, and skills implicit in a model of interpersonal competence.*

# EXTENDING THE AXIOMS

A theory of interpersonal competence is to a large extent a grand unifying theory of communication. Most contexts of communication involve extensions of the motivation, knowledge, and skills implicit in a model of interpersonal competence. To the extent that culture plays a role, it plays it through the motivation, knowledge, and skills of the interactants involved. Many models of ICC have already proffered conceptualizations, and occasionally measurement approaches, that represent differentiated instantiations of these core components. Yet the attempts to validate these models, much less to replicate validations across different research groups in different contexts, are seriously undeveloped.

If institutional assessment objectives are increasing in importance, it will be increasingly important for institutions to have coherent conceptual and operational approaches within which such objectives can be framed. Given research indicating hundreds of different concepts considered related to ICC (Spitzberg & Chagnon, 2009), which would be unwieldy and overly complex to use in an assessment context, it is important to pursue parsimonious and heuristic approaches that can bring coherence to the scholarly and pedagogical context of intercultural communication competence. The axiomatic approach developed here is intended to provide a flexible framework within which such future efforts can be extended.

## Acknowledgement

Thanks are due to the Japanese Association of College English Teachers, Kyushu-Okinawa Chapter, who invited the essay upon which this article is based: Spitzberg, B. H. (2009). Axioms for a theory of intercultural communication competence. *Annual Review of English Learning and Teaching, 14*, 69–81.

## References

Arasaratnam, L. A. (2008, May). *Further testing of a new model of intercultural communication competence.* Paper presented at the annual meeting of the International Communication Association, New York, NY.

Bennett, M. J. (1986). A developmental approach to training for intercultural sensitivity. *International Journal of Intercultural Relations, 10*, 179–196.

Berger, C. R., Karol, S. H., & Jordan, J. M. (1989). When a lot of knowledge is a dangerous thing: The debilitating effects of plan complexity on verbal fluency. *Human Communication Research, 16*, 91–119.

Berry, J. W., Kim, U., Power, S., Young, M., & Bujaki, M. (1989). Acculturation in plural societies. *Applied Psychology: An International Review, 38*, 185–206.

Bisson, M. A., & Levine, T. R. (2009). Negotiating a friends with benefits relationship. *Archives of Sexual Behavior, 38*, 66–73.

Bloom, B. S. (1956). *Taxonomy of educational objectives, handbook I: The cognitive domain.* New York: David McKay.

Brewer, M. B., & Mittelman, J. (1980). Effects of normative control of self-disclosure on reciprocity. *Journal of Personality, 48*, 89–102.

Brown, B. L. (1980). Effects of speech rate on personality attributions and competency evaluations. In H. Giles, W. P. Robinson, & P. M. Smith (Eds.), *Language: Social psychological perspectives* (pp. 293–300). Oxford: Pergamon.

Brown, D. E. (1991). *Human universals.* Philadelphia: Temple University Press.

Bugental, D. B. (2000). Acquisition of the algorithms of social life: A domain-based approach. *Psychological Bulletin, 126*, 187–219.

Byram, M. (1997). *Teaching and assessing intercultural communication competence.* New York: Multilingual Matters.

Comstock, J., Rowell, E., & Bowers, J. W. (1995). Food for thought: Teacher nonverbal immediacy, student learning, and curvilinearity. *Communication Education, 44*, 251–266.

Cozby, P. C. (1972). Self-disclosure, reciprocity and liking. *Sociometry, 35*, 151–160.

Cupach, W. R., & Spitzberg, B. H. (1983). Trait versus state: A comparison of dispositional and situational measures of interpersonal communication competence. *Western Speech Communication Journal, 47*, 364–379.

Dailey, R. M., Pfiester, A. Jin, B., Beck, G., & Clark, G. (2009). On-again/off-again dating relationships: How are they different from other dating relationships? *Personal Relationships, 16*, 23–47.

Davis, T. B., Frye, R. L., & Joure, S. (1975). Perceptions and behaviors of dogmatic subjects in a T-group setting. *Perceptual and Motor Skills, 41*, 375–381.

Deardorff, D. K. (2006). Identification and assessment of intercultural competence as a student outcome of internationalization. *Journal of Studies in Intercultural Education, 10*, 241–266.

Dillard, J., & Spitzberg, B. H. (1984). Global impressions of social skills: Behavioral predictors. In R. N Bostrom (Ed.), *Communication Yearbook* (Vol. 8, pp. 156–176). New Brunswick, NJ: Transaction.

Dunning, D., Heath, C., & Suls, J. M. (2004). Flawed self-assessment: Implications for health, education, and the workplace. *Psychological Science in the Public Interest, 5*, 69–106.

Fantini, A. E. (1995). Language, culture, and world view: Exploring the nexus. *International Journal of Intercultural Relations, 19*, 143–153.

Fletcher, G., Thomas, G., & Durrant, R. (1999). Cognitive and behavioral accommodation in close relationships. *Journal of Social and Personal Relationships, 16*, 705–730.

Gallois, C., Franklyn-Stokes, A., Giles, H., & Coupland, N. (1988). Communication accommodation in intercultural encounters. In Y. Y. Kim (Ed.), *Theories in intercultural communication* (pp. 157–185). Thousand Oaks, CA: Sage.

Griffith, D. A., & Harvey, M. G. (2000). An intercultural communication model for use in global interorganizational networks. *Journal of International Marketing, 9* (3), 87–103.

Gullahorn, J. R., & Gullahorn, J. E. (1962). An extension of the U-curve hypothesis. *Journal of Social Issues, 3*, 33–47.

Hammer, M. R., Wiseman, R. L., Rasmussen, J. L., & Bruschke, J. C. (1998). A test of anxiety/uncertainty management theory: The intercultural adaptation context. *Communication Quarterly, 46*, 309–326.

Harper, J. M., & Elliott, M. L. (1988). Can there be too much of a good thing? The relationship between desired level of intimacy and marital adjustment. *American Journal of Family Therapy, 16*, 351–360.

Havighurst, R. J. (1957). The social competence of middle-aged people. *Genetic Psychology Monographs, 56*, 297–375.

Hayes, D. P., & Meltzer, L. (1972). Interpersonal judgments based on talkativeness: I. Fact or artifact? *Sociometry, 35*, 538–561.

Heine, S. J., & Buchtel, E. E. (2009). Personality: The universal and the culturally specific. *Annual Review of Psychology, 60*, 369–394.

Heise, D. R. (1979). *Understanding events: Affect and the construction of social action.* Cambridge; New York: Cambridge University Press.

Howard Hamilton, M. F., Richardson, B. J., & Shuford, B. (1998). Promoting multicultural education: A holistic approach. *College Student Affairs Journal*, 18, 5–17.

Hunter, B., White, G. P., & Godbey, G. C. (2006). What does it mean to be globally competent? *Journal of Studies in Intercultural Education*, 10, 267–285.

Imahori, T. T., & Lanigan, M. L. (1989). Relational model of intercultural communication competence. *Intercultural Communication Competence*, 13, 269–286.

Kelley, H. H., & Michela, J. L. (1980). Attribution theory and research. *Annual Review of Psychology*, 31, 457–501.

Kim, Y. Y. (1988). *Communication and cross-cultural adaptation: An integrative theory*. Philadelphia: Multilingual Matters.

King, P. M., & Baxter Magolda, M. B. (2005). A developmental model of intercultural maturity. *Journal of College Student Development*, 46, 571–592.

Korzybski, A. (1994). *Science and sanity: An introduction to non-Aristotelian systems and general semantics* (5th ed.). Fort Worth, TX: Institute of General Semantics.

Kruger, J. (1999). Lake Wobegon be gone! The "below-average effect" and the egocentric nature of comparative ability judgments. *Journal of Personality and Social Psychology*, 77, 221–232.

Kuhn, T. S. (1970). *The structure of scientific revolutions* (2nd ed.). New York: New American Library/University of Chicago Press.

Kupka, B. (2008). *Creation of an instrument to assess intercultural communication competence for strategic international human resource management*. Unpublished doctoral dissertation, University of Otago, Otago, New Zealand.

Lonner, W. J. (1980). The search for psychological universals. In H. C. Triandis & W. W. Lambert (Eds.), *Handbook of cross-cultural psychology* (Vol. 1, pp. 143–204). Boston: Allyn & Bacon.

Lysgaard, S. (1955). Adjustment in a foreign society: Norwegian Fulbright grantees visiting the United States. *International Social Science Bulletin*, 7, 45–51.

Miller, D. T., & Ross, M. (1975). Self-serving biases in the attribution of causality: Fact or fiction? *Psychological Bulletin*, 82, 213–225.

Navas, M., García, M. C., Sánchez, J., Rojas, A. J., Pumares, P., & Fernández, J. S. (2005). Relative acculturation extended model (RAEM): New contributions with regard to the study of acculturation. *International Journal of Intercultural Relations*, 29, 21–37.

Osgood, C. E. (1969). On the whys and wherefores of E, P, and A. *Journal of Personality and Social Psychology*, 12, 194–199.

Osgood, C. E., May, W. H., & Miron, M. S. (1975). *Cross-cultural universals of affective meaning*. Urbana, IL: University of Chicago.

Patterson, M. L., & Sechrest, L. B. (1970). Interpersonal distance and impression formation. *Journal of Personality*, 38, 161–166.

Pearce, W. B., & Cronen, V. E. (1980). *Communication, action, and meaning*. New York: Praeger.

Ramaprasad, A. (1983). On the definition of feedback. *Behavioral Science*, 28, 4–13.

Rathje, S. (2007). Intercultural competence: The status and future of a controversial concept. *Language and Intercultural Communication*, 7, 254–266.

Schachter, S., Christenfeld, N., Ravina, B., & Bilous, F. (1991). Speech disfluency and the structure of knowledge. *Journal of Personality and Social Psychology*, 60, 362–367.

Schneider, C. S., & Kenny, D. A. (2000). Cross-sex friends who were once romantic partners: Are they platonic now? *Journal of Social and Personal Relationships*, 17, 451–466.

Spitzberg, B. H. (1983). Communication competence as knowledge, skill, and impression. *Communication Education*, 32, 323–328.

Spitzberg, B. H. (1987). Issues in the study of communicative competence. In B. Dervin & M. J. Voigt (Eds.), *Progress in Communication Sciences* (Vol. 8, pp. 1–46). Norwood, NJ: Ablex.

Spitzberg, B. H. (1989). Issues in the development of a theory of interpersonal competence in the intercultural context. *International Journal of Intercultural Relations*, 13, 241–268.

Spitzberg, B. H. (1993). The dialectics of (in)competence. *Journal of Social and Personal Relationships*, 10, 137–158.

Spitzberg, B. H. (1994). The dark side of (in)competence. In W. R. Cupach & B. H. Spitzberg (Eds.), *The dark side of interpersonal communication* (pp. 25–49). Hillsdale, NJ: Lawrence Erlbaum and Associates.

Spitzberg, B. H. (2007). *CSRS: The conversational skills rating scale—An instructional assessment of interpersonal competence* (NCA Diagnostic Series, 2nd ed.). Annandale, VA: National Communication Association.

Spitzberg, B. H., & Chagnon, G. (2009). Conceptualizing intercultural communication competence. In D. K. Deardorff (Ed.), *The SAGE Handbook of intercultural competence* (pp. 2–52). Thousand Oaks, CA: Sage.

Spitzberg, B. H., & Cupach, W. R. (1984). *Interpersonal communication competence*. Beverly Hills, CA: Sage.

Spitzberg, B. H., & Cupach, W. R. (1989). *Handbook of interpersonal competence research*. New York: Springer-Verlag.

Spitzberg, B. H., & Cupach, W. R. (2002). Interpersonal skills. In M. L. Knapp & J. R. Daly (Eds.), *Handbook of interpersonal communication* (3rd ed., pp. 564–611). Newbury Park, CA: Sage.

Street, R. L., Jr., & Brady, R. M. (1982). Speech rate acceptance ranges as a function of evaluative domain, listener speech rate, and communication context. *Communication Monographs*, 49, 290–308.

Thorndike, R. L. (1920). Intelligence and its uses. *Harpers Monthly*, 140, 227–235.

Ting-Toomey, S. (1999). *Communicating across cultures*. New York: Guilford.

Ting-Toomey, S., & Kurogi, A. (1998). Facework competence in intercultural conflict: An updated face-negotiation theory. *International Journal of Intercultural Relations*, 22, 187–225.

von Bertalanffy, L. (1968). *General system theory: Foundations, development, applications* (Rev. ed.). New York: George Braziller.

Wheeless, L. R., Frymier, A. B., & Thompson, C. A. (1992). A comparison of verbal output and receptivity in relation to attraction and communication satisfaction in interpersonal relationships. *Communication Quarterly*, 40, 102–115.

Wilden, A. (1972). *System and structure: Essays in communication and exchange* (2nd ed.). New York: Tavistock.

Williams, E. F., & Gilovich, T. (2008). Do people really believe they are above average? *Journal of Experimental Social Psychology*, 44, 1121–1128.

## Concepts and Questions

1. Why, when you add culture as one additional variable to communication competency, does it make the entire process of competency "far more challenging"?

2. What is Spitzberg's definition of *communication competence*? Why are the words "appropriate" and "effective" used in Spitzberg's definition?

3. According to Spitzberg, what are some common designations that "mark" culture?

4. What are the six intercultural communication models advanced by Spitzberg? What do these models have in common?

5. Why does Spitzberg believe that "People are *far, far, far,* more similar across cultures than they are different"?

6. Explain the phrase "Competence is a judgment."

7. How does Spitzberg define and explain the notion of "appropriateness" as it applies to intercultural competence?

8. Why are competence judgments related to motivation and knowledge?

9. Explain the phrase "people interact–not cultures."

# A Confucian Perspective of Communication Competence

### XIAOSUI XIAO • GUO-MING CHEN

*In the first essay in this chapter, Spitzberg examined intercultural competency in both theoretical and general terms. The second selection in this chapter looks at competency from a specific point of view. In an essay titled "A Confucian Perspective of Communication Competency,"* *competency is analyzed as it applies to Confucian teachings. The rationale behind the study is that there are major differences in how cultures perceive and attain competency during cross-cultural communication. The authors note that "from the Western perspective,*

This original essay appears here in print for the first time. All rights reserved. Permission to reprint must be obtained from the publisher and the authors. An earlier version of this essay appeared in the *Journal of Multicultural Discourse*, 4(1), 2009, pp. 61–74. Dr. Xiaosui Xiao is an associate professor in the Department of Communication Studies at Hong Kong Baptist University, Kowloon Tong, Hong Kong. Dr. Guo-Ming Chen is a professor in the Department of Communication Studies at the University of Rhode Island, Kingston, Rhode Island.

assertiveness and self-disclosure were regarded as important indicators of communication competence, while to Chinese or Japanese, being assertive and expressive may be considered detrimental to the effective interaction." Since these dissimilar perspectives can cause problems, Xiao and Chen explain and contrast the Western orientation toward competency with the one recommended by those who follow the teachings of Confucius.

The essay begins by pointing out that in the West competent communicators engage in three distinct behaviors: (a) control (influencing the outcome of the encounter), (b) adaptation (altering communication to fit the event), and (c) collaboration (having a constructive relationship with the other person). As noted, while these behaviors are appropriate by Western standards, they differ from the attributes of competency found in the Confucian perspective of communication competence. The authors suggest that the most effective technique for understanding the Confucian position on competency is to investigate its cosmological origins. This basic cosmic foundation stresses the notion that the cosmos, including human interaction, is characterized by an "organic holism and dynamic vitalism." What this means is that the universe, and all the people in it, are a grand, interrelated whole. Quoting extensively from the writings of Confucius, Xiao and Chen explore four attributes that form the core of the Confucian philosophy toward competency: (a) moral competence, (b) ability to apply the rules of moral communication, (c) ability to follow the regulative rules, and (d) the ability to exploit the constitutive rules. The authors explain how these four precepts are often made manifest during a communication encounter.

The essay concludes by returning to a comparison of the Confucian orientation toward competency with the one found in the West. The authors maintain that at the core of these differences is a moral and philosophical view of people and the world. In the West each person is born distinct, unique, and independent from all other people. Expressing this individuality is seen as a hallmark of competent communication. From the Confucian perspective, interdependence, not independence, is the chief characteristic of a competent, honorable, and ethical communicator. Hence, traits such as self-restraint, indirect expression, saving face, and reciprocity mark a competent person. The authors maintain that to participate in the new global society you must understand these dissimilar perceptions and make the necessary adaptations.

> As global society relies increasingly on interdependence and cooperation across cultures, many Western concepts and theories no longer appear adequate to explain the variety of cultural practices in the world.

## INTRODUCTION

As global society relies increasingly on interdependence and cooperation across cultures, many Western concepts and theories no longer appear adequate to explain the variety of cultural practices in the world. One of the best examples is the study of communication competence. For instance, from the Western perspective, assertiveness and self-disclosure are regarded as important indicators of communication competence, while to Chinese or Japanese, being assertive and expressive can be considered detrimental to the effectiveness of interaction. Thus, the understanding of different cultural perspectives on communication is essential to intercultural interaction. It is then the purpose of this essay to explain the concept of communication competence from the Confucian perspective, which in many ways has come to define Asian modes of communication, and to illustrate its differences from the Westerner's. The essay will first outline the Western conception of communication competence, followed by the illustration of a Confucian perspective on communication competence and its philosophical foundations. Finally, it will show comparisons between Confucian and Western perspectives on the concept.

## WESTERN CONCEPTUALIZATION OF COMMUNICATION COMPETENCE

Communication competence has been one of the most studied and debated concepts in the West. Parks (1994) identified three key issues among the numerous controversies over how communication competence should be conceptualized. The first issue concerns whether competence is to be judged from an actor's or an observer's perspective. While some scholars argued that competence can be determined by the degree of the actor's satisfaction with his or her interactive accomplishments, others argued that it can also be judged and evaluated through the eyes of the observer (Spitzberg & Cupach, 1989). From the observer's perspective, the actor's ability needs to be observed and confirmed by his or her counterpart.

The second issue regards whether competence ought to be viewed in terms of cognition or behavior. Although some scholars concentrated on the individual's ability to understand or report knowledge of how objectives can be satisfactorily achieved (e.g., Phillips, 1984), most communication scholars pointed out that competence should include both cognitive and behavioral dimensions (e.g., Wiemann & Backlund, 1980). In other words, to be competent, one must "not only 'know' and 'know how,' but also must 'do' and 'know that we did'" (Parks, 1985, p. 174).

Finally, the third issue concerns competence as a trait or state. Competence has often been seen and measured as a trait that manifests itself across time and situations (e.g., McCroskey, 1982). However, the concept was also defined as a set of specific skills used to deal with a particular problem or situation (e.g., Wiemann, 1977).

These different approaches to conceptualizing communication competence in the West share a limited number of fundamental concerns. In particular, three discerned themes run through the Western conceptualizations of communication competence: (1) control, (2) adaptation, and (3) collaboration.

First, Western scholars have generally agreed that communication is inherently purposive and goal-directed. A competent communicator must assume a keen sense of control, because "there would be no reason to communicate if we were not dependent upon others for the fulfillment of our wishes and ... these wishes or needs are fulfilled by influencing or controlling others' responses to us" (Parks, 1994, p. 592). Parks further indicated that the concern for control, whether in the sense of manipulating one's environment or influencing others' responses, was clearly embedded in most definitions of communicative competence in the West.

Second, a fundamental concern in Western communication competence is adaptability. For the effective and appropriate control of others' responses in a given situation, the communicator must understand the situational constraints on this control. The communicator must also be able to alter his or her communicative strategies in response to changing situational factors and changing responses from others (Kellermann, 1992).

Finally, the Western conceptualization of communication competence also includes the notion of collaboration. Collaboration is necessary because many of our goals cannot be accomplished without the aid of others. For this reason, a competent communicator must be capable of making and sustaining favorable relationships and interactions to achieve personal and mutual goals (Canary & Spitzberg, 1987).

In addition to these three recurring themes, *effectiveness* and *appropriateness* are the two most consistent concepts used to characterize communication competence, though communication competence has also been described in the West by various terms, including accuracy, clarity, flexibility, affection, empathy, and so forth (Chen & Starosta, 1996).

Effectiveness refers to an individual's ability to *produce intended effects through interaction*, and is measured by determining whether, and to what degree, the goals of interaction are accomplished. Effectiveness emphasizes communication skills that are composed of those verbal and nonverbal behaviors that enable people to achieve their goals in intercultural interaction. Those skills may include message skills, interaction management, behavioral flexibility, identity management, and relationship cultivation (Chen, 2007a).

Appropriateness generally refers to *the ability of an interactant to meet the basic contextual requirements of the situation* to communicate effectively. The contextual requirements usually involved verbal, relationship, and environmental contexts, which refer to the quantity, quality, relevancy, and manner of message sending. Key elements of appropriate communication include: (1) say just enough—not too little or too much; (2) don't say something that's false or speak about something for which you lack evidence; (3) relate your contribution to the topic and situation; and (4) be clear about what you are saying, and say it "with dispatch" (Wiemann & Backlund, 1980).

The following sections move to the discussion of the Confucian perspective on the cosmological origin and conceptualization of communication competence.

## CONFUCIAN PERSPECTIVE ON THE COSMOLOGICAL ORIGIN OF COMMUNICATION COMPETENCE

A thorough understanding of the Confucian perspective of communication competence requires the probing of its cosmological origin, which is characterized by an organic holism and a dynamic vitalism. According to Chen (2009), this cosmological assumption dictates that the universe, including human interaction, is a great whole, in which all is but a transitional process and the transformation of the universe is an ongoing, cyclic, and endless process. Our discussion starts therefore with Confucian cosmology and, in particular, the concept of *gan-ying,* which refers to acting on and responding in the process of communication.

### *Gan-ying* as an Organic Capacity

Clearly, in such an organic whole, interaction, or what Needham (1962) called "mysterious resonance," among its parts is essential. Ancient Chinese people used two ambiguous terms, *"gan"* (act on) and *"ying"* (answer or response) to describe this vital interconnection and interaction, and the two terms have been translated as "stimulation" and "response," respectively (Graham, 1992, p. 38). However, *gan* and *ying* differ essentially from the cause-effect process of stimulation and response in that, as Graham illustrated, "when A acts on (*gan*) B, B will not only be moved by it, but will respond (*ying*) actively" (p.38).

In Chinese society, the concept of *gan-ying* refers to a general form of interaction taking place in every aspect of a life process. It presupposes the presence and interaction of two interdependent cosmic forces of life called *yin* and *yang.* It is the mutual acting and responding of these two comic forces that fundamentally interconnects the organic parts into a harmonious whole. In this sense, *gan-ying* is a broad category that includes any psychological and biological interaction within an organic body. The category includes human communication in the sense that human speech is a response to certain internal or external acts. Zhu Xi (1986) distinguished between internal and external *gan* (act, stimulation), "When a man finishes speaking he must be silent, and when his silence ends he must speak; and this is internal *gan* (act, stimulation). But if another man calls to one from outside, this can only be called external *gan*" (p. 2438).

The concept of *gan-ying* is the foundation of the Confucian world-organism. It explains the way in which the whole universe exists and operates. Everything can be *gan* or *ying.* As the Neo-Confucian philosopher Chen Yi stated clearly, "Within heaven and earth there is nothing but *gan* (act on) *and ying* (response). What else is there?" (Cheng & Cheng, 2000, p. 198; cf. Zhang, 1999a, p. 349). The interaction between the two cosmic forces is seen as the fundamental source of life. A well-known passage from the Confucian *Classic of Changes* reads, "Heaven and Earth mesh together, and the myriad things develop and reach perfect maturity; male and female blend essences together, and the myriad creatures are formed and come to life" (1994, p. 85).

*Gan-ying,* as a cosmic process, has been viewed as a heavenly endowed ability. Living beings must be able to produce certain acts and responses to find their own position in the organic world. For Confucians, the human capacity of communication has its cosmic origin in this heavenly endowment.

### Ontological Assumption of *Gan-ying*

The dynamic concept of *gan-ying* leads to a radical ontology that assumes every living being shares the same subtle element and *qi* (vital force). This assumption provides Confucians with an ontological basis for the conceptualization of the possible interaction among myriads in the world. For instance, how can mountains and lakes possibly interact with each other? The answer is: they interact through their *qi.* According to the author of the *Classic of Changes,* "This is why Water and Fire drive each other on, why Thunder and Wind do not work against each other, and why 'Mountain and Lake reciprocally circulate.' Only in consequence of all this can change and transformation take place, thus allowing the myriad things to become all that they can be" (*Classic of Changes,* 1994, p. 122).

> *In Chinese society, the concept of* gan-ying *refers to a general form of interaction taking place in every aspect of a life process.*

The ancient Chinese practice of *feng shui* employs the *ba gua* (eight trigrams—eight combinations of three broken or unbroken lines formerly used for divination), and is grounded in the assumption of an ever-interactive and pervasive *qi* (Chen, 2007b). The application of the *ba gua* concerns the interactions among the symbols of eight basic categories of natural objects, namely, heaven, earth, lake, mountain, fire (also sun), water (also moon), thunder, and wind (also wood) to produce new meanings (Chen, 1998; Xiao, 2006).

## Epistemological Function of *Gan-ying*

The Confucian concept of *gan-ying* has epistemological implications. To the extent that all interactions are seen as taking place within a world-organism, each part of the organism, while interacting with other parts, should also be able to sense the state and the need of the whole, and be able to act or respond appropriately. Each part can act or respond in a certain way because it senses the need to do so.

From this perspective, *gan-ying* or interaction is eventually driven and guided by the interflow of sensation within the organism. This sensibility is presupposed in the concept of *qi,* which is itself sensitive. Confucians talked about the "dispositions" and "personalities" of things in dichotomous terms, such as masculinity and femininity, firmness and yielding, activeness and calmness, ardor and coolness, and so forth. With these dispositions and personalities, they are able in the *Book of Changes* and other cosmological works to explain the ways in which things act and respond and, as a result of these acts and responses, the perpetual alteration of expansion and contraction, movement and stillness, light and darkness, heat and cold, and so forth (Chen, 2008).

## Ethical and Spiritual Predisposition in *Gan-ying*

The most characteristic feature of the Confucian cosmological concept of *gan-ying* lies in its ethical and spiritual predisposition. *Gan-ying* is a wholehearted feeling or empathy toward other living beings and the organism as a whole. As such, it is not just any act and response, but rather, an ethically appropriate act and response. In light of this ethical and spiritual predisposition, Neo-Confucians saw the Confucian

ideal of *ren* (humanity, benevolence) as the universal flow of sensation that, for them, interlinked the myriad things in the world into a harmonious whole (see, especially, Zhang, 1999b). This ethical and spiritual predisposition is what fundamentally distinguishes the Confucian *gan-ying* or interaction from the mechanical notion of cause and effect or the biological notion of stimulation and response.

## THE CONFUCIAN CONCEPT OF COMMUNICATION COMPETENCE

Confucian speculation on the cosmic process of *gan-ying* or interaction sets the framework from which human communication ought to be understood and practiced by the Chinese. The Confucian concept of communication competence, therefore, should be examined from within this framework. The following section discusses the concept in terms of internal and external competence from four perspectives: *moral competence, the ability to apply the rules of moral communication, the ability to follow the regulative rules,* and *the ability to exploit the constitutive rules.*

## Moral Competence

Internally, for Confucians, communication competence is manifested as nothing less than the power of ethics, that is, the power to move the hearts of people. Ethics is itself the power of persuasion; "Right is might" infuses the Confucian classics. For instance, Confucius said,

> The noble man might stay in his chambers, but if the words he speaks are about goodness, even those from more than a thousand *li* (miles) away will respond with approval to him, and how much the more will those who are nearby do so! If he stays in his chambers and his words are not about goodness, then those from more than a thousand *li* away will go against him, and how much the more will those who are nearby do so! (*Classic of Changes,* 1994, p. 58).

A commentary on the *Classic of Changes* notes, "[T]o drum people into action all over the world is dependent on the phrases" (1994, p. 68). According to the fifth century B.C.E. Chinese literary critic Liu Xie (1983), the discursive power to move the world is derived from the words of *Dao*. Liu compared Confucius' speeches to the most brilliant sound and light, "The clapping of his wooden bell was answered for one thousand *li* around and his influence will find an echo ten thousand years from now. He expresses in literary form the light of the universe, and opens the ears and eyes of all the people" (pp. 18–19).

For Confucians, this power to move the world is not reserved for the sages only. It is embedded in the deep nature of human beings, and therefore is available to everyone. Hence, another conviction of Confucianism is that everyone has fine potential for communication and persuasive competence. To cultivate this ability, one needs not rely on outside forces, but rather only return to one's moral endowment. The question is simply whether one is morally capable of doing so or whether one can tap his or her potential to the fullest. This is questionable because Confucians also believe that after one's coming into this world, the originally pure human heart can be blocked by all sorts of material and physical desires, and consequently may lose its moral gift.

Confucianism has a third belief that provides the basis for a workable system of moral practice, that is, the belief in the likelihood of restoring one's heavenly endowed talent through a sincere process of moral cultivation. The key to understanding the feasibility of this process is the Confucian concept of *cheng* (sincerity). *Cheng* literally means being genuine and free from deceit (*Great Learning*, p. 89). In Confucianism, the concept refers to the perfect and authentic state of morality and spirit. The practicing of the virtue of sincerity can thus lead the way to one's moral nature and cosmic origin. The goal of *cheng* may appear too high to be reached by an ordinary person; however, "being sincere" is possible for anyone to reach, because one simply needs to curb one's improper or excessive desires, which according to Confucians is within anyone's capacity.

By virtue of sincerity one achieves the power of competent communication. It is believed that the mind in the state of sincerity can clearly and authentically sense the situations and needs of other beings. When one responds to the situation and needs of others with sincerity, one always does so in an appropriate and powerful fashion. The *Doctrine of the Mean* says, "He who is sincere is one who hits upon what is right without effort and apprehends without thinking. He is naturally and easily in harmony with the Way" (Confucius, 1973, p. 107). In Confucianism, such a person can stimulate heaven and earth: "There has never been a person who was completely sincere and yet did not move others. Nor has there been a person who was not sincere and yet could move others" (Mencius, 1973, p. 74).

## Ability to Apply the Rules of Moral Communication

External competence, for Confucians, refers to the behavioral aspect of competence and, specifically, to the ability to apply the rules of moral communication. Here, in terms of communication behavior, the Confucian concept of competence comes close to the Western one. Confucians emphasized the sincerity of the communicator, the free expression of the mind, and the creative application of the rules of communication.

Regarding the behavioral aspect, similar to Westerners, Confucians are as well concerned about the effectiveness and appropriateness of communication. The question is how the effectiveness and appropriateness of communication can be adequately judged from a Confucian perspective. Again, we have to discuss the fundamental basis of this judgment within the framework of the Confucian world-organism. Any words and deeds that contribute to maintaining and promoting the harmonious growth of a social body are considered effective and appropriate. Confucians have reached the final conclusion that effective and appropriate words and deeds are those that are good and sincere. However, as internal goodness and sincerity can be expressed only through words and deeds, Confucianism has also developed a system of communication rules and codes to secure and facilitate the practice of good and sincere communication. This system is *li*.

Although *li* literally means "rite" or "ceremony," its actual practice goes beyond any ordinary ritual that usually takes place in a certain time and space (Fehl, 1971). *Li*, as the way for a gentleman to engage in social interaction, has permeated every aspect of Chinese

> By virtue of sincerity one achieves the power of competent communication.

daily life. The spirit of *li* is respect and sincerity. Confucius (1979) asked, "What can I find worthy of note in a man who is lacking ... in reverence when performing the rites?" (p. 71). In addition to respect, *li* should also be conducted with sincerity. For instance, one should not ask someone else to perform a ritual of sacrifice on one's behalf, "Unless I take part in a sacrifice, it is as if I did not sacrifice" (p. 69). Moreover, even if one goes through the whole procedure in person, the sacrifice does not count if one's mind is absent. One, therefore, has to "sacrifice to the gods as if the gods were [really] present" (p. 69). From this perspective, *li* is a system of rules and codes used specifically to communicate; verbally or non-verbally, respect and sincerity. Communication competence in this regard is demonstrated by one's ability to apply these rules and codes.

Further inquiry into the dynamic functioning of *li* is important for a complete understanding of this aspect of the Confucian conception of competence. As a long-standing and effectual cultural system of communication rules, *li* serves a dual purpose of regulating and creating human interactions (Xiao, 2001). On the one hand, *li* is regularized to the extent that it provides certainty in communication and thus is a reliable code of conduct to be followed by communicators. On the other hand, *li* is open to a certain degree to allow and encourage creative interaction.

Searle's (1969) notion of regulative rules and constitutive rules can help to explain this dual function of *li*. According to Searle, there are two basic sets of rules, regulative and constitutive. Regulative rules regulate through independently existing forms of behavior, which exist independently of the rules established to regulate them. The rules of eating and drinking, for example, regulate our ways of eating and drinking, but we eat and drink in any case regardless of a given set of rules; the acts do not depend on rules. Constitutive rules, however, create new forms of behavior, such as playing chess and football, which take place only in certain settings allowed by the rules, for instance, the settings of chess and football. Thus, the activities depend on the rules. Regulative rules are prescriptive and restrictive, usually formulated in the form "If X, do Y." For instance, "When eating, do this." Constitutive rules, in contrast, allow individuals to choose what they see as an appropriate way to follow the rules. Thus, in

playing Chinese chess, one can choose to move a pawn, chariot, or any other piece, unless one faces a check. Constitutive rules are often expressed in the form "X counts as Y," for example, "You are playing chess when you ..." (pp. 33–42).

The Confucian practice of *li* necessarily involves both types of rules. That is, it includes a set of highly restrictive rules, while at the same time operating with a very limited number of constitutive rules. Accordingly, there are two types of competence. One is the ability to follow the regulative rules to meet the demands of certain human relationships and situations involving interactions. The other is the ability to exploit the constitutive rules so as to construct a status and situation that favor one's position in an interaction.

## Ability to Follow the Regulative Rules

Confucianism has formulated very specific rules, some articulated in great detail, as to how people of every rank and social status should interact with others of the same or different ranks and social status on various possible occasions. These regulative rules are derived ultimately from the belief that the organic world is a hierarchical complexity, although ontologically every part of the organism shares the same *qi* and feeling of *ren* (humanity). Therefore, every human relation demands a distinct way or pattern of communication. The way that a subject expresses respect to a monarch, for instance, differs from the way a son expresses respect to his father. One's expression is effective and appropriate only in the way that it is compatible to one's relationship with the counterpart. This is what Confucius (1979) meant when he stated, "When names are not correct, what is said will not sound reasonable; when what is said does not sound reasonable, affairs will not culminate in success" (p. 118).

Through centuries of practice, Confucian China has developed a countless number of specific rules to regulate people's acts and responses to ensure moral and sincere communication. To use a feudal prince as an example, as prescribed in the *Book of Rites,* "When a feudal prince is about to be introduced to the son of Heaven, he is announced as 'your subject so-and-so, prince of such-and-such a state.' He speaks of himself to the people as 'the man of little virtue.' If he be in mourning (for his father), he is styled 'the rightful eldest son, an orphan'; if he be taking part at a sacrifice in his ancestral temple, 'the filial son, the prince of such-and-such a state, the prince so-and-so.' If it be another sacrifice elsewhere, the style is 'so-and-so, prince of such-and-such a state, the distant descendant.'" These are only the most elementary parts of the rules of interaction for a feudal prince (1967, p. 112). Thus, the appropriate and exact application of these rules involves knowledge about the specific needs of every human relationship and every concrete situation and the ability to choose to follow the rules that correspond most closely to those needs.

> *Through centuries of practice, Confucian China has developed a countless number of specific rules to regulate people's acts and responses to ensure moral and sincere communication.*

## Ability to Exploit the Constitutive Rules

On the surface, regulative rules seem to have taken over every aspect of the Confucian pattern of communication. But underneath this regulative practice, Confucianism has, in fact, deliberately left room for individual communicators to choose what they perceive to be effective and appropriate ways of communicating their respect and sincerity, and even to construct their own identity and a favorable context for communication. This is how the Confucian *li,* as a system of moral and sincere communication, has maintained its life and charm and consequently held firm for more than two thousand years in China.

For the practice of creative communication, one then has to appeal to another set of rules. Xiao (2004) has identified *respect, sincerity,* and *reciprocity* as the three cardinal constitutive rules of *li.* This means that, put in the form "X counts as Y" or "when X, it is Y," one is already performing *li* when one respectfully and sincerely acts on and responds to others, regardless of the kind of action that is taken or the response that is made.

Usually, a person in the early stages of learning the practice of *li* needs to follow the regulative rules. After he or she comes to grasp the spirit or essence of moral communication, however, the person should no longer adhere to those external rules. Instead, he or she should be led by the spirit. The constitutive rules make it possible for individual communicators to go beyond restrictive regulations to deal with changing situations. They also allow communicators to go beyond the customary practice to convey messages of respect and sincerity in a subtle way. These rules thus operate in a higher realm of moral and spiritual cultivation. To apply the rules of respect, sincerity, and reciprocity, communicators must assume at least some degree of freedom and creativity, and that freedom and creativity can be gained only from their own state of moral and sincere cultivation.

Confucius (1979), who claimed to have followed the dictates of his own heart without overstepping boundaries, has been considered a perfect model of spiritual freedom and creativity. He did not simply comply with old rules. For example, he entered the Grand Temple and asked questions about everything. Someone remarked, "Who said that the son of the man from Tsou understands the rites *(li)*? When he went inside the Grand Temple, he asked questions about everything." On hearing this, Confucius said, "The asking of questions is in itself the correct rite" (p. 69). Asking about everything must not have been the custom in that area. Otherwise, someone could have seen its relevance to the practice of *li.* Clearly, the *li* to which the one who made the remark was referring was not the *li* of Confucius. The former concerns the following of the regulative rules of interaction inside the Temple, whereas the latter concerns the creative application of the constitutive rules of *li.* Only those who understand the spirit and the constitutive rules of *li* can appreciate Confucius' real intention here. In any case, by making himself appear ignorant, Confucius succeeded in creating for himself a humble image. He in effect was practicing what the *Book of Rites* (1967) calls the general principle of "humbling one's self and giving honor to others" (p. 65).

Another example of Confucius playing by the constitutive rules of *li* is found in the *Analects* (1979):

> In the local community, Confucius was submissive and seemed to be inarticulate. In the ancestral temple and at court, though fluent, he did not speak lightly. At court, when speaking with Counselors of lower rank he was affable; when speaking with Counselors of upper rank, he was frank though respectful. In the presence of

his lord, his bearing, though respectful, was composed ... On going through the outer gates to his lord's court, he drew himself in, as though the entrance was too small to admit him. When he stood, he did not occupy the centre of the gateway; when he walked, he did not step on the threshold. When he went past the station of his lord, his face took on a serious expression, his step became brisk, and his words seemed more laconic. When he lifted the hem of his robe to ascend the hall, he drew himself in, stopped inhaling as if he had no need to breathe. (p. 101)

What Confucius actually said to his audiences was not recorded. That is not important here. What really matters is his skillful and creative playing of different roles in front of different audiences. The role playing itself conveys a strong message of respect and sincerity.

## THE CONFUCIAN AND THE WESTERNER

The foregoing discussion suggests that there is a dual tendency in the Confucian perspective on communication—the tendency to see communication as both a natural and an ethical process. On the one hand, human communication is part of the cosmic process of *gan-ying*. On the other hand, different sorts of *gan-ying* or interaction are no less than the acting on and responding to a moral and spiritual call. From this perspective, communication competence concerns not merely a unique human ability. It actually refers to the power of both nature and ethics. Only in the light of this cosmic and ethical origin can we come to comprehend the profundity of the Confucian perspective of communication competence.

The perspective of ethics is especially important. Confucians do not believe that one can simply rely upon one's heavenly endowed capacity and thus expend little effort to learn communication. Communication, for both the Confucian and the Westerner, is something that requires diligent study and strenuous training. However, Confucians view the study of and training in communication as essentially a course of moral cultivation. Thus, in Confucian China, communication competence is always cultivated and trained in association with a broader program of moral education.

We can now reflect on the Western conception of communication competence in comparison with the Confucian perspective. The Western approaches to competence have philosophical origins, but these philosophical origins do not seem to have anything to do with the cosmic and ethical process. On the contrary, the Western conception of competence presupposes that every living being is distinct and unique in its own right, that human beings are born equal and independent of one another, and that human relationships are built externally on the basis of common interests rather than internally on the basis of predetermined organic unity or sentimental linkage.

This ontological supposition predetermines what communication has to be to make sense to Westerners. First of all, communication has to be a manipulative process to break the boundary between individual interactants, which explains why the theme of control dominates Western conceptions of communication competence. Consequently, communication is necessarily goal directed. It is not surprising that the achieving of goals, accomplishing of tasks, or solving of problem has been considered a primary motivational construct in the Western literature on competence and social skill (Greene & Geddes, 1993). This gives rise to another persistent view: that communication is self-oriented. Every communicator acts in his or her own interests, although when collaborating with others for the fulfillment of his or her goals, the communicator must also have "at least some concern for others, at least some willingness to take into account others' identities and actions" (Parks, 1994, p. 595). As a result, self-assertiveness and self-disclosure are often used to measure communication effectiveness in the West, and attributes such as consistency, integrity, clarity, straightforwardness, and honesty in expressing one's thoughts, feelings, and beliefs are traditionally regarded as important components of communication competence.

The comparison here does not suggest superiority or inferiority between the Confucians and the

> *In Confucian China, communication competence is always cultivated and trained in association with a broader program of moral education.*

Westerners regarding the way to perceive communication competence. Rather, the purpose is to explain that mainstream Chinese practices of competent communication should be understood in the light of a different set of ontological and epistemological assumptions. Emphasizing only the Western or the Confucian point of view offers no help in promoting understanding between the East or China and the West, although the Confucian perspective may provide insights for the East and the West to understand each other by means of mutual respect and sincere communication.

Finally, for future research, scholars can move one step further to specify the more concrete empirical indicators, such as self-restraint, indirect expression, saving face, reciprocity, and emphasis on particularistic relationship, of Confucian communication competence (Chen, 2002), which can be used to reify the abstract reasoning of the concept based on ethical and spiritual aspects. Moreover, how these Confucian ontological and epistemological assumptions of communication competence interact with other Chinese concepts, such as *mianzi* (face), *guangxi* (interrelation), *renqin* (favor), *yuan* (predestined relation), *bao* (reciprocity), *keqi* (politeness) and seniority, practiced in the daily interaction remains a challenging task for scholars to pursue.

# References

*Book of rites* (also *Li chi*) (1967). (J. Legge, Trans.). New Hyde Park, NY: University Books.

Canary, D. J., & Spitzberg, B. H. (1989). A model of the perceived competence of conflict strategies. *Human Communication Research, 15,* 630–649.

Chang, H.-C. (2002). The concept of *yuan* and Chinese conflict resolution. In G. M. Chen & R. Ma (Eds.), *Chinese conflict management and resolution* (pp. 19–38). Westport, CT: Greenwood.

Chen, G. M. (1998). A Chinese model of human relationship development. In B. L. Hoffer and H. H. Koo (Eds.), *Cross-cultural communication East and West in the 90s* (pp. 45–53). San Antonio, TX: Institute for Cross-Cultural Research.

Chen, G. M. (2007a). A review of the concept of intercultural effectiveness. In M. Hinner (Ed.), *The influence of culture in the world of business* (pp. 95–116). Germany: Peter Lang.

Chen, G. M. (2007b). The impact of feng shui on Chinese communication. *China Media Research, 3*(4), 102–109.

Chen, G. M. (2008). *Bian* (Change): A Perpetual Discourse of *I Ching*. *Intercultural Communication Studies, 17*(4), 7–16.

Chen, G. M. (2009). Toward an *I Ching* model of communication. *China Media Research, 5*(3), 72–81.

Chen, G. M., & Starosta, W. J. (1996). Intercultural communication competence: A synthesis. *Communication Yearbook, 19,* 353–383.

Cheng, H., & Cheng, Y. (2000). *Er Cheng yishu* [Literary remains of the two Chengs] (Vol. 15). Shanghai: Shanghai Guji.

*Classic of changes: A new translation of the I Ching as interpreted by Wang Bi* (1994). (R. J. Lynn, Trans.). New York: Columbia University Press.

Confucius (1979). *Confucius: The analects* (D. C. Lau, Trans.). London: Penguin Books.

Confucius (1973). *Doctrine of the mean.* In W. T. Chan (Ed.), *A source book in Chinese philosophy* (W. T. Chan, Trans., pp. 97–114). Princeton: Princeton University Press.

Fehl, N. E. (1971). 禮 *Li, rites and propriety in literature and life: A perspective for a cultural history of ancient China.* Hong Kong: The Chinese University of Hong Kong.

Graham, A. C. (1992). *Two Chinese philosophers: The metaphysics of the brothers Ch'eng* [Cheng] (2ⁿᵈ ed.). La Salle, IL: Open Court Publishing Co.

Greene, J. O. & Geddes, D. (1993). An action assembly perspective on social skill. *Communication Theory, 3,* 26–49.

*The great learning* (1973). In W. T. Chan (Ed.), *A source book in Chinese philosophy* (W. T. Chan, Trans., pp. 85–94). Princeton: Princeton University Press.

Kellermann, K. (1992). Communication: Inherently strategic and primarily automatic. *Communication Monographs, 59,* 288–300.

Liu, Xie [also Hsieh] (1983). *The literary mind and the carving of dragons: A study of thought and pattern in Chinese literature* (Y. C. Shih, Trans.). Hong Kong: The Chinese University Press.

McCroskey, J. C. (1982). Communication competence and performance: A research and pedagogical perspective. *Communication Education, 31,* 1–7.

Mencius (1973). *Mencius.* In W. T. Chan (Ed.), *A source book in Chinese philosophy* (W. T. Chan, Trans., pp. 51–83). Princeton: Princeton University Press.

Needham, J. (1962). *Science and civilization in China* (Vol. 2). Cambridge: Cambridge University Press.

Parks, M. R. (1985). Interpersonal communication and the quest for personal competence. In M. L. Knapp & G. R. Miller (Eds.), *Handbook of interpersonal communication* (pp. 171–201). Beverly Hills, CA: Sage Publications.

Parks, M. R. (1994). Communicative competence and inter-personal control. In M. L. Knapp & G. R. Miller (Eds.), *Handbook of interpersonal communication* (2nd ed., pp. 589–618). Thousand Oaks, CA: Sage Publications.

Phillips, G. M. (1984). A competent view of "competence." *Communication Education, 33,* 24–36.

Spitzberg, B. H., & Cupach, W. R. (1989). *Handbook of interpersonal competence research.* New York: Springer-Verlag.

Wiemann, J. M. (1977). Explication and test of a model of communicative competence. *Human Communication Research, 3,* 195–213.

Wiemann, J. M., & Backlund, P. (1980). Current theory and research in communicative competence. *Review of Educational Research, 50,* 185–199.

Xiao, X. (2001). Li: A dynamic cultural mechanism of social interaction and conflict management. In G. M. Chen & R. Ma (Eds.), *Chinese Conflict Management and Resolution* (pp. 39–50); Westport, CT: Ablex.

Xiao, X. (2004). *Li yu huaren chuanbo xingwei* [Li and Chinese patterns of communication]. In G. M. Chen (Ed.), *Theories and principles of Chinese communication* (pp. 379–405). Taipei: Wunan.

Xiao, X. (2006). *Yijing:* A self-circulating and self-justified Chinese cultural discourse. *Intercultural Communication Studies, 15,* 1–11.

Zhang, S. (1999a). *Menzi shuo* [Treatise on Mencius]. In *Zhang Shi chuanshu* [Collected works of Zhang Shi] (Vol. 1; pp. 239–393). Changchun: Changchun Chubanshe.

Zhang, S. (l999b). *Renshuo* [Treatise on humanity]. In *Zhang Shi chuanshu* [Collected works of Zhang Shi] (Vol. 2; pp. 803–804). Changchun: Changchun Chubanshe.

Zhu, X. (1986). *Zhuzi yulei* [Classified conversations of Chu Xi]. Beijing: Zhonghua Shuju.

## Concepts and Questions

1. Why do Xiao and Chen maintain that "many Western concepts and theories no longer appear adequate to explain the variety of cultural practices in the world"?

2. How would you respond to the following sentence: "Communication is inherently purposive and goal-directed"?

3. What do Xiao and Chen purport when they assert that Western communication competence "includes the notion of collaboration"?

4. How do Xiao and Chen define appropriateness as it is used in the West?

5. Explain what Xiao and Chen mean when they speak of the Confucian perspective of communication competency being "characterized by an organic holism and dynamic vitalism."

6. What is *gan-ying,* and why is it an important concept for understanding the Chinese view of communication?

7. What are Xiao and Chen suggesting when they write that for Confucians, "communication competence is manifested as nothing less than the power of ethics"?

8. Do you believe in the validity of the Confucian notion that "everyone has fine potential for communication and persuasive competence"? If "yes," why? If "no, why not?"

9. What does the phrase "external competence" mean?

# Harmony, Conflict and the Process of Argument in Chinese Societies

MICHAEL DAVID HAZEN • RUI SHI

In an essay titled "Harmony, Conflict, and the Process of Argument in Chinese Societies," Michael David Hazen and Rui Shi continue our examination of Chinese values and philosophy. In the Hazen and Shi selection, as the title indicates, the emphasis is on the values of harmony, conflict, and argument. While the authors grant the importance of

This original essay appears here in print for the first time. All rights reserved. Permission to reprint must be obtained from the authors and the publisher. Dr. Michael David Hazen is a professor in the Department of Communication at Wake Forest University, Winston-Salem, North Carolina. Rui Shi is a doctoral student in the Annenberg School of Communication at the University of Pennsylvania, Philadelphia, Pennsylvania.

harmony in Chinese culture, and even examine that value in detail, they take the stand that this fundamental value is misinterpreted by most people. Because of this false reading of harmony in Chinese interaction patterns, Hazen and Shi maintain that other key social dimensions have either been omitted or misunderstood by those who write about Chinese culture. To make their point, the authors turn to the value of conflict. Hazen and Shi write, "Due to the emphasis on harmony in communication and relationships, conflict is seen as detrimental to harmony and therefore to be avoided." The authors further note that this aversion to conflict not only takes the form of shunning interaction, but also falsely portrays the Chinese as being non-assertive. Hazen and Shi find these notions of avoidance disconcerting, since they believe conflict and argument are part of the Chinese value system. Part of Hazen and Shi's basic contention is that there is a large disparity between the expression of cultural values and the actual behaviors of the Chinese people. Their mission is to explain this inconsistency and demonstrate how conflict is manifested in Chinese interaction. To do this, the authors claim that conflict does not violate the norms associated with the value of harmony. They call this tandem relationship between harmony and conflict the "Dualistic Harmony Model." This model helps explain how harmony and conflict can work together. According to Hazen and Shi, these two seemingly opposite behaviors can work in unison because the value of harmony is multifaceted and allows room for argument when conflicts appear.

Once the authors establish that conflict is part of Chinese culture, they attempt to explain the form that conflict often takes. According to Hazen and Shi, the fusing of harmony with conflict is best explained by a body of research conducted by Tjosvold. Tjosvold introduced the concept of "constructive conflict" to describe how the Chinese fuse harmony and conflict into a workable method of dealing with private and professional problems. When "constructive conflict" is employed in Chinese interaction it is characterized by the participants "discussing views with open minds, expressing one's own views openly, considering others' views with an open mind, understanding others' concerns, working together for the benefit of both, using the other person's ideas, and communicating respect." Put into practice, the behaviors just depicted, at least in the business setting studied by Tjosvold, led to open and constructive argument. This openness produced higher levels of teamwork and increased productivity. All of these positive results were achieved without violating the harmony among members.

Hazen and Shi conclude their essay by reminding you that all cultures can have values that appear, at least at first glance, to be at variance with other values. Yet in reality, as you will see in the case of China, what appear to be conflicting values can be compatible. In short, the authors seek to remind you that value discrepancies can be misleading, since in many situations these values can be interconnected. As you move from culture to culture it is important to remember that any sweeping statements about values must allow for alternative interpretations, because values are multidimensional and contextual.

During the opening ceremony of the 2008 Beijing Olympic Games, the Chinese character *he*, harmony, was displayed on the central stage with hundreds of floating boxes. This performance before one of the largest possible audiences in the world can be taken as a manifestation of the importance of harmony in Chinese culture. Correspondingly, it is often assumed that conflict is to be avoided and that argument, especially if it is expressed in the form of disagreement, is limited. As a result of these assumptions, little research exists about the role of argument in Chinese societies. However, argument plays a fundamental role in human communication processes, and the display at the Beijing Olympics could also be taken as an argument to the world that modern China is unified and harmonious. As a result of these facts, combined with the growing importance of China in the world, the purpose of this article is to explore the role of argument in contemporary China and its relationship to harmony and conflict.

To accomplish this purpose, two steps are necessary. First, we will explain the traditional harmony model in Chinese society and examine the recent evidence relating to the various elements of the model. And second, based on the understanding gained in the first part of this article, and drawing on several bodies of recent work, we will develop a tentative framework for looking at argument processes in Chinese society.

## TRADITIONAL HARMONY MODEL IN CHINESE SOCIETY

It has been argued that harmony is the central value in Chinese society (Chen & Starosta, 1997) and that harmony is usually seen as reflected in collectivistic approaches to society. Chen (2001) based his harmony theory of Chinese communication on such Chinese concepts as humanity, appropriateness, and relationships.

Due to the emphasis on harmony in communication and relationships, conflict is seen as detrimental to harmony and therefore to be avoided (Chen 2002). As Kirkbride, Tang and Westwood (1991) put it, "conformity, collectivism, harmony and shame combine to create a social pressure and expectation which influence Chinese people to be less openly assertive and emotional in conflict situations" (p. 371). Thus, Chinese cultural values are seen as leading to a desire to preserve harmony by avoiding conflict and refraining from engaging in argument, especially when it involves disagreement (He, Zhu, & Peng, 2002).

In summary, the harmony model is seen as predicating that: (a) harmony and collectivism play a central role in Chinese society; (b) harmony leads to a desire to avoid or minimize conflict; and (c) argument, especially when it involves open disagreement, is to be avoided or muted. The following analysis will look at recent theory and research related to harmony/collectivism, conflict, and argument in China in so far as it affects our understanding of how argument works in Chinese society.

## Harmony and Collectivism

In research on cultural values, harmony is usually considered to be an aspect of collectivism. Collectivism is conceived of as reflecting a person's commitment to or integration with a group and involves deferring to the group while maintaining harmony with other group members.

The importance of harmony in China is often rooted in analyses of Chinese philosophical and historical traditions. For example, Jia (2008) sees the Chinese perspective on harmony as emerging from a foundation of Confucianism. While Confucianism has been discarded as the governing philosophy of the People's Republic of China, it is argued that the successor philosophies of Mao and Marx have continued to utilize the cultural value of harmony as a keystone of Chinese society.

*The importance of harmony in China is often rooted in analyses of Chinese philosophical and historical traditions.*

Support for the importance of harmony has been found in elements of Chinese popular culture. For example, Sun and Starosta's (2002) content analysis of 269 stories in *Twentieth Century Classical Chinese Fairy-tales Collection* found that readers were taught to adopt collectivist behaviors like getting along with others, sacrificing, and compromising for the in-group. Similarly, Song and Zhang (2008), in a study of the Chinese animation series *The Legend of Nezha*, found that values like harmony were presented in a more positive way than ones like self-interest and pleasure.

Data on the importance of harmony and collectivism in Chinese thinking are usually linked to Hofstede's research; however, his original study (1980) has no data for mainland China, only Hong Kong and Taiwan, and the data reported later for the People's Republic of China (Hofstede, 1991) is only an estimate. Subsequent studies have presented data for China but the results are mixed in several senses.

First, it is only in studies that use general, one-dimensional measures that harmony and collectivism have been found in Chinese society, and they are not as great as expected (Chen, Brockner, & Chen, 2002). Hofstede considered individualism and collectivism to be opposite ends of the same value, but many scholars now think that individualism and collectivism are really two different values (Koch & Koch 2007; Oyserman, Coon, & Kemmelmeier, 2002). Therefore, these studies may not even be measuring collectivism, but just low levels of individualism.

Second, there is evidence that collectivism may be composed of a number of components. Oyserman, Coon, and Kemmelmeier's (2002) meta-analysis of studies on collectivism and individualism revealed eight content domains that have been labeled as collectivism (relatedness to others, belonging to groups, duty to group, harmony in groups, seeking advice from others, self changes with context, hierarchy, and preference for working with groups). Studies of collectivism in China have often been measuring different things ranging from putting the group's interests first (Chen, Brockner, & Chen, 2002) to competitiveness (Green, Deschamps, & Paez, 2005) to a desire for harmony with others (Zhang, Lin, Nonaka, & Beom, 2005) to a concern for respecting hierarchy (Triandis, Chen, & Chan, 1998).

Third, when differences in what is being measured as collectivism are taken into account, some interesting data can be found. For example, Oyserman, Coon, and Kemmelmeier (2002) compared Hong Kong and the United States and found that Hong Kong was more collectivistic than the United States only when collectivism was defined in terms of (a) group harmony, (b) a focus on hierarchy and status issues, (c) group goals, or (d) the adjustment of one's self-image to the context. On the other hand, the United States was seen as more collectivistic than Hong Kong, when collectivism was defined in terms of (a) wanting to belong to one's in-group, and (b) seeking the advice of others.

Fourth, when studies use more precise standardized forms of data for country comparisons, a similar mixed pattern emerges. For example, the GLOBE study (Gelfand, Bhawuk, Nishi, & Bechtold, 2004) shows China as more on the collectivistic end of the continuum in terms of societal institutional collectivism (a form of hierarchy) but not in terms of societal in-group collectivism (a form of harmony or group identification).

What can we conclude about these ratings? The picture of harmony and collectivism in China is complex and not as simple as is thought by many.

## Conflict in Chinese Society

Our concern with conflict in this paper is based on the idea that conflict involves disagreement, and since some scholars view argument in terms of disagreement, the research on conflict in China gives us a potential window on the operation of argument processes in China. There are two questions about conflict in China that are of concern to us: (1) how much conflict exists, and (2) what are the preferred methods for managing conflict.

First, since the traditional harmony model presumes that conflict is to be avoided so as not to interfere with harmony, we would expect to find little conflict in Chinese society, and if conflict were to occur, it would be with out-groups since harmony must be maintained in the group. However, conflict seems to be part of human societies and there is some evidence for its presence in Chinese societies. For example, Koch (2005) found evidence of high levels of conflict in Hong Kong, and Koch and Koch (2007)

reported high levels of conflict in mainland China, especially among younger people. Also, Smith, Dugan, Peterson, and Leung (1998) found that Hong Kong showed a higher degree of in-group and out-group conflict than most other countries and that in-group conflict occurred more often than out-group conflict. Similarly, Nibler and Harris (2003) found greater levels of intragroup conflict in Hong Kong than in the United States. Thus, there is evidence that conflict is present in Chinese societies.

Second, when conflict does occur in Chinese societies, it might seem logical to try to resolve it by avoidance (Chen, 2002) or through such means as third-party mediators (Jia, 2002; Ma, 1992). However, the results in the research literature seem more complex. For example, Liu and Chen (2002), in a study of a state-owned plant in mainland China, found, contrary to expectations, that the preferred rank order of conflict resolution strategies was: (1) collaboration, (2) control, (3) compromise, (4) accommodation and (5) avoidance. He, Zhu, and Peng's (2002) comparison of Chinese, French, and American employees in mainland Chinese enterprises revealed that the preferred resolution strategy for all groups was integrating. Finally, Knutson, Smith, Han, and Hwang (2002) found that in two out of three situations studied, Taiwanese and American participants' most preferred strategy was integration, and their least preferred strategy was avoidance.

Why are these findings of importance to our study? If a strategy such as integrating is preferred to a strategy such as avoiding for dealing with conflict, then the amount and kind of argument that can occur in Chinese society is more complex than previously thought.

## The Relationship Between Collectivism and Conflict Resolution Strategies

There are a few studies that look at the relationship between collectivism and conflict resolution strategies. Smith, Dugan, Peterson, and Leung's (1998) previously mentioned study found that the frequency of intragroup conflict in countries, including Hong Kong, was unrelated to any cultural values including collectivism. Similarly, He, Zhu, and Peng found that "cultural values are not a strong predictor of conflict resolution styles in cross-cultural settings" (2002,

p. 144). These studies seem to indicate that collectivism and conflict resolution strategies are not related in any simple fashion.

## Argument Processes in China

The final aspect of the traditional harmony model has to do with argument processes. As stated earlier, harmony as a value in Chinese society is seen as leading to conflict avoidance, which lowers levels of assertiveness, thus de-emphasizing argumentative processes in Chinese society (Kirkbride, Tang, & Westwood, 1991). Becker states such a view when he says that since Chinese society is collectivistic, "there are tremendous barriers, social, historical, linguistic, and philosophical to the acceptance of argumentation and debate as methods for the consideration of new proposals or strategies for social political change in East Asia" (1986, pp. 89–90). However, other scholars such as Garrett have provided evidence that there was a high degree of consideration of argument in classical China, including Buddhist traditions and thinking and practice among the elites (1993). In addition, Jensen (1992) not only pointed out the use of common types of argumentative practices in ancient China and other Asian countries, but he also made clear the presence of debate in secular and monastic settings throughout China and other parts of Asia.

Part of the problem in seeing argument in Chinese societies may have to do with what is looked for. In the past, western thinking tended to equate argument with the formal structures of logic or, at least units of claims and reasons (Toulmin, Rieke, & Janik, 1979), but more recent thinking has also come to see argument as interaction between people where there is disagreement. Such types of argument are also seen as operating in everyday places such as interpersonal relationships (Meyers, Seibold, & Brashers, 1991) and organizations (Hynes 1991). O'Keefe (1977) has labeled these two views as *Argument I*, a kind of utterance that one makes, and *Argument II*, a kind of interaction or process.

While there is little data about argument processes in contemporary China, there are hints in several studies. Preston (2003), in discussing his experiences teaching argumentation to students in Beijing over a two-year period, concluded that there was no culture of "non-advocacy" among his students. In a similar fashion, Chen and Yeh, in following up on the results of an earlier study on argumentative tendencies in Hong Kong, mainland China and Taiwan, concluded that "the result is rather straightforward, showing the mainland sample to have much greater tendencies to argue and to not avoid argument than their Hong Kong and Taiwan counterparts" (2004, p. 11). In addition, there are growing signs of public argument in places such as the Internet (Qiang, 2004). Finally, studies by Tjosvold, to be discussed later, seem to suggest that argumentative interaction in organizations can have a positive impact under the right circumstances.

## A FRAMEWORK FOR UNDERSTANDING THE ROLE OF ARGUMENT IN CHINA

Our review of the nature of the Traditional Harmony Model has revealed several conclusions about the role of harmony in Chinese society. First, harmony and collectivism are central to the Chinese worldview but the research on collectivism reveals that it is a multifaceted construct and it is not totally clear what aspects of collectivism are primary in China. Second, there is evidence that there is more conflict in Chinese societies than previously thought and that Chinese strategies for dealing with conflict are similar to those in other societies. Third, there is also evidence that cultural values such as collectivism are only one factor in determining how people respond to conflict situations. And finally, argument processes have had a role in Chinese history and there are hints about its presence in current society. When this evidence about argument processes in China is combined with broadened conceptions of argument, the reality may be more complex and interesting than previously thought.

To understand the role of argument in Chinese society and to make sense out of the conclusions drawn from our review of literature, we propose to advance an exploratory framework for understanding argument in Chinese society. This framework extends the Traditional Harmony Model by integrating three new sets of research to develop a more complex understanding of how collectivism, harmony, conflict and argument relate to each other in Chinese society.

# THE RELATIONSHIP BETWEEN CULTURAL VALUES AND COMMUNICATIVE BEHAVIOR

Guo-Ming Chen, who has written extensively about the role of harmony in Chinese society, states, "As the core value of Chinese culture, harmony represents an ideal state Chinese are pursuing in daily life" (2002, p. 12). Harmony as an ideal state may not always be manifest in everyday activities in the ways expected due to a number of factors.

Matsumoto (2006) has recently contended that verbal descriptions of culture, or what he calls cultural worldviews, are not necessarily related to behaviors. He argues that things such as stereotypes, elites' use of cultural values, and social desirability can influence the expression of cultural worldviews. The danger that Matsumoto points out is that the verbal description of cultural values such as harmony may be more of an ideal than a practice.

That a gap exists between ideals and practices can be seen in a series of studies across cultures which indicate that while cultural values such as collectivism have some effect on communicative behavior, situational factors can be just as important or more so (Cai, Wilson, & Drake, 2000). Similar conclusions were made by He, Zhu, and Peng (2002) in a previously cited study about cultural values and methods of conflict resolution chosen in China.

The role of intervening factors such as those suggested by Matsumoto can be seen in a number of studies. For example, Chen (1997), in a study on group interaction in a large religious organization in Taiwan, noted that an older leader used his seniority to create conflict and influence the group, leading Chen to conclude that "Chinese decision making is a multi-facet process in which a prominent cultural value can be consciously or unconsciously used as a tool to implicitly or explicitly shake the other core values" (p. 10). In his response to Chen's paper, Starosta (1997) remarked that "If harmony is a pre-eminent value in Chinese society, how could T. Lee manipulate a meeting of church leaders to get his own way? Apparently, 'harmony' functions as a rhetorical trope or tropus: 'I am acting in the name of harmony' (even [or especially] if one is not doing so)" (p. 1). A similar view was expressed by Ma (1993) in his study of contrary-to-face-value messages (CFV), which he concludes "can be applied in a quite strategic or manipulative way as well" (p. 3) to maintain harmony.

The role of power in influencing behavior in collectivist societies was documented by Gelfand and Realo (1999). They discovered that when participants could be held accountable, the higher a person's level of collectivism, the more likely he or she was to concede to the other party in the negotiations. However, when someone would not be held accountable, the higher the person's level of collectivism, the more likely he or she was not to concede to the other party in the negotiations. While this study did not directly involve China, they did use Asian Americans as one of their collectivistic groups and they found that their results generalized across a number of collectivistic societies.

Gelfand and Realo's finding was echoed in Koch's (2005) study of Hong Kong organizations, where members reported that they avoided conflict when they feared possible repercussions. While much has changed in China, examples of four types of control by Central Chinese TV over televised international debates of university students are cited by Zhang (2002).

One way to think about the situational nature of communicative behavior in China is to look at the idea of "communication as situated accomplishment." This approach is rooted in the work of Philipsen and of Carbaugh (1990) who view communicative behavior as "artfully and inventively construct[ing] and interpret[ing] messages in situations which are massively pre-structured" but also where communication "constitutes—creates, reinforces, and transforms" situations (Stewart and Philipsen, 1985, p. 178). According to this view, culture is present in the massive pre-structuring of situations in terms of things such as norms, values, and expectations, which can constrain the arguer, but which can also serve as cultural resources that the arguer can use to achieve his or her goals. The arguer can choose to use the cultural resources in a fashion that is "in

> *One way to think about the situational nature of communicative behavior in China is to look at the idea of "communication as situated accomplishment."*

sync" with the culture, in a fashion that stretches the norms of the culture, or in opposition to the culture.

The finding of a gap between values and behavior and the forces operating in such situations can be used to generate the following possible generalizations for our framework:

1. The presence of a gap between the expression of cultural values and the behavior of people provides room for conflict and argumentative processes.

2. Cultural values and their interpretation can be used as argumentative tools within the space provided by the gap between values and behavior.

## THE DUALISTIC HARMONY MODEL

The idea that a gap between cultural values and behavior provides possible roles for conflict and argument in Chinese society can be further expanded by examining the nature of harmony as a cultural value. Leung, Koch, and Lu (2002) have proposed what they call the Dualistic Model of Harmony based on their analysis of traditional Confucian thinking, which they conclude does not encourage conflict avoidance but instead embodies disagreement and open debate. Based on their analysis, they proposed that there are two distinct forms of harmony: (1) the value perspective, which sees harmony as a goal or end in itself, and (2) the instrumental perspective, which emphasizes interpersonal harmony by avoiding relationship disintegration. These two perspectives are displayed in Table 7.1.

A closer look at each of the prototypes can provide insight into the possible links between cultural values, conflict, and argumentative behavior. The first prototype, balancing, is high in both value harmony and instrumental harmony and thus seeks to balance harmony as a goal with harmony in relationships. Parties in the conflict will seek goals based on a concern for all persons and will confront differences when necessary to reach a goal. Specific behaviors linked to this prototype are problem solving, confrontation, direct and indirect communication, mutually beneficial behavior, compromise, mediation, and face protection.

The second prototype, aligning, is high on value harmony and low on instrumental harmony and thus

**TABLE 7.1** Summary of Behavioral Relationships Between Value Harmony and Instrumental Harmony Perspectives

|  |  | Value Harmony | |
| --- | --- | --- | --- |
|  |  | **Low** | **High** |
| Instrumental Harmony | Low | Disintegrating Behavior | Aligning Behavior |
|  | High | Smoothing Behavior | Balancing Behavior |

seeks to align harmony as a goal with overt behaviors. Specific conflict behaviors associated with this prototype are problem solving, constructive confrontation, direct and respectful communication, and mutually beneficial behavior. It can be seen that both of the first two prototypes have a place for conflict, and that particular types of argumentation are part of the resulting behavior.

The third prototype, smoothing, is low on value harmony and high on instrumental harmony, and thus seeks to "smooth" interpersonal relationships while seeking one's own goals. Specific behaviors involve competition that is hidden, public conflict avoidance, superficial harmony in public, indirect communication, and face considerations.

The fourth prototype, disintegrating, is low on value harmony and low on instrumental harmony. As a result, there is no concern for harmony either as an ideal or in interpersonal relations. The resulting behavior does not promote positive interpersonal relations.

Leung, Koch, and Lu (2002) see Chinese society as more complex than is presented by the Traditional Harmony Model. This can be seen in their views about how harmony relates to methods of conflict resolution. For example, they see parallels between the smoothing prototype and conflict avoidance behavior, and between the disintegrating prototype and dominating behavior, which lead them to view both as dysfunctional in Chinese society because they would damage harmony. On the other hand, they see the balancing prototype and the aligning prototype as compatible with integrating, collaborating, or compromising approaches to conflict resolution. These views are consistent with the previously cited studies that show a preference for styles of conflict resolution such as integration or compromise in both Chinese and western societies.

There have been a series of studies that provide support for the dualistic model. For example, Koch (2005) interviewed a number of Hong Kong residents about interpersonal relations in the workplace. Respondents' accounts were significantly different from collectivist assumptions in that most people spoke of conflict and competition as common. In addition, when asked to provide behavioral explanations for conflict, they emphasized instrumental reasons rather than harmony-valuing reasons, i.e., they were trying to achieve their goals without arousing opposition.

In another study, Koch and Koch (2005) looked at the relationship between individualism-collectivism, conflict behavior and the cultural values. Unexpectedly, they found that collectivism was not significantly related to any of the types of conflict prototypes, and that instrumental harmony was not related to traditional measures of either individualism or collectivism, even though value harmony was. They also found that people with a strong sense of instrumental harmony were most likely to engage in both expressive and instrumental conflict. This suggests that the usual collectivism instruments may not measure the values most related to conflict in Chinese society. Interestingly, they also suggest that instrumental behaviors can be used as a strategy by people with either instrumental harmony or value harmony orientations to achieve their purposes.

Finally, Koch and Koch (2007) examined the relationship of collectivism and individualism to cooperative behavior in mainland China. Using separate individualism and collectivism measures, they found that students from Beijing were more individualistic than students from a regional city. Furthermore, they found that higher scores on the individualism scale predicted more cooperative behavior than higher collectivism scores. They interpreted this as meaning that the participants with high collectivism scores had higher levels of conflict with out-groups.

The Dualistic Model of Harmony and subsequent research on it suggest the following propositions for our framework:

1. Harmony as a value in Chinese society is multi-faceted, therefore leaving room for conflict about its meaning and interpretation.

2. In addition, the various meanings of harmony can be related to various forms of behavior, thus providing the potential for conflict.

3. Therefore, where conflict exists, argument becomes a tool for advancing goals and resolving the conflict.

## ARGUMENT AS CONSTRUCTIVE CONFLICT IN CHINESE SOCIETIES

In discussing their model, Leung, Koch, and Lu (2002) state that traditional East Asian values allow for the "constructive mitigation of conflict" (p. 215) and that the work of Tjosvold and his colleagues on constructive controversy provides an example of this process. Tjosvold has engaged in more than thirty studies on various aspects of conflict in Hong Kong and mainland China. An examination of his research on conflict provides a number of examples of how argument processes might work in Chinese societies.

Tjosvold's research is based on Deutsch's theory of conflict resolution (2000). Deutsch believes that cooperative goals among participants, as opposed to competitive goals, lead to a number of positive outcomes such as effective communication, helpfulness, coordination, feelings of agreement, and mutual problem solving. Deutsch's ideas have been explored by Tjosvold and others under the rubric of constructive controversy, which they define as that which: "occurs when one person's ideas, information, conclusions, theories and opinions are incompatible with those of another and the two seek to reach an agreement" (Johnson, Johnson, & Tjosvold, 2000, p. 66). In this process, when a person is confronted with another person's differing conclusions, uncertainty is aroused in his or her mind that leads to what they call epistemic curiosity, i.e., an open-minded approach to the exploration of differing viewpoints and ideas. The interaction between people then leads to an accommodation of views and the construction of a new reconceptualized conclusion that is agreed on by both parties.

Tjosvold initiated his research by asking whether this model can be translated to China, particularly in light of the traditional harmony model. However, over the last fifteen years, using a variety of research methods and a wide variety of groups in

Hong Kong, Mainland China, Singapore, and other Chinese societies, Tjosvold and his colleagues have found that "similar to research in North America, cooperative contexts were found to yield openness towards the opposing position and discussant" (Tjosvold, Leung, & Johnson, 2000, p. 481).

What is most interesting for our purposes is the role of interactive controversy and disagreement between people, i.e. argumentative processes. In Tjosvold's studies, the presence of constructive conflict is measured by looking for elements of interaction that resemble rational argumentation. For example, Tjosvold, Hui, and Sun (2004) defined constructive controversy as discussing views with open minds, expressing one's own views openly, considering others' views with an open mind, understanding others' concerns, working together for the benefit of both, using the other person's ideas and communicating respect, i.e., an integrating approach. Similarly, Yi-Feng, Tjosvold, and Peiguan (2008) asked participants whether they tried to persuade the other rationally, expressed their own positions directly, and were open minded about the other person's positions and arguments.

Initially, cooperative conflict was considered to be the opposite of approach to conflict; however, in a later study Tjosvold, Johnson, Johnson, and Sun (2006) found that competition could be constructive and was effective among Chinese employees on the mainland when there was a motive to compete and a strategy of competing fairly.

In a series of studies, Tjosvold outlined conditions under which constructive conflict would occur. For example, Tjosvold and Sun (2000) determined that affirming the other person's face at the beginning of a conflict would facilitate open disagreement and presentation of positions (constructive conflict). In other studies, he demonstrated the importance of openness, warmth in relationships (Tjosvold & Sun, 2003), persuasion (Tjosvold & Sun, 2001), and valuing relationships (Yi-Feng, Tjosvold, & Peiguan, 2008). What is suggested here is that when certain conditions, often involving elements of Chinese values, are present, constructive conflict can occur

> *Constructive conflict involving argument processes can occur in Chinese societies, especially when Chinese values such as social face and relationships are taken into account.*

in Chinese societies. Finally, Tjosvold's studies have shown that constructive conflict has positive outcomes including empowerment of employees (Tjosvold, Hui, & Law, 1998); high levels of performance in teamwork (Alper, Tjosvold, & Law, 2000); and higher levels of productivity (Chen, Tjosvold, & Liu, 2006).

In summary, Tjosvold has shown that constructive conflict involving argument processes can occur in Chinese societies, especially when Chinese values such as social face and relationships are taken into account. Thus, aspects of harmony may serve as boundary conditions that can facilitate constructive conflict when acknowledged and frustrate the development of cooperative goals when they are not. So, if a person's social face is specifically affirmed, the process of constructive conflict with its attendant argumentative processes can flourish and lead to productive outcomes in China.

The work on constructive criticism can be integrated into our framework for understanding argument in Chinese societies in the following ways.

1. Open and constructive argument processes can occur in Chinese society.

2. Argument is especially effective when it integrates elements of Chinese value systems such as the importance of face.

3. The model of argument that seems to work in China closely approximates what is considered rational argumentation.

## CONCLUSIONS

The possibilities of rational argument in China are suggested by a comparison of the following two statements:

1. Argument in organizations that can lead to good decision making is characterized by interaction over competing claims, the tension of ideas, opportunities for collective disagreement, social comparison and idea testing, a context of goodwill, and a commitment to shared procedural rules.

2. Constructive interaction in the business setting involves exploring the other's views and positions, asking questions, questioning one's own positions, mutual interest in each other's positions, enjoying competition, interacting positively with competitors, and making efforts to integrate different views.

The first statement describes the project of Willard and others to outline the productive functioning of argument in organizations (Hazen 2007, p. 3), and the second statement describes Tjosvold's conclusions about constructive conflict in China (Tjosvold & Sun, 2000, pp. 267–268). The fact that the two statements describe similar processes in organizations illustrates that, under certain conditions, argument and disagreement can operate constructively in China.

In summary, China, like every culture, encourages certain values and not others. People working within such a system can use a culture's norms to advance their interests through argument. Thus, harmony is clearly a key element in Chinese society; however, the relationship between harmony, conflict, and argument is complex, as illustrated in our proposed framework. The discrepancies between cultural values and communicative behavior, particularly as they play out in situations, mesh nicely with the insights of the Dualistic Harmony Model to provide a more complex picture of the way that argument can function in the context of harmony and conflict. The research of Tjosvold provides examples of how this process works in China.

# References

Alper, S., Tjosvold, D., & Law, K. S. (2000). Conflict management, efficacy, and performance in organizational teams. *Personnel Psychology, 53*, 625–642.

Becker, C. B. (1986). Reasons for the lack of argumentation and debate in the Far East. *International Journal of Intercultural Relations, 10*, 75–92.

Cai, D. A., Wilson, S. P., & Drake, L. E. (2000). Culture in the context of intercultural negotiation: Individualism-collectivism and paths to integrative agreements. *Human Communication Research, 26*, 591–617.

Carbaugh, D. (1990). Toward a perspective on cultural communication and intercultural contact. *Semiotica, 80*, 15–35.

Chen, G., Tjosvold, D., & Liu, C. H. (2006). Cooperative goals and leader people and productivity values: Their contribution to top management teams in China. *Journal of Management Studies, 43*, 1177–1200.

Chen, G-M. (1997, November). *Seniority and superiority: A case analysis of Chinese decision making.* Paper presented at the meeting of the National Communication Association, Chicago, IL.

Chen, G-M. (2001). Toward transcultural understanding: A harmony theory of Chinese communication. In V. H. Milhouse, M. K. Asante, and Nwosu, P. (Eds.), *Transcultural Realities: Interdisciplinary Perspectives on Cross-Cultural Relations.* Thousand Oaks, CA: Sage. Reprinted in *China Media Research, 4*, 1–13, 2008.

Chen, G-M. (2002). The impact of harmony on Chinese conflict management. In G. M. Chen & R. Ma (Eds.), *Chinese Conflict Management and Resolution* (pp. 3–17). Westport, CT: Ablex Publishing.

Chen, G-M, & Starosta, W. J. (1997). Chinese conflict management and resolution: Overview and implications. *Intercultural Communication Studies, 7*, 1–16.

Chen, L., & Yeh, J-H. (2004). *Traditional value orientations and argumentative tendencies: A study of Chinese in Hong Kong, mainland and Taiwan.* Paper presented at the meeting of the International Communication Association, New Orleans, LA.

Chen, Y-R., Brockner, J., & Chen, X-P. (2002). Individual-collective primacy and in-group favoritism: Enhancement and protection effects. *Journal of Experimental Social Psychology, 38*, 482–491.

Deutsch, M. (2000). Cooperation and competition. In M. Deutsch & P. T. Coleman (Eds.), *The Handbook of Conflict Resolution* (pp. 437–512). San Francisco, CA: Jossey-Bass.

Garrett, M. M. (1993). Classical Chinese conceptions of argumentation and persuasion. *Argumentation and Advocacy, 29*, 105–115.

Gelfand, M. J., Bhawuk, D. P. S., Nishii, L. H., & Bechtold, D. J. (2004). Individualism and collectivism. In R. J. House, P. J. Hangs, M. Javidan, P. W. Dorfman, & V. Gupta (Eds.), *Culture, Leadership and Organizations* (pp. 29–48). Thousand Oaks, CA: Sage.

Gelfand, M. J., & Realo, A. (1999). Individualism-collectivism and accountability in intergroup negotiations. *Journal of Applied Psychology, 84*, 721–736.

Green, E. G. T., Deschamps, J-C, & Paez, D. (2005). Variation of individualism and collectivism within and between 20 countries: A typological analysis. *Journal of Cross-Cultural Psychology, 36*, 321–339.

Hazen, M. D. (2007). Dissensus as value and practice in cultural argument: The tangled web of argument, con-/dis-sensus, values and cultural variations. In H. V. Hansen, *et. al.* (Eds.), *Dissensus and the Search for Common Ground*, CD-ROM (pp. 1–43). Windsor, ON: OSSA.

He, Z., Zhu, J. J. H., & Peng, S. (2002). Cultural values and conflict resolution in enterprises in diverse cultural settings in China. In G. M. Chen & R. Ma (Eds.), *Chinese Conflict Management and Resolution* (pp. 129–147). Westport, CT: Ablex Publishing.

Hofstede, G. (1980). *Culture's Consequences: International Differences in Work Related Values*. Beverly Hills, CA: Sage.

Hofstede, G. (1991). *Cultures and Organizations*. London: McGraw-Hill.

Hynes, T. J. (1991). Valuing dissensus and organizations: Being disagreeable for the good of the company. In F. H. van Eemeren, R. Grootendorst, J. A. Blair, & C. A. Willard (Eds.), *Proceedings of the Second International Conference on Argumentation* (pp. 867–874). Amsterdam: International Society for the Study of Argumentation.

Jensen, I. V. (1992). Values and practices in Asian argumentation. *Argumentation and Advocacy*, 28, 153–166.

Jia, W. (2002). Chinese mediation and its cultural foundation. In G. M. Chen & R. Ma (Eds.), *Chinese Conflict Management and Resolution*. Westport, CT: Ablex Publishing.

Jia, W. (2008). Chinese perspective on harmony: An evaluation of the harmony and peace paradigms. *China Media Research*, 4, 25–30.

Johnson, D. W., Johnson, R. T., & Tjosvold, D. (2000). Constructive controversy: The value of intellectual opposition. In M. Deutsch & P. T. Coleman (Eds.), *The Handbook of Conflict Resolution* (pp. 65–85). San Francisco, CA: Jossey-Bass.

Kirkbride, P. S., Tang, S. F. Y., & Westwood, R. I. (1991). Chinese conflict preferences and negotiating behavior: Cultural and psychological influences. *Organization Studies*, 12, 365–386.

Koch, B. J., & Koch, P. T. (2007). Collectivism, individualism, and outgroup cooperation in a segmented China. *Asia Pacific Journal of Management*, 24, 207–225.

Koch, P. (2005, May). *Conflict, collectivism and Confucianism: A study of interpersonal relationships in Hong Kong organizations*. Paper presented at the meeting of the International Communication Association, New York, NY.

Koch, P. T., & Koch, B. J. (2005, May). *Instrumental harmony in Hong Kong organizations. Re-evaluating the influence of collectivism and Confucianism on workplace interactions*. Paper presented at the meeting of the International Communication Association, New York, NY.

Knutson, T. J., Smith, V. R., Han, P-C, & Hwang, J. C. (2002). A comparison of Taiwanese and American samples on rhetorical sensitivity and conflict style. In G. M. Chen & R. Ma (Eds.), *Chinese Conflict Management and Resolution* (pp. 149–162). Westport, CT: Ablex Publishing.

Leung, K., Koch, P. T., & Lu, L. (2002). A dualistic model of harmony and its implications for conflict management in Asia. *Asia Pacific Journal of Management*, 19, 201–220.

Liu, S., & Chen, G. M. (2002). Collaboration over avoidance: Conflict management strategies in state-owned enterprises in China. In G. M. Chen & R. Ma (Eds.), *Chinese Conflict Management and Resolution* (pp. 163–181). Westport, CT: Ablex Publishing.

Ma, R. (1992). The role of unofficial intermediaries in interpersonal conflicts in the Chinese culture. *Communication Quarterly*, 40, 269(210).

Ma, R. (1993). Saying "yes" for "no" for "yes": A Chinese rule. *Journal of Pragmatics*, 25, 257–266.

Matsumoto, D. (2006). Culture and cultural worldviews: Do verbal descriptions about culture reflect anything other than verbal descriptions of culture? *Culture & Psychology*, 12, 33–62.

Meyers, R. A., Seibold, D. R., & Brashers, D. (1991). Argument in initial group decision-making discussions: Refinement of a coding scheme and a descriptive quantitative analysis. *Western Journal of Speech Communication*, 55, 47–68.

Nibler, R., & Harris, K. L. (2003). The effects of culture and cohesiveness on intragroup conflict and effectiveness. *The Journal of Social Psychology*, 14, 613–631.

O'Keefe, D. J. (1977). Two concepts of argument. *Journal of the American Forensic Association*, 13, 121–128.

Oyserman, D., Coon, H. M., & Kemmelmeier, M. (2002). Rethinking individualism and collectivism: Evaluation of theoretical assumptions and meta-analyses. *Psychological Bulletin*, 128, 3–72.

Preston, C. T., Jr. (2003, November). *Moving from stereotypes to cultural reality: Teaching the argumentation course in Beijing*. Paper presented at the meeting of the National Communication Association, Miami, FL.

Qiang, X. (2004). The rising tide of Internet opinion in China. *Nieman Reports, Summer*, 103–104.

Smith, P. B., Dugan, S., Peterson, M. F., & Leung, K. (1998). Individualism: Collectivism and the handling of disagreement. A 23-country study. *International Journal of Intercultural Relations, 22*, 351–367.

Song, Y., & Zhang, Y. B. (2008). Cultural values in Chinese children's animation: A content analysis of *The Legend of Nezha. China Media Research, 4*, 18–28.

Starosta, W. J. (1997, November). *Panel response.* Paper presented at the meeting of the National Communication Association, Chicago, IL.

Stewart, J., & Phillipsen, G. (1985). Communication as situated accomplishment: The cases of hermeneutics and ethnography. In B. Dervin & M. J. Voigt (Eds.), *Progress in Communication Science*: Vol. V (pp. 177–192). Norwood, NJ: Ablex.

Sun, W., & Starosta, W. J. (2002). A thematic analysis of the *20th Century Classical Chinese Fairy-Tales Collection*: An implication for conflict management. In G. M. Chen & R. Ma (Eds.), *Chinese Conflict Management and Resolution*. Westport, CT: Ablex Publishing.

Tjosvold, D., Hui, C., & Law, K. S. (1998). Empowerment in the manager-employee relationship in Hong Kong: Interdependence and controversy. *Journal of Social Psychology, 138*, 624–637.

Tjosvold, D., Hui, C. & Sun, H. (2004). Can Chinese discuss conflicts openly? Field and experimental studies of face dynamics in China. *Group Decision and Negotiation, 13*, 351–373.

Tjosvold, D., Johnson, D. W., Johnson, R. T., & Sun, H. (2006). Competitive motives and strategies: Understanding constructive competition. *Group Dynamics: Theory, Research, and Practice, 10*, 87–99.

Tjosvold, D., Leung, K., & Johnson, D. W. (2000). Cooperative and competitive conflict in China. In M. Deutsch & P. T. Coleman (Eds.), *The Handbook of Conflict Resolution* (pp. 475–495). San Francisco, CA: Jossey-Bass.

Tjosvold, D. & Sun, H. (2000). Social face in conflict: Effects of affronts to person and position in China. *Group Dynamics: Theory, Research, and Practice, 4*, 259–271.

Tjosvold, D., & Sun, H. (2001). The effect of influence tactics and social contexts in conflict: An experiment on relationships in China. *International Journal of Conflict Management, 12*, 239–258.

Tjosvold, D., & Sun, H. (2003). Openness among Chinese in conflict: Effects of direct discussion and warmth on integrated decision making. *Journal of Applied Social Psychology, 33*, 1878–1897.

Toulmin, S., Rieke, R., & Janik, A. (1979). *An Introduction to Reasoning.* New York: Macmillan.

Triandis, H. C., Chen, X. P., & Chan, D. K-S. (1998). Scenarios for the measurement of collectivism and individualism. *Journal of Cross-Cultural Psychology, 29*, 275–289.

Yi-Feng, N. C., Tjosvold, D., & Peiguan, W. (2008). Effects of relationship values and goal interdependence on *guanxi* between foreign managers and Chinese employees. *Journal of Applied Social Psychology, 38*, 2440–2468.

Zhang, Y. (2002). Debating with muzzled mouths: A case analysis of how control works in a Chinese television debate used for educating youths. *Media, Culture & Society, 24*, 27–47.

Zhang, Y. B., Lin, M-C., Nonaka, A., & Beom, K. (2005). Harmony, hierarchy and conservatism: A cross-cultural comparison of Confucian values in China, Korea, Japan and Taiwan. *Communication Research Reports, 22*, 107–115.

## Concepts and Questions

1. Why is there a generalized belief that harmony is an essential value in Chinese culture?

2. What is the relationship between collectivism and the Chinese value of harmony?

3. How is harmony linked to Hofstede's research on individualism and collectivism?

4. What are some of the criticisms Hazen and Shi have of current research regarding harmony? How do these criticisms help make their case that conflict and harmony can work in tandem?

5. What, according to literature reviewed by Hazen and Shi, are the usual methods employed by the Chinese to deal with conflict? Are these the same methods used in the United States?

6. What do Hazen and Shi mean when they say "argumentative interaction in organizations can have a positive impact under the right circumstances"?

7. What is the connection between harmony and avoidance in Chinese culture?

8. What do Hazen and Shi mean when they say that there is a gap between values and behavior? Can you think of some of those "gaps" in your culture?

9. What are Hazen and Shi's four prototypes? Do you think these prototypes support their claim that argument and harmony can coexist in Chinese culture?

10. How would you explain the phrase "constructive conflict"?

# The Social Construction of Demeanor through Deference Rituals

JUSTIN CHARLEBOIS

It should be apparent at this stage of the book that a competent intercultural communicator is one who has an accurate image of his or her communication partner. In addition, he or she is able to regulate each message to the profile they have constructed of the other person. Part of the adjustment and adaptation process demands an understanding of how the other person perceives their surroundings and the people in those surroundings. Our next selection, titled "The Social Construction of Demeanor through Deference Rituals," contributes to that understanding by focusing on two fundamental communication variables—interaction rituals and demeanor. Both of these variables impact the communication setting and the participants. Charlebois, drawing on the work of Erving Goffman, maintains that the manner in which people interact is not capricious or random, but rather subject to a series of patterned and learned rituals. These rituals stipulate to each person how they are to act and react in nearly all social settings—"at business meetings, at parties, or sporting events." Goffman (1963) refers to the norms constituting appropriate speech and behavior as situational proprieties. As you would expect, when the participants share a common set of norms, social action progresses effortlessly. However, when these norms clash, communication is often marked by confusion and disagreement. What Charlebois is suggesting, as he extends Goffman's hypothesis, is that when people come from different cultures, and situational proprieties are not shared, it becomes more difficult to produce successful communication.

Charlebois examines two interconnected situational proprieties of social interaction and how they can impede intercultural communication. Specifically, he discusses how a speaker might show deference to others while concurrently manifesting appropriate demeanor (proper and appropriate behavior expressed though both verbal and nonverbal messages). As noted, situational proprieties are usually rooted in culture. Hence, as people move from culture to culture they can unintentionally display a lack of respect for another person and thereby damage successful intercultural communication. To illustrate his premise Charlebois draws on the cultures of Japan and North America.

Charlebois points out that "Japan is often considered a collectivist culture society because of the importance placed on collective responsibility (rentai sekinin) and interdependence." Because of this orientation toward trust and social harmony, and the behaviors associated with these values, behaviors reflected in those values are infused into the daily life of the Japanese. One manifestation of these values is that people are "expected to give deference to others and obligated to display proper demeanor." Since the United States is considered a culture that stresses individualism, one's demeanor often takes a form different from the one found in the Japanese culture. Charlebois examines these differences in schools and the workplace. Charlebois maintains that these two opposite orientations toward deference and demeanor can result in intercultural misunderstanding. He further asserts that a "greater awareness and tolerance of socioculturally specific norms which constitute deference and demeanor could reduce instances of intercultural miscommunication ... increasing the frequency of successful intercultural encounters."

> Because of this orientation toward trust and social harmony, and the behaviors associated with these values, behaviors reflected in those values are infused into the daily life of the Japanese.

## INTRODUCTION

Social interaction is neither arbitrary nor disorderly, but is patterned by *interaction rituals* (Goffman, 1967) which specify normative ways of speaking and behaving in specific social situations such as business meetings, parties, or sports events. Goffman (1963) refers to the norms constituting appropriate speech and behavior as *situational proprieties*. When situational proprieties are shared between social interactants and they configure and orchestrate their social actions in accordance with these norms, interaction proceeds smoothly and communication is customarily successful. Conversely, if situational proprieties are not shared between speakers, or if speakers actively resist these norms, then communication may break down and miscommunication result. In the case of intercultural encounters, situational proprieties often diverge, and accordingly there is a greater risk that miscommunication will result.

The cultural basis of situational proprieties becomes strikingly apparent when we examine intercultural encounters. In these encounters, speakers draw on culturally based situational proprieties, which can be contradictory. For example, *kangaete okimasu* (I'll think about it) functions as a refusal in Japanese, while many North Americans may interpret this phrase as a potential acceptance. This ambiguous expression exemplifies non-confrontational communication, which Japanese value because it mitigates conflict and preserves social harmony which more direct communication could destroy (Davies & Ikeno, 2002; Matsumoto, 1994; Watanabe, 1993; Yamada, 1997). An increased awareness of and sensitivity toward culturally variant situational proprieties is indispensible for intercultural communicators who are aiming to reduce occurrences of miscommunication.

This essay discusses the influence of situational proprieties on social interaction and relevant implications for intercultural communication. Specifically, I discuss a

> *In the case of intercultural encounters, situational proprieties often diverge, and accordingly there is a greater risk that miscommunication will result.*

reciprocal process where a speaker pays *deference* (Goffman, 1967) to others while concomitantly exhibiting proper *demeanor* (Goffman, 1967). Since situational proprieties informing appropriate displays of deference and demeanor are situationally and culturally variant, speakers may inadvertently cause an affront in an intercultural encounter. Examples from Japanese and North American culture that illustrate the cultural basis of deference and demeanor are given. The final section of the chapter discusses the implications of these concepts for more effective intercultural communication.

## DEFERENCE AND DEMEANOR

Goffman maintains that there are certain *rules of conduct* (1967) or *situational proprieties* (1963) which constitute normative patterns of behavior in specific social situations. Rules of conduct include *obligations*, which refer to how an individual is expected to act toward others, and *expectations*, or how others are expected to act toward the individual. For example, a teacher is obligated to prepare for classes and grade papers and expects students to complete the assigned reading and submit papers on time. Obligations and expectations are like an unwritten contract which specifies normative behavior in specific social situations. Expectations and obligations are so ingrained into the fiber of daily life that members of a particular culture are often unconscious of their existence. However, expectations and obligations become apparent

> *Expectations and obligations are so ingrained into the fiber of daily life that members of a particular culture are often unconscious of their existence.*

when individuals create infractions which "characteristically lead to feelings of uneasiness and to negative social sanctions" (Goffman, 1967, p. 48). Infractions can occur in intercultural encounters where speakers' expectations and obligations differ and they unwittingly violate these norms and cause an affront.

### Deference

*Deference* is "the appreciation an individual shows of another to that other"

(Goffman, 1967, p. 77) and illustrates an *expectation*. Social actors are expected to use salutations, compliments, and apologies to pay deference to others. Although it is tempting to conflate deference with showing respect to a higher-status person, this is not always the case. For example, an individual could pay deference to a peer by saying, "I like your sweater." Compliments such as this can serve as conversational starters, which build solidarity between speakers of similar social status, and deference can also be used to establish distance between individuals. Therefore, Goffman (1967) classifies two specific forms of deference: *avoidance rituals* and *presentational rituals*, collectively termed *interpersonal rituals*.

Avoidance rituals refer to forms of deference which "lead the actor to keep at a distance from the recipient" (Goffman, 1967, p. 62) and address the recipient's need for "privacy and separateness" (Goffman, 1967, p. 67). Avoiding embarrassing topics, respecting personal privacy, and addressing someone by her or his title versus first name are examples of avoidance rituals. Most people are likely to associate deference with avoidance rituals because the commonsense usage of the term implies paying respect to someone with a higher social status. Notice, however, that privacy and separateness are universal needs which are independent of social status. Therefore, a speaker uses avoidance rituals to convey deference to recipients of different social statuses.

Some examples will better illustrate *avoidance rituals* or *deferential avoidance*. For instance, when asking a professor for a letter of recommendation, avoidance rituals are commonly used because fulfilling the request imposes upon the professor. Therefore, a polite expression such as "I know that you are really busy, but would you mind writing me a recommendation letter" is customarily employed in this situation. However, as I mentioned, avoidance rituals do not always emphasize paying someone homage, but can also accentuate individual freedom and choice.

The United States can be classified as an individualistic society because of the high value attached to

> In contrast to avoidance rituals, which honor an individual's desire for independence, presentational rituals attempt to address an individual's desire to be connected to others.

the principles of individual rights and self-reliance (Scollon & Scollon, 2001). Therefore, individual choice is venerated and evident in many aspects of everyday life. For example, when ordering a deli sandwich, individuals are provided with a wide array of choices which starts with the type of bread and extends to not only the condiments but also the type of condiments (e.g., regular or fat-free mayonnaise). Similarly, when dining out, customers specify how they want their eggs or meat cooked and are given a choice of sides to accompany their main entree. Substitutions are often allowed to further accommodate personal preferences or dietary restrictions. Providing individuals with alternatives is built on the premise of individual variation and foregrounds independence from others, which illustrates deferential avoidance.

Presentational rituals (Goffman, 1967) are a form of deference which attempt to build solidarity and establish camaraderie with others and materialize as salutations, invitations, and compliments. In contrast to avoidance rituals, which honor an individual's desire for independence, presentational rituals attempt to address an individual's desire to be connected to others. Presentational rituals are often employed when interacting with someone of a similar age and social status, but this is not always the case. For example, subordinates sometimes address their superiors by their first name. As illustrated by this example, classifications such as "presentational rituals are used between status equals and avoidance rituals between status unequals" are temporary and provisional at best. Interpersonal rituals are flexible strategies which people adapt in specific social situations.

Further examples will better illustrate *presentational rituals* or *presentational deference*. For example, complimenting a friend's new sweater or teammate's performance are examples of presentational rituals because they accentuate the acceptability and desirability of the person's behavior and accordingly build solidarity with the person. In addition to compliments, invitations, and greetings, trusting others' judgment can also be seen as a presentational ritual. For example, you might elicit your friend's opinion prior to purchasing new clothes because you trust that person. Mutual trust is an example of a presentational ritual which is related to the importance a culture or group attaches to interdependence.

Japan is often considered a collectivist society because of the importance placed on collective responsibility (*rentai sekinin*) and interdependence (Davies & Ikeno, 2002; Matsumoto, 1994; Sugimoto, 2003). Therefore, mutual trust and intergroup harmony are social values which permeate many aspects of daily life. Whereas people are presented with a seemingly endless amount of choices in North American society, Japanese society presents people with several pre-selected choices. For example, restaurants frequently offer *set menus* which includes a main dish, several side dishes, and sometimes coffee and dessert. Somewhat resembling a fast-food value meal, a customer orders *Set A*, *Set B* or simply *today's set lunch*. One set usually offers a meat main course while the other offers fish. However, unlike eating establishments in the United States, where customers are sometimes permitted to make alterations, restaurants in Japan typically proscribe substitutions of any kind. While a restaurant in the United States may allow a customer to substitute a baked potato for French fries, such an option is usually unavailable in Japan. Social conformity, not individuality, is an extolled virtue in Japanese society.

The absence of multiple choices in Japan is built upon the assumption of group homogeneity and illustrates both collectivism and mutual dependence. In collectivist Japan, a prevalent norm dictates that shared group membership entails mutual trust and interdependence (Davies & Ikeno, 2002; Matsumoto, 1994; Sugimoto, 2003). Therefore, the set menu example illustrates how a customer trusts the chef to prepare an appetizing meal. Some restaurants even offer a *makase* (leave it to me) *course* which changes seasonally and is entirely arranged by the chef. Therefore, asking the chef to modify a carefully prepared *makase* course may be considered aberrant behavior because it implies a lack of trust between customer and chef. This example illustrates presentational deference because the customer trusts the chef to prepare an aesthetically appealing and satisfying meal.

> *Demeanor is conveyed through aligning one's speech, behavior, and dress in accordance with social norms.*

## Demeanor

Presentational and avoidance rituals are examples of situated proprieties which vary by culture and social situation and change over time. Therefore, by drawing on appropriate interpersonal rituals, individuals convey to others that they have inculcated social norms and consequently present themselves as properly socialized, or possessing what Goffman (1967) terms *demeanor*.

*Demeanor* is an element of an individual's conduct which displays to others that the individual is "a person of certain desirable or undesirable qualities" (Goffman, 1967, p. 77). Demeanor is conveyed through aligning one's speech, behavior, and dress in accordance with social norms. In the United States these norms could include dressing appropriately, expressing an opinion, and using interpersonal rituals to pay deference to others. Social actors are simultaneously *expected* to give deference to others and *obligated* to display proper demeanor. Therefore, an individual who fails to give deference to others or successfully convey the possession of proper demeanor risks being labeled *socially deviant* and alienated from social interaction.

Like the concept of deference, demeanor varies by culture and social situation, and changes over time. For example, on many college campuses in the United States, it is perfectly acceptable to attend class in a relatively informal style of dress. In contrast, college students in Japan tend to come to school in designer clothes and styled hair. Norms are not only culturally and situationally specific, but also change over time. Therefore, while a more stringent dress code may have prevailed in workplaces of the past, this is not the current practice in all workplaces. These examples are meant to illustrate that norms governing what constitutes proper demeanor vary by culture and social situation and change over time. In the next section, I further discern the connection between the interrelated concepts of deference and demeanor.

## THE INTERRELATIONSHIP BETWEEN DEFERENCE AND DEMEANOR

The concepts of deference and demeanor illustrate how individuals display proper demeanor through aligning their actions with socio-culturally constructed norms which include paying deference to others through interpersonal rituals. As Goffman (1967) insightfully pointed out, demeanor is partly constructed through deference. Therefore, in many contexts in the United States, an individual displays proper demeanor through interpersonal rituals such as complimenting someone or making a polite request. Conversely, an individual displays improper demeanor through asking an acquaintance a personal question or neglecting to greet a colleague at the office.

Further examples will demonstrate the culturally and situationally specific nature of the interrelated concepts of deference and demeanor. I would like to focus attention on the familiar social contexts of school and work, in order to illustrate that despite the assumed ritualistic and mundane nature of giving deference and displaying demeanor, these concepts can and do vary by culture and social situation and change over time.

## Uchi and Soto

Prior to examining displays of deference and demeanor within specific social contexts, I would like to provide some additional information about Japanese culture. In addition to the salient cultural value of collectivism, *uchi* (in-group) and *soto* (out-group) are also indispensable concepts for anyone aspiring to delve beyond a surface level understanding of Japanese culture. *Uchi/soto* draws a clear demarcation between insiders and outsiders, and Japanese subsequently adjust their behavior depending on their interactants (Davies & Ikeno, 2002; Sugimoto, 2003). Japanese are inclined to be less candid when interacting with out-group members and more open with in-group members (Sugimoto, 2003). Broadly speaking, school affiliation forms one large in-group, but even within an individual school there are several subdivisions of *uchi* and *soto* which depend on age and group affiliation. For example, members of the freshman class form one *uchi* and consequently are expected to use appropriate *keigo* (honorific language) when speaking with upperclassmen. Even within the freshman class there are other *uchi/soto* distinctions such as members of an athletic team forming one *uchi* and members of an extracurricular club another.

This brief discussion of *uchi* and *soto* is neither meant to be exhaustive nor construct Japan as somehow inherently different from other cultures. Even in the United States, people possess simultaneous membership in multiple groups, which can construct firm boundaries between members and non-members (e.g., fraternities and sororities); however, group affiliation is more pervasive and pronounced in Japan. For example, students and company employees usually wear uniforms, sing school or company songs, and sometimes collectively engage in exercise routines (Sugimoto, 2003). Therefore, group membership is somewhat predetermined and infiltrates many aspects of daily life in Japan. The compulsory component of group membership in Japan will become more apparent in the following discussion of deference and demeanor within specific social contexts.

## Deference and Demeanor at School

There are several components of Japanese school life which illustrate the importance of presentational rituals. Commencing in secondary school, mandated uniforms clearly demarcate students' institutional affiliations. The prototypical school uniform is a black blazer and trousers for boys and navy blazer and skirt for girls. Students can be seen wearing school uniforms both inside and outside of school, which suggests that uniforms are more than a school mandate and may be a source of pride. School uniforms are an emblem which provide students with a sense of group affiliation (*shozoku*) and solidarity (*ittaikan*) (McVeigh, 2000) and therefore represent a presentational ritual.

The ritual of *kyushoku* (school lunch) epitomizes Japanese collectivism and also illustrates a presentational ritual. Instead of selling lunch in a cafeteria, Japanese secondary schools serve a preselected menu which changes daily. Significantly, the cultural practice of school lunch is more than a meal, but can be seen as a ritual which teaches students about the Japanese values of cooperation (*kyoryoku*) and collective responsibility (*rentai sekinin*). For this reason, students are required to pay the monthly fee and participate in the daily endeavor. Even more so than the previous set menu example, homogeneity and collectivism are reflected in the assumption that students eat the same menu. Hot lunches are first prepared by trained staff and then transported in large vats to individual classrooms where predetermined teams of students take turns serving their classmates. Students form a line and are served cafeteria-style by their peers. A typical school lunch consists of a main dish, side dishes, bread or rice, and milk. After all students are served and seated, students clap their hands together and proclaim in unison, *itadakimasu* (let's eat) and lunch commences. At the end of the meal, students utter, *gochisosama deshita* (I have really enjoyed the meal), and student teams perform the cleanup. These verbal expressions symbolize group affiliation and unity, addressing individuals' desire for connection with others, and therefore are illustrative of presentational rituals.

The ritual of school lunch requires the cooperation of all students and therefore illustrates a presentational ritual. Students work together on tight-knit teams where collective effort is not only desirable but also indispensable if students are to efficiently serve lunch and perform cleanup within the allotted lunch period. The various verbal and non-verbal cues that team members use, such as compliments, friendly reminders, and gestures, can be seen as presentational rituals because they emphasize group membership and build solidarity. Uncooperative students not only slow down the process, but also risk exhibiting bad demeanor. Therefore, students learn group conformity by eating the same menu as their peers and learn cooperation through working on teams.

Since Japanese society can be defined by hierarchical relationships (Matsumoto, 1994; Sugimoto, 2003), avoidance rituals are also a pervasive aspect of school life. This is strikingly apparent in age-based *senpai-kohai* (senior-junior) relationships. The terms *senpai* and *kohai* index age and clearly define the speakers' relationship. While informal hierarchies arguably exist in American schools, *senpai-kohai* relations demarcate rigid age-based boundaries between students. Underclassmen are expected to show respect, obedience, and subservience to older students (Davies & Ikeno, 2002; McVeigh, 2002; Sugimoto, 2003). Therefore,

younger students use avoidance rituals such as bowing and addressing upperclassmen with the respectful *senpai* (e.g., Tanaka *senpai*) and polite language. Failure to display appropriate deference to one's *senpai* would suggest that an individual possess improper demeanor and could incur social sanction such as bullying.

## Deference and Demeanor at Work

The workplace is another site where interpersonal rituals can be observed. Presentational rituals are observable in the formulaic expressions customarily used by employees. For example, employees start the day by enthusiastically greeting each other with "*ohayogozaimasu*" (good morning). Before leaving the company for any reason (e.g., to get lunch), an employee says *itte kimasu* (I'll go and come back) and receives *itte irrasshai* (please go and come back) as a reply from her or his co-workers. At the end of the day, an employee exclaims, "*osakini shitsureishimasu*" (I'm sorry for leaving first) and colleagues respond "*gokurosama deshita*" (many thanks for your trouble) or "*otsukaresamadeshita*" (I appreciate your hard work). Although these expressions sound unnatural when translated into English, they serve the important function of continually emphasizing shared group affiliation. Again, an employee who neglects to utter these verbal protocols risks displaying improper demeanor and could face ostracism by the group.

Avoidance rituals are most clearly evidenced by the polite language Japanese use in relation to their superiors and to out-group members such as customers. The Japanese language distinguishes between *teineigo* (polite language) and *keigo* (honorific language). *Teineigo* expresses a degree of politeness appropriate for conversing with non-intimates. For example, the prefix *o* in *ocha* (tea) upgrades the politeness level of the relatively informal *cha*. *Keigo* is more complex than *teineigo* and involves selecting appropriate honorific verb forms which convey a higher level of politeness. For example, the honorific form of the verb *iu* (speak) is *ossharu*. Therefore, a polite way to request someone's name is "*O namae wa nan to*

> *Avoidance rituals are most clearly evidenced by the polite language Japanese use in relation to their superiors and to out-group members such as customers.*

*ossharu no desu ka*" (Could you tell me your name?). In this example, replacing *iu* with *ossharu* conveys a higher degree of politeness and consequently can be seen as an avoidance ritual. Another example of *keigo* is the polite title *sensei*, which is used to address educators, doctors, or lawyers. While *teineigo* can be used to create an appropriate distance between acquaintances such as non-intimate co-workers, colleagues who feel close to each other may elect to use informal language. Conversely, *keigo* would most certainly be used when addressing a superior or customers who visit the company. These examples illustrate that even though a workplace can be considered one large in-group, there are various levels of *uchi/soto* membership which depend upon status and are reflected in language. Consequently, co-workers who are using informal language may switch to polite language when addressing their boss. Polite and honorific language expresses a degree of social distance between speakers that often reflects social status and for this reason can be seen as an example of deferential avoidance.

The above discussion has attempted to demonstrate how an individual's use of contextually appropriate interpersonal rituals demonstrates that person possesses proper demeanor. In schools, wearing a mandated uniform and cooperating during school lunch are examples of presentational deference, while addressing one's *senpai* with polite language illustrates deferential avoidance. In workplaces, formulaic expressions illustrate presentational deference, while polite language exemplifies deferential avoidance. An individual's use of these interpersonal rituals combined with attention to appearance and appropriate behavior together constitute and reflect good demeanor.

## CONCLUSION

In an era defined by rapid transportation, information technology, and globalization, intercultural encounters are becoming increasingly commonplace. These advancements enable speakers from across the globe to communicate with a relative degree of ease in both face-to-face and computer-mediated interactional contexts. The paradoxical privilege of these advancements is that long periods of face-to-face interaction are unnecessary; however, individuals acquire knowledge of situational proprieties through residence abroad and intercultural contact. As a result, individuals' access to culturally specific notions of deference and demeanor is curtailed and the chance for an intercultural misunderstanding to result is elevated.

Goffman (1967) made the insightful point that part of the reason for classifying individuals as *mentally ill* is because their behavior is viewed as transgressing contextually appropriate standards of deference and demeanor. However, incarcerating these individuals with other *social deviants* ensures that mental patients never receive access to knowledge about institutionalized social norms which govern standards of deference and demeanor. Unlike people in society, mental patients are neither always treated with deference nor aware of norms governing demeanor, and in some cases health care professionals inadvertently enable their patients by permitting deviant behavior such as outbursts which would incur social sanction outside a hospital setting.

Fortunately, mental hospitals have significantly progressed from the repressive institutions of Goffman's time. Nevertheless, there are some parallels which can be drawn between Goffman's observations and intercultural encounters today.

Speakers in intercultural encounters are similar to Goffman's mental patients in that they lack access to crucial knowledge about how to pay deference to others and consequently do not present themselves as properly demeaned. In a global marketplace, this could mean the difference between causing an offense which results in the formation of a wall that severs a potential business relationship and building a bridge that enables a relationship to unfold and prosper. The unconscious and implicit nature of situational proprieties renders them more difficult to pinpoint than grammatical or pronunciation errors. As a result, speakers can leave interactions feeling frustrated and the formation and dispersion of stereotypes can result.

I would like to suggest that greater awareness and tolerance of socio-culturally specific norms which constitute deference and demeanor could reduce instances of intercultural miscommunication. We live in an increasingly interdependent world where awareness of and respect for cultural norms is essential not only to foster better communication, but also to potentially reduce intercultural friction and strife. Therefore, one challenge facing people in this globalizing society is to expand their communication toolkits to include knowledge of social maxims constituting deference and demeanor and thereby contribute to increasing the frequency of successful intercultural encounters.

## References

Davies, R. & Ikeno, O. (2002). *The Japanese Mind: Understanding Contemporary Japanese Culture*. Rutland, VT: Tuttle Publishing.

Goffman, E. (1963). *Behavior in Public Places: Notes on the Social Organization of Gatherings*. New York: Free Press.

Goffman, E. (1967). The nature of deference and demeanor. In E. Goffman, *Interaction Ritual* (pp. 47–95). Garden City, NJ: Doubleday.

Matsumoto, S. (1994). *Nihon Bunka no Tokushitsu [The characteristics of Japanese culture]*. Tokyo: Kenkyusha.

McVeigh, B. (2000). *Wearing Ideology: State, Schooling and Self-presentation in Japan*. New York: Berg.

McVeigh, B. (2002). *Japanese Higher Education as Myth*. London: M. E. Sharp.

Scollon, R. & Scollon, S. (2001). *Intercultural Communication*. Malden, MA: Blackwell.

Sugimoto, Y. (2003). *An Introduction to Japanese Society* (2nd ed.). Cambridge, England: Cambridge University Press.

Watanabe, S. (1993). Cultural differences in framing: Americans and Japanese group discussions. In D. Tannen (Ed.), *Framing in Discourse* (pp. 176–209). New York: Oxford University Press.

Yamada, H. (1997). *Different Games, Different Rules: Why Americans and Japanese Misunderstand Each Other*. Oxford: Oxford University Press.

## Concepts and Questions

1. What does Charlebois mean when he writes, "Social interaction is neither arbitrary nor disorderly, but patterned by *interaction rituals*"?

2. What are situational proprieties?

3. How might "obligations" and "expectations" get acted out during an intercultural interaction?

4. How does Charlebois define "deference"? Can you think of an intercultural example that demonstrates deference in Japanese culture?

5. Can you think of an example of a "presentational ritual" that is found in the United States?

6. What English word best defines the Japanese notion of *rentai sekinin*? Do you believe *rentai sekinin*, as a cultural value is found in the United States?

7. How might demeanor be displayed during a communication encounter? How is demeanor often reflected in the United States?

8. How are deference and demeanor behaviors displayed in Japanese schools?

9. How are deference and demeanor behaviors displayed in the Japanese business environment?

10. How would you compare the Japanese attitude toward deference and demeanor to that of the American perception of these two values?

# Discriminating Attitudes Toward Speech

AARON CASTELAN CARGILE

*The final selection in this chapter examines some intercultural problems that can occur even if people speak the same language. In an essay titled "Discriminating Attitudes Toward Speech," you will see how the words you use, and how you express those words, can be a type of discrimination. Cargile is concerned with the way "talk" is employed as a means of singling people out and discriminating against them. As you might expect, such discrimination causes numerous intercultural difficulties. Cargile examines three major characteristics of*

This original essay first appeared in the tenth edition. All rights reserved. Permission to reprint must be obtained from the author and the publisher. Dr. Aaron Castelan Cargile is a professor in the Department of Communication Studies at California State University, Long Beach.

*speech (accents, vocabularies, and rates of speech) and how differences in these three qualities can influence interaction between people from dissimilar cultures. For Cargile, some of that influence grows out of the fact that the recipients of those language differences often attach negative images to nontraditional variations in accents, vocabulary, and rates of speed. The false assumption is that these differences somehow make the speaker inferior. As a means of overcoming these harmful attitudes, Cargile concludes his essay with some advice on how to keep these negative perceptions from obstructing effective intercultural communication.*

The term *intercultural communication* typically invokes visions of people from two (or more) different nations interacting with one another. Such a situation could be an American customs officer speaking with a Mexican tourist. In many such instances, participants may not use the same language; thus the challenge presented by differences in speech is obvious. Intercultural communication also describes interactions between people from the same nation, but from different co-cultures, as in the case of exchanges between many Asian Americans and African Americans. On these occasions, it may seem that the challenge of coping with differences in speech is minimal, if not nonexistent. Yet, it must be realized that even when people speak the same language, such as English, they don't always speak the same "language."

Consider, for example, a New York businesswoman interviewing a West Virginian job candidate who answers questions with an Appalachian drawl. She may comprehend with little, if any, difficulty what is being said; however, she may not feel completely at ease during the interaction, or afterward when she decides the person's fate of employment. Sadly, these feelings may come regardless of what the applicant has said: The applicant may be thoroughly qualified for the job, and he may answer all interview questions satisfactorily, but the words running through the businesswoman's mind may be the same as those heard by June Tyler during a closed-door meeting with a senior partner in a law firm: "be careful about hiring anyone with a mountain accent" (Pasternak, 19, p. A16). The discomfort felt by the businesswoman when faced with this fully qualified job applicant illustrates a special sort of difficulty faced by intercultural communicators—a difficulty of fair evaluation and equal treatment. Unlike more obvious difficulties of comprehension, this sort of difficulty presents a greater challenge to intercultural communication because people tend to ignore or minimize language-based prejudices.

In this example, it may be the case that the New York businesswoman is consciously aware of her decision to discriminate against the job applicant based on his Appalachian accent. Although such discrimination is illegal, many people freely admit that a Southern accent is often inappropriate and suggest that it should be abandoned in favor of other accents. For example, soon after Atlanta was awarded the 1996 summer Olympics, a column appeared in the *Atlanta Business Chronicle* encouraging citizens to "get the South out of our mouth" in order to impress the expected visitors (reported in Pearl, 1991). Unlike the open prejudice in this example, however, it is more likely that the businesswoman would not be aware of her discriminatory motives. Instead, she would likely experience only some general sense that the applicant was not quite as "sharp" as the others, and that he somehow did not "seem right" for the job, even though these impressions could unknowingly be fostered by her own prejudice against the speaker's accent. Because, as in this example, episodes of intercultural communication are often spontaneously shaped by participants' language-based prejudices, it is important that we learn to deal effectively with the challenges they present. Before this can be done, however, we must first understand both the nature of and reasons for our attitudes toward speech.

> It must be realized that even when people speak the same language, such as English, they don't always speak the same "language."

## ATTITUDES TOWARD SPEECH

Despite the previous example, skeptics might think that what we say remains far more important than how we say it. Thus, our attitudes toward speech are not "that big of a deal"; they don't ever really encourage people to act in a prejudiced or discriminatory manner, do they? Fortunately, social scientists, including linguists, psychologists, and communication scholars, have developed a field of study called "language attitudes" in order to find out if and when language influences our impressions of, and reactions to, others. It is beyond the scope of this chapter to review this entire field (see Bradac, Cargile, & Halett, 2001). Thus instead, assuming a predominantly American (U.S.) readership, I will describe some of the research investigating attitudes toward speech held by American listeners.

Although people hold attitudes toward many different features of speech (e.g., speech rate or speech style), one of the most salient features is accent. Research has shown that listeners make ready and regular judgments regarding the personal and social characteristics of speakers based simply on the way they sound. In the case of most standard-speaking Americans, they consistently prejudge others with "Appalachian," "Spanish," "German," or "African American vernacular" accented speech as less intelligent, poorer, less-educated, and less–status-possessing than standard-accented speakers (Bradac & Wisegarver, 1984; Johnson & Buttny, 1982; Luhman, 1990; Ryan & Bulik, 1982; Ryan & Carranza, 1975; Tucker & Lambert, 1969). For example, Bishop (1979) found that white female respondents evaluated African American colleagues as less responsible and less desirable co-workers when they spoke "Black" as opposed to "White" English. Similarly, Giles, Williams, Mackie, and Rosselli (1995) discovered that Anglo respondents rated the same bi-dialectical speaker as less literate and more lower class when he spoke English with a "Hispanic" accent, compared to an "Anglo" accent.

Surprisingly, though, standard-accented listeners are not the only ones who look down on many nonstandard-accented speakers. Even listeners who themselves speak with a nonstandard accent often judge others who sound like themselves to have low social standing. For example, a study by Doss and Gross (1992) revealed that African American respondents perceived same-race Standard English speakers as more competent than those who spoke African American vernacular English. As this last example suggests, the complex reality of intercultural communication is not that we think badly of *everyone* who speaks differently. Indeed, research indicates that there are some "foreign"-accented speakers who Americans *don't* perceive to be less competent or inferior (e.g., British-accented English speakers; Stewart, Ryan, & Giles, 1985). Similarly, listeners who speak with a standard accent sometimes judge nonstandard accented-speakers to be equal to standard-accented speakers along some dimensions (e.g., being "friendly" and "good natured"; see Ryan, Hewstone, & Giles, 1984). Even so, this language attitudes research demonstrates that we often prejudge others in unflattering and potentially harmful ways based on their accent alone.

## LANGUAGE-BASED DISCRIMINATION

In addition to prejudgment, our attitudes toward speech may also result in discriminatory actions against speakers. There are perhaps few contexts in which someone else's behavior is more important for our own well-being than in the courtroom or in an employment interview. In both instances, evidence shows that unfair treatment can be provoked by a speaker's use of language. For example, Seggie (1983) presented standard- or nonstandard-accented voices to listeners and told them that the speaker stood accused of one of several crimes. On the audiotapes, the speakers were heard protesting their innocence regarding the crime of which they had been accused. Listeners were then asked to make a decision regarding the probable guilt or innocence of the speaker. The results showed that standard-accented speakers were more often seen as guilty when the crime was embezzlement, whereas nonstandard-accented speakers were more often judged guilty when the crime was physical assault. Listeners thus more often associated white-collar crimes with standard-sounding defendants and crimes of violence with nonstandard-sounding defendants. Although these listeners were not actual jury members, the

> *Research has shown that listeners make ready and regular judgments regarding the personal and social characteristics of speakers based simply on the way they sound.*

results plainly suggest that people can be treated differently based on their accent alone; treatment that is particularly unfair can result in the conviction of a nonstandard-accented speaker accused of a violent crime.

In the case of a job interview, language attitudes research has extended beyond the campus laboratory to investigate the ways in which actual employees of real companies respond to accented speakers. In an important study by Henry and Ginzberg (1985), individuals with different ethnic/racial accents made telephone inquires about jobs advertised in a newspaper. Job applicants who spoke with a nonstandard accent were most often told that the jobs had been filled. Applicants with a standard accent, however, were most often invited to appear for a personal interview, even after the nonstandard speakers were informed that applications for the position were no longer being accepted! In a similar study, de la Zerda and Hopper (1979) asked employers from San Antonio, Texas, to predict the likelihood of a speaker being hired for each of three positions: supervisor, skilled technician, and semi-skilled laborer. A comparison of standard American and (Mexican American) Spanish-accented speakers revealed that standard speakers were favored for the supervisor position, whereas Spanish-accented speakers were more likely to be hired for the semi-skilled position. It would thus be doubly hard for a Spanish-accented speaker to be hired as a supervisor because he or she would not only be seen as less appropriate for this position but also as more appropriate for the lower-skilled (and lower-waged) job. Sadly, these and other results (e.g., Giles, Wilson, & Conway, 1981; Kalin & Rayko, 1978) clearly illustrate that people can not only be prejudiced against others who sound different, but they can also discriminate against these speakers in ways that may jeopardize both the speakers' livelihoods and their lives.

> *A comparison of standard American and (Mexican American) Spanish-accented speakers revealed that standard speakers were favored for the supervisor position, whereas Spanish-accented speakers were more likely to be hired for the semi-skilled position.*

## WHY DO WE HAVE DISCRIMINATING ATTITUDES

Having explored the potential dangers of attitudes toward speech, an important question to consider now is why we have these attitudes in the first place. Quite simply, attitudes exist because people have to cope with a world full of uncertainty. Life often requires us to respond to others even though we lack complete information about their character or intentions. When a uniformed stranger rings your doorbell, or a student in the library takes your chair, what are you supposed to do? Before you can respond to the person, you must first evaluate him or her. If you think the uniformed stranger is kind, honest, and responsibly doing her job as a government census worker, you should cooperate with her request for information. If you think the student is lazy, mean, and rude, you should firmly insist that he find another chair to use. Behavior demands evaluation, but we rarely, if ever, have the time, the opportunity, or the ability to base these instant evaluations on thoroughly collected or completely tested information. On what basis, then, can we behave in these situations? On the basis of prejudgments. We call on our attitudes about properly uniformed, polite, "well-spoken" individuals as a basis to evaluate and respond to the uniformed stranger at our door. And we call on our stereotypes of sloppily dressed, heavy metal music–listening, loud-talking individuals as a basis to evaluate and respond to the student in the library. Although these prejudgments may, in fact, be incorrect in these situations, without them we would have no basis for behaving spontaneously and life would quickly come to a halt.

Attitudes provide us with a sense of certainty and some basis for behavior. As such, they are absolutely natural and necessary for our survival in an otherwise uncertain world. Even so, they are especially problematic because they are mostly biased and discriminatory. As human beings, we far more often prejudge different-sounding others in unflattering ways. Although many specific reasons for this situation have been described (see Mackie, Hamilton, Susskind, & Rosselli, 1996), the underlying motive is that humans and human groups are naturally competitive; evolution has designed us with social competition in mind. We can be cooperative, obviously, but cooperation normally occurs only when it is in our interests—immediate or otherwise (see Cosmides & Tooby, 1992). Social group interaction is more often characterized by competition than cooperation (see Worchel & Austin, 1986); thus discriminatory attitudes are one way in which people maintain a competitive edge.

## DISCRIMINATING ATTITUDES IN CULTURE

Of course, the complex reality of intercultural communication is not that we are predisposed to think badly of everyone who speaks differently. As described earlier, there are occasions when we think worse of people who sound like us and better of people who sound different. How can this happen if we are supposed to develop unfavorable attitudes about *others'* ways of speaking? It usually happens when one social group dominates another to a point where competition ends. At this point, the dominant social group clearly controls the spaces in which the two groups coexist (e.g., the workplace) and often greatly influences even the subordinate group's private spaces (e.g., the home). In these circumstances, dominant and subordinate group members alike receive the dominant group's culture—the one that includes its own discriminating attitude. Consequently, members of both groups may learn to discriminate against subordinate-group speech.

In the case of the United States, the most salient social groups are those identified by race or ethnicity, and among these different groups, Anglo-Americans have clearly been dominant. As a result, mainstream American culture has socialized attitudes toward speech that favor Anglo-Americans and discriminate against all other forms of American English. For example, the CBS Evening News aired a national broadcast in which a reporter clearly passed along this bias by commenting about a program in accent reduction: "The idea is to teach them how to speak English so that it sounds like English, and not, as Henry Higgins might put it, warmed-over grits. Think of them as prisoners–prisoners of their own accent" (Fagar, 1984).

Similarly, a reporter in a regional newspaper wrote, "No matter how qualified a person is, a voice twisted by regional or ethnic influences can be a stumbling block socially and professionally" (Kerr, 1994). With ideas like these promoted not only in the media but also in school and in the workplace (see Lippi-Green, 1997), it is little wonder that many non-Anglo speakers have developed unfavorable attitudes toward their own, otherwise native, way of speaking. As one African American wrote:

> Although we were surrounded in New York by a number of poorly spoken and frequently stereotypical black … dialects, my siblings and I soon learned to hear it for what it was—the language of the street, the language of black trash. The language that went right along with Saturday-night knife fights to settle a grudge. (Hamblin, 1995, p. B8)

To make matters worse, not only do we internalize the discriminating attitudes that saturate our culture, but we also rarely give them up. Although the use of attitudes is both natural and unavoidable, they are typically used far too often, and far too long, to really benefit communicators. As discussed earlier, attitudes are useful in situations in which we must respond to others, but lack the time, the opportunity, and the ability to base our behavior on thoughtfully collected information. Sadly though, once we have developed attitudes to help get us through these pressing situations, we become lazy and use these prepackaged evaluations even when we can collect more accurate and personalized information about the person with whom we are interacting. Collecting this information is absolutely critical to fair and effective interaction, but it requires us to spend a great deal of cognitive energy; in other words, we have to think (and we all know how effortful that can be sometimes!). So instead, because it is easier, we carelessly rely on our attitudes far more often than is justifiable.

Relatedly, people also tend to rely on their attitudes far too long. By this I mean that once we have applied an attitude-based evaluation, it becomes increasingly difficult to change it despite information to the contrary because there are many different ways in which we work unknowingly to ensure the survival (and supposed accuracy) of our attitudes. For example, because attitudes affect what information we attend to (Fazio, Roskos-Ewoldsen, & Powell, 1994), we often perceive only those facts about another person that are consistent with our attitude and ignore other important, contradictory information. To illustrate, I may deem a job applicant unsuitable for a managerial position based on her accent, and then pay attention to information on her resume that supports this evaluation (e.g., lack of managerial experience), while ignoring conflicting information (e.g., high GPA or leadership experience). In this way, I can continue to rely on my original attitude-based evaluation long after I should have revised it. When this happens, we are reminded that even though attitudes are natural, the biases with which they are typically developed and applied can create substantial difficulties for fair and effective communication.

## WHAT SHOULD BE DONE ABOUT OUR DISCRIMINATING ATTITUDES?

Whether we like it or not, and whether we admit it or not, we all possess discriminating attitudes toward speech. Attitudes are an essential feature of social life, so what should responsible intercultural communicators do about them? First, the most important thing is to recognize your own attitudes toward speech. Despite the generalizations offered throughout this reading, each one of us has a distinct profile of attitudes developed over a unique life history. Figure out what your attitudes are and then notice when you use them. For example, in universities across America, students often respond unfavorably to foreign-born teaching assistants and professors. Specifically, on some campuses, more than two of five students withdraw or switch from a class when they find out their teacher is a non-native speaker of English (Rubin & Smith, 1988). In addition, many of the rest of students in classes taught by these professors make complaints of the variety that forced the state of Illinois to pass a fluency law for college instructors (Secter, 1987). Who is responsible for such student dissatisfaction? In some cases, it may in fact be an instructor with verifiably poor language skills. In many other cases, though, it may in fact be the students themselves.

On first hearing an instructor's accent, students will often unknowingly make assumptions about the instructor's personality and (language) skills based solely on their own attitudes toward foreign-accented speakers (e.g., "this teacher isn't too friendly, too smart, and he doesn't speak proper English"). The instructor may, in fact, be or do none of the things that the student assumes. Even so, because attitudes toward speech have the power to initiate selective perceptions, the students may create, in their own minds, evidence to support their views. In particular, they may "hear" the instructor make grammatical mistakes that he or she has not really made (indeed, this has been demonstrated in a study by Cargile and Giles, 1998). Students can then, in turn, point to these "mistakes" as justification for their attitudes and a reason for responding unfavorably to the instructor. Thus, a class may end up with an instructor who is in fact friendly and smart, and who speaks grammatically correct and comprehensible English, but because students have based their responses, unknowingly, on their attitudes toward foreign-accented speech alone, they may feel dissatisfied with their instruction.

As the previous scenario illustrates, in the end, the evaluations we make of others may be more a product of our own attitudes than others' behaviors. The trouble is that we rarely realize this situation, and thus act as if the other is entirely responsible for our reactions. Consequently, we must begin to manage our attitudes by recognizing their existence. Ask yourself, "Am I thinking this about the person only because of the way that he or she speaks?" You may answer "no" to this question, thus indicating that the role attitudes are playing is minimal and perhaps justified. You may, however, answer "yes,"

> On first hearing an instructor's accent, students will often unknowingly make assumptions about the instructor's personality and (language) skills based solely on their own attitudes toward foreign-accented speakers (e.g., "this teacher isn't too friendly, too smart, and he doesn't speak proper English").

suggesting that your attitudes about language use are exerting an undue and likely problematic influence on your behavior.

Once you learn to recognize the role attitudes toward speech play in your responses, a second thing to do is to seek out and integrate additional information into the evaluation process—especially when you answer "yes" to the aforementioned question. Your attitudes may lead you to believe one thing about a speaker, but your job as a responsible intercultural communicator is to test out, to the best of your abilities, whether your evaluation is accurate and appropriate. For example, in the case of a non-native English–speaking instructor, find out about his or her educational background, prior teaching experience, and real English competency through patient listening (and perhaps some careful questioning) before passing the easy, ready-made judgment that this person lacks the intelligence and ability to be a successful teacher. Of course, this kind of "fact checking" and follow-up is effortful and never easy; however, it is critical to managing our attitudes well.

Although these first two suggestions are enough to occupy all of us for a lifetime, there is a third, even more challenging, thing to do—change our discriminating attitudes. Of course, any attitude is difficult to change because it has likely developed over a lifetime and meets many our needs, like providing a sense of certainty or competitive edge. Despite this feeling, however, it is possible to remold our discriminating attitudes into *more* accurate, less biased ones.

For example, consider the teacher who is annoyed by her African American students' pronunciation of the word "ask" [a:ks]. She reprimands them for speaking "incorrectly" and justifies this action (and her attitude) by claiming that such linguistic "sloppiness" will ruin American English—a homogeneous language that assures mutual intelligibility within the United States. In response, one of her students patiently explains that the homogeneity of American English is a myth. American English resulted from a confluence of many languages, not just British English, and has always been subject to significant regional variation. Moreover, because all human languages are equally sophisticated (as Steven Pinker claims, "there is no such thing as a Stone Age language," p. 27, 1994), variation does not represent error, but instead

marks different identities within and understandings of the world. The real reason that she corrects the students, he explains, is because of her discriminatory attitudes. Otherwise, why would she preach homogeneity of pronunciation [a:sk] while accepting one variation as correct (the one associated with wealthy white Easterners [æsk]) and rejecting another as incorrect (the one associated with African Americans (a:ks])? Indeed, this is what dictionaries do!

Faced with the facts about her attitude, it is possible for the teacher to change her reactions to African American Vernacular English speakers. Rather than hearing them as "uneducated," she can relearn to hear them as claiming a place in society that is different from her own. Of course, this will require tremendous effort, patience, and practice, but it is the more accurate, less biased attitude to adopt. If we hope to follow in her footsteps of becoming responsible and fair-minded participants in intercultural interaction, we must begin, as she does, by recognizing the attitudes toward speech we currently possess. With luck, such action will set us on a path toward managing our discriminating attitudes.

# References

Bishop, G. D. (1979). Perceived similarity in interracial attitudes and behaviors: The effects of belief and dialect style. *Journal of Applied Social Psychology, 9,* 446–465.

Bradac, J. J., Cargile, A. C., & Halett, J. (2001). Language attitudes: Retrospect, conspect, and prospect. In H. Giles & P. Robinson (Eds.), *The New Handbook of language and social psychology* (2nd ed., pp. 137–155). Chichester, England: John Wiley & Sons.

Bradac, J. J., & Wisegarver, R. (1984). Ascribed status, lexical diversity, and accent: Determinants of perceived status, solidarity, and control of speech style. *Journal of Language and Social Psychology, 3,* 239–255.

Cargile, A. C., & Giles, H. (1998). Language attitudes toward varieties of English: An American-Japanese context. *Journal of Applied Communication Research, 26,* 338–356.

Cosmides, L., & Tooby, J. (1992). Cognitive adaptations for social exchange. In J. H. Barkow, L. Cosmides, and J. Tooby (Eds.), *The adapted mind: Evolutionary psychology and the generation of culture* (pp. 163–228). New York: Oxford University Press.

de la Zerda, N., & Hopper, R. (1979). Employment interviewers' reactions to Mexican-American speech. *Communication Monographs, 46*, 126–134.

Doss, R. C., & Gross, A. M. (1992). The effects of Black English on stereotyping in intraracial perceptions. *The Journal of Black Psychology, 18*, 47–58.

Fazio, R. H., Roskos-Ewoldsen, D. R., & Powell, M. C. (1994). Attitudes, perception, and attention. In P. M. Niedenthal & S. Kitayama (Eds.), *The heart's eye: Emotional influences in perception and attention* (pp. 197–216). Orlando, FL: Academic Press.

Fagar, I. (Executive Producer) (1984, October 10). *The CBS Evening News.* New York: CBS Corporation.

Giles, H., Williams, A., Mackie, D. M., & Rosselli, F. (1995). Reactions to Anglo- and Hispanic-American accented speakers: Affect, identity, persuasion, and the English-only controversy. *Language and Communication, 114*, 102–123.

Giles, H., Wilson, P., & Conway, A. (1981). Accent and lexical diversity as determinants of impression formation and employment selection. *Language Sciences, 3*, 92–103.

Hamblin, K. (1995, April 7). Speaking well has its merit. *Ann Arbor News*, Opinion Page: B8.

Henry, F., & Ginzberg, E. (1985). *Who gets the work: A test of racial discrimination in employment.* Toronto: Urban Alliance on Race Relations and Social Planning Council of Metropolitan Toronto.

Johnson, F. L., & Buttny, R. (1982). White listeners' responses to "sounding black" and "sounding white": The effects of message content on judgments about language. *Communication Monographs, 49*, 33–49.

Kalin, R., & Rayko, D. (1978). Discrimination in evaluative judgments against foreign-accented job.candidates. *Psychological Reports, 43*, 1203–1209.

Kerr, B. (1994, April 18). Voice of success silences dialect: Program helps people shed telltale tones. *Providence Journal-Bulletin*, p. B 1.

Lippi-Green, R. (1997). *English with an accent: Language, ideology, and discrimination in the United States.* New York: Routledge.

Luhman, R. (1990). Appalachian English stereotypes: Language attitudes in Kentucky. *Language in Society, 19*, 331–348.

Mackie, D. M., Hamilton, D. L., Susskind, J., & Rosselli, F. (1996). Social psychological foundations of stereotype formation. In C. N. Macrae, C. Stangor, & M. Hewstone (Eds.), *Stereotypes and Stereotyping*, (pp. 41–78). New York: The Guilford Press.

Pasternak, J. (1994, March 29). Bias blights life outside Appalachia. *Los Angeles Times*, pp. AI, A16.

Pearl, D. (1991, December 13). Hush mah mouth! Some in South try to lose the drawl. *Wall Street Journal*, p. A1.

Pinker, S. (1994). *The language instinct.* New York: Harper Collins.

Rubin, D. L., & Smith, K. A. (1988). Effects of accent, ethnicity, and lecture topic on undergraduates' perceptions of nonnative English-speaking teaching assistants. *International Journal of Intercultural Relations, 14*, 337–353.

Ryan, E. B., & Bulik, C. (1982). Evaluations of middle-class and lower-class speakers of standard American and German-accented English. *Journal of Language and Social Psychology, 1*, 51–61.

Ryan, E. B., & Carranza, M. A. (1975). Evaluative reactions of adolescents toward speakers of standard English and Mexican-American accented English. *Journal of Personality and Social Psychology, 31*, 855–863.

Ryan, E. B., Hewstone, M., & Giles, H. (1984). Language and intergroup attitudes. In J. Eiser (Ed.), *Attitudinal judgment* (pp. 135–160). New York: Springer.

Secter, B. (1987, September 27). Foreign teachers create language gap in colleges. *Los Angeles Times*, pp. AI, A26–A27.

Seggie, I. (1983). Attribution of guilt as a function of ethnic accent and type of crime. *Journal of Multilingual and Multicultural Development, 4*, 197–206.

Stewart, M. A., Ryan, E. B., & Giles, H. (1985). Accent and social class effects on status and solidarity evaluations. *Personality and Social Psychology Bulletin, 11*, 98–105.

Tucker, G. R., & Lambert, W. E. (1969). White and Negro listeners' reactions to various American-English dialects. *Social Forces, 41*, 463–468.

Worchel, S., & Austin, W. G. (Eds.) (1986). *Psychology of intergroup relations.* Chicago: Nelson-Hall.

## Concepts and Questions

1. Do you believe Cargile is correct when he asserts that people tend to like others who possess attitudes and traits similar to their own and to dislike others with dissimilar attitudes and traits?

2. What is the link between language differences and increased ethnocentrism?

3. According to Cargile, what are some examples of situations in which language accents influenced someone's perception of another person? Has accent ever

altered your perception of another person in a negative manner? Once you identified these perceptions, did you try to overcome them?

4. How might negative perceptions regarding a person's use of language influence a job interview?

5. In what settings do you most often see discrimination based on speech differences?

6. If, as Cargile asserts, it is true that not only do we internalize the discriminating speech attitudes that saturate our culture, but we also rarely give them up, how can you learn to interact successfully with people with differing speech patterns?

7. According to Cargile, how should responsible intercultural communicators manage language attitudes?

# 8

# Ethical Considerations: Prospects for the Future

*Whenever two good people argue over principles, they are both right.*

Marie Von Ebner-Eschenbach

*What is morality in any given time or place? It is what the majority then and there happen to like, and immorality is what they dislike.* **Alfred North Whitehead**

Contemporary civilization is characterized both internationally and domestically by large, increasingly diverse urban populations, which, in many respects, may be characterized as a world of strangers. Broadly speaking, one's knowledge about people from other cultures is usually rather limited, whether those people are stockbrokers in Mumbai or an immigrant family living just down the block. This lack of awareness about and ignorance of your neighbors may lead some of you to advocate or act in ways you might believe to be ethical and appropriate or beneficial to others, but which in fact may be harmful.

When interacting with others, your words and actions can affect or change their behavior, attitudes, and beliefs. The fact that your messages have such consequences confers an ethical responsibility upon you. The effects you cause might be simple or profound, short-term or long-term, immediate or delayed. Whatever the consequences of your communication, you cannot escape the fact that your actions affect other people.

Concern with the ethical dimension of communication must be a part of every intercultural encounter because your success as an intercultural communicator necessitates that you engage in ethical communication practices. Implicit in this engagement is the difficult task of knowing and understanding

> When interacting with others, your words and actions can affect or change their behavior, attitudes, and beliefs. The fact that your messages have such consequences confers an ethical responsibility upon you.

the normative behaviors common in other cultures. Brazilian anthrophilosopher Valdemar W. Setzer portrayed this difficulty when he stated, "Ethics [sic] is not definable, is not implementable, because it is not conscious; it involves not only our thinking, but also our feeling."

Unfortunately, some actions toward members of other cultures can be motivated by fear, religious differences, ethnocentrism, or racism. A recent incident involving religious differences was reported by BBC News.[1] The BBC revealed that numerous countries across Europe had been wrestling with the issue of the Muslim veil in various forms such as the body-covering *burka*, the face-covering *niqab*, or even the head scarf. Approaches to this issue have varied from country to country. French President Nicolas Sarkozy, for instance, was quoted as saying that the full veil was "not welcome" in France. Although there are no official bans on Muslim dress in the United Kingdom, some British politicians have indicated they believe veils are a symbol of an "increasingly divided Britain," they "oppress women," and they are a potential security threat. Moreover, in Austria, the Women's Minister indicated a ban should be considered in public spaces if the number of women wearing the veil increased dramatically.

Another concern of intercultural communication ethics occurs when well-intended acts have unintended consequences. For example, legislation that subsidizes U.S. soybean farmers might allow them to grow and sell their product at low prices on the world market. But that same legislation might bring economic difficulties, or even ruin, to unsubsidized soybean farmers in less-developed nations because they cannot compete against the subsidized prices. Thus, the legislation communicates disregard for the farmers in less-developed countries.

The issues of prejudice, ethnocentrism and unintended consequences are somewhat abstract problems that effective intercultural communicators must constantly confront in order to avoid conflict between their individual beliefs and customs and those of other cultural systems. This notion of differing ethical systems was borne out by the writer/publisher Elbert Hubbard when he noted that "Morality is largely a matter of geography." The author Samuel Butler summed up this position: "Morality is the custom of one's country and the current feeling of one's peers."

A few relevant culturally accepted practices that may arise from these diverse ethical perceptions include such acts as suicide bombing, female circumcision, and ethnic cleansing, as do attitudes toward the environment, the right to die, abortion, gay rights, medical ethics, animal rights, and business practices. These issues are not limited to obvious differences between national cultures but also may be found domestically in co-cultural diversity.

We now present you with four essays by prominent authors who address the topic of ethics as it applies to intercultural communication. From their knowledge and experiences, we hope that you will examine your own communicative ethics and begin to see some of the problems you must confront as you communicate with people from diverse cultures. As noted, intercultural contact raises both ethical and philosophical issues about how people from diverse cultures can live together without destroying themselves and the planet. Albert Schweitzer provided a partial answer to this problem when he specified that "The first step in the evolution of ethics is a sense of solidarity with other human beings." You are now charged with the task of deciding just what sort of interpersonal and intercultural ethics you must develop if you are to practice the art and science of intercultural communication.

## Note

1. "The Islamic veil across Europe," BBC News, 26 January 2010. Retrieved from http://news.bbc.co.uk/2/hi/5414098.stm on April 14, 2010.

# A Communicative Approach to Intercultural Dialogue on Ethics

RICHARD EVANOFF

*Richard Evanoff begins this chapter by posing the idea that there is not yet an established normative basis for intercultural ethics. He then proceeds to suggest that the best way to deal with this deficit is through communicative dialogue. He begins his essay with a brief critical review of traditional methodological approaches to ethics indicating their shortcomings in terms of dealing with intercultural situations. His review includes a discussion of empirical, theoretical, and normative approaches. He also discusses the failure of attempts to ground ethics in religion, nature, history, or reason.*

*As a solution to the shortcomings and failures he discusses, Evanoff proposes a communicative approach to the development of ethics appropriate for intercultural interaction. He believes that dialogue between members of diverse cultures must recognize that each participant is situated in a particular culture and has been socialized into certain norms. This recognition will permit the participants to reflect upon their individual norms and modify them when necessary. He also sees a communicative approach as relational, in which individual participants have relationships with others in their society. He believes that this form of communication takes place at the intrapersonal or individual level, at the social level where there is interpersonal and intergroup communication, and at the global level where international communication facilitates decision making and affects relations between nations and wider cultural groups.*

*In Evanoff's view, cross-cultural dialogue on ethics recognizes the fact that these situations are by their nature "without law" because the norms to govern behavior in such situations have not yet been created. Therefore, it is through the process of communicative dialogue that solutions can be found to the question of what people from different cultures with differing ethical traditions actually do about dealing with people from various cultures.*

The aim of this essay is to develop a communicative approach to intercultural dialogue on ethics. For this purpose ethics will be defined as critical reflection on behavior in relation to ourselves (personal ethics), others (social ethics), and the world in which we live (environmental ethics).

Three basic methodological approaches are utilized in the field of intercultural communication: (1) *empirical approaches*, which attempt to describe cultures as they are, employing both qualitative and quantitative methods; (2) *theoretical approaches*, which attempt to construct models and make generalizations about cultures based on empirical data; and (3) *normative approaches*, which attempt to solve problems in intercultural situations.

Empirical and theoretical approaches gather facts and make generalizations about, for example, how people from different cultures view marriage or conduct business. Such knowledge does not indicate, however, how problems which arise in intercultural marriages or international joint ventures might be resolved. Normative approaches involve imagining creative solutions to such problems rather than simply describing or analyzing existing values and norms. The main problem for intercultural ethics, therefore, is how normative solutions can be arrived at across cultures, given the fact that different cultures have different values and norms—a problem which is receiving increased attention both among interculturalists and in the emerging field of global ethics (see the references below).

Traditional approaches to intercultural ethics can be divided into two types: *Universalist* and *Particularist*. Universalist approaches attempt to ground ethics variously in religion, nature, history, reason, etc. These approaches largely fail, however, because there is no agreement about what is religiously

This original essay appears here in print for the first time. Used by permission of the author. Permission to reprint must be obtained from the author and the publisher. Dr. Richard Evanoff is a professor in the School of International Politics and Economics, Aoyama Gakuin University, Tokyo, Japan.

authoritative, natural, historical, or reasonable. More-over, universalists often regard their own particular culture as "universal"—a stance which is especially prevalent in Western cultures. ("Global standards," for example, are frequently American standards writ large.) Universalist approaches are connected with objective, foundational approaches to ethics, as well as to modernism, globalization, and a unilinear model of cultural development which sees all cultures as proceeding along a single line of development and converging on a single universal set of values and norms (*cf.* Fukuyama's "end of history").

Particularist approaches to intercultural ethics deny that there can be a single universal set of values and norms, and instead relativize values and norms to particular individuals and/or groups. Ethical individualism—one example of which is the notion that economic decisions should be made on the basis of individual preferences rather than on the basis of some form of collective decision making—contends that individuals are the final arbiters of value. Such a stance may be acceptable when deciding on flavors of ice cream but may be less acceptable when applied to the health, safety, and environmental impact of particular products. Cultural relativism similarly contends that since different cultural groups have different values and norms, it is impossible to formulate any values and norms which are valid across cultures. Particularism is connected with subjective, skeptical approaches to ethics, as well as to postmodernism, the preservation of local cultures and ethnic identities, and a multilinear model of cultural development which sees all cultures as proceeding along separate lines of development and diverging with respect to values and norms (*cf.* Huntington's "clash of civilizations").

It is clear that neither the universalist nor the particularist approach offer an adequate framework for intercultural ethics. While universalist tendencies can still be widely found in the fields of international politics and economics, they have been largely discredited in the field of intercultural communication, where the emphasis has been on recognizing and preserving cultural differences rather than on creating a single, homogenous "global culture." Nonetheless, cultural relativism, which is widely accepted in the field of intercultural communication, is also problematic. Although it is obvious that various cultures construct ethical systems in ways which are often incommensurable, cultural relativism does not answer the question of how conflicts between people from cultures with different values and norms can be resolved. The solution most often proposed is that we should simply "understand" and "respect" different cultures—"When in Rome, do as the Romans do."

A distinction can be made, however, between cultural *relativity* (the fact that cultures are different) and cultural *relativism* (the value judgment that different cultures must be accepted as they are). Descriptive ethics (what is *actually* done in a particular culture) cannot be equated with normative ethics (what *should* be done). To equate the two is to commit the naturalistic fallacy, i.e., the attempt to derive an *ought* from an *is*. Hatch writes, "The fact of moral diversity no more compels our approval of other ways of life than the existence of cancer compels us to value ill-health" (1983, p. 68). Cultural relativism seems progressive but is in fact conservative and tradition-bound because it obligates us to accept the values and norms of other cultures rather than giving us the opportunity to critically reflect on them and make considered decisions about which values and norms are worthy of adoption. It regards culture in "essentialist" terms (cultures have certain "essential" features which are fixed and unchanging) rather than in constructivist terms (cultures are human *constructs* and therefore susceptible to creative change). From a purely practical perspective relativism offers no solution to intercultural conflicts. Simply contending that "you have your way and I have mine" makes it impossible for people from different cultures to work together cooperatively on problems of mutual concern.

A communicative approach to intercultural ethics may offer a viable alternative to both universalism and particularism. The communicative approach recognizes that while we are each situated in a particular culture and socialized into certain norms, we are nonetheless able to reflect on those norms and change them if necessary. We are also able

> *The communicative approach recognizes that while we are each situated in a particular culture and socialized into certain norms, we are nonetheless able to reflect on those norms and change them if necessary.*

to critically reflect on the norms of other cultures and to selectively adopt (or reject) those norms which seem plausible (or implausible) to us. Such reflection results in greater objectivity, although never in pure, absolute objectivity—as humans we never have access to a "God's-eye" view of the world. Dialogue on intercultural ethics can thus be seen as taking place between specific people from specific cultures in specific contexts and in relation to specific problems. Although the context can be widened to include more than one culture, there are no "universals."

A communicative approach to intercultural ethics is also relational, seeing individuals as having relationships both with others in society and with 'the natural environment (cf. Watsuji, 1961). Ethical dialogue can take place at a variety of different levels. At the personal level there is intrapersonal communication through which decisions are made with respect to how we live our lives as individuals; at the social level there is interpersonal and intergroup communication through which decisions are made with respect to how we live together with others; at the global level there is international communication through which decisions are made with respect to the relations which exist between nations and wider cultural groups (cf. the distinction made in Apel, 1980 between micro-, meso-, and macro-domains and in Singer, 1987 between the interpersonal, intergroup, and international levels). Decisions are best made at the appropriate level. At the interpersonal level, for example, it is not necessary to formulate universal norms with respect to international marriages; such norms are more appropriately made by the marriage partners themselves and will vary from couple to couple. At the global level, however, it may be necessary to construct norms which are universal or near-universal in scope in order to address problems which cross cultural and national boundaries, such as global warming.

It can be suggested that the main principle for deciding the level at which norms should be created is related to the scope of the consequences which a particular action has. Dower has suggested the following maxim for intercultural ethics: "... where the lines of cause and effect run across nation-states, so do the

lines of moral responsibility" (1998, p. 165). If my action only affects myself, then the decision should be purely personal. If my action affects others, then those who are affected should have the right to participate in the process by which a decision is reached regarding that action (this is a simplified statement of Habermas's discourse ethics; see Habermas, 1989; 1993). For example, it may be all right for me to smoke in my own room, but not in a room full of people who find smoking objectionable; driving a car may no longer be appropriately regarded as a personal decision if the carbon dioxide emitted from my car contributes to global warming.

Finally, a communicative approach to intercultural ethics is pragmatic in that it is concerned, as mentioned previously, with solving particular problems faced by particular people in particular situations. As new problems emerge, new ethical solutions must be found; we cannot simply fall back on past ethical traditions for guidance. Ethical systems can be both abandoned and created. We no longer find slavery acceptable, for example, and we are constantly in the process of creating new ethical norms to deal with emergent problems, such as advances in medical technology and increased contact across cultures. Rather than seeing ethics as fixed and unchanging, a communicative approach sees ethics as dynamic and creative. It can be associated with an ecological model of cultural development, which recognizes that cultures may proceed along different lines of development but nonetheless co-evolve through the communicative relations they have with other cultures.

A communicative approach to cross-cultural dialogue on ethics recognizes that intercultural situations are by their very nature anomic (a-nom: "without law") because the norms to govern behavior in such situations have not yet been created. The ethical norms we are socialized into accepting as individuals usually tell us how to deal with people in our own cultures, not how to deal with people from other cultures. Therefore, the question for intercultural ethics is, given a particular problem, what should people from different cultures with differing ethical traditions actually *do* about it? Various solutions are possible: (1) *avoidance*: we can avoid having contact

> *Rather than seeing ethics as fixed and unchanging, a communicative approach sees ethics as dynamic and creative.*

with people from different cultures; (2) *adaptation:* one side is obliged to conform to the norms of the other side; (3) *confrontation:* each side insists that it alone is right: (4) *domination:* one side attempts to impose its view on the other; or (5) *dialogue:* the two sides communicate with each other about which norms should be adopted in a particular situation.

If dialogue is the preferred method for dealing with issues related to intercultural ethics, how can such dialogue be conducted? Ethnocentric approaches to cross-cultural dialogue typically take their own cultural values and norms as correct and view those of the opposite side as incorrect. Such a view rests on an Aristotelian logic which holds that if a given proposition is true, its opposite cannot be true at the same time. If individualism is "true," for example, then collectivism must be "false."

A more Hegelian, dialectical approach, however, would contend that within any point of view there are "positive" and "negative" features which can be differentiated from each other. It may be agreed that a positive feature of individualism is its emphasis on self-reliance; a negative feature is its tendency towards egoism. A positive feature of collectivism is its emphasis on cooperation; a negative feature is its tendency towards conformity. What often happens in cross-cultural criticism, of course, is that the positive side of one position is used to criticize the negative side of the other position. Self-reliance is seen as being superior to conformity and cooperation is seen as being superior to egoism. It should, however, be possible to integrate the positive features of each of the positions into a new synthesis, while discarding the negative features. Self-reliance can be combined with cooperation without contradiction, while egoism and conformity can be discarded. This new synthetic position constitutes a "third culture" which combines aspects from each of the original cultures but also transforms them in creative ways. Third cultures have the potential to provide a common ground for coordinated action across cultures and can be applied to a wide variety of cultural disputes related to value differences.

> *Ethnocentric approaches to cross-cultural dialogue typically take their own cultural values and norms as correct and view those of the opposite side as incorrect.*

## ACKNOWLEDGMENTS

This essay is based on a paper originally presented at the Aoyama Symposium on International Communication, held at Aoyama Gakuin University in Tokyo, Japan on March 5, 2005. The article summarizes research further elaborated in Evanoff, 1996; 1998; 1999; 2000; 2001; 2004; 2006a; 2006b. Slightly different versions of this article have appeared in Evanoff 2005 and 2007.

## References

Apel, K. O. (1980). *Towards a transformation of philosophy,* G. Adey & D. Frisby, Trans., (London: Routledge and Kegan Paul).

Appiah, K. A. (2006). *Cosmopolitanism: Ethics in a world of strangers.* (London: Allen Lane).

Asuncio-Lande, N. C. (Ed.). (1979). *Ethical perspectives and critical issues in intercultural communication.* (Falls Church, VA: Speech Communication Association).

Barnlund, D. C. (1979). The cross-cultural arena: An ethical void. In L. A. Samovar & R. E. Porter (Eds.), *Intercultural communication: A reader,* 4th ed., (Belmont, CA: Wadsworth), 394–399.

Booth, K., T. Dunne, and M. Cox (Eds.). (2001). *How might we live? Global ethics in the new century.* (Cambridge, UK: Cambridge University Press).

Casmir, F. L. (Ed.). (1997). *Ethics in intercultural and international communication.* (London: Lawrence Erlbaum).

Commers, M. S. R., W. Vandekerckhove, and A. Verlinden, eds. (2008). *Ethics in an era of globalization.* (Aldershot, UK: Ashgate).

Cook, J. W. (2002). *Morality and cultural differences.* (New York: Oxford University Press).

Dower, N. (1998). *World ethics: The new agenda.* (Edinburgh: Edinburgh University Press).

Eade, J., & D. O'Byrne (2005). *Global ethics and civil society.* (Farnham, UK: Ashgate).

Evanoff, R. (1996). Intercultural ethics: New ways of learning to get along with each other. In *Language and Culture in International Communication* (Tokyo: Aoyama Gakuin University Press), 145–225.

Evanoff, R. (1998). A constructivist approach to intercultural ethics. *Eubios Journal of Asian and International Bioethics,* 8, 84–87.

Evanoff, R. (1999). Towards a constructivist theory of intercultural dialogue. In N. Honna & Y. Kano (Eds.), *International Communication in the 21st. Century*. (Tokyo: Sanseido), 109–153.

Evanoff, R. (2000). The concept of 'third cultures' in intercultural ethics. *Eubios Journal of Asian and International Bioethics, 10*, 126–129.

Evanoff, R. (2001). Discussion paper on intercultural dialogue and education. UNU Workshop on the Contribution of Education to the Dialogue of Civilizations at the United Nations University, Tokyo, Japan, May 3-5. Available at http://www.unu.edu/dialogue/papers/evanoff-s5.pdf

Evanoff, R. (2004). Universalist, relativist, and constructivist approaches to intercultural ethics. *International Journal of International Relations, 28*, 439–458.

Evanoff, R. (2005). A communicative approach to intercultural dialogue on ethics. Human Dignity and Humiliation Studies website. Available at http://www.humiliationstudies.org/documents/EvanoffInterculturalEthics.pdf

Evanoff, R. (2006a). Integration in intercultural ethics. *International Journal of International Relations, 30*, 421–437.

Evanoff, R. (2006b). Intercultural ethics: A constructivist approach. *Journal of Intercultural Communication, 9*, 89–102.

Evanoff, R. (2007). A communicative approach to intercultural dialogue on ethics. In *Gaikokugo kyouiku sentaa daiichirui FD katsudou kirokushu 2003-2005* (Hiratsuka: Tokai University Press), 14–16.

Fukuyama, F. (1992). *The end of history and the last man*. (New York: Free Press).

Habermas, J. (1989). *Moral consciousness and communicative action*, C. Lenhardt & S. W. Nicholsen, Trans. (Cambridge, UK: Polity Press).

Habermas, J. (1993). *Justification and application*, C. Cronin, Trans. (Cambridge, MA: MIT Press).

Hatch, E. (1983). *Culture and morality*. (New York: Columbia University Press).

Hopkins, W. E. (1997). *Ethical dimensions of diversity*. (Thousand Oaks, CA: Sage.

Huntington, S. P. (1996). *The clash of civilizations and the remaking of world order*. (New York: Simon and Schuster).

Johannesen, R. (2002). *Ethics in human communication*, 5th ed. (Prospect Heights, IL: Waveland Press).

Kale, D. W. (1991). Ethics in intercultural communication. In L. A. Samovar & R. E. Porter (Eds.), *Intercultural communication: A reader*, 6th ed. (Belmont, CA: Wadsworth), 421–426.

Lange, H., A. Löhr, & H. Steinmann (Eds.). (1998) *Working across cultures: Ethical perspectives for intercultural management*. (Dordrecht, Germany: Kluwer Academic Publishers).

Makau, J. M., & R. C. Arnett, eds. (1997). *Communication ethics in an age of diversity*. (Urbana, IL: University of Illinois Press).

Morgan, E. (1998). *Navigating cross-cultural ethics: What global managers do right to keep from going wrong* (Boston: Butterworth-Heinemann).

Singer, M. R. (1987). *Intercultural communication: A perceptual approach*. (Englewood Cliffs: Prentice-Hall).

Watsuji, T. (1961). *Climate and culture*, G. Bownas, Trans. (Tokyo: Hokuseido).

Wiredu, K. (1996). *Cultural universals and particulars: An African perspective*. (Bloomington, IN: Indiana University Press).

Wiredu, K. (2005). On the idea of a global ethic. *Journal of Global Ethics, 1*, 45–51.

## Concepts and Questions

1. Differentiate between *empirical*, *theoretical*, and *normative* methodological approaches to solving problems in intercultural ethics. How do these approaches differ?

2. Evanoff asserts that attempts to ground ethics variously in religion, nature, history, or reason largely fail. Why is this?

3. What is the fundamental assumption of the particularist approach to intercultural ethics?

4. How does Evanoff differentiate between cultural relativity and cultural relativism? Give an example of each of these approaches to ethics.

5. How does a communicative approach to intercultural ethics differ from earlier approaches?

6. Evanoff suggests that ethical dialogue can take place at a variety of levels: the interpersonal, the social, and the global. How do these levels differ in terms of the types of ethical issues with which they deal? Give examples from your own experiences that reflect ethical issues you might consider at each of these levels.

7. Evanoff poses the question for developing intercultural ethics in the following manner: Given a particular problem, what should people from different cultures with different ethical traditions actually *do* about it? What is your answer to this question?

8. How would you engage in an intercultural dialogue to resolve issues related to intercultural ethics? What underlying assumptions would you make about the conduct of the dialogue?

9. What does Evanoff mean when he suggests that the result of communicative dialogue to establish an intercultural ethic constitutes a "third culture"?

# Worldview: The Ethical Dimension

## NINIAN SMART

*Ninian Smart, in his article "Worldview: The Ethical Dimension," continues the discussion began by Richard Evanoff leading to the development of a personal ethic for intercultural communication. Smart discusses how the ethical dimensions of a culture are a function of its worldview drawn from its religious experience, its doctrines about the universe, and the myths and historical heroes of its cultural traditions.*

*Smart recognizes modern attempts, such as the utilitarianism of John Stuart Mill and the scientific humanist community's idea that the basis of values lies in the individual human being to build ethical systems independent of religious belief. However, he holds that such ethical systems have been inadequate because ethical systems seem to "raise questions about the worldview behind [them]."*

*Smart next conducts a discussion comparing diverse religious ethics as they apply to the Christian, Muslim, Buddhist, and Hindu ethical traditions. He points out the worldview bases for these beliefs and relates their similarities and differences. Drawing from his examples, Smart concludes that "ethics is not treated in isolation, and what is right and wrong is seen in the light of a wider cosmic vision." He ends his essay by providing a normative view of what constitutes right and wrong. In considering what he believes to be right and wrong, Smart reminds you that you "live in a global city in which different cultures and worldviews interact." If one group seeks to impose its views on a group that does not share those views, the result will be conflict. Second, Smart indicates that in his view, the purpose of religion is to stress the spiritual life, and morality has to be related to such spiritual visions.*

> *Buddhists, Hindus, and Jains have a special attitude toward moral action because they believe in reincarnation. Since one may be reborn in animal or insect form, one must have a sense of solidarity with other living beings.*

## INTRODUCTION

The ethical dimension of a religion or worldview is shaped by the other dimensions, but *it* also helps to shape them. If the numinous experience revealed to early Israel and to the prophets a mysterious and dynamic deity, their moral insights suggested that this God was a good God. He demanded not just sacrifices but also contrition, not just observance of the Sabbath but also uprightness in conduct. If the mystical experience revealed to early Buddhism a realm of peace and pure consciousness, moral insight also showed that this peace was to be shared with others. and that ultimately no inner illumination not accompanied by compassion for the suffering of other living beings was worth having.

Buddhists, Hindus, and Jains have a special attitude toward moral action because they believe in reincarnation. Since one may be reborn in animal or insect form, one must have a sense of solidarity with other living beings. In the religions of the West,

From Ninian Smart, *Worldviews: Crosscultural Explorations of Human Beliefs*, 3rd ed., pp. 104–117, © 2000. Reprinted by permission of Pearson Education, Inc., Upper Saddle River, NJ. The late Ninian Smart was a Professor Emeritus in both the Department of Religious Studies at The University of Lancaster in Great Britain and the Department of Religious Studies at the University of California, Santa Barbara.

however, the dominant view has been that human beings have souls but animals do not. In theory at any rate, Indian traditions have a greater moral obligation toward animals and other living forms than has been the case in the West. But in recent times in the West a greater concern with our living environment, together with the influence of the East on our culture, has led to changes in attitudes. We see campaigns to save whales and leopards, for example. Whatever our specific attitudes, there is no doubt that the scope of morality is affected by our general worldview.

Morality is affected also by our picture of the ideal human being. The Christian looks to Christ and to the saints and heroes of the tradition. The Buddhist looks to the Buddha, the Muslim to Muhammad, the Hindu to Rama and Krishna and others, the Taoist to Lao-tse, and the Confucianist to Confucius.

So we can already see that there are ways in which the ethical dimension relates to religious experience, to doctrines about the cosmos, and to the myths and historical heroes of the traditions.

In modern times an attempt has been made to try in one way or another to set up ethics on an independent basis—[one] that is independent of traditional religious belief. But as we shall see such an attempt cannot be completely successful, because every ethical system seems to raise questions about the worldview behind it.

Thus, probably the most powerful and influential ethical system—or set of systems—in modern times has been utilitarianism, which had its chief expression in the nineteenth century through the writings of John Stuart Mill (1806–1873). Its importance lies in trying to see moral action in terms of its utility, and utility in terms of whether something helps produce human happiness or reduce human suffering. It thus shapes much of modern politics and economics in the democratic West. In the West we tend to think in utilitarian terms: to think of whether a given aspect of our institutions, such as divorce law, will bring the greatest happiness to the greatest number and the least suffering to the least number. We conduct economic policy on the basis that we should prosper in such a way that everyone can realize a reasonable degree of happiness and freedom from poverty. The American constitution speaks of the pursuit of happiness, and socialism is often based on the idea that it will banish poverty and free people for better things.

In such ways our whole Western culture is drenched with utilitarian thoughts.

This utilitarianism is often coupled with the idea, celebrated by the scientific humanist, that the basis of all values is the individual human being, and that which is most important is how individuals relate to one another. In his book *I and Thou*, the Jewish writer Martin Buber looks, as we have seen, to the deeper human relationships as the center of the meaning of life.

Somewhat opposed to the individualism of much of the West's thinking is the collectivism of the Marxist tradition. Here human behavior and economics are so closely woven together that ethics is also seen as collective: Actions are good insofar as they bring about a revolution that will consolidate socialism, or insofar as they preserve the revolution and help in the march toward an ideal society in which human beings live in harmony.

Either the study of religious ethics can deal with the facts about morality and structures of moral thinking, or else it can reflect on what is right and wrong from a normative stance. Our prime concern here is with the former approach, but I shall say something briefly about the normative questions in due course; that is, about what ethical values we might adopt.

## COMPARATIVE RELIGIOUS ETHICS

The cross-cultural study of religious ethics is sometimes called "comparative religious ethics." This is quite a recent coinage, and only in the last few years has a really systematic attempt been made to open up the field. However, there were some notable previous enterprises that dealt with ethics in a comparative way. Perhaps most important among these was the *Encyclopedia of Religion and Ethics,* edited by James Hastings before, during, and just after World War I. The *Encyclopedia,* in many enormous volumes, gave liberal and learned treatment to a host of vital themes in the study of religion and, as its title implies, included much on moral views and practices everywhere in the world.

At one level, comparative religious ethics is aimed simply at delineating the various moral systems found in societies all over the world. Sometimes it is necessary to distinguish between what are called the great and the little traditions. For instance, one can view the ethical beliefs of the Sri Lankans from the angle of the great tradition, namely, official Buddhist belief as expressed through the scriptures and the preaching of the monks. But one can also see what the actual beliefs are in the villages of the highlands (for example), where elements other than "official Buddhism" come into play. Or one could look to what the actual moral outlook is, say, of the average Italian as compared with the official teachings of the Catholic Church. Probably it is enough for us to say that just as there are many Buddhisms and many Christianities, so there are many Buddhist moralities and many Christian moralities.

When we find that there are, in fact, likenesses and differences among cultures in regard to right and wrong, we begin to ask wider questions. What accounts for these likenesses and differences? One thing we might begin to do is correlate moral values with kinds of doctrines, myths, and experiences.

But the major faiths have much in common as far as moral conduct goes. Not to steal, not to lie, not to kill, not to have certain kinds of sexual relations—such prescriptions are found across the world because such rules are necessary if there is to be a society at all. The widespread breaking of these rules would lead to chaos. Society can exist only where such wrong acts are in the minority.

However, what they mean in greater detail may vary quite a lot. In matters of sex, for example, there are varying systems. A Christian generally has only one wife, divorce notwithstanding—and for a long time in much of the Christian tradition even divorce was ruled out. A Muslim male, in contrast, may have up to four wives at one time, and divorce is built into the original legal system. As for killing, some societies allow the right of self-defense, and in war the killing of the enemy may be deemed a duty. Some religions are cautious about war or exclude it altogether, as do the Quakers; for others war is a natural means of spreading the domain in which the faith is exercised. This is notably so in the Islamic idea of the *Jihad*, or holy struggle.

The way in which the rules themselves are viewed often differs, and this means that there are different models of virtue. For the Jew and the Muslim, for instance, the rules are part of the fabric of divinely instituted law—Torah and Shari'a,

respectively. Obedience to the rules is obedience to God. In Judaism, obedience is qualified by the belief that the commandments are part of a contract or covenant between God and his people. In Buddhism the rules of morality are part of the "eightfold path" that leads to ultimate liberation. It is not that God has to be obeyed, but rather that, as part of the general effort at self-purification, it is wise to be good. The model for the monotheist is the obedient person of faith, such as Abraham. The model Buddhist is the person of superior insight.

Although Hinduism often involves belief in one divine Being, it shares with Buddhism a sense that the law or dharma is not so much something that is commanded by God, but rather that it is part of the nature of the world. The law is part of the fabric of the cosmos, so that to follow it is to follow the natural bent of things. Thus, Hinduism makes the caste system (itself controlled by dharma) an aspect of cosmic order. Moreover, the order of the world includes the way the moral fabric of things is expressed through karma. My moral acts will bear fruits both in this life and in subsequent existences. So even if ultimately—as some believe—karma is controlled by God, there is still a natural mechanism that rewards good and punishes evil. This comes to be tied in with the idea of merit: The wise person acquires merit through his or her good deeds so that he or she may be reborn in more propitious circumstances.

In order to see in more detail how belief and spiritual practice affect ethics, it may be useful to sketch the dynamics of a number of systems.

I have already alluded to the way in which in Theravada Buddhism ethical conduct is woven into the eightfold path and so becomes part of the means of attaining liberation. This helps explain why one of the five precepts of Buddhism forbids taking "drugs and intoxicants" (the word covers liquor and other things) because liquor clouds the mind and also arouses anger. The clouding of the mind must be avoided because the task of the saintly person is to cultivate clarity of consciousness and self-awareness. It is through this clarity that detached insight can be gained; such insight is liberating and can bring about ultimate decease and escape from the round of rebirth. Further, anger and allied emotions are the opposite of the peace that liberation should bring. So far, then, we can see the ban on drugs and liquor as fitting into the way a person should train himself or herself.

But not everyone is at all close to gaining nirvana. Monks and nuns are sometimes thought to be closer to attaining nirvana, but ordinary lay people may have their chance in some future life. The teaching of karma and rebirth binds together the differing layers of Buddhist society by projecting a person's career into the future beyond the grave. The ordinary person gains merit by virtuous acts in this life and hopes for some better state in the next. Indeed, the person who gives generously to the Order and follows the moral path may be reborn in a heaven. This heaven, though, is not everlasting. It is not the final goal. Here is a major difference between Buddhism and traditional Christianity. In Christianity the final judgment consigns people to heaven or hell. But in Buddhism, a person's merit is in due course exhausted, and he or she is obliged to disappear from paradise and be reborn in some other state—perhaps as a nun close to gaining nirvana. This is in accord with the Buddhist idea that all existence, including heavenly (and for that matter hellish) existence, is impermanent: Only nirvana is the Permanent, and it lies beyond existence, beyond this world and the next.

In brief, Theravada Buddhism has traditionally seen morality as part of the path that leads to nirvana, and as something that operates within a universe controlled by karma. Karma is the law of reward and penalty within the framework of rebirth, in which my status as human or animal or whatever results from my acts in previous lives. In Theravada Buddhism, morality is seen as partly a matter of being prudent—either because it helps achieve the state of final freedom and true happiness, or because at least it helps to give you a better life next time around. Morality also involves peace and, to some degree, withdrawal from the bustle of the world. This Buddhist moral code has two tiers: There is a higher, more severe, level of personal conduct for monks and nuns, and a less rigorous ethic for the laity and the mass of the people.

> *Theravada Buddhism has traditionally seen morality as part of the path that leads to nirvana, and as something that operates within a universe controlled by karma. Karma is the law of reward and penalty within the framework of rebirth, in which my status as human or animal or whatever results from my acts in previous lives.*

The ethic of Islam, in contrast, has quite a different atmosphere. For one thing, it does not (until we get to the mystical movement of inner quest known as Sufism) have two levels. It is a religion that applies equally to all men under Allah. The duality between the numinous Allah and his humble worshipers gives the latter a sense of equality and humility. Thus Islam (the word literally means "submission to God") contains a strong sense of brotherhood. It is true that, from a modern Western point of view, there is inequality for women. Islamic law and custom, stemming from the Qur'an and from the developing tradition, impose restrictions on women. Men can have up to four wives at once, but polyandry (that is, a woman having several husbands) is ruled out. Although it is not laid down in revelation, the custom of wearing the veil is widespread for women in Muslim countries. Even if women have property rights, and are protected by what in the time of the Prophet was essentially a reforming movement, some might think women's status inferior. But this is not the way orthodox Muslims view things. For them, Islamic law treats women and men as being separate and equal, because they have separate natures and functions.

The Otherness of Allah, which flows from the numinous character of the Prophet's revelations, means that all that is created is seen as coming from him; the laws by which people are supposed to live flow from him too. Thus the pattern of religious experience that was so central in the rise of Islam is consistent with, and indeed favors, the belief that there is a divinely instituted law. It happened also that early Islam saw itself as related to other revelations: So, too, in Islam there was Law, but Law with its own special features, for this was a new revelation to Muhammad that would set its seal upon the other traditions.

The emphasis on law also sprang from the strong sense of community in early Islam. Not only are all men under Allah brothers, but there is a particular community that has his blessing. The community was brought into being under the leadership of the Prophet, and before his death he succeeded in uniting a large part of the Arabs of his immediate region. The Islamic community was just embarking on those spectacular victories that stretched the new imperial power from Afghanistan to Morocco and from Spain to Iran. So the Law became the way the details of community life were defined. It covers much more than morals in the narrow sense: It embraces questions of finance, slavery, ritual, and so on.

Along with their moral teachings, religions tend to demand certain religious duties, such as keeping the Sabbath, going on pilgrimage, giving alms to the monastic order, and so on. They are religious duties rather than ethical ones in the sense that the latter directly concern people's dealings with other people. Religious duties deal especially with duties to God or duties to those who in some special way manifest religious truth. The idea behind such duties is often that they simply arise from the nature of faith: The person who loves God worships him, and this is a religious duty as well as being a result of such love. Sometimes they are seen as duties because they help bring about that kind of feeling that makes them a joy as well as an obligation. Sometimes they can be seen as a kind of exchange: The Buddhist who gives food to monks or nuns gets from them teachings that help him or her on the path toward perfection.

The importance of brotherhood and the community in Islam is seen in the requirement to give alms. The poor brother or sister is helped. The duty when called on to fight a *jihad;* or holy war, on behalf of Islam reflects the fact that Islam does not make a sharp division between Church and State. The aim is to build a society that is Islamic, and this may mean using all the levers of power, including war, against the enemies of Islam. Since Allah is, in essence, power—however much Allah may also be compassionate and merciful—it is not surprising that earthly power should be seen as a way of expressing and strengthening Allah's dominion. By contrast, Buddhism centers not on power but peace, even emptiness, and tends to have an "otherworldly" outlook. The problem of Buddhist kingship is the issue of how power can be used at all, for power may mean trampling on the lives of people, thus corrupting our consciousness and storing up bad forces of karma.

The contrast between the Islamic and Buddhist traditions comes out also in the figures of the great founders. Muhammad was not just a man of God; he was the skillful diplomat, statesman, and general. The Buddha, according to predictions at his birth, was either to become a political world-conqueror or a spiritual one. In leaving his princely palace and setting out on the quest for truth through poverty and homelessness, he gave up all worldly power. In return he gained enlightenment, and in fact helped shape the world that came after him. But there he was—the lone sage, lean from fasts, his eyes unmoving beneath the tree as he attained purity of consciousness and that inner light that for him lit up the nature of all the world and became the source of his teaching. He was diplomatic in his preaching skills, and kingly in his noble demeanor. But he was not literally either a diplomat or a politician, still less a general. Three centuries or so afterward, the Indian emperor Ashoka destroyed a neighboring people in his pursuit of wider imperial power, but he was so tormented by his aggressive actions that henceforth he tried to rule as a king of peace. At the heart of Buddhism lies a dilemma about power.

Christianity presents a third face. (And Buddhism, too, evolved a somewhat different emphasis in its later forms.) Christianity's face is that of Christ's, and he unites in himself motifs that help shape Christian ethics. Through much of Christian history, Christ basically has come in two guises: as the God who, becoming human, met death upon the Cross, and as the God who, risen into the heavens, comes to judge the living and the dead, at the dreadful and glorious end of human history. The first Christ is empty of power, in the worldly sense; the second is the essence of majesty. The one is the suffering Servant, the other the fearful Judge. All of this reflects the fact that Christians have seen Christ as both human and divine. He lives in two worlds: In our earthly world he bears the marks of humility and love, and in the other, the numinous power that belongs to the divine Being.

To some extent this ambiguity is found in the way the New and Old Testaments relate to each other. Christianity inherited much of the early Jewish tradition, but looked at it in a different way. It kept some of the old Law, notably the Ten Commandments, but it thought that Christ himself was now the pattern for living, and so his life, death, and resurrection brought in a new covenant; although Christians thought of the old covenant as part of the way God revealed himself to people—and to the people of Israel in particular—there was no need to follow the Law in the old way.

The two faces of Christ have given Christian morality a tendency toward inner struggle, thus, for the early Church, participation in warfare was wrong, as Christians sought to live a harmless and upright life. Yet the Church was the extension of God's power and had responsibility to the world God had created. When the Church came to dominate the Roman Empire, emphasis began to shift to theory of the "just" war. A war might justly be fought in self-defense; later also religious wars, known as the Crusades, became duties. Christ as judge came to be seen as the embodiment of power in the service of justice.

But at the heart of Christian morality is the ideal of *agape*, or reverential love: the love of God and neighbor. This love for other human beings extends to one's enemies, following the example of Christ, who said "Father, forgive them" from his Cross. This reverential love stems partly from the perception that every person is made in the image of the Creator and thus in the image of Christ himself.

Christian views of ethics are also much affected by the doctrine of the Fall. Judaism has not made of Genesis what the Christian tradition has. For Christianity, Adam's acts implicate the whole human race in a disaster, as a result of which human nature is corrupted. Humans are not able to be virtuous by themselves but need the help of God, through grace. The great emphasis on original sin arises from the conviction that Christ's death made a critical difference to the relationship between God and the human race. So it was clear that the greatness of Christ as "second Adam" must be reflected in the vast significance of the first Adam's act, whereby he and Eve and all of us became separated from God. The salvation in Christ presupposed the Adamic disaster. Thus, Christianity has seen human nature as unable to perfect itself by human action—only by tapping the power or grace of Christ can the Christian grow in moral stature. A major thought of the early reformers, Luther in particular, was that the Roman Catholic Church suggested that people could (and should) improve their spiritual status by going on pilgrimages,

giving to the Church and the poor, attending Mass, and so on. All of this suggested that people could gain something by performing good works, when it is only through God's grace (said Luther) that we can do anything good.

This position holds that much depends on the means of grace, that is, the way through which the Christian is supposed to receive the power of Christ. In much of mainstream Christianity, Catholic, and Orthodox, that power comes primarily through the sacraments, above all the Mass or divine liturgy. For much of later Protestantism, the chief sacrament is the Word—Christ as found in the Bible and in preaching, stirring people to holy living. The sacraments stress the divine side of Christ; preaching often brings out the human side. In the one case we receive power through the action of God in ritual; in the other case we gain power through inspiration and the example of the man Jesus.

Many of the later disputes about details of morality spring from some of these ideas and practices. The Catholic Church's defense of marriage as a life-long union and its opposition to divorce owe a lot to the notion that marriage is a divinely created sacrament. The sacrament of marriage confers God's inner grace and power on a couple and a family through the physical and social acts of living together. The Christian debate with others over abortion stems from the question of the sanctity of human life, which in turn has to do with the doctrine that the individual is made in the image of God. And Christian social action, such as that of Mother Teresa of Calcutta, stems from this same sense of reverence for others, which is part of true love, following Jesus' example.

If Christian attitudes demonstrate a tension between this world and the other, so there is a tension in Buddhism between liberation and compassion. As we have seen, there is a certain prudence about right behavior: Being good helps toward the attainment of final release, or at least toward getting a better life next time around. But compassion for the suffering of others should mean sacrificing oneself, even one's own welfare. Even nirvana may have to be put off if one is to serve their suffering fellow beings. Out of this self-sacrifice there came to be—as we have seen—a strong emphasis in Greater Vehicle Buddhism on the figure of the Bodhisattva, the being destined for Buddhahood who nevertheless puts off his own salvation in order to stay in the world to help others. There were various figures of Bodhisattvas who came to be revered and worshipped, such as the great Bodhisattva Avalokitesvara who, as his name implies, "looks down" with compassion upon those who suffer in the world. The Bodhisattva was thought to have attained such a vast store of merit through his many lives of self-sacrifice (given that he had gained enough already to be "due" for nirvana) that he could distribute this immense surplus to others to help them on their way. Thus, the otherwise unworthy faithful person could, by calling on the Bodhisattva, gain extra merit bringing him or her closer to final release from suffering. So in many ways the Greater Vehicle idea runs parallel to Christianity. But instead of the idea of love or *agape,* in Buddhism compassion is central.

Just as in Christianity "living in the world," rather than withdrawals from the world, was emphasized, so in the Greater Vehicle the sharp cleft between nirvana over there (so to speak) and worldly life here was called into question. It is possible for the Buddhist to pursue his or her ideal of imitating the Bodhisattva (indeed of *becoming* a Buddha-to-be) through living the good life in this world. Sometimes this had strange results. In medieval Japan the warrior class came to see techniques like archery and swordplay as methods which, if suitably adapted, could teach selflessness. In this manner even warfare would be a means of gaining higher insight. On the whole, however, Buddhist ethics have been eager to minimize violence.

## THE NATURE OF MORALITY

In all these examples we can see that ethics is not treated in isolation, and what is right and wrong is seen in the light of a wider cosmic vision. Yet in modern philosophy, especially since Kant in the late eighteenth century, there has been a quest to establish what Kant called the "autonomy," or independence, of morals.

Philosophers have tried to show that right and wrong can be defined independently of some wider superstructure of belief. What is right and wrong is right and wrong not because God or the Buddha says so: God or the Buddha says so because he sees what is right and wrong. What is right is right because it is right on its own account, not because God says so.

Kant thought the test of what is right and wrong is the so-called categorical imperative, to which he gave various formulations.

In essence, the categorical imperative amounted to a two-sided demand. One side holds that anything moral beings will must, to be right, be capable of being a universal law, that is, a law that all can follow. The other side holds that one should treat another human being always as an end in himself or herself and never merely as a means. Kant thought these principles were categorical, not hypothetical. A categorical imperative is absolute; it applies unconditionally. A hypothetical imperative is, by contrast, one that applies only if some condition is met. For instance, the imperative, "If you want to avoid lung cancer, give up smoking" is hypothetical, because it depends on a condition, namely that you want to avoid lung cancer. You might not care. But (according to Kant), "Do not steal" is unconditional. It applies whatever your desires are. Indeed, typically, moral imperatives run contrary to what you want. A moral demand is one that one can will to become a universal law. Thus, stealing cannot become universal without a contradiction. If people did not refrain from stealing there would be, could be, no private property; without property there would be nothing to steal. Likewise, it would be self-contradictory to imagine universal lying. If everyone lied, there could be no orderly system of communication, and language would collapse. So the very use of language presupposes truth-telling.

Kant thought also that the categorical imperative as a test of what is right and wrong is not something imposed on the individual from outside. To act morally one has to revere the moral law and apply it to oneself. So each moral person is a legislator and, in a sense, the source of morality. It is presupposed that all people, as the source of morality, are to be given reverence. Hence, the second formulation of the categorical imperative requires us to treat another person never merely as a means but also always as an end in him- or herself. So treating a person, say a prostitute, merely as a means for producing pleasure is an offense against the moral law.

All this implies that we can by reason establish what is right and wrong; morality does not have any external source, not even God. It derives, as I have said, from each person as his or her own moral legislator.

But although Kant argued for the independence of morality, and so was the forerunner of many other Western thinkers who believe that you can have "morals without religion," he thought that from a practical perspective God was presupposed by the moral law. It seems incongruous that virtue should not be matched by happiness. But in this world it is not possible for the virtuous person to gain the bliss that he or she deserves. Moreover, it is not even possible in our brief lives to achieve absolute goodness or moral perfection. We can only attain an approximation. Yet, in principle, the moral law makes absolute demands on us. Kant thought that the demands of the moral law in practice indicate that we should live on after death, and that God should in the end match our virtue with full happiness. So God and immortality are practical outcomes of the demands of the moral law. Although morality does not derive from God, we can infer a God from the moral law.

Instead of immortality, Kant could no doubt have thought of reincarnation as an alternative model of the upward striving for ultimate perfection. Had he been an Indian he might have come to very different conclusions about the presuppositions of the moral law, and karma might have taken the place of God. What appear to us as reasonable conclusions from within the perspective of our own culture may in fact look different from another cultural perspective. There are other problems with Kant's position. Not all moral rules conform to his test. Although he may rightly think that stealing and lying contain, if universalized, an inner contradiction, this does not so obviously apply (for example) to incest. We could imagine a society that does not have a strict rule against incest. Perhaps it would not break down, although it might be inferior to ours. There are also problems with the exceptions that inevitably seem to have to be made to any rule. Wouldn't stealing bread to feed a starving child be justified if there were no other way to get food? Kant's doctrines have been subject to much debate. Refinements of his approach—what might be called the logical approach—to morality have been made in modern times. But partly because of difficulties in his position, many modern philosophers have looked to consequences as holding the key to right and wrong.

In this view, known as utilitarianism, the test of a rule, an institution, or an action is whether it brings the greatest happiness to the greatest number of people and/or the least suffering to the least number. Stealing becomes wrong not only because it harms individuals, but also because it encourages people who militate against society. There are problems with the utilitarian view as well. What if sacrificing a small minority led to greater happiness for the majority? We might justify treating people merely as means if all we were interested in was worldwide happiness or suffering. Kill a person for some crime, in order to keep society orderly and make people safer and happier: Is this not treating the criminal just as a means? The next thing we know, we might treat noncriminals in the same way.

## A NORMATIVE VIEW

Already we are sliding into questions of what is normative. What is actually right or wrong? Up to now we have been trying to look at patterns of ethical thought in relation to the religious ideas and practices that shape them. What I now venture to say on what I think to be right and wrong is only one opinion (I have no special authority), and there can be many others. But it might be interesting for you to think about some of the ideas that occur to someone, like myself, who has immersed himself in the comparative study of religion and of comparative religious ethics.

The first thing to examine is that we live in a global city in which different cultures and worldviews interact. When one group seeks to impose its standards on a group that does not share the same values, conflict arises. So it seems to me that there is a great case for religious toleration, and for a

*We live in a global city in which different cultures and worldviews interact. When one group seeks to impose its standards on a group that does not share the same values, conflict arises. So it seems to me that there is a great case for religious toleration, and for a form of society in which there can be genuine plurality of beliefs and values.*

form of society in which there can be genuine plurality of beliefs and values. This toleration should breed an ethic of what might be called social personalism: I respect the social values of the other person because I respect the person in question—what another loves I love (in a way) because I love that person.

But second, it seems to me that the purport of religion is to stress the spiritual life—worship of God, a vision of the goodness of the world, the practice of meditation, a perception of the impermanence of things, and so on. Morality has to be related to such spiritual vision and life. It is true that the religions do not agree by any means and their atmospheres often greatly differ; but they still are like fingers pointing at the moon: they point to what lies beyond. This pointing to what lies beyond challenges the "worldly" notions of happiness and welfare that often enter into the calculations of modern folk, in the utilitarian tradition. True peace of spirit can (I would suggest, from a religious angle) be achieved only if one is in relationship to what lies Beyond. What is needed is *transcendental* humanism: prizing human welfare but seeing it in the light of a vision of what is eternal.

We can learn something from the tension in religion between the dynamic power of the numinous experience and the tranquility of the mystical. There is a tension, too, between the divine and human sides of Christ, and between the other worldly and this-worldly sides of insight and compassion in Buddhism. The religious person should not shrink from action in the world, and we should welcome the turbulence of human creativity and drive. But it has to have a balancing sense of peace. Thus it would seem to me that at times we cannot shrink from the use of force; society needs it to maintain order, and nations and classes may need protection from genocide and slavery. But the true aim should always be to minimize violence. As we sometimes cause pain to minimize pain, as in surgery, so we may use force to minimize violence. This attitude is often not reflected in the machismo of police forces or the nationalist hatreds of the military, although they often say that their true aim is order and peace. Force and violence are distasteful, and because they are minimally needed their excessive and common use should not be condoned.

Ultimately we need the sense of the Beyond in order to see anew the sacredness of the person. In a sense, each person is a world, a cosmos in itself. The world is alive when the cosmos and human consciousness interact, and the fields are lit up with green, the sky with blue, the birds with fluttering motion, the rain with wetness, and the sun with warmth. From my cosmos I should revere the world of others. Persons are in this way like gods: they should be treated with reverence in their creativity and joy, and with compassion in their lonely suffering. Religions give differing expressions to the overarching meaning attached to each individual. Faith helps us see the immortal dignity of each person.

Religions have often used force on people and have often been intolerant. In our own day, secular worldviews have engaged in force and practiced intolerance of human values. But perhaps because of this, the religious and secular worldviews can learn from mutual criticism.

## Concepts and Questions

1. What does Smart mean when he says, "the ethical dimension of a religion or worldview is shaped by the other dimensions, but it also helps to shape them"?

2. Give some examples of why Smart believes that ethical systems based on nonreligious principles such as utilitarianism or secular humanism are inadequate to meet the needs of an ethical system.

3. Give examples of the commonalities among major faiths regarding moral conduct.

4. How does Smart differentiate between religious duties and ethical or moral duties?

5. From Smart's perspective, how does living in a global city affect the development of an ethic for intercultural communication? What are some of the conditions that would have to exist in order for such an ethic to develop?

6. According to Smart, how does a sense of the Beyond relate to the development of an ethical system?

7. What lesson do you believe can be learned from having knowledge about religious as well as secular worldviews?

8. How easy or difficult would you find the task of building a cross-cultural ethic based on Smart's discussion of religious and secular worldviews?

9. If you were assigned to work in a foreign culture for an extended period, how easy or difficult would it be for you to construct an appropriate cross-cultural ethic?

# Cultural Diversity: A World View

THOMAS SOWELL

*Cultural diversity and its influence on communication has been a major theme throughout this book. Thomas Sowell, in his essay "Cultural Diversity: A World View," offers insight into both its importance and its limitations. One of the difficulties inherent in analyzing diversity is realizing what constitutes diversity. When we discuss such disparate topics as employee relations, entertainment, or education, the word "diversity" is frequently employed—but rarely defined. In this essay, Sowell seeks "to separate the issue of the general importance of cultural diversity—not only in the United States but in the world at large—from the more specific, more parochial, and more ideological agendas that have become associated with that concept in recent years."*

*Sowell begins by speaking about the worldwide importance and influence of cultural diversity over the many centuries of human development. He believes that the whole rise of humankind "has been marked by transfers of cultural advances from one group to another and from one civilization to another." He relates how many accepted parts of Western society had their origins in the Middle East or Asia. Such vital parts of Western civilization as paper and printing had their origins in China, and the worldwide numbering system in use today originated in India. Sowell also shows how aspects of some cultures are superior to those of other cultures. For instance, once paper and printing from China became the norm in Western society, the keeping of precious records, knowledge, and thought inscribed on scrolls disappeared because books were clearly superior. He holds that "a given culture may not be superior for all things in all settings, much less remain superior over time, but particular cultural features may nevertheless be clearly better for some purposes—not just different."*

*Sowell insists that just like civilizations, social groups differ in their effectiveness in different fields of endeavor. He then discusses the strong sociopolitical resistance to accepting the reality of different levels and kinds of skills, interests, habits, and orientations among different groups of people. To support his position, Sowell traces American immigration patterns and shows how various cultural groups have moved and developed in their new homes.*

Diversity has become one of the most often used words of our time—and a word almost never defined. Diversity is invoked in discussions of everything from employment policy to curriculum reform, from entertainment to politics. Nor is the word merely a description of the long-known fact that the U.S. population is made up of people from many countries, many races, and many cultural backgrounds. All that was well known long before the word *diversity* became an insistent part of our vocabulary, an invocation, an imperative, or a bludgeon in ideological conflicts.

The very motto of the United States—*E Pluribus Unum*—recognizes the diversity of the American people. For generations, this diversity has been celebrated, whether in comedies like *Abie's Irish Rose* (the famous play featuring a Jewish boy and an Irish girl) or in patriotic speeches on the Fourth of July. Yet one senses something very different in today's crusades for "diversity"—certainly not a patriotic celebration of America and often a sweeping criticism of the United States, or even a condemnation of Western civilization as a whole.

At the very least, we need to separate the issue of the general importance of cultural diversity—not only in the United States but in the world at large—from the more specific, more parochial and more ideological agendas that have become associated with that word in recent years. I would like to talk about the worldwide importance of cultural diversity over centuries of human history before returning to the narrower issues of our time.

The entire history of the human race, the rise of man from the caves, has been marked by transfers of

Reprinted from *The American Enterprise*, Vol. 2, No. 3, 1991, pp. 43–55. Copyright ©1991 The American Enterprise. Reprinted by permission. Dr. Thomas Sowell is the Rose and Milton Friedman Senior Fellow on Public Policy at the Hoover Institute, Stanford University, Stanford, California.

cultural advances from one group to another and from one civilization to another. Paper and printing, for example, are today vital parts of Western civilization—but they originated in China centuries before they made their way to Europe. So did the magnetic compass, which made possible the great ages of exploration that put the Western Hemisphere in touch with the rest of mankind. Mathematical concepts likewise migrated from one culture to another: Trigonometry came from ancient Egypt, and the whole numbering system now used throughout the world originated among the Hindus of India, though Europeans called this system Arabic numerals because the Arabs were the intermediaries through which these numbers reached medieval Europe. Indeed, much of the philosophy of ancient Greece first reached Western Europe in Arabic translations, which were then re-translated into Latin or into the vernacular languages of the Western Europeans.

Much that became part of the culture of Western civilization originated outside that civilization, often in the Middle East or Asia. The game of chess came from India, gunpowder from China, and various mathematical concepts from the Islamic world, for example. The conquest of Spain by Moslems in the eighth century A.D. made Spain a center for the diffusion into Western Europe of the more advanced knowledge of the Mediterranean world and of the Orient in astronomy, medicine, optics, and geometry. The later rise of Western Europe to world preeminence in science and technology built upon these foundations, and then the science and technology of European civilization began to spread around the world, not only to European offshoot societies such as the United States and Australia but also to non-European cultures, of which Japan is perhaps the most striking example.

The historic sharing of cultural advances until they became the common inheritance of the human

*We need to separate the issue of the general importance of cultural diversity—not only in the United States but in the world at large— from the more specific, more parochial and more ideological agendas that have become associated with that word in recent years.*

*Much that became part of the culture of Western civilization originated outside that civilization, often in the Middle East or Asia.*

race implied much more than cultural diversity. It implied that some cultural features were not only different from others but *better* than others. The very fact that people—all people, whether Europeans, Africans, Asians, or others—have repeatedly chosen to abandon some feature of their own culture in order to replace it with something from another culture implies that the replacement served their purposes more effectively: Arabic numerals are not simply different from Roman numerals; they are *better* than Roman numerals. This is shown by their replacing Roman numerals in many countries whose own cultures derived from Rome, as well as in other countries whose respective numbering systems were likewise superseded by so-called Arabic numerals.

It is virtually inconceivable today that the distances in astronomy or the complexities of higher mathematics could be expressed in Roman numerals. Merely to express the year of American independence —MDCCLXXVI—requires more than twice as many Roman numerals as Arabic numerals. Moreover, Roman numerals offer more opportunities for errors, as the same digit may be either added or subtracted, depending on its place in the sequence. Roman numerals are good for numbering kings or Super Bowls, but they cannot match the efficiency of Arabic numerals in most mathematical operations—and that is, after all, why we have numbers at all. Cultural features do not exist merely as badges of "identity" to which we have some emotional attachment. They exist to meet the necessities and forward the purposes of human life. When they are surpassed by features of other cultures, they tend to fall by the wayside or to survive only as marginal curiosities, like Roman numerals today.

Not only concepts, information, products, and technologies transfer from one culture to another. The natural produce of the Earth does the same. Malaysia is the world's leading grower of rubber trees—but those trees are indigenous to Brazil. Most of the rice grown in Africa today originated in Asia, and its tobacco originated in the Western Hemisphere. Even a great wheat-exporting nation like Argentina once imported wheat, which was not a crop indigenous to that country. Cultural diversity, viewed internationally and historically, is not a static picture of differentness but a dynamic picture of competition in which what serves human purposes more effectively survives and what does not tends to decline or disappear.

Manuscript scrolls once preserved the precious records, knowledge, and thought of European or Middle Eastern cultures. But once paper and printing from China became known in these cultures, books were clearly much faster and cheaper to produce and drove scrolls virtually into extinction. Books were not simply different from scrolls; they were *better* than scrolls. The point that some cultural features are better than others must be insisted on today because so many among the intelligentsia either evade or deny this plain reality. The intelligentsia often use words like "perceptions" and "values" as they argue, in effect, that it is all a matter of how you choose to look at it.

They may have a point in such things as music, art, and literature from different cultures, but there are many human purposes common to peoples of all cultures. They want to live rather than die, for example. When Europeans first ventured into the arid interior of Australia, they often died of thirst or hunger in a land where the Australian aborigines had no trouble finding food or water. Within that particular setting, at least, the aboriginal culture enabled people to do what both aborigines and Europeans wanted to do—survive. A given culture may not be superior for all things in all settings, much less remain superior over time, but particular cultural features may nevertheless be clearly better for some purposes—not just different.

Why is there any such argument in the first place? Perhaps it is because we are still living in the long, grim shadow of the Nazi Holocaust and are understandably reluctant to label anything or anyone "superior" or "inferior." But we don't need to. We need only recognize that particular products, skills, technologies, agricultural crops, or intellectual concepts accomplish particular purposes better than their alternatives. It is not necessary to rank one whole culture over another in all things, much less to claim

that they remain in that same ranking throughout history. They do not.

Clearly, cultural leadership in various fields has changed hands many times. China was far in advance of any country in Europe in a large number of fields for at least a thousand years and as late as the 16th century had the highest standard of living in the world.

Similar rises and falls of nations and empires have been common over long stretches of human history. Examples include the rise and fall of the Roman Empire, the "golden age" of medieval Spain and its decline to the level of one of the poorest nations in Europe today, and the centuries-long triumphs of the Ottoman Empire—intellectually as well as on the battlefields of Europe and the Middle East—and then its long decline to become known as "the sick man of Europe." But although cultural leadership has changed hands many times, that leadership has been real at given times, and much of what was achieved in the process has contributed enormously to our well-being and opportunities today. Cultural competition is not a zero-sum game. It is what advances the human race.

If nations and civilizations differ in their effectiveness in different fields of endeavor, so do social groups. Here there is especially strong resistance to accepting the reality of different levels and kinds of skills, interests, habits, and orientations among different groups of people. One academic writer, for example, said that 19th-century Jewish immigrants to the United States were fortunate to arrive just as the garment industry in New York began to develop. I could not help thinking that Hank Aaron was similarly fortunate—that he often came to bat just as a home run was due to be hit. It might be possible to believe that these Jewish immigrants just happened to be in the right place at the right time if you restrict yourself to their history in the United States. But, again taking a world view, we find Jews prominent, often predominant, and usually prospering, in the apparel industry in medieval Spain, in the Ottoman Empire, in the Russian Empire, in Argentina, in Australia, and in Brazil. How surprised should we be to find them predominant in the same industry in the United States?

Other groups have also excelled in their own special occupations and industries. Indeed, virtually every group excels at something. Germans, for example, have been prominent as pioneers in the piano industry. American piano brands such as Steinway and Schnabel, not to mention the Wurlitzer organ, are signs of the long prominence in this industry of Germans, who produced the first pianos in colonial America. Germans also pioneered in piano building in czarist Russia, Australia, France, and England. Chinese immigrants have, at one period of history or another, run more than half the grocery stores in Kingston (Jamaica) and Panama City and conducted more than half of all retail trade in Malaysia, the Philippines, Vietnam, and Cambodia. Other groups have dominated retail trade in other parts of the world—the Gujaratis from India in East Africa and in Fiji and the Lebanese in parts of West Africa, for example.

Nothing has been more common than for particular groups—often a minority—to dominate particular occupations or industries. Seldom do they have any ability to keep out others—and certainly not to keep out the majority population. They are simply *better* at the particular skills required in that occupation or industry. Sometimes we can see why. When Italians have made wine in Italy for centuries, it is hardly surprising that they should become prominent among wine makers in Argentina or in California's Napa Valley. Similarly, when Germans in Germany have been for centuries renowned for their beer making, how surprised should we be that in Argentina they became as prominent among beer makers as the Italians were among wine makers? How surprised should we be that beer making in the United States arose where there were concentrations of German immigrants—in Milwaukee and St. Louis, for example? Or that the leading beer producers to this day have German names like Anheuser-Busch and Coors, among many other German names?

Just as cultural leadership in a particular field is not permanent for nations or civilizations, neither is it permanent for racial, ethnic, or religious groups. By the time the Jews were expelled from Spain in 1492, Europe had overtaken the Islamic world in medical science, so that Jewish physicians who sought refuge in the Ottoman Empire found themselves in great demand in that Moslem country. By the early 16th century, the sultan of the Ottoman Empire had on his palace medical staff forty-two Jewish physicians and twenty-one Moslem physicians. With the passage of time, however, the source of the Jews' advantage— their knowledge of Western medicine—eroded as successive generations of Ottoman Jews lost contact with the West and its further progress. Christian minorities within the Ottoman Empire began to replace the Jews, not only in medicine but also in international trade and even in the theater, once dominated by Jews. The difference was that these Christian minorities—notably Greeks and Armenians—maintained their ties in Christian Europe and often sent their sons there to be educated. It was not race or ethnicity as such that was crucial, but maintaining contacts with the ongoing progress of Western civilization. By contrast, the Ottoman Jews became a declining people in a declining empire. Many, if not most, were Sephardic Jews from Spain—once the elite of world Jewry. But by the time the state of Israel was formed in the 20th century, those Sephardic Jews who had settled for centuries in the Islamic world now lagged painfully behind the Ashkenazic Jews of the Western world—notably in income and education. To get some idea of what a historic reversal that has been in the relative positions of Sephardic and Ashkenazic Jews, one need only note that Sephardic Jews in colonial America sometimes disinherited their own children for marrying Ashkenazic Jews.

Why do some groups, subgroups, nations, or whole civilizations excel in some particular fields rather than others? All too often, the answer to that question must be: Nobody really knows. It is an unanswered question largely because it is an *unasked* question. It is an uphill struggle merely to get acceptance of the fact that large differences exist among peoples, not just in specific skills in the narrow sense (computer science, basketball, or brewing beer) but more fundamentally in different interests, orientations, and values that determine which particular skills they seek to develop and with what degree of success. Merely to suggest that these internal cultural factors play a significant role in various economic, educational, or social outcomes is to invite charges of "blaming the victim." It is much more widely acceptable to blame surrounding social conditions or institutional policies.

But if we look at cultural diversity internationally and historically, there is a more basic question whether blame is the real issue. Surely, no human being should be blamed for the way his culture evolved for centuries before he was born. Blame has nothing to do with it. Another explanation that has had varying amounts of acceptance at different times and places is the biological or genetic theory of differences among peoples. I have argued *against* this theory in many places but will not take the time to go into lengthy arguments here. A world view of cultural differences over the centuries undermines the genetic theory as well. Europeans and Chinese, for example, are clearly genetically different. Equally clearly, China was a more advanced civilization than Europe in many scientific, technological, and organizational ways for at least a thousand years. Yet over the past few centuries, Europe has moved ahead of China in many of these same ways. If those cultural differences were due to genes, how could these two races have changed positions so radically from one epoch in history to another?

All explanations of differences between groups can be broken down into heredity and environment. Yet a world view of the history of cultural diversity seems, on the surface at least, to deny both. One reason for this is that we have thought of environment too narrowly—as the immediate surrounding circumstances or differing institutional policies toward different groups. Environment in that narrow sense may explain some group differences, but the histories of many groups completely contradict that particular version of environment as an explanation. Let us take just two examples out of many that are available.

Jewish immigrants from Eastern Europe and Italian immigrants from southern Italy began arriving in the United States in large numbers at about the same time in the late 19th century, and their large-scale immigration also ended at the same time, when restrictive immigration laws were passed in the 1920s. The two groups arrived here in virtually the same economic condition—namely, destitute. They often lived in the same neighborhoods, and their children attended the same schools, sitting side by side in the same classrooms. Their environments—in the narrow sense in which the term is commonly used—were virtually identical. Yet their social histories in the United States have been very different.

Over the generations, both groups rose, but they rose at different rates, through different means, and in a very different mixture of occupations and industries. Even wealthy Jews and wealthy Italians tended to become rich in different sectors of the economy.

The California wine industry, for example, is full of Italian names like Mondavi, Gallo, and Rossi, but the only prominent Jewish wine maker—Manischewitz—makes an entirely different kind of wine, and no one would compare Jewish wine makers with Italian wine makers in the United States. When we look at Jews and Italians in the very different environmental setting of Argentina, we see the same general pattern of differences between them. The same is true if we look at the differences between Jews and Italians in Australia or Canada or Western Europe.

Jews are not Italians, and Italians are not Jews. Anyone familiar with their very different histories over many centuries should not be surprised. Their fate in America was not determined solely by their surrounding social conditions in America or by how they were treated by American society. They were different before they got on the boats to cross the ocean, and those differences crossed the ocean with them.

We can take it a step further. Even among Ashkenazic Jews, those originating in Eastern Europe have had significantly different economic and social histories from those originating in Germanic Central Europe, including Austria as well as Germany itself. These differences have persisted among their descendants not only in New York and Chicago but as far away as Melbourne and Sydney. In Australia, Jews from Eastern Europe have tended to cluster in and around Melbourne, while Germanic Jews have settled in and around Sydney. They even have a saying among themselves that Melbourne is a cold city with warm Jews while Sydney is a warm city with cold Jews.

A second and very different example of persistent cultural differences involves immigrants from Japan. As everyone knows, many Japanese Americans were interned during World War II. What is less well known is that there is and has been an even larger Japanese population in Brazil than in the United States. These Japanese, incidentally, own approximately three-quarters as much land in Brazil as there is in Japan. (The Japanese almost certainly own more agricultural land in Brazil than in Japan.) In any event, very few Japanese in Brazil were interned during World War II. Moreover, the Japanese in Brazil were never subjected to the discrimination suffered by Japanese Americans in the decades before World

War II. Yet, during the war, Japanese Americans overwhelmingly remained loyal to the United States, and Japanese American soldiers won more than their share of medals in combat. But in Brazil, the Japanese were overwhelmingly and even fanatically loyal *to Japan.* You cannot explain the difference by anything in the environment of the United States or the environment of Brazil. But if you know something about the history of those Japanese who settled in these two countries, you know that they were culturally different *in Japan, before* they ever got on the boats to take them across the Pacific Ocean—and they were still different decades later.

These two groups of immigrants left Japan during very different periods in the cultural evolution of Japan itself. A modern Japanese scholar has said: "If you want to see Japan of the Meiji era, go to the United States. If you want to see Japan of the Taisho era, go to Brazil." The Meiji era was a more cosmopolitan, pro-American era; the Taisho era was one of fanatical Japanese nationalism.

If the narrow concept of environment fails to explain many profound differences between groups and subgroups, it likewise fails to explain many very large differences in the economic and social performance of nations and civilizations. An 18th-century writer in Chile described that country's many natural advantages in climate, soil, and natural resources—and then asked in complete bewilderment why it was such a poverty-stricken country. That same question could be asked of many countries today. Conversely, we could ask why Japan and Switzerland are so prosperous when they are both almost totally lacking in natural resources. Both are rich in what economists call "human capital"—the skills of their people. No doubt there is a long and complicated history behind the different skill levels of different peoples and nations. The point here is that the immediate environment—whether social or geographic—is only part of the story.

Geography may well have a significant role in the history of peoples, but perhaps not simply by presenting them with more or fewer natural resources. Geography shapes or limits peoples' opportunities for cultural interactions and the mutual development that comes out of that. Small, isolated islands in the sea have seldom been sources of new scientific advances or technological breakthroughs—regardless of

where such islands were located and regardless of the race of the people on these islands. There are islands on land as well. Where soil fertile enough to support human life exists only in isolated patches, widely separated, there tend to be isolated cultures (often with different languages or dialects) in a culturally fragmented region. Isolated highlands often produce insular cultures, lagging in many ways behind the cultures of the lowlanders of the same race—whether we are talking about medieval Scotland, colonial Ceylon, or the contemporary Montagnards of Vietnam.

With geographical environments as with social environments, we are talking about long-run effects, not simply the effects of immediate surroundings. When Scottish highlanders, for example, immigrated to North Carolina in colonial times, they had a very different history from that of Scottish lowlanders who settled in North Carolina. For one thing, the lowlanders spoke English while the highlanders spoke Gaelic—on into the 19th century. Obviously, speaking only Gaelic—in an English-speaking country—affects a group's whole economic and social progress. Geographical conditions vary as radically in terms of how well they facilitate or impede large-scale cultural interactions as they do in their distribution of natural resources. We are not even close to being able to explain how all these geographical influences have operated throughout history. That too is an unanswered question largely because it is an unasked question—and it is an unasked question because many are seeking answers in terms of immediate social environment or are vehemently insisting that they have already found the answer in those terms.

How radically do geographic environments differ—not just in terms of tropical versus arctic climates but also in the very configuration of the land and how that helps or hinders large-scale interactions among peoples? Consider one statistic: Africa is more than twice the size of Europe, and yet Africa has a shorter coastline than Europe. That seems almost impossible. But the reason is that Europe's coastline is far more convoluted, with many harbors and inlets being formed all around the continent. Much of the coastline of Africa is smooth—which is to say, lacking the harbors that make large-scale maritime trade possible by sheltering the ships at anchor from the rough waters of the open sea. Waterways of all sorts have played a major role in the evolution of cultures and nations around the world. Harbors on the sea are not the only waterways. Rivers are also very important. Virtually every major city on Earth is located on either a river or a harbor. Whether it is such great harbors as those in Sydney, Singapore, or San Francisco, London on the Thames, Paris on the Seine, or numerous other European cities on the Danube, waterways have been the lifeblood of urban centers for centuries. Only very recently has man-made, self-powered transportation like automobiles and airplanes made it possible to produce an exception to the rule like Los Angeles. (There is a Los Angeles River, but you don't have to be Moses to walk across it in the summertime.) New York has both a long and deep river and a huge sheltered harbor.

None of these geographical features in themselves create a great city or develop an urban culture. Human beings do that. But geography sets the limits within which people can operate—and in some places it sets those limits much wider than in others. Returning to our comparison of the continents of Europe and Africa, we find that they differ as radically in rivers as they do in harbors. There are entire nations in Africa without a single navigable river—Libya and South Africa, for example. "Navigable" is the crucial word. Some African rivers are navigable only during the rainy season. Some are navigable only between numerous cataracts and waterfalls. Even the Zaire River, which is longer than any river in North America and carries a larger volume of water, has too many waterfalls too close to the ocean for it to become a major artery of international commerce. Such commerce is facilitated in Europe not only by numerous navigable rivers but also by the fact that no spot on the continent, outside of Russia, is more than 500 miles from the sea. Many places in Africa are more than 500 miles from the sea, including the entire nation of Uganda.

Against this background, how surprised should we be to find that Europe is the most urbanized of all inhabited continents and Africa the least urbanized? Urbanization is not the be-all and end-all of life, but certainly an urban culture is bound to differ substantially from nonurban cultures, and the skills peculiar to an urban culture are far more likely to be found among groups from an urban civilization. (Conversely, an interesting history could be written about the failures of urbanized groups in agricultural settlements.)

Looking within Africa, the influence of geography seems equally clear. The most famous ancient civilization on the continent arose within a few miles on either side of Africa's longest navigable river, the Nile, and even today the two largest cities on the continent, Cairo and Alexandria, are on that river. The great West African kingdoms in the region served by the Niger River and the long-flourishing East African economy based around the great natural harbor on the island of Zanzibar are further evidence of the role of geography. Again, geography is not all-determining—the economy of Zanzibar has been ruined by government policy in recent decades—but, nevertheless, geography is an important long-run influence on the shaping of cultures as well as in narrowly economic terms.

What are the implications of a world view of cultural diversity on the narrower issues being debated under that label in the United States today? Although "diversity" is used in so many different ways in so many different contexts that it seems to mean all things to all people, a few themes appear again and again. One of these broad themes is that diversity implies organized efforts at the preservation of cultural differences, perhaps governmental efforts, perhaps government subsidies to various programs run by the advocates of "diversity."

This approach raises questions as to what the purpose of culture is. If what is important about cultures is that they are emotionally symbolic, and if differentness is cherished for the sake of differentness, then this particular version of cultural "diversity" might make some sense. But cultures exist even in isolated societies where there are no other cultures around—where there is no one else and nothing else from which to be different. Cultures exist to serve the vital, practical requirements of human life—to structure a society so as to perpetuate the species, to pass on the hard-learned knowledge and experience of generations past and centuries past to the young and inexperienced in order to spare the next generation the costly and dangerous process of learning everything all over again from scratch through trial and error—including fatal errors. Cultures exist so that people can know how to get food and put a roof over their heads, how to cure the sick, how to cope with the death of loved ones, and how to get along with the living. Cultures are not bumper stickers. They are living, changing ways of doing all the things that have to be done in life.

Every culture discards over time the things that no longer do the job or that don't do the job as well as things borrowed from other cultures. Each individual does this, consciously or not, on a day-to-day basis. Languages take words from other languages, so that Spanish as spoken in Spain includes words taken from Arabic, and Spanish as spoken in Argentina has Italian words taken from the large Italian immigrant population there. People eat Kentucky Fried Chicken in Singapore and stay in Hilton Hotels in Cairo.

This is *not* what some of the advocates of "diversity" have in mind. They seem to want to preserve cultures in their purity, almost like butterflies preserved in amber. Decisions about change, if any, seem to be regarded as collective decisions, political decisions. But that is not how any cultures have arrived where they are. Individuals have decided for themselves how much of the old they wished to retain, how much of the new they found useful in their own lives. In this way, cultures have enriched each other in all the great civilizations of the world. In this way, great port cities and their crossroads of cultures have become centers of progress all across the planet. No culture has grown great in isolation—but a number of cultures have made historic and even astonishing advances when their isolation was ended, usually by events beyond their control.

Japan was a classic example in the 19th century, but a similar story could be told of Scotland in an earlier era, when a country where once even the nobility were illiterate became—within a short time, as history is measured—a country that produced world pioneers in field after field: David Hume in philosophy, Adam Smith in economics, Joseph Black in

> *Cultures exist so that people can know how to get food and put a roof over their heads, how to cure the sick, how to cope with the death of loved ones, and how to get along with the living. Cultures are not bumper stickers. They are living, changing ways of doing all the things that have to be done in life.*

> *Those who use the term* cultural diversity *to promote a multiplicity of segregated ethnic enclaves are doing an enormous harm to the people in those enclaves.*

chemistry, Robert Adam in architecture, and James Watt, whose steam engine revolutionized modern industry and transport. In the process, the Scots lost their language but gained world preeminence in many fields. Then a whole society moved to higher standards of living than anyone had ever dreamed of in their poverty-stricken past.

There were higher standards in other ways as well. As late as the 18th century, it was considered noteworthy that pedestrians in Edinburgh no longer had to be on the alert for sewage being thrown out of the windows of people's homes or apartments. The more considerate Scots yelled a warning, but they threw out the sewage anyway. Perhaps it was worth losing a little of the indigenous culture to be rid of that problem.

Those who use the term *cultural diversity* to promote a multiplicity of segregated ethnic enclaves are doing an enormous harm to the people in those enclaves. Although they live socially, the people in those enclaves have to compete economically for a livelihood. Even if they were not disadvantaged before, they will be very disadvantaged if their competitors from the general population are free to tap the knowledge, skills, and analytical techniques that Western civilization has drawn from all the other civilizations of the world, while those in the enclaves are restricted to what exists in the subculture immediately around them.

We also need to recognize that many great thinkers of the past—whether in medicine or philosophy, science or economics —labored not simply to advance whatever particular group they happened to have come from but to advance the human race. Their legacies, whether cures for deadly diseases or dramatic increases in crop yields to fight the scourge of hunger, belong to all people—and all people need to claim that legacy, not seal themselves off in a dead-end of tribalism or in an emotional orgy of cultural vanity.

1. How does Sowell's treatment of the notion of diversity differ from the general usage in the United States today?

2. What are the benefits of interactions between different cultures?

3. How does cultural leadership in various fields of human endeavor change from time to time? What are the advantages and/or disadvantages of this activity?

4. Sowell asserts that some groups, subgroups, nations, or whole civilizations excel in some particular fields rather than others. What explanations does he provide to justify this assertion?

5. Sowell asserts that explanations of differences between groups can be broken down into heredity and environment. Do you agree or disagree? Why?

6. What role does geography play in developing diversity among groups?

7. Sowell differentiates between a wide view and a narrow view of diversity. What implications does he advance when people take the narrow view of diversity?

8. Do you believe, as Sowell asserts, that some people use the term *cultural diversity* to promote a multiplicity of segregated ethnic enclaves?

# The Limits to Cultural Diversity

## HARLAN CLEVELAND

*There may be a tendency among writers in the field of intercultural communication to celebrate diversity without giving thought to its potential limits. In this essay, Harlan Cleveland proposes what he believes to be limits to the importance of cultural diversity. He eloquently alerts us to some of the problems associated with cultural diversity while offering us guidance for the future. The basic problem brought about by increased cultural contact is clear for Cleveland: ethnic and religious diversity is creating painful conflicts around the world. Too often these clashes turn one culture against another in ideological disputes. When this happens, according to Cleveland, "'culture' is being used ... as an instrument of repression, exclusion, and extinction." Cleveland fears that when people see the chaos created by different cultures, they believe that their best haven of certainty and security is a group based on ethnic similarity, common faith, economic interest, or political like-mindedness. Cleveland rejects this "single-culture" hypothesis and recommends a counterforce of wider views, global perspectives, and more universal ideas. This universal view, according to Cleveland, rests in a philosophy that has civilization*
*(universal values, ideas, and practices) as the basic core for all humanity. In this analysis, culture represents the "substance and symbols of the community," while civilization is rooted in compromise and built on "cooperation and compassion." With this orientation, people can deal with each other in ways that respect cultural differences while granting essential overarching values.*

*Cleveland's optimism is clearly stated in his conclusion: "For the 21st century, this 'cheerful acknowledgment of difference' is the alternative to a global spread of ethnic cleansing and religious rivalry."*

I'm engaged just now in an effort to think through the most intellectually interesting, and morally disturbing, issue in my long experience of trying to think hard about hard subjects. I call it "The Limits to Cultural Diversity." If that seems obscure, wait a moment.

After the multiple revolutions of 1989, it began to look as if three ideas we have thought were Good Things would be getting in each other's way, which is not a Good Thing. What I have called the "triple dilemma," or "trilemma," is the mutually damaging

From *The Futurist*, March–April 1995, pp. 23–26. Reprinted by permission of the World Future Society. The late Harlan Cleveland was a U.S. assistant secretary of state, ambassador to NATO, president of the University of Hawaii and president of the World Academy of Art and Science.

collision of individual human rights, cultural human diversity, and global human opportunities. Today the damage from that collision is suddenly all around us.

In 1994, in the middle of Africa, ethnicity took over as an exclusive value, resulting in mass murder by machete. In ex-Yugoslavia (and too many other places), gunpowder and rape accomplish the same purpose: trampling on human rights and erasing human futures. Even on the Internet, where individuals can now join global groups that are not defined by place names or cordoned off by gender or ethnicity, people are shouting at each other in flaming, capital-letters rhetoric.

Look hard at your hometown, at the nearest inner city; scan the world by radio, TV, or newspapers and magazines. What's happened is all too clear: Just when individual human rights have achieved superstar status in political philosophy, just when can-do information technologies promise what the UN Charter calls "better standards of life in larger freedom," culture and diversity have formed a big, ugly boulder in the road called Future.

"If we cannot end now our differences, at least we can help make the world safe for diversity." That was the key sentence in the most influential speech of John F. Kennedy's presidency: his commencement address at American University on June 10, 1963. That speech led directly (among other things) to the first nuclear test ban treaty. For most of the years since then, we were mesmerized by the threat of strategic nuclear war, but now a big nuclear war has become the least likely eventuality among the major threats to human civilization. And that brings us face to face with the puzzle identified in Kennedy's speech: how to make diversity safe.

But is "cultural diversity" really the new Satan in our firmament? Or does it just seem so because "culture"

> *Just when individual human rights have achieved superstar status in political philosophy, just when can-do information technologies promise what the UN Charter calls "better standards of life in larger freedom," culture and diversity have formed a big, ugly boulder in the road called Future.*

> *Societies based on fear of outsiders tend toward "totalitarian" governance. Fear pushes the culture beyond normal limits on individuals' behavior.*

is being used—*as Kultur* has been used in other times and places—as an instrument of repression, exclusion, and extinction?

## AN EXCESS OF CULTURAL IDENTITY

In today's disordered world, the collision of cultures with global trends is in evidence everywhere. Ethnic nations, fragmented faiths, transnational businesses, and professional groups find both their inward loyalties and their international contacts leading them to question the political structures by which the world is still, if tenuously, organized. The results are sometimes symbolic caricatures ("In Rome, can a Moslem minaret be built taller than St. Peter's dome?") and sometimes broken mosaics like the human tragedy in what used to be Yugoslavia.

More people moved in 1994 than ever before in world history, driven by fear of guns or desire for more butter and more freedom. (This was true even before a couple of million Rwandans left their homes in terror—and some were floated out of the country as cadavers.) This more mobile world multiplies the incentives for individuals to develop "multiple personalities," to become "collages" of identities, with plural loyalties to overlapping groups. Many millions of people believe that their best haven of certainty and security is a group based on ethnic similarity, common faith, economic interest, or political like-mindedness.

Societies based on fear of outsiders tend toward "totalitarian" governance. Fear pushes the culture beyond normal limits on individuals' behavior. "To say that you're ready to *die* for cultural identity," said one of my colleagues at a workshop of the World Academy of Art and Science in Romania last year, "means that you're also ready to kill for cultural identity." Said another: "The ultimate consequence of what's called 'cultural identity' is Hutus and Tutsis murdering each other."

The fear that drives people to cleave to their primordial loyalties makes it harder for them to learn to be tolerant of others who may be guided by different faiths and loyalties. But isolating oneself by clinging to one's tribe is far from a stable condition; these days, the tribe itself is highly unstable. Differences in birthrates and pressures to move will continue to mix populations together. So ethnic purity isn't going to happen, even by forcible "cleansing."

Besides, cultures keep redefining themselves by mixing with other cultures, getting to know people who look, act, and believe differently. In today's more open electronic world, cultures also expose themselves to new faiths and fashions, new lifestyles, work ways, technologies, clothing, and cuisines.

The early stage of every realization of "cultural identity," every assertion of a newfound "right" of differences, does create a distinct group marked by ethnic aspect ("Black is beautiful"), gender ("women's lib"), religion ("chosen people"), or status as a political minority. But when members of a group, insisting on the group's uniqueness, do succeed in establishing their own personal right to be different, something very important happens: They begin to be treated *individually* as equals and tend to integrate with more inclusive communities. Traditions of separateness and discrimination are often persistent, but they are never permanent and immutable. The recent history of South Africa bears witness.

Before the fighting in Yugoslavia, the most tolerant people in that part of the world were seen by their close neighbors to be the Serbs, Croats, and Moslems living together in Bosnia and Herzegovina, with the city of Sarajevo as a special haven of mutual tolerance. The problem does not seem to be culture itself, but cultural overenthusiasm. Cultural loyalties, says one European, have the makings of a runaway nuclear reaction. Without the moderating influence of civil society—acting like fuel rods in a nuclear reactor—the explosive potential gets out of hand. What's needed is the counterforce of wider views, global perspectives, and more universal ideas.

Post-communist societies, says a resident of one of them, have experienced a loss of equilibrium, a culture shock from the clash of traditional cultures, nostalgia for the stability of Soviet culture, and many new influences from outside. What's needed, he thinks, is cultural richness without cultural dominance, but with the moderating effect of intercultural respect.

## CULTURE AND CIVILIZATION

We have inherited a fuzzy vocabulary that sometimes treats *culture* as a synonym for *civilization*. At a World Academy workshop, my colleagues and I experimented with an alternative construct. In this construct, *civilization* is what's universal—values, ideas, and practices that are in general currency everywhere, either because they are viewed as objectively "true" or because they are accepted pragmatically as useful in the existing circumstances. These accepted "truths" offer the promise of weaving together a *civitas* of universal laws and rules, becoming the basis for a global civil society.

What is sometimes called "management culture" appears to be achieving this kind of universal acceptance, hence becoming part of global "civilization." But nobody has to be in charge of practices that are generally accepted. For instance, the international exchange of money—a miracle of information technologies—is remarkably efficient, daily moving more than a trillion dollars' worth of money among countries. Yet no one is in charge of the system that makes it happen. Recently, the puny efforts of governments to control monetary swings by buying and selling currencies have only demonstrated governments' incapacity to control them.

If civilization is what's universal, *culture* is the substance and symbol of the community. Culture meets the basic human need for a sense of belonging, for participating in the prides and fears that are shared with an in-group. Both culture and civilization are subject to continuous change. In our time, the most pervasive changes seem to be brought about by the spread of knowledge, the fallout of information science and information technologies.

Civil society consists of many structures and networks, cutting across cultural fault lines, brought into being by their ability to help people communicate. They are not very dependent on public authority for their charters or their funding, increasingly taking on functions that used to be considered the responsibility of national governments. Many of these "nongovernments"—such as those concerned with business and finance, scientific inquiry, the status of women, population policy, and the global environmental commons—have become effective users of modern information technologies. In consequence, they are providing more and more of the policy initiative both inside countries and in world affairs.

Civilization is rooted in compromise—between the idea of democratic state and a strong state, between a free-market economy and a caring economy, between "open" and "closed" processes, between horizontal and vertical relationships, between active and passive citizenship. The required solvent for civilization is *respect for differences.* Or, as one of my World Academy colleagues puts it, we need to learn *how to be different together.*

Civilization will be built by cooperation and compassion, in a social climate in which people in differing groups can deal with each other in ways that respect their cultural differences. "Wholeness incorporating diversity" is philosopher John W. Gardner's succinct formulation. The slogan on U.S. currency is even shorter, perhaps because it's in Latin: *E pluribus unum* ("from many, one").

## LESSONS FROM AMERICAN EXPERIENCE

We Americans have learned, in our short but intensive 200-plus years of history as a nation, a first lesson about diversity: that it cannot be governed by drowning it in "integration."

I came face to face with this truth when, just a quarter century ago, I became president of the University of Hawaii. Everyone who lives in Hawaii, or even visits there, is impressed by its residents' comparative tolerance toward each other. On closer inspection, paradise seems based on paradox: Everybody's a minority. The tolerance is not despite the diversity but because of it. It is not through the disappearance of ethnic distinctions that the people of Hawaii achieved a level of racial peace that has few parallels around our discriminatory globe. Quite the contrary. The glory is that Hawaii's main ethnic groups managed to establish the right to be separate. The group separateness, in turn, helped establish the rights of individuals in each group to equality with

individuals of different racial aspect, different ethnic origin, and different cultural heritage.

Hawaii's experience is not so foreign to the transatlantic migrations of the various more-or-less white Caucasians. On arrival in New York (passing that inscription on the Statue of Liberty, "Send these, the homeless, tempest-tost, to me"), the European immigrants did not melt into the open arms of the white Anglo-Saxon Protestants who preceded them. The reverse was true. The new arrivals stayed close to their own kind, shared religion and language and humor and discriminatory treatment with their soul brothers and sisters, and gravitated at first into occupations that did not too seriously threaten the earlier arrivals.

The waves of new Americans learned to tolerate each other—first as groups, only thereafter as individuals. Rubbing up against each other in an urbanizing America, they discovered not just the old Christian lesson that all men are brothers, but the hard, new, multicultural lesson that all brothers are different. Equality is not the product of similarity; it is the cheerful acknowledgment of difference.

> *Civilization will be built by cooperation and compassion, in a social climate in which people in differing groups can deal with each other in ways that respect their cultural differences.*

What's so special about our experience is the assumption that people of many kinds and colors can together govern themselves without deciding in advance which kinds of people (male or female, black, brown, yellow, red, white, or any mix of these) may hold any particular public office in the pantheon of political power. For the 21st century, this "cheerful acknowledgment of difference" is the alternative to a global spread of ethnic cleansing and religious rivalry. The challenge is great, for ethnic cleansing and religious rivalry are traditions as contemporary as Bosnia and Rwanda in the 1990s and as ancient as the Assyrians who, as Byron wrote, "came down like a wolf on the fold" but, says the biblical Book of Kings, were prevented by sword-wielding angels from taking Jerusalem.

In too many countries there is still a basic, if often unspoken, assumption that one kind of people is anointed to be in general charge. Try to imagine a Turkish chancellor of Germany, an Algerian president of France, a Pakistani prime minister of Britain, a

Christian president of Egypt, an Arab prime minister of Israel, a Jewish president of Syria, a Tibetan ruler in Beijing, anyone but a Japanese in power in Tokyo.

Yet in the United States during the 20th century, we have already elected an Irish Catholic as president, chosen several Jewish Supreme Court justices, and racially integrated the armed forces right up to the chairman of the Joint Chiefs of Staff. We have not yet adjusted—as voters in India, Britain, and Turkey have done—to having a woman atop the American political heap. But early in the 21st century, that too will come. And during that same new century, which will begin with "minorities" as one in every three Americans, there is every prospect that an African American, a Latin American, and an Asian American will be elected president of the United States.

I wouldn't dream of arguing that we Americans have found the Holy Grail of cultural diversity when in fact we're still searching for it. We have to think hard about our growing pluralism. It's useful, I believe, to dissect in the open our thinking about it, to see whether the lessons we are trying to learn might stimulate some useful thinking elsewhere. We do not yet quite know how to create "wholeness incorporating diversity," but we owe it to the world, as well as to ourselves, to keep trying.

> In too many countries there is still a basic, if often unspoken, assumption that one kind of people is anointed to be in general charge.

## Concepts and Questions

1. What does Cleveland mean when he speaks of making diversity safe?

2. What does Cleveland imply when he refers to "an excess of cultural identity"?

3. How does loyalty to one's own cultural identity make it difficult to be tolerant of others?

4. What is meant by the term *cultural overenthusiasm*? How does it affect intercultural relations?

5. How does Cleveland differentiate between the concepts of *culture* and *civilization*?

6. What are the hallmarks of civilization? How can they be maintained?

7. What does Cleveland imply when he states that diversity cannot be governed by drowning it in integration?

# Index

The letters *t, n* or *f* following a page number denote a table, a note, or a figure.